THE PRINCETON HANDBOOK OF MULTICULTURAL POETRIES

THE PRINCETON HANDBOOK OF MULTICULTURAL POETRIES

T. V. F. BROGAN
EDITOR

PRINCETON, NEW JERSEY
PRINCETON UNIVERSITY PRESS
1996

Published by Princeton University Press
41 William Street, Princeton, New Jersey 08540
In the United Kingdom:
Princeton University Press, Chichester, West Sussex

EPITAPH:

No Words, No Time

Preparation of this volume was made possible in part by generous grants from the National Endowment for the Humanities and by other major foundations and private donors who value the acquisition, preservation, and dissemination of knowledge as well as the furtherance of all discourse which is reasoned, pluralist, and humane, toward the improvement of our common life.

Library of Congress Cataloguing-in-Publication Data
The Princeton Handbook of Multicultural Poetries
T. V. F. Brogan, editor
p. cm.
Articles are taken from the parent volume,
New Princeton encyclopedia of poetry and poetics
ISBN: 0-691-00168-5 (pbk. : alk paper)
1. Poetry—Dictionaries. 2. Poetics—Dictionaries.
3. Poetry—History and Criticism.
I. Brogan, T. V. F. (Terry V. F.)
II. Title.
PN1021.N392 1995 808.1'03—dc20 95-30610

This book is based on the
New Princeton Encyclopedia of Poetry and Poetics
Alex Preminger and T. V. F. Brogan, editors,
Frank J. Warnke,† O. B. Hardison, Jr.,† and Earl Miner, associate editors

Princeton University Press books are printed on acid-free paper and meet the guidelines for permanence and durability of the Committee on Production Guidelines for Book Longevity of the Council on Library Resources.

Composed in ITC New Baskerville and custom fonts.
Designed and produced by Leximetrics, Inc., South Bend, Indiana.
Printed in the United States of America.

1 3 5 7 9 10 8 6 4 2 (cloth)
1 3 5 7 9 10 8 6 4 2 (pbk)

PRE(*Till We Have Faces*)FACE:

Culture, Poetry, The Other, "Sexy Ideas," "Clerical Work," and Genuine Savagery

This is, most immediately, a book about poetry and culture(s). On a deeper level it is about life, about the meaningful rendering of life into few and memorable words that drench and abide, and—not least—about the experience of the Other. It is not about American culture, if you mean that frenzied embrace of Entertainment that stands in place of culture in *fin-de-siècle* America; quite the contrary, it is implacably about other ways and other modes. It is a book about how others have chosen to construe the world.

Nor is it a book about "theory," or politics, or ideology, or gender war, or any other topic currently fashionable in the academy, especially in the narrow and conformist ways that the academy construes thought. Rather, it is about the topics of cultural difference, gender, and social thought as they have naturally appeared in the course of the literary history of many cultures.

To read this book, therefore, should be primarily an exercise in letting go. It may also be an experience which produces, I should think, something like the pleasure of an exhibition to a weaver or painter: new vistas, new textures, whole new modes of possibility. For those who tire of the predictable, the comfortable, and the known, it offers the endless consolation that There Are Always Other Ways. It requires an openness to new forms of experience, cast, as if always, in the forms we have already devised, and it often whispers a reminder of that devising.

More specifically, this is a book which looks over, carefully and systematically but within readable scope, the poetry of 106 cultures on this planet—every culture, we think, which has any poetic tradition known well enough to be worth talking

---

C. S. Lewis, 1956—what Paul Ramsey would call a "permanently noble" book.

about. The articles are drawn without redaction from its parent volume, the *New Princeton Encyclopedia of Poetry and Poetics*, published in 1993. The signal success of that book—ten thousand copies sold in a little over a year—nevertheless did not conceal from its editors the need for smaller and more focused child-volumes on specific subject areas. The first of these, on poetics, rhetoric, genre, and criticism, appeared in 1994 as the *New Princeton Handbook of Poetic Terms*. The present volume provides, a complete survey of not poetic devices or theory but poetic history and praxis in every major national literature or cultural tradition in the world. A third volume, on poetic craft, prosody, is planned.

Our editorial principles should be stated, lest our critics chafe their hands over our illusion of objectivity. That, it happens, is not what we had in view, though it is conversely not impossible of attainment; one can, in time, learn what one is, how one thinks, and so learn to discount that when needed. In the course of our work we inspected every major reference work on literature currently available in the West, we consulted several hundred senior scholars at length, and we published requests for comment. From our research we compiled a list of 106 cultures in 92 national literatures and a much larger number of languages. Our principle of selection was but one: balance. We did not privilege older literatures over newer, so long as a tradition had some discernible oral or, better, literate artifacts for scholars to describe. We gave equal space to Western as to Eastern poetries, though we gave somewhat more weight than was strictly justified to emergent poetries and poetries which, though left only in remnants, obviously once had powerful traditions no longer or not yet known. We gave no special consideration, in these articles at least, to how well developed the theory or criticism of the tradition might be, nor to the size of the nation-state, much less the quality of the poetry (judged in foreign terms!). Our coverage of poetic history and praxis in the *New Princeton Encyclopedia* of 1993 increased by 77% over that of its predecessor volume, the *Princeton Encyclopedia of Poetry and Poetics*, last revised in 1974. Of the roughly 1.25 million words in the *NPEPP*, national-poetry surveys accounted for almost a third, or nearly 400,000 words, all reproduced here. We gave full coverage to Indo-European poetries (all the major Celtic, Slavic, Germanic, and Romance languages, as well as other obscure ones such as Hittite), the ancient Middle Eastern poetries (Hebrew Persian, Sumerian, and Assyro-Babylonian), subcontinental Indian poetries (the widest linguistic diversity), Asian and Pacific poetries (Chinese, Japanese, Korean, Vietnamese, Mongolian, and half a dozen others), continental American poetries (native Indian in North, Central, and South American regions; all the modern Western cultures), and African poetries (ancient and emergent, oral and written). We aimed, in short, to embrace in a structured and reasoned way the diversity of poetry as it is known across the globe today. In this, our aim would naturally contravene the extremities of theory presently dominating American academic discourse. But of course discourse is only chat unless it has some object, and if poetic discourse is not grounded in the minute and extensive knowledge of actual fact, it can scarcely last.

For the rest, I need only say that every article has been brought completely up to date, with a greatly augmented bibliography at the end for further reading. The authors are many of the foremost authorities in the world, and considerable editorial effort has been made to render the prose style readable throughout. We aim for an audience of general readers, journalists, students, teachers, researchers. As the midwives to these new thought-beings (so Plato on teaching), we may be excused for thinking them the most excellent children there ever were, alert, responsive; deferential yet peppy; cheerful, well groomed and unfailingly helpful; articulate and accurate in discourse; even *interesting*. See for yourself if the conceit fits not.

So, this is a book about history and culture and fact. It is overwhelmingly about other histories and cultures and facts. The premise of the book is the same as was, ever, the premise for all interrogation of the Other, namely that the blindness of the human psyche to itself being one of the thundering facts of consciousness, we learn about our selves only by learning the Other—both the otherness of our actions upon and as received by other sentient selves, and their actions upon us in response to what we in reality performed (as opposed to what we think or hope or believe, oh so fervently, we performed—fictions all). To study otherness is thus to excavate the self, with surprise, sometimes with shock, often with humility, occasionally with shame. Our actions and our faces are not known to us, so we are fools not to cleave to those things we can learn from others.

*

When I was in graduate school, one of the fixtures of the campus scene was a bag lady, a crone reduced to penury by handicap, defects of mind, and the concrescence of failings of the flesh. She got about, slowly, on crutches. She was most often seen selling trifles or begging, hunched over, her face scarcely visible. One year, the campus newspaper ran, in its opening-day issue for the Fall term, a picture of her with the following caption: "Just Because Everything Is Different Doesn't Mean Anything Has Changed."

After fierce winds of change, one wonders if anything has changed in the American academy. Some darker brown faces have replaced some very light brown ones, and a number of females have replaced males in a soundless but massive seismic-ethnic shift that will shortly invert former proportions altogether. De jure discrimination in favor of white males is replaced by de facto discrimination in favor of nonwhite nonmales. And almost everyone is unhappy. The quality of scholarship in absolute terms has declined—we may hope this will be brief—markedly. Those newly in power have shown a relish for rapid re-enactment of the traditional rituals of the power structure, i.e. cutting the throats of their opponents. The rhetoric of victimization has moved past absurd, even past offensive, especially when espoused by those who are by any reasonably standard privileged to begin with. What mostly shows is careerism. Conservatives feign innocence of the power structures of the past, conveniently forget which president tripled the national debt, and cling to a hopelessly Disneyan mythology of the Great Tradition. Radicals glorify the mythology of oppression and preach the virtues of unprincipled change while enacting swift revenge. A distanced observer might conclude only that power corrupts, or how little reason really matters, after all, or, finally, and most sensibly, it doesn't matter what you say, it only matters what you do. And what is being done, in the real world, is this: American businesses reward the loyalty of an entire generation of middle managers with the knife, proving Marx right after all about capitalism (though wrong about communism). The real world is a vastly different place from that imagined in the academy, which is why social activism in the academy seems so out of place: the purpose of the academy is to understand, and to offer to those who wish to learn and grow a synoptic vision of what is possible, leaving the choice to their reasoned judgment. To choose only one mode, and to insist on its rightness, makes of any teacher merely an advocate, a salesperson.

Does any of this matter? It used to be said that the academy was a glittering tower of civility and reasoned discourse compared with the savageries of the real world. I wonder. At a smugly Good Old Boy college, I watched a Dean desperate to reverse the college's dismal record of hiring women faculty hit upon a novel strategy: Hire A Couple and Trash the Husband. Clever idea, except that a dozen hires all ended in divorce and the women faculty thereafter left as soon as possible. Meanwhile, in the English Department, the head of the Theory Gestapo, brought in to clean out the "dead wood," led all dissenters to the career showers. He wanted, he said, "sexy ideas." He did not want "mere clerical work" (scholarship). This, we have to say, is fascism. And the fascism of the left is not automatically preferable to the fascism of the right: all fascism is deplorable. Change? Yes. Progress? Who would you ask? Is this "ideological cleansing" worse than the recent "ethnic cleansing" in Bosnia? Hard to say. Careers are ruined, lives are wrenched violently asunder, and the scars of resentment against institutional rhetoric about "family values" (secrecy, abuse, and denial, we learn, are the values of a dysfunctional family) run to the bone. Yet people walk away, alive, breathing slowly, feeling the good pressure of the wind, knowing the declination of the late afternoon sun in every season, while abroad, many die, and many more suffer, horribly. All suffering is of a piece, offensive to every conscientious person whomsoever.

The issue is not one of ideology, ascendant or descendant; ideologies come and go with surprising uniformity of fervor from their adherents, and whatever ideology is current will not last long. It's about method. It's about what you do with the people who disagree with you. If new thinking in the academy only comes down to a power struggle, its proponents merely prove themselves no better than, because no different from, their predecessors. If the academy offers us no better vision than ordinary life, the world of business, profit, and pleasure, then there is no reason to value it, or even have it. Ideas, like tools, are put to uses. Hammers are neither good nor evil, though they are used by people good and evil. The value of the idea, like the tool, depends on how it is put to use.

And what does this have to do with poetry? What voice can poetry find in modern life, in a century where an entirely different art form, cinema, is central to culture? Poetry is of course not unfamiliar with, nor even averse to real suffering. It has been said often, by Lionel Trilling perhaps best among many, that suffering is one of the chief motives for great art. It was Solzhenitsyn who said that the tragedies of literature are just laughable compared to the tragedies of real lie. Recent ethnic atrocities would seem to have brought home that fact with a vengeance. Yet in every culture known to us at all, memorable speech on subjects dear to all is given shape and pleasing order and so invested with deep and irrevocable value. If we are to go forward, now, if we are to learn, we must learn to change. And we must learn not by talking out our selves—wherein we learn nothing—but only by listening to each other, to the ways of Otherness. Hence it is with the hope that the study of speech drenched with life, and of other cultures and other ways may, even in some small way, increase our common understanding and acceptance of each other, that I offer this book.

PREFACE

The following authors, publishers, and agents granted us permission to use brief extracts from the publications listed below. We have taken pains to trace all the owners of copyrighted material used in this book; any inadvertent omissions pointed out to us will be gladly corrected in future editions:

Harry Aveling for four lines of his translation of "Nina-bobok" [Lullaby] and seven lines of "Kita adalah pemilik syah republik ini" [The Republic is Ours], two contemporary Indonesian poems, and for four lines of his translations of "Kampung Rakit" [Floating Village] and six lines from "Ini Juga Duniaku" [This Part of My World], two contemporary Malaysian poems.

Charles Bernstein for five lines of "Sentences My Father Used" from *Controlling Interests,* reprinted by permission of Charles Bernstein and ROOF Books.

Robert Bly for two lines of "Snowfall in the Afternoon" and two lines of "Waking from Sleep" from *Silence in the Snowy Fields,* copyright 1962; and four lines of "Six Winter Privacy Poems" from *Sleepers Joining Hands,* all reprinted by permission of Robert Bly.

The University of California Press for five lines of "The Box" from *Collected Poems of Robert Creeley, 1945–75,* copyright 1983; for two lines of Mounah Khouri and Hamid Algar's translation of "Two Voices" from *An Anthology of Modern Arabic Poetry,* copyright 1974; and for three lines of medieval poetry translated by J. T. Monroe from *Hispano-Arabic Poetry: A Student Anthology,* copyright 1974, all reprinted by permission of The Regents of the University of California.

Cambridge University Press for three lines from *Arabic Poetry* and three lines from *The Poems of al-Mutanabbi,* both translated by A. J. Arberry.

Carcanet Press Ltd. for five lines from "Portrait of a Lady" and eight lines of "The Red Wheel Barrow" from *Collected Poems of William Carlos Williams, 1909–1939,* vol. 1, copyright 1938; and for six lines of "Oread" and five lines of "Storm" from *Collected Poems, 1912–44,* copyright 1982 by the Estate of Hilda Doolittle.

Copper Canyon Press for an excerpt from "A Muse of Water" in *Mermaids in the Basement,* copyright 1984 by Carolyn Kizer.

The Ecco Press for an excerpt from "Meditation at Lagunitas," from *Praise,* copyright 1974, 1979 by Robert Hass.

Faber and Faber, Ltd., for two lines of "For the Time Being" and two lines of "Lullaby" from *Collected Poems* by W. H. Auden; for an excerpt from "September 1, 1939" from *The English Auden: Poems, Essays and Dramatic Writings 1927–1939;* for two lines of *The Waste Land* from *Collected Poems 1909–1962* and five lines of "Little Gidding" from *The Complete Poems and Plays, 1909–1950,* both by T. S. Eliot; for five lines of Canto II and six lines of Canto VII from *The Cantos of Ezra Pound,* copyright 1934 by Ezra Pound; for eight lines of "The Seafarer," two lines of "Homage to Sextus Propertius," four lines of "Translations and Adaptations from Heine," and three lines of "The River-Merchant's Wife" from *Personae,* copyright 1926 by Ezra Pound, reprinted by permission of the publishers.

Farrar, Straus & Giroux for an excerpt from #14 of *The Dream Songs* by John Berryman, copyright 1959, 1969 by John Berryman; for excerpts from "The Fish" and "In the Waiting Room" from *The Complete Poems, 1927–1979* by Elizabeth Bishop, copyright 1940, 1971, renewal copyright 1968 by Elizabeth Bishop, copyright 1979, 1983 by Alice Helen Methfessel; for an excerpt from "Memories of West Street and Lepke" from *Life Studies* by Robert Lowell, copyright 1956, 1959 by Robert Lowell, renewal copyright 1987 by Harriet Lowell; for an excerpt from "The Schooner Flight" from *The Star-Apple Kingdom* by Derek Walcott, copyright 1977, 1978, 1979 by Derek Walcott.

Granada and HarperCollins Publishers for four lines of "Weltende" by Jacob van Hoddes from *Modern German Poetry,* translated by Christopher Middleton; and for eight lines of "Buffalo Bill 's" from *Tulips and Chimneys* by e e cummings, edited by George James Firmage, copyright 1923, 1925, renewal copyright 1951, 1953 by e e cummings, copyright 1973, 1976 by the Trustees for the E. E. Cummings Trust, copyright 1973, 1976 by George James Firmage.

Harcourt Brace Jovanovich for five lines of "Little Gidding" from *Four Quartets,* copyright 1943 by T. S. Eliot and renewed 1971 by Esme Valerie Eliot; for two lines of *The Waste Land* from *Collected Poems 1909–1962* by T. S. Eliot, copyright 1936 by Harcourt Brace Jovanovich, copyright 1963, 1964 by T. S. Eliot; for five lines from "Praise in Summer" from *The Beautiful Changes and Other Poems,* copyright 1947 and renewed 1975 by Richard Wilbur.

Harper & Row, Publishers, for an excerpt from "Howl" from *Collected Poems 1947–80,* copyright 1955 by Allen Ginsberg.

Henry Holt and Company for two lines from "Nothing Gold Can Stay," eight lines from "Come In," three lines from "Why Wait for Science?" and two lines from "The Gift Outright," from *The Poems of Robert Frost,* ed. Edward Connery Lathem, copyright 1923, 1947, 1969 by Holt, Rinehart and Winston; copyright 1942, 1951 by Robert Frost; copyright 1970, 1975 by Lesley Frost Ballantine.

Jonathan Cape, Ltd., for two lines from "Nothing Gold Can Stay," eight lines from "Come In," three lines from "Why Wait for Science?" and two lines from "The Gift Outright," from *The Poems of Robert Frost,* ed. Edward Connery Lathem, copyright 1923, 1947, 1969 by Holt, Rinehart and Winston; copyright 1942, 1951 by Robert Frost; copyright 1970, 1975 by Lesley Frost Ballantine.

Alfred A. Knopf for six lines of "Description Without Place," two lines of "Bantam in Pine Woods," and two lines of "Not Ideas About the Thing but the Thing Itself" from *The Collected Poems of Wallace Stevens*, copyright 1954 by Wallace Stevens.

Liverwright Publishing Corporation, for five lines of "Voyages" and two lines of "Cape Hatteras" from *The Poems of Hart Crane*, edited by Marc Simon, copyright 1986 by Marc Simon; for an excerpt from "Buffalo Bill 's" from *Tulips and Chimneys* by e e cummings, edited by George James Firmage, copyright 1923, 1925, and renewed 1951, 1953 by e e cummings, copyright 1973, 1976 by the Trustees for the E. E. Cummings Trust, copyright 1973, 1976 by George James Firmage. Macmillan Publishing Company for two lines of "A Coat," two lines of "Leda and the Swan," and two lines of "The Gyres" from *The Collected Poems of W. B. Yeats*, copyright 1928 by Macmillan Publishing Company, renewed 1956 by Bertha Georgie Yeats, copyright 1940 by Georgie Yeats, renewed 1968 by Georgie Yeats, Michael Bulter Yeats, and Anne Yeats.

New Directions Publishing Corporation for five lines of Canto II and six lines of Canto VII from *The Cantos of Ezra Pound*, copyright 1934 by Ezra Pound; for eight lines of "The Seafarer," two lines of "Homage to Sextus Propertius," four lines of "Translations and Adaptations from Heine," and three lines of "The River-Merchant's Wife" from *Personae*, copyright 1926 by Ezra Pound; for six lines of "Oread" and five lines of "Storm" from *Collected Poems, 1912–44*, copyright 1982 by the Estate of Hilda Doolittle; for five lines of "The Five-Day Rain" from *Collected Earlier Poems 1940–60*, copyright 1958 by Denise Levertov Goodman; for an excerpt from "The Well" from *Poems 1960–67*, copyright 1960 by Denise Levertov Goodman; for five lines from "Portrait of a Lady" and eight lines of "The Red Wheel Barrow" from *Collected Poems of William Carlos Williams, 1909–1939*, vol. 1, copyright 1938 by New Directions Publishing Corporation.

State University of New York Press for four lines of "Lagu Biasa" [An Ordinary Song] and four lines of "Aku" [Me] from *The Complete Poetry and Prose of Chairil Anwar*, edited and translated by Burton Raffel, copyright 1970; for six lines of "Koyan Yang Malang" [Koyan the Unfortunate], by W. S. Rendra, from *An Anthology of Modern Indonesian Poetry*, translated by Burton Raffel, copyright 1968.

The University of North Carolina Press for two excerpts from *The Poems of Phillis Wheatley*, copyright 1989.

Oxford University Press, Kuala Lumpur, for four excerpts from *Modern Malay Verse, 1946–61*, edited by Oliver Rice and Abdullah Majid.

Penguin Books Ltd., for three lines of "Howl" from *Allen Ginsburg: Collected*

Poems 1947–1980, copyright 1956 by Allen Ginsberg.

Random House, Inc., for two lines of "For the Time Being" and two lines of "Lullaby" from *Collected Poems* by W. H. Auden, and an excerpt from "September 1, 1939" from *The English Auden: Poems, Essays and Dramatic Writings 1927–1939,* both edited by Edward Mendelson, copyright 1976, 1977 by Edward Mendelson, William Meredith, and Monroe K. Spears, Executors of the Estate of W. H. Auden.

The Royal Irish Academy, for four lines from *Early Irish Metrics* by Gerard Murphy, copyright 1961 by The Royal Irish Academy.

Stanford University Press, for five lines from *Japanese Court Poetry* by Robert H. Brower and Earl Miner, copyright 1961 by the Board of Trustees of the Leland Stanford Junior University.

Sterling Lord Literistic, Inc., for fourteen lines of "Black Art" from *Black Magic: Collected Poetry 1961–67,* copyright 1990 by Amiri Baraka.

Three Continents Press for "Lazarus 1962," by Khalil Hawi, translated by A. Haydar and M. Beard in *Naked in Exile,* copyright 1984; and *Bayadir al-ju* [The Thrashing Floor of Hunger], by Khalil Hawi, copyright K. Hawi, Beirut, 1965.

Zephyr Press for an excerpt from "The Muse" from *The Complete Poems of Anna Akhmatova,* translated by Judity Hemschemeyer, copyright 1989.

BIBLIOGRAPHICAL ABBREVIATIONS

Abrams	M. H. Abrams, *The Mirror and the Lamp: Romantic Theory and the Critical Tradition,* 1953.
Analecta hymnica	*Analecta hymnica medii aevi,* ed. G. M. Dreves, C. Blume, and H. M. Bannister, 55 v., 1886–1922.
Auerbach	E. Auerbach, *Mimesis: The Representation of Reality in Western Literature,* tr. W. R. Trask, 1953.
Beare	W. Beare, *Latin Verse and European Song,* 1957.
Bec	P. Bec, *La Lyrique française au moyen âge (XIIe–XIIIe siècles): Contribution à une typologie des genres poétiques médiévaux,* 2 v., 1977–78.
Bowra	C. M. Bowra, *Greek Lyric Poetry from Alcman to Simonides,* 2d ed., 1961.
Brogan	T. V. F. Brogan, *English Versification, 1570–1980: A Reference Guide with a Global Appendix,* 1981.
Brooks	C. Brooks, *The Well Wrought Urn,* 1947.
CBEL	*Cambridge Bibliography of English Literature,* ed. F. W. Bateson, 4 v., 1940; v. 5, *Supplement,* ed. G. Watson, 1957.
CBFL	*A Critical Bibliography of French Literature,* gen. ed. D. C. Cabeen, 1–; 1947–; revisions and supplements, gen. ed. R. A. Brooks, 7 v., 1968–.
Chambers	F. M. Chambers, *An Introduction to Old Provençal Versification,* 1985.
CHCL	*Cambridge History of Classical Literature,* v. 1, *Greek Literature,* ed. P. E. Easterling and B. M. W. Knox, 1985; v. 2, *Latin Literature,* ed. E. J. Kenney, 1982.
CHEL	*Cambridge History of English Literature,* ed. A. W. Ward and A. R. Waller, 14 v., 1907–1916.
CHLC	*Cambridge History of Literary Criticism,* v. 1, *Classical Criticism,* ed. G. A. Kennedy, 1989.
Corbett	E. P. J. Corbett, *Classical Rhetoric for the Modern Student,* 3d ed., 1990.
Crane	*Critics and Criticism, Ancient and Modern,* ed. R. S. Crane, 1952.
Crusius	F. Crusius, *Römische Metrik: Ein Einfürung,* 8th ed., rev. H. Rubenbauer, 1967.
Culler	J. Culler, *Structuralist Poetics: Structuralism, Linguistics, and the Study of Literature,* 1975.
Curtius	E. Curtius, *European Literature and the Latin Middle Ages,* tr. W. R. Trask, 1953.
DAI	*Dissertation Abstracts International.*
Dale	A. M. Dale, *The Lyric Meters of Greek Drama,* 2d ed., 1968.
de Man	P. de Man, *Blindness and Insight: Essays in the Rhetoric of Contemporary Criticism,* 2d ed., 1983.
Derrida	J. Derrida, *Of Grammatology,* tr. 1976.
DHI	*Dictionary of the History of Ideas,* ed. P. P. Wiener, 6 v., 1968–74.
Dronke	P. Dronke, *Medieval Latin and the Rise of European Love Lyric,* 2d ed., 2 v., 1968.
Eliot, *Essays*	T. S. Eliot, *Selected Essays,* rev ed., 1950.
Elwert	W. T. Elwert, *Französische Metrik,* 4th ed., 1978.
Elwert, *Italienische*	W. T. Elwert, *Italienische Metrik,* 2d ed., 1984.
Empson	W. Empson, *Seven Types of Ambiguity,* 3d ed., 1953.
Faral	E. Faral, *Les Arts poétiques du XIIe et du XIIIe siècles,* 1924.
Fisher	*The Medieval Literature of Western Europe: A Review of Research, Mainly 1930–1960,* ed. John H. Fisher, 1965.
Fowler	A. Fowler, *Kinds of Literature: An Introduction to the Theory of Genres and Modes,* 1982.
Frye	N. Frye, *Anatomy of Criticism,* 1957.
Gasparov	M. L. Gasparov, *Sovremennyj russkij stix: Metrika i ritmika,* 1974.
GRLMA	*Grundriss der romanischen Literaturen des Mittelalters,* ed. H. R. Jauss and E. Köhler, 9 v., 1968–.
Group Mu	Group Mu (J. Dubois, F. Edeline, J.-M. Klinkenberg, P. Minguet, F. Pire, H. Trinon), *A General Rhetoric,* tr. P. B. Burrell and E. M. Slotkin, 1981.
Halporn et al.	J. W. Halporn, M. Ostwald, and T. G. Rosenmeyer, *The Meters of Greek and Latin Poetry,* 2d ed., 1980.
Hardie	W. R. Hardie, *Res metrica,* 1920.
Hollander	J. Hollander, *Vision and Resonance: Two Senses of Poetic Form,* 2d ed., 1985.
Hollier	*A New History of French Literature,* ed. D. Hollier, 1989.
Jakobson	R. Jakobson, *Selected Writings,* 8 v., 1962–88.

ABBREVIATIONS

Jarman and Hughes	*A Guide to Welsh Literature,* ed. A. O. H. Jarman and G. R. Hughes, 2 v., 1976–79.
Jeanroy	A. Jeanroy, *La Poésie lyrique des troubadours,* 2 v., 1934.
Jeanroy, *Origines*	A. Jeanroy, *Les Origines de la poésie lyrique en France au moyen âge,* 4th ed., 1965.
Kastner	L. E. Kastner, *A History of French Versification,* 1903.
Keil	*Grammatici latini,* ed. H. Keil, 7 v., 1855–80; v. 8, *Anecdota helvetica: Supplementum,* ed. H. Hagen, 1870.
Koster	W. J. W. Koster, *Traité de métrique grecque suivi d'un précis de métrique latine,* 4th ed., 1966.
Lausberg	H. Lausberg, *Handbuch der literarischen Rhetorik,* 2d ed., 2 v., 1973.
Le Gentil	P. Le Gentil, *La Poésie lyrique espagnole et portugaise à la fin du moyen âge,* 2 v., 1949–53.
Lewis	C. S. Lewis, *The Allegory of Love,* 1936.
Lord	A. B. Lord, *The Singer of Tales,* 1960.
Lote	G. Lote, *Histoire du vers français,* 3 v., 1949–56.
Maas	P. Maas, *Greek Metre,* tr. H. Lloyd-Jones, 3d ed., 1962.
Manitius	M. Manitius, *Geschichte der lateinischen Literatur des Mittelalters,* 3 v., 1911–31.
Mazaleyrat	J. Mazaleyrat, *Éléments de métrique française,* 3d ed., 1981.
Meyer	W. Meyer, *Gessamelte Abhandlungen zur mittellateinischen Rhythmik,* 3 v., 1905–36.
MGG	*Die Musik in Geschichte und Gegenwart: Allgemeine Enzyklopädie der Musik,* ed. F. Blume, 16 v., 1949–79.
MGH	Monumenta germaniae historica.
Michaelides	S. Michaelides, *The Music of Ancient Greece: An Encyclopaedia,* 1978.
Migne, *PG*	*Patrilogiae cursus completus, series graeca,* ed. J. P. Migne, 161 v., 1857–66.
Migne, *PL*	*Patrilogiae cursus completus, series latina,* ed. J. P. Migne, 221 v., 1844–64.
Miner et al.	E. Miner, H. Odagiri, and R. E. Morrell, *The Princeton Companion to Classical Japanese Literature,* 1986.
Morier	H. Morier, *Dictionnaire de poétique et de rhétorique,* 3d ed., 1981.
Morris-Jones	J. Morris-Jones, *Cerdd Dafod,* 1925, rpt. with Index, 1980.
Murphy	J. J. Murphy, *Rhetoric in the Middle Ages: A History of Rhetorical Theory from St. Augustine to the Renaissance,* 1974.
Navarro	T. Navarro, *Métrica española: Reseña histórica y descriptiva,* 6th ed., 1983.
New CBEL	*New Cambridge Bibliography of English Literature,* ed. G. Watson and I. R. Willison, 5 v., 1969–77.
New Grove	*New Grove Dictionary of Music and Musicians,* ed. S. Sadie, 20 v., 1980.
Nienhauser et al.	W. H. Nienhauser, Jr., C. Hartman, Y. W. Ma, and S. H. West, *The Indiana Companion to Traditional Chinese Literature,* 1986.
Norberg	D. Norberg, *Introduction a l'étude de la versification latine médiévale,* 1958.
Norden	E. Norden, *Die antike Kunstprosa,* 9th ed., 2 v., 1983.
OED	*Oxford English Dictionary,* 1st ed.
Omond	T. S. Omond, *English Metrists,* 1921.
Parry	M. Parry, *The Making of Homeric Verse,* ed. A. Parry, 1971.
Parry, *History*	T. Parry, *A History of Welsh Literature,* tr. H. I. Bell, 1955.
Patterson	W. F. Patterson, *Three Centuries of French Poetic Theory: A Critical History of The Chief Arts of Poetry in France (1328–1630),* 2 v., 1935.
Pauly-Wissowa	*Paulys Realencyclopädie der classischen Altertumswissenschaft,* ed. A. Pauly, G. Wissowa, W. Kroll, and K. Mittelhaus, 24 v. (A-Q), 10 v. (R-Z, Series 2), and 15 v. (Supplements), 1894–1978.
Pearsall	D. Pearsall, *Old English and Middle English Poetry,* 1977.
PLAC	*Poetae latini aevi carolini,* ed. E. Dümmler (v. 1–2), L. Traube, P. von Winterfeld, and K. Strecker, 5 v., 1881–1937.
Raby, *Christian*	F. J. E. Raby, *A History of Christian-Latin Poetry From the Beginnings to the Close of the Middle Ages,* 2d ed., 1953.
Raby, *Secular*	F. J. E. Raby, *A History of Secular Latin Poetry in the Middle Ages,* 2d ed., 2 v., 1957.
Ransom	*Selected Essays of John Crowe Ransom,* ed. T. D. Young and J. Hindle, 1984.
Reallexikon	*Reallexikon der deutschen Literaturgeschichte,* 2d ed., ed. W. Kohlschmidt and W. Mohr (v. 1–3), K. Kanzog and A. Masser (v. 4), 4 v., 1958–84.
Reallexikon I	*Reallexikon der deutschen Literaturgeschichte,* ed. P. Merker and W. Stammler, 1st ed., 4 v., 1925–31.
Richards	I. A. Richards, *Principles of Literary Criticism,* 1925.

Saisselin — R. G. Saisselin, *The Rule of Reason and the Ruses of the Heart: A Philosophical Dictionary of Classical French Criticism, Critics, and Aesthetic Issues,* 1970.

Sayce — O. Sayce, *The Medieval German Lyric, 1150–1300: The Development of Its Themes and Forms in Their European Context,* 1982.

Scherr — B. P. Scherr, *Russian Poetry: Meter, Rhythm, and Rhyme,* 1986.

Schipper — J. M. Schipper, *Englische Metrik,* 3 v., 1881–1888.

Schipper, *History* — J. M. Schipper, *A History of English Versification,* 1910.

Schmid and Stählin — W. Schmid and O. Stählin, *Geschichte der griechischen Literatur,* 7 v., 1920–48.

Scott — C. Scott, *French verse-art: A study,* 1980.

Sebeok — *Style in Language,* ed. T. Sebeok, 1960.

Sievers — E. Sievers, *Altgermanische Metrik,* 1893.

Smith — *Elizabethan Critical Essays,* ed. G. G. Smith, 2 v., 1904.

Snell — B. Snell, *Griechische Metrik,* 4th ed., 1982.

Spongano — R. Spongano, *Nozioni ed esempi di metrica italiana,* 2d. ed., 1974.

Stephens — *The Oxford Companion to the Literature of Wales,* ed. M. Stephens, 1986.

Terras — *Handbook of Russian Literature,* ed. V. Terras, 1985.

Thieme — H. P. Thieme, *Essai sur l'histoire du vers français,* 1916.

Trypanis — C. A. Trypanis, *Greek Poetry From Homer to Seferis,* 1981.

Weinberg — B. Weinberg, *A History of Literary Criticism in the Italian Renaissance,* 2 v., 1961.

Wellek — R. Wellek, *A History of Modern Criticism, 1750–1950,* 8 v., 1955–92.

Wellek and Warren — R. Wellek and A. Warren, *Theory of Literature,* 3d ed., 1956.

West — M. L. West, *Greek Metre,* 1982.

Wilamowitz — U. von Wilamowitz-Moellendorf, *Griechische Verskunst,* 1921.

Wilkins — E. H. Wilkins, *A History of Italian Literature,* rev. T. G. Bergin, 1974.

Wimsatt — *Versification: Major Language Types,* ed. W. K. Wimsatt, Jr., 1972.

Wimsatt and Brooks — W. K. Wimsatt, Jr., and C. Brooks, *Literary Criticism: A Short History,* 1957.

GENERAL ABBREVIATIONS

Two sets of abbreviations are used systematically throughout this volume in order to conserve space. First, general terms (below) are abbreviated both in text and bibliographies. Second, within each entry, the headword or -words of the title of the entry are abbreviated by the first letter of each word, unless the word is a general abbreviation, which takes precedence. Thus in the entry, "Egyptian Poetry," that phrase is regularly abbreviated E. p., while in "English Poetry," the head phrase is abbreviated Eng. p. Both general and headword abbreviations may also show plural forms, e.g. ms. for "metaphors" in the entry "Metaphor" (and "Meter," etc.) and lits. for "literatures" in any entry.

Af.	African
Am.	American
anthol.	anthology
Ar.	Arabic
Assoc.	Association
b.	born
bibl.	bibliography
c.	century
ca.	*circa*, about
cf.	*confer*, compare
ch.	chapter
Cl.	Classical
comp.	comparative
contemp.	contemporary
crit.	criticism
d.	died
devel.	development
dict.	dictionary
diss.	dissertation
ed.	edition, editor, edited by
e.g.	*exempli gratia*, for example
Eng.	English
enl.	enlarged
esp.	especially
et al.	*et alii*, and others
ff.	following
fl.	*floruit*, flourished
Fr.	French
Ger.	German
Gesch.	Geschichte
Gr.	Greek
Heb.	Hebrew
hist.	history, histoire
IE	Indo-European
i.e.	*id est*, that is
incl.	includes, including
interp.	interpretation
Intro.	Introduction
Ir.	Irish
It.	Italian
Jh.	Jahrhundert
jour.	journal
lang.	language
Lat.	Latin
ling.	linguistics
lit.	literature
lit. crit.	literary criticism
lit. hist.	literary history
ME	Middle English
med.	medieval
MHG	Middle High German
mod.	modern
ms.	manuscript
NT	New Testament
OE	Old English
OF	Old French
OHG	Old High German
ON	Old Norse
OT	Old Testament
p., pp.	page, pages
Port.	Portuguese
Proc.	Proceedings
pros.	prosody
Prov.	Provençal, i.e. Occitan
pub.	published
q.v.	*quod vide*, which see
qq.v.	*quae vide*, both (all of) which see
Ren.	Renaissance
rev.	revised
Rev.	Review
rhet.	rhetoric
rpt.	reprinted
Rus.	Russian
Sp.	Spanish
supp.	supplement(ed)
tr.	translation, translated
trad.	tradition
v.	volume(s)

THE CONTRIBUTORS

A.B.M. Arnold B. McMillin, Professor of Russian, University of London

A.BR. Anthony Bradley, Professor of English, University of Vermont

A.E.S. Alexandrino E. Severino, Professor of Portuguese, Vanderbilt University

A.G. Albert Gelpi, Coe Professor of American Literature, Stanford University

A.G.W. Allen G. Wood, Associate Professor of French and Comparative Literature, Purdue University

A.K.R. A. K. Ramanujan, William Colvin Professor of South Asian Languages and Civilizations, University of Chicago

A.O. Ants Oras, late Professor of English, University of Florida

A.PI. Arshi Pipa, Professor of Italian and Albanian, University of Minnesota

B.B. Beth Bjorklund, Associate Professor of German, University of Virginia

B.J.F. Bernard J. Fridsma, Sr., Professor Emeritus of Germanic Languages, Calvin College

B.R. Burton Raffel, Distinguished Professor of English, University of Southwestern Louisiana

B.S.M. Barbara Stoler Miller, Samuel R. Milbank Professor of Oriental Studies, Columbia University

C.A.M. Charles A. Moser, Professor of Slavic, The George Washington University

C.A.T. C. A. Trypanis, Professor Emeritus of Greek, University of Oxford, and Fellow of the Academy of Athens

C.F. Carolyn Fowler, Professor of Africana Literature, Clark Atlanta University

C.F.S. C .F. Swanepoel, Professor of African Languages, University of South Africa

C.H.W. C. H. Wang, Professor of Chinese and Comparative Literature, University of Washington

C.J.H. C. John Herington, Talcott Professor of Greek, Yale University

C.M.E. Carol M. Eastman, Professor of Anthropology and Adjunct Professor of Linguistics, University of Washington

D.-H.N. Dinh-Hoa Nguyen, Professor of Linguistics and Foreign Languages and Literatures, Southern Illinois University

D.B.S.J. D. B .S. Jeyaraj, journalist

D.D.-H. Diana Der-Hovanessian, poet and translator

D.F.B. David Frank Beer, author

D.F.D. David F. Dorsey, Jr., Professor of African Literature and English Linguistics, Clark Atlanta University

D.K. Donald Kenrick, Romany Institute

D.KI. Dodonia Kiziria, Associate Professor of Slavic, Indiana University

D.M.L. D. Myrddin Lloyd, late Keeper of Printed Books, National Library of Scotland

D.P.B. Daniel P. Biebuyck, H. Rodney Sharp Professor Emeritus of Anthropology and Humanities, Dartmouth College

D.S.P. Douglass S. Parker, Professor of Classics, University of Texas at Austin

E.A.H. Eric A. Huberman, Assistant Professor of Sanskrit and Indic Studies, Columbia University

E.K. Edmund Keeley, Professor of English and Creative Writing, Princeton University

E.L.R. Elias L. Rivers, Professor of Spanish, State University of New York at Stony Brook

E.M. Earl Miner, Professor of English and Comparative Literature, Princeton University

E.R. Erica Reiner, John A. Wilson Distinguished Service Professor, University of Chicago

E.SP. Ezra Spicehandler, Professor of Hebrew Literature, Hebrew Union College

F.A. Fernando Alegria, Sadie D. Patek Professor Emeritus in the Humanties, Stanford University

F.J.W. Frank J. Warnke, late Professor of Comparative Literature, University of Georgia

F.L.B. Frank L. Borchardt, Associate Professor of German, Duke University

G.A. Gorka Aulestia, Professor of Literature, University of Nevada

G.F. Graham Furniss, Lecturer in Hausa, University of London

G.G.G. George G. Grabowicz, Dmytro Čyževśkyj Professor of Ukrainian Literature, Harvard University

G.L. George Lang, Research Fellow in Comparative Literature, The University of Alberta

G.S. Guy Sylvestre, Honorary Librarian and Archivist, Royal Society of Canada

G.W. George Woodcock, Professor Emeritus of English, University of British Columbia

H.G. Helena Goscilo, Associate Professor of Slavic, University of Pittsburgh

H.J.B. Henry J. Baron, Professor of English, Calvin College

H.P. Henry Paolucci, Professor of Government and Politics, St. John's University

CONTRIBUTORS

H.T. Humphrey Tonkin, President, Potsdam College, State University of New York at Potsdam

I.I. Ivar Ivask, Professor of Modern Languages, University of Oklahoma

J.B.-N. Juan Bruce-Novoa, Professor of Mexican and Chicano Literatures, University of California at Irvine

J.C.K. J. C. Kannemeyer, Senior Research Specialist, Human Sciences Research Council, South Africa

J.E.C.W. John Ellis Cherwyn Williams, Professor Emeritus of Welsh and Celtic Literature, University College of Wales, and Fellow of the British Academy

J.H. Janet Hadda, Associate Professor of Yiddish, University of California at Los Angeles

J.H.S. Joseph H. Silverman, late Professor of Spanish, University of California at Santa Cruz

J.J.R. J. J. Ras, Professor of Javanese Language and Literature, State University of Leiden

J.L. John Lindow, Professor of Scandinavian, University of California

J.L.F. John L. Foster, Professor of English, Roosevelt University

J.L.R. James L. Rolleston, Associate Professor of German, Duke University

J.M. John MacInnes, Senior Lecturer, University of Edinburgh

J.R.K. John R. Krueger, Professor of Ural and Altaic Studies, retired, Indiana University

J.S. Juris Silenieks, Professor of French, Carnegie Mellon University

J.W.JO. John William Johnson, Associate Professor of Folklore, Indiana University

J.W.R. Jarold W. Ramsey, Professor of English, University of Rochester

K.K.S. Kirsti K. Simonsuuri, Senior Research Fellow, Helsinki University

K.L. Katharine Luomala, Professor Emerita of Anthropology, University of Hawaii

K.N.M. Kathleen N. March, Associate Professor of Spanish, University of Maine

K.R. Kenneth Ramchand, Professor of West Indian Literature, University of the West Indies

K.S.C. Kang-i Sun Chang, Professor of Chinese Literature, Yale University

L.A.C.D. L. A. C. Dobrez, Director of Centre for Australian Studies and Professor of Australian, Bond University

L.A.S. Lawrence A. Sharpe, Professor Emeritus of Romance Languages, University of North Carolina

L.C. Leonard Casper, Professor of English, Boston College

L.D.L. Laurence D. Lerner, William R. Kenan Professor of English, Vanderbilt University

L.G.W. Lars G. Warme, Associate Professor of Scandinavian Languages and Literature, University of Washington

L.K.C. Lawrence K. Carpenter, Associate Professor of Linguistics and Spanish, University of North Florida

L.L.B. Linton Lomas Barrett, late Professor of Romance Languages, Washington and Lee University

L.MO. Luis Mongui, Professor Emeritus of Spanish, University of California at Berkeley

L.W. Liliane Wouters, Academie Royale de Langue et de Litterature Francaise

M.C. Miguel Civil, Professor, Oriental Institute, University of Chicago

M.D. Michael Davidson, Associate Professor of Literature, University of California at San Diego

M.E.D. Manuel E. Durán, Professor of Spanish and Catalan Literatures, Yale University

M.G.A. Mark G. Altshuller, Associate Professor of Russian Literature, University of Pittsburgh

M.GS. Manfred Gsteiger, Professor of Comparative Literature, University of Lausanne

M.MO. Massaud Moisés, Professor of Portuguese, University of São Paulo

M.-T.B. Maria-Teresa Babin, Professor Emerita of Literature, Herbert H. Lehman College, City University of New York

M.T.K. Matthew T. Kapstein, Assistant Professor of the Philosophy of Religion, Columbia University

M.U. Makoto Ueda, Professor of Japanese and Comparative Literature, Stanford University

N.A.S. Nathan A. Scott, Jr., William R. Kenan Professor of Religious Studies and Professor of English, University of Virginia

N.S. Norman Simms, Senior Lecturer, University of Waikato

P.H.L. Peter H. Lee, Professor and Chairman of the Department of East Asian Languages and Cultures, University of California at Los Angeles

P.SP. Peter Spycher, Emeritus Professor of German, Oberlin College

R.CO. Robert Cook, Professor of English, University of Iceland

R.D.T. Robert Donald Thornton, Professor Emeritus of English, State University of New York at New Paltz

R.F.L. René, Felix Lissens, Professor Emeritus of Dutch Literature and European Literatures, Universitaire Faculteiten St. Ignatius

R.G. René, Galand, Professor of French, Wellesley College

R.G.H. Russell G. Hamilton, Professor of Spanish and Portuguese, Vanderbilt University

R.H.O. Richard H. Osberg, Associate Professor of English, Santa Clara University

CONTRIBUTORS

R.L. Richard Luxton, Assistant Professor of Anthropology and Sociology, Western New England College

R.M.A.A. Roger M. A. Allen, Professor of Arabic and Comparative Literature, University of Pennsylvania

R.MCG. Robin McGrath, Professor of English, University of Alberta

R.O. Ranjini Obeyesekere, Lecturer, Princeton University

R.P.S. Raymond P. Scheindlin, Provost and Professor of Medieval Hebrew Literature, The Jewish Theological Seminary of America

R.S. Rimvydas Silbajoris, Professor Emeritus of Slavic and East European Languages and Literature, Ohio State University

S.B. Stanislaw Baranczak, Alfred Jurzykowski Professor of Polish Language and Literature, Harvard University

S.G. Stephen Gray, Professor of English, Rand Afrikaans University

S.G.A. Samuel G. Armistead, Professor of Spanish and Comparative Literature, University of California at Davis

S.H.R. Sven H. Rossel, Professor of Comparative Literature, University of Washington

S.M.N. Silvia M. Nagy, Assistant Professor of Latin American Literature, Catholic University of America

S.W. Stephen Wright, late of Addis Ababa University

T.J.H. Thomas John Hudak, Associate Professor of Linguistics, Arizona State University

T.S.H. Talat S. Halman, author

T.T. Tulku Thondup Rinpoche, Buddhayana Foundation

T.V.F.B. T. V. F. Brogan, scholar

T.W. Tibor Wlassics, William R. Kenan Professor of Italian, University of Virginia

U.W. Uriel Weinreich, late Professor of Yiddish, Columbia University

V.D. Vinay Dharwadker, Assistant Professor of Commonwealth Literature, University of Georgia

V.D.M. Vasa D. Mihailovich, Professor of Slavic Literature, University of North Carolina

V.J. Vera Javarek, late Lecturer in Serbo-Croatian Language and Literature, University of London

V.P.N. Virgil P. Nemoianu, Professor of English and Comparative Literature, Catholic University of America

W.A. William Arrowsmith, University Professor and Professor of Classics, Boston University

W.D.P. William D. Paden, Professor of French, Northwestern University

W.E.H. William E. Harkins, Professor of Slavic Languages, Columbia University

W.F. Wallace Fowlie, James B. Duke Professor Emeritus of Romance Studies, Duke University

W.J.K. William J. Kennedy, Professor of Comparative Literature, Cornell University

W.L.H. William L. Hanaway, Professor of Persian, University of Pennsylvania

W.S.A. William S. Anderson, Professor of Latin and Comparative Literature, University of California at Berkeley

W.W. Winthrop Wetherbee, Professor of Classics and English, Cornell University

THE PRINCETON HANDBOOK OF MULTICULTURAL POETRIES

A

AFRICAN POETRY.

I. IN THE INDIGENOUS EPIC TRADITION
II. IN EUROPEAN LANGUAGES
  A. *In French*
  B. *In Portuguese*
  C. *In English*

This article provides an overview of the major poetries of the African continent written in both the indigenous langs. and in the three principal European langs. For more detailed surveys, see EGYPTIAN POETRY; ETHIOPIAN POETRY; HAUSA POETRY; SOMALI POETRY; SOUTH AFRICAN POETRY; SWAHILI POETRY. See also AFRO-AMERICAN POETRY; ARABIC POETRY; WEST INDIAN POETRY.

I. IN THE INDIGENOUS EPIC TRADITION. Af. tales, proverbs, and riddles have been profusely collected since the early 19th c. But until the middle of the 20th c., epic poetry remained an unknown, ignored, or neglected topic. Some of the epic fragments which were published early escaped the attention of scholars because the information appeared in obscure journals in unfamiliar langs. (e.g. Flemish), or the data were met with skepticism because some were fragmentary and inadequately explained. Prevailing tendencies in anthropology, linguistics, and folklore focused attention on sociological, historical, or structural matters with little or no interest in Af. oral lit., let alone Af. epic lit. But this situation has changed radically, and the world of oral lit. studies is much richer for it.

The present section of this article does not consider the praise and panegyric lit. richly represented in the heroic recitations of the Ankole of Uganda, the praise poems of Rwanda and of the Luba-Kasaayi (Zaire), or the dynastic praises of the Tswana, Zulu, Sotho, and Xhosa in South Africa (see SOUTH AFRICAN POETRY). This eulogistic lit. exhibits some elements of epic poetry, but in spite of the contentions of some scholars, these praises are not mere preliminaries to the devel. of epic. Nor does the present analysis focus on the cycles of thematically and stylistically converging tales that are constructed about animal protagonists, like Sangba Ture among the Zande (Sudan), or Ananse among the Ashanti (Ghana), or the *enfant terrible* tales of the Dogon, Mande, and San (West Africa). Many of these types of tales are difficult to classify because they are built around a trickster character, like Monimambu of the Kongo, Kabundi of the Luba, or Tiya among the Ngbandi (all in Zaire), where animal and human transformations continuously interplay. Some cycles which developed around a particular heroic character may well be the scattered and incomplete fragments of a sweeping, perhaps defunct, epic trad. Neither does this discussion focus special attention on the numerous historiographic accounts (e.g. those about chief Lubango among the Sanga-Kaonde [Zambia]); such texts are interlaced with the superhuman deeds of chiefs and clan founders, who headed the migrations into a new homeland, and these chiefs' subsequent power struggles and conquests.

The problems of relating these various genres to the major epic trads. remain unsolved; a clear picture has not emerged because of the uneven geographical and cultural coverage of the available texts and the often piecemeal and idiosyncratic approach that characterizes much of the study of Af. oral lit.

The focus here, then, must be on the long oral narratives sung and recited in Af. langs. and built around a historical or mythical or historico-mythical hero and his comitatus, his extraordinary powers and feats set within a framework of marvelous events, strange encounters, tensions, and warfare. Such narratives exhibit a number of thematic and stylistic features that are uncommon or sparse in the other Af. oral genres but are common in epic texts across world cultures.

Af. oral epics have now been recorded in a wide belt of populations ranging from the Gambia and Mali to Nigeria, in West Africa, to the Bantu-speaking peoples of Cameroun and Gabon and culminating among the Bantu-speaking peoples of Zaire. Among the principal epics now well documented are those in West Africa about Kaabu among the Mandinka of The Gambia, Sundyata (also Sunjata or Sonjara) among the Mande, Kambili among the Maninka, Silamaka of the Fulani, and Ozidi of the Ijaw in Nigeria. In West Central and Central Africa, there are the epics of Akoma Mba and Zwe Nguema among the Fang of Cameroun and Gabon. In Zaire the best-known epic narratives revolve around Lianja among the Mongo, Mwindo among the Nyanga, Mubila among the Lega, and Lofokefoke among the Langa-Mbole.

Most of these texts are available in the particular Af. langs. in which they are sung and in Fr., Eng., or Dutch translations (see section II below). They range in length from about 2000 lines (Sonjara) to 10,000 and more (Mubila of the Lega). Some are recorded in different versions recited and sung by several bards over a period of time (Lianja, Mwindo, Sonjara, Kaabu). The societies in which these epic trads. flourish differ widely in their social and political structures: some are politically centralized, others are segmentary lineage organizations or even more fragmented structures; some have sweeping trads. of migration and conquest, others lack such trads. beyond the concept of local movements of groups. However, several cultural features seem to cut across many of the epic-producing groups: hunting trads. are ritually and sociologically prominent (particularly in Zaire epics, hunting and animals play a major role); profound Pygmy influences have molded their past; initiation systems (involving puberty rites and complex cycles of male and female initiations into closed associations) are extremely elaborate; and none of the groups seems to have any developed pantheon of divinities (as distinct from ancestral and nature spirits, or named forces captured from the natural environment and placed in objects by ritual experts). Distinctions frequently made by critics between heroic, historical, shamanistic, and romantic epics cannot be taken literally. In epics where the main character resembles a fictionalized hero, there are nevertheless included many, sometimes subtle, historical details. In fact, as is the case for the Mubila epic of the Lega, the entire unspoken thrust of the narrative points to a time when the unifying bwami association had not yet established itself, i.e. to a time of local migratory movements, intergroup tensions and warfare, and violence in general. In addition, most of the epic heroes rely to some extent on magical devices with which they are born or which they have acquired.

The epic trads. among the various ethnic groups are very old. It is unthinkable, as has been suggested by some scholars, that the emergence of Af. epics was linked with Islamic and European contacts. In Zaire, epics are found among populations that were not affected by Islamic intrusions and where European influences had virtually no ideological impact. Recent work among the Nyanga and Lega leads to the conclusion that Pygmies and other hunters are at the root of the epics (see Biebuyck 1978, 1992).

The epics are traditional, meaning that their original authors are unknown; only the names of the actual singers and some of their predecessors whose trads. they perpetuate have come down to us. There seem to be two categories of singers: in some of the West Af. groups that have centralized and stratified sociopolitical systems, there are professional bards who travel over wide areas at the request of sponsors. In the Bantu-speaking groups, the singers are not professional in the sense that the recitation of the epic is not their primary or sole activity. Bards like Candi Rureke among the Nyanga and Mubila Kambara among the Lega are not members of a caste or an elite group but rather simple hunters and farmers who have developed unique literary, musical, and dramatic skills. Often this is the result of a somewhat unscheduled association with a person of similar skills from whom they learned themes and techniques as companions and assistants, rather than through any formal method. The casualness of the transmission process of the great epics accounts for the fact that, in the second part of the 20th c., as the result of changing social and educational patterns, very few persons could be found who in the minds of Af. listeners still had a full grasp of the intricate trad. In Nyanga society in the mid 1950s, virtually every man and woman could adequately tell tales, but apart from a handful of men who more or less knew the integral trad., there was only one Candi Rureke left. For this reason, our perspective on the distribution and importance of the epic in the past will always be blurred.

As is clear from the limited number of versions of a single epic trad., the singers are highly creative individuals. Although they operate with set characters, themes, plots, and stylistic devices, the singers shape their texts in unique ways by rearranging and recombining elements; reinventing topoi; expanding or reducing motives, plots, themes, and characters; and showing clearcut stylistic preferences. Moreover, even the most humble singers of epics have an unparalleled mastery of their lang., as illustrated in their vast vocabulary, their precision and refinement of word choice, their creative play with names and epithets, their delicate nuancing and shading of verbal conjugations, their handling of elisions and contractions, their inclusion of aphoristic statements and onomatopoeia, and their unusual changes in word order. In a pioneering stylistic analysis of the Mwindo epic, the Nyanga linguist Kahombo Mateene has convincingly shown the importance in the narrative of nine complex style patterns widely found in world epic trads. but only sparsely present in the other Af. genres. C. Seydou has equally emphasized the unique combinations of processes at work in structuring texts for West Af. epics.

The modes of presentation of the epics differ extensively from ethnic group to ethnic group, but there are certain common features. The bard performs for an audience that responds actively with exclamations of approval or disapproval and sings refrains to the songs. The bard, who himself may play a musical instrument, is accompanied by a small group of musicians (e.g. percussionists) and eventually by one or more apprentices, one of whom may act as the most active listener, encouraging the bard through praises and helping him when he has a problem. The text may be sung in its entirety, or sung and recited, or recited with interspersed songs. Some performances include dramatic action during the recitation, the bard enacting, often, some action in which the hero is involved. In most groups, the bard is also dressed, painted, and provided with appropriate paraphernalia for the occasion; for example, he may hold certain objects that suggest the power of the hero's possessions.

The occasions on which epic narratives are traditionally performed are something of a mystery. In areas with professional bards, it is obvious that the performances could be held when the political or ritual authority asks for them or at the bard's initiative; traditionally, the appropriate context might be the coronation or death of a chief or a periodic festival when group values are validated. In other societies with nonprofessional singers, the epic (in its entirety or in installments) can be sung as part of a general rejoicing, e.g. when the inhabitants of adjoining villages celebrate the successful outcome of a big net hunt or a large group of initiates is gathered for initiation rites. It is precisely in the latter context that the present writer heard Kambara Mubila sing the great Lega epic. Among the Mongo, epics are traditionally sung only throughout the night.

Whether the texts of the epics are formulated in rhythmic prose or verse or both, they show consummate mastery of the Af. langs. Hulstaert, who published a vast number of Mongo oral texts, marvels at the extraordinary quality of the verbal skills displayed in the Lianja epic. The bards are interested not merely in the rhythmic flow of the narration following distinctive patterns of line and syllable count, they look for sound effects: alliteration, sound-imitating words, sonorous names. Their constructions are built on recurring technical and stylistic devices: an abundance of names of actors (simple generic ones and descriptive inventions) and epithets; appositives and other descriptive terms for animals, places, and objects; patronymics and group affiliations; kinship and other enumerations; formulas for spatial movements and temporal sequences; repetitions and reduplicatives; lyrical evocations; and inversions of normal word order. The bards manipulate and arrange these devices in original and unexpected ways.

The thematic structures and plots follow a pattern. The hero is born under unusual circumstances (highly variable); the mother has special status (she is a virgin, or she has an unusually long pregnancy or a very short one); the unborn hero speaks in the womb. The hero is born abruptly and in an unusual manner; he is fully ready to confront a hostile world, holding at birth weapons or other objects with magical powers. He possesses certain medicines; he has extraordinary gifts (premonition, the capacity to be reborn, to metamorphosize himself, to travel quickly over great distances, or to hear things far away). He is not necessarily physically strong, but his attributes and certain persons in his entourage or the friendship of beings of the other world make him extremely powerful. The hero has a comitatus, large or small, often comprising powerful and very active women (a mother, a wife, a twin sister, a paternal aunt). His encounters with individuals and groups—humans, animals, monsters, extraterrestrial creatures—lead to challenge, trickery, and violent actions, in the course of which the hero often infringes the basic moral principles and values of his people. In some encounters, the hero may die or succumb, then come back to life through his own will or through some magical device used by a person close to him. Some epics end *in medias res*: the hero is already back in his village, celebrating with his people; in others, the hero disappears mysteriously or dies and is succeeded by a heroic son.

The basic outline of the epics is relatively simple. The Lianja epic among the Mongo (Zaire) starts with the ancestry of the hero, then dwells (in detail) on the hero's parents. The father dies at the hands of his enemies, leaving his wife pregnant. Soon after, she gives birth to insects and other things; the hero Lianja is then born by his own volition through his mother's shin. At birth he is fully prepared for battle, possessing the typical Mongo weapons and magical objects. Right after birth, he goes in search of his father's enemies, whom he defeats. He then begins a series of journeys, accompanied by his sister Nsongo, until he reaches the Zaire River; in the meantime, many groups in his comitatus have split off and settled as separate units in the vast equatorial forest. Having reached his final destination, Lianja, accompanied by his mother and twin sister, climbs a huge palm tree and disappears forever. The concluding parts of the Lianja epic, which differ considerably from version to version, usually deal with Lianja's descendants.

As far as their contents and purposes are concerned, the Af. epics are massive ethnographic documents about institutions, customs, thought patterns, and values. Some are explicit historical documents; in others the historical realities are reduced or latent, sometimes almost nonexistent. However, in some of the Bantu epics, the hero often acts as an anti-hero, somewhat like a much admired villain who continuously infringes on values and institutions until his task is finished and he is back in his village as a wise leader. Consequently, unless the epic contents are analyzed in depth and in a broad cultural context, the real information they provide is lost. The Lega hero Mubila, for example, hears on one of his travels drum messages. He decides to investigate what they are about. When he arrives, he learns that bwami initiations of a lower order are being held and abruptly decides that he too must be initiated. The result is catastrophic: the turmoil leads to violence and death, and the implication is that, in the end, Mubila has not been initiated. For the bard, who himself was an initiate of lower bwami grade, and for the numerous male and female initiates present at the performance, the hero acts here in total ignorance of, and nonconformity with, the values and sociolegal principles inherent in bwami initiations. He acts as a stranger or as a brute emerging from an earlier period of Lega culture, when bwami did not yet exist or was gradually being introduced. The negative behavior of the hero (who, it turns out later, is not even circumcised—an essential preliminary to initiation) is a powerful warning for the listeners that nobody, not even a hero, can profanate bwami rules and values. The information which the epics are intended to provide the listeners cannot be taken at face value, simply because of the many contradictions in a hero's life and attitude.

E. Boelaert, *Nsong'a Lianja* (1949), *Lianja Verhalen,* I: *Ekofo-Versie* (1957), *Lianja Verhalen,* II: *De Voorouders van Lianja* (1958); J. Jacobs, "Le Récit épique de Lofokefoke," *Aequatoria* 24 (1961); A. de Rop, *Lianja: L'Épopé des Mongo* (1964), *Versions et fragments de l'épоépes mongo* (1978); S. Awona, "La Guerre d'Akoma Mba contre Abo Mama," *Abbia* 9–10, 12–13 (1965, 1966); J. Knappert, "The Epic in Africa," *JFI* 4 (1967); D. Biebuyck and K. Mateene, *The Mwindo Epic from the Banyanga* (1969); P. Mufuta, *Le Chant kasala des Luba* (1969); F. Oinas, "Folk Epic," *Folklore and Folklife,* ed. R. Dorson (1972); H. Pepper, *Un Mvet de Zwe Nguema* (1972); C. Seydou, *Silamaka et Poullori: Récit épique peul* (1972), *La Geste de Ham-Bodedio, ou Hama le Rouge* (1976), "A Few Reflections on Narrative Structures of Epic Texts," *Research in Af. Langs.* 14 (1983); G. Innes, *Sunjata: Three Mandinka Versions* (1974); C. Bird et al., *The Songs of Seydou Camara,* I: *Kambili* (1976); J. Clark, *The Ozidi Saga* (1977); E. Belinga, *L'Épopés camerounaise mvet* (1978); D. Biebuyck, "The Af. Heroic Trad.," *Heroic Epic and Saga,* ed. F. Oinas (1978), *Hero and Chief Epic Lit. from the Banyanga* (1978), *The Mubila Epic from the Balega* (1992); I. Okpewho, *The Epic in Africa* (1979); V. Görög et al., *Histoires d'enfants terribles* (1980); V. Görög, *Litt. orale d'Afrique noire: Bibliographie analytique* (1981); A. de Rop and E. Boelaert, *Versioms et fragments de l'épopé mongo* (1983); K. Mateene, "Essai d'analyse stylistique de l'épopé de Mwindo," *Cahiers de litt. orale* 3 (1984); G. Hulstaert, *Het Epos van Lianja* (1985); J. Johnson, *The Epic of Son-Jara* (1986); K. Kesteloot, "The Af. Epic," *Af. Langs. and Cultures* 2 (1989). D.P.B.

II. IN EUROPEAN LANGUAGES. A. *In French.* The rise of Af. p. in Fr. cannot be understood without reference to the expansion of European imperialism and culture, in particular the slave trade and subsequent colonization of Africa. Nor can the tone of that poetry be appreciated without an awareness of the intense resentment those forces evoke, and the ambiguity that putting them into Fr. might arouse.

Histories of Af. p. in Fr. usually begin in the 1930s with the Négritude movement, but its roots extend further back. The Martinican students who published *Légitime défense* in Paris in 1932 were, after all, challenging the emulation of Western cultural norms and were therefore opposed to certain earlier black writers of poetry in Fr. By the same token, these young proponents of Négritude were themselves pursuing a trad. of soul-searching and revolt exemplified by the Haitians Pierre Faubert (b. 1803) and Oswald Durand (b. 1840), and a culture which took shape in the holds of slave ships and which spoke Af. langs. and creoles before Fr.

That one cites New World writers when defining Af. p. in Fr. is thus no accident. Both Africans and Afro-Americans have had to confront the same racist oppression; they have accordingly made common cause and sought out each other for inspiration and readership, despite real differences. Hence the importance of Harlem Renaissance figures like Langston Hughes and Claude McKay to the founders of Négritude; hence that, among the three poets who two years later established a second journal, *L'Etudiant Noir,* Aimé Césaire (b. 1913) of Martinique, Léon G. Damas (b. 1912) of Fr. Guiana, and Léopold Sédar Senghor (b. 1906), only the last was from Africa itself (Senegal). This tendency towards cross-fertilization with other black lits. has made Af. p. in Fr. intercontinental in scope. Though Césaire and Senghor and later poets repeatedly demonstrate their mastery of Fr. trad., they are drawn both to Third World lits. and to direct contact with Af. lits. This desire to renew traditional oral Af. poetic practice, expressed rhetorically by the theoreticians of Négritude, has become increasingly urgent among recent poets, who are, however, more aware of the difficulties such hybrid literary forms present.

There is no exhaustive definition for the term "Négritude." Coined by Césaire in his 1939 *Cahier d'un retour au pays natal* (Return to My Native Land), it is, in his words, "the simple recognition of the fact that one is black, the acceptance of this fact and of our destiny as blacks, of our history and our culture." But there is nothing simple about this statement; its implications are manifold, and the poetry which sought to express it took many forms, from Damas' explosive *Pigments* (1937) to Césaire's virulent defense of black culture in his *Cahier* and to Senghor's lofty exaltation of Af. values beginning with *Chants d'ombre* (1945). That it is impossible to separate Af. p. from politics is obvious from the positions embraced by the founders of Négritude in the '30s, but also by the fact that the movement was so closely connected to all sides of the anti-colonial movements. It should not be surprising that the literary and political outlines of Fr.-speaking anti-colonialism took shape in postwar Paris and that a third major journal, *Présence Africaine,* was founded there by the Senegalese Alioune Diop: not until actual decolonization were Africans able to shift focus from the former metropolis, but Paris still weighs heavily upon Af. lits. in Fr.

The landmark publication of the postwar period was Senghor's *Anthologie de la nouvelle poésie nègre et malgache de langue française* (1948), with its influential preface by Jean-Paul Sartre, "Orphée noir." In Sartre's view, Négritude was but an antithesis, a second phase of reaction to white racism which, while defending the specificity of black culture, did so only in view of a final synthesis, the transition to a universal (in Sartre's version, proletarian) culture with no oppressors and, ultimately, no specificity. Sartre's perspective was at odds with that of Senghor himself, but it proved to be even more influential and set the grounds for Frantz Fanon's dialectical typology of colonial cultures in *Les Damnés de la terre* (The Wretched of the Earth, 1961), upon which most interps. of post-colonial lit. hist. repose. Indeed, it is common, though sometimes reductive, to apply Fanon's pattern of Af. p. in Fr.—i.e. to conceive of (1) a colonial period of slavish imitation of Western models, (2) a period of revolt, exemplified by Négritude, and (3) a post-colonial period in which Africans have taken control of their own culture.

As for the poets represented in the Senghor *Anthologie,* they are more complex and rewarding than any system might suggest. Though better known as a storyteller, Birago Diop (1906–89) proved himself as a poet. A brilliant talent lost at an early age, David-Mandessi Diop (1927–61) is still revered for his vehemently anti-assimilationist *Coups de pilon.* Evidence that Af. p. in Fr. extended far beyond the founding fathers of Négritude was the inclusion of the Malagasy poets Jean-Joseph Rabéarivélo (1901–37), Jacques Rabemananjara (b. 1913), and Flavien Ranaivo (b. 1914). The first of these, a unique talent who survived in utter isolation from other poets and ideologues, took his own life after producing strikingly original works.

Independence brought a sea change of sensibility to Francophone Africa. It is too simple to claim that the once-external white enemy became internal and black, for neo-colonialism and imperialism have remained major themes since the early 1960s, and condemnation of the West has by no means abated. Still, many writers did turn from the clear commitments of anti-colonialism to more ambiguous and ambitious poetic projects, and this new mood is evident in the 1966 *Présence Africaine* anthology *Nouvelle somme de poésie du monde noire,* not only among the then-younger or lesser-known voices, like Charles Nokan (pseud. Zégoua Konan, b. 1936) and J. M. Bognini (b. 1936) from the Ivory Coast, Annette M. Baye (b. 1926) from Senegal, and Yambo Ouologuem (b. 1940) from Mali, but also among established ones like B. Dadié (b. 1916) from the Ivory Coast, Edouard Maunick (b. 1931) from Mauritius, and Francis Bebey (b. 1929) and René Philombe (b. 1930) from Cameroun. Foremost among them is Tchicaya U Tam'si (1931–88), whose dense and difficult *oeuvre* combines the most contemp. poetic techniques with an anguished concern for the Congo and the ravages of colonialism, esp. in his 1962 *Epitomé.* It is against the dominating figure of Tchicaya that recent Af. Fr.-lang. poets are measured, be they his fellow Congolese Henri Lopès (b. 1937) and J. B. Tati-Loutard (b. 1939), or Cheikh Aliou Ndao (b. 1933) from Senegal. It appears, in fact, that the People's Republic of the Congo has acted in recent decades much as Paris did earlier—as a focal point and a literary clearinghouse for production in Fr. across the continent. Thus the importance of J. B. Tati-Loutard's 1976 *Anthologie de la littérature congolaise d'expression française.*

Though Négritude was a primer, Af. p. in Fr. is now neither limited to nor coterminous with it. Recent poets have been both more universal in scope and more particular. There is now a proliferation of individual national lits. in Fr. Critical studies and anthologies exist for Benin, Cameroun, the Congo, Gabon, the Ivory Coast, Senegal, Togo, and Zaire. It has seemed to some that this parceling up of a continent into national lits. may be too rash, may ignore the common heritage and political realities of the continent, and may thereby serve the interest of the elite in quest of fiefs to rule. Be that as it may, Af. p. in Fr. will doubtless continue to express the vast diversity of Africa and to offer, in doing so, some of the most exciting and moving poetry in that lang.

ANTHOLOGIES: *Poètes d'expression française,* ed. L. Damas (1947); *An Anthol. of Af. and Malagasy Poetry in Fr.,* ed. C. Wake (1965); *Anthologie négro-africaine,* ed. L. Kesteloot (1967); *Anthologie de la litt. gabonaise,* Ministère de l'Education Nationale (1978); *Anthologie de la poésie togolaise,* ed. Y.-E. Dogbe (1980); *Poèmes de demain: Anthologie de la poésie camerounaise de langue française,* ed. P. Dakeyo (1982); *Anthologie de la litt. ivoirienne,* ed. A. Kone et al. (1983).

HISTORY AND CRITICISM: L. Kesteloot, *Les Écrivains noirs de langue fr.,* 3d ed. (1967; Eng. tr. by E. C. Kennedy, 1974); S. Adotevi, *Négritudes et négrologues* (1972); D. Herdeck, *Af. Authors* (1973); R. Cornevin, *Litts. d'Afrique noire de langue française* (1976); A. S. Gérard, *Études de litt. africaine francophone* (1977), ed., *European-Lang. Writing in Sub-Saharan Africa,* 2 v. (1986); R. and A. Chemain, *Panorama critique de la litt. congolais contemporaine* (1979); *Dictionnaire des oeuvres litts. négro-africaines de langue française,* ed. A. Kom (1983); A. Huannou, *La Litt. béninoise de langue française* (1984); J. B. Kubayanda, *The Poet's Africa* (1990).

G.L.

B. *In Portuguese.* Ironically, Af. p. in Port. (also known as Lusophone Af. p.), despite the fact that it appeared first, is lesser known than its counterparts in Eng. and Fr. In 1849, José da Silva Maia Ferreira, an obscure Angolan, probably of Port. heritage, published in Luanda his *Espontaneidades da minha alma* (Outpourings from My Soul), dedicated to "Af. ladies," the first collection of poems printed in Lusophone Af. and possibly in all of the sub-Saharan region. Both the lesser status of Port. as a world lang. and the closed nature of Lisbon's Af. colonies have contributed to world ignorance of the lits. of Angola, Mozambique, Cape Verde, Guinea-Bissau, and São Tomé e Príncipe. Since the colonies achieved independence (1974–75), however, students of Af. lit. have increasingly turned their attention to these countries' unique poetries, written mainly in Port. but also (as in the case of Cape Verde, Guinea-Bissau, and São Tomé) in local Port.-based creoles.

Precursors such as Ferreira, Joaquim Cordeiro da Matta (1857–94), an early black Angolan poet, and Caetano da Costa Alegre (1864–90) from the Island of São Tomé, wrote verse modeled on European styles and themes, but often from an Af. consciousness. Some wrote verse reflecting their sense of social reformism and dedication to Republican liberalism. Beginning, however, in the 1930s in Cape Verde and in the 1950s in Angola and Mozambique, poems of cultural legitimization and growing social protest, fanned by the winds of nationalism, characterized the literary movements initiated by members of an emerging black and *mestiço* (mixed-race) intelligentsia and their Af.-born or -raised white allies.

On the largely *mestiço* Cape Verde islands in 1936, a trio of poets, Jorge Barbosa (1902–71), Oswaldo Alcântara (pseud. of Baltasar Lopes da Silva, 1907–89), and Manuel Lopes (b. 1907), founded what has come to be known as the Claridade movement, so named for the group's arts and culture journal. Under the influence of Brazilian modernism and Northeast regionalism, Barbosa first codified his islands' creole ethos. He gave artistic expression to the prevailing Cape Verdean themes of solitude, the sea, drought, and emigration with poems like "Momento" (Only a Moment):

> This our
> refined melancholy
> arising from I know not what
> a little perhaps
> from the solitary hours
> wafting over the island
> or from the music
> of the opposing sea.

In the Angolan cities of Benguela and esp. Luanda, cultural revindication erupted with thinly veiled nationalist fervor (censorship and police repression precluded outspoken militancy) among black, *mestiço*, and not a few white poets, some of whom would form the nucleus of the Movement of the Liberation of Angola (MPLA) founded in 1956. Poets like Agostinho Neto (1922–79), Angola's first president, Viriato da Cruz (1928–73), António Jacinto (b. 1924), Costa Andrade (b. 1936), and M. António (1934–89) produced poems that called for an Af. Angola. Many militant poets, in Mozambique as well as Angola, took to the bush as guerrilla fighters. Others fled into exile or paid for their militancy with imprisonment.

Throughout the 1960s and until the 1974 coup that toppled the Lisbon government, much Af. p. in Port. went underground. Militants distributed their poems clandestinely or contented themselves with seeing them published abroad. Neto, writing surreptitiously in his Port. prison cell, promised, in his poem "Havemos de voltar," that we shall return "to the sounds of the marimbas and finger pianos / to our carnival." Friends spirited this and other of Neto's poems out of Aljube prison to Kinshasa, Dar-Es-Salaam, Milan, and Belgrade where they were published in bilingual editions. Only after independence did they emerge from secrecy and "return" legitimately to Angola.

In Portugal's former East Af. colony of Mozambique, during the two or so decades prior to national independence, a few Europeans produced poetry, some of it very good, but more a conscious part of Port. lit. than of Mozambique's incipient literary expression. Starting in the 1960s, a few of these Euro-Mozambicans, most notably Rui Knopfli (b. 1933), born and raised in the colonial city of Lourenço Marques (now Maputo), sought to capture the essence of an Af.-European experience. As might be expected, however, a poetry of Af. cultural and racial essentialism, whether by black, mixed-race, or black Mozambicans, coincided with the rise of nationalism in the 1950s and '60s. Thus the *mestiço* poets José Craveirinha (b. 1922) and Noémia de Sousa (b. 1926) wrote a number of memorable poems of cultural revindication. Craveirinha, Mozambique's most celebrated poet, raised his voice with fervor in "Manifesto":

> Oh!
> My beautiful short kinky hair
> and my black eyes
> great moons of wonderment on the
>   most beautiful night
> of the most unforgettably beautiful
>   nights of the lands of the Zambeze.

Not altogether surprisingly, true Négritude poetry appeared in Lisbon. And Francisco José Tenreiro (1921–63), a *mestiço* from the island of São Tomé who lived most of his short life in Lisbon, emerged as the greatest writer of Négritude poetry in Port. Under the influence of the Harlem Renaissance, Afro-Cuban Negrism, and Francophone poets such as Senghor and Césaire, Tenreiro wrote the poems published posthumously as *Coração em África* (My Heart in Africa, 1964).

Some Angolan writers have proclaimed that their poetry was born in the struggle for liberation, while Négritude was spawned in defeat as a European-based phenomenon that had little to do with Africa. During the decade of anti-colonialist wars in Angola, Mozambique, and Guinea-Bissau, poetry became increasingly combative and tendentious. Marcelino dos Santos (b. 1929), a high-ranking member of the Mozambique Liberation Movement (FRELIMO), was at the forefront of militant poets who wrote pamphletary verse that during the protracted war served as a didactic instrument as well as a goad to political mobilization.

In the early years after independence (1975), a multiracial array of poets began seeking new forms for new content. In Angola, Manuel Rui (b. 1941) wrote, in "Poesia necessária" (Essential Poetry):

> Of new words is a country also made
> in this country so made of poems
> that production and all else to sow
> in another cycle will have to be sung.

The imperative of new discourses for new stories led Rui, along with fellow Angolans such as Arlindo Barbeitos (b. 1941), Rui Duarte de Carvalho (b. 1941), Jofre Rocha (b. 1941), and David Mestre (b. 1948), to form the basis of a new poetry. In Mozambique, Rui Nogar (b. 1933) and Luis Carlos Patraquim (b. 1953); in Cape Verde Corsino Fortes (b. 1933), Oswaldo Osório (b. 1937), and Arménio Vieira (b. 1941); in Guinea-Bissau Helder Proença (b. 1956); and in São Tomé Frederico Augusto dos Anjos (b. 1954) have all attempted, with varying degrees of success, to create such a new poetry. In Angola Carvalho has experimented with an integrated form of Af. oral expression and Brazilian concrete poetry; his compatriot Barbeitos has sought to attain that poetic measure between things and words:

in the forest
of your eyes
one sees only night
in the night
of the leopard
one sees only eyes.

By the close of the 1980s, and in spite of continuing civil war in Angola and Mozambique and of varying degrees of economic woe in all of the former colonies, Af. p. in Port. had achieved both quantity and quality. Since independence, the lang. of this poetry has accelerated its evolution into five variants of a uniquely Af. expression of potentially international appeal. Among the most promising of the cultivators of this lang. are: from Angola, Rui Augusto (b. ca. 1950), Paula Tavares (b. 1952), José Luís Mendonça (b. 1955), and Ana de Santana (b. 1960); from Mozambique, Luís Carlos Patraquim (b. 1953), Hélder Muteia (b. 1960), Armando Artur (b. 1962), and Eduardo White (b. 1964); and from Cape Verde, José L. Hopffer Almada (b. ca. 1958), who organized *Mirabilis*, an anthology of work by some 60 island poets (pub. 1991).

BIBLIOGRAPHY: *Bibliografia das lit. af. de expressão port.*, ed. G. Moser and M. Ferreira (1983).

ANTHOLOGIES: *No reino de Caliban: Antologia panorâmica da poesia africana de expressão portuguesa*, ed. M. Ferreira, v. 1: *C. Verde e G.-Bissau* (1975), v. 2: *Angola e S. Tomé e Portugal* (1976), v. 3: *Moç.* (1986); *Antologia temática de poesia af.*, ed. M. de Andrade, v. 1: *Na noite grávida de punhais* (1976), v. 2: *O canto armado* (1979); *Poems from Angola*, tr. M. Wolfers (1979); *A Horse of White Clouds*, tr. D. Burness (1989).

HISTORY AND CRITICISM: G. Moser, *Essays in Port.-Af. Lit.* (1969); R. Hamilton, *Voices from an Empire: A Hist. of Afro.-Port. Lit.* (1975), *Lit. af., lit. necessária*, v. 1: *Angola* (1981), v. 2: *Moç., C. Verde, G.-Bissau, S. Tomé e Portugal* (1983); M. Ferreira, *Lit. af. de expressão port.*, 2 v. (1977). R.G.H.

C. *In English.* With the end of the colonial period and the concomitant advance of literacy and higher education came a rapid efflorescence of Af. p. written in Eng. This poetry displays the variety to be expected in so diverse a continent, and regional styles have arisen; nevertheless, the most eminent poets have created an international community of poetic values and influences.

In general, Af. p. in Eng. eschews rhyme in favor of alliteration and assonance. Instead of metrical verse, rhythms directly governed by syntax, logic, or rhet. determine line length. Ambiguity is more often syntactic than lexical. The same austerity leads to avoidance of extended conceits unless they are buttressed by hard or sardonic reason or concrete imagery. Oral and other traditional poetry influence recent Af.-Eng. poems primarily in such fundamental elements as the poet's stance as defender of communal values; allusions to the hist., customs, and artifacts of the culture; and the architectonic features adapted from praise song, proverbial tale, epic, and prayer. Experiments in the transmutation of traditional Af. poetic forms into Eng. vary with the culture represented. The internationally published poets, of course, display a mastery of the trads. of mod. Eng. and Am. poetry; one indication of their freedom from these forms, however, is the occurrence of dramas and novels written partly or entirely in verse.

West Africa, particularly Nigeria and Ghana, has the oldest and most influential trad. of sophisticated poetry in Eng. This lyric poetry combines audacious leaps of thought and individualized expression with social responsibility; it privileges the metaphysical, religious, and social concepts of its own society rather than concepts indigenous to European cultural hist. When social protest is overt, it is usually presented with intellectual and artistic complexity rather than simplistic fervor. Exemplary Nigerian poets include Christopher Okigbo (1932–67; *Labyrinths*), John Pepper Clark (b. 1935; *Reed in the Tide*; *Casualties*; *A Decade of Tongues*; *The State of the Union*), and the Nobel Prize winner, Wole Soyinka (b. 1934; *Idandre*; *Shuttle in the Crypt*), whose plays often include poetry. Less obscure and idiosyncratic in form, allusions, and thought are the poetry of Gabriel Okara (b. 1921; *The Fisherman's Invocation*) and, from Gambia, Lenrie Peters (b. 1932; *Satellites*; *Katchikali*; *Selected Poetry*).

Among Ghanaians, experiments in the tr. and adaptation of Af. poetic forms are increasingly common, as in the works of Kofi Awoonor (b. 1935; *Rediscovery: Night of My Blood*; *Guardians of the Sacred Word*; *Ride Me, Memory*; *The House by the Sea*), Kofi Anyidoho (*Elegy for the Revolution*; *A Harvest of Our Dreams*; *Oral Poetics*), and Atukwei (John) Okai (b. 1941; *Oath of the Fontomfrom*; *Lorgorlogi Logarithms*). Closer to Western trads. of sensibility and structure are others such as Kwesi Brew (b. 1924; *The Shadows of Laughter*, *Af. Panorama*), Albert W. Kayper-Mensah (1923–80; *The Dark Wanderer*, *The Drummer in Our Time*, *Sankofa: Adinkra Poems*; *Proverb Poems*; *Akwaaba*), Kojo Laing (*Godhorse*), Frank Kobina Parkes (b. 1932; *Songs from the Wilderness*), and Joe de Graft (1924–78; *Beneath the Jazz and Brass*). Among the poets from Sierra Leone we should mention Syl Cheyney-Coker (b. 1945; *Concerto for an Exile*; *The Graveyard Also Has Teeth*) and Lemuel Johnson (b. 1940; *Highlife for Caliban*; *Hard on the Navel*).

East Af. p. is dominated by two styles. One originated in Okot p'Bitek's tr. and adaptation of his own Acholi poetry. P'Bitek (1931–82; *Song of Lawino*; *Song of Ocul*; *Song of Prisoner*, *Song of Malaya*; *Hare and Hornbill*) is probably the most widely read poet of Af. Through long rhetorical monologues usually narrated by a victim of modernization, these poems express social commentary with lucid, graphic imagery, humorous irony, and paradoxical common sense. Another such poet is Okello Oculi (b. 1942; *Orphan*; *Malak*; *Kanta Riti*; *Kookolem*). The other style, more indebted to West Af. p., uses asyndeton, subtler imagery, and more erudite allusions to convey a mordant and individualized vision of mod. life. It includes a wider range of subjects, tones, and frames of reference. Pre-eminent poets include Jared Angira (b. 1947; *Juices*; *Silent Voices*; *Soft Corals*; *Cascades*; *The Years Go By*), Richard Ntiru (b. 1946; *Tensions*), and Taban lo Liyong (*Meditations in Limbo*; *Franz Fanon's Uneven Ribs*; *Eating Chiefs*; *Another Nigger Dead*; *13 Offensives against Our Enemies*).

South Af. p. (q.v.) of necessity is most concerned with subjugation, courage, poverty, prisons, revolt, and the private griefs of public injustice. South Af. poets writing in Eng. before the 1970s were often exiles, whose works therefore also reflected British or Am. experience—e.g. Arthur Nortje (1942–70; *Dead Roots*), Cosmo Pieterse (b. 1930; *Echo and Choruses: "Ballad of the Cells"*), and esp. Dennis Brutus (b. 1924; *Sirens, Knuckles and Boots*; *Letters to Martha*; *Poems for Algiers*; *China Poems*; *A Simple Lust*; *Strains*; *Salutes and Censures*; *Stubborn Hope*). In this poetry the speaker is often an observer combining passionate concern with reflective distance, and the imagery portrays monstrous abuse in natural and social settings of oblivious serenity.

The experimental adaptation of regional Af. forms to original poetry in the Eng. lang. is best represented by the work of Mazisi Kunene (b. 1930; *Zulu Poems*; *Anthem of the Decades*; *Emperor Shaka the Great: A Zulu Epic*; *The Ancestors and the Sacred Mountain*).

The exile Keroapetse Kgositsile (b. 1938; *Spirits Unchained*; *For Melba*; *My Name Is Afrika*; *The Present Is a Dangerous Place to Live*; *Herzspuren*) and also Oswald Mbuyiseni Mtshali (b. 1940; *Sounds of a Cowhide Drum*; *Fireflames*) are forerunners of the dramatic change in and copious output of Af. p. since 1970. Written in South Af. and addressed primarily to fellow South Africans, recent poetry has a more direct militancy which nevertheless meets the dictates of both state censorship and poetic grace. It is more lyrical than hortatory. Rhythms, imagery, narrative events, and sensibility are firmly rooted in quotidian deprivations and defiance. The influence of Afro-Am. musical and poetic forms, esp. jazz, the blues, and the renaissance of the 1960s, looking back to the Harlem Renaissance is often evident (see AFRO-AMERICAN POETRY). Immediacy may be reinforced by including phrases from South Af. langs. or Afrikaans or by directly addressing the reader as a compatriot. Neither reader nor speaker is presented as impartial observer or judge. Because it is the poetry of a people seeking liberation, this poetry is marked by local detail, unromanticized factuality, emphasis on the political consequence of individual choice, and above all by the pervasive assumption that these tragedies will someday yield to victory. Major writers include Mongane Serote (b. 1944; *Yakhal'Inkomo*; *Tsetlo*; *No Baby Must Weep*; *Behold Mama, Flowers*; *The Night Keeps Winking*), Sipho Sepamla (b. 1932; *Hurry Up to It!*; *The Blues Is You in Me*; *The Soweto I Love*; *The Root Is One; Children of the Earth*; *Selected Poems*), Mafika Pascal Gwala (b. 1946; *Jol'unkomo*; *No More Lullabies*), James Matthews (b. 1929; *Cry Rage*; *Pass Me a Meatball, Jones*; *Images*; *No Time for Dreams / Feelings*), Daniel P. Kunene (*A Seed Must Seem to Die*; *Pirates Have Become Our Kings*), and Wopko Pieter Jensma (b. 1939; *Sing for Our Execution*; *Where White Is the Colour Where Black Is the Number*; *I Must Show You My Clippings*).

Politics and economics have denied wide international audience to the poetry of South Africa's Anglophone neighbors. From Malawi, David Rubadiri (b. 1930) and Frank M. Chipasula (b. 1949; *Visions and Reflections*; *O Earth Wait for Me*; *Nightwatcher, Nightsong*) have voice only through exile. Jack Mapanje (*Of Chameleons and Gods*) writes from within Malawi. Zambians like Richard A. Chima (b. 1945; *The Loneliness of a Drunkard*) and Patu Simoko (b. 1951; *Africa Is Made of Clay*) speak from within and with greater freedom. Zimbabwe has produced copious poetry reflecting both the price of liberating warfare and the consequences of victory. Pre-eminent poets include Samuel Chimsoro (b. 1949; *Smoke and Flames*), Charles Mungoshi (b. 1947; *The Milkman Doesn't Only Deliver Milk*), Musaemura Zimunya (b. 1949; *Thought-Tracks*; *Kingfisher, Jikinya and Other Poems*), Shimmer Chinodya (b. 1957), and Mudereri Kadhani.

With important national and individual differences, the poetry of Southern Africa still has a strikingly identifiable character. It is everywhere premised on an intense affinity for the land, and through that, a close union between the spiritual and physical worlds. Nature is presented as a manifestation of religious forces but is also treated with a more direct, nonsymbolic sensibility than in other Af. p. Poet and personae are more closely identified with their community through a diction which relies on direct address to reader as putative interlocutor, conversational apostrophe, quiet humor, anaphora, irony, and avoidance of strident, vitriolic or erudite effects. Esoteric lyricism and declamation are both rare. The stresses which urban cultures impose upon rural life and upon personal values and identity are common themes, as well as the systemic effects of past and current colonial hegemony. In form and themes, the poetry of this region adapts Eng. to provide sophisticated but unaffected articulation of traditional Af. worldviews in a context of rapid social change.

Despite its immense cultural and individual variety, one can hear a distinctive Af. voice in Af. p. in Eng. It maintains close identification with communal values and experience while conveying personal perceptions. A tone of responsible sincerity is everywhere demanded and achieved through elaborate technique and studied experimentation with the Eng. lang. Shared metaphysical, ethical, and aesthetic visions are sources for its vigor and originality.

BIBLIOGRAPHIES: *Bibl. of Creative Af. Writing*, comp. J. Janheinz et al. (1971); *Black Af. Lit. in Eng.* (1979), and *Supplement to Black Af. Lit. in Eng. 1977–1982* (1985), both ed. B. Lindfors; *New Reader's Guide to Af. Lit.*, ed. H. M. Zell et al., 2d ed. (1983); *Companion to South Af. Eng. Lit.*, comp. D. Adey et al. (1986).

ANTHOLOGIES: *West Af. Verse*, ed. D. Nwoga (1966); *Poems from East Africa*, ed. D. Cook et al. (1971); *The Word Is Here: Poetry from Mod. Africa*, ed. K. Kgositsile (1973); *Poems of Black Africa*, ed. W. Soyinka (1975); *A World of Their Own: South Af. Poets of the Seventies*, ed. S. Gray (1976); *Intro. to East Af. P.*, ed. J. Kariara et al. (1977); *Zimbabwean Poetry in Eng.*, ed. K. Z. Muchemwa (1978); *Af. P. in Eng.*, ed. S. H. Burton et al. (1979); *Summons: Poems from Tanzania*, ed. R. S. Mabala (1980); *Somehow We Survive*, ed. S. Plumpp (1982); *The Return of the Amasi Bird*, ed. T. Couzens et al. (1982); *A New Book of Af. Verse*, ed. J. Reed et al. (1984); *The Heritage of Af. P.*, ed. I. Okpewho (1984); *The Penguin Book of Mod. Af. P.*, ed. G. Moore et al., 3d ed. (1984); *When My Brothers Come Home: Poems from Central and Southern Africa*, ed. F. M. Chipasula (1985); *The Fate of Vultures*, ed. M. Zimunya et al. (1989).

HISTORY AND CRITICISM: A. Roscoe, *Mother Is Gold: A Study of West Af. Lit.* (1971), *Uhuru's Fire: Af. Lit. East to South* (1977); O. R. Dathorne, *The Black Mind: A Hist. of Af. Lit.* (1974); K. Awoonor, *The Breast of the Earth* (1975); R. N. Egudu, *Four Mod. West Af. Poets* (1977); G. Moore, *Twelve Af. Writers* (1980); K. L. Goodwin, *Understanding Af. P.: A Study of Ten Poets* (1982); T. Olafioye, *Politics in Af. P.* (1984); T. O. McLoughlin et al., *Insights: An Intro. to the Crit. of Zimbabwean and Other Poetry* (1984); A. Z. Davies et al., *How to Teach Poetry: An Af. Perspective* (1984); J. Alvarez-Pereyre, *The Poetry of Commitment in South Africa*, tr. C. Wake (1984); U. Barnett, *A Vision of Order: A Study of Black South Af. Lit. in Eng. (1914–1980)* (1985); R. Fraser, *West Af. P.: A Crit. Hist.* (1986); *European-Lang. Writing in Sub-Saharan Africa*, ed. A. S. Gérard, 2 v. (1986); E. Ngara, *Ideology and Form in Af. Poetry* (1990).

D.F.D.

AFRIKAANS POETRY. See SOUTH AFRICAN POETRY.

AFRO-AMERICAN POETRY. Though it did not begin to enter the established Am. canon until the 1930s, the Afro-Am. trad. in poetry reaches back into the 18th c. and may be said to have had its beginning when Lucy Terry (1728–1821), a slave owned by one Ebenezer Wells of Deerfield, Mass., composed a semiliterate poem ("Bars Fight") of 28 lines describing how Indians attacked Deerfield in August of 1746. And she in turn was followed by Jupiter Hammon (1711–86?), who spent his life as a slave of Henry Lloyd's family in Queen's Village, Long Island, New York. Hammon appears to have been a man of considerable intelligence, and one who attained some measure of prestige among the slaves in his neighborhood for his power as a preacher in their religious services. Indeed, it is the voice of the homilist that we hear in the handful of poems he produced, as they echo the Methodist hymnody on which he had been reared.

It is, however, Phillis Wheatley (ca. 1753–84) who is the major figure among Am. Black poets of the 18th c. Though in their silence about her many of the standard literary histories simply erase her from the trad., she was in fact one of the more notable writers of the Colonial period, and after the publication of her *Poems on Various Subjects, Religious and Moral* in London in 1773, she won a more substantial European reputation than any other Am. poet of her time.

Phillis was brought to the Colonies after being kidnapped by slave traders in the region today embracing the African states of Senegal and Gambia, and, as a 7- or 8-year-old child, she was purchased on a Boston dock in 1761 by the wife of a wealthy tailor, John Wheatley, in whose household she was gently and carefully reared. After little more than a year of residence with the Wheatley family, she was reading Eng. so well as to be able easily to make her way through the more difficult passages of the Bible. She began her study of Lat. at the age of 12 and was soon rendering Eng. trs. of Ovid in heroic couplets. But it was Alexander Pope who early became her great poetic model, and much of her work clearly reveals how decisive was his influence. Though hers was a poetry infinitely more sophisticated than Jupiter Hammon's, it too reflects a deep commitment to the Christian faith; her first published poem, "On the Death of the Reverend Mr. George Whitefield" (1770), expresses the hope that the people of her ancestral community will accept the Christian evangel:

> Take him, ye *Africans*, he longs for you;
> *Impartial Saviour* is his title due;
> Wash'd in the fountain of redeeming
>   blood,

You shall be sons, and kings, and
priests to God.

Her poetry is by no means much given over to racial themes, but, unlike Hammon, Wheatley did not hesitate forthrightly to express at once her devotion to liberty and her abhorrence of slavery; and both find expression in her poem "To the Right Honorable William, Earl of Dartmouth, His Majesty's Principal Secretary of State for North America":

Should you, my lord, while you peruse
my song,
Wonder from whence my love of Free-
dom sprung,
Whence flow these wishes for the com-
mon good,
By feeling hearts alone best under-
stood;
I, young in life, by seeming cruel fate
Was snatch'd from Afric's fancy'd
happy seat;
What pangs excruciating must molest,
What sorrows labor in my parent's
breast?
Steel'd was that soul and by no misery
mov'd
That from a father seiz'd his babe be-
lov'd;
Such, such my case. And can I then
but pray
Others may never feel tyrannic sway?

Given her time and her place, it was, of course, virtually inevitable that her poetic idioms should be wholly derivative from neoclassical norms, and the imitativeness of her work is not to be gainsaid. Yet one feels that Thomas Jefferson's remark, in his *Notes on the State of Virginia*, that her work is "below the dignity of crit.," reflects more than anything else—particularly when considered in relation to its immediate context in the *Notes*—how abysmal was his regular failure of imagination when Blacks were in view. For what is surely the more appropriate response to Wheatley's achievement is marveling astonishment at the swiftness and ease with which this young African's prodigious intelligence so thoroughly took possession of the New England culture of her period as to permit her becoming one unsurpassed as a poet in her moment of Am. history.

Nor was the South unrepresented in this early Afro-Am. trad., for one of its strongest exemplars is George Moses Horton, originally a slave belonging to James Horton, whose plantation was near Chapel Hill, N.C. He is thought to have been born in the year 1797 (d. 1883?), and his first volume of poems, *The Hope of Liberty*, had already been issued by 1829; a second ed. was published in 1837 under the title *Hope of Liberty—Poems by a Slave*. In 1845 his second volume, *The Poetical Works of George M. Horton*, appeared; and his third volume, *Naked Genius*, was published in 1865, the year in which Horton at last won his freedom. How he came to master the arts of reading and writing remains something of a mystery, but the pedagogic method was doubtless self-administered (as would almost certainly have had to be the case, the bestowal of literacy on slaves having been prohibited by law throughout the ante-bellum South). Though his poetry is not without a richly humorous vein and scans a variety of interests and experience, what is particularly remarkable is the passionate candor with which he speaks of the terrible indignities entailed by his servitude. Whereas Wheatley's themes generally touch not at all the human condition as it was known by Black slaves, Horton boldly expresses throughout much of his work an uncowed militancy of spirit in his cries of outrage at the cruel disadvantage suffered by his kind, and his characteristic tone is expressed in the poem "On Liberty and Slavery":

Alas! and am I born for this,
To wear this slavish chain?
Deprived of all created bliss,
Through hardship, toil and pain.

. . . .

Oh, Heaven! and is there no relief
This side the silent grave—
To soothe the pain—to quell the grief
And anguish of a slave?

These early Black poets were followed by a steady succession through the 19th c., incl. such figures as Frances Ellen Watkins Harper (1825–1911), James M. Whitfield (1830–70), and Albery A. Whitman (1851–1902). But it was not until 1896, after Paul Laurence Dunbar's third volume, *Lyrics of Lowly Life*, that a Black poet won a national audience, partly (in Dunbar's case) as a result of the endorsement offered by the novelist and critic William Dean Howells, then widely influential in Am. literary life as the editor of the *Atlantic Monthly*. Though he produced several novels and a sizable body of short stories, Dunbar (1872–1906) is today chiefly thought of as a lyricist in dialect poetry of Black peasant life. In this there is a certain irony, for his deep affection for the poetry of Keats, Shelley, and Tennyson led him to invest by far his greatest efforts in poems written in standard Eng., these making up more than half of his total poetic production. They reveal him to have been a gifted minor poet who, had his life not been cut short at 33 years of age, might well have grown very considerably in stature. But it was his dialect poems—"When Malindy Sings," "When de Co'n Pone's Hot," "Little Brown Baby," and a vast number of others—which had a great vogue in his lifetime, this so embittering him that in one of his late poems ("The Poet") he is led to say:

He sang of love when earth was young
And Love itself was in his lays.

But ah, the world, it turned to praise
A jingle in a broken tongue.

With the exception of James Weldon Johnson (1871–1938), for the Black poets after Dunbar who came to the fore in the first quarter of the 20th c.—such figures as William Stanley Braithwaite (1878–1982), Angelina Grimke (1880–1958), Georgia Douglas Johnson (1886–1966), and Claude McKay (1889–1948)—the plantation and minstrel trads. which his dialect poems had mined carried no appeal. Indeed, they felt them to make not only for sentimentality and bathos but also for a general depreciation of the dignity of the human image in Black life. Even Weldon Johnson, though he put to the finest kind of use the rhythms and intonations of Black folk sermons in his splendid volume of 1927, *God's Trombones*, was careful to liberate his material from dialectal idioms, while at the same time retaining the distinctive flavor of the Black pulpit; and he was certain that it was only by way of this kind of transformation that folk material could be made truly to fecundate a sophisticated art.

By the late 1920s an extraordinary efflorescence of talent among Black writers was bursting upon the scene, and since many of the more prominent figures—James Weldon Johnson, Claude McKay, Jean Toomer (1894–1967), Jessie Fauset (1882–1961), Rudolph Fisher (1897–1934), Arna Bontemps (1902–73), Wallace Thurman (1902–34), Nella Larsen (1891–1964), Zora Neale Hurston (1891–1960)—had one or another kind of connection with New York City's Harlem, this whole insurgency has come to be spoken of as the Harlem Renaissance. Its literary expressions were largely in the medium of prose fiction, but (apart from Johnson and McKay, who, being older, had won recognition earlier) there were three notable young poets who were a part of the movement—Langston Hughes (1902–67), Countee Cullen (1903–46), and Sterling Brown (1901–88).

Hughes was, of all the poets whom we associate with the Harlem Ren., by far the most productive, his active publishing career stretching from 1926 to 1967, the year of his death; and his *oeuvre* embraces not only 9 volumes of fiction but also 15 volumes of verse. His is a poetry predominantly devoted to the urban scene, and it is often filled with the racy rhythms of the blues and jazz:

Thump, thump, thump, went his foot
  on the floor.
He played a few chords then he sang
  some more—
"I got the Weary Blues
And I can't be satisfied.
Got the Weary Blues
And can't be satisfied—
I ain't happy no mo'
And I wish that I had died."

Indeed, his work, unmarked by cynicism or by any kind of distortion or special pleading, rehearses Black experience more richly and variously than does perhaps the work of any other Afro-Am. poet. And it is no doubt the depth of its rootedness in all the concrete materialities of Black life that accounts for the immense affection with which it has been regarded by his large and devoted body of readers.

Countee Cullen, on the other hand, was a poet whose style and orientation were very different from Hughes's. He was quite untouched, for example, by such a penchant as Hughes had for risk-taking and innovation in the handling of poetic forms; indeed, he was, as he himself said, "a rank conservative, loving the measured line and the skillful rhyme," and he appears—in such books as *Color, Copper Sun, The Black Christ and Other Poems*, and *On These I Stand*—to have been most responsive to Keats and Shelley and to such Am. traditionalists as Elinor Wylie and Robert Hillyer, finding little or nothing at all quickening in the great avatars of 20th-c. modernism. Nor, despite his plangency about the sufferings enforced upon his people, does he seem ever to have been capable of passionately identifying himself with the Black multitudes; and over and over again he permits himself a kind of self-pity (as in the following lines from "The Shroud of Color") that Hughes's robustness and unfailing sanity would never have allowed:

"Lord, being dark," I said, "I cannot
  bear
The further touch of earth, the
  scented air;
Lord, being dark, forewilled to that de-
  spair
My color shrouds me in, I am as dirt
Beneath my brother's heel; there is a
  hurt
In all the simple joys which to a child
Are sweet; they are contaminate, de-
  filed
By truths of wrongs the childish vision
  fails
To see; too great a cost this birth en-
  tails.
I strangle in this yoke drawn tighter
  than
The worth of bearing it, just to be man.
I am not brave enough to pay the price
In full; I lack the strength to sacrifice."

Then, in 1932, Sterling Brown's *Southern Road* was issued by Harcourt, Brace. Unlike Hughes, Brown, though educated at Williams College and Harvard and a member of the English faculty at Howard University, was imaginatively committed, at least in his first book, not so much to the urban scene of the Black proletariat as to the rural world of Southern Black peasants; *Southern Road* is drenched in this ethos. Also, unlike most of his contemporaries among Black poets who had discarded dialect forms, Brown chose to use the living speech of the Black demos, making it serve, in the highly nuanced uses to which he put it, an artistry which, in its dependence on folk idioms, finds its only analogue in modern poetry in the work of the distinguished Scots poet Hugh MacDiarmid.

It was most principally these three—Hughes, Cullen, and Brown—who, together with Johnson and McKay, provided the enabling examples for the Black poets whose careers began in the 1940s; and among these writers the major figures are Melvin Tolson, Gwendolyn Brooks, and Robert Hayden.

Tolson (1900–66) was the first Black poet deeply to appropriate the work of the classic 20th-c. avant-garde (Apollinaire, Pound, Eliot, Crane, Williams), though this became evident only in his remarkable *Libretto for the Republic of Liberia* (1953), commissioned by the Liberian government in 1947 as the nation's centennial poem. For in his first book, *Rendezvous with America* (1944), he was still much under the influence of such poets as Vachel Lindsay, Carl Sandburg, and Stephen Vincent Benet. And his commitment to the allusive, condensed, ironic lang. of high modernism appears to be even more resolute in his final book, *Harlem Gallery* (1965). His complex, difficult rhetoric has no doubt forfeited him the esteem of many of his Black critics, who feel it to be inapposite to the realities of Black experience, but this he was untroubled by, for though he never deserted those realities, he did not as a poet choose to present himself as merely a special case of ethnic ferment. And, for all the neglect he may as a consequence have suffered, the genuine distinction of his work is not to be gainsaid.

Gwendolyn Brooks (b. 1917) is no less preoccupied with issues of technique and craft than was Tolson, but her work is far more accessible to the general reader. Though born in Topeka, Kansas, she has spent most of her life in Chicago, and her writing is largely devoted to what she has witnessed in the daily round of the Black community there. Her earlier poetry (*A Street in Bronzeville*, 1945; *Annie Allen*, 1949—which won the Pulitzer Prize for poetry in 1950; *The Bean Eaters*, 1960) was "integrationist" in the kind of vision it embraced of how the world ought to be ordered in a multiracial society; but her 1968 book, *In the Mecca*, signalled her having taken a new turning toward the Black nationalism that was then beginning to be fostered by the holocaustal race riots that were sweeping across Am. cities. But, notwithstanding the new sternness that at this point entered her poetry, it has lost neither the shrewd, unsentimental realism nor the relish for humor that were initially a part of its great charm.

Of the poets who emerged in the 1940s—incl., as one should, not only Tolson and Brooks but also Margaret Walker (b. 1915) and Owen Dodson (1914–83)—it is Robert Hayden (1913–80) who is perhaps the most consistently interesting. Though his work searchingly renders the experience of Black Americans with that intimacy of knowledge which is born of love, he insistently refused any designation for himself other than simply that of "Am. poet." Claiming none of the easy exemptions being offered in the 1960s and early '70s by the strategists of the so-called Black Aesthetic, he took the highest kind of advantage of the whole range of expressive resources developed by the modernist movement in poetry; and "A Ballad of Remembrance," "Those Winter Sundays," "Frederick Douglass," "Runagate Runagate," "The Night-Blooming Cereus," "On Lookout Mountain," "El-Hajj Malik El-Shabazz," and a large number of other poems are among the masterpieces of modern Am. poetry. Indeed, his *Collected Poems* (1985) is one of the key poetic texts of its period, and "Middle Passage" (based in part on the 1839 insurrection on the Sp. slaveship the *Amistad*) is one of the great Am. long poems.

The turbulence in the relations between the races on the Am. scene was by the mid 1960s generating in the Black community a new pride in racial heritage so exigent that it often became a radically separatist ethnicism proposing to disengage itself not only from the Am. literary establishment but also from whatever else in the received cultural trad. might be conceived to be indelibly "Eurocentric" and "white." This undertaking found its principal expression in an immense flood of poetry from such writers as Dudley Randall (b. 1914), Margaret Danner (b. 1915), Mari Evans (b. 1923), Sarah Webster Fabio (b. 1928), Conrad Rivers (1933–68), Etheridge Knight (b. 1933), Audre Lorde (b. 1934), Sonia Sanchez (b. 1934), Lucille Clifton (b. 1936), and Nikki Giovanni (b. 1943), to mention but a few. But the immoderateness of his anger and the stringency of his expostulations made the poet and playwright Imamu Amiri Baraka (b. 1934) the presiding genius of the enterprise. The anthology of Afro-Am. p. that he and Larry Neal (b. 1937) published in 1968 (when Baraka's name was still LeRoi Jones), *Black Fire*, gave to the movement a sense of its identity and effective advertisement. And the collection of his own poetry that appeared in the following year—*Black Magic: Poetry, 1961–1967*—offered what immediately became in effect for his confreres the benchmark of authenticity. Indeed, such a poem as Baraka's "Black Art" very nicely exemplifies the violence of spirit with which the poets of the Black Arts Movement were seeking to quicken in their people a new power of self-affirmation:

> Poems are bullshit unless they are
> teeth or trees or lemons piled
> on a step. . . .
> . . . .
> We want poems
> Like fists beating niggers out of Jocks
> Or dagger poems in the slimy bellies

of owner-jews. Black poems to
smear on girdlemamma mulatto
    bitches
whose brains are red jelly stuck
between 'lizabeth taylor's toes. Stinking
Whores! We want "poems that kill."
. . . .
We want a black poem. And
a Black World.
Let the world be a Black Poem.

It may be too soon for many relative discriminations to be risked in relation to those poets who are among the more central figures of the present time, but they can at least be said to represent important achievement and large promise. Rita Dove (b. 1952), whose book *Thomas and Beulah* won the Pulitzer Prize for poetry in 1987, is surely by any reckoning in the vanguard not merely of Afro-Am. p. but of her generation at large in Am. poetry (q.v.); significantly, she, like such figures as Jay Wright (b. 1935) and Michael Harper (b. 1938), quite forswears the sentimentalities attendant upon an obsessive racial particularism and the technical indiscipline represented by the Black Arts Movement. The great charm and grace of her work result in part from an increasingly strict economy of lang. (as in the remarkable performance represented by the poems making up *Grace Notes* [1989]), from the richness of her historical imagination (as in many of the poems in *The Yellow House on the Corner* [1980] and *Museum* [1983]), and from a kind of pure attentiveness to experience that enables her easily to interweave personal and public themes.

Jay Wright's work presents, in relation to Rita Dove's, a poetry equally elegant and commanding. He emphatically asserts his fate to be that of an Afro-Am., but he happens to come out of Albuquerque, New Mexico, and thus he appears to be one who, in being originally poised, as it were, toward South America, found himself committed to a kind of borderland existence which, in his case, has resulted in a radical "de-provincializing" of the normal scene of Afro-Am. p.: the geography of that country of the spirit in which he dwells is not only hemispheric (in its extensions beyond North America to Mexico and Venezuela and Brazil) but also transatlantic, particularly in its embrace of Sp. and Af. cultures. So the explorations that are recorded in such books as *Death as History* (1967), *The Homecoming Singer* (1971), *Dimensions of History* (1976), and *The Double Invention of Komo* (1980) entail enormous complexity; and his *Selected Poems* (1987) confronts us with a lyrical talent whose range and power put us immediately in mind of Whitman and Hart Crane and Derek Walcott.

Nor can one fail to think of Michael Harper when one considers the poets of Afro-Am. descent who have moved to the fore as the century approaches its end. In such books as *Dear John, Dear Coltrane* (1970), *History Is Your Own Heartbeat* (1971), *Song: "I Want a Witness"* (1972), *Nightmare Begins Responsibility* (1975), and *Healing Song for the Inner Ear* (1985), Harper has created a body of work which, though it has won much respect and admiration, deserves to be far more widely known than it is. It is a poetry drenched in pieties, about his wife Shirley ("Shirl") and their children, her forebears and his own, his friends (e.g. Robert Hayden, Sterling Brown), various historical figures (W. E. B. DuBois, Patrice Lumumba), and many jazz musicians (John Coltrane, Miles Davis, Charlie "Bird" Parker, Bud Powell) who have all in deeply nourishing his life disclosed the real meaning of "kinship" as an affair not merely of biological accident but of the essential nature of the human condition. We are, in other words, as St. Paul says, "members one of another," and it is from this fundamental premise that his prophetic judgments of the misshapenness of the modern world spring.

Finally, if one more figure may be brought forward, Audre Lorde (b. 1934) should be spoken of, for she is one who, though originally appearing perhaps to be but yet another voice of the Black Arts Movement of the '60s and early '70s, by far outstretches the range of that moment in Afro-Am. p. She declares herself to be a "Black lesbian feminist warrior poet," but the spluttering fierceness that appears to be invoiced in this title she bestows on herself is belied by the beautiful precision and quiet eloquence of the profoundly moving poetry that we encounter in such books as *Chosen Poems Old and New* (1982) and *Our Dead Behind Us* (1986). She specializes in the contemplative lyric, and hers is a lyricism that has shaped some of the most remarkable love poems that have been written in Eng. since Graves, Roethke, and Auden. But hers is a lyricism so commodious as to be capable of talking also about the stresses and joys of being Black and being a woman, or about any of the circumstances and occasions that belong to the daily round; and the delicacy and passionateness of the lang. she supervises prompt an increasingly devoted readership to feel that she is indeed, as Adrienne Rich says, "an indispensable poet."

The numerousness of other poets whose work also deserves to be considered here—June Jordan (b. 1936), Sonia Sanchez, Margaret Danner, Ai (Florence Anthony; b. 1947), and many others—does most assuredly indicate that the Afro-Am. presence will be a major factor in Am. literary life over the coming years, and its vitality promises significant future developments that cannot now be foreseen. See also AFRICAN POETRY; AMERICAN POETRY.

ANTHOLOGIES: *The New Negro*, ed. A. Locke (1925); *Caroling Dusk*, ed. C. Cullen (1927); *The Book of Am. Negro Poetry*, ed. J. W. Johnson (1931); *Early Negro Am. Writers*, ed. B. Brawley (1935); *The Negro Caravan*, ed. S. A. Brown et al. (1941); *Am. Negro Poetry*, ed. A. Bontemps (1963); *Kaleidoscope*, ed. R. Hayden (1967); *Black Fire*, ed. L. Jones and L. Neal (1968); *Dark Symphony*, ed. J. A. Emanuel and T. L. Gross (1968); *Black Voices* (1968), *New Black Voices* (1972), both ed. A. Chapman; *The New Black Poetry*, ed. C. Majors (1969); *Black Poetry*, ed. D. Randall (1969); *Early Black Am. Poets*, ed. W. H. Robinson (1969); *Black Am. Lit.*, ed. D. T. Turner (1969); *Black Expression* (1969), *The Black Aesthetic* (1971), both ed. A. Gayle, Jr.; *The Poetry of the Negro*, ed. L. Hughes and A. Bontemps (1970); *Dynamite Voices*, ed. D. L. Lee (1971); *Afro-Am. Lit.*, ed. R. Hayden et al. (1971); *Cavalcade*, ed. A. P. Davis and J. S. Redding (1971); *Black Lit. in Am.*, ed. H. A. Baker (1971); *Black Writers of America*, ed. R. Barksdale and K. Kinnamon (1972); *Mod. and Contemp. Afro-Am.P.*, ed. B. Bell (1972); *Early Negro Writing*, ed. D. Porter (1972); *Understanding the New Black Poetry*, ed. S. Henderson (1973); *The New Negro Ren.*, ed. A. P. Davis and M. W. Peplow (1975); *Chant of Saints*, ed. M. S. Harper and R. B. Stepto (1979); *Afro-Am. Writing*, ed. R. A. Long and E. W. Collier (1985); *Collected Black Women's Poetry*, ed. J. R. Sherman, 4 v. (1988).

HISTORY AND CRITICISM: B. G. Brawley, *The Negro in Lit. and Art* (1910); V. Loggins, *The Negro Author* (1931); S. A. Brown, *Negro Poetry and Drama* (1937); J. S. Redding, *To Make a Poet Black* (1939); M. J. Butcher, *The Negro in Am. Culture* (1956); *The Black American Writer*, v. 2, ed. C. W. E. Bigsby (1969); N. I. Huggins, *Harlem Ren.* (1971); J. Wagner, *Black Poets of the U.S.* (1973); *Mod. Black Poets*, ed. D. Gibson (1973); B. Jackson and L. D. Rubin, Jr., *Black Poetry in America* (1974); A. P. Davis, *From the Dark Tower* (1974); E. B. Redmond, *Drumvoices: The Mission of Afro-Am.P.* (1976); D. Perkins, *A Hist. of Mod. Poetry*, 2 v. (1976, 1987), v. 1, ch. 18, v. 2, ch. 25; N. A. Scott, Jr., "Black Lit.—Since 1945," *Harvard Guide to Contemp. Am. Writing*, ed. D. Hoffman (1979); M. G. Cook, *Afro-Am. Lit. in the 20th C.* (1984); H. A. Baker, Jr., *Blues, Ideology and Afro-Am. Lit.* (1984), *Afro-Am. Poetics* (1988); *Black Am. Poets Between Worlds, 1940–1960*, ed. R. B. Miller (1986); H. L. Gates, *The Signifying Monkey* (1988); J. R. Sherman, *Invisible Poets: Afro-Americans of the 19th-C.*, 2d ed. (1989); B. Jackson, *A Hist. of Afro-Am. Lit.*, v. 1 (1989). N.A.S.

AKKADIAN POETRY. See ASSYRO-BABYLONIAN POETRY.

ALBANIAN POETRY. A. lit. dates from the 16th c., the oldest printed book being a missal by Gjon Buzuku (1555), the first in a long series of Roman Catholic priests and writers. Pjetër Budi, translator of a *Dottrina Christiana* (1618), was the first to add religious poems, about 800 *abab* quatrains in the national A. line, a trochaic octosyllable, often catalectic. The line occurs in two dialectal variants. The older Tosk (Southern) variant ignores stress, the ictus falling indifferently on tonic or atonic syllables, whereas the Gheg (Northern) variant is stressed on the 3rd and the 7th, with a break after the 3rd or the 4th, the metrical ictus and tonic accent usually coinciding. Budi's verse is ictic and also quantitative, a long often being resolved into two shorts. Budi's ictic and quantitative metric (Gheg differentiates between long and short vowels, whereas Tosk does not) yields to an accentual-syllabic metric in Pjetër Bogdani's *Cu-neus prophetarum* (1685), a doctrinal work interspersed with *abababcc* octaves of Italianate octosyllables.

The oldest A. poem is a Tosk hendecasyllabic octave of the Sicilian type. The *abababab* poem introduces a *Dottrina Christiana* (1592) tr. by Lukë Matranga, a Byzantine Arbëresh (Italo-Albanian) priest of Sicily, where several A. settlements existed at the time. The first collection of A. folksongs, found in the Chieuti Codex (1737), is also in Tosk. The authors, two Byzantine Arbëresh priests, were descendants of Arvanites (Greco-Albanians) who fled Morea when it was invaded by Turks. The Arbëresh verse is ictic like Budi's verse, but unrhymed. The Codex also contains religious poems in Italianate meters. Jul Variboba's *Gjella e Shën Mërisë Virgjër* (Life of St. Mary Virgin, 1762) is written in similar Italianate meters, quatrains of double pentasyllables with internal rhyme, and teems with Italianisms. The author, a Byzantine Calabro-Albanian priest, scoffs at the immaculate conception while lashing at the Church for turning the Virgin into the "Great Queen" of heaven, no longer caring for the wretched of the earth.

A byproduct of either Roman Catholic liturgy or Byzantine Arbëresh culture, A. p. includes, from the 18th c. on, a third, lay Moslem component. These poems, in Arabic script, follow oriental patterns, *aaab* or *abab* stanzas of fluctuating Tosk octosyllables, and *abab* stanzas of basically trochaic Gheg *beyts*. The major poet, Nezim Frakulla (ca. 1760), wrote a *divan* couched in Arabic and Persian nomenclature.

Thus far, A. p. is a discordant agglomeration of poetries, developing separately from different religions. Missing is a national consciousness that would bring them together. The Greek War of Independence, in which the Arvanites played an important part, was the first incentive for the birth of a national romantic poetry. Its pioneer is Girolamo De Rada (1814–1903), a Calabro-Albanian professor whose first work, *Songs of Milosao* (1836), a suite of lyrics in the unrhymed Arbëresh octosyllable, draws generously from folksongs collected by De Rada, which he deftly interweaves into a romantic story combining patriotism and *mal de siècle*. The poem was a model to younger Arbëresh poets. Gabriele Dara, Jr. (1826–85) wrote *Kënga e Sprasme e Balës* (Last Song of Bala) in the same Arbëresh meter. Italianate meters prevail in the exalted lyrics of Giuseppe Serembe (1843–91), who died insane. Antonio Santori (1819–94) wrote the first A. drama. A master of verse, Giuseppe Schirò (1865–1927) even tried Cl. meters.

In A. proper, romantic poetry flourished after

the Congress of Prizren (1878–81), marking the A. *Risorgimento.* Tosk poetry resurged with Naim Frashëri (1846–1900), a noble patriot and a mystic belonging to the Shia Bektashi sect. His popular ictic octosyllable appealed to the masses. Andon Chako (Çajupi, 1866–1930), a democratic poet, was to the Orthodox what Frashëri had been to Moslems. First among Tosks, Aleks Drenova (Asdren, 1872–1947) made use of Western metrical forms, incl. the sonnet. Fan Noli's poetic talent was spent mostly in translations—deservedly famous is his tr. of Omar Khayyám's *Ruba'iyat* (1927). Lasgush Poradeci (1899–1988) is admired for the melody of his verse.

Gheg poetry was concentrated in Shkodër. Its main representatives were Gjergj Fishta (1871–1940), a Franciscan friar, and Ndré Mjeda (1866–1937), a Jesuit. Considered by Ghegs a national poet, Fishta wrote lyric, satiric, and epic verse mostly in Western meters. His monumental *Lahuta e Malcís* (The Mountain Lute), based on North A. heroic and epic songs, is written in the popular stressed octosyllable; it recounts the battles between the North Albanians and the South Slavs during the A. *Risorgimento.* Mjeda composed lyrics set in learned meters, his sonnets (*Lissus, Scodra*) being a model of the genre. Filip Shiroka (1859–1935) wrote in exile. Among the younger generation of the Shkodër school, the most influential were Ernest Koliqi (1903–75), better known as a narrative writer, and Millosh Gjergj Nikolla (Migjeni, 1911–38). His *Vargjet e lira* (Free Verse) brought into A. lit. a *souffle nouveau,* that of social revolution. His verse, often imperfect, is nevertheless redeemed by a unique expressive power and by his original metaphors.

Contemp. A. Socialist Realism has not yet produced a poet who can compare with Migjeni. Its preeminent representative, Ismail Kadare, styled some original poems at his debut, then moved to narrative. Dritëro Agolli wrote some genuine proletarian poetry before becoming the regime's official poet. Nor is the situation better in Kosova, the Yugoslav "autonomous province" inhabited overwhelmingly by Albanians. After a promising start, due to a modicum of freedom enjoyed by Yugoslav writers, the Kosovar bark ran aground when the Kosovars, who are all Gheg, adopted for political reasons the so-called "unified literary Albanian," in fact a variant of Tosk. Because of basic phonological differences between the two dialects, their metric systems remain different.

The major living poet, Martin Camaj, is an exile who holds the Munich Albanology chair. He has published several volumes of poetry. Yet his masterpiece, *Dranja* (1981), is a suite of "madrigals" in poetic prose. It tells of the adventures of an "imperfect being," a turtle, with which the poet identifies. Written in emblematic lang., something novel in A. lit., the work succeeds in grafting the author's poetics onto the pagan mythology and ancestral customs of his Gheg highland people—a real *tour de force,* through which the poet transcends trad. while remaining faithful to his origins.

ANTHOLOGIES AND COLLECTIONS: *Rapsodie di un poema albanese,* comp. G. De Rada (1866); *Albanike Melissa—Bëlietta shqypëtare* (The A. Bee), comp. E. Mitko (1878); *Kângë popullore gegnishte* (Gheg Folk Songs), comp. V. Prennushi (1911); *Kângë kreshnikësh dhe legenda* (Heroic Songs and Legends), comp. B. Palaj and D. Kurti (1937); *Poesia popolare albanese,* tr. E. Koliqi (1957); *Chansonnier épique albanais,* tr. K. Luka (1983); *Contemp. A. Poems,* tr. B. Pogoni (1985).

HISTORY AND CRITICISM: F. Cordignano, *La poesia epica di confine nell'Albania del Nord* (1943); S. Skendi, *A. and South Slavic Oral Epic Poetry* (1954); M. Lambertz, *Die Volksepik der Albaner* (1958); G. Schirò, Jr., *Storia della letteratura albanese* (1959); A. Pipa, *A. Lit.: A Social Perspective* (1978), *A. Folk Verse: Structure and Genre* (1978); *Historia e letërsisë shqiptare* (Hist. of A. Lit.), ed. D. Shuteriqi; R. Eslie, *Dict. of A. Lit.* (1986). A.PI.

AMERICAN INDIAN POETRY.

I. NORTH AMERICAN
II. CENTRAL AMERICAN
III. SOUTH AMERICAN

I. NORTH AMERICAN. The lyric impulse in North Am. I. cultures is rich, diverse, and persistent. Since about 1960, new foundations for the understanding of the traditional forms of this impulse have been emerging in the work of linguists, anthropologists, and literary scholars—and corresponding to this renewal of interest in traditional native lyric art, there has been a remarkable flowering of poetry by Native Am. writers. Taken together, the new scholarship and the new writing have spurred a re-examination of the place of I. lit. in the Am. literary canon.

Examples of traditional Native Am. poetry and song have been recorded since Roger Williams' *Key into the Lang. of Am.* (1643), but Anglo understanding and assimilation have been problematic because the native poetries come to us from three removes, each involving severe intertextual difficulties: (1) they must be tr. into Eng. from native langs. about which, in most cases, we have only imperfect knowledge; (2) they must be rendered into texts from their original status as oral traditional songs (generally with musical settings); and (3) they must be transfigured out of the tribal contexts that shaped them into terms intelligible to modern Anglo culture.

Small wonder, then, that the study and tr. of I. lyrics have been on the whole a losing battle against the forces of ignorance and ethnocentricity, and in particular against the temptation to render such works according to Western literary assumptions. In a seminal essay, Dell Hymes has shown how well-known translations by Schoolcraft and others are vitiated by the distortions of Anglo formal and prosodic biases—in favor of regular metrics, for example, and against extensive repetition. Such studies make it clear that only through rigorous application of linguistic and ethnographic knowledge can we hope to repossess the traditional lyrics in anything like their full authenticity and expressive power. To do so is the aim of the movement known as "ethnopoetics". The full ethnopoetic program is handsomely exemplified in Evers and Molina.

In general, Am. I. traditional poetry seems to have existed in three broad functional categories. (1) As independent lyrics, "songs" per se, ranging from lullabies and love-songs to complaints, curses, war-cries, and death-songs. For the most part, such compositions appear to have been communal property, like Anglo folksongs—but in certain tribes, notably the Papago of Arizona, songmaking was a prestigious individual endeavor, and songs were identified with their composers. (2) As songs embedded in narratives, performed by raconteurs taking the part of characters who break into song, generally at moments of dramatic tension—much as Shakespeare's songs figure in his romantic comedies. For example, this mourning song is sung by Mouse at the end of a Coos story about his ill-fated marriage: "My wife! My wife! / You were so pretty, so pretty. / My heart is sad that you died. / My wife! My wife!" (3) As ceremonial poetry—works serving ritual purposes: healing, political consolidation, or propitiation of deities. Such poetry can range in length and scope from a Modoc shaman's brief incantation—"What do I suck out? / The disease I suck out"—to the immense and elaborately structured *Condolence Ritual* of the Iroquois and the *Night Chant* of the Navajo, which implicate the entire ethos of their cultures.

The most radical perception of ethnopoetic research is that *all* performative verbal forms—narrative and oratory as well as sung—is best understood as poetry, and that prose as such did not exist in native traditional verbal art. Working from tape-recorded performances of Zuni story-telling, Tedlock has found evidence of poetic lineation, indicated by regular pauses, pitch and stress changes, and so on, while Hymes' examination of Chinookan narrative texts has revealed that they are measured poetically according to a complex system of syntactic and grammatical markers.

Considered more narrowly as *lyric*, specimens of I. oral poetry share certain formal and expressive features that set them apart from Western verse. Reflecting their anonymous, collective modality, they tend to be personal and immediate without being intimate or autobiographical; the "I" of an I. lyric, rather like the "I" of traditional Eng. lyrics like "Western Wind," is universalized. A famous Pawnee song, for example, is poignant without being confessional: "Let us see, is this real / Let us see, is this real / This life I am living?" Conspicuously lacking in native lyrics is that element of *authorial irony* so pervasive in modern British and Am. poetry. Not that the native poems eschew irony—"I, even I, must die sometime / So what value is anything, I think" (Winnebago)—but it is irony as perceived in experience rather than as cultivated as a stance.

The traditional lyrics are often notable for their brevity and compression; often they seem elliptical, even fragmentary—"In the great night my heart will go out. / Toward me the darkness comes rattling. / In the great night my heart will go out" (Papago). This abrupt quality may be partly, of course, a cross-cultural phenomenon—as a Papago informant said to R. Underhill, "The song is very short because we understand so much." But a native habit of mind, an ingrained imaginative reticence, suggestive of the Oriental bias against direct declaration, is also probably at stake. A general model for such reticence existed in most tribes in the form of a taboo against directly identifying one's spirit-guide—Thunder, Elk, Wolf—as revealed in the course of solitary "power quests." One could, however, *hint* at this great secret in singing and dancing.

In structural terms, native Am. I. p. relies on relatively simple configurations—esp. repetition (with or without variation) and parallelism. In this respect, of course, the poetry reflects its oral/performative origins, esp. its association with music and singing. Whole poems were apparently meant to be sung over and over; in other cases there is extensive repetition of lines within the texts, which typically have been reduced or cut out altogether in Anglo trs., thereby obliterating the incantatory effects often achieved in the originals. One might say that if Anglo poetry generally is premised on proliferation of detail, *copia*, native traditional poetry is premised on expressive repetition.

The examples of I. p. already given illustrate its intensely visual, image-centered character: no wonder that early imagist poets and theorists like Mary Austin claimed it as a precedent and source. The ability to embody philosophical abstractions in concrete terms that Bierhorst has identified as a major achievement of Native Am. oral lit. is esp. evident in the poetry. Bound up in physical experience, its lang. is persistently figurative, not so much in formal metaphor and simile as in forms of synecdoche—concrete parts imaging and figuring complex wholes: "Wherever I pause— / the noise of the village" (Haida).

Underlying all such literary features of the traditional poetry is a magical conception of lang.—words uttered "just so" are thought to be capable of a magical instrumentality, invoking and *expressing* power in the human, natural, and supernatural realms. The Inuit word for "song," *anerca*, is also the word for "breath" and "spirit": in the traditional cultures of the Inuits and all other Native Am. peoples, song is the paramount vehicle of spiritual power. Song can make things happen, attracting good, repelling evil, or in the case of curses, drawing calamity upon one's enemies.

This belief in the magical properties of lang.,

even when the lang. is modern Am. Eng., is one of the main lines of continuity between traditional I. p. and the work of modern I. poets. They, too, are "singers for power," and most would subscribe to the declaration of N. Scott Momaday, in the course of acknowledging his debt to the Kiowa literary trad., that "man has consummate being in lang., and there only. The state of human *being* is an idea, an idea which man has of himself. Only when he is embodied in an idea, and the idea is realized in lang., can man take possession of himself."

The formal and thematic diversity of modern Am. I. p. is remarkable, and expressive of the complexity of modern I. experience, with its polarization of heroic past and deculturated present and its compulsion to find out ethnic continuities. Though many Native Am. poets do not in fact reside in their tribal homelands, most cultivate in their work a distinctive sense of ancestral and personal place, and for many there are strong *regional* identifications—with the Southwest, pre-eminently, but also with the Pacific Northwest. A pan-I. *feminist* vision is shared by a growing number of Native women writing poetry, notably Paula Gunn Allen (Laguna) and Wendy Rose (Hopi/Miwok).

Stylistically, contemp. Native Am. poetry ranges widely, from the narrative directness of Simon Ortiz (Acoma), Joseph Bruchac (Abenaki), and Maurice Kenny (Mohawk), to the imagistic, often incantatory lyricism of Linda Hogan (Chickasaw) and Joy Harjo (Creek), to the personal density and mythic allusiveness of Duane Niatum (Klallam), Elizabeth Woody, (Wasco) and Ray Young Bear (Mesquaki). Western literary influences range from Yvor Winters and the metaphysical poets (in the work of Momaday) to Whitman, Williams, Ginsberg, and Neruda—most of today's I. writers are well schooled in cl. Western lit. But the chief informing influence on the poets who are contributing to what has been aptly called the Native Am. literary renaissance seems to be their awareness of tribal poetic and narrative trads. What they self-consciously inherit of the old ways of the Native imagination, their individual 20th-c. talents are recreating and reaffirming—as in Duane Niatum's "Runner for the Clouds and Rain":

> I am the fox roaming for your changes.
> I am the salmon dreaming in the wa-
> ters of the sun.
> I am the mushroom celebrating rains.
> I am the bear dancing for the gentle
> woman.
> I am the guardian of the infant child.
> I am the carrier of the Elders' song.
> I run for the dead and the rainbow!
> (*Digging Out the Roots*, 1977)

PRIMARY TRADITIONAL TEXTS AND ANTHOLOGIES: W. Matthews, *The Night Chant* (1902); E. Curtis, *The N. Am. I.*, 20 v. (1908–24); J. Swanton, "Haida Texts and Myths," *Smithsonian Inst. Bureau of Am. Ethnology Bull.* 29 (1905); R. Lowie, *Myths and Trads. of the Crow Indians* (1918); F. Densmore, *Am. Indians and Their Music* (1926); R. Underhill, *Singing for Power* (1938); A. G. Day, *The Sky Clears* (1951); M. Astrov, *Am. I. Prose and Poetry* (1962); J. Bierhorst, *On the Trail of the Wind* (1971), *Four Masterworks of Am. I. Lit.* (1974)—Mayan, Iroquois, Navajo texts; D. Tedlock, *Finding the Center* (1972)—Zuni; J. Ramsey, *Coyote Was Going There* (1977)—Northwest; L. Evers, *The South Corner of Time* (1980)—Southwest; L. Evers and F. Molina, *Yaqui Deer Songs* (1986).

HISTORY AND CRITICISM: D. Brinton, *Aboriginal Am. Authors* (1883); E. Sapir, "Song Recitative in Paiute Mythology," *JAF* 23 (1910); M. Austin, *The Am. Rhythm* (1923); T. Waterman and E. Walton, "Am. I. P.," *AA* 27 (1925); E. Carpenter, "Eskimo Poetry," *Explorations* 4 (1958); I. Nicholson, *Firefly in the Night: A Study of Ancient Mexican Poetry and Symbolism* (1959); M. Leon-Portilla, *Pre-Columbian Lit. of Mexico* (1969); D. Hymes, *"In Vain I Tried to Tell You": Essays in Native Am. Ethnopoetics* (1983)—esp. "Some N. Pacific Poems"; D. Tedlock, *The Spoken Word and the Work of Interp.* (1983); *Smoothing the Ground*, ed. B. Swann (1983)—esp. essays by K. Kroeber; *Studies in Am. I. Lit.*, ed. P. G. Allen (1983)—esp. "The Sacred Hoop"; J. Ramsey, *Reading the Fire: Essays in the Traditional I. Lit. of the Far West* (1984); *Native Am. Discourse: Poetics and Rhet.*, ed. J. Sherzer and A. C. Woodbury (1987); A. L. B. Ruoff, *Am. I. Lits.: Intro., Bibl. Rev., Sel. Bibl.* (1990).

ANTHOLOGIES OF MODERN INDIAN POETRY: *Voices of the Rainbow*, ed. K. Rosen (1975); *Voices from Wa'Kon-Tah*, ed. M. Dodge and J. McCullough (1975); *Carriers of the Dream Wheel*, ed. D. Niatum (1975); *Many Voices*, ed. D. Day and M. Bowering (1976)—Canadian poets; *The Remembered Earth*, ed. G. Hobson (1981)—esp. Momaday, "The Man Made of Words"; *Songs from This Earth on Turtle's Back*, ed. J. Bruchac (1983); *Harper's Anthol. of 20th-C. I. P.*, ed. D. Niatum (1988).

HISTORY AND CRITICISM: A. Keiser, *The I. in Am. Lit.* (1935); K. Roemer, "Bear and Elk: The Nature(s) of Contemp. I. P.," *JES* 5 (1977); L. Hogan, "19th-C. Native Am. Poets," *Wasaja* 13 (1980); J. Ruppert, "The Uses of Oral Trad. in Six Contemp. Native Am. Poets," *AICRJ* 4 (1980); K. Lincoln, *Am. I. Ren.* (1983); A. Wiget, *Native Am. Lit.* (1985); *Survival This Way: Interviews with Am. I. Poets*, ed. J. Bruchac (1988). J.W.R.

II. CENTRAL AMERICAN. The C. Am. area presents us with a cultural and linguistic interface more complex than anywhere else in Indian America. Maya culture (600 B.C. to present day) alone comprises over 20 separate forms, which can be roughly classified into Lowland and Highland. Within the Maya area, which includes the lower half of Mexico, Guatemala, Belize, western Honduras, and parts of El Salvador, there are Nahuatl enclaves, as well as Lencan, Jicaquean, and Payan groupings with Carib-Arawak-Amazonian affiliations. South of the Maya area, the cultural and linguistic picture shades into Macro-Chibchan, a large stock with many subdivisions originating in highland South America.

To the north of the Maya, in highland central Mexico, the Aztecs (A.D. 1325–1519) inherited a long poetic trad. originating with the Toltecs. Within this Aztec trad. we find three major genres: lyric, epic, and dramatic. The lyric trad. concentrates on the major themes of Nahua religion, on war and the heroic, on philosophical speculations on the ontological basis of human life, and, to a lesser degree, on biographical accounts. The main topics of the Aztec epics concern their original pilgrimage to Anahuac, described in five pictographic sources, the *Codex Boturini*, *The Codex Aubin of 1576*, the *"Mapa de Siguenza"*, the *Codex Azcatitlan*, and *The Codex Mexicanus*. Each of these is quite divergent from the others, although certain features are common. In addition, theme poems about Quetzalcoatl and about the hist. of Tenochtitlan are prevalent. Finally, a few examples of the Aztec dramatic genre have survived, most notably the "Death of Nezahuacoyotl" in the *Cantares Mexicanos*.

The most comprehensive and detailed picture of C. Am. I. lit. is provided by the surviving Maya and Aztec texts in both pre-Columbian hieroglyphic and colonial Roman Script. The Highland Maya texts form a distinctive group; among these, the Quiché Maya Book of Counsel known as the *Popol Vuh*, the dramatic text of the *Rabinal Achi*, and the Cakchiquel Maya *Memorial of Solola* are outstanding examples of a genre of works which are simultaneously land titles, mythological recitations, dramatic enactments, and theological and philosophical elaborations. They were first composed in the 16th c. as native "readings" of earlier hieroglyphic codices now lost. Much of the content of these texts can be traced back to the Cl. Maya era of 350–900 A.D. Passages in the *Popol Vuh*, for example, explain scenes depicted on Cl. Maya pottery.

In the case of the Lowland Yucatec Maya, a series of community texts known as the *Books of Chilam Balam* (the Jaguar Priest) of surviving Maya townships such as Maní, Chumayel, and Tizimin demonstrate that a centralized Yucatec Maya literary trad. survived the Sp. conquest in 1539. These books are markedly different in emphasis from the Highland Maya texts even though they too were first composed and written down in the 16th c. They sustain the continuity of the Cl. Maya calendar into colonial times and center on documenting the social and economic effects of the arrival of the Spaniards in the peninsula and the native response to Christianity. Unlike the surviving Highland texts or the Aztec material, the *Books of Chilam Balam* are explicitly political:

> Thrice the tidings of justice of our Father,
> Descend over the multitudes of the town,
> Then a great war,
> Descends over the "white beans" of the town,
> To comprehend the true severity of everything.

The unifying center of native C. Am. poetry is the shaman's trance, used for communication with the spirit world. It is the belief that invisible spirits can be addressed and petitioned for favors which inspires the variety of poetic forms. This center is enshrined iconographically in the "uinal" cycle of 20 days at the heart of Maya and Aztec lit., in Kuna I. "ikarkana" poetry, and elsewhere.

The I. poet also works his craft to articulate individual experience, to record a vision quest, to mourn the departed, to reflect humor and to entertain, to mark the search for love and attention, to express prowess in hunting and war, to communicate a personal anecdote, to overcome the hardship of physical labor, to pass the long evenings, in short, to communicate a sense of self unbound, a "flowering." It was because poetry and song contained this unbounded self that, on becoming a subject after capture in battle, an I. warrior traditionally surrendered his personal songs as part of the tribute paid (Brotherston).

The poems of the C. Am. Indians can best be understood as special forms of dialogue in which performance is a central characteristic. Dialogue, whether it be with the gods or other men, evokes the original creation. In the opening lines of the Quiché Maya Book of Counsel, the *Popol Vuh*, the gods *Tepeu* and *Gucumatz* create the world by dialogue: "They talked then, discussing and deliberating. They agreed; they united their words and their thoughts." This is in striking contrast to the European biblical heritage with its singular Word and monologue (Burns). It also emphasizes the role that oral recitation plays in native poetic trads., even where a strong scriptural trad. existed.

C. Am. I. p. does not rely on long, detailed descriptions of context, but rather assumes that context will be manifested by other features in performance such as costume, facial expression, voice quality, phrasing, and gesture. Thus, to fully comprehend the content of a poem, an intimate knowledge of the social and spiritual context of the cultural group within which the poem was fashioned is crucial. An ethnopoetic approach that also interprets performance is necessary (see ETHNOPOETICS).

A pervasive use of parallelism and a profound dualism permeate the poetic forms of the C. Am. Indians. Rhetorical questions, prophecies, riddles, allegory, personification, question and answer sessions, insults, metaphorical strings, euphony, and onomatopoeia are also displayed. Poems vary in length from a few words to extended ceremonial presentations that might last for days. The written native texts available to us, notably the Quiché Maya *Popol Vuh*, the Yucatec *Books of*

Chilam Balam (The Jaguar Priest), and the Kuna *ikar*, are written entirely in verse and contain extensive scripts for what were dramatic reenactments of the legends of the gods and ancestors.

To the Indian, poetic ability is power. To be able to converse with the spirits in their special lang., to be able to persuade people and find agreement in counsel, and to show linguistic dexterity and a profound knowledge of custom and history are prerequisites for claiming title and rank. Because songs and poems were and are such important instruments of prestige and control, every Indian seeks to a greater or lesser extent to be a practicing poet.

ANTHOLOGIES: *General*: *The Song of Quetzalcoatl*, ed. J. H. Cornyn (1930); *First Fire*, ed. H. Fox (1978); *Image of the New World*, ed. and tr. G. Brotherston (1979). *Costa Rica*: *Leyendas y tradiciones borucas*, ed. E. S. Maroto (1979). *El Salvador*: *Mitologia cuzcatleca*, ed. M. Mendez Efrain (1979). *Honduras*: E. Conzemius, *Los Indios Payas de Honduras*, pts. 1–2, v. 19–20 (1927–28); M. Medardo, *Comizahual* (1981); *Los hijos de la muerte: el universo mitico de los Tolupan-Jicaques*, ed. A. M. Chapman, 2d ed. (1982); *Hijos del copal y la candela. Tomo 1: Ritos agrarios y tradicion oral los lencis de Honduras* (1985). *Maya, Lowland*: *The Book of Chilam Balam of Chumayel* (1933) and *The Ritual of the Bacabs* (1965), both ed. and tr. R. Roys; A. B. Vazquez, *El Codice Perez* (1939); *An Epoch of Miracles*, ed. and tr. A. F. Burns (1983); D. Boremanse, *Contes et Mythologie des Indiens Lacandons* (1986); *Jaguar Prophecy: The Counsel Book of the Yucatec Maya*, tr. R. Luxton and P. Balam (1990)—annotated. *Maya, Highland*: *Annals of the Cakchiquels*, ed. S. G. Morley and A. Recinos (1945); *Popol Vuh*, ed. and tr. D. Tedlock (1985); *Cantares Mexicanos*, tr. J. Bierhorst (1985). *Nahautl*: *Ancient Nahuatl Poetry*, ed. D. Brinton (1887). *Panama*: F. W. Kramer, *Lit. Among the Cuna Indians* (1970); *Cuna Cosmology: Legends from Panama*, tr. and ed. A. G. McAndrews (1978); J. Sherzer, *Kuna Ways of Speaking* (1986).

HISTORY AND CRITICISM: A. Tozzer, *A Comparative Study of the Mayas and the Lacandones* (1907)—highland Maya; K. A. M. Garibay, *La poesia lirica Azteca*, (1937)—Nahuatl, *Epica Nahuatl* (1945); *The Maya and Their Neighbors*, ed. C. L. Hay et al. (1948); *Handbook of Middle Am. Indians*, v. 5, ed. N. A. McQuown (1964–76); G. H. Gossen, *Chamulas in the World of the Sun* (1974); D. M. Sodi, *La Literatura de los Mayas*, 2d ed. (1978)—lowland Maya; B. N. Colby and L. M. Colby, *The Daykeeper, the Life and Discourse of an Ixil Diviner* (1981); D. Gifford, *Warriors, Gods, and Spirits from Central and South Am. Mythology* (1983); M. Leon Portilla, *Literatura de Mesoamerica* (1984); *The Southeast Maya Periphery*, ed. P. A. Urban and E. M. Schortman (1986); *Recovering the Word: Essays on Native Am. Lit.*, ed. B. Swann and A. Krupat (1987). R.L.

III. SOUTH AMERICAN. The South Am. continent was and continues to be one of the most linguistically and culturally diverse regions of the planet. The range of this exquisite complexity is constantly being expanded as continuing research and investigation yield more detailed information on various lang. groups, their speakers, and their artistic trads. The major division of the native or indigenous groups of South America is between the lowland or Tropical Forest groups and those of the Andean highlands. While focusing primarily on the Andean region due to the high civilizations that developed there and the information currently available, what follows is an attempt to treat both highland and lowland native groups. Although attempts were made in the 16th and early 17th cs. by European and Mestizo chroniclers (Cristobal de Molina, Francisco de Avila, Santa Cruz Pachacuti Yamqui Salcamaygua, Guaman Poma de Ayala) to record and transcribe the poetic trads. of different groups (such as the Naylamp legend and the Waru Chiri ms.), one must remember that the conquerors were not invited guests, nor ones who appreciated or understood the nature of the native South Am. trads. Consequently, much of the poetic record of the Conquest and Colonial periods (16th through early 19th cs.) consists of those examples that more closely matched or could be made to conform to the western European ideal. Furthermore, the majority of these examples comes from the great civilizations such as the Inca that were contacted and conquered first. As a result, the information currently available on the South Am. poetic trad. at the time of the Sp. Conquest (1532) comes from a relatively small number of sources and must represent only a small part of the poetic trads. in existence at that time.

Fortunately, since the 1970s the full range, form, and content of native South Am. p. is beginning to be clarified, due in part to more rigorous empirical studies *in situ* and to re-examination of early poetic data in light of the most recent information and methodologies. Studies of lang. in its social context and, more specifically, those dealing with ethnopoetics (the study of the indigenous interp. of native verbal art) help to illustrate not only the form and function of indigenous poetic genres but also the intricate relationship of such genres to other aspects of culture. In order to recognize the poetic nature of this oral lit., one must be aware of the parameters of what constitutes "poetry" within each particular ethnic group and of the subtlety of expression available in the non-IE langs.

The poetic genres of South Am. indigenous oral lit. consist primarily of three types: song lyrics, myths and legends, and the epic trads. of the Incas and the Chilean Mapuche. All three forms were productive and recorded in the 1500s, but only the songs, myths, and legends continue to be productive today. Now as in the early Conquest and Colonial periods (15th and early 17th cs.), much of this poetry is still produced in the Quechua (or Runa Simi "people speech") and Aymara langs.

The majority of poetic texts available today are

the lyrics of songs which are still created and performed by both Tropical Forest and Andean ethnic groups. These range from the simple repetitive chants of Chaco groups and upper Amazon shamans to the complex call-and-response song couplets of the various Tupí-Guaraní groups of Brazil. In addition to the range of forms, the uses of such songs are quite varied as well. For example, the Aymara and Jaqaru of the Andean highlands employ work songs in the cleaning of irrigation canals to make the work more enjoyable, reinforce the role of each family group in the communal work, and reassert its beneficial outcome. Among the Tapirapé, the Karajá, Nambicuara, Xingu, and the Javajé of Brazil, recreational and rhythmical work-songs are common. Love songs are used by the Quichua speakers of the upper Amazon to send messages to distant loved ones and call them back to the singer. Among the isolated Huaorani of the Ecuadorian Amazon, recreational songs usually involve spontaneous social singing. Wedding songs among the Otavalo are often spontaneous ribald entertainment and also carry socialization information both for the newlyweds and for those yet unmarried. Common to many of these ethnopoetic forms is the repetition of an underlying structure and treatment that is pan-Amazonian and/or pan-Andean.

Structurally repetitive form, which is also prevalent in myths and legends, can be easily manipulated for effect. Among the Loreto Quichua of the Ecuadorian Amazon, the structures of both the myth and the Quichua lang. allow allusions to other important themes and texts of the culture. In the excerpt below from a creation myth, the interplay of verbal suffixes with the couplet form of the myth is akin to preparing a warp for weaving:

Siluma riska nin chay wawa,
Silupi *yaykuska* ishkaynti.
(Those children went to the sky, they say,
And both of them *entered* the sky.)

Ishkaynti *yaykupi*,
Mama, washa, *katiska* nin silu punkumanta.
(When both had *gone in*,
the mother, behind [them], *followed* [them] from the sky's door, they say.)
Katipika,
chay wawakuna piñaska nin.
(Her having *followed* [them],
The children got mad, they say.)

In addition to the linguistic interplay, the repetition of "they say / one says" and other elements provides an almost hypnotic rhythm (and rhyme) not evident on the printed page. Furthermore, semantic coupling of key words in a couplet allows for an additional "rhyme of meaning" while maintaining the rhythmic integrity of the form.

In addition to songs, myths, and legends, an important epic trad. consisting of official and popular poetry also existed at the time of the Sp. Conquest and into the early Colonial period; from examples such as *Ollántay*, a drama written in verse, it is clear that this is the finest poetic trad. in South America recorded by the early European conquerors and missionaries. Poetic trads. were a vital part of Inca culture and were a repository of prescribed social behavior, mythology, and Inca revisionist history. Often such poems were composed by Inca royalty and performed before large crowds during various seasonal celebrations in the main plazas of Cuzco. As the oral lit. of an empire without a writing system, the various poetic genres were some of the few available means of passing on cultural values from one generation to the next. The early European attempt to impose elements of their own culture by utilizing manipulated versions of these trads. is evidence of the importance of their role in the Inca Empire.

The following example of an Inca hymn of supplication illustrates the religious function of poetry:

Father Wiracocha
Wiracocha of the world
Creator
Fertile procreator
In this lower world
"Let them eat, let them drink,"
Saying to those you've placed here,
Making their destinies.

While the epic narrative poems and the long poetic dramas of pre-Colombian times have been for the most part lost, the trads. of song and myth continue to be productive. Even though such ethnopoetic trads. have changed by incorporating European themes and by reflecting current social environment, the various genres available are still seen as an integral part of native culture; their successful use and performance continue to be highly esteemed.

GENERAL: *Handbook of South Am. Indians*, ed. J. Steward, 6 v. (1946–49)—surveys of many ethnic groups, incl. their lits., with excellent bibl.

ARAUCANIAN: T. Guevara Silva, *Historia de la civilización de Araucania* (1898), *Folklore araucano* (1911); F. José de Augusta, *Lecturas araucanas* (1910); B. Köessler-Ilg, *Tradiciones Araucanas* (1962); L. C. Faron, *The Mapuche Indians of Chile* (1968).

INCA AND QUECHUA: G. Poma de Ayala, *Nueva corónica y buen gobierno* (1613); E. Middendorf, *Dramatische und lyrische Dichtungen der Keshua-Sprache* (1891); P. A. Means, *Ancient Civilizations of the Andes* (1931); R. Rojas, *Himnos Quichuas* (1937); J. María Arguedas, *Canto Kechwa* (1938); *Canciones y Cuentos del Pueblo Quechua* (1949); J. Basadre, *Literatura Inca* (1938); J. Rowe, "Inca Culture at the Time of the Sp. Conquest," in Steward (above), v. 2; J. Lara, *La Poesia Quechua* (1947); J. M. B. Farfán, *Colección de Textos Quechuas del Perú* (1952); J. Lira and J. M. B. Farfán, "Himnos

Quechuas Católicos Cuzqueños," *Folklore Americano* 3 (1955); L. Cadogan, *La Literatura de Los Guaranies* (1965); G. Taylor, *Rites et trads. de Huarochiri* (1980); G. L. Urioste, *Hijos de Pariya Qaqa: La Tradición Oral de Waru Chiri* (1983); L. K. Carpenter, "Notes from an Ecuadorian Lowland Quechua Myth," *Lat. Am. Indian Lits. Jour.* 1 (1985); C. Itier, "A Propósito de Los Dos Poemas en Quechua de la Crónica de Fray Martín de Murúa," *Revista Andina* 5 (1987).

OTHER GROUPS: G. Reichel-Dolmatoff, *Amazonian Cosmos: The Sexual and Religious Symbolism of the Tukano Indians* (1971); M. de Civrieux, *Watunna: An Orinoco Creation Cycle* (1980). L.K.C.

AMERICAN POETRY.

I. THE COLONIAL PERIOD
II. NINETEENTH-CENTURY ROMANTICISM
III. MODERNIST POETRY, 1900–1945
IV. THE POSTWAR PERIOD

The often idiosyncratic strength, boldness, and ambition of Am. p. derives from two interrelated factors: its problematic and often marginalized relation to Am. society, and the lack of a defined and established literary class, culture, and audience. As a result, Am. p. developed through a dialectic between a sense of indebtedness to and derivation from British antecedents and, esp. in the best poets, a drive to resist those antecedents by conforming the trad. to peculiarly Am. circumstances or by evolving out of those circumstances the forms and motifs expressive of a distinctive sensibility. There seemed little need for arts and letters in a society of emigrants settling a harsh, alien wilderness and severing ties with the Old World while pressing the frontier ever westward to encompass the whole continent in their self-made, self-promoting prosperity. The rough-and-tumble economic expansion without the refinements of civilization allowed the Eng. commentator Sidney Smith in 1820 to sum up Am. cultural inferiority with rhetorical assurance: "In the four quarters of the globe, who reads an Am. book? or goes to an Am. play? or looks at an Am. painting or statue?"

Many besides Smith were not yet able to grasp the essential paradox of the New World: that Am. materialism and expansiveness were inseparable from a strain of introverted, self-analyzing idealism just as deep. In fact, the decade after Smith's sneer saw the beginnings of a self-conscious cultural expression and of a literary profession in the U.S. which by the early 20th c. would make Am. lit. and arts, as well as technology, recognized and imitated worldwide. Am. p.—marginalized economically but essential to psychological, moral, and religious life—played a powerful part in that act of self-creation and self-expression. Oddly, Am. poets, even those who affiliated themselves with groups and movements, conceived their task in painfully personal and private terms, yet felt their plight, however agonized, to be one connected with national destiny. Their words, however private, expressed the consciousness of their fellow Americans.

I. THE COLONIAL PERIOD. There was no poet of significant ability or accomplishment from the middle Atlantic states until Philip Freneau, nor from the Southern states until Edgar Allan Poe. But given the rigors of life on the 17th-c. frontier, the mere existence of the occasional ode, elegy, or satire is remarkable. In New England the intensities of Calvinist piety prompted a number of well-read Puritans to versify. *The Bay Psalm Book* (1640), probably the first book printed in Eng. in the New World, translated biblical texts into a plain style hammered into fourteeners. Michael Wigglesworth's *The Day of Doom* (1662), a graphic rendering of the Last Judgment in thumping quatrains, became almost equally popular. In a more personal vein, Philip Pain's *Daily Meditations* (1668) recorded his afflictions and hopes wrangling with the paradoxes of sin and salvation.

The Puritans also produced two poets of abiding importance. Anne Bradstreet (1612?–72) arrived in the Massachusetts Bay Colony on the *Arbella* in 1630 as wife of a future governor. She almost certainly heard John Winthrop's shipboard address before debarkation envisioning their settlement as a "City upon a Hill" which would illuminate the Old World, but her comment on her new situation mingled candor with humility: "I found a new world and new manners at which my heart rose. But after I was convinced it was the way of God, I submitted to it and joined the church at Boston." Amidst family chores she wrote long, conventional, didactic poems on the four elements, the four seasons, and the four ages of hist., which admiring friends caused to be published in England as *The Tenth Muse Lately Sprung up in America* (1650), the inaugural book of Am. p. But Bradstreet is best known now for her domestic poems—love lyrics to her husband, poems on the birth and death of her children, an elegy for her father, a meditation on mortality after the burning of the family house—published posthumously in 1678. The emotional depth and honesty of these lyrics convert the conceits and meters of Ren. verse into personal statements affirming love in the face of loss, faith in the face of tribulation. Our first poet could be ruefully ironic about her situation as woman in a male world of letters, but the several elegies about her attest to the warm regard she enjoyed as person and as poet.

The 1937 discovery of a 400-page ms. by Edward Taylor (1642?–1729) brought to light the work of this major poet. A Harvard graduate (with one of the largest libraries of his time) and the staunchly orthodox minister to the frontier hamlet of Westfield, Taylor wrote for his own spiritual needs rather than for publication, but preserved the poems sturdily bound in a book. The bulk of the ms. consists of two long sequences: *God's Determi-*

nations Touching His Elect, a part-lyric, part-allegorical presentation of the redemption of the elect, written in various meters and probably completed before 1690; and *Preparatory Meditations Before My Approach to the Lord's Supper. Chiefly upon the Doctrine Preached upon the Day of Administration.* The *Meditations* were written about every two months between 1682 and 1725 for the Sabbaths on which Taylor administered and received communion, and were all composed in the 6-line stanza (quatrain and a closing couplet) which Taylor learned from George Herbert. Using his Sunday sermon's scriptural text as a point of departure, the poems prepare him for the sacrament by exploring the psychology of grace and conversion, wrestling to rest his often explosive emotions, which burst out again in the next meditation. Despite Taylor's indebtedness to the Eng. metaphysical poets, we begin to hear—in the rough rhythmic emphases of his questions and declarations, the burly, clumsy colloquiality and directness of his diction, the nervy quirks and risks of his metaphorical leaps—the idiom and temper of Am. poetic speech separate itself from the more restrained and refined trad. of Eng. verse. Here is a characteristic stanza from the 23rd Meditation:

> I know not how to speak't, it is so good:
> Shall Mortall, and Immortal marry? nay,
> Man marry God? God be a Match for Mud?
> The King of Glory Wed a Worm? mere Clay?
> This is the Case. The Wonder too in Bliss.
> Thy Maker is thy Husband. Hear'st thou this?

Most of the writing in early America, however, was prose—in the 17th c., sermons, spiritual journals, tracts, letters; in the 18th c., a political focus overtaking the religious as the divisions leading to the Revolution quickened. Whatever the political differences with the mother country, the models for 18th-c. poetry were unashamedly Eng.: the neoclassicism of Pope and Swift, the pastoralism of Thomson and Gray, the hymnology of Watts—from the *Poems on Several Occasions* (1744) by Mather Byles (a Bostonian minister but also, by then, a would-be wit and man of letters) to the *Poems on Several Occasions* (1736) by a clever but anonymous "Gentleman of Virginia." The first black to become known as a poet, Phillis Wheatley (1753?–84), brought from Africa as a slave, was educated by her masters; her *Poems on Various Subjects, Religious and Moral* (1773) reflect her Eng. reading more than her African experience: her favorite book besides the Bible was Pope's *Iliad* (see AFRO-AMERICAN POETRY).

The first "school" of Am. poets was the "Connecticut Wits" of Yale and Hartford. Conservative Federalists except for Joel Barlow, they collaborated in Popean couplets on such satiric projects as *The Anarchiad* and *The Echo.* The painter John Trumbull (1750–1831) used the tetrameters of Swift and Butler's *Hudibras* for his caricatures of local types in *The Progress of Dulness* (1772) and *M'Fingal* (1782). Timothy Dwight (1752–1817), who became president of Yale, composed a ponderous epic in couplets called *The Conquest of Canaan* (1785), in which the journey of the Israelites under Joshua to the promised land can be read as the advance of the Americans under Gen. Washington to nationhood. Dwight also wrote *Greenfield Hill* (1794) in post-Miltonic blank verse to demonstrate that the new republic could yield pastoral poetry of philosophical seriousness worthy of Denham's *Cooper's Hill* and Goldsmith's *Deserted Village.* The poem concludes, as does Joel Barlow's *The Columbiad,* with a visionary prospect of America's future happiness and prosperity; both versions of paradise regained in an industrializing age represent early instances of the recurrent Am. effort to project for the unstoried nation a myth of the future commensurate with its size and ambitions. Barlow (1752–1812) had recognized the inadequacies of the Miltonic diction and heroic couplets of *The Vision of Columbus* (1787) and revised it into *The Columbiad* (1807). But *The Hasty Pudding* (1796), dedicated to Martha Washington, remains vigorous and delightful; its mock-pastoral, mock-epic couplets celebrate cornmeal mush, which New Englanders adopted from the Indians as a dietary staple.

At Princeton, Philip Freneau (1752–1832) wrote "The Power of Fancy" and co-authored "The Rising Glory of America," exhibiting early the combination of preromantic feeling and patriotic fervor which would characterize his work. He enthusiastically supported the Revolution and afterwards edited newspapers attacking the Federalists and advocating Jefferson's republicanism. His war experiences as a blockade runner and prisoner of war fueled the polemics of "The British Prison Ship" (1781). Today his public poems (e.g. "America Independent") sound bombastic; his Deistic poems on the benevolence of nature (e.g. "The Wild Honey Suckle") seem too blandly sweet; his poems about the Am. Indian (e.g. "The Indian Burying Ground") slip into patronizing sentimentality. In the heady excitement of the new republic, Freneau had high hopes for Am. lit. and for himself as the first Am. poet of stature. But despite public acclaim as the "Poet of the Revolution," Freneau spent his last years in relative obscurity and, after dying of exposure in a snowstorm, was buried under a stone inscribed "Poet's Grave."

The poetry of the Colonial period was, understandably, imitative. The question of literary nationalism—i.e., of whether Am. p. was or ought to be original or derivative, part of the European (and particularly the Eng.) trad. or a native devel. with the power of its rudeness—did not become urgent until the professionalization of lit. in the second quarter of the 19th c. Neoclassicism was not strong enough in the U.S. to precipitate a vehement romantic reaction against it. Instead, Puritan Calvinism remained sufficiently strong, both North and South, that by the time the new energies of romanticism reached Boston and New York and Charleston in the 1820s and '30s, they defined themselves not against neoclassical rules and constraints but in terms of the lingering aesthetic and epistemological assumptions of Puritanism. Thus Am. romanticism adapted the transatlantic stimulus from Coleridge and Wordsworth and Carlyle, Rousseau and Mme. de Stael, Kant and Fichte and Goethe to its own character and emphasis.

The Puritan plain style—in lit. as in architecture, dress, and worship—bespoke a deeply ambivalent suspicion of art as false, deceptive, seductive: an appeal to the carnal and the irrational, a portrayal of a fiction as a truth. In "Of Poetry and Style," Cotton Mather could still inveigh in 1726: "Be not so set upon poetry, as to be always poring on the passionate and measured pages. Let not what should be sauce, rather than food for you, engross all your application. . . . [L]et not the Circean cup intoxicate you. But esp. preserve the chastity of your soul from the dangers you may incur, by a conversation with muses that are no better than harlots." The "food" was the nourishing meat of Scripture and nature, the "sauce" the steamy smothering of style and artifice, meter and metaphor. What the Circe-muse fed you could turn you into a swine. Peter Bulkeley's Preface to a book called *Poetic Meditations* (1725) wondered whether a person could be both an "Accomplish'd Poet" and a "Great Man," since the latter peruses truth and virtue and the former is "misled by Similitude," by an "Affinity to take one thing from another," and by "Wit, . . . or, to speak more plain, an aptness at Metaphor and Allusion."

To preserve the distinction between "food" and "sauce," the Puritans contrasted two modes of perceiving, imaging, or expressing. "Types," a term derived from a method of interpreting Scripture and extended into reading the "book" of nature, reveal the spiritual truths inherent and made manifest in the phenomenal world by divine constitution. "Tropes" are mere figures of speech, similitudes and allusions gestated by the fertile fancy. Thus the great Puritan theologian Jonathan Edwards declared: "The things of this world are ordered [and] designed to shadow forth spiritual things," for "God makes the inferiour in imitation of the superiour, the material of the spiritual, on purpose in order to have a resemblance or shadow of them." Typological resemblance *presents* the God-made symbolism of objective reality, beyond the verbal skill or interpretive powers of the artist; tropological resemblance *represents* or recomposes reality in poet-made metaphors. Types present directly extrinsic truths; tropes represent indirectly imaginative inventions. Puritans used tropes, but warily. In Bradstreet and Taylor, however, typological conviction liberated and propelled their verbal and metaphorical inventiveness.

The Puritan aesthetic set the agenda for Am. p. into the 19th c. and down to the present. The hermeneutical and epistemological assumptions behind the literary distinction between type and trope, the different implications of how things come to mean and how the imagination and lang. function and participate in that process, established the poles for an ongoing dialectic that later poets would resume and resolve on their own terms.

II. NINETEENTH-CENTURY ROMANTICISM. William Cullen Bryant (1794–1878) brought the first stirrings of romanticism to Am. p. The transition from his grandfather's Federalist Calvinism to his father's Unitarianism to his own career as a nature poet and a liberal reformer sums up the declension of New England intellectual and religious life. Bryant wrote "Thanatopsis," a stoic meditation on human mortality in the round of nature, at the age of 17, and had written many of his best poems by the publication of *Poems* in 1821. His move to New York in 1825 embroiled him in the hurly-burly of journalism, crusading for labor and against slavery. His *Lectures on Poetry* (1825) argued for the possibility of an Am. art and lit. indigenous to Nature's Nation (cf. the admonitory sonnet, "To Cole, the Painter, Departing for Europe"). Despite his public activities he continued to publish poetry, meditating on landscapes from the Berkshires ("Inscription for the Entrance to a Wood," "A Forest Hymn") to the Illinois plains ("The Prairies") with a melancholy optimism. "To a Waterfowl" sets out to read as a type of God's Providence the bird's solitary flight in the twilit sky to its eventual resting place, but the imagery and hesitant rhythms reveal the difficulty of affirmation. Bryant became known as the "Am. Wordsworth," but for him the woods were not so much the manifestation of the Power that rolls through all things as a soothing, healing haven from the stresses of secular, urban living. In the end he was more like the 18th-c. meditative precursors than the visionary poet of "Tintern Abbey."

Ralph Waldo Emerson (1803–82) marks the real watershed of Am. p. After resigning his Unitarian pulpit in Boston because he could no longer adhere to the tenets of Christianity, Emerson immersed himself in Eng. and Ger. romanticism and issued his manifesto *Nature* (1836). The prophet of Transcendentalism drew many disciples, incl. Henry David Thoreau (1817–62), and he spread his message on the lecture circuit around the country, all the way to California. The "Sage of Concord" assimilated Neoplatonism, Ger. idealism, and Oriental mysticism into a Yankee conviction that individuals who trusted their powers of intuitive insight (which he called transcendental Reason) would discover in their own experience, rather than in doctrines or institutions, their harmony with nature and with the Oversoul immanent in nature. He elaborated his philosophy in *Essays* (1841, 1844) and *Representative Man* (1850).

Philosopher as poet, poet as seer ("transparent eyeball," in the phrase from the opening epiphany of *Nature*), seer as sayer: Emerson enunciated an Am. poetics so powerful that both contemporaries and succeeding generations have had to contend with it by affirmation, qualification, or denial. The three axioms laid down in the "Language" chapter of *Nature* postulated an intrinsic correspondence between words, things, and absolute truth: "1. Words are the signs of natural facts. 2. Particular natural facts are symbols of particular spiritual facts. 3. Nature is symbol of Spirit." There is a clear line from Edwards' declaration that "the material and natural world is typical of the moral, spiritual, and intelligent world, or the City of God" to Emerson's axioms. "The Poet," as Emerson expatiates in his essay of that title (1844), is the receptive and expressive medium of the Spirit in Nature, distinguished by the "power to receive and impart" his typological experience. But Emerson's unchurched experience of types rested not on the certitude of Scripture and doctrine but on the instabilities of subjective experience: "the individual is his world," he said in "Self-Reliance." That individualizing and psychologizing of experience, which is the essence of romanticism, and which was itself a result of the general decline of theological and philosophical assurance in the West and of Puritanism in the U.S., served to undermine the distinction between types and tropes; indeed, Emerson tends to use the terms almost interchangeably.

But that ambiguity was the unacknowledged subtext; what people responded to was Emerson's call to believe in "the infinitude of the private man," his affirmation of the power both of imagination to realize its perceptions and of America's natural sublimity as the source of a new poetry capable of idealizing Am. materialism and building a new society. Since realization required the seer to be also a sayer or "Language-maker," Emerson proposed an aesthetic of organicism. "Every word was once a poem. Every new relation is a new word." Consequently, organic form is not antecedent to the poem; even though the form and meaning coexist in the completed work, form does not proceed *ab extra*—i.e. from the technique of following out conventional rules and patterns—but from the impulse of the insight: "a thought so passionate and alive that like the spirit of a plant or an animal it has an architecture of its own and adorns nature with a new thing." The shape of the poem ought to be the extension of the generative experience into words.

Emerson versified his Transcendentalism in poems such as "Each and All," "Bacchus," and "Brahma"; his image of the poet in "Merlin" and "Uriel"; and his notion of organic form in "The Snow-Storm." He admitted that the pieces he collected in *Poems* (1847) and *May-Day* (1867) did not adequately exemplify the ideals he proposed, and that much of his best poetry was in his prose. Still, his rhythmic roughness and irregularity (even in metered verse), his verbal directness and freshness, often antipate the revolution in form and expression which Whitman and Dickinson would initiate. "Merlin" contrasts the authentic native poet with the imitative "jingling serenader":

> Thy trivial harp will never please
> Or fill my craving ear;
> Its chords should ring as blows the
>   breeze,
> Free, peremptory, clear.
> No jingling serenader's art,
> Nor tinkle of piano strings,
> Can make the wild blood start
> In its mystic springs.

Emerson might have been thinking of Poe (whom he called "the jingle-man") as the negative contrast to the Am. bard here. Edgar Allan Poe (1809–49), though born in Boston of traveling actors, was orphaned by the age of three and reared by the Allan family of Richmond. A Southerner by defiant choice, and a poet by aspiration, Poe struggled to support himself through journalism, writing the famous short stories and the voluminous reviews which make him the first Am. critic of stature.

A Southern strain of Calvinism not only disposed Poe to the Gothic but disabused him of the Transcendentalists' claims. The poem "Israfel" indicates his susceptibility to the idea of the exalted seer-sayer and his disillusionment with it. What can we do if "our flowers are merely—flowers," not types but phenomena in the material flux? In compensation we make flowers into tropes and, with conscious craft and calculated effect, construct from disordered nature an intricately composed artifice. The imagination functions not to discover typological truth but to devise metaphorical connection. By explicating the text of "The Raven" as a rational construction of an irrational narrative, "The Philosophy of Composition" (1846) mounts a withering attack on the supposition of ecstatic inspiration in "the so-called poetry of the so-called transcendentalists."

Emerson's distinction between poetry as the eternal verities "all written before time was" and the poem which can never adequately express those verities allowed him to judge Poe a bad poet who sometimes wrote good poems and Thoreau a poet so possessed of the spirit of poetry that he was impatient with the craft required for good poems. However, Poe's essay on "The Poetic Principle" (1848), dismissing "the heresy of The Didactic" and defining poetry as "The Rhythmical Creation of Beauty," concludes that "there neither exists nor *can* exist any work more thoroughly dignified . . . [than] this poem which is a poem and nothing more—this poem written solely for the poem's sake."

The Raven and Other Poems (1845) collected Poe's verse with an apologetic preface. Their mannered artifice represents the attempt to invent the harmony and beauty life lacks (cf. "The Conqueror Worm," "The Haunted Palace"). The woman doomed to die for her purity and beauty (cf. "Annabel Lee," "Ulalume") is the symbol of nature's failure to match the poet's ideal. "To One in Paradise" illustrates the manner and the theme:

For, alas! alas! with me
  The light of Life is o'er!
—No more—no more—no more—
(Such language holds the solemn sea
  To the sands upon the shore)
Shall bloom the thunder-blasted tree,
  Or the stricken eagle soar!

The prose poem *Eureka* (1848) was a last effort to fend off disaster by imagining a scientific cosmology. Found dying in the streets of Baltimore, Poe is the romantic genius cut down by the height of his aspirations.

Another tormented dissent from Transcendentalism after an initial fascination came from Herman Melville (1819–91). He associated with the Young America Group of literary nationalists in New York in the late 1840s and wrote fictional romances, often drawn from his adventures as a sailor and increasingly charged with philosophical and psychological themes. After abandoning fiction out of disillusion with his audience and resigning himself to obscurity as a customs inspector, Melville turned to poetry. *Battle Pieces and Aspects of the War* (1866), *John Marr and Other Sailors* (1888), and *Timoleon* (1891), the last two privately printed, were derided and forgotten, as was *Clarel* (1876), a verse novel of some 18,000 tetrameter couplets which explores through a journey-quest to the Holy Land the dilemma of Christian faith or Darwinian skepticism.

Walt Whitman (1819–92) took no note of his almost exact contemporary Melville but acknowledged Poe the romantic neurotic as the antithesis of what he wanted to make himself into. A dreamy boy from a large, mentally unstable, working-class Brooklyn family, Whitman as poet sublimated his sexual anxieties into an ideal of a joyous soul in a robust body. He left school at 15 to become a printer and journalist, editing various newspapers in Brooklyn and Manhattan during the 1840s and trying his hand for a popular audience with sentimental fiction and a temperance novel, *Franklin Evans* (1842). But nothing in the biography hints at the emergence of Whitman as poet. Later he would tell a friend about steeping himself in Emerson: "I was simmering, simmering, simmering; Emerson brought me to a boil." The poems that bubbled up were radical in technique and content. Out of Emerson's call for organic form, Whitman distilled, from translations of the Old Testament and Homer and operatic arias and recitativo, a revolution in verse technique that came to be called free verse: lines irregular in length and stresses, patterned not by meter or rhyme but by repetition of phrase and rhythm. Out of Emerson's call for an Am. seer-prophet, Whitman devised the persona whose colloquial, expansive, often exclamatory voice sounded a "different relative attitude towards God, towards the objective universe, and still more (by reflection, confession, assumption) the quite changed attitude of the ego, the one chanting or talking, towards himself and towards his fellow humanity." He was "large" and sought to "contain multitudes"—the city and countryside, the people and places of America. The opening lines of "Song of Myself," his epic of the democratic individual's consciousness struck, that expansive note from the start:

I celebrate myself, and sing myself,
And what I shall assume you shall as-
    sume,
For every atom belonging to me as
    good belongs to you.

I loafe and invite my soul,
I lean and loafe at my ease observing a
    spear of summer grass.

My tongue, every atom of my blood,
    form'd from this soil, this air,
Born here of parents born from par-
    ents the same, and their parents
    the same,

I, now thirty-seven years old in perfect
    health begin,
Hoping to cease not till death.

In July, 1855, *Leaves of Grass* appeared in a large book designed and printed by the poet. His picture as the people's Everyman provided the frontispiece, but he remained anonymous on the title page and up to the middle of the first and longest of 12 untitled poems (later "Song of Myself"), which itself erupted for 43 pages to occupy half of the book. The "Preface" of sprawling, incantatory paragraphs identified the author as the Am. bard Emerson had anticipated. Whitman sought to compensate for the shocked response of reviewers by publishing several adulatory reviews anonymously and by sending complementary copies to literati. When Emerson responded immediately with rhapsodic praise, Whitman's vocation was confirmed. The next year he published a second edition, now 56 poems, incl. "Crossing Brooklyn Ferry," with Emerson's words on the spine as advertisement.

Emerson's enthusiasm cooled, however, with Whitman's continued emphasis on the body as much as the soul and his identification of the life force with the sexual "urge." But the self-reliant Whitman maintained his independence and devoted his life ("that electric self seeking types") to the organic expansion of *Leaves of Grass* through a succession of editions, though he could not find a commercial publisher until the decade before the "Death-Bed Edition" (1891–92). Whitman revised old poems as he added new ones, reordering the sequence and groupings. With the third edition (1860) the sea-dirges "Out of the Cradle Endlessly Rocking" and "As I Ebb'd with the Ocean of Life," written during the late 1850s out of a profound but mysterious distress, explored the death theme coexistent from the beginning with the celebration of life; and the "Children of Adam" and "Calamus" sections celebrated alternatively love between men and women and love between manly comrades. The edition of 1867 added *Drum Taps*, the Civil War poems, and the Lincoln elegy "When Lilacs Last in the Dooryard Bloom'd."

By then most of Whitman's best poetry was written, but despite failing health he continued to write voluminously in verse and prose with flashes of the old power and compassion. Despite his admirers and disciples, he never received the broad audience and recognition he had hoped for as the Am. bard; but a final Preface, "A Backward Glance O'er Travel'd Roads" (1888), reaffirmed the goals and achievements that he knew had transformed modern poetry.

Though the only comment of Emily Dickinson (1830–86) about Whitman was that she had heard he was "disgraceful," the two represent complementary aspects of the Am. poet stemming from Emerson: the democratic projection of the self into nature and the city, the hermetic absorption of the world into the private self. The religion of the Connecticut River valley where Dickinson grew up as daughter of a prominent Amherst lawyer and public servant was still Congregational, not Unitarian, much less Transcendentalist. But Dickinson, the only family member not to join the local church, committed herself, in part (like Thoreau) under Emerson's inspiration, to another vocation: recording with unwavering attention the interior drama of consciousness.

Adapting the quatrain of the hymnal (and perhaps the sigla of elocution manuals) to her own purposes, Dickinson lines out, not sentence by sentence but word by word, single moments of perception and emotion. Each taut, spare poem expresses with unblinking fidelity the truth of its moment, and the accumulation of poems charts the extremes of her experience: God as present or absent, love as fulfillment or renunciation, nature as harmonious or alien. A poem beginning "The loss of something ever felt I" locates the first act of consciousness as an experience of radical bereavement, after which the individual consciousness seeks completion either through its relation to the other—nature, lover, God—or through focusing on its own integration. Though Dickinson found relation to nature, lover, or God much chancier, less assuredly typological than Emerson, this pair of separate and contrasting quatrains poses the alternatives in typically compact, gnomic terms:

Circumference thou Bride of Awe
Possessing thou shalt be
Possessed by every hallowed Knight
That dares to covet thee

Lads of Athens, faithful be,
To Thyself,
And Mystery—
All the rest is Perjury—

A recluse in her father's house by the age of 30, Dickinson maintained the independence her poetry required from the demands made on an unmarried woman in a bourgeois Victorian household. In the late 1850s she began making fair copies of poems and binding them with thread into packets which were found in a dresser drawer after her death. During the early 1860s a crisis, perhaps involving frustrated or thwarted love, precipitated an extraordinarily creative outburst: 681 poems between 1862 and '64, over a third of her 1800-odd poems. The "He" in her love poems seems to be Jesus, or a human lover (the biographical evidence is suggestive rather than conclusive), or the masculine aspect of her self—or overlays of all these. Her word for the ecstatic fulfillment of consciousness in triumphant selfhood was Immortality, sometimes expressed as a marriage, often one deferred to the next life; and despite deprivation and renunciation she experienced momentary intimations of Immortality in the upstairs bedroom which often served as images of her secluded consciousness.

In 1862 Dickinson was sufficiently confident to write to the critic Thomas Wentworth Higginson, sending three poems and asking his advice. His prompt expression of interest, she said, saved her life, but his well-intentioned insensitivity to her oddities of phrasing, rhythm, capitalization, and punctuation, as well as his caution against publication, confirmed Dickinson's sense that she would have to be content with posthumous fame. Though poems and letters began to appear after her death with some of the eccentricities normalized, the unbowdlerized collected *Poems* (1955) and *Letters* (1958) assured her place as the only woman among the great romantic poets.

Frederick Goddard Tuckerman (1821–73) was another Massachusetts recluse (living near Greenfield) whose poetry dissented from Emersonian optimism with a melancholy regret deepened by his wife's death in 1857. Though his verse appeared in magazines and in *Poems* (1860), and though he had Emerson, Tennyson, and Longfellow as admirers, Tuckerman was known during his lifetime as a botanist rather than a poet. The bulk of his work consists of five series of sonnets, notable for experimenting with that tight form and for focusing feeling in a sharply observed image, as when he depicts the soul "shooting the void in silence" like "a bird that shuts his wings for better speed." Yvor Winters called "The Cricket," Tuckerman's long meditation on the individual in nature, "the greatest poem in Eng. of the century." The other great sonneteer of the century was yet another Massachusetts recluse, Jones Very (1813–80), who infused his Puritan spirit with Transcendentalist exaltation. Visiting Very after intense mystical experiences sent him briefly into an asylum, Emerson pronounced him "profoundly sane."

The reputation of the Massachusetts poets popularly known (along with Emerson) as the "Household Poets" has diminished with time. More Victorian than romantic, they run to moralizing sentiment and prefer conventional forms to experimentation. The popularity of Henry Wadsworth Longfellow (1807–82) rivaled Tennyson's on both sides of the Atlantic. As a Harvard professor he helped to introduce Ger. lit. to the U.S., and he translated Dante. His most famous narrative poems are: *Evangeline* (1847), a tragic romance in hexameters about the exodus of Fr. Canadians to Louisiana; *The Song of Hiawatha* (1855, the year of the first ed. of *Leaves of Grass*), an epic rendering of Am. Indian legends into tetrameters imitative of the Finnish *Kalevala*; and *The Courtship of Miles Standish* (1858), a blank verse version of the famous Puritan love triangle. "The Psalm of Life" answers human mortality with a call to the work ethic, and "Excelsior" expresses a Browningesque summons to strive in the face of failure. Longfellow's chief poetic interest now lies in lyrics like "The Jewish Cemetery at Newport" and "The Cross of Snow."

James Russell Lowell (1819–91) succeeded to Longfellow's chair at Harvard and became the first editor of the *Atlantic Monthly* and a powerful liberal voice in Am. journalism. 1848 was Lowell's *annus mirabilis*, during which he published *A Fable for Critics*, a spoof of contemp. Am. writers in Popean couplets and outrageous rhymes; the first series of *The Biglow Papers*, written in a rollicking version of Yankee dialect for a down-home satire on such political issues as slavery and the Mexican War; and *The Vision of Sir Launfal*, a didactic extension of the Grail legend. "The Ode Recited at the Harvard Commemoration" of the Civil War dead (1865), written largely in one night, is perhaps his noblest poem. The literary, as opposed to medical, fame of Oliver Wendel Holmes (1809–94) rests on the several volumes of *Breakfast Table* episodes collected from the *Atlantic* and on such verse favorites of Boston local color as "Old Ironsides," "The Last Leaf," "The Chambered Nautilus," "Dorothy Q.: A Family Portrait," and "The Deacon's Masterpiece: Or, The Wonderful 'One-Hoss Shay.'"

In contrast to these Boston Brahmins, the only yeoman among the Household Poets was John Greenleaf Whittier (1807–92). Inspired by Robert Burns' Scots poetry, Whittier began to versify his Quaker piety and his Abolitionist opposition to slavery. Today "Barbara Fritchie" seems marred by flag-waving patriotism, and "The Barefoot Boy," "Maud Mullen," and "Telling the Bees" by mawkish sentiment. However, *Snow-Bound* (1866) remains a movingly nostalgic idyll of rural New England life.

Dickinson's poetry emerges from—and stands out from—the work of a number of female writers so commercially successful that Hawthorne complained enviously of the "scribbling women." The best known was Lydia Sigourney (1791–1865), the "Sweet Singer of Hartford," whose readership vied with that of the British Mrs. Felicia Hemans. Tear-jerking titles such as "Widow at Her Daughter's Funeral," "Death of an Infant in Its Mother's Arms," and "Wife of a Missionary at Her Husband's Grave" evoke the morbidity that account for Mrs. Sigourney's popularity and its decline.

The contrast between Sidney Lanier (1842–81) and Stephen Crane (1871–1900) illustrates the exhaustion of romanticism in Am. p. Born of old Virginia stock, Lanier pursued a career in both music and lit. even after service in the Confederate army and four months as a military prisoner brought on the consumption that made his remaining years a strenuous effort to stave off death. The extreme musicality of his lang. and the lush metaphorical straining for a diffuse effect indicate his admiration for Poe; in *The Science of Eng. Verse* (1880) Lanier used his knowledge of music theory and his experience as a symphony flautist to codify Poe's correlation of music and poetry into strict rules based on the assumption that the metrical foot, like the musical bar, was governed not just by pattern of stress but by syllabic duration. "Corn" and "The Symphony" established his fame in 1875 with a fiercely Southern denunciation of corrupt commerce in favor of a chivalric-agrarian ideal. "The Marshes of Glynn" and "Sunrise," the latter written in a high fever on his deathbed, express the last gasp of romantic typology as they celebrate the dying of the individual back into the sublimity of nature and nature's God. By contrast, the terse, irregular verse in Crane's *The Black Riders* (1895) and *War Is Kind* (1899), written in part in response to the angularity of Dickinson's newly published poems, extends the anti-romantic naturalism of his fiction, but Crane's tough-guy irony before man's fate in a universe of chance does not mask the wistful vulnerability, even sentimentality, of his tender heart.

Some names from the end of the century which warrant mention are: Thomas Bailey Aldrich (1836–1907) and Bayard Taylor (1825–78), genteel New York "bohemians" in search of the Ideal; the Harvard aesthetes George Santayana (1863–1952), Trumbull Stickney (1874–1904), and William Vaughn Moody (1869–1910), the last of whom came up against the brashness of Chicago when he took a post at the university there; James Whitcomb Riley (1849–1916), the "Hoosier Poet" of sentimental dialect poems; Paul Laurence Dunbar (1872–1906), son of Kentucky slaves, who wrote both dialect poems of plantation life and conventional lyrics; Lizette Woodworth Reese (1856–1935), the Baltimore schoolteacher who sang of nature and death in clean, direct lines that marked a departure from Mrs. Sigourney and her sisters; and Joaquin Miller (1841?–1913), who was born in a covered wagon on the way west and whose *Songs of the Sierras* (1871) earned him his role as swaggering bard of the Far West. But these are all decidedly minor figures. The romantic ideology which had made for the energy and experimentation of the middle years of the century had played itself out. Am. culture needed the jolt of a new ideology—modernism—to galvanize a generation of poets whose achievement rivals that of the Eng. Ren.

III. MODERNIST POETRY, 1900–1935. Edwin Arlington Robinson (1869–1935), Robert Frost (1874–1963), and John Crowe Ransom (1888–1974) are premodernists. Like their modernist contemporaries, they felt the increasing gravity and precariousness of the human predicament, as the decline of religious belief and metaphysical certitude, the subversion of Enlightenment rationalism and then of romantic intuition left the unprotected individual at risk in an indifferent universe and an increasingly violent social world. But the strongly regional conservatism of these three made them resist breaking the old forms and reject the formal experimentation that impelled modernism internationally. Robinson grew up in Gardiner, Maine, the model for his Tilbury Town. His poetry ran to long Arthurian narratives in strong blank verse: *Merlin* (1917), *Launcelot* (1920), *Tristram* (1927). But his most widely read poems are the tragic vignettes of the people of Tilbury Town—"Miniver Cheevey," "Eros Turannos," "Mr. Flood's Party"—and the ruefully melancholy sonnets about faith and doubt, such as "Maya" and "New England." Frost's tribute to Robinson applies equally to Frost himself: "His theme was unhappiness, but his skill was as happy as it was playful. . . . We mourn, but with the qualification that, after all, his life was a revel in the felicities of lang."

Frost's long career from *North of Boston* (1914) to *In the Clearing* (1962) made him revered in the U.S. and England, where he lived as a young man and learned from the pastoral, regional verse of Thomas Hardy and his friend Edward Thomas. Receiving the Emerson-Thoreau medal in 1958, he said that from Emerson he learned to write sentences crafted so close to the flesh and bone that they would bleed if cut, but he dissented from Emerson's blindness to evil and insisted that an unresolved dualism was the dialectic of nature and man. His New England pastorals—"Home Burial," "For Once, Then, Something," "Design," "West-Running Brook," "Directive"—test out the premises of Puritanism and Transcendentalism and leave the answer open. Aesthetic form provided "a momentary stay against confusion" for those provisional conclusions that allow us to persist in pitting our wits and will against ultimate defeat. Scorning free verse, Frost argued that poetic skill lay in making the dramatic tones and inflections of the speaking voice break through the strict pattern of meter and rhyme. Frost and Ransom the Tennessean admired each other's work and shared a sense of form as necessary control for the voice's ironic modulations. Ransom's "Dead Boy," "Judith of Bethulia," "Janet Waking," "The Equilibrists," and "Persistent Explorer" delineate a fallen world in which death is an omnipresent fact, transcendence a nostalgic idea, and the conflict of head and heart an impasse that paralyzes love. After *Chills and Fever* (1924) and *Two Gentlemen in Bonds* (1927) Ransom devoted himself chiefly to teaching and advocating the New Criticism (discussed below).

These poets' skepticism unsettled the typological sense of Edwards and Emerson and allowed only the double terms of trope: in Frost's words, "play's the thing. All virtue in 'as if.'" But the modernists refused to reside in ironic paradox and pressed heroically on to find the terms and means by which the imagination, even without the epistemological and metaphysical claims of romanticism, might still function as the supreme faculty of human cognition, potent enough to meet the psychological, moral, and political crises of the 20th c. Their manifestoes vehemently rejected romantic idealism and optimism. They brought to the point of rupture and release the irony which increasingly threatened to subvert romantic holism in the course of the 19th c., and thereby they reconstituted the key issue of romanticism: the validation of the imagination as the agency of individual coherence, outside systems and structures, in a secular, relativized world.

In contrast to romanticism, modernism assumed a disjunction between art and life: meaning not revealed but made. Construction was itself the cognitive act; mastery of the medium disclosed the form of perception, organic now not to the operations of nature but to the internal relations of its structure. Yet the dialectic between symbolism and imagism—the two most widely influential and persistent strains within modernist poetry—represent differing inclinations that resume in more complex formulations the distinction between tropes and types which had become cloudier and more problematic during the 19th c. As the romantic synthesis of subject and object through the agency of Spirit became harder to maintain, the destabilized focus of perception veered back and forth. Symbolism, developing out of Poe through Baudelaire and Rimbaud to Mallarmé and Valéry, exemplified the tendency to turn inward on subjective consciousness and absorb impressions of the external world into the expressions of moods and feelings of increasing subtlety. Imagism, initiated by Pound in 1912 as an alternative to symbolism, signaled the countertendency to fix consciousness in its encounter with the phenomenal world. Both symbolism and imagism are modernist rather than romantic because modernism validates subject (symbolism) and object (imagism) in the authority of the artwork rather than of Spirit. But symbolism seeks the multivalent suggestiveness of metaphor and the rich imprecision of music, where imagism seeks a clean-edged delineation of image and a painterly disposition of elements.

Ezra Pound (1885–1972) defined the image as the presentation of "an intellectual and emotional complex in an instant of time" and drew up the imagist axioms: "1. Direct treatment of the 'thing,' whether subjective or objective. 2. To use absolutely no word that does not contribute to the presentation. 3. As regarding rhythm: to compose in the sequence of the musical phrase, not in the sequence of a metronome." Direct presentation opposed romantic reflection and didacticism and mandated a rendering of the experience so that the poem rendered itself as experience. Strict verbal economy militated against emotional diffuseness. Breaking the pentameter allowed a rhythmic variety and precision unique to the particular aesthetic presentation.

In Whitman, Pound recognized the authentic Am. poetic impulse, but he took it as his vocation to educate and civilize their impulse with Old World culture. Pound's early poetry showed the influence of *fin de siècle* decadence, esp. that of early Yeats, and during the London years just before and after World War I, Pound, the energetic polemicist for modern art, apprenticed himself by writing in imitation of Gr., Lat., Provençal, Old Eng., and Chinese poetry, collected in *Personae* (1926). "Hugh Selwyn Mauberley" (1920) marked a turning point; venting his outrage at the war and a dying Eng. culture and exorcising the remnants of a decadent romanticism, he departed for Paris, and thence to Italy, and took up his life-long epic, *The Cantos*.

But how to write a historical epic which was also modern (and romantic) in locating itself in the individual consciousness? The lessons of imagism had to be extended and accommodated to temporal devel. for the longer venture. Pound felt that Amy Lowell (1874–1925) had perverted his movement with a soft-focus romantic impressionism that he dubbed "Amygism." In 1914 he wrote an essay on "Vorticism", the short-lived attempt by artists and writers around Wyndham Lewis to vitalize arts and culture in the London "vortex," and the notion of the image as vortex charged it with energetic movement and power drawn from the analogues of the machine and the whirlpool. But the big conceptual breakthrough came with Pound's absorption during the mid-teens in the notebooks of the Am. philosopher and Orientalist Ernest Fenollosa. Pound edited for publication Fenollosa's essay on "The Chinese Written Character as a Medium for Poetry," and he made Fenollosa's literal transcription of Chinese and Japanese poems into the magnificent Eng. renderings of *Cathay* (1915). Fenollosa reconnected Pound with his romantic roots by presenting ideogrammic lang. as pictographs grounded in the divinely ordained operations of nature and communicating directly without the logical and discursive machinery of parts of speech and syntax. *The Cantos* began as an extended effort, in its juxtaposition of phrases and images, at an Eng. equivalent of the ideogrammic presentation of ideas as actions.

The Cantos came out in segments throughout Pound's life, and the posthumous collection (1972) ends with Canto 120. His prose volumes include *ABC of Reading* (1934), *Guide to Kulchur* (1938), *Literary Essays* (1954), and *Selected Prose* (1973). Denounced for his anti-Semitism and sympathy with Mussolini before and during World War II, Pound was brought to Washington, D.C., in 1945 to be charged with treason, and spent 13 years in a mental hospital before returning to Italy for his final years. The ideogrammic method, historical scope, mythological references, and erudite sources of *The Cantos* are demanding, but the poem constitutes a heroic effort at resolving polarities: on the psychological level, reason with instinct, Apollonian control with Dionysian energy, archetypal masculine with feminine, sexuality with mysticism; philosophically, Gr. Neoplatonism with Confucianism; economically, individual freedom with governmental regulation of money; and historically, the record of war and violence with the possibility of building a paradisal society on earth. Beneath the modernist collage technique, the underlying romantic premises become more explicit in the course of the poem. Despite the massive egotism of the undertaking, Pound ends up insisting that the individual submit to the *Tao* and find his humble place within the eternal round of nature, that healthy economics extend the *Tao* into social organization, and that art seek to express these (typological) truths. In this ideogram from Canto 2 the union of the nymph Tyro with Poseidon presents a momentary epiphany of the sexual and metaphysical energy irradiating and resolving natural and human activity:

And by the beach-run, Tyro,
  Twisted arms of the sea-god,
Lithe sinews of water gripping her,
    cross-hold,
And the blue-grey glass of the wave
    tents them,
Glare azure of water, cold-welter, close
    cover.

William Carlos Williams (1883–1963) and Pound met at the University of Pennsylvania and remained lifelong if contentious friends. Williams teased that where Pound's word was caviar his was bread; resolutely the naturalist ("no ideas but in things"), Williams steered clear of myths and metaphysics. Critical of Pound's and more esp. Eliot's expatriation, Williams the literary nationalist committed himself as doctor and poet to poor, grimy, industrial Rutherford, next to Paterson, New Jersey ("The local is the universal"). The prose sections of *Spring and All* (1923) hail the imagination as a primal force, decreating and re-creating the world into an aesthetic invention which takes its place as an object in the world. Williams was fascinated by the experiments of Gertrude Stein (1874–1946) with words as things but shied away from her attempt to detach words from referentiality. For Williams, the art-work, though integral to itself, was not disjunct from or opposite to nature but "apposite" to it. His interest in painting and his friendship with precisionist painters like Charles Sheeler and Charles Demuth taught him to make his imagism into a kind of verbal cubism, using lineation as an analytical device to work against rather than with the syntactic groupings of words, splicing and rearranging the expected verbal relationships so as to focus maximum attention on the words themselves and the complexities of their relationships, as in:

so much depends
upon

a red wheel
barrow

glazed with rain
water

beside the white
chickens.

The many books of shorter lyrics—incl. such other favorites as "Spring and All," "The Pot of Flowers," "To a Poor Old Woman," "The Yachts," "Flowers by the Sea"—are now edited into a two-volume *Collected Poems* (1986–89). However, by the late 1930s Williams was experimenting with a longer, more complex project (*The Cantos* and Joyce's *Finnegans Wake* were two sources) published as *Paterson* in five books between 1946 and 1958 and in a single volume in 1963. Establishing the identification of the doctor-poet with his city, the poem's fragmented vignettes follow out the city's history and the human lifespan in a self-generating, self-completing open form that finds its way, then circles back on itself.

This engagement with time and history required a different sense of prosody. As Williams' *Autobiography* (1951), *Selected Essays* (1954), and *Selected Letters* (1957) show, he became obsessed in his later years with defining a measure more appropriate to the Am. idiom, and in "The Descent" he felt he discovered the principle of the "variable foot", which conceived poetic lines as musical bars having roughly the same duration but containing varying numbers of syllables and stresses like notes within the bar. He explored the possibilities of the variable foot, the lines stepped gracefully in tercets down the page in such poems—longer, more personal and meditative than the early work—as "To Daphne and Virginia" (his daughters-in-law), "For Eleanor and Bill Monahan" (old friends), "The Sparrow" (dedicated to his father), and "Of Asphodel, That Greeny Flower" (for his wife of many years).

Hilda Doolittle (1886–1961) met Pound in Philadelphia, was briefly engaged to him, and became part of his London literary circle. He gave her the *nom de plume* "H. D." and coined the term "imagist" to describe early poems of hers such as "Oread":

Whirl up, sea—
whirl your pointed pines,
splash your great pines
on our rocks,
hurl your green over us,
cover us with your pools of fir.

H. D. was drawn to Dickinson's poems as they were published in the 1920s; the two women were akin not in external circumstances but in their extraordinary sensitivity and their unswerving attendance upon recording the life of consciousness. H. D. saw her own destiny played out within the violent sexual and international politics of her time, and her autobiography turned on crucial events: the oedipal conflicts with her father and mother; the love conflicts with Pound, the Eng. poet Richard Aldington, D. H. Lawrence, and later male "initiators"; the breakup of her marriage to Aldington during World War I; the birth of her daughter by another man; the sudden advent of the Eng. novelist Bryher as the woman who rescued her from despair and death at war's end; the moments of cosmic consciousness in which she participated in life's mystery. These traumas brought her to Freud in the mid 1930s for therapy, but throughout her life real relief came from her ability to find in Gr. and Egyptian myths and mystery cults the archetypes for her own experience and then—a more remarkable achievement—to project her life into myth, in the poems of *Sea Garden* (1916), *Hymen* (1921), and *Heliodora* (1924), in the impressionistic fiction of her middle period, and in the memoirs and poetic sequences of her last phase.

The fiction taught H. D. to constellate images in a larger temporal/narrative framework, opening up form and perspective, which made possible *Trilogy* (three poems pub. separately in war-torn London and together in 1973), *Helen in Egypt* (1961), and *Hermetic Definition* (1972). *Helen*, an anti-epic told in lyrics with prose bridges, resumes the matter of Troy, which from Homer to Pound provided the theme of love and war, from the woman's perspective. It is perhaps the most ambitious poem written by a woman in Eng. and fulfills its ambition.

H. D. edited with Bryher the first selection of poems by Marianne Moore (1887–1972), though Moore's chaste modesty and reserve put her at the opposite temperamental pole. In "Poetry" her imagist dislike of metaphorical obfuscation called for "imaginary gardens with real toads in them." And Moore's Presbyterian faith gave her imagism a clear typological purpose; keying her keen eye to the mind's perceptions, she read flora and fauna as quirky, witty emblems of human virtue and weakness spun out in elaborate, elegant syllabics. The *Complete Poems* (1967) contained such admired pieces as "The Fish," "To a Snail," "In the Days of Prismatic Color," "The Mind Is an Enchanting Thing," "The Wood Weasel," and "He 'Digesteth Harde Yron'" (on the ostrich).

The declaration in 1928 by T. S. Eliot (1888–1965), already a British subject, that he was classicist in lit., royalist in politics, and Anglo-Catholic in religion would seem to sum up his distance from the Am. scene. But Eliot recognized that he combined a "Catholic cast of mind" with "a Calvinist heritage, and a Puritanical temperament" and that his Am. roots, his growing up in St. Louis and New England, were the deepest sources of his personality and poetry. Both in poetic practice and in his criticism, however, Eliot trained himself to mask the autobiographical impulse. Though he admitted that "a poet in a romantic age cannot be a 'classical' poet except in tendency," the early essays set the norms for a modernist "classicism": the need for an "historical sense" in an "impersonal" poet ("Trad. and the Individual Talent"); the "autotelic" character of aesthetic form ("The Function of Crit."); metaphorical image as the "objective correlative" of emotion ("Hamlet and His Problems"); and the crippling "dissociation of sensibility" since the 17th c. which required reintegration ("The Metaphysical Poets").

Eliot dated his poetic maturation from reading Arthur Symons' *The Symbolist Trad. in Lit.* in 1908. "The Love Song of J. Alfred Prufrock," "Preludes," and "Rhapsody on a Windy Night," and others in *Prufrock and Other Observations* (1917), the volume which Pound thought established Eliot as the poet of his generation, echo Laforgue and Baudelaire; and symbolism provided the perspective and techniques for finding in urban life the tropes to objectify the twists and turns of his acute self-consciousness. *Poems* (1920) used extreme verbal compression in tight quatrains to anatomize the conflict between sexual body and paralyzed spirit in modern society. The anxiety of Eliot's unhappy marriage precipitated *The Waste Land* (1922), which Pound helped edit into a brilliant collage of episodes in different voices and styles. So successful was Eliot's dramatization of his disillusionment and his ache for deliverance that *The Waste Land* became the most influential poem of the postwar "Lost Generation."

"The Hollow Men" (1925) was a coda to the early period, but after his conversion to Christianity, Eliot introduced, in the "Ariel" poems of the late '20s and in *Ash Wednesday* (1930), a more personal voice, now echoing Scripture, Dante, and the Book of Common Prayer to meditate on opening the concupiscent heart to redemptive grace. The essay "From Poe to Valéry" (1948) exorcised symbolism as self-enclosing, self-defeating narcissism, and "The Music of Poetry" (1942) indicated the swing from prosodic experimentation to the traditional forms and musical structure of *Four Quartets* (1943). Eliot's Calvinist sense made it difficult for him to read manifestations of the Incarnation in a sinful world, but each quartet uses a five-part structure similar to *The Waste Land* to concentrate on a place of autobiographical importance as a typological "point of intersection of the timeless / With time." "The Dry Salvages," the third Quartet, uses the Mississippi River and the Massachusetts coastline to invoke the Incarnation, while "Little Gidding" moves from the flames of the London Blitz to a fusion of Pentecostal fire and the Dantesque rose of the Paradiso:

> And all shall be well
> And all manner of thing shall be well
> When the tongues of flame are in-
> folded
> Into the crowned knot of fire
> And the fire and the rose are one.

Eliot's verse is contained in the *Collected Poems* (1963) and the *Collected Plays* (1967).

Where Eliot took his inspiration from the symbolism of Laforgue and Baudelaire, Wallace Stevens (1879–1955) took his from the symbolism of Mallarmé and Valéry, and it deepened in the course of a poetic career slowed initially by Stevens' career as an insurance lawyer and executive in Hartford, CT. "Sunday Morning" (1915) expressed in gorgeously textured blank verse a sad affirmation that the death of God obligated the mortal imagination to invest nature with the aura of paradise. Other poems in *Harmonium* (1923) aimed at a symbolist "pure poetry" whose agile wit and exotic effects of sound and color rendered discordant states of sensibility without discursive commentary, as in "Domination of Black," "The Emperor of Ice Cream," or "Bantam in Pine Woods," which begins: "Chieftain Iffucan of Azcan in caftan / Of tan, with henna hackles, halt!"

"The Idea of Order at Key West" (1934) answers the charge of escapist hedonism from Yvor Winters and Marxist critics of the '30s by demonstrating the imagination's power to satisfy the mind's "rage for order" through recomposing experience into a fiction which comprehends the flux yet reflects back on it the notion of a possible pattern. Connections and relations are not prescribed by God or nature but contrived in figures of speech. *Notes toward a Supreme Fiction* (1942) explores the tropological process under the subheadings "It Must Be Abstract," "It Must Change," and "It Must Give Pleasure." The essays in *The Necessary Angel* (1951) complement the later poems by showing how the shifting interaction between reality and the "mundo" of the imagination "help[s] us to live our lives." Here is the moral validation of the symbolist trope from "Description Without Place" (1945):

> It matters, because everything we say
> Of the past is description without
> place, a cast
>
> Of the imagination, made in sound;
> And because what we say of the future
> must portend,
>
> Be alive with its own seemings, seem-
> ing to be
> Like rubies reddened by rubies redden-
> ing.

In the later poems in the *Collected Poems* (1954) and *Opus Posthumous* (1957, 1989)—"A Primitive like an Orb," "Final Soliloquy of the Interior Paramour," "The World As Meditation"—the ironic highjinks of *Harmonium* give way to a sinuous, incantatory harmonizing of abstract lang. and recurrent archetypal figures in slow, stately pentameters. At one point Stevens wanted to call *Collected Poems* "The Whole of Harmonium."

When Hart Crane (1899–1932) gave *White Buildings* (1926) an epigraph from Rimbaud, he signaled his hope of achieving through symbolist means—synaesthesia, dense overlays of connotative and metaphorical suggestiveness, oracular apostrophe—the romantic rapture that mortality and flux denied him, as in these lines from the sequence about love and loss called "Voyages":

> Bind us in time, O Seasons clear, and
> awe.
> O minstrel galleons of Carib fire,
> Bequeath us to no earthly shore until
> Is answered in the vortex of our grave
> The seal's wide spindrift gaze toward
> paradise.

The *Letters* (1965) and essays like "Mod. Poetry" explore the efficacy of a symbolist "logic of metaphor" in a machine age. Through association with Waldo Frank's circle of literary nationalists in Manhattan, Crane embarked on an epic with the Brooklyn Bridge as its central symbol: an engineering marvel that yoked opposing shores (and, metaphorically, psychological and moral contradictions) and manifested a technological sublime to match the sublimity of the wilderness. *The Bridge* (1930) sought to elide past and present in the poet's consciousness and thus synthesize a myth or mystique strong enough to defeat *The Waste Land*'s impotent disillusionment by projecting Whitman's prophecy into an industrialized, urban America. Crane's overwrought psyche cracked under the stress of alcoholism, neurosis, and fear that *The Bridge* was a failure. "The Broken Tower" articulates the ecstatic despair that led to his suicide: he never knew whether he was a seer or a fake in seeking to break through rational categories and glimpse godhead in the compressed indirections of metaphor.

Whitman was a touchstone for others besides Crane. The Harlem Renaissance of the 1920s and '30s was the first big movement in the arts for Am. blacks and signaled their growing political and cultural consciousness. In poetry James Weldon Johnson (1871–1938) was a transitional figure; the major voices were Claude McKay (1891–1948), Countee Cullen (1903–46), and—most importantly—Langston Hughes (1902–67), who claimed to be Whitman's "darker brother" in singing his America through spirituals, jazz, and the blues. The Midwest also had its populist Whitmanesque bards: Carl Sandburg (1878–1967) with *Chicago Poems* (1916), *Smoke and Steel* (1920), and *The People, Yes* (1936); Vachel Lindsay (1879–1931) with "The Congo," "General William Booth Enters into Heaven," and "Abraham Lincoln Walks at Midnight"; and Edgar Lee Masters (1868–1950) with *Spoon River Anthology* (1915).

Other minor poets confirm, even beneath the modernist manner, the lingering romantic tenor of the period. Archibald MacLeish (1891–1982) was an expatriate aesthete in the '20s, echoing experimentalists like Eliot and Pound ("Ars Poetica" [1926], *The Hamlet of A. MacLeish* [1928]), and a social bard during the Depression and war years (*Frescoes for Mr. Rockefeller's City*, 1933); but his best poems show him to be an elegantly skilled lyric poet in the elegiac mode. e e cummings (1894–1962) played the iconoclast with his eccentric punctuation, typography, and spatial arrangement, and he talked tough in order to shock. But, as his *Complete Poems* (1972) show, he is unabashedly romantic, celebrating at once the individual's integrity and his transcendence through union with the beloved and nature. cummings' religious sense of life's sacredness goes back through his Unitarian minister-father to New England Transcendentalism. Conrad Aiken (1889–1973) flirted with imagism but found symbolism and the verbal lushness of fellow-Southerners Poe and Lanier more congenial to his introspective, sometimes psychoanalytic, sometimes philosophical mode. The lyrics of Elinor Wylie (1885–1928) and Edna St. Vincent Millay (1892–1950), dissecting the pain of love, death, and beauty in the woman's heart, are traditional in form and echo the Eng. and Am. romantics.

Another generation reformulated modernism in the '30s. Objectivism tightened further the imagist sense of the poem as constructing an encounter with things into a poem which itself has the integrity of (in Emerson's phrase) "a new thing." The chief objectivists, all proletarian in politics like Williams rather than elitist like Pound, were Louis Zukofsky (1904–78), whose indebtedness to his friend Pound, despite his Judaism and Marxism, is clear from his long autobiographical poem *A* (1979), and George Oppen (1908–84), whose *Discrete Series* (1934) intensified Williams' jagged, angular minimalism.

At the more conservative end of the spectrum,

the New Criticism translated modernist assumptions into an explicitly *literary* method of textual explication separate from biography or psychoanalysis or hist. The New Criticism studied the technical and structural properties of (in Poe's words) "this very poem—this poem *per se*" to show how the interplay of paradox, irony, tension, and sound create (again Poe) the "totality, or unity, of effect" in the (now Eliot) "autotelic" artwork. The phrase "New Criticism" was coined by Ransom to describe the critical inclination of I. A. Richards, William Empson, Eliot, and Winters. His essays in *The World's Body* (1938), *The New Criticism* (1941), and *Beating the Bushes* (1972)—many of which are collected in *Selected Essays* (1984)—called for and illustrated an "ontological crit." Through Ransom's teaching and editing and that of his students and followers, the New Criticism dominated the academic study and crit. of poetry well into the 1960s. Both Allen Tate (1899–1979) and Robert Penn Warren (b. 1905–89) were members of Ransom's Fugitives, a group of poets and economic agrarians at Vanderbilt, whose manifesto *I'll Take My Stand* (1930) defended Western humanism against the secular materialism and socialist collectivism that had corrupted the North and was corrupting their Southern homeland. Tate was deeply influenced by Poe, the Fr. symbolists, and, most obviously, Eliot. His metrical and rhyme patterns serve as a vise to contain the explosive compression of lang., metaphor, and sound effects. Like Eliot, Tate longed to shed his symbolist imagination for a genuinely symbolic one like Dante's, and his conversion to Catholicism in 1950 allowed the later poems to postulate love, human and divine, as the release from solipsistic impotence (cf. Tate's *Collected Poems* [1977] and *Essays of Four Decades* [1968]). Tate foresaw Warren's development by addressing him in "To a Romantic," for Warren's early "metaphysical" manner, characterized by New Critical tightness and paradox, gave way to a diffuse emotiveness elegizing the mortal self and the disjunction between ideals and experience (cf. *New & Selected Poems* [1985]).

Two important figures, both Californians, cast themselves as anti-modernists. Yvor Winters (1900–68) began by experimenting with both imagism and symbolism (*Early Poems*, 1966); however, in the late 1920s he concluded that both strains of modernist poetry exhibited a morally dangerous romanticism for which Emerson and Whitman were the Am. prophets and Hart Crane's breakdown and suicide the logical outcome, and he set about writing a formalist verse modeled on the Eng. Ren. as a rationally controlled reflection on morally significant experience (cf. *Collected Poems* [1978]). *In Defense of Reason* (1947) contains his essays articulating the critical norms he taught at Stanford for decades. Winters had only contempt for the poetry of Robinson Jeffers (1887–1962), who ignored both Winters and the modernist experimenters to prophesy an apocalyptic romanticism to a doomed age. The long, loose lines of his free verse, reflecting the scale of the Carmel and Big Sur landscape, identified him as a shadow-bard to Whitman. Narratives such as *Roan Stallion* (1925) and *The Double Axe* (1948) dramatize the tragedy of a human consciousness whose alienation from nature issues in neuroses and psychoses. The shorter lyrics and meditations urge, often ecstatically, the extinction of consciousness in the "brute beauty" of things which constitutes "the beauty of God," and they anticipate in the extinction of the species a return to cosmic harmony (cf. *Collected Poetry*, 1988–).

Both Winters and Jeffers rejected modernist aestheticism and insisted on value and truth extrinsic to art: Winters in a theistic humanism, Jeffers in a pantheistic inhumanism. But beyond their own work, the contradictory terms of their opposition to each other and to modernism illuminate in reverse perspective the dialectic through which imagism and symbolism resumed the old Puritan distinction between type and trope which lay at the heart of romanticism. A.G.

IV. THE POSTWAR PERIOD. The poets who came of age in the period immediately following World War II found themselves in a difficult relation to their modernist predecessors. On the one hand, the work of Eliot, Pound, Stevens, Frost, Moore, and Crane had provided younger poets with an extraordinary range of formal and thematic resources, yet this same variety also proved a stumbling block to further experimentation. It seemed to Randall Jarrell that modernism, "the most successful and influential body of poetry of this century—is dead." Such an elegiac assessment of the era masked a desire felt by many poets of this generation to have a clean slate. Innovative works such as *Spring and All*, *The Cantos*, *Stanzas in Meditation*, or *The Waste Land* had challenged the structure of traditional verse; now it was time for a stock-taking that would seize upon the liberating advantages of Fr. *vers libre* and the derived Anglo-Am. free verse but curb their excesses.

Writers born in the first two decades of the 20th c.—Theodore Roethke (1908–63), Elizabeth Bishop (1911–79), John Berryman (1914–72), Randall Jarrell (1914–65), Robert Lowell (1917–77), Howard Nemerov (b. 1920), and Richard Wilbur (b. 1921)—turned away from free verse and developed a technically complex, rhetorically difficult poetry modeled on metaphysical poets such as Donne and Herbert as well as the late modernists, John Crowe Ransom, Allen Tate, and Robert Penn Warren. Where poets of the first generation capped their careers by writing long epic or dramatic poems, postwar poets perfected a kind of reflective, ironic lyric that would become the formal model for the two decades following World War II.

T. S. Eliot's lit. crit. provided a major impetus for many of these tendencies, and his cultural crit. introduced a religio-ethical frame within which poetry could be assessed. Many of the values associated with the New Criticism—the importance of trad., the necessity for authorial detachment, the autonomy of the objective artifact—could be found in Eliot's essay, "Trad. and the Individual Talent," which became a *locus classicus* for the postwar era. Eliot's theories of impersonality were extended by the New Critics into prohibitions against intentionalism and affectivity, qualities that would turn the poem into a vehicle of personal expression rather than the site of endistanced meditation. Hence the characteristic voice in poems written during this period is arch and ironic, cautious of bardic pronouncements yet assured in its mastery of complexity and contradiction. Irony now implies more than saying one thing while meaning another; it signals that the artist is in control, able to moderate feeling by transforming it into rhetoric. In a paradox that seemed quite normal to the age, Richard Wilbur spoke of irony as being the "source . . . of what richness and honesty we may sense in a poem," as illustrated by his own example from *The Beautiful Changes* (1947):

> Does sense so stale that it must needs
> derange
> The world to know it? To a praiseful eye
> Should it not be enough of fresh and
> strange
> That trees grow green, and moles can
> course in clay,
> And sparrows sweep the ceiling of our
> day?
> ("Praise in Summer")

This poem, with its careful management of ironic tension, richly embroidered figuration, and steady iambic meters, seems destined less for sensual appreciation than for explication and exegesis. As Jarrell conceded, it was an "age of crit." in which the techniques of close reading and scientific analysis were perfected in ways that ultimately affected how poems were written. The postwar years saw colleges and universities expanding their enrollments with students on the G. I. Bill, and the curriculum needed practical critical methodologies to accommodate this influx. For the first time in history, poets in increasing numbers became teachers, and for the first time "creative writing" became part of the literary curriculum. Whereas for the first generation of modernists, poetry emerged within bohemian enclaves and expatriate communities, it now became a province of the university quarterly and the English Department classroom.

Arguably, the three poets who most typify—but at the same time challenge—the conservative tenor of the times were Robert Lowell, John Berryman, and Elizabeth Bishop. Lowell's first two books, *Land of Unlikeness* (1944) and *Lord Weary's Castle* (1946), exhibit the effects of his close relationship to his New Critical mentors, Ransom and Tate. In these works Lowell takes the metaphysical mode to an extreme, employing a gnarled, convoluted syntax and alliterative lang. to dramatize issues of incarnation and existential doubt. With *Life Studies* (1959) Lowell shocked his teachers and friends by dropping his metaphysical style and speaking in a more personal voice about his ambivalent relationship to his patrician New England family as well as about his troubled marriages, mental breakdowns, and theological anxieties. Despite Lowell's new personalism, he still maintained the formal diction and iambic cadences of his earlier work:

> These are the tranquilized *Fifties*,
> and I am forty. Ought I to regret my
> seedtime?
> I was a fire-breathing Catholic C. O.,
> and made my manic statement,
> telling off the state and president. . . .
> ("Memories of West Street and
> Lepke")

Lowell's rather archaic diction and heavy alliterations temper his confessionalism with a need to contain feeling within definite formal boundaries. In later volumes (*History*, *For Lizzie and Harriet*, and *The Dolphin* [all 1973]) he returned to a more traditional verse, working extensively in unrhymed, blank-verse sonnets.

John Berryman began by writing in the style of Auden and Yeats, but with "Homage to Mistress Bradstreet" (1956) and even more powerfully in *77 Dream Songs* (1964), he developed an idiosyncratic use of persona that permitted him a wide range of voices to dramatize various sides of his rather volatile personality. In the former poem, he collapses his own voice into that of America's first poet, speaking of his own existential malaise through Anne Bradstreet's confessions of spiritual doubt. His major work, *The Dream Songs* (1969), confronts the poet's own biography in a long sequence of lyrics, each built on three 6-line stanzas, written from 1955 until the time of his death in 1972. Despite its autobiographical content, *The Dream Songs* utilizes a complex series of personae in which mocking accusation merges with ironic self-deprecation:

> Life, friends, is boring. We must not say
> so.
> After all, the sky flashes, the great sea
> yearns,
> we ourselves flash and yearn,
> and moreover my mother told me as a
> boy
> (repeatingly) "Ever to confess you're
> bored
> means you have no
>
> Inner Resources."
> ("Dream Song 14")

Elizabeth Bishop, though less rhetorically explosive than either Lowell or Berryman, combined irregular syllabics with microscopically sharp observations to achieve a broken, tense lyricism reminiscent of Marianne Moore. She describes the skin of a fish as

> . . . hung in strips
> like ancient wallpaper,
> and its pattern of darker brown
> . . . like wallpaper: shapes like full-
> blown roses
> stained and lost through age.
> ("The Fish")

In such lines, lang. isolates and refines the image until it loses its conventional associations and becomes something exotic and even heroic. Without moralizing commentary, Bishop sees a world of vivid particulars that gain luster by her patient, at times obsessive, enumerations. In Bishop, as in her two poetic peers, formal mastery implies less the creation of seamless edifice than it does a charged linguistic and rhetorical field in which cognitive acts may be tested. Lowell's and Berryman's harsh, crabbed lang. and Bishop's enjambed, condensed lines represent a formalism impatient with its own limits, dramatizing by sheer verbal energy areas of psychological intensity that cannot yet be expressed.

Lowell's post-*Life Studies* poetry made an indelible mark on a number of writers, incl. Sylvia Plath (1932–63), Anne Sexton (1928–75), W. D. Snodgrass (b. 1926), and, to a lesser extent, John Berryman. Despite their emphasis on autobiographical materials—Plath's black comedy of suicide and patricide, Sexton's explorations of biological and psychological trauma, Berryman's brooding, self-mocking lyrics, and Snodgrass's middle-age-crisis poems—these poets reflect a much more carefully modulated response to their personal content. The strength of Plath's vehement attack in "Daddy," to take the most famous example, comes not from its specific address to her actual father, Otto Plath, who died when she was a child, but from its conscious and careful manipulation of conflicting discursive modes (childhood rhymes, holocaust imagery, obsessive repetitions) that form an "objective correlative" to her psychological condition. "Confessionalism," as M. L. Rosenthal pointed out in his inaugural essay on that movement, should be considered not as a prescriptive formula held by any one group but as a general permission felt by most poets of the period to treat personal experience, even in its most intimate and painful aspects.

If Eliot, Auden, and Frost exerted the most pervasive influence on the dominant trad. of the 1950s, Pound and Williams began to exert a like effect on an emerging avant-garde. Pound's *Cantos* had provided new interest in a historical, "open" poetry, and Williams' hard, objectivist lyrics had encouraged a poetics of visual clarity and metrical experimentation. Charles Olson's (1910–70) essay on "Projective Verse" (1950) extended their ideas with a special emphasis on the poetic line as a register of physiological and emotional contours. He sought to reinvigorate poetic lang. by what he called "composition by field," in which poetic form extends directly from subject matter and in which the line is a register of momentary attentions. According to Olson, the New Critical, autotelic poem left the poet little room for developing a historical or critical "stance toward reality beyond the poem," a stance he wanted to regain, as he felt Pound had done in *The Cantos*. He explored this stance in his *Maximus Poems* (1950–70), a long poem dwelling on the separation of individual from locale due to the ill effects of entrepreneurial capitalism.

Although Olson's essay had few adherents when it first appeared, it was a harbinger of things to come as poets sought a loosening of poetic forms and an alternative to New Critical strictures. The most public announcement of a change came from Allen Ginsberg (b. 1926), whose long poem "Howl" (1956) revived romanticism in its most vatic form and with Whitmanesque enthusiasm made the poet's specific, personal voice the center of concern:

> I saw the best minds of my generation
> destroyed by madness, starving hysterical naked,
> dragging themselves through the negro streets at dawn looking for an
> angry fix,
> angelheaded hipsters burning for the
> ancient heavenly connection to the
> starry dynamo in the machinery of
> night. . . .

Ginsberg's protest against institutional mind-control and McCarthy-era paranoia was made in what he called his "Hebraic-Melvillian bardic breath" and in a lang. as direct and explicit as Wilbur's or Lowell's was oblique. The carefully nuanced ironies of the period were jettisoned in favor of a tone alternately funny, frank, and self-protective. The fact that "Howl" received its first major critical forum in the courtroom of the San Francisco Municipal Court when its publisher went on trial for pornography added new meaning to the poem's social indictment and brought a mass readership to the work of other Beat generation writers. Many of Ginsberg's colleagues—Jack Kerouac (1922–69), Lawrence Ferlinghetti (b. 1920), Gregory Corso (b. 1930), Michael McClure (b. 1932)—provided their own critique of the era, reviving on the one hand a demotic, populist poetics inspired by Whitman and Williams, as well as the romantic, visionary work of Blake and Shelley. Performing their poetry in jazz clubs or coffee houses, occasionally accompanied by jazz, the Beat poets made the poetry reading a primary fact of postwar literary life.

The Beat movement is the most public face of a general romantic revival during the late 1950s and '60s. Whether through Olson's ideas of composition by "field," or through Robert Bly's (b. 1926) ideas of the psychological "deep image," or through Frank O'Hara's (1926–66) "personism," poets began to think of the poem not as a mimesis of experience but as an experience itself, a map of moment-to-moment perceptions whose value is measured by immediacy and sincerity rather than artistic unity. As Robert Duncan (1919–88) said, "the order man may contrive upon the things about him . . . is trivial beside the divine order or natural order he may discover in them." Duncan's remark reinvests Keats's "negative capability" with sacramental implications: the poet relinquishes order that he may discover an order prior to and immanent within experience. The older romantic idea of a synthetic creative imagination (the artist's imperative to order fragmentary reality) gives way to a poetics of "open forms" in which the poem becomes a spontaneous register of phenomenological moments. As with abstract expressionist painting during the same period, the poetics of open form stresses gestural and expressive response over reflective or meditational experience.

In the late 1950s, these general tendencies could be seen in little magazines such as *Origin, The Black Mountain Review, Yugen, The Fifties, Evergreen Review,* and, most importantly, in Donald Allen's 1960 anthol., *The New American Poetry,* which first divided the experimental tendencies of Am. p. into five groups. One group consisted of the poets associated with Black Mountain College in North Carolina, incl. Charles Olson, Robert Creeley (b. 1926), Robert Duncan, Denise Levertov (b. 1923), and Edward Dorn (b. 1929). Another group, associated with the New York art world, incl. Frank O'Hara, John Ashbery (b. 1927), Kenneth Koch (b. 1925), and James Schuyler (b. 1923). The "San Francisco Renaissance" was represented by poets such as Jack Spicer (1925–65), Robin Blaser (b. 1925), Brother Antoninus (William Everson; b. 1912), and Philip Lamantia (b. 1927). A fourth category included other West Coast writers such as Gary Snyder (b. 1930), Philip Whalen (b. 1923), and David Meltzer (b. 1937). Along with the Beats, these groups shared less a common aesthetic than a spirit of bohemian exuberance and anti-establishment camaraderie.

In a similar vein but coming from different sources, Robert Bly, James Wright (1927–80), W. S. Merwin (b. 1927), Galway Kinnell (b. 1927), Mark Strand (b. 1934), and others were developing a poetics of the psychological "deep image." Using Sp. (and to a lesser extent Fr.) surrealism as a source, they experimented with associative techniques that would circumvent discursive thought and tap into unconscious realms. Bly called his practice a "leaping poetry" which manifested "a long floating leap around which the work of art in ancient times used to gather itself like steel shavings around the magnet." Among Deep Image poets one can draw a distinction between those who create discontinuous "leaps" within a minimal, denuded landscape and those for whom the "leap" implies access to a world of numinous presence. Strand and Merwin would be examples of the first sort, creating poems in which lang. has been reduced to a bare minimum. In Wright's or Bly's poetry, conversely, the deep image serves to join quotidian, unreflective experience with realms of spiritual or natural value. Taking a walk, mailing a letter, wasting time become initiatory rites of passage into archetypal experiences. In Bly, a snowstorm transforms a barn into a "hulk blown toward us in a storm at sea; / All the sailors on deck have been blind for many years." Waking in the morning "is like a harbor at dawn; / We know that our master has left us for the day." Unlike their imagist precursors, Deep Image poets strive for clarity without relying on the criterion of verisimilitude.

Surrealism provided a common ground for another group which was initially associated with Bly and Wright but which ultimately moved in a very different direction. David Antin (b. 1932), Jackson MacLow (b. 1922), Jerome Rothenberg (b. 1931), and Armand Schwerner (b. 1927) merged a strong interest in European avant-garde movements such as dada and surrealism with the poetics of Gertrude Stein, the aesthetic theories of Marcel Duchamp and John Cage, and the theatrical "happenings" movement. In a desire to find aesthetic models that exist outside of Western trad. (or marginalized *within* it), many of these poets turned to oral and nonliterate cultures, creating along the way an "ethnopoetics" that stresses cultural and social sources of poetry.

Of course, group designations such as "Black Mountain," "Beat," or "Deep Image" do little to accommodate local variations and individual styles. O'Hara and Snyder are seldom mentioned in the same context, yet the former's desultory chronicles of New York urban life and the latter's descriptions of the natural landscape share a common interest in quotidian movement and surface detail. Poets such as Galway Kinnell or William Stafford (b. 1914) obviously share many "immanentist" or transcendentalist values with Duncan and Levertov, yet they have seldom appeared in the same anthols. or poetry readings. The anthol. "wars" of the 1960s between "open" and "closed," "raw" and "cooked," "Beat" and "square" verse served only to separate poets into warring camps and to provide confused critics with ammunition for dismissive reviews. At the same time, dissension fueled discussion, and the '60s were lively if combative years for Am. p. If there was literary warfare within periodicals, most poets of the period were united in their opposition to Am. adventurism abroad, particularly in the case of the Vietnam War. Furthermore, many of the younger generation identified a poetics of openness and innovation with the social goals of the New Left in which social action, alternate lifestyle, and cultural production were intertwined.

The emergence of political activism among poets, combined with the development of cheap, offset printing technologies, brought new constituencies into the poetry world. Increased activity in Black poetry (see AFRO-AMERICAN POETRY), Asian poetry, Native-Am. poetry (see AMERICAN INDIAN POETRY), and Chicano poetry (q.v.) coincided with the increased social consciousness among minorities during the '60s. The Black poet and playwright LeRoi Jones (b. 1934) threw off his previous Black Mountain and Beat affiliations and adopted the name Imamu Amiri Baraka to signal his alliance with the Black Nationalist movement. In similar fashion, other Black poets—David Henderson (b. 1942), Audre Lorde (b. 1934), June Jordan (b. 1936), Alice Walker (b. 1944), Michael Harper (b. 1938)—worked to foreground Black cultural experience and lang. Although alternate cultural sources became important allies in this endeavor (the use of jazz rhythms in Black writing, the use of oral chant in Native-Am. p., bilingualism in Chicano poetry), the primary formal imperatives came from the more populist, oral styles of the Beats and other new poetry movements.

Coinciding with the growth of literary communities among ethnic minorities, women writers began to write out of the social and political context of the feminist movement. Presses, reading spaces, distribution services, and anthols. provided a range of new resources for women writers, many of whom—like Adrienne Rich (b. 1931)—began their careers within the predominantly male literary community. Although "women's poetry" defines less a set of stylistic features than a historical fact, most women writers would agree with the necessity for revision as defined by Rich: "the act of looking back, of seeing with fresh eyes, of entering an old text from a new critical direction." Many of Rich's poems are just such revisions of previous texts as she sorts through the "book of myths" ("Diving Into the Wreck") to find moments in which women have been marginalized—or ignored outright. Although she began by writing poems very much in the formalist mode of the 1950s, Rich's style gradually loosened to admit her own changing awarenes of women's oppression and to express her anger at patriarchal authority.

The proliferation of poetic styles during the 1970s and '80s has, to some extent, repeated many of the tendencies of the whole modern period, though with obvious refinements. Poets have rejected the more bardic and expressive gestures—what Stanley Plumly calls "experience in capital letters"—of the 1960s in favor of a certain discursiveness, even chattiness, for which the achievement of distinctly personal realms must be accomplished through careful management of tone and diction. The dominant mode of the 1970s and '80s is a reflective lyricism in which technical skill is everywhere evident but nowhere obtrusive. The overtly romantic stance of 1960s poetry, with its emphasis on participation, orality, and energy, has given way to quiet speculation.

Within the major trad. of the 1970s and '80s one can identify three general areas of practice, all of which display a common concern with voice and tone. Among the first group, A. R. Ammons (b. 1926), John Ashbery (b. 1927), Robert Pinsky (b. 1940), Louise Gluck (b. 1943), Sandra McPherson (b. 1943), and Robert Hass (b. 1941) merge the philosophical skepticism of Wallace Stevens with the ethical, cultural concerns of Yvor Winters or Robert Penn Warren. Ashbery's poetry, perhaps the most sophisticated and complex of the group, manifests what he calls "the swarm effect" of lang. vacillating between opposing lures of "leaving out" or "putting in." His long, desultory lyrics such as "The Skaters" (1966), "Self-Portrait in a Convex Mirror" (1975), and the prose trilogy *Three Poems* (1972) record the fluctuating patterns of a disjunct consciousness. Unable to believe either in a supreme fiction or in a self-sufficient ego, Ashbery leaves "the bitter impression of absence" in lines that are often hilariously funny even as they are self-deprecating. Ammons' poetry, while similar to Stevens' treatment of philosophical issues, builds upon Frost's naturalism and his concern for the morality of "place." For Ammons, "small branches can / loosen heavy postures" ("Essay on Poetics"), and he has conducted a quiet campaign for the restorative effects of weather, seasonal change, animal life, and horticulture as they interact with the speculative intellect. Hass's poetry continues Ammons' naturalist concerns (Roethke and Rexroth are important sources as well), but builds upon subtle shifts of voice and tone. Philosophical speculation alternates with epiphanic moments as in "Meditation at Lagunitas":

> All the new thinking is about loss.
> In this it resembles all the old thinking.
> The idea, for example, that each particular erases
> the luminous clarity of a general idea. That the clown-
> faced woodpecker probing the dead sculpted trunk
> of that black birch is, by his presence,
> some tragic falling off from a first world
> of undivided light.

A second group, closely aligned with the first but extending more directly out of the "deep image" aesthetic of Bly and Merwin, would incl. poets such as C. K. Williams (b. 1936), Marvin Bell (b. 1937), Philip Levine (b. 1928), Tess Gallagher (b. 1943), Charles Wright (b. 1935), Stanley Plumly (b. 1939), and Carolyn Forché (b. 1950). In their work surrealist juxtaposition combines with a spare, sometimes minimalist style to expose unconscious or atavistic resonances in everyday events. Less inclined towards the ecstatic "leaps" of Bly and Wright, these poets prefer a more narrative progression and a considerably chastened diction. The use of long lines and prosaic speech creates a leisurely tone often at odds with the poetry's darker subject matter. In C. K. Williams' "Tar," for example, the poet reflects on the grim legacy of nuclear waste, focusing his anger through an image of children using shards of roofer's tar to scribble on sidewalks hieroglyphics of rancor and love, anathematizing the current generation's "surfeits and submissions."

A third variation on the dominant mode is what Robert von Hallberg characterizes as "The Cosmopolitan Style" and which is represented by John Hollander (b. 1929), Richard Howard (b. 1929), James Merrill (b. 1926), and Anthony Hecht (b. 1923), as well as younger poets grouped loosely under the label of "New Formalism". In this work, discursiveness becomes a foil for strategies of self-preservation and effacement. At the same time, a tendency toward conversation conflicts with the use of formal meters and complex internal and terminal rhymes. This tension can be felt in the work of Merrill, whose work often uses its own aesthetic virtuosity to mock aesthetic solutions. His poems are willfully bookish, his tone arch and urbane, derived to some extent from Auden (who appears as one of the spirit guides in *Book of Ephraim*). Merrill's reticence and detachment are calculated frames for viewing a conflicted personal hist., a condition given fullest treatment in his trilogy, *The Changing Light at Sandover* (1982). In this long poem, the poet's personal ardors, his "divine comedies," are subjected to an extraordinary anthology of literary forms, from sonnets and verse dramas to blank verse paragraphs, all subsumed under the pose of having been received during ouija board seances. Like many of his earlier poems, *The Changing Light at Sandover* is a poem about writing, a celebration of the "surprise and pleasure [of] its working-out" which offers an elaborate allegory about erotic and spiritual love in an increasingly secularized society.

Merrill is usually regarded as a principal influence on a more recent movement among younger writers known as the New Formalists and which would include Alfred Corn (b. 1943), Marilyn Hacker (b. 1942), Brad Leithhauser (b. 1953), Katha Pollitt (b. 1949), and Gjertrud Schnackenberg (b. 1953). Their renewed interest in traditional forms (as well as the possibilities of narrative poetry) has been undertaken less as a rear guard attack on debased culture (as it was for many late modernists) but as a recovery of the liberating potential of limits. In their anthology of New-Formalist verse, Philip Dacey and David Jauss stress that writing in traditional forms aims to rebalance scales that had tipped too strongly in the direction of free verse since the 1960s, leading, as a result, to a rather amorphous autobiographical lyricism in which open form became simply an excuse for sloppy practice. But the presence of pattern may be experienced as a kind of liberation, "just as a dancer might praise the limitation of gravity for making dance possible in the first place." The challenge for New Formalists has been to hide or at least diminish pattern through the use of slant rhyme, nonce forms, syllabics and expressive variants on repeated meters. At the same time, poets attempt to combine their use of regular meters and rhyme with diction drawn from contemp. life, using the idiom of urban experience, technology, and advertising to blur the usual association of traditional forms with "high" or nonstandard diction. "Form's what affirms," James Merrill says, suggesting that far from imposing a straightjacket on lang., formalism makes the saying of what is difficult a matter of ethical as well as literary choice.

All of these tendencies, whether loosely or tightly formed, could be linked by their resistance to the more autobiographical and vatic modes of the 1960s. But if the dominant trad. in recent poetry has returned to the subtleties of voice and diction that characterized the work of the 1940s and '50s, a more complex critique of expressivist poetics has come from writers gathered under the rubric "language poetry". The work of Lyn Hejinian (b. 1941), Bruce Andrews (b. 1948), Carla Harryman (b. 1952), Charles Bernstein (b. 1950), Ron Silliman (b. 1946), Clark Coolidge (b. 1939), and Barrett Watten (b. 1948) explores the degree to which the "self" and "experience" are constructs, enmeshed in social discourse. Working within a trad. that stems from Black Mountain and objectivist poetics, these poets attempt to foreground lang. as signifying system within larger social structures. Their strategies of fracturing and fragmentation open up new realms of play and semantic complexity, and their interest in the prose poem and in new forms of prose challenges the generic boundaries of lined verse. That interest can be taken as a marker of a certain *crise de vers* that haunts recent poetry in general. If "a word is a bottomless pit" (Hejinian), it is also the agency by which that pit shall be explored, and postmodern poets have taken this realization as a generative fact. Modernism foregrounded the materiality of lang. by removing it from conventional and contrived usage, making it "new" by making it strange. Late modernists from Ransom to Hecht sought to curb the excesses of linguistic and metrical "defamiliarization" by making formal control of tension and ambiguity the cornerstone of a continuing humanist enterprise. Poets of the 1960s rebelled against the limitations of that enterprise insofar as it removed lang. from voice and personal expression. If the poetry of this era sometimes became grandiose and inflated in its testimentary role, it also re-established a dialogue with the reader. As O'Hara gleefully reported, "the poem is at last between two persons instead of two pages."

It has been for the post-1960s generation to investigate how thoroughly "deep" the word is, esp. when it lacks the epistemological and ontological supports it enjoyed in previous eras. Lacking either Whitman's all-encompassing Self or the authority of Eliot's detached personae, poets have renegotiated the territory of subjectivity as an intersubjective and historical phenomenon. Whether the poet seeks to achieve ever more subtle subjective states or to deconstruct the notion of subjectivity altogether, the task must be done with the full recognition of lang.'s mediate function. What Stevens called our "never-ending meditation" is made of "A few words, an and yet, and yet, and yet—." Between these small words, something like a "post" modernism emerges.

M.D.

See also AFRO-AMERICAN POETRY; BEAT POETS.

BIBLIOGRAPHIES: *Lit. Hist. of the U.S.*, ed. R. E. Spiller et al., 3d ed. rev., v. 2, *Bibl.* (1963); K. Malkoff, *Crowell's Handbook of Contemp. Am. P.* (1973); C. Altieri, *Mod. Poetry* (1979); J. Ruppert and J. R. Leo, *Guide to Am. P. Explication*, 2 v. (1989).

JOURNALS: *AL* (1929–); *AmerP* (1983–); *APR* (1972–); *Boundary 2* (1972–); *ConL* (1960–).

ANTHOLOGIES: *Mid-Century Am. Poets*, ed. J. Ciardi (1950); *A Comprehensive Anthol. of Am. P.*, ed. C. Aiken (1944); *Oxford Book of Am. Verse*, ed. F. O. Matthiessen (1950); *Faber Book of Mod. Am. Verse*, ed. W. H. Auden (1956); *New Poets of England and America*, ed. D. Hall et al. (1957); *The New Am. P.*, ed. D. Allen (1960); *Am. P. and Poetics*, ed. D. Hoffman (1962); *Mod. Am. P.*, ed. L. Untermeyer (1962); *Am. P.*, ed. G. W. Allen et al. (1965); *An Anthol. of Am. Verse*, ed. O. Williams (1966); *Major Am. Poets to 1914*, ed. F. Murphy (1967); *Poems of Our Moment*, ed. J. Hollander (1968); *Naked Poetry, The New Naked Poetry*, both ed. S. Berg and R. Mezey (1969, 1976)—"open form" poetry; *The Poetry of the Negro*, ed. L. Hughes and A. Bontemps (1970); *No More Masks*, ed. F. Howe and E. Bass (1973); *Out of the Vietnam Vortex: A Study of Poets and Poetry Against the War*, ed. J. F. Mersmann (1974); *New Oxford Book of Am. Verse*, ed. R. Ellmann (1976); *Black Sister*, ed. E. Stetson (1981); *Longman Anthol. of Contemp. Am. P. 1950–1980*, ed. S. Friebert and D. Young (1983); *The Generation of 2000*, ed. W. Heyen (1984); *Contemp. Am. P.*, ed. A. Poulin (1985); *The Morrow Anthol. of Younger Am. Poets*, ed. D. Smith and D. Bottoms (1985); *Harvard Book of Contemp. Am. P.*, ed. H. Vendler (1985); *In the Am. Tree*, ed. R. Silliman (1986); *Lang. Poetries*, ed. D. Messerli (1986); *Strong Measures*, ed. P. Dacey and D. Jauss (1986); *Writing Red: Anthol. of Am. Women Writers, 1930–40*, ed. C. Nekola and P. Rabinowitz (1987); *The Harper Am. Lit.*, ed. D. McQuade et al., 2 v. (1987); *The Norton Anthol. of Am. Lit.*, ed. N. Baym et al., 3d ed., 2 v. (1989); *Shadowed Dreams: Women's Poetry of the Harlem Ren.*, ed. M. Honey (1989); *An Ear to the Ground*, ed. M. Harris and K. Aguero (1989).

HISTORY AND CRITICISM: W. Stevens, *The Necessary Angel* (1951); R. Jarrell, *Poetry and the Age* (1953); W. C. Williams, *Selected Essays* (1954); A. Tate, *The Man of Letters in the Mod. World* (1955); *A Casebook on the Beats*, ed. T. Parkinson (1961); G. Cambon, *Recent Am. P.* (1962); A. Ostroff, *The Contemp. Poet as Artist and Critic* (1964); R. J. Mills, Jr., *Contemp. Am. P.* (1965); R. H. Pearce, *The Continuity of Am. P.*, 2d ed. (1965); C. Olson, *Selected Writings* (1966); M. L. Rosenthal, *The New Am. Poets* (1967); H. H. Waggoner, *Am. Poets from the Puritans to the Present* (1968); D. Schwartz, *Selected Essays* (1970); R. Creeley, *A Quick Graph* (1970); R. Howard, *Alone with America* (1970)—Am. poets since mid-century; H. Bloom, *Ringers in the Tower* (1971); H. Kenner, *The Pound Era* (1971); *The Poetics of the New Am. P.*, ed. D. Allen and W. Tallman (1973); E. Fussell, *Lucifer in Harness* (1973); D. Antin, "Modernism and Postmodernism," *Boundary 2* 1 (1972–73); K. Rexroth, *Am. P. in the 20th C.* (1973); D. Levertov, *The Poet in the World* (1973); *Understanding the New Black Poetry*, ed. S. Henderson (1973); *The Craft of Poetry*, ed. W. Packard (1974); R. Mills, *The Cry of the Human* (1974); D. Stauffer, *A Short Hist. of Am. P.* (1974); A. Gelpi, *A Coherent Splendor: The Am. Poetic Ren. 1910–1950* (1987), *The Tenth Muse*, 2d ed. (1991); F. O'Hara, *Standing Still and Walking in New York* (1975); D. Perkins, *A Hist. of Mod. Poetry*, 2 v. (1976, 1987); R. Pinsky, *The Situation of Poetry* (1976); R. Wilbur, *Responses* (1976); E. Watts, *The Poetry of Am. Women from 1632 to 1945* (1977); D. Kalstone, *Five Temperaments* (1977); S. Plumly, "Chapter and Verse," *APR* 7 (Jan.-Feb. and May-June, 1978); B. Duffey, *Poetry in America* (1978); C. Altieri, *Enlarging the Temple* (1979), *Self and Sensibility in Contemp. Am. P.* (1984), *Painterly Abstraction in Modernist Am. P.* (1989); A. Rich, *On Lies, Secrets and Silence* (1979); C. Molesworth, *The Fierce Embrace* (1979); D. Hoffman, *The Harvard Guide to Contemp. Am. Writing* (1979); *A Field Guide to Contemp. Poetry and Poetics*, ed. S. Friebert and D. Young (1980); J. Holden, *The Rhet. of the Contemp. Lyric* (1980); P. A. Bove, *Destructive Poetics: Heidegger and Mod. Am. P.* (1980); H. Vendler, *Part of Nature, Part of Us* (1980), *The Music of What Happens* (1988); M. Perloff, *The Poetics of Indeterminacy* (1981), *The Dance of the Intellect* (1985), *Poetic License: Essays on Modernist and Postmodernist Lyric* (1990); C. Nelson, *Our Last First Poets* (1981), *Repression and Recovery: Mod. Am. P. and the Politics of Cultural Memory* (1990); S. Paul, *The Lost America of Love* (1981); M. L. Rosenthal and S. M. Gall, *The Mod. Poetic Sequence* (1983); A. Ostriker, *Writing Like a Woman* (1983); J. E. B. Breslin, *From Mod. to Contemp.: Am. P. 1945–65* (1984); *The L=A=N=G=U=A=G=E Book*, ed. B. Andrews and C. Bernstein (1984); R. Hass, *20th-C. Pleasures* (1984); R. von

Hallberg, *Am. P. and Culture, 1945–1980* (1985); R. Duncan, *Fictive Certainties* (1985); B. Watten, *Total Syntax* (1985); R. B. DuPlessis, *Writing Beyond the Ending* (1985); A. S. Ostriker, *Stealing the Lang.: The Emergence of Women's Poetry in America* (1986); A. Ross, *The Failure of Modernism* (1986); C. Bernstein, *Content's Dream* (1986); L. Keller, *Re-Making It New* (1987); H. A. Baker, Jr., *Modernism and the Harlem Ren.* (1987), *Afro-Am. Poetics* (1988); J. Radway and P. Frank, "Verse and Popular Poetry," *Handbook of Am. Popular Lit.*, ed. M. T. Inge (1988); *Columbia Lit. Hist. of the U.S.*, ed. E. Elliott et al. (1988); A. Shucard, *Am. P.* (1988), et. al., *Mod. Am. P. 1865–1950* (1989); M. Davidson, *The San Francisco Ren.* (1989); W. Kalaidjian, *Langs. of Liberation: The Social Text in Contemp. Am. P.* (1989); J. V. Brogan, *Part of the Climate: Am. Cubist P.* (1991). A.G.; M.D.

AMHARIC POETRY. See ETHIOPIAN POETRY.

ARABIC POETRY.

I. INTRODUCTION
II. 6TH TO 13TH CENTURIES
III. 13TH TO 18TH CENTURIES
IV. 19TH AND 20TH CENTURIES

I. INTRODUCTION. Until relatively recently, poetry has served as the predominant mode of literary expression among those who speak and write in Ar. Poetry was, in the traditional phrase, "*dīwān al-ʿarab*," the register of the Arabs, and poets had and continue to have a particular status in their own community. The Ar. word for "poetry," *shiʿr*, is derived from the verb denoting a special kind of knowledge which was believed in the earliest times to have magical or mantic properties. While poetry has afforded poets the opportunity for personal expression, it has been more often than not a *public* phenomenon, whether addressed to the tribe of ancient times, the patron during the predominance of the Caliphate and the many dynasties of the med. Islamic world, or the many political causes of the present-day Middle East.

Most histories of Ar. p. have adopted a dynastic approach based primarily on political and social devels., concentrating mainly on the poets, their role in society, and their themes. This approach serves to illustrate the close links between poetry and poetics on the one hand and divisions of the Islamic sciences on the other. However, it should be borne in mind that, while bibliographical sources provide evidence of the richness of the trad. available to us, they also make clear not only that large amounts of poetry are lost to us, but also that much more poetry remains unpublished and unassessed within the critical canon. Further, the hist. of Ar. p. has recently been undergoing a re-evaluation, based on two interlinked phenomena. First, Ar. p. itself has been going through a period of transformation and radical experimentation since the beginning of the 1950s: this process has led some critics to attempt a redefinition of what poetry is (or should be) and therefrom to initiate projects aimed at a reassessment of the corpus of cl. Ar. p. Second, critics have applied new ideas in analysis and theory—e.g. structuralism, oral-formulaic and genre theories, and metrics—to the corpus of Ar. p.

II. 6TH TO 13TH CENTURIES. A. *The Beginnings: Oral Tradition.* What have been recorded as the beginnings of Ar. p. are versions of a poetic corpus that is already highly developed in the late 5th c. A.D. The trad. is an oral one, similar to that of the Homeric poems and Serbo-Croatian songs analyzed by Parry and Lord. Thus, each poem, or rather the differing versions of each poem, represent a single, isolated yet privileged point in a long process of devel. and transmission from poet to reciter (*rāwī*). Each poem would have been performed before an audience (perhaps accompanied by music or rhythmic beat) and transmitted through generations from one "singer of tales" to another.

B. *The Poet.* The ability to improvise was (and often still is) part of the craft of Arab poets. Many occasions would arise at which they would extemporize a poem or recite a work from memory. They were important members of the tribe, in effect propagandists, whose role was to extoll the tribal virtues—bravery, loyalty, endurance, swiftness of vengeance—and to lampoon the lack of such virtues in the tribe's enemies. The various thematic "genres" used—eulogy, elegy, and satire—all concerned praise or its antithesis. The elegy (*rithāʾ*) provides some of the most moving examples of the poetic voice, as in the poems of al-Khansāʾ (d. ca. 644) for her brother, Ṣakhr, killed in tribal combat:

I was sleepless and I passed the night
  keeping vigil, as if my eyes had
  been anointed with pus, . . .
For I had heard—and it was not news
  to rejoice me—one making a report, who had come repeating
  intelligence,
Saying, "Sakhr is dwelling there in a
  tomb, struck to the ground beside
  the grave, between certain stones."
(tr. A. J. Arberry)

The poet used the different genres to depict companionship, the benefits of tribal solidarity, the beauties of women, the qualities of animals, and the joys of wine. Part of this same environment, but from a totally different social perspective, were a number of vagabond (*ṣuʿlūk*) poets such as al-Shanfarā (d. ca. 525), his companion Thābit ibn Jābir (known by his nickname, "Taʾabbaṭa Sharran"—he who has put evil under his armpit), and ʿUrwa ibn al-Ward (d. ca. 594). Ostracized from tribal society, they and their peers wrote stirring odes about their ability to withstand prolonged isolation, hunger, and thirst and their feelings of affinity with the wilder animals of the desert, as in this extract from a poem by al-Shanfarā:

To me now, in your default, are comrades a wolf untired,
A sleek leopard, and a fell hyena with shaggy mane.
True comrades, they ne'er let out the secret in trust with them,
Nor basely forsake their friend because he brought them bane.
(tr. R. A. Nicholson)

In contrast to this stark vision of life stands that of the courts of the Ghassanids, the tribe which served as a buffer between the Arabs and Byzantium, and the Lakhmids, who fulfilled the same function vis à vis Sasanid Iran from their center at al-Ḥīra (in present-day Iraq). To these courts would come not only tribal poets but also professional bards like Ṭarafa ibn al-ᶜAbd (d. ca. 565) and Maymūn al-Aᶜshā (d. 629) in search of patronage and reward for their eulogies.

C. *The Structure of the Poem.* The process of oral transmission and the later recording of poetry in written form have not preserved the stages in the early devel. of the Ar. poem. Thus we find examples of both the short, monothematic poem (*qiṭᶜa*) and the multi-sectional, polythematic *qaṣīda.* Several examples of the latter came to be highly valued, esp. by the early Muslim Caliphs and the ruling Arab aristocracy, which regarded these poems as a source and standard for the study and teaching of the cl. Ar. lang. Seven (and later ten) of the longer odes were gathered into what became the most famous collection of early Ar. p., the *muᶜallaqāt.* The *muᶜallaqa* of Imruʾ al-Qays (d. ca. 540) is the most famous poem in the collection and indeed probably in all of Ar. lit. Yet each *muᶜallaqa* manages to reflect its poet's vision of life in pre-Islamic Arabia: that of Zuhayr ibn Abī Sulmā is placed within the context of settling a tribal dispute, while the ode of Labīd (d. ca. 662), with its elaborate animal imagery and concluding aphorisms, is virtually a hymn to tribal values.

Recent analyses of some examples of the pre-Islamic *qaṣīda* have challenged the received view that its structure is fragmented, a view canonized in part by the conservative critical trad. of *ᶜamūd al-shiᶜr* ("the essentials of poetry"). It is now suggested that the choice and ordering of the various segments of these poems reflect the poet's desire to illustrate by conjunction and opposition the glaring contrasts in community life, making these elaborate poems a public event of almost liturgical significance. Thus, the *nasīb* (erotic prelude) of many poems will often be placed within the context of the *aṭlāl,* the section describing the poet's arrival at a deserted encampment. The opening lines of the *muᶜallaqa* of Imruʾ al-Qays are esp. famous: "Halt (you two) and let us weep for memory of a beloved and an abode / In the edge of the sand dune between ad-Dakhul and Hawmal." A transitional section describing a departure or desert journey allows the poet to give a description of his riding animal which is often elaborate and lengthy, and provides some of the most memorable lines from this corpus of poetry. From this interweaving of segments the poet will then turn—often by means of aphoristic sentiments—to the purpose of the poem: the bolstering of the community through praise of its virtues, criticism of contraventions of them, and sheer self-aggrandizement as a means of fostering tribal pride and solidarity.

D. *The Advent of Islam.* While the advent of Islam brought about radical changes in beliefs and customs in the society of the Arabian Peninsula, the poetic environment changed relatively little. Muḥammad himself was not averse to poetry, as sections of *Kitāb al-aghānī* make abundantly clear. Indeed, Ḥassān ibn Thābit (d. 673) is known as "the poet of the Prophet." His contemporary, Kaᶜb ibn Zuhayr, the son of the famous pre-Islamic bard Zuhayr ibn Abī Sulmā, composed a famous poem addressed to Muḥammad which illustrates the continuation of the poetic trad. into the new social context; the poem is called *al-Burda* ("The Cloak"), since, upon hearing it, Muḥammad is alleged to have placed his cloak around the poet:

I was told that the Messenger of Allah threatened me (with death), but with the Messenger of Allah I have hope of finding pardon.
Gently! mayst thou be guided by Him who gave thee the gift of the Koran, wherein are warnings and a plain setting-out of the matter.
(tr. R. A. Nicholson)

The spirit of defiance in the face of imminent danger and even death which characterizes much pre-Islamic poetry is also to be found in the odes of poets belonging to groups which broke away from the incipient Muslim community on religious grounds and fought vigorously for their conception of Islam. The poetry of the supporters of the Kharijite cause, such as al-Ṭirimmāḥ (d. ca. 723), and of the Shīᶜa, such as Al-Kumayt ibn Zayd (d. 743), is esp. noteworthy in this regard. The pre-Islamic penchant for satire of rivals and enemies finds fertile ground in the tribal squabbles which continue well into the period of the Umayyads (660–750). In a series of increasingly ribald satires (gathered into a collection known as *Al-Naqāʾiḍ*), the poets Jarīr (d. 732) and Al-Farazdaq (d. ca. 730), joined among others by the Christian poet Al-Akhṭal (d. 710), followed the pattern of earlier satirical poetry in both form and imagery and adopted rhetorical strategies characteristic of verbal dueling in the Arab world.

E. *The Emergence of New Genres.* The oral transmission of poetry continued into the Islamic period, insuring that the Arab poet's attachment to many of the themes and images of the desert lingered long after such environments were superseded by the emerging urban centers of the Muslim community. Thus Dhū al-Rumma (d. 735) was often referred to as "the last of the poets" because he continued to use desert motifs in his poems a century after the advent of Islam. Inevitably, however, the gradual process of change led to the emergence of different priorities expressed in different ways. On the political level, the changes were far-reaching. During the first century or so of Islam, Muslim armies took the religion to the borders of India in the East and across North Africa to Spain in the West. The center of Caliphal authority moved out of the Arabian Peninsula first to Damascus under the Umayyads and then to the newly founded city of Baghdad in 756 under the Abbasids. Under the impetus of this vast exercise in cultural assimilation, authors from different areas of the Islamic world began to adapt the traditional Ar. literary forms and to introduce new themes and genres.

Various segments of the *qaṣida* gradually evolved into distinct genres. The collected works of poets composed during the first century of Islam begin to contain separate sections devoted to specific categories: hunt poems (*ṭardiyyāt*) and wine poems (*khamriyyāt*)—both of these most notably in the verse of Al-Ḥasan ibn Hāniʾ (d. ca. 810), usually known by his nickname, Abū Nuwās. His wine poetry is noted not only for its disarming lasciviousness but also for the way in which he occasionally parodies the desert imagery of the earlier poetry:

> The lovelorn wretch stopped at a (deserted) camping-ground to question it, and I stopped to inquire after the local tavern.
> May Allah not dry the eyes of him that wept over stones, and may He not ease the pain of him that yearns to a tent-peg.
> (tr. R. A. Nicholson)

The blind poet, Bashshār ibn Burd (d. 783), displayed a similar impatience with Arabian conventions, though in his case it is linked to a desire to express pride in his own Persian ancestry. Another poet of the period, Abū al-Atāhiya (d. 828), is primarily remembered for his moral and ascetic poems (*zuhdiyyāt*).

One of the most remarkable devels. along these lines is that of the love poem (*ghazal*). Soon after the advent of Islam, two distinct trends appear in the Arabian Peninsula. The first, emerging from within the tribal poetic trad., placed the aloof and imperious beloved on a pedestal while the poet suffered the pangs of love from a distance, often leading to a love-death. This trad. is termed *ʿUdhrī* after the Banū ʿUdhra tribe, noted for having many such lovers, among whom was Jamīl (d. 701), one of the most illustrious exponents of ʿUdhrī poetry. Each of these love poets also carried the name of his beloved: Jamīl, for example, is Jamīl Buthayna, the beloved of Buthayna; other poets of this type are Kuthayyir ʿAzza (d. 723) and, most famous of all, Majnūn Laylā. The other trad., sensual and self-centered, developed in the cities of the Ḥijāz; it is usually associated with its most famous exponent, ʿUmar ibn Abī Rabīʿa (d. 719). With the gradual devel. of the genre the two separate strands fused, as can be seen in the works of poets such as ʿAbbās ibn al-Aḥnaf (d. ca. 807) in the East and Ibn ʿAbd Rabbihi (d. 940) in al-Andalus (as Islamic Spain was known).

F. *The Badīʿ Style: Imagery and Rhetoric.* During the Caliphate of ʿUthmān (d. 644), a generally accepted version of the Qurʾān (Koran) was established in writing, a process which set in motion many intellectual currents later to have a profound effect on poetry. Scholars in Kūfa and Baṣra (both in present-day Iraq) began to prepare the materials needed for authenticating the transmission of the Qurʾān, interpreting its text, and codifying the Ar. lang. in which the sacred text proclaims itself to have been revealed. Anthols. of poetry of different genres and from particular tribes were made, a process which involved the devel. of basic critical terms for the evaluation of literary works. A philologist of Baṣra, Al-Khalīl Ibn Aḥmad (d. 791), analysed the sounds and rhythms of the earliest poetry and set down his results as a set of meters which formed part of a definition of poetry (as "rhymed and metered discourse") which was widely regarded as canonical up to the end of World War II. This philological activity was accompanied by a gradual shift away from the predominantly oral culture of pre-Islamic Arabia toward a society in which verbal art was committed to writing.

Within this environment of compilation, authentification, and analysis, there now emerges in Ar. p. *badīʿ*, a term which literally means "innovative" but which involves a greater awareness of the potential uses of poetic imagery. The poet-Caliph Ibn al-Muʿtazz (d. 908) wrote a famous analysis of the five most significant tropes (incl. simile and metaphor) entitled *Kitāb al-badīʿ*, a work which took many of its examples from early poetry and the text of the Qurʾān. This was to be the first in an increasingly complex series of rhetorical analyses. The discussions which evolved around the subject of *badīʿ* were part of a dynamic period in the devel. of Islamic thought on religious, ethnic, ideological, and cultural issues. They also raised questions of literary taste and provoked fierce debate between proponents of the "new" (*muḥdathūn*) poets and the old. Much critical opprobrium was reserved for the poet Abū Tammām (d. 846), who was widely condemned for carrying the use of *badīʿ* to excessive lengths. At a later date, the great critic ʿAbd al-Qāhir al-Jurjānī (d. 1078) pioneered the analysis of the psychological impact of imagery on the reader and thereby accentuated the *originality* of many of Abū Tammām's ideas, a verdict gaining increasing credence in modern crit.

With the growth of the bureaucracy at the Caliph's court and the expansion of the Islamic dominions—accompanied almost automatically by the emergence of local potentates—plentiful sources of patronage became available to reward poets who would compose occasional poems. During the heyday of cl. Ar. p., many such centers existed: the Umayyads and their successors in al-Andalus; the Hamdanids in Aleppo, Syria; the Ikhshidids in Egypt; and the court in Baghdad. To all these centers poets would come in search of favor and reward. The poet who best exemplifies this patronage system is al-Mutanabbī (d. 965). He composed poems for all kinds of occasions and for a number of rulers and patrons, some of whom are eulogized and later mercilessly lampooned. Developing the use of the *badī*ᶜ style and combining a superb control of the lang. with an innate sense of the gnomic phrase, he was soon widely regarded as the greatest of the cl. Ar. poets. His *Dīwān* (collected poetry) provides us with many splendid examples of the *qaṣīda* as occasional poem; his examples of eulogy (*madīḥ*) are among the most famous contributions to a genre which was a major form of verbal art in Arab civilization:

Whither do you intend, great prince?
  We are the herbs of the hills and
  you are the clouds;
We are the ones time has been miserly
  towards respecting you, and the
  days cheated of your presence.
Whether at war or peace, you aim at
  the heights, whether you tarry or
  hasten.
(tr. A. J. Arberry, 1965)

A great admirer of al-Mutanabbī's poetry was Abū al-ᶜAlāʾ al-Maᶜarrī (d. 1057). This blind poet and philosopher began by imitating his great predecessor, but his collection of poems entitled *Luzūm mā lā yalzam* (Requirement of the Non-required), the title of which reflects the fact that he imposes strict formal rules on himself, combines consummate skill in the use of poetic lang. with some of the most pessimistic sentiments to be found in the entire Ar. canon:

Would that a lad had died in the very
  hour of birth
And never sucked, as she lay in child-
  bed, his mother's breast!
Her babe, it says to her or ever the
  tongue can speak,
"Nothing thou get'st of me but sorrow
  and bitter pain."
(tr. R. A. Nicholson)

Three poets of al-Andalus from this same period deserve particular mention: Ibn Shuhayd (d. 1035) and Ibn Ḥazm (d. 1063), both of whom contributed to crit. as well as to poetry; and Ibn Zaydūn (d. 1070), who celebrated his great love, the Umayyad Princess Wallāda, and then rued her loss to a rival at court. The Iberian Peninsula was also to contribute to Ar. p. two strophic genres, the *muwashshaḥa* and *zajal.* The origins and prosodic features of both genres are the subject of continuing and intense debate. The final strophe or refrain known as the *kharja* ("envoi") was originally a popular song in Romance or a mixture of Romance and Hispano-Ar. sung by a girl about her beloved:

My beloved is sick for love of me.
How can he not be so?
Do you not see that he is not allowed
  near me?
(tr. J. T. Monroe)

This refrain provides the rhyme scheme for the other strophes in the poem which are in literary Ar. Interspersed between them are other verses with separate rhymes. In the *zajal* genre the colloquial lang. sometimes encountered in the *kharja* of the *muwashshaḥa* is used in the body of the poem itself. With its illustrious exponent Ibn Quzmān (d. 1159) the fame of the genre spread to the East.

As the corpus of poetics and rhetoric increased in scope and complexity, poetry itself tended to become more stereotyped and convention-bound, e.g. the poetry of Ibn ᶜArabī (d. 1240), one of the major figures in Islamic theology; the mystical poet Ibn al-Fāriḍ (d. 1235); and Bahāʾ al-dīn Zuhayr, whose death in 1258 coincides with the capture of Baghdad by the Mongols, an event generally acknowledged as signaling the end of the cl. period in Islamic culture.

III. 13TH TO 18TH CENTURIES. The period between the 13th and early 19th cs. is often characterized as one of "decadence," a designation which not only reflects the distaste of subsequent critics for poetry in which a penchant for verbal virtuosity and poetic tropes prevailed, but which also serves to conceal a general lack of research. To the initial stages of the period belong such poets as al-Būṣīrī (d. 1294), who wrote a second "Burda" poem (after that of Kaᶜb ibn Zuhayr). This poem found a wide audience within the mystical circles of popular Islam much in evidence throughout the period. Concurrently in Spain Ḥāzim al-Qarṭājannī (d. 1285) was not only a major contributor to the trad. of Ar. poetics but a poet in his own right.

During much of this period the Ar.-speaking world was governed by non-Arabs, particularly the 15th–18th cs. when most of the area became part of the Ottoman Empire. The lang. of administration and official communication was Turkish, while that of literary culture, even among the Turks, was often Persian. Among the poets who composed in Ar. during this period and whose names have been preserved are the Iraqi poet Ṣafī al-dīn al-Ḥillī (d. 1349), who in addition to writing his own poetry composed a study of the *muwashshaḥa* and *zajal*, and the Egyptian, al-Idkāwī (d. 1770). Both of these poets were adept at composing verse full of embellishments, e.g. poems in which each word begins with the same letter, or each word starts with the final grapheme of the previous word. This was indeed a period of verbal artifice but also one of compilation (incl. the major Ar. dictionaries) and explication. Ibn Mālik (d. 1274) composed a poem in 1000 verses on Ar. grammar, a text which was still in use in Egyptian religious schools at the turn of the 20th c.

The limited size of the audience for the elite lit. just outlined may account for the considerable vigor of the popular literary trad. during these centuries. This is most evident in the greatest of all narrative collections, *The 1001 Nights*, as well as in other popular tales which contain large amounts of poetry in a variety of styles. And, while the trad. of popular poetry is sparsely documented, some intimations of its liveliness and variety can be gauged from the (albeit bawdy) poetry to be found in the shadow plays of the Egyptian oculist, Ibn Dāniyāl (d. 1311).

IV. 19TH AND 20TH CENTURIES. A. *The Beginnings of the Modern Revival.* The process whereby Ar. p. enters a new phase is termed *al-nahḍa* (revival). Two principal factors are involved: what one scholar has termed "the Arab Rediscovery of Europe" on the one hand, and a re-examination of the cl. trad. of Ar. poetry and poetics on the other. Esp. noteworthy figures in this revival are Rifāᶜa al-Ṭahṭāwī (d. 1873) in Egypt, and Buṭrus al-Bustānī (d. 1883), Nāṣīf al-Yāzijī (d. 1871—who was particularly inspired by the poetry of al-Mutanabbī), and Aḥmad Fāris al-Shidyāq (d. 1887) in Lebanon.

B. *Neoclassicism.* Al-Mutanabbī was also the inspiration of one of the first major figures in the neoclassical movement, the Egyptian Maḥmūd Sāmī al-Bārūdī (d. 1904), who advocated a return to the directness and purity of cl. Ar. p. and composed poetry to illustrate his ideas. Within the chronology of its own modern history, every Arab country fostered neoclassical poets, e.g. the Egyptian Ḥāfiẓ Ibrāhīm (d. 1932), the Iraqis Jamīl Ṣidqī al-Zahāwī (d. 1936) and Maᶜrūf al-Ruṣāfī (d. 1945), and somewhat later, the Palestinian Ibrāhīm Ṭūqān (d. 1941). However, critical opinion is virtually unanimous in judging Aḥmad Shawqī (d. 1932) as the greatest poet of the neoclassical school. Whether in his stirring calls to the Egyptian people, his more personal descriptive verse, or his still popular operettas, his superbly cadenced poetry seems destined to secure him a place in the pantheon of great Ar. poets. While recent devels. in Ar. p. have produced many changes, several poets have continued to compose poetry in the traditional manner, esp. Muḥammad al-Jawāhirī, Badawī al-Jabal (pseudonym of Muḥammad Sulaymān al-Aḥmad), and Al-Akhṭal al-Ṣaghīr (pseudonym of Bishāra al-Khūrī, d. 1968).

C. *Romanticism.* Signs of a reaction against the occasional nature of much neoclassical verse can be found in the works of the Lebanese poet Khalīl Muṭrān (d. 1949), although not so much in his own poetry as in his writings about poetry and particularly the introduction to his collected poems (1908). Full-blooded romanticism in Ar. p. comes from the poets of *al-mahjar* (the "emigre school"), as the Arab poets of the Americas are called. While Amīn al-Rīḥānī (d. 1940) was certainly much admired in the Middle East, the undisputed leader of the Northern group was Khalīl Jubrān [Kahlil Gibran] (d. 1931), as famous for his works in Eng. as for those in Ar.:

> Give me the flute and sing! Forget all
> that you and I have said.
> Talk is but dust in the air, so tell me of
> your deeds.
> (tr. Khouri and Algar)

Far removed from their native land, Jubrān and his colleagues, among whom were Mīkhāʾīl Nuᶜayma (b. 1889), Īliyyā Abū Māḍī (d. 1957), and Nasīb ᶜArīḍa (d. 1946), proceeded to experiment with lang., form, and mood, and in so doing introduced a new voice into Ar. p. Jubrān was also in constant touch with his fellow-countrymen in South America, among whom Fawzī Maᶜlūf (d. 1930) is the most significant figure.

In the Middle East the ideals of Eng. romanticism were vigorously advocated by three Egyptian poets: al-ᶜAqqād, Ibrāhīm al-Māzinī (d. 1949), and ᶜAbd al-Raḥmān Shukrī (d. 1958). While all three wrote poetry, the primary function of the group was to criticize the neoclassical school in favor of a new, more individual role for the poet. The 1930s and '40s were the heyday of romanticism in Ar. p. In 1932 Aḥmad Zakī Abū Shādī (d. 1955) founded the Apollo Society in Cairo, which pub. a magazine to which several poets, incl. Ibrāhīm Nājī (d. 1953), ᶜAlī Maḥmūd Ṭāhā (d. 1949), and the Tunisian Abū al-Qāsim al-Shābbī (d. 1934) made contributions. Among other important figures in the devel. of romantic Ar. p. are ᶜUmar Abū Rīsha in Syria, Yūsuf Tījānī al-Bashīr (d. 1937) in the Sudan, and Ṣalāḥ Labakī (d. 1955) and Ilyās Abū Shabaka (d. 1947) in Lebanon. As a critic Labakī also devoted his attention to the devel. of a symbolist school of poetry, much indebted to Fr. poetic theory and associated with the Lebanese poets Yūsuf Ghuṣūb and (esp.) Saᶜīd ᶜAql.

D. *The Emergence of "New Poetry": The Role of the Poet.* The period following World War II was one of political uncertainty, frequent changes of government, and revolution. The creation of the State of Israel in 1948 served as a major psychological catalyst in the Arab World. In the revolutionary atmosphere during the 1950s, the poetry of the late romantics, and in particular symbolists such as Saᶜīd ᶜAql, came to be regarded as elitist, ivory-tower lit. Along with the prevalence of such causes as Palestinian rights, nationalism (whether the

Pan-Arab or local variety), revolution, and communism came the rallying cry for "commitment" (*iltizām*). Not surprisingly, among the most prominent contributors to poetry of commitment have been a large group of Palestinian poets; particularly noteworthy are Maḥmūd Darwīsh (b. 1942), Fadwā Ṭūqān (b. 1917), and Samīḥ al-Qāsim (b. 1939). The other overriding topic of political poetry has been life among the poorer classes in both the cities and provinces of the Arab World nations: the earlier poetry of Badr Shākir al-Sayyāb (d. 1964), ʿAbd al-Wahhāb al-Bayyātī (b. 1926), and Ṣalāḥ ʿAbd al-Sabūr (d. 1982) shows this concern, as do the works of Aḥmad ʿAbd al-Muʿṭī Ḥijāzī (b. 1935) and Muḥammad Miftāḥ al-Faytūrī (b. 1930). The dark visions of Khalīl Ḥāwī (d. 1982) show a more subtle kind of commitment, tinged with bitterness, as in the prescient commentary on the Arab World in the 1960s, "Lazarus 1962":

> Deepen the pit, gravedigger,
> Deepen it to bottomless depths
> beyond the sun's orbit;
> night of ashes, remnants of a star
> buried in the wheeling abyss.
> (tr. Haydar and Beard)

The most widely read poet in the contemp. Middle East is undoubtedly Nizār Qabbānī (b. 1923), who earned enormous popularity for his several volumes of sensuous love poetry. During the 1950s he also wrote poems of social protest, such as his famous "Bread, Hashish and Moonlight"; particularly since the June War of 1967, political and social issues have been constant topics in his poetry.

With Adūnīs (pseudonym of ʿAlī Aḥmad Saʿīd, b. 1930) a different kind of commitment is encountered. After editing with his colleague, the Lebanese Christian poet Yūsuf al-Khāl (d. 1987), the journal *Shiʿr*, which has had immense influence in the devel. of a modern poetics in the Arab World, Adūnīs broke away and in 1968 founded his own journal, *Mawāqif.* He has pub. numerous poetry collections of startling originality:

> To a father who died, green as a cloud
> with a sail on his face, I bow.
> (*JArabL* 2 [1971])

Using his journal and its coterie as a conduit for his ideas, he advocates the need for "innovation," viewing the primary purpose of poetry as the use of words in new ways.

E. *Changes in Form.* Strophic Ar. p. has existed from at least the 10th c. The modern period has also witnessed other experiments, such as blank and free verse. Also noteworthy are metrical experiments within folk poetry, particularly in Lebanon where Rashīd Nakhla (d. ca. 1940) and Michel Ṭrād composed poems in strophic form and with mixed meters. In 1947 two Iraqi poets, Nāzik al-Malāʾika (b. 1923) and al-Sayyāb, initiated a break from the concept of the line as poetic unit and thus paved the way for the emergence of *shiʿr ḥurr* ("free verse"). In fact, al-Malāʾika's attempt to establish a new set of rules based on the single foot (*tafʿīla*) rather than the line (*bayt*) was soon discarded as poets began to experiment with both traditional and new quantitative patterns in their poetry. Other poets have pursued this trend even further by composing prose poetry (*qaṣīdat al-nathr*) in which the sheer conjunction and musicality of words contribute to the poetic moment: alliteration, assonance, and imagery are combined in the works of poets such as Jabrā Ibrāhīm Jabrā (b. 1919), Muḥammad al-Māghūṭ (b. 1934), and Tawfīq Ṣāyigh (d. 1971).

The Arab poet today continues to be influenced and inspired by the great cl. trad., but the stimuli provided by his own time and world are now international and of considerable variety. Thus the *qaṣīda* lives alongside the prose poem as contemp. Ar. p. draws its inspiration from both its past and present.

GENERAL REFERENCE WORKS: C. Brockelmann, *Gesch. der Arabischen Literatur,* 2 v. (1898–1902), *Supplementbanden,* 3 v. (1937–42); A. Fischer, *Schawahid Indices* (1945); *Encyc. of Islam,* 2d ed. (1954–); J. D. Pearson, *Index Islamicus 1906–1955* (1958), *Supplements* (1956–80); F. Sezgin, *Gesch. des Arabischen Schriftums,* v. 2 (1975); *The Fihrist of al Nadim,* tr. B. Dodge, 2 v. (1970); M. Alwan, "A Bibl. of Mod. Ar. P. in Eng. Tr.," *Middle East Jour.* (Summer 1973).

ANTHOLOGIES: *Ar. P. for Eng. Readers,* ed. W. A. Clouston (1881); *Ancient Ar. P.,* ed. C. J. Lyall (1885); W. S. Blunt, *Seven Golden Odes of Pagan Arabia* (1903); R. A. Nicholson, *Trs. of Eastern Poetry and Prose* (1922); *Mod. Ar. P.,* ed. and tr. A. J. Arberry (1950); *The Seven Odes,* tr. A. J. Arberry (1957); *Al-Majānī al-ḥadītha ʿan Majānī al-Ab Shaykhū,* ed. F. Afram al-Bustānī, 3 v. (1960–61); *Dīwān al-Shiʿr al-ʿArabī,* ed. Adūnīs (1964–68); *Ar. P.* (1965), *Poems of al-Mutanabbi* (1967), both ed. A. J. Arberry; *Anthologie de la litt. arabe contemporaine: la poésie,* tr. L. Norin and E. Tarabay (1967); *An Anthol. of Mod. Ar. Verse,* ed. M. Badawi (1970); *Hispano-Ar. P.,* ed. and tr. J. T. Monroe (1974); *Mawsūʿat al-Shiʿr al-ʿArabī,* ed. K. Ḥāwī and M. Ṣafadī (1974–); *An Anthol. of Mod. Ar. P.,* tr. M. Khouri and H. Algar (1974); *Mod. Arab Poets 1950–1975,* tr. I. Boullata (1976); *Women of the Fertile Crescent,* ed. K. Boullata (1978); K. Hawi, *Naked in Exile,* tr. A. Haydar and M. Beard (1984); *Majnun et Layla: l'amour fou,* tr. A. Miquel and P. Kemp (1984); *Cl. Ar. P.,* tr. C. Tuetey (1985); *Mod. Ar. P.: An Anthol.,* ed. S. K. Jayyusi (1987).

HISTORY AND CRITICISM: W. Ahlwardt, *Über Poesie und Poetik der Araber* (1856); I. Goldziher, *Short Hist. of Cl. Ar. Lit.* (1908), tr J. Desomogyi (1966); R. A. Nicholson, *Lit. Hist. of the Arabs* (1914), *Studies in Islamic Poetry* (1921), *Studies in Islamic Mysticism* (1921); Ṭ. Ḥusayn, *Al-Shiʿr al-Jāhilī* (1926)—pre-Islamic poetry and its "authenticity"; H. A. R. Gibb, *Ar. Lit.* (1926); U. Farrukh,

Das Bild der Frühislam in der arabischen Dichtung (1937); N. al-Bahbītī, *Tārīkh al-Shi'r al-ʿArabī* (1950)—hist. of early Ar. p.; M. al-Nuwayhī, *Al-Shiʿr al-Jāhilī* (n.d.)—critical approaches to pre-Islamic poetry; R. Serjeant, *South Ar. P.* (1951); R. Blachère, *Histoire de la litt. arabe*, 3 v. (1952–66); G. Gomez, *Poesia arabigoandaluza* (1952); G. von Grunebaum, *Kritik und Dichtkunst* (1955); N. al-Asad, *Maṣādir al-Shiʿr al-Jāhilī* (1956)—sources of pre-Islamic poetry; I. ʿAbbās, *Tārīkh al-Adab al-Andalusī* (1959)—hist. of Andalusian lit.; J. al-Rikābī, *Fi al-Adab al-Andalusī* (1960)—hist. of Andalusian lit.; N. al-Malāʾika, *Qaḍāyā al-shiʿr al-muʿāṣir* (1962)—issues in mod. Ar. p.; S. Dayf, *Tārīkh al-Adab al-ʿArabī*, 4 v. (1963–73)—hist. of Ar. lit., *Al-Taṭawwur wa-al-tajdīd fī al-shiʿr al-Umawī* (1974)—innovation in Umayyad poetry; J. Kamāl al-dīn, *Al-Shiʿr al-ʿArabī al-ḥadīth wa-rūḥ al-ʿaṣr* (1964)—mod. Ar. p.; E. Wagner, *Abu Nuwas* (1965); M. Ullmann, *Untersuchungen zur Ragazpoesie* (1966); I. Ismāʿīl, *Al-Shiʿr al-ʿArabī al-muʿāṣir* (1967)—mod. Ar. p.; G. Shukrī, *Shiʿrunā al-ḥadīth: ilā ayn?* (1968)—mod. Ar. p.; J. Vadet, *L'Esprit courtois en Orient dans les premiers siècles de l'Hégire* (1968); W. Heinrichs, *Arabische Dichtung und griechische Poetik* (1969); M. Bateson, *Structural Continuity in Poetry* (1970); M. al-Nuwayhī, *Qaḍiyyat al-shiʿr al-jadīd* (1971)—issues in mod. Ar. p.; R. Jacobi, *Studien zur Poetik der altarabischen Qaside* (1971); J. T. Monroe, "Oral Composition in Pre-Islamic Poetry," *JArabL* 3 (1972); M. Ṣubḥī, *Dirāsāt taḥlīliyya fī al-shiʿr al-ʿArabī al-muʿāṣir* (1972)—mod. Ar. p.; *Ar. P.: Theory and Devel.*, ed. G. von Grunebaum (1973); R. Scheindlin, *Form and Structure in the Poetry of Al-Muʿtamid ibn ʿAbbād* (1974); S. M. Stern, *Hispano-Ar. Strophic Poetry* (1974); A. Hamori, *On the Art of Med. Ar. Lit.* (1974); J. ʿAsfūr, *Al-Ṣūra al-fanniyya fī al-turāth al-naqdī wa-al-balāghī* (1974)—imagery in traditional crit. and rhet.; M. Badawi, *A Crit. Intro. to Mod. Ar. P.* (1975); J. Bencheikh, *Poétique arabe* (1975); S. A. Bonebakker, *Materials for the Hist. of Ar. Rhet. from the Hilyat al-muhādara of Hātimī* (1975); J. Stetkevych, "The Ar. Lyrical Phenomenon in Context," *JArabL* 6 (1975); S. Moreh, *Mod. Ar. P. 1800–1970* (1976); L. F. Compton, *Andalusian Lyrical Poetry and Old Sp. Love Songs* (1976); S. K. Jayyusi, *Trends and Movements in Mod. Ar. P.* (1977); R. Hitchcock, *The Kharjas: Research, Bibls., and Checklists* (1977); M. Zwettler, *The Oral Trad. of Cl. Ar. P.* (1978); K. Kheir Beik, *Le Mouvement moderniste de la poésie arabe contemporaine* (1978); Y. al-Yūsuf, *Al-Shiʿr al-ʿArabī al-muʿāṣir* (1980)—mod. Ar. p.; M. Abdul-Hai, *Trad. and Eng. and Am. Influence in Ar. Romantic P.* (1982); G. van Gelder, *Beyond the Line* (1982); *Ar. Lit. to the End of the Umayyad Period*, ed. A. Beeston et al. (1983); M. Ajami, *The Neckveins of Winter* (1984); S. Stetkevych, "The Ṣuʿlūk and His Poem: A Paradigm of Passage Manqué," *JAOS* 104 (1984); S. A. Sowayan, *Nabati Poetry* (1985); Adunis, *Intro. à la poétique arabe* (1985); M. R. Menocal, *The Ar. Role in Med. Lit. Hist.* (1988); S. Sperl, *Mannerism in Ar. P.: A Structural Analysis of Sel. Texts, 9th C.–11th C. a.d.* (1989); C. Bailey, *Bedouin Poetry from Sinai and the Negev* (1991); S. P. Stetkevych, *Abū Tammām and the Poetics of the ʿAbbāsid Age* (1991). R.M.A.A.

ARAUCANIAN POETRY. See AMERICAN INDIAN POETRY, *South American*.

ARGENTINIAN POETRY. See SPANISH AMERICAN POETRY.

ARMENIAN POETRY. Descendents of the Urartuans and Hittites, Armenians call themselves *Hai* or *Hye* and their country *Haiastan* after Haik, the legendary great-grandson of Noah. The lang. is Indo-European, and ancient Armenia may have been the cradle of the Indo-European peoples. What is today known as Armenia, one of the Soviet Republics, contains only a fraction of its ancient lands, which are now part of Turkey and Iran. A. frontiers have varied greatly as a result of repeated invasions of this region at the crossroads of East and West.

Armenia provides a perfect laboratory for the study of poetry from ancient inscriptions in cuneiform to modern times. Here one can trace the uses of poetry as incantation, benediction, celebration, and political comment; one can observe how pagan chants to the sun evolve into praises of the light of Christ, then see the same rhythms in paeans to the red dawn of Communism. From the earliest ages to the present, poetry has been a vital part of A. life. The poet, honored early as a religious leader, was expected in periods of oppression to be both conscience and witness of his time.

When Armenia became the first Christian nation in 301 A.D., ancient pagan poetry was destroyed. Only a few poems that had been transmitted orally for millennia were preserved by Movses of Khorene in his 5th-c. history. For centuries, folk poems and variations of the cycle of poems comprising the folk epic *David of Sassoun* were also handed down orally, the latter acquiring Christian characteristics after the 4th c. This is the second oldest epic recorded (pub. 1874), preceded only by the Babylonian epic *Gilgamesh* (pub. 1872). A typical folk poem is the *Groung* (Song of the Crane), written in quatrains called *hyrens* (meaning in the A. style) and sometimes attributed to the medieval troubadour Nahabed Koutchag, who wrote hundreds of *hyrens*:

> Where do you come from, crane?
> I ache to hear your call,
> to know you come from home.
> Have you any news at all?
>
> I bless your wings, your eyes.
> My heart is torn in two,
> the exile's soul all sighs,
> waiting for bits of news.

After the 5th c., when a written A. alphabet was

developed (to keep the A. church separate from the Byzantine), a strong trad. of ecclesiastical poetry evolved, incl. the work of two 8th-c. women writers, Sahakdougkt Siunetsi and Khosrovidoukht Shirag. The hymns of the church, called *sharagans* ("rows of jewels"), with rhythmic listings and musical parallelism, are best illustrated in the work of Krikor Naregatsi (Gregory of Narek, 951–1003). His cadences, insight, and mystical meditations would have earned him a central place in world lit. had he written in a more accessible lang. In Armenia his poems were put under pillows of the sick and buried with the dead. Also well known in Christian A. p. is Nerses Shnorhali (Nerses the Gracious), who used intricate rhymes, prose poems, and riddles.

The first poems about romantic love were written by Gosdantin Erzengatzi (1250–1336) and Hovhannes Erzengatzi Blouse (1230–93). Hovhannes Telgourantsi (14th c.) should also be mentioned for his love ballads and battle narratives. However, the outstanding med. poet was Frik (Katchadour Ketcharetsi), who lived during Mongol invasions (13th–14th cs.) and wrote about the injustices of the time. He was a master of the forms and techniques common to Persian poetry of the era. Other med. A. p. was produced in monasteries. The lyricism of Frik and Koutchag was a strong influence esp. on Nagash Hovnathan (17th–18th cs.) and Sayat Nova (b. 1712), who wrote songs of sentiment and consolation touched with humor and satire. His songs are A. favorites, and his life has been the subject of modern operas and films such as Sergei Paradjanov's *Color of Pomegranates.*

The Ren. in Europe, stimulated by the fall of Constantinople to the Turks (1453?), which drove Byzantine scholars to Europe, brought only darker ages for the Armenians. They became a subjugated people in their own land. Beginning only in the late 18th c., their literary Ren. was brought about by a population shift into large cities, where the A. people had the support of the church and the presence of a European colony (as opposed to the provinces, where protection against oppression was absent). In the eastern regions too, in territories under Rus. Czarist rule, a similar influx of Armenians into Tiflis, an A. cultural center, brought about a literary rebirth. Soon many A. schools in both regions were using the spoken dialects instead of the old written Krapar, which survives only in church ritual.

In the monasteries of Venice and Vienna, where many A. children were sent to study in the 19th c., the A. Mekhitarist monks were responsible for a rebirth of poetry. Poet and translator Ghevont Alishan (1820–1901) was the most influential of these monks and his students composed the poetry of the A. romantic period. Bedros Tourian (1851–72) was the first to write purely subjective poetry. He read contemp. Fr. poetry and wrote lyrics that won a large audience of admirers. But the most lyrical voice of the time belonged to Missak Medzarentz (1886–1908), whose two books, *Nor Dagher* (1907) and *Dsiadsan* (1907), have been compared to Shelley and Verlaine.

His contemporary, Raffi (Hagop Melik-Hagopian, 1837–88), when he observed the suffering in Turkish Armenia, renounced poetry for prose, following the lead of Khatchadour Abovian, called the father of modern A. lit. Another well known poet of the time, Michael Nalbandian (1829–66), died in Russia after being imprisoned for political writing. His poem "To Freedom," sung secretly both in Russia and Turkish Armenia, begins: "God of Freedom, since that day / you made life of inert clay / my first and speechless sound / while struggling to be unbound / was my cry for liberty."

The following generation in Tiflis produced Hovaness Toumanian (1869–1923), called the "poet of all Armenians," famous not only for poems, stories, and crit., but for his generosity to other writers. Also noteworthy, Avedik Issahakian (1875–1957) made wide use of legend and proverb. Vahan Derian (1885–1920) produced some of the most lyrical writing in Armenia; Medzarents and he have been called the most musical of A. poets. The most prominent poets writing at the turn of the century in Istanbul were Siamanto (Adom Yarjanian, 1878–1915), Daniel Varoujan (1884–1915), and Roupen Sevag (1890–1915). All three did much to vitalize the lang. by introducing European symbolism, social and political themes, national pride, pagan images, and, in the work of Varoujan, a new sensualism not present since the Middle Ages (he has been called "one of the most life-filled poets in Western lit."). All three are examples of the poet as leader and hero. Varoujan's "Red Soil" begins:

> Here on a plate on my desk is a gift
> a handful of soil, a clump from the
> fields
> of my fatherland. The giver thought
> he gave his heart and did not know
> he gave with it the heart of
> his forefathers.

Other poets who should be mentioned are Indra (Diran Cherakian, 1875–1921) and his student Matteos Zarifian (1894–1924).

The main influence on modern A. p. is politico-social oppression, which accounts both for poems of protest and for the absence of writing altogether. Of several periods of such oppression the worst were the Turkish massacres of 1886 and 1915; the latter not only exterminated 200 poets but also decimated the entire reading public, two million people, stopping all lit. for almost a generation.

The father of modern Soviet A. p. is Eghishe Charents (1897–1937), who gained fame at 20 with "Dantesque Legend," one of the strongest anti-violence poems in Western lit. He wrote it after the defense of Van, where he had gone as a

16-year-old soldier after the Turkish massacres had removed most of the population, incl. the nation's top writers, in Istanbul. Charents, often called the A. Majakovskij, became a stronger and more versatile writer than the Russian he admired. He died in prison. His fellow poet Gourgen Mahari (1903–69) was sent to Siberia but survived the purges. Other notable contemporaries incl. Gostan Zarian (1885–1969), another daring innovator; Kegham Sarian (1902–76), who managed to produce lyric poetry when many others succumbed to the prescribed Social Realism; and Nayirie Zarian (1900–69).

In the next generation two outstanding poets were Hovaness Shiraz (1915–85), the most popular poet of his time, and Barouyr Sevag (1924–72), whose work moves on many levels: metaphysical, political, patriotic, celebratory. Today the leading poets are Gevorg Emin (b. 1919), who is widely translated; Vahakn Davtian (b. 1923), whose early work has been compared to Yeats's and whose new poems are rooted in native soil but universal in appeal: and Hamo Sahian (b. 1914), whose work is noted for its musicality. Sylva Gaboudikian, Maro Markarian, Hratchia Hovanessian, and Saghatel Haroutunian are the leaders of the establishment. Important younger poets incl. Arevshad Avakian, Razmig Davoyan, Ardem Haroutiunian, and Hovhaness Grigorian, who, with their free floating syntax, offer fresh imagery. Yuri Sahakian's poems of social comment investigate choice and commitment, while satirist Aramais Sahagian makes playful jabs at A. life. Armen Mardirossian, Davit Hovanness, Ludvig Touryan, Ahahid Barsamian, Medakse, Henrik Edoyan, and Edward Milidonian are names most often seen in the literary journals. Among the very young and promising are Armen Shekoyan and Hrachia Saruchan.

Although A. p. may be compared to contemp. poetry worldwide, much of the love poetry is addressed to the land or lost lands across the border. Ararat, the sacred mountain of the Armenians, is a common image. Gevorg Emin in one of his Ararat poems says it is "always in sight, always out of reach, like a great love."

For an outsider the startling fact about A. p. today is the reader's involvement. Poetry is quoted in everyday life as a matter of course. Poetry books are published in huge runs and often sell out within days.

In the diaspora things are different. The only major poet to escape the genocide was Vahan Tekeyan (1878–1945), who by chance was not in Istanbul that April. His painstakingly honed sonnets have earned him a reputation as a visionary. His poems search for the affirmation and redemption that should follow tragedy, but ironically his most frequently quoted work is a bitter sonnet, "We Shall Say to God" (1917):

Should it happen we do not endure
this uneven fight and drained
of strength and agonized
we fall on death's ground not to rise
and the great crime ends
with the last Armenian eyes
closing without seeing a victorious day,
let us swear that when we find
God in his paradise offering comfort
to make amends for our pain,
let us swear that we will refuse
saying No, send us to hell again.
We choose hell. You made us know it
well.
Keep your paradise for the Turk.

Younger poets who survived or were born abroad include Aharon Dadourian and Puzand Topalian, both strongly influenced by the Fr. surrealists; Harout Gosdantian, Nighoghos Sarafian, and novelist-poet Shahan Shhnour also settled in France. Yeghivart (Jerusalem), Mousegh Ishkhan, Andranik Zarougian, and Vahe-Vahian, all orphaned children of the genocide, grew up in Syria and Beirut. Hamasdegh (H. Gelenian, 1895–1966), lived in the U.S. Today one of the leading voices of the diaspora poets belongs to Zahrad (Zareh Yaldiciyan, b. 1923) in Istanbul, who writes wry, whimsical verse. Vahe Oshagan (b. 1923) and other expatriates of Beirut, influenced by Fr. surrealists and European absurdists, now live in France or America. Many third-generation diaspora poets are writing in the lang. of the countries where they were born; hence, even though they keep A. names and themes, they belong to other lits. even while using the imagery of their ancestry. Some are doing trs., bringing the riches of A. p., locked for centuries in a difficult lang., to other cultures.

ANTHOLOGIES: *David of Sassoun*, tr. A. K. Shalian (1964); *Anthol. of A. P.*, (1978), *Sacred Wrath* (1983), both ed. and tr. D. Der-Hovanessian and M. Margossian; *Come Sit Beside Me and Listen to Kouchag* (1985), *For You On New Year's Day* (1987), both tr. D. Der-Hovanessian.

HISTORY AND CRITICISM: V. Brussov, "The P. of Armenia," tr. A. S. Avakian, *The A. Rev.* 1 (1948); H. Thorossian, *Histoire de la litt. armenienne* (1951); S. Der-Nercessian, *The Armenians* (1970); M. J. Arlen, *Passage to Ararat* (1975); D. M. Lang, *Armenia: Cradle of Civilization* (1978); C. Walker, *Armenia, Survival of a Nation* (1980); D. Der-Hovanessian and M. Margossian, "A. Lit," *Encyc. of World Lit. in the 20th C.*, rev. ed., ed. L. S. Klein, v. 1 (1981); T. Gamkrelidze and V. Ivanov, *Origins of the Indo-Europeans* (1986). D.D.-H.

ASSAMESE POETRY. See INDIAN POETRY.

ASSYRO-BABYLONIAN POETRY. Of the two main dialects of Akkadian, a Semitic lang., Babylonian (B.) and not Assyrian (A.) was used for most of the poetry. While some poetic texts survive (on clay tablets, written in cuneiform characters) from the end of the third millennium B.C., the earliest creative period can be dated from about ca. 1800 onward, the OB (Old Babylonian) period. Toward the end of the second millennium, ca. 1200 and later, new poetry is composed. Most of the poetry is known from late copies collected in the royal libraries of Tiglathpileser I (ca. 1100 B.C.) in Assur and of Assurbanipal (668–27 B.C.) in Nineveh.

Most of the texts are anonymous; only the author of the epic of the plague god Irra—who claims to have written it down from the god's dictation—and the author of the Gilgamesh Epic are known by name. Names appearing in colophons are those of the scribe, not of the poet; literary catalogues list beside titles of compositions not only personal names but also names of gods and mythological figures.

With respect to genre, the corpus may be divided into narrative, religious, and didactic poems, i.e. epics, hymns, prayers, and "wisdom lit." Purely secular poetry seems not to have been recorded in writing. Charms—against the scorpion, the toothache, or to invoke a star—are embedded in medical or magical prescriptions and suggest a pattern of folk poetry made up of short lines and often concatenated repetitions, such as

Anger advances like a wild bull
Jumps at me like a dog,
Like a lion, it is formidable in progress
Like a wolf, it is full of fury.

Verses whose lyricism would suggest love poetry, as well as first lines such as "Away, sleep! I want to embrace my lover" (cited in a literary catalogue), concern divine lovers, as in the OB poem

the women's quarter moans, the bed-
chamber weeps

wherein we were wont to celebrate the
wedding;
the courtyard sighs, the loft laments
wherein we were wont to do sweet dalli-
ance.

In an A. elegy a woman who died in childbirth complains:

I lived with him who was my lover.
Death came creeping into my bedroom,
it drove me from my house,
it tore me from my husband,
it set my feet into a land of no return.

The formal characteristic of B., as of all Semitic and also Sumerian poetry (q.v.), syntactic parallelism, evidenced in the first two examples above, is frequently combined with chiasmus, but enjambment and zeugma are rarely tolerated. Rhyme (internal or final), alliteration, onomatopoeia, anaphora, and epiphora may be used for special effect. Meter is based on stress; a line contains four measures, rarely three or five, with a syntactic break or caesura in the middle. The verse ending is trochaic (suffixes that would make the word a dactyl are truncated). Two types of acrostics, such that the initial syllable of the lines spell out a name or a pious wish, and such that each line of a strophe begins with the same sign, are also known; some of these are also telestichs.

Narrative Poetry. B. epics deal with the exploits of gods or mythological beings and are therefore often dubbed "myths." Many of these date to the OB period, although their first-millennium recensions are more complete and more elaborate—e.g. the *Story of the Bird Anzû*, who stole the Tablet of Office from the supreme god Enlil and was defeated by the god Ninurta; the story of the mythical king *Etana*, who ascended to heaven on the back of an eagle to obtain the herb for childbearing; the story of *Atra-hasis* (Exceedingly Wise), who survived the Flood brought about by the gods after they had created mankind; and the *Epic of Gilgamesh.* To the middle of the second millennium date the *Story of Wise Adapa* and of *Nergal and Ereshkigal*, which tells how Nergal came to rule the nether world together with its queen Ereshkigal. Only first-millennium recensions are known of the *Epic of Creation*, the story of the defeat of the forces of chaos by the god Marduk, who was thereby acknowledged supreme god and who created the cosmos out of the body of the primeval monster; the *Epic of Irra*, which describes the calamities that befell Babylon when the plague god Irra replaced its tutelary god Marduk; and the *Descent of Ishtar to the Nether World.*

The 19th-c. discovery of Tablet XI with its account of the Flood so closely paralleling that in the OT triggered Western interest in the *Epic of Gilgamesh.* It deals with basic human concerns of all times—friendship, and the quest for immortality, attainable only by achieving enduring fame. When Enkidu, a semi-savage created by the gods to become Gilgamesh's friend and companion, dies, Gilgamesh realizes the same fate awaits him and so begins the quest which leads him to the sole survivor of the Flood. Just as the *Odyssey* does not end with the death of Odysseus, the *Epic of Gilgamesh* ends not with the death of its hero, but as it began, with the description of the ramparts of Uruk, his lasting achievement. Some narrative poems have kings as heroes, e.g. a cycle about Sargon and Naram-Sin, who built the Akkadian empire in the late third millennium, composed in OB times and also known from later versions. Some are couched as "autobiographies," with the king narrating his own history. The lesson to be drawn from events of the past is held up to the future ruler being addressed in a sort of *envoi* at the end. The A. king Tukulti Ninurta (1243–07 B.C.) and his victory over the B. king Kashtiliash is celebrated in poems written in Assyria, reflecting A. political ideology though in the literary, i.e. B., dialect.

Religious Poetry. B. hymns address a number of gods and goddesses; they are characterized by an elevated, even *recherché* style and a vocabulary of rare terms, indicators of their learned origin and sophisticated audience. They are often divided into strophes; occasional rulings on the tablet after each distich or every 10th line may not coincide with the strophic divisions. The hymn to Shamash (the sun god and god of justice) has exactly 200 lines, divided by rulings into 100 distichs; the hymns to Ishtar, to the Queen of Nippur, and to Nabu each contain over 200 lines. Some hymns, such as the 200-line hymn to Gula, are styled in the first person, the goddess speaking her own self-praise. Some hymns are in praise of cities.

Prayers also address the deity with praise but stress the supplicant's misery and petition. Their poetic virtue lies in their description of mood and feeling. Their plaintive lyricism, in such phrases as "How wet with my tears is my bread!", "Man's sins are more numerous than the hairs on his head," or "What sin have I committed against my god?" reminds us of the penitential Psalms. Prayers to the gods of divination ask for a favorable answer to the oracle query.

Didactic Poetry comprises philosophical dialogues or monologues questioning the fairness of the fate bestowed by the god, such as the *Theodicy*, an acrostic, and the *B. Job*, consisting of four "books" of 120 lines each. Animal fables and poetic contests in which two rivals—trees, cereals—extol their own merits and belittle their opponents', hark back to a well-attested Sumerian genre.

Only a few humorous poems are known: the *Dialogue between Master and Servant*, also classed with "wisdom lit.," may be one; another is the difficult OB *At the Cleaners*, while the *Tale of the Poor Man of Nippur*, having close affinities with the *Tale of the First Larrikin* of the Arabian Nights, has perennial appeal. The *Tale of the Illiterate Doctor*, similarly situated in the Sumerian city of Nippur, draws its humor from the linguistic effects of Sumerian interspersed in the B. text.

ANTHOLOGIES: *Sumerisch-akkadische Hymnen und Gebete*, ed. and tr. A. Falkenstein and W. von Soden (1953)—good intro. and commentary; *Ancient Near Eastern Texts Relating to the O.T.*, ed. J. B. Pritchard, 3d ed. with Supp. (1969); *Les Religions du Proche Orient asiatique: Textes babyloniens, ougaritiques, hittites*, ed. and tr. R. Labat et al. (1970); *Hymnes et prières aux dieux de Babylonie et d'Assyrie*, ed. and tr. M.-J. Seux (1976).

INDIVIDUAL POEMS: O. R. Gurney, "The Tale of the Poor Man of Nippur," *Anatolian Studies* 6–7 (1956–57); C. J. Gadd, "At the Cleaners," *Iraq* 25 (1963) and A. Livingstone in *Alter Orient und Altes Testament, Sonderreihe*, v. 220 (1988); W. G. Lambert, "The Gula Hymn of Bullutsa-rabi," *Orientalia*, n.s. 36 (1967), "The Hymn to the Queen of Nippur," *Studies Presented to F. R. Kraus* (1983); W. von Soden, "Der grosse Hymnus an Nabu," *ZAVA* 61 (1971); S. A. Picchioni, *Il poemetto di Adapa* (1981); A. Schott, *Das Gilgamesch-Epos*, rev. W. von Soden (1982); J. Gardner and J. Maier, *Gilgamesh* (1984); J. V. Kinnier Wilson, *The Legend of Etana* (1985); A. Livingstone in *AOATS* 220 (1988).

HISTORY AND CRITICISM: J. Nougayrol, "L'Epopée babylonienne," *ANLMSF* (1970); O. R. Gurney, "The Tale of the Poor Man of Nippur and its Folktale Parallels," *Anatolian Studies* 22 (1972); K. Hecker, *Untersuchungen der akkadischen Epik* (1974); A. L. Oppenheim, *Ancient Mesopotamia*, 2d ed. (1977); E. Reiner, *Your Thwarts in Pieces, Your Mooring Rope Cut* (1984)—incl. originals and literary evaluations. E.R.

AUSTRALIAN POETRY. Australians possess not one but two poetic trads., one native (Aboriginal), one imported (European). The poetry of Europeans in the country goes back 200 years and at one time or another has suffered most of the disadvantages of a historically prolonged adolescence. Aboriginal poetry, on the other hand, has something like 40,000 years of continuity behind it. If there must be doubt about its future in an age of mass communication, there is none about its achievement to date. Even the randomly preserved ruins of a native oral trad. testify to its strength, subtlety, and maturity. This in spite of the difficulties involved in judging on the basis of not merely translations but translations into forms quite alien to the originals.

Aboriginal poetry is recited or sung as part of a performance or ritual which includes music, dancing, and theater and whose rationale is sacramental and religious. Though form and content are passed on from generation to generation, there is a great deal of room for improvisation and therefore variation. Clearly the reduction of this oral trad. to written Eng. texts entails considerable loss. Nonetheless, something of the quality of the original comes through in translations like T. G. H. Strehlow's of songs from Central Australia ("The ring-neck-parrots are a cloud of wings; / The shell-parrots are a cloud of wings") and R. Berndt's of the great Arnhem Land cycles associated with the earth mother Kunapipi or the ancestral sisters the Wawalag and the Djanggawul ("Although I leave Bralgu, I am close to it. I, Djanggawul, am paddling . . ."). The Berndt Djanggawul cycle describes in epic dimensions the archetypal sea journey of the parents of the tribes from the mythical Bralgu to Australia. Berndt's lovesong cycles lyrically reenact other archetypal events, e.g. the Jonah-like death and resurrection of the Wawalags, swallowed then vomited up by the python. In this case the symbolism is both sexual and seasonal, linking fertility with the monsoonal rains.

As a whole, Aboriginal oral poetry is characterized by fundamental identification of humans with the land, expressed through myth with the totemic logic analyzed by Lévi-Strauss. Chiefly it is used for initiatory, mortuary, and ritual increase ceremonies, though there are also songs for everyday purposes, not least for amusement. The impact of Aboriginal culture on white poetry has been fitful and superficial. In the 1930s the Jindyworobak group, led by Rex Ingamells (1913–55), derived inspiration from Black identification with the country. More recently, Les Murray has attempted to imitate Berndt's version of the Wonguri-Mandjigai moon-bone cycle.

From the beginning of European settlement in 1788 to the early 20th c., there was a strong white oral or partly oral trad. consisting of folksongs, ballads, and the like. To begin with, this trad. expressed the sufferings of convicts, many of them Irish, condemned to bitter hardship in an isolated penal colony. Protest songs, often treasonable in nature, were sung in defiance of authority, some of the best-known being "Van Diemen's Land," "Jim Jones at Botany Bay," and "Moreton Bay." The last of these was probably the work of Frank McNamara (b. 1811), also responsible for verses such as the grotesquely and grimly humorous "The Convict's Tour of Hell." Convict ballads elevated the figure of the outlaw and rebel, bushrangers like Bold Jack Donahoe, who scorned "to live in slavery, bound down with iron chains." They led, later in the century, to songs about other celebrated victims of the Law, Ben Hall and Ned Kelly, and to an avatar of Donahoe, "The Wild Colonial Boy."

The Gold Rush of 1851 radically altered A. society. Its songs belonged less to an anonymous folk trad. than to the stage, and by then Am. influence was as strong as that from England or Ireland. Charles Thatcher (1831–78), "The Inimitable," produced songs about the diggings which eventually passed into folklore. There were also, in the second half of the century, ballads about life on the land, focusing on squatters, poor farmers (or "cockies"), and pastoral laborers. These are characteristically stoic and often simultaneously ironic and sentimental. They range from the romantic ("The Banks of the Condamine") to work songs ("Click Go the Shears"), songs celebrating Outback life ("A Thousand Mile Away") or workers' sprees ("Lazy Harry's"), to wry or heartbroken comments on suffering and endurance ("The Old Bullock Dray," "The Cocky Farmer"). Of course the distinction between verses originating in a genuine folk trad. and literary ballads imitating that trad. is a difficult one.

From the later 19th into the early 20th c. a number of poets contributed material which became part of the general store. This included the galloping rhymes of Adam Lindsay Gordon and, after that, the ballads of Barcroft Boake (1866–92), who hanged himself by his own stockwhip, Edward Dyson (1865–1931), E. J. Brady (1869–1952), and Will Ogilvie (1869–1963). Henry Lawson (1867–1922), better known for his short stories, also wrote ballads. The most successful of all literary balladists was A. B. ("Banjo") Paterson (1864–1941), whose verse had a popularity in Australia comparable to that of Kipling in Britain. Best known are "The Man from Snowy River" and "Waltzing Matilda," which has become the unofficial national anthem. These authors published regularly in the nationalistic and radical *Bulletin,* expressing more or less consciously their sense of an A. identity and, frequently, their pride in emergent nationhood. By the time of Federation, i.e. the establishment of centralized self-government in 1901, folk ballads and their literary equivalents no longer sang of exile or revolt, though bush hardship was still a theme. Shortly after, their vogue declined, the last example of this popular genre being the work of C. J. Dennis (1876–1936).

The movement towards adaptation to a difficult new environment evident in the ballad emerges in 19th-c. poetry unconnected with the oral trad. For colonial poets the problem, whether acknowledged or not, was to transform the raw material of Australia, to *poeticize* it, and in so doing build a bridge between new and old world experiences. From the standpoint of the tourist, Barron Field eulogized the kangaroo as a divine mistake, fabulous as sphinx, mermaid, or centaur—or sooty swan and duck-mole (platypus). The persistent notion that everything was "new, new, too new / To foster poesy" was early challenged by Charles Harpur (1813–68), though with ambiguous results. Pondering the antipodean landscape like one of Caspar David Friedrich's alpine travelers, Harpur struggles to transcend the sense of the exotic. His Australia recalls Egypt, Assyria, Babylon in ruins. It is peopled by Miltonic Aborigines and viewed through the lens of the Wordsworthian sublime—tinted with 18th-c. Sensibility. Even so, there is a strength, however awkward, in work like "The Creek of the Four Graves" which is missing in the musical, nature-inspired verse of Henry Kendall (1839–82), whose melancholy warbling owes more to Eng. Victorian poetry than to the great romantics. Here too the attachment to Australia is complicated by contradictions: birds sing in September their song of May. And in the writing of the other significant colonial bard of the wilderness, Adam Lindsay Gordon (1833–70), eucalyptus trunks, like Egyptian obelisks, are carved with indecipherable hieroglyphs, native blossoms are scentless, bright birds songless.

It was not until the end of the century that poetic adaptation to the southern hemisphere became evident in the writing of poets associated with the *Bulletin.* At the same time, not all the writers of the period turned to ballads—or to "diggers, drovers, bush race-courses, / And on all the other pages, horses, horses, horses, horses." Victor Daley (1858–1905), Roderic Quinn (1867–1949), and D. M. Wright (1869–1928) created a celtic twilight Down Under; Bernard O'Dowd (1866–1953) produced a Socialist "poetry militant" inspired in part by Whitman; Christopher Brennan (1870–1932), thoroughly acquainted with European lit. from antiquity to Mallarmé, wrote a dense and sometimes profound *Livre com-*

posé. If *Poems (1913*, with its combination of romantic high-mindedness and *fin de siècle* lassitude, is difficult to appreciate as a whole, its more readable sections, such as the Nietzschean and Arnoldian "The Wanderer" sequence, represent some of the most impressive writing to emerge from Australia. The trad. of philosophical verse was carried on, rather shakily, by "William Baylebridge" (1883–1942). However, after Brennan's, the best verse of the period is that of the radical Mary Gilmore (1864–1962) and of John Shaw Neilson (1872–1942). Uneducated, dogged by poverty, Neilson is Australia's most eccentric poetic talent and, at least in the lightness and lyricism of his work, very nearly its finest.

The Great War prompted some sobering reflections in verse, but the tone of the aftermath was escapist and frivolous, dominated by nationalism gone to seed and by an equally spurious internationalism fostered by the followers of Norman Lindsay and the journal *Vision.* Hugh McCrae (1876–1958) favored satyrs and whimsy and, in his early phase, Kenneth Slessor (1901–71) followed the fashion for pseudo-jollity and the pursuit of Pan on the shores of Sydney Harbor. If the 19th-c. issue for poets had been to reconcile European poetic trads. with antipodean realities, the issue in the 20th c. was—and is—to assimilate modernity. Slessor introduced the rhythms of T. S. Eliot to A. p. in his later and best work, producing in the process what is probably the finest individual A. poem, "Five Bells."

However, even after World War II, modernism remained suspect. The Ern Malley hoax, in which the avant-garde journal *Angry Penguins* was persuaded to publish fake modernist verse, was meant to discredit experimentation and succeeded in inhibiting it for decades. In spite of this, A. p. in the 1940s, following economic depression, worldwide political upheaval, the trauma of near-invasion by the Japanese, and the intellectual shock which accompanied the assimilation of Marx and Freud, could scarcely revert to either the gum-trees-and-sheep identity of the 1890s or the Art Deco idyll of the 1920s. Whether conservative or experimental, it chose the exploration of a problematic and angst-ridden inwardness, an analogue for the previous century's exploration of *terra australis incognita.* For Francis Webb (1925–73) this search terminated in both schizophrenia and at the same time impressive work in a knotted and difficult style. For Judith Wright (b. 1915) it implied the exploration of her identity as woman, poet, and A., increasingly in relation to the fundamental presence of the land. For James McAuley (1917–76) it led from the horrors of modernity to the dubious haven of the church. For A. D. Hope (b. 1907), with McAuley the major representative of the postwar poetry establishment and the country's best-known poet, a writer less tormented than his contemporaries and at home in a witty, urbane style, it led to a reaffirmation of "classical" values and a gently ironic stance. Other poets played major parts in postwar devel., the chief of these being R. D. FitzGerald (1902–87), equally active between the wars, Douglas Stewart (1913–85), David Campbell (1915–79), J. S. Manifold (1915–85), and Rosemary Dobson (b. 1920).

By the late 1950s and early '60s, though, another poetic generation chafed under the régime of the Slessors and Stewarts. Rodney Hall (b. 1935) and Thomas Shapcott (b. 1935), themselves prolific poets, edited the *New Impulses* anthology, with its Cold War poetic manifesto of caution and doubt. This included many poets who have continued to develop their talents to the present, such as Gwen Harwood (b. 1920), Vincent Buckley (1925–88), Bruce Beaver (b. 1928), Bruce Dawe (b. 1930), Chris Wallace-Crabbe (b. 1934), David Malouf (b. 1934), Les Murray (b. 1938), and Geoffrey Lehmann (b. 1940). In the event, the new impulses of the 1950s no sooner emerged than they were overshadowed by the achievements, sometimes merely showy, sometimes substantial, of the so-called Generation of '68. The 1960s poets were young, insistent, and contemporary—though like all Australians they suffered a time-lag in the assimilation of overseas ideas. They read the Americans, listened to rock, smoked pot, marched against Vietnam, and supported a mass of underground magazines. Their anthologies were *A. P. Now, Applestealers,* and *The New A. P.*; their best poets, Michael Dransfield (1948–73) and Robert Adamson (b. 1943), the one dead of an overdose at 24, the other on the run from the law and his own personality until rescued by a hard muse.

If Dransfield, Adamson, and others like Charles Buckmaster (1951–72)—an early casualty—Richard Tipping (b. 1949), Vicki Viidikas (b. 1948), and Nigel Roberts (b. 1941) represented the romantic, often visionary, pole of a Poetry Now aesthetic, there were also more Hard-Edge practitioners such as John Tranter (b. 1943), John Forbes (b. 1950), Jennifer Maiden (b. 1949), and Martin Johnston (b. 1947). In Melbourne the most influential figure was Kris Hemensley (b. 1946), with the older Ken Taylor (b. 1930) providing guidance in the same way as Beaver did in Sydney. A separate group, incl. Laurie Duggan (b. 1949), John Scott (b. 1948), and Alan Wearne (b. 1948), held readings of their own away from the central Melbourne venue of La Mama. Inevitably a battle of the books ensued in which more conservative poets like Robert Gray (b. 1945) and Lehmann produced their own anthology, *The Younger A. Poets.* This gave prominence to the verse of the ebullient Les Murray and included poets like Roger McDonald (b. 1941) and Geoff Page (b. 1940).

At present the argument about modernity and tradition is no more settled than the older debate about nationalism and internationalism. Since the Generation of '68 and its detractors, the public has witnessed the extravagances of Performance Poets, led by the anarchist public servant, Pi O (b.

1951). Predictably, women's anthologies have appeared, as have publications of "ethnic" poetry, not all in Eng., and also of Aboriginal poetry in Eng. Where women's writing has extended the range of poetic possibilities in the 1980s, "ethnic" and Aboriginal poetry may well be in the process of doing something more fundamental: the creation not merely of new speech rhythms and vocabulary but, conceivably, of a new lang. in the making, and one suited to a multicultural society.

ANTHOLOGIES: *Djanggawul* (1952), *Love Songs of Arnhem Land* (1976), both ed. R. Berndt; *A. Bush Ballads* (1955), *Old Bush Songs and Rhymes of Colonial Times* (1957), both ed. D. Stewart and N. Keesing; *Penguin Book of A. Ballads*, ed. R. Ward (1964); *New Impulses in A. P.*, ed. R. Hall and T. Shapcott (1968); *Bards in the Wilderness: A. Colonial Poetry to 1920*, ed. B. Elliott and A. Mitchell (1970); *The New A. P.*, ed. J. Tranter (1979); *Collins Book of A. P.*, ed. R. Hall (1981); *Penguin Book of Mod. A. Verse*, ed. H. Heseltine (1981); *The Younger A. Poets*, ed. R. Gray and G. Lehmann (1983); *New Oxford Book of A. Verse*, ed. L. Murray (1986); *Penguin Book of A. Women Poets*, ed. S. Hampton and K. Llewellyn (1986).

HISTORY AND CRITICISM: *The Lit. of Australia*, ed. G. Dutton (1964); J. Wright, *Preoccupations in A. P.* (1965); *Oxford Hist. of A. Lit.*, ed. L. Kramer (1981); *Rev. of Nat. Lits.: Australia*, ed. A. Paolucci and L. Dobrez (1982); *A Possible Contemp. P.*, ed. M. Duwell (1982); H. M. Green, *A Hist. of A. Lit.*, rev. D. Green (1984–85); W. Wilde et al., *Oxford Companion to A. Lit.* (1985). L.A.C.D.

AUSTRIAN POETRY. Although A. p. is linguistically related to Ger. poetry (q.v.), there is sufficient justification for regarding it as a separate entity, since the particular ethnic, historical, and political conditions of the area combined to create a unique cultural milieu. A. ruling dynasties—the Babenbergs (976–1246) and the Hapsburgs (1278–1918)—established a strong sense of continuous trad. Its geographic location in Middle Europe made the Monarchy a meeting place between East and West, and the large Hapsburg Empire constituted a virtual melting pot of ethnic elements—Germanic, Magyar, Slavic, Jewish, and Romance. With strong ties to other Alpine lands, particularly Bavaria, and receptive to influences from Italy and Spain, the absolute center of the Empire was Vienna. Whereas the cultural trad. was consistently strong in music and theater, the poetic trad. reached a high point first in the Middle Ages and then not again until the end of the 19th c.

Med. lit. flourished in the Danube valley, although it is not entirely correct to speak of a national lit., since feudal society was regional and supranational. Ger. medieval poetry is a major trad., with a primary division between High and Low German; A. lit. represents regional variants within the High Ger. trad. Initially, the centers of culture were the monasteries, which produced religious lit. such as the *Wiener Genesis* (ca. 1060), Frau Ava's *Leben Jesu* (ca. 1125), the *Melker Marienlied* (ca. 1130–60), and Heinrich von Melk's *Memento mori* (ca. 1160). As society became more secular, groups of wandering scholars and minstrels cultivated a popular trad. that was to remain strong for centuries. The *Nibelungenlied*, a heroic epic written down around 1200 in Passau but representing the oral trad. of an earlier era, is connected to well-known localities in the Danube region, where it was very popular.

Minnesang was a European phenomenon emanating from Provence, and although its origins are disputed, scholars view the early Danubian lyrics as a somewhat indigenous movement. A well-known example is Der von Kürenberg's falcon song (ca. 1150–70) composed in the *Nibelungenstrophe*. The precourtly lyrics of Dietmar von Aist (fl. 1140–70), particularly his *Tagelieder*, exhibit a simplicity and sincerity absent in the later, more formalized verse. During the classical period of courtly lit. (ca. 1180–1250), the Viennese court was a center of cultural activity. It attracted the Alsatian Reinmar von Hagenau (1160–1210), whose elegiac verses of unrequited love represent the epitome of formal stylization. The greatest lyric poet of the time, Walther von der Vogelweide (ca. 1170–ca. 1230), also found patronage in Vienna, as well as at other courts. Walther not only perfected the high *Minnesang* but also broke through the conventions to achieve an original expression of more natural experience; he is known for his poetry of *niedere Minne* in praise of reciprocal love; and he is also known for his *Spruchdichtung* on affairs of church and state and on the transitoriness of life. This roving singer was an enlightened advocate of humanity and tolerance, and his wide-ranging oeuvre signals the height of Ger.-lang. poetry for centuries to come. Among the numerous postclassical poets, Neidhard von Reuental (ca. 1180–1246), Ulrich von Lichtenstein (ca. 1200–76?), and particularly Oswald von Wolkenstein (1377–1445) wrote poetry of lasting value.

After the decline of the Middle Ages we listen in vain for a great lyric voice, apart from the widespread folk trad., until the 19th c. Although the Ren. court of Maximilian I was an important literary center, attracting the humanist poet Conrad Celtis (1459–1508), literary developments were cut short by the wars of the Reformation; and the success of the Counter-Reformation in Austria restored the hegemony of the Catholic Church and with it Lat. as the lang. of art and learning. Jesuit drama was strong in the 16th c. until influences began to be felt from the It. *commedia dell'arte* and the Sp. court theater. Whereas the 17th-c. baroque culture produced a rich body of lyric in Protestant North Germany, the only poet of rank in the Catholic Austrian South was Catharina Regina von Greiffenberg (1633–94). Austria celebrated the age in its architecture, erecting lavish churches and palaces; and the spirit of the baroque, as well as the centrality of the Church, has remained a formative factor down to the present day. Although the 18th c. Enlightenment brought a measure of reform to the semifeudal A. society, it was too little and too short-lived to provide literary impetus. At the time when Germany produced the Classicism and romanticism of Goethe, Schiller, and the Schlegels, Austria seemed to pour its energies into music and the opera, bringing forth Haydn, Mozart, and Schubert and attracting other great composers such as Beethoven.

Modern A. lit. began in the 19th c. with Franz Grillparzer (1791–1872), who was primarily a dramatist. The leading poet of the period was the Hungarian-born Nikolaus Lenau (1802–50), whose work is characterized by melancholy, restlessness, a bittersweet lyricism, and *Weltschmerz* (19th-c. pessimism). It was the Metternich era of reactionary politics and Biedermeier society, with poetry expressing resignation and a quiet joy in small things. These traits were infused with an element of social criticism by Marie von Ebner-Eschenbach (1830–1916) and Ferdinand von Saar (1833–1906); the poetry of Anastasius Grün (1806–76) demonstrates overt political engagement. On the whole, however, A. p. was averse to confrontation with materialist culture, labor movements, and the Industrial Revolution; and currents of realism and naturalism were limited mainly to the dialect works of popular lit.

Fin-de-siècle Vienna was the scene of an unprecedented burst of creative activity, and that not only in lit. but also in music, fine art, philosophy, and psychoanalysis. It was as though latent energies had suddenly been activated precisely and paradoxically on the eve of the Monarchy. Freud is only one of the numerous figures of world renown from this era, many of whom were Jewish. Psychological observation had always been more appealing to Austrians than either philosophical abstraction or sociopolitical activism, and the time was ripe. Partly as a reaction to North German naturalism, a group of writers known as Young Vienna focused on nuances of feeling, sensual impressions, and subconscious drives in an effort to create a new aesthetic. The refined coffeehouse culture has been variously associated with impressionism, neoromanticism, symbolism, aestheticism, Jugendstil, and decadence; but no labels do justice to the supreme achievements of Hugo von Hofmannsthal (1874–1929) and Rainer Maria Rilke (1875–1926).

The precocious Hofmannsthal began publishing poetry and lyric plays at the age of 17; ten years later he stopped, and his seminal "Chandos Letter" (1902) describes a crisis of lang. that made poetry impossible. Poetry had come easily to him, as if by magic or in dream—the images he uses to express the creative power—and his early works were already masterpieces. Well-known poems such as "Terzinen über Vergänglichkeit," "Ballade des äusseren Lebens," and "Lebenslied" represent the culmination of a long trad. and demonstrate cognizance of the burden of the past as well as the transitoriness of the present. Consciousness, however, had itself become problematic, and with the loss of naiveté the self-conscious poet is torn between experience and reflection, between the affirmation and negation of life. Awareness of the social responsibility of art led Hofmannsthal to turn his attention to drama after 1902, and he is also known for his opera libretti in collaboration with Richard Strauss.

Rilke, born in Prague, seems to have lived everywhere in Europe and consequently nowhere. He is truly an international figure in terms of both creation and reception, and since his works are discussed in more detail in the essay on Ger. poetry, suffice it here to sketch an outline. Rilke's early collections of poetry, such as *Das Stundenbuch* (written 1899–1903, pub. 1905) and *Das Buch der Bilder* (written 1898–1906, pub. 1902 and 1906), reveal mystical intensity and rich imagery, although they are at times overwrought. From Rodin in Paris Rilke learned "to see," as he said, and this encounter with the visual arts resulted in *Neue Gedichte* (1907–8). In it the poet combines observation and precision with inwardness and a phenomenological sense of meaning to give new definition to the concept of *Dinggedicht.* After his prose work *Die Aufzeichnungen des Malte Laurids Brigge* (1910) Rilke wrote very little for over a decade. It was a period of existential crisis, as recorded—and poetically transformed—in his great work, the *Duineser Elegien* (written 1912–22, pub. 1923). The ensuing *Sonette an Orpheus* (1923) celebrate this transformation of the world into song. Rilke's oeuvre is so strong that virtually every subsequent poet has been compelled to deal with it; he has thus exerted great influence on the devel. of modern European poetry.

Georg Trakl (1887–1914) is a major poet whose life was cut short by the Great War. Trakl's poetry is often associated with expressionism, but in spirit it is far from the political activism of that Ger. movement or even from the emotional appeal of his countryman, the Prague-born Franz Werfel (1890–1945). Trakl depicts a world caught up in decay, destruction, and death; and whereas death had been the main theme of much of A. p., Trakl's innovation lies in his radically altered use of lang. The ruptured universe finds its correlate in free rhythms, fractured syntax, and enigmatic metaphors known as *Chiffren,* which establish an absolute relation between the incomparable realms of the referential and the ontological (as explicated among others by Heidegger). In Trakl's works the desperation of guilt and despair is expressed in a highly musical lang. of alliteration and assonance that shows the influence of Rimbaud. In the ever-varying kaleidoscopic configurations of sounds and images, all Trakl texts seem to converge in a single unitary vision.

The period between the demise of the Monarchy in 1918 and the union of Austria with Nazi Germany in 1938 was a troubled time of economic crises and political extremism, leading to World War II. There were many good writers—for whom the name Theodor Kramer (1897–1958) can stand as representative—of this "lost generation" whose lives were stymied by war and in some cases by exile or concentration camps. Despite his problematic ideological stance, Josef Weinheber (1892–1945) is a major poet whose works evince a formal mastery of style and lang., from Gr. ode forms to Viennese dialect verse. His *Adel und Untergang* (1934) thematizes the problem of art and the artist and achieves a classicism reminiscent of his model Hölderlin.

The postwar period has produced a rich body of poetry, and posterity will probably find many of its works of lasting value. The first decade is marked by traditional forms and themes in an effort to re-establish a link with the prefascist past. This traditionalism was nonetheless pluralistic, ranging from the religious mysticism of Christine Lavant (1915–73) to the sociopolitical crit. of Erich Fried (b. 1921), with the experiential humanism of Christine Busta (1915–87) and the critical skepticism of Gerhard Fritsch (1924–69) as intermediate stages. Ingeborg Bachmann (1926–73) transcended national boundaries in two lyric volumes, *Die gestundete Zeit* (1953) and *Anrufung des grossen Bären* (1956), which present spellbinding rhythms and powerful metaphors of the existential themes of time and consciousness. But the most prominent poet is Paul Celan (1920–70), who, like Rilke, is international in residence and in influence. His famous "Todesfuge" stands as a memorial to the victims of Nazi persecution, and Jewish themes recur throughout his ten volumes of poetry. Even more pervasive is the problem of lang. itself, as the poet is dispossessed of belief not only in God and man but also in the efficacy of poetic speaking. The problematic nature of lang. is evident already in *Sprachgitter* (1959), and Celan's poetry in the six volumes thereafter becomes increasingly hermetic and enigmatic, reducing utterance to near silence.

The question of lang. is important enough to serve as a gauge for tracing the devel. of postwar poetry. Reacting against what they perceived to be an outdated traditionalism, writers and artists in the mid 1950s formed the Vienna Group to proclaim a new type of art, termed "experimental." Techniques were adapted from dada and surrealism; particularly characteristic of experimental lit. are montage and collage, permutation and dislocation, and atomizing constellations and chains of discontinuous associations. Since metaphor was felt to be a mask for phony metaphysics, experimental writers stripped lang. of its mimetic intent in an effort to challenge the epistemology behind the structures. The leading poet is H. C. Artmann (b. 1921), whose wide-ranging oeuvre includes grotesque and fantastic lyrics recalling the baroque; he also introduced a sophisticated form of dialect poetry. Associated with the group were Friederike Mayröcker (b. 1924) and Ernst Jandl (b. 1925), who developed various innovative forms. Mayröcker is known for her "poetic phenomenology" that unites dreams, memories, and fantasies in a nonreferential network of associative images; and Jandl has achieved a wide public appeal with his reflectively witty concrete poetry and his visual and speech verse.

The Vienna Group had an important liberating effect on conservative A. society, and it served as a springboard for a broader group of avant-garde writers who in 1960 established a literary center in the provincial capital of Graz. The Graz Group includes, besides the illustrious Peter Handke (b. 1942), a broad spectrum of contemp. authors of varying interests, both linguistic and sociopolitical, united by a common critical stance toward the status quo in art and society. Its literary journal, *manuskripte*, is edited by Alfred Kolleritsch (b. 1931), a strong poet in his own right; his recent volumes contain opaque metaphors that examine the content and conditions of consciousness. Also strong is the Viennese poet Jutta Schutting (b. 1937), who, operating in the Wittgensteinian trad., uses lang. to question itself, as poetry investigates the presuppositions of its own existence. New developments continue to appear from both Vienna and Graz, as well as other regional centers, though in all of these developments it is evident that consciousness of trad. and critique of that trad. continue to be the central issues of postwar A. p.

ANTHOLOGIES: *Lyrik aus Deutschösterreich vom Mittelalter bis zur Gegenwart*, ed. S. Hock (1919); *Österr. Lyrik aus neuen Jhn.*, ed. W. Stratowa (1948); *Zwischenbilanz: Eine Anthol. österr. Gegenwartslit.*, ed. W. Weiss and S. Schmid (1976); *Dichtung aus Österreich*, v. 2, *Lyrik*, ed. E. Thurnher (1976); *Zeit und Ewigkeit. Tausend Jahre österr. Lyrik*, ed. J. Schondorff (1978); *Verlassener Horizont.: Österr. Lyrik aus vier Jahrzehnten*, ed. H. Huppert and R. Links (1980); *Die Wiener Moderne: Lit., Kunst und Musik zwischen 1890 und 1910*, ed. G. Wunberg (1981); *Austria in P. and Hist.*, ed. F. Ungar (1984); *A. P. Today*, ed. M. Holton and H. Kuhner (1985); *Contemp. A. P.*, ed. B. Bjorklund (1986).

HISTORY AND CRITICISM: A. Schmidt, *Dichtung und Dichter Österreichs im 19. und 20. Jh.* (1964); C. Magris, *Der habsburgische Mythos in der österr. Lit.* (1966); *Handbook of A. Lit.*, ed. F. Ungar (1973); *Kindlers Literaturgesch. der Gegenwart: Die zeitgenössische Lit. Österreichs*, ed. H. Spiel (1976); *Das junge Wien: Österr. Lit.- und Kunstkritik 1887–1902*, ed. G. Wunberg (1976); *Gesch. der deutschen Lit. vom 18. Jh. bis zur Gegenwart*, ed. V. Žmegač, 3 v. (1978–84); *Die österr. Lit.: Eine Dokumentation ihrer Literarhist. Entwicklung*, ed. H. Zeman, 4 v. to date (1979–); A. Best and H. Wolfschütz, *Mod. A. Writing* (1980); *Formen der Lyrik in der österr. Gegenwartslit.*, ed. W. Schmidt-Dengler (1981); *Mod. A. Lit.* [journal], l– (1961–).

B.B.

B

BASQUE POETRY. There is a widespread idea that the B. lang. has no lit., but the facts prove otherwise. In the last 25 years, a number of histories have been devoted to the subject; one of them, when completed, will comprise seven volumes.

B. oral lit. is extremely ancient and, moreover, very original. Within it two separate genres may be noted: the *pastorales*, a remnant of what must have been the old drama, and *bertsolarism*, B. troubadour poetry, an improvised form sung before an audience. Written lit., which began considerably later, was essentially religious until the 20th c.; praise of the B. lang. is another main theme. These texts were composed in four dialects spoken in the B. areas of France and Spain.

Linguae vasconum primitiae, the earliest book of B. p., was written in 1545 by the priest B. Detxepare. Consisting of 16 poems on religious and amorous themes, together with praise of the B. lang., it reveals the influence of the Counterreformation. Notable is its realistic diction, esp. in the dialogues between lovers. The dominant metrical form is the medieval *cuaderna via*, although the work was written in the Ren.

Oihenart (1592–1667), the first B. poet from the laity, was the outstanding poet of the 17th c. His *Atsotitzak eta Neurititzak* (Proverbs and Refrains, 1657) includes love poems as well as proverbs and refrains. The 18th c. produced no significant figure in written poetry, although oral poetry continued to be vigorous, esp. in the northern B. provinces.

The legendary poet and *bertsolari* P. Topet, "Etxahun" (1786–1862), flourished in the province of Zuberoa. One of the most original popular poets in B. lit., he wrote poems laden with highly emotional romantic emphases, in addition to violent personal satires. In the Sp. provinces of the B. country, the loss of the second Carlist War (1872–76) and the consequent loss of the old liberties were a cause of distress. This distress, however, served as a stimulus to the literary revival of the earlier 20th c., a revival anticipated in the work of F. Arrese y Beitia (1841–1906).

The earlier 20th c. saw the creation of the Academy of the B. Lang. (1918), the *Lorejaiak* (Floral Games) and poetry competitions, and the *txapelketak* or championship competitions for troubadours. N. Ormaetxea, "Orixe" (1888–1961), J. M. Aguirre, "Lizardi" (1896–1933), and E. Urkiaga, "Lauaxeta" (1905–37) were the leading poets of the time. Orixe wrote lyrical-mystical poems as well as an epic *Euskaldunak* (*The Basques*); Lizardi is considered by some to be the greatest B. lyric poet; Lauaxeta, the most modern of the group, shows in his work the influence of Fr. symbolism.

The B. lit. Ren. was cut short by the Sp. Civil War (1936–39). Lauaxeta was shot by Franco's troops, and other B. writers were imprisoned or forced into exile. For ten years after the war, publication in the B. lang. was prohibited in the Sp. area of the B. country. Among exile publications may be mentioned *Urrundik* (*From Far Away*, 1945) and *Gudarien Eginak* (The Deeds of Basque Soldiers, 1947), both by T. Monzon (1904–81).

S. Mitxelena (1918–65), in *Arantzazu* (You on the Thorn, 1949) and other works, proved to be the best interpreter of the anguish of the post-Civil War years. Other significant poets were N. Etxaniz (1899–1982) and J. I. Goikoetxea, "Gaztelu" (1908–83), who introduced modern elements into B. poetry. X. Diharce, "Iratzeder" (b. 1920) is an outstanding religious poet.

After 1950, in the B. country as elsewhere in the West, a total break from tradition manifested itself. E. T. A., the B. independence movement, appeared, and, in addition, existentialist, Marxist, and Freudian ideas began to make themselves felt. The "rupturist" poets, chief among them J. Mirande (1925–72) and G. Aresti (1933–75), broke conspicuously with the past. Mirande—antidemocratic, anti-Marxist, anti-Semitic, hostile to B. moderate nationalism—advocated violence and paganism. Against God and Church, he caused sensation by treating such themes as agnosticism, pederasty, Lesbianism, and masturbation. Aresti carried on in the southern B. area the revolution that Mirande had initiated in the northern area.

From the 1960s on, a variety of tendencies became apparent in the work of J. A. Arce, "Harzabal" (b. 1939, "spatial poetry"), M. Lasa (b. 1938), J. Azurmendi (b. 1941), and L. M. Muxika (b. 1939). B. Gandiaga (b. 1928) moved from religious to nationalistic themes, and J. M. Lekuona (b. 1927) exhibited surrealistic techniques, while X. Lete (b. 1944) denounced social and political injustice.

After the death of Franco, aesthetic rather than social elements reasserted themselves, particularly in the work of José Irazu, "B. Atxaga" (b. 1951) and J. Sarrionaindia (b. 1958). Three significant women poets—A. Urretavizcaja (b. 1947), A. Lasa (b. 1948), and T. Irastorza (b. 1961)—have addressed themselves to feminist themes.

ANTHOLOGIES: E. Zabala, *Euskal Alfabetatzeko*

Literatura (1979); K. Etxenagusia et al., *Euskal Idazleak Bizkaieraz* (1980); K. Etxenagusia, *Iparraldeko Euskal Idazleak* (1981); S. Onaindia, *Gaurko Olerkarien Euskal Lan Aukeratuak* (1981); J. Amenabar, *Euskal Poesia Kultoaren Bilduma. I: 1880–1963* and *II: 1963–1982* (1983).

HISTORY AND CRITICISM: P. Lafitte, *Le Basque et la littérature d'expression basque en Labourd, Basse-Navarre et Soule* (1941); L. Michelena, *Historia de la literatura vasca* (1960); L. Villasante, *Historia de la literatura vasca* (1961); J. Torrealday, *Euskal Idazleak Gaur. Historia Social de la Lengua y Literatura Vascas* (1977); X. Amuriza, *Bertsolaritza*, 2 v. (1981). G.A.

BELGIAN POETRY.

I. IN DUTCH
II. IN FRENCH

I. IN DUTCH (For Flemish poetry before 1585, see DUTCH POETRY). After the division of the Netherlands (fall of Antwerp to the Spanish, 1585), the southern provinces (now known as Flanders, or Flemish Belgium) lost their economic, cultural, and literary predominance. Nevertheless, although the Ren. poetry of the Netherlands was to reach its high point in the northern provinces, the renewal itself originated in the south. In the circles of the *rederijkers* one finds an interest in humanism, a gradually growing understanding of the spirit of antiquity, and a sensitivity to new moral and aesthetic ideas. Transitional figures are Lucas de Heere (1534–84) and Carel van Mander (1548–1606), in whose work one encounters new poetic forms side by side with conventional *rederijker* verse. De Heere, an admirer of Marot, introduced the sonnet into the poetry of the Netherlands and wrote odes and epigrams. Van Mander wrote sonnets in alexandrines and translated Virgil's *Bucolics* and *Georgics* into iambic verse (1597). But the spirit and form of poetry were decisively rejuvenated by Jan van der Noot (ca. 1540–95/1600), nobleman, humanist, and man of letters. Under the influence of Petrarch and the *Pléiade*, especially Ronsard, he wrote sonnets in the Fr. manner, odes, and an epic; he favored the iambic pentameter and the alexandrine; and he purified the language—all this not in a narrowly formalistic manner but with the inspiration of a true poet (*Het theatre*, 1568; *Het bosken*, 1570[?]; *Cort begrijp der XII boeken olympiados*, 1579).

In the first half of the 17th c., the Ren. found further echoes among the *rederijkers* and even, formally, in religious songbooks. Ren. elements appear in J. D. Heemssen, J. Ysermans, and the most prominent poet of the time, Justus de Harduyn (1582–1636). In his youth he celebrated the beauty and grace of his beloved in a cycle of songs, odes, elegies, and sonnets (*De weerliicke liefden tot Roose-mond*, 1613). Later, as a priest, he wrote sacred love lyrics (*Goddelicke lofsanghen*, 1620) in a more personal, less literary tone which in some songs echoes the religious lyrics of the Middle Ages.

Under the influence of the Counter-Reformation, secular poetry of all sorts was obliged more and more to yield to moral-didactic and popular poetry of religious inspiration. Its most distinguished representative was the Jesuit Adriaan Poirters (1605–74), who practiced, in *Het masker vande wereldt afgetrocken* (The World's Mask Removed, 1645), the successful genre of the spiritual emblem book: in form, an alternation of illustrations, long poems, and prose pieces, interspersed with short rhymes and verse narratives; in content, narrative, didactic, satirical, and polemic; in spirit, religious and moralistic. Elements of baroque elevation are also to be found in his work as in that of Michiel de Swaen (1654–1707), who closes the 17th c. His religious contemplative poetry suited the spiritual climate, but was distinguished from the popular-didactic poetasting of Poirters' disciples by its more individual tone and its exalted literary aims. Vondel, Cats, and the Fr. classics were his models.

The 18th c. was a period of decadence. Poetry was generally devoid of personal accents, and there were no poets capable of achieving real distinction in the kind of art prescribed by the then-dominant Fr. classical poetics (Boileau's *Art poétique*, tr. 1721). The classical ideal of regularity may be noted in the recommendations of such theorists as J. P. van Male and J. B. Bouvaert, the latter of whom also defended blank verse.

New emphases on personal feeling, national pride, and devotion to nature made themselves felt increasingly at the beginning of the 19th c. (P. J. de Borchgrave), and led to the breakthrough of romanticism, which occasioned the rebirth of Flemish lit. Karel Lodewijk Ledeganck (1805–47) and Prudens van Duyse (1804–59) directed poetry away from the classical style; it became free and spontaneous in the popular rhymes of Th. van Rijswijck (1811–49) and found an interpreter of *Weltschmerz* in J. A. de Laet (1815–91). But individuality was lacking in the climate of moderate realism which, from the 1850s on, expressed itself in scenes from the life of ordinary people (J. van Beers), songs and airs dealing with the joys and sorrows of domestic life, political and social verses, cantatas and oratorios, and epic tableaux. Strange but not very convincing are the formal-technical experiments undertaken by the so-called "taalvirtuozen" (lang. virtuosos)—Fr. de Cort and J. van Droogenbroeck—on the model of Platen and Rückert (see GERMAN POETRY). Nevertheless, some of J. M. Dautzenberg's work in this vein belongs among the best poetry brought forth in this period, along with the simple anecdotal poems of Rosalie and Virginie Loveling (*Gedichten*, 1870).

One of the most extraordinary assertions of individuality in the modern lyric is to be found in the poetry of Guido Gezelle (1830–99), a humble and learned priest remarkable for his sensuous empathy and his insights into nature as the manifestation of a divine world-order embracing man as well as the flowers, the stars, and the ants. His religious life may have brought him close to the mystical experience. Gezelle remained for a long time on the periphery of recognized poetry but is now widely acknowledged as a poet of international stature, based on his *Dichtoefeningen* (Poetical Exercises), 1858; *Kleengedichtjes* (Little Poems), 1860; *Gedichten, gezangen en gebeden* (Poems, Songs, and Prayers), 1862; *Tijdkrans* (A Wreath of Time), 1893; and *Rijmsnoer* (A Garland of Rhyme), 1897.

The young titan Albrecht Rodenbach (1856–80) wrote, in traditional meters and with neo-romantic inspiration, militant songs, epic verses, and reflective poetry. The impressionistic formalist Pol de Mont (1857–1931) fought for "art for art's sake," and Prosper van Langendonck (1862–1920) interpreted the anguish of the *poète maudit.* They anticipated the *fin de siècle* poetry of Karel van de Woestijne (1878–1929). Hypersensitive and hyperintellectual, he explored sensuous experience and the relationship between man and woman in his first volumes—*Het vader-huis* (The Paternal House), 1903; *De boom-gaard der vogelen en der vruchten* (The Orchard of Birds and Fruits), 1905; *De gulden schaduw* (The Golden Shadow), 1910. He clothes his emotions in baroque images, symbols, word-garlands, and slow rhythms. In his later, more sober verses—*De modderen man* (The Man of Mud), 1920; *God aan zee* (God at the Sea), 1926; *Het bergmeer* (The Mountain Lake), 1928—human insufficiency is a source of distress, a concern with God and eternity appears, and the poet reaches a state of renunciation and purification. Contemporary with van de Woestijne were the visionary Cyriel Verschaeve (1874–1949), the mannered Karel van den Oever (1879–1926), and the amiably stoic Jan van Nijlen (1884–1965).

In the early years of the 1920s, expressionism broke radically with the aesthetically oriented poetry of impressionism and symbolism as well as with traditional verse construction. Under the influence of Verhaeren, Whitman, Tagore, the Fr. *Unanimistes,* and, above all, the Ger. expressionists, a coming world of goodness and brotherhood was proclaimed in emotional free verse with spasmodic imagery (as in van Ostaijen, W. Moens, A. Mussche), or in moral anecdotes (M. Gijsen). Van Ostaijen (1896–1928), who stood at the beginning of this humanitarian expressionism with his volume *Het sienjaal* (The Signal, 1918), came rapidly under the spell of dada as evidenced by his *Bezette stad,* (Occupied City), 1921, and was also influenced by Apollinaire, Cocteau, and especially August Stramm's experiments with the "concentrated word." In incisive essays (e.g. *Gebruiksaanwyzing der lyriek* [Directions for the Use of the Lyric]) he formulated a theory of pure poetry based on the isolated word and on association. He realized his insights in a few late poems published in his posthumous volume, *Het eerste boek van Schmoll* (The First Book of Schmoll), 1928. V. J. Brunclair and G. Burssens took part in van Ostaijen's poetic adventure, and it had a fertilizing effect on M. Gilliams and P. G. Buckinx. Nevertheless, after the early death of Van Ostaijen the dominant force in B. p. remained traditional for a couple of decades (U. van de Voorde, R. Minne, P. Herreman, B. Decorte, K. Jonckheere).

Immediately after World War II, older conceptions of poetry as a statement of human inadequacy in an altered world were reiterated chiefly by A. van Wilderode, H. van Herreweghen, J. de Haes, Reninca (pseud. Renée Lauwers), and Chr. D'haen. The traditional line was continued, with differing accents and with the integration of new techniques, in the next generation by W. Spillebeen, W. Haesaert, G. Mandelinck, and A. van Assche. Around 1950, however, "experimental poetry" broke with the past in a spectacular manner. Its first exponents, the "Vijftigers" (Fiftiers), were grouped around the journal *Tijd en Mens* (1949–55); led by J. Walravens (*Phenomenologie van de poëzie,* 1951), these poets (H. Claus, A. Bontridder, B. Cami, M. Wauters) tried to translate a Sartrean view of life, a feeling of absurdity, chaos, *Angst,* and rebellion into an idiom related to Fr. surrealism and the lyric work of Van Ostaijen. The new idiom also was practiced by two older poets, E. van Ruysbeek and P. Le Roy, who added esoteric and mystical elements. A second wave of experimentalists, the "Fifty-fivers," published mainly in the journals *De tafelronde* (P. de Vree, A. de Roover, J. van den Hoeven) and *Gard sivik* (G. Gils, H. Pernath, P. Snoek). This movement dismissed ethical-social imperatives and metaphysical concerns in favor of a greater, sometimes exclusive, autonomy of word and image.

The most talented virtuoso of lang. and form was Hugo Claus (b. 1929), who realized and summed up the tendencies of the whole era. He built upon Antonin Artaud, practiced the erudite mannerism of Eliot and Pound, with an abundance of myths, symbols, allusions, and quotations. Claus wrote, and continues to write, pop-style and parlando-style poems as well as *Knittelverse,* satires, novels, plays, and melodramas, asserting his radical individualism in a notably varied manner.

In the Sixties, experimentation with word and sign was markedly advanced by the group around *Labris* (1962–75), by the concrete poetry of M. Insingel and Paul de Vree (1909–82), this latter a prominent author of sound poetry but more particularly of "poesia visiva," a visual poetry consisting of leftist-oriented montages of photographs, letters, and drawings (*Zimprovaties,* 1968; *Poëzien,* 1971; *Poesia visiva,* 1975). Mannerists such as N. van Bruggen and P. Conrad turned away from experimentation, as did also, in the Seventies, an entirely different movement, "neo-realism," represented by R. Jooris and H. de Coninck. Influenced by pop art and *nouveau realisme* in the visual arts, this movement showed once again an interest in undecorated reality. A counter-movement of "neo-experimentalism," placing a stronger emphasis on language and on the exploratory nature of the poem, was represented by but not limited to such foci as the journals *Morgen* (1967–72) and *Impuls* (1969–79). Among its exponents are R. de Neef, D. Christiaens, A. Reniers, L. Nolens, and H. Speliers.

The most recent trend is "neo-romanticism." As one would expect, this movement returns to inwardness, flees reality (via dream, sometimes via drugs), and cherishes tenderness, sorrow, and the unattainable. The short-lived drug addict Jottie T'Hooft (1956–77)—obsessed by a quest for absolute purity and a desire for death—opened the way for other young, if less dramatically tortured, poets like L. Gruwez.

ANTHOLOGIES: *Onze dichters*, ed. Th. Coopman and V. dela Montagne (1880); *Vlaamsche oogst*, ed. Ad. Herckenrath (1904); *De Vlaamsche jongeren van gisteren en heden, 1910–1927*, ed. Aug. van Cauwelaert (1927); *Vlaamsche lyriek 1830–1890*, ed. M. Gilliams (1937); *De Vlaamsche poëzie sinds 1918*, v. 2: *Bloemlezing*, ed. A. Demedts, 2d ed. (1945); *Breviarum der Vlaamse lyriek*, ed. M. Gijsen, 4th ed. (1953); *Vlaamse dichtkunst van deze tijd*, ed. P. de Ryck, 2d ed. (1959); *Le piú belle pagine delle Letterature del Belgio*, ed. A. Mor and J. Weisgerber (1965); *Anthologie de la poésie Neérlandaise: Belgique, 1830–1966*, ed. M. Careme (1967); *Dutch Interior: Postwar Poetry of the Netherlands and Flanders*, ed. J. S. Holmes and W. J. Smith (1984).

HISTORY AND CRITICISM: E. Rombauts, "Humanisme en Ren. in de Zuidelijke Nederlanden" and "De letterkunde der Nederlanden," *Geschiedenis van de letterkunde der Nederlanden*, ed Fr. Baur et al., v. 3, 5 (1945, 1952); A Demedts, *De Vlaamsche poëzie sinds 1918*, v. 1, *Studie*, 2d ed. 1945); M. Rutten, *Nederlandse dichtkunst van Kloos tot Claus* (1957), *Nederlandse dichtkunst Achterberg en Burssens voorbij* (1967); J. Weisgerber and A. Mor, *Storia delle letterature del Belgio* (1958); T. Weevers, *Poetry of the Netherlands in its European Context* (1960); R. F. Lissens, *De Vlaamse letterkunde van 1780 tot heden*, 4th ed. (1967); P. de Vree, *Onder experimenteel vuur* (1968); R. P. Meijer, *Lit. of the Low Countries* (1978); R. van de Perre, *Er is nog olie in de lamp der taal. Een overzicht van de hedendaagse poëzie in Vlaanderen (1945–1981)* (1982). R.F.L.; tr. F.J.W.

II. IN FRENCH. Around 1880, 50 years after B. independence, an original Francophone poetry arose. Until then only conventional voices inspired by pompous romanticism or strident nationalism were heard; this earlier poetry does not deserve further attention.

The tempestuous 1880s saw the rise of numerous reviews: *Le Jeune Belgique* (1881), which championed "art for art's sake" without the restrictions of a school, and *La Wallonie* (1886), the favorite mouthpiece of the symbolists. At the same time appeared the first publications of what we now consider classics, among which the work of Emile Verhaeren (1855–1916) comes first. Poet of Flanders, exorcist of personal torments, brawny visionary of the industrial world, he found a sentimental tone to express love. Using a wide range related to that of the symbolists and expressionists, but esp. affirming the genius of his own lang., Verhaeren is, with Maeterlinck and Elskamp, one of the three undeniably great B. poets of his time, and of these, assuredly the most powerful.

In 1889, with a collection of poetry, *Les Serres chaudes* (Hothouses), and a play, *La Princesse Maleine*, a newcomer, Maurice Maeterlinck (1862–1949) rose immediately to pre-eminence in symbolism. He represented its quintessence. An unprolific poet who wrote only one other collection, *Les Quinze Chansons* (Fifteen Songs), Maeterlinck created a theater which won him the Nobel Prize in 1911 and thereby thrust him onto the international scene. But his dramatic universe is closely linked to his poetry, and both have a crystalline transparency.

Max Elskamp (1862–1931), obscure during his lifetime, gained an audience only after World War II. Removed from theories and literary groups, he published numerous collections which reveal a profoundly original style, simple yet erudite, even archaic like a litany. He conjured up the drama of his own life. Georges Rodenbach (1855–98), associated for a long time with the symbolists, is instead an elegist in the trad. of Musset. He still moves us by his nostalgic evocations in half-tones, silences, twilights, and morbid regrets. Another elegist and symbolist, Charles Van Lerberghe (1861–1907), undertook *La Chanson d'Eve* (Eve's Song), a sequence with overtones of Mallarmé and Valéry, and the most coherent poetic work of this generation. Finally, Albert Mockel (1866–1945), founder of *La Wallonie*, exemplifies decadent symbolism. His affectations often make him unreadable, but many pages of *Clartés* (Gleams) are miraculously free of his musical theories. Some lesser figures today appear affected or *kitschy*, and need not interest us. But Jean de Boschère wrote virulent pages, Franz Hellens romantic rapture, and Paul Desmeth a constantly reworked text. Marie Nizet deserves attention as a fine poet of unrequited love, and Paul Gérardy retains a wonderful freshness.

If the hist. of Fr. poetry in Belgium covers only a century, the number of poets is nonetheless astonishing. Of the generation born around 1900, some of whose poets are still alive, the only obvious characteristic, aside from marks of dada and surrealism, is their refusal to have a poetics in common. The violent flashes of René Verboom, the discreet interrogation of Robert Vivier, the passionate vehemence of Charles Plisnier, the cosmopolitan breadth of Robert Goffin, the ironic density of René Purnoel, the musical limpidity of Maurice Carême, the delicious fantasy of Paul Neuhuys, the surrealist visions of Ernst Moerman, the militant sincerity of Albert Ayguesparse, and the futurist cadences of Georges Linze could fill an anthology, not to mention Pierre Nothomb, Robert Melot du Dy, Hélène du Bois, Robert Guiette, Eric de Haulleville, and Armand Bernier.

Four major figures emerge from this particularly brilliant constellation: Marcel Thiry (1897–1977), great sculptor of words, whose merit lies in having integrated the technology of modern life with a scholarly, even precious, vocabulary; Norge (b. 1898), also an artisan of lang., but more direct, more fleshy, uniting gravity with irony, managing adeptly both short verse and long; Henri Michaux (1899–1984), a poet with an international audience, a global explorer who charted the human abyss in *Belge en rupture* (Belgian Breaking Apart) and a linguistic man-without-a-country; and finally, Odilon-Jean Périer (1901–28), who in his short career left a perfect work with a fascinating purity.

Dada influenced several poets, but only one figure stands out clearly, Clément Pansaers (1885–1922). His writing signals the appearance of a *Belgique sauvage* (Savage Belgium) from which emerged a large part of surrealism, the entire Phantomas movement, and other avant-garde groups. As for surrealism, it was the painter Magritte who remarked, as a witticism, "There are no B. surrealists except for Delvaux and myself." In hindsight, the B. surrealists finally occupy the place they deserve, having as much dissention but more autonomy than their Fr. counterparts. They had their own humor, ferociously vitriolic, and an exemplary lucidity which came more from experience than automatic writing. The appearance of poetic collections did not constitute the essential element of their immense activity. It is impossible to name all the periodicals, brochures, tracts, or manifestoes coming from the surrealist group in Brussels connected with the review *Correspondance* (founded 1924), which included Louis Scutenaire, Paul Colinet, and Marcel Mariën, and the surrealist group of Hainaut, born of the review *Rupture* (1934), founded by the fine poet Achille Chavée.

Having left surrealism, Christian Dotremont founded in 1948 the movement Cobra (working on painting, writing, objects, the environment) and began in 1962 to experiment with logograms. At first kept underground, his approach later had an enormous influence on the "After-May '68" poets.

If there is a quality specific to Franco-B. lit., it is a corrosive humor raised to its highest point by the surrealists. It is also the attribute of *Phantomas*, a literary and pictorial review emphasizing the ludic and enlivened by the "Sept types en or" (Seven Golden Guys): Paul Bourgoignie, François Jacqmin, Joseph Noiret, Pierre Puttemans, Theodore Koenig, and Marcel and Gabriel Piqueray. *Phantomas* is perhaps the best illustration of this *Belgique sauvage*, which contrasts a little too easily with the official Belgium. It would be overly simplistic to divide B. writers into two categories: those who care about modernity and those who do not. A split nonetheless exists, which has widened since World War II and the return to traditional forms.

It is unclear if one can speak of a neoclassicism, incl. perhaps a Norge or a Thiry; in fixed forms, both poets were innovative. One may wonder if this is the case with certain conformists who present themselves as avant-garde. Trad. does not mean sclerosis, not when it is transcended by a formal rigor (Charles Bertin), an innovative metrics (Gérard Prévot), a sumptuous imagery (Ernest Delève), a blinding virtuosity (Lucienne Desnoues), a permanent metaphysical interrogation (Jean Tordeur), a jubilant registering (Jean Mogin), or a torn humanism (Roger Bodart).

The generation of 1900 is characterized by diversity. The next offers an even less coherent, indeed chaotic, range. Their work extends from the most traditional forms to forms constantly called into question, and it is difficult to situate these poets who lack a common ground. One could stress the soaring flight of feminine poetry (Andrée Sodenkamp, Jeanine Moulin, Anne-Marie Kegels); highlight a cautious approach to world harmony (Philippe Jones, Fernand Verhesen); welcome poets with an extensive register (Georges Thinès, David Scheinert), the new baroques (Gaston Compère, Hubert Juin) or fine lyric poets (Philippe Kammans, Roger Goossens); or even unite in one category unrelated writers who are concerned with serious inquiry: into forms of lang. (André Miguel), the integration of modern myths (Pierre Della Faille), or the psychoanalytical and the sacred (Henri Bauchau).

It was in the 1960s that the literary movements of the first quarter of the century fell away. Writing broke up, chose blank spaces, and rejected the facile phrase, traditional literary genres, and the aesthetics of discourse. To this general questioning appropriate to the period was added a specific malaise, the outbreak of "la Belgique de Papa" (Papa's Belgium). There resulted a stronger feeling of belonging to the Francophone world, incl. (but not limited to) France, and a greater consciousness of an identity baptized as "Belgitude."

There was an abundance of initiatives and activities. The works begun or pursued in this context remain, however, unrelated. B. poets seem to blossom in individualism. On the one hand, we see an increase in the refusal of eloquence: the concise verse of André Schmitz becomes even more concentrated in Christian Hubin, turns elliptical in Jacques Izoard, stammers with Jacques Sojcher, is sketchy with Claude Bauwens, lapidary with Marc Quaghebeur. On the other hand, Jacques Crickillon and Eugène Savitzkaya espouse fullness, while Werner Lambersy moves from minimalist poetry to vast biblical verse. Guy Goffette transcends successfully the simplicity of the everyday. Alone in his mastery of rhyme, William Cliff wrings the neck of the alexandrine, while Jean-Pierre Verheggen joyfully parodies literary stereotypes. Attentive to exactness and concision, Lilian Wouters also expresses personal truth without concessions, going as far as cruelty in the poems of *L'aloès* (Aloe, 1983). Philosophy and psychoanalysis profoundly influenced these poets. Manifest in most of them, notably Gaspard Hons, Frans De Haes, and Marc Rombaut, both disciplines are evident throughout the work of Claire Lejeune and Françoise Delcarte.

We have always known that art renews itself in cycles. Without naming the poets who have just begun in the 1980s, we can see the start of a new lyricism. One century after the rise of "La Jeune Belgique," its continuity seems assured.

ANTHOLOGIES: *Poètes française de Belgique de Verhaeren au surréalisme,* ed. R. Guiette (1948); *Lyra Belgica,* tr. C. and F. Stillman, 2 v. (1950–51); *Anthologie du surréalisme en Belgique,* ed. C. Bussy (1972); *Panorama de la poésie française de Belgique,* ed. L. Wouters and J. Antoine (1976); *La poésie francophone de Belgique,* ed. L. Wouters and A. Bosquet, 4 v. (1985–).

GENERAL WORKS: G. Charlier and J. Hanse, *Histoire illustrée des lettres françaises de Belgique* (1958); R. Frickx and R. Burniaux, *La Littérature belge d'expression française* (1980); *Alphabet des lettres belges de langue française* (1982); R. Frickx and R. Trousson, *Lettres françaises de Belgique: Dictionnaire des oeuvres,* v. 2: *La Poésie* (1988); A.-M. Beckers, *Lire les écrivains belges,* 3 v. (1985–); *Bibliographie des écrivains de Belgique* (forthcoming).

L.W.; tr. A.G.W.

BENGALI POETRY. See INDIAN POETRY.

BHAKTI POETRY. See INDIAN POETRY.

BLACK POETRY. See AFRO-AMERICAN POETRY; AFRICAN POETRY.

BRAZILIAN POETRY. B. lit., like the Portuguese lit. from which it springs and derives its main trends, at least up to the 19th c., is characterized to an unusual degree by poetic activity. The first manifestations of poetry in Brazil appear in the middle of the 16th c. with the arrival of the Jesuits, esp. José de Anchieta, (1534–97). In 1601, the publication of *Prosopopéia,* a poem of only 94 stanzas with epic intentions, inspired by Camões' *Os Lusiadas* (The Lusiads, 1572), heralds the appearance of the first B. poet, Bento Teixeira (1561–1600). In spite of its mediocrity, the poem announces the onset of the baroque school of B. p. from which arises the strong poetic personality of Gregório de Matos (1633–96). Depicting in verse the defects of colonial society, he reflects not only preoccupation with the landscape, as in his lyrics, but also concern with the human scene in his satiric poems.

During the mid 18th-c. gold rush in Minas Gerais, those who were to form the *mineira* school were born. Educated in Portugal, with some becoming members of the literary "academies" proliferating at the time, these youths wrote poetry in the academic-Arcadian fashion and, once back at home, conspired in the ill-timed, ill-fated *Inconfidência Mineira,* the earliest attempt at revolt against Portugal. Their artistic leader, Tomás Antônio Gonzaga (1744–1810), is regarded as one of Brazil's greatest lyric poets and is the author of the most popular collection of love poems in the lang., *Marilia de Dirceu* (1792). Three other names complete the quartet of the great *mineiro* lyric poets: Cláudio Manuel da Costa (1729–89), Alvarenga Peixoto (1744–93), and Silva Alvarenga (1749–1814).

Still other *mineiros* wrote epics in Brazil. The more original and sensitive epic, a major precursor of romantic Indianism, is *O Uraguai* (1764) by Basílio da Gama (1741–95). It recounts the war waged by Portugal, with Spain's aid, against the Indians of the Mission towns who rebelled at transfer from Jesuit to Portuguese rule. More truly B. in subject, but less original and less imbued with poetic genius, is *Camaruru* (1781) by Santa Rita Durão (1722–84). It is the story of Diogo Álvares, the shipwrecked sailor who discovered Bahia and became chieftain among the Indians there under the name of Caramuru (Moray). In these poems, nature varies from the bucolic, pantheistic nature of Arcady to the majestic, indigenous nature as seen through baroque, gongoristic eyes: nature stylized, not as it really is.

The *mineiros,* influenced by theories absorbed from Rousseau and other Encyclopedists, have been called preromantics. But it is only later, with political independence, that romanticism first asserts itself, firmly based, after its early steps, upon the idealized aborigine. The movement, however blurred the lines, falls into three phases:

1. The first phase, which still reflects much of the preceding Ren. and Arcadian periods, begins with *Suspiros Poéticos e Saudades* (Poetic Signs and Yearnings) by Gonçalves de Magalhães (1811–82). The best poetic talent of this first phase was Gonçalves Dias (1823–64), however. He dominates all romantic poetry through his sense of sobriety and harmony. All is balanced: love and religion, feeling for nature, patriotism, sympathy for the Indian. He, better than most, infused life into the Indian theme. One of his most famous poems is "Canção do Exílio" (Song of Exile), a delicate, poignant expression of *saudade* (yearning) for Brazil. Casimiro de Abreu (1839–60), the author of characteristically ingenuous poems, is the other good poet of the period. He died in his early twenties, shortly after the publication of *Primaveras* (Springs).

2. The second, romantic phase begins with the publication of *Obras Poéticas* (1853) by Álvares de Azevedo (1831–52) and is characterized by individualism, subjectivism, and pessimism. Least B. of all, these poets cultivated the worst habits and practices of the European decadents, and most died young. Along with de Azevedo should be mentioned Junqueira Freire (1832–55). We may add to this group of Byronic, ultra-romantic poets

the name of Fagundes Varela (1841–75), whose poetry wavers between patriotism and elegiac themes with epic overtones.

3. The *Condoreira* (from the condor, symbolic of grandeur of flight) school of social poetry (1870–ca. 1880) was linked with abolitionism and the Paraguayan War (1865–70). Now the movement bound itself more closely to B. reality while yet remaining romantic and lyrical. The great "condor" poet, Castro Alves (1847–71), developed a social conscience, turning away from native Indianism to nativist antislavery themes, so felicitously expressing contemporary sentiment that he became one of the most popular poets in Brazil. His verses exude the physical and spiritual anguish of the Negro slave, as do they also the desire of the most progressive elements in Brazil for the abolition of the Empire. His *Os Escravos* (The Slaves, 1883) contains the two poems in which he reaches supreme heights of inspiration: *Vozes de África* (Voices of Africa) and *Navio Negreiro* (Slave Ship). Chronologically, but not thematically, there is another poet of great epic inspiration whose work may be placed within this period. He is Sousândrade (1833–1902), perhaps the best of the romantics, author of *Guesa* (1888), his masterpiece.

Sated with such grandiloquent flights of lang. and with the wild subjectivism of the ultra-romantics, poets welcomed Parnassianism as a kind of panacea. Although essentially identical with the Fr. original, the movement shows some tropical modification in Brazil. Alberto de Oliveira (1857–1937), most rigidly Parnassian of the major trio, even so reflects better than the other two the lure of B. nature. Raimundo Correia (1859–1911) is more subtle, musical, pessimistic, of graver and more intense emotion. Olavo Bilac (1865–1918) shows a more facile sensibility, an evident virtuosity, and a fluent, brilliant grace of lang. Parnassianism having entered the country, symbolism inevitably followed and found many disciples, among whom Cruz e Sousa (1863–98) was the major poet reacting to the narrow materialism of the naturalists and the chill polish of the Parnassians. Even though short-lived as an organized literary movement, symbolism persists throughout the first decades of the 20th c. as a seminal influence. The mystic poet par excellence of B. symbolism is Alphonsus de Guimaraens (1870–1921), who found inspiration in the themes of his Catholic faith.

The turn of the century saw a complex of influences in B. lit.: skepticism, the sarcasm of an Oscar Wilde, the defeatist satire of an Eça de Queirós, the "barbaric" meters of a Carducci or a d'Annunzio, the ironic agnosticism of an Anatole France. Poetry was no coherent genre, had no common aim. The best poet from this period is Augusto dos Anjos (1884–1914), a poet from the Baudelairian school whose book of poems, *Eu*, has undergone innumerable editions since its publication in 1912. Constructive action came only in 1922, when a group of young poets in São Paulo organized a *Semana de Arte Moderna* (Modern Art Week) consisting of a series of concerts, lectures, and exposition of the plastic arts, the whole inaugurated with an address by the celebrated novelist Graça Aranha, who lent his support to the new movement. So began B. modernism, not to be confused with other "modernisms."

These poets, at first destructive (first phase, 1922–30) in order to be constructive later, broke with the past, stripped away Parnassian eloquence and symbolist mistiness, cast off logic together with the syntax and vocabulary of Portugal, ignored meter and rhyme in favor of absolutely free verse, extended the scope of poetry to include the most prosaic details of life, and took on a markedly national tone, reinterpreting their country's past and present by stressing the Negro elements in its formation. Among the pioneers of modernism, the principal name is Mário de Andrade (1893–1945), who in 1922 published his *Paulicéia Desvairada* (Hallucinated City), a volume of modern poems that became the bible of B. modernism, as its author came to be called the "Pope of the new creed," a role thrust upon him. Not only a poet, he was a master of modernism in music and the visual art, as well as in aesthetics and crit. Some of the first generation, like Menotti del Picchia (1892–1988) and Guilherme de Almeida (1890–1969), were converts from earlier movements; some, like Ronald de Carvalho (1893–1936), Sérgio Buarque de Hollanda (1902–82), and, greatest of these, Manuel Bandeira (1886–1968), became literary historians and critics also. Bandeira, called "the Saint John the Baptist of the new poetry" for elements in his work prior to 1922, is an independent spirit even though he shared in the establishment of modernism. He warns that the poet must first look to genuine inspiration, and only then to technique. His lang. is simple, but his concepts are not. Besides his verse, his importance lies in his rare ability to interpret B. p. to the public. The world of his poetry is the commonplace daily world, apparently unpoetic yet transmuted by his genius to lyricism.

The first generation São Paulo poets were the most radical, their liveliest leader Oswald de Andrade (1890–1954; no relation to Mário). The cult of nationalism and regionalism permeated the group, united for a time in the magazine *Klaxon* (synonym of "horn"). The ebullient Oswald de Andrade advocated what he termed "primitivism." A restless soul, he later formed the group that published the magazine *Antropofagia* (Cannibalism), a name inspired by Montaigne's famous essay. Opposing such Fr. influence, and indeed all alien "isms," Menotti del Picchia, along with Cassiano Ricardo (1895–1974), who reached the fullness of his powers only much later, Plínio Salgado (1901–75), and others, founded the *verde-amarelo* (green-yellow) group; nationalistic on an Amerindian basis, their magazine was *Anta* (Tapir), an animal which they said symbolized the barbaric original power of the land.

Modernist groups in Rio were less eager to shock the bourgeoisie and tended to be more conservative in general. A representative example would be the group of symbolist inspiration that published *Festa* (Party), to which many modernists contributed. The highest feminine poetic genius of Brazil, Cecília Meireles (1901–64), was a member. Their manifesto included four points: *velocidade* (velocity of expression, not physical speed), *totalidade* (total view of reality in all its aspects), *brasilidade* (B. nationality and reality), and *universalidade* (universality).

The next generation of modernists is nationwide in distribution, but in general their works possess similar characteristics, both philosophical and religious—or, more accurately, sociopolitical and religiomystical. Carlos Drummond de Andrade (1901–87) represents the sociopolitical trend. A master of irony, his *Brejo das Almas* (Fens of Souls, 1934) was one of the most important books of the decade. Lately this great poet has lost some of his earlier illusions about politics (e.g. belief in socialism or communism as the ideal society) but none of his reverence for poetry. Murilo Mendes (1901–75), Augusto Frederico Schmidt (1906–65), and Cecília Meireles are the finest examples of the religiomystical current. Mendes has written surrealistic poetry, metaphysical in tone; Schmidt has combined biblical inspiration and Whitmanesque rhythms; Meireles has turned to nature and Brazil's heroic past, as well as to medieval Europe, for her material. Vinicius de Morais (1913–80) and Jorge de Lima (1895–1953) must be mentioned. Despite his youth, relative to the first generation, Morais's poetic evolution has brought him closer to those older poets, although his first two books show a sustained gravity of tone in their universal themes, religion and death. Jorge de Lima, who wished to "restore poetry in Christ" and wrote the mystical *A Túnica Inconsútil* (The Seamless Robe, 1938), compellingly presents the Negro theme in *Poemas Negros* (1946). His work is profoundly Christian and wholly B., grave in tone, deliberate in rhythm, and expressed in long lines. His later works, e.g. *Livro de Sonetos* (Book of Sonnets, 1949) and *Invenção de Orfeu* (Invention of Orpheus, 1952), remain constant in feeling if they lack the proselyting force of his earlier poems. Contemporary with the oldest generation, Jorge de Lima showed himself highly versatile as he underwent successive spiritual experiences, ending with a phase of symbolic verse of personal anguish.

The poets who have appeared since 1942 can be categorized only arbitrarily. Some call themselves the "Generation of 1945," although all came on the scene either before or after that year. Amoroso Lima (pseud. Tristão de Ataíde) calls this period *Neomodernismo*, saying that modernism died in 1945. Lêdo Ivo (b. 1924), Domingos Carvalho da Silva (b. 1915), Péricles Eugênio da Silva Ramos (b. 1919), João Cabral de Melo Neto (b. 1920), and Geir Campos (b. 1924) are the principal names among these poets. Meanwhile, the older poets still living continue their creative work, although most have evolved beyond their early phases. Generally there is now a sense of discipline in the construction and polishing of the poem.

In the early Fifties, Concretism appears on the B. poetic scene, a movement based on the idea that "a poem is a graphic object." Augusto de Campos, Haroldo de Campos, and Décio Pignatari are not only the leaders of the B. concrete movement but also its best poets. With the appearance of concrete poetry a "neo-avant-garde" begins, its main trends being: (1) *poesia-experiência* (poetry as experience), whose main advocate was Mário Faustino (1930–62); (2) *instauração-praxis* (instauration-praxis), proposed by Mário Chamie (b. 1933) in 1962; and (3) *poema-processo* (poem-process), brought forth by Wlademir Dias-Pino (b. 1927). These are the most important poets, but there are others, such as Pedro Xisto, José Lino Grünewald, and Edgard Braga in the field of Concretism, and Armando Freitas Filho, O. C. Louzada Filho, and Antônio Carlos Cabral, who were interested in praxis experimentation. In the early Sixties, a group of young poets of São Paulo, incl. Álvaro Alves de Faria, Carlos Felipe Moisés, Cláudio Willer, Eduardo Alves da Costa, and Roberto Piva, published *Antologia dos Novíssimos* (Anthology of the Newest, 1962), where is notorious the influence of Fernando Pessoa, Carlos Drummond de Andrade, Murilo Mendes, and Jorge de Lima. Lindolf Bell, an inspired poet of the state of Santa Catarina, was also linked with the group. In the same year appeared in Rio de Janeiro *Violão de Rua* (Guitar of the Street) gathering poets of socialist temper, such as Ferreira Gullar, Moacir Félix, Geir Campos, José Paulo Paes, Félix de Ataíde, and Afonso Romano de Sant'Anna. During the 1970s and early '80s, the neo-avant-garde movement reduced in force considerably; a new trend began to make itself felt, political poetry, whose principal voice is Ferreira-Gullar (b. 1930), a "concrete" poet turned political. A similar evolution is evident in the poetry of Afonso Romano de Sant'Anna. José Paulo Paes has had a phase of concrete experimentation which did not, however, interrupt his deep and remarkable inclination for irony and the epigram.

Other poets who have been creating their poems independently of the tensions produced by the avant-garde and the political situation, or who can be considered latecomers, can be mentioned: Joaquim Cardozo, a poet of symbolist accent with modernist and formalist inflection; Dante Milano, a poet of classic modulation; Sosígenes Costa, author of sonnets of plastic reverberations; Carlos Nejar, a lyric poet with epic accent; Mário Quintana, an older poet in the symbolist trad.; Henriqueta Lisboa and Alphonsus de Guimarãens Filho, both also of symbolist accent; Paulo Bonfim, an heir of Guilherme de Almeida and a modernist poet of the lyrical trad. and the "Generation of '45"; Gerardo de Melo Mourão, Tiago de Melo, Geraldo Pinto Rodrigues, Alberto da Costa e Silva, and João Paulo Moreira da Fonseca, followers of the "Generation of '45" but not always obeying its rules with strictness; Armindo Trevisan and Adélia Prado, who have cultivated a lyricism of mystic inflection; and Walmir Ayala, Gilberto Mendonça Teles, Hilda Hilst, Olga Savary, Renata Pallotini, and Marly de Oliveira, whose work revives the line and the poem after years of the iconoclasm of the avant-garde. See also GAUCHO POETRY; PORTUGUESE POETRY; SPANISH AMERICAN POETRY.

ANTHOLOGIES: F. A. de Varnhagen, *Florilégio da Poesia Brasileira*, 3 v. (1850–63)—v. 1 is a historical sketch of B. letters and a pioneer work of great probity; *Antol. dos Poetas Bras. da Fase Romântica*, 2d ed. (1940), *Antol. dos Poetas Bras. da Fase Parnasiana*, 2d ed. (1940), *Apresentação da Poesia Bras.*, 2d ed. (1954), all ed. M. Bandeira—excellent intros., with crit. essay, to B. p.; *Panorama do Movimento Simbolista Bras.*, ed. A. Muricy, 3 v. (1951–52)—anthol. of B. symbolist verse with bio. and bibl. notes; *Panorama da Poesia Bras.*, ed. M. da Silva Brito, 6 v. (1959); *Mod. B. P.*, ed. and tr. J. Nist (1962)—brief but informed intro.; *Poesia do Ouro* (1964), *Poesia Romântica* (1965), *Poesia Simbolista* (1965), *Poesia Barroca*, (1967), *Poesia Moderna* (1967), *Poesia Parnasiana* (1967), all ed. P. E. da Silva Ramos; *Anthol. of 20th-C. B. P.*, ed. E. Bishop (1972); *B. P., 1950–1980*, ed. E. Brasil and W. J. Smith (1983).

HISTORY AND CRITICISM: S. Romero, *História da Lit. Bras.*, 5th enl. ed., 5 v. (1888; 1953–54)—sociological attitude causes bias, but still fundamental, though should be reevaluated in light of subsequent crit.; I. Goldberg, *Studies in B. Lit.* (1922)—a pioneer work in Eng.; A. A. Lima, *Estudos*, 6 v. (1927–33)—crit. essays on many subjects, incl. poetry, *Contribuição à Hist. do Modernismo, I: O. Pré-Modernismo* (1939), *Poesia Bras. Contemporânea* (1942); A. Grieco, *Evolução da Poesia Bras.* (1932); R. de Carvalho, *Pequena Hist. da Lit. Bras.*, 7th ed. (1944)—valuable for crit. opinions, his attitude a synthesis of Romero and Veríssimo; S. Putnam, *Marvelous Journey* (1948)—comprehensive, very readable intro. in Eng.; José Veríssimo, *Hist. da Lit. Bras.*, 3d ed. (1954)—coldly objective on art as such, with scant attention to artist or society, but still basic; M. Bandeira, *Brief Hist. of B. Lit.* tr. R. E. Dimmick (1958)—valuable despite its brevity for the insight of an active participant in B. p.; A. Bosi, *História Concisa da Lit. Bras.* (1970)—useful handbook with sharp analysis of B. poets from a sociological point of view; M. Moisés, *História da Lit. Bras.*, 3 v. (1982–85); *A Lit. no Brasil*, ed. A. Coutinho, 3d ed., 6 v. (1986)—the most ambitious attempt yet at a collaborative lit. hist. of Brazil on aesthetic principles.

L.L.B.; M.MO.

BRETON POETRY. The lang. of Lower Brittany in France (*Breizh Izel*) belongs, like Welsh and Cornish, to the Brythonic or "P"-Celtic Group, and is derived from the speech of settlers from southwest Britain who left their homeland from the 5th to the 7th c. when the Saxons were encroaching from the east. There is evidence, from Marie de France and others, that med. B. poets sang of heroes and romance, and that these lost compositions were the source of Marie's own form, the *lai*; but the earliest B. p. to survive dates from the 14th c. and consists of only a few scraps of verse. Fewer than 20 lines are all that remain of a body of popular verse in an indigenous metrical system related to that of early Welsh. The main feature is the occurrence in each line of a form of internal rhyme very similar to the *cynghanedd lusg*: "An heguen am louenas / An hegar*at* an lac*at* glas" (Her smile gladdened me, / The blue-eyed love). The native prosody survived to the 17th c., when it was superseded by the Fr. system of syllable-counting and end rhyme.

After the Treaty of Union between Brittany and France (1532), dialectal fragmentation set in, and four main dialects emerged: those of Léon, Tréguier, Cornouailles, and Vannes. Following the lead of the grammarian Le Gonidec (1775–1838), however, B. writers have endeavored to establish a cultivated literary norm, so that most works published nowadays are accessible to all contemporary readers.

Most of the verse from the 15th to the beginning of the 19th c. consists of works of religious edification, hymns, carols, a Book of Hours, and the long and dreary *Mirouer de la mort* (1519). One poem stands out: *Buhez Mabden*, a powerful meditation on death printed in 1530 but probably written a century earlier. The prophetic *Dialog etre Arzur Roe d'an Bretoned ha Gwynglaff* dates back to 1450. There are also numerous plays in verse. A few popular plays, such as the *Pevar Mab Emon* are based on chivalric romances, but most derive from the Bible and saints' lives. The influence of Fr. models is evident, with a few notable exceptions, mainly mystery plays which recount the lives of Celtic saints.

New stirrings begin with the two mock-epic poems of Al Lae (close of the 18th c.), but the real impetus comes with the rise of 19th-c. romanticism. The great event is the appearance in 1839 of La Villemarqué's *Barzaz Breiz* (Poetry of Brittany), whose contents have been shown by recent scholarship to be more ancient and more authentic than was hitherto believed. The effect was profound. A romantic vision of the B. past was created which stirred the imagination of many and led to new literary enthusiasm. Luzel was impelled to collect B. folk p., of which there were two main kinds: the *gwerziou*, usually dramatic in form, simple and direct in style, and concerned with local events and folklore; and the *soniou*, more lyrical verse, including love songs and satires.

Prosper Proux recounted his escapades with

rough humor in his native Cornouailles dialect in 1839, though by 1866 he had acquired a more "literary" (and less vigorous) expression. The Vannetais dialect was used mostly by priests who found inspiration in their faith and in their love for their native land. Esp. popular were Msgr. Joubiouz' *Doue ha mem bro* (1844) and Joakim Gwilhom's imitation of Virgil's *Georgics, Livr el labourer* (1849). From the 1850s to the 80s, only minor talents emerged. Living uprooted from the B. countryside, these poets expressed in artificial diction their love of the simple life, of the homeland, and of their inheritance which was no longer secure. This nostalgic trad. was maintained and reinvigorated in the '90s by the rich lyricism of Taldir and the more artistic Erwan Berthou, but the outstanding poet of their generation was Yann Ber Kalloc'h, killed in action in 1917. His poems, written in Vannetais and published posthumously, express strong religious and patriotic convictions enhanced by a rich and powerful imagery.

The 20th c. has seen the vigorous growth of B. literary periodicals, each with its coterie. Vannetais writers found expression in *Dihunamb*, edited by the poet-peasant Loeiz Herrieu. The *Gwalarn* group, under the leadership of Roparz Hémon, proved by far the most talented and creative. Maodez Glanndour and Roparz Hémon stand out from the group, although nearly all were gifted poets. *Gwalarn* did not survive the "Libération," but patriotic young writers launched new publications. Most did not last. The single exception was *Al Liamm*: under the guidance of Ronan Huon, it became the leading B. literary journal. In their poetry, Huon and his contemporaries Youenn Olier, Per Denez, and Per Diolier, later joined by Youenn Gwernig and Reun ar C'halan, have respected the literary standards set by *Gwalarn*. Women have also played a significant role in the survival of B. p., esp. Anjela Duval, Vefa de Bellaing, Benead, Naïg Rozmor, Tereza, and, more recently, Maï Jamin and Annaïg Renault. The journal *Brud* (now *Brud Nevez*), founded in 1957, counted one of the best contemporary poets, Per Jakez Hélias, among its first contributors. The 1960s witnessed a strong resurgence of B. nationalism. The *Union Démocratique Bretonne*, created in 1964, attracted several young militant poets: Paol Keineg, Yann Ber Piriou, Erwan Evenou, and Sten Kidna. Other poets have since come to the fore: Abanna, Alan Botrel, Yann-Baol an Noalleg, Koulizh Kedez, Padrig an Habask, Gwendal and Herle Denez, Tudual Huon, Bernez Tangi, to name but a few. Since 1974, the journal *Skrid* has welcomed new writers.

Finally, songs have always been an important part of the B. poetic heritage. This trad. has been maintained by a number of popular singers: Glenmor, Youenn Gwernig, Jili Servat, Jef Philippe, Louis Bodénès, and the internationally famous Alan Stivell. B. may be a threatened lang., but B. p. remains very much alive.

ANTHOLOGIES: *Barzaz Breiz*, ed. H. de la Villemarqué (1839); *Gwerziou Breiz Izel*, ed. F. M. Luzel, 2 v. (1868–74); *Soniou Breiz Izel*, ed. F. M. Luzel and A. le Braz, 2 v. (1890); *Barzhaz: kant barzhoneg berr, 1350–1953*, ed. P. Denez (1953); *Défense de cracher par terre et de parler breton*, ed. Y. B. Piriou (1971); *Le Livre d'Or de la Bretagne*, ed. P. Durand (1975); *Du a Gwyn*, ed. D. M. Jones and M. Madeg (1982); *Barzhonegoù*, ed. *Skrid* (1986).

SURVEYS: F. Gourvil, *Langue et Littérature bretonnes* (1952); *Istor Lennegezh Vrezhonek an Amzer-Vremañ*, ed. Abeozen [i.e. Y. F. M. Eliès] (1957); Y. Olier, *Istor hol lennegezh "Skol Walarn,"* 2 v. (1974–75); Y. Bouëssel du Bourg and Y. Brekilien, "La littérature bretonne," *La Bretagne*, ed. Y. Brekilien (1982); J. Gohier and R. Huon, *Dictionnaire des écrivains d'aujourd'hui en Bretagne* (1984).

PROSODY: E. Ernault, *L'Ancien Vers Breton* (1912); F. Kervella, *Diazezoù ar sevel gwerziou* (1965). D.M.L.; R.G.

BULGARIAN POETRY. Though B. culture is very ancient, modern B. lit.—incl. B. p.—came into its own only in the decades immediately preceding the country's political liberation in the Russo-Turkish War of 1877–78. Poetry, and esp. lyric poetry, has, however, claimed a prominent place in B. lit. in the 20th c.

Pre-liberation poets like Petko Slavejkov (1827–95) were not very prolific; moreover, they limited themselves largely to nationalistic themes. The one great poet of that epoch, Xristo Botev (1848–76), killed in the April Uprising of 1876 against the Turks, left a small group of superb lyrics in which he voiced his homeland's aspirations for freedom and other socially radical ideas.

Botev did not live to see an independent Bulgaria, but his contemporary Ivan Vazov (1850–1921) did. Vazov, who eventually achieved the status of the B. national writer, celebrated in his lyric poetry the beauties of his native land and the virtues of his people, and, in such works as the narrative poems comprising *The Epic of the Forgotten* (early 1880s), immortalized the heroes of the B. liberation. Poetry was a major component of Vazov's body of work.

By the turn of the century, the national pride expressed in Vazov's writing over the previous two decades was yielding to internationalism, forms of symbolism and modernism, and variants on individualism. Petko's son Penčo Slavejkov (1866–1912) reverted to the liberation as the subject of his ambitious but unfinished narrative *Song of Blood.* Designed as an epic of European rather than merely B. scope, the work did not measure up to its author's hopes.

Slavejkov was not a born poet, but others of his generation were, esp. Pejo Javorov (1877–1914), one of Bulgaria's finest lyric poets but a victim of metaphysical despair whose career ended in suicide, and Dimčo Debeljanov (1887–1916), the most prominent B. writer killed in World War I. Toward the end of his short life, Debeljanov's verse reflected the influence of symbolism, which took root in B. lit. quite late.

After World War I, the paths of those who had crowded the symbolist highroad before the war diverged. One group of poets brought B. symbolism to its zenith during the 1920s, when the movement had faded elsewhere. A poet's poet among this group was Nikolaj Liliev (1885–1960), who achieved great formal perfection in but a small number of poems on a narrow range of subjects. But the chief theoretician and practitioner of B. symbolism (though he had begun to publish well before 1914) was Teodor Trajanov (1882–1945). He led the battle in favor of symbolist doctrine during the 1920s through the journal *Hyperion*, which he edited; he published his best-known collection of symbolist poetry in 1929.

The other group of symbolists and modernists at war's end deserted their previous allegiances to embrace Marxism and social radicalism. This group included Ljudmil Stojanov (1888–1973), who after 1944 became a major literary power in communist Bulgaria. But most radical writers of the 1920s did not survive nearly so long as Stojanov: poets like Xristo Jasenov (1889–1925) and Geo Milev (1895–1925) perished in the wave of political repressions which swept over the country in 1923–25. Indeed, Milev was arrested for publishing a narrative poem, *September*, celebrating the anti-government uprisings of 1923 which engendered the repressions. Milev's earlier modernism left a considerable imprint on his radical poetry, which was also influenced by that of Vladimir Majakovskij. Other lyric poets of radical persuasion included Xristo Smirnenski (1898–1923), author of verse both gentle and satirical, who died very early of tuberculosis; and Nikola Vapcarov (1909–42), whose work called his countrymen to the bright future of communism and who was executed by the government for resistance activities during World War II.

Over the complicated but very interesting period between the two World Wars, a number of fine poets who were neither symbolists nor communists gathered around the leading literary journal of the day, *Zlatorog*, edited by the critic Vladimir Vasilev (1883–1963). In its pages appeared the leading B. woman poet of this century, Elisaveta Bagrjana (b. 1893), whose lyrics spoke of the modern age of machinery, steel, and concrete, but also of individual liberation from social obligations. Bagrjana wandered freely through the world; in time she also acknowledged the bonds created by love and human closeness.

Asen Razcvetnikov (1897–1951) and Nikola Furnadžiev (1903–68) joined the *Zlatorog* group in the mid 1920s after breaking with the communist movement, but their poetry of the late 1920s and early 1930s expressed a cosmic nihilism which can be traced back to poets of an earlier generation such as Stojan Mixajlovski (1856–1927), who set forth pessimistic and aristocratic views in his narrative and lyric poetry. Another characteristic poet of the period, one whose verse displayed religious overtones, was Emanuil Popdimitrov (1887–1943).

Bulgaria between the wars was an overwhelmingly peasant country which boasted a powerful Agrarian political movement. That movement, however, found little literary expression. Rural Bulgaria found its finest voice in the work of Nikola Rakitin (1885–1934), who took no interest in politics and was determined to remain close to the land. In contrast, the communist transformation of B. society after 1944 had profound repercussions in lit., esp. in the years before Stalin's death, when even Ivan Vazov was regarded with suspicion. At such a time only dedicated communist bureaucrats like Xristo Radevski (b. 1903) could flourish (he presided over the Union of B. Writers, (1949–58), whereas an idealistic communist poet like Penjo Penev (1930–59) ended by taking his own life.

The guardian of poetic integrity during the high Stalinist period was Atanas Dalčev (1904–78), whose lyric output beginning in the 1920s was very limited but of exquisite quality. During the literary repressions after 1944 Dalčev fell silent in principled protest; and thus when, in the early 1960s, it became possible to write more freely, an entire generation of technically skilled younger poets looked to him with admiration. Some among them, like Konstantin Pavlov (b. 1933), went much further than he to become genuine poetic dissidents, and therefore became very popular with young audiences. Others, like Valeri Petrov (b. 1920), specialized in poetic satire with a bite. Still others, like Blaga Dimitrova (b. 1922) or Krastjo Stanišev (b. 1933), confined themselves firmly to personal themes, or else historical topics, incl. medieval ones, which have always had a strong appeal to the B. mind, but esp. so in recent years, as B. culture has sought to recover a sense of its past. B. p. has also survived among the postwar political emigration, as in the work of Christo Ognjanoff (b. 1911), now a resident of West Germany. Poetry has always occupied a place of honor in B. letters. In the hands of the very capable contemporary generation of B. poets, it seems certain to maintain that footing into the future.

ANTHOLOGIES: *Under the Eaves of a Forgotten Village: Sixty Poems from Contemp. Bulgaria*, ed. J. R. Colombo and N. Roussanoff (1975); *Mod. B. P.*, ed. B. Bojilov, tr. R. Macgregor-Hastie (1976); *Südwinde: Neuere bulgarische Lyrik*, ed. C. Ognjanoff (1978); *Anthol. of B. P.*, tr. P. Tempest (1980); *Poets of Bulgaria*, ed. W. Meredith, tr. J. Balaban (1985).

HISTORY AND CRITICISM: D. Markov, *Bolgarskaja poezija pervoj četverti XX veka* (1959); R. Likova, *Za njakoi osobenosti na balgarskata poezija 1923–1944* (1962); *B. Poets of Our Day: Lit. Sketches*, tr. E. Mladenova and B. Tonchev (1971); C. Moser, *A Hist. of B. Lit. 865–1944* (1972). C.A.M.

BURMESE POETRY. Many B. poems have been discovered in stone inscriptions dating from A.D. 1310 onward. The passages describing the glory and achievements of kings and princes, and the noble lineage of queens and princesses, are usually in verse, as are also prayers for the donor and his friends and curses on those who damage his benefaction. These stone poems were clearly designed to be permanent records.

Side by side with these there existed another kind of poetry, less formal and more emotional in character. This was scratched with stylus on palm-leaves; the best known of the older specimens is dated A.D. 1455. From the 15th to the last quarter of the 19th c., under the patronage of Buddhist monarchs, poems of varied lengths and on varied subjects were composed by monks (Shin Thi-la-wun-tha, Shin Ra-hta-tha-ra), courtiers (Na-wa-de the First and Nat-shin-naung), or royal ladies (Mi Hpyu and the Hlaing Princess). Their poems were not addressed to posterity but to royal patrons or loved ones.

There are altogether more than 50 different kinds of poems and songs, among which the most important are: (1) *E-gyin*, historical ballads, some of which were sung as cradle songs, while others informed young princes or princesses of the achievements of their ancestors; (2) *Maw-gun*, panegyric odes, perhaps the oldest type of poem—their subjects range from the arrival at the Court of a white elephant to the conquest of Siam, and from the completion of a canal to an essay on cosmography; (3) *Pyo*, metrical versions of Buddhist and non-Buddhist stories, in narrative or expository form, transferred to a B. setting and made more vivid by small imaginative details, and homilies in verse; (4) *Lin-ga*, (Sanskrit *alaṁkāra*, ornamentation), a variety of *Pyo* but generally shorter, often used as a generic term for all kinds of verse; (5) *Ya-du*, (Sanskrit *ritú*, season), the shortest type, usually of three or fewer stanzas, dealing generally with romantic subjects such as the emotions called forth by the changing seasons, the mood of longing, and memories of loved ones.

The popular generic term for poetry in B. is *kabya lin-ga*, derived from two Sanskrit words, *kāvya*, poetry, and *alaṁkāra*, an ornamentation of sound or sense.

The primary device used to achieve verbal melody in early B. p., in which the basic number of words or syllables in the line is four, is rhyme. Vowel length and stress play virtually no part in its structure. B. is a tonal lang.; syllables are differentiated from one another not only by the consonantal and vocalic elements of which they are composed, but also by pitch and voice quality; and the lang. is largely monosyllabic—that is, broadly speaking, each syllable has a meaning and can be used as a word.

These two features—the rhyme and the number of syllables in a group—are disposed in many arrangements, but the basic scheme is to have a rhyme in the fourth syllable of one line, the third syllable of the second line and the second of the third line, while the fourth syllable of the third line will be the rhyme for the following two lines, and so on. To give an example of this "climbing" rhyme:

za-tí pon-*nyá*
gon ma-*ná* -hpyín
than-*pá* hòn-*sòn*
hpet-mé *kyòn*-thà
à-*thòn* htaung-htà.

To have this 4/3/2 scheme throughout the stanza would be monotonous, however, so B. poets introduced six other schemes: 4/3/1, 4/3, 4/2, 4/1, 3/2, and 3/1. The last line of a stanza usually has 5, 7, 9, or 11 syllables.

In other forms of verse which appeared later, the lines may consist of 3, 4, 5, or more syllables. A rhyme may be confined to two lines. And though the climbing principle persists, the rhyme schemes are less rigid and sometimes more elaborate, esp. in drama, which made its debut later than the other genres, in the "mixed style" of prose and poetry. These forms, however, are variations of the basic scheme. Embellishments of the sense are chiefly similes, metaphors, tropes, hyperboles, allusions, synonyms, and verbal gymnastics.

The last century has witnessed the advent of the printing press, the cessation of royal patronage in 1885, the intro. of Eng. education, the founding of the University of Rangoon in 1920, and the creation of the Union of Burma in 1948. During this eventful period B. p. underwent significant changes. In the 1930's an influential literary movement called *Khitsan* ("Experiment for a new age") was formed, which stressed simplicity, directness, and purity of lang. Commoners have assumed the role of poets and have to cater to a larger public with a more catholic taste. Short poems have replaced the traditional long epic.

After 1948 there was an upsurge of national pride and aspiration as well as the emergence of new political, social, and cultural environments. All these provided fertile material for B. poets. Their poems may be grouped under four categories: those (1) having the eternal themes—love and nature tinted with Buddhism—by romantic poets; (2) deprecating some malaise of society such as war, social evils, or economic exploitation—by angry poets; (3) tackling moral and spiritual problems in life—by didactic poets; and (4) advocating the need for amity among the peoples of Burma—by patriotic poets. Of the contemporary poets, two may be singled out. Nú Yin (b. 1916), distinguished by her subtle approach and sensuous lang., and Daùng Nwe Hswei (1931-85), angry, innovative, and evocative. As with the Cl. and Khitsan poets, the modern writers seldom limit themselves to one form of p. And though a few poets are attempting to popularize free verse, B. p. still retains its distinctive characteristics.

IN ENGLISH AND FRENCH: *Jour. of the Burma Re-*

search Society, Rangoon (1910), esp.: (a) Ba Han, "Seindakyawthu, Man and Poet," v. 8; (b) Po Byu and B. H., "Shin Uttamagyaw and his Tawla, a Nature Poem," v.7–10; (c) G. H. Luce, "Prayers and Curses," v. 26; (d) Hla Pe, "B. p. (1300-1971)," v. 54—incl. (1) birth, devel., scope, and nature, and (2) content and form; *BSOAS* (London), v. 12 and esp. v. 13 (art. on *Maw-gun* by Hla Pe); Maung Htin Aung, *B. Drama* (1937); Hla Pe, *Konmara Pya Zat* (1952)—pt. 1, intro. and tr., contains various rhyme schemes and forms of B. prosody; U On Pe, "Mod. B. Lit.: Its Background in the Independence Movement," *Atlantic Monthly* 201 (1958); *Minthuwun,* Eng. tr. G. H. Luce (1961)—a selection of Minthuwun's poems and prose; *Littératures contemporaines de l'Asie du Sudest,* ed. Lafont and Lombard (1974); *Lit. and Society in Southeast Asia,* ed. Tham Seong Chee (1981).

IN BURMESE: *Anthol. of B. Lit.,* ed. U. Kyaw Dun, 4 v. (1926–31); U Tin, *Kabyabandhathara Kyan* (1929)—B. prosody; Pe Maung Tin, *Hist. of B. Lit.* (1947); Ba Thaung, *Sa-hso-daw-may Athokpat-ti* [Biog. of B. Authors] (1962); Hti-la Sit-Thu, *Hnahse-ya-zú myan-ma sa-hso myan-ma kabya* [20th-c. Poets and Poems] (1985). H.PE.

BYELORUSSIAN POETRY expresses the spiritual richness and resilience of a small East Slav country set between Poland and Russia, formerly the westernmost republic of the USSR. The earliest examples of verse in B. belong to Frańcisk Skaryna (ca. 1485–ca. 1540), the Bible translator, publisher, and engraver, but he had no successors as a poet, and the panegyric genre of armorial epigrams which flourished at the end of the 16th c., particularly in the hands of Andrej Rymša, was a separate devel. More public panegyrics or "declamations" characterize the main surviving works of Simiaon Połacki (1629–80), better known for his contribution to Rus. lit., but the outstanding example of 17th-c. B. p. is the recently rediscovered *Lament* on the death of Abbot Laoncij Karpovič (1620). Although the B. lang. had enjoyed official status during the period of the Grand Duchy of Lithuania, after Union with Poland the upper classes became Polonized, leaving preservation of the vernacular to the peasantry.

Thus, the birth of modern B. p. after the B. lands had been brought into the Rus. Empire was an almost total re-birth without trad. or continuity. Paŭluk Bahrym (1813–91) is acclaimed as the first B. peasant poet, though only one poem survives. An *Aeneid* travesty, based on those of Osipov and Kotlyarevšky, enjoyed great popularity, as did another anonymous comic poem, *Taras on Parnassus* (possibly by the same author), satirizing serfdom and the Rus. and Polish literary worlds. The first half of the 19th c. is characterized by ethnographic and didactic poetry, as liberal B. landowners like Jan Čačot (1796–1847) and Vikienci Dunin-Marcinkievič (1807–84) helped to create a poetry and through it a literary lang. and concomitant national awareness. Official hostility hindered the devel. of poetry throughout the century, and in the 1890s the illegal work of Adam Hurynovič (1864–94), Ivan Łučyna (1851–97), and esp. Frańcišak Bahuševič (1840–1900) displayed anguished and often bitter sociopolitical concerns, expressed in short forms reflecting clearly the influence of folk poetry. Bahuševič, sometimes called the father of B. p., proclaimed in the intro. to his verse collection *The B. Pipe* (Krakow, 1891) the sovereign worth of the B. lang., thus inaugurating an important patriotic theme that continues to the present day.

A major boost to B. national awareness was the Vilna-based newspaper *Naša niva* (Our Field), which provided a forum for the exchange of ideas and an outlet for literary endeavor. In the cultural efflorescence associated with this publication emerged many of the greatest B. poets, whose achievement remains unsurpassed to this day, making them national classics. Particularly treasured are the highly musical lyrics of Janka Kupała (Ivan Łucievič, 1882–1942), who first appealed eloquently for the B. peasant "to be called human." In narrative and dramatic poems such as *The Eternal Song* (1908), *Dream on a Gravemound* (1910), and *Bandaroŭna* (1913), Kupała broadened the scope of B. p., drawing on Eastern and Western European models, esp. the example of Shevchenko. After the Revolution of 1917, he continued to be a national figure symbolic of the B. Ren., but most of his later work lacks élan and freshness, while a number of suppressed poems like "Before the Future" (1922) show clearly his difficulties in adapting to the country's new circumstances. His contemporary Jakub Kołas (Kanstancin Mickievič, 1882–1956) adapted more successfully, producing fine nature lyrics as well as sociopolitical poetry and some talented prose works. It is, however, in two magnificent narrative poems that Kołas's genius finds its fullest expression: *The New Land* (1911–23), an epic panorama of B. life centered on a peasant family's quest, and *Symon the Musician* (1911–25), which describes with metrical virtuosity, musical lyricism, and great psychological subtlety a musician's search for recognition and self-expression; the contrast between these masterpieces emphasizes the breadth of Kołas's achievement.

Three other poets of the *Naša niva* period deserve individual mention: Źmitrok Biadula (Samuił Płaŭnik, 1886–1941), Maksim Bahdanovič (1891–1917), and Aleś Harun (Alaksandr Prušynski, 1887–1920). Biadula wrote quirkily poignant verses, but this Jewish writer's fervent "Oath of Allegiance" (1919) is an exceptionally stirring example of B. patriotic poetry. With Bahdanovič's exiguous but highly sophisticated poetic heritage (mostly collected in *A Garland,* 1913) B. lit. made a quantum leap. Having omitted such traditional stages as Classicism, romanticism, and symbolism in its compressed literary devel., B. p. was freed from over-reliance on folk models by Bahdanovič's finely chiseled short lyrics, which introduced such hitherto-unknown forms as sonnets, octaves, and triolets. Like Bahdanovič, Harun lived many years of his life far from Byelorussia, sending his highly subjective verses to *Naša niva* from Siberian exile. His sole volume, *A Mother's Gift*, appeared during Byelorussia's brief period of national independence in 1918, but until recently suffered political suppression.

Among the many poems welcoming the post-revolutionary new life, the work of two poets stands out, both for technical quality and nihilistic vigor. Bombastic extravaganzas like "Barefoot on the Embers" (1921) and "Dance on the Gravestones" (1922) by Michaś Čarot (Michaś Kudzielka, 1896–1936) and "Assault on Form" (1922) and "In Seven-league Boots" (1923) by Michajła Hramyka (1885–1969) welcome a brash new future purged of all reminders of the past. Other poets were less extravagant, but it is only with the anti-national repression of the 1920s and late 30s that paeans to the new order automatically need to be suspected of time-serving insincerity. In the earlier years a hymn to industrialization and construction like "The Tenth Foundation" (1927) by Paŭluk Trus (1904–29) could still ring a note of genuine enthusiasm.

However, subversive strains are to be heard in the work of many poets, particularly after the suppression of the B. National Republic and the partitioning of the country into Western Byelorussia under Polish rule and Soviet Byelorussia in the East. Two of the major poets of the 1920s, Uładzimir Duboŭka (1900–76) and Jazep Pušča (Jazep Płaščynski, 1902–64), both protested against the subjugation of Byelorussia in subtly ambiguous poems depicting the lot of the B. intelligentsia; works such as Duboŭka's lyric cycle *Circles* (1925–26) and Pušča's *Letters to a Dog* (1927) and *And Purple Sails Unfurled* (1929) have not been reprinted since their first appearance.

Conditions in Western Byelorussia were equally unfavorable; many poets first began writing in prison. Kazimir Svajak (Fr. Kanstancin Stapovič, 1890–1926) published a fine book of spiritual verse, *My Lyre* (1924) (the other main religious poet was Andrej Ziaziula [Fr. Aleksandr Astramovič, 1878–1921]); and Uładzimir Žyłka (1900–33), a disciple of Bahdanovič and Harun, in addition to romantic nature lyrics, produced a convincing reply to Čačot in his major work, *Conception* (1922), which traced the various stages of the national movement. Communist poets imprisoned for their beliefs included Valancin Taŭłaj (1914–47) and Pilip Piestrak (1903–78), but by far the most outstanding was Maksim Tank (Jaŭhien Skurko, b. 1912), who combined thematic breadth with technical virtuosity and strikingly imaginative imagery in *Staging Posts* (1936), *Cranberry Blossom* (1938), and *Under the Mast* (1938); in such narrative poems as the highly symbolic *Lake Narač* (1937), *Kalinoŭski* (1938) on the 19th-c. nationalist leader; and in a brilliantly stylized folk legend, *The Tale of Vial* (1937). Tank continued to write good poetry after the reunification and represents the older generation of poets at their best. Many who came to prominence under Stalin and contributed to the revival of the panegyric genre in the late 1930s and 40s are destined for swift oblivion, but the satirical fables of Kandrat Krapiva (Kandrat Atrachovič, b. 1906) and the wide-ranging romantic lyrics of Arkadź Kulašoŭ (1914–78) retain their value, as do the brightly colored, supple nature lyrics of Natalla Arsieńnieva (b. 1903), whose West B. work was never really matched by what she wrote in the BSSR and, later still, in the USA. She was the only major poet of the B. emigration.

Although poetry has not flourished to the same degree as prose in Byelorussia, it continues to play a large part in national culture. A process of increasing sophistication continues, despite strong conservative tendencies in form, meter, lexis, and, indeed, theme, with folk influence still perceptible in the work of many poets; prosodically, the devel. has been from syllabic to syllabotonic and, most commonly, tonic verse. In the 1960s, however, much modernist experimentation appeared in the poetry of, among others, Piatruś Makal (b. 1932), Janka Sipakoŭ (b. 1936), and Ryhor Siemaškievič (1945–82), in Makal's case often used effectively in conjunction with vigorous anti-Stalinist sentiments. Other major poets in the postwar period include Danuta Bičel-Zahnietava (b. 1938), Ryhor Baradulin (b. 1935), Nił Hilevič (b. 1931), and Uładzimir Karatkievič (1930–84). A valuable publishing venture has been the "Poet's First Book" series begun in 1968. A major twin theme in the 1960s which continues today is that of Byelorussia and the B. lang., expressed most movingly in Baradulin's poem "My Language" (1963). The latter is, indeed, under constant threat of erosion, and its best chances for survival would seem to lie with B. p., for, as Harun expressed it in the first poem of *A Mother's Gift*, "the very nation is a bard."

ANTHOLOGIES: *Chrestam. novaj b. lit.*, ed. I. Dvarčanin (1927); *Antaloh. b. paezii*, ed. P. U. Broŭka (1961); *Like Water, Like Fire*, tr. V. Rich (1971); *The Images Swarm Free*, tr. V. Rich, ed. A. B. McMillin (1982); *Weissrussische Anth.*, ed. F. Neureiter (1983).

HISTORY AND CRITICISM: M. Harecki, *Hist. b. lit.* (1920); A. Adamovich, *Opposition to Sovietization in B. Lit. (1917–1957)* (1958); *Hist. b. dakastryč. lit.*, ed. V. Barysienka (1968–69); I. Ralko, *B. vierš* (1969); M. Hrynčyk, *Šlachi b. vieršaskładannia* (1973); S. Akiner, "Contemp. Young B. Poets (1967–1975)," *JBStud* 3 (1976), "Contemp. B. Lit. in Poland," *MLR* 78 (1983); A. B. McMillin, *A Hist. of B. Lit. from Its Origins to the Present Day* (1977);

Ist. b.-soviet lit., ed. I. Naumenko (1977). A.B.M.

BYZANTINE POETRY.

I. RELIGIOUS POETRY
II. EPIC POETRY
III. LYRIC POETRY
IV. VERSE ROMANCES
V. SATIRICAL VERSE
VI. DIDACTIC POETRY AND DRAMA

The majority of B. literary works labor under the Cl. Gr. linguistic and literary traditions, which smothered much of their originality. Only in religious poetry did B. lit. break fresh ground and approach greatness, and only from the 13th c. onward did it use a lang. approximating that spoken by contemporary Greeks.

The first three cs. of the Eastern Roman Empire were a period of transition from pagan Roman and Hellenistic Gr. to a Christian B. culture. This is reflected in the poetry of the time. Christian fervor appears side by side with an orgiastic love of life; hymns are composed in a Christian and pagan spirit, and grandiose *ekphraseis* (descriptions of works of art) celebrate Christian and pagan masterpieces. Of these the description of the Church of Sancta Sophia by Paul the Silentiary (fl. 563) is undoubtedly the most significant, extolling the twin grandeur of church and state around which B. life was to revolve.

I. RELIGIOUS POETRY. Originally B. religious p. used a number of Cl. Gr. meters—the hexameter, elegiac, iambic, anacreontic, and anapaestic—as can be seen from the writing of Methodius, Synesius, and Gregory of Nazianzus (4th–5th cs.). But very soon the new rhythmic meters prevailed, whose effect relied on the number of syllables and the place of the accents within a line. These, together with admiration for the martyrs and devotion to the mysteries of the new religion, gave B. religious p. a power and freshness which remained unequaled in subsequent Med. Gr. writings.

The rhythmic B. hymns fall into three periods, the first (4th–5th cs.) characterized by short hymns, the *Troparia*; the second (6th–7th cs.) by long and elaborate metrical sermons, the *Kontakia*; and the third (7th–9th cs.) by a form of hymn-cycle called *Kanon*. The second is the great period of Gr. hymnography. In its early part lived Romanos (6th c.), the most celebrated B. religious poet. Some 85 of his works have been preserved, all metrical sermons for various feasts of the Orthodox Church. They were accompanied by music, which is now lost, and were apparently rendered in a kind of recitative resembling oratorios. Romanos, being a conscientious Christian, treated his subjects exactly as the church ordained. Occasionally, however, he gives rein to his fancy, and at such times becomes grandiloquent in the style of epideictic oratory. His lang. on the whole is pure; he is rich in metaphor and imagery, and often interweaves in his narrative whole passages from Holy Scripture. His main fault is an oriental love of size, unpalatable to the modern reader.

Andrew, Bishop of Crete (ca. 660–740), initiates the third period of B. religious p. with his *Major Kanon*, a composition of huge size, in which elaboration of form results in a decline of power and feeling. The two most important representatives of this period are St. John Damascene (7th–8th cs.) and his foster brother Kosmas of Maiouma. As a hymnographer, Damascene was greatly renowned. He returned to the use of quantitative verse, even endeavoring to combine it with modern meters.

The storm of the iconoclastic controversy, which broke out in the lifetime of Damascene, brought in its wake a reaction which resulted in a new florescence of hymnography. Works (mostly anonymous) of writers of this period finally found their way into the liturgy of the Eastern Church and replaced the older hymns and metrical sermons of the days of Romanos. Of the posticonoclast poets, Symeon the Mystic (949–1022) certainly ranks highest. In B. p. he is the most important figure after Romanos, although his fervent mystical poems tend to be formless and often obscure. Moreover, he is the first person known to have used the 15-syllable line (*politikos stichos*) in personal poetry, the verse which in later years was to become supreme in the poetry of the Gr. world.

B. religious p. was to accomplish a great historical mission. It not only kept alive Gr. national and Christian feeling in the face of numerous barbarian invasions, but it also scattered to East, West, and North the seeds that later blossomed into the literatures and cultures of other peoples—the Russians, the Southern Slavs, the Romanians, the Syrians, the Copts, and the Armenians.

II. EPIC POETRY. The historical court epics of the late Hellenistic era survived in the early B. centuries. If we are to judge by their scanty remains, they had limited artistic merit. The greatest representative of the historical epic, or rather the epic encomium, and one of the most distinguished B. poets was George Pisides (7th c.). Some of his most important verse is in praise of his patron, Emperor Heraclius, whose victory over the Persians he celebrated. In the hands of Pisides new B. meters begin to take shape, in particular the B. 12-syllable iambic verse, which was to become the principal meter of subsequent Med. Gr. artverse. But the most important B. epic cycle apparently originated in the provinces of the East in the course of the 10th c. It centered on the heroic figure of Digenes (who symbolized the ideal of Med. Gr. manhood) and spread from the deserts of Syria to the Rus. steppes, even reaching the remote Gr. colonies of Southern Italy. Of this we possess today only a small number of isolated folk songs (the *Akritic Ballads*), some of great power and beauty, and half a dozen versions, ranging from the 12th to the 17th c., of a long poem now lost, the so-called *Epic of Basil Digenes Akritas.*

They all differ in lang. and style and even in the sequence of the narrative. In this epic we find Gr. and Hellenistic motifs blended with Eastern elements, as well as a number of baffling historical facts anything but contemporary.

III. LYRIC POETRY. The epigram in the Hellenistic sense of the term (the short occasional poem) was the type of lyric poetry most cultivated in Byzantium. At first it followed the late Hellenistic patterns, as the works of Agathias (6th c.), Paul the Silentiary, and others show. But from the 7th c. the new religious spirit permeates it, expressed in a predilection for churches, monastic life, and holy relics as subjects. Theodore Studites (759–826) is the most important representative in this trend. Cassia, often and unjustly called the Sappho of Byzantium, followed him in the 9th c. But the heyday of the B. epigram spans the 10th–11th cs. For it was then that John Geometres (Kyriotes), Christophoros of Mitylene, and John Mavropous flourished. They reverted to the older Hellenistic influences, and their verse displays both feeling and refined wit. The only other type of B. high lyric p. worth mentioning is the *lament*. This often takes the form of an address to the poet's soul, or of a dirge or complaint, full of the ascetic spirit of the time. It was influenced by the long and insipid autobiographical poetry of Gregory of Nazianzus, yet many important B. poets indulged in it, and it continued in the form of "a moral admonition" or "the prayer of a sinner" until the end of the B. era.

Medieval erudite poetry, permeated as it was by the ascetic spirit, did not draw on profane love for inspiration, one of the greatest sources of lyricism of all centuries. Such B. love p. as has survived is written in a more or less demotic tongue and is to be found in the love letters (the *Pittakia*) of the verse romances (see below) or in certain modern Gr. folksongs whose origins can be traced back to the Middle Ages.

IV. VERSE ROMANCES. After the fall of Constantinople to the Fourth Crusade (1204), Frankish chivalrous poetry was translated into Gr. and, influenced by this, a new type of Gr. chivalrous poetry arose. It used a more supple and lively lang. and broke away from the sterile trad. of the highbrow B. verse romances of Niketas Eugenianos (12th c.) and Theodoros Prodromos (12th c.), which blindly followed the patterns of the late Hellenistic romances of Heliodorus and Achilles Tatius. Such are *Callimachos and Chrysorrhoe, Belthandros and Chrysantza, Imperios and Margarona*, and *Florios and Platsiaflora*, all the works of unknown poets. The essence of these tales is boundless romanticism. Arduous love and the amazing fortitude of their heroes color the narrative. Yet in the hands of the B. poets Western elements are blended with Eastern, so that an oriental atmosphere of magic suffuses certain episodes, lending them a charm and a character of their own. Closely connected to these are two long biographical verse romances, *The Poem of Alexander the Great* and *The Story of the Famous Belissarios*. The first follows the pseudo-Callisthenes' life of Alexander; the second has as its subject the deeds of Belissarios, the famous general of the Emperor Justinian. To this group one should perhaps add the *Achilleis*, which treats of the life and deeds of Achilles, presenting him, however, as a medieval Western knight.

V. SATIRICAL VERSE. In the 12th c. certain satirical didactic poems appeared, permeated by a mordant B. humor, not always refined. These are generally grouped under the title of *Prodromic Poems* and are traditionally attributed to the beggar and scholar Theodoros Prodromos. Their chief interest lies in the picture of social and monastic life they give and in the type of lang. they use, in which demotic (spoken) forms abound.

VI. DIDACTIC POETRY AND DRAMA. If we exclude the epigram, perhaps no other poetic form was so assiduously and continuously practiced in Byzantium as didactic poetry. But these endless prose-in-verse creations on birds, fish, stones, vegetables, etc., are certainly not poetry in the real sense of the word, and it is very doubtful if their authors ever sought original artistic effect; information was all they wished to convey. Moreover, drama proper remained unknown in Byzantium. Such lit. as exists in dramatic form (of which the 11th-c. cento *Christus Patiens* is the most important example) was always meant to be read and not acted. The dramatic instinct of the Greeks revealed itself in the long dialogues of the *Kontakia* and in the Acclamations to the Emperors, and found ample nourishment in the pageantry of the palace ceremonies and the liturgies of the Gr. Orthodox Church. See also GREEK POETRY.

ANTHOLOGIES: *Anthologia graeca carminum christianorum*, ed. W. Christ and M. Paranikas (1872); *Byzantinische Dichtung*, ed. G. Soyter (1930); *Poeti byzantini*, ed. R. Cantarella, 2 v. (1948); *Med. and Mod. Gr. Poetry*, ed. C. A. Trypanis (1951)—bibls. for all important B. poets in the notes; *Kontakia of Romanos, B. Melodist*, ed. and tr. M. Carpenter, 2 v. (1970–72); C. A. Trypanis, *Penquin Book of Gr. Verse*, 3d ed. (1984); *An Anthol. of B. P.*, ed. B. Baldwin (1985).

HISTORY AND CRITICISM: K. Krumbacher, *Gesch. der byzantinischen Literatur*, 2d ed. (1897)—still the standard work; P. Maas, "Das Kontakion," *Byzantinische Zeitschrift* 19 (1910); Schmid and Stählin; F. Dölger, *Die byzantinische Dichtung in der Reinsprache* (1948); F. H. Marshall, "B. Lit.," in N. H. Baynes and H. St. L. B. Moss, *Byzantium* (1948); N. B. Tomadakis, *Eisagoge eis ten Byzantinen Philologian* (1952); H.-G. Beck, *Gesch. der byzantinischen Volksliterataur* (1971); H. Hunger, *Die hochsprachliche Profane Literatur*, 2 v. (1978); Trypanis; R. Jakobson, "The Slavic Response to B. P.," in Jakobson, v. 6; *Oxford Dict. of Byzantium*, ed. A. P. Kazhdan (1991).

C.A.T.

C

CANADIAN POETRY.

I. IN ENGLISH
II. IN FRENCH

I. IN ENGLISH. The first poet to write in what later became Canada was that engagingly smug Jacobean, Robert Hayman (1575–1629), a friend of Ben Jonson who in 1621 became governor of the colony of Harbour Grace in Newfoundland. He wrote of Newfoundland from a viewpoint that seemed to combine the attitudes of an early publicity agent and a slightly utopian admirer of *The Tempest*, which had been produced only shortly beforehand:

> The Aire in Newfound-land is wholesome, good;
> The Fire, as sweet as any made of wood;
> The Waters, very rich, both salt and fresh;
> The Earth more rich, we know it is no lesse.
> Where all are good, *Fire, Water, Earth and Aire*,
> What man made of these foure would not live there?

But Hayman's efforts were isolated; he had no immediate successors. The real Eng. C. poetic trad. began nearly two centuries later with Loyalists who fled the Am. revolution and settled in New Brunswick and Upper Canada, and with immigrants from Britain who began to arrive in large numbers after the Napoleonic wars. They were largely unwilling exiles who brought their preconceptions about life and poetry with them. Some, like the younger Oliver Goldsmith (1781–1861) in *The Rising Village*, tried to present the New World as materially kinder if culturally cruder than the Old, but more often they resembled Standish O'Grady (ca. 1793–1841) in his bitter invocations of the land:

> Thou barren waste; unprofitable strand,
> Where hemlocks brood on unproductive land,
> Whose frozen air in one bleak winter's night
> Can metamorphose *dark brown hares into white*!

The tendency to alternate between the elegiac (regretting a forsaken past) and the satiric (scorning an inadequate present), which characterized these poets has persisted in C. verse. But as the 19th c. continued and native-born poets appeared beside the immigrants, other strands also emerged, most notably the concept of a poetic trad. The earliest idea of the way to establish a local trad. was to turn back to previous periods in Eng. poetry, which explains the powerfully anachronistic neo-Jacobean dramas (*Saul* and *Count Filippo*) that Charles Heavysege (1816–76) wrote in his spare time as a woodcarver in Montreal, and the detached landscape poems of Charles Sangster (1822–93), which make one think of a late Augustan tinged with romanticism taking the measure of a new land. An echo of Chartist radicalism emerged in the poetry of emigrant poverty which Alexander McLachlan (1818–96) wrote, as did the first flickerings of C. nationalism in the descriptive poems in which Charles Mair (1838–1927) celebrated the western prairies.

There is a sense of something new entering C. p. with Isabella Valancy Crawford (1850–87). The diction, imagery, and metrical form of her poems are not greatly different from those of the Eng. late romantics, and if Keats had not written, and Landseer not painted, Crawford would not be quite the poet she became. What is novel in her is the way she gives herself to her poetry. Her poems grip the imagination because they are moved by frustrated passion, by the power of an inner vision that has little to do with the objective world. The bizarre hidden personality of this woman of obscure life emerges most strikingly in the way she uses conventional imagery to serve her fantasy:

> They hung the slaughter'd fish like swords
> On saplings slender—like scimitars
> Bright, and ruddied from new-dead wars,
> Blaz'd in the light—the scaly hordes.

Crawford inhabits a private world of the poetic persona. It is the so-called Confederation poets—Wilfred Campbell (1858–1919), Charles G. D. Roberts (1860–1944), Bliss Carman (1861–1927), Archibald Lampman (1861–99), and Duncan Campbell Scott (1862–1947)—who first begin to describe a recognizable Canada and in whose work the first intimations of a truly C. poetic voice can be heard. By the late Victorian era, at least in eastern and central Canada, the pioneer age had ended. Ties with the mother countries were weakening and, for the new generation, a love for the place of childhood experience was understandably more real than nostalgia for a land never seen. In giving voice to this transference of emotional allegiance, the Confederation poets at their best not only celebrated C. scenes, which Sangster and Mair had already done; they also reported with accuracy the life they harbored. Realism inevitably entered the process, as it always does when writers have to recognize the nature of the world they inhabit before they can apply to it the transfiguring processes of the imagination.

And so, in Roberts and Lampman, in Scott and at times in Carman, we see not only a strange luminous factualism in evoking the landscape, but also a new use of imagery, of lang., eventually of poetic form. It emerges in lines and stanzas more memorable, because more original, than any used before in Canada. There is that magically unprecedented line from Roberts' sonnet, "The Mowing": "The crying knives glide on; the green swath lies." And there is that final stanza of "Low Tide at Grand Pré," which has given Bliss Carman a lasting niche among C. poets:

> The night has fallen and the tide . . .
> Now and again comes drifting home
> Across these aching barrens wide,
> A sigh like driven wind or foam:
> In grief the flood is bursting home.

Modern critics find Duncan Campbell Scott the most interesting of this group because, like Roberts to an extent, but unlike the metrically conservative Lampman and Carman, he felt uneasily that a new approach to the C. land required new formal expression, and in the end went very near free verse. Already by 1905, poems like "The Forsaken," about an old Indian woman left to die in the barren land, have a broken-line pattern which shows how eager Scott was to seek in unconventional metrical forms a way of giving expression to the strange things he had seen in the C. north.

This gradual liberation of the verse of Scott and Roberts is perhaps the chief thread of continuity in C. p. in the early 20th c., for after the almost simultaneous appearance of these poets and of Carman and Lampman during the 1880s, no poet of major significance emerged until E. J. Pratt (1882–1964) published *Newfoundland Verse* in 1923. And Pratt has always seemed an anomalous figure, ushering in modernity by turning to the past. He chose epic and mock-epic forms for his major works (*Brébeuf and His Brethren, The Titanic*), and he went back to 17th-c. Hudibrastic meters to write his often heavy-handed satires, but he did explore the use of C. vernacular in verse and early recognized the importance of C. history and geography as basic subject matter.

A very different figure was W. W. E. Ross (1894–1966), who published his first book, *Laconics*, in 1930. The very title was revealing: Ross brought to C. p. a new simplicity of expression and an emphasis on imagistic clarity. His influence on his contemporaries was considerable; "Rocky Bay" is almost a model of the modern C. landscape poem:

> The iron rocks
> slope sharply down
> into the gleaming
> of northern water
> and there is a shining
> to northern water
> reflecting the sky
> on a keen cold morning.

Certainly one of the ingredients of C. modernism as it appeared in the 1930s was an imagist way of looking which, by stressing the visual, enabled poets to perceive their environment and translate their perceptions into words with an appropriateness their predecessors had never attained. Poems of this period, such as "The Lonely Land" by A. J. M. Smith (1902–80), show this process at work in a clear relationship to Ross's sharper imagism:

> This is a beauty
> of dissonance,
> this resonance
> of stony strand,
> this smoky cry
> curled over a black pine
> like a broken
> and wind-battered branch
> when the wind
> bends the tops of the pines
> and curdles the sky
> from the north.

But the poets working together in Montreal in the late 1920s and 1930s—notably Smith, F. R. Scott (1899–1985), and A. M. Klein (1909–72)—were much too polymorphous in attitude to confine themselves to imagism in their search for alternatives to the outworn 19th-c. modes most C. poets still followed. They found affinities with the Eng. poets of the 1930s and with earlier masters such as Pound and Eliot.

The C. modernist poets of this time formed interlocking groups like that centered on the *McGill Fortnightly Review* in the late 1920s (Smith, Scott, and others) and the later Montreal groups associated in the 1940s with *Preview* (P. K. Page, Patrick Anderson, Scott, Klein) and *First Statement* (Irving Layton, Louis Dudek, Raymond Souster). These groups were partly associations of convenience among poets who found it hard to get their work published in ordinary periodicals; each in his or her own way was rebelling against conventional poetics and seeking a way of expression that suited a personal vision. A vague cultural nationalism was also at large among them, but the desire to find their own voices was primary, and the movement to create a distinctive C. p. largely derived from the poets' realization that they could be fully themselves only by living in their own place and time and giving expression to the experience they knew. But paradoxically the model for giving that expression they often had to find elsewhere; for rough convenience, C. poets of this period can be divided into Anglophiles and Americanophiles.

Not only Smith and Scott were influenced by Eng. poetry of the time. Patrick Anderson (1915–79), the leading spirit of *Preview*, was a temporarily transplanted Eng. poet. Dorothy Livesay (b. 1909) dates her poetic awakening from her discovery of Auden and Spender, who showed that lyricism and a social conscience were compatible, though in the later years of her long career it is not her Marxism of the 1930s but her intense feminism that has emerged most strongly, a feminism less concerned with politics than with the intensities and ambiguities of a passionate life:

> I walk beside you
> trace
> a shadow's shade
> skating on silver
> hear
> another voice
> singing under ice.
> ("The Uninvited").

Earle Birney (b. 1904), who also began to write in the 1930s, first found a new way of talking about Canada through his study of OE poetry, whose density and power, and even diction, are strongly present in his early poems. Since then, in decades of restless experimentation, he has developed a conversational, loping rhythm that serves to convey sharp visual images and hint at their philosophic implications, as in his vivid travel poem, "Bear on the Delhi Road":

> They are peaceful both   these spare
> men of Kashmir   and the bear
> alive in their living   too
> If   far on the Delhi way
> around him galvanic they dance
> it is merely to wear   wear
> from his shaggy body the tranced
> wish forever to stay
> only an ambling bear
> four-footed in berries.

P. K. Page (b. 1916), whose intermittent career also dates from the 1940s, clearly began writing under the influence of the socially conscious British poets of the 1930s, but has moved into an extraordinarily individualized combination of verbal economy and visionary intensity; as Margaret Atwood once said, she is "both a dazzling technician and a tranced observer who verges on mysticism"; she sees indeed the technique as part of the trance.

If the *Preview* poets looked to British models for inspiration, the rival *First Statement* group initiated another recent C. trend by upholding New World poets; for them any Old World, even an Old World in revolt, was anathema. This marks the beginning of Ezra Pound's powerful if intermittent influence in Canada. Of course neither Louis Dudek (b. 1918) nor Raymond Souster (b. 1921)—much less Irving Layton (b. 1912)—appears as a mere imitator of Pound; indeed, the difference between their styles shows how each took one aspect of Pound and adapted it to his own poetic ends. Dudek is more the philosophic poet, concerned with historical issues on a global scale, and so it is the Pound of the *Cantos* whose echo we sometimes catch in a long meditative poem like *Atlantis*. An earlier, imagist Pound stands behind Souster, who adapted and refined imagism into a remarkable instrument for bringing the visible world clearly alive, while giving it a transparency through which we see the poet's mind ironically reflecting, with the thought always a consequence of the experience. Souster has written so eloquently of Toronto and its life that he has become that rare phenomenon, an urban regional poet. By contrast, Irving Layton's attachment to Pound, later to William Carlos Williams, was tenuous at most. His Dionysian attitude (one can hardly call it a philosophy), derives partly form Nietzsche and partly from Lawrence. Essentially he is a hyper-romantic, reaching a poetic extravagance and density of imagery far from anything Pound would have accepted, and at times, with luck, he can be very good. His "Tall Man Executes a Jig" is certainly one of the best poems written in Canada.

As the situation changes, up through the 1950s to the explosive 1960s, with the public attitude to poetry improving and poets becoming more self-assured, it becomes difficult to think in terms of movements. Some poets, like the austerely yet luminously religious Margaret Avison (b. 1918), were always too uncompromisingly themselves to be grouped in any meaningful way with other writers. Others, like Al Purdy (b. 1918), show in their work so broad a grasp of what it means to write poetry about Canada that they seem to epitomize a generation's experience. Yet Purdy stands, in his idiosyncratic way, quite outside categorization. He writes directly from experience; his poems often read like fragments of an autobiography. Yet there is a haunting, disillusioned love of the land in them that is more telling than any stridently nationalist verse:

> This is the country of our defeat
>   and yet
> during the fall plowing a man
> might stop and stand in a brown valley
>   of the furrows
>   and shade his eyes to watch for the
>   same
>   red patch mixed with gold
>   that appears in the same
>   spot in the hills
>   year after year
>   and grow old
> plowing and plowing a ten-acre field
>   until
> the convolutions run parallel to his
>   own brain.

Purdy's recent *Collected Poems* (1986) shows him a major C. poet by any standards. His melding of the sense of history in a new country suddenly grown old in its feelings with an awareness of place as a visual reality has enlightened younger poets, so that a kind of geohistorical trad. has come into being, represented by writers like John Newlove (b. 1938), Sid Marty (b. 1944), Andrew Suknazki (b. 1942), and, perhaps most notably, that fine rural poet of the Maritimes, Alden Nowlan (1933–83). The Western writer Patrick Lane (b. 1939) shows a remarkable evolution from a tough working poet to a philosophic poet who has movingly recorded the alienation of modern man, with compassion its only antidote.

Another strain running through recent C. p. is more concerned with the artifice of versecraft and directed to the inner landscape of memory and myth, of dream and feeling. Notable in this line have been James Reaney (b. 1926), Jay Macpherson (b. 1931), and Eli Mandel (b. 1922), poets who were once somewhat hastily classed together as a "Mythopoeic" school. Most versatile among these poets has been Margaret Atwood (b. 1939), who has also gained high reputation as a novelist and a critic, and whose work in all genres shows an extraordinary combination of mental toughness and elliptic economy. As she says in *Power Politics*:

> Beyond truth,
> tenacity: of those
> dwarf trees & mosses,
> hooked into straight rock
> believing the sun's lies & thus
> refuting / gravity.
>
> & of this cactus, gathering
> itself together
> against the sand, yes tough
> rind & spikes but doing
> the best it can

Among other poets who have in their special ways demonstrated the extraordinary variegation and enrichment of C. p. during recent decades are Leonard Cohen (b. 1934) and Gwendolyn MacEwen (b. 1941), George Bowering (b. 1935) and Michael Ondaatje (b. 1943), and perhaps most deserving of mention because her clear, spare gravity went so long unrecognized, Phyllis Webb (b. 1927), whose long verse address, "To Friends Who Have Also Considered Suicide," is a poem in intent both serious and satirical, in tone at once grave and strangely gay. It contains a whole philosophy, a whole critique of our views of existence.

> Some people swim lakes, others climb
> flagpoles,
> some join monasteries, but we, my
> friends,
> who have considered suicide take our
> daily walk
> with death and are not lonely.
> In the end it brings more honesty and
> care
> than all the democratic parliaments of
> tricks.
> It is the "sickness unto death"; it is
> death;
> it is not death; it is the sand from the
> beaches
> of a hundred civilizations, the sand in
> the teeth
> of death and barnacles our singing
> tongue:
> and this is "life" and we owe at least
> this much
> contemplation to our western fact; to
> Rise,
> Decline, Fall, to futility and larks,
> to the bright crustaceans of the oversky.

Younger Canadian poets—those born in the late 1940s and the 1950s—are now emerging into prominence, notable among them Dale Zieroth (b. 1946), Marilyn Bowering (b. 1949), and Roo Borson (b. 1952). Perhaps the most striking recent phenomenon is that of poets with strongly ethnic links and attitudes who write in Eng. In the past in Canada there were strong minor trads. in such langs. as Icelandic and Ukrainian, but now the children of immigrants tend to write in English even though they may continue to think in their parents' lang. Thus, particularly among those of It. descent—like Pier Giorgio di Cicco (b. 1949) and Mary di Michele (b. 1949)—we have notable poets who use the same lang. as their contemporaries, but continue to project their distinctive trads., filtered through the lens of C. experience.

ANTHOLOGIES: *The Book of C. P.*, 3d rev. ed. (1957), *Oxford Book of C. Verse* (Eng. and Fr.; 1960), *Mod. C. Verse* (Eng. and Fr.; 1967)—all ed. by A. J. M. Smith; *The Penguin Book of C. Verse*, ed. R. Gustafson (1959); *The New Oxford Book of C. Verse in Eng.*, ed. M. Atwood (1982); *The New C. Poets*, ed. D. Lee (1986).

HISTORY AND CRITICISM: W. E. Collin, *The White Savannahs* (1936); E. K. Brown, *On C. P.*, rev. ed. (1944); D. Pacey, *Creative Writing in Canada*, rev. ed. (1961); *Lit. Hist. of Canada*, ed. C. F. Klinck and W. H. New, 4 v. (1965–90); D. G. Jones, *Butterfly on Rock* (1970); N. Frye, *The Bush Garden* (1971); *Oxford Companion to C. Lit.*, ed. W. Toye (1983); G. Woodcock, *Northern Spring: The Flowering of C. Lit.* (1987); C. Bayard, *The New Poetics in Canada and Quebec* (1989); *Studies on C. Lit.*, ed. A. E. Davidson (1990). G.W.

II. IN FRENCH. Very few pieces of verse have reached us from the early Fr. colonial period, but it may be worthy of mention that one of the first Fr. explorers, Marc Lescarbot (1570?–1630?) is probably the author of the first poems written in and about North America (*Les Muses de la Nouvelle-France*, 1609). Much later, following the British conquest (1763), newspapermen, politicians, and clergymen resorted to verse to comment on current events; many of these pieces were collected by James Huston in his *Répertoire national* (4 v., 1848–50). They are invariably bad poetry, but they throw much light on the attitudes of the first generations of Fr. Canadians who lived under British rule. The best of the genre is Michel Bibaud's *Epîtres, satires, chansons et autres pièces de vers* (1830), the first book of verse published by an author born in Canada. More important for later poetry, though not poetry itself, is the *Histoire du Canada* (4 v., 1845–52) by historian François-Xavier Garneau, a book which played a vital role in the emergence of a Fr. C. lit., incl. poetry, by providing local writers with challenging historical subjects and patriotic themes. Without him, it is virtually certain that Fr. Can. lit. would have developed differently and somewhat later.

The later poets, Crémazie, Fréchette, and Chapman, owe much to Garneau. The earliest Fr. C. poet to achieve a certain level of excellence was Octave Crémazie (1827–79), whose poetry is generally made up of narratives inspired by historical events described by Garneau. This is largely true also of the prolific Louis-Honoré Fréchette (1839–1908), the leading Fr. C. poet of the 19th c., who, however, in addition wrote about C. nature and rural life. His major work, *La Légende d'un peuple* (1887), a series of short epics, glorifies the most popular Fr. C. heroes and historical events. Both his inspiration and style owe much to Victor Hugo: his manner is more oratorical than lyrical. The same can be said of his rival William Chapman (1850–1917), whose works are, however, less ambitious and forceful. But the overwhelming prevalence of historical themes naturally led to a reaction, as did the pervasive influence of the Fr. romantic school.

The earlier poets who turned their backs on historical subjects were (paradoxically) the historian's son, Alfred Garneau (1836–1904), a gifted minor poet who wrote mainly about nature, friendship, and death. The simple life and secular trads. of the still predominantly rural Fr. C. population are the main themes of such poets as the prolific Pamphile Lemay (1837–1918) and the delicate Nérée Beauchemin (1850–1931). It was obvious that local poets had discovered and been influenced by recent Fr. poetry, esp. the Fr. Parnassians and the symbolist school. The romantic trad. was to be maintained well into the 20th c., but new themes, trends, and techniques were introduced toward the end of the 19th c., esp. by the members of the Ecole littéraire de Montréal and some other independent poets. It is significant that at the end of the 19th c. Montréal replaced Québec City as the main center of Fr. C. lit., a fact which goes a long way in explaining how Fr. C. p. evolved from one concerned mainly with traditional values to one influenced more by the solitary and frequently disquieting life in a modern industrial metropolis. Fr. C. p. gradually became more personal and more lyrical, concerned less with historical or current events and more with inner life, with personal emotions, aspirations, sorrows, and dreams. At the same time, it also became more diversified in inspiration and more accomplished in craftsmanship.

Although the influence of such Fr. poets as Baudelaire, Verlaine, Rimbaud, and others is still visible in the works of the following generation, esp. in the poetry of the most outstanding poet of the Ecole littéraire de Montréal, Emile Nelligan (1879–1941), there is no denying that much of the new Fr. C. p. started to break away from literary colonialism. There began to be heard a distinct new voice expressing the soul of a new people. Before going out of his mind in his early twenties, Nelligan authored some of the best verse written in Canada. There is also a good deal of melancholy in the poems of the sentimental Albert Lozeau (1878–1924), but the inspiration of their contemporary Charles Gill (1871–1918) is mainly epic in his colored descriptions of the country and its legends. Lesser poets of the Ecole littéraire were Jean Charbonneau, Alphonse Beauregard, Albert Dreux (a master of free verse), Lionel Léveillé, Gonzalve Desaulniers, and Albert Ferland. The Ecole did not aim at imposing any common aims or rules; it was a forum where the most diverse poets, from the philosophical Charbonneau to the rustic Desaulniers or Ferland, could engage in dialogue. At the edge of the Ecole, one find also independent poets like Louis Dantin, Jean-Aubert Loranger, and the ultimate craftsman, Paul Morin, who drew his subjects from the most exotic themes from Italy, Spain, and the Arab world (*Le Paon d'émail*, 1911).

Between the two World Wars, most Fr. C. p. remained rather conservative, or traditional, in both form and content, much of it written in regular verse and dealing with C. themes: winter, solitude, nature, or more universal themes like love (or its absence), friendship, soul searching. There is still a great deal of romanticism in the poetry of Robert Choquette (*À travers les vents*, 1925; *Suite marine*, 1953), Simone Routier (*L'Immortel Adolescent*, 1928), Jovette Bernier (*Les masques déchirés*, 132) or Medjé Vézina (*Chaque heure a son visage*, 1934). Love is the main theme of these neo-romantic poets. The leading poet of that generation, however, Alfred Desrochers depicted with force and emotion the rude life of pioneers in a new world still largely undeveloped (*À l'ombre de l'Orford*, 1930), and a younger poet of the same vein, Clément Marchand (*Les Soirs rouges*, 1947) introduced in Fr. C. p. proletarian themes in depicting the hard times endured by city-dwellers.

Yet between the Wars there also emerged new themes and, even more so, a new style, a much freer prosody or no prosody at all, as *vers libre* gave way to poetic prose. Here the leading representatives were Hector de Saint-Denys-Garneau, Alain Grandbois, Anne Hébert, and Rina Lasnier. Although highly personal in style and substance, the work of these poets shares common features:

all four express, more or less esoterically, spiritual experiences rooted in the simultaneous realizations that the beauty of the world is constantly threatened by death, that all things are in a state of flux, and that human aspirations toward eternal bliss are mixed with the recurring misfortunes of life. There is something metaphysical about this poetry, from Garneau's *Regards et jeux dans l'espace* (1937) and Grandbois' *Iles de la nuit* (1944) to Anne Hébert's *Le Tombeau des rois* (1953) and Rina Lasnier's *Présence de l'absence* (1956). The key words of these titles are themselves very revealing of the new dimensions of this poetry: space, night, tomb, presence, absence. This is a poetry of the mind and of the soul, even if the outside world is ever-present, frequently as an enemy. These works mark the end of parochial as well as academic poetry. Henceforth, Fr. C. p. would remain modern in inspiration and style. Soon it would also proclaim the rejection of traditional values and of society itself, as an increasing number of poets would be adepts of Marxism or even anarchists (esp. at the time when Québec separatism was at its peak).

These themes have been pursued and renewed by more recent poets such as Gilles Hénault, Pierre Trottier, Paul-Marie Lapointe, Roland Giguère, Fernand Ouellette, Michèle Lalonde, Gaston Miron, and Gatien Lalointe. Although several younger poets are dealing with political and social themes and use poetry as a tool for transforming society, most recent Fr. C. p. deals with the more universal themes of love and despair, friendship and the quest for happiness. It is decidedly contemporary in matter and form.

ANTHOLOGIES: *La Poésie canadienne*, ed. A. Bosquet (1962); *Anthologie de la poésie québéçoise*, ed. G. Sylvestre, 7th ed. (1974); *La Poésie québéçoise: Anthologie*, ed. L. Mailhot and P. Nepveu (1986).

HISTORY AND CRITICISM: L. Dantin, *Poètes de l'Amérique française*, 2 v. (1928, 1934); G. Marcotte, *Une Littérature qui se fait* (1962), *Le Temps des poètes* (1969); *Mod. C. Verse in Eng. and Fr.*, ed. A. J. M. Smith (1967); *The P. of Fr. Canada in translation*, ed. J. Glassco (1970); J. Blais, *De l'ordre et de l'aventure: La Poésie au Québec de 1934 à 1944* (1975); R. Hamel, J. Hare, and P. Wyczynski, *Dictionnaire pratique des auteurs québéçois* (1976). G.S.

CARIBBEAN POETRY. See PUERTO RICAN POETRY; WEST INDIAN POETRY.

CATALAN POETRY. (This article treats poetry in Catalan, the lang. of the eastern region of the Iberian peninsula; for the poetries of the western and central langs., see GALICIAN POETRY and SPANISH POETRY.)

It has been the peculiar fate of the poetry of the Catalans that during a number of centuries it was written by them mainly in langs. that were not their own: Occitan in the Middle Ages, Castilian during the age of Sp. ascendancy. It is only since romanticism that a poetry in their own vernacular has continuously flourished in Catalonia and the C.-speaking Valencia and Balearics.

In the Middle Ages, the geographic, linguistic, and political propinquity of Catalonia and Provence, and the European prestige of Occitan poetry (q.v.), caused the Catalans to write theirs in the literary lang. of Provence, borrowing also the patterns—courtly love, satire, moralization—with the poetics of the troubadours. Most C. poets held to this practice from the 12th c. to the 15th. Guillem de Berguedà (1140–ca. 1200) and Cerverí de Girona (fl. 1250–80) are among the best of the early C. troubadours and Jaume March (1335–1410?) and Pere March (1338?–1413) among the late ones.

Relics have been found, however, of a poetry written in Catalonia in the same centuries, not in literary Occitan, but in C.: a popular, religious poetry (mainly Marian, and usually addressed to the Virgin of Montserrat), of a type still common in C. lit. Ramon Llull (1232?–1316) wrote more formal poetry in C., reaching lyric heights in his *Desconhort* (Distress) and the *Cant de Ramon* (Ramon's Song). His greatest lyric is the *Llibre d'Amic e Amat* (The Book of the Friend and his Beloved), a prose poem somewhat influenced by the Arab mystics and celebrating the ascension of Man's soul through Love toward God.

In the 14th and 15th cs. narrative poetry appeared in Catalonia, usually written in octosyllabic couplets. One might include in this type the *Spill* (Mirror) or *Llibre de les dones* (A Book about Women) by Jaume Roig (d. 1478), a book on the wiles and vices of women, written in 4-syllable couplets.

The close political ties of the Crown of Aragon with Sicily, Naples, and Italy in general soon added to the Occitan influence the influence of the It. *dolce stil nuovo*. A slight Petrarchan tinge has been noticed in the verse of Jordi de Sant Jordi (ca. 1400–24), although he was still very much a writer in the Occitan trad. Ausiàs March (1397–1459) is the heir to both troubadour and It. lyricism. Within these trads., March reveals a profound psychological insight that can transform medieval or Italianate topics into expressions of universal human emotions. His work is usually divided into songs of love, songs of death, moral songs, and spiritual songs, in all of which—as he himself said—there is no fiction, but rather truth, trouble, and solitude. Completing the trilogy of great C. poets of the 15th c. is Joan Roïc de Corella (ca. 1430–ca. 1490), a poet first of sensual love, then of pure love and finally of divine love. He was a writer of great visual and imagistic power, and also the first to introduce into C. poetics the It. hendecasyllable.

Just as it seemed that C. p. had established itself in the work of Ausiàs March and Roïc de Corella and the minor poets that followed them, a decadence set in which vitiated C. p. almost completely. In fact, from the beginning of the 16th c. to the beginning of the 19th, most C. poets abandoned C. to write in Castilian, and although the C. lang. remained the tongue of the people of Catalonia, it was used in poetry only by minor writers. The only poetic genres in C. that remained truly alive during the period were the ballad and the popular religious song, both transmitted orally by a people more attached to trad. than were the literate upper classes.

In the 19th c., with the spread of the romantic ideals of individualism and nationalism, a revival or rebirth—*la Renaixença*—of C. lit. took place. Romanticism naturally tended to foster a return to the native tongue as the means of expressing the sentiments of the people of a C. nation that was finding again its ancient pride and soul. The ode to *La Pàtria* (1833) by Bonaventura Carles Aribau (1798–1862) has often been cited as the symbolic beginning of this rebirth. Then the work of a number of poet-scholars like Joaquim Rubió i Ors (1818–99) and Manuel Milà i Fontanals (1818–84) gave it leadership and momentum. The revival in 1859 of the annual "Jocs Florals" (poetry contests) inspired a number of writers consistently to exercise their faculties in the vernacular. The instrument was finally ready and all previous efforts were crowned with the work of Jacint Verdaguer (1845–1902), a peasant priest.

After Verdaguer, no C. poet has had to apologize for the literary use of his native tongue. Verdaguer's poetry ranges from the epic in *L'Atlàntida* (Atlantis, 1877) and in *Canigó* (1886), to religious poetry, nature poetry, and the most subjective and intimate lyricism.

After Verdaguer, modern C. p., having come of age, shed its *Romantico-Renaixença* character. Joan Maragall (1860–1911) brought to it a new sense of freedom by using free verse as well as traditional forms. Maragall's poetry expresses his enjoyment of beauty, his love of life, of nature, strength, work, and creation: what is now called the "Maragallian optimism." Perhaps his best-loved books are *Pirenenques* (Pyreneean Poems), *Vistes al mar* (Views of the Sea), and *Cants* (Songs). He was the poet whose "measure was human" and could say:

> If the world is already so beautiful,
> Lord,
> when one looks at it with your Peace
> within one's eye,
> what more can You give us in another
> life?

While Maragall observed or broke the classical rules, the Balearic poets of C., Miquel Costa i Llobera (1854–1922), the author of *Horacianes* (Horatian Poems, 1906), and Joan Alcover (1854–1926), the author of *Cap al tard* (Toward the Evening, 1909) and *Poemes biblics* (Biblical Poems, 1918), reasserted the love of measure and of wisdom, the classical Mediterranean inheritance of C. culture.

The following generation of poets was heir to both the classicism of Costa i Llobera and Alcover and the vitalism of Maragall. Joan Salvat Papasseit (1894–1924) expressed the restiveness of the avant-garde. Josep Carner (1884–1969), sensuous, refined, ironic, appealed both to the critics and general readers. Carles Riba (1893–1959) brought the symbolist style to its utmost refinement in his *Elegies de Bierville* (Bierville Elegies, 1943). Both Carner and Riba went into exile after the Sp. Civil War (1936–39). Other major poets chose to stay. Among them are Josep Maria de Sagarra (1894–1961), folksy yet subtle and occasionally powerful, and Josep-Vicenc Foix (1894–1986), a great craftsman of sonnets and also a visionary poet in the surrealist line whose poems remind us of the landscapes painted by his friends Salvador Dalí and Juan Miró.

The post-Civil War generation managed to keep alive C. p. in spite of the cruel persecution of C. lang. and culture under Franco's dictatorship. Salvador Espriu (1913–82) is one of the most influential voices of the postwar period. Elegy, satire, and social crit. are fused in his work to convey dark humor and existentialist anguish. *Cementiri de Sinera* (Sinera's Churchyard, 1946) has been compared favorably with Dylan Thomas's *Under Milk Wood.* Agustí Bartra (1899–1984) spent long years in exile, where he published *L'Arbre de Foc* (Tree of Fire, 1946) and *Odisseu* (Odysseus, 1953). A poet of imagination and epic grandeur, he managed to fuse surrealism and the Cl. myths in a powerful poetic lang. During the 1960s and '70s, esp. after Franco's death and the rebirth of democracy, the image of the phoenix rising from its ashes aptly portrays the rebirth of C. p. An explosion of works by young poets dominates the literary scene. Among the outstanding new voices are Joan Brossa (b. 1919), Marta Pessarrodona (b. 1941), Narcís Comadira (b. 1942), Francesc Parcerisas (b. 1944), and Pere Gimferrer (b. 1945).

BIBLIOGRAPHIES: A. Elías de Molins, *Diccionario biográfico y bibliográfico de escritores y artistas catalanes del siglo XIX* (1889–95); J. Massó i Torrents, "Bibliografia dels antics poetes catalans," *Anuari de l'institut d'estudis catalans* (1913–14), *Repertori de l'antiga literatura catalana*, v. 1, *La poesia* (1932); J. Molas and J. Massot i Muntaner, *Diccionari de la literatura catalana* (1979).

ANTHOLOGIES: *Anthol. of C. Lyric P.*, ed. J. Triadú and J. Gili (1953); *Ocho siglos de poesía catalana: antología bilingüe*, ed. J. M. Castellet, 2d ed. (1976); *Antología general de la poesia catalana*, ed. J. M. Castellet and J. Molas (1979); *Mod. C. P.: An Anthol.*, and *Postwar C. P.*, both ed. and tr. D. H. Rosenthal (1979, 1991).

HISTORY AND CRITICISM: L. Nicolau D'Olwer, *Resum de literatura catalana* (1927); M. de Riquer, *Resumen de literatura catalana* (1947); J. Ruiz i Calonja, *Història de la literatura catalana* (1954); G. Díaz Plaja, *De literatura catalana* (1956); J. Fuster, *La poesia catalana*, 2 v. (1956), *Contra el noucentisme* (1978); J. Ruiz i Calonja and J. Roca i Pons, "Med. C. Lit." in Fisher; J. Bofill i Ferro and A. Comas,

Un segle de poesía catalana, 2d ed. (1981); A. Terry, *C. Lit.* (1972), *Sobre poesía catalana contemporània* (1985). L.MO.; M.E.D.

CHICANO (MEXICAN AMERICAN) POETRY. New Spain's northern provinces, now the U.S. Southwest, were the scene and inspiration of Sp. poetry before the Eng. colonized the Atlantic coast (see SPANISH AMERICAN POETRY). The Oñate expedition (1598) not only founded some of this country's oldest cities, it performed dramas in verse and brought Gaspar Pérez de Villagrá to chronicle the voyage in his epic poem, *Historia de la Nueva México* (1610). Among the colonizing adventures, Villagrá recorded the battle of Acoma, the first poetic rendering within the present U.S. territory of the racial and cultural conflicts that have plagued the country since the European arrival and which contemp. C. p. continues to document. Popular poetry flourished, as evidenced by the rich trad. of romances still found in New Mexico and by the *corrido,* an evolved form of romance chronicling events of communal interest, popular esp. along the Mexican-U.S. border. These traditional forms provided folkloric context and historic memory for C. poets. Cultured forms were used to a lesser extent, often by recent arrivals from Mexico or members of the educated class.

After U.S. annexation of Mexico's northern states in 1848, the Mexicans remaining in the territory continued to produce poetry, with a notable increase of written material appearing in newly founded local newspapers. Romanticism's influence was marked, as was a tendency to use verse for didactic or satirical purposes. Into the 20th c., Sp. dominated both written and oral production, and alongside poems of a personal nature there appeared poetry on themes of cultural defense and affirmation. Already in the 1850s newspapers featured poems protesting matters perennially pertinent: broken promises by U.S. politicians; discriminatory law enforcement, courts, and schools; the imposition of Eng., and socioeconomic divisions along ethnic or racial lines. Affirmation took the forms of praising Hispanic culture and, ironically, proclaiming the Mexican Am. community's loyalty to the U.S., as proven by participation in the Sp. Am. War and, later, in World War I.

In the 20th c., Eng. appeared more frequently in written poetry produced by Mexican-Americans, though community newspapers still published in Sp. poems by leading Lat.-Am. writers. During the Mexican Revolution and its aftermath (1910–36), a number of Mexican intellectuals immigrated to the U.S. and worked on newspapers; the best of Lat.-Am. *Modernista* poetry was belatedly introduced to Mexican-Am. readers during this period. The Sp. oral trad. was also bolstered by massive immigration. Yet public schooling was almost exclusively conducted in Eng., affecting both linguistic capabilities and the knowledge of a formal poetic trad. in Sp.; it is this fact which, coupled with the pro-Eng. bias of the print media, explains the increase in poetry written in Eng. by Mexican-Americans in the first half of the 20th c. Fray Angélico Chávez's *Clothed with the Son* (1939) and *Eleven Lady-Lyrics and Other Poems* (1945) were acclaimed by critics. This trend continued after World War II, a period which saw the demise of many Sp.-lang. newspapers. By the mid-1960s, when the Chicano Movement for civil rights arose, the majority of Chicanos spoke and wrote in Eng., and poetic expression was as likely to be in one as the other. Many writers attempted to mix the two (bilingualism or "code switching"), some thereby reflecting their normal speech pattern, others as a calculated political statement.

Most Chicano Movement poetry was committed to the communal struggle of the minority culture, a position reflected in its predominant themes: an identification with Mexico, esp. the pre-Columbian and revolutionary periods; a revision of U.S. history; the glorification of heroic figures; the exaltation of communal cohesion in the *barrio* (neighborhood), the family, and *carnalismo* (brotherhood); and the channeling of solidarity into political action. Its imagery spotlighted distinctively Chicano subjects, although the underlying experiences mirror those of other U.S. immigrant groups. The most significant works reveal a common structure: (1) U.S. society threatens cultural survival; (2) cultural characteristics are invested in a representative figure under direct attack; (3) that figure's images are catalogued to rescue them from destruction; (4) the poem substitutes for the threatened figure, becoming a new centering force for readers which in effect can turn individuals into a community through the shared act of reading.

Rodolfo Gonzales' manifesto, *I Am Joaquin/Yo Soy Joaquín: An Epic Poem* (1967), demanded Chicanos withdraw from U.S. social oppression into their communal traditions to rediscover their identity as survivors and warriors. Abelardo Delgado's "Stupid america" (1969) proclaimed the nation's future greatness if Chicanos were allowed to fulfill their creative potential, and the self-destruction that was the alternative. Alurista's *Floricanto en Aztlán* (Flowersong in Aztlán, 1971) proposed a hybrid of pre-Columbian philosophy and the Third-World anticapitalism as a survival strategy amid U.S. racism and class exploitation. Ricardo Sánchez' *Canto y grito mi liberación* (I Sing and Shout My Liberation, 1971) railed against U.S. life as an alienating prison. In *Perros y antiperros* (Dogs and Anti-dogs, 1972) Sergio Elizondo toured the history and geography of the Southwest to denounce Anglo-Am. encroachment and the dehumanizing character of U.S. society, positing a refuge in the C. community's love and humanity. And while Tino Villanueva's *Hay Otra Voz Poems* (There is Another Voice Poems, 1972) prefigured the introspective turn and the heightened awareness of lyric craft and tropes to come in the mid 1970s, it culminated in a declaration of the poet's dedication to communal political struggle in an interlingual lang. that is itself a metaphor of the ideological message.

This poetry's most distinctive stylistic features were (1) the predominance of narrative and mimetic over lyrical and tropical modes of expression, and (2) interlingualism, a combination of Sp., Eng., and sub-dialects. Prime exponents of the latter were José Montoya and Alurista:

Hoy enterraron al Louie
(Today they buried El Louie)
And San Pedro o sanpinche
(St. Peter or saintdamned)
are in for it. And those
times of the forties
and the early fifties
lost un vato de atolle
(a real great guy)
(Montoya, "El Louie").

mis ojos hinchados
(my swollen eyes)
flooded with lágrimas
(tears)
de bronze
(of bronze)
melting on the cheek bones
of my concern
(Alurista, "Mis ojos hinchados").

Interlingualism makes comprehension impossible for monolingual readers, while dialectal usages, like Montoya's slang, can perturb even bilinguals. Although interlingual poets of the '60s and early '70s insisted that they were simply using the community's native speech patterns, the result was poetry for initiates, unfortunately inaccessible to those Chicanos not sharing the specific linguistic context. At a simpler level, many texts were published with facing translations, e.g. *I Am Joaquin/Yo Soy Joaquín* or *Perros y antiperros*, which opened C. p. to a wider readership.

The mid 1970s brought changes. The national decline in political activism was mirrored in a poetry less ideologically or communally oriented and more personal and individualistic. Coinciding with this change, women's poetry emerged, some with a feminist perspective. Notable was an increased concern with craft. Some of the principle figures were university trained writers, exemplified by the Fresno School of C. p. groomed by Philip Levine at Fresno State University (Gary Soto, Leonard Adame, Robert Vásquez). While the use of tropes increased, narrative tendencies still predominated, reflecting their popularity in mainstream poetry.

Interlingualism has also decreased, although it still flourishes among authors who direct their work at the C. community. Blatant political statements have waned, as has the need to stress the writing's ethnic character. C. content has become more subtle, with less attempt to create uniquely C. images. More universal qualities are freely displayed. Luis Omar Salinas, known as a '60s Movement poet for his "Aztec Angel" poem, has few C. references in *Darkness Under the Tress / Walking Behind the Spanish* (1982), but his status among C. poets has, if anything, increased. Bernice Zamora's *Restless Serpents* (1976), Gary Soto's *Black Hair* (1985), and Lorna Dee Cervantes's *Emplumada* (1981) are C. texts, yet readers could easily place them within a broader framework of the U.S. experience. Many of their poems contain no Chicano references or else contextualize them to function without need of ethnic knowledge. Rafael Jesús González' "Ars poetica" (1977) ends with just such a cultural juxtaposition of universals:

the sky-eagle
devouring the earth-serpent
as a sign.
The Aztec ball player
losing the game lost his heart
to keep alive the gods.
The wells claim it:
Li Po
would die
needing it
for the moon.
("Coin, Ars poetica")

The Oriental reference is more esoteric than the Aztec ones, which are sufficiently clear for general understanding. Other poets are more subtle, as is Bernice Zamora in her parodies of Shakespeare, Robinson Jeffers, or Roethke; or Lucha Corpi, who ends her tribute to Emily Dickinson with:

We are . . . migrant
workers in search of
floating gardens as yet
unsown, as yet, unharvested.

These are specific images, yet they allude to Chicano themes of migrant work and the Aztec's founding of a promised city which probably would have received more blatant treatment a decade before.

Yet C. p. has not fully assimilated. At the community level, the 1960s-style political rhetoric still resounds, with perhaps a more profound sense of social disparity after the relatively meager progress made by the C. community since the 1970s. Some poets have infiltrated the small literary magazine network, and fewer still have published with major publishers—without the threat of Affirmative Action that prompted some houses to issue a few titles around 1970—and some poets—Gary Soto, Lorna Dee Cervantes, Luis Omar Salinas, Alberto Ríos—have been awarded significant prizes by mainstream institutions. Recognition and acceptance, however, are evidenced better, if on a limited scale, in the fact that C. p. begins to appear in major academic anthologies of Am. lit.

ANTHOLOGIES: *El ombligo de Aztlán*, ed. Alurista (1972); *ENTRANCE: Four C. Poets* (1975); *El Quetzal emplumece*, ed. C. Montalvo (1976); *Siete poetas* (1978); *Fiesta in Aztlán*, ed. T. Empringham (1981); *Contemp. C. P.*, ed. W. Binder (1986).

HISTORY AND CRITICISM: J. Bruce-Novoa, *C. Authors, Inquiry By Interview* (1980); *C. P., A Response to Chaos*; M. Sanchez, *Contemp. C. P., A Critical Approach to an Emerging Lit.* (1985); C. Candelaria, *C. P.: A Critical Intro.* (1986); W. Binder, *Partial Autobiographies: Interviews With 20 C. Poets* (1986); J. E. Limón, *Mexican Ballads, C. Poems* (1991). J.B.-N.

CHILEAN POETRY. See SPANISH AMERICAN POETRY.

CHINESE POETRY.

I. CLASSICAL
II. MODERN

I. CLASSICAL. Poetry was uniquely important in traditional China as a means of expression. From cl. antiquity (722–481 B.C.), it has been assumed that what is felt inwardly will find natural expression in words (*shi yan zhi*), an idea appearing in a chronicle in 546 B.C. This longstanding conception of poetry, which later also came to influence Japanese poetic theory, may be attributed to the Ch. consciousness of the power of writing, the notion that human configurations (*wen*) and natural patterns (*wen*) are parallel manifestations of the *Dao* or cosmic principle. From this derives the general belief that poetry, if powerfully imbued with human feeling, can bear upon political, social, and cosmic order. A standard presentation of this expressive-affective view of poetry is the "Great Preface" prefixed to China's first anthol. of poetry, the *Shi jing* (Classic of Poetry). It is in reference to this collection that the generic term for the chief form of poetry, *shi*, first appears.

Comprising 305 songs, the *Shi jing* was probably compiled sometime after 600 B.C., though its oldest parts may date as early as the 11th C. B.C. Whether or not Confucius (551–479 B.C.) himself selected the 305 poems from an earlier compilation of 3000, as alleged by the historian Sima Qian (ca. 145–85 B.C.), it is true that Confucius gave the anthol. an important place in his curriculum and that it subsequently became the fundamental text of Confucian education. The *Classic* includes folk, courtier, and dynastic songs and ceremonial hymns. All of these were originally sung and chanted. The songs cover a wide variety of subjects that reflect the daily activities of early Ch. society (before the 6th C. B.C.)—courtship, farming, hunting, feasting, war, sacrifices. These poems already evince several expressive devices basic to later Ch. p. and Ch. poetics: abundant rhyme, strong auditory effects, formal compactness, and the use of nature imagery.

The basic rhythmic unit of a Ch. poem is the single character (*zi*), and since every character is pronounced as one syllable, the number of characters in each line determines the meter. Songs in the *Classic of Poetry* are predominantly written in 4-character lines, with occasional longer or shorter lines. Rhyme schemes are fairly complex and varied at times, but the usual pattern is *abcb*. Most poems consist of short stanzas that are nearly identical in metrical structure, i.e. isometrical. The following verse, entitled "Guan ju," is the first and the best-known of the songs (every line in the original contains four characters):

"*Guan quan*," the ospreys cry
On the islet in the river:
A beautiful young girl
Is a fine match for the gentleman.

Water plants of varied length,
Left and right (we) trail them:
That beautiful young girl—
Awake, asleep, (he) longs for her.

(He) longs for her but to no avail,
Awake, asleep, (he) thinks of her.
Yearningly, yearningly,
(He) turns, tossing from side to side.

Water plants of varied length,
Left and right (we) pick them:
That beautiful young girl,
Zithers and lutes welcome her.

Water plants of varied length,
Left and right (we) sort them:
That beautiful young girl,
Bells and drums delight her.

Reduplicated sounds, such as the onomatopoetic *quan quan* in the opening line of this poem, appear frequently in the songs. Other recurrent auditory devices include alliteration and rhyming compounds, such as *cen ci* ("of varied length") and *yao tiao* ("beautiful and young"). The basic device of parallelism, based on the principle of repetition with variation, prefigures the more formalized systems of parallelism to be developed several centuries later.

Compared to Western poems, these songs are remarkably terse and compressed, esp. if read in the original, where pronouns often disappear and grammatical connections are kept to a minimum. This quality of compactness may be due to the particular nature of the Ch. lang., but more importantly, it reflects a basic aesthetic attitude typical of *shi* poetry, wherein suggestion is prized over exposition, "less" over "more." Closely related is the effect of economy and reticence achieved by an imagistic device called *xing* ("stimulus" or "metaphorical allusion"), which is used in the opening lines of most of the *Classic*'s lyric poems to connect metaphorically the natural world with the human situation. The element of *xing*, such as the brief description of the osprey in "Guan ju," intensifies the associative and allusive power of natural imagery. Because the metaphorical connection between *xing* and the human context is left unspecified, readers are provoked to infer something more, or other, as the true meaning of the poem. Thus, in Confucius' time, *xing* were alluded to by diplomats as a means of indirect reference to sensitive political situations. This explains why traditional commentators since the Han dynasty (206 B.C.–A.D. 220), instead of reading "Guan ju" as a simple love song, have developed a trad. of reading that poem, and in fact the entire *Classic* and subsequently poetry in general, as bearing moral and political significance. That is, later poets, under the influence of this long-lasting exegetical trad., would sometimes write poems to the same allegorical patterns they read in (or read into) the works of others. Recently, perhaps inspired by the revaluation of allegory in Western crit., sinologists have devoted much attention to the problem of "allegorization" or "contextualization" (P. Yu's term) in Ch. p., often citing Western treatments of Solomon's *Song of Songs* for comparison.

Whereas the *Classic of Poetry* represents the Northern roots of Ch. culture, China's second anthol., *Chu ci* (the Songs of Chu), reflects life in the Southern "colonies" around the Yangzi basin in the Warring States period (403–221 B.C.)—though recent scholarship has demonstrated that the North-South distinction should not be taken too literally. What we can be sure of is that songs in the Chu collection—which include the "Nine Songs," "Nine Changes," "Nine Pieces" ("nine" being not the number but perhaps a musical term meaning simply "many"), and a long personal lament called *Li sao* (On Encountering Trouble)—are all, in one way or another, founded on Shamanism, a religion that initially flourished in the Northern dynasty of Shang (ca. 18th–12th c. B.C.) but subsequently fell from favor there and found its permanent home in the Chu region. In terms of style and content, the Chu songs are markedly different from those of the *Classic of Poetry*: they are exuberant and colorful in imagery, inclined to erotic pursuit of water goddesses and imaginary airborne flights inspired by the practice of Shamanism. In contrast to the predominant 4-character rhythm in the *Classic*, these songs are written in a new meter, with a caesura marked by the exclamation-syllable *xi* in the middle. The two basic patterns are: (1) tum tum tum *xi* tum tum tum, and (2) tum tum tum ti tum tum *xi* tum tum tum ti tum tum (*tum* representing full words, and *ti* particles). The second pattern is known as the "Sao style," because *Li sao*, the longest poem in the anthol. and believed to have been written by the first Ch. poet recorded by name, Qu Yuan (d. 315 B.C.?), is the earliest example of it.

Qu Yuan's genius enabled him to invent not only the "Sao style" of poetry but also a striking intensity of lyricism reinforced by a symbolism of fragrant plants and flowers. He was China's Pindar, the first person to have developed a distinct individual voice in Ch. p. Poems in the "Nine Changes" and "Nine Pieces," perhaps written by later authors, are obviously influenced by *Li sao* both in form and content. But without discrediting its originality and power, one may say that *Li sao* has become famous in Ch. lit. mainly because its author represents a model of Confucian virtue for later literati to emulate. Qu Yuan was a loyal minister of Chu who drowned himself after scheming officials slandered him to the king of Chu, causing him to be rejected by his sovereign. Trad. has it that before his suicide Qu Yuan composed *Li sao* to defend his loyalty: the poem describes the poet's long fantastic journey to mythical realms and his persistent, though unsuccessful search for the "fair ladies." Its rich and varied implications have not prevented *Li sao* from being read almost exclusively as a political allegory. Perhaps this is because scholars have found it necessary to view the work as reflecting political reality in order to place it within the Confucian exegetical trad., a trad. long established by commentators of the *Classic*. Other arguments can be adduced: surely, Qu Yuan, an educated member of the Chu royal house, would have learned the conventional method of allegorical reading and might indeed have purposely composed the work as a political allegory.

The poetic genre known as *fu* (rhapsodies), which became the typical court poetry of the Han dynasty, may be regarded as deriving from *sao* poetry. The *fu* generally opens with a short introduction in prose, and the main body in verse employs a variety of line lengths (3-, 4-, 6-, or 7-character lines), end rhymes, onomatopoeia, dazzling images, occasional verbal and syntactic parallelism, lengthy enumeration of fantastic objects and place names, etc. Like *sao*, the early *fu* tends to take a panoramic, cosmological approach, focusing on imaginary celestial journeys with an aim to impress and enrapture the reader. Song Yu, supposedly a disciple of Qu Yuan, was the earliest putative author of this form. But it was Sima Xiangru (179–117 B.C.), the greatest poet of the Han dynasty, who first developed the *fu* into a major literary genre. His long *fu* on the Shang-lin Park is the symbol of a splendid age: its elaborate, if imaginary, account of rivers, hills, animals, and exotic fruits and trees in the hunting park conveys a powerful image of the Han empire during the rule of Emperor Wu. This exuberant style also characterizes, to a large extent, the numerous *fu* on capitals by later authors. Besides the panoramic *fu*, there was another type, "*fu* on objects" (*yongwu fu*), which also achieved popularity. The *yongwu fu* focuses on the description of such small objects as flowers, birds, and musical instruments, and some of the works extant today are quite brief. It is impossible to know whether these short pieces in the *yougwu* mode were parts of longer *fu* or originally intended to stand alone. After the Han there emerged gradually a particular type of "lyrical" *fu*. A case in point is Tao Qian's (365–427)

"*Fu* on Calming the Passions," a poem strongly marked by personal emotion.

In addition to *fu*, a genre called *yuefu* became important in the Han. Originally the name of the Music Bureau established by Emperor Wu to collect folksongs, *yuefu*, has been broadly applied to both ritual hymns and popular ballads, and also to literary imitations of the genre. It is said that when new music was first imported from Central Asia, many *yuefu* songs were composed for the new melodies; hence the use of irregular meters ranging from 3 to 7 characters in a line. Like folksongs everywhere, *yuefu* ballads employ devices of direct speech, dialogue, formulaic expressions, hyperbole, repetition with variations, etc. They usually present dramatic situations that have direct bearing on contemp. social realities: beautiful women resisting the advances of powerful officials, the hardships of the orphan, the abandoned wife, the old soldier. Indeed, the *yuefu* served as an appropriate genre for many authors to air social criticism anonymously. The longest of the extant *yuefu*, "Southeast Fly the Peacocks," tells of the tragic fate of a loving young couple who are forced by the man's mother to separate and who eventually take their own lives, reportedly a true story that occurred in the Later Han (A.D. 25–220). With the appearance of this long ballad, written in a 5-character rhythm, the *yuefu* became increasingly standardized in structure (though some earlier, shorter works in this genre were already composed according to the same meter). A few decades later, numerous anonymous southern *yuefu* were written in the 5-character line in quatrains. Subsequent literary imitations of this genre further developed new formal, rhetorical, and imagistic devices.

Perhaps under the influence of the *yuefu* ballads, a new verseform, the 5-character line *shi*, rose to prominence around the 2d c. A.D., largely replacing the 4-character *shi* meter dominant from the age of the *Classic of Poetry*. This 5-character line form created an overwhelming preference for fluid poetic rhythms based on an odd, rather than even, number of characters—a tendency that was to last for centuries. Among the most important features of this new form are: (1) the regularized use of a caesura after the second character, and a secondary caesura either after the third or the fourth; (2) couplets serving as independent metrical units, with the rhyme falling on the end of the second line of the couplet; and (3) independence from musical rhythms. The sudden flowering of the 5-character line *shi* inspired poets to use it as a vehicle for deep reflection and introspection. The earliest extant, though anonymous, *shi* poems written in this form, known collectively as the "Nineteen Old Poems," are dominated by subjectivity and emotion, focusing primarily on the problems of death and separation. The general tendency for *shi* poems to adopt paratactic lines and brief images gives these 19 poems the quality of restraint, thus inciting generations of commentators to view them as embodying the virtue of "gentleness and sincerity" so potently celebrated by the trad. of the *Classic of Poetry*. But it is precisely this poetics of suggestiveness that most attracted later poets. The use of the 5-character line *shi* by literati was first promoted by the poetically talented members of the Cao family (later founders of the Wei dynasty), esp. during the Jian-an period (196–220) when many first-rate poets, the Caos among them, wrote some of the finest works in the lang. The supreme value of poetry, the Jian-an literati believed, lies primarily in the individual's creative vigor (*qi*), a kind of operative energy that gives lit. immortality. Their concern with the intrinsic power of poetry led poets to become preoccupied with self-expression during the Wei-Jin era (220–316), as is eminently demonstrated by Ruan Ji's (210–63) series of 82 poems entitled "Singing of My Thoughts."

The times of the Eastern Jin (317–420) and the Southern Dynasties (420–581) were plagued by constant wars and intrigues: the Ch. government moved south in 317 after foreign invaders had taken over the north, and a constant struggle for power between great families in the south lasted nearly 300 years. But it was during this period of political disunity that Ch. poets discovered the true power of nature's beauty. Tao Qian (365–427), now customarily described as one of China's two or three greatest poets but largely overlooked during his lifetime, explores in his poetry the rustic quietude of the "farmland" (*tianyuan*). His trust in the workings of nature comes essentially from his belief that everything moves in a cyclical order and that life and death are necessary phases of nature's creation. A recluse who describes himself as living in a noisy human world yet with a detached heart, Tao Qian is deservedly the first poet to awaken in poetry the full potentiality of Daoism. The extraordinary way in which he mingles personal feelings and natural images has led later critics to use the term *qingjing jiaorong* ("fusion of feeling and scene") to describe the special quality of his poetry. But, perhaps, a more typical poet of the period was Xie Lingyun (385–433), known as the champion poet of "mountains and water" (*shanshui*) poetry. An aristocrat endowed with a strong love of landscape and travel, Xie develops a poetic style that is more visually descriptive and sensory than ever before. One senses that his elaborate use of parallelism, as if intended to capture the complementary relationship of mountains and rivers, reflects not only the Ch. ideas of the principles of the universe but also a profound influence of the earlier panoramic *fu*. But compared to earlier models in *fu*, which often detail mythical animals and fictitious objects, Xie's landscape poetry is distinguished by a descriptive realism, a desire to capture a "formal likeness" of nature. Indeed, it was the notion of verisimilitude (*xingsi*) that dominated aesthetic taste in the Southern Dynasties. The basic tenet in lit. crit. was that poetry should be characterized primarily by skillful and detailed descriptions of the natural world. In the beginning, this approach took the form of landscape poetry, as may be demonstrated by the works of Xie Lingyun and a younger poet, Bao Zhao (412?–466?). But toward the end of the 5th c., it gradually developed into a poetry focused on small objects (*yongwu shi*)—musical instruments, curtains, lamps, candles, etc.—a reflection of the literary salons of the Southern Dynasties with their intimate aestheticism and high-bred preciosity. In the 6th c., the *yongwu shi* ideal of verisimilitude was further realized in Palace Style poetry, where palace women became the main "objects" of description. An aesthetic attitude, a belief that beauty itself embodies its own *raison d'etre*, distinguishes these poems from the works of previous ages. Perhaps it is on account of this self-sufficient aestheticism, independent of moral and political considerations, that traditional critics have judged Palace Style poetry frivolous.

Parallel to the descriptive orientation was a poetic formalism that also came onto the literary horizon during the Southern Dynasties. Poets, knowing the privileged character of their poetry, began to define the boundaries of the genre: that which employs rhyme is *wen* (pure lit.); that without it is *bi* (plain writing). The main purpose of this distinction was to narrow the meaning of the classical term *wen* (patterns), which originally had a broad denotation covering both *wenxue* (lit.) and *wenzhang* (composition in general). A formal criterion such as rhyme seemed best for defining the normative boundary of this new concept of *wen*. The extent of controversy provoked by this formal revisionism was something similar to, if not greater than, the European Ren. debate over poesy. These Southern Dynasties poets also went further to experiment with tonal variations and other prosodic schemes, some of which were to evolve into important rules in Tang poetry. Shen Yue (441–513) is credited with having devised the "four tone" system, with the four tones (i.e. pitches) referring to the "level" and the three "oblique" tones ("rising," "departing," "entering"). The "level" tone corresponds to the first and second tones of today's standard Mandarin, while the "rising" and "falling" tones are distributed into the present third and fourth tones. The "entering" tone no longer exists in modern Mandarin, as it has long been redistributed among the other tones. The true significance of Shen Yue's "four tone" prosody lies in the correlation, and hence the opposition, of the "level" (O) and the "oblique" (X) tones within the individual lines—e.g. O O O X X. Ch. may have been a tonal lang. from its beginnings, but some historical linguists place the introduction of tones in the Han dynasty or later, and argue that Shen Yue's "discovery" of the four tones was in fact the observation of a new phenomenon in Ch. lang. as it called on tones (i.e. pitch) to compensate for the loss of some other phonemically distinctive features. If the tonal revolution led by Shen Yue represented a definitive break from traditional prosody, it was the talented Xie Tiao (464–499) who exhibited the true merits of this new scheme in his "New Style poetry" (*xin ti shi*), so that even hundreds of years later poets looked back to Xie Tiao as an ideal model in *shi* composition. As the successor to these early promoters of tonality, Yu Xin (512–580) combined tonal refinement and powerful lyricism in his poetry in such a way as to influence contemp. *fu* poetics, giving the *fu* genre a new formalistic outlook. This new cross-generic phenomenon is best demonstrated by the *fu, Lament for the South,* which he wrote after the fall of his dynasty, the Liang dynasty (502–57).

During the Tang dynasty (618–907), generally acknowledged as the golden age of Ch. p., the gradual codification of Regulated Verse (*lushi*)—based on the original conception of the Southern Dynasties' "New Style poetry"—brought to the Ch. trad. a whole new spectrum of poetic experience. First, the earlier "open-ended" format becomes a prescribed 8-line structure, with a level-tone rhyme falling at the end of each couplet. (Rhyme is also permissible at the end of the first line of the first couplet.) Second, the 4-couplet verse has a specific rule concerning the distribution of parallelism: the second and the third couplets are made up of parallel lines, while the last couplet is not and the first couplet usually not as well. Third, parallelism develops into an enclosed system based on symmetry, with each component in the first line matched by a grammatically similar and semantically related, yet tonally antithetical, component in the corresponding position of the second line, thus forming a perfect mirror effect. Fourth, the coherence of the poem's phonic pattern is governed by the cumulative effect of contrast (*dui*) and connection (*nian*), as in the following example:

X X O O X
O O X X O
O O O X X
X X X O O
X X O O X
O O X X O
O O O X X
X X X O O.

With its insistence, in 5-character or 7-character line forms, on a rigid tonal system and a structure of parallelism, Regulated Verse was believed to represent the perfect form of poetry. In this period the long-established quatrain form (now called *jueju*), which constituted a major portion of the popular *yuefu* ballads during the Southern Dynasties, also began to be written in a similar manner. An extended form of Regulated Verse was *pailu*, verse of unprescribed length (often several hundred lines) which observed the basic tonal patterns but was allowed to change the rhyme several times in the middle of the poem. Generally, the term "Regulated Verse" came to refer to the "new" poetry as opposed to the "Ancient Style poetry" (*gushi*) which was meant to include both old poems produced before the Tang and new poems written in the old style.

The compact and highly schematized form of Regulated Verse helped to consolidate a new aesthetics that was to become the trademark of Tang poetry: the integrity of the lyric moment. In the two middle, parallel couplets, the focus of perception is inevitably a lyric moment in which superficially referential data have been turned into static, qualitative images. Thus, the sense of subjective reality brought forth by the opening couplet is bound to be swept away by this heightened, deliberately timeless vision. Only after this momentary world of poetic reverie is over do statements of personal judgment begin to appear in the final couplet. The lyric moment is an effective poetic device for uniting the expressive and descriptive elements in poetry, and certainly a good counterweight for the prevailing objective mode so confidently celebrated by Palace Style poetry for nearly two centuries. During the 7th c., the "Four Talents" of the Early Tang were already conscious of developing a penetrating, expressive voice suited to the compactness of the new format. But it was not until the High Tang (8th c.), when Regulated Verse was hailed as an ideal form, that poets began to create a heightened lyrical vision, fully internalizing their perceptions of the natural world. Wang Wei (701–61) in particular looked up to Tao Qian as a model poet, in an attempt to convey through the new verse the effortless mingling of self and nature. One of his best-known couplets captures the completeness of a lyric moment, casual but lasting: "Walking to where the water ends, / Sitting, watching the clouds rising."

Two other High Tang poets, Li Bo (701–62) and Du Fu (712–70), have traditionally been paired together as two literary giants whose poetic styles are in sharp contrast with each other, and the evaluation of their relative merits has been a major preoccupation of critics since the Song dynasty. Li Bo is customarily viewed as a spontaneous genius, Daoist mystic, and carefree romantic, Du Fu as a meticulous craftsman, Confucian "sage of poetry," and responsible spokesman for suffering mankind. Though somewhat exaggerated, these stereotypes are not groundless: they owe much to the poets themselves, who sought to cultivate such images of self in their poetry. Their differences are clearly revealed in their respective preferences for different kinds of verse: Li Bo favored the open-ended format of Ancient Style and *yuefu* verse, with their freedom from prescribed tonal and verbal parallelism, while Du Fu, though skilled in all forms, took up Regulated Verse with particular enthusiasm, tackling great technical difficulties while pursuing formal perfection. Esp. noteworthy is Du Fu's contribution to 7-character line form of Regulated Verse in his late years, after years of living through misery and warfare, and of wandering. His typical works in this period, chief among them "Autumn Sentiments," are distinguished by an imagistic density and a complexity of symbolism which fuse personal feelings with historical allusions, thus invoking wider cultural associations and a new aesthetic sensibility.

The hist. of Ch. p. is a story of constant revival and revision. During the Middle Tang (ca. 765–835), one of the most important forms of poetry is "New *Yuefu*," an imitation of the ancient *yuefu*, written in a simple style and with an eye to expressing social criticism. The most popular poet writing in this form is Bo Juyi (772–846), even though posterity has retained as his most famous poem the "Song of Everlasting Sorrow," a romantic ballad which narrates, without overt moralization, the love story of the Emperor Minghuang and his consort Yang Guifei. In the late Tang (ca. 835–907) poets reverted to the style of complexity and density inaugurated by Du Fu's 7-character line Regulated Verse. The highly allusive and sensuous imagery of Li Shangyin's (813?–58) love poetry, which fuses reality with imagination, stands out as an effective means of expressing degrees of emotional sensitivity not previously attained in the Ch. poetic trad.

Toward the end of the Tang, a new genre, *ci* (lyric), emerged in response to the popularity of foreign musical tunes newly imported from Central Asia. At first, *ci* was regarded as a continuation of *yuefu*, but it gradually became a special trad. of composition. In contrast to the titles of *yuefu* poems, which do not refer to fixed metric patterns, *ci* titles always point to particular *ci pai* (tune patterns) for which the poems are composed. These *ci pai*, totaling about 825 if the numerous variant forms are excluded, came to be viewed as definite verse patterns. Even today, poets still write to these tune patterns, though without knowing the original melodies. This unique practice of *ci* composition is called "filling in words" (*tian ci*). *Ci* poetry is characterized often by lines of unequal length, in sharp contrast to Regulated Verse. The difference of this genre lies in its retaining—as well as refining—the major aspects of tonal metrics advanced by Regulated Verse, while varying the line lengths. The result of this crucial change is a radically new way of scansion, thus allowing also for new flexibility of expressiveness. Among some of the distinctive qualities of *ci* are: its striking intensity of emotional content, esp. that of romantic love; its mood of melancholy; and its preference for refined and delicate images. Long before Tang poets began to view *ci* as a serious poetic genre, it already flourished as a "popular song form." Songs preserved in a ms. found in a cave in Dunhuang attest to this fact. "Popular" *ci* songs were vital to the devel. of the *ci* of the literati, and, in fact, the evolution of the *ci* genre may be seen as a hist. of the intermingling of the two styles.

Although authors such as Bo Juyi had already experimented with occasional *ci*, the late Tang poet Wen Tingyun (ca. 812–ca. 870) has been regarded as the pioneer poet of the genre. His style of refined subtlety and parataxis, obviously influenced by late Tang Regulated Verse, became typical of early *ci*. The only poet during this period to break away from the overwhelming influence of Wen was Wei Zhuang (ca. 836–910). Wei's poetic voice was deliberately more direct, and thus represented a style contrary to Wen's. A few decades later Li Yu (837–978), known as one of the greatest poets in traditional China, went a step further and synthesized these two stylistic modes. The last monarch of the Southern Tang (937–75) who became a political prisoner in the Song capital from 976 until his death, Li Yu produced *ci* poems that are intensely lyrical, viewing his own personal suffering in the light of the destiny of all mankind.

Ci, however, are generally associated with the Song dynasty (960–1279), for the genre reached the height of its literary status during this period. Liu Yong (978–1053), the poet-musician, changed the direction of *ci* by boldly mixing the "popular" song style with the literati style in such a manner that it was difficult for critics to place his work in a particular stylistic category. It was Liu Yong who first borrowed the longer *manci* mode from the "popular" song trad. and transformed it into a vehicle that allowed for more complex lyrical expression. During the early Song dynasty, only Su Shi's (1037–1101) achievement in extending the poetic scope of *ci* paralleled Liu Yong's formal contributions. In Su Shi's hands, *ci* finally entered the inner circle of Song dynasty poetics and became a genre through which a poet could express the full range of his ideas and feelings. It was under his influence that *ci* began to free itself from music and became primarily a literary creation. During the Southern Song (1127–1279), poets began to explore new metaphorical complexities that tended toward symbolism, as demonstrated by the numerous *yongwu ci* (*ci* on objects), where personal feelings are expressed through small natural objects. Jiang Kui (ca. 1155–ca. 1221), Wu Wenying (ca. 1200–60), Wang Yisun (ca. 1232–ca. 1291), Zhang Yan (1248–1320), and Zhou Mi (1232–98) were representative poets in this new mode. The rise of poetry clubs during this time also served as a stimulus to the popularity of *yongwu ci*, esp. because the *yongwu* mode in poetry had always been closely connected with social gatherings. Meanwhile, during the dynastic transition from the Song to the Yuan—in what appeared to be a period of personal and cultural crisis—the *yongwu ci*, which favored implicit voice and somewhat disparate images, eventually became the perfect symbolic and allegorical medium for poets wishing to express their unwavering loyalty to the Song court and their resentment toward the Mongols. Perhaps the best examples are the 37 poems in the series of "New Subjects for Lyric Songs" (*yuefu buti*) written by 14 Southern Song loyalist poets in 1279. These poems, through the use of symbolism invoked by such objects as lotus and cicada, are believed to be allegorically related to the desecration of Song imperial tombs in 1278 by a Tibetan lama who was acting on orders from the Mongols.

A striking exchange of generic roles was noticeable during the Song: while *ci* poetry became as perfect a form for pure lyricism as Regulated Verse had been in the Tang dynasty, *shi* poetry began to slowly venture out of the pure lyrical domain. Unlike *shi* poetry in the Tang, Song dynasty *shi* had a tendency to dwell on philosophical issues and intellectual arguments. Mei Yaochen (1002–60) coined the term *pingdan* to refer to the special quality of "plainness" and "calmness" that characterizes works of his own and his contemporaries. The serene and joyful tone of Song dynasty verse, as in Ouyang Xiu's (1007–72) 800 poems, may be directly influenced by the idea of self-cultivation central to Neo-Confucian thought. Generally, *shi* poetry of this period (e.g. Su Shi; Yang Wanli, 1124–1206) is distinguished by the use of plain lang. and simple description of the details of everyday life.

During the Yuan dynasty (1280–1368), a new song form called *sanqu* emerged to become the major form of lyricism. The *sangu* is characterized by lines of unequal length, a set of prescribed tones and tunes, and an extensive use of colloquial lang. The structure of a *sanqu* is more flexible than that of a *ci* because the poet, while composing a *sanqu* to a tune, is allowed to add "padding words" (*chenzi*) to considerably extend the length of a line. But other technical requirements of this genre are highly complex and varied, often further complicated by the use of the "suite" style (*taoshu*), a device which it shares with lyric drama (*qu*). A suite is a series of songs set to the same mode, arranged according to a special sequence prescribed by the mode. The "suite" style allows a poet to compose a string of arias on a particular theme which could form part of a lyric play. But the best known *sanqu* are short ones written in the form of a single stanza, like the much admired pieces by Ma Zhiyuan (1260?–1324?).

The *shi* poetry of the Yuan, the Ming (1368–1644), and the Qing (1644–1911) Dynasties has so far been largely ignored by modern scholarship, partly because of an inappropriate, though understandable, notion of generic evolution prevailing among Ch. scholars—that the Tang dynasty was the golden age of *shi*, the Song dynasty of *ci*, the Yuan of *qu* and drama, and the Ming and Qing of vernacular fiction. While such a scheme has the advantage of viewing the hist. of Ch. lit. as a sequence of genre innovations, with each newly vital genre naturally succeeding a former period's, it nevertheless seriously distorts the real nature of generic devel. in traditional China. For, in effect, genres such as *shi* and *ci*, once created, rarely became obsolete; they continued to be used and to develop.

One considerable accomplishment of the Yuan, Ming, and Qing periods was the increasing connection of the *shi* genre with painting and calligraphy. In the Yuan, many painter-poets began to inscribe poems to their paintings with the same brush, as the crucial final step toward completing a creative process. During the Ming and the Qing, we find the same practice continuing and growing, with an unusually high percentage of poets who were also painters and calligraphers (Shen Zhou, 1427; Tang Yin, 1470–1523; Wen Zhengming, 1470–1559; Wu Weiye, 1609–72; Zhu Da, 1626–ca. 1705). The painter-calligrapher-poet trad. is the culmination of an old ideal and occasional practice existing since the Tang: the Tang poet Wang Wei is said to have produced "poems which are like paintings, and paintings like poems". And the Song dynasty poet Su Shi was an accomplished painter and calligrapher.

Another phenomenon which distinguishes Ming and Qing poets from earlier authors was their enormously ardent concern for past models and for criticism. This tendency grows out of the basic Ch. belief that the past, having accumulated so much of the civilization's wisdom, should be regarded as an enduring authority from which individual creativity must necessarily draw inspiration. To the Ming poets, who saw themselves as restoring the glories of Ch. culture after the foreign rule of the Mongols, the question was: what literary models from the past should be used in order to renew the vitality of poetry in the present? The result was the emergence of an ever-increasing number of schools and a poetry that was repeatedly redefining itself along theoretical lines (though to a much lesser degree this tendency already existed during the Song dynasty). The various schools of Ming and Qing poetry were extremely diverse in their approaches, but they can be roughly grouped into two camps: (1) those who took the High Tang poets as models, and (2) those who preferred the style of Song poetry. This Tang-Song opposition obviously seems simplistic, esp. when applied to individual authors whose stylistic preferences changed from one period of their lives to another. But most poets, given their own temperament and literary associations, seemed to have regarded themselves, or were judged by others, as belonging to one of these two camps. Thus, the Former Seven and Latter Seven Masters during the 16th c. belonged to the Tang School; so did Chen Zilong (1608–47), Wu Weiye (1609–71), Wang Shizhen (1634–1711), and Shen Deqian (1673–1769). On the other hand, Qian Qianyi (1582–1664), Zha Shenxing (1650–1727), and Li E (1692–1752) were known for their promotion of "Song dynasty style" poetry. But individualist poets such as Yuan Hongdao (1568–1610) and Yuan Mei (1716–97) stood outside these two groupings, simply preaching the importance of self-expression. In general, for poets in this period poetry had become not just a form of expression but an object of speculation and contemplation. Poetry is judged not so much according to its content as according to its handling and effect.

The 17th c. saw a renaissance of *ci* poetry which was to last until the beginning of this century. This renaissance was due largely to the efforts of the late Ming poet Chen Zilong (1608–1647), who organized the "Yunjian School of *ci*" to call attention to the unfortunate "fall" of Ming *ci* from a golden age which he located in the Southern Tang. A slightly later poet, Zhu Yizun (1629–1709), advocated the importance of elegance in *ci* writing and modeled his own work after the polished and elegant style of the Southern Song. Chen Weisong (1626–82), however, promoted the Northern Song style. Throughout the Qing many schools of *ci* arose, all searching for particular modes as models for emulation and basis for devel. The constant competition among various schools eventually made *ci* poetry a subject of serious scholarly pursuit and theoretical debate—a devel. unprecedented in the hist. of *ci*. Aside from a few individualist poets such as Nalan Xingde (1655–85) and Xiang Hongzuo (1798–1835), *ci* poets in the Qing were primarily scholars. The one critical approach that is essential to these scholar-poets is allegoresis, reading *ci* as political allegories in the manner of the Han Confucian exegesis in the *Classic of Poetry*, though now with fresh urgency—a phenomenon which obviously reflects the wide consciousness of political pressure under the rule of the foreign-born Manchus, who were always quick to root out political subversion. Thereafter, by a process we have outlined above, allegorical reading became the basis for allegorical writing. While the Qing poets advocated the use of allegory in *ci*, they eschewed an over-explicit presentation. They esp. recommended Southern Song poets as models for imitation, since these earlier authors had, in their view, mastered the poetics of implicit, imagistic association in the "*ci* on objects," by at once creating the impression of distancing and guiding readers to their intended meaning. Judged by the standards of Western poetry, their allegorical devices may seem to be only pseudo-allegorical strategies. The images are not usually connected in a goal-oriented narrative progression, nor do they refer to some philosophical or religious truth. But they are nonetheless allegories—imagistic allegories that point to historical and political truths by means of the associative power of symbolism.

Varied and diversified as it is, the Ch. poetic trad. is characterized by certain recurrent traits: (1) the use of understated but powerful imagery, whose significance lies in the implicit meaning, (2) an emphasis on the harmony of man and nature, (3) the assumption that poetry is based on personal, daily experience, (4) the feeling that individual talent is inseparable from past models,

(5) an emphasis on the individual's "creative" expression, which is not to be confused with a cult of originality *per se,* and (6) the poet's faith in being recognized by posterity. By and large, Ch. poets hope to intervene meaningfully in the life of their times, and almost always nurture a sense of cultural responsibility for the future. But the concept of "the poet" as a specialized professional of verse was absent in traditional China, where every educated Ch. was expected to have mastered the art of poetic composition. In a general sense, every educated man was a "poet," though he might not be a distinguished one. For the Ch., writing poetry was a self-inspired, self-expressive activity, not a career closed to all but poetic geniuses.

ANTHOLOGIES: *The Jade Mountain,* tr. W. Bynner and K. Kiang (1929); *The Book of Songs* (1937; 1987 ed. contains forward by S. Owen), *Ch. Poems* (1946), both ed. and tr. A. Waley; *The Book of Odes,* tr. B. Karlgren (1950)—contains Ch. text and authoritative, literal tr. of *Shi Jing*; *Poems of the Late T'ang,* tr. A. Graham (1965); *Anthol. of Ch. Lit.,* ed. C. Birch, 2 v. (1965, 1972); *Anthol. of Ch. Verse,* tr. J. Frodsham and C. Hsi (1967); *Ch. Rhyme-Prose* (1971), *Columbia Book of Ch. P.* (1984), both ed. and tr. B. Watson; *Sunflower Splendor,* ed. W. Liu and I. Lo (1975); *Among the Flowers,* tr. L. Fusek (1982); *New Songs from a Jade Terrace,* tr. A. Birrel (1982); *Wen Xuan,* tr. D. Knechtges, v. 1 (1982), v. 2 (1987); *The Songs of the South,* tr. D. Hawkes, 2d ed. (1985)—valuable background information; *Columbia Book of Later Ch. P.,* tr. J. Chaves (1986); *Waiting for the Unicorn: Poems and Lyrics of China's Last Dynasty,* ed. I. Y. Lo and W. Schultz (1986).

HISTORY AND CRITICISM: *P. and Career of Li Po* (1950); J. Hightower, *Topics of Ch. Lit.,* rev. ed. (1953), *The Poetry of T'ao Ch'ien* (1970); W. Hung, *Tu Fu* (1952); G. W. Baxter, *Index to the Imperial Register of Tz'u Pros.,* rev. ed. (1956)—with bibl. note; A. Waley, Yüan Mei *(1956); J. J. Y. Liu,* The Art of Ch. P. *(1962),* Major Lyricists of the Northern Sung *(1974),* Ch. Theories of Lit. *(1975),* Lang.—Paradox—Poetics, *ed. R. J. Lynn (1988); F. Mote,* The Poet Kao Ch'i *(1962); B. Watson,* Early Ch. Lit. *(1962),* Ch. Lyricism *(1971); J. Diény,* Les Dix-neuf Poemes Anciens *(1963); K. Yoshikawa,* An Intro. to Sung Poetry, *tr. B. Watson (1967),* Five Hundred Years of C.P., 1150–1650 *tr. J. T. Wixted (1989), with W. S. Atwell's important "Afterword"; Y. Kao and T. Mei, "Syntax, Diction, and Imagery in T'ang Poetry,"* HJAS *31 (1970), "Meaning, Metaphor, and Allusion in T'ang Poetry,"* HJAS *38 (1978); W. Schlepp,* San-ch'u *(1970); H. Frankel, "Cl. Ch. [Versification]," in Wimsatt, and* The Flowering Plum and the Palace Lady *(1976);* Studies in Ch. Lit. Genres, *ed. C. Birch (1974); A. Cooper,* Li Po and Tu Fu *(1974); C. H. Wang,* The Bell and the Drum *(1974),* From Ritual to Allegory *(1988); J. Chaves,* Mei Yao-ch'en and the Devel. of Early Sung Poetry *(1976), "Moral Action in the Poetry of Wu Chia-chi (1618–84),"* HJAS *46 (1986), "The Yellow Mountain Poems of Ch'ien Ch'ien-i (1582–1664),"* HJAS *48 (1988); D. Holzman,* Poetry and Politics *(1976); D. Knechtges,* The Han Rhapsody *(1976); H. Stimson,* Fifty-five T'ang Poems *(1976); W. Yip,* Ch. P.: Major Modes and Genres *(1976); D. Bryant, "Selected Ming Poems,"* Renditions *8 (1977),* Lyric Poets of the Southern T'ang *(1982); H. C. Chang,* Ch. Lit., *v. 2,* Nature Poetry *(1977); F. Cheng,* L'Écriture poétique Chinoise *(1977; Eng. ed. 1982); S. Owen,* The Poetry of the Early T'ang *(1977),* The Great Age of Ch. P.: The High T'ang *(1981),* Traditional Ch. P. and Poetics *(1985), Remembrances: The Experience of the Past in Cl. Ch. Lit. (1986); S. Lin, The Transformation of the Ch. Lyrical Trad.* (1978); *Approach to Lit. from Confucius to Liang Ch'i-Ch'ao,* ed. A. Rickett (1978); K. S. Chang, *The Evolution of Ch. Tz'u Poetry* (1980), *Six Dynasties Poetry* (1986), "Symbolic and Allegorical Meanings in the *Yüeh-fu pu-t'i* Series," *HJAS* 46 (1986), "The Idea of the Mask in Wu Wei-yeh (1609–1671)," *HJAS* 48 (1988), *The Late-Ming Poet Ch'en Tzu-lung (1991); Ling. Analysis of Ch. P.,* spec. iss. of *JCL* 8 (1980)—8 articles on metrics, *The Late Ming Poet Ch'en Tzu-lung* (1991); P. Yu, *The Poetry of Wang Wei* (1980), *The Reading of Imagery in the Ch. Poetic Trad.* (1987); P. Kroll, *Meng Hao-Jan* (1981); A. Davis, *T'ao Yuan-ming,* 2 v. (1983); Liu Hsieh, *The Literary Mind and the Carving of Dragons,* tr. V. Shih, 2d ed. (1983); S. Leys, *La Forêt en feu* (1983; enl. Eng. ed., 1985)—good discussion of poetry and painting; R. Egan, *The Literary Works of Ou-Yang Hsiu* (1984); S. Chou, "Allusion and Periphrasis as Modes of Poetry in Tu Fu's 'Eight Laments,'" *HJAS* 45 (1985); C. Hartman, "Poetry," in Nienhauser et al.; *The Vitality of the Lyric Voice,* ed. S. Lin and S. Owen (1986)—contains Y. Kao's important article on Regulated Verse; G. Fong, *Wu Wenying and the Art of Southern Song Ci Poetry* (1987); L. Zhang, "The Letter or the Spirit: The *Song of Songs,* Allegoresis, and the *Book of Poetry,*" *CL* 39 (1987); R. Mather, *The Poet Shen Yüeh* (1988); D. Levy, *Ch. Narrative P.* (1988); M. Fuller, *The Road to East Slope* (1990); D. R. McCraw, *Ch. Lyricists of the 17th C.* (1990).

K.S.C.

II. MODERN. Ch. p. entered a new period in 1917. Hu Shi, who had published an article entitled "Suggestions for a Reform of Lit." earlier that year, returned from America in the summer and actively began writing new poetry according to the principles he set forth. Some of his colleagues at Beijing University, notably Liu Fu, Shen Yinmo, and Zhou Zuoren, joined in the effort. While they differed from one another in goals and styles, these young intellectuals shared one conviction: new poetry should be written freely in vernacular as opposed to cl. lang. In 1920, when Hu Shi published his first collection of poems, *Changshi ji* (Experiments), he claimed that they were "verse in vernacular lang."

During the next five years (1921–26), more than 30 books of vernacular Ch. p. appeared. Many young poets were either returned students or still studying abroad, either in Japan (Guo Moro), America (Kang Baiqing, Xu Dishan, Xie

Bingxin, Wen Yido, Zhu Xiang), or Europe (Liang Zongdai, Xu Zhimo, Li Jinfa, Wang Duqing, Dai Wangshu), while some distinguished literati specializing in cl. scholarship, such as Yu Pingbo and Zhu Ziqing, also made remarkable contributions. A critic of the *Experiments* predicted that poetry written in vernacular lang. would corrupt itself presently, but few poets writing new poetry chose cl. lang. as their medium. The new poetry appeared to be emancipated completely from traditional prosody, and many formal, syntactic, and rhetorical features therein remind one of Western poetry in the hands of Goethe, Wordsworth, or Whitman. At times, even traces of such exotic forms as the Sanskrit gatha, Gr. epigram, Japanese haiku, and (esp.) the prose poems of Tagore were detectable. The most serious attempts at a new prosody were made by Wen Yido, Xu Zhimo, and Zhu Xiang, principally on the model of Eng. Victorian verse.

Major themes which concerned the poets of the early 1920s were conventionally centered on love and nature. However, some poets did treat such relatively new topics as revolt, mysticism, legends, exoticism, hallucination, and children. They proved that a different form could give new life to an old poetry, in a new cadence effective for expressing the moods of a nation continually caught up in political and cultural crises. Poets and writers organized clubs to promote ideas in response to social events. Led by Guo Moro, a group of students formed a society called "Creation" (1921) and published several magazines. Others would associate themselves with the editorial board of a journal or a literary supplement in a newspaper. A typical journal was the *Xinyue* (Crescent, 1928), initially edited by Wen Yido and Xu Zhimo, which published political comments, stories, book reviews, and lit. crit. as well as poems.

New Ch. p. experienced steady devel. over the next ten years (1927–37), until the war broke out. Amid the problems created internally by rival military forces and externally by Japanese aggression, China witnessed strong poetic creativity. The most phenomenal figure of this period was Xu Zhimo. Back from England in 1922, Xu was very active in the promotion of romanticism not only in his poetry but also in his style of living. His audacious expressions of idealism, sympathy for the poor, and contempt for hypocrisy won him loud applause across the land. Academic critics, on the other hand, praised him for his tireless pursuit of creative lang., original metaphor and imagery, and effective stanza forms. When he died in an airplane crash in 1931, he left the readers of Ch. p. an indelible image of the passionate, rebellious romantic poet. Western influence on Ch. lit. was conspicuous during this period. In poetry, there was Ger. influence on Feng Zhi; Fr. on Liang Zongdai, Li Jinfa, and Dai Wangshu; and Eng. on Xu Zhimo, Bian Zhilin, and Sun Dayu. These poets also wrote some of the most enduring, thoughtful poems of 20th-c. China. It was during the 1930s, too, that some poets began practicing a kind of free verse in excessively sweeping style, politically oriented, and often on grandiose subjects in a resounding mixture of extollment and lamentation. Ai Qing and Zang Kejia represented this tendency. Though their legitimate predecessors could include Guo Moro, who was sometimes described as "Whitmanian," they probably owed their spirited mannerism more to Yesnin and Majakovskij.

One of the most important books of poetry published before the war was *Hanyuan ji* (Han Garden, 1936), a collection of lyrical poems by Li Guangtian, He Qifang, and Bian Zhilin. This book, along with Hu Shi's *Experiments*, Guo Moro's *Nushen* (Goddess, 1921), Xu Zhimo's *Feilengcui zhi yi ye* (A Night in Florence, 1927), Wen Yido's *Si shui* (Dead Water, 1928), and Dai Wangshu's *Wo de jiyi* (My Memories, 1929), established the major types of new Ch. p. Together they formed the essence of a new trad. to be elaborated over the next two decades; they inspired the modernist movement on Taiwan during 1958–68 and set a model for young poets to restart their experimental poetry in China after 1978. These books were the six most influential sources of new Ch. p., published before the Second World War. As to the reason why Li, He, and Bian should redirect their literary styles and themes thereafter, the cause was obviously political ideology, which, though historically significant, perhaps, proved fatal to lyricism.

With the outbreak of war in July 1937 and the advance of Japanese troops across eastern China, a consensus arose among the poets to serve their country by writing propaganda into their poetry. The disputes over what Lu Xun advocated as the "Proletarian Lit. of a National Revolutionary War" and the so-called "Lit. of the United Front in Resistance to the Japanese Aggression" (1936) led to an extravagant emphasis on the political purposes of poetry at the expense of artistic quality. Instantly a great number of magazines and pamphlets were born which published pieces on the consequences of the war—separation, fear, blood, hunger, death—described in vivid emotional tones charged with sorrow and anger. These poems were called *langsong shi* (verses for oral delivery), which obviously required immediate responses from the audience in the marketplaces, temple squares, and military campgrounds where they were delivered to ensure success. Considering the fact that the majority of people at that time were illiterate, it would be rash to underestimate the contribution *langsong shi* made toward mobilizing the people against the enemy. Their simple, crude, and sentimental qualities made these verses useful on many occasions in that era and, for the same reason, made them unmemorable today.

Under such circumstances, most poets in the early 1940s neglected artistic pursuit, which was once their urgent concern during the decade

1927–37. Neither form nor thematic content was a problem any more. Then, after Mao Zedong unfolded his mandate through the "Talks at the Yan'an Forum on Lit. and the Arts" (1942), even some distinguished poets, who had been devoted to the artistic perfection of their work, changed their attitude to conform to the prescribed topics. Fortunately, there were two groups of poets who seemed able to resist the fashion: the young talents in colleges (esp. the Southwestern Associate University in Kunming), such as Mu Dan and Zheng Min; and the poets in Japanese-occupied regions, such as Feiming, Dai Wangshu, and Xin Di. Relatively unaffected by ideological pressures, they continued to merge traditional lyricism and contemporary sensibility. Enriched by their reading of Western lit., they created a style that belonged unmistakably to the 1940s, a style which can be said to identify distinctively China's "premodern" poetry.

With the founding of the People's Republic of China in 1949, many intellectuals fled the Communists to Taiwan. While the Nationalist government in Taipei, like its antagonist in Beijing, ceaselessly encouraged the writing of occasional verses for political use—a strained continuation of the partisan interference with art—the poets on Taiwan seemed freer in their literary experiments than their peers across the straits. A large number of little magazines appeared on Taiwan beginning in the early 1950s. In 1956 China launched the authoritative *Shi Kan*, a poetry journal sanctioned by the Party and graced in its inaugural issue by a group of Mao's poems in classical style. In that year, too, a "Modernist School" was formed on Taiwan without political influence from anywhere. Ji Xian, an ardent poet and editor of the magazine *Xiandai shi* (Modern Poetry), collected more than 100 poets, both Taiwanese and mainlanders, to sign a manifesto which stressed that modern Ch. p. would have to be a poetry "horizontally transplanted" from Europe but not "vertically inherited" from classical China. Amid the lasting debates that ensued, many young men and women published excellent works which not only defied political ideologies current in the civil war but also initiated a maturing modern poetry to ratify the "premodern" style of a decade earlier as the mainstream of 20th-c. Ch. lit. The controversy over "transplanting" or "inheriting" was resolved in the late 1960s as the poets came to believe that what they wrote was both *modern* and *Chinese.*

Since 1949, new poetry in China has followed a double-tracked course. Official journals publish discreet pieces which proffer political guidance and rally around the Party, while some uncomfortable voices have formed, during the last quarter of the 20th-c., a new Ch. p., sometimes called "menglong shi" (poetry in veils). The "menglong shi," which claims to have originated in the early 1970s, became known to the world only after the Cultural Revolution (1966–76), with the publication of an underground magazine *Jintian* (1978–81). The experimental nature of this poetry, which in its surrealistic and quasi-existentialist tendencies resembles the Taiwanese poetry written during 1958–68, has won many readers' confidence in the creativity of China's new literary generation. Ambiguity is the common quality of poetry in times of turmoil, as Ch. history attests, when it seeks to grow independently of political control. China is in the process of rapid social change, which poetry will certainly reflect sensitively and comment on thoughtfully, in the way it always has over the last three millennia.

ANTHOLOGIES: *Zhong-guo xin wen-xue da-xi*, v. 8, ed. Zhu Ziqing (1935); *Mod. Ch. P.*, ed. and tr. H. Acton and S. H. Chen (1936); *Contemp. Ch. P.*, ed. R. Payne (1947); *La poesie chinoise contemporaine*, ed. and tr. P. Guillermaz (1962); *20th-C. Ch. P.*, ed. and tr. K. Y. Hsu (1963); *Xien-dai zhong-guo shi xuan*, ed. M. M. Y. Fung et al. (1974); *An Anthol. of Contemp. Ch. Lit.*, v. 1, ed. P. Y. Chi et al. (1975); *Lit. of the People's Republic of China*, ed. K. Y. Hsu (1980); *Columbia Book of Later Ch. P.*, tr. J. Chaves (1986); *The Isle Full of Noises*, ed. and tr. D. Cheung (1987); *Xien-dai zhong-guo shi xuan*, ed. Y. Mu and Z. Shusen (1989).

HISTORY AND CRITICISM: K. Y. Hsu, "The Life and Poetry of Wen I-to," *HJAS* 21 (1958); C. Birch, "Eng. and Ch. Meters in Hsu Chih-mo's Poetry," *Asia Major* 7 (1959); T. T. Chow, *The May Fourth Movement* (1960); S. H. Chen, "Metaphor and the Conscious in Ch. P. under Communism," *ChinaQ* 13 (1963); M. Stolzova, "The Foundation of Mod. Ch. Poetics," *ArOr* 36 (1968); B. S. McDougall, *Paths in Dreams* (1976); D. Cheung, *Feng Chih* (1979); *Trees on the Mountain*, ed. S. C. Soong and J. Minford (1984); M. Yeh, *Mod. Ch. P.: Theory and Practice Since 1917* (1991). C.H.W.

COLOMBIAN POETRY. See SPANISH AMERICAN POETRY.

CORNISH POETRY. The C. lang., now extinct, belonged to the Brythonic or "P"-Celtic group, but had closer affinities with Breton than with Welsh. It died out in the 18th c. Apart from one long narrative poem and five plays, all on religious topics, the literary remains are meager in the extreme. Although Cornwall must have supplied to medieval romance some of the "Matter of Britain," in the extant C. lit. this rich vein is left unexploited. The earliest verse to survive is a fragment of 41 lines on a charter dated 1340, but the poem may have been copied on it some 60 years later and seems to be part of a lost play. In it a speaker gives advice on marriage (drawn from C. folklore) to a lady. The rhyme scheme is *aabccb*, with lines varying from 4 to 9 syllables. *Pascon agan Arluth* (The Passion of our Lord) is a narrative poem of 259 octaves of 7-syllable trochaic lines, the lines rhyming alternately. The earliest ms. is mid 15th c. The theme is the fasting and temptation of Christ, followed by the story of Holy Week.

The main interest of C. p. lies in the plays. These were composed by men of learning but for a popular audience and were performed in open-air theaters, the "plenys-an-gwary," spaces enclosed by circular banks of earth now known as "rounds," some of which can still be seen, e.g. at St. Just and Perranzabuloe. Three of the plays, called the *Ordinalia,* form a sequence. These are the *Origo mundi* (2846 lines), based on Old Testament history and some incongruent legendary material, the *Passio domini* (3242 lines), recounting the life and death of Christ, and the *Resurrectio domini* (2646 lines), which has a greater accretion of legend, incl. saints' lives and the death of Pilate. The rhythm is basically trochaic but stress regularity is not meticulously observed. Rhymes are often stricter to the eye than to the ear, a sure sign of learned composition. Full lines of 8 or 7 syllables can rhyme alternately, as can shorter lines or half-lines of 4 syllables, and lines of varying or equal length within the same sequence or "stanza" can conform to *aabccb* or *aabaab* rhyme schemes. More intricate patterns also occur, but otherwise such metrical features as alliteration and internal rhyme are random and not woven into a strict pattern as in Welsh *cynghanedd.*

Beunans Meriasek (The Life of St. Meriasek, 4568 lines), was discovered by Stokes in a ms. written in 1504. This play has linguistic forms which indicate a later period than the *Ordinalia,* but metrically it is similar. Local references associate it with the cult of Meriasek at Camborne, a 7th-c. saint whose legendary life forms the topic of the play. The latest of the C. plays, at least in its extant form, is *Gwreans an Bys* (The Creation of the World, 2548 lines); the earliest ms. is dated 1611. The play borrows much from *Origo mundi* but has features of its own. Lucifer and his demons revert to Eng. except when they are on their good behavior—then they speak C. The most noticeable metrical innovation is a more frequent disregard of syllable-counting. In all the plays there are passages of touching poignancy and considerable literary merit, but the quality is not sustained.

The few remaining scraps of late C. verse (mostly 17th-c.) indicate a falling away from the more strictly syllabic verse patterns of medieval C. It is uncertain whether this was merely a phase of the decay of the lang. or an increased awareness of stress as a metrical principle. A few enthusiasts in our own day have learned C., and poems in this long-neglected Celtic tongue have been written and published in recent years. A "C. Song Movement" which demanded of its participants that they should compose their own texts as well as sing traditional ones arose in the 1970s. Among the more prominent members were Richard Gendall and Anthony Snell. Other recent C. poets of note incl. the meditative D. Wall, the sensitive Brian Webb, and the ever-resourceful Tim Saunders.—*The Ancient C. Drama,* ed. and tr. E. Norris, 2 v. (1859, rpt. 1963); "Pascon agan Arluth: The Play of the Sacrament," *TPS* (1860–61), "*Gwreans an Bys,*" *TPS* (1864), "*Beunans Meriasek*" (1872; tr. M. Harris, 1977), all ed. W. Stokes, *TPS* (1860–61, 1864, 1872); H. Jenner, "The Hist. and Lit. of the Ancient C. Lang.," *Jour. of the Brit. Archaeological Assoc.* 33 (1877), *Handbook of the C. Lang.* (1904); D. C. Fowler, "The Date of the C. *Ordinalia,*" *MS* 23 (1961); R. Longsworth, *The C.* Ordinalia: *Religion and Dramaturgy* (1967); P. B. Ellis, *The C. Lang. and its Lit.* (1974); J. A. Bakere, *The C.* Ordinalia*: A Crit. Study* (1980); *The Creation of the World,* ed. and tr. P. Neuss (1983). D.M.L.; J.E.C.W.

CROATIAN POETRY. See YUGOSLAV POETRY.

CUBAN POETRY. See SPANISH AMERICAN POETRY.

CZECH POETRY. The earliest extant verse in the C. vernacular is a hymn dating from the late 12th or early 13th c. addressed to the patron saint of Bohemia, Václav ("Good King Wenceslaus"). But the 14th c. saw a great flowering of C. p., epic, lyric, and dramatic. Outstanding are an epic about Alexander of Macedon and numerous versified saints' lives, in particular a *Life* of St. Catherine of Alexandria noted for the brilliance of its imagery. These works all had Med. Lat. prototypes, but were often original in details. The lyric also came to Bohemia, chiefly from France and Italy; worthy of note is a C. variant of the Prov. *aubade.* An indigenous satiric poetry also flourished in the 14th c.; perhaps the most original example is a burlesque disputation, *Podkoní a žák* (The Groom and the Student), wherein each antagonist maintains that his life is the better. Prosodically, much of 14th-c. C. verse employs trochaic octosyllable in couplets, though the syllable count varies at times.

The Hussite period of the early 15th c. severely curtailed poetic expression, though it did produce interesting polemic poetry. Humanism brought new forms of Lat. verse, but poetic expression in the vernacular lagged behind, though the C. humanists made their native prose one of the most expressive of the written langs. of Europe. The Counter-Reformation, however, which followed the loss of C. independence in 1620, inspired the cultivation of a contemplative religious poetry of hymns and prayers remarkable for its ornate imagery and wordplay. The latter 17th and early 18th cs. witnessed the virtual death of C. national lit.; not until the latter half of the 18th c. were systematic attempts begun to revive C. as a literary lang. This movement was nationalistic and patriotic; rejecting the Jesuit baroque heritage, it reached back to the C. Protestant Humanist trad. of the 16th c. The result was that written C. as revived was somewhat archaic, and indeed has remained so until today. But conversely this unbroken bond with an ancient literary trad. has given modern C. a decided advantage over many other Central and East European literary langs. In the early 19th c., Cl. influences were strong, and a period of vacillation between quantitative and accentual systems of versification ensued. Eventually the accentually based verse triumphed, but syllable length continued to play a prosodic role.

Didactic, biblical, laudatory, and idyllic verse predominated at the end of the 18th c. in the work of A. J. Puchmajer (1769–1820). The beginning of the 19th c. brought preromanticism and a poetry dedicated to the national patriotic cause. The kinship of Czechs with the other Slavic peoples was stressed. The Slovak Ján Kollár (1793–1852), who wrote in C., produced a collection of sonnets, *Slávy dcera* (The Daughter of Sláva, 1824 and 1832), a grandiose and sometimes moving attempt to construct a Slavic mythology and foretell a happier future for the Slavic peoples. F. L. Čelakovský (1799–1852) took inspiration from Slavic folksongs for his *Ohlasy* (Echoes) of Rus. and C. folksongs (1829 and 1839, respectively).

Romanticism arrived full-blown with K. H. Mácha (1810–36), probably, in spite of his early death, the greatest C. poet. His solitary masterpiece, the narrative poem *Máj* (May), written in 1836, is Byronic in subject but remarkable for the saturated intensity of its imagery, portraying the poet's favorite romantic antitheses of youth and age, love and death. May is the time of youth and love:

> It was late evening, the first of May—
> Evening May—the time of love.
> The voice of the turtle-dove called to
> love
> Where the pine grove wafted its scent.

These are the best known lines in all of C. p. But the time of childhood innocence is fleeting:

> The fury of the times bore that season
> far away,
> Far off his dream. . . .
> The fair childhood age of the dead.

Mácha introduced iambic verse to C.: before him, modern C. verse had been exclusively trochaic (even Kollár's sonnets were in trochees), because C. has a fixed weak stress on the first syllable of each word, so that lines normally open with a stress; occasional iambic lines were considered trochaic with anacrusis. Mácha varied the treatment of the first foot of the line and, emphasizing the iambic character of the other feet, thus shaped a true iambic verse. More conservative than Mácha was his contemporary K. J. Erben (1811–70), who created the C. romantic ballad, inspired by the popular ballad of folk poetry.

The failure of the Revolution of 1848 brought an end to the independence movement and to the first wave of romanticism. Not until the 1860s did a strong new romantic movement emerge. Here once again the national cause was dominant, but now found more practical expression through the creation of popular institutions, incl. a national theater. Writers were concerned with social problems—democracy, the emancipation of women, and the correction of economic injustice, as well as national liberation. The leading poet of the period was Jan Neruda (1834–91), who strove to develop national consciousness, at times indulging in sharply ironic criticism of his too-contented countrymen. During the 1870s and '80s the nationalist tendency continued to dominate, notably in the work of Svatopluk Čech (1846–1908), a follower of the Pan-Slavist poet Kollár. Čech's style, often bombastic, at times attained real rhetorical power. In his lyrics he dealt with the political misfortunes of his people and, like Neruda, was capable of sarcasm at the national complacency.

The technical side of C. verse had suffered during this era, but the 1870s saw it rise to a new brilliance in the work of the Parnassian poet Jaroslav Vrchlický (pseudonym of Emil Frída, 1853–1912). A superb technician, Vrchlický introduced many new poetic themes and forms from abroad; in this he and his followers opposed the more nationally minded poets of the time. Vrchlický even rejected the traditionally canonical use of folk motifs and forms in C. higher poetry. He wrote voluminously, and translated from most of the European as well as the Cl. langs.; his total production exceeds 100 volumes, incl. much narrative and dramatic as well as lyric verse. A follower of Victor Hugo's evolutionary optimism, he was more limited in ideas than in form. Tending towards aestheticism and the cult of Cl. antiquity, he failed, however, to turn the current of C. p. permanently in either direction.

Vrchlický was followed by J. S. Machar (1864–1942), who sought to create a great poetic panorama of world history; like Nietzsche, he believed that history follows a spiral movement, alternately rising and falling. Machar's disciple Petr Bezruč (pseudonym of Vladimír Vašek, 1867–1958) proclaimed the sufferings of his own people, the Silesian miners; like Walt Whitman, he narrates his songs in a collective voice.

Contemporary with these "realists" were the C. symbolist poets, influenced by Fr. and Belgian symbolism and by Whitman. The greatest of these was Otokar Březina (pseudonym of V. I. Jebavý, 1868–1929), who wrote rhapsodic verse celebrating the mystic union of all people with each other and with the cosmos. Themes of decadence appear in the work of such poets as Jiří Karásek ze Lvovic (1871–1951) and Karel Hlaváček (1874–98). Viktor Dyk (1877–1931) wrote sarcastic epigrams against superficial C. patriotism and brought the C. ballad to a pinnacle in sophisticated irony. The C. symbolists, particularly Březina and Antonín Sova (1864–1928), did much to strengthen the musical aspect of C. verse and to cultivate an impressionistic visual imagery.

The achievement of national independence in 1918 was followed by a period of intense creativity. The early 1920s brought a wave of so-called proletarian poetry, expressing a warm if somewhat naive sympathy for the Soviet experiment. The leading poet of this trend was Jiří Wolker (1900–24). The late 1920s saw a sudden and violent shift to "poetism," a school of "pure poetry" which had its roots in dada, futurism, and vitalism. The poets sought to create a poetry of the joy of living, of urban life and technology, a poetry inspired by such peripheral arts as film, the circus, and the musical revue. Leading "poetists" were Vítězslav Nezval (1900–58) and Jaroslav Seifert (1901–86). But the early 1930s saw the collapse of poetism as a movement: Nezval went over to surrealism, while Seifert turned to a more personal poetry of love and sensual imagery. The interwar period also saw the cultivation of a spiritual and meditative poetry in the work of Josef Hora (1891–1945). But probably the greatest poet of this period is František Halas (1901–49), a complex writer obsessed by themes of age, death, and decay. Most of these poets were leftists in politics, but their poetry remained individualist.

World War II and the subsequent Communist coup destroyed the older poetic trad. In the spring of 1956, demands for greater freedom began to be heard, and Seifert and František Hrubín (1910–71) sharply criticized the official restrictions placed on lit. The principal poet of the 1960s was Vladimír Holan (1905–80), who published a flood of meditative, spiritualist verse, presumably written in the earlier postwar years. Seifert too found his voice again in this period; and his long and varied career was finally crowned, in 1984, by the award of the Nobel Prize for Lit., the first ever given to a C. writer.

The invasion of Czechoslovakia in 1968 by the Soviet Union and its Warsaw Pact allies dealt a new blow to C. lit and culture, a blow from which they have not yet recovered. The older generation of poets, born in the decade 1900–1910, have all died, but it is difficult to point to anyone of the first rank who has taken their place; one reason must undoubtedly be the fact that the older poets, such as Halas and Seifert, have cast a long shadow. To this we must add the fact that poetry no longer enjoys the predominance that it traditionally had in C. lit. Before World War II, poetry had always been the dominant form of C. letters; the poetic culture attained particularly high levels under symbolism, and again in the 1920s and '30s, in spite of the pervasiveness of nationalist and didactic trends and the weakness of aestheticist, Parnassian, and Classicist tendencies in modern C. lit. The native folk lyric has had a strong influence in many periods, as have the folk epics of other Slavic peoples, e.g. the Russians and Serbs. The lyric has had a stronger trad. than the epic; perhaps the lack of a native folk epos is to blame here. But the literary ballad, a mixed epic-lyric form influenced by the C. folk ballad, has been important. Dramatic poetry is on the whole weak, though there are many plays in verse. In prosodic form, binary meters are virtually exclusive in C. verse, since the lang. has a tendency to accent every odd syllable. Mixed trochaic-dactylic forms based on Cl. or native folk models are common, however, particularly under romanticism.

ANTHOLOGIES: *Česká lyra* (1911), *Česká epika* (1921), both ed. F. S. Procházka; *Mod. C. P.*, ed. P. Selver (1920); *Anthologie de la poésie tchèque*, ed. H. Jelínek (1930); *Lyrika českého obrození*, ed. V. Jirát (1940); *Mod. C. P.*, ed. E. Osers and J. K. Montgomery (1945); *Česká poesie*, pub. by Československý spisovatel (1951); *Nová česká poesie*, pub. by Československý spisovatel (1955); *The Linden Tree*, ed. M. Otruba and Z. Pešat (1963); *C. P.*, ed. A. French (1973).

HISTORY AND CRITICISM: J. Jakubec and A. Novák, *Gesch. der tschechischen Lit.* (1907); H. Jelínek, *Hist. de la littérature tchèque*, 3 v. (1930–35); J. and A. Novák, *Přehledné dějiny literatury české* (1936–39)—the most thorough survey, abridged and supplemented as *Stručné dějiny literatury české* (1946); J. Mukařovský, *Kapitoly z české poetiky*, 3 v. (1948); *Dějiny české literatury*, ed. J. Mukařovský et al., 3 v. (1959–61); J. Hrabák, *Studie o českém verši* (1959); R. Wellek, *Essays in C. Lit.* (1963); A. French, *The Poets of Prague* (1969) —poetry of the 1920s and '30s; R. Jakobson, "O Češskom stixe" and "Old C. Verse" in Jakobson, v. 5, 6; A. Novák, *C. Lit.*, rev. W. E. Harkins, 2d ed. (1986). W.E.H.

D

DALMATIAN POTRY. See YUGOSLAV POETRY.

DANISH POETRY. Rune inscriptions evidence the existence of a lost heroic poetry in Denmark, known only from Saxo Grammaticus' Lat. prose and hexameter rendering in *Gesta Danorum* (ca. 1200). *The Lay of Bjarke (Bjarkamál)*—whose heroes also appear in the Anglo-Saxon poems *Widsith* and *Beowulf*—and *The Lay of Ingjald* celebrate courage and loyalty, reflecting an aristocratic ethos that epitomizes the ideals of the Viking age.

During the Middle Ages (1100–1500), D. p. follows the European models of courtly and sacred poetry. In the *Mariaviser* (Songs to Mary) by Per Räff Lille (ca. 1450–1500), troubadour influences blend with imagery from The Song of Songs. The anonymous *Den danske Rimkrønike* (The D. Rhymed Chronicle), a hist. of the D. kings, is an important work in *knittelvers.* The dominant genre of the Middle Ages, however, is the folk ballad, which reached Denmark from France in the early 12th c. In the 16th c., poetry in the vernacular was still medieval in spirit and form, notably subject to a growing Ger. influence in the wake of the Lutheran Reformation.

In the 17th c., as the Ren. reached Denmark, efforts were made to create a national D. p. on Cl. models. Anders Arrebo (1587–1637) produced a religious epic, *Hexaëmeron* (ca. 1622; pub. 1661), describing the six days of Creation. Based on Du Bartas' *La Semaine,* it is composed partly in twice-rhymed hexameter, partly in alexandrines. The artificiality of the poem's Cl.-mythological diction is offset by descriptive details from Scandinavian nature and folk life. Following Martin Opitz' *Das Buch der Deutschen Poeterey* (A Book of Ger. Poetics, 1624), Hans Mikkelsen Ravn (1610–63) in 1649 published a manual of prosody with illustrations, making available to future poets a varied formal repertoire. Anders Bording (1619–77) is noted for his anacreontic verse, but he also single-handedly published a rhymed monthly newspaper, *Den Danske Mercurius* (The D. Mercury, 1666–77), composed in stately alexandrines. Thomas Kingo (1634–1703), a much greater poet, was able to fully exploit the new formal variety. His principal achievement is his two volumes of church hymns, still sung today, *Aandelige Siunge-Koor* (Spiritual Choirs, 1674–81). With their thematic counterpoints, sensuous imagery, and often high-strung metaphors, Kingo's hymns are unmistakably baroque in style, the highlights being his Easter hymns.

In the early 18th c., Fr. neoclassicism entered D. lit., mainly due to the activity of the Dano-Norwegian Ludvig Holberg (1684–1754). Best known for his bourgeois prose comedies, Holberg in his verse mock-epic *Peder Paars* (1719–20), influenced by Boileau's *Le Lutrin* and Cervantes' *Don Quixote,* showed himself a brilliant satirist. The rationalism of Holberg, and of the period, is counterbalanced, however, by a sentimental undercurrent, represented by Ambrosius Stub (1705–58) and Hans Adolf Brorson (1694–1764). Stub practiced a wide variety of genres, from religious lyrics to drinking songs. His concise, graceful form and light, melodious rhythms are influenced by the It. operatic aria, and his delicately picturesque style reveals rococo features. Many of the hymns of Brorson, a religious pietist, are also composed in complex meters derived from the elegant rococo aria, with its dialogue and echo effects.

D. neoclassicism was continued by a group of Norwegian authors living in Copenhagen, members of *Det norske Selskab* (The Norwegian Society), while Johannes Ewald (1743–81), a preromantic deeply influenced by the Ger. poet F. G. Klopstock, championed the claims of subjectivity. Ewald's mythological dramas on ON themes are largely forgotten, but his pietistically inspired lyric verse is very much alive. Like Klopstock, he excelled in the religious ode, exemplified by *Rungsteds Lyksaligheder* (The Joys of Rungsted, 1773), where nature description is a vehicle for the glorification of God. Ewald's pre-eminence is largely due to his ability to reconcile contraries. Extremely sensitive, acutely aware of himself as a poetic genius, and preoccupied with his own subjective experience, he possessed an admirable artistic discipline which enabled him to produce poems of great formal beauty. The only noteworthy poet of the last 20 years of the century was Jens Baggesen (1764–1826), a mercurial spirit who alternated between Cl. and romantic sensibility in accordance with the tenor of his personal experience.

The breakthrough of romanticism in D. p. was the achievement of Adam Oehlenschläger (1779–1850), whose first collection, *Digte* (Poems, 1803), was inspired by the aesthetics of the Jena school of Schelling and the Schlegels as mediated by the Copenhagen lectures of Henrich Steffens (1802). These poems signified a fierce rejection of the rationalist spirit of the 18th c., together with a rediscovery of Nordic hist. and mythology and a glorification of the creative genius who alone is capable of a unified view of nature and hist. The volume concludes with the Shakespeare-inspired *Sanct Hansaften-Spil* (Midsummer Eve Play), a lyrical comedy in *knittelvers* which satirizes the rationalist view of lit. Oehlenschläger increased his range in *Poetiske Skrifter* (Poetic Writings, 1805), which contained prose and poetry, narrative cycles, drama, lyric, and ballads and romances in varying meters. The high point of the collection is *Aladdin* (Eng. tr. 1968), a philosophical fairy-tale play in blank verse which celebrates the power of genius over chaos and evil. After 1806, Oehlenschläger's subjectivism is tempered by a growing influence from Goethe's and Schiller's objective poetry and from the Heidelberg romantic school, re-orienting his work—as well as D. lit. in general—toward national and patriotic themes. *Nordiske Digte* (Nordic Poems, 1807) included several dramas based on ON figures and themes. Worthy of mention is *Hakon Jarl*, a blank-verse tragedy modeled on Schiller's *Wallenstein.* The narrative cycle *Helge* (1814), with its impressive array of metrical forms and styles marking the subtle shifts of moods, rises to Sophoclean heights in the concluding dramatic episode, which gives a mythic perspective to the entire poem. More consistently national in inspiration was the work of another romantic, N. F. S. Grundtvig (1783–1872), who, while more of a cultural leader than a poet, created an enduring literary monument in his hymns. With their union of humanism and Christianity and their pervasive imagery from D. landscape and Nordic mythology, Grundtvig's hymns represent a unique poetic achievement.

Around 1830, D. p. moved toward greater realism and psychological diversity, its focus shifting from an idealized past to a more complex present. Johan Ludvig Heiberg (1791–1860), the theorist of *romantisme*, as this movement has been called, managed to shuttle elegantly between actuality and the dream world in his romantic plays, which dispelled the taste for Oehlenschläger's tragedies. His "apocalyptic comedy" *En Sjæl efter Døden* (A Soul After Death, 1841) is a brilliant satire of bourgeois philistinism. Christian Winther (1796–1876) typically blends lyric and narrative elements in the idyll, as in *Træsnitt* (Woodcuts, 1828), which images village life. Winther's formal virtuosity is demonstrated in the romance *Hjortens Flugt* (The Flight of the Hart, 1855), set in medieval times and employing a modified Nibelungenstrophe. The cycle of love poems *Til Een* (To Someone; 1843, 1849), in which Eros is worshiped as a divine force, is notable for its poignant lyricism. The brief lyrics of the Heine-inspired *Erotiske Situationer* (Erotic Situations, 1838) by Emil Aarestrup (1806–56), with their picturesque detail, psychological complexity, and emotional dissonance, express a distinctly modern sensibility—sophisticated and sensual—and represent a high point in D. love poetry. While the early work of Frederik Paludan-Müller (1809–76)—such as the Byron-inspired lyric-narrative poem *Dandserinden* (The Danseuse, 1833) with its felicitous ottava rima and playful irony—is fraught with aestheticism, *Adam Homo* (1841–48; Eng. tr. 1980), a three-volume novel in verse, embodies a rigorous ethical philosophy. Through its portrait of a gifted, opportunistic anti-hero who pays for worldly success with the loss of his soul, the book presents a satirical picture of contemp. D. culture. The ending, with Adam's post-mortem salvation through the Christian love of the woman he abandoned, recalls the *Divine Comedy* and *Faust.*

After naturalism was introduced by the critic Georg Brandes (1842–1927) around 1870, writers turned their attention to political, social, and sexual problems—fitter subjects for prose than poetry. Yet Brandes was important to both Jens Peter Jacobsen (1847–85) and Holger Drachmann (1846–1908), each with a distinctive profile as a poet. The sparse but first-rate lyrical production of Jacobsen, known chiefly as a novelist, was published posthumously as *Digte og Udkast* (Poems and Sketches) in 1886. Unique are his "arabesques," capriciously winding free-verse monologues—the first modernist poetry in Denmark—whose intellectual probing is veiled in a colorful ornamental lang. and evocative moods influenced by Edgar Allan Poe. The youthful *Digte* (Poems, 1872) of Drachmann more directly echoed the radical ideas of Brandes, as in the poem "Engelske Socialister" (Eng. Socialists). But soon Drachmann abandoned ideology for personal lyricism. In *Sange ved Havet* (Songs by the Sea, 1877), his best collection, the sea, whose changing moods he evokes with deep empathy, is perceived as an image of his own protean spirit. With *Sangenes Bog* (Book of Songs, 1889) radicalism reappeared, though now tempered by an awareness of age and mutability which lends a poignant existential resonance to the texts. Through his free rhythms and melodiousness, formal inventiveness, and unprecedented range of moods and attitudes, Drachmann renewed the style of romantic verse and made an extraordinary impact on subsequent D. p.

Both Drachmann and Jacobsen, as well as Baudelaire and Verlaine, influenced the neoromantic movement of the 1890s in D. p., which rejected naturalism in favor of an aesthetic demand for beauty and a mystically colored religiosity. Its program was formulated in *Taarnet* (The Tower, 1893–94), edited by Johannes Jørgensen (1866–1956), who with *Stemninger* (Moods, 1892) had introduced the dreams and visions of symbolism into D. p. Jørgensen's later poetry is marked by his 1896 conversion to Catholicism. After 1900 he further refined his condensed mode of expression, employing, like Verlaine, simple meters and rhythms to express a fervent religiosity. A more consistent follower of Fr. symbolism, as a metaphysic as well as an aesthetic theory, was Sophus Claussen (1865–1931). This is evident in his erotic poetry, where the surface sexual theme masks an underlying ontology, one of irreducible opposites. A recurrent theme of *Djævlerier* (Diableries, 1904), Eros as a demonic force, reveals Baudelaire as a primary source of inspiration. Claussen was deeply concerned with the nature of the creative process and with the poet's role. In his last major collection, *Heroica* (1925), a highlight of D. p., art and beauty are invoked as the only means of spiritual survival in a materialistic world. Notable is the poem "Atomernes Oprør" (Revolt of the Atoms), a dystopian fantasy in which Claussen shows himself the last great master of the hexameter in D. p. Other major neoromantics were Viggo Stuckenberg (1863–1905), Helge Rode (1870–1937), and Ludvig Holstein (1864–1943). While Stuckenberg's melancholy meditations on love's tragedy are executed with an exquisite sense of style, Rode's ethereal poems, with their Shelleyan affinities, verge on the ecstatic. The best of Holstein's unadorned lyrics, which are quite unaffected by symbolism, derive from his steady pantheistic vision of the unity of man and nature.

D. p. of the 20th c. encompasses diverse currents and styles, determined partly by international vogues, partly by sociopolitical events. The period before World War I replaced the introverted neoromanticism of the 1890s with realism. A Jutland regional lit. emerged, dominated by Jeppe Aakjær (1866–1930), whose melodious poetry about the nature and the folk life of his native region has remained very popular. The central poet of the period, and one of the greatest D. writers altogether, was the Nobel Prize winner Johannes V. Jensen (1873–1950). The burden of his first collection, *Digte* (Poems, 1906), a milestone in modern D. p., is a conflict between longing and a zest for life, alternating with *Weltschmerz.* Characteristic are a number of prose poems in which Jensen voices his worship of 20th-c. technology, together with a yearning for distant places and periods rendered in timeless, mythic images. After 1920 he used more traditional meters as well as alliterative ON forms. Jensen's poetry constitutes a unique blend of precise observation, philosophical reflection, and romantic vision. His innovative poetic diction, whose incongruous mixture of crass realism and refined sensuousness, of bold visionary imagery and muted lyricism, seeks to render the inexpressible flux of experience, has been enormously influential in D. p., as has his free verse influenced by Goethe and Heine.

During and after World War I, a generation of poets emerged who, inspired by Jensen and by expressionism in painting and in Ger. poetry, endeavored to create new forms of beauty. Most sensational was Emil Bønnelycke (1893–1953), whose exuberant zest for life and glorification of technology were expressed in hymnlike prose poems, but Tom Kristensen (1893–1974) was artistically more accomplished. In *Fribytterdrømme* (Buccaneer Dreams, 1920) Kristensen conveyed the restless spirit and explosive primitivism of the Jazz Age in an orgiastic display of color and sound. After a journey to the Far East, in *Paafuglefjeren* (The Peacock Feather, 1922) he adopted a more traditional style, but without overcoming his sense of malaise. In the poem "Reklameskibet" (The Show Boat, 1923), Otto Gelsted (1888–1968) from a Marxist point of view charged expressionist art with pandering to commercialism while neglecting fundamental human concerns. An admirer of Jensen, Gelsted maintained the radical-humanistic trad. in D. p. in the interwar period.

The poetry of Nis Petersen (1897–1943) and Paul la Cour (1902–56), the dominant figures of the 1930s, is also informed with humanist concerns. Petersen's anguished verse, particularly "Brændende Europa" (Europe Aflame) from *En Drift Vers* (A Drove of Verses, 1933), voices concern for the predicament of Western culture. La Cour, whose sensibility was formed by Claussen and modern Fr. poets, stressed the redemptive nature of poetry, both individually and collectively. His main collection from the 1930s, *Dette er vort Liv* (This Is Our Life, 1936), is permeated with guilt about the state of Europe, for which, like Claussen, he saw art as the only remedy. La Cour's best work, however, belongs to the '40s and after. *Fragmenter af en Dagbog* (Fragments of a Diary, 1948), which mingles philosophy, poetic theory, and verse, profoundly influenced the poets who came to maturity during the War. The surrealist Jens August Schade (1903–78) defined his attitude to the times by espousing a Lawrencean primitivism. His *Hjertebogen* (The Heart Book, 1930) contains sexually explicit love poems, along with nature impressions transformed by erotic feeling and a cosmic imagination.

Under the pressure of war and Nazi occupation, the 1940s instilled new vigor and urgency into D. p. Two distinct responses to the brutality and destructiveness of World War II were evident: an activation of political consciousness, on the one hand, and an intensive quest for a meaningful, often metaphysical *Weltanschauung,* on the other. Inspirational was the work of Gustaf Munch-Petersen (1912–38), a literary existentialist who foreshadowed postwar Modernism and, through his death in Spain fighting Fascism, became the prototype of the committed writer. Possessed by a vision of total union between conscious and subconscious, dream and reality, and stimulated by the imagism and surrealism of the Swedish and Swedo-Finnish Modernists, Munch-Petersen created a remarkable poetry that expressed a personal myth of self-making and self-liberation. Another paradigmatic poet was Morten Nielsen (1922–44), whose hard, weighty, unfinished verse oscillates between an existentialist affirmation of self and renunciation and death. Closely related to these two figures is Erik Knudsen (b. 1922), who, torn between beauty and politics—as shown by a title like *Blomsten og sværdet* (The Flower and the Sword, 1949)—increasingly used poetry as the vehicle for a Marxist critique of society.

The central poets of the 1940s, following la Cour, saw poetry as a means of personal and cultural redemption. Striving for a form that would mirror their perception of a fragmented reality, they shaped a richly symbolic style inspired by Eliot and Rilke. The absence of a shared cultural and spiritual heritage, together with messianic longings, was most convincingly expressed by a group of poets whose original forum was the journal *Heretica* (1948–53). Ole Sarvig (1921–81) and Ole Wivel (b. 1921) embody in their poetry, by way of an essentially Christian symbolism, the pattern of rebirth after cultural catastrophe. In a six-volume cycle (1943–52), Sarvig with great visionary power depicts our civilization as a wasteland. The driving force of his first collection, *Grønne Digte* (Green Poems, 1943), written in an imagist lang. related to abstract painting, is the search for a remedy to this crisis. In later volumes the crisis is overcome through an experience of God and love, a theme which reaches its zenith in his last collection, *Salmer . . .* (Hymns, 1981). A similar metaphysical orientation marks *I Fiskens Tegn* (In the Sign of the Fish, 1948) by Ole Wivel. Both Sarvig and Wivel see love and grace as the liberators from chaos. For Thorkild Bjørnvig (b. 1918), it is poetry itself which liberates. In his first, Rilke-inspired collection, *Stjærnen bag Gavlen* (The Star Behind the Gable, 1947), Eros is the predominant theme, treated with classic discipline in stanzas of great musicality and substance. In the 1970s Bjørnvig changed the focus of his poetry to deal with ecological issues.

Others pursued different paths, unaffected by ideology or metaphysical probing. The woman poet Tove Ditlevsen (1918–76) followed trad. and wrote simple rhymed verse in a neoromantic style. Piet Hein (b. 1905) in his 20 volumes of *Gruk* (1940–63; Eng. tr. *Grooks* 1–6, 1966–78) combined scientific insights with a skillful epigrammatic play of words and ideas. And Frank Jæger (1926–77), an elusive successor to Schade noted for his verbal wizardry, cultivated the idyll, though in a broken form with an ominous undertone.

During the 1960s an extroverted poetic experimentalism emerged, directed both against the materialism of the modern welfare state and against prevailing ivory-tower literary attitudes. This change was largely due to Klaus Rifbjerg (b. 1931), the most versatile D. postwar writer. Phenomenological in orientation, Rifbjerg's verse registers the chaotic plenitude of experience in technological society by means of a fractured syntax and a vast, often technical-scientific vocabulary, producing a self-reflexive polyphony of themes that constitutes its own reality. His procedure varies from one volume to another. Whereas *Konfrontation* (1960) juxtaposes, often jarringly, photographically precise observations, his principal collection, *Camouflage* (1961), draws upon cinematic montage and free association in a surrealist search for origins and an expanded, liberated self; in *Mytologi* (1970), the expansion occurs through the use of assorted masks. *Amagerdigte* (Amager Poems, 1965) and *Byens tvelys* (Twilight of the City, 1987) are written in a style of "new simplicity," matter-of-fact and reportorial. Jess Ørnsbo (b. 1932) employs a technique of startling juxtaposition similar to Rifbjerg's, adding a distinct social perspective, as in *Digte* (Poems, 1960), where a working-class district in Copenhagen forms the setting.

Two other poets, Jørgen Sonne (b. 1925) and Jørgen Gustava Brandt (b. 1929), continue the introspective approach of the 1940s. The poetry of Sonne, who is influenced by Ekelöf and Pound, is marked by intellectual complexity and formal rigor. In *Krese* (Cycles, 1963), a major work of its time, Sonne seeks to regain the pristine quality of childhood, while *Huset* (The House, 1976), more obscure, launches an ambitious mental journey into memory, fantasy, and hist. through a technique which blends observation, reflection, and visions. A similar technique is employed by Brandt, whose *Ateliers* (Studios, 1967) and *Giv dagen dit lys* (Give the Day Your Light, 1986) are characterized by the use of myths and religious symbols to express a longing for epiphany, a mystical illumination of experience.

Around 1965 there emerges a tendency toward linguistic experimentation and concretism, the use of words as building blocks possessing intrinsic value, without reference to any other reality. Already present in *Romerske Bassiner* (Roman Pools, 1963) by the Marxist poet Ivan Malinovski (b. 1926), this structuralist approach has been skillfully applied by Poul Borum (b. 1934), a practitioner of meta-poetry, and elegantly exploited by Benny Andersen (b. 1929) in his witty, thought-provoking verse based on verbal ambiguity. In the esoteric systemic texts of Per Højholt (b. 1928) and Peter Laugesen (b. 1942), lang. is transformed into intellectually challenging signs and closed symbols. The epitome of this trend is reached with *Det* (It, 1969) by Inger Christensen (b. 1935), an intricately patterned work in which the self of the reader can move from chaos to order through lang., a movement mirrored in the text itself. A related technique is employed in *Hjem* (Home, 1985) by Klaus Høeck (b. 1938), where lang. is recast into complex structures in a unique attempt to illustrate the poet's striving to define God.

The 1970s and '80s display a wide spectrum of attitudes, from poetry of commitment to neoromantic trends. The poems of Vita Andersen (b. 1944) revolve around childhood experiences and the workplace, and the collections of Marianne Larsen (b. 1951), from *Billedtekster* (Captions, 1974) to *Direkte* (1984), analyze sexual repression, class struggle, and imperialism from a feminist perspective. Less ideological, Pia Tafdrup (b. 1952) has, since her appearance in 1981, attempted to blend her experience of the erotic and of nature into images of rhythmic, sensuous beauty. More accessible are the poems of Steen Kaalø (b. 1945) and Kristen Bjørnkjær (b. 1943), who represent the same neoromantic trend, also evident in Henrik Nordbrandt (b. 1945), whose favorite settings are Greece and the Near East. Nordbrandt's *Håndens skælven i november* (The Hand's Tremble in November, 1986), with its sensitive philosophical poetry, is considered a major work of the 1980s.

The linguistic experiments of the 1960s have been continued in the '80s. Thus, F. P Jac (b. 1955), a brilliant equilibrist with words, creates a poetic universe around himself as the omniscient center, raiding the resources of the D. poetic trad. along with the repertoire of contemp. slang. A similarly eclectic approach characterizes Niels Frank (b. 1963), Bo Green Jensen (b. 1955), and Pia Juul (b. 1962), talented representatives of a quite popular postmodernism in D. p. These young poets, with their undogmatic views and enthusiasm for experimentation, will insure the continued versatility, wide scope, and high quality of D. p.

ANTHOLOGIES: *Oxford Book of Scandinavian Verse*, ed. E. W. Gosse and W. A. Craigie (1925); *The Jutland Wind*, ed. R. P. Keigwin (1944); *In Denmark I Was Born*, ed. R. P. Keigwin, 2d ed. (1950); *20th-C. Scandinavian P.*, ed. M. S. Allwood (1950); *Mod. D. Poems*, ed. K. K. Mogensen, 2d ed. (1951); *A Harvest of Song*, ed. S. D. Rodholm (1953); *Danske lyriske Digte*, ed. M. Brøndsted and M. Paludan (1954); *Den danske Lyrik 1800–1870*, ed. F. J. B. Jansen, 2 v. (1961); *D. Ballads and Folk Songs*, ed E. Dal (1967); *A Book of D. Ballads*, ed. A. Olrik (1968); *A Second Book of D. Verse*, ed. C. W. Stork (1968); *Anthol. of D. Lit.*, ed. F. J. B. Jansen and P. M. Mitchell (1971); *A Book of D. Verse*, ed. O. Friis (1976); *Contemp. D. P.*, ed. L. Jensen et al. (1977); *17 D. Poets*, ed. N. Ingwersen (1981); *Scandinavian Ballads*, ed. S. H. Rossel (1982).

HISTORY AND CRITICISM: A. Olrik, *The Heroic Legends of Denmark* (1919); C. S. Petersen and V. Andersen, *Illustreret dansk Litteraturhist.*, 4 v. (1924–34)—standard lit. hist.; H. G. Topsøe-Jensen, *Scandinavian Lit. from Brandes to Our Own Day* (1929); E. Bredsdorff et al., *Intro. to Scandinavian Lit.* (1951)—useful brief survey; P. M. Mitchell, *Bibl. Guide to D. Lit.* (1951), *Hist. of D. Lit.*, 2d ed. (1971)—best survey in Eng.; J. Claudi, *Contemp. D. Authors* (1952); F. J. B. Jansen, "Romantisme européen et romantisme scandinave," *L'âge d'or* (1953), *Danmarks Digtekunst*, 2d ed., 3 v. (1969); *Danske metrikere*, ed. A. Arnoltz et al., 2 v. (1953–54); S. M. Kristensen, *Dansk litt. 1918–1952*, 7th ed. (1965), *Den dobbelte Eros* (1966)—on D. romanticism; *Modernismen i dansk litt.*, ed. J. Vosmar, 2d ed. (1969); S. H. Larsen, *Systemdigtningen* (1971); *Nordens litt.*, ed. M. Brøndsted, 2 v. (1972); *Opgøret med modernismen*, ed. T. Brostrøm (1974); *Dansk litteraturhist.*, ed. P. H. Traustedt, 2d ed., 6 v. (1976–77)—comprehensive lit. hist.; P. Borum, *D. Lit* (1979); *Danske digtere i det 20. århundrede*, ed. T. Brostrøm and M. Winge, 5 v. (1980–82); S. H. Rossel, *Hist. of Scandinavian Lit. 1870–1980* (1982).

S.LY.; S.H.R.

DUTCH POETRY. (Belgian poetry in Dutch—i.e. Flemish—from the beginning until 1585 is treated concurrently with D. p. below; for an account of Flemish poetry from 1585 to the present, see BELGIAN POETRY, *In Dutch.*)

The earliest monuments of D. p. are the works of Hendrik van Veldeke, a Fleming who lived during the latter part of the 12th c. The absence of any older vernacular lit. may be attributed to the dominance of Lat. in both courtly and ecclesiastical circles, a dominance which persistently complicated the lit. hist. of the Low Countries. Van Veldeke, whose work has been preserved only in a MHG recension, wrote a versified life of St. Servatius and a courtly romance epic, *Eneide*, which shows the influence of Fr. courtly lit. The first great devel. of D. p. occurred in the 13th c., reaching a climax in the religious verse of the Flemish beguine and mystic Hadewych (fl. 1240). A creation of a very different sort is the beast-epic *Van den Vos Reinaerde* (Reynard the Fox), one of the finest of the genre, which may also be assigned to the early 13th c. It is an irreverent treatment of society and of epic conventions, written with wit and charm, from a decidedly nonaristocratic point of view.

These works typify the three main currents of medieval D. p.—the courtly, the religious, and the bourgeois—related at once to different classes of society and to different ways of interpreting experience. All three types of vision were to be of continuing importance in the intellectual and artistic history of the Netherlands. They were ultimately to give rise to a significant dichotomy which shaped that history, for D. p., in its later manifestations, was to tend toward extremes both of bourgeois practicality and conformity and of individualistic aestheticism and revolt. The religious impulse itself was to find a double expression—in didacticism and in unfettered mysticism.

Courtly, religious, and bourgeois elements were all combined in the work of another Fleming, Jacob van Maerlant (ca. 1235–ca. 1288), who has been called "the father of D. p.," a title he merits for productivity if for no other reason. In his early period he wrote courtly romances on the standard subjects of the aristocratic trad.—the quest for the Grail, the siege of Troy, and the legendary adventures of Alexander. Later, in his *Rijmbibel*, he treated religious themes, and he also wrote compendious works of erudition. His importance is more historical than artistic.

After the 14th c., a period of relatively little poetic activity in the Low Countries, a new poetic period began, manifesting itself first in the *rederijkerskamers* ("Chambers of Rhetoric"), bourgeois poetic associations organized in Flanders and, later, in Holland. The *rederijkers* were interested primarily in the theater, and they carried the trads. of the morality play into the Ren. *Elckerlyc* (ca. 1490), which is the source of the Eng. *Everyman*, is the most notable product of their art. The *rederijkers* also interested themselves in problems of lang. and metrics, and though it is easy to be amused by their pedantry and their obsession with the technical rules of versification, one should not underestimate their role in laying a foundation for the great literary works of the 17th c.

The influence of the It. Ren. entered D. p. in the early 16th c. in the work of the Flemings van der Noot and van Mander and the Hollanders van Hout and Coornhert. A kind of fusion of *rederijker* trad. and Ren. influence is evident in the poetry of the later *rederijkers* Visscher and Spiegel, both residents of Amsterdam, which began to assume cultural dominance after the fall of Antwerp in 1585. The 17th c., the greatest period in D. lit., was characterized by an emphasis on drama and the lyric, and in both these modes one finds a typical mixture of native trad. with themes and techniques borrowed from the It. and Fr. Ren. Pieter Corneliszoon Hooft (1581–1647) was the founder of the poetic drama in Holland. Though he was a staunch Calvinist, his imagination was fired by the southern Ren., which he had experienced on a youthful trip to Italy. His plays, though written in the rhymed alexandrines of his predecessors, follow the standard Ren. models. *Granida* is a pastoral drama in the manner of Guarini and Tasso, *Gerard van Velsen* is a Senecan tragedy, and *Warenar* is a comedy based on the *Aulularia* of Plautus.

Hooft's brilliant younger contemporary Gerbrand Adriaenszoon Bredero (1585–1618) worked more closely with the native trad. and was inspired primarily by his instinctive realism and his observant eye. *De Spaansche Brabander* (The Spanish Brabanter) is an excellent and robust comedy, but Bredero's distinctive art reaches its peak in his great *kluchten*, or farces, chief of which are *De Klucht van de Koe* (The Farce of the Cow) and *Der Klucht van de Molenaer* (The Farce of the Miller). In these works the alexandrine couplet is treated with freedom and virtuosity: the strictness of the form never seems to conflict with the raucous quality of the action or the detailed realism of the observation.

Joost van den Vondel (1587–1679), the greatest of D. poets, is also the greatest D. dramatist. Master of a poetic style which suggests Milton in its sublimity, Vondel was at the same time more clearly the heir of the writers of the morality plays than were Hooft and Bredero, for his dramatic art is always ultimately ethical and devotional in its impulse; these qualities are evident both in the early *Palamedes*, a political allegory attacking the extreme Calvinists, and in the towering works of his maturity. The dramas of his early and middle years are of many different types. *Gijsbrecht van Aemstel* is an historical and patriotic drama which, through its sympathetic presentation of Catholic ritual (a symptom of Vondel's approaching conversion to that faith), aroused the ire of the more intransigent Amsterdam Protestants. *Maagden* (The Maidens) is a dramatized saint's legend (and an example of the martyr-tragedy so fashionable during the baroque), and *De Leeuwendalers* is an idyllic pastoral drama.

Vondel's mature dramatic powers expressed themselves in a long series of remarkable biblical plays in which the spirit of the old moralities is given Sophoclean form and articulation. Particularly noteworthy are *Lucifer*, probably his masterpiece, *Adam in Ballingschap* (Adam in Banishment), and *Jephta*. The expansiveness and sublimity of *Lucifer*, both in conception and in imagery, contrast with the restrained inevitability of *Jephta*, and the contrast suggests the range of the poet's powers. Noteworthy too is his use of choruses, written in a variety of strikingly lyrical forms. The choruses of *Gijsbrecht van Aemstel* and *Lucifer* are among his finest achievements. Vondel's nondramatic production is immense—elegies, epithalamia, descriptive poetry—expressed in a wide variety of forms, many of them utilizing internal rhyme and a skillful exploitation of the diminutive endings in which the D. lang. abounds. One should also mention his political poems, his satires, his occasional pieces, and his epic, *Johannes de Boetgezandt* (John the Baptist).

Vondel's fellow-Amsterdammers, Hooft and Bredero, are also noted for their lyric poetry, in which we find an illuminating formal contrast. Hooft, the Italianate aristocrat, is a master of metrical variety. He is particularly fond of the contrapuntal interplay of rhyme and line length, as typified in the following passage:

Amaryl, de deken sacht
    Van de nacht,
Met sijn blaewe wolken buijen,
Maeckt de starren sluimerblint
    En de wint
Soeckt de maen in slaep te suijen.

Amaryl, the cover light
    Of the night,
With its bluish clouds aheap,
Makes the stars all slumber-blind,
    And the wind
Seeks to lull the moon asleep.

Bredero, on the other hand, adheres more closely to the metrics of the folksong, and at his best he achieves the lyric simplicity of that mode.

In their imagery, these three great Amsterdammers show a common love for the pictorial and the detailed, a kind of imaginative observation of the visible world which allies them to the great D. painters and serves to define one of the continuing characteristics of D. poetic trad. If Vondel has a special kinship to a painter, it is to Rubens, in the lushly baroque magnificence of his conceptions. Bredero, in contrast, has more affinity with the realistic genre painters Jan Steen and Frans Hals.

The poetry of the D. Ren. was not confined to the Amsterdam circle. To the west, around the Hague, two other poets of note were active—Jacob Cats and Constantijn Huygens. Cats is the bourgeois poet *par excellence.* His didactic verse, devoted to the ethics of practicality, codified homely advice on subjects ranging from home economics to sexual intercourse. He became the most widely quoted of D. poets, not only at home but as far afield as Sweden, but his reputation has undergone an inevitable decline. His friend Huygens is a poet of a very different sort. An admirer of John Donne and of Rembrandt, he is one of the "metaphysical poets" of Holland, particularly in his devotional poetry. Also worthy of note are the religious poets Revius, Camphuyzen, Stalpaert, De Decker, and Dullaert, as well as Maria Tesselschade Visscher, much admired by the Amsterdam circle. The last great poet of the Golden Century was Jan Luyken, whose mystical religious poetry is among the finest written in Holland.

Toward the end of the 17th c., a decline in the quality of D. p. initiated a period of relative barrenness which was to last for two centuries. The lyric trad. of Vondel declined in the hands of his disciples, and the drama, already decadent in the sensationalistic work of Jan Vos, was given its deathblow by the derivative neoclassicism preached by the literary society *Nil Volentibus Arduum.* D. p. of the 18th c. is characterized by a consistent but futile striving to escape the double bondage of an imported neoclassicism and a moribund native poetic diction. H. C. Poot and Rhijnvis Feith are the most considerable talents of this undistinquished age.

But the most significant poetic figure of Holland between 1700 and 1880 was Willem Bilderdijk (1756–1831), a perplexing figure. The paradox of his nature, at once rationalistic and romantic, Calvinistic and passionate, did not prevent him from being one of the most prolific of D. poets, though it did, probably, prevent him from fulfilling his potential. The deficiencies of his art become vices in much of the work of his disciple Da Costa and of Tollens, remembered perhaps as the most reputable poets of the most sterile age of D. p., the early 19th c. The triumph of bourgeois sensibility was complete in the Holland of the post-Napoleonic period. In such an atmosphere the romanticism which dominated European letters could find no roots, and the two D. poets of the period who may be classified as "romantics"—van Lennep and Beets—are only the palest reflections of their respective models, Scott and Byron.

As the 19th c. progressed, bolder spirits in D. artistic and intellectual circles grew indignant at the low state to which their country's poetry had sunk. With his friend, the critic Bakhuizen van den Brink, E. G. Potgieter founded *De Gids* (The Guide), a review dedicated to the revival of literary and intellectual vitality. As a poet, Potgieter was handicapped by a temperament which was too self-conscious and critical, a style which was too ponderously learned and allusive. But his example simplified the work of his successors.

The decade of the 1880s was one of the most significant in the hist. of Dutch lit., for at that time a group of gifted, iconoclastic, and energetic young poets set about reviving their country's poetry and placing it once more on the level of general European poetry. The important names of the *Beweging van Tachtig* (Movement of the Eighties) are Willem Kloos (1859–1938), Frederick van Eeden (1860–1932), Albert Verwey (1865–1937), and Herman Gorter (1864–1927). The first three, together with the critic and novelist Lodewijk van Deyssel (1864–1952) founded *De Nieuwe Gids* (The New Guide), a review which in its very name aimed at following newer paths than even the more progressive elements of the immediate past. But the work of the *tachtigers* was not entirely without forerunners: D. p. in the 1870s had received tremendous impetus from the publication of the sonnet sequence *Mathilde* by the precocious and gifted Jacques Perk (1859–81), who had reintroduced into D. p. that important form which had been neglected since the days of Hooft.

Kloos was important both as poet and critic, and his motto, "the most individual expression of the most individual emotion," summed up the aestheticism, realism, and individualism which were the artistic goals of his group. In retrospect, the achievement of Kloos and the other *tachtigers* seems more significant in ideological, cultural, and historical terms than in purely aesthetic. Some single poems, even single passages, retain their validity, and parts of their ambitious long poems—van Eeden's *Lied van Schijn en Wezen* (The Song of Appearance and Reality), for example, and Gorter's long Keatsian epic *Mei* (May)—have a freshness that does not fade. In any case, they cleared the ground and made it possible for D. p. to enter the modern age. A similar function was performed by poets in Dutch-speaking Belgium.

In their advocacy of individualism and realism, the group around *De Nieuwe Gids* had revived two of the constants of D. culture—respect for the individual and delight in accurate visual representation. Their doctrine of "art for art's sake," however, left out of account a third element of D. trad.—concern for the community, for the collective whole—which had given their nation's culture its distinctive bourgeois quality and which was expressing itself politically and economically in the achievements of late 19th-c. D. liberalism. It was on the issues of individualism and art for art's sake that the *Nieuwe Gids* group dissolved around 1890. Kloos, the intransigent individualist, remained loyal to his original ideals, but his influence steadily waned. Verwey, after a period of silence, moved toward a kind of poetry devoted more to the inner life than to external reality. Van Eeden, the most versatile member of the group, began the long spiritual pilgrimage that was to lead him through Utopian socialism to the Roman Catholic Church. Gorter, after *Mei,* devoted himself to the cause of the proletariat, expressing his communism in ultimately unsuccessful proletarian heroic verse. Eng. romanticism remained the strongest influence on the *Beweging van Tachtig*, but it was modified by Fr. and Ger. influences, notably that of Stefan George on Verwey, who was his close friend.

On the foundation laid by the *tachtigers*, the poets of the early 20th c. continued to build. The important poets between the generation of the 1880s and that of the first World War are J. H. Leopold (1865–1925), Henriette Roland Holst (1869–1952), and Pieter Corneliszoon Boutens (1870–1943). Leopold, considered by some to be Holland's greatest lyric poet since Vondel, was influenced to some degree by the *tachtigers*, but his finely organized lyrics show also the mark of his classical training. Boutens resembles Leopold in his classicism and in his introspection, but his Platonic inner vision is modified by a passionate sensitivity to external nature. He is a superb poet of nature, and none of his contemporaries has so well rendered the beauty of that flat, misty and infinitely various land.

D. p. of the 20th c. has taken an increasing share in international artistic and intellectual movements. Rilke, George, Verlaine, and Yeats were important models for such followers of Verwey as Martinus Nijhoff (who had connections with the artistic movement De Stijl) and Adriaan Roland Holst, and influences from China and India also made themselves felt. A vigorous expressionist movement, typified by the journal *Het Getij* and by the poems of Hendrik Marsman (1899–1940) dominated the poetry of the 1920s, but provoked a reaction in the more socially oriented work of the group orbiting around the periodical *Forum*, the most important members of which were the critic Menno ter Braak and the poet and novelist Simon Vestdijk (1898–1971), perhaps the most important writer of 20th-c. Holland.

Pre-eminent in D. lyric poetry of our century is Gerrit Achterberg (1905–62), who, had he written in a more widely known lang., would probably enjoy an international reputation. His achievement rests on a delicate tension among a number of elements: verbal experimentation versus a traditional sense of form, thematic limitation (virtually his sole theme is communication with a dead beloved) versus varied imagery, and colloquial vocabulary versus technical. He may be seen as a modern metaphysical poet. Other significant poets who emerged during World War II include the "moderate Surrealist" Ed. Hoornik and the Catholic Bertus Aafjes.

The 1950s witnessed a poetic revolution comparable in importance to that of the 1880s. The so-called *vijftigers* ("Fiftiers")—Remco Campert, Jan Elburg, Gerrit Kouwenaar, Lucebert (pseudonym of L. J. Swaanswijk), and Bert Schierbeek—distanced themselves from contemporary society and literary trad. alike, seeking above all immediacy, sincerity, and completeness of expression. Anti-formalist, their work is sometimes anti-intellectual. To some extent that work was anticipated by that of the short-lived Hans Lodeizen (1924–50) and the older Leo Vroman. Still, despite their experimentalism, the *vijftigers* did not abandon the concept of the poem as autonomous verbal artifact rather than as unmediated expression of the author's personality. As elsewhere in Western lit., the 1960s and 1970s saw an erosion of this concept of autonomy, as the work of many contemporaries makes clear. Among those contemporaries whose work may prove memorable may be mentioned J. Bernlef, H. van de Waarsenburg, S. Kuyper, and J. Hamelink.

D. p. of the 20th c. has, while ratifying its membership in the international world of art and thought, persistently adhered to those preoccupations which have been the historical heritage of the Dutch—the honest and vivid representation of observed reality and the untiring exploration of the delicate relationship between the individual and the community.

ANTHOLOGIES: *Zeven eeuwen*, ed. K. H. de Raaf and J. J. Griss, 4 v. (1932)—a crit. anthol.; *Coming After*, ed. A. J. Barnouw (1948); *Spiegel van de Nederlandse poëzie door alle eeuwen*, ed. V. E. van Vriesland, 3 v. (1953–55); *Een inleiding tot Vondel*, ed. A. Verwey (n.d.)—a generous selection of Vondel's works, with crit. commentary; *Dutch Interior: Postwar Poetry of the Netherlands and Flanders*, ed. J. S. Holmes and W. J. Smith (1984).

HISTORY AND CRITICISM: E. Gosse, *Studies in the Lit. of Northern Europe* (1879); H. J. C. Grierson, *The First Half of the 17th C.* (1906)—good chs. on D. p. of that period, *Two D. Poets* (1936)—studies of Hooft and Boutens; G. Kalff, *Studiën over Nederlandsche dichters der 17de eeuw* (1915); H. Robbers, *De Nederl. litt. na 1880* (1922); A. J. Barnouw, *Vondel* (1925)—a biog. in Eng.; J. A. Russell, *D. P. and Eng.* (1939); F. Baur et al., *Geschiedenis van de letterkunde der Nederlanden*, 9 v. (1939–); G. Knuvelder, *Handboek tot de geschiedenis der Nederlandsen letterkunde*, 2d ed., 4 v. (1957); T. Weevers, *Poetry of the Netherlands in its European Context* (1960); P. Brachin, *La Littérature néerlandaise* (1963); J. Snapper, *Post-War D. Lit.: A Harp Full of Nails* (1972); *A Tourist Does Golgotha and Other Poems by Gerrit Achterberg*, ed. and tr. S. Wiersma (1972); R. P. Meijer, *Lit. of the Low Countries* (1978); J. A. van Dorsten, *Op het kritieke moment: zes essays over Nederlandse poëzie van de 17de eeuw* (1981). F.J.W.

E

ECUADORIAN POETRY. See SPANISH AMERICAN POETRY.

EDDIC POETRY. See OLD NORSE POETRY.

EGYPTIAN POETRY. The ancient E. written lang. lasted for three and one half millennia, excluding its latest stage, Coptic, the lit. of which is largely distinct. The lit. under consideration here was written from ca. 2400–300 B.C. When the first connected specimens of writing appear (in tomb biographies and Pyramid Texts), the lang. is already highly developed, indicating centuries of prior devel. Major examples of lit. occur from all three Kingdoms (Old, 2755–2260 B.C.; Middle, 2134–1782 B.C.; and New, 1570–1070 B.C.) and from the Late Period (1070–332 B.C.).

The nature of ancient E. lit. has received a great deal of attention over the last quarter-century; major strides have been made in understanding the poetics underlying that lit., though no scholar should claim definitive conclusions. The widest disagreement probably centers on prosody. Though concensus is not yet possible, most scholars would probably agree with the ensuing description of E. literary style.

Ancient E. lit. (considering only those types we would today call lit., i.e. *belles lettres,* and thus excluding most of the material which is primarily liturgical, incantatory, funerary, or biographical) was almost entirely written in verse; only a few of the New Kingdom tales appear to be written in prose. Stylistically, the poetry is constructed upon a vehicle which consists primarily of verse lines occurring in pairs, the "thought couplet" (Foster). The verse line is syntactic and clausal, consisting of either a dependent or an independent clause; and the two lines together constitute a complete verse sentence. The couplets are sometimes interspersed with triplets and occasional quatrains. The couplet is not only a semantic and grammatical but also a rhetorical unit; and all the usual poetic devices of sound repetition, imagery, epithets, and figurative lang. are developed primarily within its structure. Distinct attention is paid to matters of similarity and difference, comparison and contrast (the "parallelism" of other lits.). The prosody of the verse line is still open to question, since the orthography did not reflect vowels and the pronounciation of words is not known. One scholar (Fecht), in connection with a theory of the accentuation and syllable structure of E. word groups, argues that the line consists of set numbers of *kola,* or groups of syllables, each *kolon* (colon) having one stress and based upon grammatical groupings of words. The line has also been described in terms of modern free verse (Foster). The texture of the verse line might be thought of as a combination of the rhetorical flavor of Pope's heroic couplet (lacking the end rhyme) with the cadences (or free-verse rhythms) of Whitman or the Am. modernist poets. The lit. was courtly and sophisticated, not folk; and the poets enjoyed manipulating words to the end of elegant expression.

Ancient E. lit. was also a religious lit. Secularism, agnosticism, and atheism were not options in the culture. This is not to deny various attitudes toward belief; and examples of pessimism occur ("The Man Tired of Life" and the harper's songs). Poets were conscious of genre, adding most poetic embellishment to the lyric and least to the narrative. The three dominant genres were the didactic (wisdom texts or "instructions"), the lyric (hymns and prayers), and the narrative (esp. tales; some myths). Lesser genres included the love song, epistle, lament, harper's song, and some ritual utterances.

The most prestigious genre consisted of the instructions. They have a secular flavor and were meant to convey the wisdom of life gained by a father, usually from a distinguished public career, and gathered into writing in order to pass it on to his son. Most E. lit. is now anonymous; but the instructions usually were attributed. Their authors were the great sages of the tradition: Imhotep, Hordjedef, Ptahhotep, Khety, Kaires, Ptahemdjehuty, Ipuwer, and, later, Ankhsheshonqy, as well as others. Such wisdom writings are preserved from all three Kingdoms and from the Late Period. An example is Ptahhotep's first Maxim (ca. 2330 B.C.):

> Never be arrogant because of your knowledge;
> approach the unlettered as well as the wise.
> One never can reach the limits of art;
> no craftsman ever masters his craft.
> More hidden than gems is chiselled expression,
> yet found among slave girls grinding the grain.

The lyric genre, consisting primarily of hymns and prayers, has most survivals. All the great gods of Egypt had hymns composed in their honor: Rē, Osiris, Amon, Ptah, Horus, Hapy (the deified Nile), and the Aton, among many others. A shadowy but fundamental presence behind all these (sometimes identified with one or another of them) was the Creator God, most akin to modern conceptions of the single, ultimate god of monotheism and functioning in much the same capacity, attested in Egypt as early as the 21st c. B.C. in the hymn at the conclusion of the "Instruction for Merikarē":

The generations come and go among
mankind,
and God, who knows all natures,
still lies hidden.

. . . .

Provide for mankind, the flock of God,
for He made earth and heaven for
their sake;

. . . .

They are His living images, come from
His very self.

The later "Hymn to the Sun," attributed to King Akhenaten (ca. 1340 B.C.), exhibits, as well as its monotheism, a love of nature: "How various is the world You have created, / each thing mysterious, sacred to sight, / O sole God, / beside whom is no other!"

The narrative genre is attested by several tales from both the Middle and New Kingdoms and from the Late Period. From the earliest of these come "The Shipwrecked Sailor," the magicians' tales from Papyrus Westcar, and the surviving masterpiece of ancient E. lit., "The Tale of Sinuhe." From the New Kingdom we have "Horus and Seth," "The Two Brothers," "The Doomed Prince," "Truth and Falsehood," and others. And from the Late Period come the stories of Prince Khaemwas. "The Tale of Sinuhe" (ca. 1920 B.C.) is the "autobiography" of a courtier who ran away under threat of a coup; the story consists of his slow recovery of self-respect during long years of exile in the Syria-Palestine of the 20th c. B.C. (the later "Canaan") and his eventual reconciliation with the king. At one point the aging Sinuhe prays to return home:

And may the King of Egypt be at peace
with me

. . . .

Then would my very self grow young
again!

. . . .

For now old age is come,
And misery, alone it drives me on;
my eyelids fall, my arms are heavy,
feet fail to follow the exhausted
heart.

The unknown author, in narrating a tale of over 600 verse lines, handles technical matters such as characterization, motivation, suspense, pace, and description with such surety and elegance that in this poem we certainly have one of mankind's earliest masterpieces and one of the high points of pre-Homeric lit.

A lesser genre, the love song, is esp. appealing. The poems deal with human—not divine—love and express, sometimes delicately, sometimes passionately, the full range of emotions and situations between man and woman: "My love is one and only, without peer, / lovely above all Egypt's lovely girls."

Texts are still being discovered and reconstructed (like the Middle Kingdom "Instruction of a Man for his Son") from fragments of ostraca and papyri. Though obscurities remain to hamper translation (points of grammar are still under discussion, the nature of prosody is not agreed upon, and there are still unknown words in the lexicon), E. lit. can now be translated with some confidence—it no longer needs to be "deciphered." The tradition of its translation is still very short—one century as opposed to the two millennia for translation of Gr. and Heb. texts. But soon the masterpieces of E. lit.—along with their Sumero-Akkadian counterparts—will take their rightful place at the beginning of anthologies of world poetry.

J. Towers, "Are Ancient E. Texts Metrical?," *Jour. Manchester Univ. E. and Oriental Soc.* (1936); S. Schott, *Altägyptische Liebeslieder* (1950); G. Fecht, *Wortakzent und Silbenstruktur* (1960), "Stilistische Kunst," *Handbuch der Orientalistik*, ed. B. Spuler et al., 1.1.2, *Ägyptologie: Literatur*, 2d rev. ed. (1970); M. Lichtheim, "Have the Principles of Ancient E. Metrics Been Discovered?" *Jour. of the Am. Research Center in Egypt* (1971–72), *Ancient E. Lit.*, 3 v. (1973–80); G. Posener, "Lit.," *The Legacy of Egypt*, ed. J. Harris (1971); J. L. Foster, *Love Songs of the New Kingdom* (1974), "Thought Couplets in Khety's 'Hymn to the Inundation,'" *JNES* 34 (1975), "*Sinuhe*: the Ancient E. Genre of Narrative Verse," *JNES* 39 (1980), "'The Shipwrecked Sailor': Prose or Verse?" *Studien zur altägyptischen Kultur* 15 (1988), ed., *Echoes of E. Voices: An Anthol. of Ancient E. Poetry* (1992); J. Assmann, *Ägyptische Hymnen und Gebete* (1975); W. Helck et al., *Lexicon der Ägyptologie*, 6 v. (1975–86), esp. "Metrik," "Parallelismus membrorum," "Prosodie," "Stilmittel"; W. Simpson, *The Lit. of Ancient Egypt* (1978); E. Blumenthal, *Altägyptische Reiseerzählungen* (1982); G. Burkard, "Der formale Aufbau altägyptischer Literaturwerke," *Studien zur altägyptischen Kultur* 10 (1983); E. Brunner-Traut, *Lebensweisheit der alten Ägypter* (1985); H. Brunner, *Grundzüge einer Gesch. der altägyptischen Literatur* (1986); P. Cachia, *Popular Narrative Ballads of Mod. Egypt* (1989). J.L.F.

ENGLISH POETRY.

I. OLD ENGLISH (650–1066 A.D.)
II. MIDDLE ENGLISH (1066–1500)
III. RENAISSANCE TO MODERN (SINCE 1500)
  A. *The Renaissance*
  B. *Dramatic Poetry to 1642*
  C. *The Seventeenth Century*
  D. *The Augustans*
  E. *The Romantics*
  F. *The Victorians*
  G. *Modernism*

I. OLD ENGLISH (650–1066 A.D.). Arguments for

the continuity of Eng. p. from the OE period to the ME period (1066–1500), whether technical (oral formulaism) or thematic (the Eng. "spirit" of the poetry) have elicited little critical concurrence. It is best to regard the pre-Conquest poetry of England as having its own character and identity. The 30,000 extant lines of OE poetry represent the earliest written evidence of an oral West Germanic verse trad. of the 4th–6th cs., based on alliteration and lexical stress, which gave rise to the written trads. of OE, Old Saxon, Old High German, and Old Icelandic poetry. OE poetry survived thanks to the early Christian conversion of Anglo-Saxon (AS) kingdoms and to the literacy associated with monastic culture. Christian Latinity left its impress on OE verse both in subject matter and by introducing Continental Christian and Cl. influences into native secular trads. In the minor OE corpus, runes, gnomes, maxims, proverbs, and riddles are interspersed with the scriptural and liturgical texts of formal Christianity such as renderings of *The Lord's Prayer, The Creed, The Gloria,* and a good part of the *Psalter.* Similarly, *The Descent into Hell* copies in part the apocryphal Gospel of Nicodemus, and the more important *Christ I* is based on the liturgical Advent antiphons. Associated with the Benedictine reform of the 10th c. are texts like *An Exhortation to Christian Living* and *A Summons to Prayer.* As well for heroic saints' lives like *Andreas* and *Guthlac* as for riddles or the AS Physiologus (*The Panther,* etc.), there were Med. Lat. models in such writers as Caesarius of Arles, Felix of Croyland, Avitus, Symphosius, and Lactantius.

With few exceptions, OE poetry is preserved in four great monastic codices of the 11th c. The Vercelli Book, perhaps the earliest, contains 29 pieces, incl. the *Dream of the Rood, Elene,* and *Andreas.* The Exeter Book, presented to the cathedral by Leofric, first bishop of Exeter (d. 1072), contains some of the best known of OE secular verse—*The Wanderer, The Seafarer, Widsith, Christ,* and the riddles. *Beowulf* and *Judith* comprise the larger part of MS Cotton Vitellius A.xv., now in the British Library. The Bodleian MS Junius XI (after one of its owners, Franciscus Junius) contains *Genesis, Exodus, Daniel,* and *Christ and Satan,* the so-called Caedmonian poems.

Caedmon's Hymn itself, however, the earliest OE poem which can be dated (ca. 657), is preserved in 17 mss. of Bede's *Ecclesiastical History.* Composed less than 50 years after Bishop Paulinus' conversion of King Edwin at York, *Caedmon's Hymn* fuses native AS and Christian Lat. trads. A lay brother at Strenaeshalc (now Whitby), Caedmon was unable to take his turn at verse making when the harp passed around the table until inspired by an angel in a dream. Caedmon's angelically inspired song of the creation was accounted a miracle by Bede, who records that Caedmon went on to turn into melodious verse the whole of Genesis, Exodus, and the teachings of the Apostles.

Although the attribution of the OE *Genesis* and *Exodus* to Caedmon has been firmly rejected, the Junius ms. poems are still felt to be of an early date (late 7th to early 9th c.). Critical disagreements persist, however, about the dating not only of these poems but of nearly every poem in the OE corpus. Of the biblical poems, *Exodus* augments its Vulgate source the most; *Genesis* is interesting for its inclusion of a late (9th c.) interpolation of the temptation and fall (11.235–851, *Genesis B*) that seems to translate an Old Saxon poem, a fragment of which is preserved in the Vatican Library.

In the Junius-ms. poems, Christian themes of Old Testament heroism overlap the secular AS ethic. Secular, heroic OE verse seems to have enjoyed favor even in the monastery. Nevertheless, only the fragmentary *The Battle of Finnsburh* (another version is extant in *Beowulf*) survives as an unretouched Germanic lay. Narrative materials associated with an older oral trad. persist in OE verse not only in specific allusion (e.g. reference in *Widsith* and *Deor* to Eormanric [d. 375], Ælfwine [d. 573], and Theodoric) but also in celebration of heroic conduct (aspiration to fame and glory, as in *Waldere,* or the bonds of protection and generosity, loyalty, and service between lords and thanes). The sustained vigor of secular heroic values may be seen in *The Battle of Maldon,* recorded in the *Anglo-Saxon Chronicle* entry for 991, which eulogizes Byrhtnoth's heroic defeat in the words of his follower Byrhtwold: "Resolve shall be higher, heart more bold / Spirit shall be stronger, as our strength diminishes."

Struggle is the primary motif in much of this lit.; life is accepted as fleeting. To lament the vanity of all things even while celebrating their splendor is a principal theme, esp. in the Exeter-book poems generally known as the OE elegies, among which *The Ruin, The Wanderer,* and *The Seafarer* are most renowned. In differing degree secular or Christian, the elegies exhibit a dominant pattern of loss and consolation. *The Wanderer,* e.g., uses themes of exile, ruin, and the *ubi sunt* motif to show that the only constancy is God's. More clearly didactic and perhaps even allegorical, *The Seafarer* presents the sea journey as an emblem of this world's exile from the heavenly kingdom.

In both *Widsith* and *Beowulf,* the minstrel (*scop*) sings to the harp. The discovery in the Sutton Hoo ship burial of fragments that have been reconstructed as a Ger. round harp suggests that the instrument provided formal accompaniment to poetic recitation, though much critical controversy remains. Stylistically, too, OE verse looks back to the secular AS heritage, preserving a special vocabulary, particularly certain archaic words used only in poetry. Its diction, an artificial literary *koine* with mainly West-Saxon features, is characterized by chiefly metonymic words, esp. the riddle-like kennings, e.g. "hron-rad" (the whale's road). Other devices include paronomasia, litotes, and meiosis. However, the chief stylistic devices of OE poetry are repetition, apposition, and variation, restatements of the same idea but with slightly altered connotations. Some evidence also points to formulaic composition: the beasts of battle (raven and wolf) accompany armies even when no battle occurs (as in *Exodus*), and sea-voyages are often traditionally elaborated, as in *Guthlac II,* where the Lat. original recounts only a journey by rowboat. The OE storm topos survives into ME verse.

The name Cynewulf has been worked, in runic anagrams, into the conclusions of *Juliana* and *Elene* (and also in *Christ II* and *Fates of the Apostles,* but without the "e"). Cynewulf was probably a West-Mercian cleric living in the early 9th c.; the major theme of his poems is the spiritual battle between good and evil. The most skillful of Cynewulf's poems, the epic *Elene,* recounts the *inventio crucis,* the discovery of the true Cross. Until the late 19th c., Cynewulf was also supposed the author of the *Dream of the Rood, Guthlac II, Christ I, Christ III,* and *Andreas.* Of these poems, the *Dream of the Rood,* considered the finest narrative of the Passion in medieval verse, portrays Christ as a young Germanic warrior-hero.

Beowulf, the greatest of OE poems to survive, is preserved with *Judith* in MS Cotton Vitellius A.xv. Demonstrating extensive Cl. and Christian influence, the poem draws on historical figures verified from Lat. and ON works: Gregory of Tours' *Historia francorum,* Saxo Grammaticus's *Gesta danorum,* and *Hrólfs saga Kraka. Widsith,* for instance, provides corroborating information about Hrothgar, king of the Danes. Still, *Beowulf*'s narrative materials are largely folktale (e.g. "The Bear's Son" tale motif; the "Sandhill" episode of the *Grettir Saga*) and Germanic legend, though these are given epic significance against the 6th-c. background of the Danish Scyldings and Geatish Hrethlings.

Retainer to Hygelac the Geat in the first half of the poem and, 50 years later, Geatish king for the remainder, Beowulf battles three great monsters. The first two encounters take place in Denmark where Beowulf frees Hrothgar's hall (Heorot) from the monster Grendel and then hunts down and slays Grendel's mother, who has come to Heorot seeking revenge. In the third battle, Beowulf loses his life but kills the dragon that has terrorized his people. These three battles are woven into a rich background of oration (individual speeches account for 1300 lines—40% of the total), asides, digressions, and envelope structures that contribute to recurrent, interlaced themes. The thematic structure seems to be one of contrasts: Scyld's burial at the outset and Beowulf's at the end; youth and age; heroic action and elegiac mood. If Beowulf's desire to possess the gold of the dragon's hoard is a failure of character, as some think, he yet dies the ideal Germanic prince, "gentlest, kindest to his people, and most eager for fame."

II. MIDDLE ENGLISH (1066–1500). Some OE alliterative verse continued to be written after the Norman Conquest (1066), e.g. *Durham,* an early 12th-c. *encomium urbis.* However, under the influence of the Fr. poetry brought into England by the Normans, a fresh spirit and new style characterize Early ME poetry like *The Owl and the Nightingale* (late 12th c.), whose *débat* conventions, octosyllabic line, and *courtois* vocabulary mark a clear break with the AS poetic past. Like the Med. Lat. debates (esp. *Winter and Summer*) which are its closest analogues, *The Owl and the Nightingale* generates its dialectic from the character of the contestants—the solemn Owl on her ivy-clad stump and the merry Nightingale on her bough of blossoms—although interpretations of the contest (sorrow vs. joy, duty vs. pleasure, clerk vs. minstrel) vary widely.

New literary forms proliferate in the 12th and 13th cs. A large body of religious works emerges, mostly translations and paraphrases of the Bible (e.g. *Genesis and Exodus,* ca. 1250; the 14th-c. *Rawlinson Strophic Pieces*), saints' legends (e.g. the *South Eng. Legendary,* late 13th c.; the influential *Gospel of Nicodemus,* ca. 1325), and didactic pieces such as the early *Poema morale* (ca. 1170) and the *Ormulum* (ca. 1200), an incomplete 10,000-line collection of homilies.

The earliest extant lyrics (St. Godric's Hymn, ca. 1160–70) are inspired by Lat. models, as was much of the great outpouring of later devotional verse, esp. that influenced by Franciscan spirituality. Early secular lyrics like "Sumer is icumen in" (a *reverdie*), recorded in a Reading Abbey ms. [ca. 1275] with notation for musical performance as a four-part canon accompanied by two voices) are indebted to OF and AN love lyrics, *chanson* and *pastourelle.* Macaronic verse, both secular and sacred, commonly uses Lat. and Eng., but poems mixing Fr. and Eng. or all three langs. also occur. The 14th-c. Vernon ms. preserves a fine collection of religious lyrics; secular lyrics showing importantly the influence of Fr. and Med. Lat. verse as well as the Eng. alliterative trad. are preserved in the well-known MS Harley 2253 (compiled ca. 1330). Other short verseforms worthy of note include poems dealing with contemp. conditions (e.g. the poems of Laurence Minot; the political prophecies attributed to Merlin), carols, esp. those of the 15th-c. Franciscan James Ryman, and ballads, such as those of the Robin Hood cycle preserved in Bishop Percy's Folio.

Verse is the medium for narratives of all kinds, incl. the verse chronicle (e.g. *Cursor mundi*), beast epic (*The Fox and the Wolf*), fabliau (*Dame Sirith*), parody (*The Land of Cokaygne*), natural history (*The Bestiary*), and, importantly, the medieval romance. Loosely defined as narrative poems about knightly prowess and adventure, romances were intended mostly for listening. Romances of varying types and quality appear both in AN and ME. Early Eng. romances like *King Horn* (ca. 1225) and *Havelok the Dane* (ca. 1280–1300) are preceded by AN versions; others like *Bevis of Hampton* (ca. 1300) and *Guy of Warwick* (ca. 1300) translate AN originals. Most Breton *lais* like *Lai le Freine* (early 14th c.) are also indebted to Fr. originals; some, like *Sir Orfeo*, relate adventures of the faery world. Many ME romances employ the tail-rhyme stanza, esp. those written in East Anglia in the 14th c. Chaucer's satiric *Tale of Sir Thopas* plays on the weaknesses of this verse: hackneyed phrasing, tag rhymes, ludicrous plot devices, and cardboard characters.

The romances are usually classified according to their subjects—the matter of France, the matter of Rome, and the matter of Britain. The matter of France is not well represented in ME poetry, *Ashmole Sir Firumbras* (ca. 1380) and the late alliterative *Rauf Coilyear* being the best representatives. The matter of Rome includes the popular Alexander romances (e.g. the three alliterative fragments, *Alisaunder, Alexander and Dindimus*, and *Wars of Alexander*, or the quite different *Scottish Alexander Buik* [1438] translating an OF original) and narratives of the fall of Troy like the *Gest Historiale of the Destruction of Troy* (ca. 1350–1400) and the minstrel romance the *Seege of Troye* (ca. 1300–25) which were in fact the most popular and prolific of medieval topoi. Both Chaucer and Lydgate try their hands at Troy stories.

The matter of Britain, however, furnishes the best and most popular romances in ME. King Arthur comes into Eng. p. through verse chronicle, but Layamon's *Brut* (ca. 1205), itself a tr. of Wace's AN *Roman de Brut* (the first to mention the Round Table), derives in its turn from Geoffrey of Monmouth's Lat. *Historia regum britanniae* (ca. 1130–38). Antiquarian and epic without the courtly refinement of Wace, Layamon's style mixes alliterative and rhymed verse. Layamon also introduces Celtic elements into Wace's more restrained version, incl. the prophecy of Arthur's return from Avalon. In addition to Layamon, Arthur's history is chronicled in the alliterative *Morte Arthure* and the ballad, the *Legend of King Arthur.* Of Arthur's knights, Gawain receives the most attention—witness the 12 extant ME Gawain romances. *Sir Gawain and the Green Knight*, the most widely celebrated of the Eng. Arthurian romances, links two plot motifs, the beheading game and the exchange of winnings, in a test of Sir Gawain's courtesy, courage, and loyalty.

The small, unprepossessing ms. in which *Sir Gawain* survives, Cotton Nero A.x., contains three other poems, *Cleanness, Patience*, and *Pearl*, possibly by the same author. *St. Erkenwald*, long associated with this poet (called either the *Pearl*-poet or the *Gawain*-poet), has recently been shown to have been authored by another. *Patience* and *Purity* are both homilies with biblical *exempla*; the former is an animated paraphrase of the book of Jonah, the latter, more ambitious poem ranges widely over stories of the Flood, the destruction of Sodom, and Belshazzar's feast. In *Pearl, courtois* lang. characterizes the heavenly court for which the Pearl-maiden (the poet's daughter? his own soul?) speaks. The dreamer-poet, initially anguished at the loss of his Pearl (the *pretiosa margarita* of Matt. 13.45), awakens from his dream consoled, his will reconciled with God's. Variously interpreted as elegy, *consolatio*, allegory, or dream vision, *Pearl* astonishes with its numerological and prosodic complexities: 1212 lines in 101 stanzas in groups of fives linked by refrain, concatenation, and iteration. The poem's elaborate artistry and profound emotion find no parallel in ME poetry.

Pearl aside, the Cotton Nero poems, with others whose origin is North West Midlands (e.g. the *Siege of Jerusalem* [ca. 1390]), Northern (e.g. *The Awntyrs of Arthure at the Terne Wathelyne* [ca. 1430–40]), or Scottish (e.g. *The Scottish Prophecies* [ca. 1400–50]), are written in an unrhymed, alliterative long line which is the staple meter of all those poems that have come to be loosely denominated as the Alliterative Revival (AR). Whether the form of the alliterative line was preserved in the 14th c. through an unbroken oral trad. linked to OE practice, or whether 14th c. poets shaped the line from a continuum of alliterative writing remains controversial, *Middle English*). Several other poems, like *The Pistel of Swete Susan*, combine the alliterative line with rhyme in complex stanzas. The major genres of AR poems include romances and chronicles in epic style (e.g. the *Wars of Alexander*, tr. from a Med. Lat. original), religious poetry, burlesques, satires, and allegories, many imitating Langland's *Piers Plowman.* For the most part, AR poems exhibit the same high conception of the poet's task, the same learned and bookish character, and the same concern for the social fabric as do the major Ricardian poems written in the last half of the 14th c., i.e. those by the Gawain-poet, Gower (1330–1408), Chaucer (ca. 1343/4–1400), and Langland (ca. 1330?–86?).

Of the poets working in the unrhymed alliterative long line, only Langland's name has come down to us, although the autobiographical sketch he provides in the C text of *Piers Plowman* must be regarded as suspect. In the over 50 surviving mss. of *Piers Plowman*, Skeat found evidence for three versions: a short A text, a much revised and expanded B text, and a fully revised C text (a fourth, or Z text, has also been proposed). The poem is rubricated into the *visio*, which recounts the dreaming narrator's allegorical satire of the "field full of folk"—England of the late 14th c.—and the *vita*, which recounts the pilgrimage to St. Truth through Dowell, Dobet, and Dobest.

If Langland wrote for the clerisy, however, Gower wrote for the court; his great Eng. poem, *Confessio amantis*, was commissioned by King Richard II, although later rededicated to Henry IV. Dedicated also to his friend Chaucer, Gower's *Confessio*, like *Pearl* and Chaucer's *Book of the Duchess*, may be read as a poem of consolation, since its matter is the confession by Amans of the seven deadly sins. The work also involves England's desire for justice and the common good, a theme which dominates Gower's earlier Lat. poem, *Vox clamantis.*

The chronology of Chaucer's poetry is unknown, although on the basis of internal evidence scholars have postulated an early Fr. period marked by the influence of Guillaume de Lorris and Jean de Meun (part of whose poem Chaucer translated in the *Romaunt of the Rose*), Froissart, and Machaut (whose influence may be seen in *The Book of the Duchess*). The middle or It. period, consisting of *The House of Fame, The Parliament of Foules, Troilus and Criseyde,* and *The Legend of Good Women,* is heavily indebted to Dante, Boccaccio, and, to a lesser extent, Petrarch. His late, Eng. period encompasses most of *The Canterbury Tales.*

The occasion for the first of Chaucer's major independent poems seems to have been the death (in 1368/69) of Blanche of Lancaster, wife of Chaucer's patron John of Gaunt, although the poem may have been written later in commemoration. Even this early work demonstrates Chaucer's considerable mastery of *courtois* diction and the conventions of courtly love poetry. Like *The Owl and the Nightingale,* Chaucer's *Parliament of Foules* (1380–82) plays (in part) upon the conventions of a *debat* among birds whose characters are revealed through style and idiom, but here expressed in a new verseform, rhyme royal (first tried by Chaucer in *Anelida*). Although other of Chaucer's contemporaries—John Gower, Oton de Grandson, John Clanvowe—composed valentine poems, *The Parliament* is probably the earliest, and certainly the best celebration of St. Valentine's day in Eng. lit.

By the mid 1380s, Chaucer was translating Boethius' *Consolatio de philosophia. Troilus and Criseyde, The Knight's Tale,* and *The Legend of Good Women* (written, he claims, as penance for his treatment of Criseyde) are marked by a deepening philosophical coloring and a Petrarchan lyricism. For Troilus' musing on fate in Book IV of *Troilus,* Chaucer provided a passage from Boethius (5.1–2) on necessity (a passage omitted by some scribes), and the *canticus Troili* of Book I translates Petrarch's sonnet 88, "S'amor non e." Based on Boccaccio's *Il Filostrato* and a Fr. tr., *Troilus* sets the personal fate of Troilus in love—"fro wo to wele, and after out of joie"—against the public history of Troy, radically transforming the It. story and its characters. In this work, Chaucer abandons the Fr. poets of occasional verse and seeks the company of the three crowns of Florence—Dante, Petrarch, Boccaccio—learned, philosophical poets in pursuit of fame.

When or under what influences Chaucer struck upon the idea for *The Canterbury Tales* (the frame story is a pilgrimage from London to Canterbury during which the pilgrims engage in a tale-telling contest) continue to be matters of speculation. By the late 1380s, he was working on the unfinished collection of ten extant fragments, whose tales are connected by narrative links. *The General Prologue* with which the poem opens describes the 29 (or 31) pilgrims both as satiric types on the model of *estates satire* (e.g. the hunting monk, the false pardoner) and as individuals (the monk's description suggests he has become the fat, roasted swan he so loves to eat). In many tales, the character of the teller and of the tale are carefully paired; in others the relationship seems sketchy; in a few, *The Shipman's Tale,* for instance, teller and tale are mismatched, a result of the poem's unrevised character. There is a wide variety of genres: saint's life and fabliau, allegory and romance, confession, sermon, satire, manual of penitence. Tale-telling begins in high seriousness with the Knight's Theban romance, and returns to it with *The Man of Law's Tale, The Clerk's Tale, The Prioress's Tale,* and others. Frequently, however, it degenerates into bawdy verbal attack and riposte, with the celebrated marriage debate at the center of the roadside drama. But whether engaged in personal animosity (Miller vs. Reeve, Friar vs. Summoner) or continuing debate (Wife of Bath, Clerk, Merchant, and Franklin), or commenting more subtly on recurring themes (Prioress, Canon's Yeoman), all the pilgrims touch on the great issues of the poem: love both secular and divine, justice, the power of lang., the trust necessary for community, the pilgrimage to God. Continually in print from Caxton's first ed. of 1478, Chaucer's poetry marks a significant artistic and intellectual flowering in ME—from it springs the great trad. of Eng. p.

Both in the Prologue to *The Man of Law's Tale* and in the final *Retraction,* Chaucer lists his *oeuvre,* incl. some poems, like *The Book of the Lion,* that have not survived. A number of other works, however, did survive by attaching themselves to the Chaucer canon, and these Chaucerian apocrypha give some idea of the influence Chaucer's verse exerted over the next century. Courtly poetry remains an important genre until the end of the 15th c., esp. allegorical love narratives like the *Flower and the Leaf, The Assembly of Ladies,* or Thomas Hoccleve's *Letter of Cupid,* a warning to women against false lovers and clerks. Hoccleve (ca. 1368–ca. 1430?) is chiefly memorable, however, for his tribute to Chaucer with its accompanying portrait of the poet in *The Regiment of Princes,* a manual of instruction.

Among the more accomplished of Chaucer's imitators are John Lydgate in England and Robert Henryson and William Dunbar in Scotland. Lydgate (ca. 1370–1449), a monk of Bury St. Edmunds and an untiring versifier in the amplificatory style, enjoyed both civic and royal patronage. He translated Laurent's monumental Fr. verson of *The Fall of Princes* (1431–38), for instance, at the commission of Humphrey, Duke of Gloucester. Writing in every important medieval genre, Lydgate was esteemed the greatest poet of his age, and his *Fall of Princes* continued to be admired into the Ren., where it provided material for the *Mirror for Magistrates.* Following Lydgate at least in part, Robert Henryson (ca. 1425/35?–1506?) composed *The Morall Fabillis of Esope,* but he is best remembered for his continuation of Chaucer's *Troilus* in *The Testament of Cresseid.* The other great Scottish Chaucerian or Makar is William Dunbar (ca. 1460–1520/22), a poet at the court of King James IV. He wrote occasional poems (e.g. his courtly dream vision, *The Thrissill and the Rois* [1503]), satires, and flytings, and the alliterative *Twa Mariit Wemen and the Wedo* (ca. 1508), a bawdy dialogue.

The civic or cycle plays (also called mystery plays because of guild sponsorship, or *Corpus Christi* plays for their performance on that feast date) comprise the largest corpus of ME drama, a product mainly of the 15th c. Cycles are preserved from York, Chester, and Wakefield (also called the Towneley plays), while non-cycle plays are preserved from Norwich, Shrewsbury, and London, among others. A fourth cycle, known as *Ludus coventriae* (or N-Town plays), seems to have been produced at a number of locations. Although the plays are anonymous and probably the product of several revisions, two great playwrights, the York Realist and the Wakefield Master, whose hand may be seen for instance in the First and Second Shepherds' Plays, have been identified on stylistic and metrical grounds. Several morality plays, indebted to medieval sermon trads., also survive, most notably *The Castle of Perseverance* and, at the end of the 15th c., the Eng. version of *Everyman.*

Much ME material continues to exert an influence in the 16th c. (Roger Ascham would not have objected to romances if no one was reading them), but humanism and the It. fashion give a new spur to Eng. p. after 1500; John Skelton is traditionally the last Eng. poet of that great age which precedes the Ren. R.H.O.

BIBLIOGRAPHIES AND INDEXES: *General*: *CBEL,* v. 1, *600–1660,* and v. 5, *Supp. 600–1900*; *New CBEL,* v. 1; *A Literary Hist. of England,* ed. A. C. Baugh, 2d ed. (1967). The literary histories by Pearsall, J. A. W. Bennett, H. S. Bennett, Chambers, Lewis, Greenfield and Calder, and Bolton listed below also contain bibls. *Old English*: *OE Newsletter* 1– (1967–)—annual bibl.; D. D. Short, Beowulf *Scholarship: An Annot. Bibl.* (1980); S. B. Greenfield and F. C. Robinson, *A Bibl. of Publications on OE Lit. to the End of 1972* (1980)—now the standard bibl. *Middle English*: A. H. Billings, *A Guide to the ME Metrical Romances* (1901); C. Brown and R. H. Robbins, *The Index of ME Verse* (1943), and R. H. Robbins and J. Cutler, *Supp.* (1965); W. Renwick and H. Orton, *The Beginnings of Eng. Lit. to Skelton,* 3d ed., rev. M. F. Wakelin (1966); J. B. Severs and A. E. Hartung, *A Manual of the Writings in ME, 1050–1500,* 7 v. (1967–86); W. Matthews, *Old and ME Lit.* (1968); *Eng. Drama to 1660,* ed. E. Penninger (1976); M. Andrew, *The Gawain-Poet: An Annot. Bibl. 1839–1977* (1979); R. F. Yeager, *John Gower Materials: A Bibl. Through 1979* (1981); V. DiMarco, Piers Plowman: *A Ref. Guide* (1982); J. A. Rice, *ME Romances: An Annot. Bibl. 1955–85* (1987). *Chaucer*: E. P. Hammond, *Chaucer: A Bibliographical Manual* (1908)—still important; D. D. Griffith, *Bibl. of Chaucer 1908–53* (1955); W. R. Crawford, *Bibl. of Chaucer 1954–63* (1967); A. C. Baugh, *Chaucer,* 2d ed. (1977); *Studies in the Age of Chaucer* 1–(1979–)—annual bibl.; L. Baird-Lange and H. Schnuttgen, *A Bibl. of Chaucer 1974–85* (1988).

ANTHOLOGIES: *Eng. Lyrics of the XIIIth C., Religious Lyrics of the XVth C.,* both ed. C. F. Brown (1932, 1939); *Religious Lyrics of the XIVth C.,* ed. C. F. Brown, 2d ed., rev. G. Smithers (1952); *Secular Lyrics of the XIVth and XVth Cs.,* ed. R. H. Robbins, 2d ed. (1955); *Historical Poems of the XIVth and XVth Cs.,* ed. R. H. Robbins (1959); *Early ME Verse and Prose,* ed. J. A. W. Bennett and G. V. Smithers (1968); *Med. Eng. Lit.,* ed. T. Garbaty (1984); *ME Romances,* ed. A. C. Gibbs (1988); *Alliterative Poetry of the Later Middle Ages,* ed. T. Turville-Petre (1989).

HISTORY AND CRITICISM: *General*: *CHEL*; E. K. Chambers, *The Close of the Middle Ages* (1945); C. S. Lewis, *Eng. Lit. in the 16th C.* (1954); M. Bloomfield, Piers Plowman *as a 14th-C. Apocalypse* (1962); L. D. Benson, *Art and Trad. in* Sir Gawain and the Green Knight (1965); J. A. Burrow, *A Reading of* Sir Gawain and the Green Knight (1965); V. A. Kolve, *The Play Called Corpus Christi* (1966); P. L. Henry, *The Early Eng. and Celtic Lyric* (1966); R. Woolf, *The Eng. Religious Lyric in the Middle Ages* (1968), *The Eng. Mystery Plays* (1972); W. Bolton, *The Middle Ages* (1970); B. F. Huppé, *The Web of Words: Structural Analyses of OE Poems* (1970); D. Gray, *Themes and Images in the Med. Eng. Religious Lyric* (1972); A. A. Lee, *The Guest- Hall of Eden: Four Essays on the Design of OE Poetry* (1972); S. B. Greenfield, *The Interp. of OE Poems* (1972); M. Carruthers, *The Search for St. Truth: A Study of Meaning in* Piers Plowman (1973); J. A. Burrow, *Ricardian Poetry* (1974); Pearsall—the single most useful book; W. A. Davenport, *The Art of the Gawain Poet* (1978); *ME Alliterative Poetry and Its Literary Background,* ed. D. A. Lawton (1982); E. R. Anderson, *Cynewulf: Structure, Style, and Theme in His Poetry* (1983); A. C. Spearing, *Med. to Ren. in Eng. P.* (1984); L. S. Johnson, *The Voice of the Gawain Poet* (1984); J. A. W. Bennett and D. Gray, *ME Lit.* (1986); S. B. Greenfield and D. G. Calder, *A New Critical Hist. of OE Lit.* (1986); M. Swanton, *Eng. Lit. before Chaucer* (1987); L. A. Ebin, *Illuminator, Makar, Vates* (1988); A. Renoir, *A Key to Old Poems* (1988).

Beowulf: J. R. R. Tolkien, "*Beowulf,* the Monsters and the Critics," *PBA* 22 (1936); D. Whitelock, *The Audience of* Beowulf (1951); A. Brodeur, *The Art of* Beowulf (1959); K. Sisam, *The Structure of* Beowulf (1965); E. Irving, *A Reading of* Beowulf (1968); M. Goldsmith, *The Mode and Meaning of* Beowulf (1970); *The Dating of* Beowulf, ed. C. Chase (1981); J. D. Niles, Beowulf: *The Poem and Its Trad.* (1983).

Chaucer: H. S. Bennett, *Chaucer and the 15th C.*

(1947); C. Muscatine, *Chaucer and the Fr. Trad.* (1957); D. W. Robertson, *A Preface to Chaucer* (1962); R. O. Payne, *The Key of Remembrance* (1963); B. F. Huppé, *A Reading of the* Canterbury Tales (1964); P. G. Ruggiers, *The Art of the* Canterbury Tales (1965); M. Bowden, *A Commentary on the General Prologue to the* Canterbury Tales, 2d. ed. (1967); R. M. Jordan, *Chaucer and the Shape of Creation* (1967); E. T. Donaldson, *Speaking of Chaucer* (1970); P. M. Kean, *Chaucer and the Making of Eng. P.* (1972); J. Mann, *Chaucer and Med. Estates Satire* (1973); D. R. Howard, *The Idea of the* Canterbury Tales (1976); V. A. Kolve, *Chaucer and the Imagery of Narrative* (1984). R.H.O.; T.V.F.B.

III. RENAISSANCE TO MODERN (since 1500). A. *The Renaissance.* Where should the history of modern (that is, post- medieval) Eng. p. begin? John Skelton (?1460–1529) can be seen either as the first modern or as the last medieval poet in Eng. Certainly the casual structure of his poems, the colloquial and often mischievous tone, have a strong appeal to the 20th-c. reader, and even make him look like a proto-modern in a more drastic sense of the term; but these very qualities can also be seen as belonging to a native Eng., even medieval, trad. in contrast to the more formal and Italianizing poetry of the Ren. Skelton's most popular poem is "Philip Sparrow," in which "Dame Margery" laments the death of her pet sparrow, killed by "Gyp, our cat," and which, without ever departing from the lightness of tone appropriate to the subject, introduces sexual inuendo, natural history, Cl. mythology, and an informal history of Eng. p. The poem, like much of Skelton, is written in colloquial, fast-moving dimeters, and in a tone well described (and captured) by Skelton himself in his "Colin Clout": "He chideth and he chatters, He prayeth and he patters; He clyttreth and he clatters."

With Sir Thomas Wyatt (1503–42), however, we have undoubtedly reached the Ren. Though in his own time his version of the Penitential Psalms received most attention, it is his lyrics that later ages have valued. A generation after his death, Puttenham commended him and Surrey for introducing It. polish into "our rude and homely manner of vulgar poetry," and praised them as "the first reformers of our Eng. metre and style." It. influence meant above all that of Petrarch, whose poems to Laura, filled with religious imagery and praise of the mistress for her spiritual superiority as well as her beauty, look back to earlier It. poetry, and beyond that to the "amour de loinh" of the Troubadours, and also forward, since Petrarch exercised an enormous influence on the 16th c. Wyatt's love poems, like most 16th-c. love poetry, express the laments of the unrequited or deserted lover rather than the joys of mutuality; and his sonnets introduce many of the topoi that became so popular in the Elizabethan sonnet: sexual love as a hunt, the lover as a ship running aground on the rocks. Technically, Wyatt is important for the musical quality of his lyrics: many of them were meant to be sung, and they are often self-consciously musical (e.g. "My lute, awake"). Scholars have long argued—and still disagree—whether the broken, hesitant rhythms of his lyrics result from our ignorance of 16th-c. pronunciation or are a deliberate departure from regularity in the interests of artistic expressiveness.

The name of Henry Howard, Earl of Surrey (1517–47) is regularly coupled with that of Wyatt. He too introduced It. models into Eng., and he wrote similar, but more conventional, love poems, which often seem stiff and imitative compared with Wyatt's freedom and emotional power. But he has the enormous historical importance of having introduced blank verse into Eng. (in his tr. of Books 2 and 4 of *The Aeneid*).

Several poets collaborated in *A Mirror for Magistrates* (1559–63), a long narrative poem in which various princes and other political figures tell their tragic story. It is chiefly interesting today for what it tells us about didactic views of politics in the 16th c.; also as illustrating the medieval concept of tragedy: a poem (not necessarily dramatic) that narrates the fall of a great man. It is widely agreed that the only parts of poetical interest are the *induction* and the *Complaint of Buckingham*, by Thomas Sackville (1536–1608); though rather stiffly melodramatic, these show interesting anticipations of Spenser. Sackville also collaborated with Thomas Norton on *Gorboduc* (1561), a didactic political drama in Senecan style, that could be considered the first real post-medieval Eng. play.

But if we are looking for the moment when Eng. p. most decisively emerged from the Middle Ages to the Ren., the best answer might be the publication of Spenser's *The Shepherd's Calendar* in 1579. For pastoral is an important Ren. genre, announcing an allegiance to It. poetry—the pioneering work is Sannazaro's *Arcadia* (1504)—and behind that to the ancients—the *Idylls* of Theocritus and the *Eclogues* of Virgil. Ren. pastoral idealizes rustic life and celebrates a Golden Age of simplicity and leisure. Spenser's own "aeglogues" (the pseudo-etymological spelling, to derive from goatherd, is his) are divided into plaintive, recreative (about love, often for an idealized Elizabethan), and moral ("mixed with some satirical bitterness"). Most Elizabethan love poetry makes some use of pastoral conventions, above all that of Sir Philip Sidney (1554–86) in his long, mysterious, and powerful fragment addressed to Queen Elizabeth, *The Ocean to Cynthia*, and that of the contributors to the pastoral miscellany *England's Helicon* (1600), who include, besides Sidney and Raleigh, Thomas Greene, Thomas Lodge, Robert Peele, Anthony Munday ("Shepherd Toni"), and, above all, Nicholas Breton. The trad. lives on until Marvell, the most poised and gracious of all pastoral poets, and indeed until Pope, whose Pastorals, in the best Ren. trad., were the work of his youth.

Plaintive pastorals, or pastoral elegies, often on

the death of a fellow poet, all owing something to Virgil's fifth *Eclogue*, were common in the Ren. Spenser's *Astrophel* (1586) laments Sidney, on whom Fulke Greville also wrote an elegy which is a direct statement of grief, without pastoral conventions. But the most famous pastoral elegy is Milton's *Lycidas* (1637), and the genre had an afterlife in Shelley's *Adonais* (1821; on Keats), in Arnold's *Thyrsis* (1867; on Clough), and in Yeats' "Shepherd and Goatherd" (1919; on Robert Gregory). Satirical bitterness was never common in the Eng. pastoral, though *Lycidas* does contain a fierce attack on church corruption.

In the 1590s, half a century after Wyatt introduced the sonnet into Eng., there was a craze for sonnet sequences. The originator was Sidney, whose *Astrophil and Stella,* witty, self- mocking, psychologically exploratory, and lyrically eloquent on occasion, was published posthumously in 1591; it was followed by the sonnets of Daniel, Spenser, and Drayton—Spenser has the originality of having written his to the woman he then married. The greatest of the sonneteers was of course Shakespeare, some at least of whose sonnets were written by 1598, when Francis Meres mentions his "sugar'd sonnets among his private friends." Shakespeare rehearses many of the great commonplaces of the other sonneteers, but with unsurpassed and unforgettable eloquence: the fading of beauty ("O, how shall summer's honey breath hold out Against the wrackful siege of battering days") or the immortality bestowed by the poet ("Not marble, nor the gilded monuments / Of princes shall outlive this powerful rhyme"). But Shakespeare's sonnets do not simply do better what the other sonneteers also do; they also differ in their programme. They are, in the first place, written to a man, though they use many of the topoi of compliment that other poets used to women; they exhort the young man to marry, they confess emotional dependence on him, and they hint at, without actually narrating, a quarrel between them. Indeed, when the sonnets were published in 1609, probably without Shakespeare's consent, they were by no means all sugared: they contain bitter poems of self-analysis and moral rebuke, some of them to the young man, some of them reflections on human frailty in the trad. of religious satire ("Tired with all these, for restful death I cry"). There is also a series of twenty-odd poems addressed to the misleadingly nicknamed "Dark Lady" ("black woman" is a phrase that would capture the tone better), which anatomize a degrading love with fierce self-reproach. At their most savage these poems use puns, esp. on the words "lie" and "dark," linking word-play to bitterness with an intensity unmatched in Eng. p.; thus a poem on the unhinging of judgment by passion ends with the fierce couplet: "For I have sworn thee fair, and thought thee bright, / Who art as black as hell, as dark as night."

The next major poet to take the sonnet seriously was Milton, who used it for political themes and personal (though not love) poems, and who used the Petrarchan pattern of octave and sestet rather than the three quatrains and couplet that Shakespeare had popularized. Milton's sonnets illustrate a paradox that postromantic theories of poetry as expression have difficulty coming to terms with: they seem at the same time to be poetry at the extreme of formality and conventionality, and yet poetry at its most deeply personal. After Milton the sonnet slept until its revival by the romantics, esp. Wordsworth and Keats.

Edmund Spenser (1552–99) is a central figure in Ren. poetry. His corpus is dominated by the huge, unfinished epic, *The Faerie Queene* (1589–96), which, however, did not set a fashion in Eng. p., and remains unique. It derives from the It. romantic epic of Ariosto and Tasso, with its elaborate, interweaving stories. The programme which Spenser himself announced (Epistle to Raleigh) of 12 books figuring forth the 12 moral virtues according to Aristotle, does not correspond very well to the six books we have, and some critics claim that these should be regarded as a complete poem, rounded off by an epilogue (the Mutability Cantos, which are proffered as a fragment of the seventh book). *The Faerie Queene* is probably the most complicated narrative poem in the lang., with its innumerable stories of love, pursuit, flight, and betrayal, in which fleeing maidens and pursuing knights constantly disappear down forest paths. The allegory is very complex and perhaps not meant to be completely unraveled. It is best remembered not for its structural qualities but for its famous set pieces like the Bower of Bliss (2.12), the House of Busirane (3.11–12), the Garden of Adonis (4.6), and Calidore's vision on Mount Acidale (6.10).

The Elizabethans recognized as a separate genre the epyllion or little epic, a narrative of several hundred lines with a mythological story, usually taken from Ovid. The most famous of these are Marlowe's *Hero and Leander* (unfinished at his death; "completed" by Chapman and pub. 1598), a subtle mingling of the celebratory and the ironic, richly sensuous in parts, which has left us one of the most famous lines in Eng. p., "Who ever loved that loved not at first sight?"; and Shakespeare's *Venus and Adonis* (1593), with a reluctant Adonis who owes as much to Titian as to Ovid. The publication of this poem may represent Shakespeare's attempt to establish himself as a man of letters; its sequel, *The Rape of Lucrece,* pub. the following year, is less Ovidian and more monotonous. Other epyllia are *Scilla's Metamorphosis* by Thomas Lodge (1589), which may have inspired the fashion, and *Salmacis and Hermaphrodite* by Francis Beaumont (1602).

The other poet who compasses much of the variety of Elizabethan poetry, and in a way overlapping very little with Spenser, is John Donne (1572–1631). Donne is often thought of as not being an

Elizabethan, since his witty, realistic, outrageously bold love poems have come to be regarded as the great reaction against the mellifluous charm of the Elizabethan lyric. But chronologically, Donne is as Elizabethan as Shakespeare, and his *Songs and Sonets*, mostly written in the 1590s, are contemporary with the lyrics of Thomas Nashe ("In Time of Plague"), and precede the songs of Thomas Campion, perhaps the finest of Elizabethan songwriters.

Donne shot to his position as one of the great Eng. poets in the early 20th c., with Sir Herbert Grierson's 1921 rediscovery of metaphysical poetry, and he is not likely to lose it again. His poetry was seen to offer just what the age demanded: on the one hand a direct and colloquial treatment of sexual love, in which the speaking voice replaces the idealization of the Delias and Julias of Ren. poetic convention, and on the other the famous metaphysical conceit, the delight in outrageous wit, learned ingenuity, and philosophical paradox ("She's all kings, and all princes I; nothing else is"). Now that the flush of rediscovery is over, we can see that Donne was a poet of his time. For one thing, his realistic treatment of the love relationship does not extend to the woman herself, who is as shadowy and unparticularized as any of the Delias and Julias; for another, his boldly individual public poetic personality owes a good deal to that favorite poet of the Elizabethans, Ovid. Ovid appears direct in Elizabethan poetry through the lively but clumsy tr. of the *Metamorphoses* (1565–67) by Arthur Golding, with its preliminary allegorizing epistle, and also through Marlowe's youthful tr. of the *Amores* into heroic couplets (pub. posthumously, 1597). Donne owes little to the mythological Ovid (he was even praised, in Carew's famous Elegy, for rescuing Eng. p. from the "train of gods and goddesses"), but he captures the sweet and witty Ovid (and the sour Ovid too) in his Elegies, which are closer in spirit to the *Amores* than is Marlowe's tr.

Donne's brilliant love poems are as varied in attitude as in metrical pattern (not even Hardy and Auden were more fertile in inventing stanza forms than Donne). The view of love varies from playful cynicism ("Go and Catch a falling star") through savage cynicism ("Love's Alchemy"), delight in mutual love ("The Sun Rising," "The Canonisation"), Platonic affection ("Twickenham Gardens," "The Relic"), the conquest of absence (the four Valedictions), grief at the beloved's death—or mock death ("Nocturnal on St. Lucy's Day"), and many more. Donne's verse epistles are less brilliant, yet their often conventional compliments use witty conceits that are sometimes more extravagant than those in the love poems. It is useful to think of Donne's poetry in terms of the commonplace Ren. doctrine of the three styles, high, middle, and low. His love poems move between the high and the middle styles, with occasional shocking descents into (or, more often, hints of) a coarseness in sentiment or vocabulary; his epistles use the straightforward middle style, then considered fitting for this genre; and his satires use the base style, though they are not as coarse as those of the other two satirists of the 1590s, Joseph Hall (*Vergidemiarum*, 1597–98) and John Marston (*The Scourge of Villainy*, 1598). For the Ren. critics, style derived not from the personality of the poet, but above all from decorum, that is, appropriateness to the subject: they would therefore consider it natural to associate stylistic coarseness with a genre (satire) rather than with a particular writer (though it must be added that Marston can be pretty coarse in his plays too). Satire as a genre, and coarse vigor as a quality, were neglected, even despised, in the Victorian view of the Elizabethan poets as a nest of singing birds, a view that is not yet dead; but in the 20th c., there is a more lively appreciation of the tough lang. of Donne and Marston: reading "My spirit is not puffed up with fat fume / Of slimy ale, nor Bacchus' heating grape," we might today find Marston vigorous, not just coarse and self-centered.

Donne's poetic career culminated in religious poetry, in which his love of paradox seems less of a personal quirk than a product of his Christian faith. Donne wrote two sets of religious sonnets, a linked series of thoughtful meditations on theological concepts (*La Corona*), and the violently personal "Holy Sonnets," whose emotional intensity has spoken to many modern readers who yet do not share the religious belief.

The third major figure (apart from Shakespeare) in Ren. p. is Ben Jonson (1572–1637), Cl. scholar, dramatist, epigrammatist, lyric poet. His poetry runs through all the styles, from the tender lyricism of his songs ("Still to be neat, still to be dress'd") to the coarseness of the epigrams he imitated from Martial. His greatest work is certainly in his plays, which he published in 1616 as the *Works of Ben Jonson*, thus making a claim for drama as serious lit., and not merely the script of popular entertainment—a claim posterity has endorsed.

B. *Dramatic Poetry to 1642.* We make fun of what we take seriously; so Shakespeare's mockery of pedantic genre classification in *Hamlet* ("the best players in the world either for tragedy, comedy, historical, pastoral, pastoral-comical . . . tragical-comical- historical-pastoral") may well be evidence that these classifications mattered to the Elizabethans, and that two comedies or two pastorals would for them have had more in common than two plays by the same author. Taking genre seriously need not, however, mean that the boundaries between the genres are clear-cut: it may be precisely the overlap that makes generic affiliation rewarding. In approaching Elizabethan drama by genres, therefore, rather than by authors, we may find ourselves tantalized by the existence of comical- pastoral and historical-tragical.

Three main passions provided the material of tragedy: revenge, love, and ambition. Revenge tragedy begins with possibly the most renowned of all Elizabethan plays, *The Spanish Tragedy* by Thomas Kyd (1592), which contains what came to be the stock ingredients of the genre: a ghost, several murders, a skillfully planned revenge, and an aesthetic delight in the skill of its execution. Kyd also wrote a version of the Hamlet story (which Shakespeare reworked), which has perished—thus opening the door to even more hundreds of speculations on the *Hamlet* we have. The popularity of revenge as a theme in Elizabethan drama is due, on one level, to the influence of Seneca, of whom the Elizabethans held a remarkably high opinion. The sinfulness of revenge to a Christian is mentioned in only one play, Tourneur's *The Atheist's Tragedy* (1611): "Attend with patience the success of things, / And leave revenge unto the King of Kings." Such a behest, if taken seriously, would destroy the genre, but it can lead us to ask how the Elizabethan audience responded to such plays. Did they leave their Christian scruples behind as they entered the theater, or were moral awareness and dramatic excitement held in a fruitful (if never explicitly mentioned) tension? One naturally inclines to the second hypothesis for the great plays, several of which can be read this way. There is no questioning of the ethic of revenge in *Hamlet*, but revenge is held suspended in continual tension with other themes (above all with Hamlet's own alienation and neurosis, and with his relationship with his mother). Not Hamlet but Laertes is the single-minded avenger. In Middleton and Rowley's *The Changeling* (1608), too, the dedicated avenger is a minor figure; the main theme is the moral degradation of the central character. In *The Revenger's Tragedy* (1607; probably by Tourneur, perhaps by Middleton) Vindice, the hero, takes on the persona of the avenger when he decides to go to court and is trapped by his role; his satiric gloating over the corruption of court, and his murderous gloating over the artistry of his revenge, become indistinguishable, and the resulting poetry has a resonant mingling of the moral and the decadent. In John Webster's *Duchess of Malfi* (1613), revenge emerges as a central theme only in the final act, when all has gone wrong for the heroine, and the Machiavel-figure of Bosola, in a kind of twisted repentance, turns into an avenger. These four plays, probably the finest of the revenge tragedies, are also in their different ways the most ambivalent. Other examples are Shakespeare's *Titus Andronicus* (1594) and Marston's *Antonio's Revenge* (1602) and *The Malcontent* (1604), which have many points of contact with *Hamlet*.

Since happy love and courtship are the stuff of comedy, the tragedy of love will involve either adultery or the clash between love and social obligation. The pure tragedy of adultery is found in Middleton's *Women Beware Women* (pub. posthumously, 1657) and Beaumont and Fletcher's *Maid's Tragedy* (1619). Shakespeare's three love tragedies are all different thematically. In *Romeo and Juliet* (ca. 1595) love clashes with family loyalty and the lovers are "star-crossed"; the conflict in *Othello* (1604) can be described as love versus marriage, since the blind idealization of Othello, the romantic lover, makes him susceptible to the machinations of the villain and leads him to destroy both his love and his beloved. In *Antony and Cleopatra* (ca. 1607) the lovers' adultery is secondary to the clash between their love and public duty; this play is perhaps Shakespeare's most morally ambiguous and most poetically daring. The dramatist who dealt most single-mindedly in the tragedy of love was John Ford, esp. in *Lover's Melancholy* (1629), *Tis Pity She's a Whore* (1630), a brilliantly melodramatic play about incest, and *The Broken Heart* (1633).

Ambition in its various forms is the most important of all the Elizabethan tragic themes. It is the stuff of all Marlowe's plays (*Tamburlaine, The Jew of Malta, Dr. Faustus, Edward II*; all written 1587–93) and Shakespeare's *Macbeth* (1606) and *Richard III* (1594). The central figure is always an overreacher, whose histrionic self-awareness makes him both dangerous and dramatically exciting—another example of the tension between moral and aesthetic response that is so central to Elizabethan dramatic poetry. Indeed, ambition is in some degree the theme of all history plays, a genre popular in the 1590s. Shakespeare wrote two tetralogies in this genre, the earlier (*Richard III–Henry VI*) dealing with the Wars of the Roses, and the later (*Richard II–Henry V*) dealing with earlier events: this helps to justify the cross-generic indication in the titles (*The Tragical Hist. of Dr. Faustus*; *The Tragedy of King Richard II*). Ambition is also the theme of Jonson's one great tragedy, the learned but theatrically exciting *Sejanus* (1603), as well as Shakespeare's *Coriolanus* (1608) and the works of many later tragedians, Fletcher (1579–1625), Massinger (1583–1640), and Shirley (1596–1666).

The tragedy of ambition will naturally be political. A monarch does not need to be ambitious, only an aspiring monarch; the term therefore suggests that the tragic figure will be the usurper. If the king is a good one, the usurper will be the villain (*Richard III*); if he is a tyrant, concentration on the usurper will mean that we are concerned with who is to rule (Richard II or Henry IV) rather than how. This will once again lead to ambivalence, the main figure then becoming a villain-hero, and in a sense it will lead us away from politics towards the more personal theme of succession. It is arguable that this happens in most Elizabethan political tragedy, and that Shakespeare is the only one of the dramatists who shows a real interest in the ruled as well as the rulers.

This discussion of tragedy in terms of the ruling passion has tended to direct attention to plot and theme; we can now ask whether the kind of poetry varies according to the theme. The revenge plays are often rich in sardonic and disturbing poetry, and their lang. sometimes abuts that of satire. This is most signally true of *The Revenger's Tragedy,* whose brilliant verbal effects touch on the surrealistic ("Well, if anything be damned / It will be twelve o'clock at night") and on the morally perverted ("Oh, one incestuous kiss picks open Hell"—a line that seems to wallow in its masochism, yet through the image of a scab conveys a disgust that can be seen as implicitly moral). *Hamlet* too contains powerful sardonic writing, often linked to sexual disgust: Hamlet plays the role of the satirist at times, and the lang. responds. The love tragedies, on the other hand, naturally explore many of the topoi of romantic love; *Romeo and Juliet* is filled with conceits on the relation between love and religion, or between sex and death: when Romeo claims that Juliet's body is uncorrupted because Death wants to make love to her ("The lean abhorred monster keeps / Thee here in dark to be his paramour"), the dramatic irony (we known that Juliet is not actually dead) does not detract from the brilliance of the conceit. Written in the 1590s, *Romeo and Juliet* develops conventional conceits with some originality and power; by the time of *Antony and Cleopatra,* a dozen years later, Shakespeare's poetry has grown more daring and unorthodox. The rhythm of this later play has moved far enough from the regular iambic pentameter that some of it could be taken for free verse, and the imagery relates sex and death more daringly than anything before, as in Cleopatra's line about the asp: "Dost thou not see the baby at my breast, / That sucks the nurse asleep."

Comedy can be subdivided into romantic and satiric. Romantic comedy has love as its theme, courtship as its action. It begins with lovers meeting and ends with wedding bells, using as its stock conventions love at first sight, opposition of parents, idealization of the beloved, and teasing by the friends of the lover. With love occuring at first sight, the action of the play is left to result from delaying tactics, usually parental opposition, adventure, and separation (with the heroine disguised as a boy, a convenient device, given that Elizabethan acting companies were exclusively male); the other delaying device is courtship itself, the elaborate rituals and speeches of wooing. With variations, all of Shakespeare's romantic comedies from *Two Gentlemen of Verona* (1594) to *Twelfth Night* (1601) fit this pattern. Behind Shakespeare lies John Lyly, who wrote elaborately artificial comedies of wooing which Shakespeare both parodied and learned from. The romantic comedies and tragicomedies of Beaumont and Fletcher (e.g. *Philaster,* 1611) derive from and may in turn have influenced Shakespeare, whose late comedies (*Cymbeline, A Winter's Tale, The Tempest*) move toward tragicomedy and shift attention from the young lovers to the older generation.

Satiric comedy deals with human vices and follies, esp. greed, and verges on nondramatic satire. It produced the finest dramatic writing of the age outside Shakespeare and embraces both the city comedies of Middleton and Massinger (*A Chaste Maid in Cheapside,* ca. 1613; *A New Way to Pay Old Debts,* 1622?) as well as the rich output of Jonson, who explores the humor, or dominant passion, very self-consciously in the early *Every Man in his Humour* (1598) and *Every Man out of his Humour* (1599), and implicitly in all his work. *Bartholomew Fair* (1614) and *The Devil is an Ass* (1616) mix topical satire with farce. His greatest poetry comes in *Volpone* (1605) and *The Alchemist* (1612), both outstanding for the elegance of their plotting and the brilliance of their poetry.

If we look at Ren. drama more narrowly as poetry, concentrating on style, on local verbal effects, and on verbal inventiveness, it is clear that drama produced the finest poetry of the age because of the predominance of Shakespeare. No simple summary can do justice to the variety of Shakespeare's poetic effects or the complexity of his devel., so a few pointers must suffice. His early comedies show ingenious verbal wit in formal and regular metrical patterns: *Love's Labour's Lost,* for instance, is full of lines like "Light, seeking light, does light of light beguile," where the awareness of a complicated web of meanings is immediate, even though it may take some familiarity with the text to sort out what the meanings are; and also of lines that shift suddenly in register, corresponding to the shifts between elaborate courtship rituals and sexual bluntness—so Berowne says of the heroine, "Aye, and by Heaven one that will do the deed, / Though Argus were her eunuch and her guard," allowing himself a Cl. allusion even in the midst of the insult. It is a line that could be spoken either with a cynical leer or with frank delight. If we turn from the beginning to the end of Shakespeare's career, we find a very different use of lang.—poetry that works through ellipses, contorted syntax, and mixed metaphors, sometimes of such complexity that lang. is being strained to its utmost. On occasions there is an almost perverse avoidance of the straightforward: "Sluttery to such neat excellence oppos'd / Should make desire vomit emptiness, / Not so allur'd to feed," says Iachimo, paying a compliment to Imogen's "neat excellence," and leaving her as bewildered as the audience. But this verbal restlessness is the necessary precondition for the wild fertility of lang. that distinguishes the late plays and seems to provide the only possible means of expression for Coriolanus' irascibility, Leontes' jealousy, or Cleopatra's passion. Even inarticulateness itself is expressed in Shakespeare's late poetry, as when Caliban tells how Prospero taught him "how / To name the bigger light, and how the less, / That burn by day and night"; and that inarticulateness is the necessary precondition for the physical immediacy of some of Caliban's lang., his feeling for the sounds and shapes of the magic island—a feeling that Browning responded to and extended brilliantly in "Caliban upon Setebos." For Shakespeare's greatness shows itself not only in what he wrote himself, but in how he taught other poets to go beyond him.

Shakespeare dominates, but there is striking poetic power in some of the other Ren. dramatists. Marlowe introduced into dramatic poetry a histrionic, magnificently self-conscious rhetoric ("Marlowe's mighty line") that manifests itself even in the crudities of his first play, *Tamburlaine.* The hero is a blustering warrior with scant talent save for killing, yet he expresses himself sometimes with lyric grace, other times with lines that seem to become aware of their bluster, as if the poetry both enacts the swagger and smiles at it ("Where'er I come the fatal sisters sweat"). This is an effect that passed from Marlowe to most of his followers but no later dramatist succeeded in imitating the power of Faustus' last speech before damnation, where Cl. allusion mingles with theological abstractions to express personal anguish.

The greatest verbal artist among Eng. dramatists after Shakespeare is, however, Jonson, whose satiric poetry celebrates (as does so much satire) the very qualities it attacks. Volpone's morning address to his gold, for instance, ("Open the shrine, that I may see my saint") is a religious parody of disconcerting eloquence; and the pompous Sir Epicure Mammon in *The Alchemist* disconcerts too by the way his absurd desires occasionally drop into sensuous and exquisite poetry.

The connection of Eng. p. with the stage, so deep and successful before 1642 (the year the theaters were closed), has since that date virtually ceased. Almost all the major 19th-c. poets wrote plays, few of which succeeded in the theater, and none of which has retained permanent interest; in the 20th c. there have been sporadic outbursts of poetic drama (e.g. T. S. Eliot), but on the whole Eng. drama since 1660 has been in prose.

C. *The Seventeenth Century.* The traditional way for lit. hist. to map the rich variety of nondramatic poetry in the earlier 17th c. has been in terms of the influence of Spenser, Donne, and Jonson. The "School of Spenser" includes the authors of long allegorical poems like *The Purple Island* (1633) by Phineas Fletcher and *Christ's Victory and Triumph* (1610) by his brother Giles, as well as the pastorals of Micheal Drayton (1563–1631) and William Browne (1591–1643), and that enormous piece of patriotic topography, *Poly-Olbion* (Drayton); it can also claim the young Milton, who praised the "Forests and enchantments drear, / Where more is meant than meets the ear." Donne's followers admired his wit, producing in Sir John Suckling (1609–42) charming and cynical love poems resembling the more light-hearted of the Songs and Sonnets, and in Richard Lovelace (1616–58) something more. The most self-conscious of the three groups were the "Sons of Ben," who admired and imitated Jonson's metrical polish, lyric charm, and classicism. They include Suckling and Lovelace as well as Thomas Carew (1598–1639), author of some beautiful, polished lyrics of compliment ("Ask me no more where Jove bestows, / When June is past the fading rose"), and Robert Herrick (1591–1674), one of the most loved of Eng. lyrists ("Gather ye rosebuds while ye may," "To Daffodils").

Of course such a classification must oversimplify, and almost all the poets of the age learned from all three influences, as well as from Shakespeare and directly from Lat. poetry. Herrick for instance must owe some of his pastoralism to Spenser, and can be quite as witty as Lovelace; Carew joins Jonson's polish to a subdued version of Donne's wit in a way that anticipates Marvell. The age had a common sensibility and a living poetic trad. that enabled its minor poets to write better than ever before or since.

A rather different classification recognizes a school of metaphysical poets, a term originally pejorative that later became approbatory. Richard Crashaw (1612–49) can be called "metaphysical" because of his love of paradox and his extravagant conceits: sometimes these present the central doctrines of Christianity, sometimes (as in "The Weeper"), they are simply ingenious. Crashaw has strong Continental links, esp. with the It. Marino, whom he translated, and can be considered England's one true baroque poet.

George Herbert (1593–1633) can also be linked with Donne, whom he knew, and whose love of inventing complicated stanzas he shared; his vivid creation of dramatic situations between himself and God may also owe much to Donne's poetry, both secular and sacred. Yet the most important context for Herbert's poetry is not literary but the trad. of scriptural interp. that insisted on several levels of meaning in a biblical text; the view of lang. that this supposes is central to Herbert. He is unusual among 17th-c. poets in that he wrote only religious poetry. His one volume, *The Temple,* was described by him as containing "a picture of the many spiritual conflicts that have passed betwixt God and my soul." This suggests a strong autobiographical element, and many of the poems are indeed highly personal ("The Collar," "The Pearl"); others, however, explore traditional images or scriptural texts ("Lent," "The Bunch of Grapes"). Given the habit of applying the so-called moral meaning of scripture to one's own life, and of seeing one's own experience in a wider scriptural context, each type keeps tending toward the other.

Herbert's own poetic apologia is found in the two Jordan poems, which defend simplicity and the choice of godly subject matter. They are really palinodes; and like all truly profound recantations, they enact what they reject ("quaint words and trim invention"). Modern deconstructive critics can find in Herbert a powerful statement of the position that a text undermines its assertions by its strategies, just as hunters for ambiguity can disintegrate an apparently simple line like "Shepherds are honest people; let them sing" into unfathomable ambiguities: "shepherds" could refer to priests, and the last three words could be variously emphasized (don't stop them singing; let them, not others, sing; let them sing, not quibble). It is not necessary to remove Herbert from his intellectual context in order to see how much he has to offer to modern theories of poetry.

Henry Vaughan (1622–95) has not got Herbert's superb technical skill, but he was so deeply influenced by Herbert that it is easy to confuse their poems. Vaughan's Christianity is diluted with Hermetic and Neoplatonic thought, and some of his most characteristic and striking poems arise from this, as when he contrasts the "steadfastness and state" of the nonhuman world with his own restlessness: "But I am sadly loose, and stray / A giddy blast each way." At such moments the poetry springs directly from the philosophical and theological ideas that so fascinated Vaughan. Vaughan's best-known work is "The Retreat," a charming poem about childhood that anticipates Wordsworth's Immortality Ode; but a more complex and thoughtful poetry is that in "Man," "And do they so?" "The Morning Watch," and "The Timber."

Andrew Marvell is the finest of the "metaphysicals." He mingles the cl. polish of Jonson with the wit of Donne, and the subtlety with which he deploys his knowledge of Lat. poetry embeds his work profoundly in trad. without lessening its originality. Marvell wrote mostly in tetrameter couplets, and his command of this meter is so complete that it yields a complete command over meaning too—or rather, his poems show how intimately the two skills are connected: a slight metrical nuance or semantic ambiguity can turn a very ordinary and traditional line into one of striking profundity. T. S. Eliot's famous phrase, "a tough reasonableness beneath the slight lyric grace," applies better to Marvell than to anyone else. Marvell's "To his Coy Mistress" is certainly the finest *carpe diem* poem in Eng., and his "Horatian Ode on Cromwell's Return from Ireland" is equally the subtlest political poem; while "The Garden" sums up all the ambivalences of the pastoral trad. in its polished couplets. "No white nor red was ever seen / So amorous as this lovely green" both asserts and smiles at the view that retreat from the world gives us the essence of the experiences we are avoiding.

The mid 17th c. is dominated by John Milton (1608–74), whose poetic career falls clearly into two halves. His early poems, collected in 1645, incl. "L'Allegro" and "Il Penseroso," academic exercises on the contrasting themes of mirth and melancholy, memorable for their generalized yet vivid description and their handling of myth and cl. learning. "Lycidas" was originally pub. in a volume of commemorative verses on Edward King (1637), all the rest of which is forgotten. Milton did not know King well, but by turning him into a generalized figure for the dead poet he produced a poem that was both deeply personal and deeply traditional. The longest work in the 1645 volume was the masque known as *Comus*, produced at Ludlow Castle in 1634 in honor of the Earl of Bridgewater. Masques, combining music, poetry, stage design, dancing, allegory, and compliments to members of the audience, were a popular form of entertainment at court and country houses. Jonson was the most celebrated writer of masques, and collaborated with Inigo Jones at the court of James I, but no other masque has achieved the enduring fame of this humble provincial production by a then little-known poet. The theme of *Comus* is temptation and the magical power of chastity, a didactic theme fitting the Earl's children, who took part. The monster Comus, the tempter, is both the villain and also the operative principle of the masque itself, and raises many of the issues about how moral and aesthetic judgments interact that are later raised by the figure of Satan in *Paradise Lost*.

When the Civil War came, Milton forsook poetry for political pamphleteering. When he returned to poetry, his second poetic career produced only three works. *Paradise Lost* (1667) is still the most important single poem in Eng., a Cl. epic devoted to a Christian subject. By making Satan the hero, in the conventional narrative sense, and using many of the traditional epic devices in the depiction of Hell, Milton produced a poem that in some sense refutes itself, and so offers the reader a deeply ambivalent experience. Critics have ever since tried to simplify its ambivalence, either in the direction of the romantic view that claims he was "a true poet of the devil's party without knowing it" (Blake), or in the direction of the moralistic view, that claims we should simply disapprove of Satan. To appreciate the full flavor of Milton's verse, one needs to read extended passages, but a glimpse of its complex music and its mingling of cl. allusion and personal involvement can be gained from any of the four exordia (to Books 1, 3, 7, and 9): thus in that to Book 7, he exhorts the Muse to "drive far off the barbarous dissonance / Of Bacchus and his revellers, the race / Of that wild Rout that tore the Thracian Bard / in Rhodope, where Woods and Rocks had Ears / To rapture." This expresses his lifelong fascination with the story of Orpheus. The verse enacts some of the dissonance it describes without sacrificing the music of the blank verse; it conveys the terror of the murder while also suggesting a magical quality appropriate to an ancient legend; and it inserts the full force of pagan mythology into a poem that insists on an identification of such stories with the devil. All Milton's ambivalences are present in the lines.

Paradise Regained (1671), a "brief epic," is more austere. Its choice of subject (Christ's 40 days in the wilderness) yields little action, and its choice of style yields little of Milton's verbal richness. Probably the most powerful part is the debate between Cl. learning and Christianity in Book 4 that makes explicit a conflict running not only through all Milton's work but through all Ren. culture. *Samson Agonistes* (1671), Milton's last work, pays (like *Paradise Lost*) one kind of allegiance in its subject and another in its form, the former arising from the Old Testament, the latter being that of Gr. tragedy.

D. *The Augustans.* The later 17th c. brought profound changes in Eng. society, and arguably the sharpest break in the whole history of Eng. p.: from 1660 to 1800, the map is much easier to draw. The term "Augustan," based on the claim to be the new Golden Age of the arts, corresponding to the Rome that Augustus found brick and left marble, expresses a boast made by the age itself. The arrival of Augustan poetry is conveniently shown by the shift from Dryden's "Heroic Stanzas on the Death of Cromwell" (1659), which is in quatrains, and contains some extravagant conceits that could be by Cowley or even Donne, to his *Astraea redux,* on the Restoration of Charles II (1660), which is in couplets, and altogether more bland and balanced in style. Dryden never looked back, either metrically or politically. His poetic career is divided between translation, modernization, and original composition. He Englished Virgil, Ovid, and Chaucer; most of his original poetry falls between the satiric and the didactic (*Absalom and Achitophel* [1681], *Religio laici* [1682], *The Hind and the Panther* [1687]); his most delightful poem is probably *Mac Flecknoe,* which satirizes his poetic rival, Thomas Shadwell.

Dryden has often been praised for the vigor and energy of his couplets: Pope wrote that he joined "the varying verse, the full-resounding line, / The long majestic march, and energy divine." The praise is eloquent and no doubt sincere, but is written with a matching of sound to sense that shows Pope to be an even greater master of the heroic couplet. When Dryden died in 1700, Alexander Pope (1688–1744) was only 12 years old, but was already writing, if we are to believe his own claim that "he lisped in numbers, for the numbers came"—the line is adapted from Ovid. Pope too wrote almost entirely in couplets because that was the meter thought suitable for epic, though for both Dryden and Pope the measure could as well be called the satiric couplet. Pope's career is divided in two by his tr. of Homer. Before that, his output was miscellaneous, incl. most notably the *Essay on Crit.* (1711), stating the Augustan aesthetic with clarity and consummate metrical skill, and *The Rape of the Lock* (1712), a very elegant mock-heroic whose witty surface constantly implies serious possibilities.

In the 1720s Pope, in his own words, "stooped to truth and moralized his song": his settings were now contemporary, and his satire almost unbridled. *The Dunciad* (1728–29) lacks the perfection of *The Rape of the Lock,* but it is a far more complex, extravagant, and profound mock-heroic. Its concluding vision of the triumph of the goddess Dullness has long been recognized as sublime, without ceasing to belong in a comic poem; and on a smaller scale, some of its couplets generate a lyric beauty that is both undermined and reinforced by the satiric intent ("To happy convents, bosomed deep in vines, / Where slumber abbots, purple as their vines": the impact of these lines grows even more complex if we remember that Pope was himself a Roman Catholic). The one nonsatiric poem of the later period is the *Essay on Man* (1730), a versification of many of the commonplaces of 18th-c. philosophy. The four Moral Essays, or Epistles to several persons (1731–35), are free-wheeling reflective poems, and the last two, on the use of riches, can be seen as statements of the ideal of Augustan civilization. The *Imitations of Horace* (1733–38) use the Augustan analogy with great subtlety, moving between cl. allusion and contemp. lampoon. The Prologue, in the form of an Epistle to Arbuthnot, has become the favorite among Pope's poems for its easy colloquial grace and rhythm and for its brilliantly savage portraits of Atticus and Sporus.

The other principal satirists of the 18th c. are Swift, Gay, and Johnson. Jonathan Swift (1667–1745) wrote a set of verses on his own death, whose light surface ("The Dean is dead. Pray what is trumps?") may conceal bitterness; and some poems of sexual disgust ("A Beautiful Young Nymph Going to Bed," "Strephon and Chloe") that have been read both as expressions of his own scatological obsession and as pleas for sanity—they may of course be both. John Gay (1685–1732) wrote *Trivia,* a lively mock-heroic on the art of walking the streets of London, and the very successful *Beggar's Opera* (1728), written in prose interspersed with songs that look like very conventional lyrics when read in isolation but take on a rich satiric resonance in context. Samuel Johnson (1709–84) based his two great satiric poems, *London* and *The Vanity of Human Wishes,* on Juvenal, adapting the savage indignation of the original to contemp. subject matter. They have little or no irony, and the cumulative impression of their weighty couplets shows that satire can be wholly serious and still impressive as poetry.

Augustan poetic theory, as we find it in, for instance, Pope's *Essay on Crit.* or Johnson's prose, is a consistent affair. It values the general over the particular, morality over subversion, clarity over subtlety, and explicitness over obliqueness. To the 20th-c. reader this sounds very like an anti-poetics, and we naturally ask ourselves whether poetry for the 18th c. was something quite different from what it is for us, or whether their theory did not do justice to their practice. Part of the answer may be that what we value most in 18th-c. poetry is satire and burlesque—genres that interrogate and subvert the very qualities that, in theory at least, 18th-c. critics valued so highly. Housman was no doubt making a similar point when he observed that the four finest 18th-c. poets (Collins, Smart, Cowper, Blake) had one thing in common: they were all mad.

But not all 18th-c. poetry is satire, and not all is in couplets. The Pindaric ode was a licensed departure from the preference for order and symmetry: it was supposed to be irregular in meter and full of digressions and uplifting sentiments, a kind of equivalent to the sublime in painting. Thomas Gray (1716–71) and William Collins (1721–59) both wrote such odes, though we remember Collins rather for the descriptive carefulness and tender feeling of his "Ode to Evening," and Gray above all for his "Elegy Written in a Country Churchyard," which expresses memorably many of the pastoral and elegiac commonplaces long central to Eng. p.

The half-century between the death of Pope and the arrival of Wordsworth and Coleridge is the least impressive in the history of Eng. p. It encompasses Oliver Goldsmith (1728–74), whose *Deserted Village* (1770) mingles sentimental social commentary with the pastoral trad.; William Cowper (1731–1800), author of a long blank verse reflection, *The Task* (1785), some memorable hymns, and the powerful lyric "The Castaway," which can be read as an allegory of his own mental disturbance; and Robert Burns (1759–96), Scotland's favorite poet, whose songs are still quoted and sung: "Auld Lang Syne" has become almost an unofficial Scots anthem, and "the best laid schemes o' mice and men / Gang oft a-gley" is one of the most familiar quotations in the lang. Of Burns' longer poems, *The Cotter's Saturday Night* is a sententious idealization of rural life, and *Tam o' Shanter* an uninhibited comic narrative.

George Crabbe (1754–1832) survived into the romantic period but remained an Augustan in spirit. He began with the fierce anti-pastoral *The Village* (1783) and went on to realistic, sometimes grimly humorous narratives in couplets, of which the most famous has become "Peter Grimes": the description of Peter in his depression letting his boat drift through mud-banks, along the "lazy tide," is a tour-de-force of the pathetic fallacy that has no parallel in Eng. p.

William Blake (1757–1827) was neglected during his lifetime but is now ranked with the great romantic poets. He began with a volume of graceful neo-Elizabethan lyrics, *Poetical Sketches* (1783), before turning to the deliberate naivete of the *Songs of Innocence* (1789), the complex lyricism of the *Songs of Experience* (1794), and finally the strange mythology of his Prophetic Books. To the unexpert reader, these books seem almost solipsistic in their thinking, but a great deal of scholarly work has now been devoted to them, so that those willing to study *The Four Zoas, Milton,* or *Jerusalem* with the aid of commentaries can now gain access to a coherent philosophical and even political worldview. Because Blake's poetry is obscure and at the same time immediate in its impact, there is an almost inevitable rift between the learned explicators and the readers who respond strongly and attach meanings which Blake almost certainly did not intend. A famous example is the lyric from *Milton* which asks "And was Jerusalem builded here, Amid these dark Satanic mills?" Generations of readers have taken this as a social commentary on the Industrial Revolution, but Blake scholars have arrived at no consensus regarding these mills, except to agree that they are not factories. Perhaps no poet provides better material for the modern critical argument about the relation between intention and meaning, or between meaning and significance.

E. *The Romantics.* The romantic dawn in Eng. p. is conventionally marked by *Lyrical Ballads,* published by Wordsworth and Coleridge in 1798. Most of the poems are ballads dealing with incidents and situations from common life, with simple and rustic protagonists: there is an almost anti-literary quality to them, esp. in their reliance on plain lang., as if rejecting most of the verbal resources of poetry. Wordsworth defended both his lang. and his subjects in the Preface to the second ed. (1800), which has become the most famous manifesto in Eng. p.: it attacks poetic diction and defends "the lang. really used by men," preferring "humble and rustic life" as material "because in that condition the essential passions of the heart find a better soil."

The two most important poems in *Lyrical Ballads,* however, do not seek to intensify the natural, but rather to render the supernatural natural. One is Coleridge's "Rime of the Ancient Mariner," a long sea narrative, deriving from his omnivorous reading in travel lit.: it is in ballad meter, and some of its strongest effects have the terseness of the old ballads ("Water, water, everywhere, / Nor any drop to drink"), but its exploration of extreme situations and its fascination with the exotic and the frighteningly beautiful, as in the descriptions of the icebergs and the water-snakes, make it—in the everyday sense of the term—a much more romantic poem than any of Wordsworth's. Coleridge himself described the division of labor between the two of them as one in which he was to deal with "persons and characters supernatural or at least romantic," and by his treatment "to procure for these shadows of imagination that willing suspension of disbelief for the moment which constitutes poetic faith"; and Wordsworth was to choose characters and incidents "such as will be found in every village," and to "give the charm of novelty to the things of every day." The other major poem in *Lyrical Ballads* is the poem that has come to be known as "Tintern Abbey," an account in blank verse of Wordsworth's emotional development. It claims that the maturity which hears "the still sad music of humanity" is more valuable than his passionate early enthusiasm for nature, but the greatest poetic intensity clings to the early, outgrown experiences—a pattern that is widespread in Wordsworth's finest poetry. "Tintern Abbey" is a seminal poem for the romantic movement. It resembles—and no doubt lies behind—Coleridge's series of "Conversation Poems" (the finest is "Frost at Midnight"), and above all, it foreshadows Wordsworth's masterpiece, the long autobiographical poem we know as *The Prelude.*

Wordsworth never published and never even named this poem, but he realized its importance, and tinkered with it throughout his life. It offers not a coherent psychological theory of his devel. but a series of sketches of his "spots of time"—the episodes, outwardly unimportant, that stand out in memory and helped to form him. He describes himself as "fostered alike by beauty and by fear," and far more of these memories show fear than happiness. *The Prelude* deals with memory and childhood in a way that assumes the true subject of poetry to be the self, and for this reason can be seen as a central romantic poem. It was intended as a preface to the long philosophic poem he never completed, though part of it was pub. as *The Excursion* in 1814. The first book of this contains the story of Margaret, a short bare narrative of unrelieved distress, which, for those who value the early and more radical Wordsworth, can be seen as his masterpiece in the bleak simplicity of its pathos. The later books of *The Excursion* moralize the verse and make it clear that Wordsworth is greatest as a philosophical poet when writing closest to his own experience. His true philosophical achievement was, in fact, *The Prelude* itself.

The second generation of Eng. romantics—Byron, Shelley, Keats—all died young, and were outlived by the first. George Gordon Lord Byron (1788–1824) shot to fame with *Childe Harold's Pilgrimage* (1812–18), the Grand Tour of a sensitive, brooding, passionate young man, a distinctly theatrical version of the poet himself. Today Byron's reputation rests more on a handful of polished lyrics and the long, unfinished *Don Juan* (1819–24), a witty, cynical, colloquial narrative of contemp. life.

Percy Bysshe Shelley (1792–1822) is the most Platonic and political of the romantics. His Platonism issues sometimes as a series of abstractions, sometimes as a vision of the transcendent (most famously in the image used in *Adonais,* "Life like a dome of many coloured glass / Stains the white radiance of eternity"). Most of his poems give no hint of his ardent radicalism and his hostility to the tyranny of priest and king, but those which do (*The Masque of Anarchy* [1832], "Song to the Men of England" [1839]), written with the deliberate intent of being popular, made him a people's poet throughout the 19th c. Shelley could also be intensely personal, and lyrics like the "Ode to the West Wind" or "Stanzas Written in Dejection" can be praised for their passionate feeling or condemned for their adolescent mawkishness.

John Keats (1795–1821) developed astonishingly between the lush sensuousness of his first volume, published in 1817 ("the soul is lost in pleasant smotherings"), and the maturity of his great poetry only three years later. "An artist must serve Mammon," he wrote to Shelley, rejecting all didactic views of poetry; he urged Shelley to curb his magnanimity and "load every rift [of your subject] with ore." The rich verbal texture of Keats's poetry is most apparent in his odes ("To a Nightingale," on escapism; "On a Grecian Urn," on art; "To Psyche," on ancient myth; "To Autumn," on sensuous experience of Nature). Probably no poems in the lang. have been more lingered on and more analyzed for the richness of their verbal effects than these odes: the ending of "To Autumn," for instance ("then in a mournful choir the small gnats mourn / And gathering swallows twitter in the skies") blends all the senses and "conspires" (to use Keats's own word) to imitate the bodily experiences of the watcher, while at the same time introducing, with perfect tact, the theme of death that underlies any poem on autumn. As a narrative poet, Keats took his subjects from folklore ("The Eve of St. Agnes"), from his reading ("Lamia"), and esp. from Cl. mythology: *Endymion,* his longest poem, and the two versions of *Hyperion*—the first abandoned because "too full of Miltonic inversions: Eng. must be kept up," the second also abandoned after being reworked as a more personal and homemade myth, a project similar to, but less obscure than, the complicated mythology of Blake.

Of the other romantic poets the most celebrated was Sir Walter Scott (1771–1830), now thought of as a novelist, though he began as a poet; his metrical romances of Scottish history (*The Lay of the Last Minstrel, Marmion, The Lady of the Lake*) were as popular in their day as the more exotic verse tales of Byron; but a more profound contribution to poetry is almost certainly his creative editing of the *Minstrelsy of the Scottish Border* (1802–3) and his powerful, lapidary lyric, "Proud Maisie." Walter Savage Landor (1775–1864) is the author of some exquisite tiny lyrics; and the poetry of the agricultural laborer John Clare (1793–1864) is genuinely rural, not pastoral: his choice of the title *The Shepherd's Calendar* provides one of the ironies of Eng. p., since instead of the moralizing, the courtly compliments, and the allegorical figures of Spenser, Clare fills his poem with the real awarenesses of shepherds ("the duck Waddling eager through the muck"). Clare spent much of his later life in an asylum, and this produced the most moving of his many lyrics, that beginning "I am. Yet what I am who cares or knows?"

Though the term "romantic" is universally accepted as a label for the early 19th c., there is little agreement among literary scholars about its meaning. Its main meanings can be illustrated by asking which of the Eng. poets is the representative romantic. The case for Wordsworth has already been stated: on the other hand, his belief in general truths and his faith in "that calm existence which is mine when I / Am worthy of myself" makes him very classical. Keats is the archetypal romantic if we emphasize myth and legend as material, and concrete imagery as stylistic device. Byron, who lacks the verbal genius of these two, has always seemed the archetypal romantic to Continental readers; his histrionic self-projection looks back to Goethe's Werther and Rousseau's self-image, and forward to Pushkin, Lermontov, Stendhal and Hugo.

F. *The Victorians.* Coleridge died in 1832; Tennyson published his first volume in 1830, Browning in 1833; and Queen Victoria came to the throne in 1837: so the 1830s can be considered the transition from romantic to Victorian poetry. Yet though the labels are generally used, they make an odd pair: romantic, as we have seen, attempts to describe qualities in the lit. itself (as well as in other arts), whereas "Victorian" is simply borrowed from political history It might be better to regard Tennyson and Browning as the third generation of romantic poets, and Arnold, Meredith, and the Rossettis as the fourth, rather than postulating a new phase in lit. hist. If we see the romantic movement as continuing until the advent of modernism in our own century, it would still not be as long as the neoclassical or Augustan phase. Certainly the continuity between Keats and Tennyson, between Shelley and the young Browning, between Wordsworth and Arnold, is stronger than that between the first two romantic generations. The rise of the novel to centrality in Victorian lit., and the consequent directing of the realistic impulse into that, may have helped to sustain the romanticism of Victorian poetry: George Eliot, for instance, has elements of Wordsworth and even Byron in her poetry that are much less obvious in her fiction.

Alfred Lord Tennyson (1808–92) had an ear for rhythm and an eye for nature as fine as that of any Eng. poet. Elizabeth Gaskell tells a charming story of how a gardener snorted in indignation when he read the line "black as ash-buds in March," until he looked at the ash the following spring; after that he became a devotee of Tennyson. This descriptive genius combines with a personal melancholy that gives his lyrics a characteristic emotional tone: he is both a nature poet and a highly subjective poet, a combination that came to seem natural to 19th-c. taste. His finest short poems include "Mariana," "Ulysses," and the haunting songs from his feminist/anti-feminist narrative *The Princess.* Tennyson's masterpiece is *In Memoriam,* pub. in 1850 but written over the 17 years since the death of his friend Arthur Hallam. The poem's polished quatrains return constantly to a grief so deep we may wonder about the psychology behind it; at the same time, they contain details to delight any gardener, and reflections on religious belief and the effect on it of geological discoveries. Still, Tennyson's fine poetic sensibility went with a commonplace intellect: he thought like a conventional Victorian, but felt and wrote with a rare sensibility. So, since as Poet Laureate he felt driven to write about some of the controversies of the day, his poetry offers a rare insight into the Victorian mind. He labored for many years over the *Idylls of the King,* his retelling of the Arthurian legends. They are often accused of being more Victorian than medieval. Tennyson, who admitted this, did not see it as a fault.

Tennyson and Browning are now seen as the two pillars of Victorian poetry, but recognition came much later to Browning (1812–89), who, when he married Elizabeth Barrett in 1846, was less famous than she. Browning's notorious obscurity hindered popular acceptance and still leaves his early and late work unread. He is above all the master of the dramatic monologue, some short and brilliant ("My Last Duchess," "Soliloquy of the Sp. Cloister"), some long and absorbing ("Bishop Blougram's Apology," "Mr. Sludge the Medium"). Italophiles both, the Brownings lived in Italy after their marriage, and Browning's fascination with the It. Ren. produced many of his finest works ("Fra Lippo Lippi," "Andrea del Sarto"), as well as his longest and most ambitious work, *The Ring and the Book* (1868–69), in which a sordid 17th-c. murder case is related from nine viewpoints. Among Browning's lyrics, "Two in the Campagna" can perhaps challenge Donne and Marvell for the position of the finest Eng. love poem.

Browning is a clear exception to the generalization that most Victorian poetry is romantic, exotic, and even escapist; and he is by no means the only Victorian poet to use contemp. setting and realistic treatment. Arthur Hugh Clough (1819–61) wrote two relaxed, ironic narratives about sophisticated contemp. life, *Amours de Voyage* and *The Bothie of Tober-na-Vuolich.* They are written in hexameters, scanned as much by length as by stress; as such they are one manifestation of the 19th-c. vogue for imitations of Cl. quantitative meters, and in Clough's hands the hexameter responds very readily to speech rhythm and ironic tone. *Modern Love* (1862), by George Meredith (1828–1900), is a sequence of 16-line "sonnets" about a failing marriage: the story is hinted at rather than told, and the tone varies from ironic sophistication to tragic plangency. *Aurora Leigh* (1856), a verse novel by Elizabeth Barrett Browning (1806–61), for all its occasional sentimentality and melodramatic plot, is one of the subtlest and most probing narrative poems of the age, remarkable for its proto-feminist awareness as well as its sensitive description of the Eng. landscape. Her other major work, *Sonnets from the Portuguese* (1850), is both deeply personal and deeply traditional: it expresses her love for her husband in the conventions that derive from medieval love poetry, ultimately from the troubadours; and the result is a fascinating ambivalence, depending on whether we imagine the speaker to be male or female.

The social and lit. crit. of Matthew Arnold (1822–88) has always seemed to some readers more important than his poems, but it is arguable that his earnestness, his conservatism, and his nostalgia find a more appropriate expression in verse. His reflective poetry deals directly with the spiritual crisis of the age, most movingly in "Dover Beach," indirectly in *Empedocles on Etna,* and both directly and indirectly in *The Scholar Gypsy.*

The Pre-Raphaelite Brotherhood was mainly a movement in painting; how well the term applies to poetry is questionable. Its program very clearly defined medievalism. Dante Gabriel Rossetti (1828–82), both painter and poet, was its central figure. He translated a good deal of early It. poetry, and there is a Dantesque religiosity in much of his own. His sonnet sequence *The House of Life,* somewhat more explicitly erotic than most 19th-c. poetry, led to his being denounced, along with Swinburne, as "the fleshly school of poetry". In Algernon Charles Swinburne (1837–1909), sexuality is more open, extravagant, and perverted, rendering him the nearest thing to an Eng. Baudelaire (on whom he wrote an elegy, "Ave atque vale"), but the careful cl. diction of Baudelaire's poems has nothing in common with Swinburne's incantatory lilt and excessive alliteration. Paradoxically, perhaps, the self-indulgent Swinburne is also the leading Hellenist among Victorian poets, drawing many of his subjects from Gr. mythology. Rossetti's sister Christina (1830–94) wrote simple lyrics about love, about religion (she was a devout Anglican), and a few, esp. "Twice," about both. Some feminist critics claim, with some justice, that her strange, sensuous retelling of the folktale "Goblin Market" is an imaginative achievement on a par with Coleridge's "Ancient Mariner," though it has never achieved the same fame, perhaps because of its predominantly feminine themes (virginity, menarche, anorexia). William Morris (1834–96), also a pre-Raphaelite, wrote long narratives on medieval and Norse themes, a few nostalgic lyrics (his radical politics did not lead to any poetic unconventionality), and one powerful and realistic narrative with a medieval setting, "The Haystack in the Floods."

The radical of Victorian poetry was Gerard Manley Hopkins (1844–89), whose poems were not published until 1918. A Jesuit priest, he had abandoned poetry when he entered the order, then at the suggestion of his Superior wrote a poem on the death of five Franciscan nuns in the shipwreck of The Deutschland in 1875. The Rector can hardly have expected the tortured syntax and obscure diction with which Hopkins explored his own religious experience. He then went on to produce a handful of poems, mainly sonnets, whose technical innovation had a profound influence on 20th-c. poetry: some of them celebrate nature and the God of nature ("Hurrahing in Harvest," "Pied Beauty"), while the "Terrible Sonnets" explore religious despair and the dark night of the soul. No Eng. poetry of any age wrenches lang. so violently and powerfully to fit meaning as Hopkins' profound poems of spiritual despair: his defiantly Saxon vocabulary and his sprung rhythm derive from his interest in OE, while his brilliant experimentalism anticipates much in modern poetry. In his letters Hopkins sketched a poetic theory through the concepts of "inscape" and "instress", the unifying quality of a landscape or an experience that a poem aims to capture—concepts that show the influence of Duns Scotus and his idea of *haeccitas.*

Late 19th-c. poetry is filled with the romantic love of the mysterious and the suggestive, with nostalgia, painful love, and religious longing. It is typified by the early poetry of William Butler Yeats (1865–1939), which gives little indication of his subsequent modernism. Two serious religious poems that emerge from, and never quite forsake, this world are Francis Thompson's "Hound of Heaven" (1893) and Oscar Wilde's *Ballad of Reading Gaol* (1898).

Thomas Hardy (1840–1928) is a late Victorian both in spirit and date, but because he turned to poetry after his career as a novelist was over, and then lived to so advanced an age, most of his poetry falls into the 20th c. There is astonishing variety in his shorter poems, both in form and mood, which can be leisurely or terse, colloquial or musical, and use a greater range of stanza forms—many invented by him—than any other poet in the lang. One of his most loved lyrics, a reflection on his own posthumous reputation called "Afterwards," announces its poetic individuality from the very first line in its quirky diction and meditative rhythm ("When the present has latched its postern behind my tremulous stay"). Closest to the novels in spirit are his ballads; the irony for which he is so renowned as a novelist appears in the poems as self-mockery, as cynicism, and (sometimes) as profound social commentary ("The Ruined Girl"). His finest poems are the sequence he wrote on the death of his first wife, under the general title "Veteris vestigia flammae—Traces of an Old Flame."

G. *Modernism.* A simplified view sees modernism as a reaction against this tail-end of romanticism, but the true picture is more complicated. There were several competing poetic schools in the early 20th c.: the rousing masculinity of Rudyard Kipling and Henry Newbolt; the Georgian return to the countryside (which saw itself both as a reaction against glib jingoism and as a realistic rejection of effete romanticism); and the poetry of the First World War, which began in the patriotic enthusiasm of Rupert Brooke and ended in the angry pacifism of Wilfred Owen. To many today, the more distanced and oblique response of David Jones in *In Parenthesis* (1937) is the most memorable work of World War I poetry. The Georgian anthologies, appearing from 1911 to 1922, included Walter de la Mare (1873–1956, the best of the late romantics), Robert Graves (1895–1985), and Edward Thomas (1878–1917), modern in awareness if not in technique.

The Georgians were very conscious of being Eng., and indeed there has always been a strong native trad. in 20th-c. poetry, hearkening back to Hardy and even to the Dorset dialect poet William Barnes (1801–86): John Betjeman, Philip Larkin and Ted Hughes can all be seen as belonging to it. But on the whole, modernism was an international movement, appearing in Germany as expressionism, in Russia in the work of Blok and Majakovskij, and in England as introduced from France. The seminal figures, Pound and Eliot, were both Americans, though Eliot became very thoroughly Anglicized: their poetry contains a great deal of social commentary and awareness of the ugliness of modern life, yet in many ways they derive more from aestheticism than from any trad. of social realism. T. S. Eliot (1888–1965) can be seen as the man who brought Fr. symbolism to England, both the concentrated, intellectual, gnomic poetry of Mallarmé and Valéry and the colloquial, ironic, self-conscious poetry of Corbière and Laforgue. Eliot's modernist programme derived from the claim that the Eng. metaphysicals used lang. in a way very similar to the Fr. symbolists, and issued in the famous assertion that modern poetry must be difficult: "Our civilisation comprehends great variety and complexity, and this variety and complexity, playing upon a refined sensibility, must produce various and complex results."

Eliot's very small output is certainly the most famous body of Eng. p. in the 20th c. *Prufrock and Other Observations* (1917), his first collection, opens with two dramatic monologues that owe more to Laforgue and Henry James than to Browning. Both speakers are self-conscious to the point of neurosis: J. Alfred Prufrock, in his "love-song," sees himself descending the stair "with a bald spot in the middle of my hair," and the speaker of "Portrait of a Lady" says "My smile falls heavily among the bric-a-brac." The analogy with music is central to the symbolist view of poetry, and it appears in the titles of several of Eliot's poems—"Preludes," "Five-finger Exercises," "Rhapsody on a Windy Night," and *Four Quartets*. The debt to Laforgue is most evident in "Conversation Galante," a free translation of "Celle qui doit. . ." Eliot's early poetry culminated in *The Waste Land* (1922), fragmentary and allusive in technique, deriving (Eliot claimed) from Jessie L. Weston's *From Ritual to Romance*, a Fraserian interp. of the Grail Legend as a fertility myth. Imagery from the grail story is mingled in the poem with glimpses of modern life, so that the waste land is seen not only as the land rendered barren by the curse on the Fisher King, but also as the 20th c. The poem is filled with religious symbols and with religious despair; by the time of *Ash Wednesday* (1930), which, though just as allusive in method, is much more immediately emotional in impact, Eliot had become an Anglican, and his poetry culminated in the four linked meditations of *Four Quartets* (1936–43), in which Christian symbols are introduced into the waste land: without being any less modern, they offer a more positive relation to trad., as can be seen in the sources of the titles—East Coker, the village from which Eliot's ancestors left for the New World, and Little Gidding, the Anglican community set up by Nicholas Ferrar in the 1630s. Eliot, clearly feeling he had written himself out with these poems, then turned to the stage. He wrote *Murder in the Cathedral*—in metrical verse—in 1936, and then produced a series of plays in free verse more or less disguised as prose, and with a modern setting (e.g. *The Cocktail Party*, 1948).

Eliot regarded Ezra Pound (1885–1972) as his immediate master, and dedicated *The Waste Land* to him with the phrase "il miglior fabbro" (the best craftsman). Pound's origin in aestheticism is even clearer than Eliot's, as is his debt to Browning in his early dramatic monologues. He never ceased to be a literary poet, adapting freely from many langs. (Chinese, Lat. Provençal, even OE). Pound and Eliot reintroduced into Eng. p. the Ren. idea of "imitatio," the insertion into a poem of pieces of earlier poems on the same theme, usually adapted somewhat; Pound carried this to its greatest extreme in the *Cantos*, the huge poem to which he devoted his later years.

Pound's leading Eng. follower is Basil Bunting (1900–85). His most important poem is *Briggflatts* (1966), an oblique and elusive autobiography, named after a village in his native Northumbria. "Brag, sweet tenor bull," it begins: announcing both its modernist terseness and Bunting's insistence that poetry "deals in sound."

W. B. Yeats never became a modernist to the same extent as Pound and Eliot, but he moved away from his early romanticism, partly through verbal pruning ("there's more enterprise / In walking naked"), partly through modern subject matter (esp. Ir. politics, as in "Easter 1916" and *Meditations in Time of Civil War*). His finest poems retain a concern with traditional romantic themes: religion, art, history. "A Dialogue of Self and Soul" sums up the dichotomy that runs through all his poetry. "Sailing to Byzantium" is a 20th-c. equivalent to Keats's "Grecian Urn": both poems set forth the paradox that the timelessness of art can capture the flux of living most perfectly because of its very lifelessness. Yeats was interested in a wide range of fringe religions, esoteric science, the occult, and cyclic views of history. He put these ideas into his prose work *A Vision* (1925), and used them as a basis for many of his greatest poems: his work is therefore a prime case for exploring the relation between poetry and ideas. The painstaking system of historical periods, related to the phases of the moon in *A Vision*, is compressed into terse and resonant statements about the chaos of the modern world in such poems as "The Second Coming" and "Lapis Lazuli," or such memorable couplets as "Hector is dead and there's a light in Troy. / We that look on but laugh in tragic joy," where aesthetic delight and social despair ignite each other.

Eng. p. in the 1930s grew more political: the leftwing enthusiasms of the Popular Front and opposition to fascism run through the work of Auden, Day Lewis, Spender, and MacNeice—and, rather differently, are prominent in the Scots of Hugh MacDiarmid. The Sp. Civil War was the focal conflict of the decade; a Marxist version of it is offered in Auden's "Spain 1937." W. H. Auden (1907–73), the most complex and interesting of these poets, soon left his political phase behind, and later made some attempt to suppress it when revising his early work. His three long poems, *New Year Letter* (1941), *For the Time Being* (1945), and *The Age of Anxiety* (1948), show his growing religious concern and his shift to a more psychological and anthropological stance; yet one of his most powerful political poems, "The Shield of Achilles," appeared as late as 1955. Auden's later devel. was seen as irresponsible by those who regarded him as the political conscience of the 1930s, but can equally be seen as showing a constant vitality and intellectual range. A very different view of the '30s is provided by John Betjeman (1906–83), the idol of the middlebrow public, who by the time he became the Poet Laureate in 1972 was regarded with a grudging respect by the critics, responding to his obvious verbal skill and the deep feeling under the quaint humor.

The Second World War produced surprisingly little poetry of lasting importance (though both Eliot and Dylan Thomas wrote movingly about the air raids). Little of the neoromanticism and revived surrealism of the 1940s now seems of lasting interest, except for the work of Dylan Thomas (1914–53), in whom Rimbaud seems to merge with a Welsh bardic strain. His poems, using a variety of formal verseforms, including experiments of great discipline and complexity, are at times impenetrably turgid, at other times—especially when partly autobiographical—very moving in their verbal richness. His most popular poems are the celebratory "Poem in October" and "Fern Hill," which anticipate the even more popular *Under Milk Wood* (1953), a radio play that mingles bawdiness and a nursery-rhyme magic.

The 1950s saw the rise of The Movement, as it is rather uninformatively labeled, a school of poets that valued clarity, wit, and traditional competence, and was suspicious of bardic afflatus and grand gesture. As a movement it was short-lived, and its main figures, Kingsley Amis (b. 1922), John Wain (b. 1925), Donald Davie (b. 1922), Philip Larkin (1922–86), and Thom Gunn (b. 1929), soon went their separate ways. Larkin was England's most admired poet in the 1960s, his wry melancholy and resigned awareness of the drabness of life being presented with wit and a powerful lyric gift: "Church Going" and "The Witsun Weddings," treating religion and ritual from the stance of a wryly bewildered outsider, may be considered the two most representative poems of the postwar generation. Ted Hughes (b. 1930), who became Poet Laureate in 1984, offers a strong contrast to Larkin: whereas Larkin derives from Hardy, Hughes derives from Lawrence. He is prolific, sometimes obscure, his poems crackling with verbal energy, and ceaselessly inventive. His best known volume is *Crow* (1970), which is explicitly violent and blasphemous, but it lacks the richness and subtlety of some of his shorter poems ("Hawk Roosting," "To Paint a Water-lily"), which convey the same disturbing sense of cruelty in a less blustering way.

Of the poets who rose to prominence after 1970, there is no space for a systematic survey. To group them by movements and tendencies is to risk subordinating the poetry itself to journalistic classification, but there is no real alternative if any sense of the poetic scene is to be conveyed. There has been a second "invasion" of Am. influence, esp. through the work of the "confessional" poets, Lowell, Berryman, and Sylvia Plath (who herself settled in England and married an Eng. poet), as well as through the violently modernist techniques applied to urban life—e.g. in the work of Roy Fisher (b. 1930). Adrian Mitchell (b. 1932) is a popular—and populist—poet of strong political commitment. Since the 1960s, a poetic school of astonishing richness and fertility has arisen in Northern Ireland, with the political violence endemic there since 1969 providing much of the subject matter. The leading figure is Seamus Heaney (b. 1939), whose verbal richness moves powerfully between Irish and personal themes; others are John Montague (b. 1929), Michael Longley (b. 1939), Derek Mahon (b. 1941), and Paul Muldoon (b. 1951). The work of Craig Raine (b. 1944) and Christopher Reid (b. 1949) has become known as "Martian," because of Raine's poem "A Martian sends a postcard home," a manifesto of defamiliarization, inviting us to see common objects with the eye of a Martian or small child. Many of their best poems are riddles (to which they are sometimes careful not to give the answers).

For the first time in Eng. lit. hist., women are now making a contribution to poetry as substantial as they have always made to the novel. Stevie Smith (1902–71) wrote mischievously naive poetry that verges on doggerel, but achieved a few unforgettable short poems: "Not waving but drowning" has become one of the most famous lyrics of the age. Elizabeth Jennings (b. 1926, associated with the Movement) and Sylvia Plath, who committed suicide in 1963 at the age of 32, both handle mental breakdown and inner disturbance with poise and insight; the control is less steady in Plath, who rides the whirlwind precariously, but who also wrote some very tender poems about motherhood and domestic life. More recent names include Elizabeth Bartlett (b. 1924), U. A. Fanthorpe (b. 1929), Anne Stevenson (b. 1933), Jenny Joseph (b. 1932), and Fleur Adcock (b. 1934).

Inevitably, many of the best poets fit no group. Norman MacCaig (b. 1910) combines a keen eye for nature with a brilliant verbal gift and philosophic probing, and seems at times like a blend of Hopkins and Wallace Stevens. The terse, tough religious poems of R. S. Thomas (b. 1913) are the product of a Christianity after the death of God movement. Charles Tomlinson (b. 1927) also began under the influence of Stevens, and has developed into an urbane, controlled, intelligent and at times witty poet. Peter Redgrove (b. 1932), prolific and uneven, writes in a style that is largely surrealist, or, as he would prefer to call it, erotic. Geoffrey Hill (b. 1932) has written complex, resonant poems in traditional meters (*Tenebrae*) and prose-poems (*Mercian Hymns*) that deal hauntingly with religion and hist. Keeping the classics alive is no longer the task of the privileged class in modern Britain: this can be seen in the career of Tony Harrison (b. 1937) who is at the same time defiantly provincial, writing about his working class origins in Leeds in bluntly powerful autobiographical poems, and an accomplished linguist, translating and adapting work for the stage from many langs. Even this rapid sketch of the contemp. scene should serve to show that the Eng. poetic scene is alive, well, and complicated. See also AMERICAN POETRY.

BIBLIOGRAPHIES: *New CBEL*; A. E. Dyson, *Eng. P.: Select Bibl. Guides* (1971); R. C. Schweik and D. Riesner, *Reference Sources in Eng. and Am. Lit.: An Annot. Bibl.* (1977); J. L. Harner, *Literary Research Guide* (1989), esp. sect. M.

ANTHOLOGIES: *General*: *Understanding Poetry*, ed. C. Brooks and R. P. Warren (1938–); *Poets of the Eng. Lang.*, ed. W. H. Auden and N. H. Pearson (1953); *New Poets of England and America*, ed. D. Hall et al. (1958); *Norton Anthol. of Poetry*, ed. A. W. Allison et al. (1975). *Oxford anthologies*: *Oxford Book of Eng. Verse*, ed. A. T. Quiller-Couch (1900); *Romantic Verse*, ed. H. S. Milford (1928); *Mod. Verse*, ed. W. B. Yeats (1936); *19th-C. Eng. Verse*, ed. J. Hayward (1964); *Ballads*, ed. J. Kinsley (1969); *New Oxford Book of Eng. Verse*, ed. H. Gardner (1972); *20th-C. Verse*, ed. P. Larkin (1973); *Contemp. Verse*, ed. D. J. Enright (1980); *Christian Verse*, ed. D. Davie (1982); *Traditional Verse*, ed. F. Woods (1983); *Narrative Verse*, ed. I. and P. Opie (1983); *18th-C. Verse*, ed. R. Lonsdale (1984); *Short Poems*, ed. P.J. Kavanagh and J. Michie (1986); *New Oxford Book of Victorian Verse*, ed. C. Ricks (1987); *Shakespeare*, ed. S. Wells (1987); *18th-C. Women Poets*, ed. R. Lonsdale (1989); *Oxford Anthol. of Eng. P.*, ed. J. Wain, 2 v. (1991); *New Oxford Book of 16th-C. Verse*, ed. E. Jones (1991); *New Oxford Book of 17th-C. Verse*, ed. A. Fowler (1991). *Penguin anthologies*: *The New Poetry*, ed. A. Alvarez (1962); *Religious Verse*, ed. R. S. Thomas (1963); *Elizabethan Verse*, ed. E. Lucie-Smith (1965); *Metaphysical Poets*, ed. H. Gardner, 2d ed. (1967); *Restoration Verse*, ed. H. Love (1968); *Eng. Romantic Verse*, ed. D. Wright (1968); *Victorian Verse*, ed. G. Macbeth (1969); *First World War Poetry*, ed. J. Silkin (1969); *18th-C. Verse*, ed. D. Davison (1973); *Eng. Pastoral Verse*, ed. J. Barrell and J. Bull (1975); *Contemp. British Poetry*, ed. B. Morrison and A. Motion (1982); *War Poetry*, ed. J. Stallworthy (1984).

ELECTRONIC TEXTS: *The Eng. P. Full-Text Database* (1992–94).

HISTORY AND CRITICISM: T. Warton, *Hist. of Eng. P.* (1774–81); S. Johnson, *Lives of the Eng. Poets* (1781); W. Wordsworth, Prefaces to *Lyrical Ballads* (1800, 1802) and *Poems* (1815); S. T. Coleridge, *Biographia literaria* (1817)—esp. chs. 13–16; W. Hazlitt, *Lectures on the Eng. Poets* (1818); W. J. Courthope, *A Hist. of Eng. P.* (1895–1910); Smith; W. W. Greg, *Pastoral Poetry and Pastoral Drama* (1906); *Critical Essays of the 17th C.*, ed. J. G. Spingarn (1908); R. D. Havens, *The Influence of Milton on Eng. P.* (1922); O. Barfield, *Poetic Diction* (1928); D. Bush, *Mythology and the Ren. Trad. in Eng. P.* (1933), *Mythology and the Romantic Trad. in Eng. P.* (1937), *Eng. Lit. in the Earlier 17th C.* (1945), *Eng. P.* (1952); W. Empson, *Some Versions of Pastoral* (1935), *The Structure of Complex Words* (1951), *Seven Types of Ambiguity*, 3d ed. (1953); F. R. Leavis, *Revaluation* (1936); C. S. Lewis, *The Allegory of Love* (1936), *Eng. Lit. in the 16th C.* (1954), *The Discarded Image* (1964); Y. Winters, *Primitivism and Decadence* (1937), *The Function of Crit.* (1957); J. C. Ransom, *The World's Body* (1938); W. J. Bate, *The Stylistic Devel. of Keats* (1945); Brooks; R. Tuve, *Elizabethan and Metaphysical Imagery* (1947); J. Sutherland, *A Preface to 18th-C. Poetry* (1948); G. Hough, *The Last Romantics* (1949), *Image and Experience* (1960); J. Miles, *The Continuity of Poetic Lang.* (1951), *Eras and Modes in Eng. P.* (1962); M. H. Abrams, *The Mirror and the Lamp* (1953), *Natural Supernaturalism* (1971); E. R. Wasserman, *The Finer Tone* (1953), *The Subtler Lang.* (1959); P. Cruttwell, *The Shakespearean Moment* (1954); G. Hartmann, *The Unmediated Vision* (1954), *Wordsworth's Poetry, 1787–1814* (1964); W. K. Wimsatt, Jr., *The Verbal Icon* (1954); D. Davie, *Articulate Energy* (1955), *Under Briggflatts: A Hist. of P. in Great Britain, 1960–1988* (1989); J. Press, *The Fire and the Fountain* (1955), *A Map of Mod. Eng. Verse* (1969); N. Frye, *Anatomy of Crit.* (1957), *Fables of Identity* (1963); F. Kermode, *Romantic Image* (1957), *Ren. Essays* (1971); R. Langbaum, *The Poetry of Experience* (1957), *The Mysteries of Identity* (1977); Wimsatt and Brooks; D. Perkins, *The Quest for Permanence* (1959), *Wordsworth and the Poetry of Sincerity* (1964), *A Hist. of Mod. Poetry*, 2 v. (1976, 1987); ; A. Warren, *Rage for Order* (1959); D. Daiches, *Critical Hist. of Eng. Lit.* (1960); J. Hollander, *The Untuning of the Sky* (1961), *Vision and Resonance*, 2d ed. (1985), *Melodious Guile* (1988); W. Nowottny, *The Lang. Poets Use* (1962);

The Poets and their Critics, ed. H. S. Davies (1962); I. Jack, *Eng. Lit. 1815–1832* (1963); W. L. Renwick, *Eng. Lit. 1789–1815* (1963); C. K. Stead, *The New Poetic* (1964); K. Burke, *Lang. as Symbolic Action* (1966); R. Cohen, "The Augustan Mode in Eng. P.," *ECS* 1 (1967); B. H. Smith, *Poetic Closure* (1968); H. Kenner, *The Pound Era* (1971); R. L. Colie, *The Resources of Kind* (1973); H. Bloom, *The Anxiety of Influence* (1973); L. Lerner, *An Intro. to Eng. P.* (1974); *20th-C. Poetry,* ed. G. Martin and P. N. Furbank (1975); S. Hynes, *The Auden Generation* (1976); V. Forrest-Thomson, *Poetic Artifice* (1978); P. Hobsbaum, *Trad. and Experiment in Eng. P.* (1979); B. Lewalski, *Protestant Poetics and the 17th-C. Religious Lyric* (1979); J. R. de J. Jackson, *Poetry of the Romantic Period* (1980); B. Morrison, *The Movement* (1980); A. D. Nuttall, *Overheard by God* (1980); H. Vendler, *Part of Nature, Part of Us* (1980); G. S. Fraser, *A Short Hist. of Eng. P.* (1981); E. Rothstein, *Restoration and 18th-C. Poetry, 1660–1780* (1981); Fowler; C. Ricks, *The Force of Poetry* (1984); M. A. Doody, *The Daring Muse: Augustan Poetry Reconsidered* (1985); J. H. Miller, *The Linguistic Moment* (1985); *Lyric Poetry: Beyond New Crit.,* ed. C. Hošek and P. Parker (1985); *Poetry Today: A Critical Guide to British P. 1960–1984,* ed. A. Thwaite (1985); D. Wesling, *The New Poetries* (1985); S. Curran, *Poetic Form and British Romanticism* (1986); *Poststructuralist Readings of Eng. P.,* ed. R. Machin and C. Norris (1987); G. Hammond, *Fleeting Things: Eng. Poets and Poems, 1616–1660* (1989); K. Millard, *Edwardian Poetry* (1992).

L.D.L.

ESKIMO POETRY. See INUIT POETRY.

ESPERANTO POETRY began with the first booklet on the *Internat. Lang. E.,* pub. in Warsaw in 1887 by the Polish scholar L. L. Zamenhof (1859–1917) under the pseudonym "Dr. E." ("one who hopes"). The booklet included three poems—one translated and two original—to demonstrate that this proposed second lang. for internat. use was no lifeless project but a potential living lang. Zamenhof also produced numerous E. trs., incl. *Hamlet* (1894) and the entire Old Testament. The first E. magazine, *La Esperantisto,* which began in Nuremberg in 1889, also published poetry, early poets drawing on their native trads. to establish poetic norms for E. More than 100 regular periodicals now publish tr. and original E. p. E. lit. runs to several thousand volumes, and the E. lang. is presently used or understood by several million speakers in the world. E. is a European pidgin with a simplified grammar (though inflectional endings are retained) and pronunciation but a very large vocabulary of fresh and interesting wordforms and grammatical combinations unknown in European langs., e.g. Michalski's poetic coinage *ĉielenas* (goes upwards to the sky), in which *-as* denotes the present tense, *-n* direction toward, and *-e* the adverbial ending, while *ĉiel-* is the root associated with sky or heaven, *ĉielo.* Thus *ĉiele* = in the sky; *ĉielen* = towards in-the-sky; *ĉielenas* = is towards in-the-sky.

Serious projects for universal langs. began in the 17th c. with George Dalgarno (1661) and John Wilkins (1668) and engaged the attention of Descartes, Leibnitz, and Newton. Apart from E., only Volapük (1880) and Ido ("offspring"; 1908), a modification of E., developed any significant following, now dissipated. By 1900 E. had spread beyond Poland, Russia, and Germany to Western Europe. Several collections of poems appeared, incl. three by the Czech Stanislav Schulhof (1864–1919) and the polished and musical *Tra l'silento* (Through the Silence, 1912) of Edmond Privat (1889–1962). Antoni Grabowski (1857–1921), friend of Zamenhof and skilled linguist, published an internat. anthol., *El parnaso de popoloj* (From the Parnassus of the Peoples, 1913) and a brilliant tr. of the *Pan Tadeusz* of Mickiewicz (1918). His audacious linguistic experiments prepared for the flowering of E. p. The Hungarians Kálman Kálocsay (1891–1976), in *Mondo kaj koro* (World and Heart, 1921), and Gyula Baghy (1891–1967), in *Preter la vivo* (Beyond Life, 1922), led the way. They founded the influential magazine and publishing house *Literatura Mondo* (Literary World) in 1922.

Zamenhof's interest in E. lit. aimed to create an E. literary and cultural trad., to expand and test the lang. by stretching it to its limits, and to demonstrate that it was as capable of expression as any ethnic lang. Unlike some other projects for an internat. lang. (none of which withstood the test of time), E. did not spring fully armed from its creator's head. Zamenhof's 1887 booklet contained only the basis of E.; others expanded its lexicon and discovered its latent syntactic and morphological possibilities. Kálocsay, in numerous trs. and original poetry, esp. *Streĉita kordo* (Tightened String, 1931), sought diversity: his work includes lyrics, free verse, and strict verse-forms. The Rus. Eugen Michalski (1897–1937) wrote introspective poems of startling imagery and linguistic experiment. While Privat and Kálocsay demonstrated E.'s affinities with the European trad., Michalski sought originality. But Stalinism claimed Michalski's life and silenced the talented Nikolai Hohlov (1891–1953). The figure of Kálocsay dominated the interwar years as mentor, editor, and publisher. Kálocsay and Waringhien's *Parnasa gvidlibro* (Guidebook to Parnassus, 1932) with its *Arto poetika* and glossary of literary terms and neologisms helped establish an E. trad.; in 1952, *Kvaropo* (Quartet) extended this trad. This work, by four British poets incl. William Auld (b. 1924), began a new era. Auld's *La infana raso* (The Child Rose, 1956), a poem of great variety and technical virtuosity, is widely regarded as the most impressive achievement of E. poetry to date. Auld's mentors include Michalski and the Eng.-lang. poets MacDiarmid, Pound, and Eliot. Among British contributors to E. poetry are Marjorie Boulton (b. 1930), Albert Goodheir (b. 1912), and

Victor Sadler (b. 1937), whose *Memkritiko* (1967) displays concise expressiveness and mordant irony. Poets of the generation of Auld and Boulton include the difficult and introspective Icelander Baldur Ragnarsson (b. 1930), the Brazilian Geraldo Mattos (b. 1931), and the Czech Eli Urbanová (b. 1922).

The past thirty years have seen a widening of the geographic and cultural base as increasing numbers of Chinese and Japanese poets have begun publishing. They incl. Miyamoto Masao (b. 1913), Kuroda Masayuki (b. 1909), Ossaka Kenji (1888–1969), and Ueyama Masao (1910–88). In the E. poetic trad., tr. and original work are closely linked. Trs. incl. many of Shakespeare's plays (some by Kálocsay and Auld), his sonnets (tr. Auld), Camões' *Lusiads*, Dante's *Divine Comedy*, the *Kalevala*, the *Quran*, and volumes by Goethe, Baudelaire, Sophocles, Alves, Omar Khaiyam, Tagore, and numerous others.

Because of its conciseness and suitability for linguistic experiment, E. p. has developed faster than the E. novel or drama, though over 50 original novels have appeared. E.'s lexicon has expanded vastly: Zamenhof's initial vocabulary comprised fewer than 1000 roots, from which perhaps 10,000 words could be formed. The largest contemp. dictionaries now contain 20 times that number. The lexicon remains largely European, but E. grammar and syntax resemble isolating langs., like Chinese, and agglutinative langs., like Swahili and Japanese. The future of E. poetry is promising. Younger poets such as the Brazilian Passos Nogueira (b. 1949) and the precociously talented Mauro Nervi (b. 1959) of Italy (*La turoj de l'cefurbo*, The Towers of the Capital, 1978) live in an era of increased scholarly attention to E. E. appears to have established itself as a linguistic and cultural community with its own critical norms and standards.

L. Kökeny and V. Bleier, *Enciklopedio de e.* (1933); *Gvidlibro por supera ekzameno*, ed. A. Pechan (1966); M. G. Hagler, "The E. Lang. as a Literary Medium," Diss. Indiana (1971); W. Auld, *The Devel. of Poetic Lang. in E.* (1976), *Enkonduko en la originalan literaturon de E.* (1979); V. Benczik, *Studoj pri la Esperanta literaturo* (1980); P. Ullman, "Schizoschematic Rhyme in E.," *PLL* 16 (1980); *E. in the Mod. World*, ed. R. and V. S. Eichholz (1982); *Esperanta antologio*, ed. W. Auld (1984)—anthol.; H. Tonkin, "One Hundred Years of E.: A Survey," *LPLP* 11 (1987); D. Richardson, *E.: Learning and Using the Internat. Lang.* (1988).H.T.

ESTONIAN POETRY. The E. lang., like Finnish, has the word-accent on the first syllable, is highly inflected, and tends toward polysyllabism. Its relatively small number of initial consonants favors alliteration, which, however, is unobtrusive because of the unemphatic articulation. Oral folk poetry, alive in some parts of Estonia until fairly recently and recorded in hundreds of thousands of texts, prefers an octosyllabic meter combining quantitative and accentual principles, as that of the Finnish *Kalevala.* The lines, trochaic when sung (though not when spoken), permit initial short syllables of words to be stressed only at the beginning of the verse, e.g.:

Kõlise, kõlise, keeli,
Laja vastu, laasi, suuri.

Ring, ring, tongue,
Resound, great forest.

Parallelism and periphrastic formulae—not unlike *kenningar*—abound, creating a rich, ornamental style capable of strong lyrical and dramatic effects. Written poetry since the 17th c. almost entirely discarded this form, using instead either accentual-syllabic or purely accentual meters, largely owing to Ger. influence. The numerous polysyllables, with only one clearly audible stress, often count as one long metrical foot; more frequently, however, the slight secondary stresses are exploited metrically, producing iambic or trochaic patterns, Dactylic, amphibrachic, and anapestic patterns are also frequent enough. There is considerable disinclination to use the weakly stressed inflections as rhymes. Near rhymes, permitting a fuller use of the vocabulary and surprise effects, have become more common since the 1920s.

Foreign—Baltic-Ger. and Rus.—social, economic, and political pressure slowed up the intellectual life of the Estonians until the early 19th c., when poetry, along with other cultural pursuits, began to flower. Stimulated by the romantic conception of a national genius, the leading poets of the E. national Ren. drew much of their inspiration from folklore, aided by their study of cl. antiquity, Finnish, Ger., and partly British romantic and preromantic poetry. The first notable poet, the short-lived Kristjan Jaak Peterson (1802–22), wrote inspired Pindarics. F. R. Kreutzwald's epic *Kalevipoeg* (The Kalevid, 1857–61), based on runic folk ballads, whose meter it uses, and of decisive importance as a cultural stimulus, owed much to Lönnrot's Finnish *Kalevala.* The powerful patriotic lyrics of Lydia Koidula (1843–86) with great independence developed the romantic *Lied* genre. Later in the century, political and social changes led to a less public, more intimate and more individually differentiated poetry, most impressively exemplified in the profoundly personal, tragic symbolism of the seemingly simple lyrics of Juhan Liiv (1864–1913). Symbolism in its Western form, intellectually searching, with much emphasis on a highly individualized, sophisticated style, characterizes the verse of the Noor-Eesti (Young Estonia) group, above all that of its leader, Gustav Suits (1883–1957), a revolutionary experimentalist and idealist, constantly torn between high flights of emotion and bitter, satirical skepticism. The poignancy, subtlety, formal richness, and exploratory boldness of his verse decisively affected the further course of E. p. The quiet, introspective mysticism of Ernst Enno (1875–1934), the sensitive island landscapes of Villem Grünthal-Ridala (1885–1942), influenced by Carducci, and the archaic ballads of Jaan Lôo (1872–1939) all added new wealth of language, imagery, and versification to a rapidly expanding lit. A discordant but effective note was struck by the gloomy, visionary primitivism of Jaan Oks (1884–1918).

Toward the end of the First World War, shortly before the E. declaration of independence in 1918, a new group, named after a mythological bird, "Siuru," inaugurated an era of lyrical exuberance and extreme individualism in both form and content. Its leaders, Marie Under (1883–1980) and Henrik Visnapuu (1889–1951), soon abandoned subjectivism for strenuous thought, more universal themes, and more firmly crystallized form. Marie Under, the greatest master of lyrical intensity, passed through psychological and metaphysical crises culminating in a poetry of extraordinary translucency and human insight. The eclectic but keenly picturesque aestheticism of Johannes Semper (1892–1970), the intimate dialect verse of Artur Adson (1889–1977) and Hendrik Adamson (1891–1946), and the principally Rus.-inspired experiments in melodic instrumentation of Valmar Adams (1899) preceded a temporary trend towards robust, nonphilosophic realism, which dominated the early Thirties but was followed by a strongly idealistic reaction. The deeply rooted native tendency toward symbolism, in a disciplined new form, reasserted itself in the verse of the "Arbujad" (Magicians) group, including Uku Masing (1909–1985), Bernard Kangro (b. 1910), and, above all, Heiti Talvik (1904–47) and Betti Alver (b. 1906), both intellectually among the subtlest, formally among the most brilliant of E. verse writers. Keenly aware of the great trad. of European poetry and thought, these poets sought "to enclose in slim stanzas the blind rage of the elements" (Talvik), imposing the finality of perfect expression on the emotional turbulence of a world heading toward chaos. This is equally apparent in the extreme, explosive, but fully controlled condensation of Talvik and in the more diverse output of Betti Alver, whose intense inner struggles are expressed with classical poignancy and clarity, her seriousness tempered by self-irony and sometimes also warm humor. Bernard Kangro's sensitive application of legendary and country lore added a special touch to the verse of this group.

From the Second World War up to the 1960s, which led to the Sovietization of Estonia, only the refugees were able to write freely and produce real art. Some of them, esp. Marie Under, Bernard Kangro in some of his works, and Gustav Suits in his last extensive volume of verse, have grown in breadth and depth. Though akin to the "Magicians" of the 1930s, both Arno Vihalemm (b. 1911) and Aleksis Rannit (1914–85) came into their own only in emigration. While Vihalemm has given voice to the grotesque absurdity of human existence, Rannit has chanted its sole salvation through artistic form. Kalju Lepik (b.1920), Ilmar Laaban (b. 1921), and Raimond Kolk (b.1924) comprise the first generation of exile poets. Lepik has adapted the parallelism and associative alliteration of folksong to ironic and dramatic ends; the linguistically inventive Laaban has been called the only true E. surrealist; Kolk's lyrical voice is most convincing in his dialect verse. Later exile poetry shows both the erotically charged virtuoso verse of Ivar Grünthal (b. 1924) and Ivar Ivask's (b. 1927) free-verse contemplations about being a cosmopolitan exile yet irrevocably rooted in nature, our only home. Urve Karuks (b. 1936) and Aarand Roos (b. 1940) have also made definite contributions. The revival of poetry back in Soviet Estonia was spearheaded by Jaan Kross (b. 1920) in his free-verse experiments in political frankness and by Artur Alliksaar's (1923–60) surrealist-absurdist wordplay. Their example was soon followed by the pronounced nationalist stance of Hando Runnel (b. 1938), the ecologically minded prophetism of Jaan Kaplinski (b. 1941), the polyphonic lyricism of Paul-Eerik Rummo (b. 1942), and the ironical personae employed by actor Juhan Viiding (b. 1948). Of the younger poets, Doris Kareva (b. 1958) has gained attention at home and abroad. Thanks to Gorbachev's policy of "openness," books by émigré poets have begun to be reprinted in Estonia and their work critically assessed. *Sõnarine*, a 4-vol. anthol. now in progress, promises to become the most comprehensive ever because it integrates both branches of E. lit.

ANTHOLOGIES: *An Anthol. of Mod. E.P.*, ed. W. K. Matthews (1953); *Acht E. Dichter*, (1964), *E. Lit. Reader*, (1968), both ed. A. Oras; *Contemp. East European Poetry*, ed. E. George (1985) *Kalevipoeg*, ed. J. Kurman (1982); *Ilomaile: Anthol. of E. Folk Songs*, ed. J. Kurrik (1985); *Sõnarine*, ed. K. Muru (1989–).

HISTORY AND CRITICISM: W. F. Kirby, *The Hero of Estonia*, 2 v. (1895)—on *Kalevipoeg*; M. Kampmaa, *Eesti kirjandusloo peajooned*, 4 v. (1924–36)—hist. of E. lit.; F. R. Kreutzwald, *Kalevipoeg*, 2 v. (1934–36); W. K. Matthews, "The E. Sonnet," *SEER* 25 (1946–47); E. H. Harris, *Lit. in Estonia*, 2d ed. (1953); H. Salu, *Eesti vanem kirjandus* (1953); G. Suits, *Eesti kirjanduslugu*, v. 1 (1953); A. Oras, "E. P.," *BNYPL* 61 (1957) and "Storia della letteratura estone," in *Storia delle letterature Baltiche*, ed. G. Devoto (1957); *For Ants Oras: Studies in E. P. and Lang.*, ed. V. Kõressaar and A. Rannit (1964); E. Nirk, *E. Lit.* (1987). A.O.; I.I.

ETHIOPIAN POETRY may be divided into four kinds: (1) verse written in Ge'ez (Ethiopic), a lang. which ceased to be spoken (except in the church) some four or five hundred years ago, yet has continued to be used for literary expression; (2) popular verse composed in Amharic (now the official lang. of Ethiopia), Tigrinya, Tigre, Harari, and other regional langs.; (3) modern devotional and secular poetry in Amharic; and (4) poetry written in European langs., mainly Eng.

Rhyme is the principal formal characteristic in all types of E. p. But this rhyme consists of sounds formed by the initial consonant and medial vowel of a syllable (not vowel plus final consonant, as in Eng.). If the last word of a line ends in what is ordinarily a consonant, in poetry a vowel (something between short *e* and *i*) must be sounded after it. The vowel sound alone does not constitute rhyme, however; the preceding consonant is significant, and generally one full rhyme persists for several lines before another, which differs in both consonant and vowel, begins.

Ambiguity or *double entendre* plays a more important part in traditional E. p. than does beauty of sound and rhythm. Characteristic Ge'ez verse, beginning with the classical *qene*, illustrates this quality: rhymed poems up to a dozen lines long contain intricate allusions and nuances. Even today the principles of *qene* composition require several years of study at monastic schools and a profound knowledge of the Bible, sacred legend, or dogma in order to be understood. Other Ge'ez poetry ranges from epigrammatic couplets through 9-line praise poems to long hymns—one favorite form is the *malk'e* (likeness), usually addressed to a saint and consisting of some fifty 5-line stanzas, each of which begins *salam*, and is a salutation to a different physical or moral attribute of the subject.

The earliest Ge'ez religious verse is attributed to Yared (6th c.), but surviving poems mostly date from the 15th c. or after. Patriotic sentiment and Ethiopic hymnology are often combined, as in the Ge'ez poem composed before the Battle of Adowa (1896), in which E. forces led by Emperor Menelik defeated invading Italians:

> Gomorrah and Sodom, lands of retribution, shall
> find pardon in the terrible day of battle.
> But you, base city of Rome,
> That will come upon you which did not come upon Sodom,
> For Menelik, savior of the world,
> Has sent you swathed in blood to visit Dathan and
> Abiram in the grave. . . .

Although the first poet to write in Amharic was probably Gabre Egzi'abeher (b. 1860), popular verse has been composed orally in Amharic and other regional langs. since at least the 14th c. Such verse has often been occasional, but much praise poetry has been composed by professional minstrels to honor the Emperor or to be recited at notable weddings, funerals, and other events. There are also some love songs and a variety of patriotic verse which in the latter part of the 20th c. has often taken on strong national and propagandistic tones. Like Ge'ez poetry, popular Amharic verse has often aimed at *double entendre*; puns and wordplay are more appreciated than beauty of diction. For example:

> Yimallisau inji iraññāu bāwwaqa—
> Yammichilau yallam—yās lām ka-zallaqa.

> He will bring it back, indeed, will the herdsman,
> in (the way) he knows—
> There is none (other) who can—that cow that
> has strayed.

A rustic situation is described in simple language. But it is possible to take *yas lam* not as "that cow" but as *yā-(i)islām*, "those Moslems." The couplet is now transformed: the "herdsman" stands for God; and *zallaqa* can be taken in the sense of "infiltrate." We now have a pointed comment on the infiltration into Christian Ethiopia of Moslems, whom only God knows how to send away again.

During the 20th c., Amharic has become firmly entrenched as Ethiopia's national lang. and has taken the place of Ge'ez as a respectable literary lang. Much popular Amharic verse now exists, together with more sophisticated poetic expression. The traditional rhyme system is still generally followed, but with a tendency toward shorter series of rhymes. Poems are often lengthy and didactic, with patriotism and morality as common themes. In the late 1950s, Menghistu Lemma took a step towards writing Amharic poetry in Western forms, and Solomon Deressa's 1972 poem "Legennat" (Childhood) signals the appearance of the first significant modern poetry in Amharic.

Since the 1960s, and following a short period of translations from Amharic to Eng., a body of poetry written in Eng. has appeared. Some has followed the trad. of praise poetry, first for the Emperor Haile Sellassie and then for the subsequent regime. Other themes have included social change and uncertainty about Ethiopia's place in the contemporary world. The Eng. poems of Tsegaye Gabre-Medhin are representative in that they reveal love for an ancient and proud past, a "Time-old / Highland of highlands / Ancient / Where all history ends," and yet also a dark recognition that whether it likes it or not, after centuries of isolation Ethiopia has awakened to find itself in a world where

> man swims
> In the asylum of a beatnik-bomb-age
> or hangs on
> In a sino-american wrestle world.

ANTHOLOGIES: *Matshafa qenē*, *Inē-nnā wedājochē*, both ed. H. Walde-Sellassie (1926, 1935)—the first contains 1100 Ge'ez poems, the second Amharic and Ge'ez poems; *Amāriññā qenē*, ed. Mahtama-Sellassie Walde-Masqal (1955)—over

1150 short Amharic poems; *Malk'a qubā'ē*, ed. T. Gabre-Sellassie (1955)—coll. of Ge'ez hymns called *malk'e*; *Af. Poems and Love Songs*, ed. W. Leslau and C. Leslau (1970)—incl. E. poetry, songs, and lullabies, in Eng. tr.; *Highland Mosaic: A Crit. Anthol. of E. Lit. in Eng.*, ed. P. Huntsberger (1973)—includes previously pub. works, some difficult to obtain.

HISTORY AND CRITICISM: M. Chaîne, "La Poésie chez les Ethiopiens," *Revue de l'orient chrétien*, 3d ser., 2 (1920– 21); J. M. Harden, *An Intro. to Ethiopic Christian Lit.* (1926); W. Leslau, "Chansons Harari," *Rassegna di studi etiopici* (1947); E. Cerulli, *Storia della letteratura etiopica* (1956); M. Lemma, "Intro. to Mod. E. Lit.," Af.-Scandinavian Writers' Conference, Stockholm (1967); A. S. Gérard, *Four Af. Lits.: Xhosa, Sotho, Zulu, Amharic* (1971); T. Kane, *E. Lit. in Amharic* (1975); D. Beer, "The Sources and Content of E. Creative Writing in Eng.," *Research in Af. Lits.* 8 (1977); *Lits. in Af. Langs.*, ed. B. W. Andrzejewski (1985).

S.W.; D.F.B.

F

FINNISH POETRY.

I. THE BEGINNINGS
II. THE RISE OF FINNISH POETIC LANGUAGE
III. THE MODERN PERIOD

F. p. has developed over a long history, though the oldest extant texts written in F. date only from the middle of the 19th c., and though some of its classics were initially written in Swedish. It presents a complex history of cultural and literary influence, but thematically and taken as a whole, it shows a remarkably unified inspiration from early oral trad. to contemp. modernism. F., which is not an Indo-European lang., has developed alongside the Indo-European family of langs. at the periphery of European civilization.

I. THE BEGINNINGS. A rich treasury of oral-traditional songs and tales is extant, incl. ca. 1,270,000 lines and 85,000 variants of the poetry composed in the so-called *Kalevala* meter (trochaic tetrameter in its simplest form). These are traditionally the work of anonymous singers, both men and women, but some of the principal singers are known by name, such as Arhippa Perttunen and Ontrei Malinen, both of whom were important sources for Elias Lönnrot's compilations, the epic *Kalevala* (1835, 1849), and the *Kanteletar*, a collection of lyrics and short narrative poems (1840–41). F. folk p. consists of elements dating from different periods and deriving from various cultural strata. There is evidence of the existence of a vital oral poetry before the period of Swedish expansion during the 12th c. which brought Christianity to Finland. Finno-Ugric mythology, based on animistic and shamanistic religion, is an intrinsic part of the early cosmogonic poems, magic songs, and ritual incantations of this trad. Medieval Christianity introduced new elements to F. folk p. Ballads, legends, and lamentations express both religious and secular themes. In an exquisite cycle about the birth of Christ, a F. maiden, Marjatta, a variant of the Virgin Mary, becomes pregnant by eating cranberries (F. *marja*). The religious basis of these poems, which were composed afresh by individual singers according to their poetic skill, derives from a fusion of Catholic and Gr. Orthodox beliefs.

While oral poetry survived among the illiterate and in the agrarian parts of Finland, its importance decreased as other attempts were made to forge the F. lang. into a literary medium. One such attempt is Mikael Agricola's 1548 tr. of the New Testament, an important linguistic landmark as well as one of the first literary monuments of the Protestant era. At the end of the 17th c., Lat. and Swedish-lang. poetry were composed but did not rise much above the level of conventional verse. It was not until the recovery of the oral trads. in the 18th c., inaugurated by the study of F. folk p. (e.g. Henrik Gabriel Porthan's *De poesi fennica* [1766–78]), that F.-lang. p. began to emerge from obscurity. The realization that the F. people had created poetry worthy of comparison with the *Iliad* and the *Odyssey* had an enormous impact in Finland. The following lines by Arhippa Perttunen illustrate what could be discovered on native ground:

> My own finding are my words
> my own snatching from the road
> my grinding from the grass tops
> my snapping from the heather.
> (tr. K. Bosley)

II. THE RISE OF FINNISH POETIC LANGUAGE. While Swedish-lang. poetry of European orientation dominated literary production in Finland, and while the relatively scarce examples of early F.-lang. p. belong to the didactic and exhortatory trad. of the Enlightenment, the termination of Swedish rule in 1809 brought about an altogether new situation. A few Swedish-lang. poets, such as Frans Mikael Franzén (1772–1847), whose poetry expressed a strong preromantic conception of nature and of man as divine creation, were also influential in the devel. of F. p. When the Napoleonic wars resulted in a redistribution of the northern territories of Europe, Finland fell under Rus.

rule as a virtually autonomous Grand Duchy in 1809. This situation compelled the Finns, incl. the Swedish Finns, to turn their philosophical and literary attention to questions of F. national identity. Helsinki became the center of F. cultural and literary life. The University was moved there from Turku in 1827, the F. Lit. Society was founded in 1831, and the newspaper *Helsingfors Tidningar* began to appear in 1829. J. L. Runeberg (1804–77) became the foremost Swedish-lang. poet of the time with his *Dikter* (Poems, 1830). Combining a deep feeling for simple country folk with expert knowledge of both Cl. lit. and F. oral trad., Runeberg renewed lyrical lang. with his mastery of technique. His epic poems (in hexameters), e.g. the *Elgskyttarne* (The Elkhunters, 1832), a narrative about love and hunting, demonstrate how Cl. style can be effectively used to describe humble country life. His romanticism, both lyrical and patriotic, may be seen as an important precursor of the F.-lang. p. which emerged in the 1860s.

The poet Runeberg, the philosopher and writer J. W. Snellman (1806–81), Elias Lönnrot (1802–84), and the writer and poet Zachris Topelius (1818–98) all shaped the F. national consciousness and cultural identity, but conditions were not yet ripe for the production of F. p. of merit. Lönnrot showed some genuine poetic talent in assembling the epic *Kalevala* by introducing lyric material into the narratives, adding songs, and replacing missing lines according to his vision. But the pre-eminent figure at the time was Aleksis Kivi (pseud. of Alexis Stenvall, 1834–72), primarily a playwright and novelist whose poetic achievement was not fully recognized until this century. Kivi's contemporaries considered his poetry unfinished: it was more daring and personal than anything written at the time. Many of his poems were lyrical narratives which broke away from rhyming verse and used free rhythms, creating an intensity familiar from the folk lyric.

After Kivi, there were no major poets until the end of the 19th c., though Kaarlo Kramsu (1855–95) and J. H. Erkko (1849–1906) played an important role in forging a F. poetic that could effectively express new social and historical themes. Industrialization, educational reforms, and new scientific thought were reflected in the work of F. novelists and dramatists, who explored the forms of European realism in the 1880s. Swedish-lang. poetry was mainly represented by the verse drama *Daniel Hjort* (1862) by J. J. Wecksell (1832–1907), and by the poetry of Karl August Tavaststjerna (1860–98), who reflects the new sense of alienation felt by the Swedish-speaking writers, whose minority status was becoming increasingly apparent.

National Neoromanticism was the term coined by the poet Eino Leino (1878–1926) to characterize certain currents in F. lit. and the fine arts influenced by European symbolism. It combined enthusiasm, determination, and outstanding talent in all fields: the composer Jean Sibelius, the painter Akseli Gallen-Kallela, and the architect Eliel Saarinen were all representatives of "Young Finland." A prolific poet, Leino developed an innovative technique which radically changed the F. poetic idiom. Leino put the stamp of originality on everything he wrote. While drawing upon traditional sources such as myth and folk poetry for themes and motifs, he was fully versed in European and Scandinavian lit., and translated Dante, Corneille, Racine, Goethe, and Schiller. His *Helkavirsiä* (Whitsongs, 1903, 1916) recreate the most ancient folk trads. in narrative lyrics of visionary character having a symbolic resonance that transcends the national sphere. Leino's lyrical lang. is supple and resourceful: in "Nocturne" (from *Talvi-yö* [Winter Night], 1905), the melodious lines evoke the infinite in a clearly defined space:

> The corncrake's song rings in my ears,
> above the rye a full moon sails;
> this summer night all sorrow clears
> and woodsmoke drifts along the dales.
> (tr. K. Bosley)

The inner dynamics of Leino's poetry spring from a fruitful tension between an ultra-individualistic, egocentric, amoral *übermensch* and a prophet-seer who could capture and articulate the complex spirit of his epoch. Several of his contemporaries added other elements to the vigorously developing F. poetic lang. L. Onerva (1882–1972) lent a free spirit to explorations of femininity in sensual lyric verse, while Otto Manninen (1872–1950) and V. A. Koskenniemi (1885–1964) wrote in the European classic mode. Manninen, a virtuoso poet, wrote clear, concise verse on symbolist themes and translated Homer, Gr. tragedy, and Molière. Koskenniemi, whose work now seems dated, expressed his pessimistic philosophy in tightly controlled verse inspired by ancient poetry. By 1920 F. poetic lang. had attained a variety and depth that guaranteed it a worthy place among European lits. With Finland's independence in 1917, poetry reconfirmed its central role in the expression of both individual and social sentiments.

III. THE MODERN PERIOD. While Leino has a strikingly modern timbre at times, modernism apppeared in F. p. shortly after World War I in the unique work of the Swedo-F. modernists, such as Edith Södergran (1892–1923) and Elmer Diktonius (1896–1961). Literary modernism coincided with anti-positivism in philosophy and was a reaction against 19th-c. empiricism and realism. In the 1920s, European movements such as futurism, cubism, constructivism, expressionism, and surrealism arrived in Finland almost simultaneously. Denying the ability of art to describe reality, the new poets increasingly turned away from mimetic art even as they rejected the past and everything connected with it. This was first seen in lang. experiments, e.g. in *Jääpeili* (Ice Mirror, 1928) by Aaro Hellaakoski's (1896–1952), in the poetry of

Katri Vala (1901–44), in the prose of Olavi Paavolainen (1903–64), and in the early work of P. Mustapää (1899–1973). The new generation that brought modernism to Finland formed a group called the "Firebearers," publishing albums and a journal of that name, *Tulenkantajat*. The Firebearers issued a manifesto in 1928, declaring the sacredness of art and life in tones reminiscent of the writings of the Swedo-F. modernists, but with an even greater fervor and passion. Katri Vala and Uuno Kailas (1901–33) expressed these ideals. Kailas was influenced by expressionism, while Vala, the most typical of the Firebearers, later became a politically committed leftist poet. Another literary group, "Kiila" (The Wedge), devoted itself to radical socialism after 1936. Arvo Turtiainen (1904–80), Viljo Kajava (b. 1909), and the novelist Elvi Sinervo (1912–86) were among its most important members, many of whom were imprisoned during World War II. The nation, divided by the Civil War (1918–19) following F. Independence, unified again for the effort of the Winter War, but the schism was not closed until the postwar era, as is described by Väinö Linna (b. 1920) in his epic trilogy *Täällä Pohjantähden alla* (Here under the North Star, 1959–62).

In the 1950s, poetic modernism became more sharply antitraditionalist. While drawing inspiration from both East and West, its lang., characterized by free rhythms and powerful imagery, turned hermetic. Paavo Haavikko (b. 1931), Eeva-Liisa Manner (b. 1921), Helvi Juvonen (1919–59), and Eila Kivikkaho (b. 1921) were among the most important poets, followed by other original talents such as Mirkka Rekola (b. 1931), Tyyne Saastamoinen (b. 1924), Lassi Nummi (b. 1928), and Pentti Holappa (b. 1927). Pentti Saarikoski (1937–83), whose first collection, *Runoja* (Poems), appeared in 1958, is not tied to any movement or decade. Saarikoski, a maverick genius and iconoclast, was one of the most learned of modern F. poets, as well as a translator of Homer, Euripides, Joyce, and others. With his *Mitä tapahtuu todella?* (What Is Going On, Really?, 1962) F. poetic lang. was taken to a new level where everything had to start from point zero in order to go on: the split word, the word mobile, the collage, and the explicit rejection of poetic structure all conveyed a sense of both freedom and despair. Saarikoski's work culminated in a long, free-floating philosophical poem, *Hämärän tanssit* (The Dances of the Obscure, 1983; written during the period when the poet lived in Sweden), that expresses the poet's yearning for beauty and the unification of all living things.

Haavikko and Manner, in their different ways, have been regarded as the leading F. modernists. Haavikko, director of a Helsinki publishing house, uses compelling rhythmic sequences and incantations to express, through a series of negatives, abstractions, and ironies, his skepticism about the relationship of lang. to the external world. It is an original vision, and in 1984 Haavikko received the Neustadt Prize for his achievement. Manner has explored the conflict between magical order and logical disorder, as she calls it, and has brought to F. p., from her breakthrough collection *Tämä matka* (This Journey, 1956) on, a mythical dimension, a lang. suggestive of another reality.

F. p. in the 1980s shows an unprecedented diversity; all directions seem possible. Among the poets writing in contemp. Finland are Sirkka Turkka (b. 1939), Kari Aronpuro (b. 1940), Pentti Saaritsa (b. 1941), Kirsti Simonsuuri (b. 1945), Caj Westerberg (b. 1946), and Arja Tiainen (b. 1947). Both poetry and prose occupy an important place in cultural life. Swedo-F. modernists like Bo Carpelan (b. 1926) and Solveig von Schoulz (b. 1907) have carried on the earlier modernist trad. while adding new elements. In the 1980s, one is justified in speaking of F. p. as including all verse written by Finns, whether in Swedish or F. and whether in- or outside Finland.

ANTHOLOGIES AND TRANSLATIONS: *Moderne Finnische Lyrik*, ed. and tr. M. P. Hein (1962); *Suomen kirjallisuuden antologia I–VIII*, ed. K. Laitinen and M. Suurpää (1963–75); P. Haavikko, *Sel. Poems*, tr. A. Hollo (1974); *F. Folk P.: Epic*, ed. and tr. M. Kuusi et al. (1977); E. Leino, *Whitsongs*, tr. K. Bosley (1978); *Snow in May*, ed. R. Dauenhauer and P. Binham (1978); *Territorial Song: F. P. and Prose*, tr. H. Lomas (1981); P. Saarikoski, *Sel. Poems*, tr. A. Hollo (1983); E. Södergran, *Complete Poems*, tr. D. McDuff (1983), *Love and Solitude*, tr. S. Katchadourian (1985); *Salt of Pleasure: 20th-C. F. P.*, ed. and tr. A. Jarvenpa and K. B. Vähämäki (1983); *Mod. finlandssvensk Lyrik*, ed. C. Andersson and B. Carpelan (1986); B. Carpelan, *Room Without Walls: Sel. Poems*, tr. A. Born (1987); *The Kalevala*, tr. K. Bosley (1989); *Poésie et prose de Finlande*, ed. M. Bargum (1989); *Enchanting Beasts: An Anthol. of Mod. Women Poets in Finland*, ed. and tr. K. Simonsuuri (1990).

HISTORY AND CRITICISM: E. Enäjärvi-Haavio, "On the Performance of F. Folk Runes," *Folkliv* (1951); J. Ahokas, *Hist. of F. Lit.* (1974); *Mod. Nordic Plays: Finland*, ed. E. J. Friis (1974); T. Wretö, *Johan Ludvig Runeberg* (1980); *The Two Lits. of Finland*, spec. iss. of *WLT* 54 (Winter 1980); M. Kuusi and L. Honko, *Sejd och Saga: Den finska forndiktens historia* (1983); T. Warburton, *Åttio år finlandssvensk litteratur* (1984); G. Schoolfield, *Edith Södergran: Modernist Poet in Finland* (1984); K. Simonsuuri, "The Lyrical Space: The Poetry of Paavo Haavikko," *WLT* 58 (1984); *Europe: Littérature de Finlande*, (June–July 1985); K. Laitinen, *Lit. of Finland: An Outline* (1985), *Finlands Litteratur* (1988); P. Leino, *Lang. and Metre: Metrics and the Metrical System of F.*, tr. A. Chesterman (1986).

K.K.S.

FLEMISH POETRY. See BELGIAN POETRY, *In Dutch*; DUTCH POETRY.

FRENCH POETRY.

I. MEDIEVAL
  A. *Lyric*
  B. *Narrative*
  C. *Dramatic*
II. RENAISSANCE
III. CLASSICISM
IV. EIGHTEENTH CENTURY
V. ROMANTICISM TO SYMBOLISM
VI. TWENTIETH CENTURY

It has been frequently claimed, e.g. by A. E. Housman in a Cambridge conversation with André Gide (1917), that there is in Fr. p. no trad. comparable to that of England or Germany or Italy. Housman stated that between Villon and Baudelaire—for 400 years—Fr. p. was given over to rhymed discourse in which eloquence, wit, vituperation, and pathos were present, but not poetry. Even the romantics with their abundant lyricism have been denied a place among the legitimate poets.

Gide's first answer to this challenge was to acknowledge that perhaps the Fr. as a nation do have a deficiency in lyric sentiment, but that this very deficiency accounts for the elaborate system of Fr. prosody which developed in the course of those 400 years. Strict rules of versification, acting as constraints on the poet's spontaneity, caused poetry to be looked upon in France as a difficult art form which had been more rigorously perfected there than in other countries. In answer to Housman's second question, "After all, what is poetry?" Gide turned to a definition of Baudelaire's in notes for a Preface to *Les Fleurs du mal.* "Rhythm and rhyme," Baudelaire wrote, "answer man's immortal need for monotony, symmetry, and surprise, as opposed to the vanity and danger of inspiration." This theory, whereby poetry is related to music in that its prosody springs from the deepest, most primitive part of nature, illuminates not only the entire history of Fr. p., but also Baudelaire's significant revolution in that history.

I. MEDIEVAL. The earliest extant Fr. poem is the 9th-c. *Séquence de Sainte Eulalie* (ca. 880), a brief narrative in 14 decasyllabic couplets of the saint's life and passion. In the 10th c. appears the *Vie de Saint Léger,* the earliest Fr. poem in octosyllables, the chief Fr. meter up to 1550. Three other religious poems of interest to the modern reader include the 11th-c. *Vie de Saint Alexis,* in decasyllables, with a striking episode in which Alexis, only beginning to realize his calling, commends his young bride of one day to Christ and flees the comforts of his aristocratic heritage; the 13th-c. Life by Rutebeuf of *Sainte Marie l'Égyptienne,* who led the life of a prostitute until her repentance; and the *Vers de la mort* by the Cistercian monk Hélinand de Froidmont, hallucinatory in its kaleidoscopic imagery.

A. *Lyric.* Among the earliest secular Fr. *lyric* poems are the *chansons de toile* (12th c.?), short poems probably accompanying needlework and tapestry weaving. In Southern France, a rich school of Occitan poetry, that of the troubadours, flourished during the 12th and 13th cs. In the North, the poets who followed the earlier troubadours in the 13th c. and adopted many of their forms and themes—in particular, courtly love — were known as trouvères. An innovative noncourtly poet of the 13th c. was Rutebeuf, a contemporary of St. Louis. A forerunner of Villon, he spoke directly of himself, his moral and physical sufferings, the falseness of his friends, and his unhappy marriage.

During the 14th c., the forms of the various types of poems became fixed, the most important being the ballade and the rondeau. Guillaume de Machaut (ca. 1300–77), a canon of Rheims, practically founded a school of poetry. Eustache Deschamps (ca. 1346–ca. 1406), of Champagne, was perhaps the century's most fecund poet; he composed 1500 ballades in addition to poems in all the other known genres. Alain Chartier (ca. 1390–ca. 1440) is today most famous for his *Belle Dame sans merci.* Charles d'Orléans (1391–1465) is the first Fr. poet a few of whose poems are well known today, e.g. his rondeau which begins: "The weather has left its mantle / Of wind and cold and rain."

Great poetry was first created in France by François Villon (b. 1431) from the depths of his affliction, poverty, and suffering. In his two *Testaments,* Villon illustrates the principle of Christian metaphysics that man exists by some mystery—he is unable not to exist. For Villon, as for most medieval writers, the world is only an illusion, and the one reality is his own nature. Although Villon himself had no order in his life, his poetic imagination shows that he shared his time's passion for order. This order is the two natures of man, with the supremacy of spiritual nature over temporal nature. Villon was formed not only by the genius of his race, but by the faith of his mother, of his protector, and of his age:

> Lady of heaven, queen of earth,
> Empress of the infernal swamps,
> Receive me, your humble Christian,
> That I may have my place among your
>   elect.
>   (*Dame du ciel*)

Soon after the dawn of Fr. philosophy, the poet knew, above all, the night of the world: war, famine, poverty. He sees himself in many of his characters, esp. in the role of poverty-stricken culprit. "Le pauvre Villon" betrays coquetry and narcissism. He appears neither heroic nor stoical. He is a poor lover, or, more simply, the poor man surrounded by all the legendary heroes. He is not alone because he understands the greatness of the men who lived before him, who live again in him and in his memory, and who will continue living after him. It is esp. this feeling of union with what is above time that makes Villon a poet. All the themes of the 15th c. are in his work: the Virgin, death, fortune, the martyr-lover, "la Dame sans merci," the harlot, the shepherd, the malice of priests, the vanity of this world, the flight of time. All of these themes find their purest expression in his art.

Formerly considered the wasteland of Fr. lyric p., the period of the *Grands Rhétoriqueurs*, lying roughly between Villon and Clément Marot, is now seen in its true perspective, as a time of audacious formal innovations characterized by exuberance of vocabulary, syntax, prosody, and rhet. The *Rhétoriqueurs*, esp. the greatest of them, Jean Lemaire de Belges (ca. 1473–ca. 1525), were gifted humanists who created a pre-Renaissance of sorts and who interpreted the events, customs, and ideals of the time in the light of ancient wisdom. Court poets, they were hardly refined, but spoke out vehemently against contemporary abuses, endowing modern Fr. p. thereby with some of its earliest significant satire.

B. *Narrative.* Long epic poems called *chansons de geste* and dating from the 11th and 12th cs. mark the second phase of Fr. lit. Most scholars today still accept, at least in part, Joseph Bédier's thesis (*Les Légendes epiques*) that these poems originated in churches and monasteries where the monks furnished the half-legendary, half-historical narratives glorifying their sanctuaries. The *chansons de geste* celebrating Charlemagne and the other great feudal lords form a cycle of poems, of which *La Chanson de Roland* is the acknowledged masterpiece. A single rear-guard action is sung of as an epic battle. Historical characters are converted into stylized types: Roland the rash young warrior, Charlemagne the emperor and patriarch, Olivier the wise friend and counselor, Turpin the priest-warrior. Christianity, chivalry, and patriotism are exalted. Two other cycles comparable to the *chansons de geste* deal with Celtic material or Antiquity. *Le Roman d'Alexandre* used a 12-syllable line which in time displaced the octosyllable to become the standard Fr. line, the alexandrine. The *lais* of Marie de France are short narrative poems by the first known Fr. woman poet, writing at the end of the 12th c.

The most fertile narrative poet of the 12th c. was Chrétien de Troyes. The principal author of courtly romances in Fr., he drew upon the Arthurian legends of the Round Table in his effort to reconcile the earlier warlike ideals of the *chansons de geste* with the new devotion to woman—whence such characters as Merlin, Lancelot, and Queen Guenivere. Those poets who continued Chrétien's work added poems on the Grail Legend and the story of Tristan, narrated principally by Béroul and Thomas. To the same courtly trad. may be added a charming "chante-fable," *Aucassin et Nicolette*, half prose and half verse, describing the trials inflicted by destiny on two lovers before their final happiness.

The *fabliaux* were short comic narratives characterized by immorality and coarseness. Their humor and irony had been more fully developed in *Le Roman de Renart*, a long satirical beast epic written in several parts, or "branches," probably by several poets of the 12th and 13th c. A society of animals stands for human society and presents a caricature of feudal aristocracy, clergy, and lit. themes. Renart the fox symbolizes human intelligence using trickery and ruse in order to mock authority. The multiple sources of this work are to be found in the fables of Antiquity and in European folklore.

The outstanding Fr. allegorical work of the Middle Ages is *Le Roman de la Rose*, in two parts, the first written by Guillaume de Lorris in the first half of the 13th c., the second by Jean de Meun in the second half of the same century. Guillaume de Lorris' poem is a manual of courtly love. He was familiar with Ovid's *Art of Love* and the allegories used by the *clercs* to describe the phases of love. In contrast, the second and longer part of the poem is composed in a far different style and spirit, the fictional element being a mere pretext for digressions on cosmology, life, religion, and morals. Encyclopedic and pedantic, this philosophical treatise is quite emancipated from theology. Nature is both the key to man's rights and virtues and the principle of beauty, reason, and the good. Jean de Meung's poem is the genesis of a moral philosophy which was continued, in varying degree, in the writings of Rabelais, Montaigne, Molière, and Voltaire.

C. *Dramatic.* The first form of dramatic poetry in France was the liturgical drama, closely connected with church ritual. Originally acted within the church, *drames liturgiques* were then performed outside on an improvised stage. Gradually texts became secularized. *Le Jeu de Saint Nicolas* by Jean Bodel (end of the 12th c.) represents the definitive form of religious theater—a combination of miracle and farce, with many themes and subplots. Miracle plays (*miracles*), dealing with the intercession of the Virgin, flourished esp. in the 14th c.; morality plays, satires (*soties*), and mystery plays (*mystères*) flourished in the 15th c. These last, of excessive length and demanding several days for performance, offered a popular treatment of religious history from the Creation to the time of Saint Louis. The more purely secular comic theatre comprised the pastoral play, such as *Le Jeu de Robin et Marion*, and a more complex type, half satiric, half comic, *Le Jeu de la feuillée*, both by Adam de La Halle (13th c.), as well as farces (15th c.). The masterpiece of the medieval comic theater dates from the middle of the 15th c., *La Farce de Maître Pathelin*. In character devel. and plot, it is a full-fledged comedy, a distant ancestor of Molière's art.

II. RENAISSANCE. Late 15th-c. poetry was dominated by the *Grands Rhétoriqueurs*, many of whom were attached to the Court of Burgundy. Elaborate abstractions characterized their long didactic poems; their shorter poems often depended on riddles and puns. Their influence is visible in Clément Marot (1496–1544), son of the *Rhétoriqueur* Jean Marot. Much of Marot's verse was occasional, written to praise a patron. He was a typical Ren. court poet whose gift for satire was stimulated by his contacts with the law students and lawyers of Paris (*La Basoche*), with Marguerite de Navarre, the King's sister who encouraged him, with the It. court of Ferrara (where he could give free expression to his religious and satiric themes), and with the court of Francis I. His satirical tone is varied and subtle rather than vehement. Although he continued medieval forms—the farcical, rambling, and sometimes obscene *coq-à-l'âne,* besides *rondeaux* and *ballades*—he also practiced forms that were to be developed esp. in the 17th c.: the *épître,* a long verse letter, and the *épigramme,* a short, concise poem, usually satiric and with a sting in its tail. Finally, Marot was probably the first writer of the sonnet in Fr.

Marguerite de Navarre (1492–1549) was the first important Fr. woman poet. She was not a profound theologian in her religious poetry, *Les Prisons,* but she drew abundantly on Plato and the doctrines of Christian theology. She participated in all the humanistic activities of the Ren., in philosophy, politics, and poetry; however, the sentiments which directed her life were her love of God and her quest for the Absolute.

Poetry flourished in Lyons, esp. during the reign of Francis I, in a movement which came to be called *l'école lyonnaise.* The one subject of the 3 elegies and the 24 sonnets of Louise Labé (1526–66) is love, carnal love. In the 500 lines comprising her poetic output she expresses vibrantly the causes and symptoms of her suffering without psychological subtleties. She had obviously read Petrarch, but never plagiarized his text. Far more complicated is Maurice Scève (1511–64), both in form and sentiment. Scève too wrote against a background of very conscious literary and philosophical enthusiasms. Platonism and Petrarchism had been the two current fashions in Lyons ever since their introduction by the Florentines in the 15th c. and by Marguerite de Navarre in the early 16th c. Plato's influence is even more apparent in Marguerite's religious poetry than in Scève's *Délie.* Platonism, as taught in Italy in the 15th c., esp. by Marsilio Ficino, had taken on in France the amplitude of a movement of ideas when Ficino became one of Marguerite's favorites. Scève was probably presented to her when she stopped in Lyons between April and July 1536. The title of Scève's work, *Délie,* is an anagram of the word "l'idée," but it is also the fictitious name given to the lady whom Scève loved and whom all the 449 *dizains* concern. Since each *dizain* relates one aspect or moment of the same experience, the work possesses an organic structure. Many follow the trad. of describing the particular beauties of Délie's countenance and body. But in the far more striking *dizains* where Scève analyzes the impossibility of being loved as he loves, he describes a progressive self-knowledge and self-torment which give the work its profoundest unity. The end of the long sequence of poems apostrophizes death, not as a union with the beloved but as a liberation from amorous torment. The absence of any religious philosophy gives Scève's psychology a relentless terror and bareness which is not at all characteristic of the Middle Ages and the Ren., but rather adumbrative of the modern period. Today the *dizains* of Scève are admired and studied for their difficult, often obscure symbolism.

The seven poets known as *La Pléiade* represent the most spectacular triumph of Fr. p. in the Ren. Some of their poetry is of a springlike tenderness and hopefulness, despite their awareness of life's uncertainties and the destruction of sentiment and beauty wrought by the passing of time. Their art is a union of mythology and nature—a combination of pedantic constructs and simple, heartfelt popular poetry. Rivers, woods, roses, dew, and nymphs appear everywhere in their verses, forming the natural setting for the serious themes of happiness, love, and death. Pierre de Ronsard (1524–85), the greatest poet of the *Pléiade,* left a long and varied work. His sonnets, *Les Amours,* have immortalized three women: Cassandre, Marie, Hélène. "When you are old, in the evening, by candlelight, / Seated near the fire, unwinding and spinning, / You will say reciting my verses and marvelling at them: / Ronsard sang of me when I was beautiful." His *Odes* and *Hymnes* made him the most celebrated poet in Europe. Ronsard demanded for the poet the highest position, that of *vates* (seer). The earlier poets had had a sense of professional honor; Villon had been a conscientious writer, as was Scève, with a sense of higher worldly position. But Ronsard instituted the doctrine of poetic *gloire,* a gift which the poet can bequeath and sell. In 1549, Joachim du Bellay (1525–60), the second most important member of the *Pléiade,* drew up the new poets' program and beliefs in *La Défense et illustration de la langue française.* Although Du Bellay treated the ancients with almost fanatical respect, his chief purpose was to prove that the Fr. lang. was equal in dignity to Gr. and Lat. He advised a complete break with medieval trad. and, instead, the imitation of Cl. genres: tragedies and comedies, for example, should supplant the *mystères* and *miracles* of the "Gothic" period. Du Bellay was to a certain extent responsible, in *L'Olive* (1549), for the success which the love sonnet was to have in the 16th and 17th cs. and, in *Les Antiquités de Rome* and *Les Regrets* (1558–59), for the satiric sonnet.

Two poets who wrote at the end of the century have been rediscovered in recent years. Jean de Sponde (1557–95), a Protestant who abjured his faith, as did Henri IV, left a brief work—sonnets on death and other religious poems. Because of the abundance of his metaphor and antithesis, de Sponde's name is today associated with "baroque" poetry and the metaphysical poetry of John Donne. The second discovery was of Jean de la Ceppède (1530–1622), a more prolific poet than Sponde, as witnessed by the 500 sonnets of his *Théorèmes sur le sacré mystère de notre rédemption*. The "theorem" was used by 16th-c. Fr. poets to represent the mystery of the Redemption. The symbolism and beauty of La Ceppède's sonnets seem strikingly modern: the title of Pasolini's 1968 film, *Teorema*, was probably taken from La Ceppède.

Agrippa d'Aubigné (1550–1630) was a prophet-poet as well as a soldier and memorialist. His *Tragiques* are as strongly a satiric work as Hugo's *Châtiments*. They testify to his Calvinist faith and demonstrate a close application of Scripture to the accidents of mortal existence, to the predestined significance of events of seeming chance. The seven books composing *Les Tragiques* describe France in a state of civil war. They denounce the Valois princes, the chambers of justice, and the holocausts of the century, and they reflect all the latter's styles and beliefs: Ronsard's sensitive lyricism, to a degree; a humanistic understanding of man, to a stronger degree; a biblical and apocalyptic interpretation of the day, to an overwhelming degree. D'Aubigné made an important contribution to lyric poetry in his first verse, *Le Printemps du Sieur d'Aubigné*, published long after his death. These love sonnets, begun in 1570, were inspired by Diane Salviati, the niece of Ronsard's Cassandre.

III. CLASSICISM. The Fr. classical style as it developed in the 17th c. was at times opposed by tendencies now often called "baroque." This term, more applicable to a style of architecture and sculpture than to lit., suggests a rich, almost extravagant form, with ornate and intricate flourishes. In lit., "baroque" writing has elements of fantasy and irrationality, and forms that translate the anguish of man in elaborate lang. Cl. art was, by contrast, sober, measured, and clear. The baroque taste was its opposite, and was everywhere in evidence during the years when cl. art was coming into its own.

The 20th c. has witnessed the rehabilitation of the baroque poets who, from Ronsard's decline to Boileau's rise, enriched Fr. p. with themes and forms (largely of It. origin) running counter to the coalescing cl. trad. Jean de Sponde and Aubigné in the 16th c., and Malherbe himself (in a youthful folly, *Les Larmes de Saint-Pierre*), Théophile de Viau, Saint-Amant, and Tristan L'Hermite in the 17th were the chief representatives of a movement that turned one current of Fr. p. into a contest with the indefinable, mingling religious and profane elements, building up tensions, piling up images, torturing syntax. By the unfinished ("open") character of their poems, their deliberate striving for obscure and bizarre effects, and their stretching of one image over several stanzas or an entire poem (Rubin), these solitary geniuses differed from the 17th-c. *précieux* poets, who wrote polished verses filled with the discreet allusions, witty epigrams, and short metaphors suited for an aristocratic audience.

The influence of François de Malherbe (1555–1628) dominated the poetic scene in the first half of the 17th c. His work as grammarian, poet, and critic helped to define the precepts of a Fr. art which was to be called "classical" and which occupies the central place in the history of Fr. culture. In a celebrated passage of his *Art poétique*, Boileau was later to hail the advent of Malherbe's authority in all things poetical: "At last Malherbe appeared." He was the first craftsman in the history of Fr. p. to discuss analytically, even pontifically, the rules of his craft (Abraham). He denounced erudition in poetry and the unrestrained outburst of lyricism. He purified the Fr. lang. by narrowing its range and making it capable of enunciating truths rather than personal passions. Ronsard and the other *Pléiade* poets had insisted on loftiness of theme and diction. Malherbe was the first to claim ordinary speech for poetry.

The tendencies toward bombast (*emphase*) and preciosity which had developed during the 16th and early 17th c., largely from It. and Sp. models, were opposed by Boileau (1636–1711), whose authority was strong under the reign of Louis XIV. He was a bourgeois of Paris, like Molière and Voltaire, and thus interrupted the central trad. of Fr. lit., hitherto largely aristocratic. Boileau, Molière, and Pascal represented, in their critical attitudes, a strong reaction against the *précieux* poetry of the *salons* and *ruelles*. Boileau attacked the pedantry of Chapelain and the Fr. imitation of It. models. Backed by La Fontaine, Racine, and Molière, he eventually won over to his side the public and the King himself. Imitation of nature is the highest rule for Boileau: "Let nature be our one study." But this imitation must be carried on rationally, and only insofar as nature conforms to itself, only insofar as it is universal. Hence, the law of the three unities is applicable in tragedy because it is natural and reasonable. Preciosity, which in poetry emphasized overrefined sentiment and periphrastic ornamental lang., should be condemned because it is unnatural to obscure willfully one's thought. An artist as well as a bourgeois, Boileau was also a craftsman and a painstaking theorist.

The critic Faguet claimed that a century of Fr. p. came to a close with Jean de La Fontaine (1621–95). Eclectic in the choice of his masters (he owed allegiance to Villon, Marot, and Voiture, as well as to Boccaccio and Rabelais), he converted his imitations into an art that is very much his own. His care for technical perfection he owes as theory to Malherbe, but the works themselves, *Adonis*, for example, and *Psyché*, long narrative poems, and his *Contes*, are triumphs in poetic grace, melody, and sentiment. La Fontaine recreated the genre of the fable, writing what he himself called "the 100-act comedy whose stage set is the universe." Scenes, characterizations, dialogues, all are struck off with remarkable clarity and concentration. Each fable is a dramatization. The moral value of his teaching has often been questioned, but the poems themselves appear as original creations, thanks to La Fontaine's psychological penetration and his subtle, varied use of free verse. The final lines of *Les Deux Pigeons* illustrate this art of nuance and sentiment:

> Lovers, happy lovers, do you want to
> travel?
> Do not go very far.
> Be for each other a world always beautiful,
> Always different, always new.

Pierre Corneille (1606–84) was the first poet to apply to Fr. tragedy with any lasting success the principle of the three unities. He was a major pioneer in cl. art. His poetry is vigorous but tends toward the bombastic. His lang. seems today somewhat archaic and oratorical, but he did master the alexandrine; his style has clarity and precision and a strong sense of rhythm. The poetry of his best tragedies, *Le Cid, Horace, Cinna, Polyeucte,* is a poetry of action and an intellectual lang. describing the feelings and dilemmas of the characters.

Jean Racine (1639–99) holds a high place among the religious poets of France. His choruses from *Athalie* and *Esther*, as well as his four *Cantiques spirituels,* testify to a remarkable lyric perfection. The achievement of Racine as dramatist is due in part to his theory of tragic action and to his penetration as psychologist, but in part also to his poetic gifts, the elegance of his expression, and the magic of his style. Racine's particular triumph lies in the fusion of meaning and music, of tragic sentiment and the pure sound of his alexandrine line. Racine was trained in the school of the *Précieux,* and there are elements of preciosity throughout his tragedies. But on the whole he rejected superfluous ornament and excluded unusual words from his vocabulary. When the occasion calls for it, Racine can write lines as vibrantly eloquent as Corneille's. Fr. p. was not to know again such human poignancy and such artistic simplicity and dramatic meaning until the publication of Baudelaire's *Les Fleurs du mal* in the 19th c.

Several of the major comedies of Molière (1622–73) were written in verse: *L'École des Femmes, Le Tartuffe, Le Misanthrope, Amphitryon, Les Femmes savantes.* As Racine did in the case of tragedy, Molière in his treatment of comedy fused lang. with situation and poetry with characterization. Molière's lang. is at all times vigorous, varied, and colorful. He knew the lang. of the people, the bourgeoisie, and the *Précieux.* In the high comedies, composed in alexandrines, one has the impression of listening to conversation and, at the same time, to something more substantial, thanks to the skillful syntactic organization, the lilt of the rhythm, and the resounding rhymes. Molière's style is purely theatrical—dramatic suitability of the poetic expression was his guiding rule.

IV. EIGHTEENTH CENTURY. The richest periods for lyric poetry in France were, first, the 16th c., when a renaissance of spring abundance had favored the delicate, witty songs of Marot, the sadder, more metaphysical verse of Labé and Scève, and the full maturity of the *Pléiade* poets; and, second, the 19th c., with its three so-called schools of poetry: romantic, Parnassian, and symbolist, which are but three aspects of a single devel. in modern art and sensitivity, and which continued in the major poets of the 20th c.

In the two intervening centuries, lyric poetry had been subdued or lost in other forms of writing. During the 17th c., lyric genius was always subordinated to dramatic genius. The drama of Racine's poetry had been prepared for by almost 200 years of lyric poetry, from Villon at the end of the Hundred Years' War to the advent of Louis XIV. The effusiveness and facility of lyric verse, which are its constant dangers, had been chastened and channeled in the tragedies of *Andromaque* and *Phèdre,* as, in the 19th c., the expansiveness of romantic verse would be chastised by the strict form of the Parnassians and by the severe experience of the symbol in Mallarmé's poetry.

During the 18th c., the poetic genius was taken over by the philosophers, and the exploration of self gave way to the explorations of society and of the universe. The form of poetic tragedy perfected by Racine declined rapidly, to become in the 18th c. a conventionalized, weak genre. Voltaire alone showed some competence in his imitation of Racine. The style of *Zäire,* for example, has a cl. clarity but is lacking in strong characterization. Voltaire tried all forms of poetry. His epic *La Henriade* celebrates the religious wars and the advent of Henri IV. His philosophical poems, epistles, and satires are more successful, yet they are lacking in any real sensitivity. His short poems, *Pièces de circonstance,* are perhaps his best in their elegance and wit.

Voltaire was not only the official poet of the century but also the best defender of poetry. There were many versifiers. Jean-Baptiste Rousseau (1671–1741) was called "le grand Rousseau" in order to humiliate Jean-Jacques. His *Ode et Cantates* (1723) was first published in London. Jean-Baptiste-Louis Gresset (1709–77) wrote a lighter kind of poetry in the trad. of Marot. *Vert-Vert* is a poem about a parrot brought up by nuns; as the bird moves from convent to convent it picks up the lang. of sailors. *Les Saisons* (1769), a pastoral poem by Saint-Lambert (1716–1807), was undoubtedly inspired by *The Seasons* of the Eng. poet James Thomson (1700–46). Jacques Delille (1738–1813) became famous for his translations of Virgil (*Géorgiques*), Milton (*Paradis perdu*), and Pope (*Essai sur l'homme*).

In the wake of many versifiers, André Chénier (1762–94) appeared at the end of the 18th c. as its one legitimate poet. Eventually executed by the guillotine, Chénier wrote his poems, *Les Iambes*, in prison, a work which in satiric force and vituperation takes its place beside d'Aubigné's *Tragiques* and Hugo's *Châtiments*. His extensive literary knowledge, esp. of Gr. poetry, reminds one of the Pléiade poets and their eagerness to learn from the poets of Antiquity. Chénier knew the It. poets and the Bible, the *Arabian Nights*, and the Eng. poets: Shakespeare, Young, Thomson, and Ossian. Ronsard, La Fontaine, and Chénier are the three Fr. poets who were inspired and guided by their study of Antiquity, and yet who never imitated the ancient poets in any servile manner.

V. ROMANTICISM TO SYMBOLISM. Paradoxically, the major poetic work of the 18th c. was written in prose. Its author, Jean-Jacques Rousseau, was certainly concerned with ideas, but he felt them as a poet might, and he succeeded in transmitting them to the romantic poets of the 19th c. Passages from all Rousseau's writings, but esp. his last book, *Rêveries d'un promeneur solitaire*, fixed the characteristics of the romantic temperament and gave the first fevers to a malady which was to deepen during the next hundred years. Jean-Jacques preached that man's oneness with nature was a state to be recaptured. The first stage of the new lyricism was one of "rêverie," largely narcissistic. During the first decade of romantic poetry (1820–30), and in part as a result of Chateaubriand's *René* (in poetic prose) at the turn of the century, Rousseauistic rêverie underwent an important modification. Nature continued to be the fountain of Narcissus for the romantic hero, but the traits he saw reflected in it were no longer peaceful. His dissatisfaction, vague nostalgia, tearfulness, and even sorrow had changed the visage of the self-seeking and self-reflected hero.

Lamartine (1790–1869), in his *Méditations poétiques* of 1820, expressed this new sensibility in his wanderings through nature and in his efforts to recapture moments of the past when he had experienced happiness. For Lamartine the resurrection of his memory was that of happiness and even ecstasy; his belief in the future, although indistinct, was formed in hope and optimism. It was only the terrible present for which he felt no genius. The state of disillusionment reached its most bitter expression in the verse of Alfred de Vigny (1797–1863). To the disappointment which Lamartine felt in the flux of time, Vigny added an attack on the infidelity of woman and nature herself and on the religions of the world as beneficent lies. The early romantic disillusionment thus culminated with him in undisguised pessimism. He was an uneven poet, but a forceful thinker. To his innate pessimism, Vigny opposed stoicism and a philosophy founded on work and intellection. Coldness and aloofness characterized his attitude, as well as a nobility of thought akin to that of the ancients. Although Vigny did not believe in the ultimate salvation of mankind, he did believe in the greatness of effort, the majesty of human suffering, and the achievements of philosophers and scientists. The impertinence and facility of Alfred de Musset's (1810–57) early poems changed after tragic experience with George Sand, and the "enfant terrible" of the early romantics became in his *Nuits* "un enfant du siècle," the type of the suffering poet and the victim of what has been called *pélicanisme*, after the poet's own interpretation of the pelican symbol in *La Nuit de mai*.

The position of Victor Hugo (1802–85) in the devel. of 19th-c. Fr. p. is extraordinarily important. He played a preponderant part in the gradually increasing violence of the romantic malady by the very vigor of his character and his verse. His first volumes (*Odes et ballades* and *Les Orientales*) were roughly contemporary with the first of Lamartine and Vigny, and his last volumes (*La Légende des siècles* and *La Fin de satan*) came at the time of Baudelaire and Mallarmé. During this long career, which encompassed the other more significantly brief careers of Nerval, Baudelaire, Lautréamont, Rimbaud, and Mallarmé, Hugo's philosophy or, more precisely, his cosmology developed into a form of pantheism which is the source of his best poetry. After being a mirror for the narcissistic Rousseau, a site for the anguished wanderings of Chateaubriand and Lamartine, and a distant, unconsoling splendor for Vigny, nature was sometimes raised by Hugo to a level of religious significance:

> I was alone near the waves, during a
> starry night.
> Not a cloud in the heaven, on the sea
> no sail.
> My eyes saw farther than the real
> world.

External nature, of which man is but one element, was for him a multiform manifestation of occult forces and divinity. A peculiar interpretation of the Old Testament and the Kabbala led Hugo to believe that the animation of nature, when it should be realized, would in turn animate man and solve his problems. Some of Hugo's dramas were written in verse, e.g. *Hernani, Ruy Blas, Les Burgraves*, but their value lies more in their lyricism than in their dramatic or psychological conceptions: there are many bravura passages, love dialogues, and meditations in which the dramatist is essentially a poet. (At the end of the century, in 1897, *Cyrano de Bergerac* by Edmond Rostand would represent a return to the ideals of early romantic drama. It had in its poetry many of the elements of Hugo's plays: heroism, grace, bombast, wit. The play had a tremendous success at a time when naturalistic theater was flourishing.)

Théophile Gautier (1811–72) defined in his poem *L'Art* some of the principal tenets of the Parnassian school, which grew up in opposition to the excessive subjectivity of romantic poetry. Art, he claims, finds its justification in its own intrinsic beauty and not in its relevance to morality or philosophy. Art alone has eternity, and esp. that art whose form is difficult to achieve. This doctrine of "art for art's sake" was also embraced by Hérédia and Leconte de Lisle. Traces of the same convictions are visible in Baudelaire and Mallarmé.

Hugo's pantheism had represented a moment in the hist. of man's hope and religious illumination. The prose and poetry of Charles Baudelaire (1821–67) holds out the hope of magic in nature. Baudelaire was the greatest poet of the second half of the 19th c., in the sense that *Les Fleurs du mal* (1857) was the richest source of creativeness, being both an achievement in art and a criticism for art. (In the same way, Rimbaud was to be the greatest poet for the first forty years of the 20th c., in the sense that *Les Illuminations* and *Une Saison en enfer* are the two guiding psychological documents of the period.) Baudelaire's significance lies not solely in his conception of nature as the source of sensations and the key to the world of the spirit. It lies even more preeminently in his despair over inertia and acedia, in his despair at a lack-of-feeling he felt which prevented him from willing not to sin. Hope in nature, in the whole created universe as the reflection of some half-experienced sense of unity or Divine Love, on the one hand, and, on the other, the incapacity to feel deeply enough the infractions against the laws of man and God in order to cease perpetrating these infractions, are the two aspects of Baudelaire's art, which in *Les Fleurs du mal* he calls (reversing the order) "Spleen et Idéal." This new definition of man's basic dualism and struggle with the forces of good and evil springs from the sensitivity of the 19th-c. artist. Baudelairian "idéal" was yet another expression of romantic exoticism and Hugo's hope in nature. It was the need to go to the most distant, and therefore the most purifying, parts of the world, to scenes different from the familiar, where the heart of man could be itself, unashamedly, in all of its fathomless innocence. Likewise, Baudelairian "spleen" was still another expression of romantic introspection and Vigny's pessimism:

> November, angry with the whole city,
> From its urn pours out a dark cold
> Over the pale inhabitants of the
> nearby cemetery
> And mortality over the foggy suburbs.

Spleen was the poet's incapacity to move out from himself, to disengage his spirit from the center of his dilemma, from the center of his body which had been enslaved. It was the poet's velleity and ennui which, even if they are absences and negations, may grow to uncontrollable proportions. "Idéal" in Baudelaire is often translated by the image of a sea-voyage, by *L'Invitation au voyage;* and "spleen" is often translated by the image of a closed room or cell, by a closed brain or a closed body. "Idéal" is the desire to move and to be free. "Spleen" is the horror of being unable to move and of being caught in bondage.

The poems of Arthur Rimbaud (1854–91) are the first representations of his life (*Poètes de sept ans* and *Mémoire*) and his first visions (*Bateau ivre*). His prose work, *Une Saison en enfer,* is fairly devoid of visions. It is almost a retractation, an effort to understand his past and his revolt against Christianity. It is his confession of failure. The prose poems, *Les Illuminations,* are best understood as coming after *Une Saison* in a new movement of hope and almost mystical belief in himself as poet and visionary. In the earlier works, the poet had learned his lang. of *voyant* and something concerning the failure of living as an artist. *Les Illuminations* have behind them an experience comparable to the mystic's initiation to failure. Rimbaud's example will remain that of the poet opposing his civilization, his historical moment, and yet at the same time revealing its instability and quaking torment. He is both against his age and of it. By refusing to take time to live, he lived a century in a few years, throughout its minute phases, rushing toward the only thing that mattered to him: the absolute, the certainty of truth. He came closest to finding this absolute in his poet's vision. That was "the place and the formula" he talked of and was impatient to find, the spiritual hunt that did not end with the prey seized. Rimbaud's is the drama of modern man, by reason of its particular frenzy and precipitation; but it is also the human drama of all time, the drama of the quest for what has been lost, the unsatisfied temporal existence burning for total satisfaction and certitude.

As early as Gérard de Nerval (1808–55), who incorporated the speculations of the 18th-c. *illuminés,* poetry had tried to be the means of intuitive communication between man and the powers beyond him. Nerval was the first to point out those regions of extreme temptation and extreme peril which have filled the vision of the major poets who have come after him.

The lesson of Stéphane Mallarmé (1842–98) is the extraordinary penetration of his gaze at objects in the world and the attentive precision with which he created a world of forms and pure relationships between forms. The object in a Mallarmé poem is endowed with a force of radiation that is latent and explosive. The irises, for example, in *Prose pour des esseintes,* have reached a "purity" from which every facile meaning has been eliminated. This purity is their power to provoke the multiple responses of the most exacting readers, those who insist that an image appear in its own beauty, isolated from the rest of the world and independent of all keys and obvious explanations. Mallarmé's celebrated sonnet on the swan caught in the ice of a lake illustrates this power of a metaphor to establish a subtle relationship between two seemingly opposed objects: a swan and a poet. The relationship is not stated in logical or specific terms but is suggested or evoked by the metaphor:

> Will the virginal, strong and handsome today
> Tear for us with a drunken flap of his wing
> This hard forgotten lake which the transparent glacier
> Of flights unflown haunts under the frost!

For the poet's role of magus and prophet, so histrionically played by Victor Hugo, was thus substituted the role of magician, incarnated not solely by Rimbaud (whose *Lettre du voyant* of 1871 seems to be its principal manifesto), but also by Nerval and Baudelaire who preceded him, by his contemporary Mallarmé, and by his leading disciples, the 20th-c. surrealists, 30 years after his death. This concept of the poet as magician dominates most of the poetic transformations and achievements of the last century. The poet, in his subtle relationship with the mystic, rids himself of the traits of the Hugoesque prophet, as well as the vain ivory-tower attitude of a Vigny. Emphasis on the poet as a sorcerer, in search of the unknown and surreal part of his own being, has further caused him to give up the poetry of love, esp. the facile love poetry of a Musset.

Jules Laforgue (1860–87) has been gradually assuming a place of real importance in the history of symbolism. The first constituted group of symbolist poets were active during 1880–85. The word "decadent" has been associated with them. As opposed to the symbolists, the decadents allowed in their verse the direct transcription of emotion and phenomena. There is nothing in the later Laforgue of the grand style of romantic poetry. He is concerned with depicting the shifts and variations of feeling in scenes of the modern city. The dominant mood Laforgue expresses is one of emotional starvation and emotional inhibition. The parody of his own sensibility becomes, in Laforgue's *Moralités légendaires*, the parody of some of the great myths of humanity. He recapitulates the stories of the masters—Shakespeare's Hamlet, Wagner's Lohengrin, Mallarmé's Pan, Flaubert's Salomé—and alters them in order to infuse new meanings. No such thing as a pure hero exists for this poet. He sees the so-called heroes as ordinary creatures and gives them the psychological characteristics of his Pierrots—nervousness, anxiety—and an ephemeral existence.

The first edition of Tristan Corbière's one book, *Les Amours jaunes*, appeared in 1873, which was the year of Rimbaud's *Une Saison en enfer* and Verlaine's *Romances sans paroles.* No attention whatever was paid to these three books at the time. Corbière died two years later, at the age of thirty. Not until 1883, in Verlaine's series of essays on *Les Poètes maudits*, was Corbière presented to the Paris public as a poet of importance. This first label of *poète maudit* has remained associated with his name. He refused to write poetry in accordance with traditional forms. He even refused to be a traditional bohemian. "An ocean bohemian," Laforgue once called him, since most of his life was spent in Brittany, in the towns of Morlaix and Roscoff, and since the themes of his personal suffering are mingled with the dominant theme of the sea. In many ways, Corbière was the spiritual descendent of Villon, esp. in his self-disparagement. He looked upon himself as a failure, both as a man and as a poet, and he looked upon his life as a marriage with disaster. There are strong reminiscences of Baudelaire in *Les Amours jaunes* and Baudelairian traits too in Corbière's impenetrability. There are *concetti* and antitheses almost in Góngora's style, and rhythmical innovations and patterns which Verlaine will develop. Corbière's control of his art is less strong than Baudelaire's or Rimbaud's; his revolt against order and convention is less metaphysical than Rimbaud's.

Mallarmé and Rimbaud are the greatest poets of the symbolist period. To a lesser degree, the example of Paul Verlaine (1844–96) counted also in the symbolist movement. *Fêtes galantes* (1869) evokes the delicacy and licentiousness of Watteau's paintings. His *Art poétique*, written in prison in 1873, became a manifesto for the symbolists. It insists on music, imprecision, and shading in the writing of poetry. But his influence on the devel. of Fr. p. has been slight, despite the fact that he exploited brilliantly the resources of the Fr. lang.

VI. TWENTIETH CENTURY. Verlaine's was a poetry of the heart and of pure sentiment, a trad. maintained by Francis Jammes (1868–1938), who belonged to the first generation of 20th-c. poets. Even more isolated from symbolism and the central evolution of Fr. p. stands Charles Péguy (1873–1914), celebrated between the two wars for his deeply religious poetry on Notre-Dame de Chartres and for his *Mystère de la charité de Jeanne d'Arc* (1910), a celebration echoed in turn by Geoffrey Hill in 1984. Péguy's poetry presents no linguistic or metaphorical difficulties. He is remembered as the patron-poet of peasants and as the pilgrim of La Beauce. Not until Albert Béguin's study of *Eve* in 1948 was there a critical effort to understand and explain the poetry. Péguy fashioned an alexandrine that was recognizably his own (there are ten thousand alexandrines in his work). *Eve* is Péguy's literary expression of his return to the Church, a vision of human history (as well as a poetics) which moves from the Incarnation to the Redemption in a long dialogue between the flesh (Incarnation) and the soul (Redemption), between the Fall, associated with Eve, and the Redemption, associated with Christ.

Paul Valéry (1871–1945) had listened in his early twenties to Mallarmé's conversations on poetry. In his celebrated definition of symbolism, Valéry states that the new poetry is simply trying to recapture from music what belongs to it. But in the practice of so-called symbolist poetry, he revived, and adhered to, all the classical rules of prosody. If the music of lang. is to be rediscovered and recreated, a long process of "research" is necessary into the sounds of syllables, the meanings of words, and word phrases and their combinations. The symbol in poetry establishes a relationship between things and ourselves. It is a kind of bond uniting man with the universe. Valéry appropriates some of the oldest symbols (or myths) in the world, e.g. Narcissus and the Fates, which are the titles of two of his greatest poems. Most of the poems in *Charmes* (1922) derive their title from the leading symbol: *L'Abeille* (bee), *Palme, Au platane* (planetree), *La Ceinture* (sash). Valéry is a singer of knowledge, of subterranean knowledge, where thought may be studied at its birth, in the intermediary stage between the subconscious and the conscious. His poems are metaphysical debates, as in the poems on Narcissus, where a veritable self-inquisition takes place:

> A great calm heeds me in which I listen to hope.
> In the secrets of the extinguished fountain.
> In the secrets which I fear learning.
> (*Charmes*)

At the beginning of *La Jeune Parque* (1917), we learn that some kind of metaphysical catastrophe has taken place, of which the poem develops the consequences. Valéry's fame has been built upon fragments: poems, aphorisms, dialogues, brief essays. He is the supreme example of a writer indifferent to his public, detached from any need to please his public. The dialogue which he instituted with himself and with the few great writers he turned to appears with the passage of time increasingly dramatic. *Eupalinos* as well as *Mon Faust* are comparable to the form of the Socratic dialogue, in which the resources and agility of man's conscience are explored.

Rimbaud's importance, and esp. the spiritual significance of his work, was first revealed by the poet Paul Claudel (1868–1955). Deep within a work which seems to be composed largely of revolt and blasphemy, Claudel discovered traces of a religious drama which spoke directly to him and to which he owed his return to Catholicism. The reading of Rimbaud and the religious experience he underwent at the age of 18 changed Claudel's world. These were revelations whereby he saw the world as the work of God and worthy of the poet's paean of praise. This was the genesis of his great theme of Joy, the one reality for Claudel, the one requirement for the making of an artistic work. By temperament, Claudel belongs to the race of revolutionaries and conquerors, poets like d'Aubigné and Rimbaud; but he is also like Mallarmé in his will to define poetry in its essence. From Mallarmé, Claudel learned esp. about metaphor, which is the essential element in his poetics. A metaphor is a relationship between two subjects; it may even be a relationship between God and the world. The poet's role is to apprehend the metaphors which exist in the world. This means naming each object and restoring it to its rightful place in a new ordering of the universe, in a new lexicon of the world. By naming an object, the poet gives it meaning, as God has originally done in creating the world—by naming it. The total Word, or the total poem, is therefore the universe. Each poet bears in himself a picture of the universe, a subjective maze of images which have relationships with one another. Mallarmé had followed an instinctive quest in naming various objects and seeking to understand their metaphorical meaning; Claudel goes further in willing this quest as if it were a religious obligation. Symbolism, under the guidance of Mallarmé, had been a spiritual way of understanding and celebrating the universe; in the art of Paul Claudel, it becomes a more frankly religious way of discovering, in the midst of endless variety, a secret unity. In his *Art poétique* (1903), Claudel states that metaphor is the logic of the new poetry, comparable to the syllogism of the older logic. Things in the world are not only objects to be known; they are means by which man is being constantly reborn. Claudel's plays are the most important poetic dramas in 20th-c. Fr. lit. They are concerned with human passion (*Partage de midi*) and religious themes (*L'Annonce faite á Marie*). Despite their difficult style and highly metaphorical lang., these plays reveal in production a grandeur and solemnity not found in the art of any other Fr. playwright.

It was quite appropriate that Guillaume Apollinaire (1880–1918), coming after the highly self-conscious symbolist school, would, in rebellion against such artifice, seek to return to the most primitive sources of lyricism. But by his lesson of freedom, gratuitousness, and individual morality, Apollinaire prolongs the lessons of Rimbaud and Mallarmé; like them, he considers poetic activity as a secret means of knowledge—self-knowledge and world-knowledge. The miracle of his poetry is the number of word surprises it contains and the abrupt appearances and disappearances of emotions and images. In his verses the great myths crowd close upon purely personal inventions. He calls upon his immediate knowledge of cities and ports, of unscrupulous *voyous* and popular songs, but speaks in the tone of a prophet and discoverer. The contrast between Apollinaire's extraordinary erudition, nourished on pornography, magic, popular lit., and encyclopedias, and his total simplicity as a song writer explains the profound irony pervading most of his poetry. Apollinaire's appearance, at the beginning of the 20th c., coincided with many new aesthetic preoccupations to which he brought his own inventiveness and speculative inquiry. His work joined that of the poet Max Jacob and the painters Picasso, Braque, Derain, and Matisse in a series of artistic fantasies that have gone far in shaping the modern sensibility. A farcical, festive air presided over many of the modes of art of that time, which were given the names of cubism, Fauvism, Negro art, cosmopolitanism, or erotology. Apollinaire himself was responsible for the term "surrealism." He literally became a prophet in his support of aesthetic innovations which were to become the accepted forms of the future.

Surrealism, thanks to the examples furnished by Rimbaud and Apollinaire, was to recognize that the real domain of the poet is just outside what is called the world of reason. Apollinaire had taught that the poetic act is the creative act in its fullest purity. Whatever the poet names possesses an ineffable quality; his function is precisely to explain *that,* to study what refuses to be cast into explicit lang. In this way, poetry is able to restore to lang. something of its primitive origins and mystery. Poetry like Apollinaire's does not try to fathom the supernatural or the miraculous, but simply to state the incomprehensibility of the ordinary and the commonplace. Every human expression Apollinaire saw became sphinxlike for him, and every word he overheard resembled a sibyl's utterance. His lang. has a baptismal gravity. Nascent lang., it would seem to be, rediscovering its virginity, as the poet, performing his earliest role of demiurge, calls the world to be born again by naming it.

The surrealist poets, Breton, the early Aragon, Eluard, Tzara, and Soupault, prolonged the trad. of the 19th-c. *voyant.* In the wake of Baudelaire, Rimbaud, and Mallarmé, poetry continued to be for them the effort to find a lost lang. The image or the metaphor is the result of a certain kind of alchemy. In symbolism, the alchemy had tried to go beyond the elaborate consciousness of symbolism to the very source of poetic imagination, to the sleep in which the myths of man are preserved. André Breton (1896–1966) and Paul Eluard (1895–1952), especially, have discovered (or rediscovered) the pure love of woman and sung of this love as ecstatically and vibrantly as any Ronsard. Their very intoxication with liberty seems to find an outlet in their love of woman, in their joy over their love. The human spirit's secrets were revealed to the surrealists, one after the other, in spontaneous and involuntary fashion. Their concept of woman seems to spring from the deepest part of their subconscious and to rise up to their consciousness with a primitive, almost sacred insistence. The surrealists have contributed to a rehabilitation in lit. of the role of woman as the bodily and spiritual equal of man. Love is the immediate (Eluard has entitled one of his volumes *La Vie immédiate*). The mystery of passion is a dialectic in which man makes an extraordinary request, but one which is clearly articulated in the most serious part of the surrealist program. In asking for the experience of passion, he asks for the resolution or the dissolving of the antinomy between the subject and the object, between love and death, between man and woman.

The generation of poets writing in Fr. at mid century was more dramatically allied with action—with the war and the Resistance—than the earlier poets of the century. Sartre defined the new lit. as being "engaged" (*la littérature engagée*), a term for the poetry of this generation so directly concerned with actual circumstances and events. The lesson taught by Mallarmé that there is no such thing as immediate poetry is, however, to such a degree the central legacy of modern poetry that the younger poets pass instinctively from the immediate to the eternal myths just beyond the events, the first reactions, and the first sentiments. The greatness of Pierre-Jean Jouve (1887–1976) illustrates this use of the immediate event in poetry. His universe of catastrophe is described in verse of a lofty Christian inspiration.

Existentialism, as a literary movement, did not develop any poets, with the possible exception of Francis Ponge (b. 1899), on whose work Sartre has written a long essay. His first important publication was *Le Parti pris des choses* (1942), a poetic work of great rigor and objectivity, completely lacking in any subjective lyricism.

The poetry of Jules Supervielle (1884–1960) represents a triumph in verbal simplicity in an age when poetry has not been simple. By his 1925 volume *Gravitations,* Supervielle had found his own voice, which did not vary during the next 25 years. He likes best to transcribe an inner world: thought and emotion at their birth, the speech of the blood in the veins and the beating of the heart, the land explored by the breath before it leaves the body. What he studies is mystery, that of man in the strange duality of his body and soul.

Max Jacob (1876–1944) became a well-known figure in the avant-garde circles of Paris. He incarnated the characteristics of the period: its love of parody and humor, its nonconformity, its manner of considering philosophical and aesthetic problems. After his conversion to Catholicism, his religious spirit penetrated everything. The apparition of Christ on the wall of his room in Montmarte in 1909 never ceased to count in his life (*La Défense de Tartufe,* 1919). Some of Jacob's earliest friends, notably Picasso, who called him the only poet of the period, looked upon his work as the major expression of modern poetry and art. His gouache paintings are as well known as his poems. He died in the concentration camp at Drancy in March 1944.

The cubist painters Picasso, Braque, and Juan Gris, and their friends the "cubist" poets Apollinaire and Pierre Reverdy (1889–1960), were sensitive to the changes taking place in the world. Reverdy's book *Les Épaves du ciel* was hailed by the surrealists in 1924 as the work of a master. Each of his poems forms a perfectly homogeneous and static world quite comparable to the cubist paintings of Picasso and Gris. During the last 30 years of his life, Reverdy lived as a lay associate in the Benedictine monastery of Solesmes.

Until the age of 21, Henri Michaux (b. 1899) lived principally in Brussels. His friendship with Supervielle in France helped complete the rejuvenation of poetry. He met the surrealist writers in Paris but preferred the companionship of painters: Ernst, Klee, Masson. His drawings, gouaches, and watercolors at first seemed to be contributions to his poems. But today they appear more independent, a separate means of expression. He is one of the truly authentic poetic talents who is taking his place beside those writers who investigate the strange and the unusual. The relationship that Michaux establishes between the natural and the unbelievable has created a surreal world that has become the familiar world of his poetry.

Since the middle of the century, the example and work of three poets in particular have given prestige to Fr. p. in France and abroad. During the 1950s and into the '60s, the name of Saint-John Perse (1887–1975) was revered and the poet looked upon as the worthy successor to Valéry. Throughout the '60s and well into the '70s the poetry of René Char (b. 1907) was studied with great fervor. He was often called the successor to Mallarmé and Rimbaud. In the '70s and '80s Yves Bonnefoy (b. 1923) assumed a place of eminence as the obvious successor to Rimbaud. Elected to the Collège de France in 1984 to occupy the seat vacated by the death of the critic Roland Barthes, Bonnefoy was the first poet thus honored since Valéry.

The art of Saint-John Perse (Alexis Saint Léger-Léger, or Alexis Léger) provides one of the noblest contemporary lessons on the meaning of poetry and on the role of the poet, both in his own time and in every age. Born in the Fr. West Indies, he was until 1940 a Fr. diplomat and Secretary-General of Foreign Affairs. Perse and the other poets whose trad. he continues (Baudelaire, Mallarmé, Rimbaud, Valéry, Claudel) represent extremes in their role of demiurge and in their traits of passivity to the cosmic forces. They are technicians drawing upon all the known resources of their art, upon the most modern beliefs in ancient poetic wisdom, and upon the most ancient tenets still visible in symbolism and surrealism. From his earliest poems, *Eleges* of 1910 (tr. by Louise Varèse as *Praises*), through *Anabase* of 1924 (tr. by T. S. Eliot in 1930), *Amers* of 1957 (tr. by Wallace Fowlie as *Seamarks*), and *Oiseaux* of 1963 (tr. by Robert Fitzgerald), Perse has continued to describe and analyze the condition of man in our time, the fate of man at this moment in history. His longest poem, *Amers*, is about the sea, about man submitting to the sea and forming with it an alliance. During the course of the poem the sea becomes a part of the inner life of the poet. Just as navigators take a steeple or a cliff on the mainland as a seamark (*un amer*) in their navigation, so the reader of *Amers* learns to take the marine cosmos, which is the personal universe of the poet, as a guide to the understanding of man and his work. Perse was awarded the Nobel Prize in 1960.

René Char was born in Vaucluse; the world of his poetry is rural and Mediterranean. All the familiar elements of Provence are in it: crickets and almond trees, olives, grapes, figs, oranges, branches of mimosa. The frequently used name of Heraclitus helps to fuse the Gr. spirit with the Occitan. His manner of considering the objects of his landscape, of undertaking the hardest tasks and facing the gravest risks, might be explained by the deep sense of fraternity characterizing Char's love of man and of the soil. His is not the more purely linguistic obscurity of a Mallarmé. It is more metaphorical, more surrealist, since it is lang. seeking essentially to transcribe the subconscious. The vigor of this poet's mind puts him into a separate poetic world. We are moved by the vitality of his thought, but esp. by the vitality of his concreteness. The truths of the world as he sees them are constantly demanding his allegiance. He is a poet characterized by the habit of seeing things charged with meaning—an ordered meaning regarding the relationships between nature and men. The Pléiade edition (1983) of his complete work, of one thousand pages, is a record of his achievement through more than half a century of steady writing.

All three poets (Char, Perse, Bonnefoy) are celebrants of poetry. The sacred character of this celebration is clearly visible in Bonnefoy's art, which now appears stronger than ever and in full development. He has recuperated and enriched the earlier forms of Mallarmé and Rimbaud, of Valéry and the surrealists, in his will to perpetuate the ancient lang. of poetry. His first book of poems, *Du Mouvement et de l'immobilité de douve* (1953) was tr. by Galway Kinnell in 1968. Bonnefoy studies poetry in its relationship to painting and art and has written movingly about such figures as Chagall, Balthus, Mondrian, and Giacometti. He has also translated Shakespeare. His *Ars poétique*, appearing in *L'Improbable* (1959), stresses his belief that a poem perpetuates the presence of what is going to die. Yves Bonnefoy by 1986 had become what Mallarmé was in 1896, a spokesman for poetry. For him, it is nothing less than the art of communicating about existence.

Ways of approaching the subject of poetry vary in time and with time. These ways constitute schools and movements. Today's poet in France is best characterized by an absence of any need to justify or explain his art. For a hundred years, beginning with Baudelaire in the middle of the 19th c., poetry was vibrantly justified and explained. Another poetic age began then in which the poet is the recipient of a long period of poetics, of poetic pedagogy, when he is at last free to play a more receptive role. He writes and sings poetry because it is irresistible. At this present moment in Fr. letters, when the work of poets is being examined more minutely than ever before, the poets themselves of the last two decades, Alain

Bosquet (b. 1919), Philippe Jaccottet (b. 1925), André du Bouchet (b. 1924), Yves Bonnefoy, and others, remain resolutely isolated from one another, each distinctive in his writing, each determined to think the universe for himself.

ANTHOLOGIES, TRANSLATIONS, AND INDEXES: G. Raynaud, *Bibl. des chansonniers français des XIIIe et XIVe siècles*, 2 v. (1884), partially replaced by F. Spanke, *G. Raynauds Bibl. des altfranzösischen Liedes* (1955); *Poètes d'aujourd'hui*, ed. A. van Bever et P. Léautaud, 3 v. (1929); *Petite Anthol. poétique du surréalisme*, ed. G. Hugnet (1934); *Intro. à la poésie fr.*, ed. T. Maulnier (1939); *Anthol. de la poésie fr.*, ed. A. Gide (1945); *Sixty Poems of Scève* (1949), *Complete Works of Rimbaud* (1966), both tr. W. Fowlie; *Anthol. de la poésie fr. depuis le surréalisme*, ed. M. Béalu (1952); *An Anthol. of Mod. Fr. P.*, ed. C. A. Hackett (1952); *Poètes et romanciers du moyen âge*, ed. A. Pauphilet (1952); *The P. of France*, ed. A. M. Boase (1952); *Panorama critique de Rimbaud au surréalisme*, ed. G.-E. Clancier (1953); *Poètes du 16e siècle*, ed. A.-M. Schmidt (1953); *Fr. P. of the Ren.*, ed. B. Weinberg (1954); *Mid-C. Fr. Poets*, ed. W. Fowlie (1955); *Anthol. de la poésie fr.*, ed. M. Arland, 2d ed. (1956); P. Valéry, *Coll. Works in Eng.*, ed. J. Mathews, 15 v. (1956-75), *The Art of P.*, tr. D. Folliot (1958); *Oxford Book of Fr. Verse: 18th C.–20th C.*, ed. P. M. Jones, 2d ed. (1957); *Anthol. de la poésie baroque fr.*, ed. J. Rousset, 2 v. (1961); *Penguin Book of Fr. Verse*, 4 v. (1958–61); *An Anthol. of Fr. P. from Nerval to Valéry*, ed. A. Flores, 2d ed. (1962); *Contemp. Fr. P.*, ed. A. Aspel and D. Justice (1965); *The Poems of François Villon*, tr. G. Kinnell (1965); *An Anthol. of Fr. Surrealist P.*, ed. J. H. Matthews (1966); *Anthol. poétique fr., moyen âge*, ed. A. Mary, 2 v. (1967); *An Anthol. of Mod. Fr. P., from Baudelaire to the Present Day*, ed. C. A. Hackett (1968); *Coll. Poems of St.-John Perse*, tr. W. H. Auden et al. (1971); *Fr. Individualist Poetry 1686–1760*, ed. R. Finch and E. Joliat (1971); *Chanson Verse of the Early Ren.*, ed. B. Jeffrey (1971); *Poems of René Char*, tr. M. A. Caws and J. Griffin (1976); *Anthologie des grands rhétoriqueurs*, ed. P. Zumthor (1978); G. Apollinaire, *Calligrammes*, tr. A. H. Greet (1980); *Chanter m'estuet*, ed. S. N. Rosenberg (1981); *Roof Slates and Other Poems of Pierre Reverdy*, tr. M. A. Caws and P. Terry (1981); C. Baudelaire, *Les Fleurs du mal*, tr. R. Howard (1982); S. Mallarmé, *Sel. Poems and Prose*, ed. M. A. Caws (1982); *Le Roman de Renart* (1983), *The Song of Roland* (1985), both tr. P. Terry; Y. Bonnefoy, *Poems, 1959–75*, tr. R. Pevear (1985); *La Poésie fr. du premier 17e siècle*, ed. D. L. Rubin (1986); R. Bossuat, *Manuel bibliographique de la litt. fr. du moyen âge*, 3d supp., 1960–80 (1986).

HISTORY AND CRITICISM: C. A. Sainte-Beuve, *Tableau de la poésie fr. au 16e siècle*, 2d ed. (1838); G. Paris, *La Poésie du moyen âge*, 2 v. (1885–95); F. Brunetière, *L'Evolution de la poésie lyrique au 19e siècle* (1894); H. Guy, *Hist. de la poésie fr. au 16e siècle*, v. 1, *L'Ecole des rhétoriqueurs* (1910); R. Lalou, *Vers une alchimie lyrique* (1927); E. Faguet, *Hist. de la poésie fr. de la ren. au romantisme* (1929–); Jeanroy; Patterson; M. Raymond, *De Baudelaire au surréalisme*, 2d ed. (1940); A. Beguin, *L'Ame romantique et le rêve* (1946); *CBFL*; Lote; R. Lebègue, *La Poésie fr. de 1560 à 1630*, 2 v. (1951); H. Peyre, *Connaissance de Baudelaire* (1951); J. Chiari, *Contemp. Fr. P.* (1952); W. Fowlie, *Mallarmé* (1953); J. Rousset, *La Litt. de l'âge baroque en France* (1953); R. Winegarten, *Fr. Lyric P. in the Age of Malherbe* (1954); H. Weber, *La Création poétique au XVIe siècle*, 2 v. (1956); G. Brereton, *An Intro. to the Fr. Poets* (1956); L. J. Austin, *L'univers poétique de Baudelaire: symbolisme et symbolique* (1956), *Poetic Principles and Practice* (1987); M. Gilman, *The Idea of P. in France* (1958); A. M. Schmidt, "Litt. de la Ren.," *Hist. des litts.*, ed. R. Queneau, v. 3 (1958); S. Mallarmé, *Correspondance*, 11 v. (1959–85); J. Frappier, *Poésie lyrique en France au 17e et 18e siècles* (1960); R. Dragonetti, *La Technique poétique des trouvères dans la chanson courtoise* (1960); A. Bosquet, *Verbe et vertige* (1961); W. N. Ince, *The Poetic Theory of Paul Valéry* (1961); I. Silver, *Ronsard and the Hellenic Ren. in France*, 2 v. (1961, 1987); C. A. Knudson and J. Misrahi, "Med. Fr. Lit.," in Fisher; Jeanroy, *Origines*; D. Poirion, *Le Poète et le prince* (1965); R. Finch, *The Sixth Sense: Individualism in Fr. P., 1686–1770* (1966); R. W. Greene, *The Poetic Theory of Pierre Reverdy* (1967); J.-C. Payen and J.-P. Chauveau, *La Poésie des origines à 1715* (1968); *GRLMA*; J. Lawler, *The Lang. of Fr. Symbolism* (1969); C. K. Abraham, *Enfin Malherbe: The Influence of Malherbe on Fr. Lyric Prosody, 1605–1674* (1971); U. Mölk and F. Wolfzettel, *Répertoire métrique de la poésie française des origines à 1350* (1972); M. A. Caws, *The P. of Dada and Surrealism* (1971), *The Inner Theater of Recent Fr. P.* (1972), *Presence of René Char* (1976); S. Brindeau et al., *La Poésie contemporaine de la langue fr. depuis 1945* (1973); *Order and Adventure in Post-Romantic Fr. P.*, ed. E. Beaumont et al. (1973); K. Uitti, *Story, Myth, and Celebration in OF Narrative Poetry, 1050–1200* (1973); J. J. Duggan, *The Song of Roland: Formulaic Style and Poetic Craft* (1973); J. Kristeva, *Revolution du langage poétique* (1974, tr. 1984); F. Hallyn, *Formes métaphoriques dans la poésie lyrique de l'âge baroque en France* (1975); *Sensibility and Creation: Studies in 20th-C. Fr. P.*, ed. R. Cardinal (1977); F. Ponge, *The Sun Placed in the Abyss, and other Texts* (1977)—with trs. by S. Gavronsky; M. Riffaterre, *Semiotics of P.* (1978); P. Zumthor, *Le Masque et la lumière* (1978); Bec; B. Johnson, *Défigurations du langage poétique* (1979), *A World of Difference* (1986); R. Greene, *Six Fr. Poets of Our Time* (1979); J. P. Houston, *Fr. Symbolism and the Modernist Movement* (1980); Scott; D. L. Rubin, *The Knot of Artifice* (1981); J.-P. Richard, *Onze Études sur la poésie moderne* (1981); W. Calin, *A Muse for Heroes: Nine Cs. of the Epic in France* (1983), *In Defense of Fr. P.* (1987); J. T. Naughton, *The Poetry and Poetics of Yves Bonnefoy* (1984); J. Derrida, *Signéponge/Signsponge* (1984); R. H. Bloch, *The Scandal of the Fabliaux* (1986); P. Knight, *Flower Poetics in 19th-C.*

France (1986); C. Scott, *A Question of Syllables* (1986), *The Riches of Rhyme* (1988), *Vers Libre* (1990); C. de D. Rifelj, *Word and Figure: The Lang. of 19th-C. Fr. P.* (1987); S. J. Huot, *From Song to Book* (1987); R. G. Cohn, *Mallarmé's Prose Poems* (1987); G. Chesters, *Baudelaire and the Poetics of Craft* (1988); Hollier—the most recent full history; *19th-C. Fr. P.*, ed. C. Prendergast (1990); L. W. Johnson, *Poets as Players* (1990). W.F.

FRISIAN POETRY. F., the nearest Continental relative of Eng., was once the speech of an independent and extensive maritime nation along the North Sea coast, but is today the lang. of a minority people living partly in the Netherlands and partly in Germany. It exists in three forms: East and North F., spoken in Germany, and West F., spoken in the Netherlands. Only West F., which now has legal status both in the schools and in the public life of Netherlands Friesland, has developed into a full-fledged literary lang. and *Kultursprache.*

As is the case with other Germanic peoples, lit. among the Frisians began with the songs of bards celebrating the great deeds of kings and heroes, though none of those early epics has survived. What has survived is a valuable body of F. law, the earliest dating from the 11th c., in a distinctive form marked by such literary devices as alliteration and parallelism, and often genuinely poetic in thought and feeling.

When, about the year 1500, Friesland came under foreign control, F. lost its position as the lang. of law and public life, and F. lit. sank to a low level. No great poetic figure appeared on the scene until Gysbert Japicx (1603–66), an eminent Ren. poet who with his *Rymlerije* (Poetry), published posthumously in 1668, reestablished F. as a literary and cultural lang. The 18th c. saw the rise of many followers and imitators of Japicx; however, no outstanding poetic figure came to the fore. In the 19th c., Eeltsje Halbertsma dominated the scene; much of his work is folk poetry inspired by Ger. romanticism. Another outstanding figure is Harmen Sytstra (1817–62), a romantic inspired by his country's heroic past, whose work reveals a desire to restore the old Germanic verseforms. The latter half of the 19th c. produced many folk poets, the most popular of whom were Waling Dykstra (1821–1914) and Tsjibbe Gearts van der Meulen (1824–1906), but on the whole their work is uninspired, rationalistic, and didactic. Piter Jelles Troelstra (1860–1930), with themes centering on love, nature, and the fatherland, ushered in a second romantic period.

The 20th c. ushered in a new spirit to F. p., perhaps first evident in the simple and pensive verse of J. B. Schepers, but even more clearly in the work of Simke Kloosterman (1876–1938), whose poetic art is both individualistic and aristocratic. In *De wylde Fûgel* (The Wild Bird, 1932), she gives intense and passionate utterance to the longings and disillusionments of love. Rixt (Hendrika A. van Dorssen, 1887–1979) also wrote verse characterized by emotional intensity. A first-rate poet at the beginning of the century was Obe Postma (1868–1963), whose verse has vigor, penetration, and philosophical insight. Much of it is poetry of reminiscence; still more of it is a paean to life and the good earth. Postma was the first to use free verse in F. and to use it well.

The new spirit came to full expression and ushered in a literary renaissance in the Young F. movement, launched in 1915 and led by the daring young nationalist Douwe Kalma (1896–1953). A talented poet and critic, Kalma sharply denounced the mediocrity and provincialism of 19th-c. F. letters. With him and his movement Friesland began to have an independent voice in European culture. Kalma's genius appears at its freshest in his classic *Keningen fan Fryslân* (Kings of Friesland, 2 v., 1949, 1951), a series of historical plays in blank verse featuring the F. kings and depicting the struggle between Christianity and the heathen. Kalma's lyric poetry, collected in *Dage* (Dawn, 1927) and *Sangen* (Songs, 1936) is technically skillful but often nebulous in content. His work—like that of his school—suffers from aestheticism and a poetic jargon laden with neologisms and archaisms.

Among the poets of merit who had their start in the Young F. school are R. P. Sybesma, an excellent sonneteer, and D. H. Kiestra, a poet of the soil with a vigorous talent. For decades, the most popular and widely read poet was Fedde Schurer (1898–1968), a versatile artist who preferred national and religious themes. His early poems show the influence of Young F. aestheticism; those written after 1946 are more direct, unadorned, and modern. His *Simson* (Samson, 1945), a biblical drama in verse, gained him the Gysbert Japicx Literary Prize. In 1946 he helped launch *De Tsjerne* (The Churn), the literary periodical with which most of the important names in F. letters were associated until 1968.

Around 1935 some of the younger poets, such as J. D. de Jong and Ype Poortinga, showed signs of breaking away from the Young F. movement, both in spirit and in poetic diction. Douwe A. Tamminga (b. 1909) in his *Brandaris* (Lighthouse, 1938) created his own poetic idiom, based largely on the lang. of the people which he transfigured and sublimated into pure art.

Since World War II, nearly 300 books of poetry have been pub. in Friesland. Postwar disillusionment and existential despair informed much of the poetry of the late 1940s and '50s, when biting satire and experimental forms openly declared all trads. meaningless. Among the modern voices were Anne Wadman (b. 1919) and Jan Wybenga (b. 1917), whose *Amoeben* (Amoebae) in 1953 led the way in experimental poetry. An experimentalist group led by Hessel Miedema, Steven de Jong, and Jelle de Jong started its own journal, *Quatrebras* (1954–68), and in 1961 published an anthol.

that clearly demonstrated a refusal to be restricted by conventional thought or form. Sjoerd Spanninga (Jan Dykstra, b. 1906) introduced exotic imagery from foreign cultures, esp. Oriental, through a wide variety of forms. The verse of Martin Sikkema, Freark Dam, and Klaas Dykstra was more traditional. Other older poets have continued to write: Douwe A. Tamminga's *In Memoriam* (1968), written after his son's untimely death, is a masterpiece of profound thought and feeling cast in disciplined but fluid form, and a volume of his selected works, *Stapstiennen* (Steppingstones), appeared in 1979. Tiny Mulder (b. 1921) is another distinguished poet who frequently effects a remarkable fusion of significant form and content and evinces a penetrating vision that affirms life without evading its horrors and sorrows. *Tinkskrift*, a collection of four previously published volumes, came out in 1986. Several of the younger poets show equal promise, e.g. Daniel Daen (Willem Abma), who has been not only prolific but also consistently impressive in his ability to fuse the concrete and abstract. Frequent contributions to *Trotwaer*, the successor of *De Tsjerne*, incl. Tsjebbe Hettinga, Bartle Laverman, Eppie Dam, Jacobus Quiryn Smink, and Boukje Wytsma.

ANTHOLOGIES: *Bloemlezing uit Oud-, Middel-en Nieuwfriesche Geschriften*, ed. F. B. Hettema (1887); *It Sjongende Fryslan* (1917), *De nije Moarn* (1922), *De Fryske Skriftekennisse fan 1897–1925*, 2 v. (1928–31), *De Fryske Skriftekennisse fen 1876–1897* (1939), all ed. D. Kalma; *Fiif en tweintich Fryske Dichters*, ed. F. Schurer (1942); *Frieslands Dichters*, ed. A. Wadman (1949)—excellent anthol. of poetry since 1880, with valuable intro. and Dutch tr.; *op fjouwer winen*, ed. A. R. Oostra et al. (1961)—anthol. of young experimentalists; *Country Fair: Poems from Friesland Since 1945*, tr. R. Jellema (1985).

HISTORY AND CRITICISM: C. Borchling, *Poesie und Humor im friesischen Recht* (1908); T. Siebs, "Gesch. der friesischen Lit.," *Grundriss der germanischen Philologie*, ed. H. Paul (1909); D. Kalma, *Gysbert Japiks* (1939); A. Wadman, *Kritysk Konfoai* (1951); E. H. Harris, *Lit. in Friesland* (1956); J. Piebenga, *Koarte Skiednis fen de Fryske Skriftekennisse*, 2d ed. (1957)—valuable hist.; J. Smit, *De Fryske literatuer 1945–1967* (1968); K. Dykstra, *Lyts hanboek fan de Fryske Literatuer* (1977)—valuable survey of F. lit. from its beginnings to the 1970s; survey of F. poetry 1945–84 in *Trotwaer*, no. 3–4 (1985).

B.J.F.; H.J.B.

G

GAELIC POETRY. See SCOTTISH GAELIC POETRY.

GALICIAN (OR GALLEGAN) POETRY. (This article treats primarily Sp.p. in Galician, the lang. of the western region of the Iberian peninsula; for the poetries of the central and eastern langs., see SPANISH POETRY and CATALAN POETRY.)

Spreading from the pilgrimage center of Santiago de Compostela throughout Galicia and northern Portugal, G.-Port. *cantigas* were among the earliest lyric forms in the Iberian peninsula. Their form was imposed on troubadours from non-G.-speaking regions of Spain. Most of the secular *cantigas* are preserved in the *Cancioneiro* [songbook] *da Ajuda* (mid 14th c.), *Cancioneiro da Vaticana* (end of 15th c.), and the *Cancioneiro Colocci-Brancuti* (now *Cancioneiro da Biblioteca Nacional de Lisboa*, 16th c.). King Alfonso X ("The Wise") is responsible for the religious *Cantigas de Santa Maria* (13th c.). G. poets from 1200–1350, the period of greatest achievements, incl. Martin Codax, Afonso Eanes de Coton, Bernal de Bonaval, Joan (Garcia) de Guilhade, Joan Airas, Pai Gomes Chariño, Airas Nunes, Pero Garcia, and Pedro Amigo de Sevilla, as well as others from Portugal and the rest of the peninsula. The G.-Port. school, although following Occitan models (see OCCITAN POETRY), is best exemplified by the apparently native *cantiga de amigo*, a song of melancholy nostalgia by a maiden for her absent lover.

After the death of Portugal's King Diniz (1325), the old lyric declines; from 1400 Castilian begins to replace G. as the lang. of poetry in the peninsula (see SPANISH POETRY). The bilingual *Cancioneiro de Baena* (1445) still has a few G. poems by Macias "o namorado" (fl. 1360–90), el Arcediano de Toro (fl. 1379–90), and Alfonso Alvarez de Villasandino (1340?–1428). Until the 18th c., little written G. p. has been preserved. Diego A. Cernadas de Castro (1698–1777), "el cura de Fruime," wrote bilingual occasional verse and with Manuel Freire Castrillón (1751–1820) marks the gradual rebirth of G. lit.

Romanticism brought more interest in Galicia's past and its ancient lit., folklore, and other specific features. Among others, Antolín Faraldo (1823–53) defended G. autonomy and with Aurelio Aguirre (1833–58), the "G. Espronceda," promoted literary regionalism. Francisco Añón y Paz (1812–78), "el Patriarca," is remembered for his patriotic odes and humorous compositions. Alberto Camino (1821–61), author of sentimental and elegiac verse, is a forerunner of the *Rexurdimento* (Renaissance) led by Rosalía de Castro (1837–85). The rebirth was signalled by the Floral Games of La Coruña in 1861, the winning poems of which were published in the *Album de Caridad* (1862). In 1863 Castro pub. *Cantares Gallegos* (G. Songs), the first book written in G. in the modern period. In 1880 her *Follas novas* (New Leaves) appeared. She also wrote in Castilian, but her social concerns are most obvious in G. (*Poems*, tr. A.-M. Aldaz et al. [1991]). Moreover, her themes incl. some of the earliest feminist statements in Galicia if not in the peninsula. Two of her important contemporaries were Eduardo Pondal y Abente (1835–1917), who wrote *Queixumes dos pinos* (Complaints of the Pines), and Manuel Curros Enríquez (1851–1908), forced to emigrate to Cuba after writing anticlerical verse. There he composed the nostalgic *Aires da miña terra* (Airs of My Land, 1880). Valentín Lamas Carvajal (1849–1906) sang elegiacally of the peasant life in works such as *Espiñas, follas e frores* (Thorns, Leaves and Flowers, 1875). Other poets of the later 19th c. are José Pérez Ballesteros (1883–1918), known for the 3-vol. *Cancionero popular gallego* (1885–86); Manuel Leiras Pulpeiro (1854–1912); and Manuel Lugrís Freire (1863–1940).

Among contemp. poets the lang. has become more sophisticated. Troubador trads., *saudade*, and G. patriotism are still present, while numerous foreign poetic movements have also been influential. The foremost poets of the early 20th c. are Antonio Noriega Varela (1869–1947), Ramón Cabanillas (1876–1959), Victoriano Taibo (1885–1966), and Gonzalo López Abente (1878–1963). Noriega's ruralism is close to the previous generation, but Cabanillas and López Abente reflect Sp.(-Am.) *modernismo*. Taibo's peasant themes are expression of his social commitment. The best poet of the avant-garde in Galicia was the sailor Manoel Antonio (1900–30), who collaborated with the artist Alvaro Cebreiro in the iconoclastic manifesto "Máis Alá" (Beyond, 1928). During his lifetime he pub. *De catro a catro* (From Four to Four, 1928); posthumously his nearly complete works have appeared, showing him to be a true disciple of Creationism in the manner of Huidobro. Luis Amado Carballo (1901–27) wrote a more pantheistic, vanguard poetry. Ricardo Carballo Calero, Florencio Delgado Gurriarán, Xulio Sigüenza, and Euxenio Montes also wrote avant-garde verse prior to the Sp. Civil War. Fermín Bouza Brey (1901–73), one of the best known G. writers of the postwar period, employed elements of medieval poetry; others are Alvaro Cunqueiro (1911–81), Eduardo Blanco-Amor (1897–1979),

Luz Pozo Garza (b. 1922), and María do Carme Kruckenberg (b. 1926).

Since 1976, G. p. has undergone rapid change. The proliferation of texts and critical studies led to the identification of a "Golden Age" of poetry. Some, such as X. L. Méndez Ferrín, have followed the model of Celso Emilio Ferreiro's and Lorenzo Varela's social poetry, while others have maintained Manoel Antonio's avant-garde orientation, adding a tendency to intimism (Claudio Rodríguez Fer). Several collectives have given impetus to poetic production: *Brais Pinto* (1950s), *Rompente, Alén,* and *De amor e desamor.* G. journals—*Nordés, Dorna, Escrita, A nosa terra, Nó*—have provided space for both the established writers and the new. Several anthols have appeared, and there are more women poets, among them Xohana Torres, Helena Villar, Ana Romaní, Pilar Pallarés, Xela Arias, and Helena de Carlos. X. M. Alvarez Cáccamo, M. A. Fernán-Vello, R. Fonte, M. Forcadela, and V. Vaqueiro also belong to the group of younger poets whose work is strengthening the foundation of modern G. p.

ANTHOLOGIES: *Cancionero popular gallego,* ed. J. Pérez Ballesteros, 2 v. (1942; first pub. 1886); *Escolma de poesía galega,* v. 1 (1952) and v. 2 (1959) both ed. X. M. Alvarez Blázquez, v. 3 (1957) and v. 4 (1955) both ed. F. Fernández del Riego; C. Martín Gaite and A. Ruiz Tarazona, *Ocho siglos de poesía gallega* (1972); M. V. Moreno Márquez, *Os novísimos da poesía galega* (1973); L. Rodríguez Gómez, *Desde a palabra, Doce voces* (1986); X. R. Pena, *Literatura galega medieval,* v. 2 (1986); *Festa da Palabra,* ed. K. N. March (1989)—contemp. G. women poets.

HISTORY AND CRITICISM: B. Varela Jácome, *Historia de la literatura gallega* (1951); A. Couceiro Freijomil, *Diccionario bio-bibliográfico de escritores,* 3 v. (1951–54); J. L. Varela, *Poesía y restauración cultural de Galicia en el siglo XIX* (1958); *GRLMA,* v. 2.1.C; P. Vázquez Cuesta, "Literatura gallega," *Historia de las literaturas hispánicas no castellanas,* ed. J. M. Díez Borque (1980); M. Vilanova and X. M. Alvarez Cáccamo, "Panorama de la poesía gallega de posguerra," *Camp de l'arpa* (May 1980); R. Carballo Calero, *Historia da literatura galega contemporánea. 1808–1936,* 3d ed. (1981); X. L. Méndez Ferrín, *De Pondal a Novoneyra* (1984).

L.A.S.; K.N.M.

GAUCHO POETRY. Taken literally, G. p. is the name for poetic compositions, anonymous or otherwise, which deal with the life and adventures of the Argentinean cowboy. It would be a mistake to apply the same denomination to all popular poetry produced in Sp. America.

Popular poetry, which had its origin in the Sp. *Romancero,* flourished at the end of the 18th c. and reached its peak by the middle of the 19th c. In Uruguay and Argentina, learned writers invaded the field of folk poetry and produced a number of literary imitations of the style of early *Payadores,* or singers of popular poetry. The first of these poets was the Uruguayan Bartolomé Hidalgo (1788–1822), whose famous dialogues expressed the sentiments of the G. in regard to the war of independence against Spain. He was followed by the Argentine Hilario Ascasubi (1807–75), who played an active role in the struggle against the dictatorship of Rosas and who published a number of G. ballads dealing with the siege of Montevideo (*Paulino Lucero o los gauchos del Rio de la Plata,* 1839–51). *Santos Vega, o los mellizos de la Flor* (1851, 1872), his greatest achievement in this type of poetry, tells the story of two brothers, one of whom becomes an outlaw. The main value of the poem resides in its colorful and accurate description of country and city life in mid 19th-c. Argentina. Estanislao del Campo (1834–80) followed the example of these writers and employed pure G. dialect in his *Fausto* (1866), a parody of Gounod's opera.

The greatest of the G. poems is *Martín Fierro* (1872, 1879) by the Argentine José Hernández (1834–86). A well-educated man and a writer deeply conscious of his social mission, Hernández set out to prove the moral fortitude of the G. and his right to gain a respectable position in the life of his country. Dealing with the problem of civilization and barbarism in the Am. continent, he criticized the defenders of "civilization" for their irresponsibility in ruthlessly destroying the trads. of native populations, esp. the nomad Gs. He praised the stoicism of the Sp.-Am. peasants, and with true romantic spirit he envisioned the birth of a new way of life from their epic fight in the midst of a wild continent. Encouraged by the success of his poem, Hernández wrote a second part (1879) in which he told of Martín Fierro's return from the Indian country where he had sought refuge from persecution by the city authorities. The tone of this continuation is no longer rebellious but moderately didactic. Hernández' poem owes its immense popularity in Sp. America to its virile exaltation of freedom and courage, to its forceful display of nationalism, popular wisdom, and pride in the virtues of a people who hold fast to the trad. of their homeland. The critics of yesterday and today are unanimous in considering *Martín Fierro* the highest expression of popular poetry in Sp. America.

At present G. p. is in a period of stagnation. The same may be said about popular poetry in general throughout Sp. America. But scholars and students of the subject are organizing and editing the historical texts. See also SPANISH AMERICAN POETRY.

The G. Martin Fierro, tr. W. Owen (1935); M. W. Nichols, *The G.: Cattle Hunter, Cavalryman, Ideal of Romance* (1942); *Poesía gauchesca,* ed. J. L. Borges and A. Bioy Casares, 2 v. (1955); *Antología de la poesía gauchesca,* intro. J. Horacio Becco (1972); F. E. Tiscornia, *Poetas gauchescos* (1974); F. Weinberg, *Trayectoria de la poesía gauchesca* (1977); J. B. Rivera, *Poesía gauchesca* (1977).

F.A.

GE'EZ POETRY. See ETHIOPIAN POETRY.

GEORGIAN POETRY. (This entry treats G. p. in Russian.) G. culture is one of the oldest in the region generally known today as Transcaucasia; archaeological findings in the territory date back to the third millennium B.C. During their history Georgians have often had to fight against formidable enemies—Arabs, Turks, Persians, Mongols—who numerous times invaded the country and laid waste its villages, but against all odds the nation has preserved its culture, lang., and religion. Up to the 19th c., the lit. of Georgia ws the oldest and richest of that of any of the Republics in the former Soviet Union.

The trad. of a written lit. starts in Georgia with the beginning of the Christian era (4th c.). The earliest poetic forms are to be found among liturgical psalms and hymns, initially translated from Gr. Later G. clergy developed similar forms independently, and gradually spiritual songs acquired more secular coloring, evolving into lyric poems.

During the following centuries the genre of narrative poetry emerges, influenced by the lit. of neighboring Persia. The genre reached its peak in the 12th c. during the reign of Queen Tamar (1184–1213). Among the three distinguished poets of her court—Chakhrukhadze, Ioane Shavteli, and Shota Rustaveli—the latter is unanimously acknowledged as the greatest master of G. poetic art. His epic poem *Vepkhis Tqaosani* (The Night in the Tiger's Skin) recounts the adventures of a young prince who aids his friend in search of the latter's beloved, captured by devils. Basically Christian in spirit, the narrative is nevertheless saturated with a pantheistic joy of life. The poem praises chivalrous love, heroic deeds, friendship, and loyalty to one's sovereign. Several digressions reflect codified rules of chivalrous courtship, honor, and poetic art. The poem's exceptional richness of vocabulary, powerful images, exquisite alliterations, and complex rhyming are considered to be yet unsurpassed models in G. p. The poem consists of 1576 quatrains written in the meter *shairi*, a 16-syllable verse with a medial caesura. The metrical pattern permits two types of variation in syllable-grouping: *magali* (high) *shairi* [4 / 4 // 4 / 4] and *dabali* (low) *shairi* [5 / 3 // 5 / 3]. These two types of *shairi* alternate quatrain by quatrain throughout the poem, while the rhyming pattern of each quatrain proceeds in simple monorhyme—*aaaa, bbbb, cccc*, etc.

Rustaveli's poem was viewed as a paradigm by the poets of the following four centuries, a period that marks a low ebb in the devel. of G. p. The themes and plots of *The Night in the Tiger's Skin* are borrowed and imitated in lyric and narrative poems alike, while *shairi* remained the basic meter of G. secular verse. In the 16th–17th cs., several G. kings distinguished themselves as fine poets. King Theimuraz I (1588–1662) was strongly influenced by Persian poetry. Graceful poetic images and refined vocabulary are the most prominent features of his works. Archil III (1647–1713) is known for several didactic poems in which he contemplates the destiny of his country, religion and morals, and the art of poetry. He objected to the use of Persian poetic models and tried to purify his vocabulary from foreign borrowings. But a far more radical innovator was David Guramishvili (1705–92). Although his major work, "Davitiani" (The Story of David), is written in the traditional *shairi*, in his shorter lyrics he breaks away from the canons of Rustaveli's verse and introduces a great variety of metrical forms and rhyming patterns. He too reformed the poetic vocabulary, bringing it closer to spoken lang. His love poems describe sentiments of an ordinary man rather than of an enamored knight. "Davitiani" consists of a number of short narrative poems in which the author both expresses his religious and political thoughts and recounts his tumultuous and eventful life.

The next prominent figure of G. p. is Bessarion Gabashvili (1740–91), better known as Besiki, a court poet of King Heraclius II. Love is the major theme of his remarkably elegant and sonorous lyrics. His refined images are at times too ornate, but his vocabulary is rich and innovative. Besiki frequently used an original meter later known as *besikuri* (i.e. Besikian), a 14-syllable verse of the distinct pattern 2 / 3 / 4 / 2 / 3.

At the very beginning of the 19th c., Georgia was annexed by the Russian Empire. G. nobility and intellectuals became acquainted with the lit. trads. of Russia and western Europe. Consequently, G. p. of the following decades displays the noticeable influence of romanticism. The movement is best represented by Alexandre Chavchavadze (1786–1846), Grigol Orbeliani (1804–83), and Nikoloz Baratashvili (1817–45). The poems of Chavchavadze and Orbeliani are often contemplative but never metaphysical. The poets express their pride for Georgia's heroic past or meditate remorsefully on the country's lost glory. Majestic images of nature often serve as a dramatic background for their soliloquies, permeated with pessimism and sadness. Another group of their poems, marked with vibrant sensuality, praise the earthly joys of love, friendship, and feasting. Their poetic virtuosity is best displayed in the genre of *mukhambazi*. These are predominantly love poems consisting of several 5-line stanzas of 14- or 15-syllable verses in monorhyme. Baratashvili is the epitome of G. romanticism. His poetic persona is that of a passionate rhetor and rebel challenging his destiny. In his only narrative poem, "Bedi Kartlisa" (The Fate of Georgia), he depicts with exceptional force the last devastating battle (1795) of Iraklius II against the Persian invaders. Baratashvili also significantly reformed G. versification, introducing new metrical forms and integrating into his poems new motifs and vocabulary from folksongs.

The second half of the 19th c. is marked by an

awakening of the national consciousness and increasing dissatisfaction with the oppressive policy of the czarist government. G. poets of this period adjust romantic conventions to their social and political concerns and add a good dose of satirical venom to their verses. The most prominent figure is Ilia Chavchavadze (1837–1907), the founder of a G.-lang. literary magazine, *Iveria.* An outspoken critic of the policy of Russification, he writes lyrical as well as narrative poems of patriotic appeal. Rhetorical style and strong didactic overtones emphasize the poet's civil convictions. His contemporary Akaki Tsereteli (1840–1915) enjoyed fàr greater popularity among the general public. The clarity of his images and the simplicity and sonority of his vocabulary make the satirical and political references of his poem less overbearing. Many of his love poems, often written in the genre of *mukhambazi,* have become popular songs. Another outstanding poet of the period, Vazha Pshavela (1861–1915), wrote poems in the vernacular of his native Pshavi that gave unique expressive force to his images. The tragic clash between society's moral values and pragmatic concerns is the major theme of several of his narrative poems that portray action and character of mythic and legendary grandeur.

The first decades of the 20th c. witnessed a new surge of Western influence in a proliferation of poetic schools. In 1916 a group of poets, Titsian Tabidze, Paolo Iashvili, Georgy Leonidze, Nikoloz Mitsishvili, and Valerian Gaprindashvili, published their literary magazine *Tsisperi Qantsebi* (The Blue Drinking Horns), which raised the banner of the symbolist movement in G. p. These poets experimented boldly with vocabulary and versification and adjusted Western genres to the traditional forms of G. p. They praised the intuitive and mystical sources of poetic inspiration and cultivated sensuality and intentional obscurity. Another noteworthy group known as modernists included Konstantine Gamsakhurdia, Ioseb Grishashvili, and Kote Makashvili; they published their highly refined poems in the short-lived periodical *Ilioni* (1922). G. futurists—Nikoloz Shengelaia, Simon Chikovani, Zhango Gogoberidze, and others—hastened to voice their militant aesthetic credos in their literary organ with the endemic title H_2SO_4 (1924). True to their declaration that poetry is but "a vessel of linguistic tricks," they strained the potentialities of the lang. to the breaking point, reflecting the same preoccupation with poetic means and forms as their European and Rus. counterparts.

A number of remarkable poets, Grigol Robakidze, Terenti Graneli, and Galaktion Tabidze among them, did not belong to any literary group, but their works attracted keen interest. Tabidze (1891–1959), whose images display spiritual kinship with the symbolists, is considered the most brilliant poet of the century. An acute sense of loneliness and nostalgia find poignant expression in his sonorous verse, whose graceful and subtle images are permeated with innate pessimism.

After the Socialist revolution of 1917, Georgia enjoyed a brief period of political independence (1918–21), but in February of 1921 the Red Army installed the Bolshevik government and the country was forced to enter the alliance of the Soviet Socialist Republics. Initially these cataclysmic events enhanced the creative energy of Georgian intellectuals, and various poetic groups flourished almost until 1930. But soon the ever-tightening control of censorhip forced G. poets to serve the government's demands. Some poets, mostly those of the older generation, managed to maintain high poetic standards in their rare publications, but the majority, even talented Grigol and Irakly Abashidze, produced poems distinguished only by their quasi-optimistic rhetoric and adulation of approved social causes.

By the end of the 1950s, after the official denunciation of Stalin's regime, a new generation of G. poets emerged. These poets, Anna Kalandadze, Mukhran Machavariani, Tamaz and Otar Chiladze, Archil Sulakauri, Shota Nishnianidze, Murman Lebanidze, and Tariel Chanturia, emancipated from harsh ideological restraints, expressed more freely their sentiments. They renewed experiments with metrical forms and enlarged their vocabulary, further urbanizing the themes and styles of G. p.

Since the late 1960s, some G. poets, like Lia Sturua, Besik Kharanauli and a few others, have displayed a distinct preference for *vers libre.* Sturua, an exceptionally gifted poet, is the primary force of the movement. Many young poets, however, such as Manana Chitishvili, represent a more moderate wing that continues the best trads. of G. p. with remarkable vigor, imagination, and technical artistry.

Shot'ha Rust'haveli, *The Man in the Panther's Skin,* tr. M. S. Wardrop (1912); C. Beridze, "G. P.," *Asiatic Review* (1930–31); R. P. Blake, "G. Secular Lit.: Epic, Romance and Lyric (1100–1800)," *Harvard Studies and Notes on Phil. and Lit.* 15 (1933); J. Karst, *Littérature georgienne chrétienne* (1934); *Hist. of G. Lit.* [in Georgian], ed. A. Baramidze, 6 v. (1962–78); *Georgische Poesie aus acht Jahrhunderten,* ed. A. Endler (1971); *L'avangardia a Tiflis,* ed. L. Magarotto (1982); *The Lit. and Art of Soviet Georgia,* ed. S. Dangulov (1987). D.KI.

GERMAN POETRY.

I. ORIGINS TO 1750
II. SINCE 1750

I. ORIGINS TO 1750. The emergence of an autonomous Ger. p. took place in a setting where it competed, on the one hand, with a living, highly sophisticated, and learned Med. Lat. culture and, on the other hand, with popular oral trads. often objectionable to the literate.

Charlemagne's biographer, Einhard, writes of the emperor's cultivation of his native lang., of his naming of the months and the winds in Ger., of his order to preserve in writing the *barbara et antiquissima carmina* of his people. His son, Louis the Pious, is reputed, perhaps unfairly, to have rescinded that order at the Synod of Inden (A.D. 817), reducing the written use of the vernacular to minor religious formulae. The sole survivor of these shifting policies seems to be the *Hildebrandslied* (The Lay of Hildebrand), a short narrative in irregular alliterative verse recorded at Fulda in the early 9th c. in a codex containing Old Testament materials. The *Hildebrandslied*, which has the distinction of being the oldest surviving example of heroic poetry in any Germanic dialect, is a tale of father and son on opposing sides in battle, of conflicting loyalties, and, presumably, of malevolent fate (the last lines have not survived). This poem begins the written record of Ger. p. Competitors of early date include the magical charms preserved in a 9th-c. ms at Merseburg (the *Merseburger Zaubersprüche*) of indeterminable pagan antiquity, with phrases dating back to IE times, and the fragmentary creation story in the *Wessobrunner Gebet* (The Wessobrunn Prayer) written down about the year 814 from an older source.

Like its Eng. and Scandinavian cousins, ancient oral Ger. p. employed alliteration rather than end rhyme. The written record of Ger., however, provides but few instances of alliterative verse, which did not flourish in OHG as long as in OE. The conversion to end-rhyme took place in the first hundred years of the written record, and was complete by the time of Otfried von Weissenburg's deliberately end-rhymed *Evangelienbuch* (ca. 868). His source was Med. Lat. hymnology. Such alliterative traces as survive Otfried color subsequent texts as *figurae* but no longer determine the form of poetic composition. The shift to end-rhyme points, together with the new knowledge of the identity of authors (Otfried is the first Ger. poet known by name), toward the foundation of a written vernacular lit. discrete from the dominant oral trad.

In the Carolingian period (752–911), the classes of lit. represented in the vernacular include: the poetic sermon (the *Muspilli*, in alliterative verse), gospel harmonies (the *Heliand* [The Savior] in Low Ger. alliterative verse, the *Evangelienbuch* in High Ger. rhyming verse), historical rhymed song (the *Ludwigslied* of 881), and hagiography (the *Georgslied*, ca. 896). As for Lat. written by Germans, the same period witnesses the prodigious hymnic output of Hrabanus Maurus (ca. 784–856), which seems to include "Veni creator spiritus," the lyrics of Gottschalk (ca. 805–69), a georgic (the *Hortulus*) of Walahfried Strabo (ca. 808–49), and the invention of the sequence. One heroic epic survives in Lat., the *Waltharius* (of disputed date, but probably mid 9th c.), treating the Walther of Aquitaine materials.

The Ottonian and early Salian emperors who followed (918–1056) and who brought the Holy Roman Empire to the peak of its power and prestige presided over a period of neglect of the written vernacular. Lat., however, flourished, as in the works of the Saxon nun, Hrotswitha of Gandersheim (ca. 935–ca. 973), and the "Cambridge Songs" (recorded mid 11th c.), with instances of erotic, political, and farcical verses. Wipo, author of panegyric and historiographic poems (fl. 1039), composed the sequence "Victimae paschalae laudes," which seems to have played a part in the gradual expansion of the Easter trope into full-fledged liturgical drama. Two poetic epics with contacts to the unrecorded oral vernacular survive from the late years of this period, the beast epic, *Ecbasis captivi* (The Escape of a Certain Captive), and the romance, *Ruodlieb*, which provides evidence of an indigenous courtly trad. in Germany by the mid 11th c.

A revival of written Ger. takes place in the wake of the Cluny reforms, which reached Germany around the middle of the 11th c. That revival is at the outset purely religious. Most of the poetic texts that survive treat *Heilsgeschichte* (the Hist. of Salvation), e.g. the *Summa theologiae*; *Das Anegenge* (The Beginning) of ca. 1060; *Ezzos Gesang*, sung on an ill-fated pilgrimage to the Holy Land, 1064–65; and *Das Leben Jesu* ("The Life of Jesus") by Frau Ava (d. 1127). The remaining documents are biblical, homiletic, Marian, and hagiographic. The *Annolied* (ca. 1085) survives on account of a 1639 imprint ed. by the baroque poet and critic Martin Opitz. The work begins with a universal hist. then proceeds to an idealized biography of the powerful imperial magnate Anno, Archbishop of Cologne (d. 1075). It specifically attacks the oral lit. of the time, setting its religious truth against popular fiction. The biographer of Bishop Gunther of Bamberg, who commissioned the *Ezzolied*, reports that the Bishop had a weakness for the songs about Attila and the Amelungen (the Theodoric cycle).

The theological monopoly of written Ger. appears to have held sway until the middle decades of the 12th c. Even then, such secular materials as occur do so under the patronage of the Church. The *Alexanderlied* of the priest Lamprecht (mid 11th c.) contains fabulous materials, adventures, and conquests, but only as negative exempla, instances of immoderation and the vanity of earthly striving. The immediate source is a Fr. narrative by Alberich of Pisançon, of whose original only 105 lines survive. The importance of the *Alexanderlied* lies in its indication of two trends: an expansion of the spectrum of subjects in written Ger. and an openness to other vernacular materials, chiefly but not exclusively Fr. The priest Konrad's *Rolandslied* (ca. 1170), an adaptation of an early, lost version of the *Chanson de Roland* by way of Konrad's intervening Lat. tr. illustrates the progress of these trends.

Whereas the divine direction of history still permeates the *Rolandslied*, other epics once ascribed to wandering minstrels (*Spielmannsepos*) but now thought to be the product of clerics, came on the scene for the sake, it seems, of the sheer pleasure of story-telling. These include *König Rother* (ca. 1150–60) and *Herzog Ernst* (ca. 1180). The beast epic *Ysengrimus* (ca. 1150), of Flemish provenance, provides an analogue in Lat., as do the raucous songs of the Archpoet (ca. 1161). The period also witnessed the composition of a fiercely patriotic and partisan epic in Lat., the *Ligurinus* (1187), treating the wars of Frederick I Barbarossa.

The literary flowering in written medieval Ger. (MHG) unfolded in the decades surrounding the year 1200. Both the erotic and the highly stylized conventions of refined manners that characterize courtly poetry were available in indigenous trads. even as new conventions (e.g. the *alba* or "tagelied,") and materials (Trojan and Arthurian) poured in from France (see OCCITAN POETRY). The bearers of this culture were no longer exclusively clerical but rather aristocratic or else those (the *ministerialis*) dependent on aristocratic patrons.

Still, the indigenous trads., the apparent receptiveness to influence from abroad, and the newly literate classes do little to explain the sudden arrival in Upper Austria around 1160 of the Ger. love lyric, fully formed in sophisticated meters, complex sentiment, and direct emotional appeal. The songs of Der von Kürenberg employed a stanza which the poet of the *Nibelungenlied* would soon thereafter use to write an epic. The lyrics of this first generation, including those of Dietmar von Aist and Emperor Henry VI, are still accessible to modern tastes with little or no philological training. The second generation of "Minnesänger," as they were called, "singers of romantic love"—Friedrich von Hausen, Heinrich von Veldecke, Heinrich von Morungen, and the elder Reinmar—are even more accessible. This devel. culminates in the lyrics of Hartmann von Aue, Wolfram von Eschenbach, and, above all, Walther von der Vogelweide, the supreme lyric poet of the Ger. Middle Ages (fl. 1190–1230).

Narrative poetry shared this devel., often in the same persons. Heinrich von Veldecke was credited by his great successor Gottfried von Strassburg as "grafting the first slip on the tree of Ger. p." by his adaptation of the *Roman d'Eneas* into Ger., the *Eneit*, written 1174–90. Credit for such an infusion could as well go to the anonymous author of *Graf Rudolf* or to Eilhart von Oberg for his *Tristrant* (both ca. 1170). Hartmann (fl. 1180–1210) brought over into Ger. two of the romances of Chrétien de Troyes (*Erec*, ca. 1190, and *Iwein*, ca. 1202) and wrote his own manual on courtly love (*Das Büchlein* [The Little Book], ca. 1190), as well as two *legenda* (*Gregorius* and *Der arme Heinrich* [Poor Henry], ca. 1195). Gottfried's *Tristan* (ca. 1210) raises the discussion of courtly love to its highest level and remains one of the most perplexing and provocative explorations of romantic love. Wolfram (fl. 1200–20) took Chrétien's unfinished *Perceval ou conte del graal* and transformed the Arthurian romance in *Parzival*. These three—Hartmann, Gottfried, and Wolfram—represent the first rank of Ger. narrative poets.

Their number must be joined by the anonymous author of the *Nibelungenlied* (ca. 1200). Anonymity was probably required because the work was perceived, like *König Rother* and *Herzog Ernst*, to belong to oral lit.—which, as regards its sources, it did. The Ger. written record holds nothing that anticipates the scale of the work's spectacle of honor, loyalty, treachery, and revenge. In its own time it is matched or exceeded in scope and complexity only by Wolfram's *Parzival*. The *Nibelungenlied* preserves intact the archaic value system and countless motifs from Germanic antiquity. It is, nonetheless, a work of the years around 1200, adorned with a veneer of courtliness, barely acknowledging the fabulous backgrounds of Sigfried and Brunihilde and erasing all traces of the pagan pantheon. The Church does not, however, displace the old mythology. It is a secular universe that perishes in the concluding bloodbath in the great hall of the Huns.

As the 13th c. proceeded, social change was gradually reshaping the set of common presuppositions upon which courtly culture depended. A merchant could be a hero and could instruct an emperor in piety, as in Rudolf von Ems' *Der gute Gerhart* (Good Gerhart, ca. 1225). Although Gottfried was probably of urban middle-class origin, it becomes routine for the citizen to write *belles lettres* only from the time of Konrad von Würzburg (ca. 1225–87) onward. The period immediately following the flowering is characterized by the continuing dominance of courtly conventions both formal and substantive, but with a variety of transformations and the invention or resurgence of competing forms and subjects.

In one line of devel., the courtly narrative evolved toward vast, encyclopedic poems (Heinrich von dem Türlein's Arthurian *Die Krone* [The Crown], ca. 1230, 30,000 lines; Albrecht von Scharpfenberg's *Jüngerer Titurel*, after Wolfram, ca. 1270, over 6000 six-line stanzas; Ulrich von Eschenbach's *Alexandreis*, ca. 1287, some 30,000 lines; Konrad von Würzburg's *Trojanerkrieg*, broken off by his death in 1287 at over 40,000 lines). This devel., however, seems balanced by the introduction of written short narratives in verse by such poets as Der Stricker (probably of middle-class origins, ca. 1210–50) and Wernher der Gartenaere (fl. 1246–82) with his story of social decay, *Meier Helmbrecht* (Farmer Helmbrecht).

The lyric, with its elaborate courtly decorum, was susceptible to transformations, particularly but not exclusively parody, even during the lifetime of the greatest masters. Thus Walther von der Vogelweide competed with the satirist Neidhart von Reuenthal (ca. 1190–1246), who employed peasant life as a foil to courtly conventions. As a reward, Neidhart himself was made the victim of peasant revenge throughout the vigorous subsequent trad. of farce. The vocabulary of courtly love is summoned to higher purpose in the mystical writings of Mechthild von Magdeburg (1212–80) and lives on in a poetic trad. of mysticism that extends well into the 15th c. Courtly conventions undergo further transformation in the 13th c. as Ulrich von Liechtenstein (ca. 1200–75) and Der Tannhäuser (fl. 1228–60) contort "Minnedienst" (love service), the ordeals undergone for the unattainable object of love, into the grotesque. Heinrich von Meissen, called Frauenlob (The Singer of the Lady's Praises, fl. 1275–1318) both summarizes and repudiates the trad. with a learned and highly rhetorical style, which the subsequent urban middle-class "Meistersänger" would find congenial.

The rise of the bourgeoisie in the 13th c. brought with it a certain fondness for didactic poetry treating all manner of moral and practical problems. Freidank's collection of proverbs, *Bescheidenheit,* (Wisdom, ca. 1230) and Hugo von Trimberg's *Der Renner* (ca. 1290–1300) stand out for their great popularity in the late Middle Ages, that of the latter extending well into the 18th c. This predilection also favored the continued devel. of short forms (the *Märe,* "story, tale"), easily moralized, anticipating and evolving alongside the short prose forms which come to prominence in the 15th and 16th cs. under It. and Fr. influence.

The last decades of the 13th c. also witness a revival of religious poetry. The pious returned to familiar biblical, moral, and allegorical materials, self-consciously looking back to MHG poetry of the 11th c.

In the 14th c., the great anthologies which preserve the courtly heritage are compiled in handsome mss., of which the most famous is the so-called Manesse ms. (before 1330). Compilatory works honor the memory of the Charlemagne materials (*Karlmeinet* [Little Charlemagne], ca. 1320). A pair of Strassburg citizens decided to fill in the perceived gaps in Wolfram's *Parzival* with 36,000 additional lines (1331–36). Competing genres in the middle of the 14th c. incl. vernacular liturgical poetry, "Geisslerlieder" (flagellant songs) associated with the plague years (1348–49), political poetry (Otto Baldemann and Lupold Hornburg), imperial panegyric in the court of Charles IV (Heinrich von Mügeln), and the beginnings of the minor genre of "Wappendichtung" (heraldic poetry: Peter Suchenwirt, fl. 1353–95). In the lyrics of Hugo von Montfort (1357–1423) at the end of the century, the fundamentally extramarital conventions of courtly poetry are thoroughly domesticated and applied strictly to the beloved spouse.

At the point of the apparent exhaustion of the courtly conventions, a poet and composer, Oswald von Wolkenstein (1377–1445), comes on the scene, exploring the breadth of the traditional courtly lyric, from lofty unrequited love to its bawdiest counterparts. The poet is alert to the renovations of the conventions from Italian sources, esp. Petrarch, whom he mentions by name. Oswald's obtrusive presence in many of his songs points toward a sense of self and of self-as-poet not at all in conformity with the self-effacing conventions of courtly poetry. He is the first Ger. poet (or composer) of whom a contemporary portrait survives.

Both Hugo and Oswald were of knightly class, whose dominance over the written lang. was coming to an end. An indication of the rise of popular forms is the satirical epic, set at a peasant wedding, known as *Wittenweilers Ring* (completed 1410). Sebastian Brant's widely translated *Narrenschiff* (Ship of Fools, 1494) provides evidence of how firmly entrenched the popular satirical trad. had become by the end of the 15th c.

After Oswald it is no longer possible to speak of continuity in the courtly trads. of the high Middle Ages. Attention to those trads. in the 15th c. may be characterized in the extremes as either antiquarian (Jakob Püterich von Reichertshausen, 1400–69) or revivalist (Ulrich Füetrer's *Buch der Abenteuer* [Book of Adventures], 1473–78). In between there are the countless knightly adventure stories coming into Ger. verse from Lat., Fr., and Dutch, and speaking directly to popular tastes. One translator thought enough of himself and his craft to compose a rhymed autobiography (Johann Grumelkut von Soest, 1448–1506). Among many important noble patrons of the revival, the most important is Emperor Maximilian I (1459–1519), without whose commission of the *Ambraser Heldenbuch* (the Ambras Book of Heroes) several of Hartmann von Aue's works and the *Gudrun,* a younger sister of the *Nibelungenlied,* would have been lost. The Emperor himself composed allegorical autobiographical epics (*Theuerdank* and *Weisskunig*) in a nostalgic spirit of appreciation for lost courtly trads. (or had his scribe do so in his behalf).

No fewer than five ms. anthologies of lyric poetry survive from the 15th c. In the 16th c., the number increases tenfold, with a similar number of printed books of songs for various occasions. This excludes hymnals. The lyric was an exceedingly popular form, serving all social classes and a wide array of occasions, public and private, secular and religious. The poems are largely anonymous, which led them later to be considered "folk songs," a misleading designation since many were composed for court and some evidence great sophistication. Like much of Ger. p., a few of these lyrics live on in modern times because of their link to music (e.g. "Innspruck ich muss dich lassen," set to music by Heinrich Isaak [d. 1519]).

The lyric texts of the finest Ger. poet of the 16th c., Martin Luther (1483–1546), live on in part for similar reasons, although this activity of Luther's is overshadowed by the reformer's other accomplishments. Luther addressed the Med. Lat. lyric (Notker's "Media vita in morte sumus," for "Mitten wir im Leben sind"), the courtly vernacular ("Sie ist mir lieb, die werde Magd"), the historical folksong, late med. hymnology, and the Psalms. Luther generally employed the popular four-stressed line in rhymed couplets, but also experimented with imitations of classical meters (iambic pentameters in the Ger. Sanctus, "Iesaia dem Propheten es geschah," from the Ger. mass of 1525). His early supporter, Ulrich von Hutten (1488–1523), wrote anti-papal satires, chiefly in Lat. but also in Ger. verse, and one *apologia*, "Ich hab's gewagt" (freely translating Caesar's "alia jacta est"), which was once considered the best poem in Ger. between Walther von der Vogelweide and Klopstock.

The most prolific verse writer in the period is Hans Sachs (1494–1576), who is at his best in praise of Luther ("Der Wittenbergsche Nachtigal"). Sachs, the most famous Ger. Meistersinger, may stand for Ger. vernacular lit. of the 16th c. in general: formally simple, moralizing, jocular, anecdotal—in short, popular. With the possible exceptions of satire (Sebastian Brant, Ulrich von Hutten, but also Thomas Murner's *Schelmenzunft* [Guild of Scoundrels], and *Narrenbeschwörung* [Conspiracy of Fools], 1512) and of the church hymn (Catholic, Lutheran, and Calvinist), *belles lettres* were almost exclusively in the hands of Humanists writing Lat. Conrad Celtis (1459–1508), who uncovered the works of Hrotswitha and the *Ligurinus*, wrote elegies, odes, and epigrams in imitation of the ancients. He is followed by poets of European reputation—Petrus Lotichius Secundus (1528–60), Paulus Melissus Schede (1539–1602), and Nathan Chytraeus (1543–98)—who constructed of elegies and epigrams a panegyric to Elizabeth I of England.

Toward the end of the 16th c., some signs both in criticism (e.g. Johannes Engerdus, *Prosodie*, 1583) and practice (Hans Leo Hassler, *Neue teutsche Gesang* [New Ger. Songs], 1596) point to dissatisfaction with the popular modes of expression in the Ger. vernacular. But it is not until the founding of the *Fruchtbringende Gesellschaft* (1617) in Weimar, the first of many literary societies, and the work of Martin Opitz (1597–1639), above all his *Von der deutschen Poeterei* (Concerning Ger. Prosody, 1624), that a genuine and permanent revolution overtakes Ger. p. Lat., It., Fr., and Dutch models are held up for imitation. With this devel., Lat. culture appears to triumph over "folk" trads. as the vernacular is molded to its standards, while in fact, Lat. begins to wane as the primary vehicle for lyric expression. The Ger. vernacular joins the international European style of the 17th c. known as "baroque", with its public posture and its highly rhetorical, reflective, and formalistic conventions. Perhaps precisely because of the rigidity of the forms, a remarkable amount of experimentation is undertaken, pressing the lang. for every kind of effect. The results occasionally appear bombastic or contrived to modern tastes, but many talented poets (e.g. Paul Fleming, 1609–40; Andreas Gryphius, 1616–64; Philipp von Zezen, 1619–89) employed the conventions with success. The epigram, among the strictest of the forms, had one master, Friedrich von Logau (1604–55), who continued to be quoted in many langs. into recent times.

Both the conventions and the spirit of experimentation accorded well with the requirements of the poets of mysticism (e.g. Angelus Silesius, 1624–77; Katharina von Greiffenberg, 1633–94), who on occasion (e.g. Quirinus Kuhlmann, 1651–89), so pushed lang. to the limits of expression that they seem to anticipate the experiments of the 19th and 20th cs. The new genre of the oratorio evolved out of similar experimentation (Johann Klaj, 1616–56), later carrying the Ger. hymnology of this period (e.g. Johannes Rist, 1607–67; Paul Gerhardt, 1607–76) into the churches and concert halls of the world.

The conventions of baroque poetics collapsed quite suddenly at the turn of the 18th c. The collapse was signalled by the pub. of a multi-volume retrospective anthol. (1695–1704) named by the editor, Benjamin Neukirch, for the poet Hoffmannswaldau (1617–79). The last poet to work wholly within the conventions was Johann Christian Günther (1695–1723), but his brief, brilliant, troubled career also points forward to the poetry of personal sentiment associated with the young Goethe. But the artifice and extravagance of baroque poetry offended Enlightenment theorists in Germany, both anglophile (Bodmer, 1698–1783, and Breitinger, 1701–76, who argued for "nature" and sentiment) and francophile (Gottsched, 1700–66, who argued for reason).

The rhetorical excesses, the grand theatrical panoply, and the thoroughly public posture of baroque poetry were quickly shaken off. The perspectives on nature provided by the mystical poets in particular and by the whole genre of the pastoral could not be so readily abandoned. The early "nature poetry" of the 18th c. (Brockes, *Irdisches Vergnügen in Gott* [Earthly Pleasure in God], 1721–1748; and Haller's *Alpen* [The Alps], 1729) follows in paths opened by the baroque. The same applies to the further exploration of nature, of friendship, and of wine, women, and song among the young poets who considered themselves successors of Anacreon (Hagedorn, 1708–54; Gleim, 1719–1803; Uz, 1720–96; Götz, 1721–81). They differ from their baroque predecessors by narrowing and sharpening the focus to the familiar, personal, and private. They are now perceived as immediate forerunners of the great flowering of Ger. p. that begins with the publication of the first three cantos of Klopstock's *Messias* (1748), written in Latinate hexameters but proving the Ger. vernacular tractable to any poetic task.

ANTHOLOGIES: *Deutsche Gedichte des elften und zwölfften Jahrhunderts*, ed. J. Diemer (1849); *Deutsche Dichtung des Barock*, ed. E. Hederer (1961); *Deutsche Lyrik des Mittelalters*, ed. M. Wehrli (1962); *Des Minnesangs Frühling*, ed. C. Kraus (1964); *Mittelalter*, ed. H. De Boor (1965); *Das Zeitalter des Barock*, ed. A. Schöne (1968); *Althochdeutsche Literatur*, ed. H. Schlosser (1970); *Spätmittelater, Hu-*

manismus, Reformation, ed. H. Heger (1975–78); *Die Mittelhochdeutsche Minnelyrik*, ed. H. Schweikle (1977); *All mein Gedanken, die ich hab: Deutsche Lieder des 15. und 16. Jhs.*, ed. I. Spriewald (1982).

SURVEYS AND CRITICISM, *General*: Manitius; *Reallexikon I*; G. Ehrismann, *Gesch. der deutschen Literatur bis zum Ausgang des Mittelalters* (1955–59); *Reallexikon*; K. Conrady, *Lateinische Dichtungstrad. und deutsche Lyrik des 17. Jahrhunderts* (1962); M. Walshe, *Med. Ger. Lit.* (1962); W. T. H. Jackson, "Med. Ger. Lit.," in Fisher; *Gesch. der deutschen Literatur*, ed. H. De Boor and R. Newald (1966–87); P. Salmon, *Lit. in Med. Germany* (1967); G. F. Jones, *Walther von der Vogelweide* (1968); A. DeCapua, *Ger. Baroque P.* (1973); K. Dell'Orto, "Lyric P. of the Ger. Ren.," Diss., Johns Hopkins U. (1973); H. Segel, *The Baroque Poem* (1974); J. Bostock, *A Handbook on OHG Lit.*, 2d ed. (1976); *Ren. and Reformation in Germany* (1977), *Ger. Baroque Lit.* (1983), both ed. G. Hoffmeister; W. Segebrecht, *Das Gelegenheitsgedicht* (1977); *Bibliographisches Handbuch der Barockliteratur*, ed. G. Dünnhaupt (1980); Sayce; W. Hinderer, *Gesch. der deutschen Lyrik* (1983); F. Spechtler, *Lyrik des ausgehenden 14. und 15. Jahrhunderts* (1984).

Special: K. Burdach, *Reinmar der Alte und Walther von der Vogelweide* (1928); M. Batts, *Gottfried von Strassburg* (1971); H. Bekker, *The* Nibelungenlied (1971), *Gottfried von Strassburg's* Tristan (1987); W. T. H. Jackson, *The Anatomy of Love: The* Tristan *of Gottfried von Strassburg* (1971); S. Jaeger, *Med. Humanism in Gottfried von Strassburg's* Tristan und Isolde (1977); H. Kuhn, *Minnelieder Walthers von der Vogelweide* (1982); J. Schultz, *The Shape of the Round Table: MHG Arthurian Romance* (1983); J. Goheen, *Mittelalterliche Liebeslyrik von Neidhart von Reuental bis zu Oswald von Wolkenstein* (1984); C. Jaeger, *The Origins of Courtliness* (1985); E. Haymes, *The* Nibelungenlied: *Hist. and Interp.* (1986); T. Anderson, *A Preface to the* Nibelungenlied (1987); A. Renoir, *A Key to Old Poems* (1988). F.L.B.

II. SINCE 1750. As in the 17th c., the unity of the modern Ger. literary trad. was in part consciously produced, an attempt to transcend the disunity and provincialism of mid 18th-c. Ger.-speaking societies. Friedrich Gottlieb Klopstock (1724–1803), with his rhapsodic monologues magisterially defining their own freedom, spoke for a literary culture waiting to be reborn. Until about 1750 there was no acknowledged genre of "the lyric," merely the subcategories (sonnet, song, ode, etc.) listed by Gottsched in his neoclassical *Critische Dichtkunst* (Critical Poetics, 1730). It was not until about 1850 that the lyric acquired, in a Ger. context, the dignity previously accorded to epic and drama.

Klopstock's innovations are not conceptual: his focus on Nature and God is traditional. But in his major poems, such as *Der Zürcher See* (Zurich Lake, 1750) and *Die Frühlingsfeier* (Celebration of Spring, 1764), he animates existing conventions in such a way as to transform them utterly. Thus, although Gleim had experimented inventively with imitations of classical meters, Klopstock deploys these meters seemingly effortlessly, as if they were native to the Ger. lang. And although the idea of "the sublime", derived from Longinus, was being widely promoted as preferable to didactic or descriptive nature-poetry, it is Klopstock who actually communicates sublimity through his verbal landscapes. Equally established was the ideal of friendship, of poetry affecting society through the elevating influence of the educated few. But Klopstock includes his friends expressly in the sublimity of Nature ; and his most devoted disciples, the *Göttinger Hain* which flourished in the early 1770s (Ludwig Hölty [1748–76] was the most accomplished of the group), filled poetic friendship with a new "sensibility" (*Empfindsamkeit*). Yet even as he invokes the lang. of friendship, Klopstock speaks as an inspired, necessarily isolated "bard," producing poetic truth through sheer intensity of experience. The "experience" is not subjective in any arbitrary sense; Klopstock presents himself not as a private individual but as an appointed singer, a cosmic representative of humanity.

The attribution of elevated meaning to every detail of Klopstock's world can make his intensity seem paradoxically abstract, even didactic. But the renewal of Nature was already receiving a new impetus from the theorist Johann Gottfried Herder (1744–1803), who, inspired by Bishop Percy's *Reliques of Ancient Eng. Poetry* (1765), developed a conception of the "lyrical" rooted in a new understanding of hist. Songs are, for Herder, direct expressions of a people's core experience; originally sung by bards, they survive in fragmentary form as folksongs. The definition of the folksong at this time was broad, however: Percy includes extracts from Shakespeare and other "named" poets. Herder's initiative crystallizes the key ideas of "lyric" and "nation," but with entirely different connotations from those familiar today. The nation is in no way self-contained: access to its past often involves other nations, e.g. the England, Wales, and Scotland of Herder's time. And the lyrical impulse is viewed as collective rather than private.

The quest for bardic voices was intense; the most influential of these "folk"-texts, Macpherson's *Ossian*, was revealed much later to be a forgery. But at this historical moment, the 1770s, the central project was the *creation* of a Ger. culture, not precise documentation of its past, and a genuine modern bard was ready to hand, Herder's close friend Johann Wolfgang von Goethe (1749–1832). So powerful was Goethe's personality that it is essential to recall the cultural elements blended into his poetics of nature and expressivity. The bardic voice speaks from the heart of things, but the idea of the sublime, elevating experience, as embodied in Klopstock's poetry, is vital to his speaking; so are the image of the aesthetic community and the matrix of complex metrical possibilities, deriving from Gr. and baroque models as well as from the newly prestigious folksong. What Goethe contributes to all this are two qualities decisive for all subsequent Ger. p. First, he takes the word "nature" literally: without in any way relinquishing the (inherited) sublime, Goethe pursues a lifelong quest for the organic, methodically articulating its rhythmic structures and locating the analogies to these structures in human lang. and experience. Second, he installs his own unique subjectivity at the center of his lyrical production; without abandoning the claim to representative experience (his theory of the organic sustains the claim), Goethe binds poetry to the intimate mood-shifts, the seemingly arbitrary perceptions of the private self. Goethe's poems in the 1770s range from the utter transformation of Anacreontic convention in *Mailied* (May Song) to the almost ruthless proclamation of personal autonomy in *Willkommen und Abschied* (Welcome and Farewell) and the bardic rhapsodies in emulation of Klopstock: *Ganymed, Prometheus, Wanderers Sturmlied.*

Goethe also wrote ballads in these years, the most famous of which are *Der König von Thule* (The King of Thule, 1774; sung by Gretchen in the earliest version of *Faust*) and *Erlkönig* (1782; widely known through musical settings by Schubert and Loewe). Ballads are a popular poetic form, found in the oldest Ger. lit. Herder's theory of the folksong thus provoked a flurry of ballad-writing by Goethe's young contemporaries in the so-called *Sturm und Drang* movement. The best known of these is *Lenore* (1773), a ghostly *Schauerballade* by Gottfried August Bürger (1747–94) compressing love, marriage, and death into a wild midnight ride. The blurring of the boundaries between "lyrical" expressivity and "epic" narration typifies Ger. p. at this time (the same applies to drama: Goethe's celebration of defiant genius, *Prometheus,* was originally spoken by the character Prometheus in a dramatic sketch). The lyric was to open new expressive possibilities for a lit. defining itself through images of its past.

Goethe wrote a series of ballads, notably *Die Braut von Korinth* (The Bride of Corinth), *Der Gott und die Bayadere,* and *Der Zauberlehrling* (The Sorcerer's Apprentice), in 1797 at the height of his friendship with Friedrich Schiller (1759–1805), but by then his goals had changed. In elaborately self-contained stanzas, these ballads shaped rather extreme, even perverse narratives into demonstration models of organic equilibrium. The famous "moderation" (*Mässigung*) of Goethe's genius is sometimes dated to the year 1786, when he suddenly left Weimar for Italy, later recording his discovery of "Classical" order in the *Römische Elegien* (Roman Elegies, 1788); in these 20 poems he blends a love experience into the myths, the architecture, the whole remembered imagery of Rome, playfully yet strictly deploying alternating hexameters and pentameters, the form of the Cl. elegiac distich. Returning to Weimar, Goethe began to develop a new, politically and socially stabilized fusion of the Cl. heritage with a scientific understanding of nature. Every variety of poetry was to be cultivated, incl. the epic: Goethe's *Hermann und Dorothea* (1797), an adaptation of "Germanic" values to a contemp. story of the Fr. Revolution and the resultant "refugee problem," became the model for numerous (unsuccessful) 19th-c. efforts to reinvent the Ger. verse epic.

To describe Weimar Classicism in terms of Goethe's personal devel. is both unavoidable (because of the way Goethe's personality imposed itself on Ger. lit. hist.) and misleading. Schiller was an equal partner in the collaboration until his death in 1805, and Schiller provided the central idea of this new "Classicism": *aesthetic education.* In this phrase are concentrated all the elements working productively through Klopstock and Goethe: the elevation of the individual through a fuller understanding of nature's laws as well as its "sublime" moment of grandeur, and the integration of individuals into a society governed by "beauty," i.e. the harmonious ethical functioning of the mental faculties. Schiller includes the idea of free play (*Spieltrieb*) in his vision, but it remains grave and serene nonetheless. The program is allegorized in his elegy *Der Spaziergang* (The Walk, 1795), in which self and landscape are fused at all experiential levels. Central to Schiller's experience is his contemplation of the loss of Gr. antiquity, an image of wholeness for which modernity is compelled to yearn in vain (*Die Götter Griechenlands* [The Gods of Greece], 1788). Aesthetic education can mitigate the loss, but within Weimar Classicism there remains a central contradiction, theorized by Schiller himself in 1794, between Goethe's "organic" absorption of history into his own life ("naive") and Schiller's own sense of exile ("sentimental."

A far more radical version of exile is propounded by Friedrich Hölderlin (1770–1843), a disciple of Schiller whose later path took him into such isolation that his work is neither readily describable in historical terms nor, indeed, as yet exhausted in its impact on later lit. From the repertoire of poetic possibilities, Hölderlin fashioned a vision of his role as singer-bard for an irrevocably lost world (Greece). He works from the beginning with complex Gr. meters (e.g. the Alcaic), contrasting subjective isolation with visions of natural and social fullness (e.g. *Abendphantasie* [Evening Fantasy], 1799), which speak always of the absence of the gods. The contentment of "the people" depends on their not knowing of this absence; only the singer knows, and his knowledge crowds out everything else, incl. all "moderating" hopes of aesthetic education. Hölderlin first published hymns and elegies in 1793; he is the very opposite of a hermit, being radically exposed to the immediacy of history, particularly the miseries of the wars following the Fr. Revolution. He also pursues the image of a Ger. nation, which however remains an ideal construct. In *Brod und Wein* (Bread and Wine), Hölderlin "travels" to ancient Greece in order to recapitulate the actual process of the withdrawal of the gods, of whom Jesus Christ is viewed as the last representative. Later hymns (e.g. *Patmos, Friedensfeier,* and *Germanien*) and fragments, written between 1800 and his insanity in 1806, strive to imagine a possible return of the gods.

A complexity of Ger. lit. hist. is that the decade of Weimar Classicism (1795–1805) coincides precisely with the most productive era of romanticism. Indeed Goethe was long called a "romantic" because of his paramount subjectivity. In fact there are linkages of all kinds: Goethe's study of natural phenomena, Schiller's and Hölderlin's sense of the gods as withdrawn from history—these notions are crucial to Friedrich von Hardenberg (1772–1801), who, under the pseudonym Novalis, became a major poet and theorist of romanticism. But the romantic program opposes both moderation and a Greek-centered view of culture. Novalis' *Hymnen an die Nacht* (1800) explicitly turn away from Greece towards the "Night," the mystique of death pervading medieval Christianity. The fascination with Ger. medieval culture leads to an intensive and now genuinely philological study of the Ger. past. This work culminated in the collection of folk poetry *Des Knaben Wunderhorn* (The Youth's Magic Horn, 1805–8), ed. by Achim von Arnim (1781–1831) and Clemens Brentano (1778–1842). Philological exactitude and philosophical sophistication combine to produce in the major romantic theorists, Novalis and Friedrich Schlegel (1772–1829), a very high level of linguistic self-consciousness, both serious and playful, now known as "romantic irony." From this perspective the ideal modern poetic form was the fragment, a moment of history captured and sealed in and through irony. But apart from certain texts by Novalis, Brentano, and Ludwig Tieck (1773–1853), few romantic lyrics fulfilled this imperative in practice. Brentano's most successful texts (*Sprich aus der Ferne* [Speak from Afar] and *Schwanenlied* [Swansong]) do, however, achieve an extraordinary fusion of ecstatic subjectivity with "nature" as a symbolic totality of historical time. The writer who best embodies romantic poetics is from a slightly later generation, Joseph von Eichendorff (1788–1857). Eichendorff conveys both the intensity of a moment and an ironic distance from that intensity; his lang. is consciously stylized, with its medieval landscapes, its dawns and sunsets. Sudden discontinuities, from harmony to doubt, from darkness to light and vice versa, are Eichendorff's speciality; the reader experiences simultaneously a glimpse of fullness and a sense of exile within a specifically Ger. historical landscape. *Mondnacht* (Moonlit Night), *Zwielicht* (Twilight), *Sehnsucht* (Longing): the very titles of Eichendorff's most perfect poems convey a moment of danger for the self rendered vulnerable through its openness to history and beauty. Sometimes safety is reached (*Mondnacht*); sometimes the self is sustained on the margin through intense listening to or gazing at the aesthetic heart of things.

As in Herder's thinking, romantic "nationalism" opens up the world rather than closing it off. It is the older Goethe who coins the term "world lit."; indeed, Goethe's own later poetry draws extensively on Eastern models (*West-Östlicher Divan,* 1816, a homage to the Persian poet Hafiz; *Chinesisch-deutsche Jahres- und Tageszeiten* [Chinese-Ger. Seasons of the Years and the Day], 1830). In these creative explorations Goethe joins the new romantic philology, characterized by August Wilhelm Schlegel's (1767–1845) trs. of Shakespeare (1797–1810) and his brother Friedrich's investigations of Indian thought. This multiplying of poetic possibilities persists throughout the *Biedermeier* period (1815–48), but gradually a profound intellectual division becomes evident, controlling subsequent poetic devel. It is the dualism between private and public, between the increasingly subjective dream of Nature and the immediacy of technological, political, and social change.

The major *Biedermeier* poets, Eduard Mörike (1804–75) and Annette von Droste-Hülshoff (1797–1848), do indeed struggle to renew the Goethean synthesis of self and nature, but their perceptions are defined by romantic fascination with death as well as by the micro-worlds of the organic. Both explore natural environments with an intimacy often termed "realistic"; but lacking Goethe's "scientific" premises, each develops new versions of what constitutes nature. Mörike binds his shifting moods and meditations into such rigorously closed forms that the poem's actual shape, its verbal dimension, moves from being a secondary to a primary concern. The image of the poem as quasi-organic "object," as claiming physical presence, is implicit in Mörike's *Auf eine Lampe* (On a Lamp, 1846). Droste-Hülshoff risks extreme visions of dying and the collapse of time (*Im Moose* [In the Moss], 1842), and she survives them through an overt ritualizing of the seasons as defining the human year in counterpoint with religion. That such subjectivity was endangered in this period by its own freedom, a freedom without the cultural urgency of the 18th c., becomes obvious in the lesser poets such as August von Platen (1796–1835), who renews the sonnet trad. and codifies Eastern verseforms such as the *ghazal* into a protective aestheticism; Nikolaus Lenau (1802–50), who strives to merge his consciousness with the moments and seasons of nature; and Friedrich Rückert (1788–1866), who pursues the Orientalist trend and whose gloomy *Kindertotenlieder* (Songs on the Death of Children) are so emotionally exposed and fragile that they virtually demand the support of the musical setting they eventually receive from Gustav Mahler in 1904.

The cleavage between private and public worlds is wholly visible in the work of Heinrich Heine (1797–1856); indeed, his productivity seems to depend on it. On the one hand, his mastery of inherited romantic imagery enabled him to produce the most widely read volume of "romantic" texts, the *Buch der Lieder* (Book of Songs, 1827), though most of these poems either exaggerate the "sickness" of romantically stylized love or undercut elevated sentiments with an ironic final twist. On the other hand, Heine's sensitivity to the meaning of capitalism's new technologies (rail-travel, stock exchange) was second to none. In voluntary exile in Paris from 1831 until his death, Heine wrote vivid and sarcastic journalism and some famous political poems (*Atta Troll, Die schlesischen Weber*, 1844). Yet he always declared himself a lover of beauty, mocking the compromises and earnestness apparently endemic to political commitment. Heine's double-edged style seems in retrospect to epitomize the age from which he felt so alien. Early poems from *Lyrisches Intermezzo* (1822–23) were set to music by Robert Schumann in *Dichterliebe* (A Poet's Love, 1840); arguably Schumann misses the irony, yet his delicate near-sentimentality expresses the Heine his age chose to hear. *Die Nordsee* (The North Sea, 1825–26) contains Heine's most ambitious long poems, rhapsodic invocations of seascapes and vanishing myths in which the persistent irony is both emphasized and transcended by the sheer range of historical imagination. Heine's late poems, from the "mattress-grave" of his long final illness, achieve new intensities of pain, lucidity, and self-mockery: *Morphine* (ca. 1851), *Für die Mouche* (a long dream of death amid the confusions of Western mythology, addressed to his loyal mistress, 1856).

Political poetry began to be written before 1815, at the time of the struggle against Napoleon; Ernst Moritz Arndt (1769–1860) and Ludwig Uhland (1787–1862) adapted ballad forms to the patriotic cause. As "the nation" hardened into a reactionary and repressive institution, however, political poetry took on a new oppositional sharpness with the rise of the movement *Junges Deutschland* (Young Germany) in the early 1830s. Apart from Heine, the best known poets were Anastasias Grün (1806–76), Hoffmann von Fallersleben (1798–1874), Ferdinand Freiligrath (1810–76), and Georg Herwegh (1817–75). In the period before the Revolution of 1848 known as *Vormärz* (roughly 1840 to March 1848), their voices were briefly dominant.

Two poets who were to become major writers after 1848, Friedrich Hebbel (1813–63) and Gottfried Keller (1819–90), began to publish poetry before the Revolution. Hebbel, however, who felt strongly that a political poem was no poem at all, was influential in developing a theory of the "pure" lyric after 1848. There is a sad irony in the fact that the Ger. lyric, nurtured by multiple social aspirations, should have been codified and defined at this moment of political defeat. For, esp. after 1870 with the rapid expansion of the Ger. educational system, the lyric becomes fixed in the public mind, and in the textbooks, as something refined, private, devoted to the self's interactions with nature. Because of the fluidity of the trad. to this point, it was not difficult to read this definition back into the past, venerating Goethe while stylizing his poems as, in his own phrase so vulnerable to misreading, "fragments of a great confession."

Although provincialism dominates Ger. p. between 1850 and 1890 (typified by the popular success of Emanuel Geibel [1815–84]), important poems were written, particularly by three writers better known for their fiction: Keller, Theodor Storm (1817–88), and Conrad Ferdinand Meyer (1825–98). The contradictions of the *Biedermeier* period are intensified in their work. On the one hand, the sense of experience as intimate and fragile remains primary; on the other hand, the social impotence and passivity of the private self is felt inescapably. Meyer, a master lyricist, doubted the authenticity of his own texts, revising them ceaselessly and devoting much energy to the less exposed genre of the ballad. The implicit poetics of this endangered self is a complex fusion of "pure" temporal experience with a "pure" verbal construct. The poem is to be a "thing," an object made out of time and inserted into space. The text is justified not by any moral or personal interp. of experience but by its sheer being as a text: "In poetry every thought must move as visible form" (Meyer). Storm's intro. to his 1870 anthol. of Ger. p. expresses the new institutionalization of the lyrical experience. Readers are to be stirred not to thought or action but to a more intensive registration of their own moods. Schiller's aesthetic education of mankind has become the aesthetic self-enjoyment of the educated.

If refinement, chiseled perfection, is the poetic project of the late 19th c., it becomes a reality in the work of two writers, Hugo von Hofmannsthal (1874–1929) and Stefan George (1868–1933). Hofmannsthal's few poems are such exquisite expressions of the passive self, paralyzed by the sheer weight of time past, that they seem to anticipate their own attenuation into silence. Hofmannsthal ceased writing poems in 1902 (turning to the "public" modes of drama and opera libretti for Richard Strauss) after performing a self-diagnosis in his "Letter of Lord Chandos," written in the persona of a 17th-c. Eng. nobleman. Chandos' so-called *Sprachkrise* (lang. crisis) consists in his inability to translate either inner feelings or impressions of objects and events into lang. Words have become strange and alien. In contrast, Stefan George crystallized a doctrine of pure poetry to sustain a productivity lasting from *Hymnen, Pilgerfahrten, Algabal* (Hymns, Pilgrimages, Algabal, 1890–92) through *Der Stern des Bundes* (Star of the Covenant, 1914) to a final vision of the aesthetic "nation," *Das neue Reich* (The New Empire, 1928). The Nazi attempt to co-opt this refined concept led to George's refusal even to be buried in Ger. soil (he died in Switzerland). George's poetics was nourished by his reading of Friedrich Nietzsche (1844–1900). Nietzsche's few poems intensify late 19th-c. contradictions; suspicious of lang.'s metaphorical and masking structures, he yet sought to fill every lyrical word with intensity. Following Nietzsche, Stefan George turned to Fr. models, particularly Baudelaire, whose *Fleurs du mal* he translated into Ger., and the hermeticism of Mallarmé. George sought to develop a coded symbolic lang., with a specialized orthography and a repertoire of neopagan myths, incl. beautiful youths and autumnal parks. He also built up an aesthetic "community" of disciples, the "George Circle," in resistance to contemp. vulgarity. That vulgarity, the crude voice of the cities, was beginning to find some expression about 1890 in the "monumental" naturalist style of Arno Holz (1863–1929), the ballads and impressionistic precision of Detlev von Liliencron (1844–1909), and the "applied poetry" (*angewandte Lyrik*) and cabaret songs of Frank Wedekind (1864–1918).

The dominant ideal of the poetic object, already implicit in Mörike and ever more explicit in Meyer and George, is fulfilled in the *Neue Gedichte* (New Poems, 1907–8) of Rainer Maria Rilke (1875–1926). Rilke reaches the achievement of these poems by way of the three-part collection *Das Stundenbuch* (The Book of Hours, 1899, 1901, 1903) and *Das Buch der Bilder* (The Book of Images, 1902); these volumes recapitulate the religiosity, the rhapsodic celebration of creativity, and the dream of community which are stylistic gestures reaching back to Klopstock. In the New Poems, however, Rilke crystallizes a perfect fusion of the theory and practice of "objectivity." The theory is overtly derived from the visual arts, specifically the sculpture of Auguste Rodin (for whom Rilke worked briefly as secretary) and the painting of Paul Cézanne. Poems are to achieve the sheer "presence" of these visual texts. But this is done not through mimesis, through "imitation" of a physical object. Rather, the poem obeys its own laws as a temporal art: it records the momentary glimpse binding the poet's subjectivity to an object; and it embeds that moment both in the history of civilization which has accumulated in the poet's head and in the physical, even geometric connectedness of the object to its surroundings. Rilke calls this complex relationality *Bezug*; the objects chosen are primarily aesthetic (cathedrals, statues, graceful animals), but incl. the experience of the city of Paris (children, blind men, corpses) as well as an ethical urgency (the commandment to change one's life emitted by the archaic torso of Apollo). Rilke's aim, he said, was to translate the visible into the "invisibility" of lang. and, vice versa, to bring life's invisible richness and fragility into plain view.

This equilibrium could not be sustained. In 1911–12 Rilke entered a crisis of disjunction between lang. and the zones of subjectivity and world which its task was to mediate. The crisis was reminiscent of Hofmannsthal's, but Rilke was so totally a poet that he fought his way through it. After ten years of struggle and fragmentary achievement Rilke produced the astonishing abundance of Feb. 1922, the *Duineser Elegien* (Duino Elegies) and *Sonette an Orpheus* (Sonnets to Orpheus). In these texts the world of objects is blasted open and reconstituted in a poetological dimension unique to Rilke. The bardic vocation inherited from Klopstock and mediated through Rilke's reading of Hölderlin is reborn in the gestures of the "singer" who simultaneously celebrates the world of art and nature and explores the death-realm through symbolic figures like the hero, the "young dead," and the dismembered Orpheus. This song is fused with a continuous meditation on the inadequacy of lang. as well as its transforming power. Like Goethe in his day, Rilke has had an irresistible impact on poetry in this century because of his virtual invention of a lyrical lang. The disquieting aspect of his influence derives not so much from the specifics of his subjective mythology as from the rhapsodic "overcoming" of technological, urban, and political reality. The Goethean image of harmonious nature is renewed by Rilke in the domain of sheer linguistic virtuosity. Although it is meaningless to blame Rilke for the seductions of his counter-world, his achievement has invited escapist imitation and has reactivated the struggle between nature and the city which characterized Ger. poetics before 1848.

The assault on the image of the poem as naturalized object was launched in the year of Rilke's lang.-crisis, 1911–12, by the generation known as expressionist, whose feelings towards Rilke's genius and prestige ranged from hostile to ambivalent. The publication in early 1911 of *Weltende* (End of the World) by Jacob van Hoddis (1887–1942) was widely felt to be the moment of a new poetics. The text consists of two stanzas of isolated lines, linked surreally through the passive act of reading a newspaper: "The bourgeois' hat flies off his pointed head, / the air re-echoes with a screaming sound. . . . The greater part of people have a cold. / Off bridges everywhere the railroads drop." The return of the repressed city is consummated apocalyptically in a mode of fragmentation and decay. The power of the established lang. of nature and the pure poem is such that no single counter-style is imaginable. The "grotesque" gestures of van Hoddis and Alfred Lichtenstein (1889–1914) exist in counterpoint with the "concrete" lyrics of August Stramm (1874–1915), who forced multiple meanings into single words, often neologisms.

The styles of the major expressionist poets are linked solely by the tonality of apocalypse. Georg Trakl (1887–1914) corrodes the lang. of nature poetry from within, peopling his landscapes with corpses and the streets of his native Salzburg with spots of decay; gradually his lang. uproots itself from all mimetic relations, evoking strange syntheses of corruption and purity, violence and passivity. Georg Heym (1887–1912) confronts urban life with a fanatical directness; the energy of his diseased world derives wholly from the impending moment of its disintegration. Ernst Stadler (1883–1914), on the other hand, who began publishing in 1904, strives to convert technological energy (e.g. railway trains) into imagery of Utopian transformation. His long rhapsodic lines, inspired by Walt Whitman, project a poetics that would fuse subject and object into a single rhythm of socio-political change. His was the style that became dominant: related expressionist voices incl. Franz Werfel (1890–1945), Johannes Becher (1891–1958), and Yvan Goll (1891–1950). *O Mensch* expressionism, poetry that proclaimed a "new man" in a new world, rapidly became bombastic and empty; much of the famous expressionist anthol. *Menschheitsdämmerung* (Twilight/Dawn of Humanity, 1919) has become unreadable.

A poet associated with expressionism, Else Lasker-Schüler (1869–1945) had begun publishing in 1902; her texts, with their strange linkage between religiosity, intense privacy, and surreal fantasy, suggest the deep fissures in expressionist poetics, the impossibility of a unified program such as emerged in England and France. expressionism immediately produced its ironic mirror-image, dada, with an agenda of mockery and disruption formulated already in 1916. Some dada poets, with their delight in lang. games, their open display of the processes of text construction, have become more influential than the original expressionists, esp. Hugo Ball (1886–1927), Richard Huelsenbeck (1892–1974), George Grosz (1893–1959), Hans Arp (1887–1966), and Kurt Schwitters (1887–1948). The last three of these are better known as visual artists. Fusion of the arts was a project of this generation from the outset; the composer Arnold Schönberg (1874–1951), and the painter Wassily Kandinsky (1866–1944) were both involved in the redefinition of the lyric.

It is possible to define the years 1920–70 as a unified period, its continuities all the more apparent because of the rupture of the Nazi era, 1933–45, when all major poetic voices were forced into either exile or the silence of "inner emigration." What is not possible is to discern a single dominant poetics. Rather, one must distinguish three viable styles, with distinct aesthetic energies, which major authors frequently sought to combine. The first of these, the style of "international modernism," was the last to develop in Germany because of the political catastrophes. But after 1945 its potency was correspondingly great, as poets strove to reintegrate Ger. with European culture. And the poetological essays of Gottfried Benn (1886–1956) in the 1920s had already sketched its outlines: poetic lang. functions as a counterhistorical energy, shattering banal everyday reality (Benn's word is *Wirklichkeitszertrümmerung*) in order to reassemble the pure shards of lang., technological and mythical as well as emotional, into an "absolute" poem. Benn himself, a survivor of the expressionist generation (his first collection, *Morgue*, was published in 1912), briefly succumbed to the lure of Nazism before "emigrating inwardly"; with the publication of *Statische Gedichte* (Static Poems, 1948), he became a dominant figure in the postwar literary scene. His nihilistic view of everyday life represented an extreme against which others could define their perspectives. In his influential lecture *Probleme der Lyrik* (Problems of the Lyric, 1951), Benn codified his uncompromisingly aesthetic viewpoint: acknowledging his "unfriendliness" towards the world, he nevertheless insisted that poets wrest the "truth" from history by staying as close to it as the bullfighter does the bull.

Günter Eich's (1907–72) *Inventur* (Inventory, 1946), listing the minimal possessions of a prisoner-of-war, evokes a more urgent modernism. Poetry distills, strips down experience, but reconstitutes it as a warning or prophecy, sealed off yet far from neutral (*Botschaften des Regens* [Messages of the Rain], 1955). Paul Celan (1920–70) confronts the permanent, corrosive fact of the wartime death-camps not only in his *Todesfuge* (Death Fugue, 1945) but throughout his extremely hermetic later texts (his most powerful collection may be *Die Niemandsrose* [No One's Rose], 1963). Celan's modernism has a dialectical intention: the more obscure and seemingly exclusive their imagery, the more his texts seek to open a "dialogue" (his term) with history, a dialogue directed at the repression of the death-camps' meaning in postwar consumer society, at the truth that is slipping from us. Ingeborg Bachmann (1926–73) and Hans Magnus Enzensberger (b. 1929), in their poems of the 1950s, subvert the deluded harmonies of consumerism through sardonic and uneasy allegories. A frequent presence in Enzensberger's poems is radiation, the invisible destroyer which we prefer to ignore. Other major voices of this "critical" modernism are Nelly Sachs (1891–1970), whose work is strongly focused on the death-camps; Rudolf Hagelstange (b. 1912), whose sonnet-cycle *Venezianisches Credo* (Venetian Credo, 1946) confronts Nazi degeneracy through a militant formalism; Helmut Heissenbüttel (b. 1921), theorist and practitioner of a lang. liberated from conventional syntax and revealing "reality" to be a linguistic construct ("concrete poetry,"); and Karl Krolow (b. 1915).

Krolow also has strong ties to the second major style of 1920–70, which seeks to maintain and redirect the trad. of nature poetry. Nature is no longer viewed as model or refuge. But just as Eichendorff could translate romantic clichés into a usable, transparent code, so these poets believe that the realities of 20th-c. experience can be read off from nature, using a lang. of shading and indirection. Wilhelm Lehmann (1882–1968),

Oskar Loerke (1884–1941), and Elisabeth Langgässer (1899–1950) are important exponents of this style. Their deliberately conservative texts evoke landscapes with lang. that seems to "know" the other, banal, and degraded uses to which it is put. The posthumously published poems of Gertrud Kolmar (1894–1943), written largely in the 1930s, convey powerfully the ability of natural images to illuminate a denatured society. This trad. dominated East Ger. poetics, where coded writing was widely felt to be the only "free" kind. Peter Huchel (1903–81) and Johannes Bobrowski (1917–65) traverse wintry worlds that speak silently of war and despair. Sara Kirsch (b. 1935) and Bernd Jentzsch (b. 1940) are prominent younger East Ger. poets who work in this style.

The third possibility of the years 1920–70 remained the production of an overtly political poetry, which had not achieved full stature in either *Vormärz* or expressionism. Almost single-handedly, Bertolt Brecht (1898–1956) realized this project within the modernist idiom, enabling political poetry to become central to the theory and practice of today's Ger. lit. Working eclectically, Brecht drew particularly on the ballad trad., which had been maintained in the 19th c. by regional and "storytelling" poets such as Meyer, Liliencron, and Theodor Fontane (1819–98). Brecht also adapted the epigrammatic and didactic poetics of the baroque and of China to a laconic or proverbial mode of social commentary. Not that Brecht neglected subjectivity; his long poems *Vom armen B. B.* (Of Poor B. B., 1921) and *An die Nachgeborenen* (To Posterity, 1938) present intense yet stylized autobiographical narrations, as if to reanimate Klopstock's projection of the representative self. The people Brecht represents, however, are those who have no cultural voice: soldiers who actually fight the wars, workers who actually build the palaces, and the unemployed. The complexities of publication "in dark times" meant that Brecht's poems were slow to exercise their full impact. A collection published in the Weimar Republic, *Hauspostille* (Homilies for Home Use, 1927) was followed by many poems written in exile and only gradually reassembled in the early 1950s. Important disciples were Erich Fried (b. 1921), who has specialized in the style of epigrammatic political engagement, notably at the time of the Vietnam war (*und Vietnam und,* 1966); and Wolf Biermann (b. 1936), an exiled East German, who has extended Brecht's explorations of ballad form and sought to revive poetry's ancient function through public performances.

As the modernist concept of the self-sufficient poem came to seem less viable about 1970, the goal of a political poetry became both desirable and imaginable. This does not at all mean that poems were henceforth "about" politics. Rather, a double realization was involved: that all inherited poetic lang., as mediated by the various modern styles, was the lang. of an elite; and that, in an age when everything, certainly incl. poetry, was a commodity to be bought and discarded, the poet must find ways simultaneously to confront and to evade consumerism. In practice this involved a reopening of all the issues of poetics, a guerrilla-like refusal to stay in one place. Thus Walter Höllerer (b. 1922) argued in 1965 for the merits of "long poems" as being in principle unpretentious, open to banality as well as pleasure, and shunning the preciosity and incipient commodification of the sealed-off short poem; the poems of Peter Handke (b. 1942), e.g. *Leben ohne Poesie* (Life without Poetry, 1972), seem to enact this program. Against it the case was made for brevity, for the neo-Brechtian aggressive epigram. The label "new subjectivity" was applied to poets of the 1970s because of their absorption in the details of either momentary or habitual experience, experience potentially eluding consumerist expectations. But the phrase could be (and was) reversed into "new objectivity" because these poets never stopped with the self; they always strove to locate the experienced moment within the concealed structures of a society defined and still riven by no longer acknowledged prejudices, memories, and dreams.

A specific poetological innovation of the early 1970s was the adaptation, by Jürgen Becker (b. 1932) and Rolf Dieter Brinkmann (1940–75), of the technology of camera and tape recorder to the lang. of poetry: the moment is repeatable, reversible, can be "made strange" without any premature interp. or categorization. The struggle of poets to remain both inside and outside consumer society, resisting it without retreating from it, takes many forms. Ger. p. has again become social in both premises and aspirations, though hardly in Klopstock's sense; and many writers find the agenda challenging. A few whose achievement is already significant include Christoph Meckel (b. 1935), Günter Kunert (b. 1929), Nicolas Born (1937–79), Helga Novak (b. 1935), F. C. Delius (b. 1943), Ursula Krechel (b. 1947), Jürgen Theobaldy (b. 1944), and Karin Kiwus (b. 1942). As new blends of consumerism, democracy, and nationalism erase familiar political antimonies, incl. the coded lang. employed by East Ger. poets under communism, the social imagination assigns new tasks to the lyrical subject: the poetic self recalls the humane dream of the Ger. Enlightenment—but through the *via negativa* of imagery resisting all current "representative" experience, imagery of defeat, exclusion, withdrawal. In exploring these marginal zones poets seek to renew the Utopian impulse on which poetry ultimately depends.

ANTHOLOGIES IN GERMAN: *Menschheitsdämmerung,* ed. K. Pinthus (1919)—Expressionism; *De profundis,* ed. G. Groll (1946)—non-Nazi texts, 1933–45; *Ergriffenes Dasein: deutsche Lyrik 1900–1950,* ed. H. E. Holthusen and F. Kemp (1955); *Transit,* ed. W. Höllerer (1956); *Museum der modernen Poesie,* ed. H. M. Enzensberger (1960)—international modernism; *Lyrik des expressionistischen*

Jahrzehnts, ed. G. Benn (1962); *Deutschland, Deutschland: Politische Gedichte*, ed. H. Lamprecht (1969); *17 Mod. Ger. Poets*, ed. S. S. Prawer (1971); *Deutsche Gedichte von 1900 bis zur Gegenwart*, ed. F. Pratz (1971); *Lyrik-Katalog Bundesrepublik*, ed. J. Hans, U. Herms, and R. Thenior (1978); *Ansichten über Lyrik*, ed. W. Schubert and K. H. Höfer (1980)—poetological poems and prose since Opitz; *Lyrik für Leser: Deutsche Gedichte der siebziger Jahre*, ed. V. Hage (1981); *Deutsche Gedichte 1930–60*, ed. H. Bender (1983); *Ger. P. of the Romantic Era*, ed. O. Durrani (1986); *Ger. P.*, ed. M. Swales (1987).

ANTHOLOGIES WITH ENGLISH RENDERINGS: *20th-C. Ger. Verse*, tr. H. Salinger (1952); *Penguin Book of Ger. Verse*, ed. L. Forster (1957); *Anthol. of Ger. P. from Hölderlin to Rilke*, ed. A. Flores (1960); *The Ger. Lyric of the Baroque*, tr. G. Schoolfield (1961); *Mod. Ger. P. 1910–60*, tr. M. Hamburger and C. Middleton (1962); *20 Ger. Poets*, ed. W. Kaufmann (1962); *Anthol. of Ger. P. through the 19th C.*, ed. A. Gode and F. Ungar (1964); *East Ger. P.* (1972), *Ger. P. 1910–75* (1976)—both tr. M. Hamburger; *Ger. P. from 1750 to 1900*, ed. R. Browning (1984).

POETIC FORMS: K. Viëtor, *Gesch. der deutschen Ode* (1923); G. Müller, *Gesch. des deutschen Liedes* (1925); W. Kayser, *Gesch. der deutschen Ballade* (1936), *Kleine deutsche Versschule* (1946), *Gesch. des Deutschen Verses* (1960); F. Beissner, *Gesch. der deutschen Elegie* (1941); E. Staiger, *Grundbegriffe der Poetik* (1946), tr. J. C. Hudson and L. T. Frank as *Basic Concepts of Poetics* (1991); P. Böckmann, *Formgesch. der deutschen Dichtung* (1949), *Formensprache* (1966); F. Lockemann, *Der Rhythmus des deutschen Verses* (1960); W. Hinck, *Die deutsche Ballade von Bürger bis Brecht* (1968); W. Höck, *Formen heutiger Lyrik* (1969); K. Weissenberger, *Formen der Elegie von Goethe bis Celan* (1969); J.-U. Fechner, *Das deutsche Sonett* (1969)—anthol.; G. Storz, *Der Vers in der neueren deutschen Dichtung* (1970); W. Killy, *Elemente der Lyrik* (1972); W. Freund, *Die deutsche Ballade* (1978); H. Laufhütte, *Die deutsche Kunstballade* (1979); D. Breuer, *Deutsche Metrik und Versgesch.* (1981).

CRITICISM IN GERMAN: B. Markwardt, *Gesch. der deutschen Poetik*, 5 v. (1937–67); E. Staiger, *Die Zeit als Einbildungskraft des Dichters* (1938); W. Killy, *Wandlungen des lyrischen Bildes* (1956); *Wege zum Gedicht*, ed. R. Hirschenauer and A. Weber, 2 v. (1956–63)—v. 2 on the ballad; *Die deutsche Lyrik*, ed. B. v. Wiese, 2 v. (1957); T. W. Adorno, "Rede über Lyrik und Gesellschaft" and "Zum Gedächtnis Eichendorffs," *Noten zur Literatur, I* (1958); C. Heselhaus, *Deutsche Lyrik der Moderne* (1961); *Ars poetica: Texte von Dichtern des 20. Jahrhunderts zur Poetik*, ed. B. Allemann (1966)—51 essays; W. Naumann, *Traum und Trad. in der deutschen Lyrik* (1966); A. Schöne, *Über politische Lyrik im 20. Jahrhundert* (1969); *Doppelinterpretationen*, ed. H. Domin (1969); K. H. Spinner, *Zur Struktur des lyrischen Ich* (1975); J. Theobaldy and G. Zürcher, *Veränderung der Lyrik: Über westdeutsche Gedichte seit 1965* (1976); *Naturlyrik und Gesellschaft*, ed. N. Mecklenburg (1977); *Gesch. der politischen Lyrik in Deutschland*, ed. W. Hinderer (1978); W. Rey, *Poesie der Antipoesie* (1978); W. Hinck, *Von Heine zu Brecht. Lyrik im Geschichtsprozess* (1978); *Die deutsche Lyrik, 1945–75*, ed. K. Weissenberger (1981); H. T. Hamm, *Poesie und kommunikative Praxis* (1981); S. Volckmann, *Zeit der Kirschen? Das Naturbild in der deutschen Gegenwartslyrik* (1982); *Gesch. der deutschen Lyrik vom Mittelalter bis zur Gegenwart*, ed. W. Hinderer (1983)—indispensable; H. Gnüg, *Entstehung und Krise lyrischer subjektivität* (1983); B. Sorg, *Das lyrische Ich* (1984); *Deutsche Lyrik nach 1945*, ed. D. Breuer (1988).

CRITICISM IN ENGLISH: S. S. Prawer, *Ger. Lyric P.* (1952); A. Closs, *The Genius of the Ger. Lyric*, 2d ed. (1962); J. Flores, *Poetry in East Germany* (1971); R. D. Gray, *Ger. P.* (1976); R. M. Browning, *Ger. P. in the Age of the Enlightenment* (1978); T. Ziolkowski, *The Cl. Ger. Elegy, 1795–1950* (1980); P. Bridgewater, *The Ger. Poets of the First World War* (1985); C. Waller, *Expressionist Poetry and its Critics* (1986); M. Hamburger, *After the Second Flood* (1986); J. Rolleston, *Narratives of Ecstasy: Romantic Temporality in Mod. Ger. P.* (1987); B. Peucker, *Lyric Descent in the Ger. Romantic Trad.* (1987); *Ger. P. through 1915*, ed. H. Bloom (1987). J.L.R.

GREEK POETRY.

- I. CLASSICAL
  - A. *The Preliterate Period* (CA. 2000–750 B.C.)
  - B. *The Earlier Archaic Period* (CA. 750–600 B.C.)
  - C. *The Later Archaic Period* (CA. 600–480 B.C.)
  - D. *The High Classical Period* (CA. 480–400 B.C.)
  - E. *The Fourth Century* B.C
  - F. *The Hellenistic Age* (CA. 300–21 B.C.)
  - G. *The Roman Imperial Period*
- II. MEDIEVAL. SEE BYZANTINE POETRY.
- III. MODERN

I. CLASSICAL. A. *The Preliterate Period* (ca. 2000–750 B.C.). The earliest Gr. verses preserved in writing date from the 8th C. B.C., and poetry has continued to be composed in Gr. from that time until the present day (for a view of the trad. as a whole, see Trypanis). But recent research indicates that the Gr. poetic trad. is in fact far older than the introduction of writing. The nature of the word-groups of which the Homeric epics are largely composed, as well as the content of those epics, implies a pre-existing oral trad. of heroic dactylic poetry extending back into the Bronze Age civilization of the Mycenaeans, which came to an end about 1100 B.C. The Aeolic meters that are widely used in extant Gr. p., notably by Sappho and Alcaeus, presuppose an even more ancient oral trad. of song, for they show clear affinities with the meters of the Indian Vedas; their ultimate origins may therefore date back as far as about 2000 B.C.

The introduction of an alphabet specifically adapted to the recording of Gr., which took place not later than the mid 8th c. B.C., was no doubt the most important single event in the history of Gr. p. Gr. (and European) *literature* begins here, at the point where the songs could be fixed in permanent form and transmitted to posterity. Yet for many centuries after, Gr. p. continued to bear the deep imprint of ancient oral trad., incl. two of its most distinctive characteristics: (1) its mythological and heroic content and (2) its long dependence on oral performance as the means of reaching its public. (1) Ancient Gr. p. in nearly all genres worked within a frame of reference provided by the traditional gods and the heroes of the Bronze Age. That mythic-legendary world afforded the poets both their basic story-patterns and their paradigms of conduct. Heroic epic, many forms of choral lyric, and tragedy directly represented characters and incidents drawn from that world; epinician and monodic lyric constantly evoked it as a standard against which the human condition might be measured. (2) For more than three centuries after the introduction of writing, Gr. p. continued as before to be enacted orally, often with the accompaniment of music or dancing or both, before audiences as small as dinner-parties and as large as the vast crowds at religious festivals—Plato (*Ion* 535d) mentions audiences of 20,000 for performances of epic at such festivals. Thus, Gr. p. of the archaic and high-Cl. eras combined features that may at first sight seem contradictory. It had the elaboration, finish, and durability that belong to book-poetry as opposed to oral poetry, and yet so far as its intended public was concerned it remained an oral and often even visual entertainment.

To this inheritance from the preliterate trad. may also be attributed certain other characteristics of archaic and high-Cl. Gr. p.: its richness in aural effects (the immense variety and musicality of its quantitative meters, for instance, are unmatched in any European poetry and perhaps in any poetry whatever); the prominent part it played in the cultural life of the society as a whole; and the wide range of its human appeal, particularly in its most popular genres the epic and the drama, ever since.

B. *The Earlier Archaic Period* (ca. 750–600 B.C.). Thanks (it seems) to the introduction of writing, a great number of poems dating from this period were known to the later Greeks. With the exception of the major poems attributed to Homer and Hesiod, however, most of this work survives only in quotations, summaries, and allusions, but these are enough to permit a sketchmap, at least, of a complex literary landscape. All the major nondramatic genres of subsequent Cl. poetry are already in existence, but they tend to be associated with particular geographical regions. Of these regions four stand out: Ionia, Lesbos, Sparta, and Boeotia.

The Ionic-speaking region embraced the central part of the west coast of Asia Minor and the islands that stretch from there toward Greece proper. Here the most important and longest-lasting of all Gr. and Lat. verseforms, and quite possibly of all verseforms known to man—the dactylic hexameter (– ⏑ ⏑ | – ⏑ ⏑ | – ⏑ ⏑ | – ⏑ ⏑ | – ⏑ ⏑ | – ⏑ ⏑)—seems to have achieved its definitive form. The "formulae" of which the hexameters of Homer are largely composed show elements of several Gr. dialects, but the predominant and apparently latest stratum is Ionic. It is generally inferred that the trad. of hexameter composition, after passing through the bards of at least two other dialectal regions, culminated in Ionia; and in fact the oldest Gr. trads. concerning Homer place him in Chios or Smyrna, cities that belong to this region. Ionia, then, was the probable birthplace of the two great epics that later Greece, and later Europe, perceived as the fountainhead of their lit., the *Iliad* and the *Odyssey*. Since the 18th c., a debate has raged over the genesis, authorship, unity, and dates of completion of these poems (see the fourth section of the bibl., esp. the intro. to Parry). But one certainty at least remains: from the earliest period they stood as models of the poetic art, above all for the satisfying unity of their plots and for their brilliant technique of characterization through speeches.

Also from Ionia during this period come the first examples of iambic and elegiac poetry. In both these genres the poems were relatively short monologues, predominantly concerned with war, political and personal invective, and love; but elegiac tended more than iambic to include a gnomic element, i.e. meditation and advice on various aspects of the human condition. Metrically speaking, "iambic" by the ancient Gr. definition embraced poems composed in the iambic trimeter (a three-metron or, in modern parlance, six-foot iambic line [⏑ – ⏑ – | ⏑ – ⏑ – | ⏑ – ⏑ –]) and in the trochaic tetrameter catalectic (– ⏑ – ⏑ | – ⏑ – ⏑ | – ⏑ – ⏑ | – ⏑ –). These two were to have a rich afterlife in Cl. (and to some extent later European) lit., the former as the standard verseform for dialogue in drama, the latter in comic and popular verse. Elegiac poetry was composed in elegiac couplets —a dactylic hexameter followed by a dactylic pentameter, so-called (– ⏑ – ⏑ – | – ⏑ ⏑ – ⏑ ⏑ –); this meter also was to become an enormously important medium, not least in the epigrams of the *Greek Anthology*.

The most famous and, so far as the Greeks were in a position to know, the first composer in both genres was Archilochus, of the Ionic island Paros (fl. 648 B.C.). Some Gr. authors actually put his poetry on a level with that of Homer, in its very different way; the intensity and metrical perfection of his surviving fragments seem to confirm that judgment. Archilochus was also the earliest known composer of a third variety of "iambic" poetry as anciently defined, the epode, which consisted of alternating long and short lines predominantly in iambic or dactylic meters; this was a superb instrument for invective from Archilochus to the Roman Horace. Several other iambic and elegiac poets flourished in 7th-c. Ionia, esp. Semonides, Callinus, and Mimnermus. The only distinguished elegiac poet working on the Gr. mainland during this period was Tyrtaeus (fl. ca. 640 B.C.), whose poems, composed in Sparta, survive in several extensive fragments.

The poetry of the Ionian region in all its genres is remarkable for the clarity of its expression and metrical form (the repeated line and the repeated couplet are the only options available), and for a rather sophisticated realism. For lyricism during this period, one must turn elsewhere. Gr. lyric poetry by the ancient definition was *poetry sung to instrumental accompaniment.* In practice it fell into two broad categories: choral lyric, which was normally a dance as well as a song, and might be composed in an almost infinite variety of meters and stanza forms; and solo lyric (sometimes misleadingly called personal lyric), composed for accompanied singing only, in a more limited though still extensive range of meters, and falling into short stanzas, most often quatrains. Both kinds of lyric emerge from the mists of preliteracy during this period, primarily in two centers: Aeolic-speaking Lesbos and Doric-speaking Sparta.

From the late 8th into the early 6th c., a series of choral and solo lyric poets is recorded in the isle of Lesbos. Most of them, such as Terpander and Arion, are now scarcely more than sonorous names, but Sappho and Alcaeus, who both flourished ca. 600 B.C., have left many fragments of solo lyric poetry. Both composed in approximately the same range of Aeolic lyric meters (two of the most famous Aeolic stanza forms, the "Sapphic" and the "Alcaic", are named after them), and in the same soft and musical Aeolic brogue; but in content and tone they are vastly unlike each other. For the power and beauty of her love-poetry Sappho has no peer in Gr. lit., and few in any lit. Alcaeus' songs on the turbulent politics of the island, his hymns to the gods, and above all his drinking-songs, if less elegantly crafted, were to prove of great influence on later European lyric.

Seventh-century Sparta was famed for the competitions in choral lyric at its great religious festivals, but the only one of its poets about whom anything significant is known is Alcman (second half of the 7th c.). From his numerous and in some cases quite substantial fragments it can be deduced that his choral lyrics already embodied the most striking characteristics of the choral lyric genre as it was later known. The long polymetric stanzas of his First Partheneion, for example, its extensively narrated examples from myth or saga, its gnomic passages in which the singers reflect on the universal meaning of their tale, can still find parallels in Pindar and Bacchylides a couple of centuries later.

In central Greece, Boeotia in this period saw the composition of a great number of poems; only three survive complete, the *Theogony*, the *Works and Days*, and the *Shield of Herakles*, but a fourth, the *Ehoiai* or *Catalogue of Women*, can now be restored to a considerable extent from papyrus fragments. Both the lost and the surviving poems of the Boeotian corpus were generally ascribed in ancient times to the great Hesiod, who seems to have flourished ca. 700 B.C., but most modern critics deny the authenticity of the *Shield*, and several that of the *Ehoiai*. In any case, all are composed in a medium that is virtually indistinguishable from that of the Homeric epics: the meter is the same, almost the same formulary is employed, and the same mixture of dialects is evident. But there the resemblance ends. The Hesiodic works show nothing of the architectonic skill of Homer, or of his genius for realizing character through speech. They are essentially episodic codifications of ancient lore. The *Theogony* presents the origin and history of the Gr. gods, organizing the material by generations; the *Ehoiai* followed the history of the heroic families by clans and, within clans, by generations; the *Works and Days* is a manual of the art of living, proceeding from ethical and political considerations to practical instruction in farming, navigation, and the rules of daily conduct. But this essentially catalogic principle of composition does not mean that Hesiod lacks art. Largely through the characteristically archaic techniques of ring-composition and significant repetition, he succeeds in making his topics and episodes cohere within themselves and between each other. Like Homer, Hesiod knows how to capture and hold his hearer, if by quite different means. One un-Homeric technique that appears in Hesiod for the first time in European lit. is that of the authorial "I": in the proem to the *Theogony* and through much of the *Works and Days* he builds up an impressive persona of "Hesiod," imparting both weight and liveliness to his teachings.

Much other hexameter poetry was composed in various regions of Greece during this period; the hexameter in fact seems early on to have become a kind of poetic *koine.* Particularly important in its time was the "Epic Cycle," a catena of medium-length epics by various hands that covered the entire Troy-saga. Other epics since lost are known to have told of the legendary history of Corinth, the story of the Argonauts, and the house of Oedipus. Other extant examples of early hexameter poetry are certain poems in the heterogeneous collection that has come down to us under the title of the *Homeric Hymns*: at least Hymns II (to Demeter), III (to Apollo), and V (to Aphrodite) probably belong to this period. It is a remarkable fact that by about 600 B.C. all the major nondramatic genres of Gr. p. were already in existence: heroic epic, iambic, elegiac, solo and choral lyric, and, at least in some sense, didactic (for Hesiodic poetry, though far wider in scope than the didactic poetry of later antiquity, was certainly its inspiration).

C. *The Later Archaic Period* (ca. 600–480 B.C.). The diversity of later archaic Gr. p. was great, but two general trends may be distinguished: the major poetic genres become less tied to specific regions of Greece, and lyric poetry in particular shows a growing sophistication, metrically as well as intellectually. Several of the poets who worked in this period have left names famous throughout subsequent Western lit., despite the fact that none of their books has survived intact. Composition in epic hexameters continued in many parts of Greece; some poems of the Epic Cycle and of the Hesiodic corpus, as well as several of the Homeric Hymns, probably belong to the earlier part of this period. The most significant discernible devel. is the gradual disintegration of the system of formulae characteristic of the older epics. By the late 6th c. the first tentative signs of a "literary" or "secondary" epic may perhaps be made out in the work of Panyassis of Halicarnassus.

An outstanding exponent of both elegiac and iambic poetry was the statesman Solon (fl. 594 B.C.), the earliest recorded Athenian poet. The quite substantial fragments of his work are partly gnomic or personal in content—in this conforming to Ionian precedent—but the majority address political principles and issues connected with Solon's famous reforms of the Athenian economy and constitution. Across the Aegean, Hipponax of Ephesus (fl. 540 B.C.) culminated the Ionian trad. of iambic invective and lampoon. His favorite meter was one that now appears for the first time, the *scazon* or limping iambic trimeter (⏑ – ⏑ – | ⏑ – ⏑ – | ⏑ – – ⏑). The last of the major archaic elegists, Theognis of Megara (second half of the 6th c.?), is represented by a large number of poems, predominantly gnomic in character, in the 1300-line anthology of elegiacs that somehow survived the Middle Ages and now goes under the title of *Theognidea*. Finally, the elegiac, iambic, and hexameter fragments of Xenophanes of Colophon (ca. 570–478 B.C.) open up a new dimension in poetry, the philosophic and scientific; his penetrating physical and ethnological observations and his criticism of Gr. anthropomorphic religion are expressed in lively and quite elegant verse. The two other Gr. poet-philosophers who followed him, Parmenides and Empedocles, belong rather to the history of philosophy than to that of poetry.

In lyric poetry there were spectacular developments. Recent papyrus discoveries (summarized in *CHCL* 1.6.3.) have greatly enriched our knowledge of Stesichorus of Himera in Sicily, who seems to have flourished in the first half of the 6th c. They fully confirm the ancient trads. that he composed songs very much in the epic manner, and even approaching the epic scale, and also that he adopted or perhaps invented the practice of composing choral lyric by triads (strophe, metrically responding antistrophe, nonresponding epode—), which is the most striking formal characteristic of subsequent Gr. choral lyric. Ibycus of Rhegium in south Italy (fl. ca. 535 B.C.) and Simonides of the Aegean isle of Keos (556–468) have each left superb fragments of lyric. Simonides in particular seems to have been a great innovative master, turning his hand to many different varieties of choral lyric, incl. the epinikion (which he may have originated) and the short epigram in elegiac couplets, a form which had an immense literary future before it.

Anacreon of Teos in Ionia (ca. 575–490) brought solo lyric poetry to heights of wit and technical polish that were matched in Cl. times perhaps only by the Roman poets Catullus and Horace. His many brilliant fragments sing mostly of love and wine, and only once or twice of the more somber themes of old age and death. Metrically he was not a great innovator, but he seems to have been the first poet to make extensive use of the catchy rhythm ⏑ ⏑ – ⏑ – ⏑ – ⏑, later called the Anacreontic after him. (This meter plays a great part in the extant collection of light verse datable from the Roman period that goes under the title *Anacreontea*, the poems of which had great popularity and influence in 16th- to 18th-c. Europe.)

The most momentous poetic devel. in this period was the introduction of poetic drama. Officially sponsored performances of tragedy at the Great Dionysia festival in Athens are first attested in ca. 534 B.C., and of comedy in 486. The ultimate origins of both genres, and their histories down to the time of the great Persian invasion of Greece in 480/79 B.C., are still problematic for want of adequate evidence; what is known, with some of the speculations on what is known, is collected in Pickard-Cambridge. Our extant examples of tragedy and comedy date only from the ensuing period. Scarcely more than the names survive of the two earliest recorded tragedians, Thespis and Choerilus, and not very many fragments of the third, Phrynichus (active 511–476). But it is indisputable that well before the Persian Wars, at Athens, the decisive steps had been taken toward the creation of drama. That was Athens' supreme contribution to Gr. p., a contribution that was to transform the character of ancient lit. and deeply to affect the course of Western lit. as a whole.

D. *The High Classical Period* (ca. 480–400 B.C.). After the Persian Wars, Athenian power and splendor reached their peak. The years between 479 and Athens' defeat by Sparta in 404 saw the creation of a naval empire in the eastern Mediterranean, the Periclean democracy, the erection of the great buildings and sculptures on the Acropolis—and the composition of all the surviving masterpieces of Attic tragedy. Elsewhere in Greece, choral lyric seems to have been the only poetic genre that was still practiced with great success. Our first-hand knowledge of the tragic art depends almost exclusively on the extant plays of the three most famous Attic tragedians, Aeschylus (525–456 B.C.), Sophocles (496–406), and Euripides (484–406); the earliest surviving example, Aeschylus' *Persians*, was produced in 472. On the strictly *dramatic* aspects of the art, much is to be found elsewhere (see Lesky). Viewed in the context of Gr. p., tragedy is remarkable for the manner in which it combined and consummated the achievements of so many pre-existing poetic genres. In tragic tone, in characterization through speech, and to some extent even in plot construction, the tragedians picked up and developed precedents in Homeric epic (as Aristotle implies throughout the *Poetics*, e.g. 1449b17: "anybody who can tell a good tragedy from a bad one can do the same with epics"). In metric they owed less to the epic than to iambic, solo lyric, and choral lyric. They added little to the existing repertoire of Gr. meters but combining freely metrical elements that had previously been confined to separate genres. The result, esp. in the choral odes and the arias of tragedy, is a poetry of unprecedented richness and variety in tone, tempo, and rhythm. Fifth-century Attic tragedy is thus both the starting-point of European drama and the final synthesis of all the earlier modes of Gr. p.

Probably an art of such power and wide popular appeal was bound, in time, to overshadow the traditional genres of Gr. p., and by the end of the 5th c. this process had taken place. Elegiac and solo lyric continued to be practiced until the last few decades, but only falteringly. Choral lyric alone was still able to reach great heights, but even that genre faded out of history with the death of Pindar of Thebes (ca. 518–438 B.C.). The most famous of all the choral lyricists, Pindar was master of a great range of song-types for a variety of occasions. When the Hellenistic scholars came to edit his complete poems, they grouped them under the headings of *hymns, paeans, dithyrambs, partheneia* (songs for girl-choruses), *hyporchemes* (dance-poems), *encomia, threnoi* (death-laments), and *epinikia* (victory-odes); the titles may not in every case have reflected Pindar's intent, but they give a vivid notion of the diapason of Gr. choral lyric. Of all these, only the *Epinikia*, praising the victors at the four great athletic festivals, have survived intact. Varying in length from one to thirteen triads, these odes concentrate not so much on the transient details of the athletic success as on its significance in the divine and human cosmos: the human victory is measured against mythological precedents the evocation of which—sometimes continuously, sometimes only in brief glimpses of matchless vividness—may occupy much of the ode.

Pindaric poetry is not easy reading. It may well have been more readily comprehensible in its original performance, when it was *heard* and its message was reinforced by music and choral dancing; its allusiveness, the intricacy of its word-placing and metric, and the never-failing originality and precision of its diction keep a reader in constant tension. But it is poetry of unsurpassed honesty, intensity, and profundity. Far more accessible is the choral lyric of Bacchylides of Keos, many of whose songs—mostly epinician odes and dithyrambs—have been discovered on papyri in modern times. Bacchylides was a younger poet than Pindar, but all his datable poems fall within the period 485–452 B.C., well before the end of Pindar's long career. Clarity and grace mark his poetry; his meters are simple and tuneful, his mythical narratives interestingly chosen and straightforwardly presented.

The first extant Gr. comedy is Aristophanes' *Acharnians*, produced in Athens in 425 B.C. Since antiquity it has been customary to divide the history of the Attic comic art into three phases, Old, Middle, and New. Old Comedy extended from the institution of the comic contests at the Great Dionysia in 486 B.C. until the opening decades of the 4th c., but most of our knowledge of it depends on Aristophanes' 11 surviving plays. Of all the poetry created by the Greeks, Old Comedy has the widest metrical and stylistic range and allows by far the freest play of fantasy. Its basic dialect is the local vernacular—colloquial Attic speech in all its vigor and explicitness, sexual and scatological. Further, the extant Aristophanic comedies display an extraordinary aptitude for the parody of every other poetic genre, and not least of tragedy. But Old Comedy's single most extraordinary feature was its total freedom to create characters and situations. In most Gr. p. up to that time, the basic narratives and characters were drawn from the ancient myths and sagas. The majority of Old Comic plots, however, seem to have been free fictions, some of them blossoming into poetic fantasies that might embrace Hades (as in Aristophanes' *Frogs*) or the entire universe (as in his *Birds*).

The last two or three decades of this period saw a revolutionary movement in Gr. p. and music which is known to us primarily from allusions in Old Comedy, from a partially preserved lyric text, the *Persians*, by Timotheus of Miletus (fl. ca. 450–360 B.C.), and from some of the songs in Euripides' last plays. The most remarkable technical features of this "New Music" were its total abandonment of the triadic arrangement of responding stanzas that had characterized all earlier lyric verse and the opening of a fatal split between the words and the melody of a lyric. For the first time, the evidence suggests, one syllable, instead of being set to one note, might be extended over several notes, as in modern song. These and other similarly radical innovations in the instrumentation and performance of poetry effectively meant the end of the trad. of archaic and high Cl. lyric poetry that had flourished since at least the early 7th c.

E. *The Fourth Century* B.C. The outstanding

event in Gr. lit. of this period is the triumph of prose. Prose as a literary medium had developed rather slowly in the outer regions of the Gr. world from the mid 6th c. B.C. onward. In Athens it did not establish itself until the second half of the 5th c.; only in the 4th c., and above all in the works of Isocrates, Plato, and Aristotle, did it acquire an unchallengeable position as the medium for the exploration of the deepest human concerns, philosophical, psychological, and political. Accordingly, the poet was gradually forced from his supreme role as universal teacher into the role of, at most, entertainer. The most flourishing variety of Gr. p. in the 4th c. was comedy. Aristophanes' last surviving play, the *Ploutos* (388 B.C.), is often taken to mark the transition from Old to Middle Comedy. Certainly the relative tameness of its central comic fantasy, its drastic reduction of the chorus' role, and its almost total elimination of any lyric element all seem to have been characteristics of Middle Comedy, which is conventionally dated ca. 380–320. New Comedy (ca. 320–250) is much more accessible to us, thanks to extensive papyrus discoveries over the past century. Most of these are plays by the most famous of the New Comic poets, Menander (ca. 342–291 B.C.). The New Comic plots continue the trad. of Old Comedy in that they are fictional and set in contemporary Greece, but the fictions are now much more restricted in imaginative range. On the other hand, Menander crafts exquisite plots and creates a long series of delicately shaded character studies. The predominant meter of his comedies is the iambic trimeter, occasionally varied with iambic or trochaic tetrameters. Lyric now has no place in the fabric of the comedies, although they are divided into acts (regularly, it seems, five) by pauses in the scripts marked *Khorou*—"[song] of a chorus"—apparently songs unrelated to the dramatic action, and probably not composed by the playwright. It was this last traceable phase of Gr. poetic drama, through the Lat. adaptations by Plautus and Terence, which was to provide the formal model for both the tragedy and comedy of Ren. Europe: the five-act play in iambic verse.

Noncomic poetry of the 4th c. is reduced to pitifully few fragments. Tragedies continued to be produced in large numbers at the Great Dionysia in Athens, though, perhaps significantly, the masterpieces of the three great 5th-c. tragedians now began to be performed alongside the new compositions. The New Music movement in lyric poetry (see above) had apparently run its course by the middle of the century. The epic and elegiac poems by Antimachus of Colophon (fl. ca. 400 B.C.) had their admirers in later antiquity. But on the whole, the Gr. poetic impulse that had been sustained without break from preliterate times had temporarily exhausted itself. The stage was clear for a new kind of poetry.

F. *The Hellenistic Age* (ca. 300–31 B.C.). In Athens, New Comedy—the last survivor of any of the publicly performed Cl. genres—continued in full vigor during the earlier part of this period. Elsewhere the circumstances and character of Gr. p. changed radically. The conquests of Alexander the Great (d. 323 B.C.) had extended the power, and with it the lang., of the Greeks into the Near and Middle East, a shift soon followed by a shift in the focuses of literary activity. The newly founded Gr. metropolises, above all Egyptian Alexandria, attracted talent of every kind from wherever Gr. was spoken. But the new poetic culture that arose in those vast cities, with their heterogeneous populations severed from the living traditions of the homeland, was necessarily a culture of the book; its audience was no longer the citizen in the marketplace. The result was a learned poetry of exquisite technical finish and literary allusiveness—a poetry, for the first time in this story, analogous to that of Virgil, Milton, or Eliot. At the same time, however, the Hellenistic poets were very conscious of the need to validate the new kind of poetry by ensuring the *appearance* of continuity with the older Gr. poetic trad. Many of the archaic genres were now revived in form, if transfigured in scope and tone. The most versatile of the Hellenistic poets, Callimachus (active in Alexandria ca. 280–245 B.C.), offers a good example of the process. His *Hymns* deliberately recall the Homeric Hymns of archaic Greece. Yet these Callimachean counterparts are not so much acts of piety as masterpieces of delicate wit and fantasy; and more than one of them incorporates a literary evocation of the festival at which it was to be *imagined* as delivered. Similar imitations and transpositions are to be found in Callimachus' *Iambi*, where Hipponax is an acknowledged model, and in his *Aetia*, where he invokes the precedents of Mimnermus and Hesiod.

In this general revival of the archaic genres it was impossible that Homer should be neglected, but he now elicited very diverse literary responses. To Callimachus and many other Hellenistic poets, notably Theocritus, the vast scale and heroic temper of Homeric epic were no longer achievable or even desirable, for these men aimed above all at brevity, polish, and realism. They devised their own brand of narrative poetry, the brief epic, adopting (with refinements) the Homeric medium, the hexameter, but limiting the scale to a few hundred lines. Within this space there could be no question of retelling a heroic saga; rather, the poet would illuminate a single heroic episode, bringing out its full color and detail. Examples of this form are Callimachus' fragmentary *Hekale*, Theocritus' *Idyll* 13 on Herakles and Hylas, and, at a later date, Moschus' *Europa*. A number of Hellenistic poets, however, did compose large-scale epics, though the only one that survives is the *Argonautica* of Apollonius Rhodius, a younger contemporary of Callimachus. In its versification, its lang., and its similes, this poem abundantly testifies to Apollonius' long study of Homer, yet in content and tone it is utterly un-Homeric. Apollonius' passive and hesitant hero, Jason, belongs rather to our world than to the world of Achilles and Odysseus, and the depiction in Book 3 of Medea's love for him is a breakthrough, at least in the epic context.

Hesiod was the alleged model for the many didactic poems composed in the Hellenistic period, though the wide human scope of Hesiodic poetry tended to be reduced simply to the versification of this technology or that. The most notable surviving example is Aratus' *Phainomena*, on astronomy and meteorology. The only altogether new genre created by the Hellenistic poets (or, if not created, adapted from subliterary songs and mummings of an earlier period) was pastoral poetry. The earliest known examples are the work of Theocritus, who was approximately a contemporary of Callimachus and Apollonius. The collection of his poems that has reached us under the title of *Idylls* consists of relatively short pieces, mostly in hexameters, but only a minority of them are pastorals, and one of Theocritus' most brilliant dialogue-poems, *Idyll* 15, is set in the hubbub of Alexandria itself. Both the nonpastoral and the pastoral poems display the Callimachean preference for brevity and precise detail, but in his control of verbal music Theocritus may be thought to surpass even Callimachus.

The great creative impetus of Hellenistic poetry was limited to the first half of the 3d c. B.C. Thereafter very little new ground was broken. The various genres that were then re-established or created continued to be practiced, but the surviving examples are of little poetic significance.

G. *The Roman Imperial Period.* With the battle of Actium in 31 B.C., Rome's empire over the Mediterranean and Near East was decisively established. Paradoxically, it was the *Roman* poets who henceforth most successfully exploited the legacy of Hellenistic Gr. p.; the three great poems of Virgil himself, for instance, would be inconceivable but for the precedents of Hellenistic pastoral, didactic, and epic. Though a great many poems were composed in Gr. under the Empire, none matches the work of the major Roman poets in intrinsic interest or influence on subsequent European poetry. Thus the trad. of ancient Gr. p., while competently perpetuated during this period, was gradually losing its momentum. Two slow but steady developments, one linguistic and the other social, were finally to bring that trad. to an end: a change in the pronunciation of Gr., whereby quantity is replaced by stress; and the triumph of the Christian imagination over the pagan. From about the beginning of the Christian era, the distinction in colloquial Gr. speech between long and short vowel-quantities began to disappear, and the musical pitch-accent that had prevailed since archaic times began to be replaced by a tonic stress-accent similar to that of modern Gr. or Eng. Literary Gr. p. responded only very slowly to these changes, but by the 6th c. A.D., the characteristic Byzantine versification was well established, its guiding principle no longer syllable quantity but recurrent stress accent. In this fashion Gr. p. gradually lost the superb metrical system that in the hands of Pindar, the Attic tragedians, and Theocritus had generated such an incomparable wealth and variety of verbal music. Simultaneously, Gr. p. was also being gradually distanced from pagan mythology—from the rich intellectual and imaginative resource that had provided it with its themes since the preliterate era. As a consequence of these two developments, Gr. p. was no more the same art. No absolute date can be set to that final transformation, and exceptions to the general trend can always be found: for instance, scholars continued to compose verses in quantitative Gr. meters down through the Middle Ages and Ren. But effectively the change had taken place by the end of the 6th c. A.D.

Most of the Gr. p. that survives from the Imperial Roman period falls under one of three genres: didactic, epic, and epigram. Tragedy and comedy were no longer composed, and the few known examples of lyric poetry are not very striking either in substance or metric. The didactic poets followed closely in the steps of their Hellenistic predecessors, composing versified textbooks of varying interest and merit on such subjects as geography and fishing. Epic both mythological and panegyric (i.e. celebrating the exploits of some political figure) was very widely composed. Much the most interesting example is the *Dionysiaca* composed by Nonnus of Panopolis in Egypt in the early 5th c. This story of the triumphant career of Dionysus, in 48 books (matching the total number of books in the *Iliad* and *Odyssey*), is the last major Gr. poem in hexameters.

Alone among the Gr. genres, the epigram never fell out of fashion. This kind of brief, finely worked, and pointed poem, somewhat comparable in finish and compactness to the haiku or the closed neoclassical couplet, most often took the form of one to four elegiac couplets. The earliest examples are inscriptions (*epigrammata*) on gravestones or votive objects of the archaic period. During the 5th c. B.C. the form was increasingly adapted to literary purposes, and the range of its content was extended beyond the funereal and dedicatory to many other human concerns—above all, love, humor, and wine. The great surviving corpus of epigrams, the *Greek Anthology*, put together for the most part by the 10th c. A.D., is one of the most moving and impressive of all the monuments of ancient Gr. p. Within it are found epigrams by most of the famous poets, and philosophers too, composed over a span of something like 14 centuries.

BIBLIOGRAPHIES: *L'Année Philologique: Bibliographie critique et analytique de l'antiquité gréco-latine* 1– (1927–); *The Cl. World Bibl. of Gr. Drama and Poetry* (1978); *Gr. and Roman Authors: A Checklist of Crit.*, ed. T. Gwinup and F. Dickinson, 2d ed. (1982)—covers 70 authors.

TEXTS: Bibliotheca Teubneriana series (1888–)—crit. texts without trs.; Loeb Cl. Library series (1912–)—texts, with facing trs., of all the major poets; J. M. Edmonds, *Lyra graeca*, 3 v. (1928; rpt 1952–58), *Elegy and Iambus*, 2 v. (1911; rpt 1979–82); *Callimachus*, ed. R. Pfeiffer, 2 v. (1949); *Theocritus*, ed. A. S. F. Gow, 2 v. (1950); D. L. Page, *Poetae melici graeci* (1962); M. L. West, *Iambi et elegi graeci ante alexandrum cantati* (1971–72); Oxford Cl. Texts series (1980–)—good critical texts without trs.; D. A. Campbell, *Gr. Lyric*, 4 v. (1982–)—texts with facing trs.

ANTHOLOGIES: *Oxford Book of Gr. Verse*, ed. C. M. Bowra et al. (1930); *Oxford Book of Gr. Verse in Tr.*, ed. T. Higham and C. M. Bowra (1938); D. A. Campbell, *Gr. Lyric Poetry* (1976); *An Anthol. of Alexandrian Poetry*, ed. J. Clack (1982); *Penguin Book of Gr. Verse*, ed. C. A. Trypanis, 3d ed. (1984).

GENERAL HISTORIES: F. Susemihl, *Gesch. der griechischen Literatur in der Alexandriner-Zeit*, 2 v. (1891–92); A. and M. Croiset, *Histoire de la litt. grecque*, 5 v. (1909–28); Schmid and Stählin; Trypanis; *CHCL*, v. 1.

HISTORY AND CRITICISM: D. L. Page, *Sappho and Alcaeus* (1955); A. E. Harvey, "The Classif. of Gr. Lyric Poetry," *ClassQ* n.s. 5 (1955); R. Lattimore, *The Poetry of Gr. Tragedy* (1958); T. B. L. Webster, *From Mycenae to Homer* (1959), *Hellenistic Poetry and Art* (1965); A. Körte and P. Händel, *Die Hellenistische Dichtung* (1960); Bowra; A. Pickard-Cambridge, *Dithyramb, Tragedy and Comedy*, 2d ed. (1962); G. S. Kirk, *The Songs of Homer* (1962), *Homer and the Oral Trad.* (1975); W. B. Stanford, *The Sound of Gr.* (1967); Parry; B. Snell, *Poetry and Society* (1971); F. Cairns, *Generic Composition in Gr. and Roman Poetry* (1972); A. Lesky, *Die Tragische Dichtung der Hellenen*, 3d ed. (1972), tr. as *Gr. Tragic Poetry* (1983); K. J. Dover, *Aristophanic Comedy* (1972); M. L. West, "Gr. P. 2000–700 B.C.," *ClassQ* 23 (1973); G. M. Kirkwood, *Early Gr. Monody: The History of a Poetic Type* (1974); H. F. Frankel, *Early Gr. P. and Philosophy*, tr. M. Hadas and J. Willis (1975); B. Peabody, *The Winged Word* (1975); W. G. Arnott, Intro. to Loeb ed. of Menander, v. 1 (1979)—comedy; H. White, *Essays in Hellenistic Poetry* (1980), *New Essays in Hellenistic Poetry* (1985), *Studies in Late Gr. Epic Poetry* (1987); R. Janko, *Homer, Hesiod, and the Hymns* (1982); D. A. Campbell, *The Golden Lyre* (1983); A. P. Burnett, *Three Archaic Poets* (1983), *The Art of Bacchylides* (1985); W. G. Thalmann, *Conventions of Form and Thought in Early Gr. Epic Poetry* (1984); A. W. H. Adkins, *Poetic Craft in the Early Gr. Elegists* (1985); D. S. Carne-Ross, *Pindar* (1985); J. Herington, *Poetry into Drama* (1985); *The Iliad: A Commentary*, ed. G. W. Kirk, 6 v. (1985; v. 1, on *Iliad* 1–4); G. F. Else, *Plato and Aristotle on Poetry* (1987); M. W. Edwards, *Homer* (1987); R. L. Fowler, *The Nature of Early Gr. Lyric* (1987); B. Gentili, *Poetry and Its Public in Ancient Greece*, tr. A. T. Cole (1988); G. O. Hutchinson, *Hellenistic Poetry* (1988); R. Lamberton, *Hesiod* (1988); J. M. Snyder, *The Woman and the Lyre: Women Writers in Cl. Greece and Rome* (1989); R. Hamilton, *The Architecture of Hesiodic Poetry* (1989).

PROSODY: Wilamowitz; Koster; Maas; Dale; Halporn et al.; Snell; West. C.J.H.

II. MEDIEVAL. See BYZANTINE POETRY.

III. MODERN. After the fall of Constantinople to the Turks in 1453, and until the Gr. War of Independence (1821–28), poetry flourished mainly in Gr. lands under Venetian influence. The island of Crete was the most important center. In the 16th and first half of the 17th c. it gave birth to a poetry that, though depending on It. models, has a character of its own. The masterpiece of Cretan lit. is the *Erotokritos*, an epico-lyric poem of 10,000 rhyming 15-syllable political verses composed by Vitzentzos Kornaros. The story—the chivalrous love of Erotokritos for Aretousa and their union after long and arduous adventures—follows the Frankish romance *Paris et Vienne*, but at the same time, the influence of Ariosto and of the Cretan folk song is evident.

In the remainder of the Gr. world, then under Turkish rule, the only noteworthy poems composed were the folksongs. Their heyday was the 18th c., and many folk love songs, songs of travel, lullabies, and dirges are of a remarkable beauty and freshness, superior to any poetry in Gr. since the close of the 9th c. In the 18th c. we also find the first influence of Fr. lit. upon Gr. writing in the work of Athanasios Christopoulos and John Velaras, the two most important precursors of the poetry which followed the liberation of Greece.

The liberation, finally achieved in 1828, made Athens, the capital of the country, the center of all intellectual life. It was there that the Romantic School of Athens flourished, whose founder and leading spirit was Alexander Soutsos (1803–63). He was a fervent admirer of Victor Hugo and Byron, but his exuberant romantic and patriotic writings did not capture the spirit of their models. Though he is terse and vigorous as a satirist, the great influence he exercised upon Gr. p. was not always beneficial. The other main representatives of the Romantic School of Athens—Panagiotis Soutsos, Alexander Rizos Rangavis, George Zalokostas, Theodore Orphanidis, Elias Tantalidis, and John Karasoutsas—were all slaves of an exaggerated romanticism. They use a stilted and archaic form of Gr. (the *katharevousa*) and are painstakingly patriotic. Achilles Paraschos (1838–95) is the leading figure in the last period of the school. His contemporaries George Paraschos, Angelos Vlachos, Alexander Vyzantios, Demetrios Paparrhegopoulos, Spyridon Vasiliadis, and George Vizyenos were all overshadowed by his reputation, in spite of the greater sincerity and more delicate technique of many of their works.

The Romantic School of Athens with its rhetorical profuseness, hackneyed patriotism, and stilted, purist Gr. was superseded by the New School of Athens, which resulted from a fresh assessment of Gr. national values and the linguistic movement to introduce the spoken tongue (the *demotiki,* whence "demotic") into lit. The demotic had already been successfully used by the School of the Ionian Islands, of which the greatest representative was Dionysios Solomos (1798–1857). Like other members of the Ionian aristocracy of his day he was bilingual and, having received his education in Italy, wrote his first poems in It. His early works in Gr. were short lyrics, but the War of Independence stirred him to more ambitious projects. As the years passed, his philosophic approach to art and life deepened, coming to express itself in verses of unique delicacy and balance. His is a figure outstanding in the whole of European lit. because he finally succeeded in combining harmoniously the Classical and the romantic spirit. From the *Hymn to Liberty* (the first stanzas of which became the Gr. national anthem) to the *Free Besieged,* which sings of the heroic resistance of Missolonghi, we can trace the agony and artistic achievement of a highly spiritual nature. Unfortunately, however, most of his mature work exists as only partially completed texts. In the struggle that continued from the Byzantine era between the *katharevousa* and the *demotiki* as the lang. of lit., Solomos marks a turning point. By choosing the latter he pointed the way which all subsequent Gr. p. worthy of the name was to follow. Moreover, he introduced into Gr. a number of Western metrical forms (the sestina, the ottava, the terza rima) which freed Gr. p. from the monotony of the 15-syllable verse.

Of the other poets of the Ionian School, the most important are Andreas Calvos (1792–1869) and Aristotle Valaoritis (1824–39). Calvos drew heavily on the Gr. classics to write an austere and often moralizing poetry in forms that inspired several important 20th-c. poets, such as Elytis and Karouzos. Valaoritis, though over-romantic and grandiloquent, was greatly admired in his day and became the link between the Ionian School, the "Demotic Movement," and the New School of Athens.

About 1880, a young group of poets, influenced by the violent criticism of E. Rhoides, formed the New School of Athens. They aspired to become the Gr. *Parnassians,* masters of a restrained and objective art. The central figure was Kostis Palamas (1859–1943), a man of wide reading whose works blended not only the ancient and modern Gr. trads. but also the social and spiritual convulsions of the late 19th and early 20th cs. *The Dodecalogue of the Gypsy* is perhaps his central achievement. Its hero the Gypsy musician, a symbol of freedom and art, gradually deepens into the patriot, the Greek, and finally the "Hellene"—citizen and teacher of the world. This powerful epico-lyrical work, together with *The King's Flute,* an historical epic, and *Life Immovable,* the most important of his lyric collections, confirmed his influence on such contemporary poets as George Drosinis and John Polemis and on their successors: John Gryparis in his mastery of lang., Constantine Hatzopoulos in his sense of rhythm, Miltiadis Malakasis and Lambros Porfyras in their playful charm, and Costas Crystallis in his idyllic tone. It is the poets of this generation who also introduced symbolism and free verse into Gr. p., which greatly enriched and enlivened it in the 20th c. After Palamas the most important figure of his school is undoubtedly Angelos Sikelianos (1884–1952). In his powerful verse, Gr. nature and history are seen in the light of a Dionysiac mysticism. This, together with a rich, incisive diction that brings landscape, the human form, and abstract thought into clear-cut relief, has produced some of the most striking lyrical poetry in the 20th c.

However, an equally important Gr. poet who remained untouched by the influence of Palamas was C. P. Cavafy (1863–1933). An Alexandrian both by birth and sensibility, Cavafy's major achievement was the creation of a mythical world of diaspora Hellenism dominated by irony, hedonism, and a tragic vision that celebrates those who face disaster with an honest self-awareness. The myth he created, though smaller in scale, parallels the imaginative worlds fashioned by eminent Anglo-Am. contemporaries such as Yeats, Joyce, Pound, and Eliot, and, along with his acute treatment of eroticism, eventually established his reputation as the most original and gifted Gr. poet of this century. Nikos Kazantzakis (1885–1957), well-known as a novelist, was also the author of a formidable 33,333-line modern sequel to the *Odyssey* in which the Odyssean hero, haunted by the idea of nihilism, searches for a personal belief among the various modes of thought that his new journey explores and ends in nihilism.

More significant than the poetry of Kazantzakis is that of Kostas Varnalis (1884–1974) and Takis Papatsonis (1895–1976). The former, with a strong political voice, was recognized as the last important traditional poet of his day, while the latter, esp. innovative in technique during the 1920s, wrote mystic religious poetry. The modernist movement known as the Generation of the Thirties is the most accomplished group of poets to have emerged in Greece during this century. Two of this group, George Seferis (1900–71) and Odysseus Elytis (b. 1911), were awarded the Nobel Prize in Lit. Seferis brought into Gr. p. a style, method, and vision that have often been compared to those of T. S. Eliot, and though he has been perhaps as influential in changing the course of poetry in his country as Eliot was in the Anglo-Am. trad., Seferis offers an image of the modern predicament that is deeply rooted in his own experience, in the Gr. landscape, and in Gr. lit., from Homer and the Attic tragedians through the 17th-c. Cretan renaissance and the Demotic Movement of the 19th and 20th cs. His major contributions have lain in creating a poetic lang. that is rich in nuance while spare in decoration, and a dramatic mode that makes use of mythical figures provided with a modern psyche and a contemporary habitation. Elytis was among those who introduced Fr. surrealism into Gr. p., though even in his earliest work, characterized by the yoking together of disparate images and a sometimes flamboyant lyricism reminiscent of Dylan Thomas, he projects a personal mythology that celebrates the natural and human features of his homeland. His most mature work includes the intricately constructed *The Axion Esti,* an extended secular hymn that draws on the Gr. Orthodox liturgy and the 19th-c. demotic trad. to evoke the spiritual dimension of those elements in the world of the senses that the poet feels to be most worthy of praise.

Three other poets of the same generation, Andreas Embirikos (1901–75), Nikos Engonopoulos (b. 1910), and Nikos Gatsos (b. 1912), confirmed the importance of surrealism in modern Gr. p. Embirikos was the most ambitious of the three, his use of the mode at times serving a large structure and an apocalyptic vision. Yannis Ritsos (b. 1909) and Nikiforos Vretakos (b. 1911), of the same generation, were more overtly political. Ritsos, the most prolific of the group, succeeded over the years in creating a broad if stylistically sparse poetic landscape in which the old gods no longer survive and in which their dispossessed creatures, wounded and still threatened by the tragic civilization they have inherited, move cautiously through ruined cities and across arid plains. Ritsos remains the most influential Gr. poet after Cavafy and Seferis, with wide international recognition.

The group of poets known as the First Post-War Generation found their principal resource in the Second World War and the Civil War that followed. Takis Sinopoulos (1917–81), writing in the shadow of Seferis, provided in his best work the sharpest portrait of the realities of war, attempting at the same time to enrich his vision with mythic analogies. Manolis Anagostakis (b. 1925), the most down-to-earth of the group, offered the bleakest prospect—poems in which irony is the only release from a pervasive mood of defeat, of man undone by the evil in him, often manifest through corrupt politics. Miltos Sachtouris (b. 1919) and Nikos Karouzos (b. 1926), both work in a post-surrealist mode. Sachtouris projects a nightmare image of a world that appears to have survived the destruction of humanity. Karouzos, making use of a highly personal idiom that is sometimes obscure or cryptic, draws on the pre-Socratics for philosophical sustenance, as does D. P. Papaditsas (1922–87), another post-surrealist with an esp. strong talent for promoting parallels between contemporaneity and antiquity.

The younger poets who followed these, known as the Generation of the Seventies, turned in a new direction, much under the influence of the Beat Generation in America. In style they exploited the full riches of colloquial speech, incl. imported terms. In content they called into question most orthodox beliefs and challenged most established positions, esp. those reflecting a particular political commitments. Their intention was to show the world as they truly saw it, without illusions, and to exhibit that world in a lang. as contemporary as the drifting scene they depicted. For some, this approach appeared to undervalue the traditional possibilities of poetry; for others, it appeared to rejuvenate dying modes of expression and thought by introducing vitally new, if changing, resources. The fact is that poetry has flourished in Greece in recent years as it had not since the 1930s, esp. poetry written by women, and prospects continue to be good, if still unsettled, as to who now coming to maturity will dominate the next generation. The fact is also, and more significantly, that in the last hundred years better poetry has been written in Greece than during the fourteen preceding centuries, and the Gr. p. produced in the 20th c., from Cavafy to Ritsos and Elytis, has a distinction equal to the best that has come from Greece's European neighbors.

ANTHOLOGIES: *Anthologia 1708–1933,* ed. E. N. Apostolidis (n.d.); *Poetry of Mod. Greece,* tr. F. McFerson (1884); *Songs of Mod. Greece,* tr. G. F. Abbott (1900); *Mod. Gr. Poems,* tr. T. Stephanidis and G. Katsimbalis (1926); *Eklogae apo ta tragoudia tou Hellenikou Laou,* ed. N. Politis, 3d ed. (1932); *Med. and Mod. Gr. P.* (1951), *Penguin Book of Gr. Verse* (1984), both ed. C. A. Trypanis; *Mod. Gr. P.,* tr. K. Friar (1973); *Poitiki anthologia,* ed. L. Politis, 7 v. (1975–77); *Voices of Mod. Greece,* tr. E. Keeley and P. Sherrard (1981).

HISTORY AND CRITICISM: P. Sherrard, *The Marble Threshing Floor* (1956); A. Karantones, *Physiognomies* (1960), *Eisagoge ste neoteri poiese,* 4th ed. (1976); G. Seferis, *On the Gr. Style: Selected Essays in Poetry and Hellenism,* tr. R. Warner and T. D. Frangopoulos (1966); M. Vitti, *Storia della letterature neogreca* (1971), *I Genia tou Trianda: Ideologia kai Morphi* (1979); C. T. Dimaras, *A Hist. of Mod. Gr. Lit.,* tr. M. Gianos (1972); *Mod. Gr. P.,* ed. K. Friar (1973); L. Politis, *A Hist. of Mod. Gr. Lit.,* tr. R. Liddell, 2d ed. (1975); A. Argyriou, *Neoteri poites tou mesopolemou* (1979); R. Beaton, *Folk Poetry of Mod. Greece* (1980); Z. Lorenzatos, *The Lost Center and Other Essays in Gr. P.* (1980); Trypanis; E. Keeley, *Mod. Gr. P.: Voice and Myth* (1983); G. Jusdanis, *The Poetics of Cavafy* (1987); V. Lambropoulos, *Lit. as National Institution: Studies in the Politics of Mod. Gr. Crit.* (1988); D. Ricks, *The Shade of Homer* (1989).

C.A.T.; E.K.

GUATEMALAN POETRY. See SPANISH AMERICAN POETRY.

GUJARATI POETRY. See INDIAN POETRY.

GYPSY POETRY. The G. left India some 900 years ago and migrated to Europe and, later, other parts of the world. Although generally regarded as a nomadic people, large numbers have been sedentary for many generations. Their lang., Romani, a close relation of Hindi and Punjabi, is still spoken by the majority of ethnic G. and is the vehicle of a large oral lit., chiefly folksongs, ballads, and tales. Poetry as such has only developed in this century. But there is no standard literary lang., and so each dialect has a life of its own.

The lyric first flowered in the newly founded Soviet Union, where the lang. was fostered up to 1934, after which time the Soviet government discouraged its use. Aleksandr German and O. Pankova were the outstanding names among Rus. G. writers who followed the state policy of discouraging nomadism and encouraging farm and factory work.

The Gypsies in Europe suffered alongside the Jews under Nazi persecution—a period recorded in contemporary and postwar songs and poetry such as Papusza's "Tears of Blood." Since the end of the War, increased settlement and educational opportunity at first produced writers who used the lang. of the country where they lived. These include Sandra Jayat (France), Dezider Banga (Czechoslovakia), Slobodan Berberski (Yugoslavia), and Károly Bari and József Kóvacs (Hungary), together with many in the USSR. But Romani has also developed as a written lang., though with numerous dialects. The nomadic nature of Gypsy life in the past promoted the elements of entertainment, spontaneity, and imagination in story, tale, and song. Now, greater integration with the host communities has meant the adoption of new cultural styles. In lit. the point of departure today is poetry and drama.

On a much smaller scale than before, a revival in the USSR has produced Satkevič and Leksa Manush, the latter influenced by Rus. and Fr. poets. He takes the life of his people as his main theme but looks upon that life with cold nonromantic eyes:

> Twentieth Century, what could you
> give to the Romany people?
> Perhaps some of the bright sun, to
> light their dark life.
> Or wipe the rush of tears falling from
> the women's eyes
> Or lift their singing voices with a little
> melody.
> (tr. Gillian Taylor)

In Poland emerged Papusza (Bronislaw Wajs, b. ca. 1909), who wrote abundantly for three years from 1950 until pressure from the local community to conform to the traditional role of a G. woman made her lay down her pen for some years. In Yugoslavia, where radio and periodicals foster the lang., a circle of poets developed in Skopje and the new town of Shuto Orizari, alongside a flourishing theater in Romani. Nowadays, however, the lyric writers of Kosovia are better known. Characteristic of this school is the creation of neologisms from Romani roots, rather than using loan words from Serbo-Croatian or Albanian. From a score of writers who have departed from the traditional folksongs handed down from generation to generation (and akin to those which inspired Strauss and Bartok), I will mention only three names, Dževad Gaši (b. 1958), Iliaz Šabani, and Ismet Jašarević (b. 1951). The last, in his (rhymed) autobiographical poem "Te džanel thaarako ternipe" (So that tomorrow's youth will know) tells of his hard struggle against poverty and illness.

Two poets independent of the mainstream are Ivan Nikolić and Rajko Djurić. The latter, a journalist in Belgrade, deals with philosophical concerns, which has led to his being more appreciated by educated Romanies abroad and in tr. than by his own community. G. poets in Hungary have seen their work appear both in the short-lived magazine *Rom Som* and in anthologies. Čoli Daroczi (b. 1939) takes his inspiration from Brecht and the Hungarian József Attila, while Ervin Karsai is perhaps best known for his children's poems.

In Czechoslovakia the writers in Romani are often manual workers who have had little formal education. Worthy of mention are Bartolomyj Daniel (b. ca. 1931), Tera Fabiánová (b. 1930), František Demeter (b. ca. 1947), Elena Lacková (b. 1921; also a playwright), Vojtych Fabián (b. ca. 1944), and Ondrej Pešta (b. ca. 1922).

Vittorio Pasquale writes in the less used Sinti (Sindhi) dialect, and, together with Rasim Sejdić, has been published in Italy. There are other occasional poets—Mateo Maximoff, better known for his novels in Fr. and tr. of the Bible into Romani, Dimiter Golemanov, primarily a composer of songs, Rosa Taikon (Sweden), an artist in metal, and Ronald Lee (Canada), woodcarver and novelist. But the outstanding achievement of postwar Romani poetry is the full-length verse ballad "Tari thaj Zerfi" (Tari and Zerfi) by the Lovari-dialect writer Wladyslaw Jakowicz (b. 1915), recounting the story of two lovers. It has been published in Sweden with a glossary in the Kalderash dialect, making it accessible to a wider circle of Romani speakers. Romani poets, while hampered by the lack of a standard lang. and of a regular periodical lit., are at the same time part of the wider European trad. and vital instruments in the devel. of authentic G. culture.

ANTHOLOGIES: *Volksdichtungen der siebenbürgischen und südungarischen Zigeuner,* ed. and tr. H. Wlislocky (1890); *Csikóink kényesek* (1977); *Romské Písně* (1979); *Fekete Korall* (1981); *Jaga Vatre* (1984); *Tüzpiros Kígyócska,* ed. K. Bari (1985); *Romska Narodna Poezija* (1986).

JOURNALS: *Jour. of the G. Lore Society; Études Tsiganes; Lacio Drom.*

HISTORY AND CRITICISM: G. Black, *A G. Bibl.* (1914); *Leeds Univ. Romany Catalogue* (1962); J. Ficowski, *Ciganie na polskach drogach* (1965); M. Courthiade, "Jeunes poètes roms de Cassove," *Études Tsiganes* (1982–83); J.-P. Liégeois. *Gypsies: An Illus. Hist.* (1985). D.K.

H

HAITIAN POETRY. The poetry of Haiti has exhibited two divergent tendencies: an emulation of the styles and movements of France, and an intense nationalism or racial pride. A corollary to this latter trad. of commitment is the sensitivity of H. p. to the political climate of the country. The production of poetry and the criticism of poetry have through the years been fostered to a great extent by Haiti's many literary and cultural magazines. The beginning of H. lit. is considered to coincide with the origin of the independent H. state in 1804, in the wake of the Fr. Revolution. Indeed, the first poets considered themselves the perpetuators of the ideals of that Revolution. It is not surprising therefore that the Fr.-educated poets Antoine Dupré, Juste Chanlatte, and Jean-Baptiste Romane intoned hymns and odes—replete with periphrasis, personifications, and invocations to Liberty and Independence—while Jules Solime Milscent, founder of Haiti's first significant literary magazine, *L'Abeille Haïtienne* (1817), wrote fables after the manner of La Fontaine.

With France's recognition of sovereignty (1925), poets became less intent on justifying independence, and an enthusiastic interest in the romantic movement led to a poetic production at first resembling the work of Lamartine in the case of poets such as Coriolan Ardouin and Ignace Nau. But while retaining the style of the Fr. romantics, H. poets soon began to introduce more of the tropical landscape and local ambience into their work. From the start, H. romanticism was characterized by a strong patriotism, but the patriotic current comes into its own after 1860, when poets such as Tertulien Guilbaud, Massillon Coucou, and Vendenesse Ducasse, in reaction to the numerous European and Am. detractors of the Black Republic and as apologists for Haiti's border wars with Santo Domingo, sang of the exploits of the heroes of Independence and anguished over Haiti's political and economic problems. Oswald Durand epitomizes H. romanticism, his work typically extolling the charms of the H. peasant girl but also concerned with the fate of the nation.

As the 20th c. opened, several journals, such as *Haiti littéraire et scientifique, Haiti littéraire et social* (later, *Haiti littéraire et politique*), and esp. *La Ronde,* served as forums for debate and illustration of both older romantic and newer nationalist and eclectic tendencies. Side by side with poets such as Georges Sylvain, who sought to infuse local color and a sense of the H. world-view into his rendering of La Fontaine's fables into creole (*Cric?-Crac!*), others, such as Etzer Vilaire, claimed the right to draw from all traditions in the quest for universality, while continuing to subscribe to the romantic tradition. And Léon Laleau (b. 1892) for several decades wrote carefully crafted poems ranging from delicate romanticism to complex racial awareness.

During the years 1925–27, a new group of poets emerged. Writing in *La Nouvelle Ronde* (1925), *La Trouée* (1927), and esp. *La Revue indigène* (1927), Emile Roumer, Philippe Thoby-Marcelin, Jacques Roumain, Carl Brouard, and others reacted against the Am. Occupation (1915–34), against what they perceived as a shallow portrayal of H. mores in the previous literary generation, and against the stilted formality of patriotism among some of their elders, who were reacting in their own way to the Am. occupation. Indigenism, as the movement came to be called, reaffirmed H. values and proposed to reflect them in lit. Although the theoretical writings seek a H. aesthetic, the poetry itself, while it speaks of vodun drums, peasant women, and the H. landscape, reflects the European revolutions in form and style of the first decades of the century: free verse, direct lang., surrealism, and the primacy of the image. Jean Price-Mars' critical study, *Ainsi parla l'oncle* (*Thus Spoke the Uncle,* 1928) did much to encourage greater expression of the Af. continuity in H. culture. In the early 1930s, a "new wave" of writers, among them Carl Brouard of the original *Revue indigène* group, sought to implement Price-Mars' ideas. Between 1938 and 1940, they published the journal *Les Griots,* the title of which evokes the poet-historians of Africa.

The period of the late 1940s and early 1950s was one of opened horizons. Marxism, democratic fervor, some restructuring of social institutions at home, the war and Fascism abroad, and the Négritude movement all combined to enlarge the H. poet's awareness of the common human struggle for social betterment. During the same time, race-consciousness acquired a global character which it had largely lacked in the Af.-oriented work of the 1930s. Jean Brierre, one of Haiti's most prolific poets, writes "to the memory of the lynched of Georgia" in his poem "Me revoici, Harlem" (Here I am again, Harlem): "And our footsteps across centuries of misery / Strike the same death knell on the same path." Within the same humanitarian context, poets such as René Depestre called for a revolutionary new order, Félix Morisseau-Leroy continued to validate and interpret H. culture and the ordinary folk, while others perpetuated a romantic poetry sometimes showing the influence of the newer perspective. Women (who achieved the right to vote in the 1950s and gained greater access to education) also became more vocal as poets.

With the institution of a particularly cruel and repressive dictatorship under François Duvalier in 1957, poets were among those who found it necessary to flee or take prudent leave, sometimes after torture or imprisonment. Some, such as Dépestre, energetically condemned the deterioration of Africanism into a tool of oppression in the hands of Duvalier. The exiled poets profited from cultural enrichment in Africa and North America while continuing to write of the H. experience, often using poetry as a liberating device, as in Anthony Phelps' *Mon Pays Que Voici* (This, My Country):

> The Day will come . . .
> when the dust of the pariahs
> and the sweat of the homeless
> will be no more in the new dawn
> than images without reality
> . . . .
> But patience, my son
> Sleep my child Sleep.

As the exodus continued over the next decade, the existence of an expatriate population large enough to support journals such as *Nouvelle optique* (Montréal) and *Présence haïtienne* (New York) and to justify the publication of poetry outside Haiti led to a bifurcation of H. lit. Inside Haiti, by the early 1960s, poetry and the literary magazine had been seriously impaired by repression. Nevertheless, romantic poetry continued to be produced in quantity, and several poets, such as Jeanine Tavernier Louis, Jacqueline Beaugé, René Philoctète, Rassoul Labuchin, Franck Etienne (later Frankétienne) and Marie-Ange Jolicoeur wrote poetry of substance, in much of which a social vision is evident. After the death of Duvalier in 1971, his 18-year-old son, Jean-Claude, same to power. Although repression continued, writers began to test the younger Duvalier's resolve. Magazines began to reappear, notable among them *Le Petit Samedi Soir.*

While it remains true that most H. p. has been written in Fr. (and, until recently, by members of the upper classes), a trad. of poetry in the Fr.-based creole of Haiti has also long existed, the most notable examples being by Oswald Durand, Georges Sylvain, and Félix Morisseau-Leroy. The practice of creole poetry gained ground in the 1970s and 1980s, its production swelled by younger voices such as Georges Castera Fils, Rudolph Müller, and Pierre-Richard Narcisse. Literary creole is not confined to verse, however; it has made a particular impact in the popular theater movement, in which many of the poets have participated. Creole has certainly not supplanted Fr., but it seems more and more to be viewed as a lang. capable of artistic expression.

In the years leading to the exile of Jean-Claude Duvalier in 1986, the liberating influence of poetry as a demystification (and esp. that written in creole because of its direct accessibility to the masses) was more and more exploited. Pierre-Richard Narcisse's *Dey ak lespwa* (Mourning and Hope) can serve as example: "My sun is cut into two pieces. / One for us, one for them." In the ensuing process of democratization, a freedom of expression hitherto largely unknown in H. letters came to exist, in which participated both returning exiles and those still overseas. H. p. continues to be directly related to the uncertain socio-political climate.

ANTHOLOGIES: *Anthologie d'un siècle de poésie haïtienne (1817–1925),* ed. L. Morpeau (1926); *Panorama de la poésie haïtienne,* ed. C. Saint-Louis and M. Lubin (1950); *Poésie vivante d'haiti,* ed. S. Baridon and R. Philoctète (1978).

HISTORY AND CRITICISM: D. Vaval, *Histoire de la littérature haïtienne* (1933); G. Gouraige, *Histoire de la littérature haïtienne* (1960); N. Garrett, *The Ren. of H. P.* (1963); R. Berrou and P. Pompilus, *Histoire de la littérature haïtienne,* 2d ed., v. 1-3 (1975–77); D. Herdeck, et al., *Caribbean Writers: A Bio-Bibl.-Crit. Encyclopedia* (1979). C.F.

HAUSA POETRY. In the H. lang. as spoken in Nigeria, Niger, and parts of Ghana, the single term *waka* is applied to two closely related trads., song and the writing of poetry (verse). In Nigeria, H. poets and scholars have defined the one in terms of its difference from the other. Popular song and courtly praise-singing are oral, professional, and instrumentally accompanied, displaying complex interaction between lead-singer(s) and chorus. Poetry, on the other hand, is chanted without accompaniment, and reward for performance is not usually sought; poems are composed in Roman or in *ajami* (Ar.) script and often circulate in ms. or in printed form. Song displays rhythmic regularity deriving from the drum or other instruments; poetry can be scanned according to metrical patterns of heavy and light syllables that correspond to a number of Cl. Ar. meters. In song, the words of the lead-singer are interrupted by the refrains or repetition of the *amshi* (chorus); this may occasion considerable variation in the length of "verses" between choruses. Commonly, H. p. in couplets displays end rhyme, and in 5-line stanzas end rhyme in the final line is supplemented by internal rhyme in the first four lines. It has been shown that in some cases tonal rhyme can accompany syllable rhyme.

Of the Cl. Ar. meters, nine are found in H. p. (in descending order of frequency): *kāmil, mutadārik, mutaqārib, rajaz, basīṭ, wāfir, khafīf, ramal,* and *ṭawīl.* Claims for other meters require very liberal interp. of the meter to fit the poem. The suitability of Ar. prosody as a model for the description of rhythmic regularity in H. p. has come under question both from H. scholars, who argue that rhythmic patterns have often been taken directly from song, and from other scholars who have approached the performance of H. p. using a "beat and measure" system developed in unpublished work by A. V. King on the analysis of song. The "beat and measure" system, as opposed to the "syllable and feet" system, incorporates interlinear pauses, accounts for anomalous characteristics of H. poetic rhythms, and explains the systematic use of deviations not provided for in the Cl. Ar. system (see Schuh 1988).

Modern poetry in Roman script (1903 to date) developed from the trad. of Islamic religious verse in H. *ajami* of the 19th c. Since at least the time of the Islamic *jihād* (holy war) of Shehu Usman ɗan Fodio (1804), the propagation of the faith has involved the writing of H. p. that circulated both in ms. form and, among the common people, through the performances of religious mendicants, often blind. Such poetry fell broadly into the categories of theology, praise of the Prophet, biography of the Prophet and his companions, admonition and exhortation, religious obligations, law, and astrology. While strictly religious poetry continues to be written, particularly within the brotherhood organizations, the 20th c. has seen a great broadening in themes, now covering such diverse subjects as Western education, hygiene, the evils of drink, filial piety, Nigerian geography, and many topical subjects such as the population census and the introduction of new currency. Poetry writing along with song has been an important part of the political process during the 1950s with the approach of independence (1960) and the rise of political parties in Northern Nigeria, during the civilian political eras of the early 1960s and 1980s, and during the Civil War (1967–70). To a considerable extent H. p. retains, as its most prominent characteristics, a didacticism and a concern for social issues inherited from Islamic trad. Personal lyrical expression has traditionally been restricted to the category of *madahu* (praise of the Prophet), where the lang. of deep personal devotion, longing, and desire was both legitimate and appropriate. Recently, however, love poetry, which in the past had been private, has entered the public arena through the publication of an anthology, *Dausayin Soyayya.*

Modern H. p. has been published regularly in the newspaper *Gaskiya ta fi Kwabo* (founded 1939), and prominent poets such as Aƙilu Aliyu, Mudi Sipikin, Na'ibi Wali, Salihu Kwantagora, and others have reached a wider audience by being broadcast over the radio stations of the northern states of Nigeria. Poetry-writing circles have been formed and have also had access to radio. While the majority of poets have been men, women such as Hauwa Gwaram and Alhajiya 'Yar Shehu have written on contemp. social and religious issues, following in the footsteps of the poet and translator Nana Asma'u, daughter of Shehu Usman ɗan Fodio, leader of the *jihād* of 1804, and scholar in her own right.

ANTHOLOGIES: *Wakokin Mu'azu Hadejia* (1955); *Wakokin H.* [H. P.] (1957); *Wakokin Sa'adu Zungur* (1966); Mudi Sipikin, *Tsofaffin Wakoki da Sababbin Wakoki* [Old and New Poems] (1971); *Wakokin Hikima* [Poems of Wisdom] (1975); Akilu Aliyu, *Fasaha Akiliya* [The Skill of Akilu] (1976); *Zababbun Wakokin da da na yanzu* [Selected Poems of Yesterday and Today] (1979); *Dausayin Soyayya* [The Mellowness of Mutual Love] (1982).

HISTORY AND CRITICISM: J. H. Greenberg, "H. Verse Prosody," *JAOS* 69 (1949); D. W. Arnott, "The Song of the Rains," *AfrLS* 9 (1969); M. K. M. Galadanci, "The Poetic Marriage between Arabic and H.," *Harsunan Nijeriya* 5 (1975); M. Hiskett, *A Hist. of H. Islamic Verse* (1975); S. Baldi, *Systematic H. Bibl.* (1977); D. Muhammad, "Interaction Between the Oral and the Literate Trads. of H. P.," *Harsunan Nijeriya* 9 (1979), "Tonal Rhyme: A Preliminary Study," *AfrLS* 17 (1980); R. G. Schuh, "Préalable to a Theory of H. Poetic Meter," and N. Awde, "A H. Lang. and Ling. Bibl.," both in *Studies in H. Lang. and Linguistics*, ed. G. L. Furniss and P. J. Jaggar (1988)—bibl. esp. valuable for citation of unpub. dissertations on H. G.F.

HEBREW POETRY.

- I. BIBLICAL AND MEDIEVAL
  - A. *Biblical Poetry* (1150 B.C.–150 B.C.)
  - B. *Extra-Canonical Works*
  - C. *The Mishnaic and Talmudic Period* (CA. 100 B.C.–500 A.D.)
  - D. *The Byzantine Period* (500–800 A.D.)
  - E. *Moslem Spain* (10TH–12TH C.)
  - F. *Christian Spain* (1200–1492)
  - G. *Italian*
- II. MODERN
  - A. *The European Period* (1781–1920)
  - B. *Palestinian Poetry* (1920–48)
  - C. *Israeli Poets* (1948–87)

Heb. lit. spans three millennia and ranks among the world's oldest. Heb. p. began to appear at least by the 11th c. B.C. and is still being written today. Whatever gaps disrupted this almost continual literary flow are attributable more to the loss of linking texts than to so-called "dry periods" of creativity. At times, Heb. poets were not aware of their entire literary heritage, but most often they did have both a diachronic and synchronic knowledge of at least parts of it.

In every age, incl. our own, the Heb. Bible constituted the foundation and principal component of that heritage, a major source for literary forms, symbols, rhetorical tropes, syntactic structures, and vocabulary. There has been, however, no uniformity in metrical systems: these have varied from age to age and, following the biblical period, were usually adapted from those employed in the area where the Heb. poet happened to reside (see ARABIC POETRY; JUDEO-SPANISH POETRY). In the Persian period (5th–4th cs. B.C.), Aramaic began to replace Heb. as the vernacular in Palestine, continuing as the spoken lang. long into the Byzantine period (4th–7th cs. A.D.), while Gr. prevailed in the Mediterranean diaspora. With the rise of Islam in the 7th c., Arabic became the *lingua franca* for Jews of the Middle East, North Africa, and Spain. In Christian Europe the various IE langs. were adopted. From the Middle Ages until the early 20th c., Yiddish was the vernacular used by the majority of European Jewry as the centers of Jewish population shifted to Central and Eastern Europe (see YIDDISH POETRY). The interplay of these non-Hebraic langs. and lits. with Heb., the literary lang. of the Jews, broadened and altered Heb. p., affecting its syntax, vocabulary, themes, and genres.

The scope and variety of these phenomena make it as difficult to formulate a single comprehensive definition of Heb. p. as it is to formulate one that would be valid for world poetry. Still, the definition of poetry proposed by Barbara Herrnstein Smith is sufficient to accommodate the entire gamut of Heb. p.: "As soon as we perceive that a verbal sequence has a sustained rhythm, that it is formally structured according to a continuously operating principle of organization . . . we are in the presence of poetry and we respond to it accordingly, expecting certain effects from it and not others."

I. BIBLICAL AND MEDIEVAL. A. *Biblical Poetry* (1150 B.C.–150 B.C.). The Heb. Bible (or *Old Testament*) is an anthol. of sacred texts composed over the span of at least a thousand years. While modern biblical scholars have attempted to date its separate components with reasonable conjectures, no absolute date can be ascribed to the works forming the present canon. There has been a general consensus that the most salient feature of Heb. biblical p. is that which had been already perceived by med. scholars and formulated by Bishop Lowth in 1753 as *parallelismus membrorum*, or the parallelism of cola. The poetic line is usually composed of two cola (sequences of syllables, i.e. phrases or clauses)—sometimes three or four—which are parallel to each other either completely or partially in lexis or syntax. The words of the second colon repeat in different words the meaning of the first (*synonymous parallelism*); reverse, negate, or contradict its meaning (*antithetical parallelism*); or modify it (*synthetical parallelism*). Subsequent generations of scholars have added other categories to Lowth's list. Benjamin Hrushovski best summarizes the possibilities: "It may be a parallelism of semantic, syntactic, prosodic, morphological, or sound elements, or of a combination of such elements" (*Encyc. Judaica* 13.1200). James Kugel has argued that the basic function of the parallel colon or cola is sequential: "B (i.e. the second colon) by being connected to A (i.e. the first colon), carrying it further, echoing it, defining it, restating it, contrasting with it—*it does not matter which*—has an emphatic 'seconding' character, and it is this, more than any aesthetic of symmetry or paralleling, which is at the heart of biblical parallelism" (51). Indeed, the function of the subsequent parallel colon or cola is not merely to reiterate the contents of the first synonymously or antithetically in different words, but frequently to enhance or intensify the first statement.

Following the Rus. Formalist Victor Shklovsky, Robert Alter (*Art* 10) asserts that the principle of disharmony in an harmonious context is important in parallelism: "The general purpose of parallelism like the general purpose of imagery is to transfer the usual perception of an object into a sphere of new perception, that is, to make a unique semantic modification."

Kugel maintains that the use of parallelism in biblical prose passages precludes our identifying it as the major feature of biblical poetry, leading him to deny the very existence of biblical poetry, a rather specious contention. Like most other literary devices, parallelism can be used in prose as well as verse. What distinguishes its use in biblical poetry is that it becomes the constitutive device, whereas in prose it is "subordinate to the referential (or other) function" (Waugh 68). Adele Berlin has described the "elevated style" of biblical poetry as "largely the product of two elements: terseness and parallelism. It is not parallelism *per se* but the predominance of parallelism, combined with terseness, which marks the poetic expression of the Bible" (5).

There is, however, a more strictly prosodic element in biblical poetry, namely stress. While all attempts (e.g. Sievers') to "rediscover" a numerically fixed metrical system which might underlie the biblical text have so far proven futile, any sensitive reader of the Heb. original or even its better translations cannot fail to discern cadences. Hrushovski sees in these cadences "basic units" which are "not equal," but "almost never consist of one or more than four stresses," giving as a result "simple groups of two, three or four stresses" (in Sebeok, 189).

Stress, then, reinforces the parallelistic structure. Hrushovski again: "the basis of this type of rhythm may be described as semantic-syntactic-accentuation. It is basically free rhythm, i.e. a rhythm based on a cluster of changing principles. Its freedom is clearly confined within the limits of its poetics" (*ibid.*). While the number of stresses in each colon often varies, the numbers within a larger span are often equal or similar: "The condensed, laconic nature of biblical Heb. also contributes to the prominence of each word within the line . . . the rhythm of major stresses is so strong that sometimes it may be the only support of the parallelism of two verses" (*Encyc. Judaica*, 13.1201–2).

Rhyme is occasionally employed in biblical poetry (Prov. 5:9–10), but consistent or fixed rhyme schemes are unknown in the Bible. Alliteration is a common technique: "ʾal tirʾúni *sh*eʾaní *sh*eḥarḥóre / *sh*esh*sh*ezaftani ha*sh*eme*sh*" (Song of Songs 1:6). The stressed pun frequently has an emphatic or contrastive effect: "He hoped for justice [mishpat] and beheld injustice [mispaḥ; literally, a leprous growth] / for equity [ẓədaqah] and beheld inequity" [zəʿaqah; literally, a cry of anguish] (Isa. 5:7).

Biblical poetry is replete with sophisticated tropes of every variety, incl. metaphor, simile, synecdoche, and metonymy. Psalms contains several hymns in the form of acrostics (Ps. 4, 145; Ps. 119 is an eight-fold acrostic) and several refrains (Ps. 42, 103–4, 108); Ps. 136 was probably sung antiphonally. Other techniques such as anaphora and paronomasia abound.

The Pentateuch and the Former Prophets are essentially prose works but contain the oldest strata of biblical poetry. Three types are used. (1) The short occasional poem is of very ancient provenance ("The Song of Lemekh" [Gen. 4:23], "The Song of the Well" [Num. 21:17–18], and Miriam's "Song at the Red Sea" [Exod. 15:21]—the latter may have served as the core around which Moses' "Song of Victory" [Exod. 15:1–18] was later composed). (2) A second type are the larger hymns or odes such as Moses' "Song" and "Deborah's Song" (Judg. 5), designated as *shirah* ("song," "long poem" [?]); Balaam's oracles (Num. 23:7–10, 18–25; 24:3–9, 15–24); and the song celebrating the victory over Moab (Num. 21:27–30)—this latter is designated as *mashal* (an imprecise term applied either to a poetic oration rich in allegory or metaphor [Num. 24:15 ff., for example] or later to an aphorism [much of the book of Proverbs]). (3) A third type are the early poems of blessing (Gen. 27:27–29, 39–40). These seem to mark a transition from the first type to the larger and perhaps later blessing-poems at the end of Genesis and Deuteronomy. The larger poems are sometimes called *shirah* in contrast to *shir*, but these terms are not precise: at least one shorter poem is labeled a *shirah*.

In the Former Prophets two new genres occur: David's elegy (*qinah*) over the death of Saul and Jonathan (2 Sam. 2:19–27) and Hannah's prayer (1 Sam. 2:1–10).

Few distinct poems appear in the Literary Prophets. Isa. 5:1–7 is labeled as *shirah* but follows the cadences of a prophetic peroration rather than the earlier *shirot* and *shirim*. Indeed, the peroration and oracle are the prevailing genres in these works. They employ parallelism, stresses, and other poetic conventions and are therefore sometimes defined as poetry.

It is clear that the ancient Heb. poets developed a more subtle and flexible versification and style than was elsewhere known in the ancient Near East. Nevertheless, the fundamental features of biblical poetry display a high degree of continuity with the poetry of second-millennium B.C. Canaan. Clay tablets unearthed at the Syrian coastal town of Ras Shamra beginning in 1928 reveal some of the epic and mythological poetry of the north Canaanite port of Ugarit. In a lang. closely akin to ancient Heb., three major epics and other texts employ a rather strict parallelism and a large number of Homeric-like formulae and word-pairs. Scores of the latter, such as "earth" / "dust," "head" / "pate," and "hand" / "right hand," are cognate to the same parallel usages in biblical poetry. A unique pattern known as "staircase parallelism" suggests a direct literary link between early Canaanite and biblical poetry. Ps. 92:10 ("Here, your enemies, O Lord, Here, your enemies shall perish, All doers of iniquity shall be scattered") would seem to be a demythologized variant of the following "staircase" from the Ugaritic Epic of Baal: "Here, your enemy, O Baal, Here your enemy you strike, Here you smite your adversary." However, one remarkable difference in function between Ugaritic (Canaanite) poetry and biblical poetry is that in the former, verse is used for all extant narratives, while in the latter verse never narrates at length, prose being used for that purpose.

Biblical poetry reaches its greatest sophistication in the Hagiographa (The Later Writings). The 19th-c. view that these works were all post-exilic (i.e. after 586 B.C.) is now generally rejected. Poems in the *Hagiographa* fall into five categories: (1) the epithalamia (wedding poems) of the Song of Songs (probably all pre-exilic); (2) the hymns, personal prayers, and liturgical poems of Psalms; (3) the profound religious poems which make up the book of Job; (4) the dirges composed in commemoration of the destruction of Jerusalem in Lamentations; and (5) the aphorisms called *meshalim* in Proverbs and Ecclesiastes (here differing from the earlier usage).

The poems of the Song of Songs are highly erotic and rich in passionate imagery. Probably we will never know whether they are fragments of ancient cultic hymns or simply a compendium of nuptial songs.

The Psalter towers above any anthol. of religious poetry and makes up the very core of the liturgies of church and synagogue. Scholars have divided the Psalms into various genres either by attempting to define the technical terms in their superscriptions (these are probably later than the texts themselves and may have indicated instruments or some mode or melody to which a specific Psalm was chanted) or by classifying them according to structure or content. Classification according to content has been the more successful. Gunkel's (1967), while at times forced, is useful: hymns, songs of God's enthronement, national dirges, royal psalms, lamentations, prayers or songs of thanksgiving by individuals, pilgrims' songs, victory odes, national songs of thanksgiving, songs in praise of the Torah, wisdom psalms, antiphonal psalms, and liturgies.

Lamentations, traditionally (but dubiously) attributed to Jeremiah, and certain Psalms (e.g. 137) mourn the destruction of Jerusalem and are central in the liturgy for *Tishʿah Beʾav*, the fast day commemorating the destruction of both Temples.

Robert Pfeiffer (687) speaks of the author of Job as possessing "at the same time great poetic genius and incredible erudition. His command of lang. and powers of expression are unmatched at his time; he used the greatest vocabulary of any Heb. writer." The most sublime poems in Job appear in the closing chapters of the book (28–31, 38–42).

Proverbs and Ecclesiastes form what later scholars call wisdom lit. Although they are mainly epigrammatic in structure, they contain several poems (e.g. Prov. 5 with its description of the temptress, or the paean celebrating the good wife in Prov. 31:11–31). Ecclesiastes is a masterpiece of stoic rumination. Of particular poetic intensity are the opening chapters and the devastating poem on aging with which the book closes.

B. *Extra-Canonical Works* (i.e. works not included in the Heb. biblical canon). The book of Sirach (the sole Apocryphal work even partially preserved in the Heb. original) and the Dead Sea Scrolls discovered in 1947–48 indicate that poetic activity did not cease after the canonization of the Heb. Bible in the 2d c. B.C. Most scholars ascribe the Apocryphal works to the 2d or 1st cs. B.C., and their poetry is akin to that found in the wisdom lit. The author of Sirach at times displays a remarkable fluency and originality, as when he describes the High Priest's entry into the Holy of Holies on Yom Kippur:

How glorious (he was) when he
emerged from the Sanctuary
And stepped out from inside the curtain;
Like a star shining through thick
clouds,
Like a full moon on feast days,
Like the sun combing the King's palace,
Like a rainbow seen in the cloud,
Like a lily by a flowing stream,
Like a flower of Lebanon on a summer's day
Like the fire of frankincense upon the
offering.

(50:5–9)

C. *The Mishnaic and Talmudic Period* (Roman-Byzantine, ca. 100 B.C.–500 A.D.). The lit. which has survived from the Mishnaic-Talmudic era is primarily legal or homiletic, but it contains several occasional poems celebrating important events in life: births, circumcisions, marriages, and epitaphs. These were not preserved for their aesthetic quality but because they honored important scholars. Stylistically, they mark a break with the biblical trad. Instead of parallelism, many use a four-colon line. The poems are not laced with biblical quotations, their vocabulary is a mixture of biblical and post-biblical words and their syntax is late Heb.

D. *The Piyyut* (500–800 A.D.). The Byzantine period witnessed the efflorescence of the *piyyut* (Gr. *poētēs*), a liturgical poem of a new type. Some scholars believe that it developed as a device to circumvent a decree by the emperor Justinian which forbade *deuterosis*, i.e. the teaching of the oral or Talmudic law as opposed to that in the Pentateuch. The *Hazanim* (Precentors), it is claimed, interlaced the liturgy of the synagogue with didactic hymns which expounded the prohibited teaching. Since the early *piyyut* antedates Justinian's decree, however, it is more likely that it evolved as an art form at first having the purpose of lending variety to the service and, after the liturgy was permanently fixed, simply of enriching the standardized ritual. The early authors are unknown. Unlike the *piyyutim* of the classical period, theirs were unrhymed; like the Talmudic poem, they employed word-stress and avoided parallelism. Some hymns were built around a single or multiple acrostic or reversed acrostic. Other techniques used were anadiplosis, the refrain, the repetition of a key word at the end of a colon or a stanza, and the introduction or closing of a poem with a biblical verse related to its subject.

Yose ben Yose is the first *paytan* whose name is known to us. He heads a line of major synagogue poets who wrote in Palestine between the 6th c. and the Moslem conquest of Jerusalem in 636 A.D., the more famous among them being Yannai, Simeon ben Megas, Eliezer ben Kallir, Haduta ben Abraham, Joshua ha-Kohen and Joseph ben Nisan. During the 6th c. the various *piyyut* forms became standardized and were usually inserted into key sections of the liturgy. The earliest types were the *kerovah*, which was linked to the ᶜAmidah, and the *yotzer*, linked to the *Shemaᶜ* sections of the Heb. liturgy. These varied on Sabbaths and holidays. As this lit. grew, subsections were given specific names. *Piyyutim* were also composed for festivals and fast days. An early type was the *ᶜAvodah* describing the ritual at the Temple of Jerusalem on the Day of Atonement.

While the preclassical *piyyut* confined itself to a simple style, the classical *piyyut* is almost baroque, its lang. flowery and its diction involved, favoring intricate poetic structures. Poets succeeding Yose ben Yose introduced strict rhyme schemes (fixed rhyming seems to have been introduced by either the *Paytanim* or Syrian Christian poets). In addition to the earlier acrostic forms, some classical *paytanim* signed their poems with a nominal acrostic. They were daring coiners of new words, which they constructed by assuming that Heb. was based on biliteral roots. A common poetic device was the learned allusion. Isaac, for example, is referred to as the *haᶜaqud* (the bound one). Such allusions can become very elaborate and are part of the aspect of "puzzlement" which pervades this lit.

The *piyyut* form spread to the diaspora communities of Moslem Iraq (Saadiah Gaon and his school, 11th c.), North Africa, Byzantine South Italy, and, finally, to Germany, where *paytanim* like the Qalonymos family enriched the ritual of the

Ger. Jewish (*Ashkenazi*) trad.

E. *Moslem Spain* (10th–12th c.). The establishment of the Caliphate in Spain in the 10th c. led to the rise of the highly cultivated *Sephardic* (Sp. Jewish) trad. (see JUDEO-SPANISH POETRY). For the first time since the biblical era, secular Heb. p. reappears alongside the continuing trad. of religious verse. Although we can only surmise that the *paytanim* in Byzantine Palestine were influenced by Syriac and perhaps Gr. church poetry, it is patently clear that Sp. Heb. p. was the product of an extraordinary synthesis of Jewish and Ar. culture.

The poets of the Sp. Heb. "Golden Age" were frequently court poets maintained by Spain's Jewish aristocracy who, like their Moslem counterparts, took great pride in their patronage of the arts. We know that Ḥasdai ibn Shaprut, the Jewish advisor of the Caliph ʿAbd'ul Raḥman III of Cordova (mid 10th c.) maintained a coterie of Heb. poets at his court. Foremost among them was Dunash ben Labrat, who, like many Jewish intellectuals of his day, had migrated to Spain from Iraq. Dunash adapted the Ar. quantitative meter to the needs of Sp. Heb. p., whence it became the standard for subsequent verse. But it was not just the new metric forms which were borrowed from the Arabs: Heb. poets also adopted the rules of composition fixed by the Arab rhetoricians, their rhyme patterns, and their themes. They also favored the local Sp. popular poem, the *muwashshaḥ*. Only when they wrote sacred poetry did they sometimes adhere to the *piyyut* model. More often than not, they employed the Ar. structures and techniques even in the synagogue ritual. In terms of their Heb. diction, they eschewed the cavalier way by which the *paytanim* constructed words and phrases, considering these to be barbarisms.

If the Ar. rhetoricians had insisted that the lang. of the Qurʾān was the epitome of good writing, their Heb. counterparts adhered to the biblical models, though on rare occasions they allowed themselves to draw their vocabulary from Talmudic sources. Because Heb. and Ar. were both Semitic langs., they infused Heb. words with an Ar. connotation at times.

Secular poetry was written either by poets maintained by patrons or by scholarly members of the Jewish aristocracy. One of the most common genres was the Ar. ode, the *qaṣīda*, which soon became the vehicle for occasional poems written to celebrate an important event or to praise a patron. Such poems would begin in a purely lyrical vein, describing the beauties of nature, a drinking party, or a meeting of friends, or would develop a philosophical meditation; the poet would then shift into a laudatory mode praising a patron or colleague.

The most common form of poetic line was divided into two cola. Both cola of the first line rhymed and then the same rhyme was used throughout the poem to link the end words of the second cola, i.e.

—a —a /
—b —a /
—c —a /, etc.

The poem could be of any length. Another type of poem was the stanzaic *muwashshaḥ*: each stanza was in monorhyme, the rhyme sound changing from stanza to stanza; in addition, each stanza concluded with a couplet of a new rhyme held constant throughout the poem, e.g. *aaabb cccbb*, etc. The last couplet of the poem was often written in either Ar. or Old Sp. and rhymed with the other Heb. couplets. These signatures were frequently drawn from popular song. Many other forms existed, particularly the *rubaiyat* ("quatrain"), used for love poetry, wine songs, and epigrams. Hundreds of poems from this period have been preserved.

Samuel ibn Nagrela (Hannagid, 9th–10th cs.) was a typical aristocratic poet. He was a statesman and soldier who served as prime minister of the small state of Granada. He is the author of almost every type of secular poem: wine and love songs, encomia, epigrams, dirges. Because of his military career, he wrote a great deal of war poetry, a feat never repeated by any other Jewish poet. While Samuel employed all the conventions of Ar. poetry, he often invented highly original figures of speech.

He was followed by Solomon ibn Gabirol (11th c.), a philosopher and highly gifted poet. If Samuel's personal poetry reflected the dangerous world of the soldier, ibn Gabirol's poems retold the struggle of a sickly young poet against his fate, and of his anger against the Philistines who failed to recognize his genius. Many of Gabirol's religious works give expression to his Neoplatonic philosophy. In his long poem *Keter Malkhut* (The Kingly Crown), he contrasts the glory of God the Creator with the tragic helplessness of man.

Moses ibn Ezra (11th–12th cs.) was the scion of an aristocratic family of Granada who lived to see the decline of his native city and the destruction of its affluent Jewish community. More than any other Heb. poet, ibn Ezra is an Arabophile. His work on Heb. rhet. is full of praise for the poetic genius of the Arabs. Yet he remained faithful to his own trad. Many of his religious poems form a part of the synagogue ritual, earning him the appellation of the *Sallaḥ*, the author of penitential poetry.

The greatest Heb. poet of the period was Judah Halevi (11th–12th cs.). Like Gabirol he was both philosopher and poet. Utilizing the conventions of both Heb. and Ar. poetry, he infused them with new meaning and demonstrated a linguistic agility unrivaled in postbiblical Heb. lit. Halevi also introduced two new genres: his *Zionides*, which sing of his personal longing for Zion, and his sea poems describing his voyage to Egypt from which he hoped to complete his pilgrimage to Palestine.

Sp. poets were medieval men. If their poetry was often highly sensuous and celebrated the pleasures of the flesh, at other times it reflected the somber religiosity and deep sense of sin which also permeated medieval culture. Their religious poetry indicates that they were aware of *paytanic* poetry even if they broke with its prescriptions.

Their philosophical training also led them to question the obsession of the *paytanim* with formal constructions and their paucity of original thought. Aware that they were composing poems for their community at large, the Sp. poets usually avoided complex philosophical ideas in their synagogue verse, but their religiosity is much more meditative than that of the *paytanim*. Moreover, as Kabbalah mysticism spread through Spain beginning in the 11th c., the Sp. poets introduced its early symbols and ideas into their verse.

F. *Christian Spain* (1200–1492). With the decline of Granada in the 11th c., the Golden period of Sp. Jewry ends. The centers of Jewish population shift to Christian Spain, whose monarchs unremittingly gnawed away at Moslem Andalusia. By the 15th c. the *Reconquista* was complete, and both Moslem and Jewish communities were liquidated either by exile or forced conversion.

Heb. p. in Christian Spain in the three centuries which preceded the Expulsion never equaled the quality of that attained in Moslem Andalusia. Here too a class of Jewish " nobles" served as the patrons of Heb. lit. However, class tensions often led poets to pen social satires against the powerful. Moreover, Heb. p. underwent a process of popularization, reaching a broader audience than it did in Andalusia. While the Ar. influence remained paramount, it was now transmitted through Heb. sources, since an increasing number of Jews no longer spoke Ar. The very process of translation led to a broadening of the Heb. vocabulary to include postbiblical forms and syntax. A new synthesis occurred between the Andalusian trad., which served as a formal and stylistic model, and the new Christian literary influences: troubadour and epic poetry, beast epics, allegories, and *chansons de geste* (see Pagis 1976).

The Heb. writers of Christian Spain adopted an Ar. literary form, the *maqamah*. Written mainly in rhymeprose, the *maqamah* was a picaresque compendium which contained stories, aphorisms, essays, and poems. It takes as its frame-story a dialogue between a roguish wandering scholar and his foil. The ablest of several authors of the *Maqamoth* was Judah Alharizi (12th–13th cs.).

The most important Heb. poet of 12th-c. Christian Spain was Abraham Ibn Ezra (1092–1167), a philosopher, biblical commentator, and impoverished poet, trained in the Andalusian trad., who wandered through Spain and Italy and even reached England. His poetry already manifested the peculiarities that would soon be the hallmarks of the new cultural environment: sardonic humor, realistic self-deprecation, satire, and animal allegories. His long poem *Hai ben Meqits* adopts the frame-story of a journey to the outer universe under the guidance of a mysterious mentor, a genre prevalent in the Middle East and which first appears in the Apocrypha (*Enoch*, for example). In the allegory the author (the soul) leaves his birthplace (the domicile of souls) and meets a mysterious old man (Active Intellect) who warns him against his three evil companions (Imagination, Lust, and Anger). In other poems, ibn Ezra demonstrates a penchant for realistic detail. He laments his dire poverty and his wanderings; he writes satires about his torn cloak and swarms of flies that torment him. He is the author of a charming poem about the game of chess.

Other important poets in Christian Spain were Meshullam da Piera (1st half of the 12th c.), whose poems are written in a medley of biblical, Rabbinic, and Med. Heb. styles, and Todros ben Abulafia (late 13th c.), who introduced motifs drawn from life in Christian Spain and composed a panegyric for King Alfonso X in the form of a troubadour *cançion*, using rhyme patterns hitherto unknown in Heb. p.

G. *Italian*. The It. Jewish community was established in Roman times. Although it was small in numbers, it was highly cultured and, until the 19th c., made important contributions to the corpus of Heb. p. The first It. poet known to us is Solomon of Verona (9th c.), who wrote *piyyutim* in the style of the Palestinian school which had dominated It. Heb. p. until the 12th c. Among Italy's leading *paytanim* were Shephatiah ben Amitai (d. 886) and Amitai ben Shephatiah (9th c.) of the Ahima'ats family, and also Meshullam ben Qalonymos (10th c.).

Between the 12th and 15th cs. the influence of Sp.-Heb. p.—its meter, subject matter, and structures—prevailed, but vernacular It. forms were gradually introduced, esp. the sonnet in the 14th and *terza rima* in the 15th c. The leading poets of this period were Benjamin ben Abraham delli Mansi (13th c.) and the renowned Immanuel of Rome (see below).

The final period begins at the close of the 15th c. and ends at the opening of the 20th. At first we feel the impact of the Sp. Jewish exiles who reached Italy after 1492. Religious poetry is now dominated by the Kabbalah (Jewish theosophy). Secular poetry, on the other hand, reflected the increasing contact with It. culture. More It. poetic forms are introduced: the *octava*, the *canzone*, the *canzonetta*, the madrigal, and blank verse (*versi sciolti*). Heb. poetic drama appears in the 17th c., to be followed by many such works in the 18th–19th cs. Ar. quantitative meter is soon modified by the elimination of distinction between short and long syllables so that the lines began to resemble the It. *endecasillabo* (Pagis 1976). The poet Natan Yedidiah of Orvieto (17th c.) even made an attempt to write poems in accentual meter, but the hendecasyllabic line prevailed.

Four poets stand out: Immanuel of Rome (1270?–1330?), Jacob and Immanuel Francis

(16th c.), and Moses Luzzato (18th c.). Immanuel of Rome was undoubtedly the greatest of the Italians. His *Maḥberot Immanuel* (Immanuel's Compositions) is a *maqamah* containing 28 sections, the last of which, *ha-tophet / vehaᶜeden* (Hell and Paradise), was inspired by Dante's *Divina commedia.* Immanuel first introduced the sonnet into Heb. p. His verse is amazingly supple and reflects the culture of the Ren. His bawdy verses are a rarity in Heb. letters. Immanuel composed a rhetorical work in which he described the new forms in It. verse and insisted that the *acutezza* (wit) of the poem's diction and subject matter must be primary. By this term he meant the use of *surprise,* either formally (oxymora) or conceptually (paradox), by strange and complex metaphors or uncommon conceits. In this he was faithful to the baroque school then current in Italy and Spain. Jacob and Immanuel Frances of Mantua wrote polemic satires against the supporters of Shabbatai Zevi (17th c.), the false Messiah.

Moses Hayyim Luzzato (18th c.) composed poems and allegorical closet dramas similar to the It. works of his day. His first play, *Migdal 'Oz* (Tower of Strength), was modeled after Guarini's *Pastor fido.* Luzzato combined an awareness of 18th-c. science with a deep Kabbalistic faith. His achievement lies on the border between a late Ren. and an early Modern world-view.

The Heb. p. produced by premodern Ashkenazi Jewry was almost totally religious, influenced by the Palestinian and It. schools. It consisted of liturgical hymns and dirges commemorating the massacres during the Crusades. A particular genre of martyrological poetry was the *ᶜaqedah,* which celebrated the sacrifice of Isaac as a symbol of the martyrdom of Jews. Ephraim of Bonn (12th c.) has a fine example of this genre (Spiegel, *Last Trial* 129–52), and *Netaneh toqef,* a prayer attributed to the martyr Amnon of Mainz, still holds a prominent place in the Yom Kippur liturgy.

By the 16th c., the center of Ashkenazi Jewry had moved from Germany to Eastern Europe. The Jews in the Polish-Lithuanian kingdom expressed their piety by the meticulous observation of the *halakhah* (Jewish Law) and by the study of religious texts. They inhabited a cultural milieu which rarely resorted to the arts—not even to the composition of religious hymns.

II. MODERN. A. *The European Period* (1781–1920). The bulk of the Jews of Central and Eastern Europe (Ashkenazim) drew their vernacular (Yiddish) and their religious trads. from the Ger. Jewish communities of the Rhineland. Ashkenazi Jews were more culturally isolated from their non-Jewish neighbors than were the Sp. and It. Jews. Although "court Jews" functioned in the Ger. states, they rarely played the prominent role which the Sp. grandees had played in Portugal and Spain. We know of no Ger.-Jewish patron of Heb. p.

With the rise of the *Haskalah* (Enlightenment) in the 18th c., first (and for a short time only) in Germany and then in Eastern Europe, Ashkenazim began to write belles-lettres. The early *Maskilim* (Enlighteners) advocated the "modernization" of Jewish religious and social life and resorted to Heb., the only literary lang. known to their audience, to criticize the old order and propagandize for a radical transformation of Jewish life.

In Germany, a group of *Maskilim* whose mentor was Moses Mendelssohn (1729–86) created the first Heb. periodical, *Ha-ma'asef* (The Gatherer). None of the authors of the *me'asfim* produced Heb. p. of lasting value. However, both in *Ha-ma'asef* and in individual works they published didactic, epic, satirical, and epigrammatic poems motivated by the attempt to prove that poetry of distinction could be written in Heb. and by the desire to propagate their ideology.

The early *Maskilim* turned to the Bible for their vocabulary and symbols and to Ger. lit. for subject matter and genres. They developed an euphuistic Heb. (*melitsah*) which was a mosaic of biblical verses and phrases.

By the 1820s, the *Haskalah* had penetrated into Eastern Europe, first into Polish Galicia (annexed by the Austro-Hungarian Empire), and soon thereafter into Czarist Russia. The Heb. poets of Eastern Europe wrote imitations of Ger. poetry in Heb., but except for two, Micah Josef Lebensohn (1828–52) and Judah Leib Gordon (1831–92), all had scant literary talent. The poetic activity in Germany and Eastern Europe of the latter part of the 19th c. served as the training ground which ultimately enabled Heb. writers to develop a style sufficient for the writing of a poetry of significance, a stage they had reached by the turn of the century.

Following the Czarist pogroms of the 1880s, Heb. writers despaired of the hope that Rus. society would open up to the Jews and grant them civil emancipation, thus permitting a synthesis between Rus. and Jewish culture. Jewish nationalism arose, encouraged in part by other ethnic movements which appeared in the Rus. and Austro-Hungarian Empires. Heb. poets penned sentimental verse bewailing the Jewish condition and expressing nostalgic yearnings for the ancient homeland.

During this period, Yiddish was also legitimized as a literary lang. Although at that time only a few Rus.-Jewish authors ventured to express themselves in Rus., most had the option of composing their works in Heb. or in Yiddish. Many actually wrote in both langs., and this bilingualism prevailed until World War II. The interrelation between Heb. and Yiddish lit. has recently become a major subject of interest in Heb. lit. crit. While Yiddish became the vehicle of those who dreamed of an autonomous Yiddish culture in pre-revolutionary Russia, Heb., which by the 1890s had become an adequate literary medium, quite naturally became the lang. of the Zionist writers who urged its revival as the lang. of a reconstituted Jewish commonwealth in Palestine.

Hayyim Nahman Bialik (1873–1934), the greatest figure in modern Heb. p., began publishing in 1888. He not only freed himself from the shackles of the *melitsah* but also replaced the cumbersome alexandrine meter which had been adopted by *Haskalah* poets with the accentual metrical system prevailing in Ger. and Rus. poetry. His output was relatively small: almost all of his major poems were written between 1900 and 1915. A neo-romantic lyricist, he gradually shifted from nationalist themes to personal poetry. Bialik usually employed the conventional poetic forms, but from time to time he experimented with prose poetry ("The Scroll of Fire") and wrote several works in which the cadences of the prophetic peroration override the underlying metrical pattern. These were his attempts to discover indigenous Heb. poetic forms. As a disciple of Ahad Ha'am, a positivist essayist, Bialik aimed at forging a new synthesis of the viable elements of Jewish trad. and European culture. But at the same time he had grave doubts as to whether this was possible.

His colleague Shaul Chernikhowsky (1874–1943) harbored none. Nurtured by Jewish Nietzschean ideas, he believed that symbiosis was impossible: there could be no reconciliation between modern hedonism and Jewish puritanism. He therefore sought to find links with that pre-Judaic paganism which preceded "the binding of God with the straps of phylacteries." Chernikhowsky introduced many European verseforms into Heb. and translated ancient Gr., Akkadian, and Finnish poems into Heb. Bialik and Chernikhowsky ultimately settled in Tel Aviv, but while Bialik wrote few "Palestinian" poems, Chernikhowsky composed many patriotic and landscape poems set in his new homeland. Both molded a modern Heb. poetic idiom often rooted in biblical diction, but bent it to their own needs, often giving traditional allusions an ironic twist.

B. *Palestinian Poetry* (1920–48). The school of Bialik dominated Heb. p. until the 1920s and 1930s. By then younger Heb. poets, many of whom had arrived in Israel following World War I and the Rus. Revolution, revolted against the linear and symmetrical poetry of the older poets with their traditional sources and themes. Now that Heb. had become a spoken lang., the new poetry was peppered with the vernacular. It also reflected the Socialist-Zionist ideology of the pioneer culture, which was far less "Jewish" in theme and permeated with the new Mediterranean landscape.

The prominent "pioneer" poets were Natan Alterman (1910–70) and Abraham Shlonsky (1900–73). Both were influenced by the Russian revolutionary poets Blok and Yesenin and by expressionism. The *ennui* of the disintegrating urban European culture, the destruction wrought by war, and the impending Holocaust vied with the enthusiasm for the daring novelty of the reborn homeland, its bright but uncompromising colors, its sand dunes, its sea.

A third poet broke with the Socialist-Zionist ideology and embraced a fiery quasi-racial Messianism. Uri Zvi Greenberg (1894–1981) reached Tel Aviv in the 1920s, disillusioned with European humanism. The "return" for him was a return to God's historic covenant, a rejection of the "false" morality of the gentiles and a dedication to the miracle of divine providence. Greenberg's style is often extravagantly Whitmanesque. He eschews foreign verseforms, preferring the cadences of the biblical peroration and *paytanic* verse. His vocabulary is sometimes drawn from Kabbalistic texts. *Reḥovot Hanahar* (1951; *Streets of the River*) is an overpowering volume of verse inspired by the martyrdom of the Holocaust—swinging between agonized despair and exultant, almost hysterical faith.

Heb. writers of the Palestinian generation were much more "European" than the generation of Bialik. They were an uprooted generation who wandered through the capitals of Europe, absorbing the cultures of their temporary homes. Their poetry was open to all influences: Rus. and Ger. expressionism, Rus. and Fr. symbolism, the existentialism of Rilke and George, the Freudian and Jungian views of the arts.

C. *Israeli Poets* (1948–87). With Israel's War of Independence (1948), new poets make their appearance. These were either native Israeli poets or products of the excellent Heb. school system which the Zionists had established in Eastern Europe who arrived in Palestine as young pioneers prior to the outbreak of World War II. For them, Heb. was a vibrant spoken lang. and Israel's landscape the landscape of their youth, if not their infancy. Most no longer stemmed from the traditional religious world of Eastern Europe. They were less "learned" than their forebears.

The older writers of the Israeli generation who began as junior members of the Shlonsky-Alterman school remained committed to the Socialist-Zionist ideology (Haim Guri, for example). Following the War of Independence and the mass immigration into Israel, however, many discovered that there were no facile solutions to the problems their new society faced. Once independence was attained, the egoism which had been suppressed during the struggle broke loose. Subjectivism became the rule.

Poets such as Yehudah Amichai (b. 1924), Amir Gilboa (1917–85), and Abba Kovner (1918–87) abandoned the strict metrical and verse patterns to which the older generation adhered. Amichai chose his metaphors from quotidian experience: a newspaper headline, the terms of a contract, a cliche to which he gave an ironic twist, a fragment of an old prayer. Gilboa at first had a penchant for surrealistic, childlike imagery, but as he matured he eschewed figurative lang., preferring oblique allusion and experiments with sound.

By the 1950s, Israeli culture was well on the way to Americanization. Literary influences became increasingly less Ger. or Rus.-Polish and increasingly more Anglo-Am. Natan Zach (b. 1930), the theoretically-minded poet of the 1950's and '60s, attacked what he termed the monotonous rhythms of Alterman and called for a new poetry in which line and stanza should be freed from traditional rules, and for a new diction which should have semantic significance rather than mechanical regularity. Poems should not be neatly rounded to a close but be fluid and open-ended. Figurative lang. should be used sparingly. The poet should avoid "poetic lang." and draw upon everyday speech, incl. slang. Zach also attacked "objective" or "ideological" poetry: the artist should concentrate on the subjective, existential experience of a complex modern world.

Contemp. Heb. poets are in the main secular, yet are constantly confronted by the rich religious lit. of the past, particularly their biblical heritage. Amichai can still build an ironic poem on a prayer drawn from a requiem, and T. Carmi (b. 1925) can react to a Talmudic allusion. Indeed, much poetry is evoked by tension between the sacred classics and the profane experiences of the modern poet.

Israel remains a melting pot of many cultures. Heb. p. is enriched by the interplay between them: the middle European roots of Zach, Amichai, and Pagis (1929–86); the Rus.-Polish milieu from which spring Kovner and Gilboa; the Anglo-Am. influences on Carmi, Gabriel Preil (b. 1911), who lives in New York, and Simon Halkin (1898–1987); the Mediterranean world of Mordecai Geldman; and the Maghreb world of Erez Biton.

Few women poets published during the European period, but they were quite active in Mandatory Palestine. Rahel (1890–1931) was an early "conversationalist" poet whose lyrics were clearly influenced by Rus. acmeism. Lea Goldberg (1911–70) was a sensitive and learned poet and a leading member of the Shlonsky-Alterman circle. Zelda Mishkowski (1914–84), a pious, orthodox woman, produced several volumes of imagist religious verse, a rare phenomenon in a lit. marked by its secularity. Three important contemp. women poets are Daliah Rabikowitz (b. 1935), a feminist poet whose very sophisticated *naif* poems have been widely acclaimed; Yonah Wallach (1944–85), whose verse has a decidedly Jungian bent; and Maya Bejerano, a bold experimenter with computer poetry.

Since the rise of the right wing in Israel, and particularly as a consequence of the Lebanese War, Heb. poets have reverted to political poetry. In the wake of the war, several volumes of protest poetry appeared in which poets like Zach and Rabikowitz, once the apostles of subjectivism, have participated.

BIBLIOGRAPHIES: Y. Goell. *Bibl. of Mod. Heb. Lit. in Eng. Tr.* (1968)—7500 items from 1880–1965, *Bibl. of Mod. Heb. Lit. in Tr.* (1975)—700 items since 1917 (comparative in scope); I. Goldberg and A. Zipin, *Bibl. of Mod. Heb. Lit. in Tr.* (1979–), this series providing current bibl. and extensive retroactive coverage.

ANTHOLOGIES: *In English*: *Apocrypha and Pseudepigrapha of the OT*, ed. R. H. Charles, 2 v. (1913); *Post-Biblical Heb. Lit.*, ed. B. Halper, 2 v. (1921); *The Bible*, Rev. Standard Version (1952); *A Treasury of Jewish Poetry*, ed. N. and M. Ausubel (1957); *An Anthol. of Med. Heb. Lit.*, ed. A. E. Millgram (1961); *The Mod. Heb. Poem Itself*, ed. S. Burnshaw, T. Carmi, and E. Spicehandler (1965); *Anthol. of Mod. Heb. P.*, ed. S. Y. Penueli and A. Ukhmani (1966); *Mod. Heb. P.*, ed. and tr. R. F. Mintz (1966); *The Psalms*, tr. M. Dahood (1966–70)—intro. and notes; "Israel," *Mod. Poetry in Tr.*, ed. R. Friend, (1974); *Mod. Heb. Lit.*, ed. R. Alter (1975); *The Dead Sea Scriptures*, ed. T. H. Gaster, 3d ed. (1976); *Fourteen Israel Poets*, ed. D. Silk (1976); *Contemp. Israeli Lit.*, ed. E. Anderson (1977); *Mod. Heb. P.*, ed. and tr. B. Frank (1980); *Penguin Book of Heb. Verse*, ed. T. Carmi (1981)—with intro. on prosody; "Poetry from Israel," *LitR* 26, 2 (1983); Jewish Pub. Society, *Tanakh* (1985); *Israeli Poetry: A Contemp. Anthol.*, ed. W. Bargad and S. F. Chyet (1986); *Mod. Heb. Lit. in Eng. Tr.*, ed L. I. Yudkin (1987). *In Hebrew*: *Mivḥar ha-Shirah ha-ᶜIvrit be-Italia* (1934)—Heb. p. in Italy, *Ha-Shira ha ᶜIvrit bi-Sefarad u-vi-Provence*, 2 v. (1954–56)—Heb. p. in Spain and Provence, both ed. J. Schirmann; *Mivḥar ha-Shirah ha-ᶜIvrit ha-Hadashah*, ed. A. Barash (1938)—mod.; *Sifruthenu ha-Yafah*, ed. J. Lichtenbaum, 2 v. (1962)—mod.; *Shirah Tse'irah*, ed. B. Yaoz and Y. Kest (1980)—Israeli.

HISTORY AND CRITICISM: *In English*: R. Lowth, *De Sacra Poesi Hebraeorum* (1753); G. B. Gray, *Forms of Heb. P.* (1915); S. Spiegel, *Heb. Reborn* (1930), *The Last Trial* (1967); R. H. Pfeiffer, *Intro. to the OT*, 2 ed. (1941); C. C. Torrey, *The Apocryphal Lit.* (1945)—concise handbook of Jewish postcanonical lit.; S. C. Yoder, *Poetry of the OT* (1948); *The OT and Mod. Study*, ed. H. H. Rowley (1951); M. Wallenrod, *The Lit. of Mod. Israel* (1956); M. Waxman, *A Hist. of Jewish Lit.*, 5 v. (1960); H. Gunkel, *The Psalms*, tr. T. M. Horner (1967); B. H. Smith, *Poetic Closure* (1968); S. Halkin, *Mod. Heb. Lit.*, 2d ed. (1970); D. Goldstein, *The Jewish Poets of Spain* (1971); B. Hrushovski, "Prosody, Heb.," *Encyclopaedia Judaica*, (1971–72), 13.1195–1240, and "On Free Rhythms in Mod. Poetry," in Sebeok; E. Spicehandler, "Heb. Lit., Mod.," *Encyc. Judaica* 8 (1971); I. Zinberg, *A Hist. of Jewish Lit.*, ed. and tr. B. Martin (1972–78); E. Silberschlag, *From Ren. to Ren.*, 2 v. (1973–77); J. Kugel, *The Idea of Biblical Poetry* (1981); N. Frye, *The Great Code* (1982); R. Alter, *The Art of Biblical Poetry* (1985); A. Berlin, *The Dynamics of Biblical Parallelism* (1985), *Biblical Poetry Through Medieval Jewish Eyes* (1991); R. Alter and F. Kermode, *Literary Guide to the Bible* (1987); H. Fisch, *Poetry with a Purpose* (1988); D. Pagis, *Heb. P. of the Middle Ages and Ren.* (1991). *In Hebrew*: J. Klausner, *Historiyah Shel-ha-*

Sifrut ha-ʿIvrit ha-Hadashah, 6 v. (1930–50)—mod.; F. Lachover, *Toldot ha-sifrut ha-ʿIvrit ha-Hadashah,* 4 v. (1936–48)—mod.; A. Ben-Or, *Toldot ha-Sifrut ha-ʿIvrit be-Dorenu,* 2 v. (1954–55)—contemp.; D Miron, *Arba' Panim ba-Sifrut ha-ʿIvrit Bat Yamenu* (1962)—contemp.; A. M. Habermann, *Toledoth Hapiyyut Vehashir* (1970); E. Fleischer, *Shirath Haqodesh ha-ʿIvrit Biyemei Habeinayim* (1975)—piyyut; D. Pagis, *Hidush Umasoreth beshirath Hahol ha-ʿIvrit* (1976), *Heb. P. of the Middle Ages and Ren.* (1991); E. Schirmann, *Letoldoth Hashirah vehadramah ha-ʿIvrit* (1979); L. Waugh, "The Poetic Function in the Theory of Roman Jakobson," *PoT* 2 (1980); R. Brann, *The Compunctious Poet* (1990).
E.SP.

HINDI POETRY. See INDIAN POETRY.

HISPANO-ARABIC POETRY. Opinions are divided as to whether the Ar. poetry of Spain is truly distinctive within the general field of Ar. poetry (q.v.). Some scholars point to the prominence of specific themes, such as nature and descriptions of flowers and gardens, as well as to the two types of strophic poem that originated in Spain, as evidence of the distinctiveness of H.-Ar. p.; some (Pérès, García Gómez) claim that it reflects a native Iberian trad. preserved continuously from Roman times and reemerging later in Sp. poetry (q.v.). Others point to the continuity of the forms, rhetorical patterns, and themes prevailing in Spain with those of the Abbasid Empire: most poems are monorhymed, are set in quantitative meter according to certain canonical patterns, are phrased in classical Ar., and employ the rhetorical figures associated with Abbasid neoclassical verse.

The literary dependence of Andalusia on Iraq is epitomized in the career of Ziryāb, a court singer of Hārūn al-Rashīd (9th c.), who, arriving in Spain, used the prestige of his origins to set the court fashions in poetry, music, and manners in accordance with those of Baghdad in its glory. This dependent relationship of the Muslim West on the Muslim East corresponds to the political and trade links that connected the two ends of the Mediterranean world until the establishment of an independent caliphate in Cordoba by ʿAbd al-Raḥmān III (929). But by this time the *muwashshaḥa* ("girdle poem") had already emerged as a distinctive local contribution to Ar. poetry, the only strophic form ever to be cultivated to any great extent by poets writing in cl. Ar. It is said to have been invented by Muqaddam of Cabra (9th c.).

The *muwashshaḥa* has five to seven strophes, each in two parts (*ghuṣn* [pl. *aghṣān*] and *simṭ* [*asmāṭ*]). The *aghṣān* all have the same metrical and rhyming patterns, but the rhyme sound changes from strophe to strophe; the *asmāṭ* are uniform in meter and in rhyme sound throughout the poem. The poem usually begins with an opening *simṭ*. The final *simṭ*, around which the whole poem was probably composed, is the much-discussed *kharja*. The *kharja* is either in vernacular Ar., in Romance, or (commonly) Mozarabic, a form of Hispano-Romance, and is believed to be a quotation from vernacular songs otherwise lost. Of great interest to Romance linguists as the earliest attestations of lyric poetry in any Hispano-Romance lang., the *kharajāt* are thought by some to point to the existence of an Iberian popular poetry predating the Arab conquest (711 A.D.), supporting the theory of a continuous Iberian element in H.-Ar. p.; but aside from the *kharajāt* themselves, no such poetry is extant.

The metrics of the *muwashshaḥa* may also point to Romance origin. Though the poems can be scanned in conformity with the quantitative principles of Ar. poetry, the metrical patterns only rarely correspond to the canonical ones, and the *kharja* often resists quantitative analysis altogether. The metrical principle underlying the *muwashshaḥa* is now believed by many to be syllabic (García Gómez, Monroe), though others maintain that it is quantitative, having arisen through the evolution of the *qaṣīda.* Hartmann and Stern pointed out that Eastern poets occasionally varied the *qaṣīda's* monorhyme by subdividing each of the two hemistichs with internal rhyme; the result was the pattern *bbba, a* representing the constant rhyme. When a whole poem has the *bbba* pattern, each line is a miniature stanza. Thus a subtype of the *qaṣīda* may have developed into an entirely new verse type. This shift may have occurred under the influence of Romance verseforms reflected in the *villancico* and the *rondeau,* for unlike cl. Ar. verse, the *muwashshaḥa* was sung, and Romance musical patterns seem to have played a part in shaping it.

Another class of poems thought to be derived from earlier Romance models has survived in the *urjūza* poems on historical themes by Ghazzāl ibn Yaḥya, Ibn ʾAbd Rabbihi, and others; these are long poems composed of rhyming distichs in a nonclassical quantitative meter known as *rajaz.* But neither the form nor the theme was an Andalusian invention, being rather a direct imitation of an Abbasid model, and these 9th- and 10th-c. poems do not seem to have created a lasting genre.

Though poetry is reported to have been an important feature of H.-Ar. culture, esp. in the Cordoban court, as it was throughout the Ar.-speaking world, little has survived from the 8th and 9th cs., and what has is conventional in themes, imagery, and verse patterns. But under the caliphate, Cordoba flourished as a literary center, and Andalusian poetry began to outshine that of the East. The bulk of the poetry was courtly panegyric and lampoon in *qaṣīda* form, but love poetry was extremely popular, as were descriptions of wine and wine drinking, gardens, and ascetic verse. The great names are Ibn Hānīʾ, Ibn Darrāj, and al-Sharīf al-Ṭalīq. The latter two cultivated flower poetry, which was to become a specialty of later Andalusian poets. They employ an increasingly ornate rhetorical style (*badīʿ*) that originated in the East in the 10th c. and is associated with the Abbasid master abu Tammām.

The decline of the Cordoban caliphate (1009–31) and the period of the Party Kings (1031–91) saw the greatest achievements of H.-Ar. p. Ibn Shuhaid composed a body of passionate and pessimistic verse, as well as an unusual treatise on the nature of poetry in which the narrator visits and converses with the familiar spirits of dead poets. In contrast to the prevailing doctrine of poetry as a learned craft of rhetorically ornamented speech, he propounds an idea of individual poetic inspiration. The theologian and legist Ibn Ḥazm (d. 1063) wrote mostly short love verses, more conventional in style, but embodying a spiritual ideal of love closely resembling that of the troubadours and worked out in detail in his prose treatise. Their younger contemporary Ibn Zaidūn composed a body of very individual poetry, esp. the odes arising out of his celebrated love affair with the princess Wallāda, which reflect the spiritual ideals of love developed by Ibn Ḥazm. It is from this period (late 11th c.) that *muwashshaḥa* texts are preserved.

Under the Party Kings, the city states of Spain vied with each other for pre-eminence in the arts, esp. poetry. Seville became the city of poets par excellence, boasting the presence of the mature Ibn Zaidūn, Ibn ʿAmmār, Ibn al-Labbāna, and Ibn Ḥamdīs; its last Arab ruler, al-Muʿtamid Ibn ʿAbbad, the patron of all these, was himself a gifted poet. This efflorescence of poetry was partly made possible by a policy of religious tolerance common at the Sp. courts, but the Almoravids (1091–1145) introduced a fundamentalist regime that suppressed secular arts. A few great poets, trained in the earlier period, flourished, such as the nostalgic nature poet Ibn Khafāja, Ibn ʿAbdūn, the *muwashshaḥa* poet al-Aʿmā of Tudela, and the opaque Ibn al-Zaqqāq, but it was also an age of anthologists. Nevertheless, the period saw the invention, probably by Ibn Bājja (early 12th c.), of the *zajal* and its full flowering in the works of Ibn Quzmān (d. 1160). These are strophic poems, similar to *muwashshaḥāt* in that the strophes have one element whose rhyme changes from strophe to strophe and another with constant rhyme, but the lang. is colloquial, the final *simṭ* is not different from the rest of the poem, and there may be more than seven strophes; the *asmās.t* have only half the number of lines in the opening *simṭ*. The vulgar lang. of the *zajal* complements its theme, the bawdy, colorful life of taverns and streets, observed and turned into lit. by sophisticated poets of aristocratic origin who mock the conventions of courtly love and courtly poetry. The form was probably adapted from vulgar poetry. Apparently as a secondary devel., a type of *zajal* arose resembling the *muwashshaḥa* in everything but lang. Both types are already present in Ibn Quzmān.

Under the Almohads (1145–1223) there was a revival of poetry; the great poets were al-Ruṣāfī, the converted Jew Ibn Sahl, Ḥāzim al-Qarṭājannī, whose work on the theory of poetry was also influential, and a famous woman poet, Ḥafsa bint al-Ḥājj. But the most original devel. was the mystical poetry of Ibn ʿArabī, which derived its imagery from secular love poetry and its diction from the highly metaphorical style of the age. The final phase of Islamic Spain, the Kingdom of Granada (1248–1492), produced a few important poets, incl. Ibn al-Khaṭīb, and Ibn Zamrak, whose poems embellish the Alhambra.

The similarity of some of the strophic patterns of H.-Ar. p. and the notions of love sung by the H.-Ar. poets to those of the troubadours has led some to see Ar. poetry as the inspiration of the troubadours (Nykl). The exact relationship of H.-Ar. p. to the troubadour lyric continues to be the subject of intense scholarly debate (Boaze; Menocal), as also is the problem of the *zajal's* influence on the *cantigas.*

M. Hartmann, *Das arabische Strophengedicht* (1897); A. Cour, *Un poète arabe d'Andalousie: Ibn Zaïdoûn* (1920); H. Pérès, *La poésie andalouse en arabe classique au XIe siècle,* 2d ed. (1953), Sp. tr., *Esplendor de al-Andalus* (1983); R. Menéndez Pidal, "Poesía árabe y poesía europea," *Bulletin hispanique* 40 (1938); E. García Gómez, *Un eclipse de la poesía en Sevilla* (1945), *Poemas arábigoandaluces,* 3d ed. (1946), *Todo Ben Quzman* (1972), *Las jarchas de la serie árabe en su marco,* 2d ed. (1975), *El libro de las banderas de los campeones de Ibn Saʿid al Magribi,* 2d ed. (1978); A. R. Nykl, *H.-Ar. P. and Its Relations with the Old Prov. Troubadours* (1946); A. J. Arberry, *Moorish Poetry* (1953); Ibn Ḥazm, *The Ring of the Dove,* tr. A. J. Arberry (1953); P. Le Gentil, *Le Virelai et le villancico* (1954), "La Strophe zadjalesque, les khardjas et le problème des origines du lyrisme roman," *Romania* 84 (1963)—judicious review of research to 1963; S. Fiore, *Über die Beziehungen zwischen der arabischen und der fruhitalienischen Lyrik* (1956); W. Heinrichs, *Arabische Dichtung und Griechische Poetik* (1969); Ibn Shuhaid, *Treatise of Familiar Spirits and Demons,* ed. and tr. J. T. Monroe (1971); J. M. Solà-Solé, *Corpus de poesía mozárabe* (1973); J. T. Monroe, *H.-Ar. P.* (1974); S. M. Stern, *H.-Ar. Strophic P.* (1974); M. Frenk, *La jarchas mozárabes y los comienzos de la lírica románica* (1975), *Estudios sobre lírica antigua* (1978); R. Scheindlin, *Form and Structure in the Poetry of al-Muʿtamid Ibn ʿAbbād* (1975); R. Boase, *The Origin and Meaning of Courtly Love* (1976); L. F. Compton, *Andalusian Lyrical Poetry and Old Sp. Love Songs* (1976); R. Hitchcock, *The Kharja: A Critical Bibl.* (1977); R. Boase, *The Origin and Meaning of Courtly Love* (1977); S. G. Armistead, "Some Recent Devels. in Kharja Scholarship," *La Corónica* 8 (1980); *GRLMA* 2.1.46–73; M. R. Menocal, "The Etymology of Old Prov. *trobar, trobador,*" *RPh* 36 (1982–83), *The Ar. Role in Med. Lit. Hist.* (1987); Ibn Quzman, *El cancionero hispanoárabe,* tr. F. Corriente Córdoba (1984); D. C. Clarke, "The

Prosody of the Hargas," *La Corónica* 16 (1987–88); B. M. Liu and J. T. Monroe, *Ten H.-Ar. Strophic Songs in the Mod. Oral Trad.* (1989). R.P.S.

HITTITE POETRY. The Hittites, who lived in Turkey in the second millennium B.C. and spoke an IE lang., have left a few poetic texts in the royal archives of their capital, Hattusa, modern Boghazkoy, 100 miles east of Ankara. The texts are written in cuneiform, a system of writing that the Hittites borrowed from Babylonia. It uses word signs and syllables; this causes the following difficulties for the reading of poetic texts: (1) clusters of two or more consonants at the beginning and end, and of three or more consonants in the interior of a word, had to be broken up by the addition of mute vowels; (2) the H. reading of some word signs is still unknown (such words will be rendered below by their Eng. equivalent in capitals). The IE Hittites superseded an earlier population who spoke an unrelated lang., called Hattic by scholars and for the most part undeciphered. Among the Hattic texts used by the Hittites in the cult of the gods of the land, there are some that are written in stanzas of 3 to 5 verses which are separated by horizontal rules. In contrast to these Hattic poems, H. poetic texts are not written in separate verses but rather consecutively, like prose. The oldest example is a short song contained in an historical text of the Old Kingdom (ca. 1700–1600 B.C.) and introduced by the words "Then he sings." Among texts of the New Kingdom (ca. 1400–1200 B.C.), some hymns and epics seem to be written in verse, e.g. a hymn to Istanu, the Sun God, which begins: "Istanui iskha-mi / ʾndants hannesnas iskhas" (Oh Istanu, my lord! / Just lord of judgment).

From the epic lit. of the New Kingdom we quote passages of The Song of Ullikummi. The first stanza of 4 verses, which was a prooemium of the type known from Homer, is mutilated; its last line reads: "dapiyas siunas attan Kumarbin iskhamihhi" (Of Kumarbi, father of all gods, I shall sing). The story itself begins in the fourth stanza:

11 man-tsa Kumarbis hattatar istantsani piran das
nas-kan kiskhiyats sara hudak arais
kessarats STAFF-an das
padas-sas-ma-tsa SHOES liliwandus huwan-dus sarkwit

15 nas-kan Urkisats happirats arha iyannis
nas ikunta luli-kan anda ar(a)s

11 When Kumarbi wisdom into (his) mind had taken,
from (his) chair he promptly rose,
into (his) hand a staff he took,
upon his feet as shoes the swift winds he put;

15 from (his) town Urkis he set out,
and to a cool(?) pond(?) he came.

Although both the lines and the stanzas have different length, and although it is impossible to establish a meter, it is clear from the term "song" used in the original title of the epic, as well as from the structure of the text, that we are dealing with some sort of bound lang. Occasional rhyme occurs (*das* in 11 and 13, perhaps *aras* in 16, if the *a* was pronounced; *arais* in 12 and *iyannis* in 15), but it is not systematically used throughout the text. The same is true of parallelism of the type found in the Bible: it is an occasional not an essential feature. Other devices of the epic style, such as standing epithets and repetition of standard lines and of whole passages, are common.

The Song of Ullikummi is one of a number of H. epic compositions which are based on originals in Hurrian, a non-IE lang. of north Syria and southeast Anatolia. Also of Hurrian background is an H. hymn to Ishtar, the goddess of love, with a clearly strophic structure.

H. T. Bossert, "Gedicht und Reim im vorgriechischen Mittelmeergebiet," *Geistige Arbeit* 5 (1938), no. 18, 7–10: poetic texts in H. and other Mediterranean langs., with special emphasis on rhyme, "Zur Entstehung des Reimes," *Jahrbuch für Kleinasiatische Forschung* 2 (1951–53), 233 ff.; see also *Mitteilungen des Instituts fur Orientforschung* 2 (1954) 97 ff.

TEXTS discussed here and by Bossert: E. Tenner, "Zwei hethitische Sonnenlieder," *Kleinasiatische Forschungen* 1 (1930), 387–92 —text and tr. of Sun hymns analyzed by Bossert; H. G. Güterbock, *Keilschrifturkunden aus Boghazköi* 28 (1935), nos. 10–49, —cuneiform Hattic text; p. iv on stanzas, "The Song of Ullikummi," *Jour. of Cuneiform Studies* 5 (1951), 135–61, esp. 141–44 on form, continued in 6 (1952), 8–42—text and metrical tr. of the epic, "The Composition of H. Prayers to the Sun," *JAOS* 78 (1958)—text and tr. of Sun hymn quoted above, "A Hurro-H. Hymn to Ishtar," *JAOS* 103 (1983); I. McNeill, "The Metre of the H. Epic," *Anatolian Studies* 13 (1963); C. Watkins, "A Lat.-H. Etymology," *Lang.* 45 (1969)—Old Kingdom song.

GENERAL: O. R. Gurney, *The Hittites*, 2d ed. (1954). H.G.G.

HUNGARIAN POETRY. During the centuries of H. history before the establishment of the H. state (ca. 1000 A.D.), the cultural heritage of the tribal Hs. was completely oral, so we cannot consider it to be lit. strictly speaking, but rather folklore. The poetic works of ancient H. folklore were not preserved in their original form; we have only indications of their existence, such as the shamanistic songs (*regölés*). The chronicle writers of the 11th–14th cs. who wrote in Lat. made use of the content of several ancient legends and frequently recorded them (The Legend of the Miraculous Stag, The Legend of Álmos, The Legend of the White Horse). The trad. of the pagan bards gradually mixed with that of the jugglers, entertainers of the

Middle Ages. From the beginning of Lat. lit. in Hungary until the 16th c., the H. minstrels ensured the continuity of H. poetic trad., cultivating, perfecting, and polishing the oral forms.

During the Middle Ages and Ren., poetry continued to be written in Lat., the lang. used by Janus Pannonius (János Csezmiczei, 1437–72), the first significant H. poet. His humanism found expression in a variety of forms, from satiric epigrams to elegies ("Farewell to His Country," "When He Was Sick in the Army Camp"). The H. lang. was first used for poetry during the Reformation by three disciples of Erasmus, best known for their translations of parts of the Bible: Benedek Komjáthy, Gábor Pesti, and János Sylvester. During this period the most popular form was song verse. One of the most prominent Protestant songwriters was András Baitzi (1530–50). Péter Bornemissza (1535–85) first excelled as a songwriter but later wrote plays as well as a collection of sermons. The last great literary figure of the Reformation was Gáspár Károli (d. 1591), the first to translate the full text of the Bible into H. (1590), a tr. which is still in use.

During the 16th c. the most outstanding songwriter was Sebestyen Tinódi Lantos (d. 1556); his themes revolved around the anti-Turkish struggle (*Cronica*, 1554). During the last third of the 16th c. there appeared an increasing number of versified fictitious stories, the best known of which is "Miklós Toldi" by Péter Ilosvay-Selymes. The other notable work was the "Story of Argirus," based on an unknown It. "bella istoria" by Albert Gergei. The widespread cultivation of love poetry bore fruit in Bálint Balassi (1554–94), the first great lyricist of the H. lang. Son of Protestant aristocrats, he wrote poems about his courageous battles against the Turks ("In Praise of the Outposts," "Farewell to His Homeland") as well as love poems to Anna Losonczy, whom he called Julia ("To the Cranes," "Finding Julia He Greets Her Thus"); toward the end of his life he converted to Catholicism and wrote a number of religious poems. His poetry is distinguished by the richness of its forms. Balassi produced a new verseform, known as the Balassi-Stanza. He had many followers, the most remarkable among them being János Rimay (1569–1631), who later developed his own form of expression, representing the mannerist taste of the declining Ren.

At the beginning of the 17th c., baroque culture became predominant in Hungary. The most distinguished baroque poet was Miklós Zrinyi (1620–64), scourge of the Turks. His main work is a 15-song epic, "The Peril of Szigetvár." A contemporary of Zrinyi, István Gyöngyösi (1629–1704), wrote pseudo-epics describing everyday events instead of great historical moments and written in a captivating language ("The Marriage of Imre Thököly and Ilona Zrinyi," "Phoenix Risen from his Ashes"). Throughout the 17th c. appeared a steady stream of anti-Turkish, anti-Hapsburg, popular poetry, best of which is known as *kuruc* poems ("Song of Jakab Buga"; "Come on, Palkó"; "Outlaw's Song"). Many of these poems treat the person of Ferenc Rákóczi II, leader of the Kuruc struggles for freedom (1703–11). They include the famous Rákóczi-song, which was banned in 1848; the tune is related to Berlioz's "Rákóczi March."

During the 18th c., baroque slowly gave way to Enlightenment, clearly influenced by the Fr. Revolution. The H. Jacobin movement coincided with that of the innovators of the lang., Ferenc Kazinczy (1759–1831) and János Batsanyi (1763–1845). After the tragic fall of the Jacobin movement emerged the greatest H. lyricist after Balassi, Mihály Csokonay Vitéz (1773–1805). His poetry expresses anti-feudal ideas, and his love poems to Lilla are incomparable. He has some impressionist-rococo translucence in his work besides its symbolic power and musical qualities ("To the Echo of Tihany," "To Hope," "To the Butterfly"). The H. Enlightenment, a fascinating awakening of the nation, led to changes in values, as shown in the work of the last great poet of the nobility, Dániel Berzsenyi (1776–1836; "To the Hungarians," "The Approaching Winter").

H. romanticism, also called the Reform Age, is a period of social progress headed by the liberal nobility. Ferenc Kölcsey (1790–1838), the author of the National Anthem, and Mihály Vörösmarty (1800–55) were the greatest figures of this period. Vörösmarty wrote epic poems ("The Flight of Zalán," "Csongor and Tünde") as well as lyrics to his wife ("Dream," "To a Dreamer"). His desperation over the failure of the War of Independence is ever-present in his poem "The Old Gypsy." The most extraordinary figure of the time was Sándor Petőfi (1823–48). His enthusiastic patriotism is evident throughout his works, and in his narrative poems ("The Hammer of the Village," "John the Hero") he revealed his talent for storytelling. Much of his tender lyrism is dedicated to his wife, Julia ("What shall I call Thee," "'Twas a Poet's Dream," "At the End of September") and is heavily influenced by the style of folksongs. Many of his poems are still sung by the people. Petőfi had a legendary friendship with János Arany (1817–82), who wrote more epic poetry than lyric. His most famous work is the "Toldy Trilogy"; he also wrote beautiful ballads reviving historical events ("Szondi's Two Pages," "Bards of Wales"). His elegiac sadness at the failed War of Independence appears even in idyllic poems like "Family Circle" or "To My Son." His lyrics are particularly artful in his late poems ("Autumn Bouquet"). Moving from romanticism towards realism, the great lyric poet of the 19th c. was János Vajda (1827–97). After 1849, he entered a period of pessimism. ("Lamentations 1854–56"), but later his voice acquires a new tone in love poems for Gina, a fallen woman ("Twenty Years Past").

The 20th c. opened with a new generation of

poets gathering around the literary review *Nyugat* (The West), most of whom were influenced by Fr. symbolism. Endre Ady published his first volume, a kind of fin-de-siècle parlor-poetry in which, however, his later genius is already manifested in some poems—the best are the ones describing his sorrow at the backwardness of his country ("At the Gare de L'Est," "Upward Thrown Stone," "Blood and Gold") or deal with his tormented relationship with Leda ("In an Old Wagon," "Beautiful Farewell Message"). Other poets of the same generation include Árpád Tóth (1886–1928), who classified himself as an Ady-follower ("a timid apostle of my mighty Lord"), which in fact he was not. He too evinces symbolist melancholy and a longing for a new and better world but in a quiet, pacifist way. The ill-fated Gyula Juhász (1883–1937), who was at the forefront of the Nyugat at the beginning, later slipped into the background. He carried within himself the weariness and decadence of the early 20th c., the fashionable Art nouveau. His love lyrics of hopeless desire, the Anna-cycle, are true masterpieces. The other two Nyugat poets, Babits and Kosztolányi, are examples of bourgeois humanism. Mihály Babits (1883–1941) was a poet, novelist, essayist, and moderately conservative representative of the H. intelligentsia, a great master of form, a *poeta doctus*, who contemplated with horror the detached brutality of World War I. His "Before Easter" is a masterpiece of antiwar poetry. On the other hand, Dezsö Kosztolányi (1885–1936) was a successful poet in his lifetime, a novelist, and a fashionable publicist. The child-cult of the era is mirrored in his "Laments of the Poor Little Child"—musical, tender pieces of poetry. He had no definite political views, but his playfulness and airiness became a protest in the midst of the War. Frigyes Karinthy (1888–1938) achieved wide popularity as a humorous writer, though he was the most versatile literary figure. His "The Way You Write" is a collection of superb pastiches, a satirical panorama of the literary world of his contemporaries. The only poet of war, Géza Gyóni (1884–1917), was to many critics an epigone of Petöfi.

During World War I emerged a new trend of lit. and a new generation of poets exemplified by Lajos Kassák (1887–1967). In his free verse, influenced by the It. futurists and Ger. expressionists, there was a new awareness of life. He opposed both the Social Democrats and the Communist Party and remained the most zealous propagandist of abstract lit. A significant and contradictory poet was Lörinc Szabó (1900–57); influenced by expressionism, he favored anarchical revolt against the existing order. His individualism slowly turned into self-centered isolation. This course is followed by the poetry of József Fodor (b. 1918), whose work moved in the direction of "symphonic poems." László Fenyö (1902–45), who died at the hands of the Nazis, and Lajos Áprily (1887–1978) were sensitive and accomplished poets. The mystical poetry of Jenö Dsida (1907–38) represented the Villonesque kind of fraternization with God and Death. On the other hand, Neo-Catholic lyricism is found in György Sárközi (1899–1945). József Berda (b. 1902) is the *enfant terrible* who praises in free verse the simple joys of life.

Between the two World Wars arose another generation of poets related to the Nyugat. Their poetry exhibits their depression at the rise of Fascism and also a high responsiveness to foreign cultures. A characteristic member of this generation is Sándor Weöres (b. 1913), a man of universal erudition influenced by Eastern philosophies and by T. S. Eliot, a brilliant versifier and a great master of form who created a new pattern in H. p. István Vas (b. 1910), a Socialist-sympathizer, keenly aware of the inhumanity of Nazism, protested against the barbarity of the period from the standpoint of pure reason. Zoltán Jékely (b. 1913) is a poet of romantic-mystic dream-imagery whose poetry reflects a certain melancholy, a longing for death. Gyula Illyés (1902–83), one of the leading figures of modern H. lit., started with expressionistic and surrealistic free verse during his exile in France. Upon his return to Hungary he lamented the poverty of the villagers ("Heavy Earth," "Second Harvest"). In the mid 1930s he joined the populist writers' movement ("Order Among Ruins"). After 1945 a dichotomy becomes increasingly apparent in his work: he praises the achievements of the people's democracy, while at the same time he worries about the fate of Hungary and H. culture.

The most creative poet in inter-war Hungary was undoubtedly Attila József (1905–37), a noble rival to Ady and Babits. He too visited Vienna and Paris, where he assimilated expressionism, coupling this with his highly concentrated technique of composition. He has an entire circle of surrealistic poetry ("Medals"), reality rigidified and turned grotesque. His major effort was to elevate H. working-class poetry to new heights ("Chop at the Roots"). His poems are mirrors of the increasing Nazism and his own growing psychosis ("Night in the Slums," "How It Hurts"). He took his own life at the age of 32.

After World War II, a new generation of populist poets emerged: Lajos Kónya (1914), Péter Kuczka (b. 1923), György Somlyó (b. 1920), and others. As a consequence of the social changes and Rákosi's personal cult during the 1950s, a new group of poets gathered around *Újhold* (New Moon) magazine: Ágnes Nemes-Nagy, György Rába, Sándor Rákos, István Jánosy, and János Pilinszky. They expressed their emotions and impressions in an objectified and very concise form. The greatest among them was Pilinszky (1921–81). The depth of his poetry is due to his apparent lack of poetical resources: he preferred short, epigrammatic poems, though on the other hand he also composed long poems with apocalyptic visions. The two greatest poets of our time are László Nagy (1925–78) and Ferenc Juhász (b. 1928). Their instinctive images go directly from impression to creation of a vision. Juhász wrote extensive epic poetry. His lyric mirrors the suffering of the troubled mind yet also turns towards great visions, a world-view of micro- and macrocosms. The richness of his association of ideas is quite unique, as is his extraordinary sense of rhythm. At the same time, Mihály Váci, Gábor Garay, and Mihály Ladányi tried to write a more politicized poetry without reducing the aesthetic quality of their work. They moved away from great visions to a style that is simple and direct. During the 1970s emerged a new trend, concrete poetry ; its major representative is Dezsö Tandory (b. 1938), who experiments with a new system of poetical signs of visual and musical quality sometimes at the expense of comprehensibility.

There have been several waves of emigration from Hungary during the 20th c. Western H. p. can be divided into three major groups: (1) Catholic; (2) poets in the Nyugat trad.; (3) emigrées of the Socialist period (1956). From the first group must be mentioned Béla Horváth (in Paris), influenced by the thought of Teilhard de Chardin, and Raymund Rákos (Vatican), author of several prayer books. Árpád Szélpál (Paris) represents the Nyugat trad., writing in both H. and Fr. György Faludy (England) writes a somewhat romantic "vagabond" poetry and has traveled extensively; his poetry is full of color and nostalgia. Emigration poetry is closed and introverted, a struggle to conserve a cultural identity in foreign surroundings. Tamás Tüz (Toronto) is one of the most tragic examples of this trend. In recent years there has been increasing dialogue between poets inside and outside of Hungary, leading to the creation of new modes of poetic expressionn and further enriching H. p. and culture. Political and social changes in Hungary during 1989–90 resulted in the democratic election of a new coalition government in April 1990, which eliminated all forms of censorship, thus opening endless possibilities for poetry among other forms of art. As the East-West exchange develops, hopefully more H. p. will be translated into different langs. so the world can discover the treasures of H. lit.

BIBLIOGRAPHY: *Bibl. of H. Lit.*, ed. Sándor Kozocsa (1959); A. Tesla, *An Intro. Bibl. to the Study of H. Lit.* (1964), *H. Authors: A Bibl. Handbook* (1970).

ANTHOLOGIES: *Magyar Poetry* (1908), *Mod. Magyar Lyrics* (1926)—both tr. W. N. Loew; *The Magyar Muse*, tr. W. Kirkconnell (1933); *Magyar versek könyve*, ed. J. Horváth (1942); *A Little Treasury of H. Verse* (1947); *H. P.*, ed. E. Kunz (1955); *Hét évszázad magyar versei*, ed. I. Király et al., v. 1–4 (1978–79).

HISTORY AND CRITICISM: G. Király, *Magyar ösköltészet* (1921); J. Horváth, *A Magyar Irodalmi Népiesség Faluditól Petöfiig* (1927), *A Magyar Irodalmi Müveltség Kezdetei* (1931), *A magyar vers* (1948), *Rendszeres magyar verstan* (1969)—systematic H. poetics; A. Schöpflin, *A Magyar Irodalom Története a XX. században* (1937); T. Kardos, *Középkori Kultúra, Középkori Költészet* (1941), *A Magyarországi Humanizmus Kora* (1955); G. Lukács, *Írástudók Felelössége* (1945); T. Esze, *Magyar Költészet Bocskaytól Rákócziig* (1953); J. Waldapfel, *A Magyar Irodalom a Felvilágosoás Korában* (1954); A. Szerb, *Magyar Irodalomtörténet* (1958); J. Attila, *Sa Vie, son ouvre* (1958); A. Komlós, *A Magyar Költészet Petöfitöl Adyig* (1959); M. Bucsay, *Gesch. des Protestantismus in Ungarn* (1959); V. Tóth, *A Magyar Irodalom Története* (1960); L. Könnyü, *Az Amerikai Magyar Irodalom Története* (1961); A. Sivisky, *Die Ungarische Literatur der Gegenwart* (1962); *Kis Magyar Irodalomtörténet*, ed. T. Klaniczay et al. (1965); *A Magyar Irodalom Története*, ed. M. Szabolcsi, v. 1–4 (1966); P. Rákos, *Rhythm and Metre in H. Verse* (1966); A. Karátson, *Le symbolisme en Hongrie* (1969); A. Kerek, *H. Metrics* (1971); *L'Irréconciliable: Petöfi, poéte et révolutionnaire*, ed. S. Lukácsy (1973); M. Fajcsek, *Magyarországi irodalom idegen nyelven* (1975)—incl. bibl. 1944–68; T. Ungvári, *Poétika* (1976); M. Szegedy-Maszák, *Világkép és stílus* (1980); *Vándorének*, ed. M. Béládi (1981)—H. poets in Western Europe and overseas; *Pages choisies de la litt. hongroise des origines au millieu du XVIIIe siècle*, ed. T. Klaniczay (1981); B. Pomogáts, *A Nyugati Magyar Irodalom Története* (1982); *A Nyugati Magyar Irodalom 1945 után*, ed. M. Béládi et al. (1986).

S.M.N.

I

ICELANDIC POETRY. (For I. p. prior to 1550 see OLD NORSE POETRY.) When one considers the degrading conditions in Iceland after its literary peak in the 12th to 14th cs., and esp. the period from 1600 to 1800, with its severe cold, epidemics, famines, volcanic eruptions, and harsh economic and political oppression from Denmark, it seems a miracle that there was any I. p. at all from this time. That there was, and in such excellent abundance, testifies to the extraordinary energy and love that Icelanders have devoted to poetry and the comfort and recreation they have derived from it. In perhaps no other country has poetry been so close to all the people, for there was a high rate of literacy as well as an almost universal custom of composing and memorizing and reciting verse, out of a fascination with the language's potential for intricate form and for producing an effect.

The introduction of paper in the 16th c. had more of an impact on I. p. than two other phenomena from the same period, the introduction of Danish Lutheranism and the beginning of printing (which was monopolized by the Church until 1772). Paper made it economically feasible for farmers and priests all over the country to copy manuscripts, and it was by means of these copies, as well as extensive memorization, that secular lit. was disseminated. The intensive copying and reciting activity also made for ling. and literary conservatism, with the result not only that a modern Icelander can read without difficulty his lit. from as far back as the 13th c.,but also that, at least until the recent advent of free verse, an I. poet felt a natural obligation to use alliteration according to the ancient fixed rules.

The most popular and enduring form of I. p. is the *rímur,* and it is significant that Bishop Guðbrandur Þorláksson, in an attempt to appropriate this genre for spiritual uses, commissioned *rímur* on Ruth, Judith, Esther, Tobias, and Jesus Sirach for his *Vísnabók* (Book of Poems) of 1612. This remarkable book is not only the first volume of poetry (apart from hymns) printed in Iceland, but also by its very existence a comment on the strength of I. p. Whereas in countries such as Denmark and Germany clerical writings shaped the lang., in Iceland the Church had to rise to the level of the vernacular. Earlier translations of Lutheran hymns into I. had failed miserably in this respect. Bishop Guðbrandur, recognizing the problem, enlisted the service of the best poets he knew for this volume. Many of the poems in it are anonymous, but according to the preface the chief poet was the Reverend Einar Sigurðsson (1538–1626), among whose poems is a tender lullaby on the birth of Jesus, "Kvæði af stallinum Kristi" (Poem on Christ's Cradle) in the popular dance meter, *vikivaki.* His son, the Reverend Ólafur Einarsson (1573–1659), was also a notable poet who contributed a gloomy complaint on the times to *Vísnabók.*

In a rare instance of poetic genius passing from father to son through three generations, Ólafur's son Stefán Ólafsson (ca. 1619–88) became one of the leading poets of the 17th c. He wrote, as did his father, complaints on laborers and I. sloth, as well as love lyrics and poems about the pleasures of tobacco and drink and horses.

A poet who wrote little in this light, worldly vein was the Reverend Hallgrímur Pétursson (1614–74), indubitably the major poet of the 17th c., if not of all time in Iceland. A humble man who did not, like Stefán Ólafsson, mock the common people, he was not shy about attacking the ruling classes. At one point in his masterful 50-poem cycle, *Passíusálmar* (Passion Hymns), after commenting on Pilate's error in consenting to Jesus's death, Hallgrímur adds: "God grant that those in power over us avoid such monstrous offenses" (Hymn 28). An excellent shorter hymn, "Um dauðans óvissan tíma" (On the Uncertain Hour of Death) is still sung at funerals, a good example of the role that poetry of a high order has played in I. life. Hallgrímur also wrote three *rímur* cycles and other secular poems, such as "Aldarháttur" (Way of the World), contrasting the degenerate present with the glorious period of the I. commonwealth.

Two figures stand out in 18th-c. I. p. Jón Þorláksson (1744– 1819) wrote some popular short poems, including one on a dead mouse in church ("Um dauða mús í kirkju"), and long translations of Pope's *Essay on Man,* Milton's *Paradise Lost,* and Klopstock's *Messias,* the latter two in *fornyrðislag.* Eggert Ólafsson (1726–68) was a child of the Enlightenment who, having studied natural history in Copenhagen and made a survey of Iceland, preached the beauty and usefulness of I. nature in poems such as "Íslandssæla" (Iceland's Riches) and the long *Búnaðarbálkur* (Farming Poem).

This positive attitude toward I. nature became, along with a yearning for independence, an important feature of I. romanticism, whose major poet was Jónas Hallgrímsson (1807–45). Apart from his lyrical descriptions of nature, as in "Ísland"—which begins "Iceland, frost-white mother, land of blessings and prosperity"—he is remembered for his poems on the pain of lost love and for his mastery of many poetic forms, including (for the first time in Iceland) the sonnet and terza rima. The other great romantic poet was Bjarni Thorarensen (1786–1841), who portrayed nature in similes and personifications and tended to glorify winter rather than summer, especially in his poem "Veturinn" (Winter). He also raised a traditional I. genre, the memorial poem, to a new height. Quite different from these Copenhagen-educated men was the poor folk poet and woodcarver Hjálmar Jónsson (1796–1875), known as Bólu-Hjálmar. His large body of verse includes personal invective, *rímur*, bitter complaints about poverty, and poems about death.

One of the greatest poets of the later 19th c. was Matthías Jochumsson (1835–1920), a free-thinking parson and newspaper editor who wrote excellent lyrics, hymns, and memorial poems and also made masterful translations of four of Shakespeare's tragedies.

From the abundance of good modern poets, three representatives will be mentioned here. Einar Benediktsson (1864–1940) was a powerful figure who, as a kind of latter-day Eggert Ólafsson, sought to improve Iceland by forming international corporations to mine gold and harness water power. He used lang. as he used wealth, to gain power over things, and his nature poems, like "Útsær" (Ocean), are rich with the imagery of opposing elements in nature and his view of the pantheistic force uniting all things.

Steinn Steinar (1908–58) came to Reykjavík as a poor youth in the late 1920s, and in his first collection (1934) produced poems of social protest, sympathizing with hungry workers who "don't understand / their own relationship / to their enemies." This same poem, "Veruleiki" (Reality), in free verse, goes beyond skepticism of the social order, however, to speak of the illusory nature of existence itself. This note of doubt, alienation, and nihilism became predominant in Steinn's finely pruned, paradoxical poems, the longest and most highly regarded of which is "Tíminn og vatnið" (Time and the Water), an enigmatic and symbolic meditation probably meant to be sensed rather than comprehended.

Hannes Pétursson (b. 1931) has produced sensitive and meticulously crafted lyrics on a variety of subjects including I. folklore, European places (the prison camp at Dachau, the Strasbourg cathedral), and Cl. figures like Odysseus. Hannes writes with a calm and firm voice on such themes as the emptiness of lang. and man's separation from nature. In "Stórborg" (Big City), he describes himself as sitting like a prisoner in a labyrinth of asphalt and stone from which he escapes, by the grace of a bird or trees or a fountain, "into another context, a bigger and more complex whole, a labyrinth where no one knows what lives deep inside."

BIBLIOGRAPHY: P. Mitchell and K. Ober, *Bibl. of Mod. I. Lit. in Tr.* (1975)—lists trs. of works since the Reformation period.

PRIMARY WORKS: *Bishop Guðbrand's Vísnabók 1612*, ed. S. Nordal (1937)—facsimile with valuable intro. in Eng.; *Hymns of the Passion by Hallgrímur Pétursson*, tr. A. C. Gook (1966); *Íslenzkt ljóðasafn*, ed. K. Karlsson, 6 v. (1974–78)—most comprehensive anthol.; *The Postwar Poetry of Iceland*, ed. and tr. S. Magnússon (1982).

SECONDARY WORKS: J. Þorkelsson, *Om digtningen på Island i det 15. og 16. århundrede* (1888); J. C. Poestion, *Isländische Dichter der Neuzeit* (1897)—begins with the Reformation; R. Beck, *Hist. of I. Poets 1800–1940* (1950); S. Einarsson, *A Hist. of I. Lit.* (1957); J. Hjálmarsson, *Íslenzk nútímaljóðlist* (1971); T. M. Andersson, "The I. Sagas," *Heroic Epic and Saga*, ed. F. J. Oinas (1978). R.CO.

INCA POETRY. See AMERICAN INDIAN POETRY, *South American*.

INDIAN POETRY.

I. OVERVIEW. The term "I. p." commonly refers to the immense and diverse body of usually metrical, often religious, and highly imagistic lit. produced on the I. subcontinent between about 1200 B.C. and the present. This region, which now consists mainly of India, Pakistan, and Bangladesh, is as large and varied as Western Europe. I. p. does not belong to a single, cohesive trad. but rather constitutes a constellation of numerous interacting trads. in about 20 major langs. and several hundred dialects, most of which are used widely in South Asia today.

The langs. of the I. subcontinent have preserved their poetic trads. in oral as well as written forms, using several different scripts both native and foreign. The langs. belong to four families: the Indo-Aryan (a branch of Indo-European, incl. Sanskrit, Hindi-Urdu, and Bengali), the Dravidian (the fourth largest lang. family in the world, containing 25 langs., particularly Tamil, which dates from the second century B.C.), the Austro-Asiatic (which includes many I. tribal langs.), and the Sino-Tibetan (incl. Burmese). The first two of these have dominated I. culture from the beginning. The oldest poetic trad. belongs to Sanskrit, which first achieved canonical status before 1000 B.C. and continued to flourish until the 18th c., while the youngest of the major lits. belongs to Urdu, which emerged only in the 16th c. This article covers the poetic trads. and cultural contexts in all the major Indo-Aryan and Dravidian langs., the primary subjects being Vedic, Sanskrit, Prakrit, Bengali, Hindi, Indian-English, Kannada, Marathi, Tamil, and Urdu poetry, with occasional examples from Gujarati, Malayalam, Panjabi, and Telugu. For more information on poetry in the last-mentioned set of langs., and in langs. we have not discussed—particularly Assamese, Kashmiri, Oriya, and Sindhi—the reader should consult the specialized works on these trads. listed in the bibl. (e.g. Gonda [1973–]; Zelliot; Heifetz and Narayana Rao; Sarma; Kachru).

For the greater part of the present millennium, the Indo-Aryan and Dravidian mother tongues (which are vernaculars as distinct from literary or cl. Sanskrit) have been associated with specific regions of the subcontinent along surprisingly fixed lines. In addition, particular "foreign" langs., esp. Persian (between the 13th and 19th cs.) and Eng. (since the late 18th c.), have periodically come into widespread use, thus greatly complicating the issues of linguistic, regional, national, and cultural identity, as well as of literary style, artistic quality, and poetic trad. In addition to this regional linguistic complexity, itself intensified by the universal prestige enjoyed by Sanskrit in the cl. period and Persian in the middle, there is the greater complexity resulting from the fact that, over the past 1500 years, different langs. have exploded into exemplary creativity and affected the entire I. culture without really becoming nationally spoken langs.; examples of this are Tamil in the middle period and Bengali in the modern period.

The concept of "poetry" in the different I. trads. is reflected in the various native systems of poetic genres. For about 2500 years, I. theorists and literati have often used the word *kāvya* for poetry to distinguish it from other kinds of verbal composition. In its earliest and narrowest meaning (ca. 500 B.C.), the term *kāvya* was used to characterize the poetry of the *Rāmāyaṇa*, which is epic in scope, narrative in structure, and lyrical in effect. In this sense, *kāvya* (as distinguished from the *mantras* or formulaic hymns of the Vedas) signified poetry in the *śloka* meter, with relatively unadorned diction and simplified syntax; the term therefore could also be used to describe the poetic qualities of the other major epic of the period, the *Mahābhārata*. In its somewhat wider and slightly later meaning in the late cl. period, *kāvya* signifies composition in verse, intended to create the experience of *rasa* or a particular set of poetic emotions in the audience. In this sense *kāvya* is of two basic kinds which will be further discussed below: (1) *mahākāvya*, great or major poetry, and (2) *laghukāvya*, short or minor poetry.

In its widest sense, popular around A.D. 700–1200, *kāvya* signifies the full range of imaginative composition, both in verse (*padya*) and prose (*gadya*) and mixtures of verse and prose (*miśra*). It now also includes dramatic or other texts meant for performance, which were composed in verse or prose or both and were often multilingual (in cl. Sanskrit drama, different characters speak different langs. or dialects, depending on their social and regional origins). *Kāvya* further includes prose narrative, both "fictional" (*kathā*) and "nonfictional" (*ākhyāyikā*), such as short stories, novellas and novels, moral tales, fables, biographies, and "true stories." The widest meaning of *kāvya* in the latter part of the ancient period thus coincides with the meaning of lit. itself (called *vāṇmaya* or *sāhitya*), although the term still does not cover the "total order of words" in the various langs. (Sanskrit, the Prakrits, and the several Jain langs. called the Apabhraṃśas) to which it is systematically applied. Because this conception of *kāvya* is so inclusive, I. theorists refine it by distinguishing between *dṛṣya kāvya*, poetry that has to be seen in performance to be properly understood ("drama"), and *śravya kāvya*, poetry that needs only to be heard to be fully grasped ("epic," "lyric," "prose").

In the ancient period, *kāvya* was part of several distinct "Hindu" systems of genres, two of which are worth mentioning here. The first of these systems distinguishes between *śruti* and *smṛti*. The genre of *śruti* (hearing, that which is heard) consists of texts that record "original revelation," while the much larger and more varied genre of *smṛti* (recollection, that which is remembered) contains the "received trad." that has grown up around the *śruti*. Although much of the *śruti* (the Vedic texts) and the *smṛti* (authoritative discourse on religious, philosophical, mythological, social, and political matters, such as the *Manusmṛti* and the *Dharmaśāstras*) is composed in verse, it is considered sacred and canonical and falls outside the sphere of *kāvya*. By the end of the ancient period, however, some texts admitted into the category of *smṛti* (such as the *Mahābhārata* and the *Bhagavadgītā* within it) qualify as *kāvya*. As a consequence, what *kāvya* is in any of its narrow and wider senses also depends on the other types of discourse to which it is related and from which it is distinguished.

The second major system of genres distinguishes between *itihāsa*, *purāṇa*, and *kāvya*. An *itihāsa* is a received or traditional history, such as the *Mahābhārata*, a record and explanation of past, present, and predicted future events on an epic scale. A *purāṇa*, on the other hand, is an "old text," a more popular or sectarian account of affairs in the world, and is focused on a temple or religious community. In contrast, a *kāvya* is distinguished by its aesthetic qualities and purposes, its creation of poetic emotions and pleasurable fictions. If *itihāsa* and *purāṇa* are modes of discourse "about" the world, then *kāvya* remains suspended in a realm of imaginative effect and memorable entertainment, and stands only in a potential relation to the world of everyday experience. *Itihāsa* and *purāṇa* thus shift towards *smṛti* and *śruti* to constitute a broad continuum of culturally and ideologically authoritative or "true" discourse, while *kāvya* as *vāṇmaya* or *sāhitya* (lit.) stands apart as fictive discourse (Tripp).

These and other such concepts are discussed in greater detail in recent crit. on I. p. (Dimock et al., 1974; Ingalls). Here, we shall use a mixture of I. and Western theories of poetry to describe some of the most important poetic trads. of the subcontinent over three millennia, and esp. to show how I. *kāvya* in its various senses changes, often irreversibly, and profoundly alters the ancient notion of *kāvya* itself. In our discussion of the ancient period, we shall concentrate on three different types of Sanskrit (verse) composition: (a) *śruti* or *mantra* (the Vedas); (b) *itihāsa* (the *Mahābhārata*); and (c) *kāvya* (from the epic *Rāmāyaṇa* to cl. *mahākāvya* and *laghukāvya* and their successors).

II. THE ANCIENT PERIOD (ca. 1200 B.C.–A.D. 1200). If we set aside the large lits. in the Buddhist lang. Pali and the Apabhraṃśas (the "fallen speech" varieties used by authors of the Jain religion towards the end of the ancient period), I. p. between about 1200 B.C. and A.D. 1200 was written chiefly in various forms of Sanskrit, the oldest of which (Vedic) reflects the patterns of a spoken lang. The 40 or more Prakrits that appeared later in this period probably evolved from the emerging common speech varieties of the subcontinent, and were closely related to Sanskrit in linguistic as well as literary terms.

A. *Vedic Poetry.* The Vedas, probably composed in the second half of the second millennium B.C. and redacted around 1000 B.C., contain the oldest surviving I. p. There are four Vedic collections (*samhitas*). The earliest (and best known in the West) is the *Ṛgveda* or the Veda of the Stanzas.

The *Ṛgveda* contains 1028 poems averaging ten verses in length, addressed to a wide variety of gods and treating a large assortment of themes. Among the gods it invokes in hymns, prayers, and supplications are Agni, Indra, Varuṇa, and Rudra, and among its recurrent themes are creation, birth, death, sacrifice, *soma*, earth, sky, water, dawn, night, women, and the horse of sacrifice. The verse is cryptic and the symbolism often obscure, but many of the *Ṛgvedic* poems are imagistic and disjointed, and even brilliantly surreal. The poems include natural descriptions, dramatized human and divine interactions, and condensed narratives and myths of various kinds, as well as riddles, epigrams, and spells. Although the context of these poems is ritual and the facts of performance are now complicated by the passage of time, many of them are poetically superb—strikingly fresh in imagery, dense in structure, memorable in sound and phrasing (O'Flaherty).

The second collection, the *Yajurveda* or the Veda of the Formulas, contains sacred formulas in verse which priests recite at the Vedic sacrifice. The third, the *Sāmaveda* or the Veda of the Chants, is mainly an anthol. of material found in the *Ṛgveda*. The fourth, the *Atharvaveda* or the Veda of the *atharvan* (a special kind of priest), brings together many sorts of prayers, incantations, spells, magic formulas, and songs. The Vedic verse collections are supplemented by three main kinds of later canonical discourse. The *Brāhmaṇas* are commentaries on the ritual aspects of the Vedas, while the *Āraṇyakas* are "books studied in the forests" (where early Hindu renouncers, sages, and seers seem frequently to have congregated); both are written in expository and narrative prose. The third type of discourse consists of the *Upaniṣads*, collections of "esoteric equations," which are also largely in prose, although some of the later *Upaniṣads*, produced around 500 B.C., contain some of the earliest didactic poetry, a very significant genre in the I. trad.

The four Vedas, esp. the *Ṛgveda*, and the 13 principal *Upaniṣads* have exercised an enormous influence on Hindu and I. culture, at least among the dominant castes and classes. The primary literary influences of Vedic poetry, however, have been quite specific, among which three are particularly important. First, the anonymous Vedic poets, esp. of the *Ṛgveda*, "invented" a substantial amount of the I. poetic imagery that has undergone endless variation and amplification in the various I. langs. over the succeeding 3000 years—e.g. sun, fire, rivers, horses, cows, frogs, monsoon rain, flowers. Second, the Vedic poets established a simple formal and structural principle for nonnarrative verse that dominated much I.-lang. poetry until the last quarter of the 19th c.: each verse must express one complete poetic thought. Third, Vedic poetic practice established the caesura that divides a line of premodern I. verse into two equal or unequal portions. Vedic meters provided the basis for the numerous simple and intricate meters that subsequently came to dominate Sanskrit and I.-lang. poetry (Keith; Lienhard; Dimock et al. 1974).

B. *Sanskrit Epic Poetry.* Between about 700 B.C. and A.D. 500, Sanskrit poets drew on a long trad. of bardic narrative, martial stories, and heroic tales, as well as popular accounts of specific historical events, to create the two major epics, the *Rāmāyaṇa* and the *Mahābhārata*. Although both these composite poems are traditionally attributed to specific I. authors, the latter, especially, clearly has been composed and edited collectively over a long period of time. The *Rāmāyaṇa*, attributed to Vālmīki—who may well have composed its central portion—was probably completed earlier, between about 600 and 300 B.C.; the *Mahābhārata*, attributed to Vyāsa ("the compiler"), is usually placed between about 500 B.C. and A.D. 500. The term "epic" can be applied only loosely to these works, however, for they have little in common with the conventions and structures of the Western epic trad. as defined by Homer, Virgil, Dante, and Milton. I. readers and theorists most often place the *Rāmāyaṇa* in the genre of *kāvya* (poetry, imaginative fiction) and the *Mahābhārata* in the genre of *itihāsa* (history, received trad.).

(1) The *Mahābhārata* is the longest poem in the world, running to about 100,000 verses in its canonical versions, nearly seven times the length of the *Iliad* and the *Odyssey* combined. It is divided into 18 major books (*parvans*) and concurrently into 100 minor books, each type of book being further divided into chapters (*adhyāyas*). The entire text with minor exceptions is in verse and employs a variety of meters, with the *śloka* predominating. The bulk of the poem, which would take nearly 25 days and nights to recite continuously at the rate of one verse per minute, is cast as a single dialogue between two characters, Vaiśaṃpāyana and Janmejaya. Vaiśaṃpāyana, the principal "reteller" of the story, is a student of Kṛṣṇa Dvaipāyana or Vyāsa, traditionally identified as the original author or compiler of the *Mahābhārata.* His listener and interlocutor, King Janmejaya, is a sixth-generation descendant of the principal characters of the *Mahābhārata*; it is on the occasion of a great snake sacrifice at his court that Janamejaya wishes to hear once again who his famous ancestors were and what they did.

Both outside and within this main frame of dialogue are embedded hundreds of complete, interlinked, separate, and overlapping narratives. Each of the embedded or lesser stories has its own particular teller (and sometimes its own interlocutors or listeners), so that somewhere between 300 and 400 "characters" serve as the work's "narrators within narratives." Many of the narratives nested inside the Vaiśaṃpāyana-Janmejaya dialogue are also structured as dialogues; a specific character or narrator tells a particular story or part of the main story to one or more listeners inside the fiction, so that narrator and audience, action and observation, story and dialogue become inseparable from each other and from the substance of the *Mahābhārata* throughout.

The *Mahābhārata* has at least three interrelated primary narrative lines or plots (van Buitenen, v. 1). The basic narrative framework involves over 50 major characters and spans half a dozen successive generations in an attempt to record and explain every aspect of the conflict between two branches of the Bhārata clan. The two branches are the Pāṇdavas (the sons of Pāṇdu) and the Kauravas (the descendents of Kuru), involved in a protracted struggle for power over the kingdom of Hastināpur (north of modern Delhi). The epic also includes a massive recounting of the long genealogy of the clan of the Bhāratas, mythological and cosmological accounts of all the significant events in the story, discussions of the ethics of the principal characters and their actions, and a general recapitulation (in poetic, narrative, and quasi-dramatic terms) of the entire known ancient I. world in its political, religious, philosophical, mythological, and cultural aspects. The poets of the *Mahābhārata* boldly claim: "What is found in the world is found in this book; what is not found here is not found in the world." Within its vast, epic perimeter, the *Mahābhārata* is also dialogic at the deepest level of meaning; every event, situation, and character anticipates a response and gives rise to multiple viewpoints, esp. in ethical terms, so that nothing crucial to the narrative remains unambiguous or uncontested.

Epic, heroic, and tragic in its scale and impact, the *Mahābhārata,* traditionally classified as an *itihāsa* (a received history), also refers to itself as a *kāvya,* a great poem shaped by poetic insight into the nature of the human (I., Hindu) world. But the style of the work is often plain and even rough, and not always beautiful in comparison with later Sanskrit *kāvya,* esp. cl. *mahākāvya.* The *Mahābhārata* is also ultimately anagogic in meaning (in the Dantean sense), which complicates the generic status of the poem as well as the issue of how the text is to be interpreted. In this sense, the poem is understood as a discourse on *dharma* (right conduct, ethics, duty) and the many ambiguities in the story serve to outline the ethical dilemmas that define cl. Hindu civilization.

The generic confusion of the *Mahābhārata* has no easy solution, esp. because it contains within itself the *Bhagavad-gītā,* often regarded independently as one of the great poems of world lit. The *Bhagavad-gītā,* by now translated into all major langs., is a dialogue in 18 chapters (*adhyāyas*) that takes place on the battlefield of Kurukṣetra between Lord Kṛṣṇa and Arjuna, in which the ethical dilemmas posed by civil war are debated. Together with the *Mahābhārata* as a whole, which is sometimes treated as "a fifth Veda," the *Bhagavad-gītā* has exercised an influence on subsequent life and culture on the subcontinent that cannot be explained in terms merely of the generic conventions of *itihāsa, kāvya,* or *śāstra* (van Buitenen; Zaehner; Miller 1986).

(2) The *Rāmāyaṇa,* in contrast, is a relatively homogeneous text about one-fourth the length of the *Mahābhārata.* Traditionally called a *kāvya,* the poem also describes itself as an *itihāsa,* a history of the Raghuvaṃśa, the clan of Raghu to which King Rāma belongs. In fact, I. readers most often think of the *Rāmāyaṇa* as the *ādikāvya* or the first poem in the I. literary trad., and of its traditional author, the sage Vālmīki, as the *ādikavi* or first poet. Vālmīki is said to have invented the *śloka* meter, valued as the most poetic of the ancient meters, and the *Rāmāyaṇa* is the oldest and greatest poem composed in it. But because of its religious importance, and its concern with the themes of Hindu ethics, government, and family, the *Rāmāyaṇa* is also regarded as a devotional, discursive, and normative text. Like the *Mahābhārata,* then, the *Rāmāyaṇa* is a poem rich enough to belong simultaneously to several major genres, and to be sacred and poetic in several different senses.

Unlike the *Mahābhārata,* the *Rāmāyaṇa* basically tells one continuous story in a fairly straightforward manner. The story concerns the succession to the throne of the ancient republic of Kosala (now in northeastern Uttar Pradesh), and its protagonist is Rāma, the eldest in the line of succession. Although it contains many smaller stories embedded within the story of Rāma and his wife Sītā, these narratives function as episodes within the main action rather than as digressions or elaborations of the kind found in the larger work. The central story line is complicated by the ethical issues and emotional dilemmas facing the main characters of the story: Queen Kaikeyī's ambitiousness and duplicity, her hold over Rāma's aging father King Daśaratha, Rāma's brother Lakṣmaṇa's decision to accompany Rāma and Sītā into exile, Sītā's abduction by Rāvaṇa, Sītā's faithfulness to Rāma while imprisoned in Laṅkā, and so on (Goldman et al.).

The *Rāmāyaṇa* is also very different in effect from the *Mahābhārata* because its main story is narrated in a single omniscient voice, which we associate with the implied presence of Vālmīki. The whole is organized into seven books (*kāṇḍas*) and divided into many short chapters (*sargas*), each of which tells one portion of the story progressively with sharpness, clarity, and concision. While the *Rāmāyaṇa* does not have the dialogue structure of the *Mahābhārata*, in the various Sanskrit forms in which it has come down to us it is fascinatingly self-reflexive. After a 14-year exile, Rāma returns to Ayodhyā as its rightful king. Sītā's likely violation by Rāvaṇa leads him to send her away to a hermitage in the forest which belongs to Vālmīki. There Sītā gives birth to twin sons, Lava and Kuśa, who learn and perfect the art of bardic recitation and singing. Vālmīki then teaches them—the sons of Rāma—the *Rāmāyaṇa* he has composed, and it is they who turn up at Rāma's court and sing the whole tale to the very men who are its heroes and characters. The *Rāmāyaṇa* thus contains its poet, performers, listeners, characters, and events in a closed poetic narrative of great power which is remarkably close to what W. B. Yeats called the "hermetic egg" of the poem that cannot break out of its shell.

C. *Classical Sanskrit Poetry.* Although the *Mahābhārata* and the *Rāmāyaṇa* probably continued to be edited and revised until around A.D. 500, by ca. A.D. 200 new kinds of Sanskrit poetry had begun to be composed. The new poetry, characterized chiefly by its forms, themes, and style, is usually called "classical" (as distinct from epic).

Western scholars frequently identify *kāvya* in its cl. phase as a style rather than as a genre (Keith; Seely et al.; Lienhard). This new style involved a conscious effort to create a verbal texture pleasing to both the ear and the mind. Heavily figural lang. (involving *alaṃkāra*, rhetorical embellishments or figures), strictly grammatical constructions, heavy use of nominal compounds (*samāsa*) instead of inflections, a display of learning in the arts and sciences, and a wide variety of complicated meters and verseforms all contributed to an overt show of poetic and rhetorical prowess. The cl. *kāvya* style was usually applied to subject matter provided by the earlier epics, to the creation of the specific poetic emotions (*rasas*), and esp. to the description of romantic love. In a large measure, these features gave cl. Sanskrit poetry its "impersonal" quality, analogous to the quality T. S. Eliot valorized in his theory of poetry. Among the masters of the cl. *kāvya* style were Aśvaghoṣa (2d c.), Kālidāsa (5th c.), Bhāravi (6th c.), Bhaṭṭi, Bāṇa, Kumāradāsa, Māgha, Daṇḍin, Bhartṛhari (all 7th c.), and Bhavabhūti (8th c.), as well as such later poets as Bilhaṇa, Śrīharṣa, and Jayadeva (all 12th c.). These poets and their lesser counterparts contributed to the formation and consolidation of the cl. *kāvya* style in the *mahākāvya* and *laghukāvya* genres.

(1) *Mahākāvya* (poetry in major forms) includes works that are several hundred (or even thousand) lines long, sometimes in a variety of meters. A *mahākāvya* is also referred to as a *sargabandha* poem because it is usually produced by binding together several or many *sargas* (cantos or chapters). The *mahākāvyas* by Kālidāsa, Bhāravi, Māgha, and Śrīharṣa are frequently regarded as model poems of their kind in Sanskrit poetry. The earliest surviving examples of the cl. style and the genre, however, are two *mahākāvyas* by the Buddhist poet Aśvaghoṣa (2d c.), the *Buddhacarita* and the *Saundarānanda*. The *Buddhacarita*, the complete version of which is known only through Tibetan and Chinese translations, describes in the extant Sanskrit portion the birth, childhood, and youth of Prince Gautama, leading up to the moment of his enlightenment as the Buddha. The *Saundarānanda* tells the story of how the Buddha converted his half-brother Nanda from the latter's deep love for his wife Sundarī and their worldly life together to a life of Buddhist monasticism. Both works contain numerous descriptions of natural and urban scenes, royal spectacles, amorous episodes, and theological and philosophical aphorisms—all of which were to become primary characteristics of *kāvya* over the next one thousand years.

The *mahākāvya*, however, achieved its mature form only with Kālidāsa. According to I. lore, Kālidāsa (5th c.) was originally an illiterate woodcutter but nevertheless found his genius as a poet and dramatist at the court of Candragupta Vikramāditya at Ujjain (now in Madhya Pradesh). Kālidāsa's plays include the *Śakuntalam*, probably the best known ancient I. work in the West other than the *Ṛgveda* and the *Bhagavad-gītā*. His long poem *Meghadūta* and his two *mahākāvyas*—*Kumārasambhava* and *Raghuvanśa*—represent cl. Sanskrit poetry at its most refined.

Kālidāsa's *Meghadūta* (The Cloud Messenger), though technically not a *mahākāvya*, is an elaborate conceit of the *envoi* type. Here a *yakṣa* (a nature deity or demi-god) asks a cloud to carry a message to his beloved. The poem describes the cloud's journey in detail, mixing descriptions of scenic beauty with evocations of the emotions of separation and then union (Nathan). His *Kumārasaṃbhava* (The Birth of Kumāra, the War God), a proper *mahākāvya*, describes the courtship and marriage of Lord Śiva and the daughter of the Himalayas, the goddess Pārvatī. The god of love, Kāmadeva, attempts to facilitate the union by distracting Śiva's attention while he is performing austerities; Śiva, angry, destroys Kāmadeva by opening his third eye; Pārvatī, however, succeeds where Kāmadeva failed by serving her lord faithfully; Śiva and Pārvatī marry, and on their wedding night conceive Kumāra. Kālidāsa's *Raghuvaṃśa* (The Dynasty of Raghu), his second *mahākāvya*, recounts the legends of the north-I. kings of the solar dynasty and retells the story of Rāma and Sītā.

Some of the other exemplary *mahākāvyas* in the Hindu trad., composed later, are based on material from the *Mahābhārata*. In Bhāravi's *Kirātārjunīya* (Arjuna and the Mountain Man, 6th c.) Arjuna fights a wild man who turns out to be Lord Śiva himself. Māgha's *Śiśupālavadha* (The Slaying of King Śiśupāla, 7th c.) draws on a different story from the same epic in which Śiśupāla insults Kṛṣṇa (an *avatāra* or incarnation of Lord Viṣṇu), and Kṛṣṇa then beheads him in combat. Śrīharṣa's *Naiṣadhacarita* (The Life of Nala, King of Niṣadha; 12th c.) is based on the Nala and Damayantī tale, perhaps the most famous of the stories embedded within the *Mahābhārata* (Keith; van Buitenen, v. 1). Two other significant *mahākāvyas* in the trad. from the same period are Bhaṭṭi's *Bhaṭṭikāvya* and Kumāradāsa's *Jānakīharaṇa*, the latter based on the episode of Sītā's abduction in the *Rāmāyaṇa*.

(2) *Laghukāvya*, a category of diverse poetry in minor forms, includes riddles, proverbs, and aphorisms; descriptive poems and seasonal verse; confessional poems; epigrams; erotic and love poems; devotional and religious lyrics; hymns and prayers to the natural elements; philosophical reflections and wisdom poems; verses on childhood, youth, and old age; didactic poems; imagistic observations; and even short dramatic monologues. In any of these kinds of poetry, a given piece may be in a particular metrical form or mixture of meters, often with an intricate prosodic pattern, and the category as a whole contains examples of virtually every well-known and obscure prosodic and formal variation possible in the lang. Other than brevity, the primary qualities of these poems are concreteness of imagery; exactness of description; powerful visual, aural, and emotional suggestion; refinement of expression and sensibility; and memorability. In most cases, a short poem of this kind evokes a very specific *rasa*, a poetic emotion or mood, presenting it in its purest and most concentrated form. The most highly valued *laghukāvya* verses in Sanskrit, and by extension in the Prakrit langs., are called *subhāṣita* or "well-fed, well-turned."

Much of the short lyric and didactic poetry from the ancient period of I. p., and esp. in cl. Sanskrit, is preserved in *kośas* (anthologies). A popular form of the *kośa*-style anthol. in the cl. Sanskrit period was the *śataka*, a "century" of verses. In the 7th c., four important *śatakas* of well-turned Sanskrit poems were compiled. One is the "Amaru collection" from Kashmir—attributed to a legendary author-editor, King Amaru—which served as a source for later anthols. such as Vidyākara's *Subhāṣitaratnakośa* (An Anthol. of the Jewels of Well-Turned Verses; 12th c.). The other three are attributed to the poet Bhartṛhari, who organized them thematically: the first of his *śatakas* contains love poems; the second, epigrams of worldly wisdom; and the third, poems of dispassion or renunciation. Throughout the ancient period, such *kośas* drew on two kinds of material: short poems that were explicitly written as *laghukāvya*, and complete verses or series of verses extracted from longer works, esp. *mahākāvyas*, which could stand on their own (Ingalls; Miller 1967).

Some Sanskrit poetry written at the end of the ancient period or early in the middle period falls outside the categories of *mahākāvya* and *laghukāvya*. Two 11th-c. works esp. modify the genres of I. p. in important ways. Jayadeva's *Gītagovinda*, for instance, is structured in cantos like a *mahākāvya*, but its lang. is much more lyrical than its cl. antecedents. It intersperses short religious-erotic songs between the longer movements, and its overall theme is closer to the concerns of the short religious or devotional poems written in Sanskrit through much of the cl. period. It takes up the theme of Kṛṣṇa and Radha's love and turns Radha into an object of religious devotion within the Vaiśnava poetic trad. Jayadeva's variation on the subject has proved both memorable and extremely influential in I. p., music, dance, and painting (Miller 1977). Bilhaṇa's *Caurapañcāśikā* (Fifty Poems of a Thief of Love), on the other hand, brings together a series of short poems on a single theme, a remembered clandestine affair between a poet and a princess (Miller 1971). The great cycle (or series of cycles) of Sanskrit poetry from about 1200 B.C. to A.D. 1200 thus comes to a close remarkably different from its beginning in Vedic hymns.

D. *Prakrit Poetry.* Cl. Sanskrit, as we noted above, was probably based on a variety of common speech early in the ancient period, but soon acquired the characteristics of an elite, sophisticated literary lang. and served as the "official" lang. of court and state for a very long time. The common langs. of the people of the I. subcontinent during much of the first millennium A.D., and probably a little earlier, were the Prakrit langs., which appear in written form in central India around the 2d c. Over 40 Prakrit langs. are recorded; they are classified linguistically as Middle Indo-Aryan langs.

The Prakrit langs. were put to several kinds of literary uses. In multilingual Sanskrit plays of the cl. period, for instance, the common characters and most of the women (even the queens) speak in Prakrit, while the kings and courtiers (and an occasional female mendicant) speak in the more refined Sanskrit. At the same time, many of the love lyrics of the ancient period, esp. those describing the feelings of women, are composed in Prakrit. The Prakrits, simpler in imagery, style, and emotion, seem to have been the langs. of choice for early I. song.

The most important Prakrit for lit. hist. is Maharashtri, which was used in central India in the 1st millennium A.D. King Hālā (ca. 3d c.) used Maharashtri to compose his *Sattasaī* or the *Gāthā Śaptaśadi.* It is an anthol. of about 700 short lyrics, broadly similar in content and convention to the cl. Sanskrit *laghukāvya kośas* of the kind described above. The Prakrit *gāthā,* together with the Sanskrit *kośa,* serves as the model for the collection of verses and short poems that dominates the middle period of I. p. in the Indo-Aryan vernaculars. Even in the modern period., a 20th-c. Marathi poet like P. S. Rege uses Hala's *gāthā* as a model for a collection of short, lyrical (often erotic and personal) poems.

E. *Classical and Epic Tamil Poetry.* The oldest non-Sanskrit lit. on the I. subcontinent belongs to Tamil, one of the four literary langs. of the Dravidian family found in the southern peninsular region. Early cl. Tamil lit. is called *caṅkam* lit., since it is believed to have been produced by three successive *cannkams* or academies of poets. It is represented by eight anthols., ten long poems, and a grammar called the *Tolkāppiyam* (Old Composition). Nothing of the first *caṅkam* of writers has survived; the *Tolkāppiyam* is ascribed to the second *caṅkam*; and the anthols. and long poems are all said to be the work of the third *caṅkam* and probably belong to the first three centuries of this era. Together the eight anthols. and ten long poems constitute a body of 2,381 poems ranging in length from 4 to about 800 lines; about 100 of these poems are anonymous, but the rest are the work of 473 poets known by name or by epithet (Ramanujan 1986; Hart 1979).

In the *Tolkāppiyam,* a work that is crucial for the understanding of cl. Tamil poetry, and in the anthols. themselves, this body of verse is divided into two main *tiṇais* or genres whose features are completely independent of Sanskrit poetics: *akam* (interior) poetry and *puṟam* (exterior) poetry. *Akam* poems are highly structured love poems, while *puṟam* poems are heroic poems on war, death, social and historical circumstances, the characteristics of kings, and the condition of the poets. In the anthols. both types of poems carry colophons added by later commentators. The colophon to an *akam* poem identifies its speaker with a phrase like "What she said to her girlfriend" or "What his mother said to the neighbors," while the colophon to a *puṟam* poem usually identifies its speaker, the poet, and his patron (a chieftain or king). The poems thus function like dramatic monologues in very specific situations in the interior and exterior worlds of ancient Tamil culture.

The basic conventions of the two genres derive from a taxonomy of Tamil landscapes and the cultures associated with them. Using these conventions, the *akam* genre portrays an interior landscape of love, while the *puṟam* genre portrays an exterior landscape of war. Although the two genres are distinct, they parallel each other so that love and war become part of the same universe and metaphors for one another.

The taxonomy created by the ancient Tamil poets and their commentators is comprehensive and focuses on concrete particulars. The year is divided into six seasons and the day into six parts. The Tamil country is divided into five poetic landscapes (hill, seashore, forest and pasture, countryside, and wasteland); each landscape is then named after the flower or vegetation characteristic of it (*kuṟiñci, neytal, mullai, marutam,* and *pālai* respectively) and characterized by what it contains. Thus each landscape becomes a repertoire of images for the poets, and anything in it, whether a bird or drum, tribal name or dance, can then evoke a specific feeling. A favorite device for such evocation is *uḷḷuṟai* (metonymy), in which the description of one thing evokes that of another associated with it in a particular landscape. The natural scene implicitly evokes the human scene; thus the image of bees making honey out of the *kuṟiñci* flower becomes a metonymic representation of the lovers' union.

In the *akam* genre, each of the five landscapes is matched metaphorically with the five phases of love, the times of day, and the season most appropriate to those phases: *kuṟiñci* (a white flower; hillside) is the landscape of union, at night in the cool season; *mullai* (jasmine; forest, pasture) is the landscape of patient waiting and domesticity, late in the evening and in the rainy season; *marutam* (queen's-flower; countryside, agricultural lowland) is the landscape of lovers' unfaithfulness and "sulking scenes," in the morning in all seasons; *neytal* (blue lily; seashore) is the landscape of anxiety in love and separation, at nightfall in all seasons; and *pālai* (desert tree; wasteland) is the landscape of elopement, hardship, separation from lover or parents, at midday and in summer. A similar but looser encoding of exterior situations occurs in the *puṟam* genre, where the landscapes are more inhospitable, often devastated by strife, battle, and destruction.

The *akam* poetry of cl. Tamil is found in five of the eight anthols.: the *Kuṟuntokai,* the *Naṟṟiṇai,* the *Akanāṉūṟu,* the *Aiṅkuṟunūṟu,* and the *Kalittokai.* The poems of the *puṟam* genre are collected in three anthols.: the *Puṟanāṉūṟu,* the *Patiṟṟuppattu,* and the *Paripāṭal.* Taken together, these eight anthols. and the ten long poems give us a very detailed, highly structured, and intricately encoded picture of the cl. Tamil world, in which not only is the poet's lang. Tamil, but the landscapes, personae, moods, and situations are themselves a code of signifiers for Tamil culture. For five or six generations at the beginning of the first millennium A.D. the *caṅkam* poets spoke this common lang. with a passion, maturity, originality, and delicacy which may well be unique in the ancient I. world (Ramanujan 1986).

Between ca. A.D. 300 and 900, this *caṅkam* lit. gave way to ancient Tamil epic poetry. The two main works in this trad. are the twin (interlinked) epics, the *Cilappatikāram* by Iḷaṅkō Aṭikaḷ and the *Maṇimēkalai* by Cātaṉār, which draw on cl. Tamil poetics as well as on Sanskrit models. Aṭikaḷ's *Cilappatikāram*, composed in three books, tells a story not about kings but about Kōvalaṉ, a young Pukār merchant unjustly executed for a crime he did not commit, and his wife, the virtuous Kaṇṇaki, who acquires power through her unfailing faithfulness and becomes a goddess of chastity (Daniélou 1965).

Cātaṉār's *Maṇimēkhalai* (the last part of which is missing) continues the story of the *Cilappatikāram*; the heroine Maṇimēkalai, a dancer and courtesan like her mother Mātavi, (Kōvalaṉ's mistress), is torn between romantic love and spiritual longings. While the *Cilappatikāram* gives us a detailed picture of Tamil culture—its varied religions, towns, people (a mixture of Tamils, Arabs, and Greeks), performing arts, and daily life—using Tamil *caṅkam* poetics as well as Sanskrit poetics and folklore without any particular religious commitment, the *Maṇimēkhalai* is clearly a work influenced by Buddhism (Daniélou 1989).

After about the 6th c. A.D., Tamil poetry and lit. swerved increasingly towards the phenomenon called *bhakti*, intense personal devotion to a particular god, usually either Viṣṇu or Śiva, the two principal gods of ancient and subsequent Hinduism. The earliest Tamil *bhakti* poets were the 12 Nāyaṉār saints, devotees of Śiva, whose earliest representative was the woman poet Kāraikkāl Ammaiyār. The most important Nāyaṉārs were Appar and Campantar (7th c.), and Cuntarar (8th c.). Among the major works of Śaiva *bhakti* in Tamil is the collection of hymns called the *Tiruvācakam* by Māṇikkavācakar (9th c.), for whom Śiva was lover, lord, master, and guru. The Śaiva *bhaktas* were followed by the Tamil Vaiṣṇava saint-poets, called the Āḻvārs. Among the poets who worshiped Viṣṇu, one of the earliest was again a woman, Āṇṭāḷ (8th c.). The greatest of the Āḻvār poets was also one of the last, Nammāḻvār (9th c.), who expresses poignantly the pain and ecstasy of loving God (Ramanujan 1981).

As this discussion suggests, in what we have called the ancient period, I. p. evolved along several distinct lines (within Sanskrit and outside it), passed through a number of well-defined phases (in Sanskrit, from Vedic to epic to classical; in Tamil, from *caṅkam* to epic to devotional, etc.), and came to constitute a very large and multiform body of verbal composition. This body of poetry steadily became an immense reservoir of commonplaces for subsequent I. poets to draw upon. In the middle and modern periods it also became the canon against which poets and audiences could react, as they began to create new identities in lang., style, poetic theme, genre, religious orientation, and social and political ideology. As the ancient period drew to a close, I. poets started extending the domain of poetry or *kāvya* in ways that the cl. theorists and practitioners of verse could not have envisioned.

III. THE MIDDLE PERIOD (ca. A.D. 600–1500 TO 1800). The middle period of I. p. begins at different times in the different langs. and regions of the subcontinent. In Tamil poetry, it begins around A.D. 600, well before the ancient period of Sanskrit lit. comes to an end, whereas in the case of langs. like Urdu it begins only after 1500. Broadly speaking, however, the middle period comes to a close around 1800 for most of the Indo-Aryan and Dravidian mother tongues, even though clearly modern poetry, prose fiction, and drama do not appear in many of them until after about 1860. Although the absence of definite and uniform historical closure makes generalizations extremely difficult, it is nevertheless possible to say that during the middle period as a whole, esp. between about 1000 and 1500, Sanskrit and the Prakrits cease to be the primary medium of literary composition and give way gradually to the regional mother tongues. Sanskrit has continued to be used for scholarly and ritual purposes down to the present, but the last great original poets in it, such as Jayadeva, belong to the 12th c.

This large-scale linguistic and literary shift, which seems similar to the shift from Lat. to the vernaculars in Europe near the end of the Middle Ages, goes hand in hand in India with a selective but concerted devaluation of the ancient past, and particularly with the rise of a new chauvinism focused on the Indo-Aryan and Dravidian vernaculars and their native regions. The shift also accompanies very significant changes in the political complexion of the subcontinent (the Muslims arrive to stay after about 1200 and dominate much of India until the beginning of the 18th c.). But most importantly, the shift is part of a profound evolution in religious and literary theory and practice (Ramanujan 1981).

The first mother tongue to develop the new kind of poetry was a Dravidian lang., Tamil. Among the Indo-Aryan langs., Bengali in eastern India and Marathi near the western coast were the first to be written down (ca. 1000 A.D.). Between the 10th and 14th cs., poetry appeared for the first time on a significant scale in several other linguistic media: in Assamese, Oriya, Hindi, Rajasthani, Gujarati, and Kashmiri, among the Indo-Aryan langs.; and in Kannada, Telugu, and Malayalam, among the Dravidian langs. Between the 14th and 16th cs., poetry also appeared in Panjabi and

Urdu, and by this time Arabic, Turkish, and Persian had also entered I. discourse as a result of Muslim political success on the subcontinent. By about 1600, all the native langs. mentioned had developed strong and continuous trads. of both oral and written poetry. Many of the particular genres of the middle period were associated with particular langs., social groups (esp. caste communities), and religious sects. Thus, from ca. 600–1600, more than a dozen new major lits. and trads. of poetry appeared on the I. subcontinent, gradually displacing Sanskrit, Prakrit, and cl. Tamil poetry and changing radically the constitution of the world of I. poetic discourse (Dimock et al. 1974).

What poetry is in the middle period is itself an enormous problem, since the change of medium—from three or four main ancient langs. to about 15 new regional mother tongues—involves a transformation of the very notion of poetry and its various functions. Here the problems of historical continuity and difference will be addressed by limiting the discussion to the two main areas of I. p. in the middle period: the *bhakti* movement and Islamic poetry.

A. *Bhakti Poetry.* The most prominent literary, religious, and social movement of the middle period is *bhakti* ("devotion"), which began in the far south (in the Tamil-speaking area) after the 6th c. and spread with surprising success all over the subcontinent by the 16th c. Despite the linguistic fragmentation of India in this period, *bhakti* poetry in a dozen major langs. shares a considerable number of features, while of course revealing many regional variations and peculiarities (Zelliot).

Several thousand poets, variously called *bhaktas* and *sants*, are associated with the *bhakti* movement all over South Asia, but each of the major langs. and dialects has its own particularly valued figures. Among the most significant saint-poets associated with the various kinds of *bhakti* lit. are: the Nāyaṉār devotees of Śiva, the Śrivaiṣṇava Āḻvārs, devotees of Viṣṇu in Tamil (Peterson; Cutler); the Vīraśaiva poets, esp. Basavaṇṇa, Dāsimayya, Allama Prabhu, and Mahādēviyakka, as well as the later *dāsas*, like Purandharadāsa and Kanakadāsa, in Kannada (Ramanujan 1973); Jñāneśvar, Nāmdev, Eknāth, Tukārām, and Rāmdās in Marathi (Kolatkar; Tulpule); Narasiṃha Mehtā and Mīrābāī in Gujarati, of whom the latter also belongs to the Hindi-Rajasthani trad. (Munshi; Hawley and Jurgensmeyer); Kabīr, Sūrdās, Rāidās, and Tulsīdās in Hindi (Vaudeville; Hess; Bryant; Hawley); Nānak in Panjabi (Hawley and Jurgensmeyer); Vidyāpati in Maithili and Candidās, Caitanya, and Rāmparsād in Bengali (Archer; Dimock and Levertov); and Śankardev in Assamese and Jagannāth Dās in Oriya. Over and above these individual poets, there are several sects or schools of *bhakti* poetry, each with its own tribe of saints and poets, such as the Vallabhācarya sect in the Braj Bhasa dialect of Hindi, the Dattātreya sect in Marathi, the Śaiva poets in Telugu, and the Vaiṣṇava poets in Malayalam.

Bhakti, frequently described as theism, centers on devotional poetry in which the poet expresses his or her intensely personal devotion to a particular god (or, occasionally, goddess) or seeks to be one with a god or an undifferentiated godhead. The many hundred *bhaktas* and *sants* (devotees, saint-poets) in the Indo-Aryan and Dravidian trads. of the middle period fall roughly into three categories: (1) those who worship Viṣṇu, one of his ten *avatāras* (incarnations), or one of the numerous local I. gods absorbed into Vaiṣṇava mythology over the centuries; (2) those who worship Śiva, who has no *avatāras* but may be set in different regional and transregional contexts (both Viṣṇu and Śiva are *saguṇa* ["with qualities"]); and (3) those who remain in quest of a god or godhead "without qualities" (*nirguṇa*).

The *saguṇa* poets in the various *bhakti* trads. usually oppose the *nirguṇa* poets ideologically and politically; the former often tend to be conservative while the latter tend to be radical and satiric. Among the *saguṇa* poets themselves, the Vaiṣṇavas and the Śaivas often oppose each other; and among the Vaiṣṇavas, in turn, the worshipers of Rāma and the worshipers of Kṛṣṇa (the two most popular *avatārās* of Viṣṇu in this period) frequently mock and criticize each other. The goal of theistic devotion in the middle period is the same as the goal of ritualistic brahmanism (or even Buddhism) in the ancient period, but the means—ecstatic devotion—of attaining *mukti* ("liberation" from mundane existence) are now substantially different. As this suggests, a great deal remains in common across the great historical, ideological, and linguistic divide between Sanskrit and the later vernaculars. Consequently, many of the *bhakti* poets attempt to "vedicize" themselves and to take ancient Sanskrit texts, such as the *Bhagavad-gītā* and the *Bhāgavata Purāṇa*, as palimpsests to be over-written in the new langs.

Nevertheless, during its primary devel. over six or seven centuries, *bhakti* poetry and its large accompanying lit. (mainly the lives of the poets written in verse and prose and commentaries on the poems) substantially modified, reshaped, and even rejected the brahmanism and Hinduism of the ancient period. Many of the *bhaktas* and *sants* of the middle period were low-caste or "untouchable" men and women, although some of the important poets, such as Tulsīdās in Hindi, Bahiṇābāī in Marathi, and Basavaṇṇa in Kannada, were *brāhmaṇas*, administrators, statesmen, or scholars by birth and by profession. The traditional lives of the devotees of the middle period, mostly written late in the period, are full of miraculous deeds and transformations achieved against the greatest odds. These figures thus become larger-than-life "saints" because of their powerful devotion to their chosen gods and the reciprocal grace (*kṛpā*) those gods confer upon them, a combination that constitutes a major alternative to the ritual nature of "salvation" in ancient Hinduism. The typical poet of the ancient period is a royal sage in a forest, a worldly courtier, a learned priest, or a renouncing *yogi,* while the typical *bhakta* or *sant* in the middle period frequently puts on the persona of an outcast, a rebel, a rustic, or a reformer—sometimes illiterate but practically always divinely inspired.

In general, many of the *bhakti* poets of the middle period oppose the caste system, Vedic and later Hindu ritual, the notions of pollution and untouchability, and brahmanical learning and authority. They also seriously question the ancient hierarchy of genres, attacking the legitimacy of Vedic *śruti* or revelation, the hegemonic status of the brahmanical *śāstras* as cultural codes, and the pedantry involved in a refined (esp. cl. Sanskrit *kāvya*) style. Against the authority of the received trad. or canon they pose the authority of their own immediate experience (*anubhava*), their visions, their intense personal devotion (*bhakti*), and god's privileging grace (*kṛpā*). Despite a few superficial similarities, the I. *bhakti* poets use poetic strategies and function in cultural situations that differ immensely from those of the European and Anglo-Am. trads. of religious poetry. Jñāneśvar, for instance, has little in common with his contemporary Dante.

The *bhakta* or the *sant* often claims that true poetry must be spontaneous, urgent, personal, "divinely inspired," and composed in the simpler and more genuine vernacular rather than a remote and artificial lang. of refinement like Sanskrit. *Bhakti* poets and poems therefore tend to be more immediate, colloquial, autobiographical, confessional, and dramatic than many of their cl. counterparts. But since these qualities became conventionalized early in the *bhakti* movement, the bulk of *bhakti* poetry seems fairly routine and insipid rather than inspired. Though *bhakti* stands out as a "counterculture" in the great flow of I. p., it becomes, in turn, the norm against which subsequent poetic movements define themselves. Thus, by the end of the 18th c., many of the mother tongues (such as Hindi and Marathi) develop bodies of "academic" verse written by learned poets (*paṇḍit kavis*) modeled explicitly on Sanskrit poetry and poetics, which constitute countercurrents to the stream of *bhakti* writing.

Though a large portion of the lexicon, grammar, and prosody of the Indo-Aryan vernaculars is derived in some way from Sanskrit, and Sanskrit metrical verseforms often serve as the basic models for the new poetry, *bhakti* poetry swerves away from Sanskrit *kāvya* on a significant scale in more narrowly literary terms. For instance, as already indicated, if a significant portion of epic and cl. Sanskrit poetry is impersonal and attempts to create the experience of a particular *rasa* in its audience, then much of *bhakti* poetry aims at being personal in tone and serves as immediate self-expression for its authors. Even when the *bhaktas* and *sants* claim to create a *rasa,* they call it the *bhakti rasa* or "the poetic emotion of devotion," which falls outside the conventional list of poetic emotions proper to Sanskrit *kāvya.* Such reorientations acquire meaning and power on ideological grounds as well as within the context of form and genre.

Although the ancient and middle periods are intricately interconnected, their respective poetic forms and genres differ significantly. Many poets and poetic trads. within and outside *bhakti* are so strongly associated with particular vernacular verseforms that those forms acquire the status of genres, as did the sonnet in early modern Europe. For instance, the *mangalakābya,* which lies outside the *bhakti* movement, belongs uniquely to Bengali, the *vacana* to the Vīraśaiva poets in Kannada, the *ramainī* to the Hindi poet Kabir (15th c.), and the *ovi* and the *abhaṅga* to the Marathi poets from Jñāneśvar (late 13th c.) to Rāmdās (late 17th c.). Some genre names cut across several langs., regions, and trads., e.g. the *pada* ("verses, poem, song"), the *padāvalī* (a "string" of songs, very different in structure from a modern Western poetic sequence), and the *gāthā* (an anthol. or collection of poems, modeled on Sanskrit, Pali, and Prakrit antecedents). Besides these new and often precisely differentiated forms (a Hindi *pada,* a Kannada *vacana,* and a Marathi *abhanga* cannot be confused with each other), in the middle period the mother tongues also develop their own "oral epics" and varieties of "folk song," incl. martial sagas, romances, tragic love stories, ballad-like forms, work songs, etc., all of which affect the more canonical genres of poetry. Moreover, a very high proportion of the poetic forms of the middle period is designed for performance or is integrated with some of the performative arts—music, dance, folk or popular theater, dance- drama. As far as *bhakti* poetry itself is concerned, the various religious strands in the movement bring together lyric (short) forms and epic (long) forms, and further bring these forms together with performance of various types.

One common feature of lyrical *bhakti* poetry is a refrain-like pattern that becomes prominent in singing—the opening verse of a poem, often called a *ṭeka,* is repeated after each subsequent verse. The last verse usually identifies its author explicitly in its signature line (called *bhaṇita*) or, in cases like the Kannada *vacanas,* by a unique image, metaphor, or epithet that is clearly the "signature" of that particular poet. This important feature complements the rhetorical mode of many *bhakti* poems cast as dramatic monologues, in which the poet identified speaks in a particular voice, or through a particular persona, to a god or to an immediate audience of listeners. This form of direct address makes a *bhakti* lyric different from the imagistic or descriptive lyric of the *subhāṣita* kind in cl. Sanskrit *laghukāvya,* and differentiates its rhetoric significantly from the kind of speaker-listener drama we find in cl. Tamil *caṅkam* poetry in the *akam* genre.

Some *bhakti* poems are long, and they are frequently intertextual with long poems in the ancient period of I. p. For example, the earliest long poem in Tamil *bhakti*, the *Tirumurukaāṟṟuppaṭai*, which is about the god Murugan, has six sections and draws on earlier *caṅkam* images and ancient Sanskrit mythology. Tulsīdās's *Rāmacaritamānas* in Avadhi (a major literary dialect of Hindi; 16th c.) is several thousand verses long and retells the story of the *Rāmāyaṇa*, but with all the characters now absorbed into a *bhakti* worldview. Rāma thus becomes Tulsīdās's chosen personal god. The poem is clearly epic in scope, tone, and structure, and its conventions derive from those in Vālmīki's Sanskrit *ādikāvya*, but its effect as a whole is very different: the omniscient voice of the narrator, for instance, is now interrupted by the poet-devotee's voice, expressing his devotion to the divine characters. Kampaṉ's *Rāmāyaṇa* in Tamil (12th c.) does something even more complex by accommodating the Sanskrit classic to a Dravidian lang. and its independent cl. trad.: his retelling of Rāma's story is shaped as much by the "interior" and "exterior" landscapes of *akam* and *puṟam* poetry as by the poetic conventions and emotional tones of Tamil Vaiṣṇava *bhakti* (Hart and Heifetz). All such changes connect I. p. of the middle period to the poetry and the poetics of the ancient period, but place many commonplace elements in entirely new combinations.

Many of the features of *bhakti* poetry already mentioned come together in a major poem like the Marathi *Jñāneśvarī*, one of the earliest and greatest works in the lang. of central and western India, and attributed to Jñāneśvar (13th c.), who is said to have achieved *mukti* before he turned 20. The *Jñāneśvarī* is intertextual with the *Bhagavadgītā*; it quotes each verse of the Sanskrit classic in the original lang., and then places several stanzas in Marathi before and after each quotation, thus building a new poem around and inside an old one (Tulpule).

The poetry of the *bhakti* movement coexists in the middle period of I. lit. hist. with a variety of other lits. Although *bhakti* does constitute a "counterculture" within Hindu society at this time, still it does not effectively replace older, continuing, or contemp. lits. Thus in Bengali, for instance, *bhakti* poetry inhabits a larger discursive world which also includes the genre of *mangalakābya* ("poetry of an auspicious happening"), consisting of narratives about and eulogies to local Hindu gods and goddesses, and the Bengali *mahākavya*, based on Sanskrit models (Sen). Similarly, in a Dravidian lang. like Malayalam, poetry written in the Vaiṣṇava trad. coexists with other types of poetic composition, such as the major genre of *pāṭṭu* (song), which combines linguistic and literary elements from Tamil, Sanskrit, and folk sources into a unique and complex trad. of its own after the 15th c. Moreover, *bhakti* lit. coexists with a substantial range of new court poetry, learned or academic poetry, and popular "oral epics" (Roghair; Heifetz and Narayana Rao; Blackburn et al.). In general, it also stands apart from such works and genres as the Hīr- Rānjhā tale in Panjabi, Chand Bardāī's *Prithvirāj rāso* in Hindi, Malik Muhammad Jāyasī's *Padmāvat* in Avadhi, the Buddhist *caryā- padas* in Bengali, and the *lāvaṇi* and the *powāḍā* in Marathi. Among the many such contexts of *bhakti* poetry in the middle period is the body of writing which we shall broadly call Islamic poetry.

B. *Islamic Poetry.* Islam first entered the South Asian region in the 8th c. with the conquest of Sind, and the first Islamic empire (the Delhi Sultanate) emerged early in the 13th c. Between the 13th and 18th cs., the courts of Muslim rulers, esp. in northern India, attracted refugee and immigrant men of letters from Persia and Central Asia (incl. Sufi poets) and also patronized local and regional writers who wrote in Arabic, Turkish, Persian (an Iranian relative of Sanskrit), and Urdu (a highly Islamicized version of Hindi), with the last two langs. becoming predominant. The presence of Islam on the subcontinent permanently influenced many of the Indo-Aryan langs. Modern Hindi, Marathi, and Bengali, for example, derive substantial portions of their lexicons from Arabic and Persian roots (Rypka; Sadiq).

Among the Muslim writers who played important roles in the regional lits. of the subcontinent are: Lallā (14th c.) in Kashmiri; Shāh ʿAbdul-Latīf (17th–18th cs.) in Sindhi; Wāris Shāh (18th c.) in Panjabi; Daulat Qāẓī and Ālāol (17th c.) in Bengali; and Malik Muḥammad Jāyasī, Rahīm, Manjhan (all 16th c.), and ʿUsman (17th c.) in the Avadhi and Braj Bhasha dialects of Hindi. Sufi ideas and poetics, esp. the doctrine of monotheism, clearly influenced the *nirguṇa sant* poets of north India, esp. Kabīr and the various poets in the Sikh *guru* trad. (particularly Guru Nānak, 16th c.), whose poems in a mixture of Panjabi, Hindi, Urdu, and other langs. are included in the canonical text of the Sikh religion, the *Ādigranth* or *Guru Granth Sāhib.*

The trad. of Persian writing in India, which is different from the trads. of Muslim writing in Urdu and in other I. mother tongues, goes back to the 11th c.; its first major poet was Amīr Khusrau (13th– 14th cs.), who composed poetry in Persian, Urdu, and early Hindi (Hindui or Hindavi). The most important poet in this trad. was ʿAbdul Qādir Bēdil (17th c.), who wrote 16 volumes of poetry. The I.-Persian trad. introduced the *masnavī, qaṣīda,* and *ghazal* genres into I. lit.; the *ghazal* in particular became very popular by the end of the middle period. In the 19th and 20th cs., the *ghazal* has spread, principally from Urdu models, to langs. like Panjabi and Marathi.

The poetic trads. of Urdu have their beginnings in Persian as well as in the various I. langs. of the subcontinent. Urdu poetry first appeared in central India at the courts of Bijapur and Golconda in the 16th c. In the early 18th c., Aurangabad in the Deccan became a notable center; from there, Urdu poetry spread to the courts at Delhi and Lucknow in the north, where it acquired an unusual preeminence at the end of the middle period. Two of the characteristic institutions of Urdu poetry emerged during this period: the practice of novice-poets choosing an *ustād* or master from whom they learned the craft of poetry, and the practice of poets gathering in a private or semiprivate setting to read or recite their poems (meetings called *mushāʿirahs*).

The genres of poetry that appeared in Urdu during the middle period were the *qaṣīda* (panegyrics in praise of high or holy personages); the *ḥaju* (personal and other satires; epigrams on contemporaries); the *shahr- āshūb* (poems lamenting the decline or destruction of a city and its culture); the *mars̱iyah* (an elegy for the martyred family and kinsmen of Husayn [Muḥammad's grandson]); the *masnavī* (the preferred genre for long narrative and descriptive poems); and the *ghazal* (a short, metrical, rhymed lyric on a variety of themes, esp. erotic love, Sufi love, and metaphysics). All these forms and genres in Urdu are related to specific antecedents in Persian, Arabic, and Turkish lit., and though they are not all primarily "religious" in function they are never far from the central tenets of various branches of the Muslim faith. The masters of the *qaṣīda* are Saudā and Inshāʿ (18th c.), and Zauq and Ghālib (19th c.); of the *mars̱iyah*, Mīr Anīs and Mīrzā Dabīr (19th c.); of the *masnavī*, a very widely practiced genre, Mīr, Mīr Hasan, Dayā Shankar Nasīm, and Mīrzā Shauq (18th–19th cs.); and of the *ghazal*, Mīr Taqī Mīr (18th c.) and Mīrzā Ghālib (19th c.). As these dates clearly show, the greatest phase of Urdu poetry in the middle period was the 18th through early 19th cs., overlapping with the beginning of the modern period (Ali; Ahmad; Russel and Islam; Russell).

Between ca. 1400 and 1800, *bhakti* poetry and Islamic poetry in India influenced each other extensively. The *nirguṇa sant* poets in the Hindu and Sikh trads., for example, were affected deeply by such elements in the Muslim faith as monotheism, the rejection of all forms of idol-worship, and belief in an egalitarian society; and the Muslim religious poets, esp. the ecstatic poets in the Sufi trad., were in turn affected by *bhakti* performative practices, esp. communal singing in places of worship.

Although we have described the middle period of I. p. mainly in terms of two of its components, the nature of *bhakti* and Islamic poetry, their interrelations, and their divergence from the older I. past should have indicated the kinds of change that took place on the subcontinent between about 600 and 1800. The shift from Sanskrit, the Prakrits, and cl. Tamil (as well as Pali and the Jain Apabhraṃśas) to the major Indo-Aryan and Dravidian mother tongues for literary purposes, the creation and dissemination of new genres and new principles of poetic composition, and the introduction of new beliefs, values, and worldviews added numerous features to I. p. that did not previously exist on the subcontinent. In fact, the middle period not only brought fresh resources into the common stock of I. p., but also became a part of the "traditional" I. world against which the writers of the modern period reacted. In this composite "trad.," *bhakti* poetry (but not Islamic poetry or the poetry of the folk and oral trads.) also came to be referred to as *kāvya*, thus extending the field of canonical poetry well beyond that of Sanskrit *kāvya*.

IV. THE MODERN PERIOD (SINCE CA. 1800). In the conventional view of India's lit. hist., the division between the "traditional" and the "modern" is marked by the establishment of the British colonial empire on the I. subcontinent. Two precise dates are significant: 1757, when the East India Company effectively gained control of Bengal following the Battle of Plassey; and 1818, when the British acquisition of I. territories was practically completed. In the course of the 60 years between these two dates, deeply traditional I. society began to "modernize," affecting not only the "manners and customs" of the natives but also their langs. and—often unknowingly—their lits.

A. *Colonialism and Modernization.* Western-style education first became available on a significant scale to Indians late in the 18th c. with the establishment of a number of influential missionary schools and colleges; after Macaulay's famous "Minute on Education" (1834), Eng.-lang. education became quite commonplace in the cities and towns and among the I. middle and upper classes. In the later 19th c., Indians all over the country began encountering European and Anglo-Am. literary works and reading Eng. translations of Gr. and Roman lit. and the modern European, Eng., and Am. classics. Many I. poets of the 19th c. then began consciously to imitate their Western predecessors and contemporaries, thereby creating one major kind of modern I. p. in the I. mother tongues. Thus Bengali writers started a Bengali trad. of modern epic in verse, just as Marathi poets began composing sonnets, odes, and pastoral elegies, and Hindi poets started writing romantic lyrics. These "imitative innovations" significantly changed the formal, thematic, and generic complexion of the lits. of the subcontinent. The Westernization of India under British rule also went one step further: it created the kind of poet who wanted to write poetry of the Anglo-Am. kind directly in the Eng. lang.

However, contrary to the common claim, the modernity of modern I. writing does not consist entirely in its Westernization, and I. writers did not become modern merely by imitating the qualities invented originally by European or Western writers. In many of the modern Indo-Aryan langs. the 18th and 19th cs. were largely periods of very complex and innovative interaction among the various local, national, and international trads. In Hindi and Marathi, for instance, the transitional decades between the middle and the modern periods (roughly 1775–1875) were dominated by many *paṇḍit- kavis* ("learned" or "academic" poets). These *brāhmaṇa* writers worked with Sanskrit and Persian as their cl. langs., and in the 19th c. also with Eng. as one of their official langs., but used their own vernaculars and local dialects as the actual media of literary composition. Their often voluminous poetry comes in several interlinked genres that cross the boundaries usually erected between derivative and original writing: (1) close translations of Sanskrit poems, plays, and narratives into modern I. mother tongues; (2) loose adaptations, retellings, or imitations of Sanskrit, Persian, and Arabic literary works; (3) "new" works in the modern mother tongues that basically rework old materials from the cl. langs. and from the older lit. in the mother tongues; and (4) genuinely original poems in their own langs. which explicitly adopt the norms and values of Sanskrit (and sometimes Persian-Arabic) poetics. Thus the *paṇḍit-kavis*, as the men who prepared the way for modern poetry without actually practicing it, produced works like Hindi and Marathi translations of Kālidāsa, adaptations of tales from the Arabic *Thousand and One Nights*, modern versions of old Hindi and Marathi poems and tales, and original poems modeled closely on Sanskrit erotic poetry (Dharwadker 1989, v. 2).

This mixed body of writing provided the ground in which Eng. and broadly European influences, both modern and cl., took root. The Western influences first became noticeable in the mid 19th c. when the *paṇḍit-kavis* gave way to the first two generations of writers educated in schools where Eng. was the medium of instruction and the valorized lang. The work of the new Westernized poets of these two generations falls into two main categories: (1) I.-lang. translations of Eng., Am., and some European poetry, such as the works of Shakespeare, Milton, the romantics, Thomas Hood, William Cowper, Tennyson, and Longfellow; and (2) original poems in the I. langs. that involved conscious imitation of Eng. poetic genres from the Ren. onwards, in verseforms that used Sanskrit prosodic principles and meters but had rhyme schemes, stanzaic structures, and thematic elements drawn clearly from Western models and sources. In the long run, this layer of material interacted in complicated ways with the somewhat earlier work done by the *paṇḍit-kavis*, producing mixed prosodic, formal, and generic practices that have become commonplace in the I. langs. of the 20th c. (McGreggor 1974; Schomer).

The pivotal shift from the middle to the modern period, accomplished in a surprisingly short time considering the number of langs. and cultures involved, thus brought together several lines of translation, adaptation, imitation, and original writing, as well as two very different types of poets and writers: native scholars trained in the "purely I." way (mainly in non-Western langs., incl. Persian and Arabic), and "Westernized" natives with bilingual training (mainly in Eng. and their native I. vernaculars). The historical transformation was further shaped by the print media, which introduced a factor of common access, esp. after ca. 1800, that was missing earlier. The transformation, however, was not uniform. In terms of time, the effects of modernization varied a great deal: distinctly modern I. p. appeared first in Eng. (1820s) and Bengali (1840s), and then in langs. like Marathi, Tamil, Panjabi, Gujarati, and Malayalam (1860s–90s), followed by langs. like Hindi, Urdu, and Oriya (1900s–20s) (Dimock et al. 1974; Srinivasa Iyengar; McGreggor 1974; Kopf; Schomer; Dimock 1986; Naik).

The overall effect of colonization on I. p. was thus clearly multifaceted and far-reaching: the encounter with cultures of European origin drove I. poets to experiment with varieties of poetry markedly different from anything the I. trads. themselves had invented so far; it went hand in hand with a renewed interest among I. poets in their own trads. of the ancient and middle periods, incl. Islamic lit.; and it introduced yet another literary lang. into the I. babel—Eng. These effects have continued from the early 19th c. down to the present, and the grafting of Western "influences" onto "native" sensibilities has resulted in a hybrid lit. that has broken away sharply from many of the patterns set up in I. p. over the preceding 3000 years. *Ādhunik kāvya* or *urvācīn kāvya* (modern poetry) swerves away in complicated ways from *prācīn kāvya* (ancient or old poetry), whether that of cl. Sanskrit or of the *bhakti* movement, and pushes the notion of *kāvya* or *kavitā* (poetry) across new frontiers.

B. *The Modern Poetic Genres.* The shift away from the poetry and poetics of the middle period was signaled by a concerted change in poetic forms, themes, conventions, images, metrical frames, and structural principles, as well as by radical changes in the conception of who the poet (*kavi*) is, what his or her functions are, and how his or her audience is constituted. Moreover, the new situation of the I. poet in the 19th and early 20th cs. evoked new attitudes, concerns, tones, and voices. Bengali, Hindi, Marathi, Kannada, and Tamil poets, for example, began experimenting with enjambed lines, imitations of Elizabethan blank verse, Eng. epic conventions, Miltonic similes, greater romantic lyrics, and specific European and non-I. verseforms grafted onto Sanskrit-based prosody, as well as with themes of nationalism, cultural chauvinism, and social and religious change (some of the important early modern I. poets were former Hindus who had recently converted to Christianity). This complex shift led to writing which, when placed beside I. p. of the early periods, strikes a very clearly cosmopolitan, "modern" note. However, as already suggested above, the newness of 19th- and 20th-c. I. p., whether in the native langs. or in Eng., does not emerge simply out of a rejection of the I. past.

Interestingly enough, the earliest modern poetry by writers of I. birth appeared in Eng. (in the 1820s and '30s), and not in one of the regional langs. The first I.-Eng. poet was Henry Derozio, whose sonnets and odes are virtually the earliest documents of I. nationalism. The first modern poetry in the I. langs. was written in Bengali (in the 1830s and '40s), and includes the work of bilingual poets like Michael Madhusudan Dutt, who began as a writer in Eng. and then turned to his native Bengali by conscious decision at age 35 (Srinivasa Iyengar; Parthasarathy). This is practically the earliest modern writing by non-Western writers in the world, preceding by several decades the corresponding instances in Japanese and Chinese and in the African langs. Modern I. p. in Eng. and Bengali soon gave way to a flood of similar poetry across the entire subcontinent, with self-consciously modern poetry appearing in Panjabi, Gujarati, Marathi, Tamil, Malayalam, and in the Braj Bhasha, a dialect of Hindi, from 1850 to 1900, and in Khadi Boli (modern standard Hindi), Urdu, Oriya, Dogri, Sindhi, Kashmiri, Telugu, and Kannada from 1900 to 1930. This literary expansion coincided with a number of historically and politically crucial events: the "I. Mutiny" of 1857, the subsequent dismantling of the East India Company, the formal absorption of India into Queen Victoria's Empire in 1877, the formation of the I. National Congress in 1885, and the launching of the I. freedom movement under Mahatma Gandhi's leadership at the end of World War I.

The specific poetic genres that have emerged from these developments in the colonial and postcolonial decades are worth mentioning in some detail because they demonstrate the distance modern I. p. has covered since the end of the middle period. Among the more notable modern genres are: the long philosophical or speculative poem, often epic in size and scope, which attempts to formulate a new poetic worldview (e.g. Aurobindo Ghose's *Savitri* in Eng., G. M. Muktibodh's *Andhere men* in Hindi); the nationalist or chauvinist epic, quite frequently cast as a retelling of an ancient Hindu myth or story, often from the *Rāmāyaṇa* or the *Mahābhārata* (e.g. Michael Madhusudan Dutt's *Meghanād-vadh* in Bengali, Jaishankar Prasad's *Kāmāyanī* in Hindi); the long sequence of short poems, whether religious, philosophical, satiric, or personal in theme, modeled on the Western poetic sequence as well as on premodern I. sequences (e.g. Rabindranath Tagore's *Gitanjali* in Bengali, Subramania Bharati's "prose poems" in Tamil, Arun Kolatkar's *Jejuri* and R. Parthasarathy's *Rough Passage* in Eng.); the short metrical lyric in modern rhymed stanza form, sometimes set to music, as well as the modernized lyric based on premodern I. and foreign verse-forms (e.g. Tagore's songs in Bengali, Mahadevi Varma's in Hindi, Faiz Ahmed Faiz's *ghazals* and *nazms* in Urdu, B. S. Mardhekar's and Vinda Karandikar's *abhangas* in Marathi, numerous *haikus* in Kannada, Buddhadev Bose's sonnets and Bishnu De's imitations of folksongs in Bengali); and the "free verse" poem, varying in length from a few lines to several hundred and ranging in theme from autobiographical and confessional to mythological, political, and historical (e.g. the later love poems of P. S. Rege in Marathi; the political poems of Dhoomil, Sarveshwar Dayal Saxena, and Raghuvir Sahay in Hindi; the landscape poems of Keki N. Daruwalla and the surreal poems of Arvind Krishna Mehrotra in Eng.; the poetry of bilingual poets like A. K. Ramanujan in Eng. and Kannada and Arun Kolatkar in Eng. and Marathi; protest poetry, Dalit poetry, and contemp. feminist and women's poetry in a number of langs.).

Among these, the genre of free verse poetry is esp. crucial to the changes in I. p. in all the major langs. in the late-colonial and the postcolonial periods. Modern I. poets "invented" free verse in the I. langs. in the second and third quarters of the 20th c., following the examples of the Anglo-Am. imagists and high modernists. But the freedom of free verse has meant different things in different langs.—for instance, in Bengali, freedom from the overwhelming presence of Tagore's modernity; in Urdu, freedom from the domination of the *ghazal* form in lyric poetry; in Hindi, freedom from the cloying lyricism of the early 20th-c. *ādarśavād* and *chāyāvād* poets; in Marathi, freedom from the sentimental songs of the early moderns; in Kannada and Malayalam, freedom from the rhetorical public poetry of the national freedom movement. Since the 1960s, a very high proportion of the poetry written in the various langs.—incl. Telugu, Oriya, Dogri, Sindhi, Panjabi, and Gujarati, besides those mentioned in the examples above—has appeared in free verse. Much of this poetry reveals the influence of international poetic movements that originated in Europe or the West in the 19th and 20th cs., incl. symbolism, modernism, futurism, expressionism, dada, Beat poetry, and even concrete poetry and Zen writing. Among the important Western poets of the past 200 years that I. poets working primarily in free verse (and Western forms) allude to are: Whitman, Baudelaire, Rimbaud, Mallarmé, Valéry, Apollinaire, Cesare Pavese, Vasko Popa, hans magnus enzensberger, Pablo Neruda, Nicanor Parra, Aimé Cesaire, Allen Ginsberg, and the Soviet socialist poets. As with other trads. in the world, the domination of free verse in modern I. p. since the 1940s has generally involved a major shift in poetic sensibility, from the "musical phrase" to the "colloquial phrase" as the basis of composition.

It is also noteworthy that early in the modern period (ca. 1775–1850), the colonial reconstitution of India led to the creation of specific genres of discourse which involved both colonizers and their colonial subjects in mutual tension, and altered the immediate and the future generic shapes and literary environments of I. lit. One of the striking facts about the colonial modernization in the I. case (as also in many African cases) is that a very large amount of modern I. p. is social rather than personal or confessional. For the modern I. *kavi* or poet, who is a very different person from the *bhakti* poet or the ancient I. poet described above, social poetry is so important because it exercizes his or her citizenship in the modern world. As a loosely integrated body of writing appearing in all the I. literary langs., modern I. social p. branches out into several genres, two of which are of particular significance. The first is antinationalistic or "satiric poetry," ridiculing specific aspects of I. society, history, culture, and lit., past and present. The second is nationalistic or "heroic poetry," attempting to counter the satirists by praising things Indian, concentrating on the achievements of ancient I. culture and lit. as well as on future possibilities. Satiric discourse has generated a large body of poetry in the 19th and 20th cs. criticizing particular I. beliefs, customs, and institutions such as caste, brahmanical ritual, female infanticide, widow- immolation, child-marriage, and untouchability. In contrast, the conventions of heroic discourse have enabled I. poets to retell stories from the Sanskrit and mother-tongue classics, to create new nationalistic epics, and to write about freedom from colonial rule (Dharwadker 1989, v. 2).

Broadly speaking, in the last 150 years I. p. has undergone cyclical interchanges between these two modes of writing. Between ca. 1825 and 1900, I. poets largely practiced a mixture of satiric and heroic discourse; thus Derozio in Eng., K. K. Dāmle in Marathi, Bhāratendu Harīshchandra in Hindi, and Rabindranath Tagore in Bengali, for instance, attacked certain features of I. society for being backward, exploitative, and inhuman, and at the same time also patriotically praised I. culture and values. From ca. 1900 to 1940, I. poets practiced the heroic mode, in keeping with the massive nationalist movement, esp. under the leadership of Mahatma Gandhi. In this phase, poets like Maithili Sharan Gupta and Mahādevī Verma in Hindi, Subramaniam Bhāratī in Tamil, Tagore in Bengali, Umā Shankar Joshi in Gujarati, G. Shankara Kurup in Malayalam, Bendre and Putappa in Kannada, and Muhammad Iqbal in Urdu turned explicitly to nationalistic and culturally chauvinistic themes, praising and revalorizing the content of native I. trad. and helping to transform India into "Mother India," Bengal into "Our Golden Bengal," and so on (*Daedalus*; Schomer; Dimock et al. 1974).

By about 1940, however, disillusionment with the freedom movement and its politics led to a new surge of satiric and antinationalistic poetry. With Suryakant Tripathi and G. M. Muktibodh in Hindi, B. S. Mardhekar in Marathi, and the later work of Jibanananda Das in Bengali, I. poets began once again to ridicule and attack the state of contemp. India and the hist. of I. cultural institutions. This satiric phase continued into the poetic preoccupations of the early postcolonial period (beginning with freedom from British rule in 1947), in which I. poets quite concertedly attacked the negative features of the I. past and present. Between the 1960s and '80s, social poetry in most of the langs. has arrived at yet another mixture of the satiric and heroic modes, now based on new regional, communal, ideological, and national concerns (Rubin; Jussawalla; Daruwalla; Dharwadker 1990; Dimock 1986).

The contemp. variations are most apparent in several specific phenomena: the long-term success of the Progressive (left-wing) movement in langs. like Urdu (in present-day Pakistan and Bangladesh, as well as in India), Hindi, Marathi, and Bengali (in both India and Bangladesh); "protest" movements like those involving the Hungry Generation poets in Bengali, the *pratirodhī kavis* ("oppositional poets") and *akavis* ("anti-poets" in Hindi, the Dalit poets in Marathi, the "naked poetry" writers in Telugu, and protest poets in Tamil and Malayalam; a strong upsurge of women poets in Bengali, Hindi, Marathi, Oriya, Panjabi, and Kannada; and the national prominence achieved by the poets of the 1960s and '70s in Oriya and Kannada. They are also evident in the reputations particular "modernist" poets have acquired in the various I. langs., e.g. Muktibodh, Dhoomil, Agyeya, Sahay, Saxena, Kedarnath Singh, and Shrikant Verma in postcolonial Hindi; Das, Bose, De, Nirendranath Chakrabarti, Sunil Gangopadhyay, and Subhas Mukhopadhyay in Bengali; Rege, Mardhekar, Karandikar, Kolatkar, 2Indira Sant, Mangesh Padgaonkar, Namdev Dhasal, Narayan Surve, and Dilip Chitre in Marathi; Chandrashekhar Kambar, Gopalkrishna Adiga, and K. S. Narasimhaswami in Kannada; N. Picamurti, Shanmuga Subbiah, and Gnanakoothan in Tamil; and Nissim Ezekiel, A. K. Ramanujan, Jayanta Mahapatra, Daruwalla, Adil Jussawalla, Mehrotra, Parthasarathy, Gieve Patel, Kamala Das, Eunice de Souza, Chitre, and Kolatkar in Eng. Although this list of poets and langs. (and most of the foregoing discussion) is limited to contemp. India, corresponding claims can be made for poets in Pakistan writing in Urdu, Panjabi, Sindhi, and other langs., as well as for poets in Bangladesh working in the Bengali and Urdu trads.

In the course of these fluctuations, the tensions between modernity and trad., Indianness and Westernization, have played a shaping role. Like many of their 19th-c. counterparts, 20th-c. I. poets reject certain aspects of their own past, but at the same time make use of it, achieving a modernity in which Westernization and Indianness stand in a constant and constantly productive conflict. As a result, modern I. writers, critics, and common readers now refer to all the varieties of poetry surveyed in this article as *kāvya* or *kavitā*, although they sometimes reserve the former word for the high canonical poetry of the ancient and middle periods (or, more rigorously, for only cl. Sanskrit poetry) and the latter term for the verse of the past 200 years. In its broadest 20th-c. usage, *kāvya* thus embraces a vast quantity of writing in about 20 major langs. produced over about 3000 years. As our survey indicates, the word is now capable of signifying trads. as different as those of the Valmiki *Rāmāyaṇa* and cl. Tamil *akam* and *puṟam* poetry, *bhakti* lyrics and religious epics in the middle period, Telugu "Vedas" and Bengali "mangalakābyas," Urdu or Marathi sonnets and condensed allegories in Hindi free verse, ancient Hindu Buddhist works, as well as contemp. Marxist poetry and protest poetry by former untouchables.

GENERAL: A. B. Keith, *A Hist. of Sanskrit Lit.* (1928); H. H. Gowen, *A Hist. of I. Lit.* (1931); S. N. Dasgupta and S. K. De, *A Hist. of I. Lit.* (1947); M. Winternitz, *A Hist. of I. Lit.*, 3d ed. (1962)—original Ger., 3 v., 1908–22; A. K. Warder, *I. Kāvya Lit.* (1972); *A Hist. of I. Lit.*, ed. J. Gonda, 1– (1973)—uneven but indispensible multivolume reference in progress, all langs., genres, and periods; E. C. Dimock et al., *The Lits. of India* (1974)—excellent intro.; C. Seely et al., "South Asian Peoples, Arts of," *Encyc. Britannica* (1974)—useful overview; E. Gerow, *I. Poetics* (1977); C. P. Masica, *The Indo-Aryan Langs.* (1989); *Columbia Book of I. P.*, ed. B. S. Miller et al. (forthcoming)—trs. from 15 langs.

SERIALS: *Annals of the Bhandarkar Oriental Research Institute* [*ABORI*] (1919–); *Bahuvachan* (1988–); *Harvard Oriental Series* (1883–); *Illustrated Weekly of India* (1929–); *I. Horizons* [*IndH*] (1952–); *I. Lit.* [*IndL*] (1957–); *Jour. of Asian Studies* [*JASt*] (1941–); *Jour. of South Asian and Middle Eastern Studies* (1977–); *Jour. of South Asian Lit.* [*JSoAL*] (1963–); *Jour. of the Am. Oriental Society* [*JOAS*] (1843–); *Mod. Asian Studies* (1967–); *Quest* (1950–); *South Asian Digest of Regional Writing* (1972–); *Vagartha* (1974–79); *Chandrabhaga* (1979–); *Indian P.E.N.* (1934–); *Toronto South Asia Review* (1987–).

ANCIENT PERIOD: A. A. MacDonnell, *A Hist. of Sanskrit Lit.* (1900)—useful for Vedic lit.; E. W. Hopkins, *The Great Epic of India* (1901); *The Ramayana and the Mahabharata*, tr. R. C. Dutt (1910); *The Bhagavad Gita*, tr. F. Edgerton (1944); S. N. Dasgupta and S. K. De, *A Hist. of Sanskrit Lit., Cl. Period*, 2d ed. (1962)—full inventory of the lit.; *The Shilappadikaram*, tr. A Daniélou (1965); *An Anthol. of Sanskrit Court Poetry*, tr. D. H. H. Ingalls (1965)—from Vidyākara's *kośa*, extremely influential; C. V. Narashimhan, *The Mahabharata* (1965)—handy abridgment; B. S. Miller, *Bhartrihari* (1967), *Phantasies of a Love-Thief* (1971)—on Bilhana, *Love Song of the Dark Lord, Jayadeva's Gitagovinda* (1977), *The Hermit and the Love Thief* (1978); A. K. Ramanujan, *The Interior Landscape* (1967)—important text, tr., commentary; *The Mahābhārata*, tr. J. A. B. van Buitenen, 3 v. (1973–80)—unfinished but indispensible; W. Buck, *The Rāmāyaṇa* (1974)—unreliable yet useful retelling; L. Sternbach, *Subhāśita, Gnomic and Didactic Lit.* (1974); *The Cloud- Messenger*, tr. L. Nathan (1974)—*Kalidasa*; J. Gonda, *Vedic Lit.* (1975); G. L. Hart, *The Poems of Ancient Tamil* (1975), *Poets of the Tamil Anthols.* (1979); R. Panikkar, *The Vedic Experience* (1977); B. A. van Nooten, "The Sanskrit Epics," *Heroic Epic and Saga*, ed. F. J. Oinas (1978); W. D. O'Flaherty, *The Rig Veda* (1981); S. Lienhard, *A Hist. of Cl. Poetry* (1984)—Sanskrit, Pali, Prakrit; *The Rāmāyaṇa of Vālmiki*, tr. R. Goldman et al. (1984–)—essential, in progress; *The Bhagavad- Gītā*, tr. B. S. Miller (1986)—major new tr.; *Poems of Love and War*, tr. A. K. Ramanujan (1986)—excellent, indispensible; *The Forest Book of the Ramayana of Kampaṉ*, tr. G. L. Hart and H. Heifetz (1988)—Tamil; *Maṇimekhalai*, tr. A. Daniélou (1989).

MIDDLE PERIOD: R. D. Ranade, *Mysticism in India* (1933); S. Sen, *A Hist. of Bengali Lit.* (1960); M. Mansinha, *Hist. of Oriya Lit.* (1962); *Love Songs of Vidyāpati*, ed. W. G. Archer (1963); *In Praise of Krishna*, tr. E. D. Dimock and D. Levertov (1967); K. M. Munshi, *Gujarat and Its Lit. from Early Times to 1852*, 3d ed. (1967); K. M. George, *A Survey of Malayalam Lit.* (1968); R. Russell and K. Islam, *Three Mughal Poets* (1968); J. Rypka, *Hist. of Iranian Lit.* (1968)—section on "Persian Lit. in India"; G. V. Sitapati, *Hist. of Telugu Lit.* (1968); L. H. Ajwani, *Hist. of Sindhi Lit.* (1970); *Ghazals of Ghalib*, ed. A. Ahmad (1971); *Ghalib*, ed. R. Russell (1972); *The Golden Trad.*, tr. A. Ali (1973)—Urdu; A. K. Ramanujan, *Speaking of Śiva* (1973)—Kannada, excellent; C. Vaudeville, *Kabīr*, v. 1 (1974); K. Zvelebil, *Tamil Lit.* (1974); S. Sarma, *Assamese Lit.* (1976); E. Zelliot, "The Medieval Bhakti Movement in Hist.," in *Hinduism*, ed. B. L. Smith (1976)—essential bibl.; K. E. Bryant, *Poems to the Child-God* (1978); S. G. Tulpule, *Cl. Marathi Lit. from the Beginning to 1818* (1979); B. B. Kachru, *Kashmiri Lit.* (1981); *Hymns for the Drowning*, tr. A. K. Ramanujan (1981); A. Kolatkar, "Translations from Tukaram and Other Saint-Poets," *JSoAL* 17 (1982); G. H. Roghair, *The Epic of Palnāḍu* (1982)—Telugu oral epic; *The Bījak of Kabīr*, tr. L. Hess and S. Singh (1983); J. S. Hawley, *Sūr Dās* (1984); R. S. McGreggor, *Hindi Lit. from its Beginnings to the 19th C.* (1984); M. Sadiq, *A Hist. of Urdu Lit.*, 2d ed. (1984); N. Cutler, *Songs of Experience* (1985); *For the Lord of the Animals—Poems from the Telugu*, tr. H. Heifetz and V. Narayana Rao (1987); *Songs of the Saints of India*, ed. and tr. J. S. Hawley and M. Juergensmeyer (1988); *Poems to Śiva*, tr. I. V. Peterson (1989)—Tamil; *Oral Epics in India*, ed. S. H. Blackburn et al. (1989).

MODERN PERIOD: *Collected Poems and Plays of*

Rabindranath Tagore (1956); *Green and Gold,* ed. H. Kabir (1958)—Bengali; *A Tagore Reader,* ed. A. Chakravarty (1961); *Mod. Hindi Poetry,* ed. V. N. Misra (1965); *An Anthol. of Marathi Poetry, 1945–65,* ed. D. Chitre (1967); D. McCutchion, *I. Writing in Eng.* (1969); *Poems by Faiz,* tr. V. G. Kiernan (1971)—Urdu; *Contemp. I. P. in Eng.,* ed. S. Peeradina (1972); K. R. Srinivasa Iyengar, *I. Writing in Eng.,* 2d ed. (1973); *New Writing in India,* ed. A. Jussawalla (1974); R. S. McGreggor, *Hindi Lit. in the 19th and Early 20th Cs.* (1974); *I Have Seen Bengal's Face,* ed. S. Ray and M. Maddern (1974); *Ten 20th-C. I. Poets,* ed. R. Parthasarathy (1976); *A Season on the Earth,* tr. D. Rubin (1976)—Hindi; *Considerations,* ed. M. Mukherjee (1977); D. Kopf, *The Brahmo Samaj and the Shaping of the Mod. I. Mind* (1979); *Two Decades of I. P., 1960–1980,* ed. K. N. Daruwalla (1980); *Contemp. I. Eng. Verse,* ed. C. Kulshreshtha (1980); *India: An Anthol. of Contemp. Writing,* ed. D. Ray and A. Singh (1983); K. Schomer, *Mahadevi Varma and the Chhayavad Age of Mod. Hindi Poetry* (1983); R. Tagore, *Selected Poems,* tr. W. Radice (1985); E. C. Dimock, *The Sound of Silent Guns* (1986); B. King, *Mod. I. P. in Eng.* (1987), ed., *Three I. Poets* (1991); M. K. Naik, *Studies in I. Eng. Lit.* (1987); *The True Subject,* tr. N. Lazard (1988)—Faiz; "India," *Nimrod* 31 (1988); *Contemp. I. Trad.,* ed. C. M. Borden (1989); V. Dharwadker, "The Future of the Past," 3 v., diss., Univ. of Chicago (1989); "Another India," *Daedalus* 118 (1989); "29 Mod. I. Poems," tr. V. Dharwadker, *TriQ* 77 (1990); *Another India,* ed. M. Mukherjee and N. Ezekiel (1990); *100 Mod. I. Poems,* ed. V. Dharwadker and A. K. Ramanujan (forthcoming)—14 langs.

V.D.; B.S.M.; A.K.R.; E.A.H.

INDONESIAN POETRY, like contemp. Malay poetry, is rooted in older and folk Malay poetry. *Bahasa indonesia,* the I. lang., formally divided itself from the Malay lang. in 1928; I. p. began to assume its separate course in 1917.

One of the first of the modern I. poets was Mohammad Yamin (1903– 62), an active politician. Strongly patriotic, romantic, and distinctly sentimental, Yamin was much influenced both by European (esp. Dutch) poetry and the work of Rabindranath Tagore, as well as by older and folk Malay poetry. He introduced the sonnet into I. p. His contemporaries, Rustam Effendi (1903–79), Sanusi Pané (1905–68), and Sutan Takdir Alisjahbana (1908–86), were somewhat more successful at integrating Malay, European, and oriental strands into stronger, less derivative poetry. Effendi in particular experimented with the devel. of new forms; he also tried to "find a new poetic manner" and to make *bahasa indonesia* capable of the wry, dry tone of European poetry. Pané (who also wrote in Dutch) and Alisjahbana were influenced primarily by Malay and oriental poetry. Pané had studied at Tagore's Santiniketan University. His *Puspa Mega* (Cloud Flowers, 1927) features quiet, lyrical poems of high polish but no great substance. Alisjahbana's *Tebaran Mega* (Scattered Clouds, 1936), written in memory of his first wife, is his only major work of poetry; most of his other writing is heavily European-influenced social, linguistic, and philosophical crit.

Pané, Alisjahbana, and Amir Hamzah (1911–46) jointly founded *Pujangga Baru* (The New Writer), a journal the most significant contributor to which was Hamzah, the outstanding I. poet before World War II. Scion of an aristocratic Sumatran family, he was deeply religious and just as deeply steeped in the older Malay trad. His *Nyanyi Sunyi* (Songs of Loneliness, 1937) is largely autobiographical. Chairil Anwar (see below) exclaimed: "What a bright light he shone on the new lang.," though the mystical and complex qualities of Hamzah's work sometimes make him difficult to understand. In 1939 Hamzah published a coll. of translations from other oriental lits., *Setanggi Timur* (Incense from the East).

The break with Dutch colonialism begun by the Japanese Occupation (1942–45) and formalized, on August 17, 1945, by the declaration of I. independence helped bring into being the *Angkatan 45* (Generation of '45), led by the greatest of all I. writers, Chairil Anwar (1922– 49). Others of the Generation of 45 incl. Asrul Sani (b. 1926) and Rivai Apin (b. 1927), both associated with Anwar in the tripartite *Tiga Menguak Takdir* (Three Against Fate or Three Against Takdir Alisjahbana), and Sitor Situmorang (b. 1924). Led by Anwar, these and other writers broke with romanticism; their work features blunt lang., emphatic syntax, strong components of irony and social crit., and, in Anwar's case, a passionate lyricism and strength:

> She winks. She laughs
> And the dry grass blazes up.
> She speaks. Her voice is loud
> My blood stops running.
> (*Lagu Biasa* [An Ordinary Song])
>
> When my time comes
> I want to hear no one's cries
> Nor yours either
> Away with all who cry!
> (*Aku* [Me], tr. Raffel)

His three collections, all posthumous, incl. *Deru Campur Debu* (Noise Mixed with Dust) and *Kerikil Tajam dan Yang Terampas dan Yang Putus* (two books in one: Sharp Gravel; Plundered and Broken). Many I. writers first realized the true literary possibilities of *bahasa indonesia* reading Anwar's poetry.

Anwar's effect has been almost as strong on the literary generations which have followed, though I. p. has expanded far beyond the boundaries of any one influence. Contemp. I. p. has become one of the world's most vital bodies of lit., incl. among others the work of W. S. Rendra (b. 1935), Ayip Rosidi (b. 1938), Taufiq Ismail (b. 1937), Goenawan Mohamad (b. 1942), Subagio Sastrowardoyo (b. 1924), Toeti Heraty (b. 1942), I.'s leading woman poet, Sutardji Calzoum Bachri (b. 1940), and Darmonto (b. 1942). Rendra is the senior and most noted poet of this group:

Fire has gutted the forest:
Charred logs curse at the sky
That runs across the world.

Overhead, the moon, shining with blood,
Drips orange tears from its eyes.
(*Koyan Yang Malang* [Koyan the Unfortunate], tr. Raffel)

But the range and strength of contemp. I. p. as a whole is remarkable.

Sleep, child, on the earth which never sleeps
Sleep on the grass, on the sand, on the bed
Sleep with the butterflies, the waves of the sea and the bright lights,
Which sing, slowly sing
(Goenawan Mohammad, *Nina-bobok* [Lullaby])

We are the people with sad eyes, at the edge of the road
Waving at the crowded buses
We are the tens of millions living in misery
Beaten about by flood, volcano, curses and pestilence
Who silently ask in the name of freedom
But are ignored in the thousand slogans
And meaningless loudspeaker voices
(Taufiq Ismail, *Kita adalah pemilik syah republik ini* [The Republic is Ours], tr. Aveling)

ANTHOLOGIES AND TRANSLATIONS: *Poeisi Baru*, ed. S. T. Alisjahbana (1946); *Pujangga Baru*, ed. H. B. Jassin (1962); *Anthol. of Mod. I. P.*, ed. B. Raffel (1964); *Complete Poetry and Prose of Chairil Anwar*, ed. and tr. B. Raffel (1970); *Ballads and Blues: Sel. Poems of W. S. Rendra*, ed. and tr. B. Raffel and H. Aveling (1974); *Contemp. I. P.* (1975), *Arjuna in Meditation* (1976), both ed. and tr. H. Aveling.

HISTORY AND CRITICISM: H. B. Jassin, *Chairil Anwar, pelopor Angkatan 45*, 2d ed. (1945), *Amir Hamzah, Raja Penyair Pujangga Baru* (1962), *Kesusastraan Indonesia modern dalam kritik dan esei*, 2 v. (1962); W. A. Braasem, *Moderne Indonesische Literatur* (1954); R. B. Slametmuliana, *Pöezie in Indonesia* (1954); A. Teuw, *Pokok dan tokoh dalam kesusteraan Indonesia baru*, 3d ed., 2 v. (1955); A. H. Johns, "Chairil Anwar: An Interp.," *Bijdragen tot de taal-, land-en Voklenkunde* (1964); B. Raffel, *The Devel. of Mod. I. P.* (1967); H. Aveling, *A Thematic Hist. of I. P. 1920 to 1974* (1974). B.R.

INUIT POETRY.

I. TRADITIONAL SONG AND POETRY
II. MODERN SONG AND POETRY

The Inuit (pl. form; sing. Inuk), commonly called Eskimos (a name the Inuit consider offensive), live along some five thousand miles of Arctic coastline, so comments about any one aspect of their culture are generalizations, but unlike Namerindians, the Inuit have a strong linguistic connection throughout the circumpolar world. The I. lang. belongs to the Eskalutian family, which has two branches: I., spoken in Greenland, Canada, and Alaska, and Yupik, spoken in Alaska and Siberia. Until relatively recently, I. p. belonged to oral trad. and was usually sung or chanted, often to the accompaniment of drum, choral background, or dance. Its agglutinative nature makes translation of I. p. particularly rewarding, for although a single word may require 100 characters to spell, it will contain a fully developed image.

I. TRADITIONAL SONG AND POETRY. Traditional Inuit believed in the literal power of the word (hence everyone was a singer and to some extent a poet) and thought it as imperative to work on lang. as on skins or ivory. As hunter-gatherers, they had to sing and compose in order to control the universe—to catch a seal, break a fever, or cut the weather. I. p. was very special, possessing supernatural powers, but it was also very commonplace, a part of everyday life.

Knud Rasmussen, the Greenlandic poet and scholar who collected literary material from across the circumpolar world, identified four categories of I. p.: charms, mood songs, hunting songs, and songs of derision. These four categories are not mutually exclusive, however, for they were occasionally integrated in traditional myths and legends as well as sung on their own.

A. *Mood Songs* are songs of reflection which do not involve a central story or action, but like imagist poems try to give a visual impression which involves the perception of relationships. These short poems have a strong literal meaning; they may describe a bird perched on a rock or a man waking in the morning, but tied into the simple description of the moment is a subtext concerned with the poet's emotional response to the bird or his perception of his place in the universe.

B. *Charms and Incantations*, often fragmented, incomprehensible, or in supernatural lang., are similar to nonsense verse, sound poetry, or even concrete poetry, where form dominates meaning, but they have added depth in that they have magical powers. A charm can be capable of drying blood in a wound, attracting a fish to the hook, or killing an enemy. These poems were thought by some to be so powerful that it was dangerous to give them to strangers, so words were sometimes changed before charms were offered to collectors. Simply reciting the words of a chant was often enough to put a person into a shamanistic trance. The use of obscure or archaic diction frequently makes the chants incomprehensible even to native speakers.

C. *Hunting Songs* can be reflective but are more likely to be narrative, in keeping with the subject. Rasmussen notes the difficulty of separating hunting songs from mood songs because so many touch on the joys and disappointments of the hunt; they also often use the lang. of incantation. Frequently the circumstances described in the poems are familiar to the audience, and mnemonic phrases are included to fill out the song.

D. *Derisive Songs*. Sometimes referred to as *nith* songs, drum songs, song duels, or satirical songs, these are the most interesting to readers outside the culture, perhaps because a common denominator is an ironic element of criticism. These monologues or dialogues are like medieval flytings : verbal assault is part of the game. The poet can aim the derision at himself, at another, at a group of people, or at a type of behavior. The song may only be part of an attack, or it may be a response to an attack by another singer; it may be a cheerful, loving correction or it may be a vicious assault on a reputation. The song duel, in which two singers exchange reproaches, has a judicial function in that each is allowed to voice complaints against the other in public, each is given an opportunity to respond, and the loser either acknowledges his fault or leaves the community. The song duel varies greatly from one area to another, occasionally involving boxing or head butting, and is usually also considered entertainment.

II. MODERN SONG AND POETRY. As long as the Inuit were nomadic, they had no real need for a written lang., but in the 18th c. they came in contact with European explorers, and Christian missionaries soon followed. Although writing did not develop indigenously, it was accepted quickly. Orthographies as diverse as Cyrillic, syllabic, hieroglyphic, and Roman were used across the Arctic coast as printing presses and schools were established.

Today, highly individualistic forms of I. p. such as throat music—in which the distinctive sounds are produced through gutteral, nasal, and breathing techniques—are extant, but song dueling has virtually disappeared. Although the traditional forms are seldom performed or read in the I. lang. they have gained credibility outside the culture as written translations. Modern I. p. and song is not so widely admired, but is also gaining acceptance. Most I. composers and writers now draw heavily on European musical and literary structures while still retaining some elements of the ancient forms. The themes are often different and the tone intervals are more familiar to Western ears than they would be to the ancient Eskalutians, but the lang. dictates certain rhythmic patterns peculiar only to I., so comparisons must be circumscribed. In general terms, however, poetry from the written trad. can be grouped into units similar to those Rasmussen identified in the oral modes.

A. *Mood Poems*. Still popular with both old and young authors, though now they often refer to settlement life and modern technology, these short, vivid lyrics attempt to capture emotions related to the senses, such as the joy of seeing the sun come up, the taste of meat or a steaming mug of tea, or an awareness of the passage of time. Often these brief poems will be worked into photographs, drawings, or prints so that illustration and text are indivisible.

B. *Religious Hymns and Poems*. Magic chants and incantations are no longer evident, but Christian hymns, tr. or adapted from Eng. and Danish or composed originally in I. are widely promulgated. The hymns of Rasmus Berthelsen are known throughout Greenland, while in Canada, Armand Tagoona is the best known composer of Christian songs. Occasional poems on the Incarnation or the nature of the Creator appear, but there is no significant body of lay Christian religious writings comparable in quality to that lit. which emerged from the old shamanistic beliefs.

C. *Contemporary Hunting Poems*. Although written poems about hunting are still emerging in the circumpolar world, they have taken on a romantic or spiritual importance that is quite different from those in the oral trad. While the old songs tended to be narrative and reminiscent, the new ones emerge as imaginative speculation written in many cases not by hunters but by young urban Inuit who are reluctantly tied to office jobs but regard hunting as the only fit occupation for a true Inuk. The works often urge people to return to the ways of their ancestors, or describe the need to protect the land and animals for future generations. The old hunting poems frequently explored man's sense of fragility and insecurity, with images of the land providing a sense of continuity and stability, but modern poets are more concerned with the survival of the land itself.

D. *Political Poetry*. The song duels and derisive poems generally do not exist in a pure form in modern I. p., having been banned by Christian missionaries, but certain elements have survived. The question-answer sequence, or the repeated use of the interrogative, is a feature of contemp. I. political poetry, though the respondent is as likely to be a garbage can or an alien from Mars as a snowy owl or an offended husband. The devel. of the epic is a major innovation in modern I. p.; Frederik Nielsen's trilogy on Qitdlaussuaq traces the 18th-c. I. migration from Canada to Greenland; Alootook Ipellie's long poem "The Strangers" describes the I. occupation of the Arctic from ancient times and examines the effect of European contact; Villads Villadsen's Christian epic *Nalusuunerup Taarnerani* (In Heathen Darkness) describes the death of the last Norseman in Greenland and the eventual conversion and baptism of Aattaaritaa the exorcist. The politically inspired poems are sometimes purely didactic but are more frequently satiric and ironic. Since the Inuit traditionally had no political structure, poetry has been used as an impetus to social activism by writers many of whom are politicians. There is a large body of popular music concerned with political and social issues to be found in all the I. regions. To date, there is not a wide body of I. p. available outside the culture, but inside the culture the trad. is flourishing and continues to develop.

H. Rink, *Eskimoiske Eventyr og Sagn,* 2 v. (1866–77), tr. as *Tales and Trads. of the Eskimo* (1875); W. Thalbitzer, "Old Fashioned Songs," *Phonetical Study of the Eskimo Lang.* (1904); H. Roberts and D. Jenness, *Songs of the Copper Eskimos* (1925); K. Rasmussen, *Report of the Fifth Thule Expedition, 1921–24,* 7–9 (1930–32); *Anerca,* ed. E. Carpenter (1959); *I Breathe a New Song,* ed. R. Lewis (1971); *Eskimo Poems From Canada and Greenland,* ed. T. Lowenstein (1973); *Kalaallit Taallaataat Nutaat INUIT Ny Gronlandsk Lyrik,* ed. K. Norregaard (1980); *Paper Stays Put,* ed. R. Gedalof (1980); *Poems of the I.,* ed. J. R. Colombo (1981); C. Berthelsen, *Gronlandsk Litteratur* (1983); *Alaska Native Writers, Storytellers and Orators,* spec iss. of *Alaska Quart. Rev.* (1986); *Northern Voices,* ed. P. Petrone (1988).

history and criticism: S. Frederiksen, "Henrik Lund, A National Poet of Greenland," *PAPS* 96,6 (1952), "Stylistic Forms in Greenland Eskimo Lit.," *Meddelser om Gronland* 136,7 (1954); E. Carpenter, "Eskimo Poetry: Word Magic," *Explorations* 4 (1955); H. Lynge, "The Art and Poetry of Greenland," *Greenland Past and Present,* ed. K. Hertling et al. (1971); R. Wiebe, "Songs of the Canadian Eskimo," *CanL* 52 (1972); R. McGrath, *Canadian I. Lit.* (1984); R. Pedersen, "Greenlandic Written Lit.," *Handbook of North Am. Indians, V,* ed. D. Damas (1984); C. Berthelsen, "Greenlandic Lit.: Its Trads., Changes, and Trends," *Arctic Anthro.* 23 (1986). R.McG.

IRANIAN POETRY. See PERSIAN POETRY.

IRISH POETRY.

I. POETRY IN GAELIC: 6TH–19TH CENTURIES
II. POETRY IN ENGLISH: YEATS AND THE CELTIC REVIVAL
III. IRISH POETRY AFTER YEATS

I. POETRY IN GAELIC: 6TH–19TH CENTURIES. From its origins to the present, the form and content of Ir. p. have been enmeshed with the evolution of Ir. hist. and society. Poetry in Gaelic belongs to one of the oldest vernacular lits. in Europe, extending from the 6th c. A.D. to the present. In the pre-Christian oral culture, Ir. poets (*filidh,* sing. *fili*) had for long constituted a privileged professional class; they were not only repositories of traditional knowledge but also seers and prophets with magical powers. With the displacement of their druidic religion by Christianity in the 5th c., the *filidh* apparently ceded their magical functions but maintained their identity as scholars and poets. It was the Lat. learning that accompanied Christianity that enabled Gaelic verse to be written down. The poetry of the *filidh* consisted typically of genealogies, histories, and praise for noble patrons. As Christianity was established in Ireland, the *filidh* coexisted, perhaps even intermingled with, the monastic clerics who constituted another class of learned men. The early Ir. church was organized, unusually, on a monastic structure, and such monasteries as Glendalough and Clonmacnoise were centers of learning akin to modern colleges: it was this system that gave Ireland its Golden Age in the 7th and 8th cs. Ireland became known as the island of saints and scholars, as missionary Ir. monks founded monasteries all over Europe. One official duty of clerics in the Ir. monasteries was to copy sacred texts, but they also compiled the pre-Christian lit. of Ireland—the ancient myths and epic tales which recount the exploits of the heroes Cuchulainn and Finn. They were also responsible for a body of lyric poetry, some of it as formulaic as the poetry of the *filidh,* but some charged with a fresh and numinous sense of the natural world.

The economy, precision, and delicacy of early Ir. nature poetry at its best can be seen in such delightful poems as "The Scribe in the Woods," the poem from the Fenian Cycle that begins *scel lem duib,* and "The Blackbird of Belfast Lough." Seamus Heaney gives this tr. of the latter poem: "The small bird / let a chirp / from its beak: / I heard / woodnotes, whin- / gold, sudden. / The Lagan / blackbird!" The style of poetry from the 6th to the 12th c., virtually all of it anonymous, is for the most part an intricate formalism. Complex rhyming syllabic meters gradually incorporated and displaced the technique of the earliest Ir. verse, which was cadenced and unrhymed and originated in the same IE system as did Sanskrit and Gr. verse (see Watkins). It was long thought that the rhyming, syllabic meters of Ir. verse were formed under the influence of late Lat. verse, but more recent scholarship argues just the opposite—that the versification of early Ir. p. influenced Med. Lat. verse. Certainly Lat. verse in medieval Ireland would seem to reveal the impress of Celtic models in its technique; the most famous collection of poems in this style by the Ir. Latinists is *Hisperica Famina* (7th c.). This hisperic or rhyming style was subsequently employed in the OE rhyming poem.

Bardic or Classical Ir. p. is usually dated from 1200–1600. With the Norman invasion in the 12th c. and the decline of the the monastic system, poetry became the hereditary vocation of the professional poets, inheritors of the *filidh* trad., who trained for many years in an academy and were employed by noble families, Gaelic or Norman. Before this period the distinction between *fili* and *bard* derived from the more elevated function of the *fili* as druidic prophet and seer as well as poet;

the *bard* was merely a poet or versifier who specialized in eulogy and satire. During the bardic period, however, this distinction disappears, and the term *bard* paradoxically is rarely used as the title for poet. What seems to have happened is that the once separate functions of *fili* and *bard* have merged as the *fili* shed his sacred attributes and assumed some of the functions of the *bard.* The poets of the bardic period would have been known as *filidh*; their social function and their poetry is devoid of the romanticism attached to the word "bard" in the 19th c. Some authorities would date this period earlier, from the 8th c., to coincide with the devel. of *dán díreach* ("strict verse"), the generic name for the new syllabic meters which were to be the hallmark of Ir. p. until the 17th c. Much of the verse of the bardic period is encomiastic, consisting of formal eulogies and elegies composed in the strictest of meters, court poetry written for noble patrons. Religious verse of the period is also written in this strict style.

But if virtuosity and artifice, learned lang. and ornateness were prized in all the verse of this period, there was a considerable amount of poetry in which less elaborate forms were employed. To begin with, there is a body of love poetry in the European convention of courtly love, imported into Ireland by the Normans. Pierce Ferriter (d. 1653) and Gerald Fitzgerald (d. 1398) are among the better known authors of these *dánta grádha* (love poems). There is also a category of poems on the lore of places (*dinnseanchas*), lyric and narrative verse that elaborates on the tales about Finn and Oisin, and finally, an amount of more personal poetry. If it is the somewhat less formal and more personal poetry which appeals to the modern reader, there is still a high degree of craft and technical virtuosity in such poems as Giolla Brighde MacNamee's prayer for a son (13th c.) or Gofraidh Fionn Ó Dálaigh's poem on a child born in prison (14th c.), or Muireadach Ó Dálaigh's "On the Death of his Wife," which begins "I parted from my life last night, / A woman's body sunk in clay: / The tender bosom that I loved / Wrapped in a sheet they took away" (13th c.; tr. Frank O'Connor).

With the military defeat of the Ir. Chieftains at Kinsale in 1601, the Cromwellian settlements of 1652–54, and the defeat of James II in 1690, the old Ir. social and cultural organization which supported the privileged status and function of the poet was broken. Thus much of the poetry of the 17th and 18th cs. is overtly political, a poetry of defiance, of mourning for the old order and contempt for the new. The collapse of the old order was experienced in a very personal way by the poets of the 17th c. Dáibhí Ó Bruadair (1625–98), Aogán Ó Rathaille (1675–1729), and others inherited a residual social endorsement of the aristocratic and scholarly role of the poet which in their own lifetime was suddenly withdrawn. Both went from positions of privilege and status to impoverishment and misery; Ó Bruadair ended up as an agricultural laborer.

The form and content of post-bardic poetry reflected the massive social and political upheaval of the 17th c. It is still ornate and intricate, but composed in accentual rather than syllabic verse; it employs assonance but not rhyme, uses more colloquial lang., and is dramatic in utterance. The political context obviously provided the prevailing themes of lament for Ireland's defeat and hope for its political redemption, but it probably also generated the new form of the *aisling.* Ó Rathaille is credited with inventing this political dream-vision in which a beautiful young woman, the personification of Ireland, appears to the poet, complains of her captivity and (sometimes) prophesies salvation. Perhaps the most famous of these *aisling* poems is Ó Rathaille's "Gile na Gile" (Brightness of Brightness).

With the 18th c. and the penal laws, Gaelic culture became the culture of an impoverished and oppressed peasantry. Poets were reduced to employment as hedge-school masters, minstrels, or agricultural laborers. Poetry moved closer to the people and the oral trad., and frequently employed song meter (*amhrán*). In the figures of the blind poet/musicians Turlough O'Carolan (1670–1738) and Anthony Raftery (1784–1835) may be seen the merging of literary style with folk music and ballad. Two masterpieces produced in the 18th c. are Brian Merriman's bawdy and comic *The Midnight Court* and Eibhlin Dubh O'Connell's tragic "Lament for Art O'Leary." *The Midnight Court* has affinities both with Ir. folk poetry and the European medieval poetic genre of the Court of Love; in it a court of Ir. women indict, humorously yet savagely, the various sexual failures of Ir. men. The occasion for the second poem was the murder of Art O'Leary, a casualty of the penal laws. The "Lament" is a poem of passionate grief written by the dead man's wife; it is in the keening trad., but made memorable by its sustained and moving eloquence.

There is also a large body of anonymous folk poetry written in the 17th and 18th cs. which is written mainly in accentual meters and is technically quite sophisticated. "Roisin Dubh," "Kilcash" and "Fair Donncha" are three of the better-known examples.

II. POETRY IN ENGLISH: YEATS AND THE CELTIC REVIVAL. The decline of poetry in Gaelic is obviously a result of the historical and social circumstances also responsible for the decline of the lang. in the 18th and 19th cs. By the 19th c., Eng. was rapidly becoming the vernacular lang. of Ireland, a process accelerated by the famine of the 1840s and the massive emigration that followed. While verse continued to be written in Gaelic in the 19th c., it is by and large undistinguished. The idea of Celticism was a product of Eng. romanticism, a way of explaining the difference in temperament and character of the Ir., Scots, and Welsh from the

Eng. This idea supposed the spirit of these "Celts," but esp. the Ir., to be in its essentially wild and imaginative nature utterly different from (and more interesting than) that of the stolid "Anglo-Saxons." The attempt to recover the native trad. in Ireland was fueled by this assumption of cultural difference—and superiority—to England. In the first half of the 19th c., Moore, Mangan, and Ferguson attempted in various ways to absorb and reconstitute the Gaelic trad. Although Moore's enormously popular melodies sentimentalized their originals, and his lyrics were facile if charming, he did transmit some sense of what Ir. culture had been and might be again. Mangan's "translations" (he knew little Ir.) of old Ir. poems such as "Róisín Dubh" (Dark Rosaleen) and "O'Hussey's Ode to the Maguire" somehow captured if also transformed their passionate qualities and thereby become the classic Eng. versions. Ferguson's translations from Ir. heroic and mythic material were a recovery of much that had been inaccessible but that was later to become an important part of Ir. cultural and political nationalism.

In the latter part of the 19th c., Anglo-Ir. writers, scholars, and antiquarians continued this attempt to recapture the Ir. Gaelic past and to write a distinctively Ir. lit. in the Eng. lang. William Allingham (1824–89) and William Larminie (1850–1900) are both significant contributors to this effort, but Douglas Hyde (1860–1949) and George Sigerson (1839–1925) were more influential through their translations from the Ir.

William Butler Yeats (1865–1939) was born into the Anglo-Ir. class, the Protestant landowning class that was rapidly losing its power and privilege in the late 19th c. Yeats subscribed to the efforts of the Celtic Revival; his sense of his own Irishness derived, initially, from his 19th-c. predecessors and contemporaries engaged in the enterprise of the Revival. Yeats's poetry before 1900, in such volumes as *The Wind Among the Reeds* (1899), is Ir. in its use of mythology and folklore in narrative and ballad forms, although Yeats had no first-hand knowledge of Gaelic. To a great extent, this cultural and political nationalism in Yeats and his contemporaries can be seen as a reaction to the scientific and industrial ethos of the late Victorian world. But even in this first phase of his work, Yeats's poetry cannot be dismissed as mere belated romanticism based on the notion of the superiority of things "Celtic." It is a poetry remarkable not only for its music and imagery but also for its self-conscious awareness that the quest for transcendence is unduly limiting: see, for example, "The Man Who Dreamed of Faeryland."

After 1900, in part because of Yeats's involvement in founding and running the Ir. national theater (the Abbey), the lang. of his verse became a great deal more energetic and colloquial. Most remarkably in the love poems of the volumes *In the Seven Woods* (1904) and *The Green Helmet* (1910), the stylized if beautiful rhet. of the earliest phase of Yeats's verse has been transformed into passionate and dramatic utterance: "Heart cries, 'No, / I have not a crumb of comfort, not a grain. / Time can but make her beauty over again'" ("The Folly of Being Comforted"). With the volume *Responsibilities* (1914), there is yet another change as Yeats began to write a poetry of engagement with the social and political life of his country, emerging as the chronicler of modern Ireland who spoke, in his poetry, for and about Ireland with great authority. The poems of *Michael Robartes* (1921) and *The Tower* (1928) are haunted by the nightmare of contemporary history in Ireland and Europe. It was this phase of Yeats's work, with its apocalyptic view of history, that had most in common with the work of such modernists as T. S. Eliot and Ezra Pound: "Things fall apart; the centre cannot hold; / Mere anarchy is loosed upon the world" ("The Second Coming"). In the last decade or so of Yeats's life, esp. in *Last Poems* (1936–39), the dominant note is a tragic affirmation of life defiantly expressed in the teeth of time and the worst that life can offer: "All things fall and are built again, / And those that build them again are gay" ("Lapis Lazuli").

Yeat's verseforms are the traditional ones of Eng. poetry and not the revolutionary new forms associated with Pound and Eliot: his preference is for various quatrain, sestet, and octave stanzas in iambic and trochaic measures, and he employs rhyme extensively.

Associated with Yeats and the Revival is a group of poets writing in the earlier part of the 20th c.: George Russell, also known as AE (1867–1935), Oliver St. John Gogarty (1878–1957), Padraic Colum (1881–1972), and James Stephens (1882–1950). The great folk dramatist John Millington Synge (1871–1909) is also affiliated with this group. The term "Ir. Literary Renaissance" may be employed to include the Celtic Revival and the later poetry of Yeats (which makes him not only Ireland's greatest poet, but the greatest poet of the modern world); it also includes the prose fiction of James Joyce (1884–1941), surely the greatest of the modernist prose writers, and the drama of Sean O'Casey (1880–1964).

III. IRISH POETRY AFTER YEATS. The vitality of Ir. p. after Yeats is remarkable. Poetry in Eng. may be divided, for simplicity's sake, into two categories. The first shares the broad theme of exploration of cultural identity: it reflects the individual's experience of the social life of the Ir. people in the 20th c., esp. as they emerge from a traditionally rural way of life to confront modern urban experience. This poetry is written by a very different class from the one to which Yeats belonged, and is based on a very different social experience from his. The major figures are Austin Clarke (1896–1974), Patrick Kavanagh (1904–67), Thomas Kinsella (b. 1928), John Montague (b. 1928), and Seamus Heaney (b. 1939). (Of contemporary Ir. poets only Richard Murphy hails from Yeats's Anglo-Ir. background.) This poetry by and large shares a certain sense of history, place, lang., and religion. Indeed, the theme of Ir. history as an urgent personal issue, felt in the blood, supersedes the present conflict in Ulster, and takes as its domain all of Ir. history, including the archaeological past. There is little sense of the aestheticizing of history or the creation of heroic myth that one finds in Yeats. Much of this poetry is shaped to various degrees by an awareness of Ir. lang. and lit.; except for Kavanagh, all the major figures have effected a substantial repossession of poetry in Ir. through tr. into verse in Eng. which captures more authentically the spirit of the original than did the trs. of the Revival writers. Contemporary poets have also incorporated, in various ways, this linguistic awareness into their verse in Eng. The sense of place in their poetry is frequently atavistic in its recovery of an Irishness which has been hidden from the present. The common attitude toward religion resists the oppressive aspects of the Catholic Church as a social institution in Ireland, yet the poetry is frequently imprinted with a vision of nature as sacramental, of poetry as prayer, of the artist as a sacerdotal figure.

The second category of poetry after Yeats vigorously disputes the agenda set by the first, stressing modernity rather than Irishness. There are two main groups, as well as numerous individuals: The European-Ir. poets—Samuel Beckett (b. 1906), Thomas MacGreevy (1893–1967), Brian Coffey (b. 1905), Dennis Devlin (1908–59)—constitute one group, and a number of the Ulster poets, pre-eminently Derek Mahon (b. 1941), who look to Louis MacNeice (1907–63) as exemplar, constitute the other. Both groups are possessed of a cosmopolitan sensibility, modern feelings of loss and alienation, a view of hist. informed by modern European and world hist. (rather than Ir. hist.), and a conviction that the European langs. and the classics are more significant than Ir. lang. and lit. They distrust the idea of an Ir. poet, as opposed to a poet who happens to be Ir.

The technique of Ir. p. in Eng. after Yeats, as in poetry in Eng. elsewhere in the same period, has tended to reject the traditional forms within which Yeats worked. The example of Pound and Williams (and behind both, Whitman) has been particularly liberating for Ir. poets in their struggle to emerge from Yeats's colossal shadow. But this is not the whole story. There is also, and esp. among poets from Ulster, a disposition toward a more traditional sense of form, akin to the notion of the well-made poem fostered by The Movement in Britain. There is an occasional reversion to older forms, as in Seamus Heaney's sonnet sequences; and at least one Ir. poet, Austin Clarke, has sought to import into Eng. the complicated and ornate technique of poetry in Gaelic, an undertaking which he described thus to Robert Frost: "I load myself with chains and try to get out of them." Conventional forms in Ir. may also be used unconventionally in contemporary poetry in Eng., as in the parodic appropriation of *immram* (voyage poem) and the *aisling* in the work of Paul Muldoon (b. 1951).

One index to the vitality and accessibility of recent poetry in Gaelic is the fact that it is being translated by contemporary Ir. poets who write in Eng. In the earlier generation of poets writing in Gaelic, the names to reckon with are Seán Ó Riordáin (1917–77), considered by some to be the finest poet writing in Ir. since the 18th c., Máirtín Ó Direáin (b. 1910), and Máire Mhac an tSaoi (b. 1922). The present generation includes a host of writers, from whom may be singled out Michael Hartnett (b. 1941), who also writes in Eng., Michael Davitt (b. 1950), and Nuala Ní Dhomhnaill (b. 1952). What characterizes this most recent resurgence of poetry in Gaelic is not only individual talent, but the fact that writing in Gaelic no longer precludes an acceptance of the modern world, nor does it require the employment of the strict poetic forms of the past.

If contemporary poets writing in Eng. or Gaelic do not enjoy quite the same privilege as the *filidh*, they do, like their ancient counterparts, tend to stand as a group in intimate relation to the national life of their country. By and large, they are known, respected, and listened to when they speak or write on history, society, or politics, as well as on more personal subjects. *Aosdána*, the state-supported association of writers, is obviously based in part on the conviction that the dignity and prestige enjoyed by the poets of ancient Ireland ought in some measure to be accorded to the poets of contemporary Ireland.

BIBLIOGRAPHIES: R. I. Best, *A Bibl. of Ir. Philology and of Printed Ir. Lit.* (1913); K. G. W. Cross and R. T. A. Dunlop, *A Bibl. of Yeats Crit. 1887–1965* (1971); R. Bromwich, *Med. Celtic Lit.: A Select Bibl.* (1974); M. Lapidge and R. Sharpe, *A Bibl. of Celtic-Lat. Lit., 400–1200* (1985); K. P. S. Jochum, *W. B. Yeats: A Classified Bibl. of Crit.* (1990).

ANTHOLOGIES IN ENGLISH AND TRANSLATIONS FROM GAELIC: *The Love Songs of Connacht*, and *The Religious Songs of Connacht*, ed. and tr. D. Hyde (1893; 1906); *Bards of the Gael and Gall*, ed. and tr. G. Sigerson (1897); *Sel. from Ancient Ir. P.*, ed. and tr. K. Meyer (1911); *An Anthol. of Ir. Verse*, ed. P. Colum (1922); *Love's Bitter-Sweet*, ed. and tr. R. Flower (1925); K. A. Jackson, *Studies in Early Celtic Nature Poetry*, (1935), *A Celtic Miscellany* (1951); *1000 Years of Ir. P.*, ed. K. Hoagland (1947); *Ir. Poets of the 19th C.*, ed. G. Taylor (1951); *Early Ir. Lyrics*, ed. and tr. G. Murphy (1956); *Kings, Lords and Commons*, ed. and tr. F. O'Connor (1959); *Love Poems of the Ir.*, ed. and tr. S. Lucy (1967); *The Penguin Book of Ir. Verse*, ed. B. Kennelly (1970); *The Book of Ir. Verse*, ed. J. Montague (1974); *An Duanaire 1600–1900*, ed. and tr. T. Kinsella and S. O'Tuama (1981); *Early Ir. Verse*, ed. and tr. R. Lehmann (1982); *Poets of Munster*, ed. S. Dunne (1985); *The Bright Wave*, ed. D. Bolger (1986); *The*

New Oxford Book of Ir. Verse, ed. T. Kinsella (1986); *Contemp. Ir. P.*, ed. A. Bradley (1988).

HISTORY AND CRITICISM: E. O'Reilly, *A Chronological Account of Nearly Four Hundred Irish Writers* (1820, rpt. 1970); E. A. Boyd, *Ireland's Literary Ren.* (1916); D. Corkery, *The Hidden Ireland* (1924); A. De Blacam, *Gaelic Lit. Surveyed* (1929); R. Flower, *The Ir. Trad.* (1947); M. Dillon, *Early Ir. Lit.* (1948); E. Knott, *Ir. Syllabic Poetry 1200–1600* (1957); C. Watkins, "IE Metrics and Archaic Ir. Verse," *Celtica* 6 (1963); *Early Ir. P.*, ed. J. Carney (1965); C. Donahue, "Med. Celtic Lit." in Fisher; P. L. Henry, *The Early Eng. and Celtic Lyric* (1966); P. Power, *A Lit. Hist. of Ireland* (1969); O. Bergin, *Ir. Bardic Poetry* (1970); H. Bloom, *Yeats* (1970); J. E. Stoll, *The Great Deluge: A Yeats Bibl.* (1971); T. Brown, *Northern Voices: Poets from Ulster* (1975); *Two Decades of Ir. Writing*, ed. D. Dunn (1975); R. Finneran, *Anglo-Ir. Lit: A Review of Research* (1976); D. Perkins, *Hist. of Mod. Poetry*, 2 v. (1976, 1987); S. O'Neill, "Gaelic Lit.," *Dict. of Ir. Lit.*, ed. R. Hogan et al. (1979); G. J. Watson, *Ir. Identity and the Literary Revival* (1979); R. Welch, *Ir. P. from Moore to Yeats* (1980); *The Pleasures of Gaelic Poetry*, ed. S. MacReammoin (1981); A. N. Jeffares, *Anglo-Ir. Lit.* (1982); S. Deane, *Celtic Revivals* (1985), *A Short Hist. of Ir. Lit.* (1986); D. Johnston, *Ir. P. After Joyce* (1986); P. L. Marcus, *Yeats and the Beginning of the Ir. Ren.*, 2d ed. (1987); R. Garratt, *Mod. Ir. P.* (1986); E. Longley, *Poetry in the Wars* (1986); D. Donoghue, *We Irish* (1988); R. F. Garratt, *Mod. Ir. P.* (1989).

A.BR.

ITALIAN POETRY.

I. DUECENTO: THE 1200S
II. TRECENTO: THE 1300S
III. QUATTROCENTO: THE 1400S
IV. CINQUECENTO: THE 1500S
V. SEICENTO: THE 1600S
VI. SETTECENTO: THE 1700S
VII. OTTOCENTO: THE 1800S
VIII. NOVECENTO: THE 1900S

I. DUECENTO: THE 1200S. The Middle Ages, from the fall of the Roman Empire to the 1300s, were long regarded as merely an epoch of barbarism. Modern historiography, however, has rediscovered the period from Charlemagne to the birth of the Romance vernacular lits. as a time of fervent incubation, a preparation for the cultural rebirth of the 13th and 14th cs. During this period the autonomous existence of the neo-Lat. langs. became evident. The first documents of It. lang. and lit., from the doubtful "Veronese Riddle" (9th c.) and the "Laurentian Verse" (ca. 1150) to St. Francis's "Hymn," Jacopone's poems, and the Sicilian and Tuscan love lyrics, should be examined in the light of three conditioning facts: (1) the political conformation of the It. peninsula—the constant tension between temporal and ecclesiastical power and its result, the Guelph-Ghibelline wars; (2) the influence of Fr. and Occitan literary models—the Fr. lang. precedes It. by a century or more; the delay usually being attributed to a tenacious survival of Lat., though it also owes to the absence of a central power, hence a slower evolution of feudal structures in the peninsula; and (3) the widespread religious revival beginning around the year 1000 and its vast influence throughout the 1300s.

Directly related to the latter is the monastic order founded by Francis of Assisi (1182–1226), who is also the first It. poet worthy of note. His "Cantico delle creature" (Song of the Creation), a thanksgiving hymn by and for the creature to the Creator, reflects a spirit of humility and simple faith as well as a new-found wonder at the beauty of the creation and an implicit refusal to see earthly life as a mere valley of tears. The primitive diction should not mislead the reader: Francis is a conscious creator of poetry. This can be seen in the careful structure of the hymn, in the purposeful ambivalence of word choice, and in the celebrated adjectival series which define each "member" of the grace-giving choir.

The genre of the *lauda* (the "Canticle" is also known as "Laus creaturarum"), enriched by the example of Med. Lat. liturgical lit., was endowed with high poetry by Jacopone da Todi (1236?–1306), an attorney spiritually reborn after the tragic death of his wife. Jacopone vigorously opposed the power plays of Pope Boniface VIII (Dante's arch-enemy), and was excommunicated and imprisoned by him; a number of the approximately 100 extant *laude* by Jacoponi are against the simony of the Church (e.g. "O Papa Bonifazio"). Jacopone's best poetry is inspired by his feeling of singularity and isolation in his mystical passion. "There's wisdom and rank methinks no higher / than the madness of love for the fair Messiah," Jacopone sings in "Senno me pare"; holy insanity pervades his poems. The primitive diction is, in part, poetic artifice. In "O iubelo del core" (O Heartfelt Joy), a rough-hewn *ars poetica*, the poet seems to give his program: "the tongue in your mouth stutters, / it knows not what it says." His masterpiece, the "Donna del Paradiso" (Lament of Mary), is a short dramatization of Christ's passion seen through the eyes of the Mother. Here Jacopone reaches lyric heights never before attained in It. p. The Madonna's cry to her Son, the "Lovely Lily," ("O figlio figlio figlio / figlio amoroso giglio") is supreme religious poetry, equalled only in Dante's *Paradiso*.

Jacopone had no direct following. Among Dante's indirect predecessors was the late 13th-c. flowering of religious verse in Northern Italy on the theme of the Beyond: the excessive realism of Giacomino da Verona's "Infernal Babylon" and "Heavenly Jerusalem" (620 stammering verses), and the *ex-voto*-like "Threefold Book" by Bonvesin de la Riva (1240–1313). The actual forerunners of Dante's lyric poetry were the poets of the "Sicilian School", the first matrix of It. literary trad. Centered at the Palermo court of Frederick II (1194–1250), the group devolved from the Occitan troubadour trad. It superimposed the rituals of feudal bondage and court protocol onto a concept of love, its only topic, in which the perfect submission by the Platonic lover corresponded to the heavenly perfection of the lady. The school, of vast cultural importance but wanting in invention, produced no great poetry. Among its members were Giacomino Pugliese, Rinaldo d'Aquino, and Pier delle Vigne. The reputed "inventor" of the sonnet, the notary Jacopo da Lentino (mid 1200s), is mentioned by Dante as the foremost poet of the "Magna Curia"; he was a faithful adapter of the *trouvères'* schemata of *fin amor.*

The Emperor Frederick, himself a poet, had vainly attempted to unify his Ger. and It. domains against violent ecclesiastical opposition. During his reign arose the Ghibelline (Imperial) and Guelph (Papal) factions, antagonists for over a century in It. politics. After the battle of Benevento (1266) the practice of poetry survived but was transplanted to the North. Its first noteworthy heir, Guittone d'Arezzo (1225–93), a Guelph exiled from his homeland, renewed and enriched the Siculo-Occitan trad. by extending its topics to ethical and social concerns. Guittone's hermeticism is an exasperation of the *trobar clus* of Fr. minstrelsy; his poems sound cold and artistically stifling. Although poets such as Chiaro Davanzati and the abstruse Monte Andrea shared his taste for technical complexity, Guittone had no direct disciple. His songbook is a bridge, or rather a hurdle to be overcome between the Sicilians and the first great flowering of It. lyric, the school of Dante's Sweet New Style, the Dolce stil nuovo.

The very existence of such a "school," posited only by a vague reference in *Purgatory,* is unsure. Certain, however, is a common conception of Love as "dictator" (inspirer and despot). The Bolognese judge Guido Guinizzelli (ca. 1240–76), praised by Dante as the father of the style *dolce* ("sweet," not bitterly harsh, as in Guittone) and *nuovo* ("original"), left a celebrated summary of the new amorous *ars poetica* in his *canzone*: true nobility is not of lineage but of virtue; love is a positive force: through the lady, admired from afar, the lover of "noble heart" attains spiritual perfection. Guido's Songbook (about 20 extant texts) shows a youthful vitality and a springtime acerbity, also present in Dante's *Vita nuova.* Among the numerous adepts of the Sweet New Style we can but mention Lapo Gianni, Gianni Alfani, Dino Frescobaldi, Bonagiunta Orbicciani; an anonymous Compiuta Donzella ("Accomplished Maiden"; her three sonnets show poetic skill and sincere passion); and the prolific Cino da Pistoia (d. 1336), usually characterized as a hyphen between Dante and Petrarch. The maturity of the school is represented by Guido Cavalcanti (d. 1300), Dante's "primo amico." Legend depicts him as a haughty loner, an image probably inspired by his poems (52 extant), his *ars poetica,* and theory of love. Cavalcanti's interest in the mechanics of feelings, esp. the anguish of love, gives him a "morbid and mournful" air; he seems to be an observer of his own soul. In his concept of love the image of a "real" woman stimulates the lover to create an idea of beauty which pervades his soul and, in turn, prods him to strive vainly toward the "original." Cavalcanti's masterpiece, "Ballatetta" (ca. 1300), was written in exile.

Parallel to *stilnovo* a school of jocose (or "bourgeois") poetry developed. The "Contrasto" by a Cielo d'Alcamo (1250?) is a highly artistic, lively "script" of amorous bickering, ending in bed, between a cynical minstrel and a clever country lass. The Sicilian court poets' recurrent topics (praise, submission) and artful linguistic *koinè* are the ironic subtext to this still enjoyable little masterpiece. Parody of *stilnovo* results in shrill outbursts in Cecco Angiolieri (1260–1313), the skilled Sienese sonneteer (about 100 extant poems) whose themes incl. wild quarrels with his lady (Becchina—who is no lady), tavern brawls, the sorry state of his purse, and the stinginess of his parents, who are reluctant to die. Cecco is no "It. Villon," as he has been called. His texts are meant for recital in the inn or brothel; the punchlines are ideally completed by guffaws from the guzzlers. A gentler realism inspires the sonnets of Folgòre, poet of San Gimignano (early 14th c.), reflecting the chivalric ceremonies of polite society. The frank pursuit of pleasure here is tempered by a code of behavior based on good taste. Folgòre's tenuous poetry harks back, as *stilnovo* does, to the courtly poets of Provence.

II. TRECENTO: THE 1300S. In retrospect, the first hundred years of It. lit. appear as preparation for Dante's poetry. This perception, philologically speaking, is quite correct. Aesthetically, however, a veritable chasm separates *Duecento* poetry from *The Divine Comedy.* For valid parallels one must turn to the fine arts and Giotto, or to philosophy and Thomas Aquinas.

Little is known of Dante Alighieri's life. Born in 1265 in Florence into a Guelph-leaning family of lesser nobility, he studied rhet. with Brunetto Latini. His attendance at Bologna University is doubtful; service in the wars of the *Commune* in 1289 is attested. Lasting influences upon his youth included his friendship with Guido Cavalcanti, his discovery of his own talent for poetry, and, esp., his love for a Bice Portinari, wife of the banker Bardi ("Beatrice" for the poet who remained devoted to her in her life and after her death.) Their lopsided love story is told in his youthful novel, the *Vita nuova,* but in his *magnum opus,* written to honor this young woman who died at 25, Beatrice is present from beginning to end. No mention is ever made of wife Gemma and their three or four offspring (two, Jacopo and Pietro, become exegetes of their father's work). After 1295 documents attest Alighieri's participation in the civic life of his city; in 1300 he became one of six "priori" (cabinet members) in a Florence torn between two Guelph parties: Blacks, subservient to Rome, and Whites, anti-imperial but resistant to Papal hegemony. Alighieri sided with the latter. In 1301 he was sent by his party, then in power, as ambassador to Pope Boniface VIII, who promptly detained him while the Blacks, with French and Papal help, seized power in Florence. Dante, sentenced *in absentia* to be burned at the stake, never again set eyes on his city. In exile over 20 years, he hoped at first to deserve recall on the strength of his learning: he produced works on linguistics (*De vulgari eloquentia*, a fragment in Lat.), exegesis (*Convivio*, unfinished), and political science (*De monarchia*). Scholars date the composition of *The Divine Comedy* from 1307 to the year of Dante's death in Ravenna, 1321.

The *Vita nuova* (1292–93) is a collection of poems connected by prose passages relating a tenuous love story from the meeting between Dante and Bice, both aged nine, to her death in 1290 and beyond. It is a story made up of abstract emotions, the most daring "real" event being Beatrice's one-time reciprocation of Dante's greeting. *Vita nuova* is neither autobiography nor total fiction: it is rather a typology of youthful love, pervaded by a quasi-religious, mystical solemnity and by an oneiric vagueness of detail. Poems not fit for inclusion in the "Vita," and those written after 1293, make up Dante's *Canzoniere* (or *Rime* [Songbook]). Here, besides the early and later experiments with styles and forms, we find the *canzoni* of Dante's maturity and exile; closest to the inspiration of the *Comedy* is the poem "Tre donne" (Three Women).

The 15,000 verses of the *Comedy* (for Dante, "comedy" as opposed to tragedy meant a story beginning badly but ending well; "divine" was added by posterity) took 15 years to compose. *Grosso modo*, he wrote an average of one strophe a day: 33 syllables (three hendecasyllables); hence the impression, predominant among his good readers for over six centuries, of an extraordinary density, a continually unfolding and renewed inner richness. The poet claimed at different times different purposes for his enterprise: in addition to the glorification of Beatrice and the exile's wish to show his worth, Dante seems to claim, in a letter (*Epistle* XIII) of doubtful attribution, the messianic mission "to lead the living out of a state of misery into a state of bliss." The purpose the poet did accomplish was poetic: to create with words a world which in its miraculous credibility vies with God's own creation. The reader must keep constantly in mind that the *Comedy* is a fiction, not a world, the work of a poet and master storyteller, not of the Holy Spirit. This *lapalissian* truth sets a limit to symbolic interp., even though the medieval practice of allegory is ever-present in the text. Consider, however, what distinguishes Dante's from earlier transcendental journeys. His unreadable predecessors are *all* allegory; we read Dante after seven centuries for what we find beyond his didactic purposes. Allegory is a premise of the *narratio*, flexible and often ambiguous: it is part of the plurivalence genetic to all enduring poetry. Beatrice and Virgil are, respectively, "theology" and "reason," but we believe and love them primarily because Dante "forgot," more often than not, their roles as abstractions.

The grand architecture of the poem is universally known. The *Comedy* is the fictive, visionary account of a redemptive journey through Hell and Purgatory to Paradise and God, by a pilgrim who both is and is not Dante Alighieri, guided at first by Virgil and later by Beatrice. Allegorically the trip is Everyman's progress through suffering and purgation to salvation and bliss; narratively it is an immensely, mysteriously moving story of an exploration of an unknown universe. The first realm holds the souls of the damned, distributed into nine "circles" set up according to Aristotle's categories of sin (intemperance, violence, fraud—with heresy, unknown to the Greek, thrown in). The realm of purgation is segmented into the seven deadly sins of Christian dogma (with Ante-Purgatory and Earthly Paradise bringing the number of divisions to nine). The blessed regions comprise the nine heavens of Ptolemy's geocentric universe, from the sphere of the Moon through the planets and the Sun to the fixed stars and the Empyrean, abode of all the souls happy in the sight of God. The recurrence of the number 3 and its multiples, as well as other divisions in the edifice, such as the 100 *canti*, or the strophic scheme of 3 lines of 11 syllables each—*terza rima*—or the canto and episode parallelisms and contrasts at corresponding "locations" in the three *cantiche* are the cross and delight of Dante exegesis. Hints at the Trinity?—certainly. But first and foremost, these are self-imposed "difficulties," order-creating limits with which the poet circumscribes and regulates the excesses of his boundless imagination.

Of the three canticles (34+33+33 *canti*), *Inferno* is the most dramatic and suspenseful. Memorable characters and events dominate several *canti*: Francesca's story of love and death, Farinata's "war memoirs," Chancellor Pier's suicide, Ulysses' last voyage, the prison "cannibalism" of Count Hugolin of Pisa. Purgatory is the reign of elegy, subdued sadness, and hopeful yearning: it is the *cantica* most "earthly" and peaceful. Feelings of brotherly affection dominate here; the middling tone fits well the characters on the mountainside. It is a mild crepuscular setting, in contrast to the purple-dark violence of Hell and the soul-searching beams of the last domain. *Paradise* is the triumph of Beatrice, who is a symbol and yet a real woman, with her individualized intonation, choreography, and even mannerisms. Among the blessed, absolute equality is the rule: no character should emerge; but a hymnal choir clearly cannot satisfy the playwright in Dante. The sequence of Heavens is transformed into a transcendental fireworks of growing intensity. Humanity is never absent from the rarefied mysticism signalling God's presence. And the great Saints appear in person to test, prod, warn, and guide the Pilgrim toward fulfillment. God, thanks to the magnificent intuition of Dante's genius, is depicted here not as the bearded elder of Judaeo-Christian iconography but as a blinding point of light immeasurably far and immeasurably near. In *Paradise* Dante is at his most sublime; it is the soaring flight of his mature genius.

In "Limbo" the pilgrim meets the six great poets of Cl. antiquity, and there, in a prideful aside, he reports how he was made an equal among them. Some readers detect immodesty here. In truth, Dante's claim is rather modest. Two of the six, Ovid and Lucan, through respectable storytellers, are certainly not in the same league with Homer, Horace, and Virgil (and Dante). In fact, the author of *The Divine Comedy* has in world lit. fewer than five equals: he is in that most select club which has so far admitted only Homer, Virgil, Shakespeare, and Goethe.

Dante's robust spirituality, unshaken religious convictions, and firm belief in the continuity of social structures were rooted in the apparent stability of the "old" world, the thick Ages in the Middle. The *curriculum vitae* of Francesco Petrarca (1304–74) coincides with a historical moment of accelerated change and crumbling certainties. Petrarch appears much closer to us than Dante, closer than the generation or two that actually separate these two quasi-contemporaries. The "modern" lability of Petrarch's psychic makeup is manifest in his vast correspondence, in his treatises (e.g. on "solitude," on the "remedies against Fortune"), and esp. in his Lat. "Confessions" (*Secretum*), which is a microscopic analysis of that nameless something that forever anguished his soul. Born in Arezzo of a Florentine bourgeois family in exile, Petrarch was brought up in Southern France. He studied jurisprudence at Montpellier and Bologna. On April 6, 1327, his destiny was redirected by his meeting in Avignon, Laura, the unidentified Provençal girl whom he loved in life and in death (she died of the plague in 1348) and whom he immortalized in his poetry. Petrarch is the forefather of humanism, the revival of Graeco-Roman culture that dominates the next century. His work in Lat. is immense; it (mainly the epic in hexameters, *Africa*) procured him the Poet Laureate title and crown conferred by the Senate of Rome in 1341. The uncontested arbiter of European lit., Petrarch lived the latter half of his life mainly in Italy.

Petrarch expected enduring fame from his Lat. work; immeasurably superior are his modestly titled (with affected scorn) *Rerum vulgarium fragmenta* (freely rendered, "It. bits and pieces") or *Canzoniere.* In spite of his expressed desire to burn the collection, he kept revising and perfecting the ms. to his dying day. The 366 poems (317 sonnets, plus *canzoni,* sextets, ballads, and madrigals) record the earthly (not at all merely spiritual) passion inspired by Laura, even after her "flight to heaven." This last great representative of the troubadour trad. (afterwards there will be epigones and "Petrarchism") breaks with its "Platonic" incorporeality. Some critics have doubted the very existence of Laura, assuming her to be a composite of the poetic trad. And the "love story" behind the stylized abstractions is clearly an unrequited love. But the human passion of the poet, with its ebb and flow over the years, with its emotional flotsam and jetsam of brief joys and long despair, with its cries and silences, with its phases of resignation and of rebellion, recreates, albeit perhaps *ex nihilo,* the anonymous Beloved, body and soul. A curious double process takes place: Petrarch veils and stylizes his earthly model, but the living warmth of his words makes the reader mentally recreate Laura. There is no direct description of her in the Songbook, yet we never lose sight of her.

There is something artful if not artificial in this process—the something that made F. De Sanctis remark that, while Dante was more poet than artist, Petrarch was more artist than poet. It is true, however, that readers have always privileged the poems written about Laura and the self-analytic pauses. Set aside the recantatitive opening and closing pieces as well as the few non-directly "Laura" poems, and what remains engraved in memory are the dreamy evocation of the memorable day (no. 2), the Proustian simile of the old pilgrim (16), a *solo e pensoso* walk across the fields (35), the tired prayer of the penitent (62), a lovely shape made of transparencies (90 and the famous 126), the *cameretta* [little room] of the poet (234), and, in the death of Laura, the inexorable march of days and years (272), the useless return of spring (310), and the sad song of a nightingale telling us that "nothing here below delights—and lasts" (311). A certain repetitiousness has been observed in the *Canzoniere,* but in fact the work was meant to be sampled by fits and starts, rather than by continued perusal. A monochrome uniformity is genuine in Petrarch's only other "vulgar" (i.e. It.) verse work, the later *Trionfi.* Heavily allegorical, unfinished and unrefined, these series of Dantesque *terzine* sing the "triumphs" of Love, Modesty, Death, Fame, Time, and Eternity.

Among the minor *Trecentisti* poets one should mention at least the late *stilnovista* Fazio degli Uberti, from Pisa; the courtly poet Antonio Beccari from Ferrara; the Florentine prolific polygraph, popularizer of vernacular lit., Antonio Pucci (d. 1388); and the fine author of ballads, Franco Sacchetti (d. 1400). The third component of the great *Trecento* triumvirate, Giovanni Boccaccio (1313–75), father of modern storytelling, was an uninspired but evidently inspiring versifier. Known is Chaucer's vast and undervalued debt to his *Filostrato* (1336?; the romance of Troilus in octaves) and *Teseida* (1341?, an epic, the Palamon and Arcite story). Boccaccio's own "Vita nuova" (*Commedia delle ninfe*, 1341) and allegorical vision in *terzine* (*Amorosa visione*, 1343?) influenced in turn Petrarch's *Trionfi*. There are some 100 lyric compositions also attributed to Boccaccio, counting the "day"-divider ballads from the frame of the *Decameron*. The real poetry of the *Decameron*, however, is to be looked for rather in some of the stories construed more according to the compositional norms of a poem (strophic architecture, anaphoric insistences, gigantic "rhymes," echoes and refrains) than of a short story (e.g. Zima, Federigo and his falcon, the rhythmical tale of the baker Cisti, or, esp., the wondrous ballad of Isabetta and her "pot of basil").

III. QUATTROCENTO: THE 1400S. The sudden blossoming of vernacular lit. in the 14th c. carried in it the seeds of decadence, or rather of exhausted retrenchment during the first half of the next century. Petrarch and Boccaccio (and protohumanist Dante) were indeed the fountainhead of the cultural movement called humanism, essentially an enthusiastic revival of Lat. lit. (as opposed and "superior" to It. lit.). The trend, initially a passion for Cl. learning and a rediscovery of many major texts of Lat. and Gr. antiquity, by degrees became a belief in the panacea of Cl. education, capable of "freeing" man. The main creative tenet of this new classicism was *imitatio*, theorized by Petrarch and basis for the later "Petrarchism." The new blooming of Lat. lit. highlights such well-known humanists as Pico della Mirandola, Lorenzo Valla, Coluccio Salutati, Giovanni Pontano, and Marsilio Ficino. Far from being slavish imitators, the humanists in fact ended by "dethroning the ancients from their exalted position" (Guarino, in Bondanella) by reexamining under the microscope of philology the old texts and by historicizing classicism. Humanism was nothing short of a discovery of history in the modern sense of the word.

Poetry in It. continued to be produced, marginally as it were, often in its "lower" species as imitations of popular song. The Venetian patrician Leonardo Giustinian (1338–1446) became a sort of bestseller on account of his talent for reproducing the sonorities and easy grace of the *canzonette* sung by gondoliers on the *laguna*. The same taste for the simple diction of popular genres inspired the Florentine Luigi Pulci (1432–84), but with a different result. Pulci is a "humorist" in the true sense of the word: for him life was a "harmonious mixture of sweet and bitter and a thousand flavors." His mock-heroic "epos" *Morgante*, a rewriting of the *Chanson de Roland*, is not merely a parody on the solemnities of the Fr. *chansons de geste*; it is the amusing product of a whimsical comic genius. Its rough model is enriched by characters *alive* on the page—in spite of their irrational capriciousness. In addition to the usual types, Pulci introduced Morgante, the giant, inspirer of Rabelais, the ribald monster Margutte who dies of immoderate laughter at a gross practical joke, and the amusing "logician" fiend, Astaroth, spokesman for Pulci's religious doubts and occult leanings. Byron read and translated part of this weird epic; it may have been among the inspirations for *Don Juan*.

Matteo Maria Boiardo (1441–94) made reference in a serious vein to the same material. Pulci's attitude toward the Carolingian sources had reflected popular Tuscan city-bred tastes; Boiardo brought to them the conservative provincial atmosphere of Northern courtly life. The incomplete *Orlando innamorato* (The Loves of Roland) injects Arthurian elements into the chivalric material: all-conquering love now presides over the knights' and ladies' adventures. The poem is a whirlwind of disparate episodes, unified, if at all, by overwhelming passion and vigorous action. The idiom, of strong regional flavor, hindered wide diffusion of the original; up to the 19th c. *Orlando* was read in Tuscanized remakes by Berni and others.

Florence, transformed from Dante's *Commune* into a *Signoria* under the Medicis, reacquired its cultural centrality during the second half of the century. Pulci's lord protector, Lorenzo de'Medici (1449–92; known as "Il Magnifico"), was himself a poet of great versatility. Critical appraisals of the Magnifico's poetry range from enthusiastic endorsement of his artful masquerades to viewing his output as the pastime of a statesman, the amusement of a dilettante. In truth, Lorenzo was simply one of the many skillful literati of his court. His principal merit, other than his all-important patronage, lies in his vigorous defense of literary It.: Lorenzo contributed in a decisive way to the final prevalence of the Tuscan-Florentine trad. and the decline of creative writing in Lat., almost in abeyance during the Ren.

Still, it may well be that Lorenzo's most enduring achievement was the discovery of the poetic talent of Politian (Poliziano), pseudonym of Agnolo Ambrogini (1454–94) from Montepulciano (hence the name). Politian became a leading humanist rediscoverer and editor of ancient texts. Apart from his poetry in Lat. and Gr., Politian wrote *canzoni* and other lyric poems; his masterwork is the unfinished *Stanze* ("Strophes"), the allegorical retelling, in *ottave*, of the meeting between Giuliano de' Medeci, a youth devoted to pleasure and adventure, and the nymph of unearthly beauty Simonetta (Vespucci). The airy lightness of the *Stanze* is a poetic miracle. Every octave is a contexture of reminiscences, references, and reminders (Homer, Horace, Virgil, Dante, Petrarch, and dozens of lesser classics), but the resulting quilt appears perfectly natural. Moments of noble melancholy accent the translucid text, mementos of the fragility and transience of all that is earthly. Politian is the first poet of modern times whose subject is poetry; a poet's poet, he saw lit. as the essence of life.

Composed during the last two decades of the century, the *Arcadia* of Jacopo Sannazaro (1458?–1530) has enjoyed a plurisecular fortune, cyclically renewed and, in a way, enduring into our own times of recurrent ecological lamentation. On the model of Boccaccio's *Ameto, Arcadia* is a mixture of prose tales and pastoral songs. "Antimetropolitan" yearnings (anachronistic already at inception) for a nonexistant rural simplicity, together with the immemorial myth of a lost Golden Age, inspire this early environmental manifesto. It is also a stylistic miracle: there is hardly a sentence in its loose quilt that is without a source in Cl. lit.

IV. CINQUECENTO: THE 1500S. The *Rinascimento*, the It. Ren., is the age of artistic and literary splendor between the age of humanism and the advent of baroque. Its poetic practice is pervaded by the heritage of the great *Trecento*, esp. of Petrarch (Dante was considered, by this age of refinement, a "primitive"), filtered through the classicism that prevailed in the 15th c. The *Rinascimento* is the age of Petrarchism, an age not only of servile imitation of the themes and style of the *Canzoniere*, not only the fashionable organization of one's poetic output into an ideal love story, but also an adherence to the Platonic ideal of love and to the linguistic ideal of purity, harmony, and elegance of expression, which later deteriorated into mere technical virtuosity. The patron saints of the European 1500s were Petrarch and Plato; however, Aristotle's *Poetics* was also rediscovered and deeply, at times obsessively, studied—and in part misconstrued. The tenet of *imitatio* became paramount. Literary genres were rigidly codified, just as social behavior came to be governed by a code—its great documents are Castiglione's *Courtier* and Machiavelli's *Prince*. At the threshold of this great age stands the historically important but poetically insignificant Cardinal Pietro Bembo (1470–1547), friend of Lorenzo and Politian. Bembo, as codifier of Petrarchism and Platonism, is the embodiment of the Ren. His *Rime* (Poems) are little more than textbook examples to illustrate his theories, but his treatise on the *Prose della volgar lingua* (It. Prose Style, 1525) became something of a bible for the literati of the century. This inclusive codification of literary taste and linguistic choice had a decisive influence on the diction of authors from Ariosto to Tasso.

The essence of the *Rinascimento* is best revealed in the epic romance *Orlando furioso* (The Frenzy of Roland), whose creator, one of the most likeable figures in the annals of It. lit., is Ludovico Ariosto (1474–1533). Ariosto's minor work illustrates the frustrations of a harried existence. His lyric poetry was inspired by his lifelong devotion to Alessandra Benucci, whom he married secretly so as not to forfeit ecclesiastical benefits. The *Satire* (seven *capitoli* on the model of the Horatian *sermo*) recounts his travels and reflections. The last years of his life were devoted to the definitive revision of his poem (pub. 1532 in 46 *canti*). *Orlando*, 30 years in the making, pools the experience of the minor work, the warmth and immediacy of the love poetry, the detached and smiling wisdom of the *Satire*, and the character-sketching of his theatrical pieces. The external occasion for the poem was the unfinished *Orlando innamorato*: the *Furioso* completes the story, closely following Boiardo's sources in the Carolingian epic cycle and the Celtic Arthurian legends in narrative detail, but renewing the material with poetic license. This master storyteller holds hundreds of threads in hand at once and unerringly weaves them into an immense coherent tapestry. Some critics, disturbed by the artifice of the complex plotting, posit an improbable network of allegories behind the *narratio*. The great movers of the threefold plot are Ariosto's passions: first, love conceived as an earthy emotion, frankly sensual; second, the forms of knightly behavior and of court ritual; third, an insatiable appetite for adventure. Voltaire noted that Ariosto is always "superior" to his material: he tells his story "jokingly"—taking seriously and yet mocking his inventions. Hence the frequent authorial intrusions (comments, tongue-in-cheek explanations, ironic misdirection); hence the fable-like and dreamy atmosphere around Ariosto's errant knights and ladies. Painstaking realism of detail fuses with an oneiric vagueness of context. The description of Atlante's castle and the invention of the lunar travels of Astolfo are emblematic of this attitude.

The form of the *Orlando furioso* is nothing short of prodigious. The octaves of narrative poetry—woody and lagging in Boccaccio's youthful poems, prosily stammering in Pulci's *Morgante*, loosely dressing Boiardo's laborious inventions—coincides here, for the first time in It. p., with the "breathing" of author and reader. Ariosto thinks, nay, lives in his octave, in the six (the alternately "sonorized" verses) plus two (the clinching couplet) pattern of his strophe, each one a microcosm, in its perfectly controlled and yet wondrously airy architecture, of the entire magnificent construction.

Ariosto's Petrarchan love lyrics are undistinguished products of the age, similar to myriads of contemp. songbooks. Little talent emerges from the crowd of the *Cinquecento Petrarchisti*. Monsignor Giovanni della Casa (1503–56), remembered for his *Galateo* (Book of Manners), shows a nostalgia for robust emotions and monumental imagery. Casa is an expert architect of resonant verse; his skilled enjambments still provide examples of the device in prosodic treatises. Two women poets introduce a welcome variation in a field dominated by the stylized male psychology of emotions: Vittoria Colonna (1492–1547), of aristocratic family and patroness of artists, authored a conventional songbook; Gaspara Stampa (1523–54), probably of low social standing, occasionally allows life to show through her imitative verse. Even more creatively, the feverish and disordered rhythms of a passionate existence seem to influence her songs, which are suggestive of entries in a love diary.

Intimations of the incipient baroque taste have been detected in Luigi Tansillo (1510–68). His too-easy sonorities, abuse of color, predilection for horrid landscapes, and colloquial touch seem, indeed, to point toward Marino. But more noteworthy than the lyric output of the age and its vast and forgotten epic feats (the best are Trissino's *Italy Freed from the Goths*, Alamanni's *Avarchide*, and Bernardo Tasso's *Amadigi*) is its humorous or light verse. Two cultivators of this genre had vast influence throughout the following century. Francesco Berni (1498–1535), Tuscan refurbisher of Boiardo's epic, is the wellhead of the *bernesco* poem, still jokingly cultivated in Italy—a buffoonery or "sitcom" heavy on puns. Written in an irresistibly funny It. modeled on Lat. (or a Lat. bastardized by It.), the mock-heroic epic *Baldus* by Merlin Cocai (pseudonym of the rebellious Benedictine monk Teofilo Folengo [1491–1574]) extends Pulci's *Morgante* by recounting the farcical adventures of Baldus, a descendant of Rinaldo.

The last great poetic voice of the Ren. has long been considered to be Torquato Tasso (1544–95), spiritual forerunner of baroque poetics. Most likely inheriting a psychic disorder, he became distraught by the mental effort required to produce his masterwork, the epic *La Gerusalemme liberata* (Jerusalem Delivered, 1575). Episodes of irrational behavior at the court of Ferrara and aimless excursions across the peninsula eventually led to Tasso's confinement for seven years in the dungeon asylum of Sant'Anna. Pirated editions of his poem, attacks from pedantic critics, and obsessive religious doubts exasperated his illness; he died in Rome. His minor work alone would be sufficient to give him a high rank among the Petrarchists and epic poets of his century. The *Rime* (Verses), nearly 2000 lyrics, is a workshop in which the poet perfected techniques and experimented with sentimental situations; these are interspersed with lyrics of admirable invention and masterful execution, esp. his madrigals, a genre congenial to Tasso's evanescent moods. The Petrarchan model here appears at one remove, filtered through the Petrarchists of the early 1500s—Bembo, Casa—as indeed Petrarch will be read through Tasso by the next generation of lyricists, Marino and his school. The chivalric poem *Rinaldo* (12 *canti* of *ottave*) betrays the adolescent's hand as well as features that will later govern the inspiration of his epic. Already here the war chronicle of the sources is constantly squeezed out by the courtly love. Tasso first favored the idyll, and his pastoral play *Aminta* is rightly spoken of in the same breath with his lyric output: its theatrical pretext gives way to the emotional situations and flights of pathos experimented with in the *Rime*.

Whether *La Gerusalemme liberata* is the first full poetic manifestation of the incipient baroque age (some critics hold that the very terms "baroque" and "Marinism" are misnomers for "Tassism" and "Tassomania"), or, inversely, the last bloom of the "sane" *Rinascimento* is an academic question, and interestingly, it parallels the great 17th-c. controversy (which engaged Galilei) on the relative worth of the two great narrative poems of the preceding age, Ariosto's and Tasso's. Tasso's epic, its pretext the last phase of the 1099 Crusade, has a cast made up on the one hand of lifeless historical characters and, on the other, of fictive *personae* of the poet himself, each endowed with throbbing life. To Ariosto's objectivity, detachment, and irony, Tasso opposes his subjectivity, participation, and sentimentality. All the great passionate characters of the oft-abandoned plot are facets of Tasso's psychic makeup, exhibiting the excesses and morbidity that landed their creator in Sant'Anna. The *Gerusalemme* is in this sense that *unicum*: a truly autobiographical epos. Long traverses through Aristotle's poetics and the theory of the epic preceded and accompanied the feverish composition, but the rules reaffirmed were soon discarded by Tasso's prepotent sentimental inspiration. The Crusade cedes place to the multiple, strangely disturbed love stories of the variously and wrongly assorted couples. The whole is immersed in an overheated atmosphere of gratuitous heroism, white and black magic, cliffhangers *cum* heavenly intervention, duels to the death, and battle scenes of vast confusion. In the *Orlando furioso* the goodnatured "colloquial" voice of Ludovico the Amiable constantly tended to overdub the narrator, while in the *Gerusalemme* Torquato's falsetto breaks through, fitfully as it were, to lend his creations a hundred diverse intonations of emotional disorder.

Tasso's *ottava*, ordered into obsessive parallelisms and chiastic contrasts, offers an ineffable musicality and a psychomimetic finesse never before heard. It is masterfully torn by the high drama of enjambments—much more so than Ariosto's peaceful, at times lumbering gait would allow. And yet Boileau's objection to the *clinquant du Tasse*, as well as the sometimes violent antipathy for the *Gerusalemme* shown by excellent readers, points at a fact recent Tasso crit. has placed into light: the poem is addressed to a new audience of a new age and sensibility, that of the Counter-Reformation, an age of earthshaking upheavals. This critical view allows us to reevaluate Tasso's reworking of *Gerusalemme conquistata* (Jerusalem Recovered), a text of vaster and more solemn architecture, characterized by a baroque heaviness of pace and expression and universally judged until quite recently a complete failure. The characteristics of *Gerusalemme conquistata* are in evidence in Tasso's late poem *Il mondo creato*, a ponderous account of the Creation similar in flavor to an overripe fruit.

V. SEICENTO: THE 1600S. The 17th c., a Golden Age in Góngora's and Cervantes' Spain, in Racine's and La Fontaine's France, and in the England of the metaphysical poets, was long considered to have been an age of decadence in Italy, a "century without poetry." Its dominant Tassesque aesthetics certainly revealed the exhaustion of a long-mined vein, an exasperation of the drive for outward perfection yearned for by the Ren. The age frittered away its heritage in an obsessive search for originality and "marvels." Foreign (Sp.) and Papal domination in the peninsula, the newborn religious dogmatism imposed by the Counter-Reformation, the general lowering of ethical standards owing perhaps to the riches from the New World, and the universal instability of ideas in this age of scientific revolution have all been pointed to as causes for the alleged poetic aridity of the age. In truth, an equation of the beautiful with the difficult has prevailed in all silver ages of culture (Hellenistic Greece, later Imperial Rome, our own 20th c.). The baroque age in Italy adopted the *ars poetica* of the late Ren., developing Tasso's theories and example toward a concept of poetry as a nonrational activity, and it endorsed a view of literary production and appreciation based on taste and feeling.

Giambattista Marino (1569–1625), a Neapolitan, became the high priest of the new school of writing usually called Marinism (also *Seicentismo*, conceptism, and *manierismo*). He was the theorizer and the most prolific practitioner of the poetics of *meraviglia* (of astonishment—at all costs), a style in search of the arduous and the complex. A genre loved by Marino and the *Marinisti* was poetry on art (e.g. his collection *Galleria*), a species of poetry feeding on itself (his *Lira* [Lyrics]) and pillaging all preexistent lit.—as does Marino's masterpiece the *Adone* (Adonis), in almost every one of its 40,000 verses. The poem is truly a miracle of words growing fungus-like on words and never managing to cover the void under them. The enthusiasm for the poem among Marino's contemporaries was followed by three centuries of almost total critical rejection, though *Adone* is being reevaluated.

Among Marino's contemporaries, two poets sought independence from the master: Gabriello Chiabrera (1552–1638), whose Anacreontic songs are another "reading" of Tasso, and Alessandro Tassoni (1565–1635), remembered for his mock-heroic *Secchia rapita* (The Ravished Pail, 1622). The most notable recovery of recent crit. is the poetry of the philosopher Tommaso Campanella (1568–1639), whose work closely parallels the metaphysical songs of Donne, Herbert, and Crashaw. This Calabrese monk suffered a monstrous fate, 30 years in prison (several years in the flooded underground dungeon of St. Elmo with hands and feet chained) for heresy and rebellion. Campanella's speculative output was immense, notwithstanding, and involved all branches of the *scibile*. His poems, owing to their forbidding complexity of concepts and diction, were judged by their rare readers almost devoid of interest. But today these *canzoni*, esp. the beautiful "Hymn to the Sun," composed in the depth of St. Elmo, strike us as the "missing link" in It. baroque poetry. In his translucent verses the chained poet attains the lyrical height for which Marino always strove but rarely reached.

VI. SETTECENTO: THE 1700S. The latter half of the 1600s produced a general decadence in poetry. The anti-baroque backlash came as a call to "return to nature," to observe the limits of good taste and common sense, and to renew *imitatio* and the cult of the classics. The adepts of this neoclassical revival congregated in the *Academy of Arcadia* (a loose association of literati, self-defined "shepherds"), founded in 1690 by Queen Christine of Sweden, then in exile in Rome. *Arcadia* promoted pastoral poetry, sobriety of lang., and faithfulness to trad., discarding the whole Marinist century to hark back to Sannazaro's *Cinquecento.* However, this school too in turn became the matrix of mediocre versifiers of derivative bucolic idylls. An intermittently genuine poetic voice is heard in the tenuous lyrics of the great libretto dramatist Metastasio (pseudonym of Pietro Trapassi; 1698–1782), poet-in-residence for most of his life at the Hapsburg court in Vienna. His many melodramas (e.g. *Didone abbandonata, Olimpiade, Demoofonte,* and *Demetrio*) are deservedly famous. In his *Canzonette* (Songs), Metastasio introduced a facile sentimentalism and an evanescent lyricism which he, unlike his predecessors, couched in down-to-earth lang.

Descartes' rationalism influenced practically all intellectual trends in 18th-c. Italy. The influence of the Fr. encyclopedists, Voltaire, Montesquieu, and Diderot, on the one hand, and of the Ossian craze, with the nocturnal/sepulchral fashion it brought with it, on the other, became paramount. The first civic poet of Italy, the Lombard Giuseppe Parini (1729–99), represents the sober awakening of the age leading to the earthquake of the Fr. Revolution. A seriousness of ethical purpose and a sense of mission in his social crit. distinguish this Catholic priest, editor, and schoolteacher. His early lyrics show the Arcadism prevalent at the time; his later odes from "Alla Musa" to "Messaggio" are the meditations of a political moderate. Parini is remembered, however, for his long and unfinished poem of bitter social comment, *Il giorno,* depicting one day in the life of a "giovin signore," a young man about town. The satire, ferociously allusive and resentful, and seldom attenuated by the smile of superior comprehension, seems at times shot through by a secret nostalgia for the world of fashion and elegance. Parini is the first in the history of It. p. to have obtained from the "short" hendecasyllable effects vying with those of the flexible Cl. hexameter.

The essence of pure poetry—as opposed to the practically ambitious *engagé* verse of Parini—is represented by the domineering figure of the preromantic playwright Vittorio Alfieri (1749–1803), scion of an old aristocratic family from Italy's

Piedmont region. After a stint, customary for his class, at the military academy, and the grand tour, the rich nobleman settled in the capital of Savoy to act out, as it were, Parini's recipe for the useless existence of the high-society youth of his day. Alfieri dated his conversion from 1775, with the sudden realization that the aimless, incessant agitation of his soul could be channelled into artistic creation. The first fruit of his illumination, the tragedy *Cleopatra*, was followed by a feverishly fertile decade of dramatic production (1776–86): 18 more tragedies, dramatic verse in dialogue form. The Alfierian hero, a pure revolutionary, acts out the abstract libertarian rebellion of the poet's soul, scornful of any pragmatic effort at real social progress. Alfieri's stay in Tuscany afforded him time to refine, to "Tuscanize," his Piedmontese, Frenchified linguistic and cultural background. In Paris in 1789, he was at first wildly enthusiastic about then bitterly disappointed in the Fr. Revolution. In 1792 he escaped the Terror to spend his last years in Florence writing six comedies, his violent anti-French persiflage *Il misogallo* (The Francophobe), and his celebrated *Vita* (Memoirs), with its relentlessly, almost breathlessly drawn portrait of the poet-hero.

Alfieri represents the *Sturm und Drang* of It. p. His collection of lyrics (*Rime*) amounts to a spiritual autobiography of a soul tormented by dreams of immensity. The idealized and idolized figure of the poet, alone, in haughty solitude, looms large. The Petrarchan subtext of these poems signifies a return to the source; it is the manifestation of a genuine "elective affinity" rather than the obligatory imitation of an earlier century. However, the greatest lyric poetry of this "lion of Asti" is to be found in his tragedies, texts of a lyrical essentiality, of an elliptic diction, a barebones structure, and an unrelenting pace. By critical consensus, Alfieri's most acclaimed tragic pieces, *Saul* (1882) and *Mirra* (Myrrha, 1887), are staged poems on the sublime.

VII. OTTOCENTO: THE 1800S. The Arcadian trend had sown the seeds of a rebirth of taste for Cl. ideals of beauty. In Italy these preromantic stirrings coincide with a short period of neoclassical predominance in art (Canova) and lit. concurrent with the Napoleonic age. The two movements, Arcadism of the late 1700s and neoclassicism of the early 1800s, shared an attention to form, an aesthetics based on the renewed concept of the sublime, a taste for the genuine and primordial, and a purism in the medium of art. Ippolito Pindemonte (1735–1828), remembered for his *Poesie campestri* (Rustic Verses), and Vincenzo Monti (1745–1828) were the most coherent adepts of the new trend. Monti's inborn flexibility and susceptibility to influences favored his art as a translator (his 1810 *Iliad* is a masterpiece) as well as the eclectically occasional nature of his poetic output—the centerpiece of it being his anti-republican *Basvilliana* (1791).

The poetic genius of the imperial *intermezzo* was Ugo Foscolo (1778–1827). His poetry fuses the classicist's love for perfection of form with the heritage of Parini and Alfieri and with European romanticism. Born of a Gr. mother on the Ionic island of Zante, Foscolo's classicism was, so to speak, a congenital trait in his psychic makeup. His tempestuous age provided the background for a truly romantic curriculum of wars and turbulent loves. In 1802 he published the "Vita nuova" of It. romanticism, the *Ortis* (The Last Letters of Jacopo Ortis), an epistolary novel of love and suicide inspired by Goethe's *Werther*. Foscolo's shorter poems are exemplary of the short-lived It. *Sturm und Drang*. His 12 sonnets (among them the masterpieces "Alla Musa," "A Zacinto," "Alla sera," and "In morte del fratello Giovanni") and his two major odes (1800–03) are perfect expressions of the Cl. ideal implanted in a romantic soul. His principal claim to posthumous glory should have been the *poemetto*, or three-part hymn, "Le Grazie" (The Graces), a vast corpus of fragments composed over the course of 20 years. The immaterial lightness of diction and verse can only increase our regret at the structural sketchiness of the magnificent torso. Though 20th-c. exegesis, with its bias for the fragmentary, has rediscovered this great mass of poetic wreckage, attempts at a coherent reconstruction have not been wholly convincing. The entire experience of the poet's "life in art" is the true theme of the poem.

Foscolo remains best known for his *Dei sepolcri* (Tombs, 1806), written in 295 blank verses. The theme, occasioned by the Napoleonic decree prohibiting burial within urban limits, is left behind, replaced by a poetic meditation on life and death, on the immemorial rites of burial, on fame surviving the tomb, and on the great men of the past and their sepulchers. The evocation of the nocturnal cemetery, the "triumph" in the Petrarchan sense of posthumous glory over death, the celebration of memory as a cenotaph to greatness, the motif of tears and consolation—all are close to the central topics of romanticism. In his *Sepolcri*, Foscolo emerges most cleary as the "father of It. romanticism."

The new mode of conceiving the human condition given by romanticism, with its components of Enlightenment rationalism and Restoration historicism, with its taste for the unsophisticated and primordial, and with its repertory of lugubrious themes, came of age in Italy in the 1820s. It. romantics, who first gathered around the Florentine periodical *Conciliatore* (1818–19), distinguished themselves from their fellows in Germany and England by their concern with the social and ethical role of lit. The *Risorgimento* (It. national "Resurgence," a movement which would result in 1870 in the birth of a unified modern Italy) was an important factor, mainly through the educative influence of such protagonists as the patriot Giuseppe Mazzini, the publicist Vincenzo Gioberti, and the literary historian Francesco De Sanctis.

The great models, Schiller, Byron, Chateaubriand, and Scott, had only limited direct influence on literary works. The most conventional It. romantic poet, Giovanni Berchet (1783–1851), left a thin collection of songs and ballads which is a veritable index of the items dear to European romanticism. Berchet's theoretical *Semi-Serious Letter* had a lasting impact on the reception of romantic ideology. A more interesting figure is Niccolò Tommaseo (1802–74), the blind lexicographer and Dante scholar and author of lyric poetry of "cosmic nostalgia" and a prophetic tone. The bitterness of a bleak existence inspired the Tuscan Giuseppe Giusti (1809–50), who wrote poetry marked by sarcasm and despair. His mimic talent is at its best when fixing on the page a gesture or attitude; his cerebral diction has lost its popularity. Alessandro Manzoni (1785–1873) is best known for his great novel *The Betrothed*; his verses are marginal products, but his five "Hymns" (1812–22), of deep religious inspiration, his commemorative poems, and the choral passages from his plays *Carmagnola* (1820) and *Adelchi* (1822) show the great novelist's precise diction as well as the characteristic undercurrent of *I promessi sposi*: compassion for the humble, the disinherited, and the marginal.

The realistic penchant of the romantic movement in Italy, its bias for the popular and immediate, favored the flowering of dialect poetry. The traits of dialectal speech included a down-to-earth tone, a direct documenting of life, and a built-in smile owing to the use of dialectal variation as a vehicle of low humor. The two greatest It. dialect poets lived in the heyday of the romantic *querelle*; both show the taste for the "slice-of-life," for a ready plebeian wit, and for the antiliterary spirit congenital to the realistic facet of romanticism. Carlo Porta (1775–1821) derived some of his inspiration from the decidedly nonpoetic contacts through his clerk's window in the Milan tax offices. He is one of those humble "chroniclers without pretense who end by preserving for posterity the portrait of a whole epoch" (Momigliano). His masterworks are versified *novelle*: the "disasters" of a semi-derelict (the "Giovannin Bongee" stories), the "lamentations" of a poor street fiddler (bow-legged "Marchionn"), and the tale of a streetwalker ("Ninetta del Verzee"). Porta's laughter never becomes a sneer; behind his smile one often senses the sadness of the wise. The encounter with Porta freed Giuseppe Gioachino Belli (1791–1863) from his failed attempts at It. verse and opened up the dialect of the Roman *plebs* as inspiration. A minor cleric, Belli left behind about 2000 sonnets (pub. in the 1880s) inspired by a violent anticlericalism, irreverent and often obscene. He too is a poet of metropolitan low-class life—vagrants and beggars, monks and spies, flunkeys and whores—with an infusion of prelates. His immense rogues' gallery, with its lightning-fast character sketches, infernal settings, and cynicism of expression, has been compared to Dante's characterizations in the *Inferno*. Belli's tone is more virulent than Porta's, but like Porta's, his art of portraiture, imitation of colloquial speech, and mastery of detail all point to future literary developments—to the narrative art of the naturalist school, to great Verga, and to *verismo*.

The greatest poet of modern Italy, Giacomo Leopardi (1798–1837) was born to an impoverished aristocratic family in Recanati. The poet's professed revulsion for his backward hometown and his disciplined upbringing (esp. the conservatism of his father) have been made much of in critical attempts to trace the roots of his cosmic pessimism. Recanati, however, acted as the almost exclusive locus of the poet's inspiration; there he wrote most of his poetry, and there, placed at the child-prodigy's disposal, was his father Count Monaldo's extensive library. Young Giacomo spent his adolescence in obsessive studies, amassing an astonishing amount of writing: verses, plays, and learned (though all compilative) essays and treatises, almost blinding himself in the process. Though merely the products of a pedantic youth, the early works have been shown to contain the germ of Leopardi's later and most persistent *leitmotif*: the attraction to illusions and delusions, the heroic striving toward an abstract glory marking one's passage on earth (for Leopardi, man's only existence). These motifs are recurrent in the immense notebook collection, *the Zibaldone* (1815–32). The clash of nature and reason, dominant theme of the Enlightenment, was at first given by young Leopardi a Rousseauian solution (benign nature vs. the ills brought on by human reason), but the contrary prevails in his later work: hostile nature, a "stepmother" for mankind, undermines all human endeavors. The romantic elements influencing Leopardi's system underwent a characteristic transformation: the denial of the poet's social role (and the belief in pure poetry, anticipating the "decadent" poetics to come), a materialistic worldview, a refusal of almost all nonlyric content, and a bias for the "pathetic" based on "immediacy" of feeling.

The concepts of "infinity" and "remembrance" are the cornerstones of Leopardi's best verse and are strongly present in his poetry until 1821, when the poet "escaped" from Recanati. "Rimembranze" (Recollections) and "Appressamento della morte" (Nearness of Death), written at age 18; experiments with fashionably lugubrious topics; a number of *engagé* compositions; and poetic meditations—show Leopardi's search for his poetic voice. He discovers it in the idyll "Vita solitaria" (Life of Solitude) and esp. "Sera del dì di festa" (Sunday Night). The tension is maintained through the whole (short) poem in the admirable "Alla luna" (To the Moon); however, "Infinito" (Infinite), a poem of a mere 15 lines written before the poet's flight from his family, is universally recognized as his masterwork—it is, with Dante's "Tanto gentile," the most renowned It. lyric. Its contents are of a lightness and evanescence which elude paraphrase. Its last line, with its sign of *cupio dissolvi* (the "sweetness of shipwreck"), ties Leopardi to such key texts of modern poetry as Rimbaud's "Bateau ivre" and Mallarmé's "Brise marine."

The years 1822–28, a period of uneasy independence interrupted by desperate returns to Recanati, mark an intermission in Leopardi's poetry. He fitfully produced the *Operette morali* (Little Moral Exercises, 1824), pensive and ironic dialogues on ontological questions, in this pause, a gathering of strength before his second creative period (ca. 1828–1830), an economically forced return to Recanati for 16 months of *ennui*. The cosmic meditation of "Canto notturno" (Nocturn of a Nomadic Shepherd in Asia) is "one of the supreme modern songs of existential anguish" (Perella, in Bondanella). "A Silvia" (written in Pisa, "perhaps the most poignant elegy in the It. lang."), "Ricordanze" (Memories), and "Sabato del villaggio" (Saturday in the Village) are the most characteristically Leopardian texts in his collection of *Canti* (1831), with their tone of thoughtful melancholy and disconsolate contemplation of the nullity of all things under the empty heavens. The elegy "Quiete dopo la tempesta" (The Calm After the Storm) looks for happiness in death.

The great idylls are Leopardi's true *operette morali*, meditations couched in immortal verse, liberated from the bitterness and animosity often prevailing in his prose dialogues. Leopardi lived to see his *Canti* published in a definitive edition in 1836. Their themes have a common denominator: the loss of dreams—of youth, of happiness, of heroic existence—a loss restated with calm despair in the cruel light of cold and godless reality. The meter is a kind of early free verse: discarding the strophic models of the past, Leopardi relied on a loose rhythm, now expanded freely, now suddenly restrained. While the incisive "A se stesso" (To Himself) is a pitiless spiritual self-portrait, the poet facing his bleak universe and murmuring his final renunciation, the late elegies "Amore e morte" (Love and Death) and "Tramonto della luna" (Moon Setting), as well as his last poem, "La ginestra" (The Desert Flower), seem to be not only the conclusion of an experience but also a hint at another incipient search for new directions.

The reaction to the excesses of romanticism, such as the lachrymose sentimentalism of the Prati-Aleardi school, took place in Italy under a double flag, realism and classicism. The call for a return to the sanity of everyday life as the master theme of literary mimesis was spread by a largely Lombardian group of poets known as "Scapigliati," ("the 'unkempt' ones")—a movement parallel to the Fr. *bohème*. The salient figures of the movement, the Boito brothers, Camillo and Arrigo (the latter is also remembered for his librettos), Emilio Praga, and Carlo Dossi professed an *ars poetica* based on the "slice of life." For the most part they produced "little proses in verse," unwittingly turning upside down Baudelaire's ambition of *petites poèmes en prose*.

The classicists' reaction, on the other hand, to the romantic mania for originality had at first a rather ineffectual leader in Giacomo Zanella (1820–88), who revived the minor neoclassical trad. of Monti and Pindemonte, a trend largely exhausted by mid century. The heritage of classicism in Alfieri and Foscolo, and even in the young "civic" Leopardi, was pressed into the service of anti-romanticism by Giosuè Carducci (1835–1907), a poet of vast authority who was the uncontested focal point of It. *fin de siècle* poetry. Carducci attempted to confer dignity and discipline on a field that, by his maturity, had lost or refused both. Carducci, chair of It. at Bologna, was "the last great *literatus*" Italy had. His professed ideal of a "sane, virile, strongwilled" lit. has lost most of its appeal in modern times; his reclaiming for the poet the immemorial function of *vates* has an archaic flavor. Carducci himself, after a youthful phase of loud and heathen Jacobinism, became something like a mouthpiece for the powers that were and for prevailing public opinion. His lyric production in traditional form appeared in the collections *Levia gravia* (Light and Heavy, 1861–71), *Giambi ed epodi* (Iambs and Epodes, 1867–69), and *Rime nuove* (New Verses, 1861–87). Carducci believed in the possibility of transplanting Graeco-Lat. metrics into It. versification; while probably overrated as a prosodic experiment, it makes an interesting *curiosum* out of his most discussed volume, *Odi barbare* (Barbaric Odes, 1877–89). It is likely that Carducci will survive his current eclipse by virtue of a few nonprogrammatic compositions, usually deeply autobiographical, such as his *Pianto antico* (Old Grief), about a personal loss.

VIII. NOVECENTO: THE 1900S. The last hundred years exemplify Viktor Shklovsky's observation on "schools." Apparently antithetical trends may long coexist until one of them by manifesto rises to predominance—only to cede its shortlived hegemony to its successor, which usually claims direct opposition to it but, in fact, dialectically presupposes and continues it. Thus currents as diverse as positivism and decadence, the "Voce" and the "Ronda" groups, the "Twilight" poets and the futurists, hermeticism and neorealism, not only coexist but in retrospect appear to be interdependent elements of the same whole. Two monumental figures, D'Annunzio and Pascoli, preface and condition contemp. poetry; neither strictly belongs to a "school," but each recapitulates and anticipates several.

Carducci today appears firmly rooted in the century of Leopardi and Manzoni, while the poetry of Giovanni Pascoli (1855–1912), his successor at Bologna, stretches far into our own. It foreshadows trends as distant from and seemingly alien to it as the neo-avant-garde of the 1960s and the postmodern verse of the 1980s. Pascoli is the first It. poet to "wring the neck" of eloquence. Some of his best-known pieces from *Poemetti* (1897–) and *Canti di Castelvecchio* (1903–) most surely have been swept away by the tears shed over them (e.g. "Cavallina storna" [The Dappled-Gray Pony], memorized by generations of schoolchildren). But his thin first collection, *Myricae* (1891), remains the cornerstone of modern It. p. The title "Tamarisks" hints at the "lowly shrubs" of the Fourth Eclogue, but this "last descendant of Virgil" is not merely a poet of simple rustic scenes, as his themes seem to suggest. His quaint syntax and vocabulary, invasive onomatopoeia, dialect and Lat. words, and exotic and technical terms, for example, signal the complexity underlying his deceptively simple landscapes. Pascoli's interest never fixes on the positive spectacle of human labor in the fields; his rural tableaux radiate a mysterious feeling, an almost religious stupor. G. A. Borgese recommended an impressionistic reading of Pascoli, with eyes "half-shut," and called *Myricae* the most heterogeneous book of It. p. However, a pattern in Pascoli's constructions may be discerned: a rural view is sketched out by broad brush strokes, then filtered and "un-defined" through some optical disturbance: haze, mist, fog (*tremulo* is a favorite adjective). A minimal sign of life appears, slowed at once almost to a standstill (*lento*, "slow," appears frequently in Pascoli's concordance). The cadence remains "the beating of his own heart" (Garofalo, in Bondanella)—though with the constant sinking feeling of skipped beats. At last a tiny acoustic element is added to the landscape—the chirping of a bird, the rustle of leaves, a snatch of faraway singing. That is all, but the whole remains miraculously suspenseful, suggestive not of something "else" but of itself. Even the most allegorical-seeming texts of Pascoli, e.g. his best *poemetti*, "Il vischio" (Mistletoe) and "Digitale purpurea" (Foxglove), suggest, rather than a meaning, an abstract horror, a visionary experience of Evil. The tragedy of Pascoli's life, the unsolved murder of his father in 1867, fixed his poetic age at 12: there is a sense of bewildered wonder in front of an uncomprehended world, the urge to escape, the need for refuge—a need he soon identified with poetry. In the poet's psyche, the unknown assassin assumes the features of mankind, driven on by the eternal enigma of evil. In an 1897 essay, "Il fanciullino" (The Child), Pascoli shaped this very concept into an *ars poetica*. Leopardi was the last It. poet to have, in a poetic sense, a geocentric view of man's habitat. Pascoli's universe, by contrast, is heliocentric, or rather centerless: a cold immensity in which the poet sees himself as a "tiny wanderer / lost on a star among the stars."

If Pascoli's "life in art" had few events, Gabriele D'Annunzio (1863–1938) construed his life as a work of art. A cross between Nietzsche's "superman" and Huysman's Des Esseintes (*À rebours*, 1884), this last *vates* of It. lit. devoted only his talent to his work, reserving, like Oscar Wilde, his genius for his life. In appraisals the latter crowds out the former with the memorabilia of this master self-promoter: his heroics as a flying ace, his well-publicized loves, his public switch from extreme right to extreme left, his bankrupt flight to France. "More a rhetorician than poet" (Sapegno), a "dilettante di sensazioni" (Croce), D'Annunzio titled his mature collection *Laudi* (1903–4). Composed of three parts, *Maia, Electra*, and *Alcyone*, it is a *laus vitae*, a celebration of life, in which he seems intoxicated by his own exultation: his poetry is the "inventory of his delights" (Momigliano). His extraordinary imitative skill fills his writing with disparate echoes: some from the Fr. and Eng. Parnassians and Preraphaelites, some deliberate impersonations of *stilnovo* and OF masters. This mimetic bent reflects D'Annunzio's principal characteristic, the musicality of his verse. As Debussy "paints" with music, so his friend uses words as musical notes. But D'Annunzio's music at its best is not imitative but abstract—vaguely allusive, suggestively obsessive, as in the airy curlicues of *Alcyone*, "texts without a topic." The best of D'Annunzio is often his most extreme: poems in which the thematic pretext is at its baroque flimsiest and the text an orgy of polyphony, as in "Undulna" (the nymph "regulating" the ideal line the sea "writes" on the shore), or texts in which the poet's decadent attraction to the morbid is released. D'Annunzio's art had no perceptible devel., no "early" or "late" period: his is a verse of a curious immobility.

In a 1910 article ("Poets on the Wane," in De Bernardi) Borgese defined as *crepuscolari* a group of young poets whose cult of quotidian themes and slipshod expression seemed to signal the end of a great lyric trad. The term took root without its negative connotation and today denotes a tone shared by most verse published in the decade preceding World War I. Not a formal school, "Waning Poetry" was as much a derivation from as a reaction to Pascoli's mystic rusticism and D'Annunzio's pompous alexandrinism. Given its popularity, it is probably not so much a product of its age as a producer of the contemp. fashion of skepticism and sadness. *Poems written with a pencil* (M. Moretti), *Harmonies in Gray and Silence* (Govoni), *Useless Booklet* (Corazzini), *Conversations*—the very titles of these slim volumes announce deliberate colorlessness and monotony, everyday emotions about banal objects: sleepy old gardens, hospital wards, convent walls, creaky weathervanes, bells tolling, yellowed photographs, dried flowers, nuns, invalids, beggars. These poets delight in diminutives and limited horizons: views are cut out by a small window or filtered by a dusty pane, often with some distorting defect. The most versatile member of the group was Corrado Govoni (1884–1965), who later became a futurist.

Dying at 20, a consumptive, Sergio Corazzini (1886–1907) declined the title of poet for that of a "weeping child" who "knows nothing but how to die." His free verse ebbs and flows with his desolate sobbing, and imminent death confers a vicarious authenticity on his sadness. Two poets of the first rank are customarily included here: Aldo Palazzeschi exceeds all labeling and warrants treatment apart; Guido Gozzano (1883–1916) survived tuberculosis long enough to see the success of his *Colloqui* (1911). Not since the *secentisti* did a verbless list have the evocative power of Gozzano's catalogues of "good old things in atrocious taste." Gozzano's mild irony blends with his mild yearning: he mocks what he loves and loves only what he mocks. His great trick is faking with sincerity. Gozzano's only mode is the idyll, a slightly addled idyll with its melodramatic element gone bad; the smell, voluptuously inhaled, is often that of kitsch.

Historically, "Crepuscularism" and futurism rise from the same impulse, the need to escape D'Annunzio's dominance and Pascoli's classicism. Futurism springs not from the "perception of a chaotic universe" (a formula applicable to most movements of the past thousand years) but from the adolescent rebelliousness which sustains all cyclical recurrences of *Sturm und Drang*—hence the interest in it by the New Vangard of the 1960s. It burst on the scene with the 1909 manifesto of F. T. Marinetti (1887–1944), a first-rate polemicist and a fourth-rate poet. Marinetti trumpeted activism at all costs, adventure and aggression, speed and the triumph of the Machine, destruction of the past, war as the "hygiene" of history, and scorn for women and sentiment. The very scope of its ludicrous claims killed the school; after its disintegration (1915), however, futurism was adopted by National Socialism, Marinetti becoming a sort of Poet Laureate of the regime. Still, Marinetti's poetics had a vast and, on the whole, salutary influence. His main thesis, simultaneity of impression and expression (hence fusion of object and image), influenced Apollinaire's calligrammes, dada, cubism, and Majakovskij. In Italy, futurism's best adherents soon developed in different directions, turning against its ontological claims (Lucini, Ardengo Soffici) or deriving from its libertarian impulse a ludic concept of poetry (Govoni, Palazzeschi).

Gian Pietro Lucini (1867–1914), between his early Parnassian sonnets and his late anti-futurist stance, published his theory of free verse in Marinetti's review ("Poesia," 1908) and then his *Revolverate* (Gunshots, 1909). His *Antidannunziana* (1914) satirizes D'Annunzio's superman poses. Resistance to time attests to the greatness of Aldo Palazzeschi (1885–1974), a much appreciated novelist. The production of his "poetic" decade (1905–15) differs from the humorless declamation of mainline futurists. Its wit and charm is seen in his celebrated phonomimetic "Fontana malata" (Ailing Fountain). His "L'incendiario" (The Arsonist) records the urge to break with trad.—without the obsessive need for activism or linguistic anarchy. The title of his "poetics," "E lasciatemi divertire!" (Well, I want to have fun!) describes well the zany wit of his poems. But Palazzeschi's endurance is assured by his great myths, created out of airy nothings ("Ara Mara Amara," "Oro Doro Odoro Dodoro," "Rio Bo"), and by his poems commemorating the grotesque in everyday life (Contini).

A flourishing literary culture in the years preceding World War I gave rise to a number of periodicals, many of them Florentine. The most influential, *La voce* (1908–13), was directed by the grand "impresario of culture," Giuseppe Prezzolini, who gathered together a heterogeneous group of collaborators. *La voce* became associated with nearly all the trends in vogue during its run. It offered a first forum to the best known autochthonous poetic movement in 20th-c. Italy, later called "Hermeticism." The forefather of this novel *trobar clus*, Dino Campana (1885–1932), came to notice after the "school" had gained notoriety with Ungaretti and Montale. Campana is often compared to Rimbaud and Trakl for his aimless wanderings over the world, interrupted only by his stays in mental asylums (he was permanently committed in 1918), and for his poetics of total faith in the magic of the Word. The *Canti orfici* (1914) refer to Orpheus: here poetry is a descent into Hell and a religion for initiates. The poems, marvels of fragmented verbal obsession (or drugged hallucinations), show for all that echoes of Carducci and D'Annunzio. In them syntax is not (futuristically) eliminated; it is replaced by cadences (see "L'invetriata" and the irrational "logic" of Campana's oneiric chimeras: "La Chimera" is perhaps his best known poem).

Two other influential poets who matured in the *La voce* context produced poetry in a vein related to Campana's. The existential adventure of Clemente Rébora (1885–1957), not less erratic than Campana's, took place all *within*, as a lifelong struggle with his own soul and a periodically despairing search for superior truth. Not given to theorizing, Rébora's only inspiration is his need to find the all-encompassing Word. His aptly titled *Frammenti lirici* (1913) and *Canti anonimi* (1922) record in their daring analogies, in Rébora's characteristic "imagine tesa" (taut imagery), a "sort of transcendental autobiography" of powerful originality (Contini). Camillo Sbàrbaro (1888–1967) sang the "monotonous recurrence of indifferent life," withdrawing from the bustle into his private drama. *Resine* (Amberdrops, 1911) and *Pianissimo* (1914) sound at first curiously old-fashioned—as if in the midst of a dodecaphonic revolution a humble songwriter kept on modulating his simple *lieder* on his flute—but Montale shows in *his* complex tunes the impact this withdrawn predecessor had.

The review *La ronda* (1919–23) welcomed the voices of reaction to the cult of originality in prewar poetry. Its founder, Vincenzo Cardarelli (1887–1959), advocated a return to the classics (esp. Leopardi and Manzoni), i.e. to syntax, logic, and immediate comprehension. The progress of Hermetic poetry, supported by parallel trends abroad among the Fr. and also in Eliot and Pound, proved irresistible. Its principal exponents are less typical of its program than its lesser adepts (S. Quasimodo, A. Gatto, M. Luzi, L. Sinisgalli, V. Sereni). All share the quasi-mystical concept of "poetry as life," as a magic formula capable of revealing, under the semblances of this phenomenal world, "universal reality" (Manacorda).

Giuseppe Ungaretti (1888–1970) will be long appreciated for his prosodic innovation, based on the lesson of Rimbaud's *Illuminations* and Mallarmé's "Un Coup de dès." Fragmenting the *vers libre* of his futurist beginnings, he paralleled the jocose cough of Palazzeschi's "Ailing Fountain" and Majakovskij's "staircase" poems in his trademark one-word verse (imitated even today by would-be poets). It acts as a "macroscope" for the word, harshly isolating it (Ungaretti eliminated punctuation) and transforming poetic diction into a series of fragments lit up by intermittent floodlights. In spite of disclaimers, Ungaretti is heir both to futurism and to Waning Poetry, but while these trends merely raised or lowered their volume, Ungaretti is a master of tonal modulation. His first book of verse, *Allegria* (1916; repub. 1923 with a preface by Mussolini) remains the overture to a new phase of It. p. The title of his collected poems, *Vita d'un uomo* (A Man's Life), points to his dominant theme, the sublimation of his experiences, though these, esp. in the verse of the 1930s and '40s, at times remain untranslated into poetry.

When the blurbs have yellowed and the promotion died down, Eugenio Montale (1896–1981) may well be perceived as the true heir to Pascoli. His poetry is Pascolian in its resignedly hopeless scrutiny of the "ontological mystery," its vague desire for an escape route from the "male di vivere" (both "pain of life" and "evil of living"), for a "broken seam / in the net that constrains us." Pascolian too is Montale's characteristic of transforming emotion into landscape. Pascolian is, in his epoch-making *Ossi di seppia* (Cuttlefishbones, 1925), Montale's metaphysical and baroque mythmaking, soberly desolate as it is. Much has been made of the political texts by antifascist Montale (from *Occasioni*, 1939, to *Satura*, 1971), endlessly deciphered by immense and often too-Hermetic exegesis.

Variously related to Hermeticism are four poets whose assessment is still pending: Umberto Saba (1883–1957), Cesare Pavese (1908–50), Sandro Penna (1906–77), and Pier Paolo Pasolini (1922–75). Saba was in a sense pre-hermetic; his *Canzoniere* (Songbook) "reads as a 19th-c. work" (Debenedetti). Its Petrarchan ambition signals the "only major contemp. poet wholly free from experimentalism." His simplicity and trite diction prompted critics to see in him an authentically popular poet. It slowed recognition and led Saba to publish a *Chronicle* (1948) effectually advertising his own songbook. His bias for the humble shows no trace of Gozzano's worldly irony; instead, we find warm participation, an almost childlike *amor vitae.* A typical motif is animal life related to human behavior. Pavese offered a model of anti-Hermetic poetry in his realistic and matter-of-fact *poesie-racconto* (story-poems), but the project failed both in this role and as a matrix of poetry, despite Pavese's great (but mostly extraliterary) popularity with the young. His *Lavorare stanca* (Work Makes You Tired, 1936; ineptly tr. as *Hard Labor*) is a curiosity. Interest is still inspired by this often politically and culturally "misappropriated" writer, a suicide at 42.

The populist search for the "primitive" drew another blank with Penna. "Hermetic" in a special sense ("coding" for this gay poet was a must), Penna's only topic is love, *dolce pena,* "cross and delight," "strange joy" (the last two are titles of collections). This "vigorous outsider" was also an *ermetico* in his refusal of easy legacies, in his ironclad rule of conciseness, and in his stenographic imagery. Penna sings of joy and pain with a Matisse-like luminosity of vision. His best poems, always centered on his beloved *ragazzi,* are prodigies of a balanced moment suspended in timelessness. Everything is burned off in the white heat of the poet's dogged hammering at the "right word." Penna, the self-defined "penny-a-dozen [sex]fiend" has, incongruously, an almost virginal chastity of poetic voice. Pasolini, the filmmaker, whose 1957 *Le ceneri di Gramsci* (Gramsci's Ashes) is widely acknowledged as one of the most important collections of poetry published in the postwar period, had a different and more tragic purity of voice. Paroxysms of paradox interrupt his song. The popular brand of Marxism he professed never overcame his bourgeois values. Pasolini took idiosyncrasy for ideology: the pangs of libido appear in some of his purposely controversial and perhaps less enduring pieces as the stirrings of History.

Around the critic Luciano Anceschi and his influential periodical *Il Verri* sprang into being the self-styled *Gruppo 63* (so called from its founding meeting at Palermo in 1963). Three poets associated with it are likely to mark the last decades of this century with their names: Antonio Porta (1935–89), Andrea Zanzotto (b. 1921), and Edoardo Sanguineti (b. 1930). In their verse the linguistic revolution begun by Pascoli comes full circle; his weakening of the tie between signifier and signified reaches the final stage of divorce. The movement has been compared in its sound and fury to futurism; however, the poetry initially born out of and later in some cases opposed to *Gruppo 63* is distinguished by a theoretical rigor unknown to Marinetti *et Cie.* Porta was first brought to critical notice by the collective volume *I novissimi* (1961). His poems reveal a strongly individual voice and have an eerie capacity to suggest, behind a deliberately gray diction, vast threatening conspiracies by unknown objects and persons. Porta has since gone beyond his *novissimi* origins and alliances. Some critics distinguish his poetry as the first real novelty after Hermeticism.

Zanzotto "joined" the group after the fact, as it were. His early collections, *Dietro il paesaggio* (Behind the Landscape, 1951), *Elegia* (1954), *Vocativo* (1957), and *IX Ecloghe* (1962), are characterized by traditional form (Zanzotto even wrote Petrarchan sonnets, the only 20th-c. poet to do so outside of parody). Zanzotto's arcane Arcadia suggests spectral visitations, séances of literary ghost-evoking. Lang. acts here as a trance-inducing drug. New revolutionary techniques appear with *La beltà* (Beauty, 1968) and subsequent collections of ever-increasing textual complexity.

An original member of the Palermo group, Sanguineti had anticipated in his *Laborintus* (1956) its ideological and technical characteristics. A shocked Pavese refused to consider seriously Sanguineti's early samples, and Zanzotto later called them the "record of a nervous breakdown." Sense in *Laborintus* is replaced by obsessive paranomasia. Segments read as if they were a medieval treatise on alchemy, a textbook on sociology, yesterday's newspaper, and Freud's *Traumdeutung*, all put through a shredder and reassembled at random. But Sanguineti's collected poems, *Segnalibro* (Bookmark, 1982), and esp. his *Novissimum Testamentum* (1986), rank him with the best of contemp. European poets.

Among the poets active in the last two decades, Franco Fortini and Paolo Volponi, *engagé* writers of the older generation, deserve more than a summary listing, as well as Luciano Erba, Maria Luisa Spaziani, Giovanni Raboni, Dario Bellezza, and Fabio Doplicher. Curiously, while the dialects of the peninsula had seemed doomed by 20th-c. mass education and media diffusion, poetry in dialect shows no sign of decadence. Among its practioners, heirs to Meli, Porta, and Belli, one must mention the first-rate poets Virgilio Giotti and Giacomo Noventa.

GENERAL HISTORIES: F. De Sanctis, *Storia della letteratura italiana* (1870), tr. J. Redfern, *Hist. of It. Lit.* (1968); A. Momigliano, *Storia della letteratura italiana* (1936); F. Flora, *Storia della letteratura italiana*, 4 v. (1940–41); N. Sapegno, *Compendio di storia della letteratura italiana*, 3 v. (1954); J. H. Whitfield, *A Short Hist. of It. Lit.* (1960); *Storia della letteratura italiana*, ed. E. Cecchi and N. Sapegno, v. 8–9 (1969); *I classici italiana nella storia della critica*, ed. W. Binni, 3 v. (1971–77); B. Croce, *La letteratura italiana per saggi*, ed. M. Sansone, 4 v. (1972), *Essays on Lit. and Lit. Crit.*, ed. and tr. M. E. Moss (1990); *Dizionario critico della letteratura italiana*, ed. V. Branca (1973); Wilkins; *Orientamenti culturali*: *La Letteratura italiana*: *I maggiori*, I–II; *I minori*, I–IV; *Le correnti*, I–II; *I contemporanei*, I–VI (1975–); *Dictionary of It. Lit.*, ed. P. and J. C. Bondanella (1979); *Letteratura italiana, profilo storico*, ed. I. De Bernardi et al., 3 v. (1980); M. Puppo, *Manuale critico bibliografico per lo studio della letteratura italiana* (1985).

SPECIALIZED HISTORIES AND STUDIES: E. Underhill, *Jacopone da Todi, Poet and Mystic* (1919); E. Garin, *Il Rinascimento italiano* (1941); F. Flora, *La poesia ermetica* (1947); C. Calcaterra, *Il Barocco in Arcadia* (1950); A. Momigliano, *Saggio sull'*Orlando Furioso (1952); M. Fubini, *Ritratto dell'Alfieri* (1967), "Arcadia e Illuminismo," *Dal Muratori al Baretti* (1975), *Ugo Foscolo* (1978); *Marino e marinisti: opere scelte*, ed. G. Getto, 2 v. (1954); A. Bobbio, *Parini* (1954); A. Galletti, *Il Novecento* (1954); *Lirici del Settecento*, ed. B. Maier (1960); A. Viscardi, *Storia della letteratura italiana dalle origini al Rinascimento* (1960); *Poeti del Duecento*, ed. G. Contini (1960); E. H. Wilkins, *The Life of Petrarch* (1961); J. H. Whitfield, *Leopardi's Canti* (tr. 1962), *Giacomo Leopardi* (1964); G. Santangelo, *Il secentismo* (1962); M. Bishop, *Petrarch and His World* (1963); J. V. Mirollo, *The Poet of the Marvelous: Giambattista Marino* (1963); G. Petronio, *Il Romanticismo* (1963); A. Del Monte, *Le origini* (1964); B. Maier, *Il Neoclassicismo* (1964); G. Singh, *Leopardi and the Theory of Poetry* (1964); *Complete Poems and Sel. Letters of Michelangelo*, tr. C. Gilbert (1965); T. G. Bergin, *Dante* (1965), *Petrarch* (1970); C. P. Brand, *Torquato Tasso . . . and His Contrib. to Eng. Lit.* (1965), *Ludovico Ariosto: A Preface to the* Orlando Furioso (1974); G. Pozzi, *La poesia italiana del Novecento* (1965); *Am. Critical Essays on the* Divine Comedy, ed. R. Clements (1967); *Dante's Lyric Poetry*, ed. K. Foster and P. Boyde (1967); G. Getto, *L'interpretazione del Tasso* (1967), *Carducci e Pascoli* (1977); P. Nardi, *La Scapigliatura* (1968); G. Manacorda, *Storia della letteratura italiana contemporanea* (1968); G. Contini, *Letteratura dell'Italia unita, 1861–1968* (1968); W. Binni, *Saggi alfieriani* (1969); P. Dronke, *The Med. Lyric* (1969); *Tasso's* Jerusalem Delivered, tr. J. Tusiani (1970); *Enciclopedia dantesca*, ed. U. Bosco, 5 v. (1970–78); A. Vallone, *Dante* (1971); L. Anceschi, *Le poetiche del Novecento in Italia* (1973); M. Marti, *Storia dello stil nuovo* (1973); G. Debenedetti, *Poesia italiana del Novecento* (1974); R. Griffin, *Ludovico Ariosto* (1974); *Ariosto's* Orlando Furioso, tr. B. Reynolds (1975–77); *F. Petrarch Six Centuries Later: A Symposium*, ed. A. Scaglione (1975); A. Seroni, *Il decadentismo* (1975); *Petrarch's Lyric Poems*, tr. R. Durling (1976); U. Bosco, *Petrarca* (1977); *Il Novecento*, ed. G. Grana, 10 v. (1980); *The New It. P.: 1945 to the Present*, ed. and tr. L. R. Smith (1981)—bilingual anthol.

T.W.

J

JAPANESE POETRY.

I. CLASSICAL (TO 1868)
  A. *Genres and Characteristics*
  B. *History*
II. MODERN (AFTER 1868)

I. CLASSICAL (TO 1868). This account treats poetry written in J. by those racially J. on the main archipelago. That is, it excludes Ainu and Ryukyuan poetry and J. composition in Chinese. This is the usual implicit, limited definition. The prosody of J. p. comes to consist of lines constituted by 5+7 or 7+5 morae in alternation, a mora being a formally or conceptually conceived syllable. Some modern haiku poets conceived of their poems as single lines and, like Chinese poetry, J. has been written or printed without typographical breaks for lines, except for modern editions reproducing chōka (see below). The following terms are assumed:

(1) *waka* (*yamatouta*): J. p., particularly
  (a) *chōka* ("long poem"), alternating 5- and 7-syllable lines with a last 7- added; and
  (b) *tanka* ("short poem"), of 5, 7, 5, 7, 7 syllables respectively (also used as envoys [*hanka*] for *chōka*): *kami no ku* ("upper-lines part"), the 5, 7, 5 of *tanka*, and *shimo no ku* ("lower-lines part"), the 7, 7 of *tanka*.

(2) *renga* ("linked poetry"), particularly
  (a) *renga*, using pure J. diction of *waka*; typically composed by three or four poets alternating stanzas of the upper and lower parts of *tanka* to a total of 100 (50 each), but 100-stanza units could be multiplied to 1000- or 10,000-stanza lengths; and
  (b) *haikai* ([*no, renga*; modern designation, *renku*), introducing Sinified words of lower decorum and of the same typical alternate composition and length, although the 36-stanza form (*kasen*) was most favored by Bashō.

A. *Genres and Characteristics*. Song has always been an activity of both individual and communal importance in Japan. The divinities and sovereigns in the two J. mythical histories (*Kojiki*, ca. 712; *Nihon Shoki*, 720) deliver their strongest feelings in verse. These pieces were not sung in the modern sense but were delivered in heightened voice, often as spells (*kotoage*). The court enjoyed various kinds of songs. *Kagura* were associated with Shinto and dance. *Saibara*, originally folksongs, were taken up by the court and modified by *gagaku*, stately music imported from China (lost there but preserved in Japan). *Imayō* ("present styles") incl. many kinds of song compiled around 1169. Kinds proliferate and names with them, e.g. *nagauta* and *meriyasu*, music in *kabuki*; the former is instrumentally accompanied and is fundamental to the stage; the latter is unaccompanied and was only briefly in vogue. Both kinds were also performed in pleasure quarters, where minute discriminations existed for songs. The verse portions of *nō* are cantillated in a manner approaching singing.

Comic, parodic, and satiric verse flourished ca. 1650 ff. The two major kinds were *kyōka* (*mad waka*) and *senryū*. The latter developed out of *haikai* and eventually took on the 5, 7, 5-syllabic form of opening stanzas in linked poetry. Numerous other kinds came and went as vogues.

The main line of J. p., *waka* (including esp. *chōka* and *tanka*) originated with the court but was open to all. Its earliest examples appear in *Kojiki*. It used pure J., i.e. excluded the Sinified diction increasingly used in prose. Early prosody consisted of inconsistent alternation of shorter with longer lines which gradually became settled as 5s and 7s, with hypersyllabic but not hyposyllabic lines permitted. The verse sections of *nō* and some other writing are in units of 7s and 5s; some songs are in 8s and 6s.

J. lit. seldom demonstrates the strong oppositions of its Western counterparts. Significantly, fact and fiction do not conflict, both being drawn on equally by poets. There is, however, a growing tendency for *waka* to be fictionalized. Poems might be composed to go with paintings on screens. As poetic contests (*utaawase*) became a chief venue for formal poetry, it became necessary for matching poems to be on the same topic (*dai*). Poets perspiring in August might write on "Snow in a Mountain Village," or old male poets of a young woman's love yearning. Topics were also necessary for sequences, commonly of 100 poems (*hyakushuuta*), for presentation. Informal poetry addressed to friends or lovers, or formal poetry on actual occasions, remained factual. The opening stanzas of linked poetry (see below) were required to deal with the actual setting, the rest to be fictional; but both requirements could be violated. In brief, fact is often embellished, and fiction often based on fact, with factual elements often dominant in modern poetry.

Brevity is a central feature. Poetic units not long to begin with grow shorter. The longest extant *chōka* of consequence is also the only one describing a battle, a poem by Kakinomoto Hitomaro (d. 708–15), only 149 lines long. By the late 17th c. it was common to compose opening stanzas (*hokku*) for *haikai* that were meant to stand alone, hence formally the same as modern *haiku*. No complete explanation exists for this attachment to brevity. One factor involves the closely knit nature of composing groups. The more intimately poets know each other, the less necessity and good manners require lengthiness, a fact the converse of which is the weak opposition between poet and reader. A person who is one now will be the other another time. These roles are codified in J. linked poetry, where poets compose in alternating roles as poets and audience according to complex canons. In effect, they make an integrated collection as poets-audience on the spot.

Collections are another conspicuous feature of J. p. The most prestigious, although not always the greatest, were the 21 royally commissioned *nijūichidaishū*, beginning with the *Kokinshū* (905–15) and ending with the *Shinzokukokinshū* (1439). Their typical 20-scroll form divides into halves: the first begins with the seasons (1–2 spring, 3 summer, 4–5 autumn, 6 winter) and the second with love (11–15 or so). Other scrolls involve travel (*tabi no uta*), congratulations (*ga no uta*), and complaints (*jukkai*). More and more comes to be made of a miscellaneous category in which no single topic predominates (*kusagusa no uta, zōka*), thereby allowing poets to introduce fact or avoid topics they thought timeworn. Seasonal poems open with spring's beginning and close with winter's end. Love poems present a stylized version of courtly love ; the man's view dominates early on, the woman's more thereafter. Love (*koi*) means loving or yearning for someone else, not being loved, although happy consummation (*au koi*) is treated. Love is, then, particularly agitated, and in the collections undergoes many fluctuations. Travel scrolls progress through the geography of central Japan, if not farther, and the trip never returns to the capital. There is considerable codification of topics, a tendency fully realized in the rule books (*shikimoku*) for linked poetry: haze represents spring; the moon is an autumn moon unless qualified; drizzle (*shigure*) belongs to both autumn and winter, although first drizzle (*hatsushigure*) belongs to winter.

As progressions became more skilled, associations were devised to integrate them more closely. Group associations, such as runs of anonymous poems and older (recent) poems, come first. Subtler associations involve conception (*kokoro*) or diction (*kotoba*). Conceptually, a poem on making a pillow in travel (a frequent topos) might precede one on a dream of home. The poem *de rigueur* for a man to send a woman after a love meeting might precede one where the woman wonders if her lover will come again the next evening. Frost imagery in one poem connects with withered plants in the next, or dew in one with leaves changed in color in the next (dew and frost were considered agents of change). The common association of winds with peaks could lead to a poem on wind following one on mountains. By the time of the eighth collection, *Shinkokinshū* (ordered 1201), another principle functions. Not merely selecting the best poems, compilers used lesser to set off greater to give a pleasing variety and to honor the J. aesthetic canon of asymmetry. Somewhat later, two poems might be juxtaposed with no apparent association until one realized that together they constituted an allusive variation (*honkadori*) on an older poem. Modern sequential composition (*rensaku*) offers similar forms of integration.

As these procedures imply, progressions and associations usually derive not from individual poets but from compilers, who were themselves distinguished poets. A poet with a dozen poems in a collection would find them scattered, situated according to stated or inferrable topics, progression, or association. The result is a force countervailing brevity: hence the *Shinkokinshū* can be read as a complex, varied poem of upwards of 10,000 lines. A *renga* 10,000-stanza unit (*manku*) would involve 25,000 lines. The poet Ihara Saikaku (1642–93) produced extraordinary numbers of *haikai* stanzas in a single day and night, his prodigy being 23,500 (nearly a thousand per hour, more than 15 per minute). Nobody has read this; Saikaku exhausted his scribes. Such bravado aside, the collective principle holds remarkable strength in Japan, surely the only country whose first writing system, *man'yōgana*, was named after the collection employing it, the *Man'yōshū*—although in fact it was first used in the *Kojiki* and was probably adapted from a Korean model.

In Japan verse has been unusually hospitable to prose and vice versa. Still, they are distinguished since the introduction of writing in J.: a distinct kind of *man'yōgana* was used for verse in the *Kojiki*, whose narrative in prose is interspersed with lyrics. Again, a people's rites show what they devote to the divine, and in Japan almost 30 Shinto pieces are prosimetric. Some lines are in verse, some in prose, a distinction immediately evident and ultimately baffling. Why is a line of 5 or 7, or even 4 or 8, syllables verse, whereas one of 3 or 9 is prose?

The royal collections provide two kinds of information. The second is the poet's name (or "Poet Unknown"). The first is its subject (or "Subject Unknown," not quite a title). The subject may be: (1) a flower or bird; (2) topics, e.g. "Love by the seaside"; (3) topics and occasions such as "'A distant spring view' for *The Poetry Match in Six Hundred Rounds*"; or (4) headnotes. Headnotes may show that one poem is a message or statement, the next poem a reply. Extended headnotes give a narrative setting to an exchange. In fact, with slight alteration the headnoted exchange could become an episode in the "tales of poems" genre, e.g. *The Tales of Ise*. Essentially collections of brief stories about poems, these tales show again the urge to collect, to make larger integers from smaller. Given J. poetics, readers wish to know the poet in the poem; and at court, poetry was a form of social communication. In *The Tale of Genji*, the characters exchange about 800 poems, nearly 4000 lines, alluding to yet other poems in Chinese as well as J. and to songs.

Throughout cl. J. lit., verse and prose are compatible, even if distinct and even if changing in nature over time. Poetry is the idealized member: an early term exists for J. p. (*yamatouta*), but not for prose. The term "J. lang." (*yamatokotoba*) implied idealizing of J. (as opposed to Chinese) lang. and poetry, with J. taken as the purer and truer. Chinese poetry must be written in Chinese characters; J. can be written in the cursive syllabary (*hiragana*), the standard medium of literacy for women, hence called "woman's hand," vs. the man's for Chinese. Although in practice both sexes wrote in both hands, J. p. goes back to the divinities headed by the sun goddess.

Idealizing gradually led to codifications (those for moons, haze, and travel were mentioned above), incl. poetic placenames. One visited places for poetic associations, not actual sights. In visiting Sayo no Nakayama on a clear day, one thought of the night, storms, clouds, and moon associated with the place. The Bay of Sleeves, Sode no Ura, was a godsend to poets indulging in the one excess in J. p.—superabundant tears. When *renga* master Sōgi (1421–1502) wrote of a place in Kyushu lovelier than a famous one near the capital, he rejects what he sees: what has not been celebrated in verse is, he says, no worthier of attention than poems by someone whose status is unattested by family trad. or study with a famous master.

The precedented and the customary have very strong appeal to people in traditional societies. In both Japan and China, socially esteemed art is precedented art, which is why innovation is often cast as appeal to a pristine past. Circumvention and innovation were, however, possible by experiment, and the eccentric in one generation might set precedent in another, or old Chinese precedents innovate on J. practice. All else failing, the few great innovators and exception-makers could intervene. Change in cl. and modern poetry alike also reflects engagement with, or revulsion from, valued foreign lits. (Chinese for cl., Western for modern).

The two major subjects of J. p. are nature and love. Nature has been treated in terms of the progression of seasonal phenomena, and progressively ordered so in collections. Love has been conceived of chiefly as longing, and at court involved taste more than physical beauty: lovers met in the dark. The erotic was expressed by images of wetness and women's tangled hair and symbolized by spring, dream, and color. These associations have endured. Male homosexual love became a frequent poetic topic, although not female until very recently. But a trad. of the passionate woman has endured from early times to Yosano Akiko (1878–1942). Nature tends to give assurance and love to agitate, particularly in linked poetry.

B. *History*.

Period	Genre
Oral to 13th c.	*Waka* (*chōka, tanka*)
13th–19th cs.	Linked poetry (*renga,* haikai)

J. lit. hist. is periodized, although as elsewhere the logic and terminology are inconsistent. Only two basic divisions distinguish what follows, with the second also divided in two. The dividing principle is the poetry which flourishes most, although genres of all kinds have continued to be practiced.

1. *Waka* Period. The last date assignable a *Man'yōshū* poem is A.D. 759; its first poem is assigned to Yūryaku (regnal dates unclear; he sent an embassy to China in 478). The *Kojiki* (ca. 712) may have some songs from the 3rd c. By the end of the 13th c., compilation rights for a royal collection are vested in descendants of Fujiwara Teika (1162–1241). The final four royal collections were compiled by royal order on request of the military aristocracy: power was dispersing as the nation fell into chaotic wars.

Even beyond the *waka* period proper, *waka* was associated with the divinities, with the monarchs who continued their line, and with all Japanese. *Yamatouta* is J. p. in a special sense: it is the sole literary art never on probation and from the outset the possession of all, including the illiterates.

The *Man'yōshū* selects from previous collections now otherwise lost. It includes poems from all levels of society, even a few attributed to animals. Its greatest achievement, reflecting a time over a century prior to 759, lies in the work of Kakinomoto Hitomaro (d. 708–15), a middling courtier, a kind of poet laureate, and one of the great J. poets. His occasional poems on royal affairs are public in the highest sense; his personal poems render the individual universal. Dynastic causes mingle with humane observation in his poems on the bloody Jinshin War (671), on the death of its hero Prince Takechi, and on the poet's visit to the ruined capital of the defeated rival. His poems on parting from, or mourning, wives are unforgettable. His masterpiece recounts seeing a dead man on a rocky shore after he himself has barely survived a typhoon. The world in which we die is divine—one of many kind ironies, as in the second envoy:

From open sea the waves
Break upon a rugged coast
  Become your bedding
For the pillow you have made,
And so, my lord, your rest is here.

"Become your bedding" renders a pillow-word (*makurakotoba*), an evocative fixed epithet of which Hitomaro is the unquestioned master.

His *chōka* show a skill in complex, alternating parallelism derived from Chinese practice. Otherwise he seems to ignore anything foreign. That is truer still of melodious Yamabe Akahito (fl. 724–37), who features greenery, hills, streams—whatever is "pure"—an unsullied world ignoring the suffering Hitomaro knew defined the goodness of life.

Yamano(u)e Okura (d. 785) visited China. Not surprisingly, Buddhism and even Confucianism enter *chōka* like his "Dialogue on Poverty." Emotional generalization, homely imagery, and broken syntax make his styles unmistakable. That syntax shows tellingly in the envoy to a poem mourning a son:

He is still too young
And cannot know the road to take.
  I will pay your fee.
Courier to the realms below—
Bear him there upon your back!

Ōtomo Yakamochi (d. 785) and his family are most fully represented in the collection. Perhaps the last compiler, Yakamochi sought out interesting poems from the remote and humble. His own show mastery of both poetic inheritance and new thought. He lacks the differing intensities of the other three, but his fluency and range exceed theirs.

The first of the early royal collections, the *Kokinshū* (905– 15), has poems credited to *Man'yōshū* poets, anonymous subsequent poets, and the more recent Six Poetic Sages dominated by Ariwara Narihira (825–80) and Ono no Komachi (fl. ca. 833–57), both legendary lovers. Narihira's conceptions seem to find words inadequate. Komachi's words defined her conceptions, as her famous use of pivot-words (*kakekotoba*) reveals in the double or triple meanings she infuses. The single most famous *tanka* is his:

There is no moon!
Nor is this spring the spring that was
  In those days bygone!
I myself being the sole one
Remaining the thing it was. . . .

A paradoxical poem reflecting Buddhist transience, it was known so well by later poets that its words were thought too familiar to be used for allusion.

The compilers, particularly Ki no Tsyrayuki (882–945?), defined the *Kokinshū* ethos. His generation gave Japan its first poetic, its first poetic diary, its *art.* Accommodating Chinese wit to J. sensibility, he also accommodated poetry to painting, vastly enlarging its fictional scope while retaining fact. Precisely because technique (*sama*) was his standard, he most prized the human heart (*kokoro*) as conceiver, and purity of lang. (*kotoba*) as means. His greatness towers over any single achievement, and the collection he led still affects assumptions concerning poetry's relations to the rest of life.

The next six collections imitated, then innovated on, the *Kokinshū.* Izumi Shikibu (b. 976?) was the occasion, and probably the author, of an important poetic diary. Her position in poetry was unrivaled in her time, when women created the greatest J. lit. Intense, subjective, various, and difficult, her poetry is still not adequately comprehended. After her, most of the best poets are men who extended poetic understanding, leading to the eighth royal collection, the *Shinkokisnhū,* with the profoundest poetry of these centuries.

Poetic arbiter of the age, Fujiwara Shunzei (1114–1204) imparted depth by adapting Buddhist meditation to poetry. Priest Saigyō (1118–90), beloved in Japan, and the sensitive, intense Princess Shokushi (d. 1201) are excelled in the age only by Fujiwara Teika, Shunzei's brilliant, difficult son. Poetic fiction now required learning and intellectual effort to define feeling. Many chapters have been written on two of Teika's poems:

Looking out afar,
What need is there for cherry flowers
  Or colored autumn leaves?
Along the cove the humble huts
Yielding to the autumn dusk.

  The brief spring night,
Its floating bridge of dreams
  Breaks all apart,
And from the peak there takes its leave
A cloudbank into open sky.

Teika's heirs disputed his legacies. One line offered subtle variations on the familiar, the two others new conceptions. Novelty lay in subjective manipulation through patterning, synaesthesia, and metamorphosis in seasonal poems often consisting entirely of images, in love poems without images, and in miscellaneous poems fusing the alternatives. These are represented in the 14th (*Gyokuyōshū,* 1313) and esp. the 17th (*Fūgashū,* 1349) of the 21 collections. The outstanding poets incl. the ambitious Kyōgoku Tamekane (Tamekanu, 1254–1332) and three royal figures: Fushimi (1265–1317), Eifuku Mon'in (1271–1342), and Hanazono (1297–1348). *Waka* and royalty were still associated, even after the age of *renga* had begun.

2. *Linked Poetry.* As politics turned toward chaos in the 13th c., linked poetry (*renga,* 13th–16th cs.) achieved greatness. Linked poetry employed as stanzas alternations of the *kami no ku* (upper-lines part) and *shimo no ku* (lower-lines part)—the 5–7–5 and the 7–7 syllable lines making up a *tanka.* Two or more poets usually took part in alternating composition according to elaborate rules and canons. *Renga* proper used elevated diction not unlike that of *waka,* and a 100-stanza length was most common. The nobleman Nijō Yoshimoto (1320–88) accorded *renga* premier status with a semi-royal collection, the *Tsukuba Shū* (1357). A *renga* boom had begun (even illiterates

were composing it) which lasted through the 16th c. The *renga* masters knew *waka* thoroughly; Shinkei (1406–75) composed brilliantly in both kinds. Frequently difficult, Shinkei resembles in *renga* Teika in *waka*. But the peak of *renga* came with Sōgi, who made the whole sequence rather than stanzas the aim of poetry. Caught up in wars, he fled the capital and taught *renga*, receiving teaching in classics that raised him from unknown origins to an unrivaled height as lecturer and *renga* master. Inevitably he also collected *renga*. His solo of a hundred stanzas (1499) is thought the greatest *renga* sequence, but solo composition over four months is abnormal for *renga*, so that two trios—with the noble Shōhaku (1443–1527) and Sōchō (1448–1532), son of a smith—are always praised. Sōchō's performance in *The Hundred Stanzas at Minase* sometimes lags, but perfection was subsequently achieved in *The Hundred Stanzas at Yunoyama*.

As long as *renga* was composed at court, women participated. They did less when warcamps and temples were the sites. The last impressive *renga* master, Satomura Jōha (1524–1602), made *renga* into a house art taught to the military aristocracy. Ossification had begun.

The art of *renga* can be suggested by three stanzas from the Minase sequence. Shōhaku (76) and Sōchō (77) demonstrate *renga* connectedness. Master Sōgi (78) shows how to vary, imparting beauty to desolation:

(76) Shrubs never cultivated by the owner
stand thick by the wattled door
(77) in that vicinity
the overgrown field by the hedgerow
covers the neglected hoe

In that vicinity
the overgrown field by the hedgerow
covers the neglected hoe
(78) the traveler returns dim in haze
brought by twilight in light rain.

Haikai (*haikai renga*, 16th–19th cs.) brought a lower decorum, beginning in play with diction extended by the Sinified, the humble, and the otherwise unwakalike. Conceptions were also lower. The problem was to make this mixture fundamental to human experience. It is too easy to treat Matsunaga Teitoku (1572–1653) and Nishiyama Sōin (1605–80) as frivolous predecessors of grand Matsuo Bashō (1644–94), most loved of J. poets. Actually, Teitoku effected the transition from *renga* to *haikai*, and Sōin's Danrin school had survival value in its spirited practicality. Bashō's seriousness with the low and lighthearted made *haikai* the most difficult poetic art in cl. Japan. No wonder his oeuvre is small or that he turned to an easier style when late success required frequent composition. No wonder the glory of his school ended with him.

Japan's foremost poet-painter, Yosa (Taniguchi) Buson (1716–83), led the *Haikai* Revival. Bashō sometimes nods, Buson seemingly never. Yet the common judgment seems correct: Bashō risked more of self and art, achieving a human profundity not achieved by Buson's greater accuracy and beauty. Also, by Buson's time Bashō's sequential art yielded to brilliant stanzas (cf. Shinkei) and often to separate *hokku* very like *haiku*. Kobayashi Issa (1763–1827) made a virtue of this defect by interspersing stanzas in the prose of many poetic diaries. They are moving, if not the equal of Bashō's *Narrow Road Through the Provinces*.

Two quotations must suffice to show the precarious meaningfulness of *haikai*. In *Poetry Is What I Sell* (1682), Bashō is joined for a duo by the irrepressible Enomoto (Takarai) Kikaku (1661–1707), who composes the different-seeming stanzas 34 and 35. Bashō's conclusion (36) joins Kikaku's last in violating the rule of nonrecollection in linked poetry: they echo their first two stanzas (capitals designate J. treated as Chinese):

(34) Horses may neigh at dawn like cocks
announcing freshly fallen snow
(35) poetry is what I sell
flowers not my debts concern me
so I drink all the time

Poetry is what we sell
flowers not our debts concern us
so we drink all the time
(36) as sun sets on THE SPRINGTIME LAKE
AND PLEASURE HAS BROUGHT
HOME OUR POEM.

A quite different, religious mood governs a passage in *At the Tub of Ashes*, a foursome. From Mukai Kyorai (1651–1704) (31) to Okada Yasui (1658–1743) (32) to Bashō (33), the rise in tone is remarkable; so is the skillful shift by Nozawa Bonchō (d. 1714) (34):

(31) The strolling peddler
loudly calls his wares in shortened names
as he passes by
(32) no more than cover from a shower
is human life in ceaseless flux

No more than cover from a shower
is this world in ceaseless flux
(33) sleeping at noon
the body of the blue heron
poised in nobility

Sleeping at noon
the body of the blue heron
poised in nobility
(34) trickle trickle go the waters
where rushes sway in utter peace.

Bashō's heron, head under wing, asleep on one leg, is a figure of human enlightenment. A painterly counterpart by Buson is secular, not noticeably figurative of the human, but exact in its sequence of images:

The evening breeze
blows waters to the blue heron
 whose legs are rippled.

All these quotations exemplify the opening sentence of Tsurayuki's preface to the *Kokinshū*: "The poetry of Japan takes the human heart as seed and flourishes in the countless leaves of words." E.M.

II. MODERN (AFTER 1868). Poetry since the Meiji Restoration has been dominated by three major forms:

(1) *tanka*, with the same pattern as in the cl. period, but no longer used as envoys;
(2) *haiku*, normally incl. a season word, originating in but distinct from *hokku* (first stanza of *haikai*); and
(3) *kindaishi* ("modern poetry"), particularly
(a) *shintaishi* (new-style poetry, typically consisting of 7+5 or 5+7 syllable lines and written in cl. J.) and
(b) *jiyūshi* (free-style poetry, evolved from *shintaishi* but without a fixed syllable scheme and usually written in modern J.).

Renga and *haikai* became virtually extinct in the late 19th c., surviving only among a small number of literati. *Senryū* has come to be viewed more as epigram or playful commentary than as poetry.

Like the rest of modern J. culture, poetry since 1868 has developed under the influence and stimulation of the West. It has had to respond not only to Western literary currents but to internal political and social changes caused by rapid modernization. To early modern poets, traditional verseforms seemed so outmoded that several poets, incl. Masaoka Shiki (1867–1902), went so far as to predict their total disappearance in the near future. *Shintaishi* emerged in response to the new need. Yet poets working in *tanka* and *haiku* did not give up; they endeavored to modernize those forms, and eventually succeeded in doing so.

Modernization of J. p. involved a number of innovations aimed at overcoming what early modern poets saw as the main weaknesses of cl. verse, such as brevity of form, lack of social awareness, and inability to embody sustained reasoning. One early Meiji scholar, after reading European poetry, observed: "Their poetry is closer to our prose fiction than to our poetry." The task of modern J. poets, then, was to bring poetry closer to prose, to a type of lit. flexible enough to reflect the ever-increasing complexity of modern civilization. Those who opted for *kindaishi* had little problem overcoming the deficiencies, but those who persisted in writing in premodern forms had a stiff challenge on their hands.

One scheme adopted by a number of modern *tanka* and *haiku* poets has been a method known as *rensaku* (sequential composition), in which the poet strings together two or more poems written on a common topic. The method is reminiscent of *renga* and *haikai*, except that it uses thematic rather than tonal qualities to attain structural unity and is composed by a single poet. Individual *tanka* or *haiku* grouped together would become like stanzas of a Western poem, showing progression of thought or feeling from one to the next within the group. A complex topic that cannot be done justice in a short form receives more adequate treatment by use of the *rensaku* technique. Even a topic that demands sustained thinking can be dealt with.

Other schemes devised to help overcome the brevity of traditional forms exploit visual qualities of the lang. Kawahigashi Hekigodō (1873–1937), for example, once tried what he called *ruby haiku*—*haiku* that has *furigana* (J. phonetic symbols, called "ruby" in typography) alongside Chinese ideograms. The poet would use unconventional *furigana*, so that added meaning would emerge from the surprising juxtaposition of J. syllabary and Chinese characters. Ishikawa Takuboku (1886–1912) had many of his later *tanka* printed in three lines, sometimes utilizing indentation for poetic effect:

My wife today
behaves like a woman unleashed.
 I gaze at a dahlia.

The new typographical format shocked contemp. readers, because a *tanka*, though consisting of five syllabic units and often translated as a five-line poem, had always been printed in a single or run-on line in J. Similarly, J. readers had known of *haiku* as a one-line poem, but Takayanagi Shigenobu (1923–83) began writing *haiku* like Western visual poetry:

blooming
flaming
ash's
swirling
circle
lone island's
roses

Both poets observed the 31- and 17-syllable rules, but not the line conventions of the genres.

In another attempt to modernize traditional forms, some radical poets advocated "free-style *tanka*" and "free-style *haiku*." The basis of their argument is the same as in Western free verse : the form of each poem should be determined by its unique subject matter, not by predetermined prosody. In effect, their work was short free verse, yet they insisted it was *tanka* or *haiku* on the basis of nonformal elements. For instance, Ogiwara Seisensui (1884–1976), leader of the freestyle *haiku* movement, argued that even though his poems did not follow the 5+7+5 syllable pattern they should be considered *haiku* because their subject matter was confined to nature and their structure concentric rather than linear. Such arguments did not convince many fellow poets, however, who believed that any poem that refused conventional prosody was free verse. Although free-style *haiku* gained wider support than its counterpart in *tanka*, both declined in popularity with time and all but disappeared in the second half of the 20th c. In his last years, Seisensui himself began calling his poems free verse.

Incorporating social awareness into *tanka* and *haiku* proved an easier challenge. Already in the 19th c. Shiki had shown a strong dislike for the confinements of cl. aesthetics and advocated enlargements of theme, tone, and imagery. Later poets, esp. those who came under the influence of Western naturalism, positively sought to draw on plebeian life. This trend reached a peak with proletarian *tanka* and *haiku* in the 1920s and '30s. The following 31-syllable poem by Ōkuma Nobuyuki (1893–1977) on the subject of J. Labor Day is typical:

Amidst the dust
Rising from the earth,
  A red flag—
The sight in my memory
Forever unblottable.

Efforts to link poetry to social issues went to the other ideological extreme during World War II, when many poets wrote *tanka* with ultranationalistic overtones. After the war, leftwing poetry became popular again, but this time poets were more careful not to let their political beliefs impinge on the artistic autonomy of their work. Also, the social upheaval of the postwar period wrought changes on readers' sensibilities, so that they no longer expected contemp. *tanka* and *haiku* to have *aware, sabi,* or other such traditional tones. Using the 31- or 17-syllable forms, today's poets can treat most political, social, or intellectual issues without appearing experimental or avant-garde.

All such problems that plagued *tanka* and *haiku* poets were largely unknown to those who chose to write *kindaishi,* for their verseform had all the flexibility of the Western poetry it was modeled on. Their major challenge lay in finding a way to naturalize the alien form, which had centuries of cultural trad. behind it. Esp. troublesome was the problem of lang.: Western poetry fully exploited the various musical qualities of lang., whereas modern J., mingling native and Sinified words, seemed a lang. woefully lacking in music. Devoid of accent, meter was nonexistent in J.; alliteration and rhyme were not effective poetic devices because they abounded in ordinary usage. The only usable scheme was the syllable pattern, so early poets wrote *shintaishi* in 5+7 or 7+5 syllable lines; yet repetition of such lines brought monotony in long poems. Hagiwara Sakutarō (1886–1942), who tried harder to solve the problem than most other poets, believed that the only solution would be to mix 5+7, 6+4, 8+5 and other syllable patterns in a single poem, which would be the same as writing a poem in prose. "In J.," he concluded, "the more prosaic the lang. is, the closer it approaches to verse."

Later *kindaishi* poets tried to exploit the visual features of the lang. and thereby compensate for the lack of musical quality in their work. They skillfully combined letters from the three different scripts available in their lang.: angular and seemingly artless *katakana,* cursive and graceful *hiragana,* and ideogrammic and dignified *kanji.* They would make use of *furigana* in the same way Hekigodō did in *ruby haiku.* Going beyond visual effects, they arranged words, images, and ideas in such a way as to create an "emotive rhythm," a rhythm which is more sensory than phonetic. To cite a short example, a *jiyūshi* entitled "Horse" by Kitagawa Fuyuhiko (b. 1900) consists of just one line: "It has a naval port in its intestines." This prose sentence creates no noticeable musical rhythm. Its emotional impact, however, arising almost entirely from the interplay of images and associations, is similar to that of a surrealist painting. And, in general, *jiyūshi* has become more imagistic than traditional Western poetry.

Another way in which *kindaishi* attempted to compensate for lack of inherent musical quality was by bringing in vocal and instrumental music in performance. Recordings by several early poets show that in reading *kindaishi* they sang out with a certain melody, somewhat in the manner in which *tanka* poets recite before an audience. It was as if these poets did not feel *kindaishi* would sound poetic enough when recited with the intonation of ordinary speech. Later, some famous *kindaishi* were transformed into songs by professional composers, who wrote special melodies for them. "Moon over the Ruined Castle" by Tsuchii Bansui (1871–1952) and "Coconut" by Shimazaki Tōson (1872–1943) are two notable examples. In a sense, this practice was an extension of the cl. cultural practice that had produced many instances of happy union between lit. and music. It has continued to the present day, and provides a good opportunity for the general public to come into contact with *kindaishi.*

Despite different problems confronting *tanka, haiku,* and *kindaishi,* the history of modern J. p. shows that in each of its phases there was a centripetal force bringing together a large number of poets regardless of the verseform in which they specialized. The earliest phase, extending to the first few years of the 20th c., was one of romanticism, during which time many poets worked under the influence of European romantic writers. The promoter of the movement, Kitamura Tōkoku (1868–94), wrote two long *shintaishi* inspired by Byron's *The Prisoner of Chillon* and *Manfred,* but the full potential of the new form was not revealed until Shimazaki Tōson published a collection of short lyrics called *Young Herbs* in 1897. Tōson's two predominant themes were romantic love and the anxiety of youth, and he expressed them in a delicate, exquisitely beautiful lang. that was to become a model. The theme of romantic love also found eloquent expression in the *tanka* of Yosano Akiko (1878–1942), whose *Tangled Hair* (1901) shocked contemp. readers by its bold affirmation of female sexuality. For *haiku*, Shiki published an essay called "Buson the Haiku Poet" (1897), giving lavish praise to Buson's poetry for its bright, fanciful, sometimes startling beauty.

Romanticism was succeeded by J. symbolism, most notably in *kindaishi*, after *The Sound of the Tide* was pub. in 1905 by Ueda Bin (1874–1916). This book of translations introducing the works of many Fr. symbolists made a great impact on the J. poetic scene, inspiring a new movement led by Susukida Kyūkin (1877–1945) and Kanbara Ariake (1876–1952). One reason why such difficult European poetry appealed to J. poets lay in its emphasis on the idea of "correspondence" (cf. Baudelaire), which was common in cl. J. verse. The symbolist movement reached a peak with Kitahara Hakushū (1885–1942), who, with his decadently modern sensibility and colorfully rich vocabulary, created in J. a type of poetry reminiscent of European *fin-de-siècle* lit.

Haiku poets were the least attracted to romanticism or symbolism during these years, mainly because their leader Shiki advocated in his later years the principle of *shasei* (sketch from life). This principle was advanced further by his two leading disciples, Takahama Kyoshi (1874–1959) and Hekigodō, esp. as naturalistic realism became a dominant force in J. fiction shortly after the turn of the century. Some major *tanka* poets, such as Itō Sachio (1864–1913) and Nagatsuka Takashi (1879–1915), came under the spell, too, and wrote 31-syllable poems that purported to copy life objectively. Others, like Maeda Yūgure (1883–1951) and Takuboku, focused on copying plebeian life in their *tanka*, thereby paving the way for proletarian poetry. Principles of modern European realism also attracted some *kindaishi* poets, notably Kawaji Ryūkō (1888– 1959), who published a collection of naturalistic poems entitled *Flowers on the Roadside* in 1910.

J. p. entered a new stage of maturity when its writers became more fully awakened to their modern identity. Western neo-humanism had begun to permeate the depths of J. consciousness in the early years of the 20th c., and poets gradually came to seek out their inner selves, trying to give them poetic expression. Of several major poets who did this, Takamura Kōtarō (1883–1956) was the most intensely ethical. In his first book of *kindaishi, The Journey* (1914), he powerfully asserted the potential of humanity and pleaded for elevating it to its highest level by rigorous disciplining of the self. A similar longing for exalted life pervades the *tanka* collected in *Red Light* (1913) by Saitō Mokichi (1882–1953), but life as conceived by him seems more primordial and biological, presuming a powerful force flowing in the depths of all living things. In sharp contrast, the self as seen by Hagiwara Sakutarō is lonely, ailing, and anxiety-ridden. His first book of *kindaishi* was called *Howling at the Moon* (1917), the title suggesting spiritually starved modernists forever longing for unreachable ideals. The celebration of the self did not touch *haiku* until later, possibly because the form traditionally focused on depicting external nature rather than expressing the inner self. The publication of *Katsushika* in 1930, a collection of *haiku* by Mizuhara Shūōshi (1892–1981), belatedly announced the arrival of the age of individualism in that verseform.

The 1920s and '30s saw a number of new Western ideas flowing into Japan and inducing poets to respond in varying ways. The most pervasive of such ideas was Marxism; however, except for the *jiyūshi* of Nakano Shigeharu (1902–79), few poems written by Marxist sympathizers have stood the test of time. More productive was interaction between other European movements and young *kindaishi* poets, such as between dada and Takahashi Shinkichi (1901–87); between surrealism and Nishiwaki Junzaburō (1894–1982); between imagism and Murano Shirō (1901–75); and between modernism and Kitazono Katsue (1902–78), Anzai Fuyue (1898–1965), and others. The only major poet largely free of Western influence during this period was Miyazawa Kenji (1896–1933), who turned to Buddhism and agrarianism for inspiration. Although imported ideas had less impact on poets writing in traditional forms, they still spurred the emergence of such short-lived movements as "proletarian *tanka*" and "modernist *haiku*."

After the barren years of the War, J. p. made a fresh start and, with the nation's rapid economic recovery, in time attained a new height of prosperity. Poets who established themselves in the postwar years can be classified in two categories. One was a school that stressed the social significance of poetry. Its founders were Ayukawa Nobuo (1920–86), Tamura Ryūichi (b. 1923), and other *jiyūshi* poets who in 1947 started a poetry magazine called *The Waste Land* with the aim of "discovering a ray of light in the dark empirical awareness and hopeless realization that we live in a waste land." They were joined by leftwing poets like Kaneko Mitsuharu (1895–1975), Sekine Hiroshi (b. 1920), and others, who tried to discover in the energy of the masses a hope for reclaiming the "waste land." Their poetry, unlike that of prewar proletarian poets, appealed to a wide audience because it was artistically more satisfying. *Tanka* by Kondō Yoshimi (b. 1913) and *haiku* by Kaneko Tōta (b. 1919), among many others, also showed awareness of contemp. social issues to an unprecedented degree, freely treating such topics as atomic bombing, the Tokyo Trial, and the U.S.-Japan Mutual Security Treaty.

The other school of postwar poets emphasized the importance of more universal issues. It was sometimes called the "art school" because of its high regard for the artistic perfection of the poem. Among its earliest promoters were Nakamura Shin'ichirō (b. 1918), Katō Shūichi (b. 1919), and other *kindaishi* poets, who in 1948 initiated the "matinée poétique" movement to introduce modern Fr. poetics to J. p. Although Nakamura and Katō soon stopped writing poetry, and the movement itself was short-lived, poetry concerned with basic human nature gained support when younger poets with no direct war experience began writing in the 1950s and '60s. Most prominent among these are Tanikawa Shuntarō (b. 1931) and Ōoka Makoto (b. 1931), who write meditative lyrics of serene intellect and restrained diction. Tanikawa is the first poet who has successfully transplanted the sonnet form into J. p. He and his associates have also been active as literary and social critics; their activities extend far beyond the conventional role of the poet.

What is known as "the poetry boom" arrived in the late 1960s. Perhaps the general anti-establishment attitude of the younger generation during that decade stirred interest in poetry, a medium that otherwise seemed to be becoming obsolete. Another factor may have been the ready availability of washing machines and other household appliances which freed women from many daily chores and gave them time to read and write. For whatever reason, numerous books of poetry by both old masters and new experimenters appeared. As the nation's affluence continues, "little magazines" publishing poetry have proliferated, as have books of poetry that are privately published. Poetry no longer enjoys the kind of high social prestige it once did, but it continues to fulfill its social and personal functions in Japan. M.U.

BIBLIOGRAPHIES: *The P.E.N. Club News* (1958–71); Japan P.E.N. Club, *J. Lit. in European Langs.* (1961); *Kokubungaku Kenkyū Bunken Mokuroku* [Bibliographical Materials for the Study of J. Lit.] (1971–76); J. T. Rimer and R. E. Morrell, *Guide to J. P.* (1975); *J. Lit. Today* (1976–); Internat. House of J. Library, *Mod. J. Lit. in Tr.* (1979); *Kokubungaku Nenkan* [J. Lit. Annual] (1977–); *JASt*—annual bibl.

ANTHOLOGIES AND TRANSLATIONS: Nishiyama Sōin, *Sōin Toppyaku Koi no Haikai* (1671)—J. p. on heterosexual and male homosexual love; Yosano Akiko, *Midaregami* (1904)—daring love poetry; *The Man'yōshū, 1000 Poems* (1940); R. H. Blyth, *Senryū, J. Satirical Verses* (1950), *Edo Satirical Verse Anthols.* (1961); J. Konishi, *Haiku: Hassei Yori Gendai Made* [*Haiku*: From Its Origins to the Present] (1952); T. Ninomiya and D. J. Enright, *The P. of Living J.* (1957); *Nihon Koten Bungaku Taikei* [The Great Compendium of Cl. J. Lit.], ed. I. Takagi et al., 101 v. (1957–68); K. Yamamoto, *Nihon Shiikashū* [Anthol. of J. P.] (1959); *Nihon no Shiika* [J. P.], ed. S. Itō et al., 31 v. (1967–70); H. C. McCullough, *Tales of Ise* (1968), *Kokin Wakashū* (1985), *Brocade by Night* (1985); *Nihon Koten Bungaku Zenshū* [A Full Collection of J. Lit.], 51 v. (1970–76); H. Kijima, *The P. of Postwar J.* (1975); M. Ueda, *Mod. J. Haiku* (1976); J. Kirkup, *Mod. J. P.* (1978); E. Miner, *J. Linked P.* (1979); E. Miner and H. Odagiri, *The Monkey's Straw Raincoat and Other Poetry of the Bashō School* (1981); H. Sato and B. Watson, *From the Country of Eight Islands* (1981); *The Ten Thousand Leaves*, tr. I. Levy, v. 1, *Man'yōshū*, 1–5 (1981); *Shimpen Kokka Taikan* [Newly Edited Great Canon of J. P.], 3 v. in 6 (1983–85); *Kyōka Taikan* [The Great Canon of Mad Waka], 3 v. (1983–85); L. R. Rodd, *Kokinshuū* (1984); *Waiting for the Wind: 36 Poets of Japan's Late Medieval Age* (1989), *Traditional J. P.*, tr. and ed. S. D. Carter (1991).

HISTORY AND CRITICISM: *Kindai Tankashi* [A Hist. of Mod. Tanka], ed. U. Kubota et al., 3 v. (1958); J. Konishi, "Association and Progression," *HJAS* 21 (1958), *Sōgi* (1971), *A Hist. of J. Lit.*, 5 v. (1984–), with J. version, *Nihon Bungeishi* (1985–); R. H. Brower and E. Miner, *J. Court P.* (1961), *Fujiwara Teika's Superior Poems of Our Time* (1967); K. Yamamoto, *Gendai Haiku* [Mod. Haiku] (1964); *Kōza Nihon Gendaishi Shi* [Lectures on the Hist. of Mod. J. P.], ed. S. Murano et al., 4 v. (1973); D. Keene, *World Within Walls* (1976), *Dawn to the West*, 2 v. (1984); M. Ueda, *Mod. J. Poets and the Nature of Lit.* (1983); "Himerareta Bungaku," ed. S. Yamada, spec. iss. of *Koku Bungaku Kaishaku to Kanshō* (1983)—on erotic writing and art; Miner et al., esp. parts 1, 6A, F, J, K, 7H, 8K. E.M.; M.U.

JAVANESE POETRY.

I. A.D. 732–928
II. A.D. 929–1527
III. CA. A.D. 1500–1625
IV. CA. A.D. 1578–1940

J. p. was in the beginning closely linked to religion and politics. In the Hindu-J. period, poets were members of the Brahman caste or Buddhist clergy, working either as priests and teachers in the service of the monarch or in monasteries patronized by the court.

I. A.D 732–928: the dynasty of Mĕḍang in South Central Java. Period I is dominated by Sivaite and Buddhist rulers, presumably of mixed Indian and J. blood. *Kakawin* lit. originates in this period. A *kakawin* is a sizable epic poem in Old J. composed in the metrical rules of the Indian *mahākāvya* and mostly dealing with topics borrowed from Indian mythology. The oldest dated poetry in Old J. idiom and in Indian meters is preserved in a stone inscription of 29 stanzas dated A.D 856. The oldest and largest complete poem is the *Rāmāyaṇa-kakawin*, comprising 2783 stanzas in 81 different meters and also believed to date from the 9th c. The author must have known by heart Bhaṭṭi's *kāvya Rāvaṇa-vadha*, which treats the same theme but is meant as a textbook of grammar and *alaṃkāra*.

J. art in this period adheres strictly to Indian

rules. This also applies to *kakawin* prosody. In principle the *kakawin* stanza is built up of four lines of similar length and showing the same pattern of long and short syllables. Thus the metric formula of the popular Old J. meter *śārdūlavikrīḍita,* for example, is as follows:

– – – | ⏑ ⏑ – | ⏑ – ⏑ | ⏑ ⏑ – | – – ⏑ | – – ⏑ | ⏑

Although in J. phonology vowel-length is not phonemic, the aesthetic effect of *kakawin* poetry must have been very distinctive, the text being sung, each meter to its own melody. Poetry in Java was from its inception something to be sung before an audience, not read in private.

II. A.D. 929–1527: the dynasties of Kĕḍiri, Singhasari, and Majapahit in East Java. In period II a strong tendency toward "Javanization" occurred in the plastic arts and in lit. Around A.D. 1000, the great Indian epics together with some Purāṇa's and other religious texts were translated into Old J. prose, and an efflorescence of *kakawin* lit. followed. *Kakawins* were composed for royal marriages, victories in war, and funeral rites. The authors most often used existing Indian themes but transformed them into J. stories, changing the plots radically to fit the needs of the moment and to suit the tastes of their highly placed patrons. The *Nāgarakṛtāgama* by Prapanca, a panegyric in praise of King Hayam Wuruk which contains a description of Majapahit in its heyday, is an exception, however.

Old J. must have become a dead lang., used only for literary purposes, by the end of the 13th c. if not earlier. It is not surprising therefore that the Majapahit era (1294–1527) witnessed the emergence of a new poetic trad., the *kidung* lit. A *kidung* is a sizable epic poem in Middle J., composed in indigenous meters and treating indigenous themes. Most frequently the *kidungs* contain a *ruwat* story or deal with local historical trad. or a variant of the *Panji* theme. *Ruwat* stories relate how a person or group was once freed of a curse or safeguarded against evil. They are sung or performed on the *wayang* (shadow theater) stage as part of a conjuration ceremony. *Panji* stories relate how a prince of Koripan, who is an incarnation of Vishṇu, is united after many vicissitudes with his niece, a princess of Daha (Kĕḍiri) who, being an incarnation of Śrī, was predestined to become his bride.

Kidungs ("songs") are, just as *kakawins,* sung to an audience, though on different occasions, and are composed in *tengahan* or *macapat* meters. A stanza consists of a fixed number of lines (different for each meter) of mutually different but otherwise fixed length, each ending in a certain vowel. Thus the structure of the *tengahan* meter *wukir* can be summarized in the following formula: 10–u, 6–e, 8–i, 7–u, 8–u, 8–e, 8–u, 8–a, 8–a; which means that a stanza consists of 9 lines, the first of which has 10 syllables with *u* in the final one, etc. After the downfall of the Majapahit empire in 1527, the poetic trads. in Old and Middle J. were perpetuated on the island of Bali.

III. CA. A.D. 1500–1625: the petty kingdoms on the North Coast (Pasisir). Important cultural changes occurred in Java's third period. In the prosperous cities along the North coast, a new Islamic elite had sprung up, speaking an early form of Modern J. and interested in the Arab and Indo-Persian stories that came to Java with the Qur'anic trad. The *wayang* remained popular, serving to perpetuate the Indian epic trad. Out of the *kidung* trad., new forms of poetry evolved, using the Modern J. idiom, treating new topics, and exhibiting an outspoken preference for *macapat* meters which, though technically obedient to the same rules of prosody as the older *tengahan* meters, were used in such a way that each meter with its specific melody was supposed to suggest the particular atmosphere prevailing in the canto. Included in this Modern J. p. are J. stories on topics borrowed from the international Islamic trad., original didactic poems on tenets of Islamic faith, often concerning questions of orthodox or heterodox mysticism (the *suluk* lit.), adaptations of older stories from the pre-Islamic period, wanderer stories, and compilations called *serat kanṇḍa* in which the cycles of tales forming the repertoire of the shadow theater were brought together.

IV. CA. A.D. 1578–1945: the dynasty of Mataram in South Central Java. In period IV, poetry once again became "court poetry." The new genres generated during the Pasisir period were refined. In addition, a new genre became important: the chronicle (*babad*). A modern type of *Panji* story was developed. A renewed interest in the cl. heritage led to the creation of Modern J. versions of the most important *kakawins.* New epic poems, some of them hundreds of pages long, were created, along with many shorter didactic-moralistic poems. The court poets played an important role, and even members of the royal house took an active part in poetry writing.

After Indonesian Independence in 1945, traditional J. p. ends. Western genres written in modern idiom and dealing with modern topics, such as the novel, the short story, free verse, and modern forms of the drama, all of which have developed since 1900, now hold the field.

HISTORY AND CRITICISM: E. M. Uhlenbeck, *A Crit. Survey of Studies on the Langs. of Java and Madura* (1964); C. Holt, *Art in Indonesia, Continuities and Change* (1967); T. Pigeaud, *Lit. of Java: Mss. in the Library of the Univ. of Leiden,* 4 v. (1967–80); P. J. Zoetmulder, *Kalangwan: A Survey of Old J. Lit.* (1974). J.J.R.

JUDEO-SPANISH POETRY is that poetry sung, recited, or written in the Judeo-Sp. (Judezmo, Ladino) dialect, in the various post-diasporic sanctuaries of the Sephardic Jews—North Africa (Morocco, Algeria) and the Eastern Mediterranean (the Balkans, Greece, Turkey, Israel)—after their exile from Spain in 1492. By contrast, in Western European centers such as Amsterdam, Bayonne, and Leghorn, there were Jewish authors who did not write in the Judeo-Sp. dialect but continued to form part of the Hispanic (Sp. or Port.) literary trads. (see HEBREW POETRY; SPANISH POETRY). Judeo-Sp. p. can be organized into the following generic categories: *complas* (popular religious or didactic songs), *cantigas* (lyric songs), *romansas* (traditional ballads), *endevinas* (riddles), and *refranes* (proverbs). *Complas* can be considered essentially written lit.; the other genres are oral. Following World War II, a special sub-genre of Sephardic poetry, written in Judeo-Sp. and in Fr., commemorated the tragic events of the Holocaust.

Complas (Sp. *coplas*) are strophic poems usually of paraliturgical content, by both known and anonymous authors, and are the most characteristic Sephardic genre. Typically they are sung and often are acrostic poems presenting the letters of the Hebrew alphabet or of the author's name. Since they are essentially part of a written trad., they are generally sung by men, unlike the *romansas*, which are usually performed by women. Among the most traditional *complas* are those for the festivity of Purim, composed in the 18th and 19th cs., that relate the biblical story of Esther or evoke the joys of the holiday in strophes of varying lengths, with short or long verses in zejelesque rhyme (*aaab*), often incl. a refrain. Other *complas* celebrate the festivities of Hanukkah, Passover, Pentecost, the Sabbath, the Rejoicing of the Torah, and Arbor Day. There are also dirgelike *complas* (*Quinot*) that commemorate the destruction of the Temple (70 A.D.) and other tragic events in ancient Jewish history. Other *complas* of a moralizing, admonitory bent (*complas de castiguerio*) preach the glories of God and warn against the illusory nature of worldly attractions. *Complas del felek* ("destiny") present the life and customs of late 19th- and early 20th-c. Sephardic Jewry from a satirical or humorous perspective. In *complas de Tebariá* are celebrated the praises of the city of Tiberias, of venerable sages who lived there, and of miracles concerning its Jewish population. M. Attias has published another group of poems, *Complas de 'Aliyá* ("Songs of Return to Zion"), which give voice to the Jews' longing for redemption and return to Jerusalem in all its glory. Those *complas* by Abraham Toledo, devoted to the life of Joseph and first published in 1732—part of a subgenre designated as *complas hagiográficas*—constitute for I. M. Hassán perhaps the single greatest poem in Judeo-Sp. In reworking the biblical account of Joseph's life (Genesis 37, 39–45), Toledo used numerous elements from folklore, rabbinical commentaries, and traditional life, presented with lyrical verve, lexical versatility, and rhetorical strength. In comparison with such genres as ballads and proverbs, which have strong Hispanic connections, the study of *complas* has, until recently, been gravely neglected.

Cantigas are traditional lyric songs, frequently of Hispanic origin in form and content, but, in the Eastern trad., with significant Gr. and Turkish lexical, structural, and thematic influences. Although love in all its vicissitudes is the predominant theme, there are also lyric songs devoted to various functions in the traditional life cycle: *cantigas de boda* (wedding songs), *de parida* (birth songs), and *endechas* (dirges). Many Sephardic lyric songs, esp. in the Eastern communities, are of relatively recent origin (late 19th and early 20th c.) and often consist of quatrains in couplets with assonance; some are modeled on Gr. originals and others even imported on phonograph records from Spain or Sp. America. But other lyric songs attest to a venerable Sephardic trad. going back to medieval Hispanic origins. The parallelistic rhymes of some Eastern poems and of many Moroccan wedding songs—similar to that of the primitive Sp. and Port. lyric—confirm the medieval character of the Judeo-Sp. *cantiga* trad.

Romansas (Sp. *romances*) are traditional ballads in assonating octosyllabic verse. In content they are essentially similar—in some cases, genetically related—to narrative poetry current in other European communities. No other Sephardic genre is so closely linked to its medieval Hispanic origins, and none has received as much scholarly attention. Judeo-Sp. ballads can be documented from as early as 1525 through verses used as tune indicators in Heb. hymnals. Several 18th-c. mss. are known, and numerous Eastern ballads were collected and printed in popular Heb.-letter chapbooks in the late 19th and early 20th c. There are Sephardic ballads derived from medieval Sp. and Fr. epics; others concern events in Sp. and Port. hist. or tell stories from the Bible, Cl. antiquity, or medieval romances; still others concern a variety of topoi (prisoners and captives, the husband's return, faithful or tragic love, the unfortunate wife, the adulteress, amorous adventures, tricks and deceptions). Some ballads function as wedding songs, others as dirges, still others as lullabies. Though a majority of Sephardic ballads have med. or 16th-c. Sp. counterparts, others can be shown to derive from modern Gr. narrative poetry; some were undoubtedly created in the exile communities by the Sephardim themselves. P. Bénichou's studies of oral trad. as a creative artistic process are essential to ballad crit.

Endevinas (riddles) are often rhymed and, like proverbs, should count as a part of Sephardic traditional poetry. Of all genres, the riddle has been the most gravely neglected by scholarship. Little fieldwork has been done to collect riddles, and the known Eastern repertoire is still radically limited. Nothing is presently known of the Moroccan Sephardic riddle trad. As far as origins are concerned, a preliminary assessment indicates that Eastern Judeo-Sp. riddles are about evenly divided between texts of medieval Hispanic origin and adaptations from Turkish and Gr. However, in many cases it is impossible to point to a specific origin.

Refranes (proverbs) have been abundantly collected in Heb.-letter chapbooks since the late 19th c. by the Sephardim themselves and also by Western scholars. Some Sephardic proverbs agree exactly with their Sp. counterparts, while others have obviously been taken over from Gr., Turkish, or biblical Heb. sources.

M. Attias, "Shelôshah shîrê Tsîyôn," *Shevet va-'Am* 4 (1959), *Cancionero* (1972); P. Bénichou, *Creación poética* (1968); M. Alvar, *Endechas* (1969), *Cantos de boda* (1971); S. G. Armistead and J. H. Silverman, *Folk Lit.* (1971–86), "El antiguo romancero," *NRFH* 30 (1981), *En torno al romancero* (1982), "Adivinanzas," *Philologica M. Alvar* (1983); E. Romero, "Complas de Tu-Bishbat," *Poesía: Reunión de Málaga*, ed. M. Alvar (1976), "Las coplas sefardíes," *Jornadas*, ed. A. Viudas Camarasa (1981); L. Carracedo and E. Romero, "Poesía admonitiva," *Sefarad* 37 (1977), "Refranes," *Sefarad* 41 (1981); S. G. Armistead et al., *El romancero en el Archivo Menéndez Pidal* (1978); I. Hassán and E. Romero, "Quinot paralitúrgicos," *Estudios Sefardíes* 1 (1978); P. Díaz-Mas, "Romances de endechar," *Jornadas*, ed. A. Viudas Camarasa (1981); I. Hassán, "Visión panorámica," *Hispania Judaica*, ed. J. M. Solà-Solé (1982); *And the World Stood Silent: Sephardic Poetry of the Holocaust*, tr. I. J. Lévy (1989).

S.G.A.; J.H.S.

JUDEZMO POETRY. See JUDEO-SPANISH POETRY.

K

KANNADA POETRY. See INDIAN POETRY.

KASHMIRI POETRY. See INDIAN POETRY.

KOREAN POETRY.

I. SILLA DYNASTY (57 B.C.–A.D. 935)
II. KORYO DYNASTY (A.D. 918–1392)
III. CHOSON DYNASTY (1392–1910)
IV. JAPANESE OCCUPATION (1910–1945)
V. AFTER THE LIBERATION (1945–)

Although the K. lang. belongs to a ling. family totally different from Ch., cl. Ch. was the primary written lang. of Korea until the invention of the K. alphabet in the mid 15th c. After that point, most learned men wrote both in Ch. and K., but more often in Ch. Earlier, an ingenious system was devised by the Silla people to transcribe the current spoken lang. using Ch. graphs; used from the 6th c. on, it was through this means that the extant Old K. poems, or *hyangga*, were preserved. This article, however, considers only K. poetry written in the vernacular.

There are four major native poetic forms in traditional Korea: *hyangga*, ("native song," 6th–10th c.); *pyŏlgok* or *changga* ("long song," 11th–14th c.); *sijo* ("current tune," 15th c. on); and *kasa* ("song words," 15th–19th c.). Another poetic form that flourished briefly is the *akchang* ("eulogy," 15th c.), the most representative of which is the *Songs of Flying Dragons* (1445–47), a cycle compiled in praise of the founding of the Chosŏn dynasty.

I. SILLA DYNASTY (57 B.C.–A.D. 935). *Hyangga* were written in 4-, 8-, and 10-line forms; the 10-line form comprising two quatrains and a concluding couplet was the most popular. The poets were either Buddhist monks or *hwarang*, knights trained in civil and military virtue in preparation for national service. Seventeen of the 25 extant *hyangga* are Buddhist in inspiration and content. Most *hyangga* gain their resonance through verbal felicity and symbolism. The "Ode to Knight Kip'a" (8th c.) by Master Ch'ungdam, for example, begins with a symbolic equation between the moon that pursues the white clouds and the speaker seeking the depths of his friend's mind, and concludes with a correspondence between the knight and the pine that "scorns frost, ignores snow." Like the pine tree, the knight represents the principle of growth and order, an emblem of continuity of society and culture. "Requiem" (8th c.) by Master Wŏlmyŏng uses the ancient trope comparing human generations with the scattering of leaves. The eleven devotional poems by Great Master Kyunyŏ (923–73) recall Western religious poetry in their imagery and symbolism. (As passion's flame scorches and destroys the fabric of human nature, so the ignorant mind suffers the blight of affliction.) Only the Buddha's sweet rain of truth can cause the withered soul to yield the grass of spiritual regeneration, bringing forth the golden fruit of knowledge. This harmonious state of the mind is expressed by the single metaphor of "a moonlit autumn field," the full moon of enlightenment.

II. KORYO DYNASTY (A.D. 918–1392). The interplay of Buddhist and native beliefs continued to inspire popular culture. Koryŏ lyrics, the *pyŏlgok* or *changga*, a blend of folk and art songs rooted in the indigenous culture, were composed and sung to music. Their refrains combine verbal and musical rhythms with nonsense syllables and onomatopoeic representation of the sound of the drum to create tension, suspense, and an incantatory quality. The refrain establishes the tone that carries the melody and spirit of the poem or unites a poem comprised of discrete parts. The theme of most of these anonymous poems is love, the joys and torments of which are expressed in frank and powerful language—the sadness of parting, revulsion at betrayal, renewed desire, grief at abandonment. The nameless poets were at war with time, love's chief enemy. In "Ode on the Seasons," a woman likens the stages of her love to the four seasons; in "Spring Overflows the Pavilion," a woman laments a blighted spring in her heart; and in "Winter Night" she compares the agony of desertion to a stormy night that scatters sleet and snow. But the poets say they can make the river stand still, they are content to be dissolved by fire, and they are able to transform the icy bamboo hut into a love grotto.

III. CHOSON DYNASTY (1392–1910). The *sijo*, the most popular, elastic, and mnemonic of K. poetic forms, is a 3-line poem (in tr. usually a 6-line stanza is used). The *sijo* meter is formed by an ordered sequence of metric segments comprising syllables within a set range (2–7, commonly 3–4). Each line consists of four syllable groups, with a minor pause occurring at the end of the second group and a major at the end of the fourth. An emphatic syntactic division, usually introduced in the third line in the form of a countertheme, paradox, resolution, judgment, command, or exclamation, indicates a shift to subjectivity. The interplay of sound, rhythm, and meaning is the soul of the *sijo*, the basis of its organic structure. Writers of the *sijo* in the first half of the Chosŏn dynasty were mainly the lettered class and *kisaeng*, women entertainers, while in the second half, beginning from the 18th c., they were commoners. *Sijo* are still written, an oral art for the lettered and unlettered alike. Any subject is permissible, but favored ones include praise of virtue, complaints of desertion, fear of death, the beauty of friendship, and the simplicity of rural life. A long form, called *sasŏl sijo*, evolved in the latter part of the dynasty. Written mainly by commoners, it is marked especially by onomatopoeia, a tendency to catalogue, striking imagery, and a bold twist at the end. It is frank and humorous, often satirical and running to burlesque, and explores the resources of the vernacular.

Is it a cuckoo that cries?
Is it the willow that is blue?
Row away, row away!
Several roofs in a far fishing village
Swim in the mist, magnificent.
Chigukch'ong chigukch'ong ŏsawa!
Boy, fetch an old net!
Fishes are climbing against the stream.

This is the fourth poem in the spring cycle from *The Angler's Calendar* (1651) by Yun Sŏndo (1587–1671). Yun adds two envois to the form characteristic of the fisherman's songs: a set of verbs connected with boating, and three 3-syllable onomatopoeic expressions simulating the movements and sounds of rowing. The poem opens with two lines that question the reliability of the senses of hearing and sight. Next, we see something in the distance, barely visible in the mist, but confirming the reality of the uncertain vision. The last two lines are brief and forceful, bespeaking a practical and more immediate connection with nature. In an ordered progression, then, the poem presents nature's mystery, beauty, and bounty in terms of illusory loveliness, real visual beauty, and life-sustaining reality, food from the stream. The poem not only suggests the felt transcendence of the vision, but reveals a consciousness of the transience of earthly joy and beauty. Yun Sŏndo achieves clarity and richness of vision with the simplest vocabulary and utmost economy.

The *kasa* that emerged as a new form toward the middle of the 15th c. can be compared to the Ch. rhymeprose, the *fu*. It is characterized by a lack of stanzaic division, varying lengths, a tendency toward description and exposition, at times lyricism, and by verbal, syntactical parallelism. Its norm is a group of two 4-syllable words, or alternating groups of 3 and 4 syllables, forming a line often employing syntactic and semantic parallelism.

in.seang.ŭn yu.han.han.dae
si.ram.do kŭ.ji.ŏp.ta
Life has an end:
Sorrow is endless.

Earlier examples dealt with topics such as the loyalty to the king, celebration of the virtues of retired life (Chŏng Ch'ŏl, 1536–93; Pak Inno, 1561–1643), and the sorrows of unrequited love (Hŏ Nansŏrhŏn, 1563–89). The subject matter of the 18th-c. anonymous *kasa* by women was the daily life of the middle and lower classes. The themes of later examples of definite authorship include records of officials to Tokyo and Peking, praise of institutions, the farmer's works and days, and the sorrow of banishment. From the 19th c., the *kasa* became didactic, patriotic, or nostalgic. The "Song of Seoul" (1844), which details the institutions and glories of the Chosŏn dynasty, was popular among women.

IV. JAPANESE OCCUPATION (1910–45). The "new poetry" movement dates back to the publication of "From the Sea to Children" (1908) by Ch'oe Namsŏn (1890–1957). Written in free verse, the poem's inventions include the use of 106 punctuation marks, hitherto not used in cl. poetry, stanzaic forms of unequal length, topics of the sea and children also previously little used, and onomatopoeia in the first and seventh lines of each stanza. The first collection of translations from Western poetry was *Dance of Anguish* (1921) by Kim Ŏk, the principal transmitter of Fr. symbolist poetry. Two major poets in the 1920s were Han Yongun (1879–1944) and Kim Sowŏl (1902–34). With *The Silence of Love* (1926), comprising 88 Buddhist poems, Han became interpreter of the plight of the colonized peoples by creating a poetics of absence. Kim Sowŏl, the nature and folk poet, effectively used simplicity, directness, and terse phrasing. Unfulfilled love, or unquenchable longing, permeates his work. Perhaps the most influential modern poet before 1945 was Chŏng Chiyong (b. 1903), a student of William Blake and Walt Whitman. Chŏng rendered details with imagistic precision, as in his *White Deer Lake* (1941), symbolically representing the progress of the spirit to lucidity, the fusion of man and nature. Yi Yuksa (1904–44) and Yun Tongju (1917–45), major resistance poets, perished in Japanese prisons.

V. AFTER THE LIBERATION (1945–). Major poets writing after the liberation of 1945 include Sŏ Chŏngju (b. 1915) and Pak Tujin (b. 1916). Sŏ is credited with exploring hidden resources of the lang. from sensual ecstasy to spiritual quest, from haunting lyricism to colloquial earthiness. Capable of a wide range of moods, Pak uses sonorific intricacies and incantatory rhythms, revealing a strong historical and cultural consciousness. Some poets younger than Sŏ and Pak were determined to bear witness to the events of their age; some sought to further assimilate traditional K. values; others drew variously on Western traditions to enrich their work. Hwang Tonggyu (b. 1937) has drawn his material not only from personal experience but from the common predicament of his people. In his fifth collection, *Snow Falls in the South* (1974), Hwang studies modern K. history to determine the root of the K. tragedy, esp. its division and attendant instability, in images of barbed wire besieging his consciousness and snowflakes falling from the sky. In their search for order, for what Frost called "a momentary stay against confusion," modern poets affirm their situations by bold articulation of their human condition. Like their predecessors, they do not jettison cognitive claims or social functions for poetry but give that sense of purpose and coherence that only poetry can provide. Thus they have delved into the tradition to redeem the past and to affirm the new world they have created.

ANTHOLOGIES: *Kranich am Meer: Koreanische Gedichte* (1959), *Poems from Korea: A Hist. Anthol.* (1974), *The Silence of Love: 20th C. K. P.* (1980), *Anthol. of K. Lit.: From Early Times to the 19th C.* (1981), *Pine River and Lone Peak* (1991), all ed. P. H. Lee; *Contemp. K. P.*, ed. Ko Wŏn (1970); R. Rutt, *The Bamboo Grove: An Intro. to Sijo* (1971).

HISTORY AND CRITICISM: P. H. Lee, *Songs of Flying Dragons: A Crit. Reading* (1975), *Celebration of Continuity: Themes in Classic East Asian Poetry* (1979); D. R. McCann, "The Structure of the K. Sijo," *HJAS* 36 (1976); Chŏng Pyŏnguk, *Hanguk kojŏn sigaron* [Studies in Classic K. P.] (1977); M. Sym, *The Making of Mod. K. P.* (1982); Cho Tongil, *Hanguk munhak t'ongsa* [Gen. Hist. of K. Lit.], 5 v. (1982–88). P.H.L.

L

LADINO POETRY. See JUDEO-SPANISH POETRY.

LATIN AMERICAN POETRY. See AMERICAN INDIAN POETRY, *Central American, South American*; BRAZILIAN POETRY; SPANISH AMERICAN POETRY.

LATIN POETRY.

I. CLASSICAL. Lat. p. is commonly censured as derivative. The Lat. poets wrote in meters originated by the Greeks, employed a more or less assimilated Gr. mythology as a poetic vehicle, and confined their efforts, for the most part, to genres already well established when Rome was little more than a barbarous village. Yet despite this real dependence, there remains nothing less Gr. than the masterpieces of Lat. p., whose imitation of the Gr. was never slavish, and whose trad. was a double one. On one side stood the centuries of developed Gr. lit., a lit. of infinite variety and vast achievement, supplying Lat. poets with models and sanctions, and the more valuable for being foreign without being alien. On the other stood the developing corpus of Lat. lit., steadily informing the cultural context within which a given Roman poet lived and wrote. Between these two trads. the tension was lively and fruitful for Republican poetry esp.; if earlier Lat. poetry can be generally divided between a "Romanizing" school on the one hand and a "Hellenizing" school on the other, for later poets the problem was one of preserving the double loyalty they felt without doing damage to either trad. This double loyalty was not maintained by the simple mechanical act of domesticating Gr. meters and forms or adapting them to a specifically Roman sensibility, but by the far more delicate operation of blending the strengths and virtues of both sensibilities in a common form. This marriage of two trads. was the achievement of Virgil more than any other Lat. writer; and for Virgil's followers his example loomed so large that their problem was less whether they should be Greeks or Romans than whether they should be Virgilians or something else.

Further governing the finished Lat. poem were two states of mind almost completely alien to Cl. Gr. poetry. The first was the Lat. poet's *consciousness* of his trad. and his place in it. Like the Roman historian, the Lat. poet was intensely aware of and intensely loyal to his trad.; at times his humility before his tradition's authority approaches servility. It is this intense loyalty that most nearly explains the small range and variety of Lat. p. when measured against Gr. or Eng. poetry. Trad. for the Lat. poet early acquired an enormous authority, extending to subject, conventions, form, and even rhetorical modes; it was something to be exploited, but the exploitation was an exercise in humility and craft, a constant refinement of a more or less dominant mode. Rarely does the Lat. poet rebel against his trad., though he may reject one of its modes for another. In poetry as in character the virtue of *pietas* (dutiful loyalty) is central, and *continuity* is therefore one of the dominant features of Lat. p.: in all essential respects the poetics of Virgil and the poetics of Claudian four cs. later are the same. For the same reason that Lat. p. exhibits a restricted range, it also exhibits much less flagrant sensationalism and striving after originality; yet it would be a mistake to suppose that Lat. poets were indifferent innovators or that their style is somehow impersonal. Nowhere is sensationalism of rhet. and situation more prevalent than in Lat. p., esp. in post-Virgilian verse; but it needs to be observed that formal rhetorical innovation is almost always marginal, an elaborate, sometimes frigid, refinement of the dominant rhet. of the lang. Almost never is there revolution at the core or rejection of the cardinal principles of traditional poetics. Combined with consciousness of the trad., the second dominant characteristic of Lat. p. was the passion for *utility* in lit., for its application to some patriotic or instructive end—a passion never really absent, even in the hyperesthetic pieces where the poet emphasizes its existence by his determined avoidance of it. But it is not difficult to see how the poetry that emerged from the juggling of these elements was completely different from any Gr. poetry ever written.

A. *Origins.* Traces of wholly indigenous Lat. lit. are almost nonexistent. There were rude farces in the Saturnian stress meter before the irruption of Gr. culture into Latium, but we possess no fragments. This meter, however, was employed in the first Lat. poem of which we have even the barest knowledge—a tr. of the *Odyssey* written about the mid 3d c. B.C. by Livius Andronicus, a Gr. ex-slave. He handled the jigging, heavily accented movement of his verse with little distinction, but he had the incalculable advantage of being first; his work was used as a school text for more than two centuries. His younger contemporary Gnaeus Naevius represents a further stage in the transition. His versified chronicle of the First Punic War was done in the same meter, but he seems to have owed much to Homer, while he also wrote tragedies and comedies on Attic models wherein he employed quantitative Gr. meters based on quantity rather than stress. But the towering figure of the early years is Quintus Ennius (239–169 B.C.), in the wreck of whose work we may discern the roots of most subsequent Lat. p. He wrote tragedies, comedies, didactic poems and epigrams, all largely derived from the Greeks, but his most important work was the *Annals*, an epic chronicle recording the history of Rome from the arrival of Aeneas down to Ennius' own times.

The fragments of this work—which established the dactylic hexameter as the medium of Lat. epic—still serve to illustrate the peculiar nature of Lat. p. Based openly on the Homeric poems, and in some sense a continuation of them, the work also seems to have been influenced by Hellenistic poetic histories, and it fused these two sources, separated by cs. in time and outlook, into something distinctly Roman by its dedicated patriotic and didactic bias. Ennius' somewhat older contemporary, Titus Maccius Plautus (250–184 B.C.) set a number of plays of the Gr. New Comedy into Lat., but his debt to the rough native dramatic tradition is probably quite great, as the rather tired comedy of manners of the late Hellenic and Hellenistic ages suffers a sea-change, becoming excellent bawdy farce. The 21 Plautine comedies which survive are rude, colloquial, and frankly aimed at the pit, but they are funny and vital as well.

B. *Preclassical.* The 2d c. B.C. saw Rome's first literary-philosophical coterie, a gathering of philhellenes around the younger Scipio Africanus for the purpose of serious study and adaptation of Gr. culture. Two great poets of the c. were friends and clients of Scipio. The first was Terence (Publius Terentius Afer, at work 166–59), whose six verse-comedies show a definite reaction from the "excesses" of his predecessors, such as Plautus, back to the pure Menandrean ideal of the Gr. New Comedy. The purity and beauty of Terence's Lat. is a definite landmark; but more important are the implications of his subtlety. In stressing form, expression, and relationships at the expense of strength, character, and humor itself, he clearly turned away from the general public to address the educated classes—a situation that had not occurred in Greece until the beginning of the Hellenistic Age. It was a necessary step toward grafting a sophisticated Gr. trad. onto a crude but vital Roman one. Henceforth, with few exceptions, Lat. p. was composed by learned poets for a more or less learned audience. The other great name was Gaius Lucilius (180?–102 B.C.), considered the father of satire, the only genre to which the Romans laid fair claim—though the satirical attitude has a long history in Greece, and Lucilius was well acquainted with its examples in mock-epic, comedy, and diatribe. His work, 30 books of miscellanies, or *saturae,* ranged over the experiences of educated Romans in a world that was becoming increasingly Romanized and politicized, and his strong personal statements and versatile colloquial style established the mode of Roman satire. We possess numerous fragments of his works—he fixed on the hexameter for verse-form—but none, unfortunately, of any length.

C. *Late Republican.* The lst c. B.C. witnessed the rise of rhet. and the fall of the Roman Republic, both of them events of prime importance for poetry. The first important poem of which we possess any considerable remnants was the tr. by the orator Cicero (106–43) of the *Phaenomena* of Aratus of Soli, an Alexandrian didactic work on astronomy and meteorology that combined "science," devout Stoicism, and literary art. Cicero was no great poet, but his contributions to poetic lang. and metrical polish should not be minimized. A far greater poet, who used Cicero's developments but argued passionately for Epicureanism, was Lucretius (Titus Lucretius Carus, at work 65–55). In six hexameter books he composed his remarkable poem *De rerum natura* ("On Nature"), a memorable exposition of his love of nature and its essential creativity and his passionate belief in Epicurean natural philosophy as it bears upon primary human anxieties, superstition, and the fear of death.

But the *De rerum natura* is not completely isolated. Lucretius' protest against the disturbances of politics and imminent civil war and his acceptance of the poetic challenges of didactic hexameter ally him with the interests of the revolutionary "New Poets.170 These rejected Roman politics and social issues and adopted the standards and forms of Alexandrian crit. and performance, preferring the brief, highly-wrought genres—epyllion, lyric, epigram, elegiac —to full-scale epic and didactic with their traditional themes. Our sole survivor from this learned group is Gaius Valerius Catullus (84?–54?), whose range was remarkably wide. He wrote epyllia in the Hellenistic fashion which brilliantly manifest variety and beauty of texture, care for responsion and juxtaposition, and dismay at contemporary pressures, as witnessed in *The Marriage of Peleus and Thetis,* a marvelous exhibition of unity in layered diversity. In his intenser, shorter pieces, however, he turned from Gr. practice—though not from Gr. theory—employing (like Lucilius) the full range of colloquial Lat. in experimental Gr. lyric meters to greet friends, damn enemies, and celebrate or abuse his mistress Lesbia (a name invented to evoke Sappho). These, and esp. the last group, are not the simple effusions that romantic crit. has dotingly supposed: Catullus in love is a learned poet still, and to say that he conveys the immediacy of passion more directly than any other Lat. poet is not to deny the learned intricacy of even his shortest poems.

D. *Augustan.* The Hellenizing New Poets never succeeded in making—if they ever intended—a full break with the didactic-patriotic trad., and their achievements significantly affected the superb and subtle poetry of the next age. This is best shown in the work of Rome's greatest poet, Virgil (Publius Vergilius Maro, 70–19 B.C.). His first major work was the *Eclogues* or *Bucolics*, a collection of ten pastoral poems which observe the New Poets' architectonic structure, intense attention to the word, and approved Hellenistic sources—in this case, Alexandrian Theocritus. But the difference is significant: Virgil's shepherds are not Gr., but It., and his pastorals treat overtly and covertly the way war, love, and literary politics threaten the serenity of the bucolic world. The same tendency is heightened in the *Georgics*, a poem starting from the didactic farming-poem of the Gr. Hesiod, the *Works and Days*, but transforming its agricultural poetics into a representation of human beings (particularly Romans) at the painful task of wringing a living from Nature, now gratified, now defeated, but ultimately heroic in their dedication.

This troubled dedication becomes the central focus of Virgil's *magnum opus*, the *Aeneid*. Ostensibly returning to Homeric epic, Virgil builds upon, not imitates, Homer, and his whole poem functions, in form and subject alike, to marry the hitherto divided trads. of Gr. and Roman sensibility. The achievement of the *Aeneid*'s is the willful creation of a culture, fusing apparently disparate and warring trads. into the full *mythos* of Lat. culture, and this synthesis is perfectly mirrored and supported in the almost miraculous union of form and subject. Poetry and history meet in the *Aeneid* and in the New Rome which is its subject, and the formulation is so perfect that it almost came to be final as well. Virgil, that is, almost usurps the entire trad., for his example (and the prestige of his success) was so great that it practically compelled subsequent poetry into its path and rendered it impossible by its exhaustion of the ground. The poem is strongly but realistically patriotic. It shows the New Rome of Augustus Caesar to be the product of ineluctable fate, but (in line with the New Poets) it deplores the losses to cities and people, both guilty and innocent, that imperial success entails. Aeneas, who embodies the painful dedication of the hero, finally emerges as a tragic and flawed character, and Virgil ends the epic by picturing him as a ruthless killer rather than a creative statesman. Inasmuch as Aeneas represents in mythical terms the achievements of Augustus, there can be no question about Virgil's attitude toward imperial propaganda. He and all the other Augustan poets did not scruple to distance themselves pointedly from the negative tendencies of Augustus' despotism.

Horace (Quintus Horatius Flaccus, 65–8 B.C.) is another example of restrained commitment. His earliest works—the *Epodes*—polished iambic poems based on the Gr. Archilochus—and the *Satires*—much more skillful, polished, and kindly developments of Lucilius' genre—define his mixed view of revolutionary Rome in their survey of human foibles. But in his transfer of the forms of Sappho and Alcaeus into Lat., *Odes*, Books I–III, Horace became both a great poet and the lyric voice of Augustan tensions. These lyrics (written ca. 30–23 and dedicated to Augustus' loyal aide Maecenas) treat, in various Gr. meters, in a felicity of lang. equaled only by Virgil, and in exquisitely formal precision, love and wine lightly, life and death deeply, reflecting the continuing dialogue in Rome between engagement and disengagement, Stoicism and Epicureanism.

Horace's later works consist of a fourth book of *Odes*, where this dialogue is overshadowed by the tensions of approaching old age; an important collection of ethically oriented epistles; the famous *Ars poetica*, a highly problematic versification of literary doctrines attributed to the 3d-c. Gr., Neoptolemus, which formulated for all time the basic Roman literary tenet: the successful poet must mix the useful (*utile*) with the pleasing (*dulce*); and, lastly, a Roman centennial ode.

The mixture of, or tension between, the useful and the pleasing exhibits a different and entertaining blend in another genre. Though Gr. elegiac poetry is various in theme, Roman elegy, which derived from Catullus, Alexandrian elegy, and Gr. and Roman New Comedy, was largely restricted to one theme—love—not in the light Horatian sense, but as the most important thing in the world. The spare-dictioned, deceptively simple elegies of Albius Tibullus (54?–19 B.C.) treat, with flowing structure, only of his mistress (Delia or Nemesis, significantly Gr. names), his farm, peace, and occasionally the praise of his patron, Augustus's disenchanted lieutenant Messalla. Sextus Propertius (ca. 50–after 16), the most violent and original of Augustan poets in his structure, lang., and imagery, also shows little willingness to compromise his amatory world for politics. From the intense, introspective poems on his mistress Cynthia which comprise his earliest collection, he moves to the odd sort of Roman poetry found in his fourth and last book, where, adapting an interest of Gr. Callimachus, he mixes patriotism and amatory themes. It is a mix where love often overshadows heroism or subverts it, where Roman trads. yield to a modern elegiac irony.

Propertius prepares the way for Ovid, with his much more obvious irreverence for Roman conventions and his almost total engagement with the values he perceives in love. Publius Ovidius Naso (43 B.C.–A.D.17?) utilized every bit of his formidable rhetorical training in his poetry, seeking, even at his wittiest, to elicit the underlying reality by an intense exploration of the conventional poses of the amatory elegist. Thus, in his love elegies, the

Amores and *Heroides* (verse letters cleverly imagined as written by famous women of Gr. mythology to their absent, usually faithless lovers), and even in his double-edged satirical treatments of didacticism and love-practice (*The Art of Love* and *The Remedy of Love*), he develops the unheard-of concept of equality between the partners in a love affair. But erotic poetry won him no favor with Augustus. When Ovid's greatest work, the *Metamorphoses*, potentially a patriotic epic in its size and use of heroic meter, the hexameter, turned out to be an interweaving (on the thread of "form-changing") of 250-odd stories and epyllia, which, in typical elegiac manner, exalted the individual and personal feelings at the expense of temporal and divine authority, Augustus had had enough. Ovid, already compromised by the supposed lasciviousness of *The Art of Love*, committed some accidental political indiscretion and was summarily banished to Tomi on the Black Sea—an event which brought to a premature end his *Fasti*, an irreverent elegiac poem on the Roman calendar. His last collections, the *Tristia* (Sorrows) and *Epistulae ex Ponto* (Letters from the Black Sea), return to the elegiac lament, protesting his bitter life among Latin-less barbarians but at the same time showing his independence, in spite of his suffering, as poet and man of feeling.

E. *Post-Augustan.* The last considerable age of Cl. Lat. p. shows only too clearly the cramping effects of authoritarianism and the changes made in the social life of poetry by despotism. Rhet., already a danger to poetry, now often became an end rather than a means. The literary past, both Gr. and Roman, assumed enormous prestige and became an inhibiting power—esp. the example of Virgil, whose great success with epic tended to demote other genres by comparison.

Characteristically, Silver Lat. p. exhibits a spectacle of uprooted rhet. that flourishes for its own sake or supports grandiose mythological (Gr.) structures lacking almost any social or political relevance to the times. Socially, it is the age when gifted poets beg for patronage, rich aristocrats dabble in poetry, and both types perform their works in public recitations. Many of the subjects focus on horror, perverse crimes, cosmic disorder, and the apparent triumph of evil, but they have a convenient distance as myths or long-past Roman history. In satire, however, Silver Lat. verse engages itself with contemporary immorality with great vigor and power, and its colloquial or unorthodox style combines with rhetorical techniques in an especially successful way.

Much of this poetry may be dismissed as little more than pious imitation of Virgil, as in the Virgilian pastorals of Calpurnius Siculus (under Nero) or the wretched Virgilian epic on the career of Scipio Africanus, the 17-book *Punica* of Silius Italicus (late 1st c.). Usually, however, Ovid has also exerted his influence, and the blend of Virgil, Ovid, and exuberant rhet. focused on a demonic theme appeals to the tastes of many a subsequent age, notably that of Elizabethan England and our own. The court of Nero (54–68) stimulated many poets, notably Seneca, Persius, and Lucan. Seneca, perhaps while he was tutor, then advisor to young Nero (49–63), perhaps after he prudently retired from the court, produced a series of tragedies on violent, irrational crimes from Gr. myth, which feature malevolent deities, ruthless and unpunished villains, and helpless victims—situations that negate the Stoic order and implicitly call for a new assertion of Stoic values. Aules Persius Flaccus (34–62) wrote satires saturated with Stoic conviction and a passionate appeal to the Roman conscience in a uniquely crabbed style. And Lucan (39–65), Seneca's nephew, at first a favorite then a hated rival of the artistically pretentious Nero, reacted so violently to the despotic emperor that he turned his magnificent epic, the *Civil War* (ostensibly about the conflict between Julius Caesar and the Senate in 49–6 B.C.), into a platform for shrill editorial rhet. against the political system that spawned and protected Nero. He too appeals to Stoicism and the heroic resistance to the tyranny that has enslaved Romans.

After another Civil War in 68–69, another imperial family came to power for nearly 30 years, and in its last member, the unstable and cruel Domitian, it promoted the fortunes of Statius and Martial, both men of nonRoman and unaristocratic backgrounds, and both in desperate need of patronage. Statius (ca. A.D.40–95), son of a schoolmaster, wrote much occasional verse, published in a collection called the *Silvae*, while devoting his main efforts over 12 years to his epic the *Thebaid* (on the senseless tragedy of the Seven Against Thebes). In the end, he did not feel that Rome had adequately rewarded his poetic efforts and retired to Naples to die. Martial (ca. 40–102) came to Rome from Spain, with high hopes of capitalizing on the Sp. friends of Nero, but he found himself struggling under the new dynasty, with some success though he likes to portray himself as a needy client, until the murder of Domitian in 96 put the poet in trouble with the angry men who came to power. He too was obliged to retire to his native Sp. town. But his epigrams are a fine, genial legacy of the period, sentimental or witty, often naughtily so, about life in the most brilliant and corrupt city of antiquity.

In the next "liberated" generation appears Juvenal (at work 100–30), who starts from the theme of violent Roman reaction against the tyrant Domitian but develops his own themes, Roman and general, as time passes. His tight and memorably phrased indictments of human pretense and weakness are Rome's greatest, wittiest, and angriest satires, an able use of the rhetorical techniques that had overwhelmed others' efforts. For the next three cs., Virgil, Ovid, and rhet. variously influenced Lat. p., and capable writers of Lat. verse came from all parts of the Empire to Rome or wherever the emperor made his residence. In the 3d and 4th cs., the poets began to divide over conservative Roman religion and the new Christianity. Contemporaries, Claudian from Africa was a staunch pagan, while Prudentius from Spain wrote only on Christian topics as Alaric approached, to bring Cl. Lat. p. to an end, bereft of a home, and to turn Rome into a symbolic topic for medieval poets.

See also GREEK POETRY, *Classical.*

BIBLIOGRAPHY: *L'Année philologique* 1–(1927–); *The Cl. World Bibl. of Roman Drama and Poetry* (1978); *Gr. and Roman Authors: A Checklist of Crit.*, ed. T. Gwinup and F. Dickinson, 2d ed. (1982)—covers 70 authors.

GENERAL: W. Y. Sellar, *Roman Poets of the Augustan Age,* 2 v. (1897); H. E. Butler, *Post-Augustan Poetry* (1909); T. Frank, *Life and Lit. in the Roman Republic* (1930); J. F. D'Alton, *Roman Lit. Theory and Crit.* (1931); H. J. Rose, *A Handbook of Lat. Lit.*, 2d ed. (1949); J. W. Duff, *A Lit. Hist. of Rome,* ed. A. M. Duff, 3d ed., 2 v. (1953, 1964); G. Williams, *Trad. and Originality in Roman Poetry* (1968), *Change and Decline: Roman Lit. in the Early Empire* (1978); *CHCL*, v. 2; *Nouvelle Histoire de la littérature latine,* ed. R. Herzog and P. L. Schmidt (1990).

SPECIALIZED STUDIES: P. Nixon, *Martial and the Mod. Epigram* (1927); M. M. Crump, *The Epyllion from Theocritus to Ovid* (1931); A. L. Wheeler, *Catullus and the Trads. of Ancient Poetry* (1934); H. F. Fraenkel, *Ovid: A Poet Between Two Worlds* (1945); L. P. Wilkinson, *Horace and His Lyric Poetry* (1945), *Ovid Recalled* (1955), *Golden Lat. Artistry* (1963); G. E. Duckworth, *The Nature of Roman Comedy* (1952); G. Highet, *Juvenal the Satirist* (1954); F. O. Copley, *Exclusus Amator: A Study in Lat. Love Poetry* (1956); E. Fränkel, *Horace* (1957); K. Quinn, *The Catullan Revolution* (1959); S. Commager, *The Odes of Horace* (1962); V. Pöschl, *The Art of Vergil,* tr. G. Seligson (1962); C. O. Brink, *Horace on Poetry,* 3 v. (1963–82); B. Otis, *Virgil; A Study in Civilized Poetry* (1963), *Ovid as Epic Poet* (1970); N. Rudd, *The Satires of Horace* (1966); E. Segal, *Roman Laughter* (1968); W. S. Anderson, *The Art of the* Aeneid (1969), *Essays on Roman Satire* (1982); G. Luck, *The Lat. Love Elegy* (1969); D. O. Ross, Jr., *Style and Trad. in Catullus* (1969), *Backgrounds to Augustan Poetry: Gallus, Elegy and Rome* (1975); D. West, *The Imagery and Poetry of Lucretius* (1969); M. C. J. Putnam, *The Poetry of the* Aeneid (1965), *Virgil's Pastoral Art* (1970), *Virgil's Poem of the Earth* (1979), *Essays on Lat. Lyric, Elegy, and Epic* (1982), *Artifices of Eternity* (1986); E. H. Guggenheimer, *Rhyme Effects and Rhyming Figures* (1972); D. Vessey, *Statius and the* Thebaid (1973); *Seneca,* ed. C. D. Costa (1974); J. Wright, *Dancing in Chains: the Stylistic Unity of the Comoedia Palliata* (1974); G. K. Galinsky, *Ovid's Metamorphoses: An Intro. to the Basic Aspects* (1975); F. M. Ahl, *Lucan. An Intro.* (1976), *Metaformations: Soundplay and Wordplay in Ovid and Other Cl. Poets* (1985); M. Coffey, *Roman Satire* (1976); F. Cairns, *Tibullus: A Hellenistic Poet at Rome* (1979); R. O. A. M. Lyne, *The Lat. Love Poets* (1980); R. Jenkyns, *Three Cl. Poets: Sappho, Catullus, Juvenal* (1982); M. Morford, *Persius* (1984); R. L. Hunter, *The New Comedy of Greece and Rome* (1985); H.-P. Stahl, *Propertius: "Love" and "War": Individual and State under Augustus* (1985); F. Verducci, *Ovid's Toyshop of the Heart: Epistulae Heroidum* (1985); R. Kilpatrick, *The Poetry of Friendship: Horace, Epistles I* (1986); S. Goldberg, *Understanding Terence* (1986); P. Veyne, *Roman Erotic Elegy* (tr. 1988); J. K. Newman, *Roman Catullus* (1990).

W.A.; D.S.P.; W.S.A.

II. MEDIEVAL. Early evidence of Christian Lat. poetry is sparse and random. If Commodian, who offers doctrine and exhortation in an accentual approximation of the Cl. hexameter, was indeed a 3d-c. African, he is an isolated phenomenon. Indicative of things to come are two short narratives, on Jonah and on the destruction of Sodom, written in skillful hexameters (ca. 300), and the beautiful *Phoenix* attributed to Lactantius (ca. 310), wholly pagan in detail but to the early Middle Ages plainly a celebration of the Resurrection.

A coherent Christian Lat. trad. emerges in the 4th c., deliberately conceived as an alternative to the pagan classics on which all learned Christians had been reared, but in effect an extension of the cl. trad. The *cento* of Proba (mid 4th c.) is a mere pastiche of tags from Virgil. What is innovative in Juvencus' hexameter rendering of the Gospels (ca. 330) and the freer version in Sedulius' *Carmen paschale* (ca. 430) is their ingenuity in adapting Virgilian style to Christian purposes; and Paulinus of Nola (353–431) expresses his resolve to repudiate pagan models and write a new kind of poetry in verse richly evocative of Virgil, Ovid, and Horace. Prudentius (348–405), master of many cl. styles and genres, was a brilliant original whose complex attitude toward both Christian and pagan culture we are only beginning to fathom. His *Psychomachia,* a short epic on the conflict of virtue and vice in the human soul, greatly influenced medieval iconography, and his elaborate hymns were incorporated in simplified form into the Church liturgy.

The Christian Lat. poets were to coexist with, and even displace, the great pagans in the school curriculum of the early Middle Ages, but they had few imitators. More significant for Med. Lat. poetry was the hymnody which appeared as Lat. replaced Gr. as the lang. of the liturgy. The cumbersome, dogmatic verse of Hilary of Poitiers (310–66) can hardly have had a liturgical function, and the rhythmical prose of the great *Te Deum,* despite its early and abiding popularity, was not imitated; Med. Lat. hymnody begins with Ambrose (340–97), who provided his Milanese congregation with meditations appropriate to the liturgical hours and calendar couched in 4-line strophes of iambic dimeter. Psychologically profound, and written in beautiful and surprisingly cl. Lat., the Ambrosian hymns were widely imitated and came to form the nucleus of the medieval hymnaries; their form, 4-stress lines in quatrains, has been preserved with only minor variations down to the present day, as may be seen in the Metrical Index of any hymnal.

The upheavals of the later 5th c. left their mark on the Christian Lat. trad. The bookish verse of Sidonius Apollinaris (d. 480) reflects its survival in an attenuated form in Gaul; the "epic" trad. of Prudentius and Sedulius enjoys a late flowering in the *De laudibus Dei* of Dracontius (ca. 450–500); and the verse in Boethius' *Consolation of Philosophy* (ca. 524), a prosimetrum including a range of meters imitated from Horace and Seneca, is a last manifestation of inherited familiarity with Cl. culture. The verse epistles and occasional poems of Fortunatus (535–604), charming and often brilliantly innovative, show a marked loss of syntactic and metrical fluency, though his passion-hymns *Vexilla regis* and *Pange, lingua* are among the greatest of Christian hymns. The Cl. trad. is still alive in the poems of Eugenius of Toledo (fl. ca. 650) and resurfaces with the Carolingian court poets, but new developments were also taking place. Rhyme and accentual meters begin to appear, most notably in Ir. hymnody, evidently influenced by native Celtic verseforms and the rules of rhythmical prose formulated by the Lat. grammarians, culminating in the *Altus prosator* of Columbanus (d. 597). Correct Lat. verse in quantitative meters continued to be taught in schools and written by the learned past the 16th c., but accentually measured Lat. verse is the rule after the 4th c., paving the way for the accentually based prosodies of the vernaculars (Beare). The riddles of Aldhelm (d. 709), which inaugurated a popular genre, imitate the African Lat. poet Symphosius, and the metrical life of Cuthbert by Bede (673–736) is couched in a fluent hexameter shaped by 4th-c. Christian models, but the high points of 8th-c. It. Lat. poetry are a rhythmical poem in praise of the city of Milan (ca. 738) and the accentual verse experiments of Paulinus of Aquileia (d. 802). Paulinus' somber lament on the death of Eric of Friuli (799) is an early and influential example of the *planctus*, which became a popular form and may reflect the influence of vernacular trad.

The poets who came to the court of Charlemagne brought their culture with them; much of the poetry of Paul the Deacon (d. 802) was written before he left Italy, and Theodulf (d. 821) and Alcuin (d. 804) were products of thriving schools in Spain and England. But Charles and his court inspired new poetry. Panegyric epistles by Alcuin and Theodulf, and the *Karolus Magnus et Leo Papa* (ca. 800) attributed to Einhard, celebrate Charles as the champion of political and cultural renewal, and Aachen as a new Rome. The poetry of the court includes charming occasional poems by Paul the Deacon and Theodulf's satire on the courts of law, but its finest product is the Christian Lat. pastoral, best illustrated by Alcuin's nightingale poems, his *O mea cella*, and a "Conflict of Winter and Spring," probably his, which is both a pastoral and perhaps the first example of the debate-poem or *Streitgedicht*, a form imitated in Sedulius Scotus' "Contest of the Lily and the Rose" (ca. 850) and the "Eclogue" of the pseudonymous "Theodulus" (9th–10th c.), and widely popular in later centuries, e.g. "The Owl and the Nightingale" in ME.

The later 9th and 10th c. produced further new departures. The hexameter narrative of an anonymous "Poeta Saxo" (ca. 890) celebrates the deeds of Charlemagne as an example for the Emperor Arnulf, and Abbo of St. Germain combines war poetry with moral reflections on the state of France in a poem on the Norman siege of Paris (ca. 897). The remarkable *Waltharius*, commonly attributed to Ekkehard of St. Gall (900–73) but possibly earlier, balances the impulsive and bombastic heroism of Attila against the less heroic but more sophisticated behavior of Walter of Aquitaine and his companions, providing a perspective at once sympathetic and detached on the trad. of Germanic heroism and heroic poetry that it evokes. Vernacular culture is probably reflected also in the *Ecbasis captivi* (ca. 950), a rambling beast-fable in leonine hexameters apparently written for the edification of young monks; in the mid 11th-c. *Ruodlieb*, the adventures of a wandering knight, based partly on an oriental tale, provide an early foretaste of chivalric romance.

This period was also a time of innovation in religious music, its most significant form being the sequence, sung at Mass between the Epistle and the Gospel, in which the emotional and dramatic scope of religious lyric is greatly expanded. The origins of the sequence are much debated, though the impulse it reflects is present in emotionally expressive poems like the *Versus de Lazaro* of Paulinus or the *O mi custos* of Gottschalk (ca. 825). A shaping influence (formerly thought to be the originator of the sequence) was Notker of St. Gall (d. 912), whose *Liber hymnorum* expresses a range of spiritual feeling, often in striking dramatic monologues and set forth in rhythmically parallel phrases designed for antiphonal singing. His work anticipates the religious poetry of Peter Damian and Peter Abelard and the great achievements of Franciscan hymnody.

The devel. of the secular lyric is even harder to trace, but as early as the mid 10th c. the lang. of the *Song of Songs* was being used to celebrate an idealized beloved in a way which clearly anticipates the courtly lyric of the 12th c. The mid-11th-c. "Cambridge Songs" ms. includes the sophisticated *O admirabile veneris idolum*, addressed to a beautiful boy; *Levis exsurgit Zephirus*, which dwells on the interplay of emotion and natural setting in the manner of high medieval lyric; and the magnificent *Iam dulcis amica venito*, here a passionate lovesong but found elsewhere in a form adapted to religious use. The 12th c. saw a great flowering of secular love-lyric, ranging from imitations of popular song to elaborate essays in love-psychology and *courtoisie* by poets such as Walter of Châtillon (b. 1135) and Peter of Blois (ca. 1135–1212). Many of the best of these are gathered in collections such as the early 13th-c. *Carmina Burana*, which also includes drinking songs, narrative love-visions like *Phyllis and Flora* and *Si linguis angelicis* (which anticipate the *Romance of the Rose*), and satire in the trad. of "Goliardic" verse, in which poets such as Hugh Primas (fl. ca. 1150) and the anonymous "Archpoet" of Cologne (fl. 1160s) make their own misfortunes and dissipations, real or imagined, an occasion for discussing the ills of the world.

Religious poetry, too, appears in new forms in this period. The sequence form, now evolved into accentual verse with a regular rhyme scheme, provided a model for the powerful series of *planctus* in which Abelard (1079–1142) dramatizes the sufferings of such Old Testament figures as Samson, Dinah, and the daughter of Jepthah. In the sequences of Adam of St. Victor (d. 1177–92), subtle allegorical and theological arguments appear in forms as intricate as any lyric poetry of the period, and the sonorous rhyming hexameters of the *De contemptu mundi* of Bernard of Morlas (ca. 1140) give a new force to religious satire.

Side by side with these new departures is a steadily evolving trad. of "learned" Lat. poetry based on Cl. models. Already in the late 11th c., Marbod of Rennes (1035–1123), Hildebert of Le Mans (1056–1133), and Baudri of Bourgueil (1046–1130) had produced a new, urbane poetry, Ovidian in form and manner and devoted to such topics as friendship and the cultivation of relations with noble patrons. The renewal of Cl. studies in the 12th-c. cathedral schools led to more ambitious exercises. Bernardus Silvestris' *Cosmographia* (ca. 1147) and the *De planctu naturae* (ca. 1170) of Alan of Lille, philosophical allegories in the trad. of Boethius and Martianus Capella, exhibit a new assurance vis-à-vis the great authors of antiquity. Alan's *Anticlaudianus* (1182–83), on the creation of the perfect man, announces itself as a new kind of epic, and the *Alexandreis* of Walter of Châtillon (1182), Joseph of Exeter's *Ilias* (1188–90), and John of Hanville's virtually all-encompassing Juvenalian satire *Architrenius* (1184) reflect similar ambition, while Geoffrey of Vinsauf provided a latter-day equivalent to Horace's *Ars poetica* in his *Poetria nova* (1216). Later critics such as John of Garland (d. 1258) and Hugh of Trimberg (fl. ca. 1280) could claim these writers as modern *auctores* worthy of the respect and study accorded the ancients. In addition, the 12th and early 13th cs. produced a range of school-poetry in less ambitious but widely popular forms: topical satires like the mock-visionary *Apocalypse of Golias*, aimed at ecclesiastical corruption, and the *Speculum stultorum* of Nigel de Longchamps, an elaborate beast-fable allegorizing monastic ambition; narrative imitations of ancient comedy like the *Pamphilus*, which had a lasting influence on love-narrative in several langs.; and a body of pseudo-Ovidian poetry incl. the mock-autobiographical *De vetula*, which was long considered an authentic Ovidian work.

A number of the greatest examples of medieval religious poetry date from the later 13th c., notably the *Philomena* of John Howden (d. 1275), a meditation on the power of love as exemplified in the lives of Christ and the Virgin; the hymns and sequence for the feast of Corpus Christi traditionally attributed to Thomas Aquinas (1229–74), the highest achievement of theological poetry in the trad. of Adam of St. Victor; and the work of a number of Franciscan poets, above all the *Dies irae* and *Stabat mater dolorosa* associated with the names of Thomas of Celano (d. 1255) and Jacopone da Todi (1230–1306). But in other areas the great proliferation of vernacular lit. led to a decline in the production of Lat. poetry, and the typical 13th-c. works are didactic treatises, designed to systematize and compress the materials of the traditional curriculum, secular and religious, in accordance with the needs of a newly compartmentalized system of education. Examples include the *De laudibus divinae sapientiae* of Alexander Nequam (d. 1217), an encyclopedic review of Creation as a manifestation of divine wisdom; the *Aurora*, a versified biblical commentary by Peter Riga (d. 1209); and the *Integumenta Ovidii* of John of Garland. The 14th c. produces such late flowerings as the devotional verse of the Eng. mystic Richard Rolle (d. 1349) and the powerful anatomy of the social ills of England in the *Vox clamantis* (1380–86) of John Gower, but the most significant work of this period, the Lat. verse of Dante, Petrarch, and Boccaccio, belongs to the history of the Ren.

See also BYZANTINE POETRY; MEDIEVAL POETRY.

ANTHOLOGIES AND TEXTS: MGH, *Poetae latini aevi Carolini*, ed. E. Dümmler, L. Traube, P. von Winterfeld, and K. Strecker, 5 v. (1881–1937); Migne, *PG* and *PL*—the fullest collection of texts; *Analecta hymnica*—the fullest collections of hymns; *Carmina Burana*, ed. J. A. Schmeller, 4th ed. (1907)—the only complete text, later ed. by A. Hilka and O. Schumann, though only v. 1, pts. 1–2, v. 2, pt. 1, and v. 3, pt. 1, have appeared to date (1931–71); *Early Lat. Hymns*, ed. A. S. Walpole (1922); *Med. Lat. Lyrics*, 5th ed. (1948), *More Lat. Lyrics from Virgil to Milton* (1977), both ed. and tr. H. Waddell; *The Goliard Poets*, ed. and tr. G. F. Whicher (1949); F. Brittain, *The Med. Lat. and Romance Lyric*, 2d ed. (1951); *Oxford Book of Med. Lat. Verse*, ed. F. J. E. Raby (1959); *Hymni latini antiquissimi xxv*, ed. W. Bulst (1975); *Seven Versions of Carolingian Pastoral*, ed. R. P. H. Green (1980); *Poetry of the Carolingian Ren.*, ed. P. Godman (1985)—long intro.

HISTORY, CRITICISM, AND PROSODY: Keil—collects the principal Med. Lat. grammarians and prosodists; Meyer; Manitius—the standard lit. hist.; H. Walther, *Das Streitgedicht in der lateinische Literatur des Mittelalters* (1920); Faral; Lote; Curtius; Raby, *Christian* and *Secular*; D. Norberg, *Poésie latine rythmique* (1954); Beare—good survey; M. Burger, *Recherches sur la structure et l'origine des vers romans* (1957); K. Strecker, *Intro. to Med. Lat.*, tr. and rev. R. B. Palmer (1957)—with excellent intro. and bibl., and "Mittellateinische Dichtung in Deutschen" in *Reallexikon I*; Norberg—best account of Med. Lat. prosody; Norden—artprose; A. C. Friend, "Med. Lat. Lit." in Fisher; M. R. P. McGuire, *Intro. to Med. Lat. Studies* (1964); J. Szövérffy, *Annalen der lateinische Hymnendichtung*, 2 v. (1964–65), *Weltliche Dichtungen des lateinische Mittelalters*, v. 1 (1970), *Lat. Hymns* (1989); Dronke; Lausberg—rhet.; Murphy—survey of med. rhet.; F. Brunhölzl, *Geschichte der lateinischen Literatur des Mittelalters*, 1–(1975–; Fr. tr., 2 v., 1990); P. Dronke, *The Med. Lyric*, 2d ed. (1978), *The Med. Poet and His World* (1985); C. Witke, *Numen litterarum* (1971); P. Klopsch, *Einführung in die mittellateinische Verslehre* (1972); J. Stevens, *Words and Music in the Middle Ages* (1980); *The Interp. of Med. Lat. P.*, ed. W. T. H. Jackson (1980); Brogan, 720 ff.; P. Godman, *Poets and Emperors* (1987); O. B. Hardison, Jr., *Prosody and Purpose in the Eng. Ren.* (1989)—incl. Med. Lat. W.W.; T.V.F.B.

III. RENAISSANCE AND POST-RENAISSANCE. The Ren. turned away from medieval varieties of rhythm and rhyme in Lat. p. towards versification based on a closer study and understanding of the forms of Cl. Antiquity. The result, from the 14th to the early 17th c., was not only a flood of poetry in the vernacular langs. and meters imitating Cl. themes and forms, and poetry in vernacular langs. imitating Cl. meters, but also an immense output of Lat. verse itself. Petrarch (1304–74) showed the way with hundreds of hexameters on personal and intimate themes in his three books of *Epistolae metricae* (Metrical Letters, 1333–54). Petrarch also attempted a hexameter epic on the Punic Wars, *Africa* (1338–41), left incomplete after many revisions, and 12 eclogues, *Bucolicum carmen* (Pastoral Songs, 1346–68), that allegorize his ideas on poetry and politics. Similar incursions into epic and pastoral marked the history of Lat. p. in the 15th c., e.g. the incomplete *Sforzias* by Francesco Filelfo (1398–1481) about the author's Milanese patrons; a supplementary 13th book of the *Aeneid* by the humanist Maffeo Veggio (1406–58); and ten widely admired eclogues by Mantuan (Battista Spagnoli, 1447–1516) that recall models by Virgil and Petrarch while yet evincing a distinctive piety, humor, and satire.

Further, some of the best Ren. Lat. p. appeared in Cl. forms that Petrarch did not use, such as epigram, elegy, and ode. Panormita (Antonio Beccadelli, 1394–1471) initiated Naples' Golden Age with his *Hermaphroditus* (1425), two books of licentious epigrams that out-Martial Martial. His protégé, Giovanni Pontano (1429–1503), wrote with skill in many genres, incl. four sets of elegies in the Ovidian manner, the early *Parthenopeus* for his mistress Fannia, the mature *De amore coniugali* for his beloved wife Adriana, the late *Eridanus* for young Stella, and finally *De tumulis* (Burial Mounds) for deceased loved ones.

The finest Ren. Lat. p. is supremely conscious of its imitative debt to Cl. texts, and it gains a characteristic resonance from the explicit recall of ancient poetry. At the Florentine Academy, Angelo Poliziano (1454–94) urged poets by precept and example in five verse essays, *Silvae* (Forests, 1475–86), to cultivate Cl. allusions. Poliziano himself produced some of the finest Ren. epigrams in a Cl. vein in his *Epigrammata* (1498), as did his friend and later rival Michael Marullus (ca. 1453–1500) in four books of short poems on his exile from Constantinople and his love for his mistress Neaera. But Marullus's greatest work was his four books of *Hymni naturales* (Hymns of Nature) in various meters—hexameter, Alcaic, Sapphic, iambic—proclaiming the tenets of Neoplatonic philosophy. Two high points of creative imitation were attained by the Neapolitan Jacopo Sannazaro (1458–1530): the *Piscatoriae* (Piscatorial Eclogues, 1526) that adapt to a seaside setting conventional rhetorical structures of pastorals by Virgil, Calpurnius, and Nemesianus; and an epic on Christ's nativity, *De partu virginis* (Virgin Birth, 1526), that appropriates formulas, expressions, and even whole lines from the epics of Virgil, Ovid, Claudian, and others.

The more Ren. humanists sought to recover the past, the greater they realized their distance from it. Their imitations of ancient poetry only drew attention to incontrovertible differences between pagan Classicism and Christian humanism. One consequence was an effort to develop new forms and thus expand the repertory of Lat. p. The disillusioned Venetian historian Andrea Navagero (1483–1529), e.g., destroyed his own didactic verse, but his heirs managed to publish his lively experiment in 47 pastoral epigrams, *Lusus pastoralis* (Pastoral Diversions, 1530), with great impact on both Lat. p. and the vernacular. In yet another notable departure, Girolamo Fracastoro (1483–1553), a professor of medicine at Padua, wrote *Syphilis* (1530), three books attributing the origins of venereal disease to the New World and proposing a cure.

The Reformation in the North and the Counter-Reformation in Italy accentuated the religious intensity of much Lat. p. Marcantonio Flaminio (1498–1550), e.g., renounced his own early pastoral diversions in order to devote himself to paraphrases of the Psalms in Cl. meters, *Davidis psalmi* (1546), and other *Carmina sacra* (1551). After publishing an influential versified *De arte poetica* (1527), Marco Girolamo Vida (1485–1566) composed a hexameter epic on the life of Jesus, *Christias* (1535), and a collection of Christian *Hymni* (1550).

The devel. of Ren. Lat. p. beyond the Alps followed similar patterns, confirming the use of Lat. as a truly international lang. The Hungarian poet Janus Pannonius (1434–72) and the Ger. poet

Conrad Celtis (1459–1508) wrote elegies, epigrams, hexameters, and hendecasyllables about their education in Italy and their efforts to bring humanist teachings to the North. The Fr. poet Salmon Macrin (1490–1557) graced the courts of Francis I and Henry II with a vast output of elegies, hymns, epithalamia, and assorted political verse. The Dutch poet Joannes Secundus (1511–36) displayed metrical and ling. virtuosity in odes, epigrams, epistles, and three books of elegies, but he earned fame throughout Europe for his *Basia* (Kisses), 19 voluptuous songs for a mistress named after Marullus's beloved Neaera, at once appropriating the erotic lyric from antiquity and announcing his competition with It. Ren. poets.

With the devel. of the vernaculars and the prestige of their lits. throughout Europe in the 16th c., many poets who wrote superb Lat. lyrics turned to their own langs. for more ambitious projects. Lodovico Ariosto (1474–1533) in Italy, Joachim Du Bellay (ca. 1525– 60) in France, Jan Kochanowski (1530–84) in Poland, and John Milton (1608–74) in England exemplify the trend. Notable exceptions include two 17th-c. Jesuit poets, Maciej Kazimierz Sarbiewski (1595–1640) in Poland and Jacob Balde (1604–68) in Germany, who wrote exquisite religious lyrics that accommodate scriptural poetics to Cl. meters. Though vernacular lit. finally gained ascendance, the composition of Lat. p. has survived even until our own day in schools and universities as an accomplishment proper to a Cl. scholar.

ANTHOLOGIES: *Poeti latini del quattrocento*, ed. F. Arnaldi et al. (1964)—with It. trs.; *Lateinische Gedichte deutscher Humanisten*, ed. H. C. Schnur (1967)—with Ger. trs.; *Musae reduces*, ed. P. Laurens, 2 v. (1975)—with Fr. trs.; *An Anthol. of Neo-Lat. P.*, ed. F. J. Nichols (1979)—with Eng. trs.; *Ren. Lat. Verse*, ed. A. Perosa and J. Sparrow (1979).

EDITIONS AND TRANSLATIONS: Johannes Secundus, *Love Poems*, ed. and tr. F. A. Wright (1930), and in *The Lat. Love Elegy*, ed. and tr. C. Endres (1981); G. Fracastoro, *Syphilis*, ed. and tr. H. Wynne-Finch (1935); Conrad Celtis, *Selections*, ed. and tr. L. Forster (1948); M. K. Sarbiewski, *Odes*, tr. G. Hils (1646), ed. M.-S. Roestvig (1953); J. Sannazaro, *Arcadia and the Piscatorial Eclogues*, tr. R. Nash (1966); J. Milton, *Variorum: Lat. and Gr. Poems*, ed. and tr. D. Bush et al. (1970); A. Navagero, *Lusus*, ed. and tr. A. E. Wilson (1973); Petrarch, *Bucolicum carmen*, ed. and tr. T. G. Bergin (1974), *Africa*, tr. T. G. Bergin (1977); M. G. Vida, *De arte poetica*, ed. and tr. R. G. Williams (1976), *Christiad*, ed. and tr. G. C. Drake and C. A. Forbes (1978); *Ren. Lat. P.*, ed. and tr. I. D. McFarlane (1980).

HISTORY AND CRITICISM: L. Bradner, *Musae Anglicanae: A Hist. of Anglo-Lat. Poetry 1500–1925* (1940); P. Van Tieghem, *La Lit. lat. de la Ren.* (1944); L. Spitzer, "The Problem of Lat. Ren. Poetry," *SP* 2 (1955); G. Ellinger and B. Ristow, "Neulateinische Dichtung im Deutschlands im 16. Jh.," *Reallexikon* 2.620–45; J. Sparrow, "Lat. Verse of the High Ren.," *It. Ren. Studies*, ed. E. F. Jacob (1960); W. L. Grant, *Neo-Lat. Lit. and the Pastoral* (1965); J. Ijsewijn, *Companion to Neo-Lat. Studies* (1977); W. J. Kennedy, *Jacopo Sannazaro and the Uses of Pastoral* (1983). W.J.K.

LATVIAN POETRY. The beginnings of L. p., indeed its very roots, are to be found in L. folksongs called *dainas.* Most of the dainas date from the days of serfdom and express the L. ethos that has changed little over the cs.: respect for nature, a work ethic, attitudes that edify family ties, forebearance, emotional restraint. These motifs are often found in L. p.

L. lit. proper begins in the middle of the 19th c. with the so-called National Awakening movement, a movement primarily initiated by L. intellectuals, some of them gifted poets who, inspired by the Fichtean notion of *Volksseele,* turned to indigenous sources (national history, folklore, mythology) for the inspiration and subject matter of their poetic efforts. Juris Alunāns (1832–64) inaugurates L. p. with his opuscule, *Dziesminas* (Ditties), in 1856, which set a precedent. The volume, however, is distinctly a notch above the devotional verse offered up to that time by well-meaning Ger. pastors whose knowledge of L. was very minimal. This generation of committed poets, most of them students at the University of Tartu, set the tone for what was to become known as "national romanticism." Among them: Auseklis (pseudonym of Mikelis Krogzems, 1850–79), a fiery poet much inspired by Schiller; Andrējs Pumpurs (1841–1902), who in imitation of the Finnish and Estonian national epics attempted a similar feat with his *Lāčplēsis* (The Bearslayer), though with limited success; Krišjānis Barons (1835–1923), known for his labors to collect and classify dainas, the number of which now reaches two million.

A rival intellectual impulse came with Marxism in the 1880s, precipitating a movement called the New Current and thereby an ideological schism that runs deep in L. lit. A syncretic vision, however, is profferred by Jānis Rainis (pseudonym of Jānis Pliekšāns, 1865–1929). The national past and mythology are often sources of his poetry, yet his philosophical thought extends beyond the fold of nationalism to embrace a religion of all humanity. His wife Aspazija (pseudonym of Elza Rozenberga-Pliekšāne, 1868–1943), the first L. feminist, combined in her poetry a flamboyant neoromantic nationalism with a social conscience that inveighs against social and economic injustices and bourgeois prejudices and complacency. Close to Aspazija's emotional intensity in some respects are Fricis Bārda (1880–1919) and Jānis Poruks (1871–1911), poets of lyrical moods and subtle tonalities. Other poets who became popular before World War I include Plūdonis (pseudonym of Vilis Lejnieks, 1874–1940), a master of robust rhymes and rich images, sometimes á la impressionism; Kārlis

Skalbe (1879–1945), a popular poet of simple forms, with affinities to the dainas; and Anna Brigadere (1861–1933), best remembered as the spokesperson of the humble and the young.

With L. national independence in 1918, L. p. became more susceptible to the literary currents of Western Europe. Edvarts Virza (pseudonym of Lieknis, 1883–1940) studied and translated Fr. poetry and became the official voice of the new authoritarian regime installed by a coup d'etat in 1934. His most celebrated work is an extended prose poem, *Straumēni*, that praises the virtues of bucolic life on a L. farmstead. Expressionism left an impact on Pēteris Ērmanis (1893–1969), the first L. poet to experiment with free verse. The coup d'etat brought to the fore a group of staunchly patriotic poets. Jānis Medenis (1903–61) tried to adapt folk meters to modern verse. Zinaīda Lazda (1902–61) became much admired for her lyrical landscapes, her celebration of simple life á la dainas. But there were also poets who deviated from the officially sanctioned poetics. Ēriks Ādamsons (1907–47) was an essentially urban poet, introspective and complex, ironic and refined, scornful of rural simplicities. Aleksandrs Čaks (pseudonym of Čadarainis, 1902–50) is considered the most original modernist and the one whose legacy to the following generation of poets is most felt. Forceful and iconoclastic, mocking and ironic, insisting on the importance of rhythm over rhyme, he shocked the traditionalists and fascinated the young.

In the late 1930s, as Europe was in the throes of apocalyptic events, a new generation of poets came of age. When the Soviet Armies occupied Latvia in 1944, most of them preferred to go into exile. Veronika Strēlerte (pseudonym of Rudīte Strēlerte-Johansone, b. 1912) is a poet of profound meditative moods and restrained patriotic feelings, much appreciated for her finely sculpted verse. Andrējs Eglītis (b. 1912), the widely proclaimed national bard, popular and prolific, is most celebrated for his thunderous poem, "God, Thy land is aflame." Velta Toma (b. 1912), a somewhat controversial figure for her nonconformist ideas, cultivates a forceful personal expression. Velta Snikere (b. 1920), a multifaceted personality, grafts new sensibilities of surrealist penchant onto the folkloric traditions.

Exile nurtured a new generation of poets, who share a certain aversion to loud political commitment and to emotion-drenched rhet. and a distrust for traditional poetic forms. The first cénacle was formed in Manhattan's Hell's Kitchen to become known as the Hell's Kitchen Poets. Among them: Linards Tauns (pseudonym of Arnolds Bērzs, 1922–63), an urban poet fascinated by the Babel of New York City, a visionary seeking more heightened forms of existence; Gunars Salinš (b.1924), who interweaves urban with rural images, folkloric patterns with jazz rhythms; Baiba Bičole (b. 1931) who celebrates, in rites sacred and erotic, encounters with the physical world; Aina Kraujiete (b. 1923), intellectual and erudite, given to ontological adventures, exploring alternate states of being. Outside the cénacle, but aesthetically affinitive, are Astrīde Ivaska (b. 1926), whose subtle tonalities celebrate the preciousness of lang., weaving nuance to nuance, connecting sound and sense in configurations familiar and yet original; and Olafs Stumbrs (b. 1931), whose existential anguish and loneliness subtend the satire of the social scene, much laced with black humor and sarcasm. Andrējs Irbe (b. 1924), living in Sweden, probes the ever-evanescent inner self that intimates affinities with the mysterious Nordic landscape that too escapes finality.

In the homeland, the coevals of the exiles lived on the native soil and among their people, whose lang. constantly replenishes their work. But they also created under duress, never knowing the official level of tolerance for deviation from Soviet doctrine. Vizma Belševica (b. 1931) was first hailed, then silenced, then rehabilitated for her poetry, so often characterized by ontological introspection and contemplation of the collective destinies of the L. people. Imants Ziedonis (b. 1933), prolific and immensely popular, subject to contrapuntal moods, celebrates the beauty of the land and the vitality of the people and mourns the effacement of the past through urbanization and industrialization. Ojārs Vācietis (1933–83), frequently dubbed "the L. Yevtushenko," versatile and impulsive, always managed to remain in the good graces of the Soviet authorities, while not sparing his caustic wit. Māris Čaklais (b. 1940), intensely personal and very popular among the young, combines the rustic and the refined, the spontaneous and the analytic, giving his verse a wide tonal range and a fine filigree texture. Next to these poets another generation, both abroad and in the homeland, has already come to the fore, generally more polyphonic, more acerbic, more experimental than their elders. Most recently, the advent of openness (*glasnost*) and the collapse of the Soviet Union in 1989 are not only certain to leave a lasting impact on the present and future generations but will also necessitate a revaluation of those poets whose works, long suppressed, are now being published.

ANTHOLOGIES: *Latvju modernās dzejas antologija*, ed. A. Čaks and P. Kikuts (1930); *Latviešu tautas dziesmas*, ed. A. Švābe et al., 12 v. (1952–56); *Latvju sonets 100 gados 1856–1956*, ed. K. Dzilleja (1956); *Lettische Lyrik*, ed. E. Eckard-Skalberg (1960); *Dzejas un sejas / Latviešu dzeja svešumā*, ed. T. Zeltinš et al. (1962); *Poetry from Latvia*, ed. J. Anerauds, 3 v. (1982); *Lettische Lyrik*, ed. E. Zuzena-Metuzala (1983); *Contemp. L. P.*, ed. I. Cedrinš (1984).

HISTORY AND CRITICISM: E. Virza, *La Littérature lettonne depuis l'époque de réveil national* (1926); A. Johansons, *Latviešu literatūra* (1953); J. Andrups and V. Kalve, *L. Lit.* (1954); M. Dombrovska, *Latviešu dzeja* (1966); A. Ziedonis, *The Religious*

Philosophy of Janis Rainis, L. Poet (1969); R. Ekmanis, *L. Lit. under the Soviets: 1940–1975* (1978).
J.S.

LITHUANIAN POETRY. Written lit. arose in Lithuania during the Reformation and Counter-Reformation. Before that, the poetic heritage of the nation was sustained by anonymous folk songs (*dainos*), mentioned in medieval sources. These *dainos,* of which about 200,000 have now been recorded, are best represented by lyrical love songs. The lyrical nature of poetic expression is characteristic of *dainos* in general, and it is strongly evident even in the war songs and ballads, while mythological songs are rare and epic narratives are altogether lacking. The most typical of the *dainos* exhibit numerous diminutives and employ highly developed parallelisms and a rather intricate, basically erotic, symbolism. Because the text and melody are integrally connected in the *dainos,* the rhythm is of great importance, and, as a result of the free stress in L., it is variable and often mixed. The rhyme, however, is not essential. The stanzas have mostly two, three, or four lines, either with or without refrain. Some older songs have no stanzas at all. The earliest collection of *dainos* (1825) is by Liudvikas Rėza (Rhesa, 1776–1840), the largest (4 v., 1880–83) by A. Juškevičius (1819–80); much more extensive collections are now being assembled by the L. Academy of Sciences. The trad. of folk poetry became a strong factor in the formation of the distinctly national character of L. p.

Written L. p. begins in the 16th c. with versions of canticles and hymns, incl. those of Martynas Mažvydas (Mosvidius, d. 1563), who also prepared in Königsberg the first printed L. book, *Catechismusa prasti szadei* (The Plain Words of the Catechism, 1547), a tr. of the Lutheran catechism, and prefaced it with a rhymed foreword. The most outstanding 18th-c. work was Kristijonas Donelaitis's (Donalitius, 1714–80) poem *Metai* (The Seasons, 1765–75, pub. 1818), a 3000-line poem in hexameters which exhibits in forceful lang. a keen love and observation of nature and depicts vividly the life and character of the common people. Imbued with the Pietist spirit, the poem transmits a moving sense of the sacredness of life and of the earth. At some points it can be compared with the work of James Thompson and Ewald von Kleist.

A more active literary movement appeared at the beginning of the 19th c., marked first by pseudo-classicism and sentimentalism and later by the influence of romanticism and a growing interest in L. folklore. The latter trend was particularly evident in the poetry of Antanas Strazdas, who was one of the first to merge the folksong trad. with personal expression. The next peak in the devel. of L. p. was Antanas Baranauskas (1835–1902), whose picturesque poem *Anykščiu šilelis* (The Grove of Anykščiai, 1858–59) is a veiled lament for Lithuania under the Rus. czarist regime. Baranauskas was esp. successful in creating a melodious flow of lang. using the traditional syllabic versification that is not very well suited to L. The pre-20th-c. devel. of L. p. was concluded by Maironis (pen name of Jonas Mačiulis, 1862–1932), the creative embodiment of the ideals of the national awakening and a foremost lyric poet (cf. his collection *Pavasario balsai* [Voices of Spring], 1895). His formal and structural innovations, particularly the introduction of syllabotonic versification, had great influence on the growth of the new L. p. Two other poets writing in a lyrical mode in some respects similar to that of Maironis were Antanas Vienažindys (1841–92) and Pranas Vaičaitis (1876–1901).

At the beginning of the 20th c., the general relaxation of Rus. political pressure and the ever growing cultural consciousness increased literary production and widened its horizon. New approaches were inspired by literary movements abroad. Already evident before World War I, these trends were fulfilled during the period of independence (1918–40) when L. p. reached high standards of creative art. Symbolism left a strong imprint on the early period, best represented by Balys Sruoga (1896–1947), also an outstanding dramatist; Vincas Mykolaitis-Putinas (1893–1967), later a leading novelist as well; Faustas Kirša (1891–1964); and Jurgis Baltrušaitis (1873–1944), who, after achieving distinction among the Rus. symbolists, began to publish verse in his native L. around 1930. In the 1920s, the more conservative trends were countered by modernist poets who, led by Kazys Binkis (1893–1942), formed the group *Keturi vėjai* (Four Winds). Somewhat later, neoromanticism, neosymbolism, aestheticism, and expressionism appeared on the scene, while the group *Trečias frontas* (Third Front) advocated poetry of leftist orientation.

These trends were transcended, however, by the individual achievements of the four leading poets of the second generation: Jonas Aistis (1904–73), a highly intimate poet and a master of subtle and refined expression; Bernardas Brazdžionis (b. 1907), whose poetry, sometimes stylistically innovative, sometimes rhetorical and of prophetic overtones, is a synthesis of national trads.; and Antanas Miškinis (1905–83) and Salomėja Neris (pen name of S. Bačinskaitė-Bučienė [1904–45]), both of whom have transformed the best qualities of the *dainos* into their own personal expression. The transitional features leading to the poetry of the next generation were best reflected in the verse of Vytautas Mačernis (1920–44).

The annexation of the country by the USSR during World War II was responsible for the schism that divided L. p. On the one hand, L. p. was haunted until 1989 by the paralyzing specter of Socialist Realism, and on the other, it has been learning to speak in the many modes of Western culture of many things, first of all of the pain and righteousness of exile. While some poets at home became eulogists of the Soviet system, and others, mostly of the older generation, retreated carefully into their ultimate long silence, new authors came forth to claim the favors of both the Muses and the regime and, in recent years, of the Muses alone. Eduardas Mieželaitis (b. 1919), paradoxically a loyal Communist of philosophical bent, did much to help Soviet L. p. break through to a more modern idiom. Justinas Marcinkevičius (b. 1930), also important as playwright, is perhaps the most popular poet today, speaking with great devotion, though at times with a forked tongue, of love for his country and people. Judita Vaičiūnaitė (b. 1937) sings of love in intimate urban settings and of myth in dreams of the past. Sigitas Geda (b. 1943) transforms both nature and myth into a single magical presence, his vision of the country and its soul. Marcelijus Martinaitis (b. 1936) mostly converses with his own and the nation's conscience about history, myth, and the responsibility of being human. Janina Degutytė (1928–90) is an intensely personal, lyrical poet of great integrity and noble dedication to humanity.

A number of prominent artists, writers, and intellectuals found themselves in the forefront of the national movement for independence beginning in 1989. One might say that their first obligation has become to create for themselves a free country, a fitting home for their Muse. Thus history has come full circle, returning to the situation at the end of the 19th c., when the poet's voice was also first of all a clarion for freedom.

In the West the foremost poet is Henrikas Radauskas (1910–70). He speaks in lucid and calmly measured cl. verse of the beauty of the world seen as a carnival of love and death. His loyalty, however, is not with that world but with the enchanting mysteries of poetic speech that it engenders. Jonas Aistis and Bernardas Brazdžionis continue in their previous vein, except that both have adopted a voice of outrage at their nation's destiny. Kazys Bradūnas (b. 1917) looks inward and into the past to awaken the ancient spirits of his native earth and engage them in an ongoing dialogue with Christianity and history in the native land. Jonas Mekas (b. 1922), one of the moving spirits of the "underground cinema" in New York, also writes nostalgic and pensive verse full of self-questioning and yearning for the truthful life. Algimantas Mackus (1932–64) found his own truth in a radical confrontation with the fact of exile which required him to transform all the images of hope and faith from the traditional cultural heritage into grim totems of death. Liūnė Sutema (pen name of Zinaida Katiliškienė, b. 1927) chooses the opposite task of allowing the alien world to grow into the very tissue of her soul to rejuvenate both her and the land of remembrance she carries within. Her brother Henrikas Nagys (b. 1920) embraces both emotional expressionism and Neo-romanticism. Alfonsas Nyka-Niliūnas (pen name of Alfonsas Čipkus, b. 1919), a cosmopolitan existentialist of a deeply philosophical bent, contemplates the large and bleak presence of Cosmos through the window of Western civilization.

ANTHOLOGIES: *The Daina*, ed. U. Katzenelenbogen (1935); *Aus litauischer Dichtung*, ed. and tr. H. Engert, 2d ed. (1938); *Litauischer Liederschrein*, ed. and tr. V. Jungfer (1948); *L. Folksongs in America*, ed. J. Balys (1958); *The Green Oak*, ed. A. Landsbergis and C. Mills (1962); *Lietuviu poezija*, v. 1–2, ed. V. Vanagas, v. 3, ed. K. Bradūnas (1969–71); *Litovskie poety XX veka*, ed. V. Galinis (1971); *Selected Post-War L. P.*, ed. J. Zdanys (1978); *L. Writers in the West*, ed. A. Skrupskelis (1979); *The Amber Lyre: 18th–20th-C. L. P.* (1983); *Chimeras in the Tower: Selected Poems of Henrikas Radauskas*, tr. J. Zdanys (1986).

HISTORY AND CRITICISM: B. Sruoga, "L. Folksongs," *Folk-Lore* (London) 43 (1932); J. Mauclere, *Panorama de la litt. lithuanienne contemporaine* (1938); A. Vaičiulaitis, *Outline Hist. of L. Lit.* (1942); J. Balys, *L. Narrative Folksongs* (1954); A. Senn, "Storia della letterature lituana," *Storia della letterature baltiche*, ed. G. Devoto (1957); A. Rubulis, *Baltic Lit.* (1970); R. Silbajoris, *Perfection of Exile* (1970); P. Naujokaitis, *Lietuviu literatūros istorija*, 4 v. (1973–76); *Istorija litovskoj literatury*, ed. J. Lankutis (1977); *Baltic Drama*, ed. A. Straumanis (1981).

R.S.

LUSOPHONE AFRICAN POETRY. See AFRICAN POETRY, *In French*.

M

MACEDONIAN POETRY. See YUGOSLAV POETRY.

MAGYAR POETRY. See HUNGARIAN POETRY.

MAITHILI POETRY. See INDIAN POETRY.

MALAY POETRY.

I. OLDER AND FOLK MALAY POETRY
II. MODERN MALAY (MALAYSIAN) POETRY

I. OLDER AND FOLK MALAY POETRY is highly romantic and usually derivative of Persian, Indian, Urdu, and Arabic forms, telling tales of aristocratic life and adventures. It does not possess great formal variety. The *shair*, the verseform for narrative poetry, employs monorhymed quatrains and dates from ca. 1600 A.D. In addition to romantic narrative, *shair* also record local conflicts and, in some instances, impart religious knowledge. More enduring, and therefore more important, is M. folk poetry, which is composed of three principal genres: *sesmomba* or *bahasa berirama*, a kind of unrhymed rhythmical verse usually of magical origin and utility; *peribahasa* (proverbs); and *pantun*, constructed of two couplets, rhyming *abab*, the first (known as the *sampiran*) more or less general and the second in some way a narrowing or application of the first. *Bahasa berirama* is probably the oldest of the three genres; it survives today largely in Minangkabau (Sumatran) poetry. It is chanted by a *pawang* (reciter of spells):

> Ha, you disturber of the peace,
> Noise-maker,
> Iron pins grow on my arms,
> Copper pins grow on my legs,
> I've snake poison in my beard,
> Crocodiles hold open my mouth,
> Tigers roar my roar,
> Elephants trumpet with my voice.

M. proverbs are intensely metaphorical and, because the lang. is highly compressed, can be powerfully effective. *Jang rebah, dintidih*: He that falls is pushed farther down. *Anjing ditepak kepala menjengkit ekor*. Pat a dog's head and his tail stands up. "Not even in Fr. is it possible to be so polite, or so rude, or to say such rude things with every appearance of exaggerated courtesy" (*M. Sayings*).

The most commonly employed and most influential M. folk poetry form is the *pantun* (the Eng. and Fr. spellings are "pantoum"):

> Where have you gone to, where were
> you from?
> Weeds grow taller than grain.
> What year, what month will time have
> spun
> Around to when we meet again?

Both sung and recited as well as read, the *pantun* continues to be employed in rural Malaysia and exercises a significant influence on modern M. p. (below).

II. MODERN MALAY POETRY is very different from Indonesian poetry, which like it draws from M. roots. Indonesian poetry is largely directed toward a small, highly educated, urban elite; modern M. p. seeks to be read and appreciated by all who speak Malay, whether urban or rural, and who have at most a secondary education. It is on the whole more open and accessible than Indonesian poetry, simpler and brighter in word-choice and metaphor, though also (esp. to Western tastes) much less subtle and frequently sentimental. The leading poet of contemp. Malaysia is Usman Awang (b. 1929), whose humanistic commitment and poetic bad taste is revealed in lines like "My child and all our children, / Let not their hearts be injured with weapons / Let love bloom on their faces and in their hearts / For a peaceful world, a prosperous life!" (tr. Asraf and J. Kirkup). The "Generation of the Fifties" was followed by a group of writers more interested in imagistic development (and often in religion) than in messages of social transformation. Noor S.I.: "My cup is pure / Drink, my love"; A. S. Amin: "My new life is lighted / By a friend / On the battlefield"; Salmi Manja: "The silent dusk comes alone. / The tabuh beats, the prayer call comes, / And we remember God."

The writers of the 1970s, incl. Latiff Mohidin (b. 1941), Muhhamad Haji Salleh (b. 1942), and Baha Zain (b. 1941), attempt to expand M. p. in more sophisticated directions. Baha Zain Latiff, also a visual artist, works with a vivid poetic vocabulary: "a village of rafts / Floating on the water's skin / A hundred families gathered together / Like leaves of watercress." Salleh, trained in Eng. and Am., probes the nature of M. cultural identity in a time of rapid social change: "The city builds thin walls / Around reality, / Beside canals of acid. / We cannot base civilization / On supply and demand / And old tin mines" (tr. Aveling).

None of these poets, however, has as yet solved the problems of reconciling pressing social and spiritual issues with the demands of a truly effective modern poetry. There is some hope for the future in the increased use of the M. lang. among non-M. communities, and in the government's regular and often generous support of poetry publications. Public interest, too, is high, but the outcome remains uncertain.

ANTHOLOGIES AND TRANSLATIONS: *Pantun Melayu*, ed. R. J. Wilkinson and R. O. Winstedt, 2d ed. (1955); *Kesusteraan Melayu*, ed. R. O. Winstedt, 6 v. (1958); *M. Sayings*, ed. C. C. Brown, 2d ed. (1959); *Mod. M. Verse, 1946–61*, ed. O. Rice and A. Majid (1963); *Selections from Contemp. Malaysian P.*, ed. M. H. Salleh (1978); *Malaysian P. 1975–1985*, ed. A. K. Abdullah, tr. H. Aveling (1987).

HISTORY AND CRITICISM: R. O. Winstedt, *A Hist. of Cl. M. Lit.*, 2d ed. (1961); M. T. Osman, *An Intro. to the Devel. of Mod. M. Lang. and Lit.* (1961); A. Teeuw, "The Origins of the M. *Shair*," *BKI* 122 (1966); U. Junus, *Perkembangan puisi melayu modern* (1970); A. H. Johns, *Cultural Options and the Role of Trad.* (1974); M. H. Salleh, *Trad. and Change in Contemp. M.-Indonesian P.* (1977). B.R.

MALAYALAM POETRY. See INDIAN POETRY.

MAORI POETRY. See NEW ZEALAND POETRY.

MARATHI POETRY. See INDIAN POETRY.

MEXICAN AMERICAN POETRY. See CHICANO POETRY.

MEXICAN POETRY. See SPANISH AMERICAN POETRY.

MONGOLIAN POETRY. The chief source of early M. p. is an imperial chronicle of Genghis Khan's house, the *Secret History of the Mongols* (A.D. 1240), which contains many rough-hewn verses of irregular length. Some later historical chronicles of the 17th c., such as the *Erdeni-yin Tobči* (Jewelled Summary), contain sophisticated and polished quatrains of even length and fixed form, particularly at points of direct discourse in the narrative.

The bulk of native literary expression is in the form of *üliger's,* orally transmitted verse epics, which may reach 20,000 verses in length and are recited from memory by bards. They relate the adventures of real or legendary heroes and villains such as Genghis Khan, Erintsen Mergen, Gesser Khan, and Janggar. These heroes struggle against the many-headed *manggus,* who is defeated in the end. The internal structure of the poems is quite stylized and may be diagrammed as a series of rounds between the hero and his adversary.

M. verse is alliterative (although rhyme is found in a few instances, such as the Sino-M. inscription of 1362). This alliteration chiefly occurs on the initial syllable (the entire syllable, not just the first phoneme), but internal alliteration is also found. There is no set pattern of repetition for the initial alliterating syllables. In epic poetry, alliteration is in couplets or is irregular; in lyric poetry (here used in the strict sense of the word, "composed for the lyre," hence in stanzas), it is in quatrains. The best-styled verse has 7 to 8 syllables with 3 or 4 stresses, but this is only a general guide to its construction. One may also encounter in texts the so-called graphic alliteration, by which some letters of identical shape in the Mongolian script (as t/d, o/u) may alliterate (cf. Eng. "eye rhyme").

The most characteristic formal feature is parallelism, the same idea reiterated in slightly different words in succeeding verses. This usage is very similar to the Hebraic parallelism made familiar by the Old Testament Psalms. The chief theme of M. p. has been the great epic legends, with their elaborate descriptions of heroic deeds, royal palaces, and maidenly beauty. There are also shorter poems with themes of love, nature, and religion.

One of the finest poems in M. is the *Lament of Toghon Temür,* six well-polished stanzas uttered by that ruler when he was driven from Khubilai's palace and the throne of China in 1368. In bemoaning the loss of that residence, he draws on an accretion of M. legends which were likewise used by Marco Polo in his description. This account was later taken by Purchas for his travel book, whence it filtered through Coleridge's subconscious to emerge as *Kubla Khan.*

The following free translation of M. verse employs both initial alliteration as well as end rhyme to convey the nature of the original, although rhyme is not present there. The parallelism between the stanzas will be evident.

Sitting in their hillside bowers (are)
Seven sorts of hillside flowers;
Seven sorts of stories, too,
Soon I'll say in song to you.

Garlands of the gloomy swamp,
Grow eight flowers in their pomp;
Games and gladness, eight kinds too,
Give I gladly now to you.

N. Poppe, *Mongolische Volksdichtung* (1955), "Der Parallelismus in der epischen Dichtung der Mongolen," *Ural-Altaische Jahrbücher* 30 (1958), *Khalkha-mongol'skii geroičeskii epos* [The Heroic Epic of the Khalkha Mongols], 2d ed. (1979); K. Grønbech, "Specimens of M. P.," *The Music of the Mongols* (1943); Damdinsüren, *Monggol uran jokiyal-un degeji jagun bilig orusibai* [One Hundred Extracts from M. Lit.] (1959); J. R. Krueger, "Poetical Passages in the *Erdeni-yin Tobči,* a M. Chronicle of the Year 1662," *Central Asiatic Studies* 7 (1961); F. W. Cleaves, *The Secret Hist. of the Mongols* (1982)—see also the poetic adaptation by P. Kahn (1984) of the same title; *Fragen der mongolischen Heldendichtung,* ed. W. Heissig (1983–). J.R.K.

N

NAVAHO POETRY. See AMERICAN INDIAN POETRY.

NEW ZEALAND POETRY must be seen as comprising several overlapping trads., beginning with a Maori (indigenous Polynesian) oral poetry composed of chants, songs, and choric-dance pieces. This develops alongside, and is influenced by, an intrusive Pakeha (European) presence, partly in missionary (above all, London Missionary Society and Anglican, but also Roman Catholic) hymn writing. Along with sentimental colonial imitations in Eng., there is a Maori poetry of an overt pedagogical and religious nature. Meanwhile, moving toward the 20th c., Pakeha N. Z. verse moves through partial awareness of late Victorian and Georgian conventions in Britain, and only recently, along with openness to influences from

Continental Europe and America, becomes receptive to Maori traditional content and rhythmic forms. Until the mid-1960s, British dominance maintains a false separation of Pakeha (in Eng.) and Maori (in Maori and Eng.) poetry.

Although it is essentially true that Pakeha poetry did not begin to mature until after World War I, it began to exist over a century ago. The early settlers were often cultured men, and some wrote verse, like Alfred Domett's Maori epic *Ranolf and Amohia* (1872), which imitates the more popular romantic and Victorian poets. A trad. of vernacular rhyming survived in colonial laureates like John Barr of Craigilee; but the country inherited little that was validly traditional. "Serious" verse, such as that of the journalist Thomas Bracken, was fluent but undistinguished; and the real sense of historic events—exploration, settlement, gold rushes—remained unexpressed. Even when the colonists wrote best, on the country's impressive landscapes, the work was often falsely colored by nostalgia for their Eng. "home."

The 1890s brought modest prosperity, and second-generation settlers became conscious of themselves as a people. William Pember Reeves, Parliamentarian and reformer, spoke in easy and popular verse for the idea of N. Z. as "social laboratory"; the work of Jessie Mackay and Blanche Baughan showed a stronger and more genuine talent. But, on the whole, the anxious desire for a distinctive national lit. did not begin to be realized for another generation.

Early 20th-c. Pakeha writers shared the mediocrity of contemp. Eng. poets who were often their models, but some achieved significant poetry without radical innovations of manner—Arnold Wall (1869–1966), Alan Mulgan (1881–1962), J. C. Beaglehole (1901–71), and, even more, Ursula Bethell ((1874–1945) and Eileen Duggan (1894–1972), Walter D'Arcy Creswell (1896–1960), and R. A. K. Mason (1905–71). Bethell described the Canterbury scene with virtuosity and an intense contemplative affection. Duggan evolved independently the concrete and energetic idiom of her later poems. Creswell and Mason both articulated striking attitudes toward their country: Creswell's, more highly mannered, expresses the ambivalent emotion of a kind of exasperated love affair; Mason's is that of a Roman stoic looking on the brevity of life and the fall of empires.

Although many of the poems collected in *Kowhai Gold* (1930) were still feeble, changes had begun in the 1920s. It is only roughly true to say that the achievements of modern N. Z. p. began in the 1930s, and to connect them with the depression, political ferment, and social anger of a growing community finding its place in a disturbed world. N. Z. poets came abreast of European writers—not only the younger Eng. poets (e.g. Auden, MacNeice) with whom they seemed to have most in common, but older masters such as Eliot, Pound, and Rilke. It was, however, a transformation rather than a revolution. The whole process can be seen in the work of the versatile "Robin Hyde" (Iris Wilkinson, 1906–39), which develops from the late romantic aestheticism to a contemp. idiom; another kind of example is the accomplished traditional verse of John Russell Hervey (1889–1958) and Basil Dowling (b. 1910).

From the end of World War II down to the late 1960s, there has been a conscious and sometimes factitious reaction against this "myth of insularity." In practice this means that certain writers have widened their range of reference to include more of the urban scene and to accept the influence of European and Am. poets (e.g. Baudelaire, Hart Crane, Robert Lowell, Dylan Thomas). A similar indication is the growing tendency toward the longer poem or sequence, as in Alistair Campbell's (b. 1925) *Elegy*, Keith Sinclair's (b. 1922) *Ballad of Half-Moon Bay*, or Pat Wilson's (b. 1926) *Staying at Ballisodare*. Yet this new work often represents an extension rather than an extinction of the island-myth and what it signifies, as can be seen in the poetry of Kendrick Smithyman (b. 1922), Mary Stanley, Ruth Dallas (b. 1919), and others whose work is represented in Louis Johnson's (b. 1924) annual anthology. Most of all, it appears with varied range and tone in James K. Baxter (1926–72), who combines the attitudes of the *poète maudit* and the bard. "Hemi," as Baxter was known in his last days, moved from the early romanticism of his youth to a poetry that was at once satirical and religious, and in his *Jerusalem Sonnets* and *Autumn Testament*, he creates a mystical, even apocalyptic vision of N. Z.

While some of the older British-model writers such as Allan Curnow (b. 1911), Keith Sinclair, C. K. Stead (b. 1932), and Kendrick Smithyman, continue through the Muldoon Era of the late 1970s and into the '80s, the new period is marked by increasing Am. influence, esp. after the visit by Robert Creeley (of Black Mountain fame), and in the last several years by a shift toward the word-games of postmodern poetry. Above all, it is a period marked by the assertive presence of women writers, from Lauris Edmond (b. 1924), Elizabeth Smither (b. 1941), and Riemke Ensing (b. 1939) to Marina Makarova, with her imported Slavic intensities in the University of Hawaii's Pacific Poetry Award-winning *For Yesterday* (1984). Yet some N. Z. poets move "home" to England still, like Fleur Adcock (1934), though overseas writers also establish themselves in "the land of the long white cloud," writers such as Michael Harlowe (b. 1937), Norman Simms (1940), and Don Long. These movements signal the new dynamic in N. Z. society and verse. While brash young men like Ian Wedde (b. 1946) experiment with diction to discover the discourses of a deconstructionist N. Z., the octogenarian shepherd-poet Vaughan Morgan (1907–87) creates what George Ewart Evans calls lapidary verse in "Anthoxanthum Odoratum":

After the cutting
and the tedding
and the windrowing,
after the drying
and the gathering of harvest;
after labour; not till then does the
vernal,
sweetest of all grasses,
yield the meadow scent in hay.

Maori and other Pacific Island poets also begin to move into the mainstream of N. Z. verse during this decade. Hone Tuwhare (b. 1922) had initiated the Polynesian trend with his *No Ordinary Sun* in 1964 but moved into his stride with *Come Rain Hail* in 1973 and *Something Nothing* (1974). Now one finds either the delicacies of Katerina Mataira or the harsh forcefulness of Apirana Taylor, whose *Eyes of the Ruru* (1979) leaps from street bluntness to true literary power. Samoan-born Talosaga Tolovae's *The Shadows Within* (1985) offers a subtle new blending of European and Polynesian myths with a delicate ear for voice rhythms. Listen to Tolovae echo and develop the rhythms of Hone Tuwhare in his "Poem in Spring":

Come hail
Come rain
let time and the hour rattle
the grown up children
like the wind
amongst the brittle ribs
of virgin trees.

N. Z. p. in the late 1980s is diverse and exciting, with a future brighter than at any time in the recent past. Though still a provincial trad., it nevertheless has more than its fair share of interesting poets.

ANTHOLOGIES: *N. Z. Verse*, ed. W. F. Alexander and A. E. Currie (1906), rev. without preface as *A Treasury of N. Z. Verse* (1926); *Kowhai Gold*, ed. Q. Pope (1930); *Lyric Poems of N. Z. 1928–42*, ed. C. A. Marris (n.d.); *A Book of N. Z. Verse, 1923–45*, 2d ed (1950), *Penguin Book of N. Z. Verse*, both ed. A. Curnow (1959); *N. Z. P. Yearbook*, ed. L. Johnson (1951–); *Anthol. of N. Z. Verse*, ed. R. M. Chapman and J. Bennett (1956)—comprehensive and up-to-date; *Private Gardens*, ed. R. Ensing (1977)—N. Z. women poets; *Fifteen Contemp. N. Z. Poets*, ed. A. Patterson (1980); *Oxford Book of Contemp. N. Z. P.*, ed. F. Adcock (1982); *Into the World of Light: An Anthol. of Maori Writing*, ed. W. Ihimaera and D. S. Long (1982); *Oxford Anthol. of N. Z. Writing Since 1945*, ed. M. P. Jackson and V. O'Sullivan (1983); *Penguin Book of N. Z. Verse*, ed. I. Wedde and H. McQueen, rev. ed. (1985); *Anthol. of 20th-C. N. Z. P.*, ed. V. O'Sullivan, 3d ed. (1987).

HISTORY AND CRITICISM: E. H. McCormick, *Letters and Art in N. Z.* (1940), *N. Z. Lit., a Survey* (1959); J. C. Reid, *Creative Writing in N. Z.* (1946)—two chs. on poetry; M. H. Holcroft, *Discovered Isles* (1951); J. K. Baxter, *Recent Trends in N. Z. P.* (1951), *The Fire and the Anvil* (1955); K. Smithyman, *A Way of Saying* (1965); F. McKay, *N. Z. P.* (1970); M. R. Longa, *La poesia neozelandese: delle origin inglesi a contemporanei* (1977); C. K. Stead, *In the Glass Case* (1981); N. Simms, *Silence and Invisibility* (1986), *Who's Writing and Why in the South Pacific* (1989); A. Curnow, *Look Back Harder: Critical Writings 1935–1984*, ed. P. Simpson (1987). The long-overdue *Oxford Hist. of N. Z. Lit.* is still in preparation. N.S.

NICARAGUAN POETRY. See SPANISH AMERICAN POETRY.

NORWEGIAN POETRY. At the height of the Middle Ages (ca. 1250), when the trad. of Old Norse poetry had virtually ceased to be productive, the vogue of versified Fr. romances and Occitan poetry replaced original creativity in the vernacular. The chief N. poetic monuments of the age are the folk ballads, which derived their new, nonalliterative style from troubadour verse. *Draumkvæde* (The Dream Ballad), a remarkable visionary poem, successfully blends elements of pagan and Christian myth. Petter Dass (1647–1707), the first important N. poet, remains close to folk poetry, representing a kind of people's baroque. Though indebted to the Dane, Anders Arrebo, a bishop of Trondheim whose epic *Hexaëmeron* (1661) contained descriptions of North Norway (see DANISH POETRY), Dass's *Nordlands Trompet* (The Trumpet of Nordland, ca. 1700, pub. 1739; Eng. tr. 1954) is original in style and tone. In the hymns and other poems by Dorothe Engelbretsdatter (1643–1716), the artificial lang. of the baroque is feminized through domestic imagery, and the religious feeling expressed toward Christ is tinged with a dreamy eroticism, at times lending a very engaging personal tone to her verse.

Ludvig Holberg (1684–1750) was the first N. writer to attain European stature. Holberg established an enduring conception of poetry as crit. of life and offered his countrymen, still Danish subjects, a brilliant example. However, the N. poets failed in their first ambition, namely, to create a viable poetic tragedy in the Fr. neoclassical style. Their attempts are remembered chiefly because of the parody *Kierlighed uden Strømper* (Love without Stockings, 1772) by Johan Herman Wessel (1742–85), whose ironic satire in graceful alexandrines put an end to the imitation of It. opera and Fr. tragedy. In his comic narratives Wessel effectively alternates living dialogue with rhymed epigrams. The descriptive poem was another favorite genre with the poets of this period. Like Wessel, most of them belonged to *Det norske Selskab* (The N. Society) in Copenhagen.

Whereas Denmark and Sweden had produced great romantic poetry by the first and second decades of the 19th c., respectively, romanticism reached Norway only in the 1830s and '40s. Despite the political independence of Denmark held since 1814, Norway was still under Danish cultural hegemony. In the 1830s a "culture feud" occurred between those who followed the Danish romantics and those who wanted to build a lit. on native grounds. Henrik Arnold Wergeland (1808–45), leader of the Patriots, had prodigious gifts and inexhaustible energy, which he expended on politics and popular education as well as on literary creation. His production ranges from satirical farces and cosmic dramas to intimate lyrics. As one to whom poetry meant rapture and organic form, he was the exact opposite of the Intelligentsia Party's leader, Johan Sebastian Welhaven (1807–73), a poet of quiet reflection and chiseled form who adopted the aesthetic of the Danish poet-critic J. L. Heiberg. The trads. established by these two figures have coexisted in N. p. down to the present day, though tending to converge since 1900.

Wergeland defies literary classification. While a child of the Enlightenment, he is also Norway's first great romantic poet. His vast lyric drama *Skabelsen, Mennesket og Messias* (Creation, Man and Messiah, 1830) expresses a philosophical rationalism tinged with pantheism à la Shelley. Welhaven, who found the work formless and turgid, subsequently wrote *Norges Dæmring* (The Dawn of Norway, 1834), a series of epigrammatic sonnets showing up the Patriots' uncritical cultural nationalism as well as Wergeland's artistic faults. Narrative poems such as *Jøden* (The Jew, 1842), *Jødinden* (The Jewess, 1844), and *Den engelske Lods* (The Eng. Pilot, 1844), however, escape these strictures. Wergeland's lyric genius reached its apex as he neared death, in poems like "Til min Gyldenlak" (To My Wallflower) and "Til Foraaret" (To Spring), the latter in free verse.

Romanticism underwent change in the 1840s as N. poets discovered the values inherent in their folk culture. Native ballads were collected by Jørgen Moe (1813–82) and M. B. Landstad (1802–80); the latter's *Norske Folkeviser* (N. Folk Ballads, 1853) exerted a broad influence on poetry. The pioneering work of Ivar Aasen (1813–96) in creating the New Norse lang. was another manifestation of National Romanticism. Most of the important poets—Welhaven, Vinje, Ibsen, Bjørnson—contributed to the movement. Welhaven's poetry of recollection eventually embraced the entire nation and its heritage, which he celebrated in the tone of ballad or romance, and his nature poems featured fairies and trolls of a distinctly N. character. To the romantic output of the New Norse poet Aasmund Vinje (1818–70) belongs the first authentic N. mountain poetry. National Romanticism came to full fruition with Ibsen and Bjørnson, besides Wergeland the greatest N. poets of the 19th c.

Henrik Ibsen (1828–1906) is an exponent of the Welhaven trad., both in his National-Romantic and his satirical phases. His condensed lyric poetry, often cryptically symbolic, employs a minimum of imagery. Ibsen's chief contribution to National Romanticism was the drama *Gildet paa Solhaug* (*The Feast at Solhaug*, 1856), a historical idyll influenced by the ballad. *Kjærlighedens Komedie* (*Love's Comedy*, 1862) marks the beginning of realism. Its variously rhymed, skipping iambic pentameters abound in caricature and paradox. In *Brand* (1866; Eng. tr. 1898) and *Peer Gynt* (1867; Eng. tr. 1892), the satirist blends with the National Romantic; for while exposing the faults of the N. national character, both plays envelop the N. landscape—its rivers and lakes, its mountain peaks and fabled fjords—in a romantic aura. In *Peer Gynt*, moreover, Ibsen portrays dramatic symbols of universal import. Its major theme—a selfish, morally flawed hero ultimately saved, if saved at all, through a noble woman's love—recalls the *Divine Comedy* and *Faust*. And the play's metrical variety, by contrast with the *knittelvers* used in *Brand*, produced verse capable of a vast range of effects, from idle daydreaming to physical abandon, from the lightest banter to funereal solemnity. As a group, Ibsen's verse dramas demonstrated the strengths of N. as a medium for dramatic poetry.

Bjørnstjerne Bjørnson (1832–1910) saw himself as literary heir to Wergeland. His saga dramas *Halte-Hulda* (Lame Hulda, 1858), *Kong Sverre* (1861), and *Sigurd Slembe* (1862; Eng. tr. 1888) were undertaken to give Norway a gallery of heroes matching those of the other European nations, an ambition in line with the National-Romantic program. The chief merits of these plays are historical verisimilitude and their epic tone. Bjørnson was an excellent narrative and lyric poet. *Arnljot Gelline* (1870; Eng. tr. 1917), a narrative cycle of 15 romances in various measures, is a N. counterpart to Oehlenschläger's *Helge*, Tegnér's *Frithiofs saga*, and Runeberg's *Kung Fjalar*. The imagery is rich, the diction colloquial and varied, and the meter, mostly trochaic and dactylic, attuned to the changing moods. Bjørnson's lyric poems define him as a figure of European stature. Their structure is often dramatic: "Olav Trygvason" and "Bergljot" (in *Digte og Sange* [Poems and Songs], 1870) present an entire tragic action within a few dramatically taut scenes. Worthy of special mention is "Salme II," a hymn to ever-resurgent life that marks the highpoint of Bjørnson's poetic achievement.

When, after the prose-dominated 1870s and '80s, poetry again gained prominence, it had acquired a more personal note, one attuned to nature, mysticism, and fantasy. Nietzsche, Edvard Munch, and the Fr. symbolists—largely as mediated by Danish and Swedish neoromantic poetry—were important sources of inspiration. The chief exponents of neoromantic *fin de siècle* moods were Vilhelm Krag (1871–1933) and Sigbjørn Obstfelder (1866–1900), the former expressing a rather conventional melancholy, the latter evoking bizarre moods of anxiety and wonder in a highly original form marked by pauses, repetitions, abrupt transitions, and incompleteness. Symbolist in conception, Obstfelder's poetry, with its free verse and urban imagery, anticipates Scandinavian modernism. By contrast, Nils Collett Vogt (1864–1937) possessed a robust sensibility, celebrating in dithyrambic accents an individualistic Cl. paganism à la Swinburne. New Norse poetry was revived by Arne Garborg (1851–1924) and Per Sivle (1857–1904). Garborg's *Haugtussa* (The Elf Maiden, 1895) and *I Helheim* (In Hel's Home, 1901) give voice to the dark, uncanny forces in man and nature while expressing a profound religious nostalgia. The poetry of Knut Hamsun (1859–1952) is also neoromantic in inspiration. *Det vilde Kor* (The Wild Chorus, 1904) showed Hamsun as a lyric poet of considerable range, handling national and personal themes with equal mastery. Best known is the poem "Skjærgaardsø," an exquisite lyric with mystical intimations.

About 1910 a lyric revival occurred, due in large part to Herman Wildenvey (1886–1959) and Olaf Bull (1883–1933). Inspired by Hamsun's verse, Wildenvey's *Nyinger* (Bonfires, 1907) alternates between seductive love lyrics and pantheistic nature poetry. His novel diction, mixing biblical and ballad idioms with jargon and slang, and his conversational yet musical anapestic line were apt vehicles for his troubadour talent. Bull, Wildenvey's opposite in sensibility and craft, was the leading N. poet of his time. To him, as to fellow symbolists like Rilke and Valéry, the purpose of poetry was to transmute fugitive moments of experience into what Yeats called the "artifice of eternity." "Metope" (1927), one of his most famous poems, is a moving meditation on love and destructive time. Bull's deeply personal verse is focused on the tensions of inward experience. Only through an arduously achieved perfection of form was he able to blend the disparate elements within his creative impulse: perception and memory, image and abstraction, reality and fantasy, picture and sound, spontaneous feeling and discursive thought. Starting with but few sensory data, his poems gather substance from a visionary imagination and an intellect schooled in contemp. science and philosophy. His metapoems illuminate the condition of the imagination in a world without transcendence. New Norse poetry found worthy practitioners in Olav Aukrust (1883–1929), Tore Ørjasæter (1886–1968), and Olav Nygard (1884–1924). Aukrust and Ørjasæter treated religious and philosophical themes in a national spirit using forms derived from the Edda and the ballad. Aukrust's main work, *Himmelvarden* (The Cairn Against the Sky, 1916), is a visionary poem based on a quasi-mystical experience. Its sonorous verse, vivid imagery, and mythic symbols evoke a spiritual struggle of cosmic dimensions. Both Nygard and Aukrust superbly demonstrated the evocative potential of New Norse as a poetic medium.

Though the period between the wars generated new themes and original voices, there was a dearth of formal innovation. Arnulf Øverland (1889–1968) realized his poetic mission in the wake of World War I, as evidenced in *Brød og vin* (Bread and Wine, 1919). Much of his work springs from a religiously conceived Socialist ideal, often presented in biblical symbols. *Den røde front* (The Red Front, 1937) is devoted to proletarian songs and other texts with a political message. Notable monuments to the 1930s are the poems "Guernica," inspired by Picasso's famous painting, and "Du må ikke sove" (You Must Not Sleep). His best collection, however, is *Hustavler* (House Tablets, 1929), which ranges from politics to themes such as love, death, and self. Though Øverland was awarded the national honor of dwelling in Wergeland's house after the Liberation, his restrained fervor, laconic form, and austere diction place him decidedly in the formal trad. of Welhaven and Ibsen. By contrast, Nordahl Grieg (1902–43), ceaselessly active on many fronts, is reminiscent of Wergeland. Novelist, playwright, and poet, Grieg chiefly wrote socially oriented patriotic lyrics in a style of impassioned eloquence. His greatest poetic success was the collection of war poems entitled *Friheten* (Freedom, 1943; Eng. tr. *All That Is Mine Demand*, 1944), where his rhetorical pathos is poetically justified. Gunnar Reiss-Andersen (1896–1964), whose sheer formal talent has no equal in N. p., combined a brooding introspection with sensitivity to a world in crisis. During the war he was an important spokesman for his country. One of the poems written in Swedish exile, "Norsk freske" (N. Frieze), from *Dikt fra krigstiden* (Wartime Poems, 1945), is remarkable for its imaginative scope, rhythmical virtuosity, and colorful imagery; it deserves a place beside the best poems of Grieg and Øverland.

Modernism had to wait until about 1950 to make an impact on N. p., despite the fact that in some ways Wergeland was a modernist long before Whitman's *Leaves of Grass* (1855) or before Mallarmé and Rimbaud changed the concept of poetry in Europe. Wergeland's idiosyncratic form, adapted to the changing flow of consciousness, had no counterpart in N. p. until Obstfelder. It was Welhaven's classical conception of form which prevailed, even in the 20th c.: Wildenvey, Bull, and Øverland, all very influential, were formally conservative. Their avatars were not only prolific but excelled in their craft. Inger Hagerup (1905–85) wrote condensed love lyrics reminiscent of Øverland, as well as eloquent war poems (e.g. *Aust-Vågøy*, 1941); André Bjerke (1918–85) showed his technical versatility in highly finished verse, elegantly sensuous or introspective. With the exception of Kristofer Uppdal (1878–1961), who had written some expressionist poetry early in the century, the New Norse poets were all traditionalists.

From the 1930s on, however, various features of modernism became manifest. Emil Boyson (1897–1979) mediated the poetics and the preoccupations of Fr. symbolism. Claes Gill (1910–73) knew Yeats and T. S. Eliot; an ecstatic imagist, he admired Wergeland among others. His verse disregards ordinary syntax and follows a logic of suggestion, dynamic, surprising, often paradoxical. Rolf Jacobsen (b. 1907), who received an impetus from both Fr. and Am. poetry, used free verse and technical imagery early on to evoke urban civilization in *Jord og jern* (Earth and Iron, 1933) and *Vrimmel* (Throng, 1935), but by 1951 his emphasis had shifted to the natural landscape, and in *Hemmelig liv* (Secret Life, 1954) technology is seen as a sinister force. Jacobsen is basically an imagist, and his modernism is largely limited to free verse and rapid shifts in point of view. In *Headlines* (1969) and *Pass for dørene—dørene lukkes* (Watch the Doors—The Doors are Closing, 1972), which contain much social criticism, he presents a kaleidoscope of contrasting moods, effects, and angles of vision—pathos and humor, the commonplace and the cosmic, sensory vividness and symbolic resonance. Jacobsen's poetry is quite accessible and has been widely translated.

The 1950s witnessed a debate between the traditionalists—headed by Øverland, the uncrowned poet laureate—and the modernists. The latter looked for inspiration, like Carl Keilhau (1919–57), to Rilke and modern Danish poets, or, like Erling Christie (b. 1928) and Paal Brekke (b. 1923), to T. S. Eliot. Tarjei Vesaas (1897–1970), an established New Norse novelist who had adopted a moderate modernism in his poetry, provided an important example. But the leading spirit was Brekke, whose Swedish exile during the war had exposed him to *fyrtiotalisterna*. In 1949 appeared his tr. of *The Waste Land* and other Eliot poems, along with his own first collection, *Skyggefektning* (Shadow Boxing). Brekke, also a critic and an innovative novelist, did more than anyone else to promote the new poetics. His own production is polarized between a fragmented, chaotic reality and a dream of renewed wholeness, with ironic satire as a prominent feature. He employs a richly allusive, fractured lang., with abrupt shifts in usage levels, mood, rhythm, and point of view—sentimental cliché alternating with fervent invocation, pathos with black humor, personal recollection with glimpses of a world at risk, quotidian banality with the mythic sublime. His best work, *Roerne fra Itaka* (The Oarsmen from Ithaka, 1960), is a poetic cycle in which Brekke, like Eliot, juxtaposes contemporary actuality with Cl. myth. Other important poets who responded to the new signals were Gunvor Hofmo (b. 1921), Arnold Eidslott (b. 1926), Astrid Hjertenæs Andersen (1915–85), and Harald Sverdrup (b. 1923). Hofmo and Eidslott treat religious themes; Andersen evokes erotic rapture and *participation mystique*; Sverdrup, endowed with a liberated imagination à la Dylan Thomas, celebrates the body and excoriates societal complacencies.

By 1960 the new lang. of poetry was taken for granted and many new voices were heard. Chief among them were Stein Mehren (b. 1935) and Georg Johannesen (b. 1931). Mehren is a writer of wide range—novelist, playwright, and cultural critic as well as poet. His entire *oeuvre* forms part of a philosophical-religious quest for authenticity. The problem of lang. is a central theme: how can poetic lang. mediate reality rather than merely be a reflection of consciousness? The answer, to Mehren, seems to be a quasi-mystical concept of the imagination, a transcendental aesthetic which envisages the poetic process as noetic and tropes as rooted in the reciprocal relation between subject and object in the act of cognition. In *Aurora, Det Niende Mørke* (Aurora, the Ninth Darkness, 1969) the quest theme is traced through the mythic motif of the great journey. Other noteworthy collections are *Den usynlige regnbuen* (The Invisible Rainbow, 1981) and *Corona* (1986). The work of Johannesen is sociopolitically oriented; stylistically and otherwise he is Mehren's contrary. Whereas Mehren's poems often seem like a torrential stream of images, the style of Johannesen—who was deeply influenced by Brecht—is condensed and elliptical, characterized by bizarre contrasts and mordant irony. *Ars Moriendi eller de syv dødsmåter* (Ars Moriendi or the Seven Ways of Death, 1965), his main collection, treats the seven deadly sins—modes of false, inauthentic life—within a strict, semi-scholastic format, in dialectical opposition to its often surrealist imagery.

In the late 1960s new tendencies became evident, as seen in the work of Jan Erik Vold (b. 1939). Vold began as a self-conscious experimentalist preoccupied by solipsism, and his early work includes forays into emblematic verse and concrete poetry. *Hekt* (1966), framed by a document from the Vietnam War, creates a world poised on nightmare through grotesque imagery that evokes the uncanny. Subsequently, under the influence of William Carlos Williams and contemporary Swedish poets, Vold moved toward a "new simplicity," anecdotal and confessional in *Mor Godhjertas glade versjon. Ja* (Mother Goodheart's Glad Version. Yes, 1968), almost purely visual and objective in *spor, snø* (tracks, snow, 1970), where he adapts haiku form. An older poet, Olav H. Hauge (b. 1908), who decades earlier had started out in the Aukrust mode, progressively simplified his style until, with *Dropar i austavind* (Drops in the East Wind, 1966), he was writing about everyday things in an unadorned idiom akin to his Chinese and Japanese models. Hauge became a favorite with the young poets dissatisfied with late symbolism and eager to bring poetry closer to actuality. He and Jacobsen are the grand old men of contemp. N. p. Two other poets with similar aims are Paal-Helge Haugen (b. 1945) and Kolbein Falkeid (b. 1933). The former's work has been influenced by Anglo-Am. rock music and pop poetry. *Steingjerde* (Stone Fences, 1979; Eng. tr. 1986), an autobiographical work, is notable for its narrative elements, regional color, and a mood of nostalgic recollection. Falkeid, whose poetry expresses a deep ecological concern, envisages the poem as an extension of everyday lang.; his diction has distinct anecdotal features.

In the 1970s the literary scene in Norway became intensely politicized. Several feminist poets appeared, continuing their production into the 1980s. Among important figures whose profiles were defined in the course of the decade may be mentioned Arvid Torgeir Lie (b. 1938), Eldrid Lunden (b. 1940), Annie Riis (b. 1927), Halvor Roll (b. 1929), and Arne Ruste (b. 1942). Among those whose production belongs mainly to the 1980s, the following seem very talented: Erik Bystad (b. 1952), Jo Eggen (b. 1952), Ellen Einan (b. 1931), Liv Lundberg (b. 1944), Karin Moe (b. 1945), Håvard Rem (b. 1959), and Tor Ulven (b. 1953).

N. p. today shows a variety of tendencies. Old-style lyrics flourish, but so do innovative texts that experiment with multi-media effects—"sound sculptures," "picture poems," and so forth—which blur genre distinctions. Yet the two central N. trads. of Welhaven and Wergeland persist. Satire, too, continues to hold an important place, as does national and religious pathos—all elements that have been present in N. p. from the beginning. The same applies to visionary poetry, an important strain in the work of 19th- and 20th-c. figures like Wergeland, Aukrust, Bull, and Mehren, as well as in Old Norse poetry and the medieval *Dream Ballad.* There is also a living folk poetry, made extremely popular by Alf Prøysen (1914–70). Others whose work contains elements of ballad and folksong are Einar Skjæraasen (1900–66), Jacob Sande (1906–67), Hans Børli (b. 1918), and Arnljot Eggen (b. 1923).

Finally, a special kind of poem, exemplified by Hamsun's *Munken Vendt* (The Monk Vendt, 1902) and *Driftekaren* (The Drover, 1908) by Hans E. Kinck (1865–1926), has had a deep fascination for N. writers. Dramatic in form, it has a legendary basis and a loose, episodic structure reminiscent of the picaresque. The hero, an incurable wanderer, is a great teller of tales and lives by his wits. These works adumbrate a N. epic genre. A marginal example is *Jonsoknatt* (St. John's Eve, 1933, rev. 1965) by Hans-Henrik Holm (1896–1980), a quest epic based on the ethos of National Romanticism. This ambitious, immensely difficult poem was designed as a folk epic. But the "folk" prefer more accessible fare and have received that from the troubadour poets with their simple, melodious lyrics.

WORKS AND ANTHOLOGIES: B. Bjørnson, *Poems and Songs* (1915); *Oxford Book of Scandinavian Verse,* ed. E. W. Gosse and W. A. Craigie (1925); H. Wergeland, *Poems,* tr. G. M. Gathorne-Hardy et al. (1929); *Anthol. of N. Lyrics,* tr. C. W. Stork (1942); *Norsk lyrikk gjennom tusen år,* 2d ed., ed. E. Kielland, 2 v. (1950)—comprehensive anthol.; *Norsk folkedikting,* ed. O. Bø and S. Solheim, 2d ed., 7 v. (1958–64); *Norsk lyrikk,* ed. G. Johannesen (1966); *The Literary Rev.* 12, 2 (1968–69)—N. issue; *Micromegas,* ed. F. Will, 4, 3 (1971)—New Norse issue; T. Vesaas, *30 Poems,* tr. K. G. Chapman (1971) and *Land of Hidden Fires,* tr. and intro. F. König and J. Crisp (1973); *Draumkvæde,* ed. M. Barnes (1974); *Five N. Poets,* spec. issue of *Lines Rev.,* ed. R. Fulton, 55–56 (1976); *Dannemarks og Norges poesi 1600–1800,* ed. I. Havnevik (1981); *Mod. N. Writing,* spec. iss. of *Stand* 23, 3 (1982); *Mod. Scandinavian Poetry 1900–1975,* ed. M. Allwood (1982); *20 Contemp. N. Poets,* ed. T. Johanssen (1984); O. H. Hauge, *Don't Give Me the Whole Truth,* tr. R. Fulton and J. Greene (1985); R. Jacobsen, *The Silence Afterwards,* ed. and tr. R. Greenwald (1985); *Moderne norsk lyrikk,* ed. K. Heggelund and J. E. Vold (1985).

HISTORY AND CRITICISM: E. W. Gosse, *Northern Studies* (1890); K. Elster, *Illustreret norsk litteraturhist.,* 2 v. (1923–24), "Three Lyric Poets of N.," *ASR* 13 (1925); F. Bull, "Bjørnsons lyrikk," *Streiftog i norsk litt.* (1931); F. Bull et al., *Norsk litteraturhist.,* 6 v. (1924–55); H. Beyer, *A Hist. of N. Lit.,* ed. and tr. E. Haugen (1956)—best survey in Eng.; G. C. Schoolfield, "The Recent Scandinavian Lyric," *BA* 36 (1962); W. Dahl, *Ordene og verden* (1967); H. Lie, *Norsk verslære* (1967); E. Beyer, "Et dikt mot verden," *NLÅ* (1968)—about Brekke; H. Næss, "Stein Mehren," *BA* 47 (1973), *N. Lit. Bibl. 1956–70* (1975); I. Havnevik, "Norsk lyrikk etter 1945," *NLÅ* (1974); I. Stegane, *O. H. Hauges dikting* (1974); *Norges litteraturh.,* ed. E. Beyer, 6 v. (1974–75)—most recent comprehensive lit. hist.; W. Baumgartner, "Die Dezentralisierung der n. Poesie," *Aspekte der skandinavischen Gegenwartslit.,* ed. D. Brennecke (1978); H. and E. Beyer, *Norsk litteraturhist.* (1978)—good bibl.; J. E. Vold, *Det norske syndromet* (1980); P. T. Andersen, *Stein Mehren—en logos-dikter* (1982); M. K. Norseng, *Sigbjørn Obstfelder* (1982); *Norway,* ed. S. Lyngstad, spec. iss. of *RNL* 12 (1983); S. Lyngstad, "Olav Bull," *News of Norway* 41 (1984); A. Aarseth, "The Modes of N. Modernism," *Facets of European Modernism,* ed. J. Garton (1985). S.LY.

O

OCCITAN POETRY. The root of the term O. is the word *oc*, "yes," in the lang. of medieval southern France, in contrast to OF *oïl* (Modern Fr. *oui*) and It. *si*; this triple distinction was made by Dante in *De vulgari eloquentia* (ca. 1305). The lang. has been called "langue d'oc," "Provençal," and other names since the 13th c. "Provençal" was long preferred, esp. in Eng. and Ger., but has the disadvantage that it seems to refer specifically to Provence (Lat. "Provincia romana," the region of Gaul nearest to Rome), i.e. the area east of the Rhône and home of the 19th-c. poet Mistral (see below), which is only one part of the larger area where the lang. is spoken; "Languedoc" refers to another part of the territory, west of the Rhône. "O." is free from both such misleading connotations and enjoys increasing acceptance, although it was introduced comparatively recently in both Fr. (since 1886) and Eng. (since 1940).

The annals of O. p. begin about A.D. 1000 with the *Boeci*, a fragmentary paraphrase of Boethius' *Consolation of Philosophy*, and continue to about 1050 with the *Chanson de Sainte Foy*, a saint's life. From ca. 1100–1300 were the halcyon days of the troubadours, lyric poets who sang of courtly love and a range of other subjects. Scholars debate whether William IX, Duke of Aquitaine and Count of Poitiers (1071–1126), was the first troubadour or merely the first whose works have been transmitted to us. William's eleven (or ten) extant poems include some expressing the humility and devotion of courtly love, but also others of explicit eroticism (one has been called a *fabliau*) and one in which he says goodbye to earthly power, perhaps because of an imminent departure on crusade or because he expected to die soon. The next generation included the moralist Marcabru (fl. 1130–49), who scourged the sexual license of married men and women, while in other songs he depicted encounters of the first-person narrator with a young girl; in one of these, the prototypical *pastorela*, the narrator attempts to seduce the girl but she steadfastly refuses.

In the middle years of the 12th c., Peire d'Alvernhe (fl. 1149–68) developed a theory of difficult style, or *trobar clus* (closed composition), which involved elaborate play on rhymes and sounds with obscure vocabulary and syntax; Raimbaut d'Aurenga (d. 1173) advocated such abstruseness in a debate with Giraut de Bornelh (fl. 1162–99), who defended *trobar leu*, or the easy style. Bernart de Ventadorn (fl. 1147–70?), considered perhaps the greatest love poet among the troubadours, sang with a deceptive air of simplicity about his adoration for a lady, the joy of his love and the grief of his yearning, and, less frequently, about his ecstasy in sexual fulfillment.

By about 1170 the troubadours developed a set of generic concepts. In terms of this system, the 2500-odd extant poems comprise about 1000 *cansos* or love songs; about 500 are *sirventes* or satires; about 500 are *coblas* or individual stanzas; and those remaining comprise a number of genres, incl. the *pastorela*, the *alba* or dawn poem, debate-poems such as the *tenso* and the *partimen*, and the *planh* or funeral lament.

Bertran de Born (ca. 1150–1215), whose castle of Altafort was besieged and captured by Richard Lionheart, sang of political passions with the commitment of a feudal lord dedicated to warfare as a source of moral stature. The feudal mentality also informs the *chanson de geste Giraut de Roussillon* (ca. 1150), written in an artificial blend of O. and Fr., and the parodic romance *Jaufre* (late 12th c.).

In the early 13th c., the O. region was the scene of the Albigensian Crusade, waged in the service of the pope by a Fr. leader, Simon de Montfort, against the heretical Cathars centered at Albi. According to one interpretation, the crusade destroyed the courtly society which had nourished the troubadours, and destined O. p. to inevitable decline; but it is not certain that this conflict, one among many, played so decisive a role. Peire Cardenal (fl. 1205–72) criticized the Roman Catholic Church for the failings of its unworthy priests, incl. members of the Inquisition, while expressing his own orthodox piety. Perhaps in the mid 13th c. was composed the delightful romance of *Flamenca*, whose heroine succeeds, despite the cruelty of her jealous husband, in enjoying the love of a perfect knight. Late in the century, Guiraut Riquier (fl. 1254–82) complained of the insecurity of the courtier's life and lamented that he had come among the last of the troubadours.

Though we have the melodies of only one-tenth of the troubadour poems, it is assumed that virtually all of them were set to music. The troubadour wrote both text and melody, which were performed by the joglar. Joglars and troubadours travelled widely, William IX on crusade to Syria, Marcabru and Guiraut Riquier to Spain, Bernart de Ventadorn to England, Bertran de Born to Northern France. Peire Vidal (fl. 1183–1204) ventured as far as Hungary. These travels contributed to the diffusion of the artform into other langs. such as Northern Fr., starting at the end of the 12th c.; Ger.; It., at the court of the Emperor Frederick II in Sicily; and Galician-Portuguese (see GALICIAN POETRY). The heritage of the troubadours was acknowledged by Dante and Petrarch, who extended their indirect influence throughout the Europe of the Ren. and beyond. Poets of the 20th c. who have returned to the troubadours incl. Ezra Pound, Paul Blackburn, Jacques Roubaud, and W. D. Snodgrass.

Meanwhile, a trad. of commentary on the troubadours and their songs had begun in the early 13th c. with Raimon Vidal's *Razos de trobar* (Principles of Composition) and continued with the *Donatz proensals* (Provençal Grammar) of Uc Faidit. Uc and other writers also compiled the *razos*, brief prose commentaries on individual songs, and the *vidas*, or lives of the troubadours. Around 1290 Matfre Ermengau attempted to reconcile the love sung by the troubadours with love of God in his lengthy verse *Breviari d'amor* (Breviary of Love).

During the 14th and 15th cs., O. p. fell into decline. The trad. was maintained at Toulouse by the Consistòri de la Subregaya Companhia del Gay Saber, or Academy of the Most Joyful Company of the Joyful Wisdom, which regularly awarded prizes for the best compositions in various troubadour genres. The regulations of these contests were codified in a meticulous taxonomy of troubadour practice called *Las Leis d'amor* (ca. 1341), understood as equivalent to a Code of Poetry. We are still indebted to *Las Leis d'amor* for definitions of the genres and for distinctions such as those among *coblas unissonans*, in which all the stanzas of a song have the same rhyme-sounds; *coblas singulars*, in which the rhyme-sounds change with every stanza; *coblas doblas*, in which given rhyme-sounds are maintained for two stanzas; *coblas ternas*, in which they are maintained for three stanzas; and *coblas quaternas*, in which they are maintained for four. In *coblas capcaudadas* the first line of one stanza uses the rhyme-sound of the last line of the preceding stanza, whereas in *coblas capfinidas* the first line of one stanza repeats a key word from the last line of the preceding stanza. In *coblas retrogradadas* the rhymes of one stanza repeat those of the preceding stanza but in reverse order.

On the other hand, the authority of the *Leis* has obscured evolutionary developments in troubadour practice. We are only beginning to realize that the earliest troubadours used no generic distinctions among types of song, hence that the development of the generic system requires explanation. Another fundamental evolution occurred in the practice of metrical imitation, or *contrafacture*, which only gradually became characteristic of the *sirventes* but was adopted in the *Leis* as its timeless defining trait. The elaborate rhyme-patterns of the troubadours analyzed by the *Leis*, which have attracted the scorn of critics averse to formal experimentation, are in fact only a few of the endless variations of their technique.

Only one poet of this period, Raimon de Cornet (fl. 1324–40), has left an extensive body of work incl. lyrics, verse letters, didactic texts, and two poems in Lat. The fate of O. in this period may be illustrated in the career of Count Gaston Fébus of Foix (1331–91). Although he requested the translation of an encyclopedia from Lat. into O., called the *Elucidari de las proprietatz de totas res naturals* (Elucidarium of the Properties of All Natural Things), Gaston Fébus composed his own treatise on hunting in Fr. and a collection of prayers in Fr. and Lat.—but only a single love song in O. The 14th-c. *Jeu de Sainte Agnès* shows verve in its elaboration of the traditional story and in its use of music, but two cycles of mystery plays from the 15th and 16th cs. are less successful. When the edict of Villers-Cotterêts (1539) established Fr. as the lang. of administration in the Midi, it simply recognized, and did not cause, the decline of the local vernacular.

Historians of O. p. speak of a first Ren. in the 16th c., illustrated by the Gascon Protestant Pey de Garros (d. 1581), the Provençal Bellaud de la Bellaudière (d. 1588), and Pierre Godolin of Toulouse (d. 1649); and a second Ren. in the 19th c. marked by the group of seven poets called Félibrige. Through the annual publication of the *Armana provençau* (Provençal Almanac), the group strove to reform O. spelling, to renew the lang., to compose great poetry, and to revive O. culture. The greatest of the *félibres*, Frédéric Mistral, won high praise from Lamartine for his narrative poem *Mirèio* (Mireille) and received the Nobel Prize in 1905. Despite continuing factional disputes, O. p. has grown broader in appeal during the 20th c. with the work of Max Rouquette, Bernard Manciet, and Henri Espieux. A number of contemporary figures, such as R. Nelli, C. Camproux, P. Bec, and R. Lafont, are both practicing poets and troubadour scholars. The poet and singer Claude Marti, who has recorded troubadour songs, allied O. p. with the regionalist movement during the 1970s. See also HISPANO-ARABIC POETRY; FRENCH POETRY.

BIBLIOGRAPHIES: A. Pillet and H. Carstens, *Bibl. der Troubadours* (1933); P. Berthaud and J. Lesaffre, *Guide des études occitanes* (1953), supp. by J. Lesaffre and J. Petit, *Bibl. occitane 1967–1971* (1973) and *Bibl. occitane 1972–1973* (1974); C. A. Knudson and J. Misrahi in Fisher; F. Pic, *Bibl. des sources bibliographiques du domaine occitan* (1977); R. Taylor, *La Litt. occitane du moyen âge* (1977); F. Zufferey, *Bibl. des poètes provençaux des XIVe et XVe siècles* (1981).

ANTHOLOGIES: *Trouvères et Minnesänger*, ed. I. Frank (1952); *Les Troubadours*, ed. R. Lavaud and R. Nelli, 2 v. (1960–66); *Anthol. de la poésie occitane 1900–1960*, ed. A. Lafont (1962); *Anthol. of Troubadour Lyric Poetry*, ed. A. Press (1971); *La poesia trobadorica in Italia*, ed. G. Folena and M. Mancini (1971); *La lirica religiosa en la literatura provenzal antigua*, ed. F. J. Oroz Arizcuren (1972); *La Poésie occitane*, ed. R. Nelli (1972); *Lyrics of the Troubadours and Trouvères*, ed. F. Goldin (1973); *Anthol.*

of the Provençal Troubadours, ed. R. Hill and T. Bergin, 2d ed., 2 v. (1973); *Los Trovadores,* ed. M. de Riquer, 3 v. (1975); *The Women Troubadours,* ed. M. Bogin (1976)—popularization; *Anthol. des troubadours,* ed. P. Bec (1979); *Mittelalterliche Lyrik Frankreichs, I: Lieder der Trobadors,* ed. D. Rieger (1980); *A Med. Songbook,* ed. F. Collins, Jr. (1982); *Intro. à l'étude de l'ancien provençal,* ed. F. Hamlin et al., 2d ed. (1985); M. Switten et al., *The Medieval Lyric,* 3 v. (1987–88).

TRANSLATIONS: E. Pound, *Personae* (1926); A. Bonner, *Songs of the Troubadours* (1972); W. D. Snodgrass, *Six Troubadour Songs* (1976); P. Blackburn, *Proensa* (1978).

VERSIFICATION AND MUSIC: Patterson 1.1.2; Lote; F. M. Chambers, "Imitation of Form in the Old Provençal Lyric," *RPh* 6 (1952–53); I. Frank, *Répertoire métrique de la poésie des troubadours,* 2 v. (1953–57); F. Gennrich, *Das musikalische Nachlass der Troubadours,* 3 v. (1958–65), "Troubadours, trouvères," *MGG,* v. 13; H. van der Werf, *The Chansons of the Troubadours and Trouvères* (1972); *Las cançons dels trobadors,* ed. I. Fernandez de la Cuesta (1979); P. Bec, "Le problème des genres chez les premiers troubadours," *CCM* 25 (1982); *The Extant Troubadour Melodies,* ed. H. van der Werf and G. Bond (1984); Chambers; U. Mölk, "Zur Metrik der Trobadors," *GRLMA,* v. 2.1.

HISTORY AND CRITICISM: "Prov. Versif.," *North Brit. Rev.,* 53 (1871); Jeanroy; Patterson; K. Vossler, "Die Dichtung der Trobadors und ihre europäische Wirkung," *RF* (1937); Lote; C. Camproux, *Hist. de la litt. occitane* (1953); H.-I. Marrou (under pseud. H. Davenson), *Les Troubadours* (1961); M. Lazar, *Amour courtois et "fin'amors" dans la litt. du XIIe siècle* (1964); R. Lafont and C. Anatole, *Nouvelle Hist. de la litt. occitane,* 2 v. (1970); J. J. Wilhelm, *Seven Troubadours* (1970), *Il Miglior Fabbro: The Cult of the Difficult in Daniel, Dante, and Pound* (1982); C. Marks, *Pilgrims, Heretics, and Lovers* (1975)—popularization; L. M. Paterson, *Troubadours and Eloquence* (1975); L. Topsfield, *Troubadours and Love* (1975); N. B. Smith, *Figures of Repetition in the Old Prov. Lyric* (1976); R. Boase, *The Origin and Meaning of Courtly Love* (1976); D. Rieger, *Gattungen und Gattungsbezeichnungen der Trobadorlyrik* (1976); P. Makin, *Provence and Pound* (1978); W. D. Paden, "Pound's Use of Troubadour Mss.," *CL* 32 (1980), ed., *The Voice of the Trobairitz: Perspectives on the Women Troubadours* (1989); U. Mölk, *Trobadorlyrik* (1982); J. Gruber, *Die Dialektik des Trobar* (1983); P. Miremont and J. Monestier, *La Litt. d'oc des troubadours aux Félibres* (1983); M. Mancini, *La gaia scienza dei trovatori* (1984); M. R. Menocal, *The Ar. Role in Med. Lit. Hist.* (1987); L. Kendrick, *The Game of Love* (1988); S. Gaunt, *Troubadours and Irony* (1989); Hollier; S. Kay, *Subjectivity in Troubadour Poetry* (1990); A. E. van Vleck, *Memory and Re-Creation in Troubadour Lyric* (1991). W.D.P.

OLD NORSE POETRY. The poetry of the Viking Age and medieval West Scandinavia. Although verse was composed throughout Viking Scandinavia, England, and the Western Islands, all ms. recordings are from Iceland, where they began no earlier than the end of the 12th c. Only runic inscriptions preserve alliterative lines (perhaps just rhythmic prose) from Denmark and Sweden; the most important periods are the late 10th and 11th cs. ON p. descended from common Germanic prosody but introduced a number of important innovations, of which the most important were a shift from stichic to stanzaic structure and the introduction of syllable-counting and rhyme in some meters. The stanzas have eight lines (four Germanic long lines) in nearly all meters, and there is always a syntactic break in the middle of the stanza. Stylistically, ON p. developed the metaphoric and metonymic aspects of Germanic poetry, whereas West Germanic poetry relied more heavily on variation. Nothing in ON p. approaches the length of the West Germanic epics *Beowulf* and *Heliand.* Although a few poems exceed 800 lines (e.g. *Hávamál, Lilja*), most are far shorter.

The basic formal principle is structural alliteration. In *fornyrðislag,* the meter most like what can be reconstructed for common Germanic, pairs of lines (each pair is equivalent to one Germanic long line) are linked by alliteration. It occurs in one or both of the two stressed syllables of the odd lines and regularly in the first stressed syllable of the even lines. In this system, consonants alliterate with identical consonants. Only the first consonant of a cluster is relevant for alliteration, except that *sp, st,* and *sk* function as single units. Any vowel, however, alliterates with any other vowel. Unstressed syllables and those in anacrusis are metrically irrelevant.

An important Norse innovation to this system is *ljóðaháttr,* in which the even long lines in effect are shrunk into a single line. One stress (at least) is lost, but the alliteration remains. The anonymous mythological and heroic poems are in these meters and their variations.

A second important departure was the introduction of syllable-counting. Coupled with internal rhymes, it was particularly exploited in the meter *dróttkvætt.* Besides the four pairs of lines linked by alliteration (with two alliterations required in the odd lines) and the syntactic break after the second pair, *dróttkvætt* employs a strict count of six syllables per line, with the last two forming a trochee, and with internal half-rhymes in odd lines and full rhymes in even. Here is an example:

> út munu ekkjur líta,
> allsnúðula, prúðar
> —fljóð séa reyk—hvar ríðum
> Rǫgnvalds í by gǫgnum
> (Sighvatr Þórðarson, *Austrfararvísur* 12a).

(The fair women will look out—the ladies see smoke—as we ride
furiously through Rǫgnvaldr's village.)

Here the first couplet employs vowel alliteration (the syllables út, ekk, and all); the second *r, út,* and *lít* provide half rhyme, *snúð* and *prúð* full rhyme, *fljóð* and *ríð* half rhyme, and *Rǫgn* and *gǫgn* full rhyme. The two unstressed short syllables in *munu* resolve to one syllable.

This half-stanza contains two words for "women," neither of which is the ordinary prose term. ON p. relies heavily on noun substitution for its stylistic effect, either through metonymy (e.g. *ekkjur,* literally, widows or unmarried women) or use of an elevated vocabulary (e.g. *fljóð,*) found only in poetry. The latter is an *ókennd heiti* or "unexplained appellative." If an appellative is "explained," it is part of a *kenning* (from the verb *kenna,* "teach, make known"), a figure employing two or more nouns, like "horse of the sea" for "ship." Kennings can be grammatical compounds or employ the genitive case for the determining noun ("of the sea" in the above example). It was possible to build up kennings by replacing the determining noun with another kenning ("horse of the paths of the whale"); kennings with up to six parts are attested. Given the complex metrical requirements of *dróttkvætt* and related meters and the highly inflected nature of ON, word order is far from that of ON prose. How far remains an open question.

Dróttkvætt and its numerous variations tended to be used by poets whose names survived with their work. Often such poetry was of an occasional nature. Later scholars called such poets "skalds" and their verse "skaldic."

The earliest known skald is thought to be Bragi Boddason the Old, who flourished during the latter half of the 9th c., perhaps in Norway, Sweden, or even Viking Russia. No ON p. is demonstrably older than his, and some scholars have seen in Bragi the originator of *dróttkvætt.* ON mythology has a god of poetry named Bragi. The skald Bragi and over 200 others were active from the late 9th c. through the end of the Middle Ages. During the Viking Age, they were often attached to the courts of kings or other rulers, and much of their surviving verse is encomiastic, focusing particularly on royal battles and employing the form of the *drápa.* Skalds composed verse on many other topics, however, ranging from *níð* (insults, often of a sexual nature), through love poetry, boasts, challenges, and topical comments to deep emotion (e.g. Egill Skallagrímsson's *Sonatorrek*). With the conversion to Christianity, ca. 1000 A.D., skalds began to compose on Christian topics, and these became increasingly important, although the other topics never disappeared. The major verse of the 13th and 14th cs. is mostly religious (e.g. *Lilja,* the stately poems on the Icelandic bishop Guðmundr the Good, and numerous verses on Mary and other saints), but the 13th-c. Icelandic chieftain Áron Hjǫrleifsson was the subject of at least three poems of which fragments still remain. Later religious poetry, which was often in the meter *hrynhent,* avoided the kennings and obscure diction of earlier *dróttkvætt* poetry.

The earliest written lit. in West Scandinavia was historical, and authors frequently cited individual skaldic stanzas rather than whole poems as evidence. As a result, the transmission of the early skaldic corpus is fragmentary, although some occasional stanzas (*lausavísur,* "loose stanzas") were intended to stand alone. The Icelandic family sagas contain many such verses, some of which, however, may have been composed later, perhaps even by the saga authors, and placed in the mouths of the early skalds.

Ca. 1220, Snorri Sturluson, a member of a leading Icelandic family, composed *Háttatal* ("enumeration of meters") as an encomium to the young Norwegian king Hákon Hákonarson and his guardian regent, Jarl Skúli. The poem was a metrical and stylistic *tour de force*: 101 stanzas each of which exhibited a named variation of meter or diction. It was not the first such ON poem; the Orkneyan Jarl Rǫgnvaldr Kali Kollsson and the Icelander Hallr Þórarinsson had composed their *Háttalykill* ("metrical key") during the 1140s. Snorri, however, augmented his poem with a prose commentary that has remained the foundation of ON poetics. Poem and commentary now make up the last section of a longer work, a handbook on poetics, all attributed to Snorri. Later called *Edda* (perhaps a neologism on Lat. *edo* with the sense "compose verse"), Snorri's *Edda,* now sometimes also called the "Prose Edda" or "Younger Edda," contains a Prologue, a section setting forth the mythological narratives on which many kennings are based (*Gylfaginning,* "The Deluding of Gylfi"), a section on poetic diction (*Skáldskaparmál,* "The Language of Poetry"), and *Háttatal,* the metrical catalogue and commentary. *Skáldskaparmál* is richly illustrated with examples and is a major repository of skaldic poetry. Snorri's *Edda* is not the only rhetorical work from medieval Iceland—there are four grammatical treatises, from the 12th c. through the 14th c., and the third and fourth esp. are important for poetics, but Snorri's work is in a class by itself.

In *Gylfaginning* and in the opening sections of *Skáldskaparmál,* Snorri quotes extensively from anonymous poems in *fornyrðislag* and *ljóðaháttr,* and when a ms. of such poetry turned up in the 17th c., Reformation scholars called it the *Edda* of Sæmundr Sígfússon the Learned, the 12th-c. founder of Icelandic historiography. In fact, the book dates from the later 13th c., and its written antecedents go back no further than to the end of the 12th c. Nevertheless, this ms. is still called *Codex Regius of the Poetic Edda,* sometimes also the *Elder Edda,* and its poems are termed "Eddic," as opposed to the "skaldic" poems that are mostly occasional and in *dróttkvætt* or related meters. As the existence of another ms. fragment of some of these poems shows, *Codex Regius* was a carefully planned book. It begins with *Vǫluspá*, which presents the full curve of mythic history. The following mythological poems treat, respectively, Odin, Freyr, Thor, and beings from the lower mythology (*Vǫlundarkviða* and *Alvíssmál*). Heroic poems follow. Again the redactor placed synoptic poems before those dealing with smaller aspects of the whole story. He presents, roughly speaking, two heroic cycles, those of Helgi and of the Nibelungs, from the career and death of Sigurðr through the aftermath of his demise to the final moments of death and destruction in *Hamðismál*). In all, *Codex Regius* contains some thirty poems and a lacuna whose probable contents scholars continue to debate. Another half-dozen or so Eddic poems have been found outside *Codex Regius*, and A. Heusler and W. Ranisch gathered similar verse from the mythic-heroic *fornaldarsagas* under the title *Eddica Minora*, which has by now acquired something of the status of a generic term.

Particularly in the heroic section, many of the Eddic poems tell the same or similar stories (e.g. the apparently older *Atlakviða* and younger *Atlamál*), and the role of oral trad. in their transmission remains an important research question. At least some of the poems must have been composed centuries before they were written down; each poem by now has an extensive research history discussing possible provenience. Guesses range over five centuries from Greenland to Viking Russia.

Snorri wrote his *Edda* at least in part as an attempt to defend the older skaldic style from modish dance songs, perhaps ballads. It is certain at least that ballads reached Scandinavia by the later Middle Ages, although serious recording did not begin until after the Reformation. Ballads certainly existed in Iceland, too, but there the proper heirs to the older poetry were the *rímur*.

BIBLIOGRAPHY: L. M. Hollander, *A Bibl. of Scaldic Studies* (1958); P. Schach, "ON Lit.," in Fisher; R. Frank, "Skaldic Poetry," and J. Harris, "Eddic Poetry," in *ON–Icelandic Lit.: A Crit. Guide*, ed. C. J. Clover and J. Lindow (1985).

EDITIONS: *Eddica Minora*, ed. A. Heusler and W. Ranisch (1903); *Den norsk-islandske skjaldedigtning*, ed. F. Jónsson, 4 v. (1912–15)—standard ed. of skaldic poetry; *Edda Snorra Sturlusonar*, ed. F. Jónsson (1931); *The Poetic Edda*, v. 1: *Heroic Poems*, ed. U. Dronke (1969)—with tr. and commentary; *Edda: Die Lieder des Codex Regius nebst verwandten Denkmälern*, ed. G. Neckel, rev. H. Kuhn, 5th ed. (1983)—standard ed. of Eddic poetry; *Háttatal: Edda, Part 3*, ed. A. Faulkes (1991).

TRANSLATIONS: *The Poetic Edda*, tr. H. M. Bellows (1923); *The Skalds*, tr. L. M. Hollander (1945); *The Poetic Edda*, tr. L. M. Hollander, rev. ed. (1962).

HISTORY AND CRITICISM: W. P. Lehmann, *The Devel. of Germanic Verse Form* (1956); S. Gutenbrunner, "Beiträge zur germanischen Terminologie der Metrik," *ZDP* 86 (1967): P. Hallberg, *Old Icelandic Poetry* (1975); G. Turville-Petre, *Scaldic Poetry* (1976); G. Kreutzer, *Die Dichtungslehre der Skalden*, 2d ed. (1977); R. Frank, *ON Court Poetry* (1978); K. von See, *Skaldendichtung* (1980); H. Kuhn, *Das Dróttkvætt* (1983); E. Marold, *Kenningkunst* (1983); Frank and Harris in Clover and Lindow (above). J.L.

ORIYA POETRY. See INDIAN POETRY.

P

PANJABI POETRY. See INDIAN POETRY.

PERSIAN POETRY.

I. PROSODY AND RHETORIC
II. GENRES
III. MOVEMENTS AND SCHOOLS
IV. CRITICAL TOPICS
V. POETRY AND OTHER AESTHETIC DOMAINS

P. p. is that written in the New P. lang., after the Islamic conquest of Persia in the 7th c. The formal aspects of this poetry changed little until after World War I, and the poetry written in the traditional styles is generally called "classical."

I. PROSODY AND RHETORIC. In the period preceding the Islamic era, poetry was written in Pahlavi, or Western Middle Iranian, but its prosodic system is not clearly understood. Pahlavi meters were probably based on syllable-counting combined with a pattern of stresses. Some fragments of epic and didactic verse survive. With the coming of Islam to Persia, the Pahlavi meters fell out of use and Persians began writing poetry, probably in Arabic (hereafter Ar.) at first but soon in P. as well. When they began writing in P., they used the prosody, rhet., and forms familiar from Ar. Although Elwell-Sutton has argued convincingly for P. precedents for some of the borrowed meters, the prosodic system (Ar. *ᶜarud*, P. *ᶜaruz*) of cl. P. p.—i.e. the theory of prosody, the terminology, and many of the meters used by the Persians—was borrowed from Ar. trad. The traditional *ᶜaruz* is based on 16 meters derived from patterns of vowelled and unvowelled consonants. The Arab prosodists (likewise the Persians) never conceptualized the syllable. Particular sequences of consonants and vowels were grouped into various three- or four-syllable "feet." Such "feet" were then used to build hemistichs (*miṣrāʿ*) of equal metrical length, two hemistichs forming a line (*bayt*) of poetry. Because of morphological differences and the fact that Ar. has a higher percentage of four- and five-syllable words than has P., the Ar. system of prosody did not fit the P. lang. perfectly and had to be adapted. The Persians did not use all the Ar. meters available to them, and also created a number of meters not found in Ar. poetry. P. p. has end rhyme and occasionally internal rhyme at the midpoint of a 4-foot hemistich.

The highly evolved array of P. rhetorical devices is divided into verbal devices (e.g. parallelism, paronomasia) and devices of meaning (e.g. metaphor, allusion) and bears some relation to the rhetorical systems of Gr. and Lat. poetry. Some common Western devices such as alliteration and consonance are not part of the P. rhetorical system, while others such as punning are more highly developed than in most Western poetry. Even in narrative poetry, each line should be a grammatically and syntactically complete and independent unit; enjambment is very rare.

II. GENRES. A. *Lyric Forms*. Poetic genres are defined by their content as well as form. The *qaṣīda* is a poem in monorhyme the main subject of which is other than love. By the late 15th c., prosodists were describing the *qaṣīda* as a poem having more than 15 lines, where the first two hemistichs rhyme, and then each line carries this rhyme to the end of the poem, thus: *aa*, *ba*, *ca*, and so on. Some *qaṣīdas* run to over a hundred lines. The *qaṣīda* is an occasional poem, generally meant to be declaimed in public. Subjects can include praise, congratulations, invective, celebration, elegy, or religious or philosophical meditation. Many *qaṣīdas*, following the Ar. model, begin with an amorous prelude or a description of nature, then move to the main purpose of the poem.

The principal sources of poetry in the premodern period were royal and provincial courts and Sufi centers. Poets were important members of a ruler's entourage, and poetry was part of most public and private occasions. Most court poets of the cl. period wrote *qaṣīdas*, while the mystical poets, generally not part of courtly life, tended to write fewer of these poems. Popular or folk poetry, sometimes in syllabic meters, was also produced, but little survives, and much of that is in dialects.

Qaṣīdas were written from the very beginnings of Islamic P. p. Rudaki (d. ca. 940), the earliest poet from whom we have a substantial body of work, wrote *qaṣīdas* in a fully developed style which he used with complete confidence. This indicates that a considerable trad. of P. p. preceded him, though almost none of it has survived. Other early poets who wrote mainly *qaṣīdas* were Farrokhi Sistani (d. 1037–38) and Manuchehri (d. ca. 1040), of the Ghaznavid court. Naser-e Khosrow (d. 1072–77) wrote somber, contemplative *qaṣīdas* strongly colored by his Ismaili beliefs. By the 12th c. the poetic style was beginning to change, and the *qaṣīdas* of the Seljuk period were often vehicles to display the erudition of the poet. Anvari (d. 1189–90?) and Khaqani (d. 1199) were the most prominent poets writing on secular themes during this period. After the Mongol period, as Sufi thought began to permeate P. lit. and patterns of patronage began to change, the *qaṣīdas* gave place to the *ghazal* as the most popular P. poetic form.

The *ghazal* is a monorhymed poem, the subject of which is love. Amorous preludes to *qaṣīdas* were sometimes called *ghazals* as well. By the late 15th c., the *ghazal* was described as having 7 to 15 lines, and it resembles the *qaṣīda* in its rhyme scheme. The poet generally mentions his name toward the end of the poem. If the *qaṣīda* can be considered "public" poetry, then the *ghazal* is "private" poetry. Most P. p. is meant to be performed rather than read silently, and the *ghazal*, which is intended to be sung to music in an intimate gathering, expresses best of all many of the literary and aesthetic values of the Persians. The subject of the *ghazal* is love, and the prevailing mood is one of sadness, for love is not a joyful state in P. p. Longing in separation from the beloved, the brevity of moments of union, and the pain of unrequited passion are themes that dominate the *ghazal*, and the music to which it is sung reflects this sadness perfectly. As with the *qaṣīda*, the *ghazal* displays a certain unity, the nature of which is a matter of critical debate. The ms. trad. of a cl. *ghazal* is likely to show considerable variation in both the number and order of lines, although the first two and the last lines are usually fixed. In performance, lines are often repeated and are frequently separated from each other by musical passages, giving the listener time to savor the "point" of the line and the elegance of its expression.

The *ghazal* began to flourish in the 12th c. Two distinct paths, secular and mystical (with some overlapping and deliberate ambiguity in all periods), can be traced in its devel. The secular *ghazal* continued the course of secular love poetry and had as its subject earthly love. The speaker is the male lover. The P. lang. does not formally distinguish gender, however, and unless specific male or female attributes are mentioned, the sex of the beloved is ambiguous. This causes problems when translating P. *ghazals* into Eng., and translator's decisions about the sex of the beloved often reflect the mores of the period. The customary way of portraying the lovers in *ghazals* results in the creation of conventional types and roles, where the focus is much more on the use of lang. than on the expression of personal emotion. The secular *ghazal* reached its highest level of devel. in the work of Saʿdī of Shiraz (d. 1292).

The great flowering of mystical thought which began in the 12th c. produced some of Persia's finest poetry. The first important writer of mystical *ghazals* was Sanāʾī (d. 1130–31). The scope and imagery of the mystical *ghazal* were greatly expanded by ʿAṭṭār (d. ca. 1220) and brought to their highest level by Jalāl al-dīn Rūmī (d. 1273). Rūmī's *ghazals* are ecstatic poems of spiritual love expressed in the vocabulary of earthly love, a convention familiar to Western mystical poetry. Hence mystical poetry developed an elaborate symbolic vocabulary of wine and physical beauty, along with the imagery of earthly love.

In the 14th c., the two streams of the *ghazal* began to merge, a movement which culminated in the poetry of Ḥāfiẓ of Shiraz (d. 1389–90). Using lang. in a way unparalleled in the P. trad., Ḥāfiẓ extended and combined the imagery of secular and mystical poetry and created *ghazals* with multiple levels of meaning, all simultaneously present and inseparable. Read wherever P. culture was influential, Ḥāfiẓ's *ghazals* also made a profound impression in Europe, where they inspired Goethe's *West-östlicher Divan*.

The remaining sorts of lyric poems are distinguished by form. A favorite small genre of P. p. is the *robaʾi* or quatrain. A 4-hemistich epigrammatic poem rhyming *aaaa* or *aaba*, the quatrain was written by almost all poets and by most educated persons. The *robaʾi* meters are thought to be an indigenous devel., not derived from the *ʿaruz* meters. The P. quatrain was made famous in the West by Edward FitzGerald, who translated a collection of unrelated quatrains attributed to Omar Khayyam (d. 1122) and made them into a narrative (1859, 1868, 1879). The *qeṭʿa* is a monorhymed poem except that the first two hemistichs do not rhyme. The principal strophic forms are: the *tarjiʿ band*, where *ghazal*-like stanzas are linked by the same rhyming couplet; the *tarkib band*, in which the same sort of stanzas are linked by couplets of different rhyme; and the *mosammat*, a typical form of which rhymes *aaaaax, bbbbbx, cccccx*, etc. The strophic forms are used in the same fashion as *qaṣīdas*.

B. *Narrative Poetry*. P. narrative poetry stands out among the Islamic literary trads. by virtue of its quantity, its range of subject matter, and its refinement. Written in the *masnavī* form (closed rhyming couplets), P. poetic narratives fall into the general categories of *epic, romance*, and *didactic*, subgenres produced continuously from the 10th c. to the 20th.

C. *Epic Poetry*. P. epic poetry is best exemplified by the *Shahnama* of Abu al-Qasem Firdawsī (d. ca. 1020–25). Using written and oral sources, Firdawsī cast a large part of the Iranian national legend into a poem of ca. 50,000 lines. The meter he used became so identified with the *Shahnama* that it was used for all subsequent poems in the epic style. By the time Firdawsī was writing the *Shahnama*, the P. literary lang. had become somewhat Arabicized, but Firdawsī apparently made a conscious effort at a style as purely P. as possible, and thus he is credited with preserving not only the national trad. but the P. lang. as well.

D. *Romances* were written in Persia long before the coming of Islam, and the trad. continued vigorously in the Islamic period. Produced in a courtly milieu, the P. romances had royal figures as their principal characters and emphasized the military and amorous adventures of the hero. Apart from romances within the *Shahnama*, the first important example of the genre is *Vis va Ramin* by Fakhr al-Din Gorgani (fl. 1054). Thought to be a recasting in New P. of an earlier Iranian story, *Vis va Ramin* has striking affinities with the story of Tristan and Isolde. But the most famous of the P. romance writers is Niẓāmī (d. 1209), whose five long poems were assembled into a *khamsa* (Quintet) that set a pattern imitated by many later poets. Four of these poems are romances about the lives of pre-Islamic figures: the Arab lovers Leyli and Majnun, the Iranian royal couple Khosrow and Shirin, the monarch Bahram V, and Alexander the Great. Niẓāmī was a master storyteller who wrote in a rich, complex, and subtle lang. far removed from that of Firdawsī. Niẓāmī's principal imitators were Amir Khosrow of Delhi (d. 1325) and Jāmī (d. 1492).

Horace's dictum that the poet should aim to blend instruction with delight could well have been said about P. p., whose *didactic* aspect is nowhere better developed than in extended narrative poems. *Shahnama* has its share of it, as do the romances, but there are many long poems of a deliberately didactic nature. The most popular ones are the Sufi narratives, beginning with Sanāʾī's influential *Hadīqat al-ḥaqīqa* (The Garden of Truth) and ʿAṭṭār's *Manṭiq al-ṭayr* (The Parliament of the Birds), an allegory of the soul's progress on the path to union with the Divine. The greatest of the mystical narratives is Rūmī's *Masvī-yi maʿnavī* (The Spiritual *Masnavi*), a heterogeneous poem in 27,000 lines containing Sufi philosophy and ethics, meditations, anecdotes, and tales of all kinds. A work of more secular, practical ethics is Saʿdī's *Bustan*.

III. MOVEMENTS AND SCHOOLS. The trad. of cl. P. p. was conservative, although not rigid. Great stress was laid on adherence to the canonical poetic forms, from which no deviation was allowed. Innovation, as understood today in the West, was not valued. The subject matter of poems was restricted, the stock of traditional images was relatively limited, and a sense of decorum prevailed. Poetic style did evolve, but only by refining ever more subtly the received trad. In spite of what seem to be excessive constraints, P. poets were able to achieve an unparalleled elegance and refinement of lang. in both sense and sound.

P. p. is traditionally classified in four broad period styles. The Khorasani style prevailed in Eastern Persia from the 10th c. until the 13th and is characterized by a simple and relatively unarabicized diction. After the Mongol invasion in the early 13th c., the center of P. civilization shifted to western Iran, which was more under the influence of Ar. culture and lang. than was the East. The ʾIraqi style developed here in the 12th c. and continued until sometime in the 15th c. The Safavid dynasty gained control of Persia in 1500 and succeeded in converting most of the Sunni population to Shiite Islam. Thereafter, patronage for secular court poetry declined, and many poets left Persia for the more receptive courts of central Asia and Moghul India, where P. had become the lang. of culture and diplomacy. In this period the elaborate and complicated Indian style prevailed. In Central Asia and India in particular, but also in Ottoman Turkey, P. p. flourished greatly, and indeed, Indian style poetry was still being written in the Subcontinent well into the 20th c. In the mid 18th c. within Iran, a reaction to the Indian style set in, and there was a return to writing poetry in imitation of the Khorasani and ʾIraqi styles, a movement that lasted until the Constitutional Revolution of 1906. With the Revolution and World War I came a change in the relation of the poet to society. Court patronage almost disappeared, and poets found their new audience in an expanding middle class.

The Modern style began in 1921 with the publication of Nima Yushij's long poem "Afsana" (Legend), and soon Persians began writing poetry influenced by Western styles. In this context, "modern" implies not only experiments with line length, meter, rhyme, and larger form, but the presence of an individual voice in the poem, a striving for structural unity, and personal and social concerns as subject matter. A fierce battle between modernists and traditionalists raged until after World War II, when the modern style became firmly established. Some poets threw over all restraints of form and lang. and wrote poetry that acknowledged no debt to trad.; others developed an imagery that was almost hermetic in its private symbolism. By the 1960s, voices of the generation following Nima Yushij began to be heard. Ahmad Shamlu, Mehdi Akhavan Sales, Nader Naderpur, and Forugh Farrokhzad were the leaders of this generation. Each made his or her accommodation with the past while extending the range of poetry toward the future. A younger generation, more distant from Nima, were looser with rhyme and meter, and many struggled between demands for a socially committed, activist poetry and one more private, sometimes even mystical. But the Islamic Revolution of 1979 put an end to these movements and sent many poets into exile in Europe and the United States, where an active P. literary life soon emerged.

IV. TOPICS OF CRITICAL ATTENTION. Traditional P. crit. was essentially connoisseurship, demanding highly cultivated taste in the listener and formal orthodoxy on the part of the poet. Among modern critics, P. and Western, the production of reliably edited texts has been of the first priority. Studies of the artistic devel. of individual poets writing in the cl. style are practically impossible because poems are arranged in *divans* (collections) alphabetically by the rhyme consonant, making chronological ordering almost impossible except where there are internal historical references. There has been some attention to the question of unity, particularly in *ghazals*, but it is by no means clear what, in aesthetic terms, P. poets considered to be a well-made poem. The question of the role of the poet in society occupied many critics in the 1970s.

V. POETRY AND OTHER AESTHETIC DOMAINS. Poetry was, until the 20th c., considered the primary literary medium; prose was held to be a workaday form suitable for scientific discourse but incapable of achieving the authority of poetry. Therefore prose was generally interlarded with verse, which served two main functions—either to confirm a point made in the prose or to serve as decorative embellishment. Poetry is most commonly found in the works of historians and bellettrists, and there is a special mixed genre of poetry and prose called *maqama*, of which Saʿdī's *Golestan* is the most prominent example. The relation of poetry and music has been mentioned above. Poetry and painting are closely connected by virtue of many poetic texts being illustrated with miniature paintings. Oral narrators recounting epic or religious stories, generally in verse, sometimes use large paintings as illustrations for their performance. Finally, the aesthetics of poetry and painting have some common features. For example, the worlds of the poem and the painting are often idealized and frozen in time, a garden where nature is at its most beautiful and changeless. Persons too are usually abstracted and not individualized, representing idealized beauty in a world lacking shadows. Often poetry is also used as part of decorative programs in architecture.

ANTHOLOGIES: *Sokhanvaran-i-Iran*, ed. M. Ishaque, 2 v. (1933–37); *P. Poems*, ed. A. J. Arberry (1954); G. Lazard, *Les Premiers Poètes persans*, 2 v. (1964); B. Foruzanfar, *Sokhan va sokhanvaran*, 2d ed. (1971); *Anthol. of Mod. P. P.*, ed. A. Karimi-Hakkak (1978); *LE&W* 20 (1976 [pub. 1980]).

PROSODY, RHETORIC, AND STYLISTICS: H. Blochmann, *Pros. of the Persians* (1872); F. Ruckert, *Grammatik, Poetik und Rhetorik der Perser* (1874); M. T. Bahar, *Sabk shenasi*, 3 v. (1942); M. Raduyani, *Tarjoman al-balagheh* (1949); Shams-e Qeys al-Razi, *al-Moʾjam* (1959); M. J. Mahjub, *Sabk-e khorasani* (1966); W. Heinz, *Der indische Stil in der persischen Literatur* (1973); L. P. Elwell-Sutton, *The P. Metres* (1976); F. Thiesen, *Manual of Cl. P. Pros.* (1982).

HISTORY AND CRITICISM: E. G. Browne, *Lit. Hist. of Persia*, 4 v. (1902–24), *Press and Poetry of Mod. Persia* (1914); T. Nöldeke, *Das iranische Nationalepos* (1920); Shebli No'mani, *Sheʿr al-ʿajam*, 5 v. (1935–48)—P. tr.; Z. Safa, *Hamasa sara'i dar Iran* (1954), *Tarikh-e adabiyat dar iran*, 5 v. (1956–85); E. Yarshater, *She'r-e farsi dar ahd-e Shahrokh* (1955); I. S. Braginskii, *Iz istorii Tadzhikskoi narodnoi poezii*

(1956); A. J. Arberry, *Cl. P. P.* (1958); A. Pagliaro and A. Bausani, *Storia della letteratura persiana* (1960); F. Machalski, *La littérature de l'Iran contemporain,* 3 v. (1965–80)—deals only with poetry; R. Baraheni, *Tela dar mes* (1968); M. Boyce, "Middle P. Lit.," *Handbuch der Orientalistik,* ed. B. Spuler, pt. 1, v. 4 (1968); J. Rypka, *Hist. of Iranian Lit.* (1968), "Poets and Prose Writers of the Late Saljuq and Mongol Periods," *Cambridge Hist. of Iran,* v. 5 (1968); Y. Aryanpur, *Az Saba ta Nima,* 2 v. (1971); M. R. Shafi'i Kadkani, *Sovar-e khiyal dar she'r-e farsi* (1971); A. Schimmel, *Islamic Lits. of India* (1973), *As Through a Veil* (1982); W. L. Hanaway, "P. Lit.," *The Study of the Middle East,* ed. L. Binder (1976), "The Iranian Epics," *Heroic Epic and Saga,* ed. F Oinas (1978); J. D. Yohannan, *P. P. in England and America* (1977)—bibl. of trs.; J. Clinton, "Esthetics by Implication," *Edebiyat* 4 (1979); J. S. Meisami, "Arabic and P. Concepts of Poetic Form," *Proc. of the Xth Congress of the Internat. Comp. Lit. Assoc., 1982* (1985), *Med. P. Court Poetry* (1987); H. Javadi, *Satire in P. Lit.* (1988); *P. Lit.*, ed. E. Yarshater (1988). W.L.H.

PERUVIAN POETRY. See SPANISH AMERICAN POETRY.

PHILIPPINE POETRY. A strong oral tradition—expressed as riddles and rituals in verse for planting and harvest cycles, war songs (*kumintang*), plaintive love lyrics (*kundiman*), and boat songs (*talindao*)—has kept alive the Indonesian-Malayan origins of Filipino culture. Typically, these have been characterized by quatrains built on 8-syllable lines; or 7- in the case of *tanaga,* whose core is the cryptically imagistic *talinghaga.* One of the most popular forms of entertainment during fiestas in rural Tagalog barrios is *balagtasan* (called *crissotan* in Pampango, *bukanegan* in Ilokano), spontaneous debating in verse that tests wit rather than reason. As relief during lengthy wakes, dramatic competitions in rhyme, the *duplo* and *karagatan,* are held. Losers forfeit objects which can be reclaimed only after a *loa,* a declamation similar to a riddle.

Two days are required to recite the epics of the Ifugaos, heirs to the ancient mountain rice-terraces. The *Hudhud* connects the tribal ancestors with the world's creation; the *alim* describes collective life among the gods. Muslim epics (*darangen*)—e.g. *Bantugen* and *Bidusari*—which require a week of chanting are valued for their absence of Western intrusions, whereas the Ilokano *Lam-ang* betrays the influence of 17th-c. Christian fathers. Among upland tribes scores of epics continue to assimilate modern events into ancient narratives.

No Sp. theme or form, despite 300 years of colonialism, successfully resisted local adaptation. The *pasyon,* for example, a dramatic singing of scriptural hist. at Eastertide, was originally introduced to pacify Filipinos through Christianization. Over time, however, it came to encourage nationalism because it stressed Christ's redemption of all people. Similarly, as early as the 17th c. the celebration-dance of converted Muslims inspired *moro-moro* plays (*komedya*) portraying costumed conflicts between Muslims and Christians in which religious differences gave way to poetic expression of festive tournaments and courtship. Filipinos developed extravagant translations of the Sp. *awit* (a chivalric-heroic romance in monorhymed 12-syllable quatrains) and *korido* (a legendary or religious tale in monorhymed 8-syllable quatrains). The most famous *awit, Florante at Laura* (ca. 1838), was situated in Albania in order to enable Francisco Baltazar (known as Balagtas) to describe Sp. tyranny without being censored. So effective is this concealment that the *awit* is as often remembered for the felicity of its Tagalog (the principal vernacular) as for its anticolonialism.

The elitism of Sp. rule prevented Filipinos from publishing verse in Sp. until late in the 19th c. Pedro Paterno's *Sampaguitas y Poesias Varias* (1880), the first collection of a Filipino-Sp. poet, had to be printed in Europe. More permanent has been Jose Rizal's "Mi Ultima Adios," a patriotic lament composed in Manila the day before his execution in 1896, an event which ironically helped provoke the revolution he had tried to prevent. For a time Rizal had lived in Spain with other Filipino *ilustrados* of the Propaganda Movement, which attempted, through Marcelo del Pilar's satirical verses, for example, to halt the Foreign Office's oppression in the colony.

Fernando Ma. Guerrero, in *Crisalidás* (1914), carried on Rizal's libertarian views in Sp. but turned them against the new occupying force, the United States, which could not decide on a date for the islands' independence. For the same purpose, Tagalog was used by Jose Corazon de Jesus (called "Batute" for his romantic poems) when he wrote his 443-stanza allegorical narrative, *Mga Gintong Dahon* (The Golden Leaves, 1920) against Western imperialism.

In 1940, Manuel L. Quezon as first president of the Commonwealth awarded national prizes for lit. in Sp., Tagalog, and Eng. Zulueta da Costa's prize poem, *Like the Molave,* praises the nation about to be born in the declamatory style of Walt Whitman. Even simpler are the short poems of Carlos Bulosan, about troubled migrant workers like himself on the West Coast of the United States and, later, his wartime hymns. Far more experimental are the imagery and internal rhymes of Jose Garcia Villa, an expatriate in New York whose self-assertions find radiant expression, often compared with William Blake's, in *Have Come, Am Here* (1943) and *Volume Two* (1949). The latter contains his "comma poems," with spaces between words replaced by a regular filigree of commas, to enforce a stately and incandescent measure. Wordplay as encrusted correlatives of the perceiver's sensibility occurs as well in Virginia Moreno's "batik poems," Ophelia Alcantara Dimalanta's *Montage* (1974), and Edith Tiempo's *The Tracks of Babylon* (1966).

In Tagalog the counterparts of these opposing poetics—the socially committed and the resplendently self-expressive—have been Amado V. Hernandez, whose *Isang Dipang Langit* (A Measure of Sky, 1961) and *Bayang Malaya* (Free Land, 1969) describe the struggle of a labor leader, later a political prisoner, to liberate the peasantry from poverty; and Alejandro G. Abadilla, whose free-verse *Piniling mga Tula ni AGA* (Selected Poems of AGA, 1965) is a protest in the name of personal independence.

Such contrasts signify the multiple heritage of the Filipino writer and, sometimes, bilingual skill. "Mestizo" poems by Rolando Tinio try to combine Asian and Euroamerican heritages by alternating lines in different langs. or providing a pastiche of langs. in a single line. *Sitsit sa Kuliglig* (Chitchat with a Cricket, 1972) and *Dunung-Dunungan* (Pretending Knowledge, 1975) include reminiscences of Tinio's childhood in Manila's slums and complaints against the neo-colonialism which keeps the Filipino economically dependent. Other writers have produced poems or books in alternating langs. Alejandrino Hufana supplemented the epic portraits in *Poro Point* (1961) and his long narrative *Sieg Heil* (1975) with occasional lyrics and Ilokano lullabies. To Cirilo Bautista's early volumes—*The Cave* (1968), an Orphic descent into the "minotaur" caves of Lascaux in the Pyrenees; *The Archipelago* (1970), a chronicle of the *conquistadores*; and *Telex Moon* (1981)—have been added *Sugat na Salitâ* (Wounds of Words, 1986). Marra Pl. Lanot devotes a third of *Passion and Compassion* (1981) to poems of social protest in Filipino, the national lang. Her themes typify the liberal-radical defiance of writers during the dictatorial rule (1965–86) of Ferdinand Marcos. A variety of such poems appear in the multilingual volume, *Versus*, edited by Salanga and Pacheco (1986).

No poet writes in more langs. or on more diverse themes then Federico Licsi Espino, Jr., whose chapbook output has been prolific, exemplified by *In Three Tongues* (1963), *Dark Sutra* (1969), and *In the Very Torrent* (1975). Among persons working in Filipino, Virgilio S. Almario (Rio Alma) ranks foremost, as his translations into Eng., *Selected Poems 1968–1985*, (1987), demonstrate. His *Doktrinang Anakpawis* (Worker's Manifesto, 1979) sacrifices nothing of difficult art to its identification with the oppressed and impoverished. More understated and conversational but equally nonconformist politically are Jose F. Lacaba's poems in *Mga Kagilagilalas na Pakikipagsapalaran* (Feats of Chance, 1979).

Ricaredo Demetillo, almost alone, has regularly resisted the trend to identify ethnic pride with either the national lang. or the eight dominant vernaculars. Since *No Certain Weather* (1956), he has published only in Eng., incl. the spiritual pilgrimage *La Via* (1958); the epic encounter of dissidents from Brunei with pygmy aborigines on Panay in the 13th c., *Barter in Panay* (1961), *The Heart of Emptiness in Black* (1974); the crosscultural mural of literary and visual artists, *Masks and Signatures* (1968); and his meditations on morality, in *The Scarecrow Christ* (1973) and *Lazarus, the Troubadour* (1974).

Politicization of P. p. has been inevitable, given centuries of uneasy acquiescence to foreign rule. Poetry served resistance movements determined to achieve national self-definition. Critics and anthologists memorialize these efforts over and above hundreds of transitory love lyrics, even when suffering and loss animate both. Yet only occasionally have they failed to distinguish between naked manifesto and poetic merit; and despite recurrent appeals for the exclusive use of Filipino, the cosmopolitanism of so many writers due to the confluence of cultures regularly demonstrates the Filipinos' ability to adapt opportunities from abroad to their own perceived needs.

ANTHOLOGIES: *New Writing from the Philippines*, ed. L. Casper (1964); *Walong Dekada ng Makabagong Tulang Pilipino*, ed. V. Almario, (1981); *P. Lit.*, ed. B. and C. N. Lumbera (1982).

HISTORY AND CRITICISM: V. Almario, *Ang Makata sa Panahon ng Makina* (1972); O. Dimalanta, *The P. Poetic* (1976); R. Ileto, *Pasyon and Revolution* (1979); *Salimbibig*, ed. J. Galdon (1980); *Balagtasismo vs. Modernismo*, ed. V. Almario (1984); B. Lumbera, *Tagalog Poetry, 1570–1898* (1986); L. Casper, *Firewalkers* (1987); R. Demetillo, *Major and Minor Keys* (1987); D. L. Eugenio, *Awit and Corrido: P. Metrical Romances* (1987).

L.C.

POLISH POETRY.

I. THE MIDDLE AGES
II. RENAISSANCE
III. BAROQUE
IV. ENLIGHTENMENT
V. ROMANTICISM
VI. POSITIVISM AND NEOROMANTICISM
VII. THE INTERWAR PERIOD AND THE WAR YEARS
VIII. THE POSTWAR PERIOD

I. THE MIDDLE AGES. As a consequence of Poland's adoption of Christianity in its Western form in A.D. 966, Lat. served as the dominant literary lang. for at least three centuries. Some oral folk poetry in P. must have existed at this early stage, but nothing has been preserved in written form. Oddly enough, the first recorded poem in P. is the most refined literary product of the entire medieval period. "Bogurodzica" (Mother of God), an anonymous religious hymn from the 13th c. preserved in a 15th-c. ms., consists of two stanzas with a highly complex parallel construction and sophisticated verse structure.

Throughout the 14th and 15th cs., P. p. is characterized by a prevalence of religious topics.

Within devotional poetry, the epic is still poorly represented: "Legenda o św. Aleksym" (The Legend of Saint Alexis), e.g., is unexceptional verse hagiography, drawing on foreign sources and rather primitive in form. By contrast, devotional lyricism flourished in numerous Lenten and Easter songs, Christmas carols, and hymns to the Virgin, mostly adaptations from Lat. Some of these poems are quite innovative. "Żale Matki Boskiej pod Krzyżem" (Lament of the Mother of God at the Foot of the Cross), a first-person monologue, forsakes allegorical commonplaces for an individualized point of view and emotional intensity. "Pieśń o Męce Pańskiej" (Passion Song) represents an early attempt at syllabic regularity. As a rule, however, the verse structure of medieval P. p. is based on a loose system of relative syllabism, with uneven lines equal to clauses and approximate rhymes.

Secular P. p. of the Middle Ages, far less abundant, consists of poems and fragments written for various purposes with similarly various aesthetic results. Some of them are merely mnemonic devices, while others are didactic and satiric; there are several timid attempts at erotic poetry as well. The most interesting lay poem of the period is the 15th-c. "Rozmowa Mistrza ze Śmiercią" (A Dialogue between Master and Death); one of many variations on the medieval theme of *memento mori*, it stands out by virtue of its vivid, if macabre, imagery and humor.

II. RENAISSANCE. Western European humanism had its representatives in Poland as early as the second half of the 15th c., but only the 1560s ushered in the "Golden Age" of the P. Ren. Meanwhile, a few transitional figures emerged. The first P.-lang. poet whose identity is at least partly established is Biernat of Lublin (ca. 1465–ca. 1529). His major poetic work is *Żywot Ezopa* (The Life of Aesop, ca. 1522), the first part of which is a rhymed account of the life of the legendary slave, while the second part presents the collection of fables. Another early humanist, this time much closer to the Ren. mentality, is Mikołaj Rej (1505–69), traditionally called the father of P. lit. A country squire with almost no formal education, he wrote in P., not in Lat. Rej's exclusive use of the vernacular was deliberate: it had much to do with the awakening of a sense of national identity in the beginnings of the Ren. His poetry is mostly didactic, descriptive, or satiric; it ranges from enormous versified treatises or dialogues to brief epigrams. As a poet, Rej undeniably lacks subtlety and artistic balance; his strengths are his passion for the particulars of life and his robust style.

Against the background of his predecessors, but also of his contemporaries, the work of Jan Kochanowski (1530–84) appears as the culmination of the P. Ren. as well as one of the crowning achievements of all Slavic poetry before the 19th c. An educated humanist, Kochanowski was indebted to the Cl. heritage as well as to contemporary It. and Fr. lit., but he gave his writing a national specificity and personal perspective. The bulk of his mature work is written in P., which he raised almost single-handedly to the rank of a literary lang. His P. output consists of the collections *Fraszki* (Trifles, 1584), *Pieśni* (Songs, 1586), and *Treny* (Threnodies, 1580); a masterly poetic adaptation of the Psalms, *Psałterz Dawidów* (1578); several epic poems; and a Cl. tragedy in verse, *Odprawa posłów greckich* (The Dismissal of the Grecian Envoys, 1578). If the Anacreontic *Fraszki* and Horatian *Pieśni* present Kochanowski as an orderly and well-balanced mind that enjoys the *aurea mediocritas* of everyday life, his *Treny* is marked by a radically different tone. This sequence of laments over the death of his little daughter encompasses a wide range of shifting feelings, from utter despair and doubt to final reconciliation with God's decrees; the poet's usually lucid and tranquil style acquires a pre-baroque complexity and tension.

Kochanowski's influence on subsequent phases of P. p. was both enormous and varied. Perhaps his most durable legacy was his contribution to the devel. of P. verse. The revolution he carried out consisted in replacing the remnants of the medieval system of relative syllabism with a strictly syllabic system, incl. exact rhyme, stabilized caesura, and paroxytonic cadence. This rigor allowed him the freedom to employ enjambment and thus create an interplay between syntax and verse structure. In addition, he was able to introduce a bewildering variety of meters and stanza patterns. Despite the 19th-c. success of the more songlike syllabotonic system, Kochanowski's syllabism remains one of the basic verse systems of P. p.; only since the beginnings of the 20th c. has it been rivaled seriously by tonic verse and *vers libre*.

As early as the second half of the 16th c.—that is, at the zenith of the Ren.—some literary innovations were already foreshadowing the arrival of the baroque. Mikołaj Sęp Szarzyński (1550–81), who died three years before Kochanowski, was a full-fledged baroque poet *avant la lettre*. His only collection, *Rytmy abo wiersze polskie* (P. Rhythms or Verses; pub. posthumously in 1601), has been rediscovered only in recent decades, after centuries of oblivion. Szarzyński did not write much, but what he wrote reveals an extraordinary personality, a profoundly metaphysical poet. In particular, a handful of his religious sonnets, in which tortuous syntax, violent enjambment, and oxymoronic imagery portray a mind torn asunder by spiritual torment, bear comparison with the best of John Donne or George Herbert.

These two giants, Kochanowski and Szarzyński, dwarf the other poets of the P. Ren., yet several are not without artistic merit. Sebastian Grabowiecki (ca. 1543–1607) was an author of refined devotional lyricism. Sebastian Fabian Klonowic (ca. 1545–1602) wrote descriptive and didactic poems that abound with picturesque details. Szymon Szymonowic (1558–1629) left behind a collection of half-bucolic, half-realistic *Sielanki* (Idylls, 1614), an important link in the evolution of the pastoral genre.

III. BAROQUE. In P. p. of the 17th c. the new baroque style soon evolved into two different manners, sociologically demarcated by the cultural horizons of a royal or aristocratic court on the one hand and, on the other, those of the petty gentry's manor. While court poetry, more cosmopolitan, strongly resembled the Western European baroque of Marino and Góngora, the latter manner, often called the Sarmatian Baroque, was much more provincial and conservative.

The "Westernized" brand of the P. baroque had its most brilliant exponent in Jan Andrzej Morsztyn (1621–93). A courtier and political intriguer, he was close to Fr. libertinism in outlook, and he considered his writing a kind of entertainment (his two collections of poems were never published in his lifetime). His chief concern in poetry was not so much "worldly happiness" *per se* as its inherent self-contradictions. In particular, the paradoxes of love are illuminated in Morsztyn's poetry by a wide variety of striking conceits, in which there is as much frivolity as metaphysical fear. Beside him, the P. "line of wit" was represented by, among others, Daniel Naborowski (1573–1640), perhaps the most typical Marinist among poets of the early baroque, and J. A. Morsztyn's distant relative Zbigniew Morsztyn (ca. 1627–89), author of erotic poetry as well as devotional emblems.

While the court poets excelled in lyric and epigrammatic forms, the Sarmatian baroque was more diversified in its choice of genres and styles, which ranged from brief songs and lyrics to immense epic poems. The lyric branch is best represented by Szymon Zimorowic (ca. 1608–29), whose only book, *Roksolanki* (Ruthenian Maidens, 1654), appeared many years after his premature death. An ingeniously composed sequence of songs or lyric monologues by different speakers, the collection sounds the psychological mysteries of love with subtle simplicity. Kasper Miaskowski (ca. 1550–1622) was the most gifted representative of early baroque poetry of nature.

The middle and late phases of the Sarmatian baroque were characterized, however, by the poets' taste for moralism, didacticism, satire, and historical epic. The poet who exemplified all of these inclinations was Wacław Potocki (1621–96), a provincial nobleman who, in the seclusion of his country manor, wrote an immense amount of verse, incl. the epic *Wojna chocimska* (War of Chocim, 1670) and the collections *Moralia* (1688) and *Ogród . . .* (A Garden; pub. only in 1907). Samuel Twardowski (ca. 1600–61) was another poet who wrote in this vein, producing a historical epic, a mythological tale in verse, and a poetic romance. Krzysztof Opaliński (1609–55) can be considered the most prominent representative of the satirical bent in baroque poetry. Finally, Wespazjan Kochowski (1633–1700) was the central figure of the late baroque; his collection of lyrics and epigrams, *Niepróżnujace próżnowanie* (Unleisurely Leisure, 1674), surpasses the average production of those years in its technical finesse, and his long poem in biblical prose, *Psalmodia polska* (P. Psalmody, 1695), is an early manifestation of messianic P. historiosophy.

The first 60 years of the 18th c. marked a catastrophic decline in P. culture. P. p. of this period, still continuing the line of the Sarmatian baroque, was becoming increasingly monotonous in its treatment of devotional topics and its reliance on worn-out conceits. The last great triumph of baroque style—a much belated one, to be sure—occurred in 1768, when the so-called Confederacy of Bar, a gentry rebellion, produced a wave of anonymous religious and patriotic verses.

IV. ENLIGHTENMENT. In the mid 1760s, however, new tendencies began to occupy the center of the cultural stage. Under the reign of the last P. king, Stanisław August, the ideology of the Enlightenment rapidly gained ground along with a renewal of interest in Western (esp. Fr.) literary novelties. In poetry, the last decades of the 18th c. marked a resurgence of neoclassicism. The purification of lang. went hand in hand with a return to discipline and clarity in writing. Cl. genres, incl. descriptive poems, mock epics, odes, epistles, satires, fables, parables, and epigrams, were revived and cultivated.

Among the circle of poets close to the royal court, the most outstanding was Bishop Ignacy Krasicki (1735–1801). In 1778 he published anonymously his *Monachomachia*, a mock epic in ottava rima ridiculing the obscurantism and indulgence of monks. As a satiric poet, he reached his climax in *Satyry* (Satires, 1779–84), a series of penetrating ironic observations on contemporary morals which, thanks to brilliant dialogue and dramatic monologue, succeeded in being didactic without indulging in intrusive rhetoric. Another of his masterpieces is the collection *Bajki i przypowieści* (Fables and Parables, 1779), in which the old genre of the animal fable acquires a new form close to the epigram and characterized by clarity and conciseness as well as a bitter and disillusioned, if humorous, vision of humanity.

Another great master of witty verse was Stanisław Trembecki (1739?–1812). A libertine and courtier, he wrote political odes honoring the King and obscene erotic poems with equal ease. His highest achievements are his poetic fables, his rococo anacreontics, and his descriptive poem *Sofiówka* (Sophie's Garden, 1806).

By and large, though, poets of the P. Enlightenment pursued the stylistic ideals of either strict neoclassicism or preromantic sentimentalism. A good example of the former is the work of Bishop Adam Naruszewicz (1733–96); its belated extension can be seen in the conservative and rigid stance of the last generation of neoclassicists, incl.

Kajetan Koźmian (1771–1856), Ludwik Osiński (1775–1838), and Alojzy Feliński (1771–1820). During the first decades of the 19th c., Sentimentalism, on the other hand, surfaced in the works of Franciszek Dionizy Kniaźnin (1750–1807) and Franciszek Karpiński (1741–1825), who, in their songs and eclogues, offered many fine examples of simple and emotionally direct lyricism. Another link between the Enlightenment and romanticism can be discerned in the work of the versatile writer Julian Ursyn Niemcewicz (1758–1841), the first to popularize the ballad through both his translations and his original poetry.

V. ROMANTICISM is a pivotal epoch in P. lit. hist. The historic upheavals beginning with the final partition of Poland in 1795 created a sociopolitical situation in which lit., and particularly poetry, became a substitute for other means of shaping the nation's mentality. The term *wieszcz* (a bard, but also a prophet) came into being to denote the new role of the poet as spiritual leader. However, one of the most conspicuous features of P. romanticism is the enormous disparity between a few great "bards" and hundreds of minor poets, both for artistic innovation and actual influence. It is also significant that all the giants of P. romanticism achieved their prominence in exile; their works, of unprecedented value to the cultural survival of the oppressed P. nation, were written and published mostly in Paris.

The period of greatest achievement in romantic poetry is framed by the dates of two abortive insurrections against Czarist Russia, 1830–31 and 1863. But the starting point of P. romanticism in a broader sense is 1822, the year that saw the debut of Adam Mickiewicz (1798–1855). Mickiewicz began to write as a student at the University of Wilno and immediately became the central figure of the rapidly emerging romantic movement. His early work still owed a great deal to the spirit of the Enlightenment: "Oda do młodości" (Ode to Youth), for example, is a peculiar combination of Cl. rhet. and the new *Sturm und Drang* ideology. Well read in Goethe, Schiller, and Byron, Mickiewicz soon developed his own romantic style. His first volume, *Ballady i romanse* (Ballads and Romances), was an audacious manifestation of a specifically P. version of early romanticism in which references to native folklore helped to introduce elements of fantasy and the supernatural and to express the "living truths" of the heart. Mickiewicz's debut was hailed as a literary breakthrough by his own generation, but it met with ridicule from his elders the Classicists. The ensuing strife between the romantics and the Classicists was fueled by Mickiewicz's subsequent publications during the 1820s. Two tales in verse, *Grażyna* (1823) and *Konrad Wallenrod* (1828), two parts of the poetic drama *Dziady* (Forefather's Eve, 1823), and the exquisite sequence of *Sonety krymskie* (Crimean Sonnets, 1826), all offer an entirely new set of values, such as frenetic love, the tragic loneliness of the hero, and individual sacrifice.

Mickiewicz's leading role at this stage becomes apparent when contrasted with the output of other early romantics. Antoni Malczewski (1793–1826) left behind only one major work: the Byronic tale in verse, *Maria* (1826). Bohdan Zaleski (1802–86) was an author of serene, songlike imitations of folk poetry. Seweryn Goszczyński (1801–76) gained notoriety as a bard of social protest.

Esp. after the 1831 defeat of the November Insurrection, when many P. intellectuals, incl. Mickiewicz, settled in France as political refugees, Mickiewicz's position of leadership became indisputable. His theme of patriotic struggle and heroic sacrifice now acquired new, metaphysical dimensions, while in his poetic art he constantly sought new forms of expression. Part 3 of *Dziady* offered a new vision of Poland's destiny as well as a new step in the devel. of romantic drama; the work is a masterpiece of innovative construction, style, and versification. Only two years later, Mickiewicz published a completely different book, yet another masterpiece, *Pan Tadeusz* (1834), a Homeric epos on the poet's homeland, the P.-Lithuanian province at the time of the Napoleonic wars, in which nostalgia and sorrow mix with warm humor and discreet irony. In the subtlety of its narration (the interplay of the narrator's identification with and distance from the reality presented) and its stylistic richness, *Pan Tadeusz* remains to this day the crowning achievement of P. epic poetry. After its publication, Mickiewicz, increasingly absorbed in mystical soul-searching and political activity, lapsed into silence as a poet, interrupted only by the brief sequence of the so-called Lausanne poems (written in 1839), purely lyric in character and strikingly innovative in their use of indirect symbolic lang.

Mickiewicz's fellow-exile and main rival, Juliusz Słowacki (1809–49), was less appreciated by his contemporaries. Yet his voluminous output spans a great many genres from lyric poems to poetic dramas to tales in verse and visionary epics, and his plays are a crucial factor in the evolution of P. romantic poetry as well as theater. Written mostly in verse, they experiment with both versification and dramatic construction; their settings are variously realistic, historical, legendary, dreamlike, or symbolic. In his poems, Słowacki felt equally at ease in epic description or in lyric confession, in complex stanza patterns or in biblical prose. His book-length poem in ottava rima, *Beniowski* (1841), is a magnificent example of the genre of the "poem of digressions" and of romantic irony, close in its style to Byron's *Don Juan* and Puškin's *Evgenij Onegin*. The last, "mystical" period in Słowacki's short life yielded an immense (even though unfinished) poem, also in ottava rima, *Król-Duch* (King-Spirit, 1847), a mythopoetic vision of P. destiny shown through consecutive reincarnations of the nation's spirit. Sélowacki's significance lies not only in his matchless technical virtuosity but also in that in his last phase he was an early forerunner of modern trends in poetry, incl. symbolism. Characteristically, his fame grew rapidly in the 1890s and 1900s.

Critical opinions, concerning the other two poets of the 19th-c.'s "great four" have become diametrically opposed in the 20th c. Zygmunt Krasiński (1812–59), for some time labeled "the third bard," today is admired mostly as an author of fascinating letters and two excellent political plays. Possessing a perspicacious and complex mind, Krasiński nevertheless lacked both Mickiewicz's poetic force and Słowacki's craftsmanship.

The posthumous reputation of the work of Cyprian Kamil Norwid (1821–83) presents a stark contrast with Krasiński's diminishing appeal. Forgotten and isolated in his lifetime and rediscovered only several decades after his death, today he is considered the philosophic and artistic harbinger of modern P. p. One generation younger than Mickiewicz, Norwid developed his art both under the influence of and as a polemic with P. romanticism. He replaced the prevalent attitude of nationalistic messianism with his original version of humanistic universalism, a concept of modern man as heir to the great civilizations of the past. From this perspective, Norwid attempted to dissect the most essential problems of contemp. history, politics, and culture. Although he employed a wide variety of genres and forms, he was most successful in his brief lyrics, distinguished by their highly intellectual content. In particular, his collection of 100 such poems titled *Vade-mecum* (written before 1866 and never published in his lifetime) offers an amazingly modern model of semantically dense and ironic poetry.

In contrast to the four great emigrés, among the multitude of "domestic" poets of the 19th c. only a few authors achieved some distinction—Kornel Ujejski (1823–97) with patriotic poems, Ryszard Berwiński (1817–79) with a call for social revolution and with ironic observations on contemp. morals, Teofil Lenartowicz (1822–93) with lyrics based on stylistic references to folklore, and Władysław Syrokomla (1823–62) with verse tales employing the voice of a peasant speaker.

VI. POSITIVISM AND NEOROMANTICISM. The 1863 defeat of the January Insurrection generated a distrust of romantic ideology and undermined the authority of romantic "bards": the ensuing epoch of positivism was a programmatically antipoetic age. In lit. there was a general shift toward realistic and naturalistic fiction and drama; only a few names of relative significance emerged in the field of poetry. Adam Asnyk (1838–97) left behind a number of lyrics, postromantic in style and ranging from the erotic to the philosophic. Maria Konopnicka (1842–1910) was one of the most vocal proponents of social reform in the spirit of positivism; her poetry written in defense of the oppressed is characterized by its skillful use of folklore and its introduction of a speaker from the lower classes. In the last decade of the 19th c., the prosaic epoch of positivism gave way to another era of poetry. This new trend, variously called Young Poland, modernism, or neoromanticism, was strongly influenced by Western European symbolism and the philosophy of Schopenhauer and Nietzsche, but it also gave expression to specifically P. problems. The most influential exponent of the new "decadent" mood was Kazimierz Przerwa Tetmajer (1865–1940), who in his lyric poems published in the 1890s set up an emotional model for the whole generation of Young Poland—a norm of sensitivity consisting of pessimism, individualism, and distrust of any dogma. Other poets of this period underwent a more complicated devel. Jan Kasprowicz (1860–1926), for example, started with naturalistic depictions of peasants' poverty and after intermediary stages of symbolist spleen and expressionist rebellion ended as a serene poet of reconciliation with God and the world. From the technical point of view, his late poems are an important contribution to "tonism," a system of accentual versification based on an equal number of stresses rather than syllables.

Stanisław Wyspiański (1869–1907), best known as a prolific playwright, was perhaps the most romantic of all poets of Young Poland. His visionary, half-romantic, half-symbolist plays refer to both P. history and contemp. events, mingling mythological or legendary figures with historical or present-day characters. Tadeusz Miciński (1873–1918), also an innovative dramatist, was the author of an important collection of poems, *W mroku gwiazd* (In the Darkness of Stars, 1902), in which he anticipated expressionism. Leopold Staff (1878–1957) lived long enough to participate in three consecutive literary epochs; within Young Poland, he represented a trend opposing "decadence" and favoring Cl. lucidity.

The greatest poet of Young Poland emerged quite unexpectedly when the epoch was already in decline. Bolesław Leśmian (1878–1937) published his first collection only in 1912, and his next two books appeared as late as 1920 and 1936. Nevertheless, he must be considered a belated symbolist, and only the striking originality of his lang. obscures this genetic link. Leśmian's poetic style is a direct consequence of his philosophy. A follower of Bergson, he saw the world as a field of incessant conflict between inert Matter and the creative force of Spirit; since this conflict cannot be resolved, the world is always *in statu nascendi.* The task of poetry is to convey this instability. Its rhythm should express the world's *élan vital,* and its imagery should reflect reality's metamorphoses. The poet himself should assume the cognitive stance of primeval man, whose act of perception creates, as it were, the world perceived.

VII. THE INTERWAR PERIOD AND THE WAR YEARS. The 20 years of Independent Poland (1918–39) can be visualized as a gradual turn from light to darkness, from initial optimism and hope to final catastrophe. This change found its reflection in the evolution of poetry. The tone for the first decade of the interwar period was set by an explosion of new, mostly avant-garde programs and a multitude of poetic groups, periodicals, and even cabarets around 1918. Many of these initiatives were ephemeral, but some of them developed into influential trends. There was, however, only one poetic group that managed to hold sway over public opinion for two decades, if not longer. The five poets who formed a group called Skamander—Julian Tuwim (1894–1953), Antoni Słonimski (1895–1976), Jan Lechoń (1899–1956), Jarosław Iwaszkiewicz (1894–1980), and Kazimierz Wierzyński (1894–1969)—owed their popularity to the fact that their poetry was original and innovative while also far more comprehensible than the works of their avant-garde contemporaries.

Skamander's only program consisted of rejecting traditional concepts of poetry's "duties" and enjoying artistic freedom; accordingly, the group abandoned all neoromantic conventions and turned to contemp. reality and a refreshingly direct style. But the differences among the five poets were to increase as their work developed. Tuwim soon became a master of verbal magic and explosive lyric force. Słonimski's poetry was rationalistic, discursive, and rhetorical. Lechoń, obsessed with P. history, combined references to the romantic trad. with a Cl. style. Iwaszkiewicz, after his brief fascination with expressionism, chose aestheticism as his principal attitude.

Wierzyński, initially a joyful vitalist, was to reach his peak in his bitter post-1945 poetry, written in exile and much modernized in form. Within the wide circle of Skamander's influence, some other poets followed their individual paths. Władysław Broniewski (1897–1962) managed to combine his Communist ideology with close ties to the P. romantic trad. In her concise, aphoristic poems, Maria Pawlikowska (1891–1945) aimed to formulate modern woman's perspective on the theme of love. Jerzy Liebert (1904–31) was an original poet of religious experience.

While Skamander dominated the poetic scene, numerous avant-garde groups propounded more radical programs of new poetry. The P. futurists, incl. Bruno Jasieński (1901–39) and Aleksander Wat (1900–67), did not win a great following, but they prepared the ground for the program of the so-called Cracow Avant-garde, the most prominent representatives of which were Tadeusz Peiper (1891–1969) and Julian Przyboś (1901–70). As opposed to the futurists' poetic anarchism, the Cracow Avant-garde advocated constructivism and rigor based on metaphor and syntax.

The 1930s, marked by economic, political, and ideological crisis, brought about the so-called Second Avant-garde—not so much a poetic group as a new generation of poets who prophesied the approaching global catastrophe. Konstanty Ildefons Gałczyński (1905–53), who later was to become one of the most popular P. poets, did so by use of the grotesque and mockery. Józef Czechowicz (1903–39), initially a poet of idyllic provincial landscapes, in his later poems expressed his Catastrophist fears using his own avant-garde technique of metaphoric condensation. Czesław Miłosz (b. 1911), the greatest living P. poet and the winner of the 1980 Nobel Prize for Lit., underwent a complicated evolution from his prewar Catastrophism to his present poetry of metaphysical theme and polyphonic construction.

The atrocities of World War II confirmed the premonitions and predictions of Catastrophist poetry; the theme of "Apocalypse come true" was central to the work of a new generation of poets, most of whom died young as underground fighters or soldiers in the 1944 Warsaw Uprising. Such was the fate of Krzysztof Kamil Baczyński (1921–44), who left behind a brilliant lyric oeuvre, visionary and symbolist in style.

VIII. THE POSTWAR PERIOD. After the end of World War II and the imposition of Communist rule in Poland, many of its poets worked in exile. Despite a censorship ban, a great deal of emigré lit. found its way into the country and enjoyed a remarkable popularity, to mention only the examples of Miłosz, Wierzyński, and Wat. Those poets who have remained in Poland or have been repatriated faced a situation of more or less limited freedom of speech until the 1980s. In spite of that, post-1945 P. p. scored many artistic successes. Tadeusz Różewicz (b. 1921) offered a new, ascetic style employing "the anonymous voice" of a survivor. After the years of Stalinism (1949– 55), one of the first harbingers of the approaching "thaw" in cultural policy was the publication in 1955 of Adam Ważyk's much-discussed "Poemat dla dorosłych" (Poem for Adults), followed by similarly "revisionist" poems by Mieczysław Jastrun (1903–83) and others.

The year 1956 marked the beginning of a genuine eruption of new names, trends, and poetic programs. The poetry of the late 1950s and 1960s was characterized by the coexistence of a strong current of ironic moral reflection, as found in the works of Zbigniew Herbert (b. 1924), Wisława Szymborska (b. 1923), Artur Międzyrzecki (b. 1922), Julia Hartwig (b. 1921), Wiktor Woroszylski (b. 1927), and Stanisław Jerzy Lec (1909–66), and an equally powerful trend of linguistic experimentation, exemplified by Miron Białoszewski (1922–83), Tymoteusz Karpowicz (b. 1921), Witold Wirpsza (1918–85), and Jerzy Ficowski (b. 1924). Stanisław Grochowiak (1934–76), Tadeusz Nowak (b. 1930), and Jerzy Harasymowicz (b. 1933) contributed to the post-1956 "liberation of imagination" by building their private worlds of imagination and fantasy. Ernest Bryll (b. 1935) offered his own version of a return to the romantic trad., and Jarosław Marek Rymkiewicz (b. 1935) propounded his program of modern neoclassicism.

In the early 1970s, a new generation of P. poets came to the fore, drawing upon the experiences of both the older "moralists" and "linguists" in order to find a new poetic lang. for antitotalitarian protest and existential reflection. Ryszard Krynicki (b. 1943), Ewa Lipska (b. 1945), Adam Zagajewski (b. 1945), Julian Kornhauser (b. 1946), and Stanisław Barańczak (b. 1946) are representative of this trend, joined in the 1980s by promising younger poets such as Jan Polkowski (b. 1953) and Bronisław Maj (b. 1953).

ANTHOLOGIES: *Od Kochanowskiego do Staffa*, ed. W. Borowy (1930); *Poeci renesansu*, ed. J. Sokołowska (1959); *Zbiór poetów polskich XIX wieku*, ed. P. Hertz, 7 v. (1959–75); *Five Cs. of P. P.*, ed. and tr. J. Peterkiewicz and B. Singer (1962); *Poezja polska 1914–39*, ed. R. Matuszewski and S. Pollak (1962); *Poeci polskiego baroku*, ed. J. Sokołowska and K. Żukowska, 2 v. (1965); *Poezja polska*, ed. S. Grochowiak and J. Maciejewski, 2 v. (1973); *Poezja polska XVIII wieku*, ed. Z. Libera, 2d ed. (1976); *Poezja Młodej Polski*, ed. M. Jastrun (1976); *Kolumbowie i współcześni*, 2d ed. (1976), *Ze struny na strune* (1980), both ed. A. Lam; *Antologia polskiego futuryzmu i Nowej Sztuki*, ed. Z. Jarosiński and H. Zaworska (1978); *Średniowieczna pieśn religijna polska*, ed. M. Korolko, 2d ed. (1980); *Świat poprawiac—zuchwałe rzemiosło*, ed. T. Kostkiewiczowa and Z. Goliński (1981); *Postwar P. P.*, ed. C. Miłosz, 3d ed. (1983); *Poeta pamieta*, ed. S. Barańczak (1984); *P. P. of the Last Two Decades of Communist Rule*, ed. S. Baranczak and C. Cavanagh (1992).

HISTORY AND CRITICISM: J. Krzyżanowski, *P. Romantic Lit.* (1930), *A Hist. of P. Lit.* (1980); W. Borowy, *O poezji polskiej w wieku XVIII* (1948), *O Norwidzie* (1960); W. Weintraub, *The Poetry of A. Mickiewicz* (1954), *Rzecz czarnoleska* (1977); M. Kridl, *A Survey of P. Lit. and Culture* (1956); C. Zgorzelski, *O liryce Mickiewicza i Słowackiego* (1961); K. Wyka, *Pan Tadeusz*, 2 v. (1963); M. R. Mayenowa, *Strofika: praca zbiorowa* (1964), *O sztuce czytania wierszy*, 2d ed. (1967); J. Trznadel, *Twórczośc Leśmiana* (1964); J. Sławiński, *Koncepcja jezyka poetyckiego Awangardy Krakowskiej* (1965); *Obraz literatury polskiej XIX i XX w.*, 11 v. (1965–79); H. Zaworska, *O nowa sztuke* (1965); J. Błoński, *M. Sep Szarzyński, a poczatki polskiego baroku* (1967), *Odmarsz* (1978); K. Wyka, *Modernizm polski*, 2d ed. (1968), *Rzecz wyobraźni*, 2d ed. (1977); S. Jaworski, *U podstaw Awangardy* (1968); M. Podraza-Kwiatkowska, *Młodopolskie harmonie i dysonanse* (1969), *Symbolizm i symbolika w poezji Młodej Polski* (1975); M. Janion, *Romantyzm* (1970); M. Giergielewicz, *Intro. to P. Versification* (1970); Z. Łapiński, *Norwid* (1971); I. Opacki, *Poezja romantycznych przełomów* (1972); J. Kwiatkowski, *Klucze do wyobraźni*, 2d ed. (1973); G. Gomori, *C. Norwid* (1974); A. Witkowska, *A. Mickiewicz* (1975); T. Kostkiewiczowa, *Klasycyzm, sentymentalizm, rokoko* (1975); C. Zgorzelski, *O sztuce poetyckiej Mickiewicza* (1976); A. Sandauer, *Poeci czterech pokoleń* (1977); J. Stradecki, *W kregu Skamandra* (1977); *Słownik literatury polskiego Oświecenia*, ed. T. Kostkiewiczowa (1977); M. Dłuska, *Studia z historii i teorii wersyfikacji polskiej*, 2d ed., 2 v. (1978); S. Barańczak, *Etyka i poetyka* (1979), *A Fugitive from Utopia* (1987); J. Ziomek, *Renesans*, 4th ed. (1980); M. Klimowicz, *Oświecenie*, 4th ed. (1980); H. Markiewicz, *Pozytywizm*, 2d ed. (1980); J. Pelc, *J. Kochanowski* (1980); C. Hernas, *Barok*, 4th ed. (1981); M. Głowiński, *Zaświat przedstawiony* (1981); M. G. Levine, *Contemp. P. P., 1925–75* (1981); E. Balcerzan, *Poezja polska w latach 1939–65*, v. 1 (1982); *Poeci dwudziestolecia miedzywojennego*, ed. I. Maciejewska, 2 v. (1982); R. Przybylski, *Klasycyzm* (1983); C. Miłosz, *The Hist. of P. Lit.*, 2d ed. (1983); B. Carpenter, *The Poetic Avant-garde in Poland, 1918–39* (1983); T. Nyczek, *Powiedz tylko słowo* (1985); *Poznawanie Miłosza*, ed. J. Kwiatkowski (1985); F. W. Aaron, *Bearing the Unbearable: Yiddish and P. P. in the Ghettos and Concentration Camps* (1990). S.B.

POLYNESIAN POETRY. Cultural and linguistic homogeneity, both in poetry and prose, is sufficiently marked, despite interisland diversity, to designate Polynesia a distinctive cultural area of the Pacific. This area extends south from the Tropic of Cancer, which passes through the Hawaiian Islands, and east of the 180th meridian, except for New Zealand and Tuvalu (formerly called Ellice Islands). Westward in Melanesia and Micronesia are scattered P. enclaves. Because Polynesia, like these other areas, was nonliterate prior to European contact, knowledge was mainly transmitted orally and by demonstration, usages which are both of continuing importance. An exceptionally verbal society, Polynesia elevated oral art to a high level of beauty and subtlety. The limited number of sounds in P. langs. also shaped P. verbal style, with Hawaiian having the fewest (five long and five short vowels and only eight consonants—*p, k*, glottal stop, *h, m, n, l, w*). Consequently, poets used numerous homonyms, puns, repetitions, reduplication, and alliteration, and, unlike modern listeners, enjoyed frequent reiterations of sound. Grammar also favored repetition.

The earliest knowledge of P. p.—its themes, styles, forms, functions, performances, and composers—that came from late 18th-c. Western explorers provides a baseline for charting post-European change and retention. Initially Western culture—Christianity, literacy, printing, mores, technology, and political organization—introduced by 19th-c. missionaries, settlers, colonial officials, and voyagers stimulated poetic creativity by adding new concepts and symbols without, however, the traditional art losing its indigenous identity. Although the subsequently increasing Westernization led to cultual attenuation of the traditional, more than "memory culture" of poetics survived. With modifications to allow for foreign stimulus, the past tense used here to characterize P. p. can frequently be replaced by the present tense.

POLYNESIAN POETRY

Poetry, integral to personal life from birth to death and to both religion and entertainment, was frequently entwined with ritual, vocalization, and dance to express values, give aesthetic pleasure, transmit knowledge, and affirm the affinity of human beings with nature and the supernatural. P. cultural traits of personifying nature with gods and spirits (many regarded as ancestors) and of reacting emotionally to changing aspects of landscape led to minute observation, vivid description, and extensive naming of places and natural forces.

The value given to artistic and imaginative manipulation of lang. within recognized patterns ensured that any individual with creativity, a good memory, and a good voice could win social and material rewards. Fame was not limited by sex, age, occupation, or social position either in a populous, class-structured archipelago or a small, less formally organized atoll. A bard of commoner status received gifts from audiences and, even better, might be added to a chief's retinue. Chiefs and chieftesses, however, were the most prolific composers, priding themselves on their poetic talent and erudition. Their elite status, assuring them of recognition and opportunity for performance, made poetry a predominantly aristocratic art. Oral trad. and publication have preserved texts of poems, many composers' names, and information about styles of delivery, circumstances of composition, and the significance of elliptical allusions.

Poetry and music being inseparable, each adding power to the other, a poet composed text and melody at the same time. Each category of poetry had its characteristic modes of rhythmic oral delivery, the principal modes being song or recitative, with variations and combinations of each. Hawaiians, for example, distinguished between an *oli* and a *mele* but adapted a poem to either. An *oli* was a dignified recitative, most often a solo, with limited gestures and occasional percussion accompaniment, for dirges, prayers, eulogies, and genealogies, each class with its special *oli* style. The basic style was a rapid, guttural, vibrating monotone on a single pitch that required a strong, deep voice trained to hold the breath through long phrases often ending with a trill. Continuity of sound was essential because breath carried the *mana*-filled words, and a break or hesitation except at appropriate places was believed unlucky in a secular poem and fatal in a sacred. A *mele* was sung or chanted to the accompaniment of dance (*hula*), pantomime, and instruments (not always the three together); a subtype was performed either with or without dance for love songs, name songs honoring individuals, or genital chants celebrating their generative powers. A *mele*, customarily performed with a chorus whose leader sang solo parts, had marked, repeated rhythmic patterns if danced and a wider range of pitch and freedom than the *oli*. Missionary hymns brought melody, which Polynesians called *hīmeni* and combined with old styles of delivery for new poems, not necessarily sacred, but not danced. While music changed as Westerners introduced their folk and work songs, texts retained many traditional themes and devices. The same was the case in other achipelagos beside the Hawaiian.

A new poem that met an audience's approval was performed repeatedly and might become a classic passed on for generations. Change came, however, from variations and distortions in delivery and from other poets combining the new poem with existing poems, adding or eliminating verses, replacing proper names, and adapting the poem to different social uses. The recurrence of certain themes, images, phrases, and lines was not considered plagiarism because poets shared the same culture, formulaic lang., and poetic diction; genius lay in fresh and innovative rearrangement or reinterpretation.

Islands frequently restricted rights of performance, esp. if the poem was a gift or part of the intangible treasure of a chiefly lineage. It could be performed only in the owner's presence or with permission, and at death was bequeathed to a relative. A 101-line poem was the condolence gift ("My poem is but poor yet take it") that Chief Fisherman Ulamoleke, a petty Tongan chief, composed and chanted to his bereaved friend Falepapalangi, a renowned professional poet, who thanked him by immediately repeating the entire poem.

Samoan chiefs (but not commoners) could sing a *solo* (the Samoan term for a recitative epitomizing a myth or legend) of the subcategory *fa'ali'i*—royal, concerning a royal lineage. A politically important trad., for example, centered on Sanalālā: when his canoe was swept to sea from Tonga to Samoa, his father's land, his Tongan mother, Chieftess Fitimaupaloga, composed a 21-line *solo fa'ali'i* considered "exceedingly beautiful." A chief was much admired when he sang it with a plaintive cadence while accompanying himself on a type of drum only certain chiefly families could use (Freeman). The first three lines of its introduction below are repeated as epilogue:

> See the morning cloud arise.
> Where in that crimson cloud
> Is Oneata's lovely bay?
> The bay where is my child,
> My child makes my heart breathless.

Illustrated are such common P. poetic devices as inspiration from nature and place; irregular but rhythmic lines; repetition of sounds, words, and syllables; and (peculiarly in western P.) deliberate rhyming and terminating sets of lines with a certain sound.

Hawaiian, Marquesan, and Tuamotuan ruling families owned sacred creation and genealogical chants which only senior males and high priests could intone in consecrating a chief's primary wife's firstborn son and on other occasions. Numerous resemblances with other chants elsewhere prove the chants share the same P. heritage. Their fundamental function concerned procreation and the continuity of life through the chief, on whom, as the closest link to the gods, the fertility of nature and people depended. Starting with creation, a chanter connected the infant to his divine and earthly kin and thereby confirmed his rank, privileges, taboos, territory, and power. Because words had power to produce action, an error or hesitation negated a sacred chant.

An example is the Hawaiian *Kumulipo* (Origin in Deepest Darkness), a 2,102-line masterpiece of the type called *ku'auhau*, "pathway-lineage," property of the family of Kalākaua and his sister Lili'uokalani, the last rulers in the 19th c. of the monarchy established by Kamehameha I in 1795. When priests ca. 1700 A.D. chanted the *Kumulipo*, each name activated the latent *mana* (supernatural power) of High Chief Keawe's son and heir, named Lono-i-ka-makahiki because he was born during the annual Makahiki festival for Lono, god of peace and prosperity. It may have been recited in 1779 over Captain Cook as the returned god Lono.

Over half of the chant lists genealogical pairs. Of its sixteen odes the first seven are in the period of Pō (Darkness, Night) when earth emerged and generating couples bore named descendants in each class of plant and animal species of sea, sky, and land. The remaining nine odes are in the era of Ao (Light, Day, Reason) when gods, demigods, and their sacred descendants were born. The chant carried the spark of life and *mana* down to Lono-i-ka-makahiki, who would continue this ancestral line. Hawaiians differ on the inner meaning (*kaona*) of the chant. A political interpretation is that it symbolizes migration, population growth, and the rise of rival chiefs who established branch family lines and seized lands. A favored *kaona* is that the child's development parallels that of the cosmos, born from night and ocean; conception, birth, and early growth occur in Pō, and adolescence and sexual and social maturity in Ao. Here is the prologue to Ode One:

At the time when the earth became hot
At the time when the heavens turned
about
At the time when the sun was darkened
To cause the moon to shine
The time of the rise of the Pleiades
The slime, this was the source of the
earth
The source of the darkness that made
darkness
The source of the night that made
night
The intense darkness, the deep dark-
ness
Darkness of the sun, darkness of the
night
Nothing but night
The night gave birth. . . .
(Beckwith)

A secular text and sometimes its music might come to a poet during dreams, visions, trances, and solitude, aided by supernatural beings after prayers and offerings. Narrators of prose sagas used supernatural, legendary, and fictitious characters as surrogates to pour out poems, more stable over time than the plots. The New Zealand fairy folk Patupaiarehe sang in an archaic dialect, and the Hawaiian goddess Hi'iaka, the most prolific poet of all, composed incomparable *mele*, *ole*, and other forms during a journey (a favorite P. device for unifying songs) for her sister Pele, volcano goddess. Chants in sagas about pan-Polynesian mythical or legendary chiefs like Rata and Tahaki are sometimes attributed to other characters in the plots.

Poets composed alone, with a companion, or in a group. Each poet in a conclave, composing at a chief's order for a special event, contributed lines which after revision became part of the whole that everyone memorized so as to preserve. A Hawaiian ruler who had his *haku mele* (weavers of songs) compose name chants celebrating his expected child's ancestry, then perform them widely, believed, as did others, they contributed to a favorable outcome.

Among numerous festivals that central Polynesians held between 19th-c. wars was Chief Poito's dusk-to-dawn entertainment to please two gods of Mangaia Island. For a year, six poets worked on 20 songs and presentations while the people raised food for guests. In the local style the poets structured solos and choruses with an introduction, "foundation," "offshoots," and finale. Some required drums and precision choreography with as many as 200 performers. In Pukapuka three villages set aside a festival day to face each other in poetic contests with old and new insulting songs and dances.

Eastern P. chiefs and priests, who were educated in sacred houses of learning, excelled in technical skill at composition and erudition. Marquesan and Mangarevan masters served rulers as organizers and directors of ceremonies, determined official versions of sacred chants and history, and recited the most sacred parts of chants. A Marquesan tribal Master of Chants, outranked only by the ruler and the inspirational priest, might be deified at death. Nonetheless, if another tribe's Master challenged him, he had to compete successfully before an audience, exhibiting his learning, quickness in composition, and ability in other oral arts at the risk of losing his title or even his life. Many P. islands had such contests of wit and learning.

A Samoan chief's talking chief, also a master of ceremony and subject to challenges from a rival, upheld his chief's and village's prestige, esp. on official visits to other villages, by his command of the complex art of oratory, learning, composition, and knowledge of procedure and etiquette due each titled man present. Tonga, on the other hand, had a class of professional poets, generally untitled but with status roughly equivalent to a ruler's ceremonial attendants. A poet, though honored, was entirely dependent on his patron chief, and usually insecure even as to his life. At one time contests between poets became so bitter they had to be discontinued.

Travelling entertainment troupes, dependent on the largesse of chiefs and donations from audiences, danced and sang popular songs and put on humorous skits at public gatherings and festivals. Islands like Mangareva and the Cook Islands and Marquesas had informally organized groups, mostly young people with an older leader. Hawaiian hula troupes, more organized, underwent taboo-regulated education in schools, each with its own customs but all emphasizing prayers and invocations to gods and goddesses. Most organized of all was the progressively graded Arioi Society of male and female entertainers serving the god 'Oro in the Society Islands; all except members of the highest grades in inherited positions had to kill children born to them or leave in disgrace (Luomala).

One cannot generalize as yet for all Polynesia as for New Zealand about differences between men's and women's compositions. Maori women, who as a group predominated as composers, were more likely than men to compose songs about frustrated love ("Would I were a broken canoe that might be mended") and short, informally arranged, intensely personal laments with simple but appealing imagery ("Like the tides within Tirau forever rising and falling / Is my wild lamentation within Houhangapa"). Maori men were more likely to compose longer, more formally structured laments, filled with elaborate imagery to emphasize that the whole tribe had lost a great man ("like a star shining apart in the Milky Way," or "a sheltering rata tree from the north wind"). That men composed most of the priestly songs may apply to Polynesia as a whole; however, little is known about compositions by priestesses (Ngata; Mead). See NEW ZEALAND POETRY.

The West has fostered both retention and change through its printing press, transportation, education, and lang. Foreigners, the first to collect and publish traditional lore in island langs., occasionally translated and discussed it in their national langs.—Eng., Fr., or Ger. Vernacular newspapers and magazines since the 19th c. have published literate islanders' collections of "old" lore and their creations of novels, plays, and poems combining traditional and Western themes. Festivals of song and dance reviving older forms and inspiring new that were once limited to a single island or archipelago now bring audiences, composers, and performers from an increasingly wider area; air travel has made them pan-Pacific. An elite group of University-educated literary artists that emerged during the 1960s and 1970s, consciously or not, draws inspiration from oral art to write creatively in Eng. and to develop a Pacific-wide "new lit."

Collections of texts of chants, most with translations, some with music, and all with ethnographic discussion, appear in the bulletins, memoirs, and special publications of the Bernice P. Bishop Museum (Honolulu) and in the journals, memoirs, and Maori texts of the P. Society (Wellington). See Bishop Museum *Bulletin* 8, 9, 17, 29, 34, 46, 48, 95, 109, 127, 148, 158, 183, *Memoirs* IV, V, VI, *Special Pubs.* 2, 51, 61; P. Society *Memoirs* 3, 4, 5, 41; *Maori Texts*: A. T. Ngata, *Nga Moteatea*, Part I (1959), and A. T. Ngata and P. Te Hurinui, Part II (1961); *MANA*, Univ. South Pacific Publ. (1973–).

W. W. Gill, *Myths and Songs from the South Pacific* (1876), *Historical Sketches of Savage Life in Polynesia* (1880); M. W. Beckwith, Intro., *The Hawaiian Romance of Laieikawai* (1919), *The Kumulipo, a Hawaiian Creation Chant* (rpt. 1972); S. H. Elbert, "Chants and Love Songs of the Marquesas, Fr. Oceania," *Jour. P. Society* 56 (1947), "Hawaiian Literary Style and Culture," *Am. Anthropologist* 53 (1951); J. D. Freeman, "The Trad. of Sanalālā," *Jour. P. Society* 56 (1947); M. K. Pukui, "Songs (Meles) of Old Ka'u, Hawaii," *JAF* 62 (1948); D. Christensen and G. Koch, *Die Musik der Ellice-Inseln* (1964); S. M. Mead, "Imagery, Symbolism, and Social Values in Maori Chants," *Jour. P. Society* 78 (1969); B. Mitcalfe, *Maori Poetry: The Singing Word* (1974); M. McLean and M. Orbell, *Traditional Songs of the Maori* (1975); N. B. Emerson, *Unwritten Lit. of Hawaii: Sacred Songs of the Hula* (rpt. 1977), *Pele and Hiiaka, a Myth from Hawaii* (rpt. 1978); Subramani, *South Pacific Lit. from Myth to Fabulation* (1985); K. Luomala, *Voices on the Wind: P. Myths and Chants*, rev. ed. (1986). K.L.

PORTUGUESE POETRY. P. lit. has its origins in the *cantigas* which arose in Galicia toward the end of the 12th c. In the earliest period, Galician and P. p. cannot be satisfactorily separated (see GALICIAN POETRY). Gradually the center of gravity of this common poetry moves south with more identifiable P. names among the *trovadores* (troubadours of upper classes), *segreis* (lower-born, paid composers), and *jograis* (musicians of humble birth) represented in the three great *cancioneiros*. Although these collections contain much monotonous verse revealing poverty of ideas and highly conventional vocabulary, there are poetic gems of clearly personal inspiration and technical perfection, esp. among the *cantigas de amigo* based on indigenous folk *cossantes* rather than on Occitan types. Some of the better known P. poets are Joan Zorro, Vasco Gil, Joan Soares Coelho, Airas Perez Vuitorom, Lourenço Jogral, King Diniz (1261–1325) and his natural sons Afonso Sanches and Pedro Conde de Barcelos. After the death of Diniz, who was the most prolific, the Galician and P. langs. gradually separate, and the troubadouresque tradition declines.

Much of the poetry written during the 15th c. is contained in the *Cancioneiro Geral* (General

Songbook, 1516), published by Garcia de Resende (1470?–1536) with compositions by nearly 300 poets. This court poetry shows greater metrical variety and more sophisticated form than the Galician-P. compilations. Sp. influence predominates—some poems are in this lang. (Indeed, most P. poets up to the 18th c. are bilingual.) Much space is devoted to such trivia as poetic competitions, collective poems on ladies, petty satire, and poetic glosses of more social or sociological than literary interest. There are, however, Garcia de Resende's *Trovas* on the death of Inês de Castro; João Roiz de Castelo Branco's *Cantiga, partindo-se* (Song of Parting); the satirical work of Alvaro de Brito Pestana; Duarte de Brito, who reveals some It. influence; and poets who became famous later in the 16th c. One of these, Gil Vicente (1465?–1536?), the father of P. theater, included in his popular drama many lyric passages, *cantigas de amigo,* and other songs of medieval and folk inspiration in Sp. and P.

Resende's *Cancioneiro* already shows some Italianate influences, but Francisco Sá de Miranda (1495–1558), after his stay in Italy (1521–26), introduced into Portugal the sonnet, *canzone,* Dante's tercets and Ariosto's ottava rima, and many Ren. features that characterized the *Quinhentistas* (poets of the 1500s). Sá de Miranda was a painstaking craftsman, but the moral tone and formal innovations of his work are more important than its artistic qualities. His friend Bernardim Ribeiro (1482–1552), author of a highly sentimental pastoral novel *Menina e moça* (Young and Maiden), favored bucolic poetry and wrote the first eclogues in P. (*Jano e Franco,* etc.). This form would be greatly exploited for the next century, perhaps most successfully in the *Trovas de Crisfal* by Cristóvão Falcão (1518–57?).

The Ren. imitation of Cl. genres inspired Luis de Camões (ca. 1524–80), author of the greatest literary epic of the Iberian Peninsula, *Os Lusíadas,* and the outstanding P. lyric poet of all time. His *canções* and sonnets show a rare mastery of form and inspiration:

> My sweet soul who departed so soon,
> discontent with this life,
> rest eternally in heaven
> and let me live always sad on this earth!

The Lusiads, in ten ottava rima cantos, is perhaps the most typically national of all epics. Vasco de Gama's memorable expedition to India (1497–98) represents the principal subject; the hero of the poem is the P. people. Historical events (the founding of the P. kingdom, the battle of Aljubarrota, the death of Inês de Castro, etc.) and legendary ones (the "Twelve of England"), episodes from voyages (the fictitious Island of Love), and, through prophecy, Lusitanian accomplishments of the 16th c. are all magnificently described. The mingling of pagan mythology and Christianity, prosaic lines, and abuse of Cl. allusions in this poem have been criticized, but they are amply compensated for by the grandeur of conception, quotable lines, sincere patriotism, erudition, and reflections of the personal experiences of a very eventful life.

Other contemporaries still popular are two brothers, Diogo Bernardes (ca. 1530–1605?) and Frei Agostinho da Cruz (1540–1619). Bernardes wrote religious verses and bucolic poems that show a sincere love for P. nature in their descriptions of the Lima River. Agostinho destroyed his profane verse but left some profoundly religious songs.

The 17th c. could not but represent an anticlimax. In literary terms, its chief distinction lies in the great prose that contributed to the devel. of the modern P. lang. The poetry, much of which was collected in the five-volume *A Fénix Renascida* (1716–28), suffered from excesses inspired by Sp. Gongorism and *culteranismo.* Francisco Rodrigues Lobo (1580?–1622), however, continued the Ribeiro trad. with simple, gentle, yet colorful eclogues. Sóror Violante do Céu (1601–93), a Dominican nun, was much admired for her ingenious conceits imbued with mystic fervor, occasionally in a somewhat incongruous fashion. Francisco Manuel de Melo (1608–66), bilingual in Castilian and P., is better in prose, but has left eclogues and epistles of technical excellence. Throughout the century there were many epics, but all were overshadowed by Camões' work. Perhaps in no other country has such a large part of the national poetic effort gone into the production of epics.

The best poetry of the 18th c., particularly from the latter half, is produced by Arcadians who rejected Sp. influence of the 17th c. in favor of Fr. neoclassicism. The poetry from this period that is still remembered owes its reputation more to style and philosophical content than to its lyric qualities. Many of the poets belonged to the "Arcadia Lusitana" (or "Acad. Ulissiponense," from 1756) or the "Nova Arcádia" (from 1790). Each poet adopted the name of a shepherd celebrated in antiquity, and often such pseudonyms became better known than the real names. Pedro António Correia Garção (1724–72) is remembered for his reforms and for elegant poems such as *A cantata de Dido.* Nicolau Tolentino de Almeida (1740–1811) is the principal satirical poet. The most personal love lyrics of the century were written by a poet claimed by both Portugal and Brazil, Tomás António Gonzaga (1744–1810). His *Marília de Dirceu,* a lyric exception among many volumes of moralizing neoclassic verse of the age, has enjoyed exceptional popularity, as demonstrated by the great number of editions (probably second only to Camões). This is due not only to its melodiousness and sincerity, but also to the poet's romantic personal tragedy, his involvement in the Minas Conspiracy in Brazil (1789) and subsequent exile to Mozambique, which frustrated his love for "Marília." Among the New Arcadians, José Agostinho de Macedo (1761–1831) attracted contemporary attention by his irregular life and his bitterly polemic and philosophic verse. More important was Manuel Maria Barbosa du Boccage (1765–1805), a bohemian whose life has given rise to many *piadas* (anecdotes) but whose production includes, among much that is trivial, contentious, satirical, and improvised, sonnets of a perfection to be found only in Camões and Antero de Quental.

Romanticism in Portugal borrowed many features from France and elsewhere but represents a less spectacular break with the 18th c. than in other countries. Politically, events in Portugal tended to make its proponents patriotic and liberal. The beginning of the movement is usually dated from 1825, with the publication of *Camões,* an epic on the neglect of genius, by João Batista da Silva Leitão de Almeida Garrett (1799–1854). Almeida Garrett's neoclassical background prevented him from falling into romantic excesses. He contributed to literary nationalism with his collection of ballads, *Romanceiro* (1843). His best lyric verse is contained in *Folhas caídas* (Fallen Leaves, 1853)—ardent, elegant poetry among the best love songs in the lang. He is more restrained and more modern than many contemporaries. With his interest in the national past, his politically liberal enthusiasms, his great versatility, and his mastery of all genres, Almeida Garrett personifies P. romanticism, coming as close to being a one-man movement as is possible. Contrasting with him in personality and works, Alexandre Herculano (1810–77) wrote his best poetry in *A harpa do crente* (The Harp of the Believer, 1838), imbued with an austere, Christian spirit. Herculano, best known for his histories and historical novels, is a master of the lang. but produced more prosaic poetry than Garrett.

Another romantic, António Feliciano de Castilho (1800–75), remained more detached from the political agitation of the time because of his blindness. He, too, began as a neoclassic and possesses formal perfection with occasional inspiration. Usually, however, he must substitute mastery of lang. and patient craftsmanship for imagination and sensibility.

Among the "ultra-romantics," Soares de Passos (1826–60), translator of Ossian, is characterized by an emotive melancholy and morbid imagination. João de Deus (Ramos, 1830–96) combines some of the best features of the romantics with bourgeois sentiment and optimistic unselfishness. His effervescent *Campo de flores* (Field of Flowers, 1869, 1893) expresses best *o amor português*: fresh, chaste, and simple love.

The reaction against Castilho, who had come to represent all that was trivial and traditional in romanticism, gave rise to the "Questão Coimbrã" (1865), a pamphlet war led by Antero de Quental (1842–91), Teófilo Braga (1843–1924), and other Coimbra students. Although interested in liberal political and philosophical ideas, they also were more fertile in genuine poetry. Antero's *Sonetos* are unique in P. lit., presenting a diary of the poet's pessimism and his agonized struggle to attain a faith reconciling materialism and the spirit, a struggle the failure of which culminated in his suicide. Abílio Manuel Guerra Junqueiro (1850–1923), occasionally reminiscent of Victor Hugo in his fiery rhetoric, attacks church and state in *A velhice do Padre Eterno* (The Old Age of the Eternal Father, 1885) and *A Pátria* (The Motherland, 1896), but shows some transition to symbolism in *Os simples* (1892) with episodes from the simple, virtuous life of country people. Also often iconoclastic and satirical, António Duarte Gomes Leal (1848–1921) has genial moments when he avoids the declamatory. José Joaquim Cesário Verde (1855–86), in the posthumous *Livro de Cesário Verde,* has left a collection of increasing popularity. His chief quality is an adaptation of naturalism or realism to poetry, painting in concrete details the monotony of bourgeois life, with some inclination to the unusual and grotesque.

António Nobre (1867–1900) lived and published his *Só* (Alone, 1892) in Paris and was familiar with current literary movements there, but he is intensely P. in his introspective subjectivity. His suffering is communicated with gentle sensitiveness and almost morbid *saudade.* Sebastianism, P. folklore, a wealth of images, and metrical freedom lend to his work an enduring fascination. Fausto Guedes Teixeira (1872–1940) and Augusto Gil (1873–1929) may be compared in their tenderness and simple lyric qualities.

Some of these poets display traits of Fr. symbolism, but usually Eugénio de Castro (1869–1944) is given credit for introducing this movement and Sp.-Am. modernism into Portugal. Castro, who became the country's best known poet abroad, prefaced his manifesto to *Oaristos* (Intimate Dialogues, 1890). He advocated greater freedom of form, varied and often eccentric vocabulary, unusual rhymes, alliteration, and emphasis on the aesthetic and sensual rather than the social uses of poetry. Beginning as a refined and aristocratic poet for the elite, in *Horas* (1891) and *Salomé e outros poemas* (1896), he later became more restrained and national in such works as *Depois da ceifa* (After the Harvest, 1901) and *Constança* (1900). Camilo Pessanha (1867–1926) wrote the delicate, symbolistic *Clépsidra* (1920). Through his long residence in Macao he learned to translate Chinese poetry and to endow his own work with an exquisite imagination, a musicality and formalistic daring greatly admired by the next generation. From Olhão in the extreme south came João Lúcio (Pousão Pereira, 1880–1918), who has some admirable moments, esp. when singing of his native region. Joaquim Pereira Teixeira de Vasconcelos ("Teixeira de Pascoaes," 1878–1952) invented Saudosism to epitomize the Lusitanian genius, a melancholy and pantheistic solidarity with all things. From his nationalistic theories sprang the traditionalist *Renascença Portuguesa,* a society organized in Oporto in 1910 to promote public awareness and civic-mindedness. Its mouthpiece was the journal *Águia.* Florbela Espanca (1894–1930), "Sóror Saudade," continues to enjoy great popularity because of the formal perfection of her sonnets, which depict personal tragedy, unfulfilled yearnings, and a deep despair.

With the publication of the Vanguard journal *Orpheu* (1915), P. p. underwent a total renewal. Instead of nationalistic isolationism, the journal proposed internationalism; instead of traditional forms and themes, its poetry incorporated such European literary trends as futurism and cubism. Launched by a group of young poets, some still symbolists, *Orpheu* revealed an innovative quality due principally to the work of three poets: Fernando Pessoa (1888–1935), Mário de Sá-Carneiro (1890–1916), and José de Almada Negreiros (1893–1970). These poets broke away from the lyrical trad. to embrace the dramatic. Showing an overriding commitment to poetry, they directed their talent toward technical experimentation and their boundless energy against the fossilized, well-entrenched writers whose work reflected parochial nationalism. Because their poetry was iconoclastic, the young modernists of *Orpheu* were for many years identified with scandalous, insane behavior.

Fernando Pessoa is the most extraordinary poet of *Orpheu* and the most astonishing P. poetic phenomenon of this century. His influence dominated the next three generations of poets and continues to be felt. Wanting to deviate from traditional lyricism, he stepped outside the self into four poets, one designated by his own name, the others by other names, each with a unique style and a particular philosophical outlook, a different way of looking at the world. Yet in spite of the multifaceted self, Pessoa's poetry is a composite whole, the totality made clear by each contributing self.

Mário de Sá-Carneiro (1890–1916), the other dominant poetic figure to emerge from *Orpheu,* is known by two books of poetry, *Dispersão* (Dispersion, 1914) and *Indícios de Ouro* (Traces of Gold, 1937), both revealing an extraordinary inventiveness combined with exquisite images. Pessoa is the fabulous architect of a poetic cathedral, each altar exhibiting on all sides contrasting magical glass windows of luminous brightness. Sá-Carneiro, on the other hand, is more instinctive and musical as he creates in a sheaf of metaphors the myth of his deep-felt despondency. By contrast, José de Almada Negreiros (1893–1970), better known as a painter than as a poet—his poetry was confined to the *Orpheu* period—is visibly exterior. He wrote long, free-verse poems criticizing P. society, venting his spleen against social hypocrisy and pseudo-intellectualism. The youngest of the group, his combativeness and public posture was the most outrageous; behind the pose, however, loomed a great talent, manifested not only in poetry but also in painting and fiction.

The next movement centered on the magazine *Presença* (1927–40), begun by a group of young students at the University of Coimbra who valued lit. above political militancy through the arts. As such, they reverted to the model set by *Orpheu,* resurrecting that journal from oblivion and ostracism. The most important poet of the group was José Régio (pseudonym of José Maria dos Reis Pereira, 1901–69), also an important novelist, dramatist, and critic. As a poet, Régio dwells on deep, psychological probings, as in *Poemas de Deus e do Diabo* (Poems of God and the Devil, 1925), which dramatizes the conflict between good and evil. Miguel Torga (b. 1907), another *presencista,* reaffirms in his poetry the hegemony of the visible self as he grapples tortuously with the question of Christ's presence on earth; his mysticism is rooted in the crags and arid valleys of Northern Portugal, the harsh, inhospitable region of his birth. Adolfo Casais Monteiro (1908–72) also emphasizes the telluric, intimating the intangible at times without pursuing it. Monteiro and esp. Carlos Queiroz (1907–49) already reflect the impact of Pessoa's poetry, whose influence began to mold every major movement and poet in Portugal after 1943–49, when his posthumous works began to be known.

After *Presença* ceased publication in 1940, world events as well as internal politics demanded that poets become politically committed. The Neorealist movement had as its principal representatives Carlos de Oliveira (b. 1921) and Manuel da Fonseca (b. 1911), whose poetry reflected social problems and national folk themes. One of the few poets whose work derives from a trad. preceding the Pessoa phenomenon, Vitorino Nemésio (1902–78) depicts the P. scene through surrealist imagery in precise, careful lang. Pessoa's legacy is particularly noticeable in the surrealist poets Alexandre O'Neill (1924–86) and Mário Cesariny de Vasconcellos (b. 1923). The former uses colloquialisms and slang to express vociferously a satirical poetic bent; the latter is an exceptional, intellectually profound poet, as seen in the much anthologized "You are Welcome to Elsinore." *Cadernos de Poesia* (Poetry Notebooks), a poetic movement popular in the 1940s, brought together poets who, besides admiring Pessoa, read the Anglo-Am. poetry of Pound and Eliot. Of these, the better known are: Eugénio de Andrade (b. 1923), whose poems are metaphorical and intensely musical; Sophia de Mello Breyner (b. 1919), who depicts in images of singular beauty the transcendence of things real; and Jorge de Sena (1919–78), who taught for 18 years in the United States and was a novelist and short-story writer as well as a critic and poet. His poetry is erudite, sometimes passionate, other times delicate, but marred by bitter denunciation.

In the 1950s, P. p. continued its fascination with Pessoa, esp. with the poems subscribed by the self, which conceptualize the ineffable. The magazine *Árvore* (1951–53) introduced two important poets who, following Pessoa, pursued luminous transcendence, albeit with a greater degree of emphasis on linguistic innovation. António Ramos Rosa (b. 1924) attempts to capture a fragmented reality through words, ultimately the only reality. Egito Gonçalves (b. 1922), on the other hand, much more telluric than visionary, wavers between eroticism and social commitment, love and satire. Still tied to surrealism, Herberto Helder (b. 1930) blends surrealistic metaphors to the point of losing sight of any referent.

Concretism is represented in Portugal by E. M. de Melo e Castro (b. 1932), whose poems reflect the emphasis placed by recent poets on the intricacies of the text.

ANTHOLOGIES: *Poems from the P.*, ed. A. F. G. Bell (1913); *Portugal—An Anthol.*, ed. G. Young (1916); Antero de Quental, *Sonnets and Poems*, tr. S. G. Morley (1922); E. de Castro, *Dona Briolanja and Other Poems*, tr. L. S. Downes (1944); L. Vaz de Camões, *The Lusiads*, tr. W. C. Atkinson (1952); *The Oxford Book of P. Verse*, ed. A. F. G. Bell, 2d ed., ed. B. Vidigal (1953); *P. Poems with Trs.*, ed. J. B. Trend (1954); *Líricas portuguesas*, 1st ser., ed. J. Régio (n.d.), 2d ser., ed. J. Cabral de Nascimento (1945), 3d ser., ed. J. de Sena (1958); *Presença da literatura portuguesa*, ed. A. A. S. Amora, M. Moisés, and S. Spina, 2d. ed., 5 v. (1967); *Contemp. P. P.*, tr. J. Longland (1966); *Contemp. P. P.*, ed. H. Macedo and E. M. de Melo e Castro (1978); J. de Sena, *The Poetry of Jorge de Sena*, ed. F. G. Williams (1980); E. de Andrade, *Inhabited Heart*, tr. A. Levitin (1985); F. Pessoa, *Selected Poems*, tr. E. Honig and S. M. Brown (1986).

HISTORY AND CRITICISM: T. Braga, *História da litteratura portugueza* (1896–)—many vols. deal specifically with different phases of poetry; A. F. G. Bell, *Studies in P. Lit.* (1914), *P. Lit.* (1922; P. tr. 1931); *Historia da literatura portuguesa ilustrada*, ed. A. Forjaz de Sampaio et al., 4 v. (1929–42)—lavishly illustr., with bibl.; Le Gentil; F. de Figueiredo, *A épica portuguesa no século XVI* (1950), *Lit. portuguésa*, 3d ed. (1955)—also available in Sp.; J. G. Simões, *Fernando Pessoa* (1950), *Itinerário histórico da poesia portuguesa* (1964); G. Le Gentil, *La littérature portugaise*, 2d ed. (1951)—the best brief intro.; H. V. Livermore et al., *Portugal and Brazil, An Intro.* (1953)—with bibls. of studies by E. Prestage and A. F. G. Bell and of trs. from P. to Eng.; *Dicionário das literaturas portuguesa, galega e brasileira*, ed. J. do Prado Coelho (1960)—entries on individual poets and works, versification, and movements; T. R. Hart, "Med. P. Lit.," in Fisher; *Portugal and Brazil in Transition*, ed. R. Sayers (1966); A. J. Saraiva and O. Lopes, *História da lit. portuguesa*, 5th ed. (1967); H. Cidade, *Lições de cultura e lit. p.* (1968); T. F. Earle, *Theme and Image in the Poetry of Sá de Miranda* (1980), *The P. of António Ferreira* (1988); *The Man Who Never Was*, ed. G. Monteiro (1982); L. N. Rodrigues, *Garrett and the Eng. Muse* (1983); F. Bacarisse, "A Alma Amortalhada," *Mário de Sá Carneiro's Use of Metaphor and Image* (1984), N. Andrews, Jr., *The Case Against Camões* (1988); T. F. Earle, *The Muse Reborn: The Poetry of António Ferreira* (1988).

L.A.S.; A.E.S.

PRAKRIT POETRY. See INDIAN POETRY.

PROVENÇAL POETRY. See OCCITAN POETRY.

PUERTO RICAN POETRY. The historical devel. of the art of poetry in Puerto Rico dates back to the Taino Indians. On his second voyage in 1493, Columbus discovered Puerto Rico, which was called *Borinquen* by the Indians. The Sp. chroniclers described the *Areyto* of the Tainos as a choral ritual of magical and aesthetic significance. Oral poetry, songs, and dances merged in recitation, movement, and music. In the 16th c., *Areyto* remnants mingled with folklore and popular poetry brought by Spaniards and Africans to their new home.

The *Sixth elegy* of Juan de Castellanos' (1522–1607) *Elegías de Varones Ilustres de Indias*, dedicated to Juan Ponce de León and his conquest of Borinquen, is comparable to Ercillas' *La Araucana*. The impact of the Golden Age on the cultural life of Puerto Rico centered on the seven years that Bishop Bernardo de Balbuena (1561–1627) lived on the island until his death. His work and his library in San Juan were so esteemed that Lope de Vega mentioned this fact in *Laurel de Apolo*. The first native poet, the priest-scholar Francisco de Ayerra y Santamaría (1630–1708), spent his adult life in Mexico. Found in his elaborate baroque poetry is an exceptional sonnet dedicated to Sor Juana Inés de la Cruz at her death.

By the mid 19th c., poetry had emerged as the preferred medium for expression of the creative spirit in the island's artistic and literary life. Youth collected their own prose and poetry in anthologies called *aguinaldo*, *album*, or *cancionero*. Poets recited and improvised verse in public and official gatherings. Founded in 1876, the *Ateneo Puertorriqueño* became an intellectual center. Neoclassical and romantic poets lectured, recited, and celebrated *juegos florales*. The influence of Sp. and Latin-Am. poetry was pervasive in the late 19th c.: romanticism dominated, from the most passionate nuance to the most subtle and refined. Themes of love and patriotism flourished in the works of such talented writers as Alejandro Tapia y Rivera (1826–82), Lola Rodríguez de Tío (1843–1924), and José Gautier Benítez (1851–80). Tapia exalted the past in *La Sataniada*, the most extensive P. R. poem of the 19th c. The 30 cantos in 8-line stanzas are reminiscent of Espronceda's *El Diablo Mundo*. Lola Rodríquez de Tió, the first recognized outstanding woman writer, created love poetry and patriotic verse charged with vigor and fire. As a political exile, she lived in Caracas, New York City, and finally in Cuba until her death. Among her contributions to her homeland's culture are the revolutionary lyrics of *La Borinqueña*, the national anthem. Gautier Benítez excelled in writing love and patriotic verse similar to the verse of

Byron and Bécquer. His lyrical expressions of nostalgic absence and joy at the return to the shores of Borinquen attest to his essential romanticism.

At the turn of the century, the impact of the Sp.-Am. War (1898), with the subsequent transferral of Puerto Rico from the colonial orbit of Spain to that of the U.S., created social and artistic unrest. This "fear and trembling" gave the poetry of the pre-World War I period (until 1918) a special character within the prevalent modernismo. The struggle to preserve the vernacular and to survive as a Sp.-Am. cultural entity gave poetry a strongly romantic accent. Even so, the poets adopted the aesthetic credo, metrical innovations, and stylistic freedom that the Nicaraguan master Rubén Darío was disseminating in his new verse throughout the Sp.-speaking world. Among the first innovators of P. R. p. was José de Diego (1866–1918), celebrated both for his patriotic and love poems: in 1915 he became the torchbearer in defense of the Sp. lang.

Modernismo denounced the perils of colonialism under the new master, while searching for universal values. Examples abound in the poetry of Luis Lloréns Torres (1878–1944), Virgilio Dávila (1869–1943), Evaristo Ribera Chevremont (1896–1976), and Luis Palés Matos (1899–1959). Lloréns Torres, together with Nemesio Canales (1878–1923), the prominent author of *Paliques*, founded the literary magazine *Revista de las Antillas* in 1913. This opened the way for the avant-garde movements following World War I. The defense of Hispanic roots and the ideal of Antillean union dominated the work of thinker-patriot Eugenio María de Hostos (1839–1903). In turn, these thoughts inspired some of Lloréns' best poems: "Song of the Antilles" and "Mare Nostrum." Besides those major works he wrote *décimas* and *coplas* of extraordinary beauty, reviving "criollo" motifs in a search for identity. Virgilio Dávila chanted the beauties of country life and smalltown tempo with a sense of humor and graceful criticism in *Pueblito de Antes* (1916) and *Aromas del Terruño* (1917). Introducing post- and ultra-modern tendencies from Spain, Ribera Chevremont's poetry offers a new transition. *Tú, Mar y Yo y Ella* (1946) and *El Hondero lanzó la piedra* (1975) are two of his best books.

The avant-garde movements had captured the minds and imaginations of the poets around 1930. Luis Palés Matos, outstanding exponent of Afro-Antillean themes, created the masterpiece *Tun Tun de Pasa y Grifería* (1937), considered as significant as the Cuban poetry of Ballagas and Nicolás Guillén. Palés devised his own mythology of black culture which exploits onomatopoeic rhythms with magical cadence and carries a satirical, social protest. He identifies Caribbean islands with subtlety and refinement:

Cuba—ñáñigo y bachata
Haití—vodú y calabaza
Puerto Rico—burundanga.

The movement and dance of the "African soul" in the Caribbean is expressed in some of his poems:

Calabó y bambú bambú y calabó
Es el sol de fuego que arde en Tum-
buctú
Es la danza negra de Fernando Poo
El alma africana que vibrando está
En el ritmo gordo del mariyandá.

The avant-garde movements, short-lived but impressive, followed the pattern set by European and Latin-Am. ultra-modern trends. Ultraism, cubism, dada and many other philosophical, artistic, and anti-artistic tendencies (like existentialism) have left their mark on 20th-c. P. R. p. Some of the more significant are: "Noismo," based on the concept of negation; "transcendentalismo," suggesting the metaphysical; "atalayismo," boldy emphasizing the extravagant side of every possible idea.

According to the ideology, imagination, and personality of the writer, a variety of lang. and a search for originality typify 20th-c. P. R. p. Prominent scholar-poet José A. Balseiro (b. 1900) published his first books under the influence of Rubén Darío. His favorite themes have been love, art, music, and a sentimental patriotism. His *El Ala y el Beso* (1983) has the charm of a classic and the surprise of a youthful approach to life. In his youth, Luis Muñoz Marín (1898–1980), politician and creator of the "Estado Libre Asociado" (Commonwealth status), wrote excellent poems in Eng. and Sp. denouncing misery and social injustice.

The Nationalist Party, led by Pedro Albizu Campos, has generated since the 1930s a political poetry of protest and denunciation of colonialism. Many poets wrote in defense of the poor, demanding social justice. Francisco Manrique Cabrera (1908–78), in *Poemas de mi Tierra, Tierra* (1936), stressed a "neocriollismo," characterized by a telluric and mysterious symbiosis with the soil, the "tierra, tierra" of one's birth with its strongly patriotic and emotive overtones. Juan Antonio Corretjer (1908–85), in *Amor de Puerto Rico, Alabanza en la Torre de Lares* and other books, expressed his militant, Marxist ideas and his ideological fusion of history, geography, and patriotism within a comprehensive poetical whole.

Women came to the fore as excellent poets in the 1930–50 period. Clara Lair's (1895–1973) passionate accent compares to the erotic frenzy of the Uruguayan Juana de Ibarbouru and the Argentinian Alfonsina Storni. *Arras de Cristal* (1937) and *Trópico Amargo* (1950), together with *Cuaderno* (1961), represent her best work. Julia de Burgos (1914–53) combines a telluric, "neocriollista" love of nature with a patriotic and cosmic love of freedom. She expresses in tender, brave accents the struggles of a person suffering love, loneliness, and death in tragic circumstances. Her famous poem *Rio Grande de Loíza* is a biographical song in which self and river are intertwined through symbolic myth. Critics laud her books: *Poemas en Veinte Surcos* (1938), *Cancíon de la Verdad Sencilla* (1939), and *Mar, tú y Otros Poemas* (1954).

Since 1960, there has been a rich output of anthologies, literary reviews, and performances. So-called "canta-autores" sing their poems to the accompaniment of music, popularizing their own work and that of the past. The quantity and quality of creative lyrical minds, whose militant voices mingle in gradations of artistic and humanitarian themes, form a pattern of multiple tones and meanings. They include the denunciation of colonialism and identification with "Third World" struggles and Latin-Am. woes.

Francisco Matos Paoli (b. 1915), author of *Elogio de la Locura* and candidate for both the Nobel and Cervantes Prizes, is the most prolific 20th-c. poet to date. His lang., his faith, the metaphysical search for the unknown, and his total dedication to poetry deserve the high esteem he commands. Paoli's best known book is *Elogio de la Locura.* Luis Hernández Aquino (1907–88), a scholar, linguist, and poet, writes about hist. and the Sp. and Taino components of the P. R. identity. He founded *Bayoán,* one of the finest poetry reviews (1950–51, 1961–65), and wrote *Isla para la Angustia,* one of the best books of contemporary P. R. p.

Some P. R. poets have done their work in the U.S., esp. in New York City. Though some may have spent most of their lives there, they continue to write in Sp. and to express their attachment to the homeland. Among the best are: Diana Ramírez de Arellano (b. 1919), Juan Avilés (b. 1904), Clemento Soto Vélez (b. 1905), and Graciany Miranda Archilla (b. 1910). A younger generation, known as "Neo-Ricans," write poetry in Eng. and mixed Sp. and Eng. similar to that published by the Chicanos. This new speech pattern exploring new areas of expression is characteristic of Víctor Hernández Cruz (b. 1949) and of Pedro Pietri (b. 1944), who has written movingly about the New York Puerto Ricans in *P. R. Obituary.* One of the best translators of Eng. poetry to Sp. is César A. Portala (b. 1914), a P. R. poet also living in New York.

Vehicles for post-1950 poetry and crit., the new but short-lived reviews represent a chain of aesthetic and ideological stages that trace the process of poetic devel. in modern P. R. The most important are: *Bayoán* (1950–51, 1961–65); *Guajana* (1962–66); *Mester* (1966); *Orfeo* (1954–56); *Pegaso* (1952); *Versiones* (1966); *Ventana* (1975); *Alero* (1982–86); and *Mairena* (1979–87). Other general magazines open to poetry and poetics have been *Asomante, Sin Nombre,* and *Zona de Carga y Descarga.* Probably the best critic of poetry, and a poet himself, is Juan Martínez Capó (b. 1923). Author of *Viaje* (1961), for years he has maintained a regular weekly article in one of the leading newspapers, *El Mundo.*

Since 1980, the younger and older generations have upset the age barrier, establishing and maintaining a closer relationship in public recitals and literary meetings. Consequently, the discussion of "poetry and poetics" has broadened in scope. *En Una Sola Torre (50 años de Poesía Puertorriqueña)* (1986) includes a great variety of poets. Among them is the work of Angela María Dávila (b. 1944), author of *Animal Fiero y Tierno* (1977). Also represented is 90-year-old Manuel Joglar Cacho (b. 1898), author of such works as *La Sed del Agua* (1965), *Soliloquios de Lázaro* (1956), and *Cien Campanas en una Sola Torre* (1986). Martínez Capó considers this "exceptional anthology" of "diverse context" a magnificent compendium of 50 years of P. R. p. The influences on current P. R. p. are many, but chiefly Sp. poetry of the generation of 1927 (Lorca, Alberti, Alonso, et al.) and Latin-Am. poetry from Darío onward (Neruda, Vallejo, Borges, et al.). Furthermore, today's poetry, in lang. and in theme, reflects the impact of modern technology on an unwary humanity, drug addiction, the women's liberation movement, and obscenity. Contemporary P. R. p. lends itself to a wide range of critical approaches. See also SPANISH POETRY; SPANISH-AMERICAN POETRY.

ANTHOLOGIES: *The P. R. Poets,* ed. A. Matilla and I. Silén (1972); *BORINQUEN,* ed. M. T. Babín and S. Steiner (1974); *Poesía militante Puertorriqueña,* M. de la Puebla (1979); *Herejes y mitificadores: Muestra de poesía Puertorriqueña en los Estados Unidos,* ed. E. Barradas y Rafael Rodríguez (1980); *Inventing a Word: An Anthol. of 20th-C. P. R. P.,* ed. J. Marzán (1980); *Antología de la poesía de la mujer Puertorriqueña,* ed. T. Ortiz (1981); *Antología general de la poesía Puertorriqueña: Tradición y originalidad,* ed. L. Ríos (1982); *En una sola torre (50 años de poesía Puertorriqueña)* (1986).

HISTORY AND CRITICISM: L. H. Aquino, *Movimientos literarios del siglo XX en P. R.* (1951), *Nuestra aventura literaria* (1966); J. R. de Alvarez, *Literatura Puertorriqueña: Su proceso en el tiempo* (1983); J. E. González, *La poesía contemporánea de Puerto Rico, 1930–60* (1986). M.-T.B.

R

RAGUSAN POETRY. See YUGOSLAV POETRY.

ROMANIAN POETRY. The earliest surviving texts of R. p. date from the 17th c. In the 17th and 18th cs., R. p. is chiefly of three kinds. The first is religious poetry, esp. verse translations of biblical books.

Thus Dosoftei, a learned Moldavian clergyman, translated the *Psalms* (1673) in rhymed couplets of variable length that indicate equally the influence of R. oral folk verse and of classicist Polish poetry. The second is occasional poetry following Western models—elegies, odes, pattern poetry, and epigrams. The most prominent example is by the historian and statesman Miron Costin, whose *Viata lumii* (The World's Life, ca. 1672) is a meditation on the vanity of life and the mutability of fortune, written in rhymed couplets of 12 or 13 syllables in irregular meter. The third kind is represented by a wide variety of historical chronicles in verse that flourished in the 18th c. in the southern principality of Wallachia. These are often polemical, always picturesque, and undoubtedly circulated orally.

The 18th c. also witnessed the culmination of oral folk verse, references to and quotations from which are found already in the 15th and 16th cs. They express in a variety of genres the existential horizon and emotional universe of a stable agrarian society. While steeped in a religiosity that combines a simplified Christianity and a broad pantheistic sacrality, this poetry also preserves some traces of a pre-Roman pagan mythology. Heroic trads. are rendered not in epics but rather in short ballads. The bulk of folk poetry consists of *doinas*, lyrical expressions of love, loneliness, grief, and yearning, or, less often, glee, carousal, or revolt. Broader visions are provided by the myth of master-builder Manole, who sacrificed his and his wife's life to the achievement of a unique building, and particularly by *Miorita*, which is often said to embody a R. folk-philosophy. It tells the story of a migrant shepherd who, upon hearing his companions' plot to murder him, does not defend himself but rather turns the occasion into a grand reconciliation with nature, the stars, and the animals. The popularity of folk poetry declined toward the end of the 19th c., and it had virtually disappeared by the middle of the 20th.

The end of early R. lit. was marked by Anton Pann (1796?–1854), who synthesized the oral, didactic, and mythical-historical modes in a mock-naive style. The decisive turn of R. p. towards Western values and forms occurred in the last two decades of the 18th c. The Wallachian nobleman Ienache Văcărescu (1740?–93) and his two sons wrote gracious and erotic Anacreontic verse on Gr., It., and Fr. models. At almost the same time, in Transylvania, Ion Budai-Deleanu (1760?–1820) wrote a satirical mock-epic of the medieval struggle against the Ottoman empire.

The first half of the 19th c. in R. p. is characterized by the simultaneous assimilation of Enlightenment, neoclassical, romantic, and Biedermeier forms and ideas, which led to a number of interesting combinations. Dimitrie Bolintineanu (1819–72) and Grigore Alexandrescu (1814–85) wrote historical ballads, satires, fables, and elegies much influenced by Lamartine and Byron. Vasile Alecsandri (1821–90) combined the fervent struggle for democratic reform and national unity common to the generation inspired by the ideals of 1848 radicalism with poetic serenity, a smiling Epicureanism, and a search for classical balance. He excelled in patriotic verse, natural description, poetic drama, and adaptations of the newly recovered oral trad.

The greatest 19th-c. R. poet was Mihai Eminescu (1850–89), who was influenced by the Ger. romantics and by the philosophies of Kant and Schopenhauer. Unfortunate love, social marginality, intense nationalism, mental illness, and early death no less than his towering poetic achievement soon turned Eminescu into a mythic figure. He gave to R. p. the modern form of its poetic lang. Eminescu's poetry (melancholy meditations on history, society, sentimental love, and allegory) is founded on a deeper level of mythical cosmology, irrational vision, and subjective pantheism. Eminescu's unpublished work contains huge fragmentary epics that describe the universe as emerging out of the lamentations of universal or divine self-consciousness; he also evoked the pre-Roman society of the Dacians as a pristine, luxuriant, and crystalline world of which later history is but a series of deformed copies. Eminescu's radical conservatism was the wellspring for all later forms of nationalism in Romania.

For three decades after Eminescu's death, two poetics schools vied for primacy. One was symbolism, which appeared largely under Fr. influence; its most important representative was Alexandru Macedonski (1854–1920), a flamboyant artist who believed fervently in aesthetic perfection; his poetry abounds in images of precious stones, fabulous mirages, and morbid obsessions. Ion Minulescu (1881–1944), an able manipulator of grandiloquent images and sentimental intimations, continued the movement. The other school was the populist and idyllic movement mainly advocated by the journal *Semănătorul*. Its proponents emphasized the use of simple lang. and drew their inspiration from national trads. and local themes. The best poets in this trad. were George Cosbuc (1866–1918), who also produced a superb tr. of Dante's *Divine Comedy*; Octavian Goga (1881–1938), whose best verse expresses a kind of primeval suffering; and Stefan O. Iosif (1875–1913).

The unification of all R. provinces following World War I and the beginnings of capitalist democracy favored an unparalleled growth of poetic diversity and power. The R. high modernists strove to combine trad. and innovation; the influence of Ger. expressionism and of Fr. modernists such as Valéry and Mallarmé can often be recognized in them. George Bacovia (1881–1957) expressed a universal hopelessness through his austere and obsessive verse, full of images of rain, mud, illness, and provincial dreariness. His poems, inspired by Moldavian towns, evoked a symbolic universe of humidity and putrefaction. Ion Barbu (1895–1961), a mathematician, wrote obscure, semantically packed, tightly structured verse exploring philosophical propositions; for him, the formal order of poetry outlined "a purer, secondary game." In other poems Barbu indulged his voluptuous pleasure in the verbal thickness of a lush and lurid Balkan world, with its jesters, whores, and sages. Lucian Blaga (1895–1951), philosopher, diplomat, and professor, inquired poetically into the connections between natural reality and transcendent mystery; he evolved from Dionysian rhapsodic tones to praise of the agrarian order as a suggestion of cosmic harmony. Tudor Arghezi (1880–1967) renewed the discourse of R. p. by mixing metaphysics and realism. He is particularly impressive for his astounding thematic range, from pamphleteering virulence, coarse violence, and sexuality to the worlds of children and of wrestling with religious faith and doubt.

In the same generation there were able traditionalists such as the cultivated neoclassicist Ion Pillat (1891–1945); the natural mystic Vasile Voiculescu (1884–1963); Adrian Maniu (1891–1968), who clothed a decadent weariness in the mock-simplicity of folk iconography; and the late neoromantic Alexandru Philippide (1900–79), whose poems abound in cosmic visions and historical nightmares. Among the many nationalist poets of the age, the most prominent was Aron Cotrus (1891–1957), whose messianic thunderings were couched in rolling free verse and a racy, sonorous vocabulary.

At least as vital and effective was the group of bewildering experimentalists, surrealists, and avant-garde radicals who eventually came to influence even Western European poetry. Best known among them was the founder of dada, Tristan Tzara (1896–1963), but of comparable distinction were Benjamin Fondane (1898–1944), Ilarie Voronca (1903–46), and Gherasim Luca (b. 1913), all of whom emigrated to France. Gellu Naum (b. 1915) and Sasa Pană (1902–81) were among the chief animators of poetic anarchism, which they aligned with leftist political attitudes. Camil Baltazar (1902–77) with his fluid and melodious verse and his morbid yearning for paradisal innocence, as well as Ion Vinea (1895–1964) with his jazzy rhythms and strident prose inserts, strove to bring experimental poetry closer to the mainstream and to endow it with more finished forms.

The poets who emerged in the later 1930s and '40s had to suffer the trauma of war and of repeated political upheavals. Some of the early Existentialists, like Vintilă Horia (b. 1915) and Stefan Baciu (b. 1918), chose exile. Others had to accept long periods of silence. They can be roughly grouped into the Bucharest and the Sibiu schools. The former is exemplified by Ion Caraion (1923–86), Geo Dumitrescu (b. 1920), D. Stelaru (1917–71), and Constant Tonegaru (1919–52), all ironic pessimists who clamored for adventurous vitality and the demolition of philistine prejudices. Among them Caraion is remarkable for the unrelenting and ferocious darkness of his images. The Sibiu group, exemplified by Radu Stanca (1920–62), the abstractionist Ion Negoitescu (b. 1921), and above all Stefan Aug Doinas (b. 1922), eloquently pleaded for the autonomy of culture and the humanizing role of aesthetic production. Doinas is a consummate craftsman in a wide range of genres and forms, an admirable translator of poetry (e.g. *Faust*), a poet of intense metaphoric creativity, and the author of ethical satire and Neoplatonic visionary evocations.

The establishment of a Communist regime in 1947 which suppressed artistic freedoms led to more than a decade of poetic barrenness. Typical of the cliché-ridden and sloganeering versification of the 1950s is Mihai Beniuc (b. 1907). The lyrics of Nina Cassian (b. 1924) often escape banality through their mixture of bantering cynicism, intelligent feminism, and erotic intensity. However, only the more liberal 1960s brought a revival of poetry. Nichita Stănescu (1933–83), a poet with an extraordinary capacity for the transfiguration of everyday reality, became the standard-bearer of a generation devoted to experiment and to a metaphorical version of reality free from ideological interference. Ioan Alexandru's (b. 1941) best verse moved from the cruelty of tragic naturalism toward a kind of religious harmony. Ion Gheorghe (b. 1935) managed to alternate crass primitivism and oracular obscurities with sophisticated lang. games. Mircea Ivănescu (b. 1931) wrote self-analytic elegies in which stream-of-consciousness techniques are applied with lucid irony. Marin Sorescu (b. 1936) dealt in parody and in the jocular debunking of habit. Leonid Dimov (b. 1926) inaugurated an "onereic" movement based on dream imagery and associations of verbal music. Despite adverse political pressures, the feeling that the maintenance of high aesthetic standards is crucial for national survival encouraged the continuation of these efforts, either in the direction of lyrical purity, as in the poems of Sorin Mărculescu (b. 1936) and Ana Blandiana (b. 1942), or in the more open discontent and ethical rage of Ileana Mălăncioiu (b. 1940), Mircea Dinescu (b. 1950), and the dissident Dorin Tudoran (b. 1945). Many of these poets were in the forefront of the 1989 anti-Communist revolution. A new generation emerged soon thereafter, led by the postmodernist Mircea Cartarescu (b. 1955) and the cynical, street-wise Florin Iaru (b. 1955) and Ion Stratan (b. 1954).

Two things should be added. One is that poetic and aesthetic values occupied a much more prominent place in R. culture than in the West: lit. was a respected mode of conveying wisdom and social values. The greater poets and movements were flanked for two centuries by hundreds of minor authors, and only an awareness of these can suggest the thick texture of R. p. The other is that the R. territory was hospitable to lit. written by numerous ethnic groups—Hungarian, Serbian, Saxon Ger., Bukowina Jewish, and others. Important literary figures such as Nikolaus Lenau and Paul Celan, besides others mentioned above, originated here and can thus round off our understanding of the landscape of R. p.

ANTHOLOGIES: *Rumanian Prose and Verse,* ed. E. D. Tappe (1956); *Anthol. of Contemp. R. P.,* ed. R. McGregor-Hastie (1969); *46 R. Poets in Eng.,* ed. S. Avădanei and D. Eulert (1973); *Antologia poeziei românesti,* ed. Z. D. Busulenga (1974); *Petite anthologie de poésie roumaine moderne,* ed. V. Rusu (1975); *Poezia română clasică,* 3 v., ed. A. Piru (1976); *Mod. R. P.,* ed. N. Catanoy (1977); *Poesia romena d'avanguardia: Testi e manifesti da Urmuz a Ion Caraion,* ed. M. Cugno and M. Mincu (1980).

HISTORY AND CRITICISM: E. Lovinescu, *Istoria literaturii romane moderne* (1937); B. Munteano, *Mod. R. Lit.* (1939); G. Călinescu, *Istoria literaturii române* (1940); G. Lupi, *Storia della letteratura romena* (1955); V. Ierunca, "Litt. roumaine," *Histoire des litts.,* ed. R. Queneau, v. 2 (1956); K. H. Schroeder, *Einführung in das Studium des Rumänischen* (1967); C. Ciopraga, *La Personnalité de le litt. roumaine* (1975); *Scriitori români,* ed. M. Zaciu (1978); V. Nemoianu, "The Real R. Revolution," *The World and I* 6 (1991). V.P.N.

ROMANSH POETRY. See SWISS POETRY.

ROMANY POETRY. See GYPSY POETRY.

RUMANIAN POETRY. See ROMANIAN POETRY.

RUSSIAN POETRY. The birth of Rus. lit. may be traced to the 11th c., but written texts in verse (i.e. characterized by rhyme and rhythm) first made their appearance relatively late, in the 17th c. By contrast, Rus. folklore, which obviously predated recorded literary texts, in certain genres had always been framed in verse. Although relying on diverse rhythms, Rus. folklore is by and large tonic, i.e. it has approximately the same number of stresses in each poetic line. As a rule, Rus. folklore lacks rhyme, and like other national folklores was performed to musical accompaniment, its vocal nature largely determining its rhythmic structure. Such are the numerous ceremonial songs (chanted for harvests, weddings, and divination) which comprise the most poetic part of Rus. folklore. Historical songs, rooted in concrete historical events, are a comparatively late phenomenon. The best-known folklore genre is the folk epic (*bylina,* q.v.), which recounts the exploits of famous warriors (*bogatyri*) who gathered around the Kievan Prince Vladimir much as the Knights of the Round Table did around King Arthur. These heroes regularly sallied forth to battle enemy invaders and fight dragons, and for other exploits of quest and adventure.

Elements of rhythmic organization and poetic lyricism surface in lit. written long before the 17th c., most notably in one of the earliest works, *Slovo o polku Igoreve* (The Lay of Igor's Campaign, 1185). This masterpiece tells of the unsuccessful campaign of a northern prince, Igor of Novgorod-Severskij, against nomad tribes, of his captivity, and his return to his beloved wife. The text consists of separate, lyrically embellished episodes, e.g. a description of the battle, the lament of Igor's wife Jaroslavna, and Igor's flight. A wealth of poetic devices—epithets, metaphors, similes, repetition—as well as the rhythmic nature of the prose in which it is written allies this medieval Rus. text with poetic rather than prosaic forms. *Slovo* exerted a broad influence on Rus. art in the 19th and 20th cs., particularly poetry, music, and painting.

From the 13th to the 16th cs., Rus. lit. overwhelmingly favored prose, with occasional forays into poetry. To this category belong mainly liturgical songs as well as folk verse, usually satiric and farcical (so-called *skoromošiny*), which also penetrated written lit. Epistolary prose of the 16th and 17th cs., which played on readers' emotional responses, is constructed on the principle of syntactic parallelism, whereby the subject (or the most significant word) is consistently placed at the beginning or end of every sentence. Such a structure leads to the creation of a kind of case rhyme based on inflectional suffixes, a system that generates root rhymes and approximate rhymes.

These developments prepared the reader for formal written verse, which emerged in the middle of the 17th c., transplanted into Russia from Poland via the Ukraine. This imported system of versification was called syllabic verse (*virši*), the basic features of which are three: (1) isosyllabism (11- and 13-syllable lines being most widespread); (2) double (*parnaja*) rhyme, as a rule feminine, that resulted from the Polish influence, for in Polish the stress of each word invariably falls on the penultimate syllable; and (3) caesura, normally after the 5th or 6th syllable. The undisputed master of Rus. syllabic verse was Simeon Polockij (1629–80), a monk from Byelorussia who subsequently became Tsar Alexis Mikhailovich's closest associate. Paronomasia and unexpected rhymes mark Polockij's refined and luxuriously ornate verses. His noteworthy successors in syllabic poetry incl. Sylvester Medvedev (1641–91) and Karion Istomin (mid 17th c. to 1717 or 1722). A memorable 17th-c. work in syllabic verse is Petr Buslaev's *poema* (verse epic) entitled "Umozritel'stvo duševnoe . . . o pereselenii v večnuju žizn' . . . baronessy Stroganovoj" (Spiritual Speculations . . . About Baroness Stroganova's . . . Removal to Eternal Life, 1734). Couched in beautiful Rus., it emanates a palpable sense of sorrow and an inspired exaltation in its depiction of Christ. The syllabic trad. in the 18th c. ends with the works of Antiox Kantemir (1708–44), who systematized syllabic verse and introduced an obligatory caesura; more important still are his innovations in poetic lang. and thematics. A proponent of Petrine reforms, Kantemir produced satires against such subjects as ignorance, drunkenness, and court intrigue, taking Cl. and contemp. Fr. authors, esp. Boileau, as models.

The Petrine reforms gave rise to new forms of cultural life and a rapid if turbulent rapprochement with the West. This process resulted in the growth of a new, Europeanized lit. that introduced genres and styles of poetry previously unknown in Russia. In this area Vasilij Trediakovskij (1703–69) played a crucial role. His treatise "Novyj i kratkij sposob k složeniju Rossijskix stixov" (A New and Short Method of Rus. Versification, 1735) rejected the syllabic system, replacing it with the principles of syllabotonic verse, which serve as the foundation of modern Rus. versification. Based on the regular alternation of accented and unaccented syllables, the revised system clearly took account of and built on the quintessential nature of the Rus. lang. Trediakovskij, however, did not pursue his notions to their logical conclusion, confining his reforms to the trochee and to poems in short lines. Nevertheless, he created the Rus. hexameter, into which he translated Fénelon's prose novel, *Les Aventures de Télémaque.* The hexameter is used even today for anthological verse and Cl. trs. In spite of success in individual enterprises, however, Trediakovskij lacked the poetic skill to embody his theories in practice. Neither his contemporaries nor his immediate successors appreciated his brilliant, innovative ideas, and they ridiculed his verses.

It took the great scientist, scholar, and poet Mixail Lomonosov (1711–65) to complete Trediakovskij's reforms, a task he was splendidly equipped to execute. With Trediakovskij's ideas as a point of departure, and adapting the model of Ger. prosody, Lomonosov codified an elaborate system of syllabotonic versification (q.v. in Terras). His system provided a theoretical foundation for the inclusion in Rus. prosody of all the meters found to this day: the iamb, the trochee, the dactyl, the amphibrach, and the anapest. Lomonosov also developed the "three styles" system, establishing a generic hierarchy of styles. The degree to which a style was "elevated" depended on the presence in it of archaic, solemn, Church Slavonic diction. Such a lexicon became the basic component of the "high style," which was mandatory for odes and heroic epics (*geroičeskie poemy*); in the "middle style," reserved for tragedies, satires, and lyrics, only the Slavonicisms shared by Church Slavic and Rus. and accepted in general use were admissible; the "low style," suitable for comedies and songs, had to limit itself to purely Rus. vocabulary. Although rarely observed *in toto,* this system nonetheless served as the foundation for Rus. classicism. Lomonosov's favorite genre was the ceremonial ode, where he preached enlightened absolutism and in striking, vivid imagery glorified the Rus. Tsars, esp. Peter I, and the greatness of Russia. Probably his highest poetic achievement remain the two "Razmyšlenija o Bož'em Veličestve" (Meditations on the Greatness of God), where the poet and scholar merge to offer a grandiose vision of the universe, the beauty of the northern lights, and the magnificence of the sun. His poetic legacy also includes verse tragedies, an unfinished epic about Peter the Great, and spiritual odes (his versions of the Psalms), the last representing a peak in his creative output.

Lomonosov's literary foe, Aleksandr Sumarokov (1717–69), is the most thoroughgoing classicist in the history of Rus. p. In his bitter polemics against Lomonosov, he accused the latter of excessive grandiosity, over-reliance on metaphor, and the interpolation of improbable imagery in his odes. He himself wrote in a lang. that was clear and simple for the time. Sumarokov created the Rus. verse tragedy, and with justifiable pride called himself the Rus. Racine. His tragedies (*Xorev,* 1747; *Dmitrij Samozvanec* [Dmitry the Pretender], 1771) usually appropriated subjects and plots from Russia's national history, a practice which violated classicist norms. In all other respects, however, Sumarokov strictly observed cl. rules: he abided by the unities, pitted love against duty as the central conflict, had his heroes deliver speeches advocating Enlightenment philosophy, and maintained a purity of style and genre. Unlike Boileau, Sumarokov in his treatise *Epistola o stixotvorstve* (Epistle on Writing Poetry, 1747) stressed the significance of the song in the system of cl. genres. In transforming the song into a lyric poem that most often described tragic love, Sumarokov became the creator of the Rus. love lyric.

Classicism became firmly established in the works of Sumarokov's successors. In 1779, Mixail Xeraskov published the first complete Rus. epic poem, *Rossiada,* about Ivan the Terrible's conquest of Kazan. The genre of burlesque, which enjoyed special popularity in Russia, is best represented by V. Majkov's epic *Elisej, ili razdražennyj Vax* (Elisei, or Bacchus Enraged, 1771), which parodies the *Aeneid* while depicting the life of Moscow's drunkards. I. Bogdanovič's elegant epic *Dušen'ka* (1783) recounts with sly irony the amorous adventures of Eros and Psyche, who on Rus. soil become Dušen'ka ("soul" in Rus. is *duša*). The fable, a genre demanding the "low style," also thrived during this period, reaching its apogee with Sumarokov, whose fables admittedly sometimes abused colloquial or vulgar lang. Another popular fabulist, Ivan Xemnicer (1745–84), likewise possessed considerable skill, but the fable truly found its master at the beginning of the 19th c., when all the other cl. genres had virtually disappeared, in Ivan Krylov (1768/9–1844). For the first time in Rus. lit., the narrators of his fables spoke a lively colloquial Rus. while embodying typical traits of the Rus. national character.

Soon after consolidating itself in the school of Sumarokov and his followers, Rus. classicism rapidly eroded, losing the clarity and precision characteristic of the movement. This process was accelerated by Gavrila Deržavin (1743–1816), considered by many the supreme poetic genius of the 18th c., whose work already contains elements of preromanticism. Although Deržavin called all his poems odes, they altogether lack the majestic grandeur of the genre, its "high" style, and its special lexicon. Boldly mixing lexical levels, Deržavin placed the high and the low side by side. Thus in the famous ode "Felica" (1783), Deržavin describes Catherine II engaged in her official state activities, contrasting her with the nobles engrossed in the most commonplace occupations: drinking coffee, trying on new clothes, searching for fleas in their hair. In his philosophical poems Deržavin meditates on the ineluctability of death and the chilling horror of its approach, as for instance in "Na smert' knjāzja Meščerskogo" (On the Death of Prince Meshchersky, 1779), which shows the influence of Edward Young's *Night Thoughts.* The apogee of Deržavin's philosophical verse is the ode "Bog" (God, 1784). Translated into numerous European langs., it envisions man as the center of the universe, the link connecting heaven and earth whose being synthesizes both the spiritual principle and brute matter: "I am a tsar—I am a slave, I am a worm—I am God."

The transition from the 18th c. to the 19th and to new literary tendencies is best represented by Nikolaj Karamzin (1766–1826), the founder of Rus. Sentimentalism and its most ardent spokesman. Although more a prosaist than a poet, Karamzin nonetheless composed verses that played a significant role in the devel. of Rus. lyric. In a lang. free of archaisms, Karamzin's poems sketch the complexity of man's inner world, which his successors and imitators in the early part of the 19th c. explored more thoroughly and with greater intensity.

The first decades of the 19th c., deservedly called "the Golden Age of Rus. lit.," issue in part from the work of Vasilij Žukovskij (1783–1852), one of the best Rus. lyric poets and Karamzin's most inspired successor. Žukovskij's autobiographical, elegiac poetry treats unhappy love, the death of one's beloved, and the hope for a meeting beyond the grave, all in a tone of wistful melancholy. Nature appears in a similarly despondent light in Žukovskij's poems, which repeatedly emphasize evenings, sunsets, mists, and the moon, for Žukovskij strives less to capture surroundings than to share with the reader a mood of doleful, pensive gloom. With Žukovskij, for the first time in Rus. p., the word acquires multiple meanings and shades that are more essential than its basic denotation. In his search for the suggestive, polysemous word, Žukovskij foreshadows the symbolists. The most popular part of his legacy consists of his ballads, the most famous of which is *Svetlana,* a Russified version of Burger's ballad *Lenore.* Žukovskij's most enduring contribution to Rus. letters remains his innumerable trs. of European and Eastern poets, e.g. Goethe, Schiller, Scott, Byron, Homer's *Odyssey, The Mahabharata, The Shahname,* and many others.

The other major poet of the Golden Age, Žukovskij's contemporary, Konstantin Batjuškov (1787–1855), lapsed into insanity in 1822 and remained so for the rest of his life. He left behind a small collection of poetry and several prose experiments. Unlike Žukovskij's verse, Batjuškov's is vivid, buoyant, permeated with light, and rather erotic, traits esp. evident in his anthology verse, where Batjuškov strives to depict the color, physicality, and object-studded concreteness of the ancient world he reconstructs. In his efforts to find the precise, expressive poetic word, Batjuškov clearly anticipates the acmeists. The fragile hedonism of a fictitious antiquity. however, does not save Batjuškov from a profound pessimism: in his world, fleeting passion, pleasure, and beauty yield to tragedy, evil, and death. Marked by a mellifluous euphony unique in Rus. p., Batjuškov's poems suggest the influence of It. verse, which he knew intimately.

Opposition to the Karamzinian school came from the Archaists, among whom numbered the later Deržavin; Nikolaj Gnedič, the translator of the *Iliad*; and Sergij Širinskij-Šixmatov, the author of two epic poems. They formed a group called The Society of Lovers of the Rus. Word (Beseda liubitelej russkogo slova; 1811–16), at meetings of which they made speeches and read from their works. The Society published a journal containing its members' creative efforts. Karamzin's followers, who included Batjuškov and Žukovskij, founded, in opposition to the Society, a humorous counterpart called Arzamas, which disbanded once the Society ceased to exist. The Archaists did not consider smoothness and melodiousness poetic virtues; in their view, the expressiveness of poetic lang. required heavy, awkward rhythms, archaic polysyllables, and complex syntax. These notions were articulated and put into practice in the interesting though ponderous verses of Aleksandr Radiščev (1742–1802), whose predecessors were Trediakovskij and Semën Bobrov (1762–1810), author of philosophical odes and darkly romantic descriptions of nature. Other opposition to and polemics with Žukovskij came from P. Katenin (1792–1853), author of folkloric ballads (*Ol'ga, Ubijca* [The Murderer], *Lešij* [The Forest Spirit]), and Wilhelm Kjuxelbeker (1797–1846), a poet, dramatist, and literary critic.

The Golden Age and Rus. p. as a whole reached their apogee in the work of Aleksandr Puškin (1799–1837), who not only deserves the title of genius but belongs in the select company of the four or five geniuses (along with Dante, Shakespeare, and Goethe) who herald the efflorescence of a new European lit. Puškin's oeuvre assimilated the poetic achievements of the 18th and early 19th cs. and set the course for Rus. lit. thereafter. It is not surprising that a bona fide cult of Puškin remains active even in contemp. Rus. cultural life, a cult that surpasses the veneration for Tolstoj and Dostoyevsky. If in his early works Puškin proved to be the heir and pupil of Žukovskij, Batjuškov, and Deržavin, his verses nevertheless showed such mastery and finish that they instantly proclaimed him the foremost poet of his era. His period of apprenticeship culminated in 1820 with the mock heroic poem *Ruslan i Ljudmila* (Ruslan and Liudmila).

Puškin's Southern exile (1820–24), when he was banished from Petersburg for his political verses, coincided with the romantic period of his creativity. His so-called "Southern" or "Byronic" *poemy* portray the romantic hero fleeing civilization for such exotic climes as the Caucasus and a gypsy camp. The structure of these narratives indeed recalls Byron's Oriental tales, but Puškin's romantic hero proves spiritually and morally bankrupt when confronted with the sincere, passionate emotions of representatives of the primitive world (*Kavkazskij plennik* [The Prisoner of the Caucasus], *Cygany* [The Gypsies]). In the later *Poltava* (1828), Puškin synthesized the historical *poema* with a romantic love narrative, while glorifying the achievements of Peter I. The theme of Peter becomes central in Puškin's masterpiece, the epic *Mednyj vsadnik* (The Bronze Horseman, 1833), which dramatizes the Petersburg flood of 1824. Puškin depicts the conflict between the state, symbolized by the statue of Peter I, and the individual—the simple, modest man whose happiness is destroyed at the ruler's command. While acknowledging the claims of the individual and his right to happiness, Puškin's *poema* shows the inevitable conflict between that right and the demands of the state.

During his Southern exile Puškin also embarked on his most ambitious work, which he completed only seven years later (1823–30): his verse-novel *Evgenij Onegin* (Eugene Onegin). At the center of the novel, which charts the tragic fate of the Rus. intelligentsia, stands the disillusioned, skeptical, Byronic hero Onegin, incapable of finding either occupation or happiness. After killing his friend, the young romantic poet Lenskij, in a duel, Onegin travels and finally discovers love, only to have his impassioned declaration spurned, at which juncture the novel breaks off. With the luckless heroine of the novel, Tat'jana, originates the series of pure, strong, young Rus. women whom Turgenev later immortalized. The extremely simple plot of *Eugene Onegin* is amplified by numerous "lyric digressions" which enable the author to participate in the novel both as one of its personae and as commentator. For this work Puškin created the special "Onegin stanza", a quatorzain with a complex rhyme scheme reminiscent of the Eng. sonnet.

As part of his increasing absorption with history, Puškin in 1825 wrote *Boris Godunov*, a tragedy in blank verse assessing the role of the populace in historical cataclysms. A particularly productive period of Puškin's creativity was the autumn of 1830. Forced by cholera quarantine to remain at his estate in Boldino, Puškin completed in an amazingly short span a series of superb works, incl. his "little tragedies": "Mozart and Salieri" ("Mocart i Salieri"), "The Stone Guest" ("Kamennyi gost'"), "The Covetous Knight" ("Skupoj ryear'"), and "The Feast during the Plague" ("Pir vo vremja čumy"). These highly condensed scenes investigate fatal passions such as love, greed, and envy, exploring the tragic, irreconcilable contradictions and polarities of human existence: love and death, inspiration and toil, age and youth. Finally, Puškin bequeathed to Rus. lit. a fund of lyric poetry on a broad range of themes, among them love, nature, and philosophical issues. Each of these masterpieces, which he wrote throughout his life, represents a different psychological situation for the articulation of which Puškin unfailingly finds the single word that perfectly meets the requirements of the moment or scene. That word may belong to any lexical or cultural level, be it colloquial, bookish, archaic, or vulgar. As an entity Puškin's poetry cannot be identified with any poetic system or movement such as romanticism or realism. Always comprehensible to any educated native speaker (hence their ostensible simplicity and accessibility), his poems at the same time defy translation into a foreign lang. precisely on account of the impossibility of locating the perfectly equivalent word, the *only* suitable word, within another linguistic system.

Puškin died prematurely in a duel without having realized many of his plans and, really, his seemingly limitless potential. Around him had clustered a group of gifted poets usually called the Puškin Pleiad, comprising primarily his friends Evgenij Baratynskij, Anton Del'vig, Petr Vjazemskij, Nikolaj Jazykov, and several others. Of these, the most formidable poet was indisputably Baratynskij (1800–44), whose epic *Eda* (1824) implicitly criticized Puškin's brand of romanticism: it replaced exotic gypsies and Circassian damsels with a Finnish peasant girl, and the enigmatic romantic hero with a commonplace officer-seducer. His other well-known *poema*, *Bal* (The Ball, 1828) has as its heroine a society beauty who poisons herself because of an unfortunate romance. Puškin himself thought highly of Baratynskij's *poemy*, which contrasted dramatically with his own. As a lyric poet, Baratynskij began with meditative elegies that usually mourned irretrievable happiness and juxtaposed the lyric protagonist's past with his melancholy present. Pessimism becomes the dominant note in Baratynskij's mature lyrics, so much so that in "Poslednij poet" (The Last Poet, 1835) he perceives civilization as inimical to beauty; contemp. society leaves the poet no option but to die in disillusioned isolation. Particularly imposing is Baratynskij's tragic masterpiece "Osen'" (Autumn, 1837), which juxtaposes the death of nature in autumn to the autumn of human life. Baratynskij reinforces the dark, morose ponderousness of his reflections with complex syntactic constructions and an intentionally archaic lexicon which contrast sharply with the unusual lightness of Puškin's verse.

Mixail Lermontov (1814–41) essentially also belongs to the Puškin Pleiad, though critical opinion has traditionally assigned Lermontov the role of Puškin's successor and placed him on a par with Puškin in the history of Rus. lit. Lermontov's short and luckless life (military service, Caucasian exile, death by duel at age 26) allowed him little opportunity to realize fully his poetic talent. Although he attained instant fame in 1837 with his poem on Puškin's death, his active literary career lasted only four years, during which he produced the most memorable instances of the quintessential Rus. romantic *poema*: *Pesnja pro kupca Kalašnikova* (Song of the Merchant Kalashnikov, 1838), which borrows from folklore for its dramatic story of love and death in the time of Ivan the Terrible; *Mcyri* (The Novice, 1840), the final confession of a fugitive novice that in structure and rhythm recalls Byron's *Giaour*; and *Demon* (1829–41), an operatic account of the fatal love of the spirit of evil for the beautiful Tamara. A profound and sweeping disillusionment imbues Lermontov's lyrics—disillusionment with his generation, himself, and life at large (e.g. "Duma" [Ballad], "Poet" [The Poet]). In a world that is "dreary and dismal," bereft of love, populated by a cruel and vicious humanity intent on brutalizing the poet-prophet, death offers the only deliverance. Lermontov's verse is energetic and abrupt, "an iron verse, steeped in bitterness and malice." This energy gains additional force in several poems from the masculine rhymes of Lermontov's iambic tetrameter. Ternary meters, however, occur much more often in his poetry than in Puškin's.

The next important stage in the history of Rus. p. finds its most gifted representative in Fedor Tjutčev (1803–73). A lyric poet of genius as well as a government official and diplomat, a salon wit, and one of the most educated men of his time, Tjutčev wrote very little and published even less: his collected poems, which embody his soul's innermost secrets, his *sancta sanctorum*, fill only a single slender volume. Tjutčev's philosophical poems reveal a Schellingian pantheism which conceives of nature as an organism animated by a spirit incomprehensible and inaccessible to humankind:

> Nature is not what it seems to you,
> It is no blind nor soulless image—
> It has a soul, and freedom too,
> It has love, it has a language.

The boldness of Tjutčev's metaphors stems from his metaphorical perception of the universe. Thus in his "documentary description" of his vision, summer lightning is God's stern pupils shining through his heavy lashes, the Earth's head is crowned with the sun, and its feet are washed by spring waters; the poet sees the gentle smile of fading autumn. Love lyrics which are decidedly tragic in concept and mood occupy a special place in Tjutčev's oeuvre, doubtless owing to the poet's protracted liaison with a much younger mistress who died of consumption. For Tjutčev, love is the manifestation of elemental forces; it dooms human life, unavoidably leading to death—a tragic conception of passion that has affinities with Turgenev's in his fiction. Tjutčev infuses his descriptions of his beloved's last moments and her departure from life with searing, inexpressible pain, and locates that heart-wrenching loss within a general landscape of human suffering. Technically, Tjutčev expanded the traditional rhythmic system of Rus. p., partly through an increased use of the trochee (as opposed to the iambic meters favored by Puškin's school), and esp. through his conscious violation of the rhythmic structure of syllabotonic versification. His unorthodox shifts in rhythm as an artistic device prepared the ground for the *dol'nik*, a tonic meter widely used at the beginning of the 20th c.

Although chronologically Tjutčev's poetic output spills over into the 1860s, it nevertheless brings the Golden Age to a close. Interest in verse diminished perceptibly in the 1850s as it was ousted by prose, which rapidly gained dominance as a genre. Both literary theory and crit. of this period enthusiastically embraced the principle of utilitarianism, viewing lit. as a useful means of enlightening the common people and liberating them from social repression. Such a pragmatic approach to lit. esp. characterized the crit. of Nikolaj Černyševskij and Nikolaj Dobroljubov, who derived their ideas from Comte and Feuerbach. Predictably, "ideological" prose fiction could fulfill the utilitarian task better than poetry, which at best was regarded as second-rate material for propaganda. Nikolaj Nekrasov's (1821–78) phrase, "You may not be a poet, / But be a citizen you must," became the slogan of this influential literary camp with its leftist political values.

Nekrasov, by birth a member of the landowning class, a brilliant publisher and editor, a successful gambler, and a wealthy snob late in life, was the sole authentically talented poet in this group. At the same time, Nekrasov was a man with a tragic and morbid attitude to life, which found expression in his portrayal of peasant and urban poverty and condignly earned him fame as a popular poet of the people. Given to calling his muse bloody and "horsewhipped," Nekrasov chronicled the sufferings of Rus. peasant women, crushed by hard physical labor in addition to their husbands' drunkenness and beatings ("V doroge" [En Route], 1845; "Trojka," 1846). He immortalized the denizens of city slums exhausted by hunger and cold ("Edu li noč'ju" [Whenever I drive at night], 1847; "Vor" [The Thief], 1850), the forced laborers at their harrowing toil ("Železnaja doroga" [The Railroad], 1864), the unfortunate sick peasants who lacked all rights ("Neszataja polosa" [An Unharvested Strip], 1854; "Razmyšlenija u paradnogo pod"ezda" [Musings in the Main Driveway], 1856), and the soldier flogged to death by his superiors ("Orina, mat' soldatskaja" [Orina, A Soldier's Mother], 1863). In his huge epic poem *Komu na Rusi žit' xorošo* (Who Is Happy in Russia, 1865–77), Nekrasov attempted a comprehensive canvas of Rus. life in the post-Emancipation 1860s. Several successful sections aside, the poems as a whole failed to cohere and disintegrated into separate units. Nekrasov's poetry tends toward simple rhythms, it favors ternary meters, and it does not aim for metrical variety; consequently, his verses often lapse into a monotonous uniformity of rhythm.

Poets of the 1850s–70s who could legitimately be called members of the "Nekrasov school" include the critic Dobroljubov, who produced poor poetry; the satirist and witty parodist D. Minaev, author of feuilletons in verse; M. Mixajlov, renowned for his revolutionary activities and his civic and political verse, who was the originator of "prison" poetry and left excellent trs. of Heine; the satirical poet V. Kuročkin, who earned a reputation for his trs. of Béranger; the self-taught merchant's son I. Nikitin, who concentrated on peasant life; I. Surikov; and several other lesser figures.

The "art for art's sake" school that stood in opposition to the Utilitarians did not so much defend "pure art" as reject a pragmatic approach to lit. and argue in favor of varied thematics. The most talented and "purest" lyricist among them was Afanasij Fet (1820–92), a follower of Schopenhauer, whose *World as Will and Representation* he translated. According to Fet, the "real" world and the world of poetry and beauty are two utterly unrelated realms. An officer and highly successful landowner in everyday life, Fet, when transported into the sphere of the sublime, became an inspired poet. The poet's task, he maintained, is to perceive the beauty which lies beyond the commonplace purview of the average being and to reveal that beauty to others. Love and nature are the most frequent themes in his lyrics. Fet's nature poems celebrate the alluring, festive beauty of the natural world in its manifold aspects: velvet night, mysterious dawn, dense forest, silver snow, trilling birds, delicate butterflies. Where other poets dwell on the psychological complexity of love relationships, Fet confines himself to the selective mention of a few details from which the reader must deduce the portrait of the beloved or recreate the situation. A momentary impression captured by the poet expands in the reader's mind into a poetic scene which reminds us simultaneously that beauty is transitory and that poetry can only suggest the inaccessible, ideal beauty of a world beyond our reach. Fet's substitution of synecdochic detail for the whole and the musicality of his verse, achieved through systematic alliteration and assonance, make him the first Rus. impressionist poet, whom the symbolists revered as their most important forerunner. Boldly innovative in rhythm, Fet combined diverse meters in a single poem, alternated very long lines with extremely short ones (sometimes consisting of only one word) within a stanza, and followed a stanza in binary meter with one in ternary. All these devices paved the way for the dissolution of syllabotonic versification that took place in Rus. p. at the turn of the century.

Other talented proponents of anti-utilitarian tendencies in the mid 19th c. include Fet's friend Aleksej K. Tolstoj (1817–75), Jakov Polonskij, (1810–97), Apollon Majkov (1821–97), Lev Mej (1822–62), Karolina Pavlova (1807–93), and others. They strove to fuse musicality with reconciliation in their depiction of reality, created beautiful nature and love lyrics, and rediscovered historical and folklore themes. A decisive force in the battle against the utilitarian school was exerted by anthology verse. Characterized by vividness and visual plasticity, anthology verse flourished in the 1850s and 60s, being a genre favored by almost all the poets of the "art for art's sake" movement. It comprised the most significant part of Nikolaj Ščerbina's (1821–69) output.

Despite the decline of interest in poetry in the 1850s at the hands of the utilitarian critics, by the 1860s–70s the "art for art's sake" school had raised poetry to new heights, laying the groundwork for its luxuriant flowering at the turn of the century, when their contributions were reassessed and assimilated. The 1880s, however, witnessed once again a sharp decline in Rus. p. The civic ardor of the utilitarian school ended with the most popular poet of the 1880s, Sëmen Nadson (1862–87), who died from consumption. A sense of doom, a resentment against middle-class satiety and crass vulgarity, and a hatred for "the kingdom of Baal" dominate Nadson's verses, which show talent but suffer from uniformity of both theme and rhythm. Although the "pure art" school as a whole proved more fecund, its representatives in the 1880s paled by comparison with its pioneers. Their ranks included Aleksej Apuxtin (1840–93), with his intimate romances and lyrics in a gypsy vein, Konstantin Slučevskij (1837–1904), and Konstantin Fofanov (1862–1911). These men stood on the threshold of Rus. symbolist poetry, when the brilliant new era of Rus. culture dawned—an era that lasted to 1917 and came to be known as the "Silver Age."

Symbolism, which became the most influential poetic current of this period, found its theoretical underpinnings in the ideas of the Neoplatonic philosopher Vladimir Solov'ëv (1853–1900). At the heart of Solov'ëv's eschatological system rests the idea of the World Soul, the Eternal Feminine, the Feminine Cosmic Source, which can only be attained in the sphere of art. Through the perception of art alone, asserted Solov'ëv, can one come into contact with other worlds. Hence, in the symbolist scheme semantics become unstable and intentionally polysemous (it is no accident that the symbolists cited Žukovskij and Fet among their forerunners).

Considered the founder of symbolism, Valerij Brjusov (1873–1924) willingly fulfilled his role as the movement's theoretician, leader, and publisher. From 1893–95 he pub. three collections entitled *Russkie simvolisty* (Rus. symbolists). His own poetry, which is distinguished by picturesqueness and cold craftsmanship, has a rational, declarative cast and reveals Brjusov's technical adventurousness: he tried his hand at every known poetic genre and all the meters and stanza forms common to world poetry. Two of Brjusov's predecessors who actually realized symbolist ideas were Konstantin Bal'mont (1867–1942), a brilliant master of musical verses and superb rhythms who emigrated in 1920, and Fëdor Sologub (1862–1927), whose pessimistic poems juxtapose the doomed real world of mortality with the beautiful imaginary world of "the Star of Oilay" or "the Star of Mair."

During the second phase of Rus. symbolism, which began ca. 1900, several outstanding poets of various ages joined the by-then-dominant movement. Among the older symbolists one finds Vjačeslav Ivanov (1866–1949), who left the Soviet Union in 1924, and Innokentij Annenskij (1856–1909). The immensely erudite Ivanov became the movement's most outstanding theoretician. His skillfully archaized, allusive verses, which draw attention to their bookishness and the complexity of their rhythmic structure, make considerable demands on their reader. Like Ivanov, Annenskij came to literature relatively late; the majority of his poems were not published in his lifetime. Permeated by unrelieved pessimism, these lyrics repeatedly dwell on death, expressed in images borrowed from the finely perceived details of everyday life. Ancient Greece appears in a guise of equally inconsolable gloom in Annensky's four tragedies, based on motifs from ancient myths. Younger symbolists of the second generation incl. Andrej Belyj (1880–1934) and Aleksandr Blok (1880–1921). A splendid poet and prosodist, Belyj also shone as a prose writer and critic. His major collections of poetry, *Zoloto v lazuri* (Gold in Azure), *Pepel* (Ashes), and *Urna* (The Urn), reflect the abstruse complexity of the symbolist worldview. Both the ideal expanse of the azure and purple sky and the brutal ordinariness of the earth, with its cities and villages, are described in almost Nekrasovian tones (indeed, Belyj dedicated *Pepel* to Nekrasov). The philosophical principles of Baratynskij's and Tjutčev's lyrics find a new meaning and are assimilated into symbolism in Belyj, whose poetry brims with neologisms and shows true originality in stanza construction, whereby an individual word, emphasized through intonation, serves as the basis of a rhythmic pattern and becomes a line of the poetic text. Subsequently, these experiments by Belyj influenced the efforts of Majakovskij and Cvetaeva to break new poetic ground.

A genius whose oeuvre constitutes the summit of poetic achievement in the early 20th c., Aleksandr Blok divided his collected lyrics into three volumes. In the first, which contains the famous collection of "Stixi o Prekrasnoj Dame" (Verses about the Beautiful Lady), true to the philosophy of Solov'ev, Blok exalts the ideal world of beauty, light, and worship of the Deity wherein resides his mystic beloved, the incarnation of the World Soul, the Eternal Feminine. In the second volume, the poet "moves from the divine realm to that of the creatures," abandoning the churches and temples, the poetic *terems* (halls or towers) and azure skies, for the poeticized world of swamps and northern forests populated by evil spirits, phantasmal Petersburg, and winter blizzards. The poet's lyrical devel. culminates in the third volume with a sense of tragic, inconsolable despair that admits of no solution, even in death. Blok was the first poet of the era to write a *poema*, "Dvenadcat'" (The Twelve), about the October Revolution, which he was prepared to accept regardless of the blood, devastation, and terror, for he perceived in the cataclysm a new and purifying beginning. The twelve rebels of his narrative simultaneously appear as twelve apostles, ahead of whom walks the figure of Christ, a symbol of the blessing given to the imminent world. Blok appreciably extended the rhythmic possibilities of Rus. verse, making extensive use of *dol'niki.* The hallmarks of Blok's poetry are polysemous diction, melodiousness, and expressiveness. One other excellent poet and critic belonging to the youngest generation of symbolists is Vladislav Xodasevič (1886–1939), a substantial part of whose creative activity took place in emigration.

The second decade of the 20th c. witnessed a reaction to the vagueness of symbolist poetry in the emergence of a counter-movement. Mixail Kuzmin (1875–1936), a poet who portrayed scenes (e.g. of the Rus. 18th c.; of Egypt during the Hellenistic era) in extremely vivid and sensual images, called for "beautiful clarity" in poetry. A literary group headed by Nikolaj Gumilëv (1886–1921), later executed for his participation in an anti-Bolshevik plot, answered that summons. Calling themselves "acmeists," the group's members decried the symbolists' neglect of the material world. To acmeism belong two of the greatest 20th-c. Rus poets: Anna Axmatova (1889–1966) and Osip Mandelštam (1891–1938). Both poets observed faithfully acmeism's principles of clarity and plasticity, its pictorial tendencies, and its grounding in material culture. In *Rekviem* (Requiem), pub. in the Soviet Union only in 1987, Axmatova captured in mercilessly clear and expressive verses the horrors of the Stalinist terror of 1937. In one of her last works, *Poema bez geroja* (Poem Without a Hero), she incarnated in masterly rhythms the twilight of the Silver Age on the eve of the October Revolution. Denounced by the Party's Central Committee in 1946, Axmatova became the focus of attacks by politically conservative critics. The course of her poetic devel. ran parallel to Mandelštam's, who perished in Stalin's camps. Both moved thematically from paeans to the beauty of the Ancient and European worlds (esp. the dazzlingly beautiful and cold Petersburg) to the keen-sighted and unsparing depiction of the cruelty, desolation, and vulgar mediocrity of post-Revolutionary Rus. life. One of the last poets "reared on acmeism" was Dmitrij Klenovskij (1893–1976), the majority of whose works were written in emigration. With some reservations, one could include Georgij Ivanov (1894–1958) among the younger acmeists. His fine lyrics matured from *recherché* exoticism to the tragic nostalgia of his later years in emigration.

An essential role in the poetic life of the Silver Age was played by the futurists, who gave prominence to the acoustic aspect of words. Rejecting all earlier achievements in Rus. and world poetry, they elaborated the theory of the "self-oriented" (*samovitoe*), i.e. self-significant word, devoid of all semantic associations. On its basis they created a "trans-sense" (*zaumnaja*) poetry: a poetry free of semantic significance, possessing only sound value. Their ideas link the futurists with dada and other avant-garde tendencies not only in poetry but also in the visual arts. The supreme futurist poet and theoretician was Velimir Xlebnikov (1885–1922), a master of experimental verse which richly illustrates his faculty for creating words. One of the most accomplished of the futurist poets was Vladimir Majakovskij (1894–1930), who resembled other futurists insofar as his rejection of the past logically forced him to accept the October Revolution, which he actively supported through his artistic work. Majakovskij's maximalist temperament and hyperbolic tendencies led him to extremes of dedication, so that by the 1920s his poetry became purely propagandistic. His political jingles evinced none of his earlier lyrical powers. After Majakovskij's suicide, Stalin proclaimed him the best poet of the Soviet era, an assessment which still obtains in official Soviet culture. Majakovskij wrote predominantly accentual verse in which the main rhythmic unit becomes the word (a single accent), which itself can comprise a whole line; hence the "ladderlike" effect of Majakovskij's verses on the printed page. To some degree the influence of his rhythms is discernible in contemp. poetry, esp. that of Voznesenskij and Evtušenko.

In contrast to the emphatically urban futurists, their contemporaries Nikolaj Kljuev (1885–1937) and Sergej Esenin (1895–1925) found inspiration almost exclusively in the countryside. Kljuev, who perished in the camps, produced heavily ornamental poetry, dense with imagery derived from the religious beliefs of the Schismatics and patriarchal peasant life. Esenin, whose popularity continues to rise steadily, was Majakovskij's major rival during the 1920s. In melodious verses that suggest Blok's influence, Esenin sang the beauty of nature, peasant life (often in idyllic tones), and Christianity, which he perceived as the peasants' religion. After the Revolution, however, his verses acquired a tragic tone as he mourned the fall of peasant Russia; the degeneration of love into lechery; and the fate of the poet, whose final refuge is the tavern. Sincere despair, which led him to suicide, sounds unmistakably in his last poems, "Moskva kabackaja" (The Moscow of Taverns) and "Čërnyj čelovek" (The Black Man).

The original and remarkable gifts of Marina Cvetaeva (1892–1941) have their roots in Blok and Axmatova, but the devel. of those gifts was disrupted by the Revolution and Cvetaeva's emigration in 1922. Her energetic poems, packed with inner tension, in broken rhythms of short lines and frequent enjambment, were created in unbearably trying circumstances, amidst poverty, constant travel, and misery exacerbated by Cvetaeva's cheerless temperament. An organic synthesis of Rus. folklore, 18th-c. odic rhetoric, and Deržavin, Puškin, the futurists, Goethe, and Rilke [her favorite poets], her verses won Cvetaeva an enormous audience in Russia in the 1960s. Returning to her homeland in 1939, Cvetaeva could not endure the conditions of her personal life (her daughter's arrest and her husband's execution) and committed suicide.

If poetic life in Russia remained fairly active during the 1920s, that continuation was due largely to inertia. Literary societies and unions arose and disbanded in rapid succession. A partial list of the organizations that proliferated during this period includes Proletcult, devised to forge a proletarian poetry independent of former trads.; LEF (Majakovskij and Aseev), which rejected art in the name of fact; the romantic *Pereval* (Divide) group, with Mixail Svetlov and Eduard Bagrickij; Kuznica (the Smithy), which included M. Gerasimov, V. Kirillov, and S. Rodov, who glorified the proletariat and the "metallic world of machines"; the imagists, incl. Esenin, Vadim Šeršenevič, and Anatolij Mariengof, who in their polemics with futurism emphasized the imagistic nature of the poetic word; and the "Oberjuty," an avant-garde group that founded a theater of the absurd and produced surrealist and expressionist poems. Almost all the members of the group (Daniil Xarms, Nikolaj Olejnikov, Aleksandr Vvedenskij, Nikolaij Zabolockij, and others) were suppressed—and some were shot—in the 1930s. The year 1932 saw the elimination of these and all other groups when, by government decree, the Union of Soviet Writers was established as the sole legitimate writers' association. During the ensuing two decades Rus. p. ground to a standstill. Genuine poets fell silent, wrote "for the drawer" (with no hope of publishing their work), or undertook translation.

Such was the fate of the consummate poet Boris Pasternak (1890– 1960). Although initially allied with the futurists, Pasternak essentially continued the trads. of the Rus. and Ger. philosophical lyric (Tjutčev and Rilke). Laden with profound and complex imagery, his poetry has the intensity of passionate love lyrics. Despite various attempts to engage in postrevolutionary public life (he wrote a *poema* about the 1905 Revolution, for example), Pasternak remained an individualist to the core, and the government never succeeded in wooing him to its side. For a long stretch after the formation of the Writers' Union, Pasternak kept silent, translating Goethe, Schiller, and Shakespeare and working on the novel *Doctor Zhivago*, the last section of which is a verse cycle that draws richly on religious themes and motifs. Pub. in Italy in 1957, the novel earned Pasternak the Nobel Prize the following year. But this unleashed a campaign of vituperative Soviet persecution against Pasternak that eventually pressured him into refusing the award. These events undermined Pasternak's already uncertain health, and he died of cancer in 1960.

The "thaw" ushered in by Stalin's death in 1953 facilitated a renascence in Rus. p. that lasted almost two decades. Young poets entered the literary ranks to form the poetic avant garde of the Sixties. Adrej Voznesenskij (b. 1933) instantly drew readers' attention through his unexpected rhymes, his virtuoso deployment of metaphor, and the boldness and originality of his ideas. In articulating his hatred for despotism (a typical concern after Stalin's death), his poems regularly pitted tyrants against such artists and "masters" as Rus. architects, Goya, Gauguin, Blok, and Rublev. Although as individuals they perished, their art and art in general triumphed, thus achieving a moral victory over tyranny. Voznesenskij's poetry evidences his fascination with constructivism in architecture, with cybernetics, and with modern physics, and juxtaposes the complex rhythms of the modern world with the banality of everyday existence.

The complicated form of Voznesenskij's poems and his attraction to the technocratic tendencies of the West briefly made him the idol of the Rus. intelligentsia. His constant rival, who matched him in popularity and reached a wider audience, was Evgenij Evtušenko (b. 1933). Formally quite primitive (in rhythm, syntax, and imagery), his poems suggest affinities with Majakovskij. Yet his best works not only boast a topicality and dynamic power, but boldly touch on topics forbidden in the Soviet press: Stalinism, anti-Semitism, Party bureaucracy, corruption, bribery, and sex.

The sensational success of Voznesenskij and Evtušenko overshadowed other poets whose talents compared with and perhaps even outstripped that of the two celebrities, for whom public adulation abated at the close of the 1960s. That decade was uncommonly wealthy in talents that emerged suddenly after 30 years of incubation or repression. Of these the most memorable incl. Bella Axmadulina (b. 1937), author of subtle and profound philosophical verse; Aleksandr Kušner (b. 1936); Nikolaj Rubcov (1936–71), who died prematurely, leaving a body of nature lyrics; and Viktor Sosnora (b. 1936), who wrote on Rus. history. Alongside these poets appeared the exponents of a new genre: "bards" who sang their verses to guitar accompaniment. Tape recorders expedited the rapid dissemination of their poems. Of the bards, the most eminent are the subtle lyricist Bulat Okudžava (b. 1924), the keen satirist Aleksandr Galič (1918–77), and the tragic poet and actor Vladimir Vysockij (1938–80). To this group also belongs Novella Matveeva (b. 1934), who composes verses full of philosophical reflection and unexpected romantic imagery.

With the 1970s, the topicality and political subtext that marked the poetry of the previous decade receded into the background. A wholesale rejection of both classical and official Soviet culture now manifested itself in the works of poets belonging to this "barracks" school of poetry, whose spiritual fathers were the futurists and the Oberjuty. Nine large volumes of undigested raw material containing the verse, crit., diaries, and reminiscences of these poets were recently pub. by Konstantin Kuzminskij. Whereas the works of Gennadij Aigi (b. 1934) regularly reveal his debt to the futurist trad., the career of Naum Koržavin (b. 1925), now living in emigration, reflects a definite shift from anti-Stalinist political verse to philosophical musings on the meaning of life and the poet's calling. Among the contemp. poets whose literary powers matured only in emigration, Aleksej Cvetkov (b. 1947) and Baxyt Kenžiev (b. 1950) deserve mention. In the United States they encountered poets working in the cl. mode: Igor' Činnov (b. 1909), Ivan Elagin (1918–87), and Nikolaj Moršen (b. 1917).

In general, poetry jettisoned politics and ideology to reclaim once more the sphere of spiritual values and to explore the immemorial issues of

God, truth, and moral fortitude. This devel. resulted in the belated recognition of Arsenij Tarkovskij (b. 1907), whose philosophical poetry, with roots extending to the trad. of Deržavin and Tjutčev, became the reading of choice for the spiritual elite of the 1970s. But the foremost poet of the decade is unquestionably the Nobel Prize winner (1987), Iosif Brodsky (b. 1940), tried and sentenced to exile in 1965 for social parasitism and forced to emigrate in 1972. Brodsky's completely apolitical poetry examines universal problems, to which he seeks solutions partly by drawing analogies between the contemp. world and past cultures, whether biblical Judea, Homeric Greece, ancient China, Cl. Rome, England in the 17th c., or Russia in the 18th.

This submersion in world culture, together with a tangible feel for the past and present, makes Brodsky an heir and successor to the acmeist trad. (Axmatova had a high opinion of his verses). That trad. surfaces also in the works of other poets who are Brodsky's contemporaries and friends. They appropriate from late acmeism not only its preoccupation with concrete objects but also its profoundly religious orientation, as demonstrated in the fine poems of Oleg Oxapkin (b. 1944), Dmitrij Bobyšev (b. 1936), Jurij Kublanovskij (b. 1947), Elena Švarc (b. 1948), Vasilij Betaki (b. 1930), and several others. Calling themselves the poets of "the Bronze Age," they stress their links with Petersburg culture, which passed through a Golden and then a Silver Age. At the same time, the Bronze Age presages in apocalyptic fashion the dawn of the Iron Age, with its subculture and its computers, when, they fear, no room will be left for poetry.

See also ARMENIAN POETRY; BYELORUSSIAN POETRY; GEORGIAN POETRY; UKRAINIAN POETRY.

ANTHOLOGIES: *Specimens of the Rus. Poets*, tr. J. Bowring, 2 v. (1821–23); *Russkaja poezija*, ed. S. A. Vengerov, 1–7 (1893–97))—best and most complete anthol. of the 18th c.; *Russkaja poezija XX veka*, ed. I. S. Ezov and E. I. Samurin (1925); *Na Zapade: Antologija russkoj zarubežnoj poezii*, ed. J. P. Ivask (1953)—widest selection of Rus. p. in exile; *12 poetas rusos XIX–XX*, ed. V. Vinogradova (1958); *Anthologie de la poésie russe*, ed. K. Granoff (1961); *The Heritage of Rus. Verse*, ed. D. Obolensky (1965)—with literal prose trs.; *Russkie poety: Antologija v četyrex tomax*, ed. D. D. Blagoj et al. (1965–68); *Mod. Rus. P.*, ed. V. Markov and M. Sparks (1966)—with verse trs.; *The New Rus. Poets 1953–1968*, ed. G. Reavey (1968); *Fifty Soviet Poets*, ed. V. Ognev and D. Rottenberg (1969)—in Rus. and Eng.; *Russkaja sillabičeskaja poezija XVII–XVIII vv.*, ed. A. Pančenko (1970); *Ten Rus. Poets* (1970)—in Rus. with biographies and commentaries in Eng.; *The Silver Age of Rus. Culture*, ed. C. and E. Proffer (1971); *Rus. P. Under the Tsars*, ed. R. Burton (1971); *P. from the Rus. Underground*, ed. J. Landland et al. (1973)—bilingual; *The Blue Lagoon*, ed. K. K. Kuzminsky and G. L. Kovalev, v. 1–5 (1980–86); *Third Wave: The New Rus. P.*, ed. K. Johnson and S. M. Ashby (1992).

HISTORY AND CRITICISM: A. N. Sokolov, *Očerki po istorii russkoj poemy 18 v. i pervoj poloviny 19 v.* (1956); *Istorija russkoj poezii*, ed. B. P. Gorodeckij, v. 1–2 (1968–69)—fullest hist. of Rus. p. to 1917; R. Silbajoris, *Rus. Versification* (1968)—studies three 18th-c. theories; V. Žirmunskij, *Teorija stixa* (1968); B. Ejxenbaum, *O poezii* (1969); M. J. Lotman, *Analiz poetičeskogo teksta* (1972, tr. 1976 as *Analysis of the Poetic Text*), *Struktura xudožestvennogo teksta* (1975, tr. 1977 as *The Structure of the Artistic Text*); A. M. Pančenko, *Russkaja stixotvornaja kul'tura XVII veka* (1973)—on the emergence of Rus. p.; L. Ginzburg, *O lirike*, 2d ed. (1974); *Mod. Rus. Poets on Poetry*, ed. C. R. Proffer (1976); E. Etkind, *Materija stixa* (1978); D. Brown, *Soviet Rus. Lit. Since Stalin* (1978); V. Veidle, *Embriologija poezii* (1980); E. J. Brown, *Rus. Lit. Since the Revolution* (1982); *Istorija russkoj sovetskoj poezii, 1917–41; 1941–80*, ed. V. Buzik et al., v. 1–2 (1984)—incomplete and tendentious; G. Struve, *Russkaja literatura v. izgnanii*, 2d ed. (1984); F. Peter, *Poets of Mod. Russia* (1983); G. S. Smith, *Songs to Seven Strings* (1984); M. Altshuller and E. Dryža Kova, *Put' otrečenija: Russkaja literatura 1953–68* (1985)—essays on Rus. p. of the 1950s and '60s; G. A. Gukovskii, *Lomonosov, Sumarokov, and the Sumarokov School*, Soviet Studies in Lit., v. 21,1–2 (1984–85); Terras, esp. s.v. "Bylina," "Poema," "Versification, Historical Survey"; B. P. Scherr, *Rus. P.* (1986)—prosody; D. Lowe, *Rus. Writing Since 1953* (1987)—short but valuable survey of contemp. Rus. p.; *Cambridge Hist. of Rus. Lit.*, ed. C. A. Moser (1989); E. Bristol, *Hist. of Rus. P.* (1991); V. Terras, *Hist. of Rus. Lit.* (1992).

WORKS ON INDIVIDUAL WRITERS: B. V. Tomaševskij, *Puškin*, 2 v. (1956, 1961); R. A. Gregg, *Fedor Tiutchev* (1965); R. F. Gustafson, *Imagination of Spring: The Poetry of Afanasy Fet* (1966); S. S. Birkenmeyer, *Nikolaj Nekrasov* (1968); H. Troyat, *Pushkin* (1970); J. West, *Rus. Symbolism: A Study of Vyaceslav Ivanov and the Rus. Symbolist Aesthetic* (1970); A. Cross, *N. M. Karamzin: A Study of his Literary Career (1783–1803)* (1971); B. Dees, *E. A. Baratynsky* (1972); B. M. Žirmunskij, *Tvorčestvo Anny Axmatovoj* (1973); O. R. Hughes, *The Poetic World of Boris Pasternak* (1974); I. Z. Serman, *Konstantin Batyushkov* [in Eng.] (1974), *Mikhail Lomonosov: Life and Poetry* (1988); D. Blagoj, *Mir kak krasota: O "Večernix ognjax" A. Feta* (1975)—the best study of the nature of Fet's lyrics; A. Haight, *Anna Akhmatova: A Poetic Pilgrimage* (1976); G. McVay, *Esenin: A Life* (1976); I. M. Semenko, *Vasily Zhukovsky* [in Eng.] (1976); B. Christa, *The Poetic World of Andrey Belyi* (1977); A. Pyman, *The Life of Aleksandr Blok*, 2 v. (1979–80); E. D. Sampson, *Nikolay Gumilev* (1979); B. M. Eikhenbaum, *Lermontov: A Study in Literary-Historical Evaluation* (1981); *Lermontovskaja enciklopedija*, ed. V. A. Manujlov (1981); V. Terras, *Vladimir Mayakovsky* (1983); J. D. Grossman, *Valery Bryusov and the Riddle of Rus. Decadence*

(1985); J. Karabičevskij, *Voskresenie Majakovskogo* (1985)—the only strongly negative study of Majakovskij, which criticizes the Soviet canonization of the poet; S. Karlinsky, *Marina Tsvetaeva* (1985); P. Gromov, *A. Blok, ego predšestvenniki i sovremenniki* (1986); J. G. Harris, *Osip Mandelstam* (1988); V. Xodasevič, *Deržavin* (1988); R. Iezuitova, *Žukovskij i russkaja literatura ego vremeni* (1989); V. Polukhina, *Joseph Brodsky: A Poet of Our Time* (1989).

M.G.A.; tr. H.G.

S

SANSKRIT POETRY. See INDIAN POETRY.

SCOTTISH GAELIC POETRY. The origins of S. G. p. are naturally identical with those of Ir. (see IRISH POETRY), since both langs. derive from a common Celtic source. This identity is preserved in classical or "bardic" poetry, which continued to be written without significant regional variation in both countries, up to the 17th c. in Ireland and up to the 18th in Scotland (which held the cultural status of a province vis-á-vis the mother country). This fact, as well as the destruction of mss., has to be considered when noting the comparative paucity of poems of S. provenance or authorship. Nevertheless, there are poems connected with Scotland extant from as early as the 11th or 12th c. Identity is constituted by the same literary dialect, the same expression of "heroic" values, the same metrical forms (although G. is a stressed lang., cl. poetry, based on Med. Lat. verse, observes regularity of syllable count), the same rigorous and complex rules of ornamentation. Not all poems of course conform to this austere standard. Poetry which utilizes an easier, modified technique is fairly common, whether written by members of the hereditary caste of learned men who had undergone the arduous training of the bardic schools or by members of the aristocracy who had not but at least had some facility for composing competent verse. All these features of style are admirably displayed in the earliest and principal compilation of cl. verse to have survived in Scotland, the Book of the Dean of Lismore (ca. 1512–26). It also provides a fair sample of the range and variety of the themes of bardic verse: encomia of court poets for their patrons, satire, religious poetry, "ballads" of Fionn and Oisein, (formally, the G. "ballad," in this context, belongs with the rest of bardic poetry), moral and didactic verse, and poetry in the *amour courtois* trad. This last genre, Continental in origin, mediated by the Anglo-Normans but grafted on a native root, establishes the European dimensions of the poetry, as do other kinds influenced directly by Lat. The excellence of bardic verse lies in its highly developed lang., in its sophisticated and allusive style, and above all in the elaborate and subtly modulated music of its intricate metrical patterns. Its limitations, on the other hand, inhere neither in subject matter nor technique but rather in a formalism of conventions inseparable from the office of the professional poet, that of public panegyrist to the great men of his society.

The cl. poets were by definition literate; their counterparts, the vernacular poets, on the whole were not, and with some exceptions their work has been recovered from oral trad. by 18th-c. and later collectors. But too much can be made of this disjunction. Vernacular poets continue to express many of the attitudes of cl. poetry. Irregularly stressed meters, derived from the syllabic versification of literate poets, survived demotically. Among regularly stressed meters, one of the most interesting, because it is restricted to Scotland and closely associated with vernacular panegyric, is the so-called Strophic meter (minimally, two-stress lines followed by a three-stress line, though extensions and elaborations occur). The two great early practitioners of this form whose work has survived, Mairi Nighean Alasdair Ruaidh (ca. 1615–1707) and Iain Lom (ca. 1620–1710), are not innovators. Although the latter is exercised by national issues, both are clan poets composing in a panegyric trad., and both clearly have the security of established practice behind them—perhaps stretching back to a point anterior to the introduction of Lat. learning. The rhetoric of their verse at its best has a splendidly affirmative quality.

The anthology known as the Fernaig Ms., compiled between 1688 and 1693, contains distinctive examples of poems (religious, political, elegiac, etc.) that help to point the steps, in style and lang., between cl. and vernacular verse, while oral poetry, in many ways the demotic mainstream throughout, has continued to be composed up to the present.

The ballads traditionally attributed to Oisein son of Fionn exist in both literary and oral form. James MacPherson's spurious "translations" of these (pub. 1760–65) are loosely based on, among other sources, collections made from oral recitation, beginning in the early 18th c. The Ossiànic Controversy itself stimulated further collections of all kinds of poetry and music. The first phase of this continued into the early 19th c.; thereafter, important collections were made intermittently throughout the 19th and 20th cs.

In the 18th c. a fresh dimension was added to the scope and expressiveness of S. G. p. by Alexander MacDonald (1700–70), the perfervid nationalist and poet of the "Forty-Five," and by Duncan Bán Macintyre (1724–1812), the hunter-poet. A highly educated man drawing on all the resources of G., MacDonald is the outstanding figure of his age. The resonant verse of John MacCodrum (1693–1779) seems more of the 17th c. by comparison, but the controlled, detailed naturalism of Macintyre's *Praise of Ben Dorain* embodies a movement away from clan poetry. These two were completely oral poets, as was Rob Donn (1714–78), the best satirist in vernacular G. The poetry of William Ross (1762–90) manifests a wider sensibility which certainly owes something to his learning in Eng. and in the Cl. langs. Ross's tender, anguished love poems merit a special place in the history of G. lit.

G. verse fell to its nadir in the 19th c. when the breakup of G. society due to Eng. intrusion and forced emigration partially destroyed the G. spirit. Moreover, a good deal of the published work of the time is the product of urbanized Gaels influenced by romanticism and other alien conventions. Yet an appreciable body of vigorous oral poetry continued to be composed, in which the verse of Mary MacPherson of Skye (1821–98) is notable.

The hist. of the Gaels in Scotland has left a profound impression on G. p. Anglicization of the S. dynasty in the 11th c. and the destruction of the Lordship of the Isles in the 15th are two markers in a process of ethnocide which produced a seige mentality. This stimulated the devel. of panegyric praising the caste of aristocratic warrior-hunters who protected and rewarded their people. Organized in sets of conventional images or formulas which work as a semiotic code, panegyric is not only a form but a pervasive style in G. p., particularly ca. 1600 to 1800, but its workings are traceable even in contemp. poetry. G. p. has suffered from being largely excluded from the great innovative movements of post-medieval Europe. Much less important, but equally significant, is the fact that a great deal of G. p. appears to have been sung or chanted. Partly because it was mainly an oral poetry and partly because verse and not prose has always been the primary literary medium of G., a strong, supple, rich lang. has been evolved, capable of immense diversity in form and mood.

This lang. has been triumphantly recharged in the 20th c. Iain Rothach (1889–1918) is the first strong new voice, and Somhairle MacGill-Eain (b. 1911) the doyen: his work marks a revolution in G. writing. George Campbell Hay (1915–84) rehabilitates the subtle movement of the older meters; Ruaraidh MacThomais (b. 1922) introduces and develops *vers libre*, a departure of great interest in G. metrics; Domhnall MacAmhlaigh (b. 1930) is a pioneer in the same field. Iain Mac a' Ghobhainn (b. 1928) can be both avant-garde and traditional. Younger poets, e.g. Aonghas MacNeacail (b. 1942), Maoilios Caimbeul (b. 1944), and the sisters Catriona (b. 1947) and Morag (b. 1949) NicGumaraid have made notable contributions. A remarkable devel. is the writing of G. by non-native speakers, among whom William Neill and Fergus MacKinlay are outstanding. All these poets write from a bicultural background with an intense awareness of the 20th-c. universe. In that sense G. p., in the movements of almost a century, has been made modern.

ANTHOLOGIES: *Ortha nan Gaidheal: Carmina Gadelica*, ed. A. Carmichael, 5 v. (1928–54); *G. Songs of Mary MacLeod*, ed. J. C. Watson (1934); *S. Verse from the Book of the Dean of Lismore* (1937), *Bardachd Gháidhlig: Specimens of G. P. 1550–1900*, 4th ed. (1976), both ed. W. J. Watson; *The Songs of John MacCodrum* (1938), *The Blind Harper: An Clarsair Dall*, both ed. W. Matheson (1970); *Heroic Poetry from the Book of the Dean of Lismore*, ed. N. Ross (1939); *The Songs of Duncan Ban Macintyre*, ed. A. MacLeod (1952); *Orain Iain Luim*, ed. A. MacKenzie (1964); *Hebridean Folksongs*, ed. J. L. Campbell and F. Collinson, 3 v. (1969–81); *Poems and Songs by Sileas MacDonald*, ed. C. Ó Baoill (1972); *Nua-bhardachd Ghàidhlig*, ed. D. Macaulay (1976); *Highland Songs of the Forty-Five*, ed. J. L. Campbell, 2d ed. (1984).

HISTORY AND CRITICISM: D. Thomson, *The G. Sources of MacPherson's "Ossian"* (1952), *An Intro. to G. P.* (1974), *The New Verse in S.G.: A Structural Analysis* (1974), *The Companion to G. Scotland* (1983), "G. Literary Interactions with Scots and Eng. Work," *Proc. 1st Internat. Conf. on the Langs. of Scotland* (1986); J. MacInnes, "The Oral Trad. in S. G. P.," *SS* (1968), "The Panegyric Code in G. P. and its Historical Background," *Trans. Soc. G. Inverness* (1976–78); I. Grimble, *The World of Rob Donn* (1979); S. Maclean, *Ris a' bhruthaich* (1985); W. Gillies, "The Cl. Ir. Poetic Trad.," *Proc. 7th Internat. Congress of Celtic Studies* (1986); *Sorley Maclean Critical Essays*, ed. R. J. Ross and J. Hendry (1986). J.M.

SCOTTISH POETRY. S. p. has been written in Welsh, Gaelic, Lat., Lallans (Scots), and Eng.; here the concern is for only the last two and their admixture. Because Lallans from Northumbrian Anglian is undeveloped, it has steadily lost ground to Eng. (of the 1200 separate poems submitted to *New Writing Scotland* no. 5 [1987], for example, "a bare sprinkling" is in Lallans); nevertheless, just how much freshness, range, color, and memorability it can still command is clear in *Sterts & Stobies* (1986), the Scots poems of R. Crawford and W. N. Herbert, as well as in the poetic prose of W. L. Lorimer's brilliant tr. of *The New Testament in Scots* (1983).

The Scots poet today, whether always in Eng. (MacCaig) or always in Lallans (Mackie), will reveal himself as a Scotsman when he reads aloud, for many features of pronunciation are common. Like his countrymen he is likely to disclose something of shrewdness, sentiment, common sense, patriotism, piety, and democracy; and he is likely to respect nature, facts, industry, reticence, loyalty, and literacy. For his verse he will favor alliteration, music, obloquy, nostalgia, the standard Habbie, the bob and wheel, the narrative in octosyllabic couplets, and single malt whisky.

The main sources of early S. p. are three 16th-c. mss.: Asloan, Bannatyne, and Maitland Folio; however, Andrew of Wyntoun's rhymed *Cronykil* (1424) is the source for what is possibly the oldest surviving fragment (ca. 1286)—eight octosyllabic lines rhyming *abababab*, of which the last three have now epitomized Scotland's history for 700 years: "Crist, borne in virgynyte, / Succoure Scotland, and ramede, / That is stade in perplexitie." Several unskilled romances like *Sir Tristrem* ("Thomas the Rhymer's"?) followed these verses before 1374–75, when Barbour composed *The Bruce*, Scotland's first literary achievement. A superb story of freedom narrated with infectious enthusiasm, this "factional" romance, based on the Fr. medieval romance, introduces a new subject matter: Scotland. Barbour, the poet-chronicler, seldom slackens his pace through 20 books of octosyllabic couplets; when he does, it may be for such captivating digression as explaining how a warrior's tears differ from a woman's, but more often it is to show that he is remembered in Scotland because he himself remembers his countrymen's "hardyment," with such lines as "And led thair lyff in gret trawaill, / And oft, in hard stour of bataill, / Wan eycht gret price off chewalry, / And was woydyt off cowardy."

In 1424, Scotland crowned James Stewart after his 18-year imprisonment in London. As James I (1394–1437), he described Chaucer and Gower to his court as "Superlative poetis laureate" and under their influence composed "The Kingis Quair." Here rhyme royal, conventional allegory of lover and rose, matter from Boethius, and ME all contend that this James is the first and last "S. Chaucerian." The mid-15th c. claims Sir Richard Holland's *The Buke of the Howlat*, an ingenious beast epic examining Scotland's court life. The late 15th c. claims Blind Harry's extravagant *The Wallace*, an epic romance in heroic couplets extending Barbour's nationalism; *Cockelbie's Sow*, an anonymous country tale with alliterative play in irregular 3- and 5-beat couplets; and the anonymous, amusing *Rauf Coilyear*, a satiric anti-romance on the theme of a king (Charlemagne) among unaware rustics. The 13-line stanza of *Rauf* (nine long and four short lines of black letter) parodies the old alliterative stanza of *Sir Gawain and the Green Knight*. Last, the anonymous descriptive pieces "Christ's Kirk on the Green" and "Peblis to the Play" start a trad. of rustic brawl that finds new life in the 20th-c. merrymaking of Garioch's "Embro to the Ploy." Other poems in this trad. like Fergusson's "Leith Races" and Burns' "Holy Fair" adapt the "Christ's Kirk" stanza of ten lines, 4/3/4/3/4/3/4/3/1/3 rhyming *ababababcd*, the last as refrain.

Nowhere are the post-World War II advances in S. studies more apparent than with respect to S. p. of the 15th c., "The Aureate Age," the high creativity of the "S. Chaucerians" or "makars." Influences upon these superior poets are today known to have been not only Eng. but also directly Fr. and It. as well as native. At the forefront were Henryson and Dunbar.

Robert Henryson (1425?–1506?) drew upon several medieval literary forms (lyric, ballad, pastoral) for his delightful "Robene and Makyne," arguing "The man that will nocht quhen he may, / Sall haif nocht quhen he wald." "The Annunciation" is unusual as religious verse of the Middle Ages in that its appeal is to intellect through paradox; "Orpheus and Eurydice," the most famous of the shorter love poems, masterfully illustrates cl. narration of romance material under Fr. and It. influences. The 13 beast fables after Aesop and Saint Cloude are uncompromisingly Scottish. Skillfully, Henryson reveals personality by gesture and remark; delicately, he controls narrative rhythm in a blend of entertaining story and central moral. Political questions within the allegory (e.g. "The Tale of the Lion and the Mouse") present the poet as a democrat in the line of Lindsay, Fergusson, and Burns. The fable "The Preiching of the Swallow" and *The Testament of Cresseid*, both in rhyme royal, are Henryson's two finest poems, full of his charity, humanity, and high-mindedness. Central to the *Testament* is the question, Why do men made in the image of God become "beistis Irrational"? This beautiful, moving tragedy of sin Henryson develops with the originality of a great mind, permitting him, in contrast to Chaucer, freedom to invent his own ending.

William Dunbar (ca. 1460–ca.1513) was priest and poet at the court of James IV. Strong Fr. and Occitan influences upon a variety of lyric forms are apparent in his 80-odd poems, never long. The temperament is European, the craftsmanship superb in its intricacies, linguistic virtuosity, and harmony of sound and sense, the tone variously personal, witty, exuberant, eccentric, blasphemous, manic-depressive: "Now dansand mery, now like to dee." Dunbar's favorite subjects are himself, his milieu, woman (dame, widow, Madonna), and Catholic Christianity. Some poems, like "The Goldyn Targe," a dream allegory, and "Ane Ballat of Our Lady," belong to the poetry of rhetoric and the court; thus they are replete with the favorite phrase "me thocht," internal rhyme, and aureate diction ; other poems, such as "The Flyting of Dunbar and Kennedie" and "The Tretis of the Twa Mariit Wemen and the Wedo" (the first blank verse in Scots, strongly alliterative), belong to the poetry of ribald speech. Satires of this order are central to Dunbar's work and the truest measure of his restoration of the vernacular.

Bishop Gavin Douglas (1475?–1522) and Sir David Lindsay (1490?–1555?) complete the makars' roll. More learned than either Henryson or Dunbar, Douglas focused his dream vision *The Palace of Honour* on the nature of virtue and honor in educating a young poet and, therewith, acknowledged indebtedness to such It. humanists as Poggio-Braccilini and Petrarch. Douglas' *magnum opus* is his tr. of the *Aeneid*, also in heroic couplets, the first tr. of a classic into Scots and a major source for Surrey's *Aeneid*, the first Eng. blank verse. Its prologues, notably that to Book VII, reveal an individual voice, a wealth of lang., and the typical Scots poet's eye for nature. Sir David, Lyon King-at-Arms and promoter of Knox, intellectual revolutionary and early defender of writing for Iok and Thome in the maternal lang., has made his reputation as the most popular Scots poet before Burns primarily on *Ane Pleasant Satire of the Thrie Estaitis*, a morality play or propaganda drama with Lady Sensuality and Flattery as the leads. Blending comedy and common sense, Lindsay gives answer to What is good government? in sophisticated verseforms: bob and wheel, 8-line stanzas of iambic pentameter in linking rhyme for formal speeches, and exchange of single lines in couplets of stichomythia.

With the Wedderburns' *Gude and Godlie Ballatis* and the songs of Alexander Scott, national Scotland approached the death of the Eng. queen, Elizabeth I (1603), the Union of the Crowns (James VI of Scotland crowned James I of England), and the loss of court and courtly lang. Such loss, together with the King James *Bible*, the splendor of Spenser and Shakespeare, and the victories of Covenanting Puritans, makes it impossible to name one Scots poet of high distinction during the entire 17th c., not excluding Alexander Montgomerie (1545?–1610?), poet of *The Cherry and the Slae*, dream vision and allegory; any other member of King James' "Castalian band"; or William Drummond of Hawthornden (1585–1649), who showed with some success what a Scotsman could compose in Eng. No longer a court lang., Scots lived on as the vernacular of folk lit.: ballad and song.

S. ballads represent an oral trad. (see Buchan) of anonymous narrative songs arising in the late Middle Ages to flourish in the 16th and 17th cs., and to be collected in the latter 19th c. by Child. Chief subjects are violent history ("Oterborne"), tragic romance ("Clerk Saunders"), and the supernatural ("Tam Lin"). The vernacular is simple and stark, grimly realistic and fatalistic. The vividly dramatic story unfolds through unity of action, characterization, and the relentless pace of the ballad meter, but never wholly. Formula, epithet, incremental repetition, refrain, alliteration, and question-and-answer advance the plot. Colors are primary; images are violent ("The curse of hell frae me sall ye beir / Mither, mither"), tender ("O waly, waly! but love be bony / A little time, while it is new"), eerie ("The channerin worm doth chide"), and beautiful ("And she has snooded her yellow hair / A little aboon her bree").

Ballads aside, the period from 1603 to World War I produced poets who chose literary Eng. as their medium because they thought it was impossible to use Lallans and be taken seriously. So James Thomson (1700–48), poet of *The Seasons*, Robert Blair, and James Beattie used standard Eng. for their remembered works. Sir Walter Scott (1771–1832) retained the vernacular of the ballads he collected and improved for his *Minstrelsy* but chose Eng. for his long poems (*The Lady of the Lake*) and for the excellent songs in his novels ("Proud Maisie"). Byron and Campbell were Scotsmen, but are better left to Eng. letters. Later poets such as James Thomson (1834–82) and Robert Louis Stevenson again chose Eng. for *The City of Dreadful Night* and *A Child's Garden of Verses*. Poetry in Lallans, however, was alive—just barely—as the 1707 Union of Parliaments reduced Scotland to a "region" of Great Britain.

James Watson's *Choice Collection* in two vols. (1706–09) includes Semple of Beltrees' mock elegy "Epitaph of Habbie Simson" (ca. 1650) in a stanza which gives name to the "standard Habbie," better known as the Burns stanza; Hamilton of Gilbertfield's "Bonny Heck" has the same stanza for the last words of a dying greyhound distantly related to Henryson's talking animals and anticipating Burns' "Poor Mailie's Elegy." These poems are in Lallans. So, too, are such works of Allan Ramsay (1685–1758) as his invention of the verse epistle (usually in tetrameters), his burlesque elegy on a church treasurer who could smell out a bawd, his poetic drama *The Gentle Shepherd*, many of the songs in his *The Tea Table Miscellany*, and all of the older Scots poems in his *The Ever Green*. Ramsay's prosody becomes Robert Fergusson's (1750–74); Fergusson's, Burns'. Within a vernacular revival these three poets compose their satires, genre poems, epistles, and comic narratives, principally in six verseforms: common measure with its variant, ballad meter, octosyllabic couplets, heroic couplets, the standard Habbie, "Christ's Kirk," and "Cherrie and the Slee." Among the third of Fergusson's 100-odd poems in Lallans is his masterpiece, "Auld Reekie," realistically describing everyday life in Edinburgh, "Whare couthy chiels at e'ening meet / Their bizzin craigs and mou's to weet."

More and more, except in the S. household where "The Cotter's Saturday Night" and "To a Mouse" hold sway, the measure of Robert Burns' (1759–96) high accomplishment has become the satires like "Holy Willie's Prayer," *The Jolly Beggars*, the narrative "Tam o' Shanter," and the hundreds of songs. The cantata *The Jolly Beggars* has his characteristic merits of description, narration, dramatic effect, metrical diversity, energy, and sensitivity to the beauties inherent in S. words and music. Otherwise, hearing a song like "Scots wha hae" or "Ca' the Yowes," each showing masterful skill at uniting words and music, will unforgettably illustrate this genius. To Burns under the S. Enlightenment we owe the perpetuation of S. folksong. How rich this heritage is has been the further study of those like Sharpe, Duncan, and Greig in the 19th c. and Henderson and others at the School of S. Studies in the 20th. By contrast, literary songs from the 18th c. to the 20th tend toward sentimentalism, whether Jean Elliot's "Flowers o' the Forest," Lady Nairne's "Caller Herrin," or verses by Violet Jacob, Marion Angus, and Helen Cruickshank.

Seldom does 19th-c. S. p. better James Hogg's (1770–1835) "sad stuff." Slavish imitations of Burns strike low, nor rise by the *Whistle-Binkie* (fiddler's seat at merry-makings) anthol. or the couthy sentimentality of Kailyard (a type of fiction from about 1880 of rural life, dialect, and sentiment; see James M. Barries' *A Window in Thrums* or Ian Maclaren's, pseud. for Rev. John Watson's, verse epigraph). Industrialization and the Calvinist ethic of profitability and genteel respectability bring poets to their knees. At century's close, however, Robert Louis Stevenson (1850–94) composes poems like "The Spaewife" in a literary Scots, the precision of which opposes the Kailyard; "blood and guts" John Davidson (1857–1909) experiments in Eng. with new myths, symbols of science's dethroning religion; and the founder of the S. Ren. grows as a lad in Langholm.

In the 1920s, Christopher Grieve (1892–1978) took the pseudonym "Hugh MacDiarmid" as he abandoned Eng. versifying to become a makar in Scots. Created under the banner "Back to Dunbar!," early lyrics like "Empty Vessel" excel in clarity and power of Scots, intensity of passion, audacity of imagery, and originality of movement and rhythmical pattern. Such verses as the following sing:

> Mars is braw in crammasy,
> Venus in a green silk gown,
> The auld mune her gowden feathers,
> Their starry talk's a wheen o' blethers,
> Nane for thee a thochtie sparin,
> Earth, thou bonnie broukit bairn!
> —*But greet, an' in your tears ye'll droun*
> *The haill clanjamfrie!*
> (*The Bonnie Broukit Bairn*)

MacDiarmid's masterpiece is *A Drunk Man Looks at the Thistle* (1926), a long sequence of poems in the form of a dramatic monologue. Unity derives from the protagonist, who rhapsodizes on love and death and meditates on Scotland and the world. MacDiarmid's "synthetic" Scots presents difficulties, esp. in longer poems like *To Circumjack Cencrastus*, which become more and more a poetry of fact (statement and argument) and Marxist. Doubtful that Scots is adequate to propagate socialism, MacDiarmid reverts to Eng. as early as 1955.

Others in Eng. and Scots, though not makars, add luster to the S. Ren. extending into the 1960s. "The three skeeliest Lallans makars" around MacDiarmid are Robert Garioch (1908–81), Sydney Goodsir Smith (1915–75), and Alexander Scott (b. 1920). Scott's glitter and glower show in his humorous "Paradise Tint"; Smith's "lemanrie" informs his *Under the Eildon Tree*; and Garioch's full vocabulary marks his scintillating *Sixteen Edinburgh Sonnets* after the Belli *romanesco* originals. Skillful, too, are William Soutar's (1898– 1943) "whigmaleeries" (fantasies) and his bairn rhymes *Seeds in the Wind*, with the lyrical "O luely, luely, cam she in." Three poets in Eng. surpass others: Norman MacCaig (b. 1910), who now wears the mantle of Scotland's *eminence grise*; Iain Crichton Smith (b. 1928) within the S. Ren.; and Edwin Muir (1887–1959), without. MacCaig, like G. S. Fraser (1915–80) and T. Scott (b. 1918), begins with the tortured syntax and private imagery of the Apocalypse Movement but develops a romantic-classic stance and Edinburgh Doric for his habitual checking-up on appearance and reality (e.g. "Spraying Sheep"). Closest to him is Alexander Young (1855–1971). Crichton Smith, with roots in Lewis Gaeldom, creates finished verses with recurrent figures of island and old woman on his favorite theme of being alone. Muir's most famous line is "Burns and Scott, sham bards of a sham nation." Scotland's first great metaphysical poet, a symbolist for whose *The Labyrinth* (1949) Kafka, Freud, and Jung are important, Muir "gloriously" (T. S. Eliot) breaks new ground in his mythical romances on the Fall, published as *One Foot in Eden* (1956).

Today some poets experiment: with ON and OE (G. M. Brown [b. 1927]); with Chinese or Japanese forms (Crichton Smith, D. Glen [b. 1933], and K. White [b. 1936]); with surrealism (D. Black [b. 1941]); with psychiatry (K. Morrice [b. 1924]); with feminism (Liz Lochhead [b. 1948] unapologetically in "Laundrette" and Tessa Ransford with a feminist rage in "In the Fishmonger's"); with Euclidian figures (A. Mackie [b. 1925]); with a view to performance (T. Leonard [b. 1944] in the phonetic spellings of Glasgow dialect); with "sound" poetry (G. MacBeth [b. 1932]); and with MacDiarmid's "aggrandized" Scots as flyting (hilariously rendered in R. Crawford [b. 1959] and W. N. Herbert [b. 1961]). Two others experiment with unusual versatility: I. H. Finlay (b. 1925) with the neo-modernism of "poem-prints," "poem-gardens," and "concrete" poetry (e.g. "Star/steer" carved in slate); and E. Morgan (b. 1920) with his "instamatic," "emergent," and "concrete" poems like "Loch Ness Monster's Song." Some poets translate foreign poetry into Scots or Eng. poetry: R. Fulton, some 14 v.; Morgan, from eight foreign langs. into Scots; A. Reid (b. 1926), from Neruda and Borges into Eng. Some poets sing more traditionally: in Eng., the prize-winning D. Dunn (b. 1942) in his narrative elegies (1985); Valerie Gillies (b. 1948) in her animal poems like "The Salmon Loup"; in Scots, A. Mackie in the exceptionally fine *Clytach* (1972); and Sheena Blackhall in "Heelstergowdie" (1986); and C. Rush (b. 1944), in a poem opening in Eng. and closing in Scots, *A Resurrection of A Kind* (1985). See also SCOTTISH-GAELIC POETRY.

ANTHOLOGIES AND TEXTS: *The Scots Musical Museum*, ed. J. Johnson, 6 v. (1786–1803); *Bishop Percy's Folio Ms.*, ed. J. Hales and F. Furnivall, 3 v.

(1867–68); *Eng. and S. Popular Ballads*, ed. F. J. Child, 5 v. (1883–98); *The Bruce*, ed. W. W. Skeat, 2 v. (1894); *Scott's Minstrelsy of the S. Border*, ed. T. Henderson, 4 v. (1902); *Works of Sir David Lindsay*, ed. D. Hamer, 4 v. (1931–36); *Works of Gavin Douglas*, ed. D. F. C. Coldwell, 4 v. (1957–64); *Honour'd Shade*, ed. N. MacCaig (1959)—anthol. of mod. S. p.; *Trad. Tunes of the Child Ballads*, ed. B. Bronson, 4 v. (1959–72); *Collected Poems of Edwin Muir* (1965); *Oxford Book of S. Verse*, ed. J. MacQueen and T. Scott (1966); *Poems and Songs of Robert Burns*, ed. J. Kingsley, 3 v. (1968); *Contemp. S. Verse*, ed. N. MacCaig and A. Scott (1970); *Made in Scotland*, ed. R. Garioch (1974); *Coll. Poems of S. G. Smith* (1975)—intro. Hugh MacDiarmid; *Complete Poems of Hugh MacDiarmid 1920–76*, ed. M. Grieve and W. R. Aitken, 2 v. (1978); *Mod. S. Verse 1922–77*, ed. A. Scott (1978); *Poems of William Dunbar*, ed. J. Kinsley (1979); *Poems of Robert Henryson*, ed. D. Fox (1981); *Akros Verse*, ed. D. Glen (1982)—nos. 1–49; *Complete Poetical Works of Robert Garioch*, ed. R. Fulton (1983); R. Crawford and W. N. Herbert, *Sterts & Stobies* (1986); *Twelve More Mod. S. Poets*, ed. C. King and I. C. Smith (1986); *An Anthol. of S. Women Poets*, ed. C. Kerrigan (1991).

HISTORIES AND STUDIES: T. F. Henderson, *S. Vernacular Lit.* (1900); A. Mackenzie, *Historical Survey of S. Lit. to 1714* (1933); J. Speirs, *The Scots Lit. Trad.* (1940); *S. P.*, ed. J. Kingsley (1955); K. Wittig, *The S. Trad. in Lit.* (1958); T. Crawford, *Burns* (1960)—best study of poems; D. Craig, *S. Lit. and the S. People* (1961); K. Buthlay, *Hugh MacDiarmid* (1964); D. Daiches, *The Paradox of S. Culture* (1964), *Lit. and Gentility in Scotland* (1982); T. Scott, *Dunbar* (1966); F. Collinson, *Trad. and National Music of Scotland* (1966); T. C. Smout, *A Hist. of the S. People 1560–1830* (1969), *A Century of the S. People 1830–1950* (1986); H. M. Shire, *Song, Dance and Poetry of the Court of Scotland under King James VI* (1969); A. M. Kinghorn, *Middle Scots Poets* (1970): D. Buchan, *The Ballad and the Folk* (1972); *Hugh MacDiarmid: A Crit. Survey*, ed. D. Glen (1972); R. D. S. Jack, *The It. Influence in S. Lit.* (1972), *S. Lit.'s Debt to Italy* (1986); *Robert Burns*, ed. D. Low (1974); R. Fulton, *Contemp. S. P.* (1974); M. Lindsay, *Hist. of S. Lit.* (1977); R. Knight, *Edwin Muir* (1980)—best study; G. Kratzmann, *Anglo-S. Lit. Relations 1430–1550* (1980); W. R. Aitken, *S. Lit. in Eng. and Scots* (1982)—excellent bibl.; J. MacQueen, *Progress and Poetry 1650–1800* (1982); *Scotch Passion*, ed. A. Scott (1982)—the erotic poetry; *The New Testament in Scots*, tr. W. L. Lorimer (1983); C. Kerrigan, *Whaur Extremes Meet* (1983)—study of MacDiarmid's work; R. Watson, *Lit. of Scotland* (1984); *Concise Scots Dict.*, ed. M. Robinson (1985)—intro. is Aitkins' excellent "A Hist. of Scots"; W. Scheps and J. A. Looney, *The Middle Scots Poets: A Ref. Guide* (1986); *The Hist. of S. Lit.*, ed. C. Craig, 4 v. (1987–); F. Stafford, *The Sublime Savage: James Macpherson and the Poems of Ossian* (1989); D. Glen, *The Poetry of the Scots* (1991). R.D.T.

SEPHARDIC POETRY. See JUDEO-SPANISH POETRY.

SERBIAN, SERBO-CROATIAN POETRY. See YUGOSLAV POETRY.

SIAMESE POETRY. See THAI POETRY.

SINDHI POETRY. See INDIAN POETRY.

SINHALESE POETRY. See SRI LANKAN POETRY.

SKALDIC POETRY. See OLD NORSE POETRY.

SLOVAK POETRY. Until the 19th c., the Slovaks had virtually no lit. in their own lang.; Lat. and Czech served as written langs., and only sporadic attempts were made to write in S. The 17th c. saw what may be regarded as the beginnings of a national lit. in two great hymnals, the Protestant *Cithara sanctorum* (1636) and the Catholic *Cantus catholici* (1655). The first collection contained mostly Czech hymns, but a few were S. and employed vernacular expressions. The lang. of the *Cantus catholici* represented an attempt by the Jesuits of the University of Trnava to write in Western S. dialects. Throughout the later 17th c. and most of the 18th c., the baroque period in Slovakia, poetry continued to be predominantly religious or didactic.

Neoclassicism dominated S. lit. from the end of the 18th c. up to 1840. A new attempt to standardize S. was made at this time by Anton Bernolák (1762–1813), a Catholic priest; Bernolák's S. was similarly based on Western S. dialects. His follower, Ján Hollý (1785–1849), wrote ponderous epics on patriotic historical subjects, drawing heavily for inspiration on antique poets. The failure of Bernolák's S. to win acceptance, however, doomed Hollý's work to oblivion. More successful was Ján Kollár (1793–1852), who wrote in Czech. His great sonnet cycle, *Slávy dcera* (The Daughter of Sláva, 1824), laments the impotence of the Slavic peoples but predicts their future greatness.

Not until the 1840s and the first romantic generation was a standard S. lang. created that would endure. Based on Central S. dialects, and hence more widely acceptable, it was largely the work of two Protestant nationalists, L'udovít Štúr (1815–56) and J. M. Hurban (1817–88). The romantic poets who surrounded Štúr were strongly influenced by the S. folksong; ardent patriots, they largely defined national lit. by its use of popular speech and folk forms. They finally solved the question of prosody; hitherto both quantitative and accentual systems of versification had been employed. Now, on the model of the S. folksong, the romantics adopted accentual verse.

The romantic generation included a number of significant poets. Andrej Sládkovič (pseudonym of Ondrej Braxatoris, 1820–72) created a historical epic, *Detvan* (1853), an idyllic but partly accurate description of S. peasant life. Janko Kráľ (1822–76), the greatest of the romantics, produced ballads interesting for their use of Oedipal themes. Ján Botto (1829–81) eulogized the famous bandit of the Carpathians who had become a symbol of liberty to the common people in *Smrť Janošíka* (The Death of Janošík, 1862). Ján Kalinčiak (1812–71) also treated S. historical subjects, but with more realistic detail.

S. hopes for liberty were shattered by the failure of the Revolution of 1848. As the century wore on and Hungarian rule became more severe, a mood of hopelessness set in. Svétozar Hurban Vajansky (1847–1916) and Pavol Országh (1849–1921), who wrote under the pseudonym of Hviezdoslav, were the greatest poets of the era. Hurban Vajanský, the son of J. M. Hurban, was a romantic, but with a vein of irony and satire new to S. lit. Hviezdoslav was a Parnassian poet, whose translations from Shakespeare, Goethe, Puškin, and others provided a new stimulus. In keeping with his cosmopolitanism, he avoided the hitherto dominant tone of the folksong. Hviezdoslav was a lyric, epic, and dramatic poet; his masterpiece is probably the *Krvavé sonety* (Bloody Sonnets, 1919), which mirror the horror of World War I. His late poetry became increasingly disillusioned, though he lived to see Slovakia win freedom.

Symbolism, or *Moderna* as the Slovaks called it, had its chief poet in Ivan Krasko (pseudonym of Ján Botto, 1876–1958), the son of the older Botto. Krasko shares Hviezdoslav's pessimism, but his poetry is more modern in its use of the lexicon and its subtle introspective moods. Janko Jesensky (1874–1945) cultivated a cosmopolitan satire relatively unique in S. p. Among younger writers of the interwar period, Emil B. Lukáč (1900–79) was a complex and contradictory religious poet influenced by Paul Claudel. Ján Smrek (pseudonym of Ján Čietek, 1899–1982) was a vitalist who delighted in sensual descriptions of female beauty. He also flirted with poetism, an indigenous Czechoslovak poetic movement (see CZECH POETRY) which arose in the late 1920s and which contained traits of futurism and dada. Another poetist was Laco Novomesky (1904–76), a Communist journalist noted for his many ideological reversals; he was imprisoned in 1951 for nationalist "deviation" but released in 1956. Ultimately he was rehabilitated, to play the role of the outstanding poet in a period largely without poetry, in which role he is perhaps emblematic of a politically troubled and changing time.

The principal foreign influences on S. p. have been those of Czech, Ger., and Rus. lit. Like Czech, S. has a fixed stress on the first syllable of the word, which facilitates the use of trochaic meters. Still, iambic verse—usually with considerable freedom in the opening foot of the line—is very common, and in fact more popular than trochaic in the second half of the 19th c. Ternary meters are virtually impossible in S. because the stress tends to fall on every odd syllable. Dactylic feet may alternate with trochees, however; such purely tonic rhythms were popular under the influence of classical meters and of native folksongs, both in the romantic era and again in modern times.

The severity of the national problem in Slovakia and the political role played by many S. writers have given S. p. a strongly nationalistic coloring. Those poetic forms are popular in which national ideas can be expressed or implied: narrative poetry, the popular song, and the reflective lyric. Traditionally poetry dominated prose in S. lit., but since World War II this situation has been reversed and prose is now absolutely dominant.

ANTHOLOGIES: *Slovenská poesie XIX. století*, ed. Fr. Frýdecký (1920); *Sborník mladej slovenskej literatúry*, ed. J. Smrek (1924); *Slovenské jaro; ze slovenskej poesie, 1945–1955*, ed. C. Stitnicky (1955); *An Anthol. of S. P.*, tr. I. J. Kramoris (1947)—bilingual; *The Linden Tree*, ed. M. Otruba and Z. Pešat (1963); *Antológia staršej slovenskej literatúry*, ed. J. Mišianik (1964).

HISTORY AND CRITICISM: S. Krčméry, "A Survey of Mod. S. Lit.," *SEER* 6 (1928); M. Bakoš, *Vývin slovenského verša* (1939); A. Mráz, *Die Lit. der Slovaken* (1942), "Dejiny slovenskej literatúry," *Slovenská vlastiveda*, 5 (1948); *Dejiny slovenskej literatúry*, ed. A. Mráz et al., 3 v. (1958–65); J. M. Kirschbaum, *S. Lang. and Lit.* (1975). W.E.H.

SLOVENE POETRY. See YUGOSLAV POETRY.

SOMALI POETRY. Somalia has been called a nation of poets because of the extensive use of verse in social intercourse by these East African people. S. poetic trad. employs poetry for discussing politics, expressing love, sending secret messages, conducting family and clan business, and bantering between the sexes. Until the mid 1950s, S. p. was totally oral. Even after 1972, when a Roman script was introduced, most poetry continued to be composed and performed orally. Printed poetry is rare, to be found only in a few books published by government agencies and daily newspapers. Some religious poetry is written in Arabic, and one S. poet in the Négritude trad., Wm. J. F. Syad, has emerged.

The S. poetic trad. ranges from verbatim memorization of complex forms to formulaic and improvised composition (simultaneous composition and recitation) of simpler forms. Specific poems in complex genres are attributed to named poets, and the roles of poet and reciter/memorizer, though overlapping, are separate. Some reciter/memorizers, like Ḥussein Dhiqle, have gained prestige in their own right. Ḥussein was the spokesperson for Sayid Maḥammad 'Abdille Ḥassan, called the "Mad Mullah" by his British enemies. This S. national hero, religious leader, and warrior was a brilliant poet of classical verse, which aided his 20-year holy war against foreign colonials early in the 20th c.

Generic differentiation in S. p. is accomplished by a combination of scansion rules, function, topic, and musical setting. The genre of highest prestige is the *gabay*, which functions in political discourse, social debate, religion, and philosophical contemplation. Next in prestige are the *jiifto* and *geeraar*, which deal with similar subjects but have different scansions and recitation melodies. These three genres are used by men; the *buraambur* is used by women for many of the same functions. These four genres are practiced and disseminated with an attempt at verbatim memorization and are composed of irregular strophaic stanzas recognizable by prolonged notes at the end of the last word in each strophe.

Work songs are less complex and include an element of formulaic composition. Each defined type of work among the nomads (ca. 44% of the population) has its own genre and range of topics. Camels are watered two times per trip to the wells, and two genres of *hees geel* accompany these tasks. Different genres of *hees maqal* are associated with the separate tasks of taking baby sheep and goats to wells and herding them from one campsite to another. Separate genres of *hees adhi* are employed for the same two tasks associated with adult sheep and goats. Women weave three varieties of mats, and different genres are recited during each task (*hees harrar, hees alool, hees kebed*). The pounding of grains (*hees mooye*) and the churning of milk (*hees haan*) also have specific genres. These poems set rhythm and work pace and function socially as indirect modes of communication between the sexes. In one *hees adhi*, for example, a woman sings to her ram admonishing him for choosing the wrong husband for his kid. Metaphorically she is admonishing her own husband for arranging the marriage of their daughter to a man of whom she does not approve.

While work genres of the same meter are widespread throughout Somalia, recreational genres are regional and tend to be composed via improvisation. Many genres are employed for dancing when young men and women are permitted to mix. A popular genre in the North is the *dhaanto*, where the *hirwo, wiglo*, and *belwo* were popular in the past. Having the same function, all four genres scan identically; they are differentiated by their melodies. Over 15 other dance genres have been identified; these are employed as media for dance gestures and modes of expression by creative poets who gain considerable prestige if they prove skillful.

In contrast to the quantitative scansion of classical S. poetry, the *heello* has gained prestige since the 1950s and is recited by both men and women. Modeled first on Indian, then European song modes, it is lyric in nature and accompanied by European musical instruments. Topics are similar to those assigned to the *gabay*, along with many others considered too frivolous for classical verse. The *heello* is complex in structure; hence its composition tends to be similar to that of the *gabay*. Diffusion is accomplished by means of radio and tape recorder as well as oral memory.

Memorization of S. p. is made possible by strict rules of prosody. Scansion patterns, the text of the poem, and musical accompaniment minimize the effects of faulty memory. Minor variation sometimes occurs from one reciter/memorizer to another, but changes are made so the text will scan properly. Classical poetry scans with a quantitative system involving a relationship between syllables and vowel length. The smallest units are short vowels which have the temporal equivalence of one *mora*; long vowels, as in words like *gabadh* (girl) and *koob* (cup), have two morae. *Ilaah* (God) has three, and *daanyeer* (monkey) has four. Morae fit into metric slots called *semes. Monosemes* hold short vowels, but *disemes* hold either two short vowels or one long unless a genre rule requires a long vowel. Monosemic or disemic boundaries may not be crossed by long vowels. The configuration of semic patterns in part defines the genre. Syllables also play a role, and three different relationships can be isolated. Open set moro-syllabic relationships allow as many syllables as morae on a line. Closed sets allow only one syllable per seme. Semi-closed sets designate specific numbers of morae and syllables but allow too many disemes, so short vowels are forced into some disemes while long vowels are forced into others.

The scansion pattern of the *gabay* will illustrate the intricacies of classical poetry. The following line is from *Jiinley* (Poem Alliterating in "J"), by Sayid Maḥammad 'Abdille Ḥassan:

⏑‖⏊|⏊ | ⏑‖⏊ | ⏑¦⏑| ⏑‖⏊
Ḥuseenow jikraar lama hadlee,
⏊ | ⏑ ‖ ⏊ | ⏑¦⏑ |⏑‖
jaalkay baad tahay e.

O Ḥussein, do not speak with obstinance,
for you are my comrade.

The *gabay* is a tetrameter. Feet are demarcated by double bars, semes by single bars, and open and semi-closed moro-syllabic relationships by broken bars. Anacrusis is allowed (the breve before the first double bar). The pattern within each foot is diseme + diseme + monoseme, and a caesura falls between the first and second disemes in the third foot. An open set moro-syllabic relationship occurs in the first hemistich, where any diseme may hold one long vowel or two shorts. In the second hemistich the relationship is semi-closed, specifying eight morae and six syllables. Since there are three disemes, one must hold two short vowels, but the poet may chose which diseme so to treat. Throughout the entire poem only one alliteration is allowed, at least one instance of which must occur in each hemistich. The manipulation of semic configurations and moro-syllabic relationships constitutes the manner Somalis use to expand their generic repertoires. When these patterns are rearranged, new genres are created.

Published collections of S. p. feature mostly verse of the nomads, but poetic activity among those who work the land is equally common. Research is carried out in the National Academy of Sciences and Arts and at the S. National University, where investigation of unclassified genres is conducted.

B. W. Andrzejewski and I. M. Lewis, *S. P.* (1964); B. W. Andrzejewski, "Poetry in S. Society," *Sociolinguistics*, ed. J. B. Pride and J. Holmes (1972), "The Poem as Message: Verbatim Memorization in S. Oral P.," *Memory and Poetic Structure*, ed. P. Ryan (1981); J. W. Johnson, "The Family of Miniature Genres in S. Oral P.," *Folklore Forum* 5 (1972), *Heellooy Heelleellooy: The Devel. of the Genre Heello in Mod. S. P.* (1974), "S. Prosodic Systems," *Horn of Africa* 2 (1979), "Recent Researches into the Scansion of S. Oral P.," *Proc. of the 2d Internat. Congress of S. Studies*, ed. T. Labahn (1984), "Set Theory in S. Poetics," *Proc. of the 3d Internat. Congress of S. Studies*, ed. A. Puglielli (1988); Jaamac Cumar Ciise, *Diwaanka gabayadii Sayid Maxamed Cabdulle Xasan* (1974); Abdillahi Derie Guled, "The Scansion of S. P.," *Somali and the World*, ed. Hussein Mohamed Adam (1980); Said Sheikh Samatar, *Oral P. and S. Nationalism* (1982); *Lit. in Af. Langs.*, ed. B. W. Andrzejewski et al. (1985); F. Antinucci and Axmed Faarax Cali, "Idaajaa," "Poesia orale somala: storia di una nazione," *Studi Somali* 7 (1986). J.W.JO.

SOUTH AFRICAN POETRY.

I. IN AFRIKAANS
II. IN ENGLISH
III. INDIGENOUS

I. IN AFRIKAANS. With the exception of a few sporadic examples in the late 18th and first half of the 19th c., the first Afrikaans poetry in South Africa dates from the last quarter of the 19th c., when the first real attempts were made to raise Afrikaans—which up to that time had been the lang. of conversation at the Cape of Good Hope for more than a century, developing out of 17th-c. Dutch—to the level of a written lang. The themes of this early Afrikaans poetry were limited by the close bonds with the South Af. fatherland in general and the Afrikaner in particular and dealt with the life of ordinary Afrikaans burghers and their folklore. The poets aimed at encouraging the people to fight for their rights and at inspiring, teaching, and entertaining them. The poems are very often oratorical and programmatic in nature and make use of a labored style. In effect, the literary products of this period are based principally on a subculture, given the writers' isolation from foreign influence, although there are imitations of Scottish examples (Burns) and early 19th-c. Dutch poetry.

After the Anglo-Boer War (1899–1902), during which time very little attention was paid to lit., a number of younger writers saw it as their task to develop Afrikaans as an instrument through which the deepest emotions of the individual and of the people could be expressed. The Anglo-Boer War, South Af. landscape, and religious experience—all exemplified in the work of Jan F. E. Celliers (1865–1940), Totius (pseudonym of J. D. du Toit, 1877–1953), and C. Louis Leipoldt (1880–1947)—were important stimuli to poetry immediately after 1900. Apart from strictly metrical poetry there were experiments with free verse, and apart from poems written in stanzas and the sonnet, the dramatic monologue was practiced. The poets of this generation were influenced by Dutch, Ger., Eng., and Fr. models, but the influence is neither significant nor conclusive and was very seldom contemporary.

The poets of the third generation, with Toon van den Heever (1894– 1956) as the most important, do not, on the whole, achieve the standard of the previous generation, although there is greater individualism present in their writings, and love and eroticism are introduced as themes. Two older poets who produced their best work at this time are Eugène N. Marais (1871–1936) and A. G. Visser (1878–1929).

Around 1930 a new generation of poets, who display a far greater professionalism than their predecessors, began to publish. The new artists—of whom N. P. van Wyk Louw (1906–70), Uys Krige (1910–87), W. E. G. Louw (1913–80), and Elisabeth Eybers (b. 1915) are the most important—perceive poetry as a conscious task and, unlike their predecessors, claim the right to explore all areas of human life. Initially their poetry was focused on the inner life and was self-analytic and confessional, but the danger of an exaggerated withdrawal from the outside world was counteracted by devel. toward a more oblique poetry, although Krige's work shows a greater receptiveness to external stimuli from the beginning. This movement toward objectification found its strongest expression in Van Wyk Louw, who, in addition to a new type of psychological ballad and dramatic monologue, wrote the modern epic *Raka* (1941), which explores the tension between two contrasting characters. Later he produced one of the most important volumes of Afrikaans poetry, *Tristia* (1962). In Eybers' work, the world of the woman and the bond between her and her family is explored. Her later poetry, written in the Netherlands, is stripped of every external embellishment and has a new vital quality. In contrast to the poets who wrote after the Anglo-Boer War, the "Dertigers" (the Afrikaans poets of the Thirties) are more receptive to Dutch, Ger., and Eng. poetry.

In the Forties, a fifth generation of poets, initially influenced strongly by the "Dertigers," made their debut. From the beginning, however, the war, the city, and a new social consciousness were more strongly present in their poetry, qualities which gave rise to a harsher and sharper-edged verse. Of these poets, the work of Ernst van Heerden (b. 1916) catches the reader's attention as the struggle of a sensitive and defenseless person against the modern world, whereas G. A. Watermeyer (1917–72) practiced a new type of melodious verse; and compassion for the Jew and the Colored appears in the works of Olga Kirsch (b. 1924) and S. V. Petersen (b. 1914). The most important poet of this generation is D. J. Opperman (1914–85), who explores the world with a virtually mystic urge to identify with all earthly things. His poetry has a concentrated verbal economy which finds expression in the compact metaphor and the short-circuited image. He writes a cryptic type of poem with successive layers of meaning; he uses the sonnet, quatrain, cycle, soliloquy, and epic (*Joernaal van Jorik*, 1949) with great expertise. He achieves an intricate unity in volumes such as *Blom en baaierd* (Flower and Void, 1956) and *Komas uit 'n bamboesstok* (Comas from a Bamboo Stick, 1979).

Since the mid 1950s, several important poets have made their appearance. Peter Blum (b. 1925) initiated this renewal with poetry in which rhythmical abandon, startling imagery, and an anti-sentimental, demasking tone catch the reader's attention. Adam Small (b. 1936) writes strongly satirical, derisive, and sometimes bitter political poetry. In her best work, Ingrid Jonker (1933–65) prefers a free verse similar to that of Éluard and the Dutch experimentalists of the Fifties. The most important new talent is that of Breyten Breytenbach (b. 1939), who shows his mastery of Afrikaans in his originality and in his amazing power to convey images through a daring exploitation of the face value of words. After Breytenbach, the most important poet is Wilma Stockenström (b. 1933), with her meaningful exploration of the dry, harsh Af. landscape, written in tersely figurative and barbed lang. A reaction to the too-amorphous free verse of the Sixties also appears in a number of poets who received their grounding in the art of poetry from Opperman (e.g. Antjie Krog, Lina Spies, Fanie Olivier, Marlene van Niekerk) or who built on his trad. through wordplay and linguistic legerdemain (J. C. Steyn, T. T. Cloete), whereas Sheila Cussons, whose poetry has a mystical element, is the most important exponent of Roman Catholicism in Afrikaans.

ANTHOLOGIES: *Afrikaans Poems with Eng. Trs.*, ed. A. P. Grové and C. J. D. Harvey (1962); *Penguin Book of South Af. Verse*, ed. J. Cope and U. Krige (1968), ed. S. Gray (1989); *Groot verseboek*, ed. D. J. Opperman, 9th ed. (1983).

HISTORY AND CRITICISM: R. Antonissen, *Die Afrikaanse letterkunde van aanvang tot hede*, 3d ed. (1965); R. Antonissen et al., "Afrikaans Lit.," *Standard Encyc. of Southern Africa*, v. 1 (1970); G. Dekker, *Afrikaanse literatuurgeskiedenis*, 12th ed. (1972); J. C. Kannemeyer, *Geskiedenis van die Afrikaanse literatuur*, 2 v. (1978–83), *Die Afrikaanse literatuur, 1652–1987* (1988); *Perspektief en profiel*, ed. P. J. Nienaber, 5th ed. (1982). J.C.K.

II. IN ENGLISH. South Africa first appears in Eng. poetry in the work of Donne, Milton, and Dryden, in the wake of the Port. Luis de Camões, who mentions the Cape of Good Hope as a passage to be rounded on the sailing route to the East. Anonymous British visitors there, wintering from service in India, brought occasional poetasting to its shores, which in 1820 became substantially colonized by Eng. speakers. The first South Af. Eng. poet as such, Thomas Pringle (1789–1834), emigrated from Scotland to the Eastern Frontier and adapted Scottish border ballads and the Wordsworthian reverie for lyrics such as "Afar in the Desert," which still opens many anthologies today. Pringle also established *The South Af. Literary Journal* in 1824.

The semi-permanent warfare between Dutch speakers, indigenous blacks, and the British in 19th-c. South Africa gave rise to an alternate popular trad. of anti-emancipationist verse in the person of Andrew Geddes Bain (1797–1863), who in the Victorian era used his polyglot resources for humorous purposes. His successor, Albert Brodrick (1830–1908), wrote of the diamond fields and gold fields and of the early process of industrialization.

The Anglo-Boer War of 1899–1902, which became a media event (incl. the first newsreels), was also the first round of a poet's battleground that extended into World War I. Rudyard Kipling (1865–1936) on the jingo side advocated Imperial progress, while South Af.-born poets like Beatrice Hastings (1879–1943) in *The New Age* defended home rule. Black poets, particularly in multilingual newspapers, began a trad. of protest against deprivation of human rights which persists to the present day.

After the Union of the Southern Af. states in 1910, Natal produced two major poets whose careers developed around the cultural magazine *Voorslag* in the 1920s: Roy Campbell (1901–57) and William Plomer (1903–73). Both eventually settled in Europe to pursue right-wing and left-wing politics, respectively. Campbell's early *The Flaming Terrapin* (1924) combined imagist and symbolist influences to assert a futuristic Af. life-force, while Plomer's successive volumes from 1927 maintained a democratic, satirical view of the segregated south.

After World War II many returning soldier-poets, such as Anthony Delius (b. 1916) and Guy Butler (b. 1918), asserted a "stranger to Europe" view of their local culture with a white Af. sense of belonging in the subcontinent. This in turn produced the journals, societies, and academic discipline which now make South Af. Eng. poetry an independent channel of the British mainstream.

With the accession to power of the Afrikaner apartheid government in 1948, Eng. as a cultural medium moved into an oppositional role which has produced a lit. of resistance written by blacks and whites alike. The banning or forcing into exile of many poets in the 1960s, such as Dennis Brutus (b. 1924) and Mazisi Kunene (b. 1930), further fragmented the poetry into an international diaspora whose links to the internal scene are increasingly tenuous. But in 1971, with the publication of *Sounds of a Cowhide Drum* by Mbuyiseni Mtshali (b. 1940), a period of intense internal publication commenced, notably in the work of Sipho Sepamla (b. 1932) and Mongane Serote (b. 1944), sometimes known (after the June 1976 uprising) as "Soweto poets."

During the 1980s, South Af. Eng. poetry has remained a central literary activity in journals as diverse as *Contrast* and *Staffrider*, incl. many nonnative Eng. lang. poets. More general and specialist anthologies have appeared in this decade than in all previous South Af. history combined, and the secondary lit. too is now sophisticated.

The leading poet of the present, Douglas Livingstone (b. 1932), who published his first slim volume (*Sjambok*) in 1964, produced his *Selected Poems* in 1984. With its metaphysical style, his work displayed an openness to British and Am. poetic developments while being regional in its documentary range and subject matter. Other poets with substantial oeuvres incl. Lionel Abrahams (b. 1928), Stephen Gray (b. 1941), Jeni Couzyn (b. 1942), and Christopher Hope (b. 1944). Jeremy Cronin (b. 1949), following the less linguistically purist direction of a Bain, has brought the freedom songs of a romantic like Pringle into a new synthesis.

At one end of the spectrum, poetry serves as a protesting and educational instrument for black liberation, while at the other, Eng. is seen as a continuous medium of aesthetic conciliation and negotiation among the many other lang. experiences of Southern Africa.

ANTHOLOGIES: *Centenary Book of South Af. Verse*, ed. F. C. Slater, 2d ed. (1945); *A Book of South Af. Verse*, ed. G. Butler (1959); *Penguin Book of South Af. Verse*, ed. J. Cope and U. Krige (1968); *Return of the Amasi Bird: Black South Af. P. (1891–1981)*, ed. T. Couzens and E. Patel (1982); *Mod. South Af. P.* (1984), *Penguin Book of Southern Af. Verse* (1988), both ed. S. Gray; *Paperbook of South Af. Eng. P.*, ed. M. Chapman (1986).

HISTORY AND CRITICISM: G. M. Miller and H. Sergeant, *A Critical Survey of South Af. P. in Eng.* (1957); M. van Wyk Smith, *Drummer Hodge: The Poetry of the Anglo-Boer War* (1978); M. Chapman, *South Af. Eng. P.: A Mod. Perspective* (1984); *Companion to South Af. Eng. Lit.*, ed. D. Adey et al. (1986); M. Van Wyk Smith, *Grounds of Contest: A Survey of South Af. Eng. Lit.* (1989). S.G.

III. INDIGENOUS. Poetry in the indigenous Af. langs. of southern Africa is conveniently classified into an *oral* and a *written* (i.e. modern) component.

A. *Praise poetry* is an acclaimed mode of expression in the oral trad. In the Xhosa and Zulu languages (Republic of South Africa) such poetry is known as *izibongo*, in Southern Sotho (Lesotho and Republic of South Africa) as *dithoko*, in Setswana (Botswana and Republic of South Africa) as *maboko*, and in Northern Sotho (Republic of South Africa) as *direto*. In the langs. of the northern parts, however, such as Shona (Zimbabwe), and Tsonga and Venda (Republic of South Africa), heroic praise poetry does not exist as extensively. It is a poetry of celebration of kings, national leaders, and war heroes. Basically eulogistic, the poems are broadly comparable to the panegyric in other trads., though with more laudatory than narrative objectives. The poems are composed on the spur of the moment by the heroes themselves or recited by personal or national bards. The occasion of recitation varies from just after personal feats and victorious battles to national gatherings of various kinds.

Also in existence are *clan praises*. These occur fairly extensively, though not exclusively, in the langs. of the northern parts of the region. In Shona they are known as *nhétémbo dzorúdzi*, in Venda as *zwikhodo*, and in Tsonga as *swiphato*. In Xhosa they are called *isiduko*, in Zulu *izithakazelo*, and in Southern Sotho *diboko*. These are praises of specific clans or their branches, but may also incl. praises of other subjects such as clan initiates, animals, Af. beer, and divining bones.

Another oral type was developed after the discovery of minerals, when thousands of Af. laborers went to the South Africa mines. In Southern Sotho this is called *difela tsa ditsamayanaha* (songs of the "country travelers"), and in Xhosa *izibongo zasezimayini* (mine praises). A mixtures of nostalgia, aggression, and satire, this type relates the experiences of the novice migrant worker finding himself in foreign circumstances.

B. *Modern poetry* shows various generic and technical features of the oral trad. along with other influences of the same kind from foreign, mainly Eng., lit. Although these genres have been developing since the early 20th c., most are still transitional. Experimentation with imported devices such as end rhyme was less successful than the adaptation of devices carried over from the oral trad. such as repetition, parallelism, enumeration, and a wide register of imagery. In later years a kind of free verse developed, the potential and direction of which are still being explored. The output of modern poetry in most lits. is impressive, with the literary poets venturing on a variety of types, such as modern praises, shorter epics, ballads, elegies, sonnets, and satires. In Xhosa these poets incl. Mqhayi, Jolobe, Burns-Ncamashe, Yali-Manisi, and Qangule (who also writes verse drama); in Southern Sotho, Ntsane, the Khaketlas, Mokhomo, Mohapeloa, Lesoro, Maphalla, and Masiea (who also writes verse drama); in Zulu, Vilakazi, the Ntuli brothers, Msimang, Khumalo, and Dlamini; in Northern Sotho, Mamogobo, Matsepe, Matlala (who also writes verse drama), and Lentsoane; in Setswana, Seboni, the Kitchin brothers, Magoleng, and Shole Shole; in Tsonga, Masebenza, Nkondo, Marhanele, and Magaisa; and in Venda, Tsindane, Nemukovhani, and Sigwavhulimu. Mod. poetry in Swati (Swaziland and

Republic of South Africa) started to emerge in the 1980s, with Mkhatshwa (verse drama), Zwane, and Luphoko the pioneers.

Most of the taxonomy sketched here also applies to the poetry of neighboring states such as Lesotho, Swaziland, Botswana, Zimbabwe, and even beyond.

Praise Poems of Tswana Chiefs, ed. I. Schapera (1965); *Izibongo: Zulu Praise Poems*, ed. T. Cope (1968); D. P. Kunene, *Heroic Poetry of the Basotho* (1971); *Lithoko: Sotho Praise-Poems*, ed. M. Damane and P. B. Sanders (1974); *Shona Praise Poetry*, ed. A. C. Hodza and G. Fortune (1979); P. S. Groenewald, "Die pryslied, prysgedig, prysdig, prysvers," *Studies in Bantoetale* 7 (1980); C. T. Msimang, "Imagery in Zulu Praise-Poetry," *Limi* 9 (1981); M. I. P. Mokitimi, *A Literary Analysis of Lifela tsa litsamaya-naha Poetry* (1982); A. S. Gérard, *Comp. Lit. and Af. Lits.* (1983); J. Opland, *Xhosa Oral Poetry: Aspects of a Black South Af. Trad.* (1983); C. F. Swanepoel, *Sotho Dithoko tsa Marena: Perspectives on Composition and Genre* (1983); J. M. Lenake, *The Poetry of K. E. Ntsane* (1984); D. B. Z. Ntuli, *The Poetry of B. W. Vilakazi* (1984); L. Vail and L. White, *Power and the Praise Poem* (1991); *Musho: Zulu Popular Praises*, ed. and tr. L. Gunner and M. Gwala (1992). C.F.S.

SOUTH AMERICAN POETRY. See BRAZILIAN POETRY; GAUCHO POETRY; SPANISH AMERICAN POETRY.

SPANISH AMERICAN POETRY. This entry covers poetries written in Sp., the lang. of those areas in the Western hemisphere which, after their independence from Spain in the first half of the 19th c., came to be known as nation-states—i.e. Argentina, Chile, Colombia, Cuba, Ecuador, Guatemala, Peru, Uruguay, and Venezuela. For a survey of the indigenous poetries of this area see AMERICAN INDIAN POETRY. The poetry of the Portuguese-speaking part of South America is treated s.v. PORTUGUESE POETRY and BRAZILIAN POETRY.

Sp. Am. p. shall be described here as a powerful stream in a constant process of changes, actions, and reactions, revealing, as well, essential constants that, considered from the proper perspective, suggest a fundamental unity. This stream had its origins in the cl. trad. of the Sp. and It. Ren. At first it was written by Spaniards for Spaniards. The Am. setting appeared only as an exotic world to captivate the fancy of Europeans. As some of the soldier-poets stayed in America, however, a strange sense of attachment and loyalty to the New World developed in their writings. Soon they began to express the saga of the Am. Conquest with a social consciousness which was not entirely European, but rather the result of humanism tested under the forces of war and death. These soldier-poets, of whom Alonso de Ercilla (1533–94) is the most eminent example, could not bring themselves to follow the fashion of It. epic poetry. They had no need to make up adventures in America. The poet had hardly anything to invent. He was fighting not only Indians but his own allies as well, and quite often he wrote his poems to secure royal favor, to promote the cause of a kind patron, or to thwart a personal enemy. Male protagonists were real, indeed, but heroines were a luxury with which he could dispense; romance was used sparingly and only to break the monotony of narrative. Touched by the self-sacrificing attitude of the Indian people and by the un-Christian exploitation of which they were victims, these poets glorified the Indians, presenting them to the European readers of the 16th and 17th cs. as pure and noble creatures driven to desperation by the evil ambitions of Western civilization. The Black Legend thus was born and the foundations laid for the idealization of primitivism to be expounded by the philosophers of the 18th c.

Sp. Am. epic poetry of the 16th and 17th cs. thus differed somewhat from the epic poetry of the European Ren. Indeed, one could say that a poet such as Ercilla actually developed an original form of epic which might be described as follows: his poem has no individual hero, since the poet sings the birth of a nation, exalting the people both of Spain and of America; Ercilla devotes a great deal of space to the narrative of his own adventures; and the intention is more political and social than purely artistic. From a literary viewpoint, Ercilla's epic blends the direct realism of primitive poetry and the artistic flair of the It. *Romanzi.* Ercilla's masterpiece, *La Araucana* (Araucana), is divided into three parts which appeared separately in 1569, 1578, and 1589. He had a school of imitators; among them, one is still remembered by critics: Pedro de Oña (1570–1643?), a Chilean, whose poem *Arauco domado* (Arauco Subdued) appeared in 1596 but who is more appreciated now for the lyric quality of *El Vasauro* (The Golden Vase).

There was another kind of soldier in the Sp. conquest of America, just as fearless and determined as the heavily armored Conquistador: the missionary. Between the cross and the sword the Am. Indian found his way into the literary world of Western civilization. Since the priest-poet could not deal directly with contemp. wars, he wrote sacred verse on subjects taken from the Middle Ages and ancient history.

The best examples of this type of epic produced in Sp. America are: *La Cristiada* (Cristíada) by Fray Diego de Hojeda (1570–1615), an Andalusian by birth who lived and died in Peru; and *La grandeza mexicana* (The Greatness of Mexico, 1604) by Bernardo de Balbuena (1561–1627), a contemporary of Góngora, who lived in Mexico. Balbuena praised the splendor of the Mexican vice-royalty in cl. tercets, thus providing the basis for Sp. Am. baroque poetry. Relegated to obscurity by the popular success of Ercilla, the priest-poets increasingly withdrew into the learned isolation of their monasteries to engage in rhetorical contests. They opened their hearts and minds to the intellectual pyrotechnics of the great Góngora, the Sp. master of euphuism, vying with each other in expressing deep concepts in a syntax laden with Gr. and Lat. complexities. Testimony to these contests is Carlos de Siguenza y Góngora's (1645–1700) *Triunfo parténico* (Athenian Triumph), and proof of Góngora's predominance among the Sp. Am. baroque poets is the *Apologético en favor de don Luis de Góngora* (Apology for Góngora, 1662) by the Peruvian Juan de Espinosa Medrano (1632–88). It is obvious that these and other poets of the period did have an inkling of what Góngora was attempting: they knew that in his rhetorical labyrinth he was creating a poetic lang. of his own and, with it, a world of fantasy that stood defiantly against the logic of cl. realism. But in general his disciples failed him.

One alone approached him in depth of thought and poetic power: Sor Juana Inés de la Cruz (1648–95), the Mexican nun who excelled in every literary genre she attempted. She produced comedies, dramas, and religious plays; she wrote an autobiographical essay, *Respuesta a Sor Filotea de la Cruz* (Reply to Sor Filotea de la Cruz, 1691), that stands even today as a model of independent thinking and brilliant argumentation; she wrote graceful *villancicos* in a popular vein; she emulated the great euphuistic poets of Spain, Góngora and Calderón in *Primero sueño* (First Dream), and produced a highly sophisticated interp. of a subconscious world built into a complex poetic structure; she wrote of love with an insight and a profound understanding which have made her critics wonder if real passion might not have been the reason for her religious seclusion. One example may give the reader an idea of the excellence of her love sonnets, which the critics have compared to those of Lope de Vega and Shakespeare:

Love, at first, is fashioned of agitation,
Ardors, anxiety, and wakeful hours;
By danger, risk, and fear it spreads its
 power,
And feeds on weeping and on supplica-
 tion.

It learns from coolness and indiffer-
 ence,
Preserves its life beneath faithless ve-
 neers,
Until, with jealousy or with offense,
It extinguishes its fire in its tears.

Love's beginning, middle, and its end
 are these:
Then why, Alcino, does it so displease
That Celia, who once loved you, now
 should leave you?

Is that a cause for sorrow and remorse?
Alcino mine, no, love did not deceive
 you:
It merely ran its customary course.
(tr. S. G. Morley)

Colonial Sp. Am. baroque poetry was a hothouse flower, nursed by artifice and killed by artifice. Far away from the literary academies and the solitude of the cloisters, a new poetry was slowly coming into being: a rough, impetuous song of mountains, pampas, rivers, and seas. This poetry was the Am. descendant of the Sp. *Romancero.* Old Sp. ballads were on the lips of the Conquistadors and, used as they were in the manner of proverbs, served to illustrate many a decision and to give a historical twist to local incidents. Hernán Cortés was quick to quote an old ballad, if we are to believe his historian, Bernal Díaz del Castillo. Perpetuated by oral trad., these ballads underwent colorful modifications and eventually came to express the Am. spirit that was treasuring them. From the great variety of subjects in the Sp. *Romancero,* Sp. Am. people chose those that esp. appealed to their imagination and worked on them with exuberance. They made and remade the adventures of Charlemagne, El Cid, Los Infantes de Lara, Conde Alarcos, and Juan de Austria. They memorized the deeds of famous bandits and invented new outlaws, romantically brave, full of vengeance against the Sp. masters and the wealthy creoles. This was the birth of the so-called Gaucho poetry, which reached its peak in the second half of the 19th c. and produced at least one masterpiece: José Hernández' (1834–86) *Martín Fierro* (1872, 1879).

The young scions of wealthy Sp. Am. families, who had the fortune to study in France, Spain, and England, absorbed the political and literary effervescence created by the romantic movement. They were joined by the exiles in Paris and London who plotted the overthrow of the Sp. rulers in America. Shortly after, Napoleon's invasion of Spain brought about the political independence of Sp. America, and as the new republics were coming into existence, the political and literary expatriates started their journey home.

Romanticism took root in Sp. America without the structure of a movement. Poets wrote romantic poems without realizing they were doing so. A Cuban, José María Heredia (1803–39), brought up in the best neoclassical trad., wrote *En el Teocalli de Cholula* (On the Ancient Temple of Cholula, 1820) ten years before the romantic movement was launched in Spain. His themes were idealization of the Mexican landscape, decadence, and death. Heredia searches for the expression of ideal beauty, but his words are only approximations lost among mysterious echoes in an atmosphere of melancholy and disillusionment. *Niagara* is generally recognized as his best poem: Heredia's description of the waterfall, eloquent and impassioned, his masterly blending of landscape and mood—solitude, homesickness, an invocation to God—make this poem a true example of the best Sp. Am. romanticism.

Two other poets also contributed to the introduction of romanticism to Sp. America: José Joaquín Olmedo (1780–1847), born in Ecuador and author of *A la victoria de Junín: canto a Bolívar* (To the Victory at Junin), and Andrés Bello (1781–1865), the eminent Venezuelan humanist whose poem *Silva a la agricultura de la zona tórrida* (The Agriculture of the Torrid Zone), though of dubious artistic merit, is truly Am. in subject matter and intent. The expression of both these poets is strictly bound to classical norms, but the love for their homeland, their deep lyrical feeling for the beauties of the Am. landscape, their exaltation of Am. heroes, their use of Am. Indian diction, transcend rhetorical limitations to give their compositions an undeniable romantic meaning.

Sp. Am. romanticism blossomed in the second half of the 19th c. Its success as a school was strengthened by the presence of a number of distinguished Sp. poets who had come to America seeking wealth and honor. Among these, two should be remembered for the influence they had on their contemporaries: José Joaquín de Mora (1783–1864), who settled down as a teacher in Chile and traveled extensively in America before returning to Spain, and the famous José Zorrilla, who spent some time in Mexico. Soon, Sp. Am. poets realized that romanticism as a school was a thing of the past in Europe. They knew that Fr. poetry was already undergoing a transformation which would soon crystallize in Parnassianism and symbolism. The reluctance of some writers to recognize the romantic nature of their poetry produced an odd situation: Bello and the Argentine Domingo Faustino Sarmiento urged the creation of a truly Am. literary style; Bello was identified as a classicist and Sarmiento as a defender of romanticism. But Bello had been a powerful factor in the establishment of romanticism not only as a poet but as a translator as well, and Sarmiento had savagely ridiculed romanticism in his newspaper articles. In fact, both were arguing for the same thing, only from different viewpoints: they wanted a lit. that would reflect the genius of the New World, a forceful expression which would inspire its people to create their own civilization. Bello had an eclectic mind and wished to benefit from the classical heritage as well as from modern achievements; above all, he had complete faith in the genius of Spain. Sarmiento, on the other hand, believed that Spain had run its course and that Sp. Americans should sever all ties with her and open their minds to the fresh and invigorating influence of France.

The younger poets, whether following Bello or Sarmiento, emulated models which sang in a surprisingly similar key: Zorrilla or Espronceda, Chateaubriand or Lamartine or Hugo. Sp. Am. poets suddenly discovered themselves at odds with bourgeois society; they fought tyranny, went into exile, longed for the homeland, felt bitter and rejected, sang the glories of Greece, Poland, and Mexico in their struggles for independence, and even evoked the Middle Ages, although historical interest led them more often to a colorful Indian past; they took the ocean as a symbol, twilight as the emblem of their melancholy; they wrote legends and historical plays—in a word, they produced romanticism. They are too numerous to list; few are remembered today as good poets, but among them one should mention the Cubans Gabriel de la Concepción Valdés (1809–44) and Gertrudis Gómez de Avellaneda (1814–73); the Argentines Estéban Echeverría (1805–51), José Mármol (1817–71), Olegario Andrade (1839–82), and Rafael Obligado (1851–1920); the Peruvian Manuel González Prada (1848–1918); the Mexican Manuel Acuña (1849–73); and the Uruguayan Juan Zorrilla de San Martin (1855–1931). Of these, some are regarded with particular interest: Echeverría, for example, the author of *Elvira o la novia del Plata* (Elvira or the Argentine Bride, 1832), an early romantic poem; Gómez de Avellaneda, who won literary fame in Spain as the author of passionate poems such as "Al partir" (Departing); González Prada, a revolutionary poet and forceful polemicist; and Zorrilla de San Martin, whose poem *Tabaré* (1888) is one of the landmarks of Sp. Am. romanticism. One cannot neglect the work of two major Colombian poets: José Eusebio Caro (1817–53), a masterful painter of landscapes, a philosopher and moralist of pungent originality; and Gregorio Gutiérrez González (1826–72), the author of a bold regionalist poem, *Memoria sobre el cultivo del maíz en Antioquia* (Memoir on the Cultivation of Corn in Antioquia, 1866), whose delicate sentimentalism has been compared to that of Bécquer.

Gradually the romantic fever subsided, and the poets who began to write in the last third of the 19th c. showed a growing concern for refinement and sophistication. Eloquence is toned down. The desire to escape reality becomes a search for the exotic and the decadent. No longer do the expatriates weep for a distant homeland; they enjoy the foreign places they visit and write about them with elegance and a sort of playful irresponsibility. They are still romantic, of course, and many refuse to go the way of damnation singing its praises. Instead, they pine away in touching *nocturnos*. Two of them are good poets in a dated sort of way: Julián del Casal (1863–93), a Cuban, and José Asunción Silva (1865–96), a Colombian. What makes these poets different from their romantic predecessors is only the sophistication of the symbolism they borrowed from Fr. lit. They wrote short bits of melancholy amorousness, whereas their predecessors wrote vast cascades of passionate lamentations. They show little concern for historical events, except that they condescend sometimes to attack the United States for its budding imperialism in Sp. America. If they feel at odds with society, they do not confront it but escape from it, sometimes literarily and sometimes literally by committing suicide, as in the case of Silva. The most socially conscious of them, the Cuban José Marti (1853–95), is the least modernistic and, at the same time, the most universal. Better than most of his contemporaries, Marti represents the Am. effort to establish the image of a new man and a new society in Western lit. His poetry, *Ismaelillo* (1882), is innovative in a popular manner, eloquent without being emphatic, and profoundly individualistic. In contrast, the Mexican Salvador Díaz Mirón (1853–1928) continues to be romantic in his love poems and neoclassical in his descriptions of nature. Much of his poetry is still rooted in the Libertarian trad. so much admired by Rubén Darío. *Lascas* (Rock Chippings, 1901) is considered his best book, a fine example of refinement in form and subdued sentimentalism. Some important critics believe that another Mexican, Manuel Gutiérrez Nájera (1859–95) played an essential role in introducing the main features of *modernismo* into Sp. Am. p. Musicality, a power to suggest the hidden meanings in everyday life, a natural sense of mystery, and predestination add substance to his poetry.

By the end of the 19th c., a new poetic movement was developing in Sp. America. Its leader was the Nicaraguan Rubén Darío (1867– 1916). At a very young age he left his native land, lived for a while in Guatemala and El Salvador, and settled for a few years in Santiago, Chile. Here he came into contact with writers who introduced him to the work of Fr. symbolists. Under strong Fr. influence he published a book of poems and short stories, *Azul* (Azure, 1888), which immediately garnered him an international reputation. At the turn of the century, his books—*Prosas profanas* (Lay Hymns, 1896), *Cantos de vida y esperanza* (Songs of Life and Hope, 1905), *El canto errante* (The Wandering Song, 1907)—became the Bible of the new poets, and his name was revered. Critics and historians of Sp. Am. lit. have written scores of books dealing with *modernismo* (q.v.—Sp. modernism). This poetic trend, which lasted to about 1920, could be described as the Sp. Am. expression of Fr. *Parnasse* and *Symbolisme.* In the beginning it represented an escape from reality (exoticism was then one of its main features), and later it turned its attention to America, influenced somewhat by Walt Whitman. From Parnassianism it inherited a fastidious concern for beauty of form; from symbolism it learned to subdue emotions, replacing exclamation by suggestion, and also it inherited a liking for pure fantasy and an interest in the aesthetic of decadence. From Gongorism, which Darío revived in all its splendor, *modernismo* took a fondness for intricate and brilliant imagery. Putting all this together was the fascinating miracle wrought by Darío. He made people think that a "new civilization" was being born, but today one realizes that with Darío an old historical fact found its affirmation in the work of art: Sp. Am. "new civilization" was the blossoming of European culture, mainly Fr. and Sp., in the midst of a continent whose natural forces and soul were still unknown entities. Darío awakened many a dream in the minds of Sp. Am. intellectuals. His magic touch sent his disciples away with the dangerous notion that they too were demigods. After his disappearance, *modernismo* faded in the winds of our materialistic age like a cloud of golden dust.

A number of poets who achieved distinction following in the steps of the Nicaraguan master include the Argentine Leopoldo Lugones (1874–1938), an eloquent, rather overpowering poet in whose works—*Las montañas del oro* (The Golden Mountains, 1897), *Los crepúsculos del jardín* (Twilights of the Garden, 1905), *Lunario sentimental* (Sentimental Lunar Poems, 1909), and *Poemas solariegos* (Poems of the Homestead, 1928)—one finds an amazing blend of all the major literary currents of the 19th c. and strong anticipations of avant-garde schools such as Ultraism ; Amado Nervo (1870–1919), the refined, gently religious, amiable Mexican, a genuine romantic, author of *Serenidad* (Serenity, 1914), *Elevación* (Elation, 1917), and *Plenitud* (Plenitude, 1918); Luis G. Urbina (1868–1934), also a Mexican, sentimental, ironic, surprisingly original in his treatment of subjects considered prosaic in his own time (*Lámparas en agonía* [Lamps in Agony], 1914; *El glosario de la vida vulgar* [Glossary of Everyday Life], 1916); Rufino Blanco Fombona (1874–1944), Venezuelan, a brilliant, colorful poet too strongly bound by the likings of his epoch (*Pequeña ópera lírica* [Small Lyrical Works], 1904; *Cancionero del amor infeliz* [Songbook of Unhappy Love], 1918); Julio Herrera y Reissig (1875–1910), Uruguayan, undoubtedly the greatest poet of modernism after Darío, a true representative of contemp. Sp. Am. baroque, deeply preoccupied with the creation of a poetic lang. that would combine the best elements of Gongorism, symbolism, and Parnassianism—he is the real link between the poetry of the 19th and 20th cs. in Sp. Am. and a forerunner of Huidobro's creationism ; Ricardo Jaimes Freyre (1868–1933), Bolivian, exquisite in his already outmoded exoticism, a true master of versification (*Castalia bárbara* [Barbarian Castaly], 1899; *Los sueños son vida* [Dreams are Life], 1917); Guillermo Valencia (1872–1943), Colombian, a poet of profound pictorial sense whose classical aloofness, in the midst of a period when color and brilliance were used with naive profuseness, is proving to be the reason for his survival among the most respected literary figures of his country (*Ritos* [Rites], 1898; enl., 1914); José Santos Chocano (1875–1934), Peruvian, a bombastic versifier and self-styled interpreter of the Am. world (*La selva vírgen* [The Virgin Jungle], 1901; *Alma América* [Soul-America], 1906); José María Eguren (1874–1942), another Peruvian, who made his reputation as a poet by being subtle and subdued in contrast to Chocanos's grandiloquence; and the Chileans

Manuel Magallanes Moure (1878–1924) and Carlos Pezoa Véliz (1879–1908). Today it seems obvious that the Mexican Enrique González Martínez (1871–1952) was the outstanding figure among this group. One of the poems in his book *Los senderos ocultos* (The Hidden Paths, 1911)—"Tuércele el cuello al cisne" (Wring the Swan's Neck)—sounded the death knell for *modernismo.*

Some poets, too young to accompany Darío as disciples but too old to overtake the avant-garde forces, found themselves stranded with the remnants of modernism. A few of them became excellent poets, but as a group they represent a lost generation. The best known among them are: the Uruguayan Carlos Sabat Ercasty (1887–1982), the Chileans Angel Cruchaga Santa María (1893–1964) and Juan Guzmán Cruchaga (1895–1979), the Mexicans Ramón López Velarde (1888–1921) and Juan José Tablada (1871–1945), the Colombian Porfirio Barba Jacob (1883–1942), and the Puerto Rican L. Lloréns Torres (1878–1944). Cruchaga Santa María and López Velarde deserve special mention; each in his own way established an important link with the baroque poetry of midcentury Lat. America: Cruchaga as a sensuous mystic very close to the early Neruda, and López Velarde, the author of "Suave patria" (Soft Motherland), as the forerunner of a conversational type of lyric poetry which would reach its climax with César Vallejo and Nicanor Parra.

In a place by themselves one should mention four women poets who transformed the lit. of Lat. America: Gabriela Mistral, Delmira Agustini, Alfonsina Storni, and Juana de Ibarbourou. These women helped to bring about a social revolution of far-reaching effect; they fought for the social and psychological emancipation of Sp. Am. women. The Chilean Gabriela Mistral (1889–1957), who won the Nobel Prize in 1945, became the living banner of a movement for child welfare, for women's rights, and for social laws to protect the Indians. It has been said that the Nobel Prize may have been given to her as a reward for an entire life devoted to defending the poor and the outcast, and that her glorification of motherhood convinced the Swedish Academy of the true universality of her poetry. To the students of Sp. Am. lit. her greatness reaches beyond the limits of mere philanthropy: in her three most important books, *Desolación* (Desolation, 1922), *Tala* (Land Clearing, 1938), and *Lagar* (Grape-Crushing Vat, 1954), Mistral created a style solidly realistic, direct, and forceful, deeply religious in a biblical sense, and oddly rural in its vocabulary; her lang. offered a sharp contrast to the decadent elegance of modernism. The Uruguayan Delmira Agustini (1886–1914) began writing before she was 17 years old. Her prescience of a violent death—she was killed when she was 28—her yearning for an all-satisfying love, her passionate descriptions of masculine beauty, her direct and voluptuous allusions to the sexual act, were taken by the critics as the daring but innocent poetic exercises of a gifted adolescent. But when her poems appeared in book form—*El libro blanco* (The White Book, 1907)—Darío and his disciples recognized that a major new poet had arrived. Not a shade of artifice mars the pathos of her sensuous pleas. Touched by the sublime emotion of a real artist, the crude reality of her naked figures assumes classical aloofness. In the Argentine poet Alfonsina Storni (1892–1938), the tragic story of Delmira Agustini is repeated. After a nightmarish life of loneliness and economic strain, she committed suicide. Sex flashes violently in her metaphors (*Ocre* [Ocher], 1925). But she lacks the natural refinement of Agustini and her poetry, after pounding on the emotions of the reader who senses the coming unhappy climax, falls to earth in a mixture of bewilderment and anguished, almost cynical defeat: *El mundo de siete pozos* (The World of Seven Wells, 1934), *Mascarilla y trébol* (Mask and Clover, 1938). The Uruguayan Juana de Ibarbourou (1895–1979), on the other hand, devotes her wholesome life to singing of motherhood and youth, of maturity and the strain of a vanishing existence (*Las lenguas de diamante* [The Diamond Tongues], 1919; *Raíz salvaje* [Savage Root], 1920; *La rosa de los vientos* [Sextant], 1930). With her the revolutionary period of women's poetry in Sp. Am. comes to an end. Mention of these women brings one to the threshold of contemp. Sp. Am. p. However, their turbulence remains. With the rhetoric of passion drastically diminished, and finally eliminated, this poetry goes on changing directions, finding existentialism on the way, baring the roots of its linguistic search, coming to rest in a form of conversational expression of love, loneliness, and sadness. In Uruguay one senses a reaction against the serenity of Ibarbourou; new voices arise, avoiding emphasis through the use of an oral lang., in the poetry of Idea Vilariño (b. 1920), Ida Vitale (b. 1923), and Circe Maia (b. 1932). Vilariño's books—*La suplicante* (The Suppliant, 1945), *Cielo, cielo* (Heaven, Heaven, 1947), *Por aire sucio* (Through Dirty Air, 1950), *Poemas de amor* (Love Poems, 1957), and *No* (1980)—reach a surprisingly wide audience. Vitale's best known works are: *Oidor andante* (Walking Listener, 1972) and *Jardín de Sílice* (Silicon Garden, 1980); among Maia's books one should mention: *En el tiempo* (Within Time, 1958) and *Presencia diaria* (Daily Presence, 1974).

The poetry by women of other Lat. Am. countries shows a similar tendency to deemphasize the rhetoric of sentimentalism. A few names have gained international recognition: the Mexican Rosario Castellanos (1925–74), author of *Al pie de la letra* (To the Letter, 1959), *Lívida luz* (Livid Light, 1960); the Salvadorean Claribel Alegría (b. 1924), with books such as *Vigilias* (Vigils, 1953), *Acuario* (Aquarium, 1955), *Aprendizaje* (Apprenticeship, 1970), and *Sobrevivo* (Surviving, 1978); and the Argentine Olga Orozco (b. 1922), with *Desde lejos* (From Afar, 1946), *Las muertes* (Deaths, 1952), *Los juegos peligrosos* (Dangerous Games, 1962), and *Cantos a Berenice* (Songs for Berenice, 1977).

In the maturing of the new schools that came after Darío, France again played an important role, for it was the spirit of dada that killed the nostalgic decadence of Darío's late disciples, and it was surrealism and creationism that provided the aesthetic ideas which brought Lat. Am. poets closer to Spain's Generation of 1927 (see SPANISH POETRY) and to Ultraism. Contemp. Sp. Am. p. seems to have come into its own through the combined action of four main factors: the work of Mistral, Agustini, Storni, and Ibarbourou mentioned above; the reaction against Darío; a critical examination and revision of poetic lang.; and the search for mythical forms of realism led by Pablo Neruda and César Vallejo.

The reaction against Darío's *preciosité* came around 1920. Mexican *Estridentismo*, the Whitmanism of Armando Vasseur and Sabat Ercasty, the sensual pessimism of Barba Jacob, and the metaphorical values of ancestral regionalism led the movement against a "modernist" revolution which in less than 30 years had already become reactionary. These poets abandoned the objective or "representational" approach to nature; they gave up rhyme and, briefly, even punctuation. They created a new form of exoticism: the escape into abstraction. The most brilliant of these poets was the Chilean Vicente Huidobro (1893–1948). In his country he was followed by a gifted group of poets, among them: Rosamel del Valle (1901–63), Humberto Díaz Casanueva (b. 1908), Juvencio Valle (b. 1906), and Eduardo Anguita (b. 1914). Huidobro involved himself in a dramatic search for a creative lang., claiming that the poet should not imitate nature but should assume instead the role of a true creator, whence the name for his brand of poetics, *Creationism.* As a poetic speaker he was a king of metaphors. His readers could not fail to detect irony in his efforts. This irony and his playfulness in proposing his theories hurt his literary reputation. At the end, far away from the fireworks of the avant-garde, Huidobro wrote deep, meditative poetry about the mysterious symbols of the ocean and of the passing of time—*El cuidadano del olvido* (Citizen of Forgetfulness, 1941) and *Ultimos poemas* (Last Poems, 1948); his most famous work continues to be *Altazor* (Altazor, 1931).

In the early 1930s, another Chilean directed a rebellion against abstract poetry: Pablo Neruda (1904–73), whose poetry evolved from the melodious symbolism of *Veinte poemas de amor y una canción desesperada* (20 Poems of Love and a Song of Despair, 1924) to an astonishing glorification of the most prosaic elements of reality. Slowly and deliberately he proceeded to destroy all that Sp. modernism considered sacred. In conceiving the monumental chaos which constitutes the essence of *Residencia en la tierra* (Residence on Earth, 1925–35), Neruda has expressed, as no one had done before, the metaphysical anguish of the Sp. Am. man, his terrors, his superstitions, his sense of guilt imposed on him by religious teachings and the broken trad. of his Indian forefathers, his loneliness in the midst of a strange civilization that he does not understand and cannot appreciate, his consternation before nature that crushes him with its untamed jungles, oceans, and mountains, his decadence coming as the result of exploitation, malnutrition, alcoholism, poverty, and disease. *Residencia en la tierra* is an expression of the psychological and social drama affecting great numbers of Sp. Am. people today. From this surrealistic statement of the decadence of the Western world, Neruda moved towards a politically committed poetry, beginning with *España en el corazón* (Spain in My Heart, 1937), a book inspired by the Sp. Civil War, followed by *Las furias y las penas* (The Furies and the Sorrows, 1939), *Nuevo canto de amor a Stalingrado* (New Song of Love for Stalingrad, 1943), and *Canto general* (General Song, 1950).

Neruda strongly believed in identifying his personal life with his creative work. After the Sp. Civil War he joined the Chilean Communist Party and was elected senator. Toward the end of his life he became a candidate for the presidency of Chile. However, he was never a strictly political poet; *Canto general*, a masterpiece of surrealistic mythology, contains anecdotal material together with some of the most profound lyrical poetry ever written by Neruda ("Alturas de Macchu Picchu" [Heights of Macchu Picchu], "El gran océano" [The Great Ocean]). All during his most active political life Neruda never ceased writing great love poetry (*Cien sonetos de amor* [A Hundred Sonnets of Love], 1959) and delicate, ingenious miniatures such as his *Odas elementales* (Elementary Odes), 1954. After winning the Nobel Prize (1971) and serving as Chilean Ambassador to France, Neruda returned to Chile in 1972. He died the following year during the bloody military coup in which President Salvador Allende was killed. Neruda left several books that were published posthumously; in them one finds remarkable expressions of Neruda's materialistic philosophy of life and death together with touching autobiographical remembrances.

When César Vallejo (1892–1938), the great Peruvian poet, began to publish his mature work, Darío's modernism was dead. Vallejo's formal break with modernism, however, did not mean a direct return to reality, but a move from Darío's abstractions to another kind of abstraction, a world of violent myths, sometimes oneiric, sometimes the result of furious sadness. Perhaps one could describe Vallejo's poetic vision as a particularized counterpart of Neruda's apocalyptic imagination in *Residencia en la tierra.* Vallejo, like Neruda, had avoided the *Ultraísta* movement. His Neosymbolism, erotic and regionalistic, gained in solitude a moribund, existential sediment. This explains why Vallejo is so different from the boisterous playfulness of the Peninsular and Lat. Am. avant-garde poets of the 1920s. This approach to mythology, so characteristic of Andean pathos, is accomplished by Vallejo not by losing, but rather by improving his conversational, eccentric attitude in the face of poetic fact. His colloquial phrases in *Los heraldos negros* (The Black Harbingers, 1918), *Trilce* (Trilce, 1922), and *Poemas humanos* (Human Poems, 1939) are given the suggestive power of *leitmotif;* they work as magical formulae. Numbers, at random, do likewise. This is Vallejo's road toward an essential reality, toward a unifying image of man facing the processes of life and death: Vallejo equates opposite terms. To do this he uses several devices, two of which are fundamental in his poetry: the false passage of time, and the nostalgic feeling for persons and things from the standpoint of a living death. To understand man, he is saying, we must detect the skull behind the smile. Life, thinks Vallejo, is a great death, great because of the size of the deceit involved. In spite of this pessimism, Vallejo's poetry has been interpreted as an expression of Christian faith, and even as a form of socialistic humanism. Young poets of the second half of the 20th c. particularly venerate Vallejo.

At the present time, Jorge Luis Borges (1899–1986) might be more famous as a writer of short-stories and essays than as a poet; however, it is entirely possible that in the years to come he will be remembered for his poetry. Works such as *Fervor de Buenos Aires* (Fervor for Buenos Aires, 1923), *Luna de enfrente* (Moon Across the Street, 1926), and *Cuaderno San Martín* (San Martin's Notebook, 1929) are being rediscovered as if miraculously untouched by time. Borges describes reality in terms of essential existence, bordering on metaphysical truth. Yet he works with humble objects and artifacts—an old house, a backyard, a guitar, knives, flowers, portraits—in which he uncovers myths, ancestral roots, unmovable and perennial. He asserts the unreality of time—"Poema conjectural" (Conjectural Poem)—as he perceives the reality of death. Things and beings revolve around this sense of duality. For Borges, poetry is an instrument of knowledge and understanding; it is not magic, nor historical prophecy. The poet discovers his cadences as he enters daily life wisely unaware of the mysteries that surround him. Borges avoids all traces of artificiality, having early in his career abandoned his sophisticated attempts at *ultraísmo.* For many years he pruned his early works in order to destroy every possible link with the avant-garde. At the end, almost completely blind, he dictated his poems, usually impeccable sonnets, full of wisdom, simple charm, and a sort of courtly, innocent love. Buenos Aires, the city of his birth, shines in his poems: Borges describes it as "my home, its familiar neighborhoods, and, along with them, what I experienced of love, of suffering, and of misgivings." In "Casas como ángeles" ("Houses like Angels") he writes:

> I think of the pale arms that make evening glimmer
> and of the blackness of braids: I think of the grave delight
> of being mirrored in their deep eyes, like arbors of the night.
>
> I will push the gate of iron entering the dooryard
> and there will be a fair girl, already mine, in the room.
> And the two of us will hush, trembling like flames,
> and the present joy will grow quiet in that passed.
>
> (tr. Robert Fitzgerald)

This devotion to themes of nostalgia in the heart of the overpowering city, not far from the Argentine plains full of passionate history, was also characteristic of a group of Borges' contemporaries: Ricardo Molinari (b. 1898), Eduardo González Lanusa (b. 1900), Francisco Luis Bernárdez (1900–79), Leopoldo Marechal (1900–70), and Raúl González Tuñón (1905–74). The subtleties of creationist abstraction were maintained by Enrique Molina (b. 1910).

Mexican poetry during this period was untouched by the portentous events of the Mexican Revolution, which had deep effects on the novel, on painting, and on music. The leading poets were suspicious of foreign influences and extremely reluctant to allow themselves any enthusiasm for lately arrived *isms.* Curiously loyal to Sp. trad. and cl. form, poets experimented, however, with subjects of varied and profound significance. Carlos Pellicer (1899–1977; *Material poético* [Poetic Materials], 1962) encompassed a world of music and color in highly stylized form. José Gorostiza (1901–73) explored in depth the metaphysical projections of Mexican culture (*Muerte sin fin* [Death Without End], 1939), and Xavier Villaurrutia (1903–50) made of his love poetry the epitome of exquisite sophistication (*Nocturnos* [Nocturns], 1933; *Décima muerte* [Tenth Death], 1941). Salvador Novo (1904–74) played with grandiose themes of Mexican history (he was the official *cronista* of Mexico City), but his poetry also reveals tenderness and pathos (*Poesía* [Poetry], 1961). See also CHICANO POETRY.

The last brilliant flashes of the Sp. Am. avant-garde are to be found in the poetry of Jorge Carrera Andrade (Ecuador, 1902–76), Luis Cardoza y Aragón (Guatemala, b. 1904), Emilio Adolfo Westphalen (Perú, b. 1911), Vicente Gerbasi (Venezuela, b. 1913), José Lezama Lima (Cuba, 1910–76), and Efraín Huerta (Mexico, 1914–82).

At this point the historian might feel tempted to include Nicolás Guillén (b. 1902) among the poets reacting against the elitism of *Ultraísmo.* That would be only partly right. Guillén was above the polemics of the avant garde. He created a powerful poetic movement that became characteristic of the Caribbean world. With Guillén, black poetry ceased to be an exotic pastime to become the expression of an oppressed people struggling for social liberation. Guillén's poetry is not just "political"; it is great art that combines the refined intricacies of old Sp. ballads with the fascinating rhythms and cadences of African music and dance. Some of his books (*Motivos de son* [Motifs for Cuban "Sones"], 1930; *Cóngoro Cosongo* [Congoro Cosongo], 1931; *El son entero* [Complete "Sones"], 1947) are already classics in Sp. Am. p. To the acknowledgment of the baroque poet and novelist Lezama Lima, we should add the names of Eliseo Diego (b. 1920) and Cintio Vitier (b. 1921), who represent the link between pre- and post-revolutionary poetry in Cuba. Both appeared at a time when philosophical and even religious currents dominated the literary world in Havana. After the revolution in 1959, they remained in Cuba and now are looked upon as leaders by a younger generation.

When Octavio Paz (b. 1914) assumed the leadership of his generation in Mexico, the whole poetry of Sp. America once again underwent rebellion and change. But this time the main issue was *language*: prose writers and poets felt the urgency of doing away with the dated rhetoric of the avant garde. Short-story writer Julio Cortázar, novelists such as Juan Rulfo, Gabriel García Márquez, Elena Garro, and Enrique Molina, and poets like Nicanor Parra (b. 1914), Alfredo Cardona Peña, Germán Belli, Alí Chumacero, Mario Benedetti, Olga Orozco, Jaime Sabines, Homero Aridjis, Ernesto Cardenal, Enrique Lihn, Jorge Tellier, and others sound the alarm and engage in a passionately critical consideration of literary lang. The return to vernacular, unrhetorical, direct lang. is thoroughly established. Anti-poetry is born, led by Parra's outrageously funny and merciless attack against the capitalist establishment in *Poemas y antipoemas* (Poems and Antipoems, 1954). His conversational, ironic discourse serves as a cover for a bitter condemnation of society and, more recently, of nature's destruction by man. Parra absorbed a tone of controlled desperation in his careful readings of British poetry, particularly T. S. Eliot. He owes some of his surrealistic populism to earlier Sp. Am. poets, such as Pablo de Rokha (1894–1968), a Chilean, author of *Gran temperatura* (Great Temperature, 1937) and *Canto del macho anciano* (Song of an Ancient Male, 1965) among many books, and León de Greif (1895–1976), one of the leading figures in contemp. Colombian poetry (*Obras completas* [Complete Works], 1960). Parra's counterpart in Chilean poetry is Gonzalo Rojas (b. 1917), whose expression of profound existentialist density has gained in importance and projection in recent years (*Oscuro* [Dark], 1977; *Del relámpago* [On Lightening], 1981).

Paz stands at the opposite extreme of Parra. His poetic discourse is surrealistic in form but philosophical in content. His preoccupation with the soul and the fate of his people lends an almost tragic tone to his poetry. Paz's impact on Sp. Am. p. has grown steadily. His roots are in Fr. surrealism (*Libertad bajo palabra* [Freedom on My Own Word], 1935–57; *Salamandra* [Salamander], 1958–61); but philosophically he has delved deeply into Oriental trads., as if he were slowly tracing a path from ancient religions through pre-Colombian cosmogonies toward modern existentialism. Following in Paz's footsteps, José Emilio Pacheco (b. 1939) has gained a solid reputation as a poet, essayist, and translator (*Los elementos de la noche* [Night Elements], 1963; *Islas a la deriva* [Aimless Islands], 1976; *Desde entonces* [Since Then], 1980).

As we approach the end of the 20th c., Sp. Am. p. reflects a movement from surrealism and conversationalism toward an explicit discourse of philosophical desperation, sometimes attributed to national conditions of ruin and pessimism, sometimes to struggles of social liberation, but most often to individual anguish. Neruda's voice continues to be heard, but young poets close their ears to his cosmic clamor; they are drawn to more strong, direct, down-to-earth statements. Their discourse seems rough in its directness but is filled with loneliness and tenderness as well. Some of these new voices are already rising above the chorus of small presses and little magazines, establishing a solid international reputation: in Central America, the Salvadorean Roque Dalton (1933–75; *Taberna y otros lugares* [Tavern and Other Places], 1969); in Peru, Antonio Cisneros (b. 1942; *Canto ceremonial contra un oso hormiguero* [Ceremonial Song Against an Anteater], 1968; *Crónica del Niño Jesús de Chilca* [Chronicle of the Chilca Child Jesus], 1981); in Chile, Jaime Quezada (b. 1942; *Las palabras del fabulador* [The Fabulist's Words], 1968; *Huerfanías* [Orphan Themes], 1985), and Raúl Zurita (b. 1951; *Purgatorio* [Purgatory], 1979; *Anteparaíso* [Ante Paradise], 1982).

Looking back over the second half of the 20th c. the reader knows that she has seen the rise and end of a rich and splendid trad. of baroque poetry. In the twilight of this period, a few names became firmly established in Western lit. The move now is back to fundamental poetic statements in the midst of decisive social changes.

See also PORTUGUESE POETRY; BRAZILIAN POETRY; SPANISH POETRY; CHICANO POETRY.

ANTHOLOGIES: *Antol. de poetas hispanoamericanos*, ed. M. Menéndez y Pelayo, 4 v. (1893–95)—mostly 19th c.; *Antol. de la poesía española e hispanoamericana*, ed. F. de Onís (1934); *La poesía chilena nueva*, ed. E. Anguita and V. Teitelboin (1935); *Indice de la poesía uruguaya contemporánea*, ed. A. Zum Felde (1935); *Indice de la poesía argentina contemporánea*, ed. J. González Carbalho (1937); *Indice de la poesía ecuatoriana contem-*

poránea, ed. B. Carrión (1937); *Orbita de la poesía afrocubana,* ed. R. Guirao (1938); *Indice de la poesía peruana contemporánea,* ed. L. A. Sánchez (1938); *Nuevos poetas venezolanos,* ed. R. Olivares Figueroa (1938); *Anthol. of Contemp. Lat. Am. P.,* ed. D. Fitts (1942)—Sp. and Eng. texts; *Twelve Sp. Am. Poets,* ed. H. R. Hays (1943)—Sp. and Eng. texts; *Indice de la poesía paraguaya,* ed. S. Buzó Gómez (1943); *La poesía mexicana moderna,* ed. A. Castro Leal (1953); *Cien años de poesía en Panamá,* ed. R. Miró (1953); *Antol. de la poesía hispanoamericana,* ed. G. de Albareda and F. Garfias, 10 v. (1957–); *Anthol. of Mexican Poetry,* ed. O. Paz, tr. S. Beckett (1958); *Antol. de la poesía chilena contemporánea,* ed. R. E. Scarpa and H. Montes (1968); *Con Cuba: An Anthol. of Cuban Poetry of the Last 60 Years,* ed. N. Tarn (1969); *New Poetry of Mexico,* ed. O. Paz and M. Strand (1970); *Antol. de la poesía hispanoamericana contemporánea: 1914–1970* (1971), *Antol. crítica de la poesía modernista hispanoamericana* (1985), both ed. J. O. Jiménez; *Penguin Book of Lat. Am. Verse,* ed. E. Caracciolo-Trejo (1971); S. Yurkievich, *Fundadores de la nueva poesía latinoamericana* (1971); *Lat. Am. Revolutionary Poetry: a Bilingual Anthol.,* ed. R. Marquez (1974); *Antol. crítica de la poesía tradicional chilena,* ed. I. Dolz Blackburn (1979); *Poesía peruana, antol. general,* ed. A. Romualdo et al, 3 v. (1984); *Woman Who Has Sprouted Wings: Poems by Contemp. Lat. Am. Women Poets,* ed. M. Crow (1984); *Muestra de poesía hispanoamericana del siglo 20,* ed. J. A. Escalona-Escalona, 2 v. (1985); *Antol. de la nueva poesía femenina chilena,* ed. J. Villegas (1985); *Poets of Chile: A Bilingual Anthol., 1965–1985,* ed. and tr. S. F. White and J. A. Epple (1986); *Three Women Poets: Louise Labe, Gaspara Stampa, and Sor Juana Ines de la Cruz,* ed. F. J. Warnke (1987); *A Sor Juana Anthol.,* tr. A. S. Trueblood (1988)—intro. by O. Paz.

HISTORY AND CRITICISM: A. Torres-Ríoseco, *Rubén Darío: casticismo y americanismo* (1931); J. E. Englekirk, *Edgar Allan Poe in Hispanic Lit.* (1934); A. Alonso, *Poesía y estilo de Pablo Neruda,* 2d ed. (1951); S. Rosenbaum, *Mod. Women Poets of Sp. America* (1945)—excellent bibl.; P. Henríquez Ureña, *Literary Currents in Hispanic America* (1945); M. del Carmen Millán, *El paisaje en la poesía mexicana* (1952)—esp. 19th c.; F. Alegría, *Walt Whitman en Hispanoamérica* (1954), *La poesía chilena* (1954); M. Henríquez Ureña, *Breve historia del modernismo* (1954); E. Anguita, *Antol. de Vicente Huidobro* (1954)—fine critical intro.; R. Fernández Retamar, *La poesía contemporánea en Cuba* (1954); F. Dauster, *Breve historia de la poesía mexicana* (1956); Unión Panamericana, *Diccionario de la lit. latinoamericana* (1958–); A. Rama, *Rubén Darío y el Modernismo* (1970); C. Fernández Moreno, *América Latina en su lit.* (1972); *A Woman of Genius: The Intellectual Autobiography of Sor Juana de la Cruz,* tr. M. S. Peden (1982); J. A. Escalona, *Muestra de poesía hispanoamericana del Siglo XX,* 2 v. (1985); F. Schopf, *Del Vanguardismo a la Antipoesía* (1986); O. Paz, *Sor Juana,* tr. M. S. Peden (1988); G. Kirkpatrick, *The Dissonant Legacy of "Modernismo"* (1989); F. W. Murray, *The Aesthetics of Contemp. Sp.-Am. Social Protest Poetry* (1990). F.A.

SPANISH POETRY. (This article treats primarily Sp. p. in Castilian, the lang. of the central region of the Iberian peninsula; for the poetries of the western and eastern langs., see GALICIAN POETRY and CATALAN POETRY.)

I. THE EARLIEST LYRICS
II. THE MEDIEVAL EPIC
III. MONASTIC POETRY
IV. POETRY OF THE 14TH CENTURY
V. THE REIGN OF JUAN II
VI. THE REIGN OF FERDINAND AND ISABELLA
VII. RENAISSANCE POETRY (16TH CENTURY)
VIII. BAROQUE POETRY (17TH CENTURY)
IX. NEOCLASSICAL POETRY (18TH CENTURY)
X. ROMANTIC AND POSTROMANTIC POETRY (19TH CENTURY)
XI. THE 20TH CENTURY

I. THE EARLIEST LYRICS. Sp. p. originated, no doubt, simultaneously with the Sp. lang. itself or, more precisely, with those Romance dialects which developed on the Iberian peninsula during the Middle Ages (see SPANISH PROSODY). The dialects began, of course, not as written but as spoken langs.; hence the first Sp. p. was, naturally, oral poetry. Only almost indecipherable fragments of this poetry have been preserved, transcribed in Ar. or Heb. letters, as refrains (*kharjas*) appended to longer, more learned poems (*muwashshahana*) written as early as the 11th c. by Moorish or Jewish poets of southern Spain (see HEBREW POETRY). The dialect of the *kharjas,* known as Mozarabic, reflects the earliest stage of a recognizably Sp. lang. These *kharjas,* which antedate even the lyric poems of the Occitan troubadours, are predominantly love songs, snatches of lamentation in which girls bewail the absence of their lovers; the poetic intensity of these fragments, tremulously chaste in the Heb. poems, more sensual in the Ar. ones, can still be felt by the Sp. reader, despite one or two archaic words of Semitic origin:

> My heart is leaving me.
> Oh God, I wonder whether it will return?
> My grief for my beloved is so great!
> He is sick: when will he be well?

Such fragments are the only survivors of a body of oral poetry which must have been common to most communities of the Iberian peninsula. The first Sp. p. recorded in the Lat. alphabet, that of the 13th-c. Galician-Portuguese *cancioneiros* or collections of songs, includes *cantigas de amigo* which are quite similar to the *kharjas* in theme; in the traditional folk poetry of Castile, as well, the *villancicos* or refrain carols, deriving from the Hispano-Ar. *zéjel,* are frequently *Frauenlieder* of a similar sort.

II. THE MEDIEVAL EPIC. The oldest monument of Sp. lit. is the anonymous *Poema del Cid* or *Cantar de Mío Cid*; written about 1140, it is the best surviving example of the Sp. medieval epic. Like the Fr. *chansons de geste,* the *Poema del Cid* reflects feudal customs of Germanic origin which may be traced back to the Visigothic period; it also shows signs of the direct influence of Fr. literary models and, perhaps, of certain Ar. sources as well. The word "cid" itself is of Ar. origin and means feudal lord, which is the title of the poem's hero, Rodrigo Díaz de Vivar, a well-documented historical personage who, exiled by Alfonso VI of Castile and Leon between 1079 and 1099, took the city of Valencia from the Moors in 1089. Given a degree of historicity and of geographical precision which clearly distinguishes this poem's level of realism from the fantasy of Fr. epics such as the *Chanson de Roland,* the *Poema del Cid* is essentially the dramatic depiction of a relatively restrained and modest type of feudal hero.

Written in lines of variable length (14-syllable lines predominate) divided into hemistichs, with assonance at the ends of the lines, the poem was evidently composed for dramatic oral recitation by a *jongleur* or professional court entertainer. It begins with the pathos of the hero's unjust exile. But Rodrigo Díaz is always a faithful vassal to the king, sending him booty from each of the battles that he wins in Moslem land. After taking Valencia, he is restored to the good graces of the king, who honors him by sponsoring his daughters' marriages to two Leonese noblemen. But the sons-in-law turn out to be as decadent and cowardly as they are proud. When they beat and abandon their wives, the Cid does not take vengeance into his own hands, but appeals to the king for justice to be administered in accordance with law. His second vindication is even more glorious than his first.

The sober understatement of this epic poem's style reflects the orderly, measured character of its hero. Thus, the first major work in the history of Sp. p. has none of the baroque exuberance or picaresque cynicism which are often considered typical of Sp. lit.; it is, in fact, quite classically subtle in its balanced avoidance of all extremes.

Other Sp. medieval epics certainly existed which can be reconstructed from later chronicles and ballads, but the original versions are for the most part lost. Among the surviving texts are a 13th-c. clerkly reworking of an epic on Fernán González and the much later *Mocedades de Rodrigo,* in which the Cid is depicted, not as an austere feudal vassal but as an arrogant, fiery youth. It is this later, more romantic Cid who was to become famous in ballads and plays.

III. MONASTIC POETRY. In the 13th c., the scholarly poet of the cloister begins to compete with the *jongleur* of the feudal court. He replaces the militaristic Romanesque virtues of feudal society with the Gothic virtues of devotion to Our Lady, the saints, and the Mass. His sources are not recent Sp. history or oral legends but Lat. manuscripts: the Bible, the lives and miracles of the saints, even legends of Cl. antiquity. And he uses not a loose oral meter but a fixed stanzaic form known as *cuaderna vía* : four 14-syllable lines (*alejandrinos*; cf. *alexandrine,* q.v.), all ending in a single true rhyme.

Gonzalo de Berceo (ca. 1200–65) is the best representative of this poetic school. A secular priest and confessor of La Rioja, he was closely associated with the important monasteries of San Millán de la Cogolla and Santo Domingo de Silos. His works deal exclusively with religious subjects: lives of saints, theology, the Virgin Mary. His *Milagros de Nuestra Señora* (Miracles of Our Lady), for example, consist of 25 brief stories, each telling of a miracle wrought by the Virgin's intercession. These stories are almost all adapted from standard Lat. sources common to most of medieval Europe. Berceo's poetic achievement was to popularize and humanize these legends by retelling them in Castilian, the local lang. of the people. His style is simple and clear to the point of being almost prosaic, but his attitude of childlike faith and his rustic images are often charming and occasionally quite lyrical. A spirit of Christian egalitarianism and a sense of humor contributed to a 20th-c. revival of Berceo's popularity as a poet.

Somewhat different, though of the same metric genre and period (the first half of the 13th c.), is the *Libro de Alexandre,* doubtfully attributed to a Leonese cleric, Juan Lorenzo "Segura" de Astorga. Following Lat. and Fr. sources, it reveals Alexander the Great in the medieval guise of a legendary hero. It is encyclopedic in scope, combining Cl. reminiscences, exotic fantasies, mythology, evocations of the springtime garden of love, and moral didacticism. It is definitely more sophisticated than Berceo's works, and more formally polished in style. Other poems of this school are the *Libro de Apolonio,* the *Poema de Yusuf* (the story of Joseph based on the Koran rather than on the Old Testament and written in Ar. rather than Lat.), and the *Vida de Santa María Egipcíaca.*

IV. POETRY OF THE 14TH CENTURY. It is significant that Spain's greatest medieval poet lived south of the Guadarrama Mountains, that is, not in the more soberly European Old Castile of Burgos and the Cid but in the Mozarabic New Castile of Toledo. Juan Ruiz (ca. 1283–1350), probably born in Alcalé de Henares, no doubt studied at the episcopal seminary of Toledo; here the archbishop, primate of Spain, maintained a strongly clerical center of studies in the midst of a peculiarly Sp. goliardic atmosphere of taverns and Moorish dancing girls. Though ordained and made Archpriest of Hita, Juan Ruiz conveys in his poetry this Mozarabic atmosphere as he assimilates to it his readings in the Med. Lat. lit. of Europe, ranging from the Bible and the Breviary to preachers' moral fables and aphorisms to goliardic love songs and Ovid's erotic poems.

Though his great poem, the *Libro de buen amor*

(The Book of Good Love), is written chiefly in the same *cuaderna vía* stanzas that Berceo had used in the previous century, it really belongs to a different genre altogether. It is, in fact, *sui generis* so far as European lit. is concerned; its peculiar autobiographical and didactic form has been related by María Rosa Lida to the Semitic *maqamat,* a genre cultivated by various Hispano-Hebraic authors preceding Juan Ruiz. In a general way its picaresque tone and content might remind the Eng. reader most of the contemporary Chaucerian *Wife of Bath's Tale.* Its essentially equivocal nature allows the author to play constantly between poles which are usually considered to be mutually exclusive: personal experiences and adaptations from Lat. sources, moral didacticism and irrepressible humor, ascetic fervor and erotic fever. The author seems simultaneously to be a priest and a sidewalk *jongleur.*

When one analyzes more literally the objective content of the *Libro de buen amor,* one can distinguish from the basic plot, which is a series of erotic adventures told in the first person, several elements which are more or less loosely attached: moral fables, adaptations of Ovid's *Ars amandi* and of the 12th-c. Lat. comedy *Pamphilus,* burlesque allegories associated with Lent and Easter, assorted satires, and a few lyric poems, mostly devoted to the Virgin. The work is, in sum, Spain's poetic synthesis of Gothic culture, a crudely human comedy worthy of comparison with Dante's refined divine one, full of the joy and pathos of life under the shadow of death, and permeated by a deeply ironic humor and childlike sense of playfulness.

There is only one poem worthy of note in the second half of the 14th c.: The *Rimado de palacio* by the solemn Basque Chancellor Pero López de Ayala (1332–1407). This "palace rhyme" is primarily political in its emphasis; it is austerely, severely moralistic as it fiercely satirizes contemporary decadence of church and state.

V. THE REIGN OF JUAN II. Lyric poetry as an independent genre developed much later in Castilian than in Galician-Portuguese or Catalan, the western and eastern languages of the peninsula. Early Catalan poetry is, in fact, part of the history of the troubadour lyric, the linguistic difference between Occitan and Catalan being relatively slight. In the west, lyric poetry written in the Galician-Portuguese dialect included both the *cantigas de amigo,* related to the folk poetry in the early Mozarabic *kharjas,* and more sophisticated love poems stemming from the direct influence of the Occitan troubadours. Thus the cult of courtly love entered Sp. lit.; even poets who spoke Castilian as their native dialect used Galician for writing lyric poetry during the 13th and most of the 14th cs. The scholarly Alfonso X of Castile (1221–84) wrote his 430 *Cantigas de Santa María* in Galician, evincing a wide range of metrical virtuosity *à la provençale.* But between 1350 and 1450 the center of Sp. lyric poetry shifts from Galician to Castilian; the first collection of Castilian lyrics, the *Cancionero de Baena,* is dated 1445. In this collection the troubadour style predominates, but the allegorical and philosophical influence of It. poetry, particularly Dante, is also apparent.

The two major prehumanistic poets of Juan II's reign are Íñigo López de Mendoza, first Marquis of Santillana (1398–1458), and Juan de Mena. Santillana was a leading figure of the northern Castilian nobility, involved militarily in the civil wars of Juan II's reign. His youthful lyrics include witty *dezires,* courtly *canciones,* and pseudo-rustic *serranillas* (*pastourelles*); the latter, based on the encounter of traveling knight with mountain lass, are delightfully sophisticated variations of a popular genre. More ambitious is his *Comedieta de Ponça* (1436), an elaborate allegorical narrative in the It. trad. An interesting product of Santillana's final 20 years are 42 sonnets, the first to be written in any lang. other than It.; they reveal the influence of the "dolce stil nuovo" and of Petrarch. A final category of poetry includes mature works treating of moral, political, and religious themes; typical is *Bias contra Fortuna* (ca. 1450), in which the semilegendary philosopher-statesman of ancient Greece engages in Stoic debate with an arbitrary and tyrannical Fortune.

Juan de Mena (1411–56), born in Cordova the son of a leading family of converts from Judaism, is the typically scholarly humanist of southern Spain; he studied at the University of Salamanca and at Rome and was named Lat. Secretary at the court of Juan II. His poetry is of two types: troubadour love poetry as it had developed in Spain, marked by scholastic "wit," psychological subtleties, and a strong tendency to use pseudoreligious hyperbole; and politico-moral poetry such as *La coronación,* a difficult allegory in which literary personages are presented as though either in Hell or in Paradise, with the Marquis of Santillana crowned as perfect knight in both arms and letters. Mena's most ambitious poem is the *Laberinto de Fortuna,* consisting of almost 300 *arte mayor* stanzas. In it the poet visits the crystal palace of Fortune; allegorical wheels and planetary circles lead to the culminating vision of Jupiter and Saturn, representing Juan II and his minister Don Álvaro de Luna, prophesying the achievement of national unity. His rhet. grandiloquence, Latinized vocabulary, aesthetic use of Cl. allusion, and emphatic nationalism make of Juan de Mena the most significant herald of the Ren. in 15th-c. Sp. p.

One other poem of this period deserves special mention: the *Coplas por la muerte de su padre* of Jorge Manrique. This elegy for the death of his father is one of the most perfectly controlled poems in Sp. lit.; its classical flow of simple lang. makes it a perennial favorite of the Sp.-speaking world. Its themes are late medieval commonplaces: the transience of earthly life (the "Ubi sunt" theme) and a compensating Christian faith in eternal life. But at the hands of Jorge Manrique they receive a molding of verbal expression that is inimitable:

> . . . how swiftly pleasure leaves us; how,
> when we recall it, it grieves us; how, in
> our opinion, any time past was better
> than now.

VI. THE REIGN OF FERDINAND AND ISABELLA. With the marriage of Ferdinand of Aragon and Isabella of Castile, the political unity of the peninsula (except for Portugal) was achieved; religious unity was achieved in 1492 by the expulsion of all unconverted Jews and by the capture of Granada, the sole remaining Moslem kingdom on Sp. soil. The Middle Ages were receding; in art and in education the It. Ren. was clearly arriving. But in poetry it was still a transitional period. The Hispanized troubadour lyric continued without great change. Religious poetry took on a more sentimental coloration in the works of the popular Franciscan poets Íñigo de Mendoza and Ambrosio Montesino. The most important devel. was a new interest on the part of literate poets in the folk trad.; *villancicos* (refrain-carols) and *romances* (ballads) were now collected, elaborated upon, and published. All of the above elements may be observed in the great folio *Cancionero general*, first published by Hernando del Castillo in 1511 and revised several times during the 16th c. This late medieval corpus of poetry continued to exert an influence upon Ren. poets of succeeding generations, even into the 17th c.

The ballads or *romances* are especially interesting and important in the history of Sp. lit. The semilyrical fragments deriving from national epics such as the *Poema del Cid* maintained an epic meter: 16-syllable lines divided into 8-syllable hemistichs with continuous assonance at the ends of the lines. (In modern editions the hemistichs are usually printed as complete octosyllabic lines, and the assonance thus appears only at the ends of the even-numbered lines.) Similar ballads grew out of Carolingian, Arthurian, Moorish, and other romantic or popular stories. They were published first in small groups as broadsides; these were gradually collected and reprinted as small volumes; finally, in 1600, a voluminous *Romancero general* was published. Famous Golden Age plays were based upon the more popular cycles; everyone seems to have been familiar with the *romances*, for they were constantly cited and alluded to. The ballad genre has been familiar to every generation, from the Golden Age to the romantics and the neopopularists of Lorca's generation; and the oral trad. has lived on into the 20th c. among the more isolated communities of Spain, the Sephardic Balkans and North Africa, and Sp. America.

VII. RENAISSANCE POETRY (16TH CENTURY). In 1526, at the court of Charles V in Granada, the Venetian ambassador Andrea Navagero suggested to the courtier-poet Juan Boscán (ca. 1490–1542) that he try his hand at writing sonnets and other It. forms in Sp. With the encouragement and collaboration of his friend Garcilaso de la Vega (1503–36), Boscán's experiment was successful; a new type of poetry eventually took root in Spain, marking a distinct shift in poetic sensibility. The success of this revolution was due largely to the superior aesthetic gifts of Garcilaso, who not only assimilated It. metric forms (the hendecasyllabic line in sonnets, *canzoni, terza rima, ottava rima, rima al mezzo*, and blank verse), but also captured an essential part of the It. Ren. spirit in his poetry: a sensuous, metaphoric flow of bucolic, erotic, and mythological themes expressing a new sense of beauty in grief and in idealized Cl. scenes and landscapes. Despite his many stylistic debts to Virgil and Sannazaro, to Petrarch and Ovid, Garcilaso's Sp. p. (he also wrote Lat. odes) strikes a new note which belongs to him alone.

> Near the Tagus River in sweet solitude
> there is a thicket of green willows
> all covered over and filled with ivy
> which climbs the trunk to the top
> and so weaves and enchains it up there
> that the sun cannot penetrate the verdure;
> the water bathes the greensward with sound,
> making joyful the grass and the human ear.

The poetry of Boscán and Garcilaso was published posthumously in a single volume in 1543 and was republished many times during the 16th c. Garcilaso's poetry was first published separately in 1570; it was treated as a humanistic classic by being annotated by a professor at the University of Salamanca in 1574 and by the scholar-poet Fernando de Herrera of Seville in 1580. Thus Garcilaso's 35 sonnets, five odes, two elegies, one epistle, and three eclogues became the foundation of a Ren. trad. of poetry in Spain. Very little poetry has been written in Sp. since the 16th c. that has not been influenced to some extent by that of Garcilaso de la Vega. We could list innumerable 16th-c. poets belonging to Garcilaso's new school: Diego Hurtado de Mendoza (1503–75), Hernando de Acuña (1520?–80), Baltasar del Alcázar (1590–1606), Francisco de Figueroa (1536–1617?), Francisco de Aldana (1537–78), Gutierre de Cetina (1520–57?), et al. There was a more or less serious movement of nationalistic resistance against the new It. meters, headed by Cristóbal de Castillejo (1490?–1550); even his own poetry, however, while avoiding the new meters, frequently reflects the Ren. spirit much more than it does the spirit of the Sp. 15th c.

Christianity and the Ren. join forces in the poetry of the Augustinian friar Luis de León (1527–91) and of the reformed Carmelite monk San Juan de la Cruz (1542–91). Luis de León was a biblical scholar and professor at the University of Salamanca. In his vigorously classical odes he manages to fuse the satirical rusticity of Horace with a soaring Neoplatonic Christianity which at times approaches true mysticism. Because of its explicit philosophical content, his poetry often receives more serious attention than does that of Garcilaso; it seems to reconcile the Greco-Roman and the Hebraic-Christian trads. and certainly reaches more than once the heights of truly great Cl. poetry. Much more ethereally mystical is the even smaller body of lyrics by San Juan de la Cruz. His major poem, the *Cántico espiritual,* draws directly upon the Song of Solomon and indirectly upon Garcilaso's eclogues; the resultant imagery, tremulously sensual, lends itself to an extended allegory of the soul's mystic love for God. Nowhere else in Western poetry is erotic intensity so essential to the expression of an overwhelming religious experience; St. John of the Cross is without doubt one of the few great mystic poets. Just after a climactic moment, he writes these lines:

> I stayed there forgetting myself,
> I leaned my face over the Beloved;
> everything stopped and I let myself go,
> leaving my cares
> forgotten among the lilies.

At the same time, on a lower plane, poets continue to use the traditional Sp. meters, esp. the octosyllable. Scholastic wit of a 15th-c. sort is revived for religious purposes in the *Conceptos espirituales* (1600) of Alonso de Ledesma (1562–1623).

The most serious attempt to continue Garcilaso's trad. was that of his annotator Fernando de Herrera (1534–97), the central figure of a school of poets developing in Andalusia, principally in Seville. His voluminous notes to Garcilaso's works are, in fact, a poetic manifesto of a Neoplatonic sort. Herrera declares that erudition is necessary for great poetry, that the Sp. lang. is as richly expressive as the It., and that the poetic genius expresses divine reality. His Cl. learning is inexhaustible; in his notes he writes veritable histories of the poetic genres and uses a large Gr. vocabulary in making rhetorical analyses. Thus his *Anotaciones* (1580) are a major contribution to Ren. poetics, second in Spain only to the Aristotelian *Filosofía antigua poética* (1596) of A. López Pinciano.

Having taken minor orders, Herrera devoted his entire life to scholarship and poetry. He wrote several heroic odes or hymns on national themes; their grandiloquent echoes of the Old Testament define Herrera's organ voice. But the social center of his life was the literary *tertulia,* or salon, of the Count and Countess of Gelves; here Herrera found it natural to focus his poetry, in the manner of Petrarch, upon the lovely young countess. These sonnets, odes, and elegies, in which he exquisitely suffers and delights, reflect primarily a literary experience within an aristocratic, scholarly setting; they won for him among his contemporaries the title of "the Divine," when in 1582, a year after the countess's death, he published them with the modest title of *Algunas obras de Fernando de Herrera.* Other members of this Andalusian school of poets are Luis Barahona de Soto (1548–95), Pedro de Espinosa (1578–1650), Francisco de Rioja (1583–1659), and Francisco de Medrano (1570–1607).

Mention should here be made of Ren. epic poetry. Spain has nothing to compare with Portugal's *Lusiadas* (1572), but the epic of the conquest of Chile, *La Araucana* (1569–90) by Alonso de Ercilla (1533–96?), can still be read with interest and pleasure. Worthy of note is the literary treatment of the Indian chieftain Caupolicán as a "noble savage."

VIII. BAROQUE POETRY (17TH CENTURY). From among the dozens of considerable poets of 17th-c. Spain, we can select for special attention the three who are generally considered greatest: Luis de Góngora (1561–1627), Lope de Vega (1562–1635), and Francisco de Quevedo (1580–1645). Among them they represent the main trends of Sp. lyric poetry during the second half of the Golden Age. Góngora, like Juan de Mena, was born in Cordova and, like Herrera, took minor orders entitling him to an ecclesiastical benefice; in Cl. erudition and aristocratic intellect he was second to neither of his Andalusian predecessors, rivaling Garcilaso himself as a major creative figure of Sp. p. In a sense he continues and elaborates upon Garcilaso's trad., carrying each of his stylistic traits to its ultimate poetic consequences, achieving an aesthetic purity almost devoid of any quotidian human emotion deriving from such common themes as love, religion, or politics.

Like Lope and Quevedo, Góngora cultivated poetry not only of the Ren. trad. in Italianate meters, but also of the more med. folkloric trad. in octosyllables and other short lines. His *romances* and *villancicos* (or *letrillas*) show a thorough familiarity with the more popular themes and meters; Góngora characteristically polishes and elaborates upon them, however, in such a way that we could never mistake his exquisite poems for those of the anonymous trad. His burlesque and satirical poems are equally polished. And his sonnets achieve a final formal perfection, whether heroic, funereal, erotic, or burlesque in theme. His most ambitious Cl. poems are quite difficult to read, both because of their unusual syntax and because of the intellectual complexity of their metaphors, conceits, and mythological allusions. His masterpieces in this style are baroque pastorals: the *Fábula de Polifemo y Galatea,* based on Ovid's Polyphemus, and the *Soledades,* the plot of which is more original, though hardly a line is without Cl. allusions. This style of his, traditionally labeled *culteranismo* or *cultismo,* though widely imitated in Spain and Sp. America, has never been surpassed:

> Sicily in its mountains never armed a beast with such ferocity nor shod it with such wind that it might either fiercely or swiftly save its many-colored skin: it is already a jacket, that former mortal terror of the woods, for him who with slow step brought back the oxen to his shelter, treading the doubtful light of day [i.e. twilight].

The world of Góngora's major poems is a material world of solid substances and glittering colors in which the poet, using words, attempts to rival the artificiality of nature, of *Natura Artifex,* herself. It is no accident that a taste for this poetry has been revived in the 20th c. by Spain's most sophisticated modern poets.

Lope de Vega, the creator of Spain's lyrical Golden Age theater, was also a very productive poet; his sonnets alone number 1600 or more. He also wrote many long narrative poems, of which his Tassoesque *Jerusalén conquistada* is perhaps the most noteworthy. Between 1604 and 1637 five important collections of his lyric poems were published; they are not so polished as those of Góngora, but they are full of variety, spontaneity, and flowing grace. His odes, eclogues, elegies, and sonnets belong to Garcilaso's Cl. trad., with light baroque elaborations of all sorts; he occasionally attempts to rival even Góngora. His poems actually do surpass Góngora's in personal emotion, if not in erudition and technical skill. At the other pole, Lope's folkloric lyrics are unexcelled; unlike Góngora's, they are often indistinguishable from those of the anonymous trad. And his ability to fuse these two trads., the learned and the popular, is similarly unsurpassed. No other poet could compete with Lope de Vega's facile abundance; he was indeed a veritable phenomenon, "Nature's monster."

Finally, Francisco de Quevedo, though his poetry too is extremely various, represents chiefly a severe moralistic trend, an awareness of universal human corruption, in Spain's baroque poetry. An incisive satirical wit characterizes most of Quevedo's poetry, which at times is quite obscene; his colloquial puns and other witticisms are often very funny in a grim sort of way. His profoundest lyrical note is struck when he faces death with Stoic desperation:

> Now fearfully within the heart
> resounds the final day;
> and the last hour, black and cold,
> draws near, filled with terrible shadows. . . .

The literary power of Quevedo's love poetry has been rediscovered in recent years. To the worn courtly and Petrarchan conventions he added a new dimension of existential anguish deriving from his awareness of time and death, epitomized in his masterpiece, a sonnet entitled "Love Constant Beyond Death":

> My eyes may be closed by the final shadow which will take away from me the bright day, and this soul of mine may be freed by an hour indulgent to its anxious longing; but it will not, on the further shore, leave the memory in which it used to burn; my flame is able to swim across the cold water and disobey a harsh law. A soul which has been imprisoned by no less than a god, the veins which have supplied the moisture to so great a fire, the marrow which has gloriously burned: it will leave its body, not its [loving] anguish; they will be ash, but it will have feelings; they will be dust, but dust which is in love.

The element of fire (love, suffering, life) engages in a desperate battle for survival against water (extinction, oblivion, death); despite all evidence the poet-lover asserts the invincibility of his passionate will, even when buried in the element of earth (ashes, dust, the dead body). The octet affirms in general terms what the sestet repeats in psychological and physiological detail, ending emphatically with the word "enamorado." This sonnet belongs to a cycle of 64 sonnets dedicated "A Lisi," a high point in the neo-Petrarchan trad. of Sp. love poetry.

It is traditional, though inaccurate, to list Spain's 17th-c. poets either as *cultista* followers of Góngora (Jáuregui, Bocángel, Espinosa, Soto de Rojas, Villamediana, Polo de Medina, et al.) or as *conceptistas* like Quevedo (the Argensola brothers, Esquilache, the anonymous author of the *Epistola moral a Fabio*). As a matter of fact, Cl. erudition and mythological allusions, the trademarks of *culteranismo,* were almost universal in 17th-c. poetry; and few poets completely avoided indulging in puns, conceits, and other forms of baroque wit. The question is, with regard to each poet, how he developed an individual style as he made use of the available popular devices. The modern critic can usefully study the poetics of the period: the *Libro de erudición poética* (1611) by L. Carrillo y Sotomayor; the *Discurso poético* (1623) by J. de Jáuregui; and, above all, the *Agudeza y arte de ingenio* (1642), in which the great Jesuit *conceptista* Baltasar Gracián (1601–58) cites Góngora far more than any other poet. Among 17th-c. epic poems, perhaps two are worthy of mention here: *La Christiada* (1611), based on Christ's Passion, by Diego de Hojeda (1571?–1615), and *El Bernardo* (1624), on a national epic hero, by Bernardo de Balbuena (1568–1627).

IX. NEOCLASSICAL POETRY (18TH CENTURY). With the Bourbon dynasty replacing the Hapsburgs in the 18th c., the Fr. neoclassical standards of Ignacio de Luzán's *Poética* (1737) rejected the baroque poetry of Góngora and Quevedo, advocating a return to the cl. "good taste" of Garcilaso. But there seemed to be few new creative poets. Nicolás Fernández de Moratín (1737–80) emphasized moral, social, and political utilitarianism in his verse, while continuing to imitate Cl. models in his metrical experiments. A more personal preromantic note appears in José Cadalso (1741–82), whose *Ocios de mi juventud* is somewhat influenced by Edward Young. Juan Meléndez Valdés (1754–1817) was the best representative of a new enlightened lyricism in which modern science and social utility entered the Platonic universe of cl. poetry, with a special emphasis on music and sensuousness. His poetry had a strong influence on the following generation of N. Alvarez de Cienfuegos (1764–1809) and Manuel José Quintana (1772–1857).

X. ROMANTIC AND POSTROMANTIC POETRY (19TH CENTURY). The romantic movement, like neoclassicism, came into Spain from outside; it was the Germans and the Eng. who helped Spaniards to rediscover and appreciate anew their own *romances* or ballads and Golden Age lyrics. This leads eventually to the publication of the *Romances históricos* (1841), new poems by the Duke of Rivas (1791–1865), in which national legends and atmospheres are nostalgically evoked in colorful pictures. More passionately romantic and lyrical was José de Espronceda (1808–42), an active Byronic personality rife with political and amorous escapades. His *Poesías líricas* (1840) are filled with emotions which are violent, if not profound, and with the sound and rhythm of a renovated poetic lang.; his erotic and libertarian impulses are often colored with a rebellious, nihilistic Satanism. The best example of this is his Don Juanesque *Estudiante de Salamanca,* full of vitality and technical virtuosity. Greatly influenced by Rivas and Espronceda was José Zorrilla (1817–93), whose romantic stage version of the Don Juan story is full of similar poetry and is still played annually. With Zorrilla the romantic movement put roots deep into Sp. history. Zorrilla wrote verse facilely and in tremendous quantities; by the time he died, he had become himself a national monument to romanticism, a 19th-c. Lope de Vega.

The only Sp. poet of the 19th c. whose works can still be read without condescension in the 20th is Gustavo Adolfo Bécquer (1836–70). Bécquer combines the clear ideas and ineffable sentiments of a late romantic Platonism with a mathematical rigor of stanzaic form; his characteristic figure is anaphora, emphasizing an inexorable parallelism leading up to a climactic conclusion. Whereas modernist and postmodernist poets scorned as formless sentimentalists or dead rhetoricians other romantic and bourgeois poets of the 19th c., they looked back to Bécquer as a founding father, the first truly modern poet of Spain. His 76 short *Rimas* (1871) are marked by a simplicity and musicality of lang. reminiscent of folksong; their inner dream-world of sentiment is, however, more ethereal, sophisticated, deliberately artistic. A constant theme is the ineffability of love, despair, memories, and all profound emotional values.

> Can it be true that when sleep touches
> our eyes with its rose-colored fingers,
> our spirit flees the prison it inhabits
> and soars away in haste?

Perhaps two non-Castilian poets, writing in dialects revived literarily by romantic regionalists, are remotely comparable in quality to Bécquer: Rosalía de Castro (1837–85), writing in Galician, and Jacinto Verdaguer (1845–1902), writing in Catalan. Rosalía de Castro, along with Bécquer, because of her clear sense of form and feeling, and her metrical experiments, has been one of the few 19th-c. poets to be praised and imitated by modernist and postmodernist poets. More widely read than any of these, however, were two postromantic, solidly bourgeois poets, the prosaic humorist Ramón de Campoamor (1817–1901) and the rhetorical idealist Gaspar Núñez de Arce (1832–1903); with these two, Sp. lyricism reached a nadir from which it was to rise only under the impulse of Ruben Darío's *modernismo.*

XI. THE 20TH CENTURY. Ruben Darío (1867–1916) was born in Nicaragua, but his poetic innovations reached every corner of the Sp.-speaking world. His cult of beauty, evinced in his metrical experiments, in his Parnassian sensuousness, and even in his Verlainean religiosity, amounted to a stylistic revolution hardly less important than that of the 16th c. Yet Spain's first great poet in the 20th c. was not a modernist; in fact, Antonio Machado (1875–1939) seems to illustrate, as an Andalusian living in somber Castile, a reaction against all that was showy and external in Darío, a deliberate turning within, a searching for his own unknown God. His style is simple, apparently almost prosaic at times; yet there are always deep inner resonances. Even his landscapes have their true existence, not in the world of geography, but upon the contours of the soul. His most typical symbolic scene is that of a fountain trickling in a deserted square at sunset:

> The embers of a purple twilight
> smoke behind the dark cypress grove.
> In the shadowy arbor is the fountain
> with its winged nude Cupid of stone
> silently dreaming. In the marble basin
> reposes the still water.

His first volume of poems, entitled *Soledades* (1903), was written between 1899 and 1902, a period dominated by the impressive *Prosas profanas* (1896) of Rubén Darío. Anticipating in some ways the latter's *Cantos de vida y esperanza* (1905), Machado in his *Soledades* was less concerned with the direct representation of sound, color, and other physical sensations; he sought a poetry of subtle inner responses to the images of an outer world. In this respect he represents the introspection of the peninsular Generation of 1898, as opposed to the spectacular sensuousness of Rubén

Darío's internationally important *modernismo.* More directly related to Darío is the poet of transition who stands between modernism and Lorca's generation, Juan Ramón Jiménez (1881–1958). A perfectionist like Valéry, Jiménez spent his life working on his poetry, stripping it of all nonessentials, seeking forms of expression to reflect as precisely as possible the subtle shadings of his emotional world. In 1956 he received the Nobel Prize both for his own work and, vicariously, for that of two Sp. poets no longer living at that time, Antonio Machado and Federico García Lorca.

Lorca (1899–1936) is the most widely known member of the major constellation of 20th-c Sp. poets who reached maturity during the 1920s. With Alberti (b. 1902) he represents primarily the Andalusian, folkloric tendency: a popular intuitive genius of great lyrical power, fusing in his poetry elements drawn from many currents within the Sp. cultural heritage, ranging from childlike ingenuousness to the sophistication of a Góngora. Lorca's anguished poems on urban dehumanization and the loss of myth make of his *Poeta en Nueva York* (1940) a cultural monument for all Hispanic exiles in the United States. More cosmopolitan and intellectual members of the same group are the Castilians Pedro Salinas (1892–1952) and Jorge Guillén (1893–1985). Salinas was above all a love poet, reducing his whole world to an intense relationship of dialogue between an I and a Thou: "In order to live I have no need / of islands, palaces, towers. / What an immense joy it is / to live in our pronouns!"

Guillén's perfectionism is reminiscent of Juan Ramón Jiménez. He owes something no doubt to Rimbaud and other Fr. poets, but his poetry as contained in *Cántico* (definitive ed., 1950) is his own creation, an attitude of boundless joy and wonder at existence in this world—though in his later years his poetry took on a somewhat more anguished, less exuberant tone. Two other important members of Lorca's generation have continued to write influential poetry in Spain since the Civil War: Dámaso Alonso (b. 1898) and Vicente Aleixandre (1900–85). Aleixandre released the Freudian subconscious in mythic images of love and violence climaxing in *Sombra del paraíso* (1944); he returned to everyday life in *Historia del corazón* (1954). In Franco Spain he encouraged many younger poets with his support. Alonso, Spain's leading philologist and analyst of poetry, initiated a distinctly existentialist movement in Sp. p. with his *Hijos de la ira* (1944), which, with its God-forsaken anguish at human suffering and social injustice, echoes in modern terms certain notes of the Heb. Psalms.

During and after the Civil War, many new poets have found readers in Spain; poetry in fact was less stunted by the Fascist Franco regime than either drama or fiction. One very promising poet, Miguel Hernández (1910–42), died in prison; a country boy with very little formal education, he read Sp. baroque poetry for himself and wrote some highly original verse. He was a link between Lorca's generation, Quevedo's and Neruda's poetry, and the socially committed poets of the Franco era.

Given the large number of good Sp. poets who have been writing since the Civil War, it is convenient to group them in terms of influential magazines, series of editions, and anthologies. A relatively conservative group of poets who had participated actively in the Civil War published in the postwar review *Escorial*: Luis Felipe Vivanco (b. 1907), Leopoldo Panero (b. 1909), Luis Rosales (b. 1910), Dionisio Ridruejo (b. 1912). The younger poets tended to gravitate toward two poles. The more neoclassical and orthodox ones, following the lead of the *Escorial* poets, incl. José García Nicto (b. 1914), Rafael Morales (b. 1919), José María Valverde (b. 1926), and others, entitled their review *Garcilaso* A more baroquely existentialist group looked rather to Quevedo and *Hijos de la ira* for guidance, gravitating around the review *Espadaña*: Gabriel Celaya (b. 1911), Blas de Otero (b. 1916), Leopoldo de Luis (b. 1918), Vicente Gaos (b. 1919), Carlos Bousoño (b. 1923), Eugenio de Nora (1923). In the younger generation as a whole there is a definite reaction against the aestheticism of Juan Ramón Jiménez and the Lorca generation; their poetry is often directly concerned with questions of social justice.

In 1943, José Luis Cano (b. 1912), himself a poet, established the Adonais series of monthly poets, with annual prizes and occasional anthols. (1953, 1962); for 20 years this was the major center for current Sp. p. More recently, other series, esp. Visor editions, have become more important. Critical moments in the history of postwar Sp. p. were marked by the publication of certain anthols., particularly the one based on a survey by Ribes (1952), three controversial collections edited by Castellet (1962, 1966, 1970), and those of Batlló (1968, 1974), José Olivio Jiménez (1972), and Jiménez Martos (1972). Buenaventura's anthol. of Sp. women poets appeared in 1985.

The Andalusian Luis Rosales, who had published a collection of sonnets (*Abril*, 1935) before the Civil War, created a highly personal love poetry in *La casa encendida* (1949), combining lyric and narrative modes with free verse, colloquial lang., and surrealist images. A voice fully representative of an antithetic poetry of social anguish and realism was that of the prolific Basque Gabriel Celaya (born Rafael Múgica), bursting with indignation and disgust in *Tranquilamente hablando* (1947) and *Las cosas como son* (1949). Blas de Otero (1916–79) moved from religious anguish in the trad. of Unamuno and Alonso toward a similar social and political poetry in *Pido la paz y la palabra* (1955), a veritable Sp. Communist Manifesto in moving verse. Carlos Bousoño, a distinguished literary critic who worked with Alonso and analyzed Aleixandre's poetry in his doctoral dissertation, began as a poet with *Subida al amor* (1945) and has remained faithful to a metaphysical ideal. José María Valverde, on the other hand, moved from neoclassical and religious to socially committed poetry with *La conquista de este mundo* (1960) and *Años inciertos* (1961).

Major poets who began to publish somewhat later, in the 1950s, incl. Gloria Fuertes (1918–81), Ángel González (b. 1925), Carlos Barral (b. 1928), Jaime Gil de Biedma (b. 1929), José Ángel Valente (b. 1929), Francisco Brines (b. 1932), and Claudio Rodríguez (b. 1934). Among these there was for over 20 years a strong cosmopolitan group centered in Barcelona and writing in Castilian, with the support of the critic Castellet and important publishers. Carlos Barral with his *Metropolitano* (1957) and Jaime Gil de Biedma with *Moralidades* (1966) were perhaps the most representative and important members of this group. Ángel González, from Oviedo, cultivated an ironic detachment culminating in *Procedimientos narrativos* (1972). Brines, from Valencia, published in 1984 a retrospective collection of his own work entitled *Ensayo de una despedida (1960-1977)*, in which meditation on everyday scenes leads to impassioned imagery.

The following constitute a later and even more heterogeneous group: Félix Grande (b. 1937), Carlos Sahagún (b. 1938), Pedro Gimferrer (b. 1945), Antonio Colinas (b. 1946), Guillermo Carnero (b. 1947), Antonio de Villena (b. 1951). Gimferrer, a bilingual Catalan-Castilian poet and critic, achieved a notable and influential success in Castilian with his *Arde el mar* (1966), reflecting his absorption of readings from Lorca to Eliot. Carnero, from Valencia, writes only in Castilian; he has moved from baroque imagery to an exemplary sober discipline in *El azar objetivo* (1975).

A 15-year gap, 1961–76, divides the poetic oeuvre of María Victoria Atencia (Málaga) into two parts. In his prologue to her *Ex libris* (1984) Carnero has testified to the literary maturity of her second period, beginning with *Marta & María* (1976). In the new post-Franco Spain, the poetic voices of women, long absent, are beginning to be heard.

See now BASQUE POETRY; CATALAN POETRY; CHICANO POETRY; GALICIAN POETRY; HEBREW POETRY; HISPANO-ARABIC POETRY; PORTUGUESE POETRY; SPANISH AMERICAN POETRY.

ANTHOLOGIES: *Contemp. Sp. P.* (1945), *Ten Centuries of Sp. P.* (1955), both ed. E. L. Turnbull; *The Heroic Poem of the Sp. Golden Age,* ed. F. Pierce (1947); *Antologia de la poesía lírica española,* ed. E. Moreno Báez (1952); *Antología consultada de la joven poesía española,* ed. F. Ribes (1952); *Sp. Lyrics of the Golden Age,* ed. P. D. Tettenborn (1952); *Penguin Book of Sp. Verse,* ed. J. M. Cohen (1956); *Floresta lírica española,* ed. J. M. Blecua (1957); *Poesía española,* ed. D. Marín (1958); *Veinte años de poesía española (1939–1959)* (1962), *Un cuarto de siglo de poesía española (1939–1964)* (1966), *Nueve novísimos* (1970), all ed. J. M. Castellet; *Ren. and Baroque Poetry of Spain,* ed. E. L. Rivers (1964); *Antología de la nueva poesía española* (1968), *Poetas españoles poscontemporáneos* (1974), ed. J. Batlló; *Diez años de poesía española (1960–1970),* ed. J. O. Jiménez (1972); *La generación poética de 1936,* ed. L. Jiménez Martos (1972); *Textos medievales españoles,* ed. R. Menéndez-Pidal (1976); *Antología de la poesía española (1900–1980),* ed. G. Correa (1980); *Las diosas blancas: antología de la joven poesía española escrita por mujeres,* ed. R. Buenaventura (1985).

HISTORY AND CRITICISM: A. Coster, *Fernando de Herrera* (1908); H. A. Rennert and A. Castro, *Vida de Lope de Vega* (1919); A. F. G. Bell, *Luis de León* (1925); J. Cano, *La poética de Luzán* (1928); K. Vossler, *Lope de Vega und seine Zeit* (1930); J. Baruzi, *St. Jean de la Croix* (1930); A. Valbuena Prat, *La poesía española contemporánea* (1930); E. Joiner Gates, *The Metaphors of Luis de Góngora* (1933); F. Lecoy, *Recherches sur le Libro de buen amor* (1938); R. Menéndez Pidal, *La España del Cid* (1939), *Le epopeya castellana a través de la literatura española* (1946), *Los origenes de las literaturas románicas* (1951); E. A. Peers, *A Hist. of the Romantic Movement in Spain* (1940); W. E. Colford, *Juan Meléndez Valdéss* (1942); A. del Río, *Pedro Salinas* (1942); J. Guillén, "La poética de Bécquer," *Revista Hispanica Moderna* 8 (1942); E. Honig, *García Lorca* (1944); M. Menéndez y Pelayo, *Antología de poetas líricos castellanos* (1945); J. Casalduero, *Jorge Guillén: Cántico* (1946); P. Salinas, *Jorge Manrique, o tradición y originalidad* (1947); G. Díaz-Plaja, *Historia de la poesía lírica española* (1948); R. Lapesa, *La trayectoria poética de Garcilaso* (1948); M. R. Lida de Malkiel, *Juan de Mena, poeta del prerrenacimiento español* (1950), *Two Sp. Masterpieces: The Book of Good Love and The Celestina* (1961); G. Brenan, *Lit. of the Sp. People* (1951); D. Alonso, *Poesía española* (1952), *Poetas españoles contemporáneos* (1952), *Estudios y ensayos gongorinos* (1955), *De los siglos oscuros al de oro* (1958); A. Castro, *La realidad histórica esp.* (1954); F. Cantera, *La canción mozárabe* (1957); E. Asensio, *Poética y realidad en el cancionero peninsular de la edad media* (1957); R. Lapesa, *La obra literaria del marqués de Santillana* (1957); C. D. Ley, *Sp. P. Since 1939* (1962); O. H. Green, *Spain and the Western Trad.* (1963–); J. E. Keller, "Med. Sp. Lit.," in Fisher; J. Lechner, *El compromiso en la poesía española del siglo XX,* 2 v. (1968–75); F. Grande, *Apuntes sobre poesía española de posguerra* (1970); V. García de la Concha, *La poesía española de posguerra* (1973); J. L. Cano, *Lírica española de hoy* (1974); F. Rubio, *Las revistas poéticas españolas (1939–1975)* (1976); M. E. Simmons, "The Sp. Epic," *Heroic Epic and Saga,* ed. F. J. Oinas (1978); *Historia y critica de la literatura española,* ed. F. Rico, 8 v. (1980); A. L. Geist, *La poética de la generación del 27* (1980); A. Carreño, *La dialéctica de la identidad* (1982); A. P. Debicki, *Poetry of Discovery* (1982); S. Daydí-Tolson, *The Post-Civil War Sp. Social Poets* (1983); Navarro; M. H. Persin, *Recent Sp. P. and the Role of the Reader* (1987); *After the War,* ed. J. Wilcox (1988).

E.L.R.

SRI LANKAN POETRY covers work in three langs.: Sinhala poetry, which dates to the 1st c. A.D.; Tamil poetry, which developed a distinctly S. L. identity in the 20th c.; and English poetry, of which a small but significant body of work now exists dating mainly from the mid 20th c.

I. SINHALA POETRY
II. TAMIL POETRY
III. ENGLISH POETRY

I. SINHALA POETRY. A. *The Ancient Period* (1st–9th cs. A.D.). A few rock inscriptions of unrhymed couplets and a more substantial body of graffiti poems from Sigiriya are all that survive. The graffiti are short lyrics in a variety of metrical forms expressing the varied responses of visitors to the magnificent rock fortress of Sigiriya.

B. *The Classical Period* (10th–19th cs.). The earliest extant complete poems are from this period. The *Siyabaslakara*, a 10th-c. treatise on rhet., the *Sasadāvata* (Birth Story of the Hare, 12th c.), the *Muvadevdāvata*, (Birth Story of the Deer), and the *Kavsilumina* (Diadem of Poetry, 13th c. A.D.) are the major works. They are in unrhymed couplets or *gī* (lyric) verse and are strongly influenced by classical Sanskrit theories of poetics.

By the mid 14th c., a literary form known as the *sandēsa* (message poem), in four-lined, end-rhymed stanzas, becomes popular. The author sends a message, usually through a bird, to a god or religious dignitary asking blessings. The form allows the poet to describe the towns, villages, landscape, shrines, rituals, and festivals encountered en route and the poems are thus of considerable literary and sociological interest. The *Mayura* (Peacock), the *Tisara* (Goose), and the *Sělalihini* (Mynah) *Sandēsas* are 15th-c. works. The *Kāvyasēkara*, the *Guttila Kāvya*, the *Budugunālaṃkāraya* and *Lōvādasaṃgrahaya* are other Buddhist works of this period.

From the 16th c. onward, the Portuguese, Dutch, and British in turn gained increasing control of the island. Literary activity declined. Although the poets of the Mātara School (late 18th c.) kept the trad. nominally alive, nothing of significance appears until the 20th c.

C. *The Modern Period* (20th c.). Nationalistic movements around the turn of the century stimulated literary activity again, much of it Buddhist, classicist, revivalist, and didactic. The 20th c. also saw the growth of a secular poetry, nationalist in theme and traditional in form. By the Thirties, Munidāsa Kumāranatunge had begun a movement for lang. reform, termed *Hela*, to rid Sinhala of Sanskrit influences. Kumāranatunge's critical writings had considerable impact, and his poems for children introduced a new simplicity into Sinhala poetry.

The major breakthrough came with the introduction of free verse (*nisandäs kavi*). G. B. Senanayake had experimented with unrhymed verseforms as early as 1945 in his poems in *Paligānīma* (Revenge). However, it was Siri Gunasinghe in *Mas Lē Näti Äta* (Bones Without Flesh or Blood, 1956), *Abhiṇikmana* (Renunciation, 1958), and *Ratu Käkulu* (Red Buds, 1962) who established and popularized the form. Gunasinghe together with others such as Gunadasa Amerasekera and Wimal Dissanayake, who were part of the literary world of the University of Peradeniya in the Fifties, became known as the Peradeniya poets. Influenced by the literary theories of Am. New Criticism, they were at first criticized as Westernized ivory tower aesthetes, but their work soon gained acceptance. Their writings gave a new vitality and flexibility to the lang. Ediriweera Sarachcharanda, the foremost critic and theorist for the group, also revolutionized the theater with his poetic dramas *Manamē* (1956) and *Siṃhabāhu* (1958).

The Seventies saw a fresh burst of poetic activity by writers whose works reflect a strong social concern. However, their evocative use of lang. and the control and confidence with which they draw on classical and folk as well as foreign literatures, give their work an energy that overrides the didacticism. Mahagama Sekera's *Heṭa Irak Pāyayi* (Tomorrow a Sun Will Rise, 1971), *Nomiyami* (I Will Not Die, 1973), and *Prabuddha* (1976); Parakrama Kodituwakku's *Akīkaru Putrayakugē Lōkayak* (The World of a Disobedient Son, 1974) and *Aluṭ Minihek Äviṭ* (A New Man Has Come, 1976); and Monica Ruwanpathirana's *Tahanam Dēsayakin* (From a Forbidden World, 1972) and *Obē Yeheliya Äya Gähäniya* (Your Friend, She is Woman, 1975) are some of the important works of this group.

The dynamic energy of the Seventies slackens perceptibly by the Eighties. The civil war, disturbing and demoralizing but strangely distant because fought in the North, leaves hardly any mark on the poetry. The creative impetus seems to shift away from poetry to drama. R.O.

II. TAMIL POETRY. While the Tamil presence in Sri Lanka goes back to very early times, Tamil lit. gained a distinct Sri Lankan identity only much later. The earliest reference to a S. L. Tamil poet is in the *Sangam* lit. of the 3d c. A.D., where verses attributed to Putatēvanar with the prefix *Elathu* (Lanka) appear. In 1310 A.D., *Caracotimalai* by Pōcaraca Panditār was presented in the court of the Sinhala king Parākramabāhu III at Dambadeniya. These are the only references for the early period.

The flourishing Tamil kingdom in the Jaffna peninsula (14th–17th cs.) gave rise to several poetical works. The best known was *Rakuvamcam* by Aracakēcari, the poet laureate. Under colonial rule the proselytizing activities of Christian missionaries spawned a genre of religious poetry which was given further impetus by the introduction of printing.

Early S. L. Tamil poetry had traditionally been seen merely as an extension of Indian Tamil writing, but by the 1940s a renaissance occurred, when many young poets began to emphasize their S. L.

identity. A distinctly different Tamil poetry soon evolved. Nantāran, Kantacami, and Mahakavi are important poets of this period. An emphasis on simplicity, colloquial meters, and concrete visual images is the hallmark of this Lankan Tamil poetry.

When Sinhala was made the official lang. in 1956, a new political consciousness evolved among the Tamils. Three schools of poetry emerged. The first was nationalist, in support of a Tamil Federal state. The second group called themselves "Progressives," were influenced by left-wing ideologies, and advocated a radical transformation of S. L. society, both Sinhala and Tamil. The third refused to be identified with either group and wrote a very individualized poetry. Modern forms such as free verse were introduced, and poets and poetry proliferated.

By the 1970s, Tamil political aspirations for a separate state led to guerilla war. Thereafter, the experience for S. L. Tamil poets was blood, tears, violence, battle, exile, death, and life amidst death. The new "war poetry" reflected these realities. S. L. Tamil poetry now charts its own course and is totally different from Indian Tamil writing unexposed to such experiences. The major poets of the 1980s are Jeyapālan, Cēran, Celyan, Yēcuraca, Vicayēntran, and Vilvaratinam.

Love and war had been the basic themes of early Sangam lit. Once Tamil military exploits ceased after colonial conquest, war poetry died out. The trad. has been revived in the past decade. However, new political developments after the Indo-Lankan peace accord may evoke yet other changes in S. L. Tamil writing. D.B.S.J.

III. ENGLISH POETRY in Sri Lanka develops its own identity in the mid 20th c. The poetry of the past two decades clearly reflects a growing confidence and maturity. Lakkdasa Wikkramasinghe in his pioneering work boldly experimented with the rhythms of Lankan Eng. *Lustre Poems* (1965) has a dynamic energy, while later works such as *The Grasshopper Gleaming* (1976) show his growing control of his medium. Patrick Fernando's *Selected Poems* (1984) is more formal in style. He is an accomplished poet at ease in the Eng. lang. Yasmine Gooneratne's *Word, Bird and Motif* (1971) and *Lizard's Cry* (1972) reveal her flair for the satiric mode, where her control of tone and sensitivity to the nuances of words have full play. Anne Ranasinghe's *Poems* (1971) and *Plead Mercy* (1975) provide sharp insights into a range of personal experiences that bridge two worlds. Basil Fernando in *A New Era to Emerge* (1973) and Jean Arasanayagam in *Apocalypse* (1983) and *A Colonial Inheritance* (1985) write movingly of the current realities of S. L. life. The readership for Eng. poetry in Sri Lanka is small but influential. It also has the potential of an international readership. R.O.

GENERAL: M. Wickramasinghe, *Mod. Sinhalese Lit.*, tr. E. R. Sarachchandra (1949); C. E. Godakumbura, *Sinhalese Lit.* (1955); K. S. Sivakumaran, *Tamil Writing in Sri Lanka* (1964); R. Obeyesekere, *Sinhalese Writing and the New Critics* (1974); K. Sivathamby, *Tamil Lit. in Eelam* (1978).

ANTHOLOGIES: *Poetry from the Sinhalese*, tr. G. Keyt (1939); *Sigiri Graffiti*, ed. and tr. S. Paranavitarne (1955); *An Anthol. of Cl. Sinhalese Lit.*, ed. C. Reynolds (1970); *Poetry of Sri Lanka*, ed. Y. Gooneratne, *JSAL* v. 12 (1976); *Mod. Writing in Sinhala*, ed. R. Obeyesekere and C. Fernando (1978); *Marantul Valvōm [We live amidst Death]: A Collection of Tamil War Poetry 1977–1985* (1985); *Sinhala and Tamil Writing from Sri Lanka*, ed. R. Obeyesekere, *JSAL* v. 22 (1987). R.O.; D.B.S.J.

SUMERIAN POETRY. Written in cuneiform script, S. texts of an undeniably poetic nature first appear around 2600 B.C. S. lit. is preserved in a large number of clay tablets, most of them school exercises, since the training of administrative scribes included learning traditional poetry. Most of the preserved texts date from the 18th c. B.C. or shortly before, although some of them are copies of poems attested in tablets dating from the Ur III dynasty (2112–2004 B.C.) or even earlier. Tablets written after the 18th c., when S. had become an extinct lang., are mostly compilations of excerpts of earlier texts or imitations of them and were used in liturgical services in Mesopotamian temples until the 2d c. B.C.

Copious native lexical compilations allow the meaning of S. words to be determined with a precision unusual in ancient langs., but our present knowledge of S. phonology lacks the precision necessary to determine metrical patterns with confidence. In particular, vowel quality and quantity, as well as the accentual system, remain largely unknown. Attempts to find metrical patterns based on vowel length and stress should therefore be viewed with skepticism. The number of syllables, however, presents definite regularities. Large portions of poems (rarely entire ones) are written in lines of 8+5 syllables, but other types of verse are also known; fillers and alterations of the normal morphological forms keep the syllable count within the intended limit. Alliteration and assonantal rhyme are known, but sparingly used. A strophic type common in laudatory hymns consists of two identical sections, the first preceded by a descriptive epithet or by nothing, the second by the name of the praised one. From a song to the Moon god, patron of dairies:

en šu sikil-la dug.šakìr-e hé du$_7$
níg šu-dug$_4$-ga-zu an-ra ^{d}en-líl-ra
ša-mu-un-ne-sag$_9$
^{d}nanna en šu sikil-la dug.šakìr-e hé du$_7$
níg šu-dug$_4$-ga-zu an-ra ^{d}en-líl-ra
ša-mu-un-ne-sag$_9$

Oh Lord, you made the butter churn
fit the pure hands,

you made your foods a delight for
Heaven and for [the god] Enlil.
Oh Moon, oh Lord, you made (etc.).

A favorite form of strophe consists of a fixed frame with slots filled by members of a lexical set (e.g. parts of a sacred boat or plants grazed by sheep) accompanied by descriptive or laudatory phrases. Some copies of hymns contain rubrics of uncertain meaning, but they are probably musical since several start with the word for "chord" or "string." Very late copies of liturgical poems occasionally include notations that may be intended to guide the recitation or singing of the text. Several native designations identify the various poetic genres. In most cases they seem to refer to the performance of the poem or its function rather than its formal structure (note, however, *šìr-gíd-da*, "long song").

S. poetic lang. is characterized by various types of parallelism, refrains, repetitions, and figurative speech. Stereotyped images, formulaic passages, and traditional expressions are among its major components. Internal analysis, confirmed by textual history, indicates that S. p. existed primarily as oral trad. With very rare exceptions, the poems are anonymous. A compilation of songs in praise of the shrines of the major cities is attributed to Enheduanna, daughter of king Sargon (2334–2279 B.C.), and some self-laudatory songs are said to have been composed by the kings themselves. No term for "poet" is known. The texts were intended for public recitation by the *nar*, "musician," or, in the case of cultic songs, by the *gala*, "cantor," rather than for private reading.

The most extensive poems are narrative. Some deal with legendary heroes from the city of Uruk; five belong to the epic cycle of Gilgamesh (episodes from them were later included in the Akkadian Gilgamesh epic) and three to the cycle of Lugalbanda and Enmerkar. Others are mythological texts about divine beings (e.g. "Inanna's Descent into Hades," "Dumuzi's Dream," "Birth of the Moon God"). Poems that should be considered court lit. include royal hymns—known for practically all kings of the Ur III, Isin, and Larsa dynasties (21st to 18th c. B.C.)—and contests (*a-da-mìn*) between personifications of natural entities (e.g. "Winter and Summer," "Tree and Reed," "Silver and Copper"). Songs in praise of deities or temples are particularly numerous. The goddess Inanna is the central figure in many of the narratives. Political events inspired laments over the destruction of cities; the oldest refers to the destruction of Nippur by Naram-Sin, ca. 2230 B.C., the most recent to a similar event during Ishme-Dagan's reign, ca. 1940 B.C. After the 16th c. B.C., liturgical laments over the destruction of shrines are the dominant form of lit. Other types of texts include agricultural songs, a lullaby from the end of the 3d millennium B.C., dirges for individuals, poetic letters, and love songs. It is difficult at times to decide if a text, e.g. a didactic one, should be considered poetry or prose. The average length of a poem is 300–400 lines; but epic texts can be longer and there are much shorter poems, esp. among hymns and songs. What contributes to making S. p. interesting, besides its early date, is the presence in it of forms and themes (e.g. the Flood) that are echoed in the Bible.

ANTHOLOGIES IN TRANSLATION: S. N. Kramer, *Ancient Near Eastern Texts*, ed. J. B. Pritchard (1969); M. Cohen, *S. Hymnology* (1981); D. Wolkstein and S. N. Kramer, *Inanna Queen of Heaven and Earth* (1983); T. Jacobsen, *The Harps that Once* (1987).

STUDIES: M. Bielitz, "Melismen," and W. Heimpel, "Observations on Rhythmical Structure," *Orientalia* 39 (1970); H. Sauren, "Zur poetischen Struktur," *Ugaritische Forschungen* 3 (1971); H. Limet, "Essai de poétique," *Alter Orient und Altes Testament* 25 (1976); C. Wilcke, "Formale Gesichtspunkte," *Assyriological Studies* 20 (1976); M. Civil, "Feeding Dumuzi's Sheep," *Am. Oriental Series* 67 (1987). M.C.

SWAHILI POETRY. S. p., traceable to Ar. models of Islamic verse, developed as an African poetic form in 19th-c. coastal East Africa. Earlier S. mss. go back to the early 18th c., with the earliest, *al-Hamziya*, a S. version of the Ar. poem *Umm al-Qura* (Mother of Villages [Medina]), in *takhmis* (long-measure verse) form, actually presented as a S. interlinear tr. of the Ar. version. *Takhmis*, a term derived from the Ar. "to make five," denotes 3-line stanzas with 2 original hemistichs added, rhyming *aaab*. Sheikh Saiyid Abdallah bin Nasir (ca. 1720–1820), a Saiyid (Muslim) from Hadramawt as was the author of *al-Hamziya*, used the *takhmis* form in the renowned story of the legendary hero Liyongo. This S. poetic form later gave rise to quatrain (*shairi*) and serenade- or praise-song (*t'umbuizi*) forms. The most important prosodic features of S. p. are rhyme and fixed patterns of syllabic measure. The earliest extant *t'umbuizi* are in indeterminate long measure of at least 15 syllables.

Another early S. poetic form, *tendi*, has lines of four short hemistichs; the first three rhyme together and the fourth carries a rhyme repeated as the terminal rhyme of each stanza. *Tendi* (singular form *utendi*) are long narrative poems embodying oral trad. and circumstantial accounts of historical and contemp. events. For the S. people, *the* vehicle of hist. is poetry. Early S. p. was written in Ar. script, accommodating Swahili's extra vowels and non-Ar. consonants by adding diacritics to the Ar. characters. Other versions of the exploits of Liyongo have been done in this form which in modern times has been used to document, for example, the struggles for independence in Kenya and Tanzania, and the Maji-Maji rebellion of 1905.

The most popular S. verseform for short themes of topical interest is *shairi*, originally chanted on the island of Lamu in the context of traditional *gungu* dances. Akin to the quatrain in form, *shairi* contrasts with the indigenous *mavugo,* celebration songs without patterned rhyme or meter. *Shairi* are sung at the "great national dances of the Mombasi S.," such as the procession to the groom's house on the eve of a wedding, the celebration of the S. new year in Mombasa, and at the *gungu* marriage dance itself. *Shairi* may be as short as one line or as long as 19. Each line is self-contained in such a way that longer poems ingeniously reiterate the same theme through riddles, wordplay, and homonymy. The *shairi* form is most often associated with the poet Muyaka bin Haji al-Ghassaniy (1776–1840) of Mombasa, who is credited with extending S. p. to commentary on contemp. events, i.e. with secularizing the genre.

Perhaps the S. poet most widely known in the West is Shaaban Robert (1909–62). Ironically, though his poetry is conventional and adheres to traditional forms, he extended the range of S. lit. by borrowing Western forms such as the essay, novella, and autobiography. 20th-c. S. p. continues to be conservative; some is still written in Ar. script. Julius Nyerere, while President of Tanzania, brought poetry into the political arena by encouraging poets such as Mathias Mnyampala (1919–69) to stage public performances of S. song p. (*ngonjera*), hoping that such poetry would teach "good conduct, indigenous culture, and national politics."

As a poet himself, Nyerere brought innovative practices to S. p, introducing enjambment and modes of free verse that had been frowned upon by traditional S. poets, who saw free verse (*guni*) as defective. More recent poets eschew the negative aspects of such creativity and, like Nyerere, admit unconventional rhyme schemes and odd numbers of syllables, departing from the conventionalized norms of the 19th c. In the late 1960s, a new breed of poet began to emerge, exemplified by Mnyampala, who began to incorporate foreign terms in his works even within traditional forms—to the extent of producing *shairi* of three Eng. lines and a fourth in broken Ar.

S. song p. of the nationalist public type of *ngonjera* exists alongside poetry chanted in S. musical clubs, which is topical, deeply allusive, and close to oral trad. The female singer Siti binti Saad (1880–1950) was widely known for her singing and compositional abilities in that mode.

Ahmad Nassir bin Juma Bhalo (1937–) of Mombasa is a S. poet whose poetry is within the traditional mode, yet its performance and composition on the radio is contemporary. His works are chanted by a professional singer to a melodic pattern based on Ar. modal scales. The verses are gnomic, the poet's responsibility oratorical. Bhalo may be seen to be influenced by both Muyaka and Shaaban Robert, yet his works were written to be read and sung. Notable among the modern poets who, with Mnyampala, have departed from the strictures of Muyaka's *shairi* form are E. Kezilahabi and Ibrahim Hussein, who present their own themes, personal sentiments, and philosophies.

One other form of S. p. is the *wimbo* (sonnet, ballad, lyric, hymn). Such lyric S. p. may be in *shairi* meter or use 12-syllable lines with a caesura occurring after either the 4th or (most commonly) the 6th syllable. (Some *wimbo* have 16-syllable lines.) *Wimbo* are *never* written. They may preserve oral trads. or be composed for contemp. events (e.g. the *mavugo* wedding songs), but in either case they represent a form of oral S. p., while the more classical forms were written to be sung. According to Allen (1971), "the composer thought in the tune and the sense follows the tune," while at the same time the music of the poetry is secondary to the form and content. The musical demands on S. p. are thus less than those of text. Music is used to heighten the effect of the poetry—indeed, *tendi* are often thought of as heightened speech—which is frequently sung by an unaccompanied soloist using a nasal tone and a narrow range of pitches. A single melody can be used for many *tendi.*

One fact often overlooked about S. p. is the importance of women in most S. verse. One of the most revered poems is that by Mwana Kupona (d. ca. 1860), written by a woman for her daughter and intended to be read by women as a guide to proper behavior. Women scholars have also been instrumental in preserving classical S. p. mss., since when such mss. exist they are held by the women of the house. Most oral trad. is in the heads of women, and it is the women who are acclaimed for the best recitations (Allen).

Permeating all forms of S. p. is the notion that recitation is appropriate when a suitable occasion arises. Poetry is an impromptu part of S. life, not dependent on formal settings yet appropriate to them (as in celebratory contexts). Features of S. p. such as rhyme extend to jokes and riddles as well as *wimbo.* S. p. is also an instrument used to comment upon society's problems. It may be composed by anyone, and most people can and do so when they need to. It is common to see *shairi* in the daily papers, submitted in the trad. of "letters to the editor" as 4-line stanzas beginning with phrases such as "Give me a space in your daily, editor" (*unipe nafasi mwako gazetini mhariri*). The noted political scientist Ali Mazrui, commenting on the integral role of poetry in S. daily life, tells of letters he received from people who had heard that two of his sons had gone blind: these letters were in the form of topical *shairi.* He responded appropriately by composing his "Ode to the Optic Nerve."

The recent signs of S. p. adapting in form, content, and lang. to modern modes of presentation (e.g. newspaper and radio) indicate that the genre remains vital. Tightly constrained cl. verse-forms seem to be giving way to more flexible ones. The now-common use of Roman script is conducive to the introduction of words from Eng. and other langs. As both Kenya and Tanzania evolve their national cultures, it is likely that S. p. will continue to be a prime mode of literary expression by coastal people. The incorporation of *tendi* within genres such as drama, where aspects such as dialogue make it natural, may be expected to increase. Indeed, S. p. may be expected to be incorporated increasingly in the other literary forms to which S. writers are now turning their attention.

COLLECTIONS: Muyaka bin Haji, *Diwani ya*, ed. W. Hichens (1940)—collected works; A. Nassir, *Poems from Kenya*, ed. L. Harries (1966); *Waimbaji wa Juzi* [Singers of Yesteryear], ed. A. A. Jahadhmy et al. (1966); J. W. T. Allen, *Diwani ya Shaaban*, ed., (1968), *Tendi*—6 examples of cl. S. verseforms with tr. and notes (1971); M. Shabaan et al., *Malenga wa Mvita*, ed. S. Chiraghdin (1971); *Islamic Poetry*, ed. and tr. J. Knappert (1971), *An Anthol. of S. Love Poetry* (1972); *Muyaka*, ed. M. H. Abdulaziz (1979)—19th-c. popular S. p; *Johari za Kiswahili* (1960)—series of edited *tenzi* pub. by the East African Lit. Bureau.

HISTORY AND CRITICISM: L. Harries, *S. P.* (1962), "S. Lit. in the National Context," *RNL* 11 (1971); J. Knappert, *Traditional S. P.* (1967); *Uchambuzi wa Maandishi ya Kiswahili* [Analysis of S. Writings], ed. F. Topan (1971); "Intro." to Spec. Iss. on S. Verbal Arts, ed. C. M. Eastman, *RAL* (1986). C.M.E.

SWEDISH POETRY. Very little is known about the earliest S. p., since none has been recorded. Rune inscriptions show, however, that *fornyrðislag*, the Edda stanza, was known, and possibly also *dróttkvætt*, the cl. skaldic verseform. An extensive oral poetry existed, comprising pagan hymns and mythological verse. There may be traces of Sweden's heroic poetry in *Beowulf* and in the skaldic poem *Ynglingatal.*

The chief monuments of medieval S. p. are the folk ballads, at their height in the 13th and 14th cs. The S. ballad approximates the Scottish in spirit and structure. The versified chronicles, from *Erikskrönikan* (Eric's Chronicle, 1320–21) to *Stora rimkrönikan* (The Great Rhymed Chronicle, ca. 1500), are important productions in *knittelvers.* Of the known poets, Tomas af Strängnäs (d. 1443) adumbrated a national trad. with his patriotic lyrics, like *Frihetsvisan* (The Song of Freedom). The 16th c. (1511–1611) produced mostly didactic poetry, typified by the first S. attempt at drama, the biblical play *Tobiae comedia* (ca. 1550) ascribed to Olavus Petri (1493–1552).

In the 17th c. (1611–1718), S. poets aimed to create a vernacular lit. matching the achievements of antiquity. With his epoch-making allegorical-didactic epic *Hercules* (1648; pub. 1658), Georg Stiernhielm (1598–1672) demonstrated the aptness of S. for hexameter verse. Stiernhielm nationalized the Greco-Roman gods and introduced vivid personified abstractions, thereby avoiding excessive artificiality. The resultant merging of Classicism and Gothicism—S. nationalism—was to remain a shaping force in S. p. until the end of the 19th c. Stiernhielm's art was broadly realistic, a trait that may derive from his acquaintance with Dutch poets, esp. Jacob Cats. He also introduced the sonnet, composed in alexandrines, a practice abandoned only by the romantics. Samuel Columbus (1642–79), who with Urban Hiärne (1641–1724) and others made up the first S. literary coterie, was Stiernhielm's chief follower, but his lyric verse, such as *Odae Sveticae* (1674), is more melodious. Intimately personal as well as national was the inspiration of Lars Wivallius (1605–69), first in a fairly continuous line of unschooled singers whose popular lyrics have enriched S. p. He was followed by Lars Johansson, or Lucidor (1638–74), whose forte was the convivial song, where he provides a link between Wivallius and Bellman, the 18th-c. virtuoso of the genre.

Baroque poetry found a practitioner in Gunno Eurelius Dahlstierna (1661–1709), whose allegorical epic *Kunga Skald* (The King's Poem, 1697) introduced ottava rima into S. p., also characteristically in alexandrines. The poem, however, lacks narrative unity, and the uneven marinistic style fails to sustain the mood. Later, Samuel Triewald (1688–1743) advocated Fr. neoclassicism, while the Finn Jacob Frese (1691–1729) became Sweden's first significant subjective poet. Frese's Christian epic *Passionstankar* (Thoughts on the Passion, 1728) expresses profound religious feeling. As transformed by the romantics, Frese's introspective lyricism became an enduring trad. in S. p. Johan Runius (1679–1713) was a virtuoso rhymer celebrating bourgeois jocundity. Triewald, Frese, and Runius represent the chief styles of the upcoming century: Fr. neoclassicism, sentimental romanticism, and S.-Carolinian poetic realism.

In the 18th c., neoclassic principles were *de rigueur* both in epic, with its obligatory alexandrines, and in drama. Olof von Dalin (1708–63) produced both a tragedy and an epic in the prescribed style, but modern readers prefer his ballads and epigrammatic satires. In the 1750s Hedvig Charlotta Nordenflycht (1718–63) established a literary *salon* in order to further refine the poetic standards of Dalin. Its principal habitués were Finnish-born Gustaf Filip Creutz (1731–85) and Gustaf Fredrik Gyllenborg (1731–1808). Creutz's *Atis och Camilla* (1761) is a lovely pastoral poem. Gyllenborg was more didactic; his best work, *Människans elände* (The Misery of Man, 1761), shows traces of Rousseau. The poetry of Carl Michael Bellman (1740–1809) is peculiarly individual as well as national. It exhibits a wide gamut of moods, from burlesque humor to dark melancholy; but Bellman is best known, and loved, for his *joie de vivre.* He was also a superb narrator and created an unforgettable gallery of comic types.

The Gustavian Age (1772–1802) was *par excellence* the age of Enlightenment and of Fr. artistic taste, enforced by such literary societies as *Utile Dulci* and *Svenska akademien* (The S. Academy, est. 1786). But a preromantic movement inspired by

Rousseau, Eng. preromantics, Klopstock, and *Sturm und Drang* acquired considerable influence. The satirist Johan Henrik Kellgren (1751–95), initially an advocate of neoclassicism, with *Den nya skapelsen* (The New Creation, 1789) expressed a profound idealism foreshadowing the romantic age. By contrast, Anna Maria Lenngren (1755–1817) was the voice of common sense, treating everyday subjects in a simple style that makes her verse readable even today. Among preromantic Gustavians, Bengt Lidner (1757–93) demonstrated an impressive formal virtuosity in *Grevinnan Spastaras död* (The Death of Countess Spastara, 1783), and the Finn Frans Michael Franzén (1772–1847) developed an imaginative, musical poetic idiom, which he used in *Människans anlete* (The Human Countenance, 1793) as the vehicle of an aesthetic-religious idealism.

The 19th c. initiated a great period in S. p. Ger. romanticism and philosophical idealism were the dominant influences. Through Germany, S. poets became acquainted with Shakespeare and Ren. Fr. and It. authors. Accordingly, the new poetry was exceedingly varied in form. The first group of romantics belonged to *Auroraförbundet* (The Aurora League), founded at Uppsala in 1807. Its members came to be called Phosphorists, from the name of their periodical, *Phosphoros* (1810–13). Per Daniel Amadeus Atterbom (1790–1855), who was inspired by the Jena school of romanticism, emerged with *Blommorna* (The Flowers, 1812–37) as the chief Phosphorist poet. His most ambitious work, *Lycksalighetens ö* (The Isle of Bliss, 1824–27), is an allegorical fairytale play which embodies the confict between aestheticism and an ethical ideal. With its imaginative fervor and cl. form, the poetry of Erik Johan Stagnelius (1793–1823), one of the most gifted S. poets, is related to Phosphorism. The lyric cycle *Liljor i Saron* (Lilies of Sharon, 1821–23) alternates between world-weary mysticism and erotic passion. His greatest work, *Bacchanterna* (The Bacchae, 1822), treats the fate of Orpheus in Cl. Gr. style, dramatizing the contrast between spiritual rapture and sensual intoxication. Known for his ability to convey intense feeling and to concretize abstractions, Stagnelius—who epitomizes the subjective mode in S. p.—has been very influential.

The second group of S. romantics were associated with *Götiska förbundet* (The Gothic League), which called for a national literary revival. Its head, Erik Gustaf Geijer (1783–1847), treated regional subjects in a simple style. It was Esaias Tegnér (1782–1846), one of the foremost S. poets, who came closest to realizing the Gothicist program. Drawing upon the Heidelberg school of romanticism and Ger. classicism, Tegnér achieved a new national poetry. His most important works are *Nattvardsbarnen* (The Children of the Lord's Supper, 1820), a religious-didactic narrative in hexameter verse influenced by Goethe's *Hermann und Dorothea*, and *Frithiofs saga* (1825), his greatest achievement. Despite a lack of historical verisimilitude, the virile, courtly character of Frithiof became an instant idol. The poem is a free rendering of an Old Icelandic saga. Its form, a cycle of 24 romances in various meters, is modeled on Oehlenschläger's *Helge*. Tegnér shows remarkable skill at evoking the changing moods of the story by varying the stanzaic forms and metrical patterns. In his masterful handling of Homeric hexameter, he was a worthy heir to Stiernhielm. The 1830s and 1840s produced only one original romantic, Carl Johan Love Almquist (1793–1866), a bizarre and exotic writer inspired by Byron whose poems are notable for their free-verse qualities and emotional wizardry. His chief work, *Törnrosens bok* (The Book of the Briar Rose, 1832–51), contains lyric, narrative, and dramatic pieces—and prose. His *Songes*, with their artless form, suggestive music, and gripping tone, link Almquist with Stagnelius, both forerunners of poetic modernism in Sweden.

In the sensibility of the great Finnish poet Johan Ludvig Runeberg (1804–77), realism and romanticism go hand in hand. Of his narrative poems may be mentioned *Elgskyttarne* (The Elkhunters, 1832), in hexameters, and the somber *Kung Fjalar* (1844), his best work, in which influences from Nordic myth, Ossian, and Cl. antiquity are merged. But the verseforms, modeled on Nordic meters, are his own creation. Runeberg is best known for his immortal *Fänrik Ståls sägner* (The Tales of Ensign Stål, 1848–60), a narrative-lyric cycle. *Idyll och epigram* (1830–33), with its laconic verses in trochaic meter, contains strikingly original lyrics.

After two relatively barren decades, in the 1870s Carl Snoilsky and Viktor Rydberg ushered in a period of new creativity. Snoilsky (1841– 1903) belonged to *Namnlösa Sällskapet* (The Nameless Society, est. 1860), whose realistic poetic program was inspired by Runeberg and contemp. Norwegian poetry. His *Dikter* (Poems, 1869) demonstrates great versatility and a joyous love of life and freedom. But his later poetry is richer, combining, as in "Afrodite och Sliparen" (Aphrodite and the Knife-Grinder, 1883), social awareness with personal moods. Through his blend of romantic idealism, Cl. form, and national inspiration, Rydberg (1828–95) became a successor to Stiernhielm and Tegnér. With *Dikter* (1882, 1891), however, his reflective poetry acquired a distinctly modern note. "Den nya Grottesången" (The New Song of Grotti, 1891), launching fiery imprecations against industrial slavery, typifies his later work.

The best poet of the 1880s was August Strindberg (1849–1912), who had a first-rate lyrical talent. By its flair for actuality and its free, careless rhythms, Strindberg's poetry effected a break with the late romantic style. His bold imagery was to be much emulated in the 1890s. *Dikter på vers och prosa* (Poems in Verse and Prose, 1883) and *Ordalek och småkonst* (Word-Play and Minor Art, 1902–05) contain a world of impressions, moods, and visions. Urban scenes coexist with family idylls, while poems like "Chrysaëtos" and "Holländarn" (The Dutchman, 1902) resonate with chords of passion. With its irregular rhythm and scientific imagery, his hymn to the female body in "The Dutchman" was significant for the future. Like Stagnelius and Almquist, Strindberg helped pave the way for the poetic modernism of the postwar period. Of other poets of the 1880s, Ola Hansson (1860–1925) renounced realism in an attempt, inspired by Poe, Nietzsche, and Mallarmé, to penetrate beneath appearances. This endeavor was facilitated by a superb sense of rhythm.

In the 1890s, S. p. experienced a veritable renascence. Though the new poets adhered to the minute observation and psychological analysis of the naturalists, the renascence was decidedly neoromantic: beauty, imagination, and self were apotheosized. Moreover, the decade evinced, by its interest in regional poetry and historical subjects, a desire to rediscover its roots and redefine the nation's identity. The poets practiced a variety of forms and, in romantic fashion, aimed to create a grand style.

Four figures—Heidenstam, Levertin, Karlfeldt, and Fröding—were the vehicles of this poetic renewal. With his first collection, *Vallfart och vandringsår* (Pilgrimage and Wander-Years, 1888), Verner von Heidenstam (1859–1940), originally a painter, created an epoch in S. p. Its impressionistic, richly visual style replete with baroque images and daring coinings—Heidenstam later called it "imaginative naturalism"—would have been impossible without the example of Strindberg. In *Dikter* (1895)—supported critically by *Renässans* (Renascence, 1889) and *Pepitas bröllop* (Pepita's Wedding, 1890), both of which repudiated "shoemaker realism"—his central themes appeared: the glories of the imagination, of his native region, and of his country. These were also the basis of *Ett folk* (One People, 1920), a narrative cycle celebrating a S. ideal of chivalry and heroism. Oscar Levertin (1862–1906) was the most romantic of the new poets. The main themes of his work, love and death, are treated in a richly textured style influenced by the Eng. Pre-Raphaelites. Erik Axel Karlfeldt (1864–1931) was the voice of his native region, Dalecarlia, whose landscape, people, and customs he presented in *Fridolins visor* (Fridolin's Songs, 1898) and *Fridolins lustgård* (Fridolin's Pleasure Garden, 1901).

Gustaf Fröding (1860–1911) is one of the greatest lyric poets of Sweden. Already *Guitarr och dragharmonika* (Guitar and Concertina, 1891), critically prepared for by his essay *Om humor* (On Humor, 1890), evidenced a mature talent. It was precisely its brilliant and contagious humor that made this collection stand out. *Nya dikter* (New Poems, 1894) also contained serious, even somber poems, such as "Bibliska fantasier" (Biblical Fantasies), with their dark *Weltschmerz.* But only in *Stänk och flikar* (Splashes and Rags, 1896) and *Nytt och gammalt* (New and Old Pieces, 1897) does Fröding lay bare his soul—in Nietzschean visions, paeans to pagan beauty, and intimate confessions like "Narkissos." Here also, in "Sagan om Gral" (The Story of the Grail), he makes his first attempt at a catharsis of life's paradoxes by means of metaphysical humor. Fröding is the last great figure in the S. trad. of spontaneous realistic verse which originated in Wivallius. His broad appeal is chiefly due to his naked intensity and the innate skill with which he exploits the lyric potentialities of the S. lang. This lang., with its undulating rhythm, rich modulation, and great variety of expressive vowel sounds, is admirably suited for lyric poetry, and not surprisingly the strength of S. p. lies precisely in this genre. S. is esp. effective for expressing moods of passion and grotesque humor, and Bellman and Fröding demonstrate a prodigious aptitude for both. The latter could produce the subtlest nuance of melody, tone, and mood by conjuring with rhyme, rhythm, and sound effects.

The writers who appeared after 1900 inherited the realism of the 1880s along with neoromanticism, but they worked out their own forms of expression. Bo Bergman (1869–1967) created a new style marked by clarity, a colloquial idiom, and simple rhythms. With *Marionetterna* (The Puppets, 1903) he initiated an urban poetry in the modern manner. Vilhelm Ekelund (1880–1949) showed a preference for unrhymed verse and free rhythms *à la* Pindar, Hölderlin, and Strindberg in his reflective verse. Anders Österling (1884–1981) adopted in *Idyllernas bok* (The Book of Idylls, 1917) a moderate poetic realism inspired by the Eng. Georgians.

World War I imbued S. p. with pessimism and religious questing. In *Ångest* (Anguish, 1916), Pär Lagerkvist (1891–1975) expressed moods of anxiety in an unadorned, unrhythmical verse of striking novelty. His manifesto *Ordkonst och bildkonst* (Verbal and Pictorial Art, 1913) had announced a radical modernism related to Ekelund's experiments and to expressionism in painting. Anticipating the Swedo-Finnish Modernists, Lagerkvist inaugurated the modernist movement in S. p. The evolutionary humanism of Erik Blomberg (1894–1965), whose Faustian lyric confession *Den fångne guden* (The Captive God, 1927) inspired younger writers, became an important rallying-point for poets in an age of religious skepticism. During the 1920s the melancholy idyll, related to Österling's poetry, was the dominant genre. In the work of Erik Lindorm (1889–1941), a proletarian poet of city life, the bourgeois idyll was dissolved. Birger Sjöberg (1885–1929), a troubadour of disillusion, introduced a new spirit and style. Sjöberg's *Kriser och kransar* (Crises and Laurel Wreaths, 1926) expressed postwar anxiety in an idiom using slang and jargon in discordant counterpoint with more conventional diction.

The definite breakthrough of modernism—the devel. of which constitutes a central movement in 20th-c. S. p.—came with the appearance in 1929 of the anthol. *Fem unga* (Five Young Poets), two of whose contributors, Harry Martinson (1904–78) and Artur Lundkvist (b. 1906), should be noted. These writers, whose program found a nonliterary complement in a primitivism inspired by D. H. Lawrence and Freudian psychology, reinforced Lagerkvist's emphasis on immediacy of poetic expression by demanding the use of objective visual imagery, a doctrine derived from the Am. imagists. The poetry of Karin Boye (1900–41), while spiritually akin to primitivist modernism, is fraught with idealism and an uncompromising ethos. Gunnar Ekelöf (1907–68), who started as a surrealist, further elaborated the modernist technique by employing musical principles of poetic structure, nonlogical syntax, and verbal telescoping *à la* James Joyce. Three other important poets, known for their militant humanism during the 1930s, were Hjalmar Gullberg (1898–1961), Johannes Edfelt (b. 1904), and Bertil Malmberg (1889–1958). Though none was a programmatic modernist, both Gullberg and Edfelt practiced Sjöberg's disturbing reversals in rhythm and idiom; and when drawing upon the cl. trad., they used it in a characteristically modern manner, namely to reinforce their somber probings of the contemp. psyche and political scene through ironic contrast.

During the 1940s the modernist movement, headed by Erik Lindegren (1910–68) and Karl Vennberg (b. 1910), advanced on a broad front. It encompassed the programs and techniques of both the "pure" and the "engaged" poets of the 1930s. The pressure of the war situation and impulses from Kafka, Eliot, and Rilke combined to produce a poetry marked by dissonance and anguished pessimism—in Lindegren's words, a "catharsis of impotence." The poets' disillusionment and skepticism are illustrated by what Vennberg termed a choice "between the indifferent and the impossible." Epochal was Lindegren's *Mannen utan väg* ("The Man Without a Way," 1942; Eng. tr. 1969), a cycle of sonnets broken up into couplets in which the disorder of the war years is expressed in explosive images. Of *fyrtiotalisterna* ("The Poets of the Forties"), one may mention Werner Aspenström (b. 1918), Sven Alfons (b. 1918), Bernt Erikson (b. 1921), Ragnar Thoursie (b. 1919), and Stig Carlson (1920–71). The tortured individualism and existentialist questionings of these poets were expressed in experimental modes that evoked charges of obscurity from the general public.

The generation of poets emerging after the war returned to a more concrete reality, with everyone seeking a new point of departure. The result was a poetry of great diversity. One trend was toward either the idyllic-romantic, as in the work of Bo Setterlind (b. 1923), or toward nature description, as in the early work of Folke Isaksson (b. 1927). Linguistic sophistication and semantic irony predominated in the meta-poetry of Göran Printz-Påhlsson (b. 1931) and Majken Johansson (b. 1930), members of a group of poets at the University of Lund who excelled in the cultivation of unusual forms such as the sonnet and the villanelle. The irony and bitter pessimism of Sandro Key-Åberg (b. 1923) and the posturings of Lars Forssell (b. 1928) as jester or clown concealed a search for commitment and ideological identification. The theatricality of Forssell's poetry sharpened the satire, and in his cabaret songs, patterned after Fr. *chansons*, he found an effective vehicle for his political engagement. Östen Sjöstrand (b. 1925) emerged as a religious mystic whose poetry is often couched in the idiom of the natural sciences; with Lindegren's later work, it shares a striving toward the condition of music, an attempt to express the absolute. The unobtrusive formal perfection of the poetry of Tomas Tranströmer (b. 1931) and his sure instinct for the liberating metaphor placed him in the forefront of the new generation of poets when he made his appearance in 1954. Subsequent works, such as the collections *Hemligheter på vägen* (Secrets on the Way, 1958), *Mörkerseende* (Night Vision, 1970; Eng. tr. 1971), and *Östersjöar* (Baltics, 1974; Eng. tr. 1975), confirmed his position as one of the most significant, and most translated, of modern S. poets.

In the years following mid-century a number of well-established poets presented some of their most important works. Pär Lagerkvist crowned his long poetic career with *Aftonland* (Evening Land, 1953; Eng. tr. 1974), a summation of familiar themes—childhood memories and metaphysical probings—from the writings of this self-styled "religious atheist." Harry Martinson had already earned a unique position in S. lit. by his unsurpassed nature poetry and his sweeping vision encompassing microcosm and macrocosm at one glance. In 1956 he published the space epic *Aniara* (Eng. tr. 1963), in which the poet saw himself as "a medium and reporter from his own time." Science fiction and allegory in one, the poem offers a chilling vision of a technological future gone astray and a nostalgic celebration of the earth, with an implied warning against its potential destruction at the hands of man. Hjalmar Gullberg presented a whittled-down verse of stark simplicity in his last collection of poetry, *Ögon, läppar* (Eyes, Lips, 1960).

Gunnar Ekelöf's stature as the central figure in Scandinavian poetry became indisputable with the publication of *En Mölna-elegi* (A Mölna Elegy, 1960; Eng. tr. 1985) and his last three collections, which form a "Byzantine triptych": *Diwan över Fursten av Emgión* (Diwan on the Prince of Emgion, 1965), *Sagan om Fatumeh* (The Tale of Fatumeh, 1966), and *Vägvisare till underjorden* (Guide to the Underworld, 1967; Eng. tr. 1980). By means of avatars and archetypes, the poet offers in these works a learned summation of the human experience, a simultaneous view of humanity's past and present, of myth and history. Like Martinson's

Aniara, Ekelöf's poetry abounds in literary allusions. Thanks to the efforts of such poets as Ekelöf and Forssell, official recognition was given to the poetic genius of the popular troubadour Evert Taube (1890–1976), whose songs extolling love, the S. summer, and seafaring adventures made him a worthy successor to Bellman.

The poets of the 1960s placed a strong emphasis on communication, with a growing demand for reader participation in "creating" a poem. The period was characterized by a distrust for established social and linguistic structures and a questioning of the ability of traditional poetic lang. to break through these structures. Anti-symbolic, non-metaphoric "concretism" even enlisted electronics and cybernetics to create a new lang. The parallels with pictorial pop art were obvious, as shown in the work of the poet and painter Carl Fredrik Reutersvärd (b. 1934). Göran Palm (b. 1931) advocated a "new simplicity," making poetry an instrument for exploring a tangible sociopolitical reality locally as well as globally. Sonja Åkesson (1926–77) offered a woman's perspective on everyday life, viewing its trivialities and absurdities with humor and irony. The new political awareness was a dominant aspect of the works of Åke Hodell (b. 1919), Erik Beckman (b. 1935), and Björn Håkanson (b. 1937). It found its emblematic expression in the poem *Om kriget i Vietnam* (About the War in Vietnam, 1965) by Göran Sonnevi (b. 1939). Sonnevi's poetry is typical of the period in its blend of concrete observation and abstract theory, of radical activism and acute linguistic awareness.

Whereas the common political concerns of the 1960s offered a somewhat misleading appearance of unity to the poetry of that decade, the 1970s and 1980s present a picture of great diversity. The nakedly reductive poetry of Lars Norén (b. 1944) and the verbal experiments of Bengt Emil Johnson (b. 1936) in his extensive poetry of the four seasons represent conspicuously different approaches. A tentative distinction could be made between two temperaments, both of which find a voice in the most recent S. p.: romantic, musical, and verbally opulent in the works of Tobias Berggren (b. 1940) and Niklas Rådström (b. 1953); intellectual, learned, and reflective in those of Lars Gustafsson (b. 1936), highly theoretical and conscious of critical fashions in those of the "postmodernist" Ulf Eriksson (b. 1958). Traditionally, poetry is the S. literary genre *par excellence*. There is every indication that it will continue to be so.

ANTHOLOGIES: *Oxford Book of Scandinavian Verse*, ed. E. W. Gosse and W. A. Craigie (1925); *Anthol. of S. Lyrics from 1750–1925*, ed. C. W. Stork (1930); *Mod. S. P.*, ed. C. D. Locock (1936); *S. Songs and Ballads*, ed. M. S. Allwood (1950); *Lyrikboken*, ed. T. Nilsson (1951)—illustrated; *40-talslyrik*, ed. B. Holmqvist (1951); *Masterpieces of S. P.*, ed. F. Ahlberg (1952); *50-talslyrik*, ed. B. Holmqvist and F. Isaksson (1955); *Barocklyrik* (1962), *Rokokolyrik*, both ed. B. Julén (1962); *Eight S. Poets*, ed. and tr. F. Fleisher (1969); *Friends, You Drank Some Darkness*, ed. and tr. R. Bly (1975)—poems by Martinson, Ekelöf, and Tranströmer; *Svensk dikt från trollformler till Lars Norën*, ed. L. Gustafsson (1978)—comprehensive; *Mod. S. P. in Tr.*, ed. G. Harding and A. Anselm Hollo (1979); *Contemp. S. P.*, ed. and tr. J. Matthias and G. Printz-Påhlsson (1980).

HISTORY AND CRITICISM: E. W. Gosse, *Northern Studies* (1890); H. Schück, *Hist. de la litt. suédoise* (1923); O. Sylwan, *Den svenska versen från 1600-talets början*, 3 v. (1925–34), *Svensk verskonst från Wivallius till Karlfeldt* (1934)—versification; L. Maury, *Panorama de la litt. suédoise contemporaine* (1940); C. A. D. Fehrman, *Kyrkogårdsromantik: Studier i engelsk och svensk 1700-talsdiktning* (1954)—comparative study, summarized in Eng.; I. Holm and M. von Platen, *La litt. suédoise* (1957); A. Gustafson, *A Hist. of S. Lit.* (1961); R. B. Vowles, "Post-War S. P.," *WHR* 15 (1961); G. C. Schoolfield, "The Recent Scandinavian Lyric," *BA* 36 (1962); E. N. Tigerstedt et al., *Ny illustrerad svensk litteraturh.*, 5 v. (1967)—standard lit. hist. with annotated bibl; G. Brandell and J. Stenkvist, *Svensk litt. 1870–1970*, 3 v. (1974–75); L. Gustafsson, *Forays into S. P.* (1978); S. H. Rossel, *A Hist. of Scandinavian Lit, 1870–1980* (1982); B. Olsson and I. Algulin, *Litteraturens Historia i Sverige* (1987).

S.LY.; L.G.W.

SWISS POETRY.

I. OVERVIEW
II. IN GERMAN
III. IN FRENCH
IV. IN ITALIAN
V. IN RHAETO-ROMANSH

I. OVERVIEW. Contrary to an old and popular cliché employed in books on the hist. of S. lit., the production of poetry in this small country has been extremely prolific and diverse, particularly in the 19th and 20th cs. Thus we arrive at the not very original conclusion that even within such a spatially and temporally limited area encyclopedic "completeness" is an utopian notion and that, therefore, we have to content ourselves with giving mostly positions and developments or, as Werner Weber says, with looking for "indications of the whole in individual phenomena." As to the existence of a specifically "Swiss" p., this question cannot be answered here. In the S. Confederacy, with its four langs., the types of relationships between culture and lit. are quite different from one another, and some authors (for example, the "globetrotter" Blaise Cendrars) may more aptly fit into international categories than into those applying to a small country.

Chronologically, the evolution runs from the medieval Minnesingers in the Ger.- and Fr.-speaking parts of Switzerland (Rudolf von Fenis, Johannes Hadlaub, Steinmar, Oton de Grandson) to the poetry of "the children of Marx and Coca-Cola," a phrase echoing Jean-Luc Godard which was used by Daniel Walter (b. 1953) as the title of one of his texts. The poets themselves perceive an arc extending from metaphysical meditations via the wordplays of *lettrisme* to couplets expressing *engagé* criticisms of established society. Philippe Jaccottet (b. 1925) likens the labor of a poet to the night watch of a herdsman ("Le Travail du poète" in *L'Ignorant*, 1958):

> The task of a look becoming weaker by
> the hour
> is not to go on dreaming or shedding
> tears,
> but to be on the watch like a shepherd
> and to summon
> all those who risk getting lost by falling
> asleep.
> (tr. P. Spycher)

The "house poet of Basel," Berthold Redlich, is considerably less ambitious; for a commission he produces rhymed love letters, speeches, and advertisements, and he recommends himself like this: "Sensible people dial his number / For it frees you from a poet's worries!" There is room for opposites and, moreover, for absurdities in a "post-modern" society that regards itself as pluri-cultural and that lives by the rules of consumerism. To the extent that the functions of poetry are (still?) separate ones, "high poetry" can be characterized as the concern of a specific, linguistically and intellectually educated reading public which constitutes a small share of the public targeted by advertising- and everyday-poetry. A connection between both of them is established, among other things, by "concrete poetry", whose protagonist Eugen Gomringer (b. 1925 in Zurich), perhaps the internationally best known representative of more recent S. p., writes in his "23 Points about the Problem of 'Lit. and Society'" (1958; in his collection *Worte sind Schatten*, 1969): "no longer being adequate for our changing times, classic-humanistic organicism has been superseded by what Max Bense has called 'synthetic rationality.'" Logically enough, Gomringer defines the "new poem" as an "object for use." It is true that "concrete poetry" takes an extreme position (some people have thought they recognized something typically Swiss in its mechanically puzzled-out quality). But the question of just how shopworn that which we designate here as "classical-humanistic organicism" was and has a general relevance, the more so since this cultural trad. put its firm stamp on the style and thematics of "bourgeois" poetry between ca. 1850 and 1950. In 1950, the year in which he died, Werner Zemp, a poet writing in this Classical-romantic trad., deplored what he perceived as the new antagonism of the technological mind with the soul: "Day after day we have to watch precious things getting irretrievably lost!" (Letter of April 3, 1959, in Zemp's *Das lyrische Werk, Aufsätze, Briefe*, 1967). Zemp was a *poeta doctus*, combining lyrical production with critical reflection, a combination that is represented throughout Switzerland by important writer-critics (Max Rychner [1897–1965] embodies it perfectly; below, in the Fr.-speaking section, see Georges Nicole and Pierre-Louis Matthey [1893–1970]; in the It.-speaking section, see Giorgio Orelli [b. 1921] and Adolfo Jenni [b. 1911]; in the Rhaeto-Romansh-speaking section, see Andri Peer [1921–85]). Only rarely does this inclination find expression in poetological programs, or, even less likely, in manifestoes; the distinctly preferred form is that of essays about other writers. One can say that the lyrical production of Switzerland is unprogrammatic, but also that the poets are keenly aware of the universality of poetry. A fairly unique case is that of the adoptive Genevan George Haldas (b. 1917); his literary output, beginning with the essay *Les Poètes malades de la peste* (1954), is accompanied by a steadily increasing diaristic one in which poetological reflection plays a significant role.

The break with cultural trad. in the course of the 1950s, notably in the Ger.-speaking part of Switzerland (considerably less so in the Fr.-speaking part, where writers continue cultivating a kind of inwardness that derives from romantic sources, among them Ger. ones), manifested itself not only in a new conception of form, which was influenced by the West European and Am. modernism and by the West Ger. "Kahlschlag" (forest-clearing) lit., but also in the abandonment of the traditional S. themes of the poetry of the Alps and of idyllic nature. The transformation of a centuries-old rural society into a modern, urbanized, service-job society has had a revolutionary effect on the writers' views of life. It would be wrong, however, to regard this transformation as a total one and thus to overlook (modernized) re-establishments of relationships with the poetry of earlier generations. The roots of a specifically S. modernity have been discovered in the works of Robert Walser (1878–1956), Hans Morgenthaler (1890–1928), and Adrien Turel (1890–1957); in the recently edited texts of the outsider, the ostracized "sick man" and "naive" painter Adolf Wölfli (1864–1930), an overwhelming wealth of linguistic "picture puzzles" has come to light. And the often radical social engagement of many contemp. poets is, in the last analysis, part of a S. trad. of political poetry that can be traced back through Gottfried Keller and Juste Olivier to the folk- and war-songs of the late Middle Ages.

Lyrical speech means participation in a global lang.; at the same time, poetry is the lang. of subjectivity and thus, at least potentially, of marginality. The consensus of a certain kind of elitist poetry, but also that of a certain kind of stereotyped patriotic poetry, could deceive the reader about its subjectivity and marginality. Contemp. poetry rejects this consensus and takes up the counter-rhetoric of both its own lit. and foreign lits. It has never completely escaped the threat of a new conformity (which frequently was a thematic, but also, given its adoption of fashionable lyrical understatement and discontinuity, a formal one). The freedom for poetic production and the freedom of the critically selective reader have never been as great as they are now. Reflecting this new freedom is "Jenseits von heute," by Hans Schuhmacher (b. 1910) in his *Meridiane* (1959):

It's lovely today.
A lot lies in ruins
And new things
Are not yet in use.
Anything may happen.

ANTHOLOGIES AND COLLECTIONS: *Lesebuch schweizerischer Dichtung,* ed. S. Lang (1938); *Bestand und Versuch: Schweizer Schrifttum der Gegenwart,* ed. B. Mariacher and F. Witz (1964); *Textbuch der Gruppe Olten I, II* (1975, 1976); *Schweizer Lyrik des zwanzigsten Jahrhunderts,* ed. B. Jentzsch (1979); *Neue Schweizer Literatur* (1980); *Anthol. of Mod. S. Lit.*, ed. H. M. Waidson (1984).

HISTORY AND CRITICISM: G. de Reynold, *Histoire littéraire de la Suisse au XVIIIe siècle,* v. 1, 2 (1909, 1912); E. Jenny and V. Rossel, *Gesch. der schweizerischen Literatur* (1910), *Histoire de la litt. suisse* (1910); F. Ernst, *Die Schweiz als geistige Mittlerin von Muralt bis Jacob Burckhardt* (1932), *Gibt es eine schweizerische Nationalliteratur?* (1955); C. Clerc et al., *Panorama des littératures contemporaines de Suisse* (1938); T. Greiner, *Der literarische Verkehr zwischen der deutschen und welschen Schweiz seit 1848* (1940); G. Locarnini, *Die literarischen Beziehungen zwischen der italienischen und der deutschen Schweiz* (1946); K. Schmid, "Versuch über die schweizerische Nationalität," *Aufsätze und Reden* (1957); G. Calgari, *Storia delle quattro letterature della Svizzera* (1959), *Die vier Literaturen der Schweiz* (1966); F. Jost, "Y a-t-il une litt. suisse?," *Essais de litt. comparée I: Helvetica* (1964); K. Marti, *Die Schweiz und ihre Schriftsteller—die Schriftsteller und ihre Schweiz* (1966); D. de Rougemont, *La Suisse ou l'histoire d'un peuple heureux* (1969); P. Nizon, *Diskurs in der Enge* (1970); *Der Schriftsteller in unserer Zeit,* ed. P. A. Bloch and E. Hubacher (1972); M. Gsteiger, "Litt. et nation en Suisse romande et en Suisse alémanique," *RLC* 216 (1980), ed., *Die zeitgenössischen Literaturen der Schweiz* (1980); A. Muschg, "Gibt es eine schweizerische Nationalliteratur?" *Ich hab im Traum die Schweiz gesehn,* ed. J. Jung (1980); *Die Viersprachige Schweiz,* ed. J. C. Arquint et al. (1982); G. Steiner, "What is 'S.'?" *TLS* 7 (1984); *Mod. S. Lit.: Unity and Diversity,* ed. J. L. Flood (1985).

II. IN GERMAN. If we disregard the Med. Lat. sequences (Notker Balbulus of St. Gall died in 912) and the Minnesingers of the 12th–13th cs., mentioned earlier (the *Manessische Liederhandschrift,* created in the 14th c., probably compiled in Zurich, is the most famous specimen of its genre in the Ger.-lang. territory), the origins of Ger.-S. p., i.e. the poetry written in the Ger.-speaking part of Switzerland, are to be found in the mostly anonymous political and ecclesiastic poems of the late Middle Ages (*Das Sempacherlied,* end of the 14th c.; *Das Tellenlied,* ca. 1474; the spiritual poetry of Heinrich von Laufenberg, 15th c.); but it was not until the 18th c. that a theoretically underpinned, genuinely "S." p. emerged (J. J. Breitinger's *Critische Dichtkunst* [1740] with a foreword by J. J. Bodmer, put forth fundamental theories guided by models of Eng. lit.). Yet Albrecht von Haller's *Versuch schweizerischer Gedichte* (1732), containing "Die Alpen," had already won European fame for the "land of the herdsmen," partly due to V. B. von Tscharner's Fr. tr. This, along with the prose poems of Salomon Gessner (1730–88, *Idyllen,* 1756), disseminated throughout the Continent the image of a mythic rural society and of an alternately heroic and idyllic Nature. The *Schweizerlieder* (1767) of the theologian and physiognomist J. C. Lavater (1741–1801) were intended to reactivate the legacy of the national history in the style of preromantic ballads, while the *Gedichte* (1793) of J. G. von Salis-Seewis discreetly transposed the elegiac lyricism of the Ancien Régime to a Helvetic mode. Political poetry, represented by Niklaus Manuel (1484–1530), and satire, represented by Pamphilus Gengenbach (1480–1525) and Johannes Grob (1643–97), recede into the background during the time of upheaval between revolution, restoration, and regeneration. Not until young Gottfried Keller (1819–90) began to write did political poetry re-awaken, influenced by the political age 1815–48; Keller, creator of nature poems, festive and patriotic poems ("O mein Heimatland!") came to be viewed as an exemplary S. national writer, yet next to, or in, his rhetorical faith in progress, overtones of sorrow and hopelessness are not to be ignored. His fellow S. and contemporary, Conrad Ferdinand Meyer (1825–98), is the creator of an original variant of European symbolism, of a poetry of escapism and isolation, turning to hist., nature, and the world of ballads for his subjects. Heinrich Leuthold (1827–79) was a remarkable translator and was close to the Munich Circle of Writers; his poetry was also one of escapism and isolation.

Carl Spitteler (1845–1924), whose *Olympischer Frühling* (1900–10) is the fruit of his anachronistic attempt to write verse epics about a somewhat modernized mythical world, and Josef Victor Widmann (1842–1911), author of idyllic poetry, point forward to the 20th c.—that is, to a tension between the trad. of *l'art pour l'art* and what the expressionistic S. poet Karl Stamm (1890–1914) called "the start of the heart's journey," and between bourgeois life and marginality. Werner Zemp (1906–59), Siegfried Lang (1887–1971), and Urs Martin Strub (b. 1910) belong to the former tendency; Albin Zollinger (1895–1941), Albert Ehrismann (b. 1908), and Max Pulver (1889–1952) to the latter. The period after the Second World War saw a revitalization of the production of poetry running from the *lied*-like melodies of Silja Walter (b. 1919) to the pointed modernism of Alexander Gwerder (1923–52) and the wordplay of Eugen Gomringer (mentioned above). Rainer Brambach (1917–86), Gerhard Meier (b. 1917), Walter Gross (b. 1924), and Erika Burkart (b. 1922) among many have striven for, and achieved, a synthesis.

Dialect poetry does not simply exist face to face with poetry in standard Ger.; in most cases the former complements the latter. Whereas the earlier authors of dialect poetry, e.g. Gottlieb Jakob Kuhn (1775–1849), Meinrad Lienert (1865–1933), Alfred Huggenberger (1867–1960), and Josef Reinhart (1875-1957), prefer subjects taken from the peasant homeland, the "modern dialect" movement has articulated modern changes in lang. and society in a new form of dialect poetry (Kurt Marti [b. 1921], Ernst Eggimann [b. 1936], and others). The poetry of the cabaretists and the folksingers (Max Werner Lenz [1887–1973], Alfred Rasser [1907–77], Mani Matter [1936–72]), who often combine dialect with standard lang., warrants special mention.

ANTHOLOGIES AND COLLECTIONS: *Schwyzer Meie: Die schönsten schweizerdeutschen Gedichte,* ed. G. Thürer and A. Guggenbühl (1938); *Gut zum Druck: Literatur der deutschen Schweiz seit 1964* (1972), *Mach keini Schprüch: Schweizer Mundartlyrik des 20. Jahrhunderts,* both ed. D. Fringeli (1972); *Kurzwaren: Schweizer Lyrik,* ed. Zytglogge-Verlag, 5 v. (1975–88); *Fortschreiben: 98 Autoren der deutschen Schweiz,* ed. D. Bachmann (1977); *Belege: Gedichte aus der deutschen Schweiz seit 1900,* ed. W. Weber (1978); *Gegengewichte: Lyrik unserer Tage aus dem deutschsprachigen Raum der Schweiz,* ed. H. Schaub (1978).

HISTORY AND CRITICISM: J. Baechtold, *Gesch. der deutschen Literatur in der Schweiz* (1892); J. Nadler, *Literaturgesch. der deutschen Schweiz* (1932); E. Ermatinger, *Dichtung und Geistesleben der deutschen Schweiz* (1933); M. Blöchlinger, *La Poésie lyrique contemporaine en Suisse allemande* (1947); A. Bettex, *Die Literatur der deutschen Schweiz von heute* (1950); A. Zäch, *Die Dichtung der deutschen Schweiz* (1951); M. Wehrli, "Gegenwartsdichtung der deutschen Schweiz," *Deutsche Literatur in unserer Zeit,* ed. W. Kayser et al. (1959); W. Günther, *Dichter der neueren Schweiz,* 3 v. (1963–87); *Schweizer Schriftsteller im Gespräch,* ed. W. Bucher and G. Ammann (1970–71); *Der Schriftsteller und sein Verhältnis zur Sprache dargestellt am Problem der Tempuswahl,* ed. P. A. Bloch (1971); E. Pulver, "Die deutschsprachige Literatur der Schweiz seit 1945," *Die zeitgenössischen Literaturen der Schweiz,* ed. M. Gsteiger (1980); *Helvetische Steckbriefe: 47 Schriftsteller aus der deutschen Schweiz seit 1800,* ed. W. Weber et al. (1981).

III. IN FRENCH. From the Minnesingers to Haller and Lavater to Frisch and Dürrenmatt (of the two world-famous contemporaries, only Dürrenmatt has written some poetry on very rare occasions), the lit. of the Alemanic part of Switzerland has moved forward in a fairly close symbiosis with "cultural" Germany. Conditions in the *Romandie,* the Fr.-speaking part of Switzerland, however, are distinctly different. On the one hand, the Romandie has made outstanding contributions to Fr. lit. (e.g. Rousseau), and its consciousness of belonging to a larger linguistic and cultural realm has always been keen—indeed, at times too keen (which may, in part, explain the almost total disappearance of its original Franco-Provençal dialects)—but the relationship between the "motherland" and the small "cultural provinces," which have clung to their political autonomy and to their preponderantly Protestant orientation, has only recently become more relaxed. For a long time, Fr.-lang. S. lit. has existed as a mere footnote to Fr. lit. Apart from the examples of folk poetry (cf. the famous "Ranz des vaches," written in dialect) and from Oton de Grandson (mentioned earlier), no attempts at poetry were made until the 18th c., when Fr. idyllic poetry was adopted (*La Vue d'Anet* by the Bernese writer S.-L. von Lerber, 1723–83), or when contemp. Ger.-S. "national lit." was emulated (*Poésies helvétiennes* by the Vaudois Philippe-Sirice Bridel, 1757–1845). Romantic poetry, which was nonexistent in the Ger.-speaking part, was cultivated in the Romandie; its (none too original) practitioners, Jacques Imbert-Galloix (1807–28), Frédéric Monneron (1813–37), and Etienne Eggis (1830–67), show not only the continuing influence of the Ger. romantic mind in the 20th c. (the distinguished critic Albert Béguin confirmed this influence in his book *L'Ame romantique et le rêve,* 1937) but also the tragic isolation and introversion which has frequently been branded as the "original sin" of the Romandie lit. In the works of Louis Duchosal (1862–1901), Edmond-Henri Crisinel (1897–1948), and of the superior master of forms Pierre-Louis Matthey (1893–1970), the search for poetic expression has its quasi-religious correlate in the search for the meaning of isolation and loneliness, and, conversely, the feeling of being existentially threatened turns into devotion to pure art. Edouard Tavan (1842–1919) carries this devotion most skillfully to an extreme; Alice Chambrier (1861–82) pours it into rather sentimental molds; Henry Spiess (1876–1940) translates the contrast between the intellect and the senses into melodious cadences. All of these poets are close or distant literary brothers and sisters or descendants of Henri-Frédéric Amiel (1821–81), the gifted poet and translator and author of the unique *Journal intime* (first ed. in part, 1923; ed. complete, 1976ss.): being wedged between grace and nausea, between exaltation and world-weariness, they write their verses in order to convert their individual destiny to myth. There is no dearth of patriotic subjects, of realistically drawn nature images, and, above all, of examples of traditional poetry about the Alps in the 19th and early 20th c.—for example, in the poetry of Juste Olivier (1807–76) and Henry Warnery (1859–1902); paradoxically, the outsider Amiel is also the author of "Chant de guerre helvétique," which is a celebration of the patriotic uprising of 1857.

Calvin's legacy, Rousseau's love for nature, the experience of a tragic sense of life, and the cult of form remain powerful influences on the poetry of the "Renaissance des lettres romandes," which emerged at the time of the First World War, although these influences assume new dimensions. The novelist C.-F. Ramuz (1870–1947) wrote only a few poems (*Le petit village*, 1903), and Gonzague de Reynold (1880–1970) does not venture beyond patriotic rhetoric; but in the lyrical work of Gustave Roud (1897–1976), metaphysical inquiry crystallizes into structures of perfect linguistic unity. The title of his late volume of poetry, *Campagne perdue* (1972), signals a change in the traditional picture of poetry in the Romandie; yet as much as ever, regional and cantonal subjects retain their place (Geneva, Vaud, Neuchâtel, Valais, Fribourg); and in an exemplary way, Alexandre Voisard (b. 1930) contributed to the debate on the desirable size and shape of the new canton of Jura through his long poem *Liberté à l'aube* (1967). The Jura also appears in the works of Werner Renfer (1898–1936), tragically broken in those of Francis Giauque (1934– 65), and in the manner of balladry in those of Jean Cuttat (b. 1916). Corinna Bille (1912–79) and Maurice Chappaz (b. 1916) depict a time of change in their Valais when it was still partly archaic and idyllic, partly drawn into technological progress; Georges Haldas (b. 1917) and Vahé Godel (b. 1931) represent urban poetry and the cosmopolitan scene of Geneva. Anne Perrier (b. 1922), Jacques Chessez (b. 1934), and Jean Pache (b. 1933) combine a sense of trad. with the avantgardism typical of the Vaudois; the most prominent of them is Philippe Jaccottet (b. 1925), who lives in France. Finally, we should take note of cosmopolitan S. such as Nicolas Bouvier (b. 1929), one of the distant disciples of the Franco-Swiss writer Blaise Cendrars (1887–1961). These examples illustrate the richness and the multidimensionality of the poetry of a so-called "small" lit. which is by no means small.

ANTHOLOGIES AND COLLECTIONS: *Chants du Pays: Recueil poétique de la Suisse romande*, ed. A. Imer-Cuneo (1883); *Anthol. des poètes de la Suisse romande*, ed. E. de Boccard (1946); *Ecrivains de Suisse française*, ed. C. Guyot (1961); *Anthol. jurassienne*, ed. P.-O. Walzer, v. 1–2 (1964); *Anthol. romande de la litt. alpestre*, ed. E. Pidoux (1973); *A Contre temps: Huitante textes vaudois de 1980 à 1380* (1980); *Rencontres poétiques internationales en Suisse romande, Yverdon-les-Bains*, ed. L. and R.-L. Junod (1984); "Anthol. lyrique de poche," *La Litt. de la Suisse romande expliquée en un quart d'heure*, ed. B. Galland (1986)—incl. hist. and crit.; "Poèsie aujourd'hui," *Écriture* 30 (1988).

HISTORY AND CRITICISM: P. Godet, *Histoire littéraire de la Suisse française* (1890–95); V. Rossel, *Histoire littéraire de la Suisse romande des origines à nos jours* (1903); P. Kohler, "La litt. de la Suisse romande," *Histoire de la litt. française*, ed. P. Kohler et al., v. 3 (1949); M. Weber-Perret, *Écrivains romands 1900–1950* (1951); A. Berchtold, *La Suisse romande au cap de XXe siècle: Portrait littéraire et moral* (1964); *Pourquoi j'écris*, ed. F. Jotterand (1971); J. Chessex, *Les Saintes Écritures* (1972); M. Gsteiger, *La Nouvelle litt. romande* (1978); J.-P. Monnier, *Écrire en Suisse romande entre le ciel et la nuit* (1979); J.-C. Potterat, *L'Ombre ab souk, études sur la poèsie romande* (1989).

IV. IN ITALIAN. One of the topoi of historians of S. lit. is that of prefacing any discussion about the It.-speaking part of Switzerland with a reference to the precarious state of this third national lang. As a matter of fact, the influx of (primarily Ger.-speaking, incl. S.) "foreigners" into southern Switzerland constitutes a serious cultural problem. It is all the more surprising to see how interesting and diverse the poetry of a minority (about 300,000 inhabitants in the canton of Ticino and in the It.-lang. valleys of the Grisons) actually is, esp. in the second half of the 20th c. Up until Francesco Chiesa (1871–1973), the founding father of the more recent lit. of the Ticino, who was a classicist in his poetry (*Calliope*, 1907), there had been only a few memorable poets: Francesco Soave (1743–1806), the translator of Gessner and Young; Giampiero Riva (1696–1785); and Angelo Nessi (1873–1932), who resided in Milan for the better part of his life (the ties of southern Switzerland with the It. province of Lombardy are close). Giuseppe Zoppi (1890–1952) wrote traditionally helvetic lyrical prose about the Alps; Valerio Abbondio (1891–1958) was an author of elegies. It is the "post-Chiesa generation" that has brought about a real flowering of poetry; this generation has received support from small literary publishing houses, periodicals, and the radio and television networks of southern Switzerland, but also, increasingly, recognition from Italy. Its best-known member is Giorgio Orelli (b. 1921); an adherent of Italy's school of hermetic poetry, he has distinguished himself as a translator of Goethe, and in his search for precise poetic ciphers, he manages to build the dissonances of modern life into his depictions of nature in his homeland (*Sinopie*, 1977). The It.-speaking Grisonian Remo Fasani (b. 1922), a *poeta doctus*, addresses the phenomenon of the destruction of nature by civilization, particularly forcefully in his recent works (e.g. *Pian San Giacomo*, 1983). Generally, we can say that the It.-lang. poetry of modern times has changed from an idyllic genre to one of mundane life and social criticism. Angelo Casè (b. 1936), Alberto Nessi (b. 1940), Amleto Pedroli (b. 1922), Aurelio Buletti (b. 1946), and contemp. dialect poets like Ugo Canonica (b. 1918) and Sergio Maspoli (b. 1920) fit into this pattern, whereas Adolfo Jenni (b. 1911), Federico Hindermann (b. 1921), and Grytzko Mascioni (b. 1936) are more interested in artistic matters.

ANTHOLOGIES AND COLLECTIONS: *Scrittori della*

Svizzera italiana, 2 v. (1936); *Scrittori ticinesi dal Rinascimento a oggi*, ed. G. Zoppi (1936); *C'è un solo villaggio nostro: Scrittori della Svizzera italiana*, ed. P. R. Frigeri (1972); *Südwind: Zeitgenössische Prosa, Lyrik und Essays aus der italienischen Schweiz*, ed. C. Castelli and A. Vollenweider (1976); *Rabbia di vento: Un ritratto della Svizzera italiana attraverso scritti e testimonianze*, ed. A. Nessi (1986); *Svizzera italiana*, ed. G. Orelli (1986).

HISTORY AND CRITICISM: P. Fontana, "L'ultima generazione di Scrittori della Svizzera italiana e l'eredità di F. Chiesa," *Il Veltro* 11 (1967); A. Vollenweider, "Die italienischsprachige Literatur der Schweiz seit 1945," *Die zeitgenössischen Literaturen der Schweiz*, ed. M. Gsteiger (1980); R. Fasani, *La Svizzera plurilingue* (1982); "Litt. de Suisse ital ienne: Recueil d'articles," *Études des lettres* 4 (1984); G. Orelli, "Scrivere nella Svizzera italiana," *Versants* 6 (1984); D. Janack-Meyer, "Aspetti culturali di una minoranza linguistica," *Quaderni Grigionitaliani* (1987); *Lingua e letteratura italiana in Svizzera: Actes du Colloque de Lausanne*, ed. A. Stäuble (1987).

V. IN RHAETO-ROMANSH. The position of Rhaeto-Romansh or Grisons-Romansh, the fourth national lang. of Switzerland (linguistically related to the Romansh of the It. Dolomites and Friuli, but geographically and culturally separate and confined to parts of the canton of Grisons) is in several respects a singular one: Romansh is the lang. of a small minority (about 50,000 people). Almost without exception this minority speaks Ger. as a second lang.; it does not have a common written lang., but is split into a number of regional groups (Ladin, Surselva, Central Grisons)—it was only a short time ago that apparently successful efforts were made towards the creation of a unifying idiom, which was to be called *Rumantsch Grischun*. This lang. of an archaic-Alpine peasant culture is seriously threatened with extinction but nevertheless possesses a strong vitality in the midst of an industrial and postindustrial society. Therefore, a hist. of Rhaeto-Romansh lit. (incl. poetry) can never really be completely detached from the struggle for linguistic survival and cultural identity.

In early times, the epic *Chanzun da la Guera dal Chastè da Müsch* (Song of the War of Müss) by Giav Travers (1483–1563) and a rich body of oral lit., from which the *Canzun da Sontga Margriata* (Song of St. Margareta) have to be singled out; in the age of the Reformation and the Counter-Reformation, there were primarily religious texts, e.g. the Psalm translations by Johann Grass (1683) and the church hymns by Balzar Alig (1674). In the 19th c., the epoch of the "renaissance of Rhaeto-Romansh," a partly folksong-like, partly elegiac poetry, arises because of Gian Battista Sandri (1787–1857), Conradin de Flugi (1787–1874), Chasper Po (1856–1936), and others. Gion Antoni Huonder (1824–67) wrote "Pur suveran" (The Sovereign Peasant), Gudench Barblan (1860–1916) a poem about his mother tongue ("Chara lingua de la mama" [Dear Lang. of My Mama]), Zaccaria Pallioppi (1820–73) philosophical poetry, and Giachen Hasper Muoth (1844–1906) historical ballads. Folklore and Alpine nature remain chief subjects in the poetry of Gion Cadieli (1876–1957) and Rudolf Lanz (1854–1927) among others. Caspar Decurtins (1855–1916) gathered together the literary legacy in a bulky anthology.

The revival of Rhaeto-Romansh lit. was initiated by three eminent writers: Peider Lansel (1863–1943), Alexander Lozza (1880–1953), and Gian Fontana (1897–1935). Lansel, the most original of them, strongly advocated reading older poetry, too. In the 20th c., the traditionalists are Chasper Ans Grass (1900–63), Artur Caflisch (1893–1967), Giatgen Michél Uffer (1883–1965), Sep Modest Nay (1892–1945), Duri Gaudenz (b. 1929), and others. The satirist Men Rauch (1888–1958), Curo Mani (b. 1918), Tista Murk (b. 1915) have turned to the modern forms of the universal lang. of poetry; even more daring are Flurin Darms (b. 1918) and Hendri Spescha (1928–83), but the true model is the poetry of Andri Peer (1921–85), who also wrote essays on the problems of being a contemp. writer. Ranging from the pedagogical ethos of Gion Deplazes (b. 1918) to the aggressive criticism of progress by Theo Candinas (b. 1929) and Armon Planta (b. 1917), these poets express their awareness of living in a world of radical change. A formal correspondence to this awareness is furnished on the one hand by poets such as Felix Giger (b. 1946), with his broad brushstrokes, and on the other Leta Semadeni (b. 1946) with his concise notation. Hardly anybody, however, has equaled the utterly unpretentious, perfect modernity of the Engadinian Luisa Famos (1930–74).

ANTHOLOGIES AND COLLECTIONS: *Rätoromanische Chrestomathie*, ed. C. Decurtins, 12 v. (1896–1919); *Musa Rumantscha: Anthol. poetica moderna*, ed. P. Lansel (1950); *The Curly-Horned Cow: Anthol. of Swiss-Romansh Lit.*, ed. R. R. Bezzola (1971); *Rumantscheia: Eine Anthol. rätoromanischer Schriftsteller der Gegenwart*, ed. Quarta Lingua (1979).

HISTORY AND CRITICISM: J. Pult, "Die rätoromanische Literatur," *Romanische Philologie*, ed. G. Rohlfs, v. 2 (1952); G. Mützenberg, *Destin de la langue et de la litt. rhétoromanes* (1974); I. Camartin, *Rätoromanische Gegenwartsliteratur in Graubünden* (1976); R. R. Bezzola, *Literatura dals Rumauntschs e Ladins* (1979); L. Uffer, "Die rätoromanische Literatur der Schweiz: Ein Ueberblick bis heute," *Die zeitgenössischen Literaturen der Schweiz*, ed. M. Gsteiger (1980). M.GS.; tr. P.SP.

T

TAMIL POETRY. See INDIAN POETRY; SRI LANKAN POETRY.

TELUGU POETRY. See INDIAN POETRY.

THAI POETRY. Poetry dominated T. lit. until the early 20th c., when prose also became widespread. Noted for rhyme and sound play, T. p. is written in syllabic meters in five major verseforms: *rāī*, *khlōng*, *kāp*, *chan*, and *klọn*. The T. (Siamese) lang. presently has five tones which also form part of the metrical requirements. The king and court poets used these forms nearly exclusively until 1932, though in many cases the works are anonymous.

The earliest verse appeared during the Sukhothai period (ca. 1240–1438). Sukhothai reached a high level of civilization, but extant poems are few; the only significant extant text is *Suphāsit phra ruang*, a series of moral maxims written in *rāī* and credited to King Ramkhamhaeng (ca. 1279–98). These stanzas have an indefinite number of 5-syllable lines linked by rhyme. Melodious and concise phrases, suggestive of poetry, also appear in inscriptions from the period.

The Ayutthaya period (1351–1767) saw the rise of classics in *rāī*, *khlōng*, *kāp*, and *chan*. *Khlōng*, like *rāī*, originally appeared when T. had only three tones. *Khlōng* consists of 5-syllable lines grouped into stanzas of two lines (*khlōng sọng*), three (*khlōng sām*), and four (*khlōng sī*). The *kāp* stanzas, probably borrowed from Khmer, include *yānī* with two 11-syllable lines, *surāngkhanāng* with seven 4-syllable lines, and *chabang* with one 4-syllable line between two 6-syllable lines. Indic in origin, the *chan* meters were adapted from meters found in Sanskrit and Pali during this period.

One of the earliest and most difficult Ayutthayan works is *Ōngkān chāēng nam* (The Water Oath), a composition used by officials to reaffirm their loyalty to the king. Throughout the era, Buddhist themes dominate many compositions. In 1482, King Traylokkhanat (1448–88) commissioned a royal version of the *Vessantara Jataka*, the Buddha's life prior to his last birth on earth. This version, the *Mahāchāt kham luang*, consists of passages in Pali followed by T. translations into *rāī*, *khlōng*, and *chan*. Important compositions with historical themes began with *Lilit yuan phāī* (ca. 1475). Written in *lilit*, a combination of *rāī* and *khlōng*, this poem describes the victories of King Traylokkhanat. The popular *nirāt* genre, in which the poet compares his lover's features to the beauties of nature, also developed about this time. During the reign of King Narai (1656–88), the court became a major center of poetry production, and the era came to be known as the Golden Age of T. lit. Probably the most famous of Narai's court poets was Sri Prat. In and out of favor with the king because of his sharp wit, he composed the famous *Kamsuan sī prāt*, a *nirāt* describing his journey to his place in exile. The *chan* meters gained prominence with the adaptation of Buddhist birth stories into verse such as the *Samutthakhōt kham chan* and *Sua khō kham chan*. Probably the most famous work from this period, although some scholars date it in the reign of King Traylokkhanat, is the *lilit* classic *Phra lọ*, the tragic romance of Prince Phra Lọ and two princesses from a neighboring kingdom. Literary output declined after Narai, however, due to war and internal strife. Notable works from the end of the Ayutthaya period incl. a collection of boating songs in *kāp*, *Kāp hāē rua*, and a description in *chan* of the king's journey to a Buddhist shrine, *Bunnōwāt kham chan*. In 1767 the Burmese destroyed Ayutthaya.

The establishment of the new capital at Bangkok revived literary production at court, this time primarily in *klọn*, which probably first appeared during the Thonburi period (1767–82). Since then it has been the favored T. verseform, with two types used regularly: *klọn hok* with six syllables per line and *klọn pāēt* with eight. The 4-line *klọn* stanzas are famous for rhyme schemes and rhyme links that often continue for thousands of stanzas. Hoping to recreate lost works, Rama I, Phra Phutthayotfa (1782–1809), the first king at Bangkok, organized a royal composition committee that produced the *Rāmakian* (the T. version of the Indian classic, the *Rāmāyaṇa*) and parts of *Inau* and Dālang (romances based on the Javanese Panji cycle introduced through Malaysia). Rama II, Phra Phutthaloetla (1809–24) continued the literary revival with another version of the *Rāmakian* and a complete version of *Inau*, much of which, it is thought, he composed himself. Sunthorn Phu (1786–1856), arguably Thailand's greatest poet, used *klọn* for many *nirāt* poems and for the long imaginative romance *Phra aphaimanī*. Prince Paramanuchit (1790–1853), monk, poet, and Indic classicist, contributed textbooks on the *chan* meters, the final part of *Samutthakhōt kham chan*, and *Lilit talēng phāī*, a glorification of the battles of King Naresuan. Khun Phum (1815–80), the leading woman poet of the 19th c., produced satirical poems of biting wit in her famous literary salons. Traditional narrative poetry continued into the 20th c. in compositions by Prince Bidyalongkarana (1876–1945); one of his most noted works is *Sām krung*, a history of the three T. capital cities, Ayutthaya, Thonburi, and Bangkok.

The 1932 revolution gave Thailand a constitutional monarchy; and court-dominated poetry thereafter ceased. Post-1932 poetry differed from classical works in its brevity, its lyricism, and its emphasis upon crit. and instruction. Many of these changes resulted from the efforts of Chao Phraya Thammasakdimontri, known as Khru Thep (1876–1943), a journalist-poet. Later, in the 1940s and '50s, Assani Phonlachan (b. 1918) sought to de-emphasize the importance of rhyme and sound in T. p. At the same time, Chit Phumisak (1932–65), a political idealist, helped launch the "Art for Life's Sake" movement, which attacked individuals and even whole political systems; Phumisak criticized cl. T. p. for not meeting the needs of the people. Other poets such as Prakin Xumsai, writing as Ujjeni (b. 1919), and later Naowarat Pongpaiboon (b. 1940) emphasized nature, love, and emotion along with social crit. The 1960s saw much experimentation with verseforms, incl. free verse (*klọn plāū*). During this time the poet-painter Angkarn Kalayanapongse (b. 1926), probably the most respected of contemp. poets, developed his themes and style. Often described as a nature poet, he finds expressions of universal messages in nature, art, and the past. The fluid political climate of the early 1970s revived protest and socialist themes. The student uprising of October 14, 1973, the return to democracy, and the subsequent suppression on October 6, 1976, have provided the themes for much of T. p. up to the present. Naowarat Pongpaiboon has emerged as the most eloquent chronicler of these events ("Mere Movement," "The Day that Killed the Dove," "From Sunday to Monday: October 14, 1973"). Political and social crit. continue to serve as major themes of T. p. today, and poets continue to use both cl. and a variety of experimental verseforms.

ANTHOLOGIES AND TRANSLATIONS: *Magic Lotus, a Romantic Fantasy* (1949), *The Story of Phra Abhai Mani* (1952), *The Story of Khun Chang and Khun Phan* (1955), all ed. and tr. P. Chaya; *Khun Chang, Khun Phèn: La Femme, le héros et le vilain*, tr. J. K. Sibunruang (1960); P. na Nakhōn, *Prawat wannakhadī T.* (1964); R. Jones and R. Mendiones, *Intro. to T. Lit.* (1970); *Sang Thong*, tr. F. S. Ingersoll (1973); *Ramakien*, tr. J. M. Cadet (1982); *Mere Movement*, tr. N. Pongpaiboon (1984); *A Premier Book of Contemp. T. Verse*, ed. M. Umavigani et al. (1985); *Phādāeng Nāng Ai: A Thai-Isan Folk Epic in Verse*, tr. W. Tossa (1990).

HISTORY AND CRITICISM: H. H. Prince Bidyalankarana, "The Pastime of Rhyme-making and Singing in Rural Siam," *Jour. of the Siam Soc.* 20 (1926), "Sebha Recitation and the Story of Khun Chang Khun Phan," *Jour. of the Siam Soc.* 33 (1941); P. Schweisguth, *Étude sur la litt. siamoise* (1951); P. Anuman Rajadhon, *T. Lit. and Swasdi Raksa* (1953); P. Purachatra, "Thailand and Her Lit.," *Diliman Rev.* 6 (1958); J. N. Mosel, *A Survey of Cl. T. P.* (1959), *Trends and Structure in Contemp. T. P.* (1961); K. Wenk, *Die Metrik in der Thailändischen Dichtung* (1961), *Sunthọn Phū—ein T. Literat* (1985); T. H. Bofman, *The Poetics of the* Ramakian (1984); T. J. Hudak, "Poetic Conventions in T. *chan* Meters," *JAOS* 105 (1985), "The T. Corpus of *chan* Meters," *JAOS* 106 (1986), *The Indigenization of Pali Meters in T. P.* (1990). T.J.H.

TIBETAN POETRY. The T. term for poetry is *snyan-ngag* (Sanskrit *kāvya*), "ornamental lang.," and for poet is *snyan-ngag-mkhan* (Sanskrit *kavi*). *Snyan-ngag* is characterized by the use of rhetorical ornament (*don-rgyan*, Skt. *arthālaṃkāra*) and phonetic ornament (*sgra-rgyan*, Skt. *śabdālaṃkāra*). It may be in either verse or prose, and there is little deliberate use of rhyme. Colloquially, however, Tibetans speak of *rtsom* (literally "composition") to refer to poetic verse in particular. T. verse typically consists of quatrains, with lines of 5 to 15 syllables, and in very ornate verse sometimes more. Shorter lines are characteristic of archaic and folk poetry, while translations of Sanskrit poetry and poetry influenced by Sanskrit models use lines of 7 or more syllables. The lines are most often metrically regular and generally trochaic, with a final syllable added when the line contains an odd number of syllables. Parallel syntax is often employed, one or more syllables being repeated at the beginning, middle, or end of each line, or the same syllable within a single line. Tropes include various sorts of simile (*dpe-rgyan*) and metaphor (*gzugs-rgyan*), and the use of stylized literary synonyms (*mngon-brjod*).

The indigenous T. poetic genres, little influenced by translated lit., include folksongs (*glu*, songs of varied meter, and *gzhas*, dance-songs of four 6-syllable lines), epic and bardic verse (*sgrung-glu*), and versified folk oratory (*tshig-dpe/ mol-ba*). These are generally unwritten but have informed T. lit. in several respects. The inspiration of folksong, for instance, permeates the poems of the Sixth Dalai Bla-ma (1683–1706), as in this example, in the characteristic trochaic trimeter of the dance-song:

> If I follow my girl friend's heart,
> Life's religious wealth will run out;
> If I adhere to single retreat,
> I'll be running against my girl's heart.

The subject matter of T. folksong may include love, politics, grief, nature, or activities such as grazing, sowing and harvesting, or construction work. Literary redactions of Tibet's epic and bardic trads. are represented by manuscript and printed versions of the popular tales of King Gesar (*ge-sar sgrung*). Folk oratory, on the other hand, has seldom been recorded, though its colorful rhet. occasionally punctuates T. yogic songs and biographies.

The T. script and literary lang. developed in the 7th c. A.D., early literary effort being primarily devoted to tr., particularly of Indian Buddhist lit. During the 13th c. this translated lit. was canonized in the form of two great collections, the *Kanjur* (*bka'-'gyur*, "translated pronouncements") in roughly 100 volumes, consisting of the discourses attributed to the Buddha, and the *Tanjur* (*bstan-'gyur*, "translated treatises") in roughly 200 volumes, consisting of the writings of later Indian scholars and sages. These incl. much verse, providing enduring examples for T. writers. The latter collection also includes trs. of Sanskrit treatises on the "lang. sciences" (*sgra-rig, śabdavidyā*)—grammar, synonymy, poetics (above all the *Mirror of Poetics, Kāvyādarśa*, by Daṇḍin), metrics, dramaturgy—the basis for all later T. literary education.

As in India, verse was often the vehicle for works on philosophy and doctrine (*lta-ba/grub-mtha'*). While highly technical works were versified for mnemonic reasons, poetic elaboration of Buddhist doctrine employed scriptural figures of speech, as in this example from the work of Klong-chen Rab-'byams-pa (1308–63):

> Life is impermanent like clouds of
> autumn,
> Youth is impermanent like flowers of
> spring,
> The body is impermanent like borrowed property,
> Wealth is impermanent like dew on
> the grass.

Many of Tibet's major religious writers composed outstanding doctrinal verse, incl. Tsong-kha-pa (1357–1419), 'Jigs-med Gling-pa (1729–98), and Shar-rdza Bkra-shis rgyal-mtshan (1859–1935).

Gnomic verses (*legs-bshad*) modeled on aphorisms from Indian books of polity (*nītiśāstra*) found their greatest exponent in Sa-skya Paṇḍita (1182–1251), whose *Treasury of Aphoristic Gems* (*legs-bshad rin-po-che'i gter*) is cited proverbially. Other famed aphoristic collections are those of Paṇ-chen Bsod-nams grags-pa (1478–1554) and Mi-pham rnam-rgyal (1846–1912). Ethical and spiritual instructions (*zhal-gdams*) may adhere closely to doctrinal models, or to the conventions of gnomic verse; but they may also make powerful use of colloquialisms and elements of folksong, as do the *Hundred Admonitions to the People of Ding-ri* (*ding-ri brgya-rtsa*) of Pha-dam-pa Sangs-rgyas (12th c.), by origin an Indian yogin, and the *Thirty-seven Skills of the Bodhisattva* (*rgyal-sras lag-len so-bdun-ma*) by Rgyal-sras Thogs-med bzang-po (1295–1369).

The complex ritualization of T. religion has encouraged the devel. of ritual and devotional verse (*cho-ga, gsol-'debs*). Accomplished academic poets, such as Paṇ-chen Blo-bzang chos-rgyan (1570–1662), author of a popular *Worship of the Guru* (*Bla-ma mchod-pa*), have contributed here, as have inspired "treasure-discoverers" (*gter-ston*), whose revelatory verses are chanted daily by devout Buddhists throughout Tibet.

Verse narratives (*rtogs-brjod*) may be fables or legends, histories or hagiographies (*rnam-thar*). Such works are sometimes reminiscent of Indian Purāṇic texts, as is the *Testament of Padmasambhava* (*Padma bka'-thang*), redacted by O-rgyan Gling-pa (b. 1323), or may be modeled on exceedingly ornate Sanskrit *kāvya*, as are the *Narrative of the Lord of Men* (*Mi-dbang rtogs-brjod*) and other writings by Mdo-mkhar Tshe-ring dbang-rgyal (1697–1763).

Drawing thematic inspiration from the Apabhraṃśa songs of the Indian Buddhist tantric masters, and imagistic and metrical resources from indigenous bardic and popular verse, the Buddhist yogins of Tibet created an entirely distinctive family of verseforms collectively known as *mgur*, yogic songs. The greatest author of *mgur* was the inspired sage Mi-la-ras-pa (1040–1123), famed as Tibet's national poet. Here he sings of his foremost disciple, Ras-chung (b. 1084):

> He's gone off riding a fine steed:
> Others' steeds are skittish,
> But Ras-chung's steed doesn't shy.
> On the stallion of thought's vital wind,
> My son Ras-chung, he's gone riding off.

The poetry anthol. was not a well-developed form in Tibet, perhaps owing to the emphasis on the collected works of individual authors and yogins; commentaries on Buddhist doctrine often make such extensive use of quotations that they amount to anthologies in any case. Nonetheless, mention must be made of the extraordinary *Ocean of Songs of the Bka'-brgyud School* (*bka'-brgyud mgur-mtsho*), originally compiled by the eighth Karmapa hierarch, Mi-bskyod rdo-rje (1507–54), an anthol. of masterpieces of the *mgur* genre.

Indian erotic lore was known primarily through Buddhist tantric lit., and frankly erotic imagery is often used symbolically in religious verse, less frequently in secular verse. A modern author, Dge-'dun chos-'phel (1894–1951), has composed an original and highly amusing *Treatise on Love* (*'dod-pa'i bstan-bcos*), inspired by the *Kāma Sūtra*, but in some respects also reminiscent of Ovid's *Art of Love*.

Owing to the stability of the T. cl. literary lang., the form and lexicon of T. poetic composition as represented in the most recent authors differ little from models dating back a millennium. The secularizing and colloquializing tendencies of contemp. T. journalism have gradually begun to influence T. literary activity in other spheres, so that we do see some evidence of very recent poetic experimentation. Any attempt to assess such devels. at present, however, would be premature.

FOLK VERSE AND BARDIC TRADITIONS: R. A. Stein, *L'épopée tibétaine de Gesar dans sa version lamaïque de Ling* (1955), *Recherches sur l'épopée et le barde au Tibet* (1959); G. Tucci, *T. Folk Songs*, 2d ed. (1966); N. N. Dewang, "Musical Trad. of the T. People: Songs in Dance Measure," *Orientalia Romana: Essays and Lectures*, v. 2 (1967); M. Helffer, *Les Chants dans l'épopée tibétaine de Ge-sar d'après le livre de la Course de cheval* (1978); B. Nimri Aziz, "On Translating Oral Trads.: Ceremonial Wedding Poetry from Dingri," *Soundings in T. Civilization,* ed. B. N. Aziz and M. Kapstein (1982).

TRANSLATIONS: J. Bacot, *Three T. Mysteries* (1924); G.-C. Toussaint, *Le Dict de Padma* (1933); E. Conze, *The Buddha's Law Among the Birds* (1955); *The Hundred Thousand Songs of Milarepa,* tr. G. C. C. Chang, 2 v. (1962); J. Bosson, *A Treasury of Aphoristic Jewels* (1969); R. A. Stein, *Vie et chants de 'Brug-pa Kun-legs le Yogin* (1972); S. Beyer, *The Cult of Tārā* (1973); Longchenpa, *Kindly Bent to Ease Us,* tr. H. Guenther, 3 v. (1975–76); *The Rain of Wisdom,* tr. Nālandā Tr. Committee (1980); K. Dhondup, *Songs of the Sixth Dalai Lama* (1981); L. G. Wangyal, *The Prince Who Became a Cuckoo* (1982).

HISTORY AND CRITICISM: P. Poucha, "Le vers tibétain," *ArO* (Prague) 18 (1950), 22 (1954); J. Vekerdi, "Some Remarks on T. Prosody," *AODNS* 2 (1952); K. Chang, "On T. P.," *CAsJ* 2 (1956); E. G. Smith, Intros. to *Encyclopedia Tibetica,* v. 3–5 (1969); R. A. Stein, *T. Civilization* (1972), ch. 5.

T.T.; M.T.K.

TURKISH POETRY.

I. EARLY TURKISH POETRY
II. DIVAN (CLASSICAL) POETRY
III. RELIGIOUS OR TEKKE POETRY
IV. INDIGENOUS FOLK POETRY
V. EUROPEANIZATION OF TURKISH POETRY

I. EARLY TURKISH POETRY. Some early lyrics (found in Chinese tr.) and vestiges of oral epics seem to lend credence to the speculation that poetic sensibility among the Turks of Central Asia probably dawned before the birth of Christ. However, the actual beginnings of the T. poetic trad. lie in the period between the late 9th and mid 11th c. A.D., when T. tribes moved into and settled parts of Anatolia, which was under the influence of Islam and of Arab and Persian cultures. These *Oğuz* Turks brought with them a dialect already rich in expressive resources and a developed popular lit. By the end of the 11th c., however, the Turks had converted to Islam in huge numbers and embraced its prevalent culture, incl. its philosophy and lit. Out of this assimilation came the first poetic work of stature that clearly bears the imprint of the new literary orientation, *Kutadgu Bilig* (Wisdom of Royal Glory, ca. 1069–70) by Yusuf Khass Hajib. Composed in *aruz* (Arabic-Persian quantitative prosody), this mirror for princes, consisting of about 6500 couplets, is a vast philosophical treatise on government, justice, and ethics. Written about the same time, Kasgarlı Mahmut's *Divan ü Lügat-it Türk* is a lexicon and compendium of the T. lang. and its major dialects which includes many specimens (some fragmentary) of pre-Islamic and early Islamic T. p.

From the end of the 13th c., when the Ottoman state came into being, through the mid 19th c., three main trads. of T. p. evolved: (1) Persian-influenced *Divan* (classical) poetry, (2) religious or *Tekke* poetry, and (3) indigenous folk poetry. From the mid 19th c. up to the present day, T. p. has undergone an extensive European orientation.

II. DIVAN (CLASSICAL) POETRY. *Divan* poetry (also called Court poetry), whose course ran almost parallel to the glories and decline of the Ottoman Empire, spanned more than six centuries. Composed by and for an intellectual elite mostly affiliated with the Court, its main vehicle of expression was the Anatolian T. dialect. From beginning to end, cl. T. p. remained under the dominance of Persian and Arabic poetry. It tried to emulate the meters, stanzaic forms, and mythology used by Persian and Arab poets, as well as a substantial portion of their vocabulary. To suit the metric requirements of *aruz, Divan* poets often deliberately distorted T. vowels or employed words of Arabic and Persian origin which lent themselves better to *aruz. Divan* poetry also used the major verseforms of Persian and Arabic lit., e.g. *ghazal* and *qaṣīda, mas̱navi, rubâi, tuyuğ, Şarkı* (originally *murabba*), *musammat,* and *tarih* (chronogram).

Form reigned supreme over *Divan* poetry. Content, most *Divan* poets felt, was the autonomous substance of a literary trad. whose concepts and values were not to be questioned, let alone renovated. They considered originality fortuitous at best, and preferred to achieve perfection in craftsmanship. Despite the tyranny of form, prominent *Divan* poets often attained a profound spirituality, a trenchant sensitivity, an overflowing eroticism. Perhaps no *Divan* poet can be said to show a broad range of poetic sensibilities. Tradition sanctioned not range, but depth. Between the given extremes of the continuum of subject matter, the masters, i.e. Fuzulî, Baki, Şeyh Galip, and others, achieved an impressive profundity of passion expressed with gripping power—from self-glorification to self-abnegation, from agony to ebullient joy, from fanatic continence to uninhibited hedonism. Islamic mysticism, as the soul's passionate yearning to merge with God, formed the superstructure of this poetry. In the hands of the first-rate poets, the *Divan* trad. produced a corpus of exquisite lyric and mystic poetry which has steadily retained its impressive literary significance.

Early *Divan* masters were Seyhî (d. ca. 1431), Ahmedî (1334–1413), Ahmet Paşa (d. 1497), Ahmed-i Dâî (15th c.), and Necati (d. 1509). Many of the Sultans were accomplished poets, incl. Mehmed, who crushed Byzantium, and Selim II (d. 1574). The most prolific among them was Süleyman the Magnificent (d. 1566) who composed close to 3000 verses. The greatest figures of the *Divan* trad. emerged in the period of the Ottoman Empire's grandeur. Fuzulî (1494–1556) stands as the most impressive creative artist of cl. T. lit. He composed three *Divans* (major collections of poems), one in T., one in Arabic, and one in Persian, in addition to several *mesnevîs* (verse narratives). His masterpiece *Leylâ vü Mecnun* is a *mesnevî* of close to 4000 couplets in which Fuzulî made a philosophical and dramatic exploration into worldly and mystic love. Perhaps no other poet exerted as much influence on the *Divan* poetry of the following centuries. Among his most memorable lines: "I wish I had a thousand lives in this broken heart of mine / So that I could sacrifice myself for you once with each life." Fuzulî chose to write his T. poems in the *Azerî* dialect in the manner of Nesimî (d. 1404). Baki (1526–99) achieved wide fame for the aesthetic perfection of his secular *ghazals* and *qaṣīdas* in lines and couplets which often have an epigrammatic concentration; his best-known line has become a proverb among Turks: "What endures in this dome is but a pleasant sound." Hayalî (d. 1557) and Taşlıcalı Yahya Bey (d. 1582) attained renown for their craftsmanship and sensitive lyricism. Rûhi-i Bağdadi (d. 1605) composed a *Terkib-i Bend,* which still stands as a masterpiece of social and philosophical satire with a strong moral concern. The supreme satirist of the *Divan* trad., however, was Nef'i (1582–1635), who, in his masterful *qaṣīdas,* courageously lampooned hypocrisy and affectation. Şeyhülislâm Yahya (1552–1644) produced refined *ghazals,* while Nailî (d. ca. 1666) won renown for his delicately elegant lyrics. Intellectual exploration and social commentary abounded in the poetry of Nâbi (1642–1712). Nedim (d. 1730) sang the joys of living and the beauties of nature (particularly in the city of Istanbul). He contributed to *Divan* poetry a lilting, entrancing style derived mainly from the colloquial Istanbul T. of his day. The last master of *Divan* poetry was Şeyḫ Galip (1757–99), who, in addition to a superb *Divan,* produced *Hüsn ü Aşk* (Beauty and Love), an allegorical work of passionate mysticism. Although the cl. trad. continued until the early part of the 20th c., after Şeyh Galip it produced no figure or work of significance.

III. RELIGIOUS OR TEKKE POETRY. Religious poetry flourished among the mystics, Muslim clergy, and the adherents of various doctrines. Members of the *tekkes* (theological centers) were particularly prolific in such poetry, which drew upon and overlapped both *Divan* and folk trads. Ahmet Yesevî (d. 1166) and Ahmet Fakih (d. ca. 1250) were early masters. Perhaps the greatest figure of religious lit. was the poet-saint Mevlânâ Celâleddin-i Rumi (1207–73), who wrote a six-volume Persian *mesnevî* of nearly 26,000 couplets about the ways of mysticism. In the late 13th and early 14th c., Sultan Veled (Mevlânâ's son), Âşık Paşa, and Gülş ehrî achieved distinction. The most renowned T. masterpiece to come out of the religious trad. was *Mevlid-i Şerif* (1409), composed by Süleyman Çelebi (d. 1422). An adulation of the Prophet Mahomet, this poem is chanted as a requiem among Muslim-Turks. Two folk poets, Kaygusuz Abdal (15th c.) and Pir Sultan Abdal (16th c.), have made substantial contributions to T. religious poetry. Their poetry represents the Alevî-Bektaşi movement (long considered heretical) and is a deviation from and reaction against some of the tenets of traditional Islam.

IV. INDIGENOUS FOLK POETRY. Parallel to *Divan* poetry, T. folk poetry has run its own evolutionary course. Its roots lie in the pre-Islamic epic trads. of the peripatetic T. tribes. Although most of these epic poems were lost in whole or part, one major epic entitled *Oğuznâme* reveals that Turks had a developed poetic faculty long before they fell under the influence of the Persian and Arab cultures. The *Dede Korkut Tales* of the Oğuz tribes contain poems in rather free renditions which also stand at the source of the folk trad. Folk poetry has been created and kept alive to our day by the *ozans, saz şairleri* (poet-musicians), and *âşıks.* It has voiced, in its spontaneous, sincere, and often matter-of-fact fashion, the poetic sensibilities of the uneducated classes, in contrast to cl. poetry, which was composed and read by the intellectual elite. In indigenous verseforms, e.g. *türkü, koşma, mani, destan, semai,* and *varsaği,* mostly extemporized and sung to music, replete with assonances and inexact rhymes, and composed in simple syllabic meters, folk poetry gave voice to the themes of love, heroism, the beauties of nature, and, at times, Islamic mysticism. Unsophisticated and unpretentious, it evolved a serene realism, an earthy humor, and a mellifluous lyric quality. The trad. still remains alive in Turkey's rural areas, as well as among urban devotees of lit., and has exerted an appreciable influence on the T. p. of modern times. In fact, many versifiers of the late 19th and 20th c. have adopted the vivid rhythms and much of the vocabulary and idiom of folk poetry.

A genius who emerged in the 13th c. came to dominate folk verse: Yunus Emre (d. ca. 1321). Employing both folk prosody and *aruz* meters, he created an impressive corpus of poems (some now lost) rich in philosophical content, intensely mystical, steeped in the best folk idiom, melodious, and full of vivid imagery and fresh metaphor. Later centuries witnessed the first-rate works of Karacaoğlan (ca. 1606–80), a poet of love and pastoral beauty, Âşık Ömer (d. 1707), Gevherî (d. ca. 1740), Dadaloğlu (1785–1868), Dertli (1772–1845), Bayburtlu Zihni (d. 1859), Erzurumlu Emrah (d. 1860), and Seyrani (1807–66).

V. EUROPEANIZATION OF TURKISH POETRY. The decline of the Ottoman Empire reached a critical point by the middle of the 19th c. Younger T. intellectuals started seeking the Empire's salvation in technological devel., political reform, and cultural progress fashioned after European models. The so-called *Tanzimat* (Transformations) of the 1840s aimed at realizing some of these far-reaching changes. A new orientation toward Europe (France, in particular) brought the younger poets into contact with the aesthetic theories and verseforms of Fr. poetry. While *aruz* was not abandoned, T. poets experimented with forms, rhythms, and styles. A reaction set in against words of Arabic and Persian origin. Poetry acquired a social awareness and a political function in the hands of some poets who endeavored to gain independence from external political domination. Ziya Paşa (1825–80), Şinasi (1826–71), and Namik Kemal (1840–88) emerged as champions of nationalism. Recaizade Ekrem (1847–1914) and Abdülhak Hâmit Tarhan (1852–1937) echoed the Fr. romantics. The latter, a prolific poet and author of numerous verse dramas, gained stature as a ceaseless renovator. His poetry, which covered a wide range of topics, had a philosophic bent as well as dramatic impact.

In the late 19th and early 20th c., under Sultan Abdülhamit's suppression, most T. poets retreated into a fantasy world of innocent, picturesque beauty where, in a mood of meek sentimentality and lackadaisical affection, they attempted to forge the aesthetics of the simple, the pure, and the delectable. Their lyric transformation of reality abounded in new rhythms and imaginative metaphors expressed by dint of a predominantly Arabic-Persian vocabulary and an appreciably relaxed *aruz.* A Fr.-oriented group of poets referred to as *Servet-i Fünun,* after the literary magazine they published, became prominent on the literary scene. Its leader Tevfik Fikret (1867–1915) also wrote angry political poems against the Sultan's despotism and the Empire's crumbling institutions. His poetry represented a new direction for the formal and conceptual progress of T. p.

During the same period, *Divan* poetry was continued by a few minor poets. Folk poetry maintained much of its vigor and exerted considerable influence on many younger poets striving to create a pervasive national consciousness and purify the T. lang. by eliminating Arabic and Persian loanwords. Ziya Gökalp (1875–1924), social philosopher and poet, wrote poems expounding the ideals and aspirations of T. nationalism. Mehmet Emin Yurdakul (1869–1944) and Rıza Tevfik Bölükbaşi (1869–1949) used folk meters and forms as well as an unadorned colloquial lang. in their poems. Mehmet Âkif Ersoy (1873–1936), a meticulous craftsman and a deft master of *aruz,* wrote mainly of T. glory and of Islam's *sumnum bonum.* Eşref (1846–1912) emerged as Turkey's best satirical poet of the past hundred years. The *Fecr-i Âti* movement contributed in some measure toward the creation of a poetry that Turks could claim as their own.

The T. Republic came into being in 1923. It consolidated national unity and moved swiftly to eliminate Islamic elements from T. life. Emphasis was placed on Westernization, including the introduction of the Lat. alphabet. In the early part of the Republican era, poetry served primarily as a vehicle for the propagation of nationalism. Younger poets branded *Divan* forms and meters as anathema. Native verseforms and syllabic meters gained popularity. Intense efforts were undertaken toward a systematic purification of the lang. The group *Beş Hececiler* (Five Syllabic Poets)—Faruk Nafiz Çamlibel (1898–1973), who was equally adept at *aruz,* Orhan Seyfi Orhon (1890–1972), Enis Behiç Koryürek (1898–1949), Halit Fahri Ozansoy (1891–1971), and Yusuf Ziya Ortaç (1896–1967)—produced simple, unadorned poems celebrating love, the beauties of nature, and the glories of the T. nation. Other poets, however, shied away from chauvinism and evolved individualistic worldviews and styles. Symbolism attained success in the consummate poetry of Ahmet Hâş im (1884–1933), who employed *aruz* freely. Neoclassicism gained considerable popularity under the aegis of Yahya Kemal Beyatlı (1884–1958). A supreme craftsman, Beyatlı wrote of love, nostalgia for the Ottoman past, the beauties of Istanbul, and the metaphysics of life and death in poems memorable for their refined lang. and melodiousness. Necip Fazıl Kısakürek (1905–83) engaged in teleological explorations into modern man's agony. Ahmet Muhip Dıranas (1909–80) and Ahmet Hamdi Tanpınar (1901–61) wrote some of the most refined lyric poems to come out of their generation.

From the 1920s onward, modern poetry was dominated by Nazım Hikmet (he sometimes used Ran as his last name; 1902–63), who was an exponent of the Communist ideology. It was Hikmet who introduced free verse as adapted from Majakovskij. Thanks to the extensive translation of his love lyrics and revolutionary poems, he became the most famous T. poet in the world. His profound influence on his disciples in Turkey remains potent decades after his death.

In the years following World War II, poets furthered their earlier innovations, incl. *vers libre* imported from France. After surrealism cast a brief spell on the literary scene, a new school emerged setting forth what may be defined as poetic realism. Introduced by Orhan Veli Kanık (1914–50), Oktay Rifat (1914–88), and Melih Cevdet Anday (b. 1915), and subscribed to by others, incl. Bedri Rahmi Eyuboğlu (1913–75) and Cahit Külebi (b. 1917), this doctrine placed the poet in the center of society and made poetry's function utilitarian. In the late 1940s, most T. poets served as standard-bearers of the social problems of their day. Poetry became a vehicle for the expression less of subjective experience than of objective truth. Written in free verse (occasionally in folk forms and meters), postwar poems drew on all that was alive, vivid, and colorful in the T. idiom. The critic Nurullah Ataç (1898–1957) played a major role in setting the directions of modern poetry in the 1940s and 1950s. In the same period, Cahit Sitkı Tarancı (1910–56) produced impeccable lyrics. Fazıl Hüsnü Dağlarca (b. 1914) emerged as a superior poet of impressive range. His is the poetry of philosophical quest, and it displays a wealth of metaphor and a sonority almost unequalled in

20th-c. T. p. Behçet Necatigil (1916–79) writes poems rich in intellectual substance, while Salâh Birsel (b. 1919) interfuses ingenious verbal patterns and sonic capers.

The abstract movement (sometimes referred to as "meaningless poetry") which held sway from the mid 1950s onward sought to mobilize the imaginative resources of the T. lang. and created a new obscurantism. While İlhan Berk (b. 1916), Attilâ İlhan (b. 1925), Turgut Uyar (1926–85), Edip Cansever (1928–86), and Cemal Süreya (b. 1931) expanded the horizons of metaphor and melody in their highly complex poems, the social realists, during various spurts of freedom from the early 1960s on, took up the battlecries of social justice. Because Turkey's literary establishment is enamored of its own cultural legacy as well as the aesthetics of other nations, contemp. T. p. stands as a remarkably rich synthesis which embraces aspects of the *Divan* and folk trads., the prevalent themes of world poetry, and the myths and values of diverse civilizations. It is both authentically national and self-assuredly universal.

ANTHOLOGIES AND SELECTIONS: E. J. W. Gibb, *Ottoman Lit.: The Poets and Poetry of Turkey* (1901)—awkward trs.; *The Star and the Crescent*, ed. D. Patmore (1946); F. H. Dağlarca, *Selected Poems* (1969); O. V. Kanık, *I am Listening to Istanbul* (1971), *The Book of Dede Korkut* (1972); *Penguin Book of T. Verse*, ed. N. Menemencioğlu (1978)—excellent selections; *Yunus Emre and His Mystical Poetry* (1981), *Contemp. T. Lit.* (1982), both ed. T. S. Halman; Yusuf Khass Hajib, *Wisdom of Royal Glory*, ed. and tr. R. Dankoff (1983); N. Hikmet, *Sel. Poems* (1987); *Süleyman the Magnificent-Poet*, ed. and tr. T. S. Halman (1987).

HISTORY AND CRITICISM: E. J. W. Gibb, *A Hist. of Ottoman Poetry*, 6 v. (1900–1909)—the classic study; F. Köprülü, "Ottoman T. Lit.," *Encyclopaedia of Islam*, v. 4 (1934); A. Bombaci, *Storia della letteratura turca* (1956)—excellent general survey; T. S. Halman, "Poetry and Society: The T. Experience," *Mod. Near East: Lit. and Society*, ed. C. M. Kortepeter (1971); W. G. Andrews, *An Intro. to Ottoman Poetry* (1976), *Poetry's Voice, Society's Song: Ottoman Lyric Poetry* (1985); I. Basgöz, "The Epic Trad. among Turkic Peoples," *Heroic Epic and Saga*, ed. F. J. Oinas (1978). T.S.H.

U

UGARITIC POETRY. See HEBREW POETRY.

UKRAINIAN POETRY. The history of U. p. can be divided into three major periods, made all the more distinct by sharp discontinuities between them. Underlying and producing these discontinuities are profound shifts in U. society; not only do basic political and social structures disappear, to be replaced by entirely new ones, but, at least until the modern period, U. literary and historical consciousness does not succeed in bridging these changes.

The first period, from the beginnings in the 10th–11th c. to roughly the 14th c., coincides largely with the lit. of Kievan Rus', which by general consensus is taken as the common patrimony of the East Slavs—the Ukrainians, Byelorussians, and Russians. The second, middle period, from the late 16th to the late 18th cs., reflects primarily the poetics of the baroque and witnesses a flowering of U. lit. and culture, even though later the bookish and church-dominated character of this lit. came to be seen as a fatal flaw, given 19th-c. U. sociopolitical development, and the entire period underestimated or even dismissed from the canon. The third period, from the beginning of the 19th c. to the present, coincides with the birth of the modern U. nation and the emergence of contemp. literary U. based on the vernacular. Because of the strong populist current underlying this political and cultural revival, the idea and content of "U. lit." was often identified, throughout the 19th and even into the 20th c., with this third period alone.

In the course of the early modern (17th–18th cs.) and modern periods poetry has consistently played a dominant role. However, the privileged place of poetry in the system of genres of U. lit. must be seen as reflecting the concrete circumstances and limitations within which it existed; through much of the 18th and 19th cs., for example, U. lit. survived practically without institutions (publishing houses, a press, the theater) and without a social consensus as to its validity, to its "right to life" alongside the Imperial Rus. lit., and indeed for some decades in the face of official proscription. While such strictures were highly deleterious for prose and drama, however, poetry not only survived but grew, establishing trads. and a certain hegemony.

The question of the role of poetry in old U. (Kievan) lit. is made particularly complex by the characteristic diffuseness and interpenetration of genres in that lit. In general, from this period there are no extant works that point to distinct poetic genres, let alone to theories of poetics, histories of or commentaries on poetry, and so on. This absence is striking in view of the fact that Byzantine lit., which served as a primary if not always immediate model for the old Kievan lit., had a rich gamut of poetic genres. We can, however, speak of poetry in Old U. lit. in terms of (1) the oral trad., (2) translated and "borrowed" lit., and (3) verse elements in the original lit. The first of these, with which histories of U. and Rus. lit. traditionally begin, is complex and surrounded by much confusion. The major misconception is that Old U. oral lit. is to be identified with folklore, with the creativity of the folk; in fact, as in various other analogous situations, this lit., while oral, was most probably a product of a court or "high" trad. which only over the centuries "sank" into the repertoire of folklore. The actual evidence for this oral poetry, moreover, is only indirect. Whether as the epic cycle of *byliny* (U. *staryny*) which depict the Kievan context and setting, but which were preserved only in the northern Rus. territories, or as the broad gamut of ritual poetry related to the agricultural cycle and various pagan rites, the actual texts date only from the 18th–19th cs., so that conclusions about the range and function of oral lit. in this earliest period must remain speculative.

Verse as such is found in the various translations and adaptations of Byzantine liturgical lit., particularly hymnography (see BYZANTINE POETRY). These hymns influenced contemp. Kievan texts and even had an impact on the bookish versification of the 16th–18th cs. By general consensus the major poetic work of this period is the *Igor Tale* (*Slovo o polku Igoreve*) describing a relatively minor and unsuccessful military campaign of 1185. Putatively written sometime in the early 13th c., it was discovered and published at the turn of the 19th c. Although some doubts remain, its authenticity has been argued on both linguistic and historical grounds. Its syncretic form, mixing military and cautionary tale, lyrical moments with dynastic programme (which some, ahistorically, prefer to read as "patriotic" fervor) is also taken as proof of its authenticity. Its sonorous, vivid lang. and imagery, its deft many-stranded narrative of rhythmic prose, have made of the *Slovo* for all the modern East Slavic lits. the quintessential poetic correlative of Kievan Rus'.

The period of the 14th to the late 16th c. is remarkable and still puzzling for its dearth of cultural and literary texts; the ravages of the Mongol invasion, the Tartar raids, the peculiar cultural stasis during the Lithuanian domination of the U. lands, and the movement of Orthodox churchmen and sees north of Muscovy only partially explain this lacuna. A major exception to this bleak picture is the emergence sometime in the 16th c. of a new form of oral poetry, the *duma* (pl. *dumy*), which supplanted the older *staryny* and was to have a strong impact on much of subsequent U. p. Though oral (the *dumy* were sung by wandering, often blind singers), this was not a narrowly folkloric genre—its perspective encompassed all of U. society. The *dumy*, reflecting elements of heroic epic, ballad, and elegy, are above all "sacred songs" conveying profound social and historical experiences. The latter are highlighted in cycles of *dumy* dealing with wars with the Turks and Tartars, and then later with the 17th-c. wars of liberation from Poland. Apart from introducing a vibrant new form, the *dumy* also establish the pattern of a popular poetry that can lay claim to being more "authentic," closer to the national experience, than any bookish form.

At the end of the 16th c., U. society and culture undergo a remarkable revitalization, which culminates in the mid 17th c. with an autonomous Cossack state that, with changing fortunes, was to last more than a century. Under the impact first of Ren. ideas, but soon thereafter of the still more pervasive baroque, U. p. proceeds to expand its repertoire of genres, and with the establishment of ever more centers of learning, esp. the Mohyla Academy in Kiev (founded in 1632), it finds a self-confidence that allows it to compete with the highly developed and sophisticated Polish poetry of the time. Nevertheless, a characteristic feature of Middle U. lit. is its bilingualism: throughout the 17th and early 18th cs., it is written in U. or in Polish, depending on theme or genre or projected audience. By the mid 18th c. this bilingualism—again reflecting a concrete social and political reality—becomes U.-Rus. In both cases the choice of the other lang. reflects not a hedging of the writer's U. identity but rather the conventions of the literary system.

The earliest poetry of this period, beginning from the 1580s and '90s, is syllabic in meter, in genre emblematic and heraldic. Throughout the first part of the 17th c., U. p. is represented mainly by panegyric, historical, and didactic verse. The poetry of praise in particular reflects the emergence of new cultural centers and leaders, such as Jelisej Pletenec'kyj, archimandrite of the Caves Monastery in Kiev (e.g. *The Image of Virtue*, 1618), or the metropolitan Petro Mohyla (e.g. the *Eucharisterion*, 1632, or the *Euphonia*, 1633), who establishes an Academy that is not only the mainstay of the cultural efflorescence of 17th-c. U. but the major center of learning in the Slavic Orthodox world. The genre system at this time is still not crystallized, with historic narrative often merged with lament or polemic (e.g. *The Lament of Ostrog*, 1636), or the didactic with the lyrical (e.g. Kyryl Trankvilion Stavrovec'kyj's *The Much-Valued Pearl*, 1646). The panegyric mode itself may be infused with dramatic elements, as in Kasjan Sakovyč's eulogy of Hetman Sahajdačnyj (1622).

By the second half of the 17th c. U. p. shows a relatively broad range of forms and a differentiation into "high" genres (reflecting baroque poetics) and popular genres. In the former, such important poets as Lazar Baranovyč and esp. Ioan Velyčkovs'kyj, while writing in both bookish U. and Polish, and while still predominantly reflecting religious themes, give a new depth to national self-expression. The popular genres in turn—fables, satires, and Christmas and Easter verse—are mostly anonymous and close to the vernacular. At times, as in the poetry of the wandering monk

Klymentij Zinovijev, with its encyclopedic overview of U. life and customs (incl. a large collection of proverbs), they are an invaluable mirror to a whole epoch.

The early 18th c. witnesses the maturation of U. school drama—in the works of Feofan Prokopovyč, Lavrentij Horka, Manujil Kozačyns'kyj, and Mytrofan Dovholevs'kyj. Prokopovyč's tragicomedy *Vladymir* (1705), the best known of these, exemplifies the didactic poetics of this genre, as the historical theme—the Christianization of Kievan Rus'—becomes a vehicle for political satire and for the apotheosis of the U. hetman, Mazepa. After the defeat of Mazepa in 1709, Prokopovyč became the prime ideologue of the new Rus. state founded by Peter I; his departure for St. Petersburg epitomizes the massive movement of U. scholars, clergyman, and writers to Russia at the beginning of the 18th c. In broad historical terms the growth and centralization of the Rus. empire signal in the course of the 18th c. the ever-greater provincialization of Ukraine. In poetry two significant developments accompany this. On the one hand, there is an ever more conservative and hidebound reliance in books of poetics on the norms and conventions of the baroque (which in Russia is quickly abandoned—beginning with Prokopovyč himself—for neoclassicism). On the other hand, as a function of the new laws promulgated by Peter I prohibiting the publication of books in U., U. lit. was forced to go underground, to exist only in ms. form. Various genres did, however, survive: lyric poetry, puppet plays, burlesque verses, dialogues and verse satires. Paradoxically, at the end of the 18th c. there appears the most significant talent of premodern U. lit.—the peripatetic mystic philosopher and poet Hryhorij Skovoroda (1722–94). His book of devotional poetry, *The Garden of Divine Songs*, synthesizing Cl. and biblical, mystical and folk elements, remains the highpoint of 18th-c. U. p.

Modern U. p. is traditionally dated with the appearance of Ivan Kotljarevs'kyj's *Enejida* of 1798, a travesty of Virgil's *Aeneid.* Finding its analogue to the fall of Troy in the destruction of the last Cossack stronghold (the Zaporozhian Sitch), marking the end of U. autonomy in the 18th c., the *Enejida* focuses on the wanderings of a band of Cossacks, and in the course of its six cantos provides an encyclopedic and loving account of U. provincial life and customs. Mixing an energetic optimism, satire, nostalgia for the past, and above all broad humor, the poem became a rallying point for a new U. lit. in the vernacular. Although he abandoned the old syllabic versification in favor of the iambic tetrameter that was then ascendant in Rus. poetry, Kotljarevs'kyj did draw on a broad range of comic and burlesque devices characteristic of 18th-c. U. p. In fact, his example was almost too successful, in that for over three decades U. p. came to be dominated by the burlesque mode.

In this period even talented poets like Petro Hulak-Artemovs'kyj (1790–1865) paid their dues to this trad. (popularly called "Kotljarevščyna")—in his case by writing travesties of Horace's Odes. Beginning with the 1820s, however, U. romantic (or more precisely, preromantic) poets, like Lev Borovykovs'kyj, Amvrozij Metlyns'kyj, and Mykola Kostomarov (1817–85—who later became a major U. and Rus. historian and spokesman for the U. cause), introduced an entirely new poetics: in conjunction with the ethnographic historical and antiquarian work of such scholars as I. Sreznevskij, M. Bodjans'kyj, and M. Maksymovyč, the focus of this poetry fell on the turbulent Cossack past and on the wealth of U. folklore.

A similar literary and cultural revival was initiated in the mid 1830s in western Ukraine, then under Austria-Hungary. Led by such young clergymen-poets as Markian Šaškevyč (1811–43), Ivan Vahylevyč (1811–66), and Jakiv Holovac'kyj (1814–88), the so-called Ruthenian Trinity, it sought to legitimize the vernacular lang., to rediscover historical and ethnic roots, and to advance cultural and national autonomy.

A sea change in the range and depth—and status—of U. p. was effected by the first true romantic, Taras Shevchenko (1814–61). Born a serf and freed only at the age of 24, Shevchenko virtually at once came to be lionized by both U. and Rus. society as a uniquely powerful and inspired poet. Arrested in 1847 in connection with the secret *Brotherhood of Saints Cyril and Methodius* and exiled for ten years, he returned in ill health but with poetic powers unimpaired. Seen as a martyr and bard even in his lifetime, Shevchenko became upon his death the animating spirit of the U. national movement, and indeed the object of a popular cult to this day. Shevchenko's poetry, traditionally called the *Kobzar* (the Minstrel) after his first slim collection of 1840, divides along the lines of intimate lyric poetry (with a range of folkloric stylizations); political poetry, with powerful excoriations of social and national oppression, particularly by Tsarist authority; and narrative poems, incl. historical poems and ballads. All of these modes are unified and guided by structures of mythical thought which basically project a movement from the present state of victimization—personal as well as collective—to a redeemed and purified humanity, where "on the renewed earth / there will be no enemy, no tempter, / but there will be a son and a mother, / and there will be people on this earth."

Pantelejmon Kuliš (1819–97), friend and critic, exegete and rival of Shevchenko, also significantly broadened the range of U. p.—by new historical themes, expanded formal concerns, and, not least, translations of Shakespeare and the Bible, of Byron and other Western poets. Many of Shevchenko's successors tended to be overshadowed however, and their voice distorted by his Muse. This was particularly true of the fine western U. poet Jurij Fed'kovyč (1834–88). Of those who resisted the pull of Shevchenko's model the most important were two poets on the borderline of romanticism and realism, Stepan Rudans'kyj (1834–73) and Jakiv Ščoholiv (1823–98).

Generally, poetry in the latter half of the 19th c. was strained by the weight of perceived realist obligations and, more concretely, by official Rus. edicts of 1863 and 1876 banning the publication and importation of U. books. A poet who exemplifies both the call of national, civic duty and the thrust of an authentic, personal poetry is the western U. Ivan Franko (1856–1916). A man of indefatigable energy, prose writer and dramatist, critic, translator and scholar as well as poet, Franko too became the conscience of his people. His poetry covers a broad gamut—exhortatory, historical, satiric, lyrical, and confessional, this last is by far the most successful.

The period of modernism, generally from the 1890s to World War I, witnessed the differentiation of the U. literary marketplace and the emergence of poetry for a more select public. One of the first to turn to European and universal historical and philosophical themes was Larysa Kosač-Kvitka (pen name, Lesja Ukrajinka; 1872–1913); her drama (much more than her lyric poetry) serves to establish these concerns in U. p. Her masterpiece, *The Forest Song,* draws its inspiration from folklore and psychological introspection.

On the eve of World War I there appeared the symbolist poetry of Oleksandr Oles' (1878–1944), Mykola Voronyj (1871–1942), and Mykola Filjans'kyj (1873–1938), an anticipation of the outstanding poet of the 20th c.—Pavlo Tychyna (1891–1967). At first a symbolist and spirited supporter of the U. national revolution, and at the end of his life an orthodox spokesman for the Soviet system, Tychyna underwent a complex evolution, but in his early and mature poetry, at least, remains the most innovative and influential poetic voice of his time.

In the 1920s, with the establishment of Soviet rule in Ukraine and esp. the official policy of "Ukrainization," U. lit. for the first time since the 17th c. enjoyed the support of a state; its growth and energy were spectacular, as manifested in the proliferation of separate movements, particularly the neoclassicists, with such outstanding poets as Maxym Ryl's'kyj (1895–1969), Mykola Zerov (1890–1930?); and the futurists, with Myxajl Semenko (1892–1930?), the theorist and impresario of the movement, and Mykola Bažan (1904–83), who began as a futurist but quickly outgrew it to become, by virtue of his intellectualism and historicism, the second most important U. Soviet poet of the century. Adding to the variety, ferment, and sheer breadth of expression of U. p. in the 1920s and early '30s were the constructivists (e.g. Valerjan Polishchuk), neoromantics (e.g. Oleksa Vlyz'ko), and others who belonged to no formal organization or movement—such as Jevhen Pluzhnyk or esp. Volodymyr Svidzins'kyj (1885–1941), master of lyrical, almost mystical introspection.

But by the 1930s the Stalinist terror had crushed the national and cultural revival, and hundreds of writers perished in camps and purges. With Soviet U. p. reduced to silence or the empty rhet. of paeans to Stalin and the Party (most poignant when written by such as Tychyna, or indeed Ryl's'ky and Bažan), the poetic scene shifted to western Ukraine, then under Poland, or to Poland itself, and Czechoslovakia, where various poets and writers had emigrated, fleeing the Bolsheviks. Though in the inter-war period the literary climate there was often obscured by nationalist fervor, such poets as Jevhen Malanjuk, Oleksa Stefanovyč, Oksana Ljaturyns'ka, and others did make distinct contributions, the greatest being that of Bohdan Ihor Antonych (1909–37). Beginning with formal experimentation and a fascination with the rich imagination of his native Carpathian (Lemko) region, he attains in his mature poetry an expressive power and metaphysical and symbolic complexity that put him in the forefront of 20th-c. European poetry.

Immediately after World War II, U. p. had a short period of intense activity in the emigration, beginning with the Displaced Person camps in Germany, where long-repressed energies came to fruition in a multitude of publications. Outstanding among a range of poets of the middle generation were Oleh Zujewskyj and Vasyl Barka. Each, in rejecting the rhet. of the earlier emigré generation, tended toward a hermetic difficulty, Zujewskyj by searching for a pure poetry without emotional and even semantic signposts, and Barka by a baroque lang. and religiosity. The highpoint of U. emigré poetry, however, was the informal "New York Group" that arose in the late 1950s and lasted to the early 1970s. Emma Andijevs'ka, Jurij Tarnawsky, Bohdan Boychuk, and Bohdan Rubchak, all of them born between the wars, but very much attuned to the West, gave to U. p. a new and valuable avant-garde cast.

Even though decimated in the 1930s and then long repressed, Soviet U. p. remained in the mainstream. A major revival occurred in the early and mid 1960s with the appearance of such significant young poets as Vasyl' Symonenko, Lina Kostenko, Mykola Vinhranovs'kyj, Dmytro Pavlychko, and the most talented of them, Ivan Drach. Their common concern for authenticity and lyric intensity was amplified by historical and ethical concerns. In contrast to the rather traditional poetics of his contemporaries, the poetry of Vasyl Holoborod'ko moved toward the surreal and fantastic; for this very reason it was largely not published and had only a limited impact. This is all the more true of such dissident poets as Vasyl' Stus and Ihor Kalynets. Most significantly, however, the liberalization of Soviet society then political collapse of the Soviet Union in the 1980s had a profound and positive effect on the general climate of U. p.—in its rehabilitation of victims of repression and of historical memory as such, in its galvanization of various established poets, in its reassertion of the social and historical role of U. p., and above all in its facilitation of the emergence of a new generation of poets in the U. republic.

ANTHOLOGIES: *The U. Poets*, ed. and tr. C. H. Andrusyshen and W. Kirkconnell (1963); *Xrestomatija davn'oji ukrajins'koji literatury*, ed. O. I. Bilec'kyj (1967); *Koordynaty*, ed. B. Boychuk and B. T. Rubchak (1969); *Antolohija ukrajins'koji liryky*, ed. O. Zilyns'kyj (1978); *Ukraijins'ka literature XVIII st.*, ed. O. V. Myšanyč (1983); *Antolohija ukrajins'koji poezii*, ed. M. P. Bažan et al. (1984).

HISTORY AND CRITICISM: G. Luckyj, *Literary Politics in the Soviet Ukraine 1917–1933* (1956); *Istorija ukrajins'koji literatury*, ed. J. P. Kyryljuk et al. (1967–71); D. Čyževs'kyj, *A Hist. of U. Lit.* (1975); G. Grabowicz, *Toward a Hist. of U. Lit.* (1981); Terras. G.G.G.

URDU POETRY. See INDIAN POETRY.

URUGUAYAN POETRY. See SPANISH AMERICAN POETRY.

V

VEDIC POETRY. See INDIAN POETRY.

VENEZUELAN POETRY. See SPANISH AMERICAN POETRY.

VIETNAMESE POETRY. Early V. p. developed on the basis of both cl. poems by Buddhist monks and Confucian scholars and numerous folk verses sung by minstrels and peasants at rural festivals. The genre used most often in popular verse is the six-eight (*lục-bát*) couplet form, a V. innovation in which a line of six monosyllabic works is followed by a line of eight. This form can comprise a number of tonal iambs or anapests, with both final and medial rhyme, as shown in the first four lines of *The Tale of Kiêu*, with *o* representing either of the two flat or even tones, *x* one of the four sharp or oblique tones, and *R* a rhyme:

o o o x o oR1
Trăm năm trong cõi nguòi ta
x o x x x oR1 x oR2
Chu tài chu mênh khéo là ghét nhau
x o x x x oR1
Trai qua môt cuôc bê dâu
x o o x o oR2 x oR3
Nhung þiêu trông thây mà þau þón lòng

A hundred years—in this life span on earth
Talent and destiny are apt to feud
You must go through a play of ebb and flow
And watch such things as make you sick at heart

Such couplets are found in proverbs and sayings, work songs, love songs, children's songs, lullabies, and riddles. But the alternation of hexasyllables and octosyllables can continue almost without limit, the number of lines reaching several thousand in the case of such long narratives as *The Tale of Kiêu* by Nguyen Du, *The Story of Phan Trân* by Dô Cân, and *Lục Vân Tiên* by the blind poet Nguyên Đ'inh Chiêu. A variation of the six-eight meter is preceded by two lines of seven words, thus engendering the "double-seven six eight" (*song-thât lục-bát*) meter, used in elegies and ballads and typified by Phan Huy Ich's or Đoàn Thị Điêm's tr. of *The Song of a Soldier's Wife* (a poem first written in cl. Chinese by Đăng Trân Côn), or Marquis Ôn-nhu's *The Plaint of an Odalisque*. All those moving pieces, first meant to be chanted, later became limited blockprint editions circulated among friends and connoisseurs and printed in *chu nôm*, the demotic script which in the 11th c. assimilated Ch. characters to transcribe individual V. words.

The same gentry scholars who created such popular stories in vernacular V. verse, several of whom remained anonymous, often authored prodigious poetic compositions well crafted in Ch. itself. Whichever lang. they used, their clear preference was for the 8-line stanza (*bát cú*), sometimes reduced to a quatrain called *tú tuyêt*, with each line containing either 7 words (*thât ngôn*) or 5 (*ngu ngôn*) and obeying the rules of Ch. prosody (see CHINESE POETRY). The 254 poems left by Nguyên Trãi in the 15th c., the collection composed by Emperor Lê Thánh-tông and the court ministers who clustered around him as the "28 constellations" in his Tao-þàn Academy, and the pastorals of Nguyên Binh Khiêm all reveal features of V. culture in a distinctly native rhythm—the caesura falling after the third syllable of the seven in the line rather than after the fourth, as in T'ang poems—as well as native imagery, allusions, and metaphors.

With the ascendancy of the Roman script (*quôc-ngu*), invented in the 17th c. by Western missionaries, both Ch. and "southern" characters lost their hold on V. education and culture. By 1918, the year the old-style literary examinations were abolished, the new romanization designed to facilitate assimilation of Fr. culture and the newborn press rapidly stimulated literary output among Fr.-trained writers. Thê Lu, Luu Trọng Lu, Chê Lan Viên, Huy-Thông, Xuân-Diêu, and Huy-Cân began to write "new poetry," an innovative genre launched by Phan Khôi in 1932, turning away from Ch. versification with its rigid rules for tonal harmony and parallelism, and utilizing new rhythms (e.g. 8-word lines) and new rhymes, as well as alliterative and assonantal reduplication and sound symbolism. Poets in and around the literary group Self-Reliance (*Tụ-lục*) exhorted love, individual freedom, and the beauty of Nature in stanzas that were first printed in the group's magazines *Phong-hoá* and *Ngày nay* before appearing in book form.

Romanticism and lyricism took full advantage of the musicality of the lang. in poems by the original Nguyên Khăc Hiêu, who experimented with verse in 3-word and 5-word lines; by Trân Tuân Khai, who succeeded in combining the old and the new; and by Quách Tân, who sounded like a Nguyên Khuyên, a Trân Tê Xuong, or a Đông-hô, who exuded love of the countryside. This trad. of modern poetry couched in plebeian terms was quickly followed by such talented writers as Nguyên Bính, Đinh-Hùng, Vu Hoàng-Chuong, and Bàng Bá Lân, who overnight became the idols of a city youth attuned to their newly expressed sensibilities. Whereas Buddhist, Confucian, and Taoist themes still dominated a segment of 20th c. V. p., new ideals of liberty and happiness crowded compositions by a new generation who, north of the 17th Parallel, concentrated on anticolonial and socialist topics or who, south of the demarcation line, lamented the moral decay, broken families, and disrupted careers that they readily blamed on the war years. Women, who figure prominently in the literary scene, inherited the trad. begun by female poets such as Đoàn Thị Điêm, Hô Xuân-Huong (well-known for her erotic imagery through clever double entendre) or Nguyên Thị Hinh (known as "Lady Thanh-quan" and noted for her sober and elegant cl. verse).

In content dependent on the social context and expressing a painful conflict between traditional (i.e. Sino-Vietnamese) and foreign (i.e. Western) elements, and in form rising above the old constraints to ingenious inventiveness, modern V. p. steadily increases its riches, whether inebriated with "achievements" of socialism inside the country or, since 1975, despondent over the travail of the emigrés' separation from the motherland, writers who yet express their nostalgia in prolific creations in expatriate publications around the world.

ANTHOLOGIES: Vietnam P.E.N. Center, *Poems and Short Stories* (1966); *Anthologie de la poésie vietnamienne*, ed. Chê Lan Viên (1969); *The War Wife: V. P.*, tr. K. Bosley (1972); *A Thousand Years of V. P.*, ed. and tr. Nguyên Ngọc Bích (1975); *The Heritage of V. P.*, ed. and tr. Huynh Sanh Thông (1979); *Le Chant vietnamien: Dix Siècles de poésie*, ed. Nguyên Khăc Viên (1981); *Fleurs de pamplemoussier: Femmes et poésie au Vietnam*, ed. Huu Ngọc and Françoise Corrèze (1984).

HISTORY AND CRITICISM: Trân Trọng Kim, *Viêt-thi* (1956); Duong Đình Khuê, *Les Chefs d'oeuvre de la littérature vietnamienne* (1966); Xuân-Diêu, "V. p. over the past 30 years," *Lotus* 26 (1975); Duong Đình Khuê and Nicole Louis-Hénard, "Aperçu sur la poésie vietnamienne de la décade prérevolutionnaire," *BEFEO* 65 (1978); Nguyên Tiên Lãng, "Panorama de la poésie contemporaine vietnamienne," *Littératures contemporaines de l'asie du sud-est*, ed. Lafont and Lombard (1984); M. Durand and Nguyên-Trân Huân, *Intro. to V. Lit.* (1985); Công-huyên-tôn-nu Nha-Trang, "The Role of Fr. Romanticism in the New Poetry Movement in Vietnam," *Borrowings and Adaptations in V. Culture*, ed. Truong Buu Lâm (1987). D.-H.N.

W

WELSH POETRY has a history spanning 14 centuries, from the odes of Taliesin and Aneirin in the 6th c. to the odes of the poets who now compete for the chair every year at the Royal National Eisteddfodau of Wales. We deduce from Gildas' diatribe on the bards of Maelgwn, King of Gwynedd (d. ca. A.D. 547) that theirs was a trad. which, derived through the Celts from Indo-European peoples, accorded bards a special role—on account of the magical powers attributed to them—in relation to their rulers. They were expected to call into being and to praise in those rulers the qualities most needed to fulfill their functions, esp. prowess and valor in battle. In short, bards were assigned a sacral role in the life of their people.

During the early period of its history W. p. was composed and handed down orally. Most of the extant poetry written before the death of the last W. princes in 1282–83 is preserved in the *Black Book of Carmarthen, The Book of Aneirin, The Book of Taliesin, The Book of Hendregadredd*, and the *Red Book of Hergest*, ms. volumes the first of which was written ca. 1260, the last toward the end of the 14th c. The oldest poetry, that composed from the beginning of the W. lang. to the end of the 11th c. (although more has been preserved from the earliest century than the later ones) is usually called *Yr Hengerdd* (the Old Song), and its composers are called *Y Cynfeirdd* (the Early Bards).

The Book of Taliesin, written in the first half of the 14th c., purports to contain the poems of Taliesin, but it is obvious that there are two Taliesins, one historical and the other legendary. Most of the twelve poems, mainly panegyrics, which can be attributed to the historical Taliesin are addressed to Urien, who ruled ca. 575 over Rheged, a realm including parts of modern Galloway and Cumbria.

The Book of Aneirin (second half of the 13th c.) opens with the statement in W., "This is the Gododdin. Aneirin sang it." The Gododdin, originally the name of a people in northeast England and southeast Scotland, is a long poem celebrating the bravery of a war-band sent to recapture a stronghold from the English about the year 600 A.D., although the date lacks any archaeological backing. They fought almost to a man, gloriously but unsuccessfully. Aneirin eulogizes them for the most part individually, so that the poem comprises a series of elegies. More importantly, though, the poem contains evidence that the Britons of southern Scotland had poets who practiced the same poetic art to celebrate the heroic deeds of the dead and the quick as that of the Britons of Wales or the W., so that we have here the reason why the poetry of Taliesin and Aneirin was appropriated as traditionally their own by the poets of Wales. Further, there is very little linguistically to distinguish the earliest poetry produced in Wales from that of ancient northern England and southern Scotland. It was sung to exalt the rulers on whose heroic qualities the survival of the people depended, and it used the same poetic embellishments, endrhyme to link lines and, within the line, the repetition of the same consonant or vowel sounds, i.e. incipient *cynghanedd.*

By the middle of the 9th c., Powys, the kingdom adjoining Gwynedd in north Wales, was hard pressed by the Eng. Its struggle is reflected in the work of a bard or school of bards who composed a series of dramatic stories woven round the 6th-c. figure of Llywarch Hen (Llywarch the Old), his kin, and the 7th-c. prince of Powys, Cynddylan, although the stories reflect the emotions aroused by contemporary events on the borders of Powys. At one point in the saga, Llywarch Hen urges his son Gwên to go into battle against the Eng. invaders. Gwên goes and, like his brothers before him, is killed on the dyke. There follows a magnificent elegy in which the father mourns the last and the best of his sons. Whether there was once a prose framework to these poems, composed of monologues and dialogues, is still disputed, but it seems reasonable to assume its existence, and to assume also that the W., like the Irish in the West and the Hindus in the East, followed a practice, dating from Indo-European times, of using prose for ordinary narrative and verse for the expression of strong emotion and moments of heightened tension. On the other hand, W. lit., like Irish, has no early verse epics.

The W. kingdoms found themselves in a state of endemic warfare not only against the Eng. but among themselves. Since they were slow to accept primogeniture inheritance, internecine dynastic feuds were frequent, and W. bards could not fail to be propagandists. Some of them claimed powers of vision and prognostication; in times of dire distress, these donned the role of prophesying victory against the Eng. foe. The most remarkable W. prophetic poem, *Armes Prydain,* (The Prophecy of Britain), composed about 930 A.D., foretold that the W. would be joined by the Cornishmen, the Bretons, the Britons of Strathclyde and the Irish, incl. the men of Dublin (the Danes), to overthrow the Eng. and banish them across the sea whence they had come. Although in the W. trad. the legendary Taliesin and the equally legendary Myrddin (Merlin) were the seers *par excellence,* and as such were credited with many anonymous prophecies, internal evidence suggests that *Armes Prydain* was composed by a monk in one of the religious houses of south Wales. Vaticinatory poems appear throughout the Middle Ages and were esp. numerous in the form of *cywyddau* (plural of *cywydd,* sometimes referred to as *cywyddau brud,* prophetic *cywyddau*) during the Wars of the Roses.

At one time it appeared that the Normans would conquer Wales as easily as they had conquered England, but the W. rallied and preserved their independence more or less intact until 1282–83. The national revival, which secured the survival of the W. under their princes, manifested itself also in a fresh flowering of poetry. The poets of the princes, sometimes called the *Gogynfeirdd* (the "not so early" bards, to distinguish them from their predecessors the *Cynfeirdd*), sang in much the same way Taliesin had sung, but they were not content simply to imitate their predecessors; they developed a much more complex poetic style and a more sophisticated system of *cynghanedd,* sometimes called *cynghanedd rydd,* ("free" *cynghanedd,* to distinguish it from *cynghanedd gaeth* or "strict" *cynghanedd,* which the bards of the nobility later evolved). Their poetry indicates that they formed a kind of order in which the *pencerdd,* the master craftsman who had won his position in competition, taught one or more apprentices in a school of *ars poetica.* According to some accounts, the function of the *pencerdd* was to sing the praise of God and the king. Next in order of rank stood the *bardd teulu,* originally the bard of the king's household-troops; apparently he was expected to sing to these troops before they set off for battle, but he could also be called to sing to the queen in her chamber.

Among the foremost of these *Gogynfeirdd* were Gwalchmai (ca. 1140–80), Cynddelw (ca. 1155–1200), Llywarch ap Llywelyn (ca. 1173– 1220), and Dafydd Benfras (ca. 1220–57). Their range of themes was not large, and their poetry dazzles by the intricacies of its *cynghanedd,* the superb command of lang., and the wealth of literary and historical references rather than by any individuality of thought. If the *Gogynfeirdd* borrowed their themes and much of their technique from the *Cynfeirdd,* they succeeded by their ingenuity in elaborating the former and refining the latter, in producing poems remarkable for originality of expression. After the defeat of the W. princes their patrons, they were saved from extinction partly by the resilience of their guild, though mostly by patronage from the newly emergent nobility. It is thus appropriate that they should now be called "Poets of the Nobility," *Beirdd yr Uchelwyr.*

In the reorganization following 1282, W. society finally had to shed its heroic-age features: no wars were allowed, and martial prowess and valor ceased to have their old value. The poets as well as the nobility had to reassess their function, the former becoming more of a craft guild than an order. The *cywydd* (*deuair hirion*) superseded the *awdl* as the favorite meter, "strict" *cynghanedd* took the place of "free" *cynghanedd,* and entertaining the nobility became more important than exalting it. The effects of foreign influences were mediated mainly by the new religious orders and by a few *clerici curiales,* esp. Einion Offeiriad, whose "bardic grammar" sought not only to impose order on the practice of the poets but also to give it a new intellectual framework. Einion's is the earliest extant attempt at a metrical analysis of W. p. His division of "meters" into the three categories of *awdl, cywydd,* and *englyn,* subject to the modifications by Dafydd ab Edmwnd in 1450 (who arranged the "24 meters" into these three classes) became the accepted forms of "strict-meter" poetry and has remained so to this day.

Dafydd ap Gwilym (fl. 1320–70) perhaps owes a great deal of his indisputable brilliance as a poet to the fact that he had inherited the poetic craft of the *Gogynfeirdd* and was able to adapt it to popularize the *stil nuovo.* He wrote *awdlau* in the old style, but by grafting the embellishments associated with them, *cynghanedd,* on the lower-order verseform, the *traethodl,* he made the resulting *cywydd deuair hirion* into a meter which the new poets of the nobility took pride and delight in using and which won the favor and patronage of the nobility. Dafydd addressed *cywyddau* to his patron Ifor ap Llywelyn (fl. 1340–60), celebrating his generosity so much that he became renowned as "Ifor the Generous," henceforth the exemplar of all bardic patrons. But Dafydd's fame rests ultimately on his *cywyddau* to women and his masterly expression in them of his love of women and of nature. He must have recited or sung these *cywyddau* to small audiences for their entertainment. One of his favorite strategies is to picture himself in a false or undignified situation, making himself the butt of his audience's laughter. Thus he describes in a *cywydd* how one night in an inn he tried to make his way in the dark to the bed of a girl whose favour he had bought in advance by wining and dining her, only to strike his leg against a stool and his head against a trestle table, knocking over a huge brass pan in the process, and creating such a din that the household woke up and began to search for him as an intruder. It was only through the grace of the Lord Jesus and the intercession of the saints, he tells us, presumably with tongue in cheek, that he escaped detection, and he begs God for His forgiveness. But he describes such situations with such wit, invention, verbal dexterity, and technical skill that one must conclude that the audience's enjoyment of the theme was secondary to its enjoyment of the expression, and that the poet's extensive use of *dyfalu,* etc., presumes a high degree of literary appreciation on the part of his listeners.

It was inevitable that Dafydd ap Gwilym should set the stamp of his poetry on that of his younger contemporaries and immediate successors, and that, once the shock of his originality and exuberance had been absorbed, the trad. should reassert itself, albeit in modified form. The poets retained their guild organization, their way of transmitting knowledge of the poetic craft, and sundry privileges. But they and their patrons had become aware of the world outside Wales—the influences of the Hundred Years War must not be underestimated—and some at least had become conscious that the eulogies that bound poet and patron could be interpreted as sycophancy. A poet of strong conscience, such as Siôn Cent in the first quarter of the 15th c., could not fail to feel this tension, and his vivid pessimism and gloomy *Weltanschauung* made him condemn the traditional W. Muse as deceitful and proclaim his own as the "true" or Christian Muse. But Siôn Cent had few followers. The bardic institution was strong enough to withstand his influence, as well as the disastrous effects of the Owain Glyndwr Rebellion and the Black Death. Indeed, there is evidence that, contrary to expectation, Wales shared, albeit to a lesser extent, the prosperity which England enjoyed in the 15th c.—the Black Death seems to have put greater wealth in the hands of fewer people—and the poets shared in the prosperity of their patrons. The result is that the century 1435–1535, the *grand siècle* of W. p., is remarkable not only for its large number of poets but also for the very high standard achieved by many of them. The poets were sufficiently self-confident to assemble in *eisteddfodau*—first in Carmarthen (about 1450) and then in Caerwys (1523)—to make improvements in their metrical and *cynghanedd* systems. Dafydd ab Edmwnd is the poet esp. associated with the first *eisteddfod,* and Tudur Aled with the second, but other great names are not lacking: Dafydd Nanmor, Guto'r Glyn, Lewis Glyn Cothi, and Gutun Owain. Such poets (and the work of many has survived) broadened the themes of praise to include the more domestic and civilized: dynastic marriages, well-built mansions with gardens, excellent tablefare, and material as well as cultural wealth.

After 1282 perhaps the most important date for W. p. is 1485, the year Henry VII acceded to the throne of England, though the implications of that event became apparent only gradually. The most immediate result was that the W. nobility found even greater opportunities for advancement in England, so that many of them abandoned their role as patrons of the W. Muse. And there were a number of others whose contact with the Reformation and the Ren. made them eager to bring their native culture into line with that of England and the Continent. This meant that W. poets should abandon their guild organization, make the secrets of their craft accessible to the general public, and, more important still, assimilate the new learning proffered by the recently invented printing press, esp. knowledge of the art of rhetoric. Above all, a purpose other than praise, esp. unwarranted praise, had to be found for the W. Muse. Most of these points were raised in the famous debate of 1580–87 between Archdeacon Edmwnd Prys and the poet Wiliam Cynwal, and in the open letter which Siôn Dafydd Rhys addressed to the poets in 1597. Some efforts were indeed made to help the W. poets adjust to the new circumstances: descriptions of the W. poetic art and handbooks of rhetoric were published. Of special interest is the description of the poetic art published by Dr. Gruffydd Robert of Milan, a Roman Catholic in exile: he advocated a relaxing of the rules of "strict" *cynghanedd* and the adoption of the "free" accentual meters for epic poetry.

But it was extremely difficult to abandon a poetic trad. and practice that had endured for a thousand years, and very few W. poets found it possible to take up the new learning. Deprived of patrons, the poets found themselves devoid of incentive either to teach or to learn the art which hitherto had been handed down from generation to generation. Grufydd Phylip of Ardudwy, who died in 1666, was the last of the "old" or professional poets. Henceforth their art was to be kept alive by amateurs drawn from the clergy or the ranks of the gentry. Edmwnd Prys showed what could be achieved, but by the end of the first quarter of the 18th c., the old trad. seemed dead.

In some mss. written after 1550, poems in the free accentual meters began to appear side by side with poems in the strict meters. There is no reason to suppose that the free accentual meters had not been previously used; they would not have been considered worthy enough to be copied into ms. collections with the more professional strict-meter poems. Their presence in increasing numbers in the mss. implies that they were becoming more esteemed. It is usual to distinguish two kinds of free accentual meters, one old and native, the other new and borrowed, although some of the embellishments of the strict meters were added to both. The newly borrowed accentual meters were based on those of Eng. songs set to popular airs. There is, for instance, a W. ballad dated 1571 to be sung to the tune "Adew my pretty pussie." The practice of composing W. lyrics to musical airs, native and borrowed, continued throughout the 18th and 19th cs. and persists to this day.

Wales experienced two revivals in the 18th c. The religious or Methodist revival is important in the history of W. p., indirectly because it helped to extend literacy among the people and directly because it gave an impetus to the composition of hymns and hence to other kinds of poetry as well. William Williams, "Pantycelyn" (1717–91), wrote a long poem, "Theomemphus," in which he describes the spiritual experiences of a soul caught up in the Methodist revival, as well as hundreds of hymns. "Pantycelyn" has every right to be regarded as the father of the modern W. lyric. A later hymnwriter, Ann Griffiths (1776–1805), rivals him only in the emotional intensity of her expression.

The literary revival is associated with the "Morrisian" circle, whose leading members—Lewis Morris (1701–65), Goronwy Owen (1723–69), and Evan Evans ("Ieuan Fardd," 1731–88)—were not only poets but also scholars, and as such drew much of their inspiration from the contemporary Eng. literary scene. The Ossianic productions of the Scot Macpherson had stimulated general interest in the ancient popular lits., and the "Morrisian" circle were anxious to demonstrate the antiquity of the W. poetic trad. Evans, their finest scholar, searched for material in the libraries of the landed gentry. Though most of the material he collected remained unpublished, his *Specimens of the Poetry of the Antient W. Bards* marked an important milestone in the rediscovery of the W. poetic trad. It also anticipated the publication of the *Myvyrian Archaiology of Wales* in 3 v., of which v. 1 (1801) was until modern times the only printed source for the texts of the work of the *Cynfeirdd* and the *Gogynfeirdd*.

Goronwy Owen, the "Morrisian" circle's most accomplished poet, was so enamored of the W. strict-meter trad. that he could not bring himself to call anything else poetry. He was prepared to accord every praise to Milton's compositions, but since they were not written in *cynghanedd* he could not call them poetry. Yet at the same time he was too much of a classical scholar not to accept that the most significant poetic genre was the heroic epic. Much to his disappointment, the W. poetic trad. could not boast a heroic epic in strict meter. This deficiency he attempted to supply by writing *Cywydd y Farn Fawr* (The *Cywydd* of the Great Judgment); he also left a legacy of critical ideas, esp. the principles that poetry should follow strict rules of composition and that it could be judged according to criteria derived therefrom.

Later *eisteddfodau* were, in the early 19th c., meetings at which small groups of poets delivered themselves of impromptu verses to test their skill and to entertain a few bystanders. The *eisteddfod* has since developed in several ways. The range of the competitions held has been extended to include music and the other arts, but one feature has remained constant: the highest honor is still accorded to the poet who can produce the best long poem in strict meters. When it could no longer be maintained, following Goronwy Owen, that poetry without strict meters was impossible, the second highest honor was accorded to the poet who could produce the best long poem in the free accentual meters or even in free verse. The presupposition for all these poetic competitions remained Owen's tenet, that poetry is composed according to certain rules, so that success in following these rules can be measured and judged. On the whole, poems in the strict meters lent themselves better than those in the free accentual meters to this kind of competition: indeed, the two categories invited different kinds of criticism. Still, both sorts of poems tended to have common characteristics: they are predominantly objective, impersonal, descriptive, formal in structure, and stylized in diction.

Although W. literary culture in the 19th c. had remarkable achievements to its credit, incl. the work of Evan Evans ("Ieuan Glan Geirionydd," 1795–1855), John Blackwell ("Alun," 1707–1840), and Robert Williams ("Robert ap Gwilym Ddu," 1766–1850), it had no firm base in a well-established educational system. Schooling did not become compulsory until the end of the century, and even then only scant attention was paid to the W. lang. One of the results was a curious lack of self-confidence shown even by the most talented poets, an inability to recognize what they could do best and a failure to persevere and develop it when they achieved success. This is true of Ebenezer Thomas ("Eben Fardd," 1802–63), who wrote the best *eisteddfodic awdl* of the century in strict meter, *Dinystr Jerusalem* (The Fall of Jerusalem), for the Welshpool *Eisteddfod* of 1824 and then, dissatisfied with his success in the strict meters, wrote a long mediocre poem on the Resurrection (*Yr Adgyfodiad*) in the free accentual meters.

As a poet, critic, and editor, William Thomas ("Islwyn," 1832–78) concentrated in his mature years on poetry in the strict meters, but his major contribution to W. p. was made as a young man, when he wrote two long poems entitled *Yr Ystorm* (The Storm). They show a young man struggling to express thoughts and emotions vaguely understood in words only rarely adequate, but they leave the reader with a feeling that in better circumstances and with more persistence he could have developed into a finer poet. Islwyn was claimed as the "Father" of a group of poets calling themselves the "New Poets." They believed that they were breathing new life into the W. poetic trad. by eschewing the strict meters in favor of the free accentual meters for long philosophical poems. But the nebulous nature of their thought is betrayed in their equally nebulous lang., which is often extremely bombastic.

John Morris-Jones (1864–1929) had a clearer vision than the "New Poets" of what was needed. He undertook the task of restoring the literary standards of classical W. On the one hand, he was able to standardize the orthography, to restore the syntax, and to purify the idiom of the lang. On the other, by emphasizing the entire span of the W. poetic trad. from its beginnings, he was able to reveal its greatness and to uncover some of the forgotten secrets of the prosody underlying that greatness. As a professor and author of both the standard grammar of the lang. and the definitive description of its prosody, his authority was unassailable, but he was also a successful poet in both strict and free meters, and hence a constant adjudicator at the national *eisteddfodau* of his time. He took the W. nation to school. And he was fortunate in his brilliant disciples, some even more generously gifted at poetry than he. His influence is most obvious in the work of T. Gwynn Jones, W. J. Gruffydd, and R. Williams Parry. The next generation of poets—T. H. Parry-Williams, D. Gwenallt Jones, Waldo Williams, Saunders Lewis—also benefited from his work on the lang. but developed their own ideas of poetic diction and form. Although many mastered the art of the strict meters, their most outstanding contributions have been in the free accentual meters. Some, notably Euros Bowen, have developed *vers libre* in which a form of *cynghanedd* is almost essential. Euros Bowen, Bobi Jones (R. M. Jones), and Gwyn Thomas are the most prolific, most diverse, and most significant poets of their generation.

There has recently been a remarkable increase in the popularity of the strict meters among the youngest generation of W. poets, foremost of whom is Alan Llwyd. This is perhaps because television and radio have provided a platform for poetry as entertainment, esp. poetry in the strict meters. Teams drawn from the W. counties compete with each other in composing poems in the strict meters, the *cywydd*, the *englyn*, as well as lyrics in the free accentual meters; their meetings are recorded for broadcasting, and successful teams compete again at the *National Eisteddfod* in *Y Babell Lên*, the Literary Pavilion. Such has been the success of these meetings that a Strict Meter Society (*Cymdeithas Cerdd Dafod*) has been established with more than a thousand members, publishing a monthly periodical called *Barddas* and several volumes of poetry and criticism each year.

See also BRETON POETRY.

BIBLIOGRAPHIES: G. O. Watts, "Llyfryddiaeth Llenyddiaeth Gymraeg," *BBCS* 30 (1983); C. Donahue, "Med. Celtic Lit.," in Fisher; R. Bromwich, *Med. Celtic Lit.: A Select Bibl.* (1974); *Llyfryddiaeth Llenyddiaeth Gymraeg*, ed. T. Parry and M. Morgan (1976).

ANTHOLOGIES: *Poems from the W.* (1913), *W. Poems of the 20th C.* (1925), both ed. H. I. Bell and C. C. Bell; *The Burning Tree* (1956), *Presenting W. P.* (1959), both ed. G. Williams; *Oxford Book of W. P.*, ed. T. Parry (1962); *Med. W. Lyrics* (1965), *The Earliest W. P.* (1970), *20th-C. W. Poems* (1983), all ed. J. P. Clancy; *The Gododdin*, ed. K. Hurlstone Jackson (1969); *The Poetry of Llywarch Hen*, tr. P. K. Ford (1974); *Dafydd ap Gwilym: A Selection of Poems*, ed. R. Bromwich (1982); *Dafydd ap Gwilym*, tr. R.

M. Loomis (1982); *W. Verse*, ed. T. Conran, 2d ed. (1986)—long intro. and useful appendices; *Early W. Saga P.*, ed. J. Rowland (1990).

HISTORY AND CRITICISM: H. I. Bell, *The Devel. of W. P.* (1936); G. Williams, *An Intro. to W. P.* (1953); Parry, *History*; Jarman and Hughes, esp. the articles by Bromwich, Lewis, and Rowlands; Stephens; B. Jones and G. Thomas, *The Dragon's Pen* (1986); R. Bromwich, *Aspects of the Poetry of Dafydd ap Gwilym* (1986).

PROSODY: J. Loth, *La Métrique galloise*, 2 v. (1900–2), but see the rev. by Morris-Jones in *ZCP* 4 (1903), 106–42; Morris-Jones—still useful, indexed by G. Bowen, *Mynegai i Cerdd Dafod* (1947); R. M. Jones, "Mesurau'r canu rhydd cynnar," *BBCS* 28 (1979); A. T. E. Matonis, "The W. Bardic Grammars and the Western Grammatical Trad.," *MP* 79 (1981); "Appendix on Metres" in Conran (above). J.E.C.W.

WEST INDIAN POETRY refers to poetry written in the Eng. which has evolved as the lang. of the formerly British possessions in the Caribbean area. This poetry is essentially a 20th-c. phenomenon. Most of the verse written in the West Indies before 1900 is minor British poetry using the tropical landscape only as a different setting for epic and pastoral or as a new source of the picturesque. The people in this exotic garden, the slaves, were either ignored or marginalized by British poets. Indeed, little was done to give formal education to the slaves before Emancipation in 1834. By the early 20th c., however, post-Emancipation efforts to provide universal elementary education had begun to produce literates from all races and classes. These island-born writers regarded the landscape as more than just a setting; nascent nationalisms in all the islands began to affect the form and esp. the content of literary productions.

The first important W. I. poet, Claude McKay (Jamaica, 1890–1948) was a cultural nationalist. He wrote in dialect as well as in Standard Jamaican, drawing upon country life and folk trads. (*Songs of Jamaica*, 1912), and his experience of the city where he served as a policeman (*Constab Ballads*, 1912). McKay's emigration to the United States in 1912 enhanced his literary achievement and he continued writing as a W. I. poet, but at home he had no influence during his lifetime. So the visible shapes of W. I. p. came from the practice of more conventional authors who had little use for dialect or the folk heritage. The efforts of the early 20th-c. practitioners have been preserved in four period anthologies (McFarlane 1929 and 1949, Cameron 1931, and Clarke 1943).

These pioneers produced a dependent colonial poetry that looked loyally to the Mother Country ("For England is England, who mothers my soul") and saw no conflict between that and loving the "little green island far over the sea." They took their support and models from the Victorians, from the romantics, and from the Victorian watering down of the romantics. They turned out stiff imitations of accepted models, favoring the sonnet, blank verse, and, esp. in Jamaica, the doubly imported villanelle. Like most Eng. poets of the time they wrote in fixed forms, and they believed that certain subjects were poetic and others not, even certain words were inherently poetic, while others (e.g. dialect) were not fit for expressing "Great Thoughts." They saw their "landscape" but they wrote about "Nature."

By the late 1930s, the artificial poetry of what has been variously called "the Caribbean pastoral trad." and "poetry for recitation" was coming to an end. The trad. begun by Edward Cordle (*Overheard*, 1903), enlarged by the emigré Claude McKay, and kept ebullient and alive by Louise Bennett (see *Selected Poems*, 1982) would soon animate W. I. writing.

On the social scene, responses to the Depression of the Thirties were colored by racial and cultural ideologies derived from movements like Pan-Africanism, Garveyism, the Rus. Revolution, and the Harlem Renaissance ; the whole process was to be accentuated by the harsh experience of World War II. In writing (incl. the calypso), there was a definite turning away from Nature to social issues. Landscape was rediscovered and used to reflect the human struggle. There was a departure from conventional forms and poetic diction, an exuberant indulgence in dialect, and a reckless plunge into declamation and a free verse so free it sometimes became only angry prose. The new subject matter included history, historical processes, and a wide range of folk material not hitherto considered literary. This period of social protest and racial affirmation embraced the use of the lang. of the streets, forced a rapprochement between writing and the speaking voice, and instituted a free trade between poetry, dialect verse, folksong, and calypso. The calypso is a highly rhythmic secular song on topical matters which developed among the slaves and has flourished in the 20th c., esp. in Trinidad and Tobago, as a medium for social commentary, satire, and lyricism. Dance and music are integral to its performance by a bardic figure and chorus who usually generate enthusiastic audience participation.

The 1940s and early '50s saw the establishment and flourishing of important periodicals: in Jamaica, *Focus*; in Barbados, *Bim*; in Guyana, *Kyk-Over-Al*; in Trinidad, *The Beacon*. These periodicals, the BBC's radio magazine *Caribbean Voices* (Figueroa 1970), and two anthologies (1954, 1958) are the key sources for the poetry of the 1940s and 1950s. There were many fine poems in this period, but few authoritative and lasting voices. This was as much a result of the plain fact that there was no outstanding talent as that there was no audience, and no particular value placed on W. I. p. except by the practitioners themselves ("the unknown, the abortive poets") and a small reading circle. Of the poets writing in this period, George Campbell (b. 1918; *First Poems,* 1945), Una Marson (1905–65; *Heights and Depths,* 1932), M. G. Smith (b. 1921), H. A. Vaughan (b. 1901), Frank Collymore (1893–1980; *Selected Poems,* 1971), A. J. Seymour (b. 1914; *Selected Poems,* 1965), E. McG. Keane (b. 1927; *L'Oubli,* 1950), and Wilson Harris (b. 1921; *Eternity to Season,* 1954) were considerable and are still very much in the trad.

Three others achieved greater heights. Eric Roach (1915–74) was born in Tobago; his work is immersed in the peasant life and in history, incl. the Af. connection. His experiments with dialect and the speaking voice were controlled by a careful concern with craft. A. L. Hendricks (b. 1922; *On This Mountain,* 1964, and other volumes) is another poet of substance; Hendricks' wit, elegance and lyricism have not been duly appreciated, and the smooth surface of his verse is muscled (not bulgingly enough for some) by a deeply native inspiration. Hendricks is one of the few Jamaicans to show the sea-consciousness that seems to characterize the southern Caribbean writers. But the most outstanding poet of the period was the Guyanese, Martin Carter (b. 1927; see *Poems of Succession,* 1977). Carter's involvement in social and metaphysical issues, his apparently instinctive control of free verse, and his ability to retain the dialect tone (its harshness as well as its lyricism) combine to make his compressed epic, "University of Hunger," perhaps the best single poem ever written by a W. I.

At last, in the 1960s W. I. p. came of age with the establishment of the international reputations of the Barbadian, Edward Brathwaite (*The Arrivants,* 1973), and the St. Lucian, Derek Walcott (*Selected Poems,* 1964), both born in 1930. Brathwaite's great subject is Africa and the Af. heritage. His world is made up of all the places where the Af. has set foot and laboring hand. His rhythmic poetry draws inventively upon folk and urban experience, and he makes brilliant use of the wide range of forms to be found not only among New World descendants of Africans, but also in Africa itself. Walcott, playing a more subdued music, is the W. I. poet of landscape and the sea. His themes are personal—love, death, loss—and his sociocultural vision is of the meeting of cultures which engendered the newness of the New World:

> I'm just a red nigger who love the sea,
> I had a sound colonial education,
> I have Dutch, nigger and English in
> me,
> and either I'm nobody, or I'm a nation.
> ("The *Schooner* Flight," from *The Star-Apple Kingdom* [1979])

In the works of Walcott and Brathwaite the formalist attitude of the early practitioners fuses at last with the dialect line introduced by Cordle and McKay. The fallout has been widespread. At last there were native masters who belonged to and were defining a trad. Poetry in the West Indies, now shown to be a possible profession, suddenly became popular. The new generation, represented by Mervyn Morris (b. 1937; *The Pond,* 1973 and other volumes), Dennis Scott (b. 1939; *Uncle Time,* 1973 and other volumes), Anthony McNeill (b. 1941; *Reel from "The Life Movie,"* 1972), and Wayne Brown (b. 1944; *On the Coast,* 1972), is alive to social, political, and cultural issues but feels no necessity to proclaim or advertise its West Indianness. Still, these poets write in the shadow of Walcott (*Another Life,* 1973) and Brathwaite (*Mother Poem,* 1977; *Sun Poem,* 1982), who continue strongly as contemporaries.

But while the dialect trad. and the formalist attitude have been fusing (there are stunning experiments by Walcott and Brathwaite), there has also emerged a trend toward a more democratic and instant performance poetry sometimes referred to as "rapso" or "dub." Some of this is akin to those combinations of music, drumming, and poetry that are by now reasonably familiar. But the new trend unites elements of traditional orality (which uniquely are alive in Caribbean societies) with the new or secondary orality opened up by the devel. and spread of electronic media (Smith 1987). This phenomenon draws upon the popular calypso and reggae music and marks an important area of collaboration between the recent island poetry and the Black British poetry now being written by descendants of West Indians in the U.K. (Johnson 1978).

This account of a rich and diverse poetic scene would be incomplete without noticing the recent upsurge in women's poetry. In Jamaica, women's poetry can be traced back to the troubled Arabella Moulton-Barrett, Una Marson, and Barbara Ferland (b. 1919), and it would be possible to find similar figures in the other territories. But regardless of whether or not we can so construct a trad., the work of Dionne Brand (*Fore Day Morning,* 1978), Claire Harris (*From the Women's Quarters,* 1984), Judy Miles (b. 1942), and Grace Nicholls (*I is a Long-Memoried Woman,* 1983), to mention only a few, suggests that W. I. p. is once more about to transform itself.

ANTHOLOGIES: *Voices from Summerland,* ed. J. McFarlane (1929); *Guianese Poetry 1831–1931,* ed. N. E. Cameron (privately pub. in Guyana, 1931); *Best Poems of Trinidad,* ed. A. M. Clarke (1943); *A Treasury of Jamaican Poetry,* ed. J. McFarlane (1949); *Anthol. of Guianese Poetry,* ed. A. J. Seymour (1954); *Anthol. of W. I. P.,* Federation Commemoration Issue of *Caribbean Quart.* 15,2 (1958); *Caribbean Voices,* ed. O. R. Dathorne (1967); *Breaklight,* ed. A. Salkey (1971); *Caribbean Voices,* ed. J. Figueroa (1971); *Jamaica Woman,* ed. P. Mordecai and M. Morris (1971); *Seven Jamaican Poets,* ed. M. Morris (1971); *Caribbean Poetry Now,* ed. S. Brown (1984); *Penguin Book of Caribbean Verse in Eng.,* ed. P. Burnett (1986); *The New Brit. Poetry,* ed. Allnutt et al. (1988); *W. I. P.*, ed. K. Ramchand and C. Gray (1989).

HISTORY AND CRITICISM: E. Baugh, *W. I. P. 1900–1970* (1971); G. Rohlehr, "W. I. P.: Some Problems of Assessment," *Bim* (1976); L. Brown, *W. I. P.* (1978); K. Ramchand, "Parades Parades: Modern W. I. P.," *SR* (1979). K.R.

X

XHOSA POETRY. See AFRICAN POETRY; SOUTH AFRICAN POETRY.

Y

YIDDISH POETRY.

I. PRE-19TH CENTURY VERSE
II. THE 19TH CENTURY
III. THE TWENTIETH CENTURY

Y. is the lang. of Eastern European Jewry and that culture's offshoots the world over. It is commonly believed to date back at least a thousand years, with its roots in Western Europe. Modern Y. p. exhibits every subject and technique known in the lits. of Europe and America and derives an extra measure of cosmopolitanism from a readership distributed over five continents. But out of its combined prehistory and history of nearly a millennium, only two or three generations have witnessed this unrestricted flourishing. In traditional Ashkenazic culture, it was rather study—the continuous interp. of basic Talmudic law in the light of changing conditions of life—that absorbed the creative passions of the society. Literary expression in the Western sense was unimportant, and Jewish poetry of the premodern period (both Y. and Heb.) is marked, for all its diversity, by a generally ancillary character.

Then, with the revolutionary upheavals in East European Jewry in the late 19th and 20th c.—urbanization, industrialization, internal migration and emigration, political organization and eventual civic emancipation, attended by widespread secularization and "Europeanization" of Jewish culture—Jewish poetry in both langs. was lifted to the very top of the cultural values of Judaism. It attracted a body of talent which in previous centuries would have been otherwise engaged, and, in accordance with the increased receptivity of its writers and readers to outside influences, it quickly managed to catch up with common European accomplishments. Y. p. "in one grand leap landed in the general 20th c." (Harshav). Even in its treatment of specifically Jewish themes in an imagery full of traditional allusions, Y. p. became avowedly and factually part and parcel of modern European and Am. poetic culture.

I. PRE-19TH CENTURY VERSE. The origins of Y. lit. have been lost, but early contemp. references to it as well as the developed poetic technique of the oldest dated works so far discovered (A.D. 1382) indicate a prehistory antedating the extant evidence. Prior to the 19th c., Y. lit., the bulk of which is in verse, was written in an idiom based predominantly on Western Y. dialects, a standardized lang. which was preserved without interruption in Western Europe until about 1800, then superseded by a rapidly evolving new standard on an East European interdialectal base. The influence of medieval Ger. poetic trads. and a stylistic irradiation from intentionally literal translations of the Bible caused literary Y. to be highly stylized, and only a weak reflection of contemp. colloquial speech.

Scholars originally theorized that much of this verse was meant for oral performance by professional minstrels or laymen, esp. since, even after the introduction of printing, the tune was often specified at the beginning or end of a work. More recently, however, convincing arguments have been advanced against the so-called *shpilman* theory. Epic poems both of the general European repertoire (King Arthur, Gudrun, etc., with specifically Christian references deleted) and on Old Testament themes (e.g. Samuel or the Sacrifice of Isaac) are extant in 14th- and 15th-c. recensions which show relatively strict meters and, generally, "long-line" stanza-structure of the type *xaxa xbxb.* There is now reason to believe that the European epics are translations or transcriptions of Ger. originals and that the works based on Jewish themes were written by scribes or other well-educated writers (Shmeruk).

Two verse novels by Elye Bokher (E. Levita, 1469–1549) strikingly bridge the gap between original Jewish works and borrowed secular ones. Using It. sources, Bokher created his own versions in which Jewish elements are freely integrated with the primary material. In addition, he introduced ottava rima into Y. well over a century before it was attempted in Ger. poetry. Elye Bokher also seems to have been the first to use accentual iambs in any European poetry.

The metrical structures of epic poetry were not carried forth elsewhere in Y. verse. This is evident in collections of 16th- and 17th-c. popular songs (which reflect a convergence of traditional with current Ger. models), in religious lyrics, in the many verse chronicles and dirges describing historical events, and also in satirical or moralizing occasional pieces, where the meters decrease in regularity until the number of syllables per measure of music varies widely and sometimes grows quite high. Y. p. of early modern times thus corresponds in its free-accentual basis to most contemp. Ger. verse. Drawing on the Heb. liturgical trad., Y. verse sometimes made use of the acrostic and ornamental extravagances such as making all lines of a reasonably long poem end in the same syllable.

II. THE 19TH CENTURY. Through most of the 19th c. the folksong flourished, and the recitative improvisation, narrative (on biblical subjects), and moralizing poem remained productive genres. Meanwhile Y. lit. made a new beginning, centered this time in Eastern Europe and carried by the emigrations toward the end of the century to England, the United States, and the far corners of the earth. The new writers were stimulated mostly by the *Haskalah* (Enlightenment) movement, which encouraged familiarity with European (esp. Ger. and Rus.) lit. and made Jewish writers increasingly self-conscious about the underdeveloped state of their langs., Y. and Heb., for the purposes of social crit., philosophy, and secular education.

While Heb. lit. toyed with a biblical manner, Y. writers explored the cultural framework offered by the folksong, which was noticed at last after a "submerged" existence spanning centuries, during which it was neither recorded nor reflected in lit. The Y. folksong favored an *xaxa* stanza and a free-accentual meter (usually 4 stresses per line) in which, compared with Ger. folksong, the use of unstressed syllables to fill the musical measures was increased, probably as a result of the Slavicized prosodic structure of the lang. However, more European standards of song construction and phrasing introduced more elaborate rhyme schemes (*abab* and *aabccb* became widespread), and strict syllabotonic meters became *de rigueur* in the theater and in quasi-theatrical songs. The rising labor movement furnished a new public for song verse, but also for declamatory verse—an additional factor conducive to regular syllabotonic meters.

In the 1890s Y. p. hit its stride at last. Though it lagged noticeably behind the development of prose—particularly the shorter forms—it now became the vehicle of truly lyrical expression, as exemplified by S. Frug (1860–1916), I. L. Peretz (1852?–1915), and M. Rosenfeld (1862–1923). These authors, who had all complained about the lexical and stylistic inadequacy of Y., now laid the foundations of modern Y. p. by efforts to master a lyrical viewpoint and experiments with a variety of imagery and structural patterns.

IV. THE 20TH CENTURY. The existence of a new intelligentsia with secular education, some of it acquired in Y.-lang. schools, cast Y. p. in this period of its culmination into the mainstream of contemp. world trends. Y. lit. now showed itself more sensitive than ever to developments in other lits. with which it was in contact. There were the interest and the formal means to attempt modernism along Am., Ger., and Rus. lines. At the same time, in the Y. poetic culture there appeared genuine internal responses to innovation. The group *Di Yunge* (Young Ones) in America (M.-L. Halpern [1886–1932], Mani Leyb [1883–1953], Z. Landau [1889–1937], and others) early in the century reacted to the political tendentiousness and rhetoric of the labor poets by trying to write poetry that would be "more poetic" in diction and subject matter and more individuated in its sentiments.

Dedicated to "art for art's sake," the poets of *Di Yunge* emphasized the expression of aesthetic experience even while supporting themselves as laborers: "thank goodness I'm not a cobbler who writes poems, / But a poet who makes shoes" (Mani Leyb). *Di Yunge* cherished a vision of Y. lit. in which a monolingual reader could be a well-educated world citizen. To this end, they turned some of their energies to translation and to introducing "exotic" themes, such as Christianity and sexuality, into Y. p.

Di Yunge called forth the protest of *In zikh* (The Introspectivists), a group (A. Leyeles [1889–1966], J. Glatstein [1896–1971], and N. B. Minkoff [1893–1958], among others) which, avowedly inspired by Yehoyosh (1872–1927) and influenced by contemp. Eng. and Am. poetry, denied in principle a distinction between the intellectual and the emotional and opened wide the door of its poetry to all themes, all words, all rhythms, no matter how free or regular, so long as they embodied the personal experience of the poet. As expressed in its manifesto of 1920, the *In zikh* poets saw no theoretical reason to identify themselves as Jewish artists other than that they were Jews and wrote Y. Moreover, although they accepted syllabotonic meters as a possibility, they were in fact convinced that free rhythms were the surest vehicle for achieving poetic truth. Finally, they had no fear of exposing their deepest psychic realities, embracing free association as their chief poetic method.

As the cumulative effect of a growing corpus of poetry made itself felt, the demands for originality pushed Y. poets onto new paths. Assonance as a substitute for rhyme was explored (e.g. by P. Markish [1895–1952] and other Soviet poets). Sonnet sequences and works in the more difficult Romance fixed forms were successfully created (e.g.

L. Naydus [1890–1918]). Syntactic parallelism, etymological figures, and consonance were mobilized to recreate biblical Heb. effects in a new Jewish medium. Epic poems, verse novels, and verse drama (esp. by H. Leivick [1888–1962]) were produced and acclaimed. Interest in Old Y. p. was awakened, and several writers attempted new works in 16th-c. lang. The poems of S. Etinger (1800–56), a forgotten modernist, were published posthumously. The folksong reappeared, but this time in subtly stylized forms (e.g. by Halpern and I. Manger [b. 1901]).

Post-World War I regional constellations such as the expressionist group *Di Khaliastre* (the Gang) in Warsaw (U. Z. Greenberg [d. 1896–1981], Melech Ravitch [d. 1976], and others) and *Yung-Vilne* (Young Vilna) in Vilna (notably Chaim Grade [1910–82] and A. Sutzkever [b. 1913]) set themselves specialized tasks against a common literary background. The sweet awareness of a poetic trad. being formed was reflected in poetic allusions to well-known poems. A standardized literary lang. came into use in which dialectal rhymes and expressions grew ever rarer.

In this period, the "discovery of the mother tongue," now emancipated in its functions, was completed. Poets by the scores, following the major writers of the late 19th c., learned to use the Y. lang. to its full extent. Y. prosodic structure, Germanic but remodeled presumably along Slavic lines, was employed to create easy triple and even paeonic meters. The refreshing syntax of conversational folk Y. was channeled into poetry (notably by E. Shteynbarg [1880–1932]). The pernicious etymologizing approach of the past was dead: words were used according to their precise Y. phonology and semantics, without reference to—and sometimes in defiance of—their form and meaning in the stock langs. Sound frequencies typical of a particular component of Y. were forged into a new poetic device, making it possible, for instance, to suggest "Slavicness," and hence village earthiness, by an accumulation of *z* and *c* sounds (thus M. Kulbak [1896–1940]), or "Germanness" by emphasizing *a* and final *e* sounds (e.g. Glatstein).

At the same time, the idiom of traditional Jewish study was annexed to the modern literary lang.; it found use not only when required by the subject (as in the poetry of M. Boraisho [1888–1949], A. Zeitlin [1899–1974], or Grade), but also in thematically unspecialized writing, where it functions simply as a flexible abstract vocabulary. Above all, the many derivational patterns of Y. grammar were exploited for the enrichment of the lang. New coinages abounded, and some, like *umkum* (violent death) and *vogl* (restless wandering), have become common elements of the lang. The poetry of Glatstein and Sutzkever is particularly rich in novel derivations.

With the genocide of six million Jews by Germany and her Axis collaborators, Jewish cultural life in most of Eastern Europe was virtually destroyed; what was left received a second devastating blow through Stalin's ban of Y. culture and the elimination of Y. writers in the USSR after 1949, culminating in the August 12, 1952 murder of the Y. poets Markish, D. Hofshteyn (b. 1889), L. Kvitkob (b. ca. 1890), and I. Fefer (b. 1900), among others. The Holocaust of the war years naturally became the central theme of Y. lit. not only in the Nazi-made ghettos, but globally. However, after 1948, the rebirth of a Jewish state in Israel opened new subjects, descriptive, psychological, and ethical, to Y. p.; there an active Y. cultural life rapidly developed, incl. publication of *Di goldene keyt* (The Golden Chain), the premier Y. literary journal.

The technical brilliance of Y. p. did not diminish in the postwar period. In its rhythmic features, however, postwar writing seems to have retreated from the experimentation of the previous period. As Leyeles put it: "When there are no bounds to suffering, create, through pain, a ritual fence [i.e. a preventive measure] of rigorously restrained patterning."

What might be called the second generation since the catastrophic events of the Holocaust and Stalinism reveals a shift in the balance of Y. verse. Whereas actual poetic output is shrinking, scholarship has reached new levels of sophistication and intensity. This phenomenon is directly related to the decimation of the Y.-speaking community and hence the number of native speakers of Y. Those poets who remain, such as Sutzkever, B. Heller (b. 1908), and G. Preil (b. 1910), must contend with the problem of creating in a lang. whose future is, at best, uncertain: "During daytime a funeral, at night a concert / And inevitably, I go to both" (Sutzkever). Scholarly research, by contrast, has been increasingly active, and undertaken more and more by those who are not native speakers of Y. Their work, encompassing a wide variety of perspectives, e.g. historical, social, feminist, psychoanalytic, and comparative, highlights the tremendous vitality of the poetic corpus, even if the number of poets living today is small. One major outcome of recent studies and anthologies is the greater recognition and appreciation of Y. women poets. See also HEBREW POETRY.

ANTHOLOGIES: *Antologye: finf hundert yor yidishe poezye*, ed. M. Bassin, 2 v. (1917); *Yidishe dikhterins: antologye*, ed. E. Korman (1928); *Naye yidishe dikhtung*, ed. Y. Paner and E. Frenkl (1946); *Dos lid iz geblibn*, ed. B. Heller (1951); *Mivhar Shirei Y.*, tr. into Heb. by M. Basuk (1963); *A shpigl af a shteyn*, ed. Kh. Shmeruk (1964)—focuses on murdered Soviet writers; *A Treasury of Y. P.*, ed. I. Howe and E. Greenberg (1969); *Selected Poems of Jacob Glatstein*, tr. R. Whitman (1972); M.-L. Halpern, *In New York: A Selection*, ed. and tr. K. Hellerstein (1982); *Am. Y. P.: A Bilingual Anthol.*, ed. B. and B. Harshav [Hrushovski] (1986); *Penguin Book of Mod. Y. Verse*, ed. I. Howe et al. (1987)—Y. and Eng.

HISTORY AND CRITICISM: L. Wiener, *Hist. of Y. Lit. in the 19th C.* (1899); M. Weinreich, *Bilder fun der yidisher literatur-geshikhte* (1928); D. Hofshteyn and F. Shames, *Literatur-kentenish (poetik)*, 2 v. (1927–28); M. Erik, *Di geshikhte fun der yidisher lit.* (1928); Z. Reyzen, *Leksikon fun der yidisher lit.*, 4 v. (1928); Y. Tsinberg, *Di geshikhte fun der lit. bay yidn*, v. 6 (1935); N. B. Minkoff, *Yidishe klasiker poetn*, 2d ed. (1939), *Pyonern fun yidisher poezye in amerike*, 3 v. (1956); Y. Mark, "Y. Lit.," *The Jews*, ed. L. Finkelstein, v. 2 (1949); N. B. Minkoff and J. A. Joffe, "Old Y. Lit.," and S. Niger, "Y. Lit. of the Past 200 Years," *The Jewish People Past and Present*, v. 3 (1952); B. Hrushovski [Harshav], "On Free Rhythms in Mod. Y. P.," *The Field of Y.*, ed. U. Weinreich, v. 1 (1954), "The Creation of Accentual Iambs," *For Max Weinreich on his 70th Birthday* (1964), *The Meaning of Y.* (1990); *Leksikon fun der nayer yidisher literatur*, 8 v. (1956–); U. Weinreich, "On the Cultural Hist. of Y. Rime," *Essays on Jewish Life and Thought*, ed. J. L. Blau (1959); S. Liptzin, *The Flowering of Y. Lit.* (1964), *The Maturing of Y. Lit.* (1970); I. Howe, *World of Our Fathers* (1976), ch. 13; J. Hadda, *Yankev Glatshteyn* (1980); Kh. Shmeruk, *Prokim fun der yidisher literatur-geshikhte* (1988); R. Wisse, *A Little Love in Big Manhattan* (1988); F. W. Aaron, *Bearing the Unbearable: Y. and Polish P. in the Ghettos and Concentration Camps* (1990). U.W.; J.H.

YORUBA POETRY. See AFRICAN POETRY.

YUGOSLAV POETRY. (This article surveys the poetries written in the regions of Ragusa, Dalmatia, Serbia, Slovenia, Croatia, and Macedonia in the country formerly known as Yugoslavia.)

The natural aptitude of the Y. peoples for poetic invention throughout their history is demonstrated by the wealth and beauty of their folk poetry. This poetry is of two kinds, "heroic" or epic, and lyric. The lyric poems, in lines of varying lengths and meters, express every emotion and every aspect of the life of the people. There are ritual and ceremonial songs, dirges, love songs, work songs, and songs sung to accompany dancing or various celebrations. The majority of the epic (heroic) songs relate events from the country's past. Mythological or semi-legendary themes occur in those of earlier origin: the more recent the ballad the more authentic its subject. The ballads with historical subjects deal for the most part with the struggles against the Turks. The cycle describing incidents connected with the disastrous battle of Kosovo in 1389 has the greatest aesthetic value and is the most moving. Metrically, a regular line in the majority of the epic ballads is decasyllabic, with a caesura after the fourth syllable and a clear tendency toward trochaic distribution of stresses and with a quantitative close: ⏑ ⏑ – ⏑ . (When stressed, the ninth syllable is usually long, and the eighth and seventh are short.) The basis of Y. epic meter is thus both stress and quantity and has been a matter of detailed study. There is little or no rhyme.

Y. folk poetry was virtually unknown outside of the country until the field studies in Yugoslavia of Milman Parry and Albert B. Lord in the 1930s and 1950s and the publication of the results of their findings. Parry and Lord (after Parry's death, Lord and David E. Bynum) recorded many oral folksongs, on the basis of which they formulated their theories about the characteristics, structure, and formulas of South Slavic folksongs. They applied their theories about the formulaic idioms to other ancient and medieval epics, which, in turn, has led to a continuing discussion about the basic nature of folk poetry, becoming an indispensable part of the genre's study today.

As regards written verse, the earliest consisted principally of 13th- and 14th-c. translations of hymns and other poems of an ecclesiastical nature. The liturgical verse of the Orthodox Church, influenced by Byzantium, was mostly translated from Gr. and was written in Serbian recensions of Old Church Slavonic in the Cyrillic alphabet. That of the Roman Catholic Church, in the Glagolitic alphabet, was similar in character, but Catholic religious verse not purely liturgical was also written in the vernacular. The earliest extant records of this poetry date from the 15th c.

When the cultural development of the peoples of the interior was suppressed under foreign domination, conditions were favorable for the cultivation of lit. only in the free republic of Dubrovnik (Ragusa) and elsewhere in Dalmatia. Here poetry began to flourish in the 15th c. under the influence of the It. Ren. The Petrarchan lyric was imitated in Dubrovnik first by the "troubadour" poets Šiško Menčetić (1457–1527) and Džore Držić (1461–1501), of whom the latter was less imitative and more sincere. These poets favored a slightly modified form of the *strambotto* as well as the Petrarchan sonnet. The conceits employed by the It. lyricists were introduced with ingenuity into this poetry, which yet retained some indigenous elements and certain reminiscences of folk ballads. Love is the predominant motive, but other themes such as patriotism and religion occur. The meter is usually a dodecasyllabic line with internal rhyme, but an octosyllabic line is also employed by certain subsequent poets. Songs of a similar character, sung by shepherds, were introduced into the "pastoral novel" *Planine* (The Mountains) by Petar Zoranić (b. 1508?) of Zadar. Another aspect of It. influence is seen in imitations of Florentine carnival poetry. Of these, *Jedjupka* (The Gypsy) by Mikša Pelegrinović (1500?–26) of Hvar, has the greatest charm and originality. The earliest epic was *Judita* (1501) by Marko Marulić (1450–1524) of Split. Using the dodecasyllabic line, and in verse in which fashionable adornments are not absent, he relates the biblical story of Judith, suggesting an analogy between its background and his own country's perils. Other notable poetic works of the 16th c., in the same meter, are *Robinja* (The Slave-girl) by Hanibal Lucić (1485?–1553) of Hvar, the earliest secular dramatic work in Croatian lit., though a narrative poem in dialogue form rather than a drama; and *Ribanje i ribarsko prigovaranje* (Fishing and Fishermen's Talk) by Petar Hektorović (1487–1572), also of Hvar. Although this poem, describing a fishing expedition, is to some extent reminiscent of It. piscatorial eclogues, it is one of the most original and realistic works of the period. Folk-epic songs sung by fishermen in the poem represent the earliest written record of Y. traditional poetry. The lyrical, contemplative, and epic poetry of Mavro Vetranović (1482–1576), often with a moralizing purpose, was relatively free from foreign influences but generally of little aesthetic value. New metrical forms, imitated or adapted from It. lyrics, were introduced to Ragusan poetry by Dinko Ranjina (1536–1607) and Dinko Zlatarić (1558?–1613?), whose work as translators of Gr. and Lat. verse also reflects the Ren. revival of interest in Cl. lit. in Italy.

With the work of Ivan Gundulić (1589–1638), Ragusan lit. is generally considered to have reached its "Golden Age." The influence of the Ren. had given way to that of the Counter-Reformation; national consciousness, a moral purpose, religious feeling, and philosophical meditations—elements found scattered among the works of most of his predecessors—are supreme in those of Gundulić. His *Suze sina razmetnoga* (The Tears of the Prodigal Son), in 3 cantos, is a confession of sin and a meditation on the transitoriness of earthly things. In his greatest work, the epic *Osman*, a poem inspired by his faith in the Slavs and in Christianity, Gundulić weaves a complex pattern of incidents around his central theme—an event in the contemporary war between the Poles and Turks. The epic is akin to those of Tasso and Ariosto, with stylistic traits of Marinism. It is composed in quatrains of octosyllables rhyming *abab*.

The Ragusan love lyric continued to flourish in the verse—with characteristics of Marinism—of Stijepo Djurdjević (1579–1632), best known for his satirical *Derviš*, describing the emotions of an elderly dervish in love; and in the exquisite, concise, and erotic poems of Ivan Bunić (1591–1658?). Both Bunić and the last great Ragusan lyricist, Ignjat Djurdjević (1675–1737), in whose work the baroque influence predominates, also treated the subject of the repentant Mary Magdalene in longer works inspired by Gundulić.

As lit. slowly revived elsewhere in the Y. lands, verse was at first put to practical uses. Employing the convenient decasyllabic line of the epic folk-ballads, Andrija Kačić-Miošić (1704–60), of central Dalmatia, wrote a chronicle of the South Slavs, and Matija Reljković (1732–98), a Slavonian, composed his admonitory poem *Satir* (The Satyr). The Serb Jovan Rajić (1726–1801) composed, among other works, an allegorical-historical epic *Boj zmaja s orlovi* (The Battle of the Dragon with the Eagles) in the artificial *rusko-slovenski* lang. cultivated by Serbian writers of his period. The didactic element, characteristic of the lit. of this time, is present in the pseudo-classical lyric poetry of the Serb Lukijan Mušicki (1777–1837). Meanwhile the foundations of Slovene poetry were laid by Valentin Vodnik (1758–1819), the first Slovene poet to write in the vernacular.

With the romantic movement came the revival of poetic composition as an art and the inspiration derived from the indigenous folk poetry, vast collections of which were made in the first half of the 19th c. by Vuk Karadžić (1787–1864), to whom future Serbian and Croatian writers were also indebted for his linguistic reforms. The folk-poetry element is a characteristic of the work of Sima Milutinović (1791–1847), whose epic and lyric poetry glorifying the Serbs is a mixture of realism and fantasy. It is also a characteristic of the work of the great Serbian poet, Petar Petrović Njegoš (1813–51), Prince-Bishop of Montenegro. Njegoš's lyric and epic poetry, composed in intellectual isolation, expresses his intense patriotism and his groping for a solution to the philosophical problems which tormented him. His *Luča mikrokozma* (The Torch of the Microcosm) treats a subject similar to that of Milton's *Paradise Lost*; his greatest work, *Gorski vijenac* (The Mountain Wreath), is an epic in dramatic form and a synthesis of aspects of Montenegrin life. The epic *Smrt Smail-Age Čengica*, by the Croat Ivan Mažuranić (1814–90), also in the style of the epic songs, graphically and powerfully depicts the sufferings of Montenegrins under Turkish oppression. The sonnet was introduced to the Croatian lit. of the period by Stanko Vraz (1810–51), who wrote also in the style of the folk ballads. Both he and Petar Preradović (1818–72) composed moving love lyrics at a time when poetry in Croatia comprised mainly patriotic verse.

New inspiration was brought to Serbian poetry by the fresh, spontaneous lyrics of Branko Radičević (1824–53). The meter is again often that of the folk ballads, but the themes are very diverse. Lyric poetry became the principal literary product of young Serbian writers after the middle of the century: Jovan Jovanović Zmaj (1833–1904) wrote simple and moving personal lyrics, later pouring out verses commenting on contemp. events; Djura Jakšić (1832–78) composed patriotic verse whose stridency contrasts with the melancholy tone of his emotional poems, e.g. his poignant *Na Liparu* (In the Lime-grove). The last of the great Serbian romantic poets was Laza Kostić (1841–1910), a translator of Shakespeare and composer of Shakespearean verse dramas and of lyric poetry.

The work of Slovenia's greatest poet, France Prešeren (1800–49) showed for the first time the potentialities of Slovene as a literary lang. His sonnets, sincere expressions of emotion, are examples of perfect harmony of form and theme. The cultivation of lyric poetry in various forms continued in Slovenia. That of Fran Levstik (1831–87) is sincere and expressive; Josip Stritar (1836–1923) skillfully experimented with various meters and poetic forms. This concern with form is seen also in the lyrics of Simon Gregorčič (1844–1906), expressing his love of nature and his longing to promote tolerance. The influence of folk poetry is evident in the lyrics of Simon Jenko (1835–69), a poet of patriotism, nature, and love; and the historical ballads which Anton Aškerc (1856–1912), nationalist and social critic, made the vehicle for expression of his principles were sometimes composed in the decasyllabic line; but no one meter can from this period onward be considered characteristic of Y. verse.

In Croatia, Silvije Strahimir Kranjčević (1865–1908) wrote with great violence or pathos, his work reflecting his nationalistic, socialistic, and anticlerical views, and his pessimism and bitterness. Meanwhile the Croatian critic A. G. Matoš (1873–1914), himself a poet, demanded complete freedom of expression in poetry, which should be untrammelled by any tendentious elements and in which aesthetic value should be of supreme importance. To his teaching were added lessons in form and technique derived from the Parnassians. Prominent among Matoš's contemporaries, the Croatian "modernists," were the poets Dragutin Domjanić (1875–1933), Vladimir Vidrić (1875–1909), and Milan Begović (1876–1948). Ljubo Wiesner (1885–1951) and Nikola Polić (1890–1960) were among those who continued the trad. of the subjective, aesthetic lyric, and an outstanding Croatian lyricist, Tin Ujević (1891–1955), with verse of great diversity of subject, emotion, expression, and form, may be counted as a disciple of Matoš. The eminent Croat Vladimir Nazor (1876–1949), optimistic and exuberant, expressed an intense love of all forms of life and nature in lyric verse and in epics with legendary or historical themes.

In Serbia, Vojislav Ilić (1860–94), a pure lyricist, provided examples of poetic technique for future poets. The works of a trio of lyric poets, Aleksa Šantić (1868–1924), a writer of patriotic and emotional verse; Jovan Dučić (1871–1943), whose lyrics, exquisite in phrasing and form, show the influence of the Parnassians, and Milan Raki'c (1876–1938), equally a perfectionist but a poet of profounder ideas and emotions, represent some of the best and purest in Serbian poetry of the next decades. Meanwhile there appeared a great Serbian lyricist of another school, Vladislav Petković-Dis (1880–1917), a poet of dreams and despair, to whom the sincere expression of emotions was of more importance than a studied perfection of form. Characteristics of the decadent movement in Serbian poetry before the First World War are found also in the melancholy verse of Sima Pan durović (1883–1960); Veljko Petrovič (1884–1967) wrote verse of sympathy for the victims of social injustices as well as vigorous patriotic verse. Pessimism is characteristic of the lyrics of Dušan Vasiljev (1900–24), the poet of revolt. One of the most prominent 20th-c. Serbian poets, Miloš Crnjanski (1893–1977), expresses his emotions and disillusionment in verses of great originality of both form and theme. The poetry of Rade Drainac (1899–1943) and of the poetess Desanka Maksimović (b. 1898) is also intimate, subjective, and emotional; but while that of the former may be bitter in tone, that of the latter is sensitive and delicate, and notable for its beauty and purity of expression. Oskar Davičo (b. 1909), a consummate craftsman, began as a surrealist in the late 1920s and has remained vitally present ever since. In postwar Serbian poetry, the most prominent poets are Vasko Popa (b. 1922) and Miodrag Pavlović (b. 1928). In his cyclical poetry Popa combines traditionalism and new myths, offering a new vision of man and universe. Pavlović also creates new myths out of old Serbian legends in contemplative, erudite, and stunningly crafted poems. Stevan Raičković (b. 1928) is down-to-earth and nature-bound, a pure lyricist, while Ivan V. Lalić (b. 1931) writes intellectual, neoclassical, masterfully refined poems. Branko Miljković (1934–61) created an influential body of poetry of intense contemplation and heightened lyricism. Of the younger generation, Ljubomir Simović (b. 1935), Borislav Radović (b. 1935), and Matija Bećković (b. 1939) epitomize a large group of gifted poets.

Miroslav Krleža (1893–1981), the dominant figure in contemp. Croatian lit., has composed ballads and lyrics, many of which are indictments of social injustice, most of them vigorous and intense. Of other Croats, Ivan Goran Kovačić (1913–43) will be remembered chiefly as a poet of the Second World War for his impressive cycle *Jama* (The Pit). Gustav Krklec (1899–1980), Dobriša Cesarić (1902–77), Nikola Šop (1904–82), and Dragutin Tadijanović (b. 1905) contribute to the wealth of 20th-c. Croatian lyric poetry, remarkable for its variety, spontaneity, and originality. The work of Krklec has been described as a "lyrical monologue" reflecting the varying emotions of the poet's life; Cesarić, without striving after unconventional forms of expression, has written works of great aesthetic value; Šop, earlier known for his sensitive religious lyrics, has now turned his attention to longer philosophical works inspired by poetic visions of space; the spontaneous and sincere lyrics of Tadijanovič express his dreams and emotions, his love of nature, and his nostalgia for the simple life. In the postwar generation, the works of Jure Kaštelan (b. 1919)—whose style has been compared with that of Walt Whitman—and of Vesna Parun (b. 1922), while still subjective, are concerned with more general human problems. Of other important postwar Croatian poets, Zvonimir Golob (b. 1927) is an image-maker influenced by Sp. and South Am. poets; Slavko Mihalić (b. 1928) meditates on the fate of the individual in a modern society, blending simplicity, precision, and lyrical fluency; and Milivoj Slaviček (b. 1929) poeticizes a running dialogue with his fellow man and with himself about the basic questions of existence. In the next generation, Ivan Slamnig (b. 1930), a diligent experimenter, blends black humor, seriousness, and strong intellectualism. Vlado Gotovac (b. 1930) writes a terse, hermetic, yet authentically lyrical poetry of ideas, while Antun Šoljan (b. 1932), influenced, like Slamnig, by Eng. and Am. poetry, creates clear images and parables, revealing an intense inner life. Daniel Dragojević (b. 1934), also a creator of parables and images with philosophical, religious, and visual-artistic undertones, leads a welter of promising young poets.

Oton Župančič (1878–1949), the greatest Slovene poet of the 20th c., turned from the early influence of the symbolists to the composition of lyrics which are striking in their originality and variety in form and phrasing. His influence is seen in the work of Alojz Gradnik (1882–1967). Between the wars, social criticism was the concern not only of Slovene prose writers but of poets; outstanding among the latter were Anton Podbevšek (b. 1898) and Mile Klopčič (b. 1905). Župančič and the poet-dramatist Matej Bor (b. 1913) composed verse inspired by World War II. Other prominent Slovene poets are Srečko Kosovel (1904–26), Edvard Kocbek (1904–81), and Miran Jarc (1900–42), one of the foremost exponents of expressionism. Of the younger generation, Ciril Zlobec (b. 1925), Tone Pavček (b. 1928), Dane Zajc (b. 1929), Gregor Strniša (1930–87), and Kajetan Kovič (b. 1931) have established themselves as the leading poets. Zlobec mixes lyrical sensitivity with a concern for prosaic problems. Zajc depicts the loneliness and alienation of modern man beset with fear of the futility of existence. Strniša created highly articulate allegories, metaphors, and dream sequences. Kovič combines sensitive contemplation, intellectual vigor, and radical experimentation. More recently, Veno Taufer (b. 1933), influenced by modern Eng. poetry, exhibits surrealist and neo-expressionist traits, while Tomaž Šalamun (b. 1941), the most vocal and iconoclastic among younger poets, writes associative poetry, using its seeming chaos as a freeing agent to drive his points home.

The youngest of Y. lits., Macedonian, has existed underground for centuries but came into full bloom only after World War II. Among pioneers, Kosta Racin (1908–43) deserves a place of honor for his sincere and emotional poems about the fate of his countrymen. The three founders of contemp. Macedonian poetry are Slavko Janevski (b. 1920), Blaže Koneski (b. 1921), and Aco Šopov (1923–83). The picturesque and boldly imaginative poetry of Janevski is complemented by Koneski's direct, intimate, and meditative poetry and by Šopov's subtle lyricism and intense sensitivity. The next generation, represented by Mateja Matevski (b. 1929) and Gane Todorovski (b. 1929), extends the horizons, as do Radovan Pavlovski (b. 1934) and Bogomil Djuzel (b. 1939), two of the many promising younger poets. In a time of bitter ethnic and regional warfare, contemp. Y. p. nevertheless continues to be characterized by unabating vitality, modern idiom, freedom of expression, variety, experimentation, and openness to world poetry.

ANTHOLOGIES: *Heroic Ballads of Serbia*, tr. G. R. Noyes and L. R. Bacon (1913); *Serbian Songs and Poems*, tr. J. W. Wiles (1917); *Kossovo: Heroic Songs of the Serbs*, tr. H. Rootham (1920); *Ballads of Marko Kraljevic*, tr. D. H. Low (1922); *Antologija novije hrvatske lirike*, ed. M. Kombol (1934); *Anthologie de la poésie yougoslave des XIXe et XXe siècle*, tr. and ed. M. and S. Ibrovac (1935); *The Revolt of the Serbs against the Turks, 1804–1813*, tr. W. A. Morison (1942); *Srpske narodne pjesme*, ed. Vuk Karadžić, 1–4 (1953–58); *Antologija novije srpske lirike*, ed. B. Popović, 9th ed. (1953); *The Parnassus of a Small Nation, An Anthol. of Slovene Lyrics*, tr. and ed. W. K. Matthews and A. Slodnjak (1957); *Antologija dubrovačke lirike*, ed. D. Pavlović (1960); *An Anthol. of Mod. Y. P.*, ed. J. Lavrin (1962); *Novija jugoslavenska poezija*, ed. V. Popović (1962); *Antologija srpskog pesništva*, ed. M. Pavlović (1964); *Contemp. Y. P.*, ed. V. D. Mihailovich (1977); *Marko the Prince: Serbo-Croat Heroic Songs*, ed. and tr. A. Pennington and P. Levi (1984); *Serbian P. from the Beginnings to the Present*, ed. M. Holton and V. D. Mihailovich (1988).

HISTORY AND CRITICISM: J. Torbarina, *It. Influence on the Poets of the Ragusan Republic* (1931); D. Subotić, *Y. Popular Ballads* (1932); A. Slodnjak, *Geschichte der slowenischen Literatur* (1958); A. Kadić, *Contemp. Croatian Lit.* (1960), *Contemp. Serbian Lit.* (1964); M. P. Coote, "Serbocroatian Heroic Songs," *Heroic Epic and Saga*, ed. F. J. Oinas (1978); S. Koljević, *The Epic in the Making* (1980).

V.J.; V.D.M.

Z

ZULU POETRY. See AFRICAN POETRY.